C0-BUW-668

The Developing Person

Through the Life Span

Christian Pierre, *Beachside Generations* (front cover), *Friends* (back cover) The artist Christian Pierre has lived in several cultures and has experienced many of life's vicissitudes, yet her paintings are luminous and expressive. Note the joy and thoughtfulness reflected in these scenes, showing people appreciating butterflies, infancy, and music in brilliant, colorful places. This is a metaphor for using this textbook: Study and learn, of course, but also enjoy every page, every idea, and every age of life.

The Developing Person

Through the Life Span

SIXTH EDITION

Kathleen Berger

Bronx Community College
City University of New York

WORTH PUBLISHERS

Publisher: Catherine Woods

Senior Sponsoring Editor: Jessica Bayne

Developmental Editors: Cecilia Gardner, Randee Falk

Executive Marketing Manager: Renée Altier

Associate Managing Editor: Tracey Kuehn

Art Director, Interior and Cover Designer: Barbara Reingold

Production Editor: Vivien Weiss

Layout Designer: Paul Lacy

Senior Illustration Coordinator: Bill Page

Illustrations: Todd Buck Illustration and TSI Graphics, Inc.

Photo Editors: Meg Kuhta, Bianca Moscatelli

Photo Researcher: Julie Tesser

Production Manager: Barbara Anne Seixas

Composition: TSI Graphics, Inc.

Printing and Binding: R.R. Donnelley & Sons Company

Cover Art: Christian Pierre, *Beachside Generations* (front) and
Friends (back)

Library of Congress Cataloging-in-Publication Data

Berger, Kathleen Stassen.

    The developing person through the life span / Kathleen Stassen

    Berger.-- 6th ed.

        p. cm.

    Includes bibliographical references and indexes.

    ISBN 0-7167-5706-0

        1. Developmental psychology.   I. Title.

    BF713.B463 2004

    155--dc22

                                      2003064337

ISBN: 0-7167-5706-0 (hardcover) (EAN: 9780716757061)

        0-7167-9159-5 (paperback) (EAN: 9780716791591)

        0-7167-0387-4 (complimentary) (EAN: 9780716703877)

© 2005, 2001, 1998, 1994, 1988, 1983 by Worth Publishers

All rights reserved.

Printed in the United States of America

First printing 2004

Worth Publishers

41 Madison Avenue

New York, NY 10010

www.worthpublishers.com

Credit is given to the following sources for permission to use the photos indicated:

Part Openers

1. Laura Dwight, pp. ix, 1

2. Gary Connor/Index Stock Imagery, pp. x, 118, 119

3. Johner/Photonica, pp. x, 194, 195

4. Len Rubenstein/Index Stock Imagery, pp. xi, 262, 263

5. Antonio Mo/Taxi/Getty Images, pp. xii, 338, 339

6. Gary Connor/PhotoEdit, pp. xii, 410, 411

7. Mark Richards/PhotoEdit, Inc., pp. xiii, 488, 489

8. Mark Gilbert/Stone/Getty Images, pp. xiv, 572, 573

Chapter Openers

1. Tony Savino/The Image Works, p. 2

2. Laura Dwight/Corbis, p. 32

3. David M. Phillips/Photo Researchers, Inc., p. 58

4. Stephanie Rausser/Taxi/Getty Images, p. 90

5. Lisi Dennis/The Image Bank/Getty Images, pp. 120, 193

6. Jacques Charlas/Stock Boston/PictureQuest, pp. 146, 193

7. Johner/Photonica, pp. 170, 193

8. Elizabeth Crews, pp. 196, 261

9. Tom Hood, The Daily Courier/AP Photo, pp. 216, 261

10. Deborah Davis/PhotoEdit, Inc., pp. 236, 261

11. Osamu Koyata/Pacific Press Service, pp. 264, 337

12. Ellen B. Senisi, pp. 288, 337

13. Sean Sprague/The Image Works, pp. 312, 337

14. Alan & Linda Detrick/Photo Researchers, Inc., pp. 340, 409

15. Lauren Greenfield, pp. 362, 409

16. David Grossman/The Image Works, pp. 384, 409

17. Pierre Tostee, pp. 412, 487

18. Karen/Corbis Sygma, pp. 434, 487

19. Tom Stewart/Corbis, pp. 458, 487

20. Lilly Doug/Botanica/Getty Images, pp. 490, 571

21. Arlene Collins/The Image Works, pp. 518, 571

22. Tony Anderson/Taxi/Getty Images, pp. 542, 571

23. Kent Meireis/The Image Works, pp. 574, 667

24. Xinua-Chine Nouvelle/Gamma Liaison, pp. 604, 667

25. Lawrence Manning/Corbis, pp. 632, 667

Ep. Steven M. Stone/Picture Cube, p. Ep-0

About the Author

Kathleen Stassen Berger received her undergraduate education at Stanford University and Radcliffe College, earned an M.A.T. from Harvard University and an M.S. and Ph.D from Yeshiva University. Her broad experience as an educator includes directing a preschool, teaching philosophy and humanities at the United Nations International School, teaching child and adolescent development to graduate students at Fordham University, teaching undergraduates at Montclair State University in New Jersey and at Quinnipiac University in Connecticut as well as inmates earning a paralegal degree at Sing Sing Prison.

For the past 35 years Berger has taught at Bronx Community College of the City University of New York, recently as the elected chair of the Social Science Department. She has taught introduction to psychology, child and adolescent development, adulthood and aging, social psychology, abnormal psychology, human motivation, and, of course, life-span development. Her students—who come from many ethnic, economic, and educational backgrounds and who have a wide range of interests—consistently honor her with the highest teaching evaluations. Her own four children attended New York City public schools, one reason that she was elected as president of the Community School Board in District Two.

Berger is also the author of *The Developing Person Through Childhood and Adolescence* and *The Developing Person Through Childhood*. Her three developmental texts are currently being used at nearly 700 colleges and universities worldwide in four languages. Her research interests include adolescent identity, sibling relationships, and bullying, and she has contributed articles on developmental topics to the *Wiley Encyclopedia of Psychology*. Berger's interest in college education is manifest in articles published in 2002 by the American Association for Higher Education and the National Education Association for Higher Education. She continues to teach and learn with every semester and every edition of her books.

Brief Contents

Contents

Part I

The Beginnings 1

Part IV

The School Years 263

Part VII

Middle Adulthood 489

Preface

Development happens, ready or not. Every year brings gains and losses, continuity and discontinuity, constantly discovered and reported by the scientists, and then described and understood by you and me. Between the fifth and sixth editions of this textbook, not only did the World Trade Center disappear from my neighborhood but my mother, my father, and my husband died. Yet there were gains. Among them, I taught in California, Ohio, New Jersey, Texas, and Connecticut, all places I had never taught before. Now I am again in the Bronx, teaching life-span development again to students of various backgrounds and ages.

Development is not only about our personal gains and losses but also about the gathering of new research and theory. Worldwide, the birth rate is falling and the life span increasing, which has led to increased attention to each newborn and each centenarian. More babies are not just surviving but thriving, with less malnutrition, more breast feeding, less neglect, and more intellectual stimulation than ever before. Most older children are in school, learning more deeply as well as for a longer time than earlier cohorts. Teenagers and young adults wait to marry and have children, and their middle-aged parents have altered the context of marriage, the workplace, and retirement. Each of these changes affects us all.

Globalization has also altered our understanding of the human experience. People in all cultures, of all ethnic groups, from all backgrounds, grow and develop in ways specific to their culture, their ethnicity, their personality, and their birthplace, yet universal verities—love, work, family, attachment, death—are the foundation of life for all of us, expressed in hundreds of variations. As the global economy changes the human experience, the Human Genome Project reveals genetic similarities and differences among humans not imagined before.

This book could easily be thousands of pages long if it were to reflect all that developmentalists believe is crucial for everyone to understand, but it must be manageable for students to read (and carry!) in one semester. Just as there is more that I hope to accomplish each day than I actually do, deciding what to delete is always the most difficult part of writing. But this is a task I've undertaken with more determination in this edition than ever before.

Since the very first edition, I have tried to make this book reflect the values of my own classroom—high standards and clear expectations. But effective learning does not occur unless the instructor follows through with enthusiasm, humor, and intellectual honesty, as I know from my own teaching. I try to apply this philosophy to textbook writing as well.

The best developmental textbooks integrate theory and practice with such powerful clarity that they make students think deeply about the long-term implications of the research and concepts, and simultaneously enable students to master the specific facts and applied skills required of practiced professionals. There should be no gap between theory and practice; they need each other. This vision describes the high standards I hold; I hope these standards as well as my enthusiasm for the field and my humor are evident in this book. If so, I thank my heroes and mentors. These include not only my own gifted professors who studied directly with Erikson, Piaget, and Skinner but also researchers whom I admire from the cool distance of the printed page: Ainsworth, Baltes, Bem, the

Coles, Garbarino, Gardner, the Gibsons, Lightfoot, Olweus, Plomin, Rutter, Schaie, Vygotsky, Whitborne, Zigler—and many more (which explains why the bibliography is longer than any comparable book's)—plus the thousands of peers and students who continue to teach me.

I expect every student to learn and understand. Specific current issues—adult attachment, ageism, alcohol abuse, Alzheimer's disease, amniocentesis, anorexia, apprenticeship, assisted reproduction, asthma, attention-deficit disorder, bilingual education, breast feeding, birth abnormalities, bulimia, brain development, bullying, and many, many more—are defined and delineated fairly, raising questions that have no easy answers. More important, controversies are put into context: Genetic, cultural, historical, ethnic, and economic influences are never ignored.

New Features

A number of aspects of this edition may be singled out for special mention:

- *Even stronger integration of theory and practice*   The five theories introduced in Chapter 2—psychoanalytic, behaviorism, cognitive, sociocultural, and epigenetic—are applied many more times in the book, from explanations of how babies learn language to how adults can combat secondary aging. We all must become accustomed to alternative perspectives. Nothing is quite so practical as a good theory, as my mentors taught me, and nothing about development is a mere abstraction. In this new edition, more than ever, theoretical insights are connected to practical issues. This link is evident throughout, notably in the "Especially for . . ." questions in the margins and through features in the new "Thinking Like a Scientist" and "A Case to Study" series, which help readers see how the experience of each developing person illustrates theories and applications.
- *Up-to-date research*   Every year brings new concepts and research. The best of these are integrated into the text, including hundreds of new references on many topics—among them, challenges to Piaget's theories, origins of infant language, causes of emotional regulation, genetics of Alzheimer's disease, and impact of stereotype threat.
- *Streamlined presentation*   In talking with faculty who have been using this book, I realized that over five editions, this book had grown, becoming too long. This edition is shorter by almost 100 pages, and each topic is more explicitly linked to the next.
- *New learning features*   With every edition, changes in the narrative are made to enhance readers' understanding of what scientists do. Readers are offered many opportunities to test their observational and analytical skills. The new "Thinking Like a Scientist" and "A Case to Study" features illuminate core ideas, from recognizing child neglect to planning a good death. In addition, there are more observational quizzes for photographs, and some quizzes for graphs and tables have been added to ensure that quantitative data will be examined at the detailed level required for solid science. I've also added a medial summary at the end of each major section to allow students to pause and reflect on what they've learned. These and other pedagogical elements of the text reflect recent research in learning strategies.

Ongoing Features

Many characteristics of this text have been acclaimed since the first edition and have been retained in this revision:

- *Language that communicates the excitement and challenge of the field*   An overview of the science of human development should be lively, just as children and adults are. Consequently, each sentence has been crafted to convey tone as well as content. More summarizing and transitional statements are provided, in order to clarify the logical connection between one idea and the next. Sentences are shorter and less daunting, although I still choose some vocabulary words that will expand comprehension. Chapter-opening vignettes are more evocative, to bring students into the immediacy of development from the very first paragraph.

- *Coverage of diversity*   Cross-cultural, international, multiethnic, rich and poor, male and female—all these words and ideas are vital to appreciating how we all develop. Studies of various groups make it clear that we are all the same, yet each of us is unique. From the discussion of the cultural context in Chapter 1 to the coverage of religious beliefs about dying in the Epilogue, each chapter refers to the vast possibilities in human cultural experience. New research on family structures, immigrants, bilingualism, and ethnic variations in disease are among the many topics that are presented, always with respect for human diversity, throughout the book. Below are just a few of the places where you can find discussions of culture and diversity in this new edition.

Defining culture, pp. 10–14
Family sleeping arrangements as an example of cultural traits, pp. 12–14
Ethnicity and culture, p. 14
Sociocultural theory, pp. 45–46
Applications of sociocultural theory, p. 53
Cultural variations in birth, pp. 109–111
International and domestic diversity in low birthweight, pp. 104–105, 113
Cultural variations in motor skill development, pp. 134–136
Ethnicity, culture, and SIDS, pp. 139–141
Malnutrition worldwide, pp. 142–143
Cultural variations in language development, pp. 160–161
Temperament and caregiving across cultures, p. 176
Sociocultural theory and the social context of infant development, p. 177
Cultural variations in parental and familial roles in child rearing,
    pp. 186–187
Ethnic variations in growth patterns, pp. 197–198
Learning across cultures, p. 221
Culture and context as influences on theory of mind, p. 223
Cultural and social context for early childhood language acquisition
    (including coverage of bilingualism), pp. 228–230
International differences in preschool education, pp. 231–233
Cultural influences on emotional development, p. 242
Worldwide prevalence of rough-and-tumble play, p. 244
Parenting styles, pp. 246–250
Sociocultural theory and gender role development, p. 257
In Person: Two Children of Mexican Heritage Living in California, p. 266
Culture, ethnicity, and physical development in middle childhood,
    pp. 269–271
Brain and motor skill development, p. 273
Culture and the IQ test, p. 275
Cultural and cognitive development in the school years, p. 292
Criticism of Kolhberg's stages from international perspectives, pp. 293–294
Schooling and cultural values, pp. 301–302, 304–308
Bilingual education, pp. 308–309

- *Up-to-date coverage*   My students as well as my children keep me current through their questions and concerns. I learned from my mentors' curiosity, creativity, and suspicion; as a result, I am eager to read but ready to analyze thousands of journal articles and books on everything from abuse to zygosity. The recent explosion of research in neuroscience and genetics has challenged me, once again, first to understand and then to explain many complex findings and speculative leaps.

- *Topical organization within a chronological framework*   The book's basic organization remains unchanged. Four chapters begin the book with coverage of definitions, theories, genetics, and prenatal development, used not only as a developmental foundation but also as the structure for explaining the life-span perspective, plasticity, nature and nurture, multicultural awareness, risk analysis, the damage–repair cycle, family bonding, and many other concepts that yield insights for all of human development. The ensuing seven parts correspond to the major periods of development. Each part contains three chapters, one for each of the three domains: biosocial, cognitive, and psychosocial. The topical organization within a chronological framework is a useful scaffold for student understanding of the interplay between age and domain as they themselves actually experience it. Linking science to everyday life is one way to expand cognition. The chapters are color-coded with tabs in the margins: The pages of the biosocial chapters have green tabs, the cognitive chapters have blue tabs, and the psychosocial chapters have orange tabs.

■ *Relevant features*   In some books, boxes are tacked on to make the text seem more current or multicultural than it really is. In this edition, four series of deeper discussions appear as integral parts of the text, and only where they are relevant. These features include two series that readers have particularly liked in earlier editions (called "Changing Policy" and "In Person") and two that are new to this edition (called "A Case to Study" and "Thinking Like a Scientist").

■ *Pedagogical aids*   Each chapter ends with a chapter summary, a list of key terms (with page numbers indicating where the word is introduced and defined), and three or four applications, or exercises designed to let students see how important concepts apply to everyday life. Terms are defined in the margins where they are introduced (in boldface) in the text and again in a glossary at the back of the book. The outline on the first page of each chapter and the system of major and minor subheads facilitate the widely used survey-question-read-write-review (SQ3R) approach. New to this edition are the section-ending medial summaries designed to scaffold student retention. Observational quizzes inspire readers to look more closely at data and photographs, and the "Especially for . . ." questions in the margins apply concepts to real-life careers and social roles.

Examples of an "Especially for . . . " question, an Observational Quiz for a graph, and an Observational Quiz for a photograph are presented below and on the next page.

Especially for Doctors and Nurses If you had to choose between recommending various screening tests and recommending various lifestyle changes in a 35-year-old, which would you do? (See answer, page 511.)

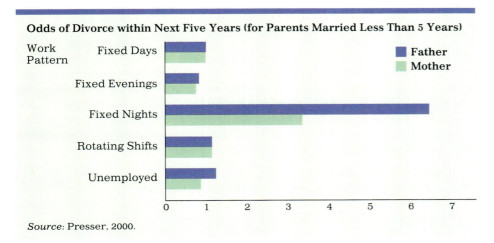

Odds of Divorce within Next Five Years (for Parents Married Less Than 5 Years)

Work Pattern

- Fixed Days
- Fixed Evenings
- Fixed Nights
- Rotating Shifts
- Unemployed

■ Father
■ Mother

Source: Presser, 2000.

FIGURE 19.3 Parents' Work Schedules and the Risk of Divorce Both the wife's and the husband's work schedules affect their chances of getting divorced. To interpret this graph, you need to know that the odds of divorce are set at a baseline of 1.0 for those who are working "fixed days" (that is, most work hours occur between 8 A.M. and 4 P.M.). The odds of divorce for other couples are higher or lower than 1, depending on whether the risk is greater or less than that of the fixed-days group.

   This study was longitudinal, measuring work schedules of 3,476 married couples over five years. Of those who initially had been married less than five years, 21 percent had divorced; of those who had been married more than five years, 8 percent had divorced.

? *Observational Quiz* (see answer, page 484): Looking closely at the graph, can you say what effect parental unemployment has on a marriage with small children?

■ *Photographs, tables, and graphs that are integral to the text*   Students learn a great deal by studying this book's illustrations, because Worth Publishers encourages authors to choose photos, tables, and graphs, to write captions, and to alter designs to better fit the words—not vice versa. As one result, photos and captions are instructional, supplementing and extending the text. Appendix A furthers this process by presenting at least one chart or table per chapter, containing detailed data for further study.

Learning Is Fun The original purpose of the Head Start program was to boost disadvantaged children's academic skills. The most enduring benefits, however, turned out to be improved self-esteem and social skills, as is evident in these happy Head Start participants, all crowded together.

? *Observational Quiz* (see answer, page 234): How many of these children are in close physical contact without discomfort or disagreement?

Content Changes for the Sixth Edition

Human development, like all sciences, builds on past learning. Many facts and concepts must be restated in every edition of a textbook—stages and ages, norms and variations, dangers and diversities, classic theories and fascinating applications. However, the study of development is continually changed by discoveries and innovations, so no paragraph in this sixth edition is exactly what it was in the fifth edition, much less the first. Extensive updating is evident on virtually every page. Highlights appear below.

Chapter 1: Introduction
■ Greater emphasis on cultural contexts of development
■ New subsection ("Who Sleeps with Whom?") provides a detailed example of how lifestyle patterns are affected by cultural values
■ A Case to Study: "This Sense of Liberation" (about a boy growing up on a Georgia farm)

Chapter 2: Theories of Development
■ Updated and expanded coverage of epigenetic theory
■ Greater emphasis on sociocultural theory, especially on the work of Lev Vygotsky
■ Applications of theory to real-world examples, including hyperactivity and sexual orientation
■ Thinking Like a Scientist: What Is a Mother For? (Harlow's surrogate mothers)
■ In Person: My Beautiful, Hairless Babies (the ethological perspective on why I adore my children)

Chapter 3: Heredity and Environment
- Expanded discussion on the interaction between genes and environment in senility and Alzheimer's disease
- Changing Policy: Too Many Boys? Too Many Girls?
- Thinking Like a Scientist: The Human Genome Project
- A Case to Study: "What Do People Live to Do?" (a young couple's quandary over their Down syndrome fetus)
- Changing Policy: Decisions and Values (some of the ethical dilemmas brought up in genetic counseling)

Chapter 4: Prenatal Development and Birth
- Updated international data on low birthweight, exposure to teratogens, and infant mortality
- Changing Policy: AIDS and Alcohol as Teratogens

Chapter 5: The First Two Years: Biosocial Development
- New research on sleep
- Expanded discussion of brain growth, including expansion, pruning, sculpting, and the development of the cortex
- New coverage of early infant cognition
- Updated information on infant nutrition, including breast feeding and malnutrition
- Heavily revised section on public health issues and initiatives worldwide, with specific coverage of immunization and sudden infant death syndrome
- A Case to Study: Toni's Well-Child Visit (identifying the signs of early deprivation)
- Thinking Like a Scientist: Plasticity and Young Orphans (Romanian adoptees)

Chapter 6: The First Two Years: Cognitive Development
- Research-based challenges to Piaget's theories of early cognition
- Expanded coverage of information processing
- New treatment of the effects of culture on language acquisition
- Revised section on theories of how infants learn language
- Thinking Like a Scientist: Object Permanence Revisited

Chapter 7: The First Two Years: Psychosocial Development
- Expanded coverage of temperament, including coverage of epigenetic theory
- More on development of emotions and social context (synchrony, social referencing)
- Expanded treatment of infant day care includes cross-cultural approaches to day care
- A Case to Study: Parents on Autopilot (a boy's need to develop social connections)

Chapter 8: The Play Years: Biosocial Development
- Coverage of the significance of brain development, especially the prefrontal cortex (with implications for education)
- Updated section on injury control and prevention
- Revised discussion of the incidence and prevention of child maltreatment
- A Case to Study: The Neglect of Neglect: A 2-Year-Old Boy

Chapter 9: The Play Years: Cognitive Development
- Expanded coverage of Vygotsky's theory
- More explanations and data on theory of mind
- New insights into language development, including the role of cognition
- Enhanced coverage of bilingual education
- The pros and cons of early-childhood education (including the qualities of good pre-K programs)

Chapter 10: The Play Years: Psychosocial Development
- Importance of emotional regulation and emotional intelligence
- New cross-cultural comparisons of parenting practices
- Expanded section on the influence of violent TV and video games on young children

Chapter 11: The School Years: Biosocial Development
- Coverage of cultural variations in obesity
- New treatment of the importance of brain development to coordination and body movement
- New research on autism, ADHD, and ADD
- In Person: Two Children of Mexican Heritage in California
- A Case to Study: Billy: Dynamo or Dynamite?

Chapter 12: The School Years: Cognitive Development
- Expanded coverage of Piagetian and Vygotskian theory
- New research on information processing in the school years, emphasizing the importance of brain development
- New international data on children's understanding of logic
- New criticisms of Kohlberg's theory of moral development
- Various approaches to teaching reading and mathematics (including ideological controversies)
- New discussion of educational standards
- Thinking Like a Scientist: How Does Class Size Affect Learning?

Chapter 13: The School Years: Psychosocial Development
- Updated research on ways to treat and discourage bullying
- New coverage of family functions and structures
- New discussion of resilience in school-age children
- Thinking Like a Scientist: Intervention to Stop Bullying: Impossible?

Chapter 14: Adolescence: Biosocial Development
- New research on timing of puberty, including the impact of genes, stress, and evolution
- New material on risks of teenage sex

Chapter 15: Adolescence: Cognitive Development
- Coverage of intuitive and analytic modes of cognition
- Revised discussion of adolescent risk taking regarding school, jobs, and sex
- Expanded section on school
- Thinking Like a Scientist: Piaget's Balance Experiment

Chapter 16: Adolescence: Psychosocial Development
- Updated coverage of adolescent depression, suicide, and rebellion
- Restructured discussion of adolescent romance and sex
- Expanded treatment of the importance of parents and peers in social development
- In Person: Talking to My Children About Marriage and Parenthood

Chapter 17: Early Adulthood: Biosocial Development
- New section on psychopathologies (depression, schizophrenia, and antisocial behavior, especially male violence) in early adulthood
- New coverage of gender differences in health status
- A Case to Study: Julia: "Too Thin, As If That's Possible"

Chapter 18: Early Adulthood: Cognitive Development
- New discussion of the impact of stereotype threat on cognition
- New coverage of culture and cognition
- Updated material on contemporary college students

- Thinking Like a Scientist: Reducing Stereotype Threat
- In Person: Faith and Tolerance

Chapter 19: Early Adulthood: Cognitive Development
- New coverage of the impact of culture on courtship and marriage
- Expanded discussion and new research on same-sex unions
- Updated coverage of domestic violence
- Reorganized and expanded section on marital roles includes new research on dual-earner families and single parents
- A Case to Study: Linda: "Her Major Issues Were Relationships and Career" and Linda Again: "A Much Sturdier Self" (impact of identity on early adult development)

Chapter 20: Middle Adulthood: Biosocial Development
- Updated discussion of menopause, including new research on hormone replacement therapy
- New research on the effects of diversity on health
- Increased emphasis on health habits that can moderate secondary aging
- Thinking Like a Scientist: World Health and the Tragedy of the Commons

Chapter 21: Middle Adulthood: Cognitive Development
- New emphasis on life-span changes and fluctuations in intelligence
- New section on culture and cognition
- New coverage of the impact of stress on coping
- In Person: An Expert Parent

Chapter 22: Middle Adulthood: Psychosocial Development
- New research on marriage and divorce
- Updated material on caregiving in middle age
- New coverage of international trends in nest-leaving
- New coverage of culture and grandparenting, including custodial grandparents
- Research on scaling back and retirement
- Changing Policy: Income and Age

Chapter 23: Late Adulthood: Biosocial Development
- Updated material on compensation strategies
- New biological theories of aging
- New section contrasting ageism in various nations
- Increased emphasis on health habits that can prevent or moderate secondary aging
- In Person: "Do I Want to Live to 100?"

Chapter 24: Late Adulthood: Cognitive Development
- Updated material on normative memory changes in aging
- New research on risk factors for Alzheimer's disease and current treatments
- Thinking Like a Scientist: Neuroscience and Brain Activity

Chapter 25: Late Adulthood: Psychosocial Development
- New coverage of diversity in elder-care practices and values
- Deeper discussion of caregiving, including the psychological impact on both caregiver and care receiver
- Updated coverage of widows and widowers and growing old alone
- A Case to Study: Mrs. Edwards, Doing Just Fine
- Changing Policy: Between Fragile and Frail: Protective Buffers

Epilogue
- New coverage of culture and dying
- Updated treatment of palliative care, the hospice movement, and euthanasia
- A Case to Study: "Ask My Son and My Husband"

Appendix A: Supplemental Charts, Graphs, and Tables
- Quantitative data (in chart, graph, or table form) for further exploration, keyed to each chapter

Appendix B: More About Research Methods
- New section on how research validity can be enhanced (through representative sampling, and use of a comparison group)
- Hints about using the Internet for research

Appendix C: Three Research Assignments

Supplements

As an instructor myself, I know the importance of good supplements. I have been known to reject a textbook adoption because the company had a bad record on ancillaries and service. Fortunately, Worth has a well-deserved reputation for the quality of such materials—for both professors and students. With this edition you will find:

Exploring Life-Span Development: A Media Tool Kit

This CD series (also available for instructors on VHS and DVD) was prepared by a talented team of instructors including Lisa Huffman, Ball State University; Tom Ludwig, Hope College; Tanya Renner, Kapiolani Community College; Stavros Valenti, Hofstra University; and Catherine Robertson, Grossmont College. Combining video, animations, self-tests, and interactive exercises, the Exploring Life-Span Development Media Tool Kit offers students hands-on, interactive learning. These activities range from investigations of classic experiments (like the Visual Cliff and the Strange Situation) to observations on children's play, adolescent risk-taking, and successful aging. The student tool kit includes more than 60 interactive video-based student activities, quizzes, and flashcards tied to every chapter of the book. The instructor tool kit includes more than 350 video clips and animations, along with teaching tips and discussion starters.

Journey Through the Life Span Observational Videos

Bringing observational learning to the classroom, this new life-span development video allows students to watch and listen to children and adults as a way of amplifying their reading of the text. Students will be able to observe children from birth through death, in day-care centers, in schools, homes, nursing homes, and hospices and from a multitude of cultures and communities across the globe (Africa, Europe, Latin America, and Asia). Some of the most noted experts in development—Patricia Greenfield, Charles Nelson, Barbara Rogoff, and Carolyn Rovee-Collier—talk about their work in areas ranging from the biology of early brain development to bereavement. This three-video set also includes more than six hours of footage, including one hour of observational clips without narration. An instructor's observation workbook provides teaching and activity tips, while a student workbook helps students sharpen their observational skills and relate text material to real-life settings.

The Scientific American Frontiers Videos for Developmental Psychology

This remarkable resource provides instructors with 17 video segments of approximately 15 minutes each, on topics ranging from language development to nature–nurture issues. The videos can be used to launch classroom lectures or to emphasize and clarify course material. The Faculty Guide by Richard O. Straub (University of Michigan) describes and relates each segment to specific topics in the text.

Life-Span Development Telecourse

This new Life-Span Development TeleWeb Course, *Transitions Throughout the Life Span* developed by Coast Learning Systems and Worth Publishers, will teach the fundamentals of life-span development. The course also explores the variety of individual and developmental contexts that influence development, such as socioeconomic status, culture, genetics, family, school, and society. Each video lesson includes specific real-life examples interwoven with commentary by subject matter experts. The course includes 26 half-hour video lessons, a Telecourse Study Guide, and a Faculty Manual with test bank. The test bank is also available electronically.

Instructor's Resource eLibrary (IReL)

The Instructor's Resource eLibrary brings together all of the existing text and supplementary resources in a single, easy-to-use Web interface. This searchable, Web-based integrator includes materials from the textbook, the *Instructor's Resources,* and electronic supplements, including PowerPoints, and video clips. Through simple browse and search tools, instructors can quickly access virtually any piece of content and either download it to their computer or create a Web page to share with students.

Instructor's Resources

This collection of resources written by Richard O. Straub has been hailed as the richest collection of instructor's resources in developmental psychology. This manual features chapter-by-chapter previews and lecture guides, learning objectives, springboard topics for discussion and debate, handouts for student projects, and supplementary readings from journal articles. Course planning suggestions, ideas for term projects, and a guide to audiovisual and software materials are also included. New to this edition are additional media teaching suggestions.

Study Guide

The Study Guide, by Richard O. Straub helps students evaluate their understanding and retain their learning longer. Each chapter includes a review of key concepts, guided study questions, and section reviews that encourage students' active participation in the learning process; two practice tests and a challenge test help them assess their mastery of the material.

PowerPoint Slides

A number of different presentation slides are available on the Web site or on a CD-ROM. There are two prebuilt PowerPoint slide sets for each text chapter—one featuring chapter outlines, the other featuring all chapter art and illustrations. These slides can be used as is or customized to fit individual needs. Catherine Robertson (Grossmont College) has also produced a set of slides featuring tables, graphs, and figures.

The Worth Image and Lecture Gallery

Using Worth's Image and Lecture Gallery, located at www.worthpublishers.com/ilg, instructors can browse, search, and download illustrations from every Worth title and prebuilt PowerPoint presentation files for specific chapters, containing all chapter art or all chapter section headings in text form. Users can also create personal folders on a personalized home page for easy organization of the materials.

Overhead Transparencies

This set of 100 full-color transparencies consists of key illustrations, charts, graphs, and tables from the textbook.

Test Bank and Computerized Test Bank

The test bank prepared by myself, Bob Rainey (Florida Community College at Jacksonville), and Jill Saxon includes at least 80 multiple-choice and 50 fill-in, true-false, and essay questions for each chapter. Each question is keyed to the textbook by topic, page number, and level of difficulty. The Diploma computerized test bank, available for Windows and Macintosh, guides instructors step-by-step through the process of creating a test, and allows instructors to add an unlimited number of questions, edit questions, format a test, scramble questions, and include pictures, equations, and multimedia links. Online testing is also available through the system.

Companion Web Site

The companion Web site (www.worthpublishers.com/berger) is an online educational setting for students and instructors. It is free and does not require any special access codes or passwords. Student resources include: chapter outlines; learning objectives; Internet exercises; annotated Web links, sample essay question; case study question; online quizzes with immediate feedback and instructor notification; interactive flashcards and frequently asked questions about developmental psychology. For instructors, the Web site includes a full array of teaching tools, such as PowerPoint slides, syllabus posting, an online gradebook, and links to various resources, including WebCT, Blackboard, and the Worth Image and Lecture Gallery.

Thanks

I'd like to thank those academic reviewers who have read this book in every edition and who have provided suggestions, criticisms, references, and encouragement. They have all made this a better book. I want to mention especially those who have reviewed this edition:

Jackie Adamson, *South Dakota School of Mines & Technology*
Dais Akiba, *City University of New York, Queens College*
Dan Bellack, *Trident Technical College*
Cynthia Berg, *University of Utah*
Judy Berger, *John Abbot College*
Katherine A. Black, *University of Hartfod*
Laura Bradley Yurko, *Asheville Buncombe Technical Community College*
Susan Brashaw, *Superior College*
Deborah Burke, *Pomona College*
Liza Cariaga-Lo, *Yale University*
Judith B. Chandler, *Furman University*
Steven Cockerham, *East Tennessee State University*
Pamela Costa, *Tacoma Community College*
Nancy Darling, *Bard College*

Lisabeth F. DiLalla, *Southern Illinois University School of Medicine*
Karen L. Fingerman, *Purdue University*
Katherine J. Follett, *Elon University*
Karen Friedlen, *Mt. Mary College*
Tony Gary, *Mississippi Delta Community College*
Joanna Gonsalves, *Salem State College*
Robert Hansson, *University of Tulsa*
Laurie Hirohata, *Kapiolani Community College*
Debra Hollister, *Valencia Community College*
Patricia Jennings, *University of California, Davis*
Jenessa Johnson, *West Virginia University*
Michelle Karnes, *D'Youville College*
Michelle Kelley, *Old Dominion University*
Veena Khandke, *University of South Carolina—Spartanburg*

Judith Levine, *Farmingdale State University*
Laura Levine, *Central Connecticut University*
Marva L. Lewis, *Tulane University*
Paul Macaruso, *Community College of Rhode Island*
Micheline Malow-Iroff, *City University of New York—Queens College*
Jerry Marshall, *Green River Community College*
T. Darin Matthews, *The Citadel*
Mary Kay Mulligan, *Eastern Shore Community College*
Christopher K. Randall, *Troy State University—Montgomery*
Thomas G. Reio, Jr., *University of Louisville*
Olaf Reis, *University of California, Santa Cruz*
Carrie Rothstein-Fisch, *California State University—Northridge*
Stephanie Rowley, *University of Michigan*

Lana Rucks, *Sinclair Community College*
Gloria Russo Wassell, *Cornell University*
Anita L. Saunders, *Alfred University*
Desi Shipp Hacker, *Norfolk State University*
David Shwalb, *Southeastern Louisiana University*
Elizabertha G. Simo, *Houston Community College—Northwest*
Frederick M. Smiley, *Cameron University*
Michael E. Sonntag, *Lander University*
Carol Staben-Burroughs, *Montana State University*
Joyce Tang Boyland, *Alverno College*
Stacy D. Thompson, *Oklahoma State University*
Constance Toffle, *West Virginia University*
Robin West, *University of Florida*
Keith E. Whitfield, *Pennsylvania State University*
Loriena A. Yancura, *University of California, Davis*

In addition, I wish to thank those instructors who participated in our online survey. We've tried to apply the insights gained from their experiences working with the fifth edition to make this new edition better.

Yiling M. Chow, *North Island College*
Rose De Luca, *Bay State College*
Robin Freyberg, *Rutgers University—Livingston*
Rea Gubler, *Southern Utah University*
Sheila Guidry, *Auburn University—Montgomery*
Lisa Hager, *Spring Hill College*
Roderick D. Hetzel, *LeTourneau University*
Richelle Hoekstra-Anderson, *Mid-State Technical College*
Judith M Horowitz, *Medaille College*
Scott L. Horton, *University of Southern Maine*
Linda Layton, *Northcentral Technical College*
Wendy L. Mills, *San Jacinto College North*

John T. Nixon, *State University of New York—Canton*
Sonia K. Ochroch, *Community College of Philadelphia*
Robert R. Rainey Jr., *Florida Community College at Jacksonville*
Jonathan E. Roberts, *Armstrong Atlantic State University*
Jonathan Schwartz, *Yeshiva University*
Elizabeth C. Sites, *Liberty University*
Cindy Stevenson, *Walla Walla Community College*
Christie Suggs, *Wallace Community College*
Riley H. Venable, *Texas Southern University*
Laura M. Wasielewski, *Saint Anselm College*
Doni P. Whitsett, *University of Southern California*
Bernadette Wise, *Iowa Lakes Community College—South*

The editorial, production, and marketing people at Worth Publishers are dedicated to meeting the highest standards of excellence. Their devotion of time, effort, and talent to every aspect of publishing is a model for the industry. I particularly would like to thank: Renée Altier, Jessica Bayne, Cele Gardner, Tracey Kuehn, Meg Kuhta, Bianca Moscatelli, Babs Reingold, Barbara Seixas, and Vivien Weiss.

Dedication

To my daughters, Bethany Ruth Berger, Rachel Stassen-Berger, Elissa Aria Rivka Berger, and Sarah Ariel Martha Berger. They were little girls when I began writing (except Sarah, who was not yet conceived), and they have supported and sustained me all these many years, especially since January 28, 2003, when their father died. I love them now, more than ever.

Kathleen Stassen Berger

New York, February 2004

The Developing Person

Through Childhood and Adolescence

Part I

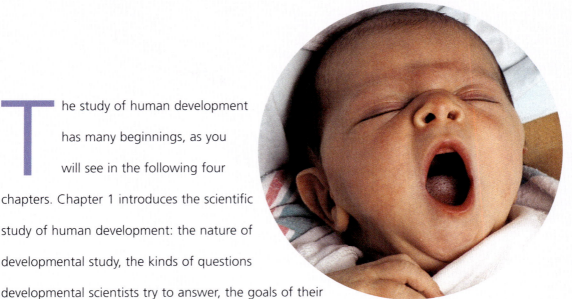

The study of human development has many beginnings, as you will see in the following four chapters. Chapter 1 introduces the scientific study of human development: the nature of developmental study, the kinds of questions developmental scientists try to answer, the goals of their study, and some of the research methods they use to understand human development within specific family, social, cultural, and historical contexts. Chapter 2 explains how theories organize and guide our study of human development. You will be introduced to some major theories—three grand theories and two emergent ones.

Chapter 3 traces the interaction of hereditary and environmental influences. Each human being develops in accordance with chemical guidelines carried on the genes and chromosomes. Interacting with the environment, genes influence everything from the shape of your toes to the swiftness of your brain waves. Personality traits, many diseases, and biological growth are also partly genetic. Understanding the fundamentals of gene–environment interaction is essential to understanding human development.

Chapter 4 details the beginning of human life, from the fusing of sperm and ovum to make one cell to the birth of a developing person, a totally dependent individual who can nevertheless see, hear, and cry, and is ready to engage in social interaction. Those prenatal days are the foundation for the decades that follow, and this chapter introduces some concepts that are fundamental throughout our study of the life span.

The Beginnings

Introduction

scientific study of human development
The science that seeks to understand the ways in which people change and remain the same as they grow older.

You are about to begin a fascinating journey paralleling that of life itself, in which you will follow human development from beginning to end, from the moment of conception to the final breath. This chapter will help you make that journey, providing you with signposts (definitions) and essential equipment (methods), including a working compass (ethics).

Fascinating though this journey is, you may be reluctant to start this book, especially because it includes 100 pages or so on late adulthood and death. Fear not. Life at every stage is exciting; learning about old age is helpful. Socrates understood this when he said:

> I enjoy talking with very old people. They have gone before us on a road by which we, too, may have to travel, and I think we do well to learn from them what it is like.
>
> *[Quoted by Plato, in* The Republic*]*

If this aphorism from an ancient Greek philosopher is not convincing, the lessons of these 25 chapters may be. Keep an open mind.

Studying the Life Span: Five Characteristics

The **scientific study of human development** *seeks to understand how and why people—all kinds of people, everywhere—change, and how they do not change, from conception until death.* Three elements of this definition are crucial.

First, developmental study is a *science*. It depends on theories, data, analysis, critical thinking, and methods similar to those used in every science, from physics to economics. The goal of developmental science is to understand *how and why*, to discover the processes of, and the reasons for, development. We use the scientific method to ask and answer "How?" and "Why?"

Second, the focus is on *all kinds of people,* young and old, rich and poor, male and female, of every ethnicity, background, sexuality, culture, nationality, and so on. The challenge is to describe the universalities (beyond the obvious ones of birth and death) and the differences (beyond the fact that each new conception contains a unique genetic code), and then to describe these universalities and differences in ways that simultaneously distinguish and unify us. For example, when you first meet someone, you recognize that person as human (universal) and as a member of his or her sex and generation (differences within universals; we all have a sex and an age). But when you think about yourself or someone you know well, you realize how much deeper and more particular each individual is. Developmental scientists seek to convey both: the generalities and the specifics.

life-span perspective A view of human development that takes into account all phases of life, not just childhood or adulthood.

The third, and pivotal, element of this definition is *change from conception to death*. *Development* means "change over time," and thus the study of human development requires focusing on all the changes of human life, from the very beginning to the very end.

To further understand this definition, we consider the **life-span perspective**. The life-span perspective is a way of studying human development that takes into account every moment of life, including the first seconds after conception and the years after age 100. This perspective recognizes a "reciprocal connection" between the study of childhood and the study of adulthood (Baltes et al., 1998), linking one chronological period and another. Both *continuity* (as with biological sex and temperament) and *discontinuity* (as with language abilities and health habits) from one time to the next are always evident.

The life-span perspective highlights the fact that even continuity includes change; for example, being female (a lifelong trait) has very different implications for newborns, adolescents, and adults. At the same time, obvious discontinuity nonetheless builds on previous events, as when the babbling infant becomes the adult author.

The life-span perspective emphasizes five distinct characteristics (Baltes et al., 1998; Smith & Baltes, 1999; Staudinger & Lindenberger, 2003):

multidirectional A characteristic of development, referring to its nonlinear progression—gains and losses, compensations and deficits, predictable and unexpected changes.

multicontextual A characteristic of development, referring to the fact that each human life takes place within a number of contexts—historical, cultural, and socioeconomic.

multicultural A characteristic of development, which takes place within many cultural settings worldwide and thus reflects a multitude of values, traditions, and tools for living.

multidisciplinary A characteristic of development encompassing the idea that dozens of academic disciplines contribute data and insight to the science of development.

plasticity A characteristic of development that indicates that individuals—including their personalities as well as their bodies and minds—change throughout the life span.

- **Multidirectional.** Change occurs in every direction, not always in a straight line. Gains and losses, predictable growth and unexpected transformations, are all part of the human experience, evident at every age and with every type of development.
- **Multicontextual.** Human lives are embedded in many contexts, including historical conditions, economic constraints, and cultural traditions.
- **Multicultural.** The science of development recognizes there are many cultures—not just internationally but also within each nation—each with a distinct set of values, traditions, and tools for living.
- **Multidisciplinary.** Numerous academic fields—especially psychology, biology, sociology, and education, but also neuroscience, economics, religion, anthropology, history, medicine, genetics, and many more—contribute data and insight to the science of development.
- **Plasticity.** Every individual, and every trait within each individual, can be altered at any point in the life span. Change is ongoing, although neither random nor easy.

We will now elaborate on each of these five characteristics in turn.

Multidirectional

The study of human development is the study of change; it is dynamic, not static. Developmentalists sometimes analyze each millisecond, as when a barely perceptible change in a newborn's face reflects a parent's fleeting glance. Such moments are fascinating in themselves and also reflect past time (such as the birth process) and predict future events (such as the attachment between parent and child). Thus, each tiny change is embedded in other changes.

Not only milliseconds, but also decades can be analyzed and compared, as several notable scientists have done, again seeing reflections of the past and predictions for the future. The patterns of late adulthood, for instance, depend partly on an individual's personality at age 20, partly on whether he or she has a supportive spouse, and partly on recent events such as retirement (Vaillant, 2002). Similarly, visual and auditory sharpness at age 70, 80, and 90 are connected to earlier health; they also predict mental alertness 10 years later (Baltes, 2003).

In studying change over time, developmentalists have discovered that each aspect of life (physical health, intellectual growth, social interaction) is multi-

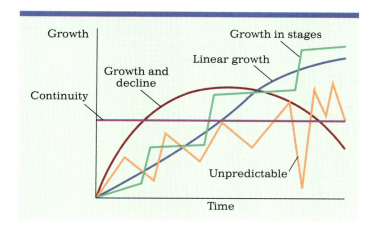

FIGURE 1.1 Patterns of Developmental Growth Many patterns of developmental growth have been discovered by careful research. Although linear (or near-linear) progress seems most common, scientists now find that almost no aspect of human change follows the linear pattern exactly.

directional; any direction—up, down, stable, or erratic—is possible. There is evidence for simple growth, radical transformation, improvement, and decline, as well as for continuity—day to day, year to year, and generation to generation. This diversity is not surprising, once we take into account the elaborate genetic codes that lay the foundation for human growth; the countless particular experiences that shape and refine development; and the multiple influences of family, school, friends, and community—all within ever-changing social and cultural contexts.

Figure 1.1 illustrates some of these many kinds of change. Linear change (the blue line, showing a smooth, gradual increase) is the easiest to envision and measure, but true linear change is unlikely to occur in human life. Development speeds up, slows down, and follows various trajectories; the specifics depend on which aspect of development, in whom, at what age, is being described.

Development is the result of **dynamic systems,** which make measuring change even more complex (Lerner, 1998; van Geert, 2003; Yoshikawa & Hsueh, 2001). "Dynamic" refers to the continual change within each person and each social group; "systems" highlights the systematic connection of each change to other developments in every individual and every society. Let us look at an example of dynamic change.

dynamic systems A process of continual change within a person or group, in which each change is connected systematically to every other development in each individual and every society.

Physical Growth

Body size increases very quickly in the early prenatal hours. Growth slows down as birth approaches and then it temporarily reverses: Newborns lose about 10 percent of their body weight by day 4. Throughout childhood children grow, but not linearly: Growth is fastest at night, when the child is sleeping; height is added faster in summer, weight in winter. Over the years, older children grow more slowly than younger children, but young adolescents experience a sudden growth spurt that slows down as adulthood approaches. Adults stop growing in height and are quite steady in weight as well, unless they overeat or starve. In late adulthood, weight and height normally decrease slowly, with the loss of muscle (greater in men) and bone (greater in women). Sudden weight loss in adulthood is a sign of sickness, not healthy aging. Obviously, for height and weight, as for every kind of change, the path is not linear.

We have described the purely maturational changes in body weight. In addition, as anyone who has stepped on a scale more than once is aware, fluctuations in body weight are affected by many other changes: in appetite, nutrition, family, stress, exercise, culture, food supply, and even climate. Historical changes have powerful effects as well, as shown by the recent emergence of what the United Nations describes as an "epidemic of obesity" in many countries, quite unlike the starvation that was—and in some places still is—a problem. Weight is part of a dynamic system, interacting with other parts of that system and other systems, as are height and every other aspect of growth.

Effects, Large and Small

A small change may have a very large effect, precisely because every change is part of a dynamic system. The potential power of a small change is called the **butterfly effect**, after a 1972 speech by weather expert Edward Lorenz titled "Predictability: Does the Flap of a Butterfly's Wings in Brazil Set Off a Tornado in Texas?" The idea is that, just as a final drop of water might make an overfull glass suddenly spill over, so a small increase in wind in the Amazon might be the final force that triggers a new weather direction resulting in a storm hundreds of miles away. The possibility that small input may result in large output applies to human thoughts and actions as well as to the natural sciences. A tiny change, a small gesture, a single spoken word may have a profound effect on a person's development (Masterpasqua & Perna, 1997).

Closely related is a seemingly opposite idea: A large change may make no perceptible difference. For example, a group of 87 young refugees from war-torn Bosnia, aged 4 to 6 (all of whom had fled their homes and most of whom had been shot at, lost family members, seen dead bodies, and been very hungry), were surprisingly "high on positive characteristics and low on psychological symptoms and problems" (Dybdahl, 2001, p. 1225). The ordeal had much more impact on their mothers, but the aid workers observing the children reported that "the majority managed to cope and function in everyday life" (p. 1226).

Exactly how and why these children emerged relatively unscathed requires further research. It also remains to be seen how these children will develop over time. Because families are dynamic systems, a child's positive coping may restore a mother's psychic balance, further protecting the child, or a mother's ongoing distress may eventually damage her child. For both mother and child, whether or not the father died or survived may also affect their well-being.

The fact that these preschoolers had few problems makes sense when other research is considered. In general, young children can cope with difficult experiences as long as their parents are nearby and supportive. A close bond to a loving caregiver protects against adversity of many kinds, including illness, poverty, and even war (Burlingham & Freud, 1942). In this example, continuity (the mother–child bond) was more powerful than the horrific changes the children experienced, rendering a seemingly large disruption much less unsettling than one might think. The point is that scientific research on human development highlights both the direction and the intensity of change, sometimes with unexpected results.

Much of the research in human development has practical applications, and this research is an example. Fifty years ago, parents were forbidden to visit their hospitalized children, for fear they would bring germs that would make the children sicker. Many children died alone, in hospitals, as a result. Now family members are encouraged to stay with their ill children, and more children recover.

Multicontextual

Humans develop in many contexts that profoundly affect the way they develop. A small contextual change can become the butterfly's wing beat that produces a major shift, even a massive disaster. Contexts include the physical context (for example, climate, noise, urbanization), the family context, and many more. In this chapter, we highlight three aspects of the *social context*, that is, of the society or the social setting, that impact each person throughout life—specifically, the historical, socioeconomic, and cultural contexts.

---

butterfly effect The idea that a small action or event (such as the breeze created by the flap of a butterfly's wings) may set off a series of changes that culminate in a major event (such as a hurricane).

Especially for Nurses How can a person's body temperature be considered multidirectional?

The Historical Context

All persons born within a few years of one another are said to be a **cohort,** a group of people whose shared age means that they travel through life together. (Once the term *cohort* included only people born in the same region and social class as well as the same era, but, with increasing globalization and democratization, *cohort* is now a more inclusive term.) The people in a particular cohort, in other words, are subject to the same history—with the same prevailing assumptions, important public events, technologies, and popular trends. People of the same age tend to be affected similarly; those significantly older or younger may be affected differently or not at all. You can confirm this by asking members of other generations of your family about deficit spending, or smoking marijuana, or the appropriate use of a cell phone. Marijuana smoking, for example, is much more acceptable to those who were born around 1950 than it is to those born in 1930 or 1970, largely because of cohort differences during late adolescence.

As profound economic, political, and technological changes occur over the years, basic concepts about how things "should be" are influenced by how things *were* before the changes occurred. Scholars have discovered that our most cherished assumptions about how things should be are not always generally accepted. Instead, such an assumption is likely to be a **social construction,** an idea built more on shared perceptions than on objective reality. As social shifts occur, social constructions also change, sometimes cohort by cohort.

Right now, for example, perceptions about the role of computers in society are shifting. The oldest cohorts tend to see the Internet as a source of problems—pornography, social isolation, obesity, crime. The middle cohorts consider computers as powerful tools to be mastered. The youngest cohorts think of them as appliances, no more remarkable than toothbrushes or televisions; they want fast, colorful, and audible computers of their own. Each cohort is partly correct; each has its own social construction. In fact, new inventions, from the radio to the automobile and probably even the first campfire or plowed field, have always been judged by the older generations who grew up without them as corrupting the youth, who no longer do things the traditional way (Wartella & Jennings, 2000).

The impact of the historical context varies with age. For example, people tend to remember best and most fondly the events that happened to them in adolescence and early adulthood (Berntsen & Rubin, 2002) and tend to forget or reinterpret childhood deprivation (Vaillant, 2002), so that growing up during a difficult period such as the Great Depression is very difficult from experiencing it as an adult. Take the story of Jimmy, a farm boy in rural Georgia, who breathed red dust continuously in his un-air-conditioned home, who got splinters in his

cohort A group of people whose shared birth year, or decade, means that they travel through life together, experiencing the same major historical changes.

social construction An idea that is built more on shared perceptions of social order than on objective reality.

"You'd better ask your grandparents about that, son— my generation is very uncomfortable talking about abstinence."

Changing Values To some extent, the experiences and values of late adolescence influence each cohort for a lifetime. Maturity does not usually change those values, but at least it can make each generation realize the limitations of its historical context.

bare feet at school, and who would have died of blood poisoning if he hadn't been so eager to help his father in the fields. He tells this story with fond nostalgia in the following Case to Study feature.

A Case to Study

"This Sense of Liberation"

My most persistent memory as a farm boy was of the earth. There was a closeness, almost an immersion, in the sand, loam, and red clay that seemed natural, and constant. The soil caressed my bare feet, and the dust was always boiling up from the dirt road that passed fifty feet from our front door, so that inside our clapboard house the red clay particles, ranging in size from face powder to grits, were ever present, particularly in the summertime, when the wood doors were kept open and the screen just stopped the trash and some of the less adventurous flies. . . .

There is little doubt that I now recall those days with more fondness than they deserve. . . . From as early in March until as late in October as weather and my parents permitted, I never wore shoes. The first warm days of the year brought not only a season of freshness and rebirth, but also a time of renewed freedom for me, when running, sliding, walking through mud puddles, and sinking up to my ankles in the plowed fields gave life a new dimension. I enjoyed this sense of liberation. . . .

There were some disadvantages to bare feet. There was always the possibility of stepping on old barbed wire or a rusty nail, with the danger of tetanus. Another problem was at school. The pine floors were not sanded and polished but rough, the dust kept down by regular applications of used motor oil. We soon learned to pick up our feet with each step, because splinters were prevalent and a threat to bare feet that slid for even an inch across the surface.

Our most common ailments were the endemic ground itch, ringworm, boils and carbuncles, and sties on our eyes, plus the self-inflicted splinters, cuts, abrasions, bruises, wasp or bee stings. . . . On different occasions, I had both arms and three ribs broken, but my most memorable injury was just a small splinter in my wrist. . . . My arm was swollen only slightly, but I couldn't bend my wrist or move my fingers without intense pain, so I stayed at home instead of going to the field. One day, after our noon meal,

as Daddy was leaving to go to work, he said, "The rest of us will be working while Jimmy lies here in the house and reads a book." I was stricken by his remark, knowing that he was disgusted with me when he called me "Jimmy" instead of "Hot." . . . My good reputation as a worker was important to me, and my father's approval was even more precious.

Not knowing what to do, I went out into the pasture near our home, ashamed of my laziness while my Daddy had to work even harder than usual. Desperate for a cure, I finally put my hand against a fencepost with my fingers upward, wrapped my belt tightly around it, and then slowly raised my arm to force my wrist to bend. All of a sudden, to my delight, there was a big eruption of pus, in the midst of which was a half-inch piece of blackened wood. I ran back to the house, got on my bicycle, pedaled it as fast as possible to the cotton field, and reported to Daddy for work. When I showed him the splinter, he smiled and said, "It's good to have you back with us, Hot."

[Carter, 2001, pp. 15, 29, 78–82]

PHYLLIS PICARDI / STOCK SOUTH / PICTUREQUEST

A Clapboard Home Long grass now covers the loam and red clay that 80 years ago felt liberating to the boy named Jimmy. He sometimes slept with the farm family who lived here, although his own home was larger, with more windows, a stone's throw away.

The impact of the historical context can be profound. Compare Jimmy's early life with that of most children in Georgia today: They live in climate-controlled comfort, buy many pairs of shoes at the local mall, and are far more likely to stay in school (only one child in ten graduated from high school in the United States a century ago, compared with about nine in ten today). Indeed, children are far more likely to survive: The child death rate was 100 times greater when Jimmy was a boy than it is today.

The Socioeconomic Context

When social scientists study the second major contextual influence, the socioeconomic context, they often focus on **socioeconomic status,** abbreviated **SES** and sometimes called "social class" (as in middle class or working class).

Socioeconomic status is not determined by income alone. Rather, a family's SES is most accurately measured through a combination of factors, including education, income, neighborhood, and occupation of head of household. (In the past, the father's occupation was the crucial one; now either parent's occupation may be used.) The SES of a family consisting of, say, an infant, an unemployed mother, and a father who earns $12,000 a year would be low if the wage earner is an illiterate dishwasher living in an urban slum but high if the wage earner is a postdoctoral student living on campus and teaching part time.

The point of this example is that SES reflects more than money: It includes all the associated advantages and disadvantages, opportunities and limitations, and relates to past history and future prospects as well as to present status. Although poverty obviously limits access to high-quality housing, medical care, education, and so on, other factors may make the situation better or worse.

The larger social context and people's perception of their SES can have an effect. Some scholars find that low SES is more debilitating if the family lives in a community or nation where the gap between high and low SES is large, because this adds to the psychic burden of those on the bottom of the ladder (Keating & Hertzman, 1999).This is debatable, but all social scientists agree that income is only part of SES.

Not only may disparity in income be more important than absolute level, but change in income may be more important as well. For example, one study of impoverished families whose income improved over three years—although their income was still below average—found that the children did as well in school as middle-class children did (Dearing et al., 2001). The rising income had a more beneficial effect than the actual amount might indicate. Thus, SES is always an influential part of the social context, but the specifics are complex.

Families and Neighborhoods

Low income is a rough but useful indicator of poverty, and poverty is a rough but useful indicator of severe problems (abuse, sickness, drug addiction). Yet it is apparent that some low-income families and some low-income neighborhoods raise children and support adults who are psychologically strong, physically healthy, and successful in many ways. What characterizes such neighborhoods and families?

One crucial variable for a neighborhood is *collective efficacy,* which occurs when neighbors create a functioning, informal network of people who show concern for each other and their block. Such actions as getting rid of trash on the street, repairing broken windows, watching to keep the children safe, and so on are a better measure of the emotional and physical health of the people in a neighborhood than average income (Cohen et al., 2000; Sampson et al., 1997). Religious institutions sometimes enhance collective efficacy, so social scientists looking at neighborhoods assess whether churches, temples, and mosques serve most of the people. Schools, clinics, and stores can also enhance, or undercut, collective efficacy.

LIBRARY OF CONGRESS

Why Not Put the Children to Work? The current view of childhood as a special period given over to formal education and play is a fairly recent one. As late as 1900, one out of every five children between the ages of 10 and 16 in the United States worked, often at dirty and dangerous jobs in factories, mills, and mines. These "breaker" boys, who usually started their work at age 10, had the task of picking out slate and rubble from crushed coal as it came down chutes from giant processors. Their hours were long; their environment was choked with coal dust; and their pay was less than a dollar a day.

socioeconomic status (SES) An indicator of a person's social and economic standing, measured through a combination of family income, educational level, place of residence, occupation, and other variables.

Response for Nurses (from page 6): Body temperature is not constant; it rises or falls with time of day, age, activity level, as well as illness. Body temperature is typically higher in the morning, while studying in one spot, and in old age!

Don't Go There Not just poverty but neglect and crime are evident in this scene on Chicago's South Side. In communities where incomes are low but the residents care about the neighborhood, abandoned cars are towed away, not stripped, and empty buildings are rebuilt, demolished, or at least boarded up, not left with broken windows for rats and drug addicts to enter.

culture The specific manifestations of a social group's design for living, developed over the years to provide a social structure for the group members' life together.

Families benefit from such neighborhoods, and supportive relationships within a family are also crucial. Even if parents are poor, with little formal education, they can be good parents. The quality of parenting is the single most important predictor of a resilient child, which is a child who can overcome many hardships (Duncan & Brooks-Gunn, 2000; Wyman et al., 1999).

Similarly, in adulthood, family support is a better predictor of health and happiness than any objective measure of physical health or personal income (Schneider & Davidson, 2003; Vaillant, 2002). Family respect and cohesion may be the explanation for a surprising statistic from California, the most ethnically and economically diverse state in the United States. Non-Hispanic whites have the highest average SES, but, of those Californians who reach age 70, the average non-Hispanic white dies at age 85, the average Hispanic at 90, and the average Asian-American at 94 (Hayes-Bautista et al., 2002).

The Cultural Context

Culture affects each human at every moment. Precisely because culture is so pervasive, just as a fish does not know it is surrounded by water, people are usually unaware of their culture until they are separated from it or it is challenged. When social scientists use the term **culture,** they refer to the countless specific manifestations of a social group's "design for living." The social group can be citizens of a nation, residents of a region within a nation, members of an ethnic group, or even students in a college community. Any group can have its own culture, which includes values, technologies, customs, clothes, dwellings, cuisine, and patterns of behavior, especially social behavior. For example, do you call professors by their first names? Why or why not? The reasons are cultural.

Culture includes all the decisions that people make, from whether to cover their mouth when they laugh to what to eat for breakfast. Culture is dynamic, changing as people do, and it is also supportive, allowing each person to move

Cherish the Child Cultures vary tremendously in their views of such seemingly personal matters as ideal family size. China's "one-child" policy urges every family to limit reproduction in order to shrink the country's population and to expand its economy.

?*Observational Quiz* (see answer, page 12): What three signs suggest that this community enjoys this boy?

forward through life without spending too much time on every little detail. People tend to think about and question their culture only when a specific aspect seems harmful or when they realize that members of another culture do things differently. To better see how people are influenced by their culture without realizing it, consider where and with whom children from different cultural backgrounds sleep. Most parents never give this much thought; they just put the children to bed. Social scientists traveling around the world discovered that sleeping places are cultural, not natural.

Who Sleeps with Whom?

Suppose you are asked to arrange the sleeping places for a family of six moving into a new apartment. The family consists of a husband and wife, two daughters aged 15 and 2, and two sons aged 6 and 9; the apartment has a living–dining room, a kitchen, one bathroom, and two bedrooms. Think a moment and take a look at Figure 1.2 before reading on.

Have you come up with an arrangement? If you are from an Asian or African culture, you probably see two easy solutions: Either the males sleep in one bedroom and the females in the other, or everyone sleeps in one bedroom, perhaps on mats on the floor, with the other room becoming a reading, studying, and computer room. The close quarters do not pose a problem for people from the many cultures where the company of others, awake or asleep, is preferred (Schweder et al., 1998).

> If you are from a [Western] culture . . . , however, you believe in the ritualized isolation of children during the night, the institution of "bedtime," and the protection of the privacy of the "sacred couple" upheld by a cultural norm mandating the exclusive co-sleeping of the husband and wife.
>
> *[Schweder et al., 1998, p. 873]*

Most Western cultures teach that husband and wife must sleep together, without the children, that infants need to sleep in separate cribs (Nakamura et al., 1999), and that 15-year-olds are already young men or women who need some privacy. Consequently, from this perspective, this family has a problem without a solution—except the one suggested by one of my students: "They must move."

This example highlights an important point. People in a given culture justify their practices as preferable to other possibilities (Westerners might connect communal sleeping with sexual abuse; Easterners might see isolated sleeping as child neglect), but the dynamic connections between practice and culture are far deeper than such justifications suggest. Each culture endorses certain parental strategies—for sleeping, talking, feeding, disciplining, encouraging, playing, and so on—that guide children to develop abilities, values, and expectations that are well suited for the place and time in which they are living. Thus, children who sleep with their parents are being taught to depend on their parents for warmth and protection; children who sleep alone are being taught to become independent of their families. Both practices seem to result in reasonably healthy young adults.

Multicultural

You can see from the preceding discussion that a multicultural approach to the study of human development is useful. Comparing several cultures always makes it much easier to notice which developmental patterns are universal for all humans and which ones depend on the social context. Comparisons can also provide insights into the effects of various practices. These points will become apparent from two examples.

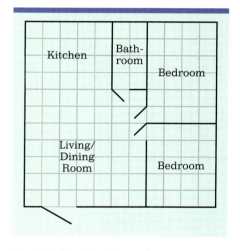

FIGURE 1.2 Who Sleeps Where? A six-person family needs to sleep in the apartment diagrammed here. We have a mother, father, two daughters ages 2 and 15, and two sons ages 6 and 9. Can you figure out where each person should sleep?

Especially for Parents If you think 1-year-olds should not sleep in their parents' room, why do you think that?

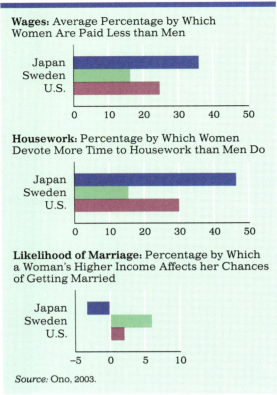

Wages: Average Percentage by Which
Women Are Paid Less than Men

Japan
Sweden
U.S.

0   10   20   30   40   50

Housework: Percentage by Which Women
Devote More Time to Housework than Men Do

Japan
Sweden
U.S.

0   10   20   30   40   50

Likelihood of Marriage: Percentage by Which
a Woman's Higher Income Affects her Chances
of Getting Married

Japan
Sweden
U.S.

−5   0   5   10

Source: Ono, 2003.

FIGURE 1.3 Marry the Rich One? In every nation, women earn less than men and do more housework than men, on average, and in every nation, wealthier men are more likely to marry. The surprise revealed by multicultural data is that, in nations that are closer to sexual equality, women who earn more are more likely to marry, but where the sexes are farther from equality, higher-earning women are less likely to marry.

Response for Parents (from page 11): If you think the child should be in a separate room because the parents need privacy, keep in mind that people can have sex in many places and times other than in their shared bedroom at night. If you think this will teach the child, at a young age, to be independent, your reasoning is plausible: The child is likely to learn not to depend on the parents for warmth and comfort while sleeping.

❗Answer to Observational Quiz (from page 10): At least four adults are smiling at him; he is eating an apple that was brought to the market for sale; he is allowed to sit on the table with the food. If you noticed another sign—his new green sandals—give yourself bonus credit.

Too Rich to Marry?

Worldwide, the richer they are, the more likely men are to marry. A leading theory of marriage is that women seek to marry "good providers"—men who are relatively stable, established workers—while men seek to marry "good housewives"—women who will give them supportive homes and healthy children (Becker, 1981). Are these patterns universal—characteristic of humans regardless of culture? In the current historical context, where gender equality is more widely accepted than it once was, has the gender divide implicit in this theory narrowed at all? It is true that the average groom is still several years older than the average bride, and that fact seems to support the idea that women seek to marry "good providers."

The question then arises: Do women become less desirable marriage partners as they earn more income, presumably becoming less dependent on a husband and less likely to focus on being "good housewives"? A multicultural study of three prosperous nations found that, in general, higher income reduced marriage prospects slightly for women in Japan, increased them slightly for women in the United States, and increased them significantly for women in Sweden (Ono, 2003) (see Figure 1.3). These differences reflect the fact that in many ways, Japanese women experience the least gender equality, Swedish women the most, and American women a level of equality between the other two groups. Thus culture, rather than a universal human pattern, seems to be the crucial factor here, as only a multicultural analysis could have shown.

Now we return to the example of sleeping arrangements, with a multicultural comparison of practices within one nation.

The Children's House

An unusual sleeping arrangement was once common in hundreds of *kibbutzim* (the plural of *kibbutz*) in Israel. A kibbutz is a kind of farming commune whose members share work, meals, income, and child care. Children originally spent several hours each day with their parents but slept in a separate "Children's House" with other children and without adults. (The adults took weekly turns monitoring the children by intercom, in case an emergency arose during the night.) In the communal culture of the kibbutzim, the idea was that this practice would encourage all the children to become loyal to their "brothers and sisters" on the kibbutz, as well as to their biological parents. After about 20 years, however, the practice was changed, first in a few kibbutzim, then in others, primarily because the parents wanted their children with them at night.

The resulting differences in children's experiences created an opportunity to compare the effects of different sleeping practices, as one researcher did (Scharf, 2001). Three groups of 16- to 18-year-olds from more than a dozen kibbutzim were studied: 33 had spent all their nights away from their parents; 34 had begun life sleeping in Children's Houses but had switched before age 6 to sleeping near their parents; and 33 had always slept near their parents. This study also included a fourth group of 31 adolescents who had never lived on a kibbutz but had been raised in the city in their parents' homes and were thus more representative of the mainstream Israeli culture.

The researcher evaluated these four groups of adolescents, particularly their emotions regarding their parents (see Figure 1.4). Many in the group of teenagers who had always slept apart from their parents, especially the boys, had difficulty talking about and relating to their family members (Scharf, 2001). Other research on kibbutz-raised children who slept apart from their parents found similar results (Aviezer et al., 1994).

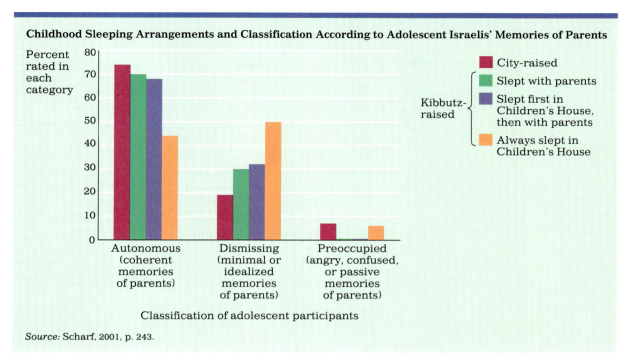

Childhood Sleeping Arrangements and Classification According to Adolescent Israelis' Memories of Parents

Legend:
- City-raised
- Kibbutz-raised: Slept with parents
- Kibbutz-raised: Slept first in Children's House, then with parents
- Kibbutz-raised: Always slept in Children's House

Y-axis: Percent rated in each category

X-axis categories: Autonomous (coherent memories of parents); Dismissing (minimal or idealized memories of parents); Preoccupied (angry, confused, or passive memories of parents)

Classification of adolescent participants

Source: Scharf, 2001, p. 243.

FIGURE 1.4 **The Cost of Early and Continuing Nighttime Separation from Parents** The adolescent participants' tape-recorded reminiscences about their parents were rated by trained researchers who did not know which of the four sleeping arrangements the participants had experienced in childhood. The youngsters were rated as autonomous, dismissing, or preoccupied, according to the criteria established for the Adult Attachment Interview. Those who, as children living on a kibbutz, had slept in a Children's House rather than near their parents were least likely to be rated as autonomous. Overall, the three groups of kibbutz-raised children were more likely to be rated as dismissing, with distorted memories of their parents, than were the city-raised participants.

Note that the crucial factor was not the kibbutz culture in general, but the specific cultural practice of sleeping away from parents during childhood, as the comparisons made clear. Virtually all Israeli kibbutzim now encourage parents to have their children sleep near them. The Children's Houses are empty at night (Oppenheim, 1998), in part because a new cultural practice that once seemed to make logical sense turned out to have unanticipated negative consequences.

Ethnicity, Race, and Income

Much confusion arises when people—both scientists and nonscientists—refer to ethnic groups, racial groups, and income classes, as these categories can overlap in complicated ways. Because multicultural research is so important, and ethnicity can be an important cultural category, we need to untangle these three categories.

Briefly, an **ethnic group** shares certain attributes, almost always including ancestral heritage and often including national origin, religion, and language. (*Heritage* refers to customs and traditions passed down to the present; *national origin* means country of birth or ancestors' birthplace.) An ethnic group, in other words, has a culture, and someone born into an ethnic group may choose to identify with the group and be a part of its culture.

People can belong to more than one culture—they can follow more than one life design. In multiethnic nations such as the United States and Canada, many individuals function well within the majority culture (the national culture), within the culture of their own ethnic group, and, for that matter, within regional, school, and other cultures as well.

Especially for Social Scientists Can you think of any cultural assumptions that might have led to the now-universal practice in Israel of having kibbutz children sleep near their parents?

ethnic group A collection of people who share certain attributes, almost always including ancestral heritage and often including national origin, religion, customs, and language.

Especially for Immigrants Why might it be unwise for you to abandon the customs of your native culture?

race A social construction by which biological traits (such as hair or skin color, facial features, and body type) are used to differentiate people whose ancestors came from various regions of the world.

Response for Social Scientists (from page 13): Researchers as well as leaders in Israel assume that children should have strong relationships with their parents. Could this assumption itself be a social construction?

Ethnic categories have their basis in history, sociology, and psychology, not in biology. The term **race,** in contrast, is intended to categorize people biologically— on the basis of genetic differences and variations in appearance (skin, hair, eyes, and body structure). However, the concept of race is problematic, and social scientists prefer not to use racial categories: There are no clear-cut racial groups, and differences among people supposedly of the same race are greater than average differences among people of different races. Ethnicity and culture affect development in many ways; race in and of itself does not (Bamshad & Olson, 2003), unless others react to a person's "race" and the person responds.

Social scientists have only recently realized that race is a distorted concept. In 1970, the U.S. census categorized people as white, black, and other. Three new categories were added in 1980: "Asian and Pacific Islander," "American Indian, Eskimo, Aleut," and "Hispanic, may be of any race" (Hispanics also had to choose "white" or "black"). In the 2000 census, "Asian" was separated from "Native Hawaiian and Pacific Islander," and, for the first time, people were allowed to check "more than one race." The 2010 census will, undoubtedly, change the categories again. Suffice it to say that, although much traditional research used racial categories, the term *race* is less and less used, and less useful, in social science.

To further complicate matters, SES variations tend to follow ethnic variations, so that developmental patterns reflect both income and ethnic influences (U.S. Bureau of the Census, 2002). For example, only 5 percent of Hispanics in the United States live alone, but almost 15 percent of European-Americans do. Is this cultural, in that Hispanics value family closeness and interdependence, or is it income-related, in that Hispanics earn only about 60 percent as much as European-Americans and hence fewer single adults and widows can afford their own apartments? Among African-Americans, the elderly only rarely live in nursing homes. Is this because of respect for the elderly within the culture or because social services within the majority culture discriminate against those who are poor, making early death more likely and admission to nursing homes more difficult for low-income people, many of whom are nonwhite? Answers are difficult; researchers are very cautious about ascribing any particular result to ethnicity or income.

Multidisciplinary

The study of human development requires insight and information from many disciplines, because each person develops simultaneously in body, mind, and spirit. Development is thus often divided into three domains—the biosocial, cognitive, and psychosocial—that roughly correspond to biology, psychology, and sociology. This textbook follows that division, with three chapters covering each age period. Many other disciplines are also reflected throughout. As one expert explains: "The study of development is a huge community enterprise that spans generations and many disciplines" (Moore, 2002, p. 74). Human beings develop not only in various domains but also within multifaceted contexts and cultures. This means that if we hope to understand human development or the development of any given person, we need facts and insights from several disciplines.

Consider one family in a Michigan town where unemployment was rampant. Richard and Oracene Williams found themselves with too little money and, soon, too many children. They were far from being a conventional family, as shown by the unconventional names of their daughters—Isha, Lyndrea, Yetude (from Oracene's first marriage), Venus, and Serena (Richard's biological children)—by their willingness to move across the country to Los Angeles, and by the father's determination to craft his two youngest daughters into tennis stars. When Venus was 4 and Serena 3, they began playing tennis. Fifteen years later, they were among the world's top five women players, each having been ranked number one at some point. By 2003, in the Grand Slams, the most prestigious tournaments in tennis, Venus had won four singles titles and Serena six, they had won six women's doubles titles together, and they had each also won two mixed-doubles titles.

Is this story astonishing? Of course it is. However, drawing on many disciplines, developmentalists can gain insights into Venus and Serena's success:

- Biologists would note that physical strength among practiced athletes peaks at about age 20—right around the age at which Venus and then Serena rose to the top of women's tennis.

- Sociologists would note that this family chose a different path from the beginning and that their drive and dedication enabled Venus and Serena to practice tennis many hours a day.

- Psychologists would add that teenagers who are unusually talented (athletes, musicians, mathematicians, or whatever) are characterized by two traits: (1) evident genetic strength and (2) at least one parent who enables them to succeed, providing lessons, practice time, motivation, and equipment even if it means sacrificing necessities (as the Williams family did).

- Family therapists note that siblings typically support and challenge each other (Volling, 2003). As the youngest, Serena used to lose to Venus: Surely some of her present power comes from her wish to defeat her older sister.

SEAN GARNSWORTHY / GETTY IMAGES

Double Winners In the 2003 Australian Open, Venus *(left)* and Serena *(right)* Williams won the women's doubles championship, their fourth consecutive Grand Slam tournament final. The sisters' tennis-playing prowess is awesome, but not incredible to any developmentalist who takes a multidisciplinary approach to their family history. When 3-year-old Serena first hit a tennis ball to 4-year-old Venus, she was on her way to being ranked the world's number one women's player in 2003; Venus earned that honor in 2002.

More broadly, a combination of nature and nurture (further discussed in Chapters 2 and 3) is evident for every shining young talent, from Johann Sebastian Bach to Drew Barrymore. Developmentalists from every discipline notice family traits—both good and bad—echoed from generation to generation. Human variations are endless, but they are not totally unpredictable.

This means that a discerning scientist could have predicted success for the Williams sisters by the time they were 10. Of course, hindsight is always keener than foresight, and understanding what factors helped Venus and Serena become such good tennis players does not diminish the awe inspired by their victories. They are an inspiration to other families, who now understand that talented children need parental help if they are to become prodigies or superstars.

The most interesting question is, What next? Superstars must be unusually flexible and dedicated to stay at the top for more than a few years. One reporter quoted Serena: "I'm an actress, I'm a model, and an athlete . . . I prefer to put tennis third" (Tebbutt, 2003). Developmentalists, using many disciplines to focus on this family, would find Serena's statement neither troubling nor surprising; no one makes the same choices at age 15, 20, and 30.

Plasticity

The final characteristic emphasized by the life-span perspective, plasticity, or the capacity to change, is a particularly encouraging one. The term *plasticity* denotes two complementary aspects of development. Human traits can be molded into different forms and shapes (as plastic can be) yet people maintain a certain durability (again, like plastic).

Plasticity provides both hope and realism—hope because change is possible, and realism because people must build on what has come before. Genes, families, cultures, and experiences—those are the raw material from which humans mold and shape their lives. People can overcome handicaps and reexamine values, but

Response for Immigrants (from page 13): Because cultures develop for reasons, a custom that seems superficial and old-fashioned in your new country may be part of an interdependent design for living; changing one custom may affect many other aspects of your life. This does not mean that change is bad; it simply means that aspects of both the old culture and the new culture should be examined before being adopted or discarded.

they cannot ignore them. No matter what directional path a person follows, the journey begins at some particular point and then proceeds up, down, or straight ahead. To better understand the hope and limits of plasticity, consider another case study, this one of my nephew David.

In Person

My Nephew David

In the spring of 1967, in rural Kentucky, an epidemic of rubella (German measles) struck two particular victims—my sister-in-law, who had a rash and a sore throat for a couple of days, and her 4-week-old embryo, who was damaged for life. David was born in November, with a life-threatening heart defect and thick cataracts covering both eyes. Other damage included minor malformations of the thumbs, feet, jaw, and teeth, as well as of the brain.

The historical context was crucial. Had David been conceived a decade later, widespread use of the rubella vaccine would have protected him from damage. Had he been born a few years earlier, he would have died. Indeed, some doctors expected David to live briefly as a severely retarded child requiring custodial care. But in 1967 the new miracle of microsurgery saved his tiny heart and his life.

My brother is a professor and his wife is a nurse; their cultural and socioeconomic contexts encouraged them to seek outside help rather than accept their fate. They asked advice from a teacher at the Kentucky School for the Blind. She knew that development is plastic and that early guidance can help individuals overcome disabilities, because she had seen this happen in many other people. She told them to stop blaming themselves and stop overprotecting David. If their son was going to learn about his world, he had to explore it.

For example, rather than confining David to a crib or playpen, they were to provide him with a large rug for a play area. Whenever he crawled off the rug, they were to say "No" and place him back in the middle of it. He would learn to use his sense of touch to decide where he could explore safely without bumping into walls or furniture. They followed this advice.

Nonetheless, progress was slow. Rubella had damaged much more than David's eyes and heart. At age 3, he could not yet talk, chew solid food, use the toilet, coordinate his fingers, or even walk normally. An IQ test showed him to be severely mentally retarded. Fortunately, however, although most children with rubella syndrome have hearing defects, David's hearing was normal.

By 1972, when David turned 5, the social construction that children with severe disabilities are unteachable was being seriously challenged. David's parents found four schools that would accept a child with multiple handicaps. In accordance with the family's emphasis on education, they enrolled him in all four. He attended two schools for children with cerebral

palsy: One had morning classes, and the other—40 miles away—afternoon classes. (David ate lunch in the car with his mother on the daily trip.) On Fridays these schools were closed, so he attended a school for the mentally retarded.

On Sundays he spent two hours in church school, which was his first experience with "mainstreaming"—the then-new idea that children with special needs should be educated with normal children. Particularly in the church community, the cultural-ethnic context of northern Kentucky benefited David: Accepting the disabled and helping neighbors are basic Appalachian values.

At age 7, David entered a public school, one of the first severely disabled children to be mainstreamed. His motor

Three Brothers Studying the development of other people is fascinating in many ways, not the least of which is that no human is untouched by understanding the personal story of another. I have learned many things from David, shown in this recent family photo with his two older brothers, Bill *(left)* and Michael *(right)*. One is the role of siblings: Bill and Michael protected their younger brother, but David also taught them, making them more nurturant than most young men in their community. I know this firsthand—these boys were the closest thing my daughters had to big brothers, and they tolerated teasing that some older cousins would have put a stop to.

skills were poor (among other things, he had difficulty controlling a pencil); his efforts to read were limited by the fact that he was legally blind; and his social skills were seriously impaired (he pinched people he didn't like, hugged girls too tightly, cried and laughed at inappropriate times).

By age 10, David had skipped a year of school and was a fifth-grader. He could read—with a magnifying glass—at the eleventh-grade level and was labeled "intellectually gifted" according to tests of verbal and math skills. Outside of school he began to learn a second language, play the violin, and sing in the choir.

David now calls his college experience an "adversity," and certainly many of his peers and professors were unprepared for a student like him. He sometimes seemed to learn *too* well, asking precise questions and remembering numbers and words that most students would forget. He sometimes took offense at inadvertent slights. But he finally graduated with a double major in Russian and German. He studied in Germany to refine his translating skills and now earns his living as a translator (a choice that may have grown from David's need to listen carefully, since he cannot see social nuances of facial expressions). His latest report is that he is

> generally quite happy, but secretly a little happier lately, especially since November, because I have been consistently getting a pretty good vibrato when I am singing, not only by myself but in congregational hymns in church. [He explained vibrato:] When a note bounces up and down within a quarter tone either way of concert pitch, optimally between 5.5 and 8.2 times per second.
>
> *[David, 2002]*

Amazing. David is both knowledgeable and happy, and he continues to develop his skills. He also has a wry sense of humor. When I told him that I wasn't progressing as fast as I wanted to in revising this text, even though I was working very hard every day, he replied, "That sounds just like a certain father I know." As his aunt, I have watched David defy many pessimistic predictions. The rubella damage will always be with him, limiting his development. But David is a testimony for plasticity as well: No human is entirely or inevitably restricted. Contexts, for good or ill, always matter.

The Person Within the Context

The five characteristics of human development emphasized by the life-span perspective all point toward the same conclusion: No one is exactly like the statistically "average" person of his or her cohort, socioeconomic status, or culture. Each person is guided in divergent directions by many contextual influences, whose power varies from individual to individual, age to age, situation to situation, and family to family. Moreover, each person has unique genes and experiences, and each might defy easy predictions. David was not expected to survive and thrive, but he did; the daughters of low-income African-Americans were not expected to become the best in tennis, but the Williams sisters did; a rural Georgia lad was not expected to become president of the United States, but Jimmy Carter did. People can and do develop in ways that defy expectations; they can even help change the contexts that have shaped them.

This is illustrated by another passage from Jimmy Carter's autobiography. He grew up in a southern community in the 1930s where racial segregation was accepted without question. He was white, and A.D., his best friend, was black. He writes that sometimes

> Daddy let A.D. and me go to Americus to see a movie by ourselves. We had to walk up the railroad to Archery, find the little red leather flag left for the purpose, and stick it upright in a hole in the end of a crosstie. The engineer would see the signal and stop so we could board in front of the section foreman's house. It cost fifteen cents each, and we parted company during the ride to sit in the seats marked "white" and "colored." When we arrived in Americus we walked together to the Rylander Theater and separated again, A.D. paying his dime at a back entrance and sitting in the high third level while I went in to sit either downstairs or in the first balcony. Afterward, we would go back home, united in friendship though physically divided on the segregated train. Our only strong feeling was one of gratitude for our wonderful excursion; I don't remember ever questioning the mandatory racial separation, which we accepted like breathing.
>
> *[Carter, 2001, pp. 95–96]*

Life After the Prime At age 57, Jimmy Carter lost his bid for reelection as president of the United States. However, he has demonstrated in the subsequent decades that an active, productive life can continue through late adulthood. He has published 14 books; led delegations worldwide to promote peace, democracy, and adequate housing; and won the Nobel Peace Prize in 2002, at age 78. He is shown here on his historic visit to Cuba that same year—the first U.S. president, in or out of office, to visit Cuba since the communist Castro regime came to power in 1959.

CRISTOBAL HERRERA / AP PHOTO

Not the Usual Path Despite her age, this woman has set out to walk the Appalachian Trail from Maine to Georgia. If we use a life-span perspective, this is not a surprise, because she always enjoyed exercise and the outdoors, and covering the trail's entire 2,160-mile length was her lifelong ambition.

When they got older, both Jimmy and A.D. fought against racial segregation, which they had come to believe was very wrong. But their childhood historical and cultural context had created a racist social construction that was "accepted like breathing." They came to understand that segregation was wrong in part because contexts were changing. Obviously, the political and social events of the 1950s and 1960s opened their eyes, as it did for most Americans. Perhaps Jimmy's personal experiences and scientific training (he studied engineering in college) enlightened him sooner than other people. As Paul Baltes, the founder of life-span developmental study, reminds us, "We need to keep in mind that the future is not something we simply enter, the future is also something we help create" (Baltes, 2003, p. 38). Jimmy Carter, among many others, changed the culture.

Human development is a science that seeks to understand how people change throughout their lives. Each life is a dynamic system, characterized by change that is multidirectional. Every social context has an impact on the development of each person. For example, historical and socioeconomic conditions make some paths through life much more attractive than others and close off other directions completely. Similarly, culture is pervasive, affecting choices from the first sleeping and eating patterns to family formation and adult work, although people tend to be unaware of cultural influences unless these are highlighted in some way. Because a multicultural approach makes contrasts and similarities more evident, it is an integral part of the life-span perspective. Developmental study is also multidisciplinary, drawing on biology, psychology, and sociology, as well as on other disciplines. Plasticity is possible at every stage of life, which means not only that change can always occur but also that change builds on prior developments.

Developmental Study as a Science

Because the study of human development is a science, it is based on objective evidence. Because it concerns human life and growth, it is also laden with personal implications and applications. This interplay of the objective and the subjective, of the universal and the individual, of young and old, of past, present, and future makes developmental science a challenging, fascinating, and even transformative study. Of all the sciences, the study of human development is perhaps the most dynamic, unpredictable, and interdisciplinary. It also may have the most noble goal: "explaining, assessing, and promoting change and development" (Renninger & Amsel, 1997, p. xi). In other words, developmental scientists seek not only to understand and measure human change but also to use their knowledge to help all people develop their full potential.

This lofty goal is of vital importance. Everyone has heartfelt opinions about how children should grow, why they turn out as they do, and where and when adults should find work or romance or religion. By definition, opinions are subjective and tend to be biased, or influenced, by our particular backgrounds and experiences. The goal is universal; the methods vary.

The Scientific Method

scientific method An approach to the systematic pursuit of knowledge that, when applied to the study of development, involves five basic steps: Formulate a research question, develop a hypothesis, test the hypothesis, draw conclusions, and make the findings available.

To the scientist, faithful to the evidence and eager to advance knowledge, there is as much joy in being "wrong" as right (Hofer, 2002). Scientists ask questions and seek answers, always examining what has been taken for granted. The **scientific method,** as it applies to developmental study, involves four basic steps and sometimes a fifth:

1. *Formulate a research question.* On the basis of previous research or a particular theory or personal observation, pose a question about development.

2. *Develop a hypothesis.* Reformulate the question as a **hypothesis,** which is a specific prediction that can be tested.

3. *Test the hypothesis.* Design and conduct a research project that will provide evidence—in the form of data—about the hypothesis.

4. *Draw conclusions.* Use the evidence to support or refute the hypothesis. Assess any limitations of the research (including limitations related to the particular participants) and any alternative explanations for the results. Suggest further research.

5. *Make the findings available.* Publishing the research is often the fifth step in the scientific method. It involves describing the procedure and results in sufficient detail that other scientists can evaluate the conclusions or replicate the research. **Replication** is the repetition of a scientific study, using the same procedures on another group of participants, to verify or refute the original study's conclusions.

hypothesis A specific prediction that is stated in such a way that it can be tested and either confirmed or refuted.

replication The repetition of a scientific study, using the same procedures on another group of participants, to verify or refute the original study's conclusions.

Research Methods

Between the questions developmental scientists ask (steps 1 and 2) and the answers they find (steps 4 and 5) lies their methodology—the specific strategies or methods used to gather and analyze data and test hypotheses. These strategies are critical because "the ways that you attempt to clarify phenomena in large measure determine the worth of the solution" (Cairns & Cairns, 1994). In other words, *how* research is designed affects the *validity* (does it measure what it purports to measure?), *accuracy* (are the measurements correct?), *generalizability* (does it apply to other populations and situations?), and *usefulness* (can it solve real-life problems?) of the conclusions.

Some general strategies to make research valid, accurate, and useful are described in Appendix B. The major theories of human development, which give rise to many research questions, are explained in Chapter 2. Now we turn to four methods of testing hypotheses: observations, experiments, surveys, and case studies. Remember, the overall goal is to find evidence that answers questions and to do so in a way that minimizes biases and other potential problems.

Observation

Often hypotheses regarding human development are first examined via **scientific observation**—that is, observing and recording, in a systematic and objective manner, what people do. Observations often occur in a naturalistic setting, such as at home, in a workplace, or on a public street. Typically, the observing scientist tries to be as unobtrusive as possible, so that the people being studied (the research participants) act as they normally would.

Observation can also occur in a laboratory. In this setting, the scientists sometimes are not visibly present at all; they may sit behind one-way windows that allow them to peer, unnoticed, into the experimental room, or they may record data with a video camera placed on the wall. In the laboratory, scientists study many aspects of behavior, such as the rate and duration of eye contact between infant and caregiver, the patterns of dominance and submission that emerge as an entire family discusses its vacation plans, the heart rate and brain activity of a man watching a frightening movie.

Observation has one major limitation, however. It does not indicate what causes the behavior we observe. We may notice that one 11-year-old sneaks a beer and another does not, but observation does not tell us *why* there is this difference between these two youngsters.

scientific observation A method of testing hypotheses by unobtrusively watching and recording participants' behavior either in a laboratory or in a natural setting.

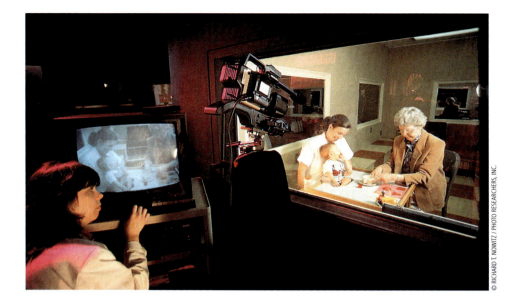

© RICHARD T. NOWITZ / PHOTO RESEARCHERS, INC.

Do Not Disturb: Science in Progress Does any 6-month-old understand that cups go on saucers, that circles are not squares, and that mothers know the answers when a child does not? In this laboratory observation, one scientist elicits the answers while another videotapes the results for later analysis.

correlation A number indicating the degree of relationship between two variables, expressed in terms of the likelihood that one variable will (or will not) occur when the other variable does (or does not). A correlation is *not* an indication that one variable *causes* the other.

Correlation and Causation The preceding brings up an important distinction between establishing correlation and proving causation. Naturalistic observation provides no definitive answers about causes. The data can prove that certain variables correlate with other variables, not that one causes another.

A **correlation** exists between two variables if one variable is more (or less) likely to occur when the other occurs. For instance, in the United States, young adolescents who abuse alcohol are more likely to be male than female and more likely to be non-Hispanic white (European-American) than black (African-American) (Johnston et al., 2001). Thus, there are correlations between drinking and being male and European-American. But why? Are hormones, upbringing, advertising, or peer pressure the reason? Are African-Americans protected by genes or religion? All are logical hypotheses. Correlation indicates a connection, but it does not specify the reason for that connection.

The Experiment

experiment A research method in which the researcher tries to determine the cause-and-effect relationship between two variables by manipulating one variable (called the *independent variable*) and then observing and recording the resulting changes in the other variable (called the *dependent variable*).

independent variable In an experiment, the variable that is introduced or changed to see what effect it has on the dependent variable.

dependent variable In an experiment, the variable that may change as a result of the introduction of or changes made in the independent variable.

An **experiment** is a method that scientists use to try to determine causation. In the social sciences, experimenters typically expose a group of people to a particular treatment or condition to see if their behavior changes as a result. For example, they might provide healthy breakfasts in school for low-income children, to see if over time the children's scores on achievement tests improve.

In technical terms, experimenters manipulate an **independent variable** (the treatment or special condition). They note how that change affects the specific behavior they are studying, which is called the **dependent variable.** Thus, the independent variable is the new, special treatment; the dependent variable is the response (which may or may not be affected by the independent variable).

Finding out which independent variables affect which dependent variables, and how great that effect may be, is the purpose of an experiment. By measuring a dependent variable before and after an independent (experimental) variable is imposed, and assessing changes, researchers are often able to show a link between cause and effect. If breakfast (independent variable) improves achievement (dependent variable), then a causal link can be established. This is the reason experiments are performed: No other research method can so accurately pinpoint what leads to what.

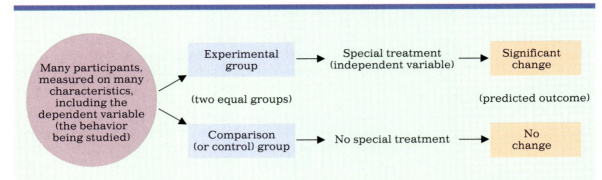

Procedure:

1. Divide subjects into two groups that are matched on important characteristics, especially the behavior that is the dependent variable of this research.

2. Give special treatment, or intervention (the independent variable), to one group (the experimental group).

3. Compare the groups on the dependent variable. If they now differ, the cause of the difference was probably the independent variable.

4. Publish the results.

FIGURE 1.5 How to Conduct an Experiment

? *Observational Quiz* (see answer, page 23): Does the experimental group always change?

experimental group In an experiment, the participants who are given a particular treatment.

comparison group In an experiment, the participants who are not given special treatment but who are similar to the experimental group in other relevant ways. (Also called the *control group*.)

Note, however, that an experiment conducted in this way could be misleading: Maybe something else improved the test scores. Another group must be measured. Thus, in a typical experiment (as diagrammed in Figure 1.5), two groups of participants are studied: an **experimental group,** which is given a particular treatment (the independent variable), and a **comparison group** (also called a *control group*), which does not get the special treatment but is similar to the experimental group in other ways (such as age, ethnicity, SES).

In the study of the Bosnian refugees mentioned on page 6, data were collected on a dozen variables for all the mothers and children (dependent variables). Half of the mothers were then given special counseling (the independent variable) to help them cope with their children's reactions to their wartime experiences. These women's children constituted the experimental group. The other mothers received no counseling; their children were the comparison group.

After five months, all the children were examined again. Few significant differences were found between the experimental and comparison groups of children. (*Significant* and *insignificant* are statistical terms that indicate the likelihood that the results did or did not occur by chance. In this study, most improvements—in mental health, in achievement, and so on—were so slight, and the total number of children involved was so small, that most changes were insignificant; that is, they could have happened by chance.) The only significant changes were biological: The children in the experimental group gained more weight over the five-month period than the other children did (Dybdahl, 2001).

In trying to understand why the counseling sessions did not improve emotional health, the author speculates that the treated mothers talked with the comparison-group mothers, so that all benefited. In order to verify this explanation, the intervention would have to be repeated with new groups who were kept separate from each other. It is also possible that counseling did not help the children because they did not need help. Remember, they were surprisingly unscathed by the civil war. Or perhaps the mothers did not benefit from counseling. Other research finds that counseling after a psychological trauma is often ineffective (McNally, Bryant, & Ehlers, 2003).

With all experiments, questions remain. First, to what extent do the findings from an artificial experimental situation apply in the real world? A major problem with many experiments is that the controlled situation, with the scientist manipulating the independent variable, is different in important ways from normal, everyday life. This problem has led many developmental scientists to do field research (as with the Bosnian children), but then the results are rarely as clear as in a laboratory.

In addition, in most experiments (except those with very young children) the participants know they are research subjects. Participants may attempt to produce the results they believe the experimenter is looking for, or, especially if they are adolescents, they may try to undermine the study. Even if the participants do not react in either of these ways, almost all are more nervous than they otherwise would be. As discussed in detail in Chapter 24, this is a particular problem for the elderly, who perform less well when they think an experiment will "prove" they are becoming senile.

Ideally, an experiment avoids these pitfalls by relying on natural conditions, which become the independent variable. Natural conditions can create an experimental and a comparison group. In the study of the kibbutz children, the independent variable was children's sleeping conditions (either near or apart from their parents), and the dependent variable was the adolescents' emotional relationships to family members. This study was a *natural experiment*, recommended as the most accurate and ethical way to conduct developmental research on children (Bronfenbrenner, 1979). However, for some research questions, such as those on perception or memory, artificial conditions are best to prove or disprove a hypothesis.

The Survey

survey A research method in which information is collected from a large number of people by personal interview, written questionnaire, or some other means.

A third research method is called the **survey.** Information is collected from a large number of people by personal interview, written questionnaire, or some other means. This is an easy, quick, and direct way to obtain data. Surveys are especially useful when scientists want to learn about children, because an obvious way of doing so is to ask parents or teachers.

Unfortunately, getting valid data through an interview or questionnaire is more difficult than it seems, because these methods are vulnerable to bias from both the researcher and the respondents. The questions can be biased, and the particular phrasing can lead people to answer in a particular way. For example, far more people are in favor of allowing a woman to "terminate an unwanted pregnancy" if her partner agrees than of letting a couple "kill an unborn child." In addition, many people who are interviewed may respond inaccurately or with answers that they think will make them seem wise or good.

The Case Study

case study A research method in which one individual is studied intensively.

Finally, a **case study** is an intensive study of one individual. Typically, the case study is based on interviews with the person regarding his or her background, current thinking, and actions; it may also utilize interviews of people who know the individual. Additional case-study material may be obtained through observation, experiments, and standardized tests, such as personality inventories and intelligence tests. (A true case study is much more detailed than the excerpts presented in the feature called "A Case to Study" in this book.)

Case studies have been called the "bedrock" of psychological research (Coleman, 2002); they provide a wealth of detail, which makes them rich in possible insights. Many developmentalists prefer case studies precisely for that reason: The complexity of a human life is easier to comprehend through the rich *qualitative,* or descriptive, information of a case study than through the sheer numbers of a *quantitative* study. Nonetheless, a careful quantitative study is more objective, at least in some ways. The collection and interpretations of case-study information reflect the biases as well as the wisdom of the researcher. Moreover, even when a case study is carefully collected and interpreted, the conclusions apply with certainty to only one person. The case study has two important uses:

- To understand a particular individual very well
- To provide a provocative starting point for other research

No confident conclusions about people in general can be drawn from a sample size of 1, or even 10 or 20, no matter how deep and detailed the study is; yet, without case studies and our own personal experiences, the study of development would be dry and irrelevant for most of us.

> The scientific method is designed to help researchers answer questions with carefully collected evidence. In general, all scientists gather data and draw conclusions based on the data they find. They report their methods, findings, and conclusions so that other scientists can build on their work or question their results. There are many ways to gather developmental data, and each method compensates for the weaknesses of the others. Researchers can observe people in naturalistic or laboratory settings, or they can experimentally elicit reactions under controlled conditions or take advantage of unusual natural experiments. They can survey hundreds or even thousands of people, or interview a smaller number of people in great depth, or study one life in detail. Each method brings researchers closer to the issues and answers. Together the methods can either support or refute hypotheses and theories.

Studying Changes over Time

Remember the definition on page 3: The scientific study of human development seeks to understand how and why people—all kinds of people, everywhere—change, and how they do not change, from conception until death. Accordingly, for research to be truly developmental, it must be able to deal with things that change and continue *over time*.

Developmental scientists use the methods just described—observations, experiments, and so on—but they add another dimension to measure developmental change. More specifically, they design their research so that it includes time, or age, as a factor. Usually they accomplish this with one of three basic designs: cross-sectional, longitudinal, or cross-sequential (see Figure 1.6).

Cross-Sectional Research

The most convenient, and thus more common, way to include age in a developmental study is by designing **cross-sectional research.** In a cross-sectional study, groups of people who differ in age but share other important characteristics (such as level of education, socioeconomic status, and ethnic background) are compared. Cross-sectional design seems simple enough, but it is very difficult to ensure that the various groups being compared are similar in every important background variable except age. Let's look at a simple, hypothetical example of cross-sectional research.

Suppose a group of 10-year-olds are found to weigh 11 pounds (5 kilograms) more than a comparable group of 6-year-olds. It seems reasonable to conclude that during the four years between ages 6 and 10, children gain an average of 11

! *Answer to Observational Quiz* (from page 21): No. Note the word *predicted*. The hypothesis is that change will occur for the experimental group and not the control group, but the reason for doing the experiment is to discover whether that prediction does indeed come true.

cross-sectional research A research method in which groups of people who differ in age but share other important characteristics are compared.

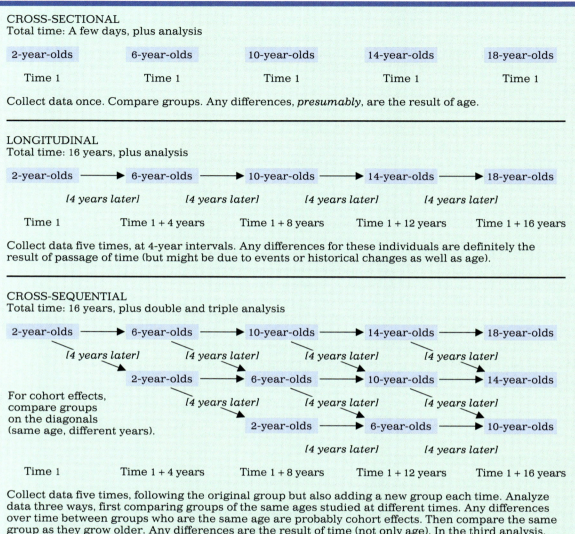

CROSS-SECTIONAL
Total time: A few days, plus analysis

| 2-year-olds | 6-year-olds | 10-year-olds | 14-year-olds | 18-year-olds |
| Time 1 | Time 1 | Time 1 | Time 1 | Time 1 |

Collect data once. Compare groups. Any differences, *presumably*, are the result of age.

LONGITUDINAL
Total time: 16 years, plus analysis

2-year-olds ⟶ 6-year-olds ⟶ 10-year-olds ⟶ 14-year-olds ⟶ 18-year-olds

[4 years later]   *[4 years later]*   *[4 years later]*   *[4 years later]*

Time 1   Time 1 + 4 years   Time 1 + 8 years   Time 1 + 12 years   Time 1 + 16 years

Collect data five times, at 4-year intervals. Any differences for these individuals are definitely the result of passage of time (but might be due to events or historical changes as well as age).

CROSS-SEQUENTIAL
Total time: 16 years, plus double and triple analysis

2-year-olds ⟶ 6-year-olds ⟶ 10-year-olds ⟶ 14-year-olds ⟶ 18-year-olds

[4 years later]   *[4 years later]*   *[4 years later]*   *[4 years later]*

     2-year-olds ⟶ 6-year-olds ⟶ 10-year-olds ⟶ 14-year-olds

For cohort effects, compare groups on the diagonals (same age, different years).

[4 years later]   *[4 years later]*   *[4 years later]*

         2-year-olds ⟶ 6-year-olds ⟶ 10-year-olds

[4 years later]   *[4 years later]*

Time 1   Time 1 + 4 years   Time 1 + 8 years   Time 1 + 12 years   Time 1 + 16 years

Collect data five times, following the original group but also adding a new group each time. Analyze data three ways, first comparing groups of the same ages studied at different times. Any differences over time between groups who are the same age are probably cohort effects. Then compare the same group as they grow older. Any differences are the result of time (not only age). In the third analysis, compare differences between the same people as they grow older, *after* the cohort effects (from the first analysis) are taken into account. Any remaining differences are almost certainly the result of age.

FIGURE 1.6 Which Is Best? Cross-sequential research is the most time-consuming and most complex approach, but it also yields the best information about development. This is one reason why hundreds of scientists conduct research on the same topics, replicating one another's work—to gain some of the advantages of cross-sequential research without having to wait all those years.

pounds. However, even such an obvious conclusion might be wrong. It could be that the particular 10-year-olds in the study were better nourished throughout their lives than the particular 6-year-olds or that they had some other relevant characteristic that was not accounted for. Certainly, if the 10-year-old group compared with the 6-year-old group included more boys than girls or more Africans than Asians, the weight difference would reflect sex or ethnicity as well as age.

Of course, good scientists try to make cross-sectional groups similar in every major background variable. Nevertheless, even if two cross-sectional groups were identical except for age, they would still reflect cohort differences because each age group was born in a different historical period. In this example, even four years could make a difference in the typical diet, as new snacks are introduced each year and schools change exercise programs.

More broadly, factors in any domain could change over four years. In a biosocial domain, a particular childhood disease might have emerged or been eliminated or levels of nutrition could have changed (e.g., because of a war or

Compare These with Those The apparent similarity of these two groups in gender and ethnic composition makes them candidates for cross-sectional research. Before we could be sure that any difference between the two groups is the result of age, we would have to be sure the groups are alike in other ways, such as socio-economic status and religious affiliation. These two groups are not exactly the same, but we cannot tell whether the cross-sectional differences are significant or not.

changes in welfare policy). In the cognitive domain, popular opinion about ideal weight could have changed in such a way as to make children weight-conscious, leading many of them to undereat. Finally, in the psychosocial domain, how children in a society spend their time changes.

These differences are not merely speculative. For example, between 1950 and 1954, children's television watching increased from zero to an average of almost three hours a day, causing children to be less active and thus to gain weight. Any historical pattern could affect average weight, and thus cross-sectional results would be deceptive because they ignore cohort differences.

Longitudinal Research

To help discover whether age itself is the reason for an apparent developmental change, scientists undertake **longitudinal research,** studying the *same individuals* over a long period of time. Because longitudinal research compares information about the same people at different ages, it eliminates the effects of background variables, even those that researchers are not aware of. If we know how much children weighed at age 6 and how much the same children weigh at age 10, it is easy to figure out how much weight they gained during the four intervening years.

Longitudinal research is particularly useful in studying development over a long age span (Elder, 1998). It has yielded valuable and sometimes surprise findings on many topics, including the following:

- *Adjustment to divorce.* The negative effects linger, but not for everyone (Hetherington & Kelly, 2002).
- *The role of fathers in child development.* Even 50 years ago, fathers were far more influential regarding their children's future happiness than the stereotype of the distant dad implies (Snarey, 1993).
- *Prevention of teenage delinquency.* One factor is patient parenting at age 5, using conversation rather than physical punishment to correct the child's behavior (Pettit et al., 2001).

Notice that these effects can be understood only by looking at the same individuals.

longitudinal research A research method in which the same individuals are studied over a long period of time.

ALL: MARK ANTMAN / THE IMAGE WORKS

Nathaniel Becomes Nat Longitudinal research shows how people change and how they remain the same over time. Babies *(a)* mostly stay in one place and stare, in contrast to 2-year-olds *(b)*, who actively explore everything. Nine-year-olds *(c)* learn the health habits their culture teaches them, but 13-year-olds *(d)* cherish their privacy so much that Nat (which he prefers over his given name, Nathaniel) would probably never allow his father to photograph him brushing his teeth. At 18 *(e)* and 28 *(f)*, it is obvious that this red-haired, bespectacled young man is still the thoughtful and bemused person he was at 6 months; but changes are obvious as well, not only in hair and glasses but also in attitude.

Longitudinal research that includes repeated measurement at regular intervals can uncover not only change but also the process of change. Do children learn to read suddenly, by "breaking the code," or gradually? The answer could not be found by simply comparing preliterate 4-year-olds and fluently reading 8-year-olds. However, following children month by month reveals the answer: Reading is usually a gradual process, although certain aspects can be grasped quite suddenly (Adams et al., 1998). Does the correlation among happiness, longevity, and a supportive marriage occur because happy, healthy people are more likely to marry, or because marriage itself aids health? Longitudinal research finds that both are true (Vaillant, 2002).

You will learn the results of many longitudinal studies throughout this book. Nevertheless, this design, too, has some serious drawbacks. Over time, some subjects may withdraw, move far away, or die. These changes can skew the ultimate results if those who disappear differ from those who stay in the study (more rebellious? of lower SES?). In addition, the research itself may affect those who remain (who might "improve" over a series of tests, for example, only because they become increasingly familiar with the questions), and this may limit the applicability of the study's findings. Cohort effects are inevitable. For this reason, historical trends in nutrition, education, and travel mean that "new generations reaching later life are soon to differ considerably from our present image . . . in . . . vigor, income, interests, expectations and geographical mobility, and in their experience of family life" (Wadsworth, 2002). As you can see, longitudinal research shares some of the limitations of cross-sectional research.

Perhaps the biggest problem of all is that a longitudinal investigation is very time-consuming and expensive. It involves far more commitment from scientists and funding agencies than does cross-sectional research.

Cross-Sequential Research

Cross-sectional research and longitudinal research each have advantages that tend to make up for the other's disadvantages. Scientists use the two together in various ways (Hartman & George, 1999). The simplest is **cross-sequential research** (also referred to as *cohort-sequential* or *time-sequential* research) (Schaie, 1996). With this design, researchers follow several groups of people of different ages (a cross-sectional approach) and over the years (a longitudinal approach).

Using cross-sequential design, we can compare findings for a group of, say, 50-year-olds with findings for the same individuals at age 30, as well as with findings for groups who were 50 a decade or two earlier and groups who are 30 years old now. Cross-sequential research thus allows scientists to disentangle differences related to chronological age from those related to historical period. Researchers using this method are like prospectors for gold, sifting through other elements to find genuine nuggets of age-related development (see Figure 1.6).

cross-sequential research A hybrid research method in which researchers first study several groups of people of different ages (a cross-sectional approach) and then follow those groups over the years (a longitudinal approach). (Also called *cohort-sequential* or *time-sequential research*.)

The Ecological-Systems Approach: A Synthesis

From a life-span perspective, the usefulness of combining many methods, seeking to understand the developing person within many contexts and dynamic systems, is apparent. No person can be thoroughly studied in isolation.

Urie Bronfenbrenner deserves credit for this recognition. Referring to attachment (discussed in Chapter 7), Bronfenbrenner (1977) noted the limitations of laboratory research: "Much of contemporary developmental psychology is the science of the strange behavior of children in strange situations with strange adults for the briefest periods of time" (p. 513). He recommended an **ecological-systems approach** to the study of human development. Just as a naturalist studying an organism examines the *ecology,* or the interrelationship between the organism and its environment, Bronfenbrenner argued, developmentalists likewise need to examine all the systems that surround the development of each person.

ecological-systems approach Research that takes into consideration the relationship between the individual and the environment.

Among the systems Bronfenbrenner described were *microsystems* (elements of the person's immediate surroundings, such as family and peer group), *exosystems* (such local institutions as school and church), *macrosystems* (the larger social setting, including cultural values, economic policies, and political processes), and *chronosystems* (the historical conditions). A fifth system, the *mesosystem,* involves the connections between microsystems; for example, the communication processes between a child's parents and teachers form a mesosystem (Bronfenbrenner & Morris, 1998).

In scientific research, it is difficult to incorporate all the systems, just as it is hard to use all methods and strategies of research simultaneously. As an example, Table 1.1 lists attributes of microsystems and exosystems that support the safety of a child at three developmental periods: infancy, childhood, and adolescence. Obviously, no single study could investigate all these factors. The goal, however, is ultimately to study all the systems that might affect development over time. Bronfenbrenner was a pioneer in recognizing this goal.

> In order to study how humans change over time, researchers have refined three strategies. Cross-sectional research compares groups of people of various ages, to see how the variable in question is affected by the variable of age. Longitudinal research follows the same individuals over a long period of time, making it easier to detect intra-individual differences and to notice sudden shifts that might occur. Finally, cross-sequential research combines the first two. No matter which research strategy is used, an ecological-systems approach considers all contexts and systems that affect development.

TABLE 1.1 Factors that Promote Safety and Security

INFANCY

Family/Home:
Strong emotional bond between infant and caregiver
Use of positive reinforcement by caregiver to promote prosocial behavior
High caregiver awareness and knowledge of home safety measures
Active supervisory style by parent
Absence of home hazards

Community:
Presence of parental support networks
High population awareness of indicators of child abuse and neglect
Home visitation programs
Environmental protections (e.g., reduced lead exposure)

CHILDHOOD

Individual:
Development of social skills and ability to regulate emotions
Involvement in activities that promote positive attachments and prosocial norms
Acquisition of early academic skills and knowledge
Impulse control (e.g., crossing a street to retrieve a ball)
Frequent use of personal protection (e.g., bike helmets, safety seats)

Family/Home:
High awareness and knowledge of child management and parenting skills
Caregiver participation in child's education and social activities
Frequent parent protective behaviors (e.g., use of child safety seats)
Presence of home safety equipment (e.g., smoke alarms, cabinet locks)

School/Peers:
Promotion of home–school partnerships
Availability of enrichment and tutoring programs
Social norm development for protective behaviors (e.g., wearing helmets)
Absence of playground hazards
Management support for safety and injury prevention
Injury reduction and safety promotion policies and programs

Community:
Availability of prosocial activities for children and their parents
Active surveillance of environmental hazards
Effective prevention policies in place (e.g., pool fencing)
Commitment to emergency medical services for children and trauma care
Adoption of safety culture

ADOLESCENCE

Individual:
Involvement with prosocial peers
Building friendships
Developing a sense of self-identity
Using personal protective equipment often (e.g., seat belts)
Refusal-skills training for alcohol and drug use

Family/Home:
High awareness and knowledge of adolescent management and parenting skills
Monitoring access to lethal weapons
Caregiver participation in adolescent's education and social activities
Active involvement in teen driving contracts and monitoring
Installation and frequent testing of smoke alarms

Schools/Peers:
Availability of programs to facilitate entry into the workforce
Availability of instruction in problem solving, refusal skills, and anger management
School safety policies and programs (e.g., bike helmet use, firearms hazards)
Frequent contact with positive peer modeling

Community:
Low availability of lethal weapons and alcohol
Availability of safe places for adolescents to socialize
Policies that support enforcement of safety laws
Effective emergency medical services and trauma care
A commitment to environmental safety

Source: Sleet & Mercy, 2003, pp. 87–88.

Age and Ecological Systems At every age, a person develops within an ecosystem, with factors that vary by age and context. Thus, safety in adolescence is encouraged by friendship with constructive peers and by an absence of guns—quite different from infancy, in which guns and friends are much less important, but laws prohibiting lead paint are crucial.

Ethics and Science

Every scientist must be concerned with the ethics of conducting and reporting research. At the most basic level, researchers who study humans must ensure that the participants are not harmed and that participation is voluntary and confidential. Each academic discipline and professional society involved in the study of human development has a **code of ethics,** or set of moral principles.

code of ethics A set of moral principles that is formally adopted by a group or organization.

In developmental studies, the need to protect the participants is especially obvious with children, but the same principles apply no matter what age the person is (Gilhooly, 2002). These include respecting all participants, explaining the purposes and procedures of the study, obtaining written permission ("informed consent"), and allowing the participants to stop at any time. The most important principle is to never harm the participants, avoiding not only physical harm but also psychological distress.

The possibility of distress varies with a participant's age and condition (Thompson, 1992). A young child may become upset by a few minutes of separation from a caregiver; older children are susceptible to loss of self-esteem and sensitive to violations of privacy; parents of adolescents may not want anyone to ask their offspring anything about sex, drugs, or discipline.

Often, the studies with the greatest potential benefit involve the most vulnerable groups, such as women who have been abused or children who have been suspended from school. Ironically, some groups (women, children, drug addicts) were excluded as subjects of research into drug treatments for AIDS because experimental drugs might have done them unexpected harm; as a result, the first effective AIDS treatments had never been tested on the people who might need them most (Kahn et al., 1998). This example shows that the benefits of research need to be considered as well as the costs.

The Implications of Research

Once an investigation has been completed, additional ethical issues arise concerning the reporting of research findings. An obvious breach of scientific ethics is to "cook" the data, arranging the numbers so that a particular conclusion seems the only logical one.

This can occur unintentionally, which is one reason replication is so important. Deliberate deception regarding the data is cause for ostracism from the scientific community, dismissal from a teaching or research position, and, in some cases, criminal prosecution. Further, *"in reporting results, . . . the investigator should be mindful of the social, political, and human implications of his [or her] research"* (Society for Research in Child Development, 1996).

What does "mindful" of implications mean? An example makes it clear. A storm of controversy was evoked by a study of college students who had become sexually involved with adults before reaching the legal age of consent (Rind et al., 1998). The study, a *meta-analysis* (which is a compilation of data from many other sources), correctly reported that the consequences depended on many factors. However, talk-show hosts, various special-interest groups (on all sides), and political candidates condemned the study—not because of its results, but because of their own misinterpretation of it. Some felt that the article, and the American Psychological Association which published it, condoned teenage sex or sexual abuse—the absolute opposite of the truth. Such misinterpretation occurred for many reasons, but one reason was that the authors and editors were not sufficiently mindful of the inferences that other people might draw:

> Scientists are committed to verifying their claims in terms of the logic-based system of thinking. . . . Scientists sometimes forget that media personalities, elected

Especially for Future Researchers What question in child development do you think needs to be further investigated? What do you think the problems with such research might be?

politicians, and many others operate under very different rules from psychologists and other scientists. . . . Like it or not, scientists operate not only within a scientific context but also a societal one.

[Sternberg, 2002, pp. 193, 194]

In another research project, a group of college students who listened to Mozart before taking a cognitive test scored higher than another group who heard no music (Rauscher et al., 1993; Rauscher & Shaw, 1998). This "Mozart effect" was also misinterpreted; the governor of Georgia ordered that all newborns receive a free Mozart CD in order to improve their intelligence, and Florida passed a law requiring every state-funded infant day-care center to play classical music. The actual initial study was irrelevant to infants, and the results could not be replicated (McKelvie & Low, 2002; Nantais & Schellenberg, 1999; Steele et al., 1999).

As these examples demonstrate, even when the scientific method is carefully used and proper safeguards for the subjects are in place, ethics requires a concern for implications. Hasty generalizations are often false, so researchers must take special care to explain their findings. Scientific methodology and integrity are the bases of our study of human development, and that is all the more reason to make sure the implications are carefully interpreted.

Response for Future Researchers (from page 29): Almost any issue that you care about is a valid subject for research, partly because scientists work best if they truly want to learn the answers. Beyond the problems of time, money, and protection of participants, the crucial question is whether you are prepared to obtain results that contradict your own social constructions. Some of the best and bravest scientists surprise themselves as well as their culture.

What Should We Study?

Every reader of this book should consider the most important ethical concern of all: Are scientists doing enough to study the issues that are crucial to human development?

■ Do we know enough about human sexual urges and actions to prevent sexually transmitted diseases, stop unwanted pregnancy, halt sexual abuse, and cure infertility?

■ Do we know enough about stress, poverty, and prejudice to enable humans to be happier and healthier?

■ Do we know enough about angry children to prevent a child from becoming a bully, a delinquent, and then a violent criminal?

■ Do we know enough about retirement to predict who will benefit and how?

The answer to all these questions is a resounding *NO!* Sometimes, even when we think about ethical particulars such as informed consent and confidentiality, we forget about this larger ethical concern.

Ethics means far more than taking care of research participants and reporting research carefully and honestly. It also means choosing to investigate topics that are major concerns for the human family. Many examples of scientific findings that have enhanced human development are given throughout this book. However, people suffer because many questions have not been answered, or even asked. The next cohort of developmental scientists will continue this work, building on what is known. Read on.

There are ethical issues at every stage, from designing studies so that participants will not be harmed to accurately reporting results. Perhaps the most difficult ethical question is how to explore the pressing policy questions of the day. The issues that most need answers tend to be the most difficult to explore objectively. For those interested in human development, those issues are precisely where further research is needed.

SUMMARY

Studying the Life Span: Five Characteristics

1. The study of human development is a science that seeks to understand how people change over time. Sometimes these changes are linear—gradual, steady, and predictable—but more often not.

2. The life-span perspective reminds us that development is multidirectional, multicontextual, multicultural, multidisciplinary, and plastic. *Plasticity* means that change is always possible but never unrestricted: Childhood becomes the foundation for later growth.

3. Development is the product of dynamic systems. Any one change affects an interconnected system, and any one person affects all the other people in a family or social group.

4. Change may be small or large, caused by something seemingly insignificant, like the flap of a butterfly's wings, or something large and pervasive, like a civil war. Development can seem to be continuous, or unchanging, for a period of time, and then a massive transformation can suddenly occur.

5. Each individual develops within unique historical, cultural, and socioeconomic contexts. Because each person has unique genes and experiences, contexts do not determine an individual's development, but they always influence it.

Developmental Study as a Science

6. The scientific method leads researchers to question assumptions and gather data to test conclusions. Although far from infallible, the scientific method helps researchers avoid biases and guides them in asking questions.

7. Among the research methods used by scientists are observation, experiments, surveys, and case studies. Each method has strengths and weaknesses.

8. The most reliable conclusions can be drawn when similar results are found in replications using various methods with many subjects in diverse cultures. Well-designed experiments are useful but difficult to conduct in studying human development, unless natural circumstances happen to create an experimental group.

9. Many statistical methods further scientific research. One is correlation, a number that indicates how two variables are connected (but does not prove that one variable causes the other). Another tool is determining significance, which indicates the degree of possibility that a particular result occurred by chance.

Studying Changes over Time

10. To study growth over time, scientists use three strategies: cross-sectional research (comparing people of different ages), longitudinal research (studying the same people over time), and cross-sequential research (combining the first two methods).

11. Further synthesis is the goal of the ecological-systems approach, which takes into account various components of the individual's environment.

Ethics and Science

12. Ethics is crucial in all sciences, perhaps especially in developmental research when children are involved. Not only must participants be protected, but results must be clearly reported and understood.

13. Appropriate application of scientific research depends partly on the integrity of the scientific methods used but even more on careful explanation and interpretation of the conclusions. The most important ethical issues are whether the critical questions are being asked, and whether the needed research is being conducted.

KEY TERMS

scientific study of human development (p. 3)
life-span perspective (p. 4)
multidirectional (p. 4)
multicontextual (p. 4)
multicultural (p. 4)
multidisciplinary (p. 4)
plasticity (p. 4)
dynamic systems (p. 5)
butterfly effect (p. 6)

cohort (p. 7)
social construction (p. 7)
socioeconomic status (SES) (p. 9)
culture (p. 10)
ethnic group (p. 13)
race (p. 14)
scientific method (p. 18)
hypothesis (p. 19)
replication (p. 19)

scientific observation (p. 19)
correlation (p. 20)
experiment (p. 20)
independent variable (p. 20)
dependent variable (p. 20)
experimental group (p. 21)
comparison group (p. 21)
survey (p. 22)
case study (p. 22)

cross-sectional research (p. 23)
longitudinal research (p. 25)
cross-sequential research (p. 27)
ecological-systems approach (p. 27)
code of ethics (p. 29)

APPLICATIONS

1. It is said that culture is pervasive but that people are unaware of it. List 30 things you did *today* that you might have done differently in another culture. (You might list what you did in one column and what you might have done in another.)

2. Is socioeconomic status an important context? How would your life be different if your parents had much less, or much more, education and income than they actually do?

3. Design an experiment to test a hypothesis you have about human development. Specify the hypothesis. Then describe the experiment, including the sample size and the variables. (Look first at Appendix B, at the back of this book.)

Chapter Two

Theories of Development

As we saw in Chapter 1, the scientific effort to understand human development usually begins with questions. One of the most basic is: How do people develop into the persons they ultimately become? Each theory emphasizes particular aspects of the human experience. The following five questions are each central to one of the theories described in this chapter:

- Do early experiences—of breast-feeding or bonding or abuse—linger into adulthood, even if they seem to be forgotten?
- How important are specific school experiences in human intelligence?
- Can a person develop moral values without being taught them?
- Does culture elicit behavior, so that, for example, violent criminals are more common in one place than another, in China or Canada, or in crowded cities or on quiet farms?
- If your parents or grandparents suffer from depression, schizophrenia, or alcoholism, will you develop the same condition?

For every answer, more questions arise: Why or why not? When and how? And, perhaps more importantly, so what? In other words, what implications and applications arise from the answers?

What Theories Do

Each of the five questions listed above is answered by one of the five major theories described in this chapter. Thousands of other questions, related to hundreds of thousands of observations, arise from the study of human development. To frame various questions, and to begin to answer them, we need some way to determine which facts are relevant. Then we need to organize those facts to lead us to deeper understanding. In short, we need a theory.

A **developmental theory** is a systematic statement of principles and generalizations that provides a coherent framework for understanding how and why people change as they grow older. Developmental theorists "try to make sense out of observations . . . [and] construct a story of the human journey from infancy through childhood or adulthood" (Miller, 2002, p. 2). Such a story, or theory, connects facts and observations with patterns and explanations, putting the details of life into a meaningful whole. Further, as one scientist quipped, "Nothing is as practical as a good theory." To be specific:

- Theories form the basis for hypotheses, a "point of departure" for individual scientists (Renninger & Amsel,

developmental theory A systematic statement of principles and generalizations that provides a coherent framework for studying and explaining development.

1997, p. ix). Formulating the right questions is much more difficult than finding the right answers. Theories suggest the questions.

- Theories generate discoveries: "New facts change the theory, and changes in the theory generate new experiments and thus new facts" (Miller, 2002, p. 4).
- Theories offer insight and guidance for everyday concerns by providing a coherent view of human development. If a teenager shouts "I hate you" to his father, the father should interpret this outburst before reacting.

Hundreds of theories are relevant to developmental science. Several are called **grand theories**, because they offer "a powerful framework for interpreting and understanding . . . change and development of all individuals" (Renninger & Amsel, 1997, p. ix). Many are **minitheories;** they explain only a part of development or apply only to some individuals (Parke et al., 1994). And a few are **emergent theories;** they may become the new systematic and comprehensive theories of the future.

This distinction of *grand, mini-,* and *emergent* theories is best understood by referring to the multidisciplinary aspect of the life-span perspective. The grand theories of human development originated in the discipline of psychology, focusing particularly on childhood. (Two of the grand theorists, Sigmund Freud and Jean Piaget, depicted the final stage of human development as beginning in adolescence and continuing throughout adulthood.)

By contrast, the discipline of sociology focused on social groups and studied age norms and family structures over the "life course" (Mayer 2003). This led to several minitheories (such as activity theory, disengagement theory, and exchange theory) that center on some aspect of adult development; it also led to spinoffs of the grand theories.

The multidisciplinary life-span approach has meant additional cross-fertilization among disciplines. Historical events (notably, increasing globalization and immigration) and genetic discoveries have also given rise to emergent theories. These new theories have not yet gelled into grand theories, but they are insightful, current, and in a sense broader than theories that drew only on psychology.

This chapter will focus on three grand theories—psychoanalytic, behaviorist, and cognitive—and two emergent theories—sociocultural and epigenetic. Throughout the remaining chapters of the book, these five theories will be further described when they are relevant, as will many minitheories. Remember that theories are useful because they provide a framework and perspective. There will be times in our study when an organizing framework will be essential.

Grand Theories

In the first half of the twentieth century, two opposing theories—psychoanalytic theory and behaviorism (also called learning theory)—began as theories of psychology and later were applied to human development. By mid-century, cognitive theory had also emerged, and it gradually became the dominant seedbed of research hypotheses. All three theories are "grand" in the sense that they are comprehensive, enduring, and widely applied.

Psychoanalytic Theory

Psychoanalytic theory interprets human development in terms of inner drives and motives, many of which are irrational and unconscious (hidden from awareness). These basic underlying forces are viewed as influencing every aspect of a person's thinking and behavior, from the smallest details of daily life to the crucial choices of a lifetime. Psychoanalytic theory also sees these drives and mo-

grand theories Comprehensive theories that have traditionally inspired and directed thinking about development. Psychoanalytic theory, behaviorism, and cognitive theory are all grand theories.

minitheories Theories that focus on some specific area of development and thus are less general and comprehensive than the grand theories.

emergent theories Theories that bring together information from many disciplines but that have not yet cohered into theories that are comprehensive and systematic.

psychoanalytic theory A grand theory of human development that holds that irrational, unconscious drives and motives, many of which originate in childhood, underlie human behavior.

tives as the foundation for the stages of development that every human experiences in sequence. Each stage entails specific developmental tasks, from establishing human bonds in infancy to attaining emotional and sexual fulfillment in adulthood.

Freud's Ideas

Psychoanalytic theory originated with Sigmund Freud (1856–1939), an Austrian physician who based this theory on his clinical work with patients suffering from mental illness. He listened to their accounts of dreams and fantasies, as well as to their "uncensored" streams of thought, and constructed an elaborate, multifaceted theory. According to Freud, development in the first six years occurs in three stages, each characterized by sexual interest and pleasure centered on a particular part of the body. In infancy, that body part is the mouth (the *oral stage*); in early childhood, it is the anus (the *anal stage*); in the preschool years, it is the penis (the *phallic stage*). Then come *latency* and, beginning at adolescence, the *genital stage*. (See Table 2.1 for descriptions of the stages in Freud's theory.)

Freud maintained that at each of these stages, sensual satisfaction (from stimulation of the mouth, anus, or penis) is linked to major developmental needs and challenges. During the oral stage, for example, the baby not only gains nourishment through sucking but also experiences sensual pleasure and becomes emotionally attached to the mother, who provides this oral gratification. During the anal stage, pleasures related to control and self-control—initially with defecation and toilet training—are paramount.

One of Freud's most influential ideas was that each stage includes its own potential conflicts. Conflict occurs, for instance, when an adult tries to wean a baby from the beloved bottle (oral stage) or a society tries to direct an adolescent's sexual urges (genital stage). According to Freud, how an individual experiences and resolves these conflicts—especially those related to weaning, toilet training, and sexual curiosity—determines that individual's lifelong personality and patterns of behavior. An adult may not know it, but the fact that he or she smokes cigarettes (oral) or keeps careful track of money (anal) or is romantically attracted to a much older partner (phallic) signifies unconscious problems rooted in a childhood stage.

Erikson's Ideas

Freud had many followers who became famous psychoanalytic theorists in their own right. Although they all acknowledged the importance of unconscious, irrational forces and of early childhood, each expanded and modified Freud's ideas. The most notable of these neo-Freudians was Erik Erikson (1902–1994), who formulated his own version of psychoanalytic theory.

Erikson spent his childhood in Germany, his adolescence wandering through Italy, and his young adulthood in Austria. Just before World War II, he arrived in the United States, where he studied Harvard students, children at play, and Native American cultures. These varied experiences helped Erikson understand the significance of cultural diversity and of the shifts that occur in adulthood.

Freud at Work In addition to being the world's first psychoanalyst, Sigmund Freud was a prolific writer. His many papers and case histories, primarily descriptions of his patients' bizarre symptoms and unconscious sexual urges, helped make the psychoanalytic perspective a dominant force for much of the twentieth century.

Childhood Sexuality? The girl's interest in the statue's anatomy may reflect simple curiosity, but Freudian theory would maintain that it is a clear manifestation of the phallic stage of psychosexual development, when girls are said to feel deprived because they lack a penis.

What's in a Name?—Erik Erikson As a young man, this neo-Freudian changed his last name to the one we know him by. What do you think his choice means? (See caption to photo below.)

Erikson proposed eight developmental stages covering the entire life span, each characterized by a particular challenge, or *developmental crisis* (see Table 2.1). Although Erikson described two opposites at each crisis, he recognized that there is a wide range of outcomes between these extremes. For most people, development leads to neither extreme but to something in between.

As you can see from Table 2.1, Erikson's first five stages are closely related to Freud's stages. Erikson, like Freud, believed that problems of adult life echo unresolved conflicts of childhood. For example, an adult who has difficulty establishing a secure, mutual relationship with a life partner may never have resolved the crisis of early infancy, *trust versus mistrust*. However, Erikson's stages differ significantly from Freud's in that they emphasize people's relationships to their family and culture, not only to their sexual urges.

In Erikson's theory, the resolution of each developmental crisis depends on the interaction between the individual and the social environment. In the stage of *initiative versus guilt,* for example, children between ages 3 and 6 often want to undertake activities that exceed their abilities or the limits set by their parents. Their efforts to act independently leave them open to pride or failure, with the resolution of the crisis depending partly on how they go about seeking independence, partly on the reactions of their parents, and partly on their culture's expectations. As an example, some cultures *encourage* assertive 5-year-olds, seeing them as creative spirits who know their own minds, whereas other cultures *discourage* them, seeing them as "rude" or "fresh." Children internalize, or accept, these responses from their parents, peers, and cultures. Even in late adulthood, one older person may be quite bold and outspoken while another is always fearful of saying the wrong thing, because of their diverging resolutions of the initiative-versus-guilt stage of early childhood.

Developmentalists owe a debt of gratitude to Freud as well as to the neo-Freudians who extended and refined his concepts. Many psychoanalytic ideas are

Who Are We? The most famous of Erikson's eight crises is the identity crisis, during adolescence, when young people find their own answer to the question "Who am I?" Erikson did this for himself by choosing a last name that, with his first name, implies "son of myself" (Erik, Erik's son). Although the identity crisis is universal, particulars vary from place to place and time to time—with each cohort distinguishing itself from the slightly older cohort in some way.

?*Observational Quiz* (see answer, page 38): Where and when do you think this photograph was taken?

TABLE 2.1 Comparison of Freud's Psychosexual and Erikson's Psychosocial Stages

Approximate Age	Freud (Psychosexual)	Erikson (Psychosocial)
Birth to 1 year	*Oral Stage* The mouth, tongue, and gums are the focus of pleasurable sensations in the baby's body, and sucking and feeding are the most stimulating activities.	*Trust vs. Mistrust* Babies learn either to trust that others will care for their basic needs, including nourishment, warmth, cleanliness, and physical contact, or to lack confidence in the care of others.
1–3 years	*Anal Stage* The anus is the focus of pleasurable sensations in the baby's body, and toilet training is the most important activity.	*Autonomy vs. Shame and Doubt* Children learn either to be self-sufficient in many activities, including toileting, feeding, walking, exploring, and talking, or to doubt their own abilities.
3–6 years	*Phallic Stage* The phallus, or penis, is the most important body part, and pleasure is derived from genital stimulation. Boys are proud of their penises, and girls wonder why they don't have one.	*Initiative vs. Guilt* Children want to undertake many adultlike activities, or fear the limits set by parents and feel guilty.
6–11 years	*Latency* This is not a stage but an interlude, during which sexual needs are quiet and children put psychic energy into conventional activities like schoolwork and sports.	*Industry vs. Inferiority* Children busily learn to be competent and productive in mastering new skills or feel inferior and unable to do anything well.
Adolescence	*Genital Stage* The genitals are the focus of pleasurable sensations, and the young person seeks sexual stimulation and sexual satisfaction in heterosexual relationships.	*Identity vs. Role Diffusion* Adolescents try to figure out "Who am I?" They establish sexual, political, and career identities or are confused about what roles to play.
Adulthood	Freud believed that the genital stage lasts throughout adulthood. He also said that the goal of a healthy life is "to love and to work."	*Intimacy vs. Isolation* Young adults seek companionship and love with another person or become isolated from others because they fear rejection and disappointment. *Generativity vs. Stagnation* Middle-aged adults contribute to the next generation through meaningful work, creative activities, and/or raising a family, or they stagnate. *Integrity vs. Despair* Older adults try to make sense out of their lives, either seeing life as a meaningful whole or despairing at goals never reached.

widely accepted today—for example, that unconscious motives affect our behavior and that the early years are a formative period of personality development.

Behaviorism

The second grand theory arose in direct opposition to the psychoanalytic emphasis on unconscious, hidden urges. Early in the twentieth century, John B. Watson (1878–1958) argued that if psychology was to be a true science, psychologists should study only what they could see and measure: human behavior, not human thoughts and hidden urges. In Watson's words:

> Why don't we make what we can *observe* the real field of psychology? Let us limit ourselves to things that can be observed, and formulate laws concerned only with those things. . . . We can observe behavior—what the organism does or says.

[Watson, 1924/1998, p. 6]

Especially for Teachers Your kindergartners are talkative and always moving. They almost never sit quietly and listen to you. What would Erik Erikson recommend?

Especially for Teachers Same problem as above, but what would a behaviorist recommend?

An Early Behaviorist John Watson was an early proponent of learning theory, and his ideas are still influential today.

behaviorism A grand theory of human development that focuses on the sequences and processes by which behavior is learned. (Also called *learning theory*.)

conditioning According to behaviorism, any process in which a behavior is learned. See *classical conditioning* and *operant conditioning*.

classical conditioning The process by which a neutral stimulus becomes associated with a meaningful stimulus, so that the organism responds to the former stimulus as if it were the latter. (Also called *respondent conditioning*.)

operant conditioning The process by which a response is gradually learned via reinforcement or punishment. (Also called *instrumental conditioning*.)

!Answer to Observational Quiz (from page 36): The signs suggest Asia, and the fact that overt rebellion is difficult in a small Asian town suggests a large city. If you guessed Tokyo, score one correct. A sharp eye on the T-shirt and an accurate memory of when Mohawk hairstyles were in fashion would give you another correct answer—probably 1992.

According to Watson, if psychologists focus on behavior, they will realize that anything can be learned. He said:

> Give me a dozen healthy infants, well-formed, and my own specified world to bring them up in and I'll guarantee to take any one at random and train him to become any type of specialist I might select—doctor, lawyer, artist, merchant chief, and yes, even beggar-man and thief, regardless of his talents, penchants, tendencies, abilities, vocations, and race of his ancestors.
>
> *[Watson, 1924/1998, p. 82]*

Other psychologists, especially from the United States, agreed. They found it difficult, using the scientific method, to verify the unconscious motives and drives identified by Freud (Uttal, 2000). They developed **behaviorism** to study actual behavior, as objectively and scientifically as possible. Behaviorism is also called *learning theory* because of its focus on how people learn specific behaviors and develop new patterns, step by step.

Laws of Behavior

Laws of behavior are said to apply to every individual at every age, from newborn to octogenarian. These laws provide insights into how mature competencies are fashioned from simple actions and how environmental influences shape individual development. In the view of behaviorists, all development involves a gradual process of learning, and, therefore, development does not occur in specific stages linked to age or maturation (Bijou & Baer, 1978).

Learning occurs through **conditioning,** as a particular response comes to be triggered by a particular stimulus. There are two types of conditioning: classical and operant.

Classical Conditioning A century ago, Russian scientist Ivan Pavlov (1849–1936) began to study the link between stimulus and response. While doing research on salivation in dogs, Pavlov noted that his experimental dogs began to drool not only at the sight of food but also, eventually, at the sound of the approaching attendants who brought the food. This observation led him to perform his famous experiment in which he taught a dog to salivate at the sound of a bell.

Pavlov began by ringing the bell just before presenting food to the dog. After a number of repetitions of this bell-then-food sequence, the dog began salivating at the bell's sound even when there was no food nearby. This simple experiment was one of the first scientific demonstrations of **classical conditioning** (also called *respondent conditioning*).

In classical conditioning, an organism (any type of living creature) comes to associate a neutral stimulus with a meaningful one and then responds to the former stimulus as if it were the latter. In Pavlov's original experiment, the dog associated the sound of the bell (the neutral stimulus) with food (the meaningful stimulus) and responded to the sound as though it were the food itself. That response was a conditioned response to the bell (which became a conditioned stimulus), which meant learning had occurred.

Operant Conditioning The most influential North American proponent of behaviorism was B. F. Skinner (1904–1990), who agreed with Watson that psychology should focus on the scientific study of behavior. Skinner also agreed with Pavlov that classical conditioning explains some types of behavior. However, Skinner believed that another type of conditioning—**operant conditioning** (also called *instrumental conditioning*)—plays a much greater role in human behavior, especially in more complex learning.

In operant conditioning, the organism learns that a particular behavior produces a particular consequence. If the consequence is useful or pleasurable, the organism will tend to repeat the behavior to produce the consequence again. If

A Contemporary of Freud Ivan Pavlov was a physiologist who received the Nobel Prize in 1904 for his research on digestive processes. It was this line of study that led to his discovery of classical conditioning.

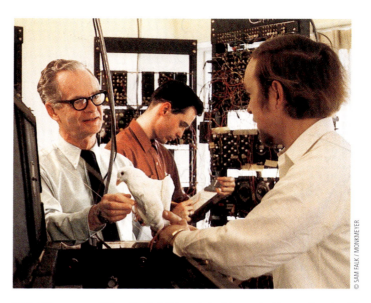

Rats, Pigeons, and People B. F. Skinner is best known for his experiments with rats and pigeons, but he also applied his knowledge to human problems. For his daughter, he designed a glass-enclosed crib in which temperature, humidity, and perceptual stimulation could be controlled to make her time in the crib enjoyable and educational. He wrote about an ideal society based on principles of operant conditioning, where, for example, workers in less desirable jobs would earn greater rewards.

the consequence is unpleasant, the organism will tend not to repeat the behavior. Pleasant consequences are sometimes called "rewards," and unpleasant consequences are sometimes called "punishments." Behaviorists hesitate to use those words, however, because what people commonly think of as a punishment can actually be a reward, and vice versa. The true test is the *effect* a consequence has on the individual's future behavior, not whether it is intended to be a reward or a punishment. For example, a child who misbehaves in school may be "punished" by being suspended from school, but if the child hates school, suspension is actually a reward for misbehaving.

Once a behavior has been conditioned (learned), animals (including humans) continue to perform it even if pleasurable consequences occur only occasionally. Almost all of a person's daily behavior, from socializing with others to earning a paycheck, can be understood as a result of operant conditioning. For instance, when a baby first gives a half smile in response to a full stomach, a mother might smile back. Soon the baby is conditioned by the mother's responsive smile to give a bigger smile, and the mother encourages the smile by picking the baby up. As time goes on, the baby becomes a smiling toddler, a cheerful child, an outgoing adolescent, and a friendly adult—all because of early operant conditioning and periodic reinforcing.

In operant conditioning, the process of repeating a consequence to make it more likely that the behavior in question will recur is called **reinforcement** (repeating a consequence to make the behavior *less* likely is called *punishment*) (Skinner, 1953). A consequence that increases the likelihood that a behavior will be repeated is therefore called a *reinforcer*. The mother's early reinforcement produces a socially responsive, smiling adult.

The study of human development has benefited from behaviorism. That theory's emphasis on the causes and consequences of observed behavior has led researchers to see that many behavior patterns that seem to be genetic, or to result from deeply rooted emotional problems, are actually learned. And if something

Response for Teachers (from page 37): Erikson would note that the behavior of 5-year-olds is affected by their developmental stage and by their culture, and therefore you might design your curriculum to accommodate active, noisy children.

Response for Teachers (from page 37): Behaviorists believe that anyone can learn anything. If your goal is quiet, attentive children, begin by reinforcing a moment's quiet or a quiet child, and soon all the children will be trying to remain attentive for several minutes at a time.

reinforcement The process in which a behavior is followed by results that make it more likely that the behavior will be repeated. This occurs in operant conditioning.

Especially for Older Brothers and Sisters
Psychologists believe that the best role models for
children are older siblings and other people they
know well and see daily, rather than sports stars or
political heroes. Why?

is learned, it can be unlearned, which is a very hopeful message. This realization
has encouraged scientists to find ways to eliminate particular problem behaviors—among them temper tantrums, phobias, and addictions. They analyze all
the reinforcements, punishments, and past conditioning and then break the
stimulus–response chains that sustained the destructive actions, substituting
new patterns.

Like any good theory, behaviorism has also been a source of hypotheses for
many scientific experiments, such as those described in the following Thinking
Like a Scientist.

Thinking Like a Scientist

What Is a Mother For?

Because theories help organize perceptions, they make it
easier for scientists to interpret their observations. True scientists welcome not only findings that confirm a theory but
also data that disprove them.

Both behaviorism and psychoanalytic theory originally
assumed that the reason children love their mothers is that
the mothers satisfy basic hunger and sucking needs. In
other words, they held that "the infant's attachment to the
mother stemmed from internal drives which triggered activities connected with the libations of the mother's breast. This
belief was the only one these two theoretical groups ever
had in common" (Harlow, 1986).

The hypothesis, derived from both theories, was that love
of mother resulted from maternal feeding. Harry Harlow, a
psychologist who studied learning in infant monkeys, observed something that made him question this hypothesis:

> We had separated more than 60 of these animals from their
> mothers 6 to 12 hours after birth and suckled them on tiny
> bottles. The infant mortality rate was a fraction of what we
> would have obtained had we let the monkey mothers raise
> their infants. Our bottle-fed babies were healthier and heav-
> ier than monkey-mother-reared infants. . . . During the
> course of our studies we noticed that the laboratory-raised
> babies showed strong attachment to the folded gauze dia-
> pers which were used to cover the . . . floor of their cages.
>
> [Harlow, 1986, p. 103]

In fact, the infant monkeys seemed more emotionally attached to the cloth diapers than to their bottles. This observation was contrary to the two prevailing theories, since
psychoanalytic theory would predict that the infant would
love whatever satisfied its oral needs, and behaviorism that
the infant would become attached to whatever provided reinforcing food. Harlow set out to make a "direct experimental analysis" via his monkeys.

Using monkeys to study emotional processes in humans
may seem a stretch to some people, but not to Harlow, who
had been trained as an experimental psychologist. He believed that "the basic processes relating to affection, includ-

HARLOW PRIMATE LABORATORY, UNIVERSITY OF WISCONSIN

Clinging to "Mother"   Even though it gave no milk, this "mother" was
soft and warm enough that infant monkeys spent almost all their time holding
on to it. Many infants, some children, and even some adults cling to a familiar
stuffed animal when life becomes frightening. According to Harlow, the reasons
are the same: All primates are comforted by something soft, warm, and familiar
to the touch.

ing nursing, contact, clinging, and even visual and auditory
exploration, exhibit no fundamental differences in the two
species" (Harlow, 1958).

Harlow provided infant monkeys with two "surrogate"
(artificial) mothers, both the right size, with a face that included obvious eyes. One surrogate was made of bare wire,
and the other was covered by soft terrycloth. He divided his
monkeys into two groups. One group was fed by a bottle put
through the chest of the cloth "mother"; the other by a bottle
put through the chest of the wire "mother."

To collect his data, Harlow measured how much time each baby spent holding on to one or the other of the two surrogates. The monkeys who had a cloth mother that provided milk clung to it and ignored the wire mother. However, even the babies that fed from the wire mother preferred the cloth mother, going to the wire mother only when hunger drove them to do so. In short, no attachment to, or love for, the nourishing wire mother could be observed, but the cloth mother seemed to win the infants' affection whether or not it provided food (see Figure 2.1).

Harlow then wondered whether the cloth surrogate mothers might also reassure infant monkeys when frightening events occurred, just as a real mother does when a scared youngster runs to her. He set up another experiment, putting an unfamiliar mechanical toy into a cloth-reared infant monkey's cage. The monkey immediately sought comfort from its cloth mother, clinging to it with one hand and then timidly exploring the new object with the other.

Wire mothers provided no such reassurance. Monkeys who were exposed to the same stress with only the wire mother's presence showed signs of fright—freezing, screaming, shivering, hiding, urinating. It seems, then, that mothering is not primarily about feeding, but about touching, comforting, and holding, which Harlow called "contact comfort" or "love" (Harlow, 1958).

Harlow's research is a classic example of the use of theories. Although his study disproved an aspect of both behaviorism and psychoanalytic theory, that is not the most significant point. Remember, theories are meant to be useful, not necessarily true. (If they were known to be true in every aspect, they would be scientific laws, not theories.) In this example, because he knew what the psychoanalytic and behavioral theories said about love and comfort, the baby monkeys' interactions with the gauze diapers caught Harlow's attention. That led to closer observation, a hypothesis, a clever series of experiments, and some amazing results.

Both psychoanalytic theory and behaviorism were revised and expanded in response to Harlow's experiments and to other evidence. Advice to caregivers changed as well: Crying infants should be picked up and cuddled, even if they are not hungry. The result has been much more cradling and less crying—all because a scientist compared a theoretical prediction with his own observations and performed ingenious experiments to test his hypothesis.

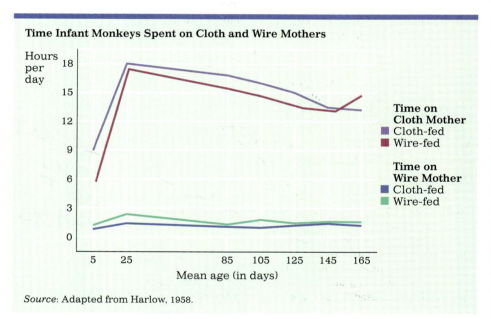

Time Infant Monkeys Spent on Cloth and Wire Mothers

FIGURE 2.1 Softer Is Better During the first three weeks of Harlow's experiment, the infant monkeys developed a strong preference for the cloth-covered "mothers." That preference lasted throughout the experiment, even among the monkeys who were fed by a wire-covered mother.

? *Observational Quiz* (see answer, page 45): At five days, how much time did the wire-fed monkeys (compared with the cloth-fed monkeys) spend on the cloth mothers?

Source: Adapted from Harlow, 1958.

Social Learning

Originally, behaviorists sought to explain all behavior as arising directly from a chain of learned responses, the result of classical and operant conditioning. However, every grand theory is sufficiently comprehensive and thought-provoking that later scientists revise and extend it. One revision of behaviorism, based on thousands of studies, arose from evidence that all creatures appreciate the touch, warmth, reassurance, and example of other, similar beings. This

Social Learning in Action Social learning validates the old maxim "Actions speak louder than words." If the moments here are typical for each child, the girl in the left photo is likely to grow up with a ready sense of the importance of this particular chore of infant care. Unfortunately, the boy on the right may become a cigarette smoker like his father—even if his father warns him of the dangers of this habit.

? *Observational Quiz* (see answer, page 45): What shows that these children imitate their parents?

social learning theory An application of behaviorism that emphasizes that many human behaviors are learned through observation and imitation of other people.

modeling In social learning theory, the process in which people observe and then copy the behavior of others.

self-efficacy In social learning theory, the belief that one is effective; self-efficacy motivates people to change themselves and their contexts.

evidence led to **social learning theory** and to the recognition of a third type of learning (see Figure 2.2). Humans, even more than other animals, learn many behaviors by observing the behavior of others, without personally experiencing any reinforcement. Humans also strive for the feelings of pride and acceptance that other people can give.

An integral part of social learning is **modeling,** in which people observe behavior and then copy it. For children, parents are the first models. Modeling is not simply imitation, because people model only some actions, of some individuals, in some contexts. For example, you undoubtedly know some adults who tend to repeat their parents' behavior patterns but others who strive to never repeat certain of their parents' behaviors. Thus, some adults who were physically beaten in childhood might be abusive to their children, but others might be very careful to "never lay a hand" on them. From a behaviorist perspective, both reactions confirm social learning. They testify to the power of the original example. Generally, modeling is most likely to occur when the observer is uncertain or inexperienced (which explains the readiness of children to use modeling) and when the model is someone admirable and powerful, nurturing, or similar to the observer (Bandura, 1986, 1997).

Human social learning is connected to people's perceptions and interpretations of what they observe (in this, social learning theory incorporates part of cognitive theory, which is explained in the next section). It is also related to self-understanding, self-confidence, social reflection, and feelings of **self-efficacy,** the belief that one is effective. All of these have cognitive roots and consequences. For example, in an individual, self-efficacy is associated with high aspirations and achievement (Bandura et al., 2001). As you learned in Chapter 1, *collective efficacy* prompts family and community systems to join together to work for improvements (Sampson et al., 1997). As these examples suggest, social learning theory and, more generally, behaviorism encourage action, because modeling and conditioning can change an individual, a social group, or even a culture.

? *Response for Older Brothers and Sisters* (from page 40): An older sibling is an ideal role model because he or she has survived or—better yet—succeeded within the same family and community context in which the younger child lives but has human weaknesses that are also apparent. By contrast, distant role models are portrayed as unusually skilled or fortunate, with no weaknesses—unless a particular foible reaches the headlines and causes children to lose faith in the former hero.

FIGURE 2.2 Three Types of Learning Behaviorism is also called learning theory, because it emphasizes the learning process, as shown here.

Learning occurs through:

■ **Classical conditioning** Through association, neutral stimulus becomes conditioned stimulus.

■ **Operant conditioning** Through reinforcement, weak or rare response becomes strong, frequent response.

■ **Social learning** Through modeling, observed behaviors become copied behaviors.

Cognitive Theory

The third grand theory, **cognitive theory**, focuses on the structure and development of thought processes and understanding. A person's thinking and the expectations that result from a particular understanding affect the development of attitudes, beliefs, values, assumptions, and behaviors, according to cognitive theory. Cognitive theory is the dominant perspective in contemporary psychology, used by therapists as well as scientists, many of whom have developed minitheories. One significant version of cognitive theory is called *information-processing theory,* and an effective treatment for depression is cognitive therapy; both of these offshoots of cognitive theory are discussed later.

Now we will delineate the stages and processes of the original grand cognitive theory, which was pioneered by Jean Piaget (1896–1980). Although originally trained in the natural sciences, Piaget became interested in human thought processes when he was hired to field-test questions for a standard intelligence test for children. Piaget was supposed to find the age at which most children could answer each question correctly, but it was the children's wrong answers that intrigued him. *How* children think is much more important and more revealing of mental ability, Piaget concluded, than *what* they know. Moreover, understanding how people think makes it possible to understand how they interpret their experiences and how they construct their values and assumptions.

Piaget maintained that there are four major periods, or stages, of cognitive development: the *sensorimotor* period, the *pre-operational* period, the *concrete operational* period, and the *formal operational* period (see Table 2.2). These periods are age-related, and, as you will see in later chapters, each period has features that permit certain types of knowing and understanding (Piaget, 1952b, 1970a, 1970b).

Movement from one period to another is propelled by the human need for **cognitive equilibrium**—that is, a state of mental balance. Each person attempts to make sense of new experiences by reconciling them with his or her existing understanding. Cognitive equilibrium occurs when new experiences "fit" one's present understanding, whether this fitting involves a baby's discovery that new objects can be grasped in the same way as familiar objects or an adult's explanation of shifting world events as consonant with his or her political philosophy. However, when a new experience does not fit existing understanding, the individual falls into a state of *cognitive disequilibrium,* an imbalance that initially produces confusion. As Figure 2.3 illustrates, disequilibrium leads to cognitive growth, as the person modifies old concepts to fit the new experience. According to Piaget, cognitive adaptation occurs in two ways:

- Reinterpreting new experiences so that they fit into, or *assimilate* with, the old ideas

- Revamping old ideas so that they can *accommodate* the new experiences

YVES DEBRAINE / BLACK STAR

Would You Talk to This Man? Children loved talking to Jean Piaget, and he learned by listening carefully—especially to their incorrect explanations, which no one had paid much attention to before. All his life, Piaget was absorbed with studying the way children think. He called himself a "genetic epistemologist"—one who studies how children gain knowledge about the world as they grow up.

cognitive theory A grand theory of human development that focuses on the structure and development of thinking, which shapes people's attitudes, beliefs, and behaviors.

cognitive equilibrium In cognitive theory, a state of mental balance in which a person is able to reconcile new experiences with existing understanding.

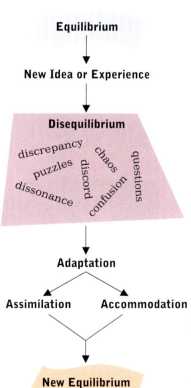

FIGURE 2.3 Challenge Me Most of us, most of the time, prefer the comfort of our conventional conclusions. According to Piaget, however, when new ideas disturb our thinking, we have an opportunity to expand our cognition with a broader and deeper understanding.

TABLE 2.2 Piaget's Periods of Cognitive Development

Age Range	Name of Period	Characteristics of the Period	Major Gains During the Period
Birth to 2 years	Sensorimotor	Infants use senses and motor abilities to understand the world. Learning is active; there is no conceptual or reflective thought.	Infants learn that an object still exists when it is out of sight (*object permanence*) and begin to think through mental actions.
2–6 years	Preoperational	Children use *symbolic thinking,* including language, to understand the world. Thinking is *egocentric,* causing children to understand the world from their own perspective.	The imagination flourishes, and language becomes a significant means of self-expression and of influence from others.
6–11 years	Concrete operational	Children understand and apply logical operations, or principles, to interpret experiences objectively and rationally.	By applying logical abilities, children learn to understand concepts of conservation, number, classification, and many other scientific ideas.
12 years through adulthood	Formal operational	Adolescents and adults think about abstractions and hypothetical concepts and reason analytically, not just emotionally.	Ethics, politics, and social and moral issues become fascinating as adolescents and adults take a broader and more theoretical approach to experience.

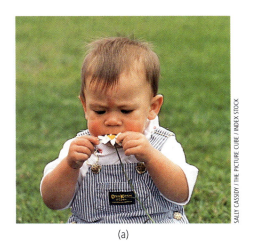

(a)

(b)

How to Think About Flowers A person's stage of cognitive growth influences how he or she thinks about everything, including flowers. *(a)* To a baby, in the sensorimotor stage, flowers are "known" through pulling, smelling, and perhaps tasting. *(b)* A slightly older child might be egocentric, wanting to pick and eat the vegetables now. *(c,d)* At the adult's formal operational stage, flowers can be part of a larger, logical scheme—either to earn money or to cultivate beauty. Thinking is an active process throughout the life span.

(c)

(d)

Assimilation is easier, because it does not require much adjustment. But accommodation is sometimes necessary, and it produces significant intellectual growth.

If a friend's argument reveals cognitive inconsistencies in your opinions, if your favorite chess strategy fails, if your mother says something you never expected her to, you will experience cognitive disequilibrium. In this last example, you might *assimilate* your mother's words by deciding she didn't mean what she said. Intellectual growth would occur if, instead, you *adapted* your previous conception of your mother to *accommodate* a new, expanded understanding of her.

Ideally, when two people disagree, or when they surprise each other by things they say, adaptation is mutual. For example, parents are often surprised by their grown children's ideas. If the parents are able to grow intellectually, they revise their concept of their offspring, accommodating as they come to a more comprehensive perspective. The children, too, might need to accommodate a new understanding of their parents, probably including increased respect. The point of this example is that cognitive growth is an active process, dependent on discordant ideas and challenging experiences, not on maturation (the focus of psychoanalytic theory) or repetition (as in behaviorism).

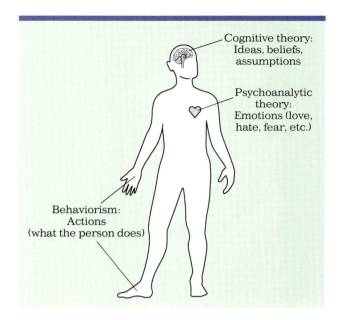

FIGURE 2.4 **Major Focuses of the Three Grand Theories**

The three grand theories originated almost a century ago. Each was pioneered by men who are still recognized for their ability to set forth psychological theories so comprehensive and creative that they are called "grand." Each grand theory has a different focus: emotions (psychoanalytic theory), actions (behaviorism), and thoughts (cognitive theory) (see Figure 2.4). The methods they used also differ. Psychoanalytic theory relied heavily on case studies in order to uncover hidden drives; behaviorists conducted experiments in order to find the laws of learning; cognitive theorists asked questions and analyzed unexpected answers. All the grand theories are intriguing, but they are also limited, not as comprehensive as they once seemed to be. These limitations become apparent when we look at two emerging theories.

! *Answer to Observational Quiz* (from page 41): Six hours, or one-third less time. Note that later on, the wire-fed monkeys (compared with the cloth-fed monkeys) spent equal, or even more, time on the cloth mothers.

! *Answer to Observational Quiz* (from page 42): The obvious part of the answer is that the girl is diapering her doll and the boy is pretending to smoke a cigarette, but modeling goes far beyond that. Notice that the girl has positioned her doll exactly as her mother has positioned the baby, and that the boy's blue-jeaned legs are posed casually, just like his father's.

Emergent Theories

Unlike the grand theories, the emerging theories are multicultural, multidisciplinary, and multimethod. For all these reasons, they are particularly pertinent to a life-span perspective on human development.

Sociocultural theory draws on research in education, anthropology, and history; epigenetic theory arises from biology, genetics, and neuroscience. In part because of their scope and recency, neither emergent theory has developed a comprehensive, coherent explanation of how people change over the entire life span. However, as you will now see, both provide significant and useful frameworks for the science of human development.

Sociocultural Theory

In Chapter 1, we saw that humans develop within social contexts. Although "sociocultural theory is still emerging" (Rogoff, 1998, p. 687), it takes this idea one step further. The central thesis of **sociocultural theory** is that human development results from dynamic interaction between developing persons and

sociocultural theory An emergent theory that holds that human development results from the dynamic interaction between each person and the surrounding social and cultural forces.

The Founder of Sociocultural Theory Lev Vygotsky, now recognized as a seminal thinker whose ideas on the role of culture and history are revolutionizing education and the study of development, was a contemporary of Freud, Skinner, Pavlov, and Piaget. Vygotsky did not attain their eminence in his lifetime, partly because his work, conducted in Stalinist Russia, was largely inaccessible to the Western world and partly because he died young, at age 38.

apprenticeship in thinking In sociocultural theory, the process by which novices develop cognitive competencies through interaction with more skilled members of the society, often parents or teachers, who act as tutors or mentors.

guided participation In sociocultural theory, the process by which a skilled person helps a novice learn by providing not only instruction but also a direct, shared involvement in the learning process.

A Temporary Support Structure Scaffolds support workers as they construct a new building or repair an existing one, such as the California state capitol in Sacramento, shown here. Similarly, expert teachers erect educational scaffolds, using hints, ideas, examples, and questions to support the novice learner until a solid cognitive structure is formed.

their surrounding society and culture. According to this theory, society and culture are not simply external variables that impinge on the developing person; they are integral to development (Cole, 1996).

Along with the examples of the power of contexts and particularly culture given in Chapter 1, consider this further example: What do you do if a 6-month-old baby starts to fuss? You could find a pacifier, turn on a musical mobile, change the diaper, give a bottle, pick up the baby and walk around, sing a lullaby, offer a breast, shake a rattle, or close the door so the noise won't bother anyone. Each of these is a "right thing to do" according to parents in some cultures but not in others. Few parents are aware that their response to a baby's cry is shaped by their culture, yet this is precisely the case, according to sociocultural theory.

Cultures provide not only the practices but also the tools and theories. For instance, some cultures have no pacifiers, bottles, or mobiles—or even diapers or doors. The lack of those objects profoundly affects parents and infants, in ways that echo lifelong. Possessions and privacy are valued much more by some adults than by others, because of their early cultural experiences.

Guided Participation

The major pioneer of the sociocultural perspective was Lev Vygotsky (1896–1934), a psychologist from the former Soviet Union. Vygotsky was particularly interested in the cognitive competencies that developed among the culturally diverse people of his huge nation, including such skills as the proper use of tools in an agricultural community and the appropriate use of abstract words among people who had never been to school. In his view, these competencies develop from interactions between novices and more skilled members of the society, who act as tutors or mentors in a process called an **apprenticeship in thinking** (Rogoff, 1990, 1998).

The implicit goal of an apprenticeship in thinking is to provide the instruction and support that novices need so that they can acquire whatever knowledge and capabilities their culture values. The best way to accomplish this goal is through **guided participation:** The tutor engages the learner in joint activities, offering not only instruction but also direct involvement in the learning process.

This active apprenticeship is a crucial concept for sociocultural theory, which holds that each person depends on others for learning.

Note the centrality of social interaction, quite different from either a student's own discovery or a teacher's lecture. In guided participation, neither student nor teacher is ever passive; each learns from the other, through the words and activities that they engage in *together* (Karpov & Haywood, 1998). This is one crucial difference between sociocultural theory and the grand theories of the past: "Cognitive development occurs in and emerges from social situations" (Gauvain, 1998, p. 191). Adults learn from children as well as vice versa, and both adults and children learn as much from their peers as from older or younger individuals.

The concept that a culture's patterns and beliefs are social constructions (as explained in Chapter 1) is easy for sociocultural theorists to understand. The reality that something is socially constructed does not reduce its power or importance; quite the opposite. Values are among the most potent forces, shaping the development of every member of the culture. This point was stressed by Vygotsky, who himself was a teacher and argued that mentally and physically disabled children can learn (Vygotsky, 1925/1994). If people believe that "every child can learn," they are likely to find a way to teach every child.

The Zone of Proximal Development

According to sociocultural theory, *what* people need to learn depends on their culture, but *how* they learn is always the same, whether they are learning a manual skill, a social custom, or a language. Cultural context, the behavior of others, and guided participation are always part of the process.

For learning to occur, a teacher (who can be a parent or peer as well as a professional) draws the learner into his or her **zone of proximal development**, the skills that the learner can master with assistance but cannot yet perform independently. Through sensitive assessment of the learner's ability and capacity for growth, the teacher engages the student's participation, guiding the transition from assisted performance to independent achievement. The teacher must avoid two opposite dangers, boredom and failure. Some frustration is permitted, but the learner must be actively engaged, never passive or overwhelmed (see Figure 2.5).

To make this abstract-seeming process more concrete, let's take a simple example—a father teaching his 5-year-old daughter to ride a bicycle. He probably

Especially for Nurses Using guided participation, how would you teach a young child who has asthma to breathe with a nebulizer?

zone of proximal development In sociocultural theory, the range of skills that a learner can exercise and master with assistance but cannot yet perform independently. According to Vygotsky, learning can occur within this zone.

FIGURE 2.5 The Magic Middle Somewhere between the boring and the impossible is the zone of proximal development, where interaction between teacher and learner results in knowledge never before grasped or skills not already mastered. The intellectual excitement of that zone is the origin of the joy that both instruction and study can bring.

Learning to Ride Although they are usually not aware of it, children learn most of their skills because adults guide them carefully. What would happen if this father let go?

Especially for Teachers Following Vygotsky's precepts, how might you teach reading to an entire class of first-graders at various skill levels?

epigenetic theory An emergent theory of development that emphasizes the interaction of genes and the environment—that is, both the genetic origins of behavior (within each person and within each species) and the direct, systematic influence that environmental forces have, over time, on genes.

preformism The belief that every aspect of development is set in advance by genes and then is gradually manifested in the course of maturation.

begins by slowly rolling her along, supporting her weight while telling her to keep her hands on the bars and her feet on the pedals, to push the right and left pedals in rhythm, and to look straight ahead. As she becomes more comfortable and confident, he begins to roll her along more quickly, noting out loud that she is now able to keep her legs pumping in a steady rhythm. Within another lesson or two he is jogging beside her, holding on to just the handlebar. When he senses that, with a little more momentum, she could maintain her balance by herself, he urges her to pedal faster and slowly loosens his grip. Perhaps without her even realizing it, she is riding on her own.

Note that this is not instruction by rote. Learning must be active: No child learns to ride a bike by memorizing written instructions. Social and cultural skills are almost impossible to transmit unless the teacher has mastered them: If a father intellectually understands the general principles but does not know how to ride, he is best advised to let his bike-riding wife do the instructing.

Learning must also be individualized. Some children need more assurance than others; instruction is modified for the particular learner. A parent needs to listen and sense exactly whether more support or more freedom is needed at each moment, so the process is constantly adjusted.

Such excursions into and through the zone of proximal development are commonplace, not only in childhood but throughout life. Ideally, the learning process follows the same general pattern in all instances: The mentor, sensitively attuned to the learner's ever-shifting abilities and motivation, continually urges the learner on to new levels of competence, while the learner asks questions and shows signs of progress that guide and inspire the mentor. The particular skills and processes vary enormously from culture to culture, but the overall social engagement is the same.

Sociocultural theorists have been criticized for overlooking developmental processes that are not primarily social. Vygotsky's theory, in particular, has been viewed as neglecting the role of genes in guiding development, especially with regard to neurological maturation in mental processes (Wertsch, 1985; Wertsch & Tulviste, 1992). The other emerging theory, which we will now discuss, begins with genetics.

Epigenetic Theory

Epigenetic theory emphasizes the interaction of genes and the environment, an interaction that is seen as dynamic and reciprocal (Gottlieb, 2003). Such interaction is in sharp contrast to a traditional idea of **preformism,** according to which everything is set in advance by genes and then is gradually manifested in the course of maturation.

Epigenetic theory is the newest developmental theory, but it incorporates several established bodies of research. Many disciplines of the natural sciences—including biology (especially the principles of evolution), genetics, and chemistry—provided a foundation for epigenetic theory. Many psychologists, including Erikson and Piaget, described aspects of their theories as epigenetic, recognizing that development builds on genes but is not determined by them.

With, On, and Around the Genes

What, then, is new about this theory? One way to understand that is to consider the theory's name, which is derived from the root word *genetic* and the prefix *epi. Genetic* refers to the entire genome, which includes the particular genes that make each person (except monozygotic twins) genetically unique as well as the genes that all humans have shared for thousands of years.

Although some scientists in the nineteenth century were fascinated by heredity, most contemporary social scientists downplayed the importance of genes (Wahlsten, 2003). Epigenetic theory avoids both extremes. The *genetic* in *epigenetic* acknowledges the powerful instincts and abilities that arise from our biological heritage. All psychological as well as all physical traits, from bashfulness to blood type, from moodiness to metabolism, from vocational aptitude to voice tone, are influenced by genes. Even the timing of developmental change is genetic: Humans walk and talk at about 1 year, and reach reproductive maturity in early adolescence, because genes switch on those abilities (unless something is terribly wrong). Thus, half of epigenetic theory is the recognition of genes.

The other half is equally important if we are to avoid exaggerating the power of genes (Singer, 2003). The prefix *epi* means "with," "around," "before," "after," "on," or "near." Thus, *epigenetic* refers to all the surrounding factors that affect the expression of genetic instructions. Some are stress factors, such as injury, temperature, and crowding. Some are facilitating factors, such as nourishing food, loving care, and freedom to play. These and other factors arise from the environment in which the organism develops. Epigenetic theory puts the two halves together in one word to signify the inevitable interaction. This is illustrated by Figure 2.6, which was first published in 1992 by Gilbert Gottlieb, a leading proponent of epigenetic theory, and has been redrawn and reprinted dozens of times since (Gottlieb, 2003).

Obvious and direct epigenetic effects are easier, and more ethical, to find in lower animals than in people. For example, the shape of an animal's face and the color of its fur are the result of genetic factors, but some species develop abnormal facial features or change the color of their fur depending on environmental conditions. Even biological sex can be epigenetic: Experimenters incubated a clutch of alligator eggs at various temperatures. At about 32°C all the baby alligators became male, and below that temperature all became female (Ferguson & Joanen, 1982).

Many other epigenetic factors have been shown to affect human body and brain development (Dawson et al., 2000). One expert explains, "Brain development is not just a genetic process but an epigenetic one" (Johnson, 1999). Even identical twins, who have identical genes, are born with different brain structures. Other differences develop as they grow, because of epigenetic factors (Finch & Kirkwood, 2000).

As development progresses, most people move along the course set by earlier genetic–environmental interactions, partly because development becomes less plastic. However, a new context may change epigenetic patterns that are already in place, illustrating the power environmental factors can have. Consider, for example, drug addiction. A person's potential to become addicted is genetic. That potential is realized—a genetically vulnerable person becomes an addict or

THE NEW YORKER COLLECTION © 1998 WILLIAM HAEFELI FROM CARTOONBANK.COM

"Isn't she marvelous? Our own little bundle of untapped potential."

The Epigenetic Perspective Although these parents may not realize it, their words echo the essence of epigenetic thought—that each human is born with genetic possibilities that must be nurtured in order to grow.

Response for Nurses (from page 47): You would guide the child in the zone of proximal development, where teacher and child interact. Thus, you might encourage the child to prepare the nebulizer (by putting in the medicine, for instance), and then breathe through it yourself, taking turns with the child.

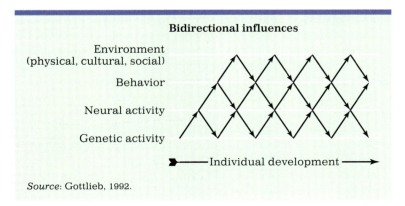

Bidirectional influences

Environment (physical, cultural, social)

Behavior

Neural activity

Genetic activity

Individual development

Source: Gottlieb, 1992.

FIGURE 2.6 An Epigenetic Model of Development Notice that there are as many arrows going down as going up, at all levels. Although development begins with genes at conception, it requires that all four factors interact.

Response for Teachers (from page 48): First of all, you wouldn't teach them "to read"; you would find out where each child was and what he or she was capable of learning next, so that instruction would be tailored to each child's zone of proximal development. For some this might be letter recognition; for others, comprehension of paragraphs they read to themselves. Second, you wouldn't teach the whole class. You would figure out a way to individualize instruction, maybe by forming pairs, with one child teaching the other; by setting up appropriate computer instruction; or by having parents or ancillary teachers work with small groups of three or four children.

selective adaptation The idea that humans and other animals gradually adjust to their environment; specifically, the process by which the frequency of particular genetic traits in a population increases or decreases over generations, depending on whether the traits contribute to the survival of the species.

alcoholic—if the person repeatedly consumes an addictive substance. Thus, addiction is the outcome of the interaction of genes and environment. However, as one team of researchers explains:

> Within the epigenetic model, each intermediary phenotype [genetic manifestation] is an outcome as well as a precursor to a subsequent outcome contingent on the quality of person–environment interactions. . . . Indeed, sudden shifts . . . can occur. In this regard, it is noteworthy that 86 percent of regular heroin users among soldiers in Vietnam abruptly terminated consumption upon return to the United States (Robins, Helzer, & Davis, 1975). In effect, a substantial change in the environment produced a major phenotype change.
>
> *[Tarter et al., 1999, p. 672]*

A crucial aspect of this theory is that genes never function alone; their potential cannot be actualized unless certain "epi" factors occur. For example, many psychological disorders, including schizophrenia, autism, antisocial personality, and depression, have a genetic component. But none are purely genetic; all are epigenetic (Reiss & Neiderhiser, 2000; Rutter & Sroufe, 2000; Sanchez et al., 2001). As one example, the rate of severe depression is higher among people who inherit a particular variant of a particular gene (called the short allele of 5-HTT). However, even people who have this variant are not likely to become depressed unless they are maltreated as children *or* experience stressful events as adults (Caspi et al., 2003).

A more familiar example is height. Each person is genetically programmed to grow to a certain height. Overeating and stretching will not add height. However, a child who is malnourished will be several inches shorter than genetic potential would have allowed. Thus, on an individual level, the genes for height combine with influences from the early environment.

Genetic Adaptation

So far we have focused on how epigenetic factors affect the development of individuals. Epigenetic factors also affect entire species. Over time, in a process called **selective adaptation**, genetic traits that increase the ability of members of a species to survive and reproduce become common, while those that are destructive become rare. That is, some genes are *selected* to pass from one generation to the next, because the individuals with those traits are likely to survive to adulthood and then have offspring, who will inherit their traits (Ellison, 2001). Environmental changes affect which traits increase the chances of survival. Selective adaptation is, in this way, an epigenetic process.

Epigenetic effects are most readily apparent in animals. For example, as a result of selective adaptation, some animals develop camouflage, or markings and coloration, that protect them from predators by allowing them to blend into their surroundings. More generally, the design of the bill (for birds) or teeth (for mammals) develops to enable the creature to get food from the environment; a long, pointed bill can pry insects out of the bark of trees, for instance.

In humans, too, epigenetic effects are apparent in particular populations. As an example, many people are lactose intolerant (cow's milk makes them sick), but in regions where dairy farming was introduced thousands of years ago, a genetic enzyme that makes cow's milk digestible gradually allowed people to tolerate milk and thus improved their chances for survival. As a result, this genetic variant gradually became widespread in the human population, especially in Europe.

The interaction between genes and environment affects survival. If a species' gene pool does not include variants of crucial genes that can adapt to certain conditions, the entire species will eventually die out. About 90 percent of all species that ever existed have become extinct, because animals that could not adapt to changes in their environment died and were not replaced (Buss et al.,

1998). Humans have adapted well despite changing conditions, in part because genes for social impulses and language help humans learn from one another.

It is apparent that humans adapt, selectively, to various climates, diets, and social groups. Look at the Inuit, whose body type, hair, and social instincts are well suited for survival in a subzero climate; or the Zulu, who have opposite characteristics because of an opposite climate. Selective adaptation is less apparent when it involves personality traits (such as shyness or aggression) in highly mobile populations, but epigenetic theory suggests that adaptation and selective expression occur in these genes as well.

Humans, in many ways, adapt successfully. Consider height again. As a species, humans are taller than chimpanzees (the animals who are genetically closest to people) because carrying things while walking long distances is easier with long legs and grasping arms and hands. Consequently, height was adaptive because it increased mobility, enabling humans to establish homes in distant fertile regions. Humans are almost unique among mammals in their survival in every part of the world.

One unusual characteristic of humans is a long childhood, with the young dependent on their parents for a decade or more. For humans to survive, selective adaptation requires adults to spend years in child rearing, because the child must spend years in brain maturation. This parental investment occurs because parents have a natural inclination, triggered by birth, to love their offspring—as I can attest.

ethology The study of patterns of animal behavior, particularly as that behavior relates to evolutionary origins and species survival.

In Person

My Beautiful, Hairless Babies

The epigenetic approach focuses on both the "micro" interactions of genes at the individual level and the "macro" genetic systems that have developed within the species over time. In the latter respect, epigenetic theory builds on a well-established theory called *ethology* (Hinde, 1983). **Ethology** is the study of patterns of animal behavior, particularly as that behavior relates to evolutionary origins and species survival.

The ethological perspective has particular relevance for infancy. Many of the instinctive behaviors of young infants and their caregivers tend to promote survival (Marvin, 1997).

Infant Instincts
Infants come into the world already equipped with social predispositions and social skills that help ensure their nurturance and development. For example, they can distinguish the sounds and rhythms of speech, recognize the facial expressions of fear and pleasure, and distinguish one person from another by smell, touch, and sound. Despite being so obviously immobile and helpless, human infants are genetically programmed to display reflexes—including grasping, clinging, crying, and grunting—that summon adults or keep them nearby.

In the beginning, infants accept help from anyone—a good survival strategy in the centuries when women regularly died in childbirth. By the time they are able to crawl,

however, infants have become emotionally attached to their specific caregivers as well as fearful of unfamiliar situations.

Over the course of human history, infants who stayed near nurturing and protecting adults were more likely to survive. Hence, selective adaptation produced infants who are receptive to anyone at first and who become very attached to one or two people by age 1.

Adult Impulses
Correspondingly, caregiving adults are genetically equipped to nurture babies. Logically, no reasonable adult would ever put up with being a parent. It is irrational to endure the sleepless nights, dirty diapers, and frequent cries of a baby. Fortunately, however, genetic impulses are not logical. Humans are programmed to cherish and protect children.

As the mother of four, I have been surprised by the power of this programming many times. With my first-born, I asked my pediatrician if my Bethany wasn't one of the most beautiful, perfect babies he had ever seen.

"Yes," he said, with a twinkle in his eyes, "and my patients are better looking than the patients of any other pediatrician in the city."

With my second newborn, the hospital offered to sell me a photo of her—hairless, chinless, and with swollen eyelids—at 1 day old; I glanced at it and said "no." The photo didn't look at all like her—it made my beautiful Rachel look almost ugly. I was similarly enamored of my third and fourth. For the fourth, however, a new thought came to me: I am not only a woman who loves her children; I am a woman who loves her sleep. In the predawn hours, as I roused myself yet again to feed my fourth baby, I asked myself how se-

lective forgetting had allowed me, once again, to choose a disruptive addition to my life that was guaranteed to deprive me of my precious slumber. The answer, of course, is that some genetic instincts are even stronger than the instinct for self-preservation.

Open Wide Caregivers and babies elicit responses from each other that ensure survival of the next generation. The caregiver's role in this vital interaction is obvious, but ethology has shown that infants starve if they do not chirp, meow, whine, bleat, squeal, cry, or otherwise signal hunger—and then open their mouths wide when food arrives. Both the baby birds and 5-month-old Jonah obviously know what to do.

UNEP / SAY BOON FOO / THE IMAGE WORKS

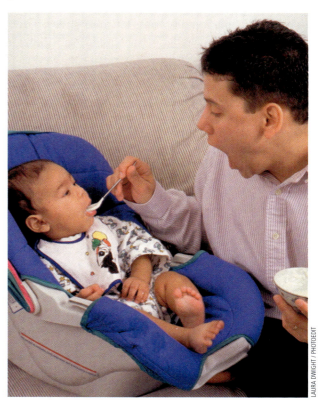
LAURA DWIGHT / PHOTOEDIT

?*Observational Quiz* (see answer, page 54): In some ways, babies all look alike, as ethological theory points out. What are three similarities among the babies above and the infant monkey on page 40?

The two emergent theories seem to point in opposite directions. Sociocultural theory looks outward, to the overarching social, historical, and cultural patterns that affect communities, families, and, ultimately, individuals. Epigenetic theory begins inward, with thousands of genes, and then incorporates the factors that directly affect the expression of those genes. Both emergent theories, however, combine insights, data, and methods from many academic disciplines and take into account current research and techniques of analysis unavailable to earlier generations. Both are innovative and exciting, useful for contemporary scientists who are eager to discover new aspects of human development.

What Theories Can Contribute

Each of the theories presented in this chapter has contributed a great deal to the study of human development, focusing on one aspect and thus adding to our understanding of the life span (see Table 2.3).

TABLE 2.3 Five Perspectives on Human Development

Theory	Area of Focus	Fundamental Depiction of What People Do	Relative Emphasis on Nature or Nurture?
Psychoanalytic	Psychosexual (Freud) or psychosocial (Erikson) stages	Battle unconscious impulses and overcome major crises	More nature (biological, sexual impulses, and parent–child bonds)
Behaviorism	Conditioning through stimulus and response	Respond to stimuli, reinforcement, and models	More nurture (direct environment produces various behaviors)
Cognitive	Thinking, remembering, analyzing	Seek to understand experiences while forming concepts and cognitive strategies	More nature (person's own mental activity and motivation are key)
Sociocultural	Social context, expressed through people, language, customs	Learn the tools, skills, and values of society through apprenticeships	More nurture (interaction of mentor and learner, within cultural context)
Epigenetic	Genes and factors that repress or encourage genetic expression	Develop impulses, interests, and patterns inherited from ancestors	Begins with nature; nurture is crucial, via nutrients, toxins, and so on

- *Psychoanalytic theory* has made us aware of the importance of early childhood experiences.
- *Behaviorism* has shown the effect that the immediate environment can have on learning, step by step.
- *Cognitive theory* has brought a greater understanding of how intellectual processes and thinking affect actions.
- *Sociocultural theory* has reminded us that development is embedded in a rich and multifaceted cultural context.
- *Epigenetic theory* emphasizes the interaction between inherited forces and immediate contexts.

In order, these five theories present us with: the unconscious processes, the environment, the intellect, the culture, and the genes. No comprehensive view of development can ignore any one of these factors.

Each theory has had its critics. Psychoanalytic theory has been faulted for being too subjective; behaviorism, for being too mechanistic; cognitive theory, for undervaluing genetic differences; sociocultural theory, for neglecting individuals; and epigenetic theory, for neglecting society. Today most developmentalists prefer an **eclectic perspective.** That is, rather than adopt any one of these theories exclusively, they make selective use of them. The state of research in human development has been accurately characterized as "theoretical pluralism" because no single theory fully explains the behavior of humans as they go through life (Dixon & Lerner, 1999).

eclectic perspective The approach taken by most developmentalists, in which they apply aspects of each of the various theories of development rather than adhering exclusively to one theory.

The Nature–Nurture Controversy

Whatever the limitations of particular theories, time and time again, as we study the life span, we find that theories provide understanding and insight about myriad experiences and events. It is easy to be dazzled, whipsawed, and confused about human development if we do not have some perspective to guide us. One illustration is the dispute that has echoed through every decade of developmental study: the nature–nurture controversy (Dixon & Learner, 1999; Singer, 2003).

Nature refers to the influence of the genes that each person inherits from his or her parents at the moment of conception. **Nurture** refers to all the environmental influences that come into play after conception, beginning with the mother's

nature A general term for the traits, capacities, and limitations that each individual inherits genetically from his or her parents at the moment of conception.

nurture A general term for all the environmental influences that affect development after an individual is conceived.

!Answer to Observational Quiz (from page 52): Sparse hair (or fur, or feathers), big heads, and evident responses to their caregivers.

health during pregnancy and including all the individual's experiences in the outside world—in the family, the school, the community, and the culture at large.

The nature–nurture controversy has taken on many names, among them *heredity versus environment* and *maturation versus learning*. Under whatever name, the basic question remains: How much of any given characteristic, behavior, or pattern of development is the result of genes and how much is the result of experiences? Note that the question is "How much?" not "Whether" or "Which ones?" All developmentalists agree that nature and nurture interact to produce every specific trait; no characteristic develops as an exclusive response to either nature or nurture. Yet the specifics are hotly debated—and theories can help.

Theoretical Perspectives on Hyperactivity and Homosexuality

Consider two very different issues: the basis of hyperactivity and the basis of homosexuality. How, and to what extent, are nature and nurture involved in each case?

Some children seem always active, running around or restless even when they should be still. They are impulsive, unable to attend to anything for more than a moment. This is called *attention-deficit/hyperactivity disorder,* or AD/HD (American Psychiatric Association, 2000). Is AD/HD more a matter of *nature* (born into the child) or *nurture* (a product of the home, school, and society)?

There is evidence for both possibilities. Several facts support the argument that "nature" (genetic inheritance) is responsible:

■ AD/HD children are usually boys.
■ AD/HD children often have close male relatives with the same problem.
■ AD/HD children are typically overactive in every context.
■ AD/HD children often calm down when they take stimulants, such as Ritalin, Adderall, and even coffee.

The last fact convinces many: Since biochemical treatment works, the cause of AD/HD must be biochemical—that is, essentially, nature.

There is also evidence that "nurture" is the cause:

■ The rate of AD/HD diagnosed in the United States has increased from less than 1 to more than 5 percent over the past 50 years. Genes do not change that fast; a rapid increase in any problem suggests an environmental cause. There is dispute as to what that cause might be. Urban life, television, lead, refined sugar, and food additives have all been suspected.
■ Rates of AD/HD are much higher in some classrooms than in others. This suggests that teachers who are not adept at classroom management and curriculum structure may elicit AD/HD in their students.
■ No biological test, such as of blood chemistry or brain structure, reliably distinguishes AD/HD children from normally active children.

This last fact is persuasive to many. If there is no biological marker, the essential cause must be nurture.

Now let us look at the nature–nurture controversy related to sexual orientation. Most social scientists once assumed that homosexuality was the product of nurture, variously attributed. Psychoanalytic theory held that it originated in early childhood, caused by a weak father and an overbearing mother. Behaviorists thought that people learned sexual behavior, as they learned everything else, through reinforcement and punishment. Cognitive theory suggested that, because people's thoughts and ideas determine their actions, some people's thoughts led them to rebel against family and society by experiencing homosexual impulses. Sociocultural theory led to an awareness that some cultures accept homosexuality much more readily than others (some societies expect everyone to be homosexual during adolescence; others are horrified at the thought of homosexuality). The frequency of homosexuality follows cultural expectations—another argument for the role of nurture.

When researchers began to test hypotheses based on these theories, nurture was revealed as less crucial in causing homosexuality. First, surveys found that most people have sexual thoughts and impulses that they do not act on. Indeed, many people with homosexual impulses have heterosexual interactions, including marriages (Masters & Johnson, 1966). A distinction can be made between sexual *orientation,* which concerns a person's erotic inclinations and thoughts, and sexual *expression,* which involves a person's sexual activities. Thus, a culture's attitude (nurture) can and does affect sexual behavior but does not necessarily affect the incidence of sexual orientation, which could be mainly a matter of nature.

Building for the Future The proud parents beam as their 19-month-old son uses blocks to make a tall building. Erik Erikson and other psycho-analytic theorists would be happy, too: Erikson observed that boys build towers and girls create circular enclosures. Psychoanalytic theorists might not be so happy, however, with these parents' sexual orientation.

Second, no evidence was uncovered that parental relationships and personality characteristics play a role. Psychoanalytic theory seems in error.

Third, children raised by homosexual couples (either adopted or the biological offspring of one of the parents) are found to be heterosexual or homosexual in the same proportions as children raised by heterosexuals. This suggests that children do not learn their sexual orientation from their parents' example.

Other lines of research suggested more of a role for nature than for nurture, which theoretically was involved, but which the evidence did not support. For example, several genetic analyses found linkages in homosexuality among close relatives (especially monozygotic twins, and uncles and nephews) (Bailey et al., 2000), and prenatal hormones were found to affect a fetus's eventual sexuality (Collaer & Hines, 1995).

Both hyperactivity and homosexuality are discussed later in this text. Now is not the time to decide whether nature or nurture causes either of them. In fact, for those who take a "developmental perspective," choosing nature or nurture is a "dangerous quagmire." According to two psychologists:

> Those who dichotomize sexual orientation into pure biological or social causation fall into a dangerous quagmire. To deny any role for biology affirms an untenable scientific view of human development. Equally harsh and deterministic would be to deny the significance of the environment.
>
> *[Savin-Williams & Diamond, 1997, p. 235]*

On many issues with policy implications, people have diametrically opposed opinions based on emotions, not data. For example, some say that society, by restricting play and imposing excessive homework, makes boys hyperactive and then medicates them rather than deal with the underlying problems through school reform or culture shifts. Others say that, just as we give insulin to children with diabetes, it is cruel not to give Ritalin to children with AD/HD.

Similarly impassioned opinions arise when homosexuality is discussed, or, for that matter, birth defects, school curricula, divorce laws, nursing home regulations, and so on. In the many issues that somehow relate to the nature–nurture debate, ideology often adds to the complexity and polarization of opinion. As one scholar, using the example of aggression, points out: "Individual differences in aggression can be accounted for by genetic or socialization differences, with politically conservative scientists tending to believe the former and more liberal scientists the latter" (Lewis, 1997, p. 102).

As a result, "opinions shift back and forth between extreme positions" (Singer, 2003, p. 438). Because opposite opinions can lead to contradictory and even harmful policies, it is critical to separate assumptions from facts, to put something between opinions and conclusions. How can we get past extremes, resist the pull of political views, overcome the confusion of assumptions? Theories!

Theories suggest hypotheses, investigation, and, finally, answers, substituting some objective research for personal assumptions. For instance, although it is now known that the parental relationship is not the cause of homosexuality, this conclusion could not be drawn until researchers tested the psychoanalytic hypothesis. Theories as such are not true or false, but they serve to move the scientific process forward.

In later chapters, as you encounter elaborations and echoes of the five major theories and various minitheories, you will no doubt form your own opinion as to the validity and usefulness of each. Probably you will also take an eclectic view—one that chooses the best from each theory—to guide your exploration. You may even begin to devise a coherent, comprehensive, systematic approach of your own.

> Theories—grand, mini-, or emerging—are very practical. Many issues related to human development—including, for example, the origins of hyperactivity or of homosexuality—stir up impassioned opinions and at the same time have practical implications, which require objective research. Theories help scholars and others find their way through the thicket of political and personal assumptions. Most scholars remain open to various theoretical perspectives, choosing to be eclectic in their approach rather than tied to any one point of view.

SUMMARY

What Theories Do

1. A theory provides a framework of general principles that can be used to guide research and explain observations. Each developmental theory interprets human development from a somewhat different perspective, but all developmental theories attempt to provide a context for understanding how individual experiences and behavior change over time. Theories are practical in that they aid inquiry, interpretation, and research.

Grand Theories

2. Psychoanalytic theory emphasizes that human actions and thoughts originate from powerful impulses and conflicts that often are not part of our conscious awareness. Freud based psychoanalytic theory on the idea that sexual urges arise during three stages of childhood development, called the oral, anal, and phallic stages. Parents' reactions to conflicts associated with these urges have a lasting impact on the child's personality.

3. Erikson's version of psychoanalytic theory emphasizes psychosocial contexts, wherein individuals are shaped by the interaction of personal characteristics and social forces. Erikson described eight successive stages of psychosocial development, each of which involves a developmental crisis.

4. Behaviorists, or learning theorists, believe that the focus of psychologists' study should be behavior, which can be observed and measured. This theory seeks to discover the laws that govern the relationship between events and the reactions they produce.

5. Behaviorism emphasizes various forms of conditioning—a learning process. In classical conditioning, a neutral stimulus becomes associated with a meaningful stimulus, and eventually the neutral stimulus alone produces the response first associated with the meaningful stimulus. In operant conditioning, certain responses, called reinforcers, are used to make it more likely that certain behaviors will be repeated.

6. Social learning theory recognizes that much of human behavior is learned by observing the behavior of others. The basic process is modeling, in which we first observe a behavior and then repeat it. Generally, the person being observed is admirable in some way or the behavior is one that the observer is motivated to repeat.

7. All theories lead to research that tests various hypotheses. Harlow's studies of mother love among baby monkeys revealed that comforting contact was more important than food in establishing the mother–infant bond.

8. Cognitive theorists believe that a person's thought processes have an important effect on his or her understanding of the world and thus on his or her development. Piaget proposed that an individual's thinking develops through four age-related periods.

9. Piaget believed that cognitive development is an active and universal process. Curiosity is guided by the search for cognitive equilibrium, which is a person's ability to explain a new situation with existing understanding. When disequilibrium occurs, people develop cognitively by modifying their understanding to cover the new situation.

Emergent Theories

10. Sociocultural theory explains human development in terms of the guidance, support, and structure provided by culture. For Vygotsky, learning occurs through the social interactions that learners share with more knowledgeable members of the society who guide learners through the zone of proximal development.

11. Epigenetic theory begins by noting that genes are powerful and omnipresent, potentially affecting every aspect of development. This theory also stresses an ongoing interaction between the genes and environmental forces, which can range from prenatal toxins to long-term stresses. This interaction can halt, modify, or strengthen the effects of the genes, both within the person and, over time, within the species.

What Theories Can Contribute

12. Psychoanalytic, learning, cognitive, sociocultural, and epigenetic theories have each contributed to the understanding of human development, yet no one theory is broad enough to describe the full complexity and diversity of human experience.

13. Each theory provides a useful perspective; none are complete in themselves. Most developmentalists are eclectic, adopting aspects of various theories rather than following any single theory.

14. Every theory can shed some light on issues such as the nature–nurture controversy, which centers on how much influence heredity and the environment each have on human development. All researchers agree, however, that both factors influence all aspects of development to some extent.

KEY TERMS

developmental theory (p. 33)
grand theories (p. 34)
minitheories (p. 34)
emergent theories (p. 34)
psychoanalytic theory
  (p. 34)
behaviorism (p. 38)
conditioning (p. 38)

classical conditioning (p. 38)
operant conditioning (p. 38)
reinforcement (p. 39)
social learning theory (p. 42)
modeling (p. 42)
self-efficacy (p. 42)
cognitive theory (p. 43)
cognitive equilibrium (p. 43)

sociocultural theory (p. 45)
apprenticeship in thinking
  (p. 46)
guided participation (p. 46)
zone of proximal development
  (p. 47)
epigenetic theory (p. 48)
preformism (p. 48)

selective adaptation (p. 50)
ethology (p. 51)
eclectic perspective (p. 53)
nature (p. 53)
nurture (p. 53)

APPLICATIONS

1. Developmentalists sometimes talk about "folk theories," which are theories developed by ordinary people, who are usually unaware that they are theorizing. Choose three common sayings, such as "A penny saved is a penny earned" or "As the twig is bent, so grows the tree." Explain the theory that each saying reflects.

2. The nature–nurture debate can apply to many issues. Ask three people to tell you their theory about what factors create a criminal. Identify which of the five theories described in this chapter is closest to each of these explanations.

3. Behaviorism has been used to change personal habits. Think of a habit you'd like to change (e.g., stop smoking, exercise more, use less bad language). Count the frequency of that behavior for a week, noting the reinforcers for it. Then, and only then, try to learn a substitute behavior by reinforcing yourself for it. Keep careful records, and report your results. Why did you succeed or fail in changing your habit?

Chapter Three

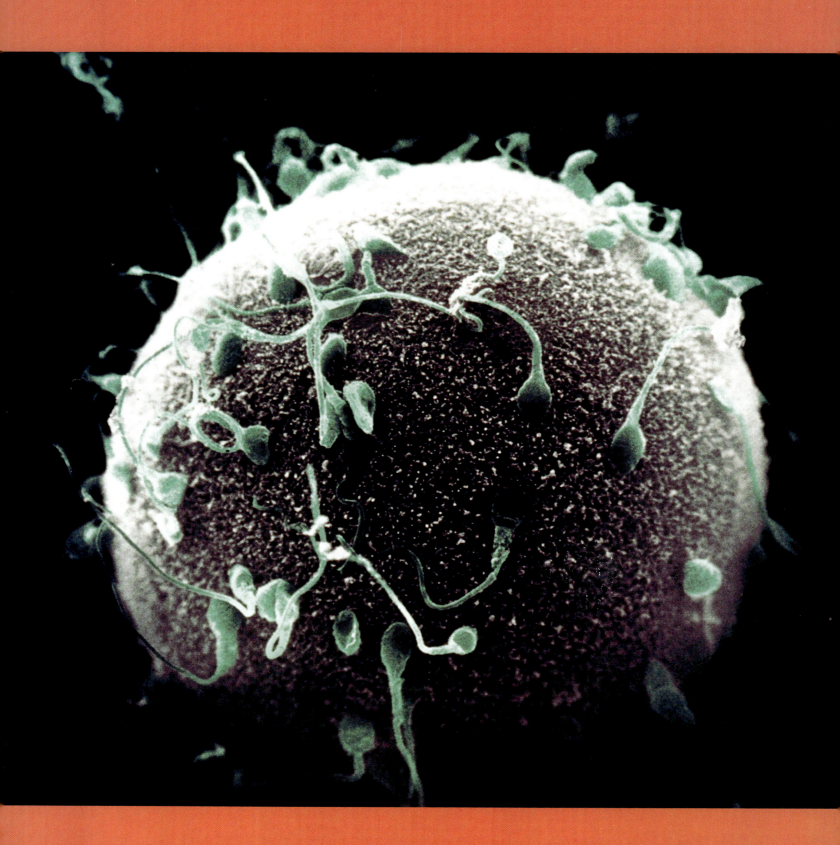

Heredity and Environment

DNA (deoxyribonucleic acid) The molecular basis of heredity, constructed of a double helix whose parallel strands consist of both pairs held together by hydrogen bonds.

chromosome A carrier of genes; one of the 46 molecules of DNA (in 23 pairs) that each cell of the body contains and that, together, contain all human genes.

Genes play a leading role in the drama of human development. Prospective parents want to know what traits their children will inherit; physicians sometimes question patients about close relatives and distant ancestors; scientists have been working for decades to decode the human genome; and all students of human development realize that "once we take development seriously, we must also take genetics seriously" (Pennington, 2001). Yet, in many ways, genes are a mystery—pervasive and powerful, yet also hidden and elusive.

One day when I arrived to pick up my daughter Rachel from school, another mother pulled me aside. She whispered that Rachel had fallen on her hand and that Rachel's little finger might be broken. My daughter was happily playing, but when I examined her finger, I saw that it was crooked. Trying to avoid both needless panic and medical neglect, I took Rachel home and consulted my husband. He smiled and spread out his hands, revealing the same bent little finger. Aha! An inherited abnormality, not an injury. But why had I never noticed this before?

That bent little finger is one small example of millions of genetic surprises in human development. This chapter anticipates and explains some of the many mysteries of the human genetic code, going behind the scenes to reveal not only what genes are but also how they work and some of the ethical issues raised by our growing knowledge of them. We begin with the basics.

The Genetic Code

As you learned in the preceding chapters, a person is much more than a set of genetic instructions. Development is always dynamic, ongoing, and interactional. Each person is unlike anyone who has gone before. One of the many miracles of development is that just four chemicals are the basic building blocks of the genetic code.

What Genes Are

To reveal the secrets of the genetic code, we need to review some basic biology. All living things are made up of tiny cells. The work of these cells is done by *proteins*. Each cell manufactures these proteins according to instructions stored at the heart of each cell in molecules of **DNA (deoxyribonucleic acid)**, the famed double helix. Each molecule of DNA is called a **chromosome**, and these chromosomes contain the instructions to make all the proteins a living being needs.

genome The full set of chromosomes, with all the genes they contain, that make up the genetic material of an organism.

gene The basic unit for the transmission of heredity instructions.

This enormous and complex packet of instructions is the **genome.** There is a genome for every species; the human genome is the code for making a human being.

Each human has 23 pairs of chromosomes in each cell (except for reproductive cells). One member of each pair is inherited from each parent. The instructions in these 46 chromosomes are organized into units called **genes.** Every gene is a separate section of the chromosome, and each contains the instructions for a specific protein. A protein is made up of a long string of chemical building blocks called *amino acids.* So the recipe for a protein consists of instructions for stringing together the right amino acids in the right order.

These instructions are written into our DNA using the genetic code, in various combinations of four chemicals: adenine (A), thiamine (T), guanine (G), and cytosine (C). As Figure 3.1 shows, each molecule of DNA is made up of two strands of these chemicals, twisted around each other into a double helix. The two strands are connected by "rungs" so that the double helix looks like a twisted ladder. Each rung is made up of a pair of these chemicals, which combine in only four ways: A-T, T-A, G-C, and C-G. These pairs are arranged in groups of three called *triplets.* Each triplet is the genetic code for a particular amino acid. A gene is the series of triplets corresponding to the string of amino acids that make up one particular protein.

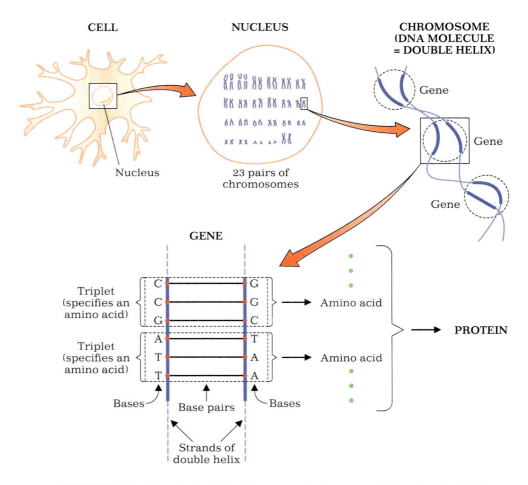

FIGURE 3.1 How Proteins Are Made The genes on the chromosomes in the nucleus of each cell instruct the cell to manufacture the proteins needed to sustain life and development.

Our genome contains about 30,000 genes, allowing cells to make the proteins that help make each person unique and sustain our development. As one expert explains, if each triplet is considered a word, this sequence of genes is

> . . . as long as 800 Bibles. If I read the genome out to you at the rate of one word per second for eight hours a day, it would take me a century. . . . This is a gigantic document, an immense book, a recipe of extravagant length, and it all fits inside the microscopic nucleus of a tiny cell that fits easily upon the head of a pin.
>
> *[Ridley, 1999, p. 7]*

This quotation captures some of the immensity of the genetic code, but it does not explain another amazing part of human genetics—how our genes work together to make human beings.

The Beginnings of Human Life

Human development begins at conception when a male reproductive cell, or *sperm* (plural: *sperm*), penetrates the membrane of a female reproductive cell, or *ovum* (plural: *ova*). Each reproductive cell, or **gamete,** contains 23 chromosomes (in other words, the chromosomes in gametes are not paired, as they are in other cells).

The particular member of each chromosome pair that appears in a given sperm or ovum is random; some gametes have one member of a pair, and some have another. This means that one person produces 2^{23} different gametes, more than 8 million versions of the 23 chromosomes.

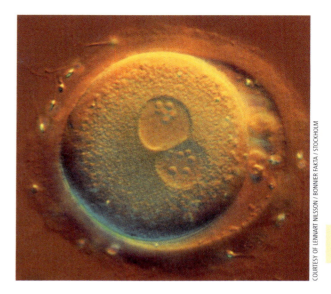

COURTESY OF LENNART NILSSON / BONNIER FAKTA / STOCKHOLM

The Moment of Conception This ovum is about to become a zygote. It has been penetrated by a single sperm, whose nucleus now lies next to the nucleus of the ovum. Soon, the two nuclei will fuse, bringing together about 30,000 genes to guide development.

Zygote and Genotype

When a sperm finds its way through the fallopian tubes to the ovum, only its head actually makes it inside the ovum's membrane. For the first hour or so, the sperm's head creeps toward the nucleus of the ovum. When the two finally meet, their nuclei fuse and a new living cell called a **zygote** is formed: Two reproductive cells have literally become one, and the 23 chromosomes from the father match up with the 23 chromosomes from the mother—so that the zygote contains 46 chromosomes arranged in pairs. The genetic information contained on these 46 chromosomes constitutes the organism's genetic inheritance, or **genotype,** which is set at conception and endures throughout life.

gamete A reproductive cell; that is, a cell that can reproduce a new individual if it combines with a gamete from the other sex.

zygote The single cell formed from the fusing of a sperm and an ovum.

genotype An organism's entire genetic inheritance, or genetic potential.

OMIKRON / PHOTO RESEARCHERS, INC.

Mapping the Karyotype A *karyotype* portrays a person's chromosomes. To create a karyotype, a cell is grown in a laboratory, magnified, and then usually photographed. The photo is cut into pieces and rearranged so that the matched pairs of chromosomes are lined up from largest *(at top left)* to smallest *(at bottom right, fourth box from the left).* Shown in the last two boxes at bottom right are the two normal possibilities for the 23rd chromosome pair: XX for a female and XY for a male.

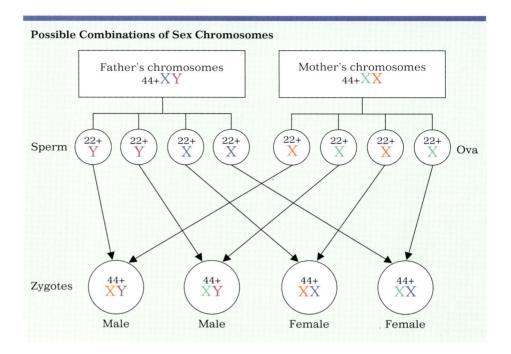

Possible Combinations of Sex Chromosomes

FIGURE 3.2 **Determining a Zygote's Sex**
Any given couple can produce four possible combinations of sex chromosomes; two lead to female
children, and two to male. In terms of the future
person's sex, it does not matter which of the
mother's Xs the zygote inherited. All that matters is
whether the father's Y sperm or X sperm fertilized
the ovum. However, for X-linked conditions it matters a great deal, because typically one, but not
both, of the mother's Xs carries the trait.

allele A slight, normal variation of a particular gene.

23rd pair The chromosome pair that, in humans,
determines the zygote's (and hence the person's) sex, among other things.

XX A 23rd pair that consists of two X-shaped chromosomes, one from the mother and one from
the father.

XY A 23rd pair that consists of one X-shaped chromosome from the mother and one Y-shaped
chromosome from the father.

spontaneous abortion The naturally occurring
termination of a pregnancy before the fetus is
fully developed. (Also called *miscarriage*.)

Sex Determination and Sex Ratio

In 22 of the 23 pairs of human chromosomes, the two chromosomes are very
closely matched. Each chromosome of the pair contains hundreds of genes in the
same positions and sequence. This match is not absolutely identical because
some genes come in several slight, normal variations called **alleles.**

The **23rd pair** is a different case. In females, the 23rd pair is composed of
two large, X-shaped chromosomes. Accordingly, it is designated **XX.** In males,
the 23rd pair is composed of one large, X-shaped chromosome and one much
smaller Y-shaped chromosome. It is designated **XY.**

Because a female's 23rd chromosome pair is XX, every ovum that her body
creates will contain either one X or the other—but always an X. And because a
male's 23rd pair is XY, half of his sperm will contain an X chromosome and half
will contain a Y. The Y chromosome (but not the X) contains a gene (called SRY)
that directs a developing fetus to make male organs. Thus, the critical factor in the
determination of a zygote's sex is which sperm reaches the ovum first—a Y sperm,
creating a male (XY), or an X sperm, creating a female (XX) (see Figure 3.2).

Although only one chromosome determines sex, strictly speaking, sex determination is not always entirely the result of a race between an equal number of X
and Y sperm. Rarely, a man carries a gene that renders either his X or Y sperm
immobile, so he fathers only sons or only daughters. Occasionally a woman's
uterus is unusually acid or alkaline, giving either X or Y sperm an advantage.
Further, in a stressful pregnancy, XY embryos are more likely than XXs to be ex-
pelled in a **spontaneous abortion** (also called a *miscarriage*).

For the total population, these factors even out, and the natural sex ratio at
birth is close to 50/50. The actual current sex ratio in the United States is about 52
males to 48 females. Minor ethnic variations are apparent: Chinese-Americans
have the most males, at 55/45, and Hawaiian-Americans have the fewest, at 50/50
(Martin et al., 2001).

Historically, wars and diseases sometimes killed most of a given population
before they could reproduce, with girls more likely to survive than boys. When
the sex ratio became markedly imbalanced, some cultures encouraged men to
take multiple wives and thus to father more children, replacing and maintaining

the population. If the total population was not shrinking, other societies simply favored males, practicing female infanticide (a practice so common that the Koran explicitly forbade it) or allowing men to divorce or even kill wives who had no sons (as did England's King Henry VIII). Scientific knowledge has settled some of these ethical questions but has also raised new ones, as the following Changing Policy feature makes clear.

Changing Policy

Too Many Boys? Too Many Girls?

Over the course of history, billions of women ate certain foods, slept a certain way, or prayed to have the boy or girl they wanted. Today, we know that no postconception diet or action can alter the sex of the developing embryo.

However, knowledge does not change desires; it only changes the means used to attain them. In China, between 1990 and 1993, prenatal testing of embryos led to abortions of millions of female fetuses as well as to international adoption of thousands of infant girls who were not wanted by their biological parents. In India, in the state of Punjab in 1999, only 79 females were born for every 100 boys; this imbalance is evidence that prenatal testing and then abortion of developing females occurred in about 25 percent of all pregnancies (Duggar, 2001). In Nepal, women are much more likely to use contraception after the birth of a son than a daughter (Leone et al., 2003).

Sperm-sorting techniques have long been used with cattle, if either beef or milk is the desired product, but is still experimental with humans. This possibility (along with the reality of selective abortion) raises the question of whether sex selection is a private choice or a public issue. Worldwide, men are particularly likely to prefer sons over daughters. Consider the social consequences if only half as many girls as boys were born.

In family life
- Fewer single mothers, more never-married men
- Weaker family ties overall (because women maintain the family network)
- More children per woman, fewer children per man
- More children with learning disabilities, hyperactivity, conduct disorders
- Fewer adolescents with depression, eating disorders

In economic life
- More engineers, architects, billionaires
- Fewer teachers, secretaries, widows living alone
- Less demand for fashionable clothes, household furnishings, kitchen equipment
- More violent crimes, police, judges, prisons

In health care
- More accidental deaths, suicides, homicides
- Fewer specialists in gerontology, gynecology, chronic illness
- More people suffering from drug and alcohol abuse
- Fewer nurses, health aides

In community life
- More spectators and participants at sports contests
- Fewer people at libraries and churches
- More wars and more votes for conservative policies
- Fewer day-care centers and fewer votes for liberal policies

Do you object to the *community life* category, because culture, not biology, determines interest in sports, religion, or voting? You are right to do so. However, the same objection applies to every item. Chromosomes do not determine behavior directly; culture can adjust to remedy problems. For example, if more nurses were needed, salaries and training could be made more attractive to men.

The Ethics Committee of the American Society for Reproductive Medicine (2001) permits selective use of human sperm sorting, especially to avoid a genetic disease. What do you think?

Multiple Zygotes

Although every zygote is genetically unique (i.e., has a unique genotype), not every newborn is. In some pregnancies, the growing cluster of cells splits completely apart in the early stages of development, creating two or four or even

Any Monozygotic Twins Here? Sometimes twins are obviously dizygotic, as when they are of different sexes or, like the girls on the right, differ notably in coloring, size, and perhaps visual acuity. However, sometimes dizygotic twins can look a lot alike, just as two siblings born a year or two apart can share many physical characteristics.

?Observational Quiz (see answer, page 67): What do the similarities and differences of the boys in the left photo suggest about their zygosity?

monozygotic twins Twins who have identical genes because they were formed from one zygote that split into two identical organisms very early in development.

dizygotic twins Twins who were formed when two separate ova were fertilized by two separate sperm at roughly the same time. Such twins share about half their genes, like any other siblings.

eight identical, independent zygotes. These multiple zygotes can then become multiple births—**monozygotic twins** (identical twins) or monozygotic quadruplets and so on, so named because they originate from one (*mono*) zygote. Because they originate from the same zygote and have the same genotype, monozygotic multiple births share identical genetic instructions for physical appearance, psychological traits, vulnerability to diseases, and everything else.

About a third of twins are monozygotic; the rest are **dizygotic twins.** Dizygotic twins (also called fraternal twins) begin life as two separate zygotes created by the fertilization of two ova at roughly the same time. (Usually, only one ovum is released at a time, but occasionally, two or more ova are available for fertilization.) Although dizygotic conceptions may occur as frequently as one in every six pregnancies, usually only one twin develops past the embryo stage.

Dizygotic births occur naturally about once in every 60 births, with considerable variation among ethnic groups. (Women from Nigeria, for example, spontaneously produce dizygotic newborns about once in every 25 births; women from England, once in 100; and women from Japan, once in 700 [Gall, 1996]).

Age is also a factor: Women in their late 30s are three times as likely to have dizygotic twins as women in their early 20s (Mange & Mange, 1999). The reason is that, as menopause approaches, ovulation becomes irregular, with some cycles producing no ova and others multiple ova.

Dizygotic twins share no more genes than any other offspring of the same parents; that is, they share about 50 percent of the genes governing individual differences. They may look quite different from each other. Or they may look a great deal alike, just as nontwin brothers and sisters sometimes do, but genetically they are only half alike. For example, about half the time, one dizygotic twin is a boy and the other is a girl.

Duplication, Division, and Differentiation

At conception, when the sperm and ovum combine into a zygote, they form a complete set of instructions for creating a person. This creation is far from straightforward, involving complex processes of duplication of genetic information, cell division, and differentiation of cells into different types. Life begins with a single cell, but the process becomes increasingly complex as development proceeds (Johnston & Edwards, 2002).

Duplication and Division

Within hours after conception, the zygote begins the first stages of growth through a process of *duplication* and *division*. First, the 23 pairs of chromosomes duplicate, forming two complete sets of the genetic code for that person. Then these two sets move toward opposite sides of the zygote, and the single cell within the zygote splits neatly down the middle. The zygote's outer membrane now surrounds two cells, each containing a complete set of the original genetic code. These two cells duplicate and divide to become four; these four, in turn, duplicate and divide to become eight; and so on.

When you (or I, or any other person) were born, your original zygote had become about 10 trillion cells. By adulthood, those cells had become more than 100 trillion. But no matter how large the total number, no matter how much division and duplication occur, each cell (except gametes and some cells of the immune system) carries an exact copy of the complete genetic instructions inherited by the one-celled zygote. This explains why DNA testing of any body cell, even one from a drop of blood or a snip of hair, can identify "the real father," or "the guilty criminal," or "the long-lost brother."

Differentiation

The fact that every cell in the embryo contains the developing human being's complete genetic code does not mean that any cell could become a person—far from it. At about the eight-cell stage, a third process, *differentiation*, is added to duplication and division. Cells begin to specialize, taking different forms and reproducing at various rates, depending on where in the growing mass of cells they are located. As one expert explains it, "We are sitting with parts of our body that could have been used for thinking" (Gottlieb, 2002, p. 172). Very early in development, cells change from being able to become any part of a creature to being able to become only one part—an eye or a finger, for instance.

Genes also affect this process. Some genes code for proteins that switch other genes on and off, making sure that the other genes produce the right proteins at the appropriate times. These **on–off switching mechanisms** continue lifelong, instructing cells to repair damage, to take in nourishment, to multiply, to atrophy, and even to die. Certain genes switch on at particular ages, propelling maturation of specific parts of the brain important in physical and cognitive development, such as the ability to think about abstractions or to plan ahead (Plomin et al., 2001).

But keep in mind that "genes merely produce proteins, not mature traits" (Gottlieb, 2002, p. 164). In other words, particular genes may instigate body and brain formation, but genetic expression also depends on the influence of other genes and the environment. A zygote might have the genes for becoming, say, a musical genius, but that genetic potential will not be realized unless additional genes and factors in the environment permit that trait to develop. A distinction is made between *genotype*—which, as you learned earlier, is the sum total of genes inherited by a person—and **phenotype**—that is, the person's actual appearance and behavior, which are the result of both genetic and environmental influences.

Gene–Gene Interactions

Conception brings together genetic instructions from both parents for every human characteristic. Exactly how do these instructions influence the specific traits that a given offspring inherits? The answer is quite complex, because most traits are both **multifactorial**—that is, influenced by many factors, including factors in the environment—and **polygenic**—that is, affected by many genes.

Almost all important traits are the result of interactions among several genes (Hoh & Ott, 2003). On–off switching mechanisms, as mentioned, are one type of gene–gene interaction. Among the other types are two patterns of genetic interaction, additive and dominant–recessive.

Additive Genes

Some genes are said to be **additive genes.** When genes interact additively, the trait reflects fairly equal contributions of all the genes that are involved. The

on–off switching mechanisms Processes in which certain genes code for proteins that switch other genes on and off, making sure that the other genes produce proteins at the appropriate times.

phenotype A person's actual appearance and behavior, which are the result of both genetic and environmental influences.

multifactorial Referring to inherited traits that are influenced by many factors, including factors in the environment, rather than by genetic influences alone.

polygenic Referring to inherited traits that are influenced by many genes, rather than by a single gene.

additive gene A gene that, through interaction with other genes, affects a specific trait (such as skin color or height).

Skin Color Is Inherited But . . . Using "black," "white," "red," and "yellow" to denote human skin color is misleading, because humans actually have thousands of skin tones, each resulting from the combination of many genes, and none of them are one of these four colors. Depending on which half of each parent's skin-color genes children happen to inherit, each child can be paler, ruddier, lighter, darker, more sallow, more olive, or more freckled than either parent. This is particularly apparent in many African-American families, like this one, whose ancestors came from at least three continents.

dominant–recessive pattern The interaction of a pair of alleles in such a way that the phenotype reveals the influence of one allele (the dominant gene) more than that of the other (the recessive gene).

dominant gene The member of an interacting pair of alleles whose influence is more evident in the phenotype.

recessive gene The member of an interacting pair of alleles whose influence is less evident in the phenotype.

X-linked Referring to a gene that is located on the X chromosome.

many genes that affect height, hair curliness, and skin color, for instance, usually interact in an additive fashion. Indeed, an estimated 100 genes each contribute a small amount to affect height (Little, 2002).

Consider an unlikely couple. A tall man whose parents and grandparents were all very tall marries a short woman whose parents and grandparents were all very short. Assume that every one of his 100 height genes is for tallness and that hers are all for shortness. The couple's children will inherit tall genes via the father's sperm and short genes via the mother's ova. Because the genes affecting height are additive, the children will be of middling height (assuming that environmental influences, such as nutrition and physical health, are adequate). None of them will be as tall as their father or as short as their mother, because each has half the genes for tallness and half for shortness, averaged together. (In fact, my father was very tall and my mother quite short, and my brother and I are in between.)

In actuality, most people have both kinds of ancestors—relatively tall ones and relatively short ones—so children are often taller or shorter than either parent. My daughter Rachel is of average height, shorter than either my husband or me. However, she is taller than either grandmother. Rachel inherited her grandmothers' shortness genes from our genotypes, even though it is not apparent in our phenotypes. Our three other children are taller than Rachel, especially our youngest, Sarah, who is two inches taller than I am. She obviously inherited quite different genes from us than Rachel did.

How any additive trait turns out depends on all the contributions of whichever genes (half from each parent) a child happens to inherit. Every additive gene that is part of a person's genotype has some impact on the phenotype. I myself am tall because my father was very tall; I would have been even taller if my mother had not been so short. I also would have been taller if only one of the chromosomes in my 23rd pair had chanced to differ. If I were XY (that is, male) instead of XX, I would be 3 to 4 inches taller, because male hormones add several inches of height.

Dominant and Recessive Genes

Less common than additive genes are nonadditive genes, in which the phenotype shows the influence of one gene much more than another's. In one kind of nonadditive pattern, alleles interact according to the **dominant–recessive pattern**. When a pair of alleles interact according to this pattern, the resulting phenotype reveals the influence of one allele, called the **dominant gene**, more than that of the other allele, called the **recessive gene.**

Sometimes the dominant gene completely controls the characteristic and the recessive gene is merely carried, with no influence evident in the phenotype. In other instances, the outcome reflects *incomplete dominance,* with the phenotype influenced primarily, but not exclusively, by the dominant gene.

Many physical characteristics are expressed according to the dominant–recessive pattern. Blood types A and B are both dominant and type O is recessive, leading to a complex relationship of genotype and phenotype in blood inheritance (see Appendix A, p. A-3.) Brown eyes are also said to be dominant over blue eyes, and many genetic diseases are recessive. However, even with eye color and many diseases, additive interactions are also apparent.

A special case of the dominant–recessive pattern occurs with genes that are **X-linked,** located on the X chromosome. If an X-linked gene is recessive—as are the genes for most forms of color blindness, many allergies, several diseases, and some learning disabilities—the fact that it is on the X chromosome is critical. Recall that males have only one X chromosome. Thus, whatever recessive genes a male happens to inherit on his X chromosome cannot be counterbalanced or dominated by alleles on a second X chromosome—he has no second X. So any recessive genes on his X chromosome will be expressed. This explains why traits carried on the X chromosome can be passed from mother to son but not from father to son (since the Y chromosome does not carry the trait) (see Table 3.1). This also explains why males have more X-linked disorders, such as color blindness.

More Complications

As complex as the preceding descriptions of gene–gene interaction patterns may seem, they make these patterns appear much simpler than they actually are. That is because, to be able to discuss interaction at all, we are forced to treat genes as though they were separately functioning "control devices." But, as we have noted, genes merely direct the creation of 20 amino acids, the combinations of which produce thousands of proteins, which then form the body's structures and direct its biochemical functions. The proteins of each body cell are continually affected by other proteins, nutrients, and toxins that influence the cell's functioning (Masoro, 1999).

Not only is it the case that "no gene operates in a vacuum," but each gene "basically interacts either directly or through its protein product with many other genes or gene products" (Peltonen & McKusick, 2001, p. 1226). The outcome of this interaction is difficult to predict. In fact, a small change in one factor may be inconsequential or may cascade to create a major anomaly. The outcome depends on dozens of other factors, many of which are not yet understood (Kirkwood, 2003).

In the dominant–recessive pattern, a dominant gene—even one that is completely dominant—might not actually "penetrate" the phenotype completely (i.e., might not be completely expressed). Such incomplete penetrance may be caused by temperature, stress, or some other nongenetic factor. Similarly, in the additive pattern, some genes may contribute substantially more than others, because they are partially dominant or because their influence is amplified by other genes. For

!*Answer to Observational Quiz* (from page 64): They are almost certainly monozygotic. Their similarities include every obvious genetic trait—coloring, timing of tooth loss, thickness of lips, and shape of the ears and chin. Their differences include exactly the kinds that might be imposed by parents who have trouble distinguishing one child from the other—the color of their eyeglass frames and the length of their hair.

Especially for History Students Some genetic diseases may have changed the course of history. For instance, the last czar of Russia had four healthy daughters and one son with hemophilia. Once called the royal disease, hemophilia is X-linked. How could this rare condition affect the monarchies of Russia, England, Austria, Germany, and Spain?

TABLE 3.1 The 23rd Pair and X-Linked Color Blindness

X indicates an X chromosome with the X-linked gene for color blindness

23rd Pair	Phenotype	Genotype	Next Generation
1. XX	Normal woman	Not a carrier	No color blindness from mother.
2. XY	Normal man	Normal X from mother	No color blindness from father.
3. XX	Normal woman	Carrier from father	Half her children will inherit her X. The girls with her X will be carriers; the boys with her X will be color-blind.
4. XX	Normal woman	Carrier from mother	Half her children will inherit her X. The girls with her X will be carriers; the boys with her X will be color-blind.
5. XY	Color-blind man	Inherited from mother	All his daughters will have his X. None of his sons will have his X. All his children will have normal vision, unless their mother also had an X for color blindness.
6. XX	Color-blind woman (rare)	Inherited from both parents	Every child will have one X from her. Therefore, every son will be color-blind. Daughters will be only carriers, unless they also inherit an X from the father, as their mother did.

Inheritance of an X-Linked Recessive Trait
The phenotypes on lines 1 and 2 are normal because their genes are normal. Those on lines 3 and 4 are normal because the abnormal X-linked gene is recessive and the normal gene is dominant. Those on lines 5 and 6 are color-blind because they have no dominant, normal X.

Response for History Students (from page 67): Hemophilia is a painful, episodic disease that once (before blood transfusions became feasible) killed a boy before adulthood. Though rare, it ran in European royal families, whose members often intermarried, which meant that many queens (including Queen Victoria) were carriers of hemophilia and thus were destined to watch half their sons die of it. All families, even rulers of nations, are distracted from their work when they have a child with a mysterious and lethal illness. Some historians believe that hemophilia among European royalty was an underlying cause of the Russian Revolution of 1917 as well as the spread of democracy in the nineteenth and twentieth centuries.

Human Genome Project An international effort to map the complete human genetic code.

much of their research, geneticists rely on mice that have been carefully inter-bred so that almost no genetic differences can be found between one mouse and another. Yet mice with almost identical genotypes perform differently from one lab to another—evidence for the power of small variations in alleles or of the environment (Walstein, 2003).

Further, certain genes behave differently depending on whether they are inherited from the mother or the father. This parental "imprinting" or "tagging" involves hundreds of genes (Hurst, 1997). Some of the genes that influence height, insulin production, and several forms of mental retardation affect a child in different ways—even in opposite ways—depending on which parent they came from.

Genetic Diversity

One of humanity's striking features is that each person differs in multiple ways from all the others. As one team of scientists explains: "All organisms vary in subtle and profound ways that involve every aspect of biological systems, including morphology, behavior, physiology, development and susceptibility to common disease" (Glazier et al., 2002).

Mechanisms of Genetic Diversity

Given that each human sperm or ovum contains only 23 chromosomes, how can every conception be genetically unique? You already know that about 8 million chromosomally different ova or sperm can be produced by a single individual, which means that any couple can produce 64 trillion different children.

What's more, just before a chromosome pair in a man's or woman's body divides to form gametes, genes from corresponding segments of the pair are randomly exchanged, altering the genetic composition of both pair members. Through the vast number of unpredictable new combinations it produces, this *crossing-over* of genes adds greatly to genetic diversity.

Another important mechanism of genetic diversity is *mutation,* the alteration of genetic information caused by environmental factors, from radiation to toxic chemicals. Most mutations are lethal, preventing zygotes from developing into a viable fetus. The few zygotes that do survive may thrive and live long enough to reproduce, changing the species over the centuries.

Outsiders might see superficial family resemblances in siblings. Every parent knows, however, that each child is unlike the others. It is no exaggeration to say that every zygote is unique. No wonder it is sometimes said that the parents of one child believe in nurture but the parents of two or more children believe in nature (Wright, 1998).

Health Benefits of Genetic Diversity

Genetic diversity safeguards human health. One surprising example relates to infection by the human immunodeficiency virus (HIV), which leads to AIDS. Infection by HIV can be prevented by sexual abstinence or "safe sex," and death from AIDS can be postponed by a sophisticated drug regimen; nonetheless, AIDS is devastating, highly infectious, and increasingly deadly in many nations. However, a few people who are exposed to HIV, even repeatedly exposed, never catch the virus, because a small difference in the code of one gene prevents the virus from infecting their cells (Little, 2002). Other genetic differences probably also allowed some humans centuries ago to survive the plague, or tuberculosis, or other scourges. Genetic diversity thus maintains the species, although obviously not every individual. As the Thinking Like a Scientist feature explains, the **Human Genome Project** is expanding our understanding of the connections between genetic makeup and disease.

Thinking Like a Scientist

The Human Genome Project

Thousands of geneticists are working to decipher the genomes of various living things. Recent successes in genetic mapping have included yeast, nematodes, rice, fruit flies, and, most notably, humans, through the Human Genome Project.

In the year 2000, two drafts of the human genome were published, a scientific feat that merited front-page headlines in newspapers throughout the world. Although still incomplete, these drafts are enormously useful for locating genes responsible for certain disabilities and for revealing three astonishing facts:

- All living creatures share genes. For example, the eyes of flies, mice, and people all originate from the Pax6 gene; the gene that produces legs for a butterfly is the same gene for the four legs of a cat, the many legs of a centipede, and the two legs of a person.
- The more closely related the organisms, the more genes they have in common. For example, humans and chimpanzees have 99 percent of their genes in common.
- Humans have only about 30,000 genes, not the 100,000 estimated a decade ago.

From these surprises, several useful research directions emerged. First, it has become obvious that a few special genes are crucial as "regulator" genes, which direct the other genes in numerous ways. For example, the distinction between your legs and those of other creatures is the result of a regulator gene that advises the leg gene to make legs of a particular shape and number (Pennisi & Roush, l997). Thus regulator genes, which guide growth and development throughout the body, account for most of the genetic differences between humans and other animals.

Second, because differences that once seemed large are dwarfed by the similarities among all living things, researchers can develop treatments for problems that once seemed intractable. For example, every mammal embryo is genetically commanded to make seven neck bones (Barnett, 1998). Because of the influence of other genes, those seven bones in a whale's neck become flat, thin disks, in a giraffe's neck become elongated, and in a human's neck are in between. To learn about the causes and repair of human neck injuries, scientists can study the neck of any mammal.

Research on small mammals can find causes and treatments for most human illnesses, including the many forms of cancer, mental illness, and blood disorders (Demant, 2003;

Little, 2002). Many research methods—including interbreeding (for genetic purity), cross-breeding (to isolate genes), knocking out genes (disabling a gene to learn which gene does what), and experimenting with drugs (to discover intended and unintended effects)—are impossible with people and would take years with most mammals; but the results from applying these methods to mice have already revealed much about human diseases.

For example, a promising treatment for diabetes comes from an experiment on mice, whose insulin production was first destroyed, then re-created, via insertion of two genes (Kojima et al., 2003). In another example, genetic predisposition is evident for almost every type of cancer, which also means that genetic protections are apparent. Two strains of mice can differ 100-fold in their susceptibility to particular cancers (Demant, 2003).

TEK IMAGE / SCIENCE PHOTO LIBRARY / PHOTO RESEARCHERS, INC.

Reading the Code A small segment of a DNA molecule is sequenced into bands, with one color for each of the base pairs. These pairs direct the synthesis of enzymes and proteins that, in turn, direct the formation of a living creature. One small change in a gene might result in a physical anomaly or a mental quirk. A few hundred different genes might result in a giraffe instead of a whale.

To summarize, genes are everything and nothing—everything in that they are the raw materials from which a creature is developed, and nothing in that genes are merely sequences of chemicals that produce tens of thousands of proteins, which direct the formation and function of trillions of cells—all of which are dependent on nutrients and other factors in the environment. The particular genotype a person happens to inherit influences almost every characteristic, although specifics are not usually evident from the phenotypes of both parents. However, genotype is only one part of the story. Human diversity is guaranteed by the process of gamete formation and then conception. When a sperm fertilizes an ovum, forming a new zygote, that zygote is unlike any ever conceived before.

From Genotype to Phenotype

To grasp the complexity of genotype and phenotype, consider a pair of quotations. The results from two decades of research confirm that virtually every psychological characteristic is genetically influenced. In the words of one geneticist:

> The results were consistently striking, albeit slow to be accepted. Genes were shown to influence virtually every aspect of human personality, temperament, cognitive style, and psychiatric disorder. The effects of heredity were substantial, typically representing 30 to 70% of total variation, and highly replicable across societies and cultures. The long reach of genes extended from a friendly disposition to xenophobia, from bipolar disease to bedwetting, from getting married to keeping a job.
>
> *[Hamer, 2002, p. 71]*

At the same time, these studies reinforce another, equally important conclusion: Virtually every psychological characteristic and personal trait is also affected by the person's environment (Bouchard, 1994, 1997). Nature always interacts with nurture, and vice versa. As four leading researchers explain:

> The first message is that genes play a surprisingly important role throughout psychology. The second message is just as important: Individual differences in complex psychological traits are due at least as much to environmental influences as they are to genetic influences.
>
> *[Plomin et al., 2001, p. 323]*

As you learn more about the interactions among genetic and nongenetic influences, remember to distinguish between a person's genetic inheritance—his or her genetic *potential*—and the actual *expression* of that inheritance in the person's physiology, physical appearance, and behavioral tendencies. The sum total of all the genes a person inherits, the *genotype* (the genetic potential), is present in each zygote. The sum total of all the actual, expressed traits is the person's *phenotype* (the combination of genetic potential and expression). The phenotype is what can be observed by looking at a person, by analyzing the person's body chemistry, and by noting the person's behavior. Thus, physical traits (such as bushy eyebrows) and nonphysical traits (such as a hunger for excitement) are parts of the phenotype.

We all have many genes in our genotypes that are not expressed in our phenotypes. In genetic terms, we are **carriers** of these unexpressed genes; that is, we "carry" them in our DNA and can pass them on to our sperm or ova and thus to our offspring. When a zygote inherits a gene that was only carried (not expressed) by one parent, the zygote will have that gene in the genotype. That gene may then be expressed in the phenotype or may simply be carried again, with a chance of affecting the next generation.

carrier A person whose genotype includes a gene that is not expressed in his or her phenotype but can be passed on to his or her children.

Environment affects every human characteristic. Even physical traits are influenced by the environment: height by nutrition, muscles by exercise, coloring by sun and dye, and so on. Psychological traits are even more readily influenced by the social context—family, school, community, culture.

To make this point clear, we look at behavior genetics, which helps us understand the complex genetics and subtle environmental influences behind human behavior. Then we look at three examples: the influence of the environment on traits that are sometimes said to be "genetic"—Alzheimer's disease, schizophrenia, and alcoholism.

Behavior Genetics

The multifactorial and polygenic complexity of our character traits is particularly apparent from research in **behavior genetics,** the study of the genetic origins of psychological characteristics (Plomin et al., 2001). These include personality traits, such as sociability, assertiveness, moodiness, and fearfulness; psychological disorders, such as schizophrenia, depression, and attention-deficit/hyperactivity disorder; and cognitive traits, such as memory for numbers, spatial perception, and fluency of expression.

Mental retardation, for example, has been studied in great depth and detail. Virtually every type of inheritance pattern—including additive, dominant–recessive, X-linked, polygenic, and multifactorial—is evident in at least one of the major types of mental retardation. More than 100 distinct genetic disorders have mental retardation as one symptom (Little, 2002). No wonder it is difficult to be precise about the influences of genes on behaviors.

Similar complexity probably exists for all aspects of personality and intellect, although many areas have not yet been studied in great detail. It is known that every behavioral tendency is affected by many genes, some interacting in the dominant–recessive mode, some additive, and some with puzzling patterns not yet understood. Almost every behavior pattern can be caused by several different sets of genes, so it is incorrect to assume that any one phenotype is the consequence of any one genotype (Rutter & Sroufe, 2000). Moreover, a given genotype can often lead to dramatically different phenotypes, especially given the profound influence of culture (Hardy et al., 2002).

Thus, when we say something is "genetic," we do not mean that its genetic origins are substantial, fixed, or unalterable. We mean that it is part of a person's basic foundation, affecting many aspects of life but determining none (Johnston & Edwards, 2002). As one expert put it, "A gene is a framed canvas upon which the psychological environment paints the person" (Brown, 1999). Every trait, action, and attitude of every living organism has a genetic component: Without genes, no behavior could exist. But without environment, no gene would be expressed.

Senility Caused by Alzheimer's Disease

Normal aging does not inevitably bring senility, as is explained in detail in Chapter 24. Briefly, normal aging slows down intellectual activity, with working memory, in particular, losing speed and power over the years. However, even at age 100, most people remember past experiences and well-learned skills (from verbal expression to piano playing) quite well. By contrast, those who are senile suffer from widespread and devastating memory loss as well as other signs of illness.

The kind of senility most common and most feared is Alzheimer's disease, which occurs when a protein called amyloid B accumulates in the brain, leading to the dysfunction and death of brain cells and disrupting the mind. Some reports imply that Alzheimer's is entirely genetic, but this is the case only when the disease is "early onset," typically beginning before age 50.

behavior genetics The study of the genetic origins of psychological characteristics, such as personality patterns, psychological disorders, and intellectual abilities.

CORBIS / THE PURCELL TEAM

Shyness is Universal Inhibition is a psychological trait that is influenced by genetics. It is more common at some ages (late infancy and early adolescence) and in some gene pools (natives of northern Europe and East Asia) than others. But every community includes some individuals who are unmistakably shy, such as this toddler in Woleai, more than 3,000 miles west of Hawaii.

Much more common is "late-onset" Alzheimer's disease, which is becoming increasingly prevalent as more people live to age 80 and beyond. Is late-onset Alzheimer's genetic? As you can probably guess from all you have read so far, the answer is "yes and no." Each person has a pair of ApoE genes, which come in three common alleles, called ApoE2, ApoE3, and ApoE4. Version 2 makes Alzheimer's disease less likely, version 3 is neither facilitating nor protective, and version 4 makes it more likely.

Within the United States, the overall genetic frequency among European-Americans seems to be about 15 percent ApoE2, 60 percent ApoE3, and 25 percent ApoE4. This means that about 40 percent of European-Americans have at least one ApoE4 gene; for Hispanic-Americans, the corresponding figure is somewhat lower, about 30 percent; for African-Americans it is lower still, about 20 percent. (These are approximations; researchers will soon refine these estimates and will indicate rates for Asian-Americans and Native Americans as well as for people from other parts of the world.)

Compared to someone without ApoE4, a person with one ApoE4 gene is two to five times as likely to develop Alzheimer's disease and a person with two ApoE4 genes (one from each parent) is five to ten times as likely (Selkoe & Podlisny, 2002). However, the risk of senility seems to level off at about age 85, and some people over age 90 with two copies of the gene are still not senile. Apparently, the gene increases the risk but does not cause the disease.

This is crucial, because it is easy to overestimate the role of genes in almost any condition known to be genetic. Indeed, one team of scientists proposed to assess everyone at about age 50, using family history, genetic markers, and blood chemistry in order to "estimate, first crudely and later more accurately, the likelihood an individual will develop Alzheimer's disease" (Selkoe & Podlisny, 2002, p. 90). But such "accurate" predictions are not possible, and most researchers think it unethical to test healthy people for ApoE4 genes, because prediction and prevention are not certain (Post, 2001).

Other health indicators, including hypertension, diabetes, and high cholesterol, make all kinds of brain disease more likely in old age (Deary et al., 2003). Diet, exercise, not smoking, weight control, and proper medical care (e.g., controlling blood pressure) help the mind as well as the body.

Being mentally alert as well as physically healthy also staves off senility. Cognitive habits developed early in life can make a difference, too. In the Nun Study, a longitudinal study of women who chose to become nuns in the Catholic Church, researchers analyzed essays the nuns had written 60 years earlier. A typical sentence in one essay was:

> After I finished the eighth grade in 1921 I desired to become an aspirant at Mankato but I myself did not have the courage to ask the permission of my parents so Sister Agreda did it in my stead and they readily gave their consent.

A typical sentence in another was:

> After I left school, I worked in the post office.

Researchers who did not know the health outcomes of these women scored the essays for emotional density, particularly the use of positive emotional words. The first essay scored high (*desired, courage*) and the second scored low. In general, nuns who became senile were less emotionally expressive. Thus, the Nun Study suggests that one factor in the development of Alzheimer's disease in old age is the level of emotional expression in childhood—a factor that is much more nurture than nature (Snowden, 2001).

All these factors that help to prevent Alzheimer's disease—such as normal blood pressure, intellectual activity, and emotional expression—are themselves partly genetic. But it seems obvious from this example that nongenetic influences are also crucial. The same point applies, as you will see, to two other "genetic" disorders, schizophrenia and alcoholism.

Schizophrenia

Psychopathologies—including depression, antisocial behavior, phobias, and compulsions, as well as virtually every other neurotic or psychotic disorder—are genetically based traits that are also subject to strong environmental influence. For example, relatives of people with schizophrenia have a higher-than-normal risk of developing the illness themselves. To be specific, the rate of schizophrenia is about 1 percent in the population overall but about 12 percent when a parent or full sibling is schizophrenic (Plomin et al., 2001). If one monozygotic twin develops schizophrenia, about two-thirds of the time the other twin does, too. (Rutter, 2002).

Viewed another way, however, the same statistics reveal the importance of the environment: One-third of monozygotic twins whose twin has schizophrenia are not themselves afflicted, nor are about 88 percent of offspring of a parent with schizophrenia. Many people diagnosed with schizophrenia have no close relatives with the illness, and most close relatives of schizophrenics do not themselves develop the disorder.

Using genetic and epidemiological techniques, scientists are advancing in the treatment and prevention of schizophrenia. It is now known that genes that predispose for schizophrenia occur on chromosomes 1, 5, 6, 10, 13, 15, and 22 (McGuffin et al. 2001). None of these genes act alone: Some people with the genes do not develop schizophrenia; some people without these genes do.

Obviously, schizophrenia is multifactorial, with environmental elements—possibly a slow-acting virus, head injury, inadequate oxygen at birth, or other physical insult—playing a pivotal role (Cannon et al., 1999). One predisposing factor appears to be birth during late winter, probably because some virus that is more prevalent in late fall or early winter can affect a vulnerable fetus (Mortensen et al., 1999). But birth date has only a small effect, as does almost every other genetic or environmental influence. A cascade of factors causes mental illness of any kind and causes every other behavior as well.

Alcoholism

At various times, drug addiction, including alcoholism, has been considered a moral weakness and a personality defect (Leonard & Blane, 2000). Alcoholics were once locked up in jails or in mental institutions. Entire nations even tried to stop people from drinking by making alcohol illegal, as the United States did during the Prohibition era, from 1919 to 1933. People who are not alcoholics have long wondered why some people just can't stop drinking to excess, and alcoholics have kept trying and failing to limit themselves to one or two drinks.

Now we know that some people's inherited biochemistry makes them highly susceptible to alcohol addiction. Anyone can abuse alcohol, but each person's genetic makeup creates an addictive pull that can be overpowering, extremely weak, or something in between.

This biochemical origin helps to explain the prevalence of alcoholism in some ethnic groups, such as those from the British Isles and from northern Russia. In multiethnic cultures such as the United States, the groups with the highest rates of alcoholism are those with high rates in their ancestral homeland.

The likely explanation is a biochemical reaction passed down through the generations. Biochemistry allows some people to "hold their liquor" and to drink too much; it causes others, notably many East Asians, to sweat and become red-faced after just a few sips. This embarrassing response, particularly for women,

Especially for College Students Who Enjoy a Party You wonder if one of your male friends is an alcoholic, because he sometimes drinks too much. He may be OK, though, because he can still talk clearly after drinking twice as much as you do. What should you ask him?

All Alcoholics? Probably Not Farm workers in Provence, France, pause for a meal—complete with bread, wine, glasses, and a tablecloth. Habitually drinking alcohol alone is a sign of alcoholism; drinking with friends and food is not. Of course, cultural pressure to drink creates problems, which is one reason France has a high rate of cirrhosis, but this might not be a pressure group: One of the two bottles contains water.

Response for College Students Who Enjoy a Party (from page 73): Your friend's ability to "hold his liquor" is an ominous sign; his body probably metabolizes alcohol differently from the way most other people's do. Alcoholics are often deceptive about their own drinking habits, so you might ask him about the drinking habits of his relatives. If he has either alcoholics or abstainers in the family, you should be concerned, because both are signs of a genetic problem with alcohol. Ask him whether he can have only one drink a day for a month. Alcoholics find such restricted drinking virtually impossible.

is an incentive to avoid alcohol (McGue, 1995). Some people become sleepy, others nauseated, others aggressive, and others euphoric when alcohol hits their brains, and each person's reaction increases or decreases the eagerness to have another drink.

Selective adaptation (see Chapter 2) is part of the explanation for this ethnic variation. For centuries in the British Isles, and indeed most of Europe, beer and wine were actually healthier for people than water, because the fermentation process killed many of the harmful bacteria that thrived in drinking water. Thus, being able to drink alcohol in quantity was adaptive. East Asians had a different solution to the problem of bacteria: They boiled their water and drank it as tea. About half of all Asians lack the gene for an enzyme necessary to fully metabolize alcohol because their ancestors didn't need it.

Alcoholism is not simply a biochemical reaction; it is psychological as well as physical. Addictions correlate with certain personality traits that are evident in only some people who have the gene for metabolizing alcohol; these traits include a quick temper, a readiness to take risks, and a high level of anxiety. These traits are both genetic and environmental.

Thus, alcoholism is polygenic, with almost every alcoholic inheriting a particular combination of biochemistry-affecting and temperament-affecting genes that push him or her toward abusive drinking. Originally, women were less likely to be pushed, because families and cultures pulled them in the opposite direction. Now that women in many cultures are free to follow their genetic impulses, they seem as susceptible to inherited alcoholism as men are (Heath et al., 1997).

Culture still counts. If a person with a strong genetic tendency toward alcoholism spends a lifetime in an environment where alcohol is unavailable (in a devout Islamic family in Saudi Arabia, for example), the genotype will never be expressed in the phenotype. Similarly, if the person lives in a nation where alcohol is readily available (such as the United States or Japan) but belongs to a religion that forbids it (Mormon or Seventh-Day Adventist, for instance) or a gender that virtually never gets drunk (Japanese women), they are likely to escape their genetic destiny.

In any example of human behavior, complex interaction is evident. As one biologist explains:

At every stage of development, from moment to moment, the growing organism is interacting with a varying environment; and the form of each interaction depends on the outcome of earlier interactions. This process is indescribably complicated—which is why it is never described and rarely even acknowledged. The extreme of intricacy is reached in human development, for the conditions which we and our children experience are often the products of deliberate, sometimes intelligent, choice.

[Barnett, 1998]

On a practical level, genes affect every trait—whether it be something wonderful, such as a wacky sense of humor; something fearful, such as a violent temper; or something quite ordinary, such as the tendency to get bored. However, the environment affects every trait as well, in ways that change as maturational, cultural, and historical processes unfold, with an impact that can be chosen or changed, depending on the people and society. Genes are always part of the tale, influential on every page, but they never determine the plot or the final paragraph.

Chromosomal and Genetic Abnormalities

We now give particular attention to chromosomal and genetic abnormalities. Chromosomal abnormalities occur when a zygote's cells have more or fewer chromosomes than the usual 46. Genetic abnormalities occur when one or more of the person's 30,000 or so genes code for a protein that can cause serious problems or fails to code for a protein needed to prevent problems.

There are three reasons why chromosomal and genetic abnormalities are the focus of attention here:

- Disruptions of normal development provide insight into the complexities of genetic interactions.
- Knowledge of the origins of chromosomal and genetic abnormalities suggests how to limit their harmful consequences.
- Misinformation and prejudice compound the problems of people who are affected by such abnormalities.

Chromosomal Abnormalities

A gamete with more or fewer than 23 chromosomes, which could create a zygote with chromosomal abnormalities, can occur for many reasons, some genetic and some environmental (such as the parents' exposure to excessive radiation). However, the variable that most often correlates with chromosomal abnormalities is maternal age. According to one estimate, a 20-year-old woman has about 1 chance in 800 of carrying a fetus with Down syndrome, a 39-year-old woman has 1 chance in 67, and a 44-year-old woman has 1 chance in 16 (see Appendix A, p. A-3, for details).

Other chromosomal abnormalities are less common than Down syndrome, but virtually all follow an age-related pattern (Snijders & Nicolaides, 1996). About half of all fetuses with these abnormalities are aborted spontaneously and others are aborted by choice, so fewer infants with chromosomal abnormalities are born than these statistics might suggest. Paternal age is also important, with chromosomal abnormalities increasing when the father is over age 40 (Crow, 2003).

Some chromosomal abnormalities occur after gametes fuse to form a zygote if duplication does not occur correctly. Some cells in the zygote may end up with more or fewer than 46 chromosomes; the result is a person who is **mosaic**—that is, who has a mixture of cells, some normal and some with the incorrect number of chromosomes.

LAURA DWIGHT

Not Too Old to Have a Healthy Baby The only age group to have an increase in birth rate over the past decade is women over 39. While older couples have a higher risk of conceiving an embryo with chromosomal abnormalities, modern medical care and prenatal monitoring can help them produce a healthy baby.

mosaic Referring to a condition in which a person has a mixture of cells, some normal and some with the incorrect number of chromosomes.

Chromosomal miscounts can also occur in nonmosaic, or "full," forms, in which all the cells have an abnormal number of chromosomes. This situation can be traced back to gamete formation: Sometimes when gametes are formed, the 46 chromosomes divide unevenly, producing a sperm or an ovum that does not have exactly 23 chromosomes. If such a gamete fuses with a normal gamete, the result is a zygote with more or fewer than 46 chromosomes.

Although this pattern is common—occurring in as many as half of all conceptions (Borgaonkar, 1997)—most such zygotes do not even begin to develop. Most of the rest never come to term—usually because a spontaneous abortion, or miscarriage, occurs. Even if the fetus survives pregnancy, birth is hazardous: About 5 percent of stillborn (dead-at-birth) babies also have more than 46 chromosomes (Miller & Therman, 2001).

Out of about every 200 births, one baby survives with 45, 47, or, rarely, 48 or 49 chromosomes. The chromosomal abnormality leads to a recognizable *syndrome,* a cluster of distinct characteristics that tend to occur together. The cause can be three chromosomes (a condition called a trisomy) at one location instead of the usual pair.

If the problem occurs at the 23rd pair, there is more variation: Not only can trisomies occur but four or even five chromosomes instead of two can be present, or—the only example of a human surviving with fewer than 46 chromosomes—a person can have only one chromosome, an X, at the 23rd location.

Down Syndrome

Down syndrome is the most common extra-chromosome condition. A third chromosome is present at the 21st pair, which is why Down syndrome is also called trisomy-21. Most embryos with trisomy-21 die. A few decades ago, almost all surviving Down syndrome infants died in early childhood, but advances in treatment mean that now most survive well into adulthood (though seldom into old age).

Some 300 distinct characteristics can result from the presence of that extra chromosome. No individual with Down syndrome is quite like another, either in symptoms or in their severity. (One reason is that some Down syndrome individuals are mosaic, having some cells with 46 chromosomes and others with 47.) Despite this variability, most people with trisomy-21 have certain specific facial characteristics—a thick tongue, round face, slanted eyes—as well as distinctive hands, feet, and fingerprints. Many also have hearing problems, heart abnormalities, muscle weakness, and short stature.

In terms of neurological development, almost all individuals with Down syndrome experience mental slowness. Their eventual intellectual attainment varies: Some are severely retarded; others are average or even above average. Usually—but not always—those who are raised at home and given appropriate cognitive stimulation progress to the point of being able to read and write and care for themselves (and often much more). Those who are institutionalized tend to be, and to remain, much more retarded because they lack the intellectual stimulation of family life (Carr, 1995).

Many young children with trisomy-21 are unusually sweet-tempered; they are less likely to cry or complain than other children. Temperament may be a liability, however. If a Down syndrome child is more passive than others, that characteristic produces a slower learning rate and a lower IQ as time goes on (Wishart, 1999).

Earning His Daily Bread This man with Down syndrome works in a cafeteria and, by all reports, is a steady, conscientious employee.

? *Observational Quiz* (see answer, page 80): Visible are four signs of Down syndrome; not visible (and perhaps not present) are at least four other signs. Name all eight.

MACPHERSON / MONKMEYER

People with Down syndrome age faster than other adults. For them, the ailments of old age usually begin at about age 30 (Hassold & Patterson, 1999). By middle adulthood, they "almost invariably" develop Alzheimer's disease, which severely impairs their limited communication skills and makes them much less compliant (Czech et al., 2000). They are also prone to a host of other problems more commonly found in older persons, including cataracts and certain forms of cancer. Consequently, their mortality rate begins to rise at about age 35, and their life expectancy is lower than that of other mentally retarded adults and much lower than that of the population as a whole (Strauss & Eyman, 1996).

This generally pessimistic description, however, does not reflect the actual experience of many individuals with Down syndrome. It is true that all have language difficulties and many have other serious medical problems. But they may still become happy, proud, and successful young adults. One gave the following advice to others:

> You may have to work hard, but don't ever give up. Always remember that you are important. You are special in your own unique way. And one of the best ways to feel good about yourself is to share yourself with someone else.

> *[Christi Todd, quoted in Hassold & Patterson, 1999]*

Abnormalities of the 23rd Pair

As already explained, every surviving human has at least one X chromosome in the 23rd pair; an embryo cannot develop without an X. However, about 1 in every 500 infants either is missing a sex chromosome (thus the X stands alone, which produces a girl with Turner syndrome), or has two or more other sex chromosomes in addition to the first X. These abnormalities usually impair cognitive and psychosocial development as well as sexual maturation. The specifics depend on exactly which chromosomes are on the 23rd site.

The presence of abnormal sex chromosomes may go undetected until a seemingly normal childhood is followed by an abnormal puberty, particularly for a boy who has *Klinefelter syndrome,* XXY. Such a boy will be a little slow in elementary school, but it is usually not until puberty—when his penis does not grow and fat begins to accumulate around his breasts—that his parents wonder if something is seriously wrong. In many cases, treatment with hormone supplements can alleviate some of the physical problems, and special education may remedy some of the deficits related to cognitive functioning—another example of the influence of nurture on nature.

Genetic Abnormalities

Relatively few people are born with abnormal chromosomes. However, everyone carries abnormal genes that could produce serious diseases or handicaps in the next generation (see Table 3.2). These genes are usually recessive or additive (an additive abnormal gene can give rise to multifactorial disorders, in which the effect of the gene is expressed only if specific other genes are also present in the person's genotype) and are influenced by the environment as well. Most of the 7,000 *known* genetic disorders are dominant, since the effects of a dominant gene are apparent in the person's phenotype.

With a few exceptions, dominant disorders are not seriously disabling because people with disabling dominant disorders are unlikely to have children and thus are unlikely to pass their genes on. One exception is *Huntington's disease,* a central nervous system disorder caused by a genetic mutation—this time more than 35 repetitions of the "word" CAG (cytosine-adenine-guanine)—that remains inactive until adulthood, by which time a person could have had children.

TABLE 3.2 Common Genetic Diseases and Conditions

Name	Description	Prognosis	Probable Inheritance	Incidence*	Carrier Detection?†	Prenatal Detection?
Albinism	No melanin; person is very blond and pale.	Normal, but must avoid sun damage.	Recessive.	Rare overall; 1 in 8 Hopi Indians is a carrier.	No	No
Alzheimer's disease	Loss of memory and increasing mental impairment.	Eventual death, often after years of dependency.	Early onset—dominant; after age 60—multifactorial.	Fewer than 1 in 100 middle-aged adults; 40 percent of all adults over age 85.	Yes, for some genes; ApoE4 allele increases incidence.	No
Breast cancer	Tumors in breast that can spread.	With early treatment, most are cured; without it, death within 3 years.	BRCA1 and BRCA2 genes seem dominant; other cases, multifactorial.	1 woman in 8 (only 20 percent of breast cancer patients have BRCA1 or BRCA2).	Yes, for BRCA1 and BRCA2.	No
Cleft palate, cleft lip	The two sides of the upper lip or palate are not joined.	Correctable by surgery.	Multifactorial.	1 in every 700 births; more common in Asian-Americans and American Indians.	No	Yes
Club foot	The foot and ankle are twisted.	Correctable by surgery.	Multifactorial.	1 in every 200 births; more common in boys.	No	Yes
Cystic fibrosis	Mucous obstructions, especially in lungs and digestive organs.	Most live to middle adulthood.	Recessive gene; also spontaneous mutations.	1 in 2,500; 1 in 20 European-Americans is a carrier.	Sometimes	Yes, in most cases.
Diabetes	Abnormal sugar metabolism because of insufficient insulin.	Early onset (type I) fatal without insulin; for adult onset (type II), variable risks.	Multifactorial; for adult onset, environment is crucial.	Type I: 1 in 500 births; more common in American Indians and African-Americans. Type II: 1 adult in 10.	No	No
Deafness (congenital)	Inability to hear from birth on.	Deaf children can learn sign language and live normally.	Multifactorial; some forms are recessive.	1 in 1,000 births; more common in people from Middle East.	No	No
Hemophilia	Absence of clotting factor in blood.	Death from internal bleeding; blood transfusions prevent damage.	X-linked recessive; also spontaneous mutations.	1 in 10,000 males; royal families of England, Russia, and Germany had it.	Yes	Yes
Hydro-cephalus	Obstruction causes excess fluid in the brain.	Brain damage and death; surgery can make normal life possible.	Multifactorial.	1 in every 100 births.	No	Yes

*Incidence statistics vary from country to country; those given here are for the United States. All these diseases can occur in any ethnic group. When certain groups have a high or low incidence, it is noted here.

†Studying the family tree can help geneticists spot a possible carrier of many genetic diseases or, in some cases, a definite carrier. However, here "Yes" means that a carrier can be detected even without knowledge of family history.

Name	Description	Prognosis	Probable Inheritance	Incidence*	Carrier Detection?[†]	Prenatal Detection?
Muscular dystrophy (13 diseases)	Weakening of muscles.	Inability to walk, move; wasting away and sometimes death.	Duchenne's is X-linked; other forms are recessive or multifactorial.	1 in every 3,500 males develops Duchenne's.	Yes, for some forms.	Yes, for some forms.
Neural-tube defects (open spine)	Anencephaly (parts of the brain missing) or spina bifida (lower spine not closed).	Anencephalic—severe retardation; spina bifida—poor lower body control.	Multifactorial; defect occurs in first weeks of pregnancy.	Anencephaly—1 in 1,000 births; spina bifida—3 in 1,000. More common in Welsh and Scots.	No	Yes
Phenylketo-nuria (PKU)	Abnormal digestion of protein.	Mental retardation, hyperactivity; preventable by diet.	Recessive.	1 in 10,000 births; 1 in 100 European-Americans is a carrier; especially Norwegians and Irish.	Yes	Yes
Pyloric stenosis	Overgrowth of muscle in intestine.	Vomiting, loss of weight, eventual death; correctable by surgery.	Multifactorial.	1 male in 200, 1 female in 1,000; less common in African-Americans.	No	No
Schizo-phrenia	Severely distorted thought processes.	No cure; drugs, hospitalization, psychotherapy relieve symptoms.	Multifactorial.	1 in 100 people develop it by early adulthood.	No	No
Sickle-cell anemia	Abnormal blood cells.	Possible painful "crisis"; heart and kidney failure; treatable with drugs.	Recessive.	1 in 500 African-Americans; 1 in 10 African-Americans and 1 in 20 Latinos is a carrier.	Yes	Yes
Tay-Sachs disease	Enzyme disease.	Apparently healthy infant becomes weaker, usually dying by age 5.	Recessive.	1 in 4,000 births; 1 in 30 American Jews and 1 in 20 French-Canadians are carriers.	Yes	Yes
Thalassemia	Abnormal blood cells.	Paleness and listlessness, low resistance to infections.	Recessive.	1 in 10 Greek-, Italian-, Thai-, and Indian-Americans is a carrier.	Yes	Yes
Tourette syndrome	Uncontrollable tics, body jerking, verbal obscenities.	Often imperceptible in children; worsens with age.	Dominant, but variable penetrance.	1 in 250 births.	Sometimes	No

Sources: Briley & Sulser, 2001; Klug & Cummings, 2000; Mange & Mange, 1999; McKusick, 1994; National Academy of Sciences, 1994; Shahin et al., 2002.

!*Answer to Observational Quiz* (from page 76): Four visible signs: round head, short stature, large hands, slanted eye sockets. Not visible: mental retardation, heart abnormalities, muscle weakness, thick tongue.

fragile X syndrome A genetic disorder in which part of the X chromosome is attached to the rest of it by a very thin string of molecules; often produces mental deficiency in males who inherit it.

Especially for Young Adults What genetic disorders are prevalent in your family?

Another dominant disorder that can be severe is *Tourette syndrome,* which is quite common but variable in its effects. About 30 percent of those who inherit the gene for Tourette syndrome exhibit recurrent uncontrollable tics and explosive outbursts of verbal obscenities. The remaining 70 percent experience milder symptoms, such as an occasional twitch that is barely noticeable and a postponable impulse to speak inappropriately. A person with mild Tourette's might curse and tremor at home but behave normally in public.

One genetic disorder is sex-linked, because it is carried on the X chromosome. For this reason, males are more likely to be severely affected, although females can be affected as well, which makes it not exactly recessive. That condition is called **fragile X syndrome.** It is caused by the mutation of a single gene on an X chromosome, with the result that the gene has more than 200 repetitions of the "word" CGG (cytosine-guanine-guanine) (Plomin et al., 2001). (Some repetitions are normal, but not this many.) The mutation involved in fragile X syndrome intensifies as it is passed from one generation to the next, with more CGG repetitions.

Of females with the fragile X gene, about one-third show some mental deficiency but the rest are normal (perhaps because they also carry one normal X chromosome). Of males who inherit a fragile X chromosome, about 20 percent are normal, about 33 percent are somewhat retarded, and the rest are severely retarded. The cognitive deficits caused by fragile X syndrome represent the most common form of inherited mental retardation (many other forms are not inherited). In addition to cognitive problems, the fragile X is often associated with inadequate social skills and extreme shyness (Dykens et al., 1994; Hagerman, 1996).

The wide range of effects produced by this disorder and the pattern of inheritance are somewhat unusual. However, the more we learn about other abnormal genes, the more diversity we find. For example, schizophrenia, as you have already learned, is genetic in origin; but some people with genes that predispose for schizophrenia do not develop the disorder, and twins with identical genes may develop different behaviors (Plomin et al., 2001).

Recessive and multifactorial disorders are less likely to be recognized than dominant disorders but actually claim many more victims, largely because they can pass unchecked (and unnoticed) from carrier to carrier for generations. As a result, carrier status can easily become widespread in a population. Among the more commonly known recessive disorders are cystic fibrosis, thalassemia, and sickle-cell anemia. As many as 1 in 12 North Americans is a carrier for one or another of these three. Each of these became widespread because, although the double recessive was lethal, the single recessive was protective. For example, carriers of the sickle-cell trait are less likely to die of malaria. Their descendants—who include 10 percent of all African-Americans—are carriers of a gene that is no longer needed for protection.

Most genetic research has been done in Europe and North America. Undoubtedly, many other dominant and recessive conditions are prevalent in Asia, Africa, and South America that have not yet been named and described (Wright, 1998).

As you read earlier in this chapter, most genes are neither dominant nor recessive. It follows that most diseases are partly genetic, in complex patterns, influenced by circumstances after birth. This is true for every condition known to affect human health, including heart disease, cancer, strokes, and diabetes.

Diabetes has been studied extensively. It is known that type II diabetes (the most common type, also called *adult-onset diabetes*) is genetic and that some ethnic groups (e.g., African-Americans, Hispanic-Americans, and members of many Native American peoples) are much more likely to become diabetic than is the U.S. population as a whole. However, it is also known that diet is pivotal. Diabetes does not begin unless a person is genetically vulnerable *and* has more body fat than is considered ideal for someone of that age and height (Acton et al., 2002). Once again, nature and nurture interact.

People's concerns and fears about having chromosomal or genetic abnormalities and about passing them on to their children affect them deeply. Read one personal account. In it, Martha raises the questions that underlie this entire chapter: What is a person, and why do people live as they do?

A Case to Study

What Do People Live to Do?

John and Martha, who were in their 20s and graduate students at Harvard, were expecting their second child. Martha was four months pregnant, and her initial prenatal screening revealed abnormally low levels of alpha-fetoprotein (AFP). A low AFP level could indicate that her fetus had Down syndrome. To recheck the AFP results (Down syndrome is rare when the parents are under 35) and to allow time for a more definitive test called amniocentesis, another blood test was immediately scheduled.

John met Martha at a café after a nurse drew the second blood sample, before the laboratory reported the new levels. Later, Martha wrote about their conversation.

"Did they tell you anything about the test?" John said. "What exactly is the problem?" . . .

"We've got a one in eight hundred and ninety-five shot at a retarded baby."

John smiled, "I can live with those odds."

I tried to smile back, but I couldn't. . . . I wanted to tell John about the worry in my gut. I wanted to tell him that it was more than worry—that it was a certainty. Then I realized all over again how preposterous that was. "I'm still a little scared."

He reached across the table for my hand. "Sure," he said, "That's understandable. But even if there is a problem, we've caught it in time. . . . The worst case scenario is that you might have to have an abortion, and that's a long shot. Everything's going to be fine."

. . . "I might *have to have* an abortion?" The chill inside me was gone. Instead I could feel my face flushing hot with anger. "Since when do you decide what I *have to* do with my body?"

John looked surprised. "I never said I was going to decide anything," he protested. "It's just that if the tests show something wrong with the baby, of course we'll abort. We've talked about this."

"What we've talked about," I told John in a low, dangerous voice, "is that I am pro-choice. That means I decide

whether or not I'd abort a baby with a birth defect. . . . I'm not so sure of this."

"You used to be," said John.

"I know I used to be." I rubbed my eyes. I felt terribly confused. "But now . . . look, John, it's not as though we're deciding whether or not to have a baby. We're deciding what *kind* of baby we're willing to accept. If it's perfect in every way, we keep it. If it doesn't fit the right specifications, whoosh! Out it goes.". . .

John was looking more and more confused. "Martha, why are you on this soapbox? What's your point?"

"My point is," I said, "that I'm trying to get you to tell me what you think constitutes a 'defective' baby. What about . . . oh, I don't know, a hyperactive baby? Or an ugly one?"

"They can't test for those things and—"

"Well, what if they could?" I said. "Medicine can do all kinds of magical tricks these days. Pretty soon we're going to be aborting babies because they have the gene for alcoholism, or homosexuality, or manic depression. . . . Did you know that in China they abort a lot of fetuses just because they're female?" I growled. "Is being a girl 'defective' enough for you?"

"Look," he said, "I know I can't always see things from your perspective. And I'm sorry about that. But the way I see it, if a baby is going to be deformed or something, abortion is a way to keep everyone from suffering—*especially* the baby. It's like shooting a horse that's broken its leg. . . . A lame horse dies slowly, you know? . . . It dies in terrible pain. And it can't run anymore. So it can't enjoy life even if it doesn't die. Horses live to run; that's what they do. If a baby is born not being able to do what other people do, I think it's better not to prolong its suffering."

". . . And what is it," I said softly, more to myself than to John, "what is it that people do? What do we live to do, the way a horse lives to run?"

[Beck, 1999, pp. 132–133, 135]

The second AFP test came back low but in the normal range, "meaning there was no reason to fear that Adam had Down syndrome" (p. 137).

Genetic Testing and Genetic Counseling

Until recently, after the birth of a child with a serious or even fatal disorder, couples blamed fate, not genes or chromosomes. They often went on to have more children, who might have the same problem or be carriers of it.

genetic counseling A process of consultation and testing that enables individuals to learn about their genetic heritage, including conditions that might harm any children they may have.

Today, many couples worry about their genes even before they marry. Almost every adult has a relative with a serious disease that is partly genetic. **Genetic counseling** can help relieve some of these worries, although its outcome also requires careful decision making by the prospective parents. In general, prenatal, preconceptual, or even prenuptial genetic testing and counseling are recommended for:

- Individuals who have a parent, sibling, or child with a serious genetic condition that is known to be either dominant or recessive
- Couples who have a history of early spontaneous abortions, stillbirths, or infertility
- Couples who are from the same ethnic group or subgroup—particularly if the couple are close relatives
- Women age 35 or older and men age 40 or older

The Process of Genetic Counseling

The genetic counselor begins by constructing the couple's family histories, charting patterns of health and sickness over the generations, particularly with regard to early deaths and unexplained symptoms. The counselor then explains specific conditions based on age, ethnicity, and genetic history, and discusses what testing might accomplish and what the options will be if testing reveals high risk of serious conditions. The couple then decides whether to proceed with genetic testing, pregnancy, or both.

Response for Young Adults (from page 80): The only incorrect answer would be "none," because every family has some genetic traits that could be harmful.

Some tests provide information before conception. In addition, over the past 30 years, researchers have developed prenatal tests to detect whether abnormalities are present (Goetzel & D'Alton, 2001). Six are described in Table 3.3, from routine to highly unusual.

There is an interesting paradox here. Genetic counselors, scientists, and the general public usually believe it best to proceed with testing before and during pregnancy because some information is better than none. However, high-risk individuals (who are most likely to hear bad news) do not necessarily agree, especially if the truth might jeopardize the marriage, health insurance coverage, or the chances of parenthood (Duster, 1999). If the genetic tests would reveal only

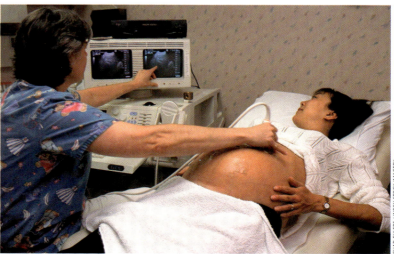

There's Your Baby For many parents, their first glimpse of their future child is an ultrasound image. The outline of the fetus's head and body are visible once an expert points them out. Measuring the width of the head is the best way to estimate fetal age, and the presence of more than one heartbeat is the first signal that a multiple birth is expected.

? *Observational Quiz* (see answer, page 84): What two signs indicate that the ultrasound procedure is not painful?

CHAD EHLERS / INDEX STOCK IMAGERY

TABLE 3.3 Some Methods of Genetic Testing

Test	Description	Uses, Risks, and Concerns
Alpha-fetoprotein assay	A sample of the mother's blood is tested for the level of alpha-fetoprotein (AFP).	• AFP level is an indicator of neural-tube defects, multiple embryos (both cause usually high AFP), or Down syndrome (with low AFP). • The test itself is not risky, but non-normal AFP levels indicate that additional testing is needed. • About 10 percent of all pregnant women exhibit high or low AFP, but 98 percent of these are false alarms, called "false positives," which cause much needless worry. • It is also possible for AFP to produce a "false negative," suggesting no problem when there is actually a defect.
Ultrasound (sonogram)	High-frequency sound waves are used to produce a "picture" of the fetus.	• Sonograms reveal problems such as a small head or other body malformations, excess fluid accumulating on the brain, Down syndrome, and several diseases (for instance, of the kidneys). • Sonograms also estimate fetal age, reveal multiple fetuses, determine the position of the placenta, and indicate fetal growth. • No known risks, unlike the X-rays that it has replaced.
Amniocentesis	About half an ounce of the fluid inside the placenta is withdrawn. The cells are cultured and analyzed.	• Amniocentesis detects chromosomal abnormalities and other genetic and prenatal problems. • The amniotic fluid also reveals the sex of the fetus. • Amniocentesis cannot be safely performed until midpregnancy (at least 14 weeks), and it takes a week or more before results are known. About once in 200 pregnancies, amniocentesis causes a spontaneous abortion.
Chorionic villi sampling	A sample of the placental tissue that surrounds the fetus is obtained and analyzed.	• CVS provides the same information as amniocentesis but can be performed earlier, at about the 10th week of pregnancy (Goetzel & D'Alton, 2001), which makes it easier for the couples to abort if they choose. • Compared to amniocentesis, CVS is more likely to cause a spontaneous abortion.
Pre-implantation testing	After in vitro fertilization, one cell is removed from each zygote at the four- or eight-cell stage and analyzed.	• Pre-implantation testing requires in vitro fertilization (IVF). Ova are surgically removed from a woman and fertilized by sperm. The resulting zygotes are tested. Those zygotes without the feared condition are inserted into the woman's uterus, where they have about one chance in four of becoming an embryo and a baby.
Gamete selection	Ova and/or sperm are screened to select ones that are free of particular problems.	• Gamete selection also requires in vitro fertilization (selected ova are fertilized with selected sperm) but avoids the rejection of viable zygotes. • Every gamete (and every human) carries genes for some harmful conditions, so gamete selection is useful only if particular conditions are likely and genetic tests are accurate.

Sources: Goetzel & D'Alton, 2001; Peterson, 2001.

the risk to the adult, not to a prospective child, most high-risk adults say they would rather not know about their own fate. For instance, most people who have a 50/50 risk of developing Huntington's disease refuse to be tested (Peterson, 2001). Only when they are contemplating parenthood do they want to know their own genetic status.

A Basis for Decision

If testing can reveal that they might bear a child with a serious disorder, many people would like to know what to expect. Of course, odds are risk assessments, not guarantees. If both partners have a recessive gene for sickle-cell anemia, for instance, and the couple plans to have several children, then all of them, some of them, or none of them *could* have the disease. Probability laws tell us that one child in four will be afflicted, two in four will be carriers, and one in four will not even be a carrier; but each new pregnancy is a new risk. Once a fetus is

Genetic Counseling in Action Early in genetic counseling the prospective parents typically view a chart, such as the one held by the female counselor, that helps them understand inheritance patterns and risks. The counselors also look for signs that the two individuals will be able to understand and mutually decide on their next steps.

? *Observational Quiz* (see answer, page 86): At least one sign that these two prospective parents will face their dilemma together is evident. What is it?

developing, tests can predict whether or not it will have sickle-cell anemia. However, as this chapter has emphasized, the interactions among a person's genes and between genes and numerous factors in the environment make each developing person somewhat unpredictable. In this case, some people with sickle-cell anemia suffer and die young, but others live satisfying lives. Counselors can present probabilities and hopes; they cannot promise or decide.

Clearly, genetic testing is a tool, not an answer. Novices need guidance to make effective use of this tool. Some genetic counselors are better guides than others. More and more genetic counselors are needed, and current college students might consider this profession. Imagine yourself as the counselor in the following actual episode.

> After having a newborn die with a trisomy, a pregnant couple disagreed about amniocentesis. The woman wanted it, but the man didn't. The husband asked the counselor, *"Well, what are we to do?"*
>
> The counselor answered, *"It's not my problem. I am not you. You'll have to come to some resolution with your conscience and work it out with your wife."*
>
> [Kessler, 2000, p. 154]

A better answer was suggested by an expert on genetic counseling: "When you ask me 'What are we to do?' what do you see as the problem?" (Kessler, 2000, p. 156). This challenge causes the couple to think about many aspects of their situation: their religious beliefs, their relationship, what it would be like to experience the death of another newborn, which risks they are willing to accept, their feelings of shame and guilt, how they feel about raising a child with medical or psychological problems. Any one of these might be the core issue; a good counselor helps the couple explore any issues that are important to them.

Fortunately, the results of genetic testing do not usually end a marriage or a couple's hopes of becoming parents. Some couples may learn that only one partner carries a harmful recessive trait and therefore none of their children will have the disease. Others may learn that their risk of bearing a child with a serious illness is not much higher than that of any other couple.

! *Answer to Observational Quiz* (from page 82): The woman's smile and her hand holding her belly. She is relaxed and focused on her fetus, not on herself.

Alternatives

Even if both partners are carriers of a serious condition or are at high risk because of their age or their family history, they still have many alternatives, as

Figure 3.3 indicates. Some may avoid pregnancy and, perhaps, plan to adopt. Some might choose a reproductive alternative such as artificial insemination with donor sperm, in vitro fertilization with a donor ovum, gamete selection by first screening the woman's ova, or in vitro fertilization using the parents' own gametes followed by genetic testing of the cell mass before it is inserted into the uterus. If testing during pregnancy reveals serious problems, a couple can consider abortion or begin gathering information that will help them deal with the issues they may face after the child is born.

Some may decide to postpone pregnancy until promising treatments—either postnatal or prenatal—are further developed (treatments have already made a dramatic difference for those with sickle-cell anemia, cystic fibrosis, and various other conditions). Of prenatal treatments, *genetic engineering,* the altering of an organism's genetic instructions through the insertion of additional genetic instructions, is the most innovative. The same procedures are also called *gene therapy* by those who emphasize their benefits (Paterson, 2001). Whether called engineering or therapy, the procedures have not yet proved feasible on a large

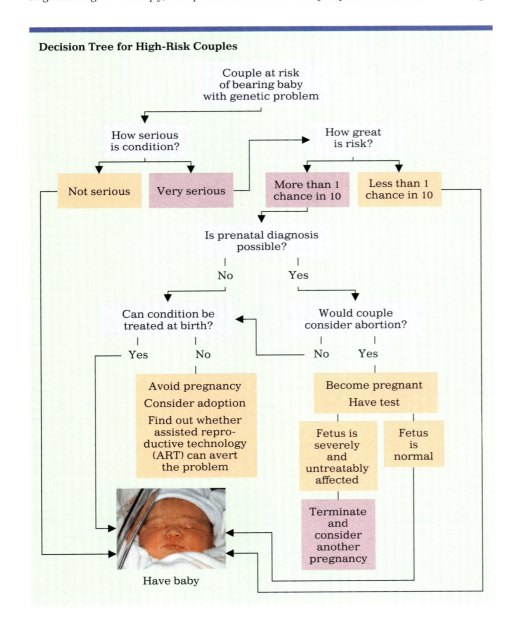

Decision Tree for High-Risk Couples

FIGURE 3.3 At-Risk Decision Making With the help of a genetic counselor, even couples who know they run a risk of having a baby with a genetic defect might decide to have a child. Although the process of making that decision is more complicated for them than it is for couples with no family genetic illness and no positive tests for harmful recessive genes, the outcome is usually a healthy baby. Genetic counselors provide facts and alternatives; couples make decisions.

!Answer to Observational Quiz (from page 84): They are holding hands.

Especially for a Friend A female friend asks you to go with her to the hospital, where she is planning to be surgically sterilized. She says she doesn't want children, especially because her younger brother recently died of sickle-cell anemia, a recessive disease. What, if anything, should you do?

scale, primarily because, as you have learned throughout this chapter, genetics is far more complex than was once believed:

> Few other disciplines in medical research have offered as much hope for success and received as much criticism for failure as the field of gene therapy. It is now clear that early investigators underestimated the influence of genetic individuality on the response of cells . . ."
>
> *[Liu et al., 2003, p. 679]*

Obviously, decisions about conception are not based simply on genetic analysis. Two couples with identical odds of conceiving zygotes with the same condition may make quite different choices—depending on their age, ethnicity, religion, finances, ethics, personal relationship, and the number and health status of any other children they may have.

Counseling begins with objective facts but ends with a very personal decision. Social values, religious beliefs, and even genetic counselors themselves may come into conflict with genetic knowledge, which, as the following feature highlights, raises dilemmas that few people have thought about.

Changing Policy

Decisions and Values

As you have seen, the process of genetic testing is far less neutral and objective than it may appear to be. Indeed, most genetic counselors believe that being value-neutral is neither necessary nor desirable (Mahowald et al., 1998). And it is a high priority that patients be allowed to make their own decisions. But this can create thorny dilemmas. For example, what would you advise in the following four cases?

1. A pregnant couple are both achondroplastic dwarfs, a genetic condition that affects appearance but not intellect. They want genetic analysis of their fetus, which they intend to abort if it would become a child of normal stature.

2. A 40-year-old woman chooses to be tested and hears bad news: She has the BRCA1 gene, which gives her about an 80 percent chance of developing breast cancer before age 70, and perhaps ovarian or colon cancer as well. She refuses to believe the results and insists that no one tell her family, including her mother, her four sisters, and her three daughters. Several of them probably have the gene and may be in the early stages of cancer without knowing it.

3. A 30-year-old mother of two daughters (no sons) learns that she is a carrier for hemophilia. She requests pre-implantation analysis, demanding that only male embryos without her hemophilia-carrying X chromosome be implanted. This means that female zygotes, only half of which might be carriers, would be given no chance to develop.

4. A couple has a child with cystic fibrosis. They want to know whether they both have the recessive gene or whether their child's condition was a spontaneous mutation (as is often the case). If the latter is true, they could have another child with very little risk of cystic fibrosis. During testing, the counselor learns that the wife has the gene but the husband does not—and also realizes that the husband is not the biological father of the child.

[adapted from Science News, 1994]

Many college students are tempted to break confidentiality for dilemmas 2 and 4 and to refuse to test the clients in dilemmas 1 and 3. What would you do?

In the United States, genetic counselors try to follow two ethical guidelines.

- The results are kept confidential, beyond the reach of insurance companies and out of public records.
- The final decision is made by the clients, not by the counselor, whose job is to provide facts and options, not to impose values and conclusions.

A problem arises in interpreting these guidelines, however. Should test results be kept confidential even from other family members who are directly affected? And should a client be allowed to make a decision that the counselor believes is unethical? Most counselors answer "yes" to both questions, but many members of the public answer "no."

The ideal is to reserve testing for suspected cases of serious, well-understood conditions, for which diagnosis is quite accurate, treatment or prevention is available, and ethical guidelines are clear (Peterson, 2001). Unfortunately, diagnosis, especially of unusual chromosomal abnormalities, is often uncertain. Many pregnant couples are faced with puzzling results (either positive or negative) or ambiguous findings.

Members of the medical profession usually decide which tests should be done and when, and doctors are influenced by culture, as all humans are. As a consequence, nations differ in the use of prenatal testing.

Doctors also vary widely in the way they present prenatal tests to prospective parents. For instance, in one British hospital that required doctors to offer genetic tests to all pregnant patients, one doctor spoke to a patient of the "tremendous amount of heartache if we get a false positive" (quoted in Heyman & Henriksen, 2001, p. 100). Another told a patient to ask herself, "How do I feel about having a Down syndrome baby?" (p. 145) and then work back from there to decide about getting tested. Not surprisingly, the patient of the first doctor decided to have no genetic tests, and the second doctor's patient had amniocentesis.

Couples with identical results often make opposite decisions. For example, when told their fetus has an XXY on the 23rd chromosome (Klinefelter syndrome), about half of all couples abort and half carry the fetus to term (Peterson, 2001).

> When sperm and ova combine, the resulting zygote always carries some genes for susceptibility to various syndromes, abnormalities, or diseases. Perhaps as often as half the time, the total number of chromosomes is not the usual 46. If the zygote has a serious chromosomal miscount, chances are it will be too defective to begin to grow, much less become a full-term infant. The main exceptions are Down syndrome (trisomy-21) and abnormalities of the 23rd pair, which allow offspring to live and develop for many years.
>
> Although all humans have several serious genetic ailments on their genotypes, usually they do not appear in the phenotype. As a result of selective adaptation, few newborns with evident severe problems survive and reproduce, rarely passing the genes on to another generation. Less severe problems (such as the gene for Tourette syndrome), dominant diseases that do not appear until middle age (such as Huntington's disease), and recessive diseases that enhance survival if only one gene is inherited (such as sickle-cell anemia) are exceptions; they can be passed on because carriers are likely to have offspring.

Conclusion

As for Martha and John, even though their second AFP test indicated that their fetus was unlikely to have Down syndrome, Martha still had a gut feeling that something was wrong. She volunteered for amniocentesis and got bad news: Her fetus had the extra chromosome of Down syndrome after all. She decided not to abort and gave birth to Adam. Years later, when Martha was talking to a group about her decision to continue her pregnancy, a woman in the audience said that she had been in the same situation but had made the "wrong" decision. Martha replied that there was no right or wrong decision; every decision about prenatal testing is difficult, and each choice has costs (Beck, 1999). (We return to John and Martha in Chapter 4.)

A child with special needs is ultimately the primary responsibility of the parents. Doctors, neighbors, teachers, and political leaders have opinions, and certainly can offer help, but the mother and father are the ones who must pound on

Response for a Friend (from page 86): Ask her to go with you to a genetic counselor for testing instead. She may not even be a carrier of the sickle-cell trait (you know she doesn't have the disease, so she has one chance in three of not being a carrier). Even if she is a carrier, she can have a child with the disease only if the father is also a carrier. Further, many women decide in their 30s that they want to have a child after all; urge your friend not to do anything irreversible.

a child's chest to loosen mucus (cystic fibrosis), hold a small body still for the injection (diabetes, hemophilia), and ignore the stares or comments of strangers (almost all disabilities). They are also the ones who kiss their children goodnight and watch them dream. Finally, they are the ones who hope that each newborn will become a toddler, a preschooler, a school-age child, a teenager, and, ultimately, an adult who lives to a happy, healthy, and productive old age.

The rest of this book describes the ongoing process of development and growth filled with problems and promise. As you read and deepen your understanding, try to answer Martha's question: What do people live to do, the way a horse lives to run?

SUMMARY

The Genetic Code

1. Genes provide the foundation for all development, instructing the living creature how to form the body and brain, and then how to behave. For humans, about 30,000 genes, located in precise positions on 46 chromosomes, direct development.

2. Human conception occurs when two gametes (an ovum and a sperm, each with 23 chromosomes) combine to form a zygote, 46 chromosomes in a single cell. Soon that cell begins to duplicate, divide, and differentiate, following genetic instructions to form an embryo, which eventually becomes a genetically unique human being.

3. The sex of the embryo is determined by whether a Y sperm or an X sperm penetrates the ovum, creating either an XY (male) or XX (female).

4. Usually only one human zygote develops at a time. Twins occur if that one zygote splits into two separate beings (monozygotic, or identical, twins) or if two ova are fertilized by two sperm (dizygotic, or fraternal, twins).

5. Genes interact with one another in various ways, sometimes with each contributing to development (additive genes), sometimes in a dominant–recessive pattern, and sometimes with codes that are switched on or off by other genes or by factors in the environment.

From Genotype to Phenotype

6. The environment interacts with the genetic instructions for every trait, even for matters of physical appearance. Behavior genetics is the study of how genes affect behavior. It is apparent that behavior is almost always multifactorial and polygenic.

7. Environmental influences are particularly crucial for such conditions as Alzheimer's disease, schizophrenia, and alcoholism. Some people are particularly susceptible, for genetic reasons, to each of these, but factors that are nongenetic also influence these and probably every condition.

Chromosomal and Genetic Abnormalities

8. Often a gamete has fewer, or more, than 23 chromosomes, creating a zygote with fewer or more than 46 chromosomes. Such a zygote almost never develops into a baby.

9. If there are three chromosomes at the 21st site, that fetus may be born with Down syndrome; if the odd number of chromosomes occurs at the 23rd pair, again the baby may be born. In such cases, the person has a number of special problems but can live a nearly normal life.

10. Some genetic abnormalities are both protective and harmful. In such cases, the gene can become frequent in a population. This has occurred with the gene for the sickle-cell anemia trait, which protects carriers against malaria but also causes a debilitating anemia.

11. Almost everyone is a carrier for genetic abnormalities, but usually those conditions are recessive (not affecting the phenotype), mild, or do not emerge until late adulthood.

12. Genetic testing and counseling can help many couples learn whether their future children are at risk for a chromosomal or genetic abnormality. Various types of prenatal testing can also reveal possible problems.

13. The final decision about future pregnancies is made by each couple. Genetic testing can give rise to ethical dilemmas, and couples, counselors, and cultures tend to favor some options over others.

KEY TERMS

DNA (deoxyribonucleic acid) (p. 59)
chromosome (p. 59)
genome (p. 60)
gene (p. 60)
gamete (p. 61)
zygote (p. 61)
genotype (p. 61)
allele (p. 62)

23rd pair (p. 62)
XX (p. 62)
XY (p. 62)
spontaneous abortion (p. 62)
monozygotic twins (p. 64)
dizygotic twins (p. 64)
on–off switching mechanisms (p. 65)
phenotype (p. 65)

multifactorial (p. 65)
polygenic (p. 65)
additive gene (p. 65)
dominant–recessive pattern (p. 66)
dominant gene (p. 66)
recessive gene (p. 66)
X-linked (p. 66)
Human Genome Project (p. 68)

carrier (p. 70)
behavior genetics (p. 71)
mosaic (p. 75)
fragile X syndrome (p. 80)
genetic counseling (p. 82)

APPLICATIONS

1. Pick any trait of yours, and explain all the possible influences that nature *and* nurture have on it. For example, if you have a short temper, show what inherited traits and what learned habits might be the reasons.

2. As you may have read, many men want to have at least one son. Interview several men to find out if they follow this pattern. If they give the socially acceptable answer ("It does not matter"), probe deeper to ask what differences there are between boys and girls, and what fathers should do for sons and daughters. Your task is to listen and take notes—not disagree. In your paper, you can analyze the implications of what you heard.

3. Draw a genetic chart of your biological relatives, going back as many generations as you can, listing all serious illnesses and causes of death. Include ancestors who died in infancy. Do you see any patterns that might indicate what genetic susceptibility you have? If so, how can you avoid the consequences? If you cannot, why not?

Chapter Four

Prenatal Development and Birth

Wonder and worry, worry and wonder. Expectant parents wonder: Will the baby be a boy or a girl? One baby or two? What name to choose? What color hair, eyes, and skin? What shape head, nose, and chin? When and how will birth occur, with what help, from whom? Expectant parents worry, too, praying that their baby will be healthy.

My close friend Judy was a high school history teacher who always emphasized the contrast between the broad generalities of the human experience and the local particulars. When she was pregnant with her first child, she rubbed her bulging belly and told her students: "According to international statistics, this is a Chinese boy." Judy was right—at least in a sense. A majority of fetuses are male (about 52 percent) and more are Chinese than any other ethnicity (about 30 percent). So, given these statistical generalities, Judy's statement was accurate.

Of course, given Judy's local particulars (genes, age, sonogram), I was not at all surprised when she gave birth to a healthy European-American girl. Judy herself seemed awestruck, repeatedly recounting tiny details, as if no baby like hers had ever happened before. Again, she was right.

This example illustrates the dual themes of this chapter, which describes human development from conception through birth. Every topic in the chapter—embryonic development, damage from teratogens, low birthweight, medical assistance, mothers and fathers, and so on—is directly relevant to the world's 200 million pregnancies every year. Yet each pregnancy and birth is unique and never proceeds exactly as anticipated. This chapter includes many significant generalities and crucial variations. Learn all you can, and then, if you become a parent, expect to be awed by your personal miracle.

From Zygote to Newborn

The most dramatic and extensive transformation of life occurs from the beginning to the end of prenatal development. To make it easier to study, this awesome process is often divided into three main periods. The first two weeks of development are called the **germinal period;** the third through the eighth week is the **embryonic period;** the ninth week until birth is the **fetal period.** (Alternative terms are discussed in Table 4.1.)

TABLE 4.1 Timing and Terminology

Popular and professional books use various phrases to segment pregnancy. The following comments may help to clarify the phrases used.

- *Beginning of pregnancy:* Pregnancy begins at conception, which is also the starting point of *gestational age.* However, the organism does not become an *embryo* until about two weeks later, and pregnancy does not affect the woman (and cannot be confirmed by blood or urine testing) until implantation. Paradoxically, many obstetricians date the onset of pregnancy from the date of the woman's last menstrual period (LMP), about 14 days *before* conception.

- *Length of pregnancy:* Full-term pregnancies last 266 days, or 38 weeks, or 9 months. If the LMP is used as the starting time, pregnancy lasts 40 weeks, sometimes expressed as 10 lunar months. (A lunar month is 28 days long.)

- *Trimesters:* Instead of *germinal period, embryonic period,* and *fetal period,* some writers divide pregnancy into three-month periods called *trimesters.* Months 1, 2, and 3 are called the *first trimester;* months 4, 5, and 6, the *second trimester;* and months 7, 8, and 9 the *third trimester.*

- *Due date:* Although doctors assign a specific due date (based on the woman's LMP), only 5 percent of babies are born on their exact due date. Babies born between three weeks before and two weeks after the due date are considered "on time." Babies born earlier are called *preterm;* babies born later are called *post-term.*

germinal period The first two weeks of development after conception; characterized by rapid cell division and the beginning of cell differentiation.

embryonic period Approximately the third through the eighth week after conception, the period during which the basic forms of all body structures develop.

fetal period The ninth week after conception until birth, the period during which the organs of the developing person grow in size and mature in functioning.

implantation Beginning about a week after conception, the burrowing of the organism into the lining of the uterus, where it can be nourished and protected during growth.

Germinal: The First 14 Days

You learned in Chapter 3 that the one-celled zygote, traveling slowly down the fallopian tube toward the uterus, begins to duplicate and multiply (see Figure 4.1). At about the eight-celled stage, differentiation begins. The early "stem" cells take on distinct characteristics and gravitate toward particular locations, foreshadowing the types of cells they will become.

About a week after conception the multiplying cells (now numbering more than 100) separate into two distinct masses. The outer cells form a shell that will become the *placenta* (the organ that surrounds and protects the developing creature), and the inner cells form a nucleus that will become the embryo.

The first task of the outer cells is to achieve **implantation**—that is, to embed themselves in the nurturant environment of the uterus. Implantation is far from automatic. At least 60 percent of all natural conceptions and 70 percent of all in

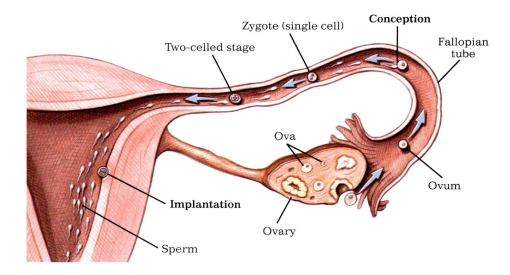

FIGURE 4.1 The Most Dangerous Journey In the first 10 days after conception, the organism does not increase in size because it is not yet nourished by the mother. However, the number of cells increases rapidly as the organism prepares for implantation, which occurs successfully about a third of the time.

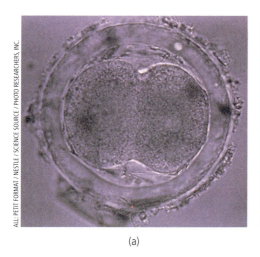

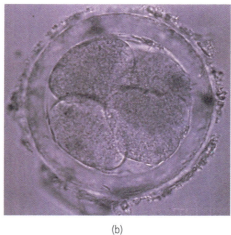

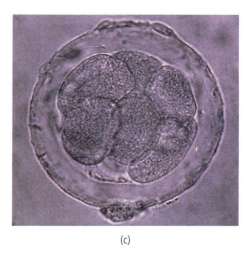

(a) (b) (c)

vitro conceptions that are inserted into the uterus fail to properly implant (see Table 4.2). Most new life ends even before the embryo begins to form or the woman suspects she is pregnant.

Embryo: From the Third Through the Eighth Week

The start of the third week after conception initiates the *embryonic period,* during which the formless mass of cells becomes a distinct being—not yet recognizably human but worthy of a new name, **embryo.** The first sign of a human body structure appears as a thin line down the middle of the new embryo, which becomes the neural tube by 22 days after conception and eventually develops into the central nervous system, including the brain and spinal column (Larsen, 1998).

The head begins to take shape in the fourth week, as eyes, ears, nose, and mouth start to form. Also in the fourth week, a minuscule blood vessel that will become the heart begins to pulsate, making the cardiovascular system the first to show any activity. By the fifth week, buds that will become arms and legs appear,

First Stages of the Germinal Period The original zygote as it divides into *(a)* two cells, *(b)* four cells, and *(c)* eight cells. Occasionally at this early stage, the cells separate completely, forming the beginning of monozygotic twins, quadruplets, or octuplets.

embryo The name for the developing organism from about three through eight weeks.

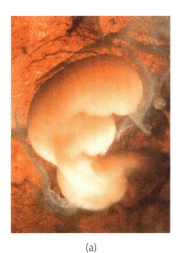

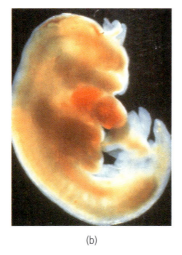

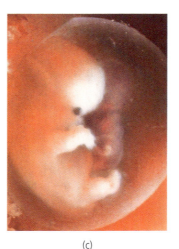

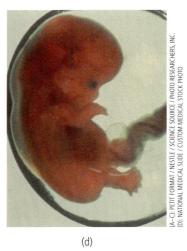

(a) (b) (c) (d)

The Embryonic Period *(a)* At 4 weeks past conception, the embryo is only about ⅛ inch (3 millimeters) long, but already the head (top right) has taken shape. *(b)* At 5 weeks past conception, the embryo has grown to twice the size it was at 4 weeks. Its primitive heart, which has been pulsing for a week now, is visible, as is what appears to be a primitive tail, which will soon be enclosed by skin and protective tissue at the tip of the backbone (the coccyx). *(c)* By 7 weeks, the organism is somewhat less than an inch (2½ centimeters) long. Eyes, nose, the digestive system, and even the first stage of toe formation can be seen. *(d)* At 8 weeks, the 1-inch-long organism is clearly recognizable as a human fetus.

TABLE 4.2 Vulnerability During Prenatal Development

The Germinal Period
At least 60 percent of all developing organisms fail to grow or implant properly and thus do not survive the germinal period. Most of these organisms are grossly abnormal.

The Embryonic Period
About 20 percent of all embryos are aborted spontaneously, most often because of chromosomal abnormalities.

The Fetal Period
About 5 percent of all fetuses are aborted spontaneously before viability at 22 weeks or are stillborn, defined as born dead after 22 weeks.

Birth
About 31 percent of all zygotes grow and survive to become living newborn babies.

Sources: Bentley & Mascie-Taylor, 2000; Moore & Persaud, 1998.

fetus The name for the developing organism from eight weeks after conception until birth. When it is born—even preterm at 22 weeks or post-term at 41 weeks—it is called a baby.

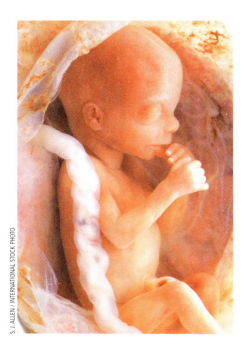
S. J. ALLEN / INTERNATIONAL STOCK PHOTO

and a tail-like appendage extends from the spine. The upper arms and then fore-arms, palms, and webbed fingers appear. Legs, feet, and webbed toes, in that order, emerge a few days later, each having the beginning of a skeletal structure (Larsen, 1998). Then the fingers and toes separate (at 52 and 54 days after conception, respectively).

At the eighth week after conception, the embryo weighs just one-thirtieth of an ounce (1 gram) and is about 1 inch (2½ centimeters) long. The head has become more rounded, and the features of the face have formed. The embryo has all the basic organs and body parts (except sex organs) of a human being, including elbows and knees.

Fetus: From the Ninth Week Until Birth

The organism is called a **fetus** from the ninth week after conception until it is born. This period involves tremendous change, from a tiny, sexless creature smaller than the final joint of your thumb to a 7½-pound, 20-inch-long boy or girl.

The Third Month

Although chromosomes determine sex, not until the third month do the sex organs take discernible shape. Then, if the embryo is male (XY), the SRY gene on the Y chromosome signals the development of male sexual organs; with no such signal (XX), the fetus develops female sex organs (O'Rahilly & Muller, 2000).

By the twelfth week, the genital organs are fully formed and are sending hormones to the developing brain. Although most functions of the brain are gender-neutral, some sex differences in brain organization occur in mid-gestation (Cameron, 2001).

At the end of the third month, the fetus has all its body parts, weighs approximately 3 ounces (87 grams), and is about 3 inches (7.5 centimeters) long. Early prenatal growth is very rapid, and there is considerable variation from fetus to fetus, especially in body weight. The numbers given above—3 months, 3 ounces, 3 inches—have been rounded off for easy recollection. (For those on the metric system, "100 days, 100 millimeters, 100 grams" is similarly useful.)

The Middle Three Months: Preparing to Survive

In the fourth, fifth, and sixth months, the heartbeat becomes stronger and the digestive and excretory systems develop. Fingernails, toenails, and buds for teeth form, and hair (including eyelashes) grows. Amazing as all that is, the brain is even more impressive, increasing about six times in size and developing many new neurons (in a process called *neurogenesis*) and synapses, or connections between neurons (*synaptogenesis*), in the middle trimester. This process continues for years, as you will see in later chapters (Bourgeois, 2001; Takahashi et al., 2001), but the entire central nervous system first becomes responsive and sentient during mid-pregnancy. By full term, human brain growth is so extensive that the *cortex* (the brain's advanced outer areas) must fold into layers in order to fit into the skull (see Figure 4.2).

The Fetus At the end of 4 months, the fetus, now 6 inches long, looks fully formed but out of proportion—the distance from the top of the skull to the neck is almost as large as that from the neck to the rump. For many more weeks, the fetus must depend on the translucent membranes of the placenta and umbilical cord (the long white object in the foreground) for survival.

?Observational Quiz (see answer, page 96): Can you see eyebrows, fingernails, and genitals?

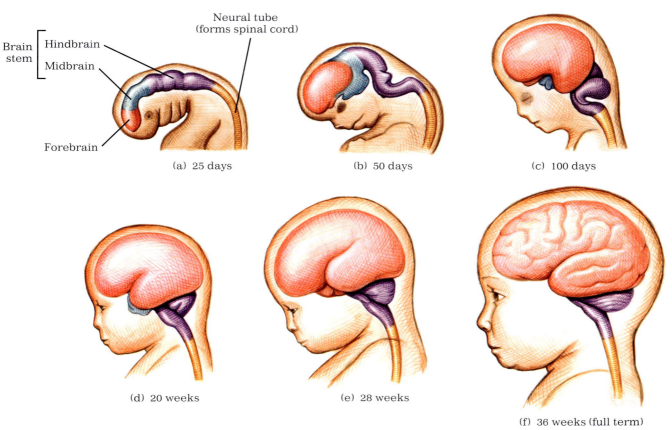

Source: Adapted from Cowan, 1997, p. 116.

FIGURE 4.2 **Prenatal Growth of the Brain** Just 25 days after conception *(a)*, the central nervous system is already evident. The brain looks distinctly human by day 100 *(c)*. By the 28th week of gestation *(e)*, at the very time brain activity begins, the various sections of the brain are recognizable. When the fetus is full term *(f)*, all the parts of the brain, including the cortex (the outer layer), are formed, folding over one another and becoming more convoluted, or wrinkled, as the number of brain cells increases.

Advances in fetal brain functioning are critical in attaining the **age of viability** (the age at which a preterm newborn can survive), because the brain regulates basic body functions, such as breathing and sucking. Viability begins at about 22 weeks after conception. Babies born before 22 weeks rarely survive more than a few days, because even the most sophisticated respirators and heart regulators cannot maintain life without some brain response. At 26 weeks, the survival rate improves to about 50 percent, although 14 percent of these survivors are severely mentally retarded and 12 percent have cerebral palsy (Lorenz et al., 1998).

At about 28 weeks after conception, the brain-wave pattern includes occasional bursts of activity, resembling the sleep–wake cycles of a newborn (Joseph, 2000). Similarly, because of ongoing brain maturation, the heart rate becomes regulated by body movement (speeding up during activity, slowing during rest) between 28 and 32 weeks (DiPietro et al., 1996). Largely because of this neurological awakening, the odds of survival are much better for a preterm infant who is at least 28 weeks old.

Weight is also crucial to viability. By 28 weeks, the typical fetus weighs about 3 pounds (1,300 grams), and its chances of survival have increased to 95 percent. However, little Pearl, born in Florence, Italy, in February 2002, weighed just 10 ounces and survived—the smallest newborn ever to do so. Fetuses that small are usually less than 20 weeks old and are stillborn. Pearl had four advantages: her sex (girls have better survival odds), her birth process (elective cesarean,

age of viability The age (about 22 weeks after conception) at which a fetus can survive outside the mother's uterus if specialized medical care is available.

TOM CARTER / PHOTOEDIT, INC.

Should They Have Stopped at Two? A third child will soon join this family. Most families in China and Italy have one child; most families in Africa have four; and most families in the United States, like this one, have two.

? *Observational Quiz* (see answer, page 98): What three things in this photograph suggest that this couple will cope well with a third child?

which puts no stress on the fetus), her birthplace (an advanced medical center), and her fetal age (27 weeks). The obstetrician was "completely taken aback" by her weight, but her maturity helped her survive (D'Emilio, 2002).

The Final Three Months: From Viability to Full Term

Attaining the age of viability simply means that life outside the womb is *possible*. Each day of the final three months of prenatal growth improves the odds, not only of survival but also of a healthy and happy baby. A viable preterm infant born in the seventh month is a tiny creature requiring intensive hospital care and life-support systems for each gram of nourishment and for every shallow breath. By contrast, after nine months or so, the typical full-term infant is a vigorous person, ready to thrive at home on mother's milk—no expert help, oxygenated air, or special food required.

The critical difference is maturation of the respiratory and cardiovascular systems. In the last three months of prenatal life, the lungs begin to expand and contract, exercising the muscles that are involved in breathing by using the amniotic fluid surrounding the fetus as a substitute for air, and the valves of the heart go through a final maturation.

! *Answer to Observational Quiz* (from page 94): Yes, yes, and no. Genitals are formed, but they are not visible in this photo. That object growing from the lower belly is the umbilical cord.

The fetus usually gains at least 4.5 pounds (2,000 grams) in the third trimester, increasing body weight to about 7½ pounds (3,400 grams) at birth (see Table 4.3). This weight gain ensures that the developing brain is well nourished; severe malnutrition in the second or third trimester reduces the future child's ability to learn (Georgieff & Rao, 2001).

TABLE 4.3 **Average Prenatal Weights***

Period of Development	Weeks After Conception	Weight (Nonmetric)	Weight (Metric)	Notes
End of embryonic period	8	⅟₃₀ oz.	1 g	A birthweight less than 2 lb. (1,000 g) is considered extremely low birthweight (ELBW).
End of first trimester	13	3 oz.	100 g	
At viability (50–50 chance of survival)	24	22 oz.	600 g	
End of second trimester	26–28	2–3 lb.	1,000–1,300 g	Less than 3½ lb. (1,500 g) is very low birthweight (VLBW). Less than 5½ lb. (2,500 g) is low birthweight (LBW).
End of preterm period	35	5½ lb.	2,500 g	Between 5½ and 9 lb. (2,500–4,500 g) is considered normal weight.
Full term	38	7½ lb.	3,400 g	

*To make them easier to remember, the weights are rounded off (which accounts for the inexact correspondence between metric and nonmetric measures). Actual weights vary. For instance, a normal full-term infant can weigh between 5½ and 9 pounds (2.5 and 4 kilograms); a viable infant, especially one of several born at 26 or more weeks, can weigh less than shown here.

The relationship between mother and child intensifies during the final three months, for fetal size and movements make the pregnant woman very aware of the fetus. In turn, her sounds, smells, and behavior become part of fetal consciousness. Beginning at the 28th week, the fetus hears many sounds, including the mother's heartbeat and her voice, as well as a door slamming or a car backfiring—sounds that cause a startled jump inside the uterus (Aslin & Hunt, 2001). If the mother is unusually stressed, the fetal heart beats faster and body movements increase (DiPietro et al., 2002). In addition, hormonal changes caused by the pregnancy may be related to the mother's increased feelings of attachment to the developing person (Fleming et al., 1997).

Especially for Fathers-to-Be When does a man's nongenetic influence on his children begin?

Before we proceed, let us take stock of the rapid growth of these first, hazardous months. In two weeks of rapid cell duplication, differentiation, and finally implantation, the organism transforms itself from a one-celled zygote to a many-celled embryo. The new embryo soon develops the beginning of the central nervous system (3 weeks), a heart and a face (4 weeks), arms and legs (5 weeks), hands and feet (6 weeks), fingers and toes (7 weeks) while the inner organs take shape. By 8 weeks, all the body structures, except male and female organs, are in place. Fetal development then proceeds rapidly, including mid-trimester weight gain (about 2 pounds or 1,000 grams) and brain maturation, which make viability possible by about 22 weeks. Lung and heart maturation in the final three months and 5 more pounds (about 2,300 grams) make the 35- to 40-week-old newborn a survivor, born "on time," ready for life.

Risk Reduction

Now we will describe some of the many toxins, illnesses, and experiences that can harm a developing person in the months before birth. If this topic alarms you, keep two facts in mind:

- Despite the many dangers to the developing organism, the large majority of newborns are healthy and capable.
- Most hazards can be avoided or their effects reduced.

Thus, prenatal development should be thought of not as a dangerous period to be feared but as a natural process to be protected. The goal of *teratology,* the study of birth defects, is to increase the odds that every newborn will have a healthy start. **Teratogens** are substances (such as drugs and pollutants) and conditions (such as severe malnutrition and extreme stress) that increase the risk of prenatal abnormalities. These abnormalities include not only physical problems that are obvious at birth but also more subtle impairments in learning and behavior.

Teratogens that can harm the brain, and thereby make a child hyperactive, antisocial, learning-disabled, and so on, are called **behavioral teratogens.** About 3 percent of all fetuses are born with major structural anomalies, and 2 percent are born with minor problems (Green, 2001). Another 10 to 20 percent will develop behavioral difficulties that could be related to behavioral teratogens.

teratogens Agents and conditions, including viruses, drugs, chemicals, stressors, and malnutrition, that can impair prenatal development and lead to birth defects or even death.

behavioral teratogens Teratogens that can harm the prenatal brain, affecting the future child's intellectual and emotional functioning.

risk analysis The process of weighing the potential outcomes of a particular event, substance, or experience to determine the likelihood of harm. In teratology, risk analysis involves an attempt to evaluate all the factors that increase or decrease the likelihood that a particular teratogen will cause damage.

Determining Risk

Teratology is a science of **risk analysis,** of weighing the factors that affect the likelihood that a particular teratogen will cause harm. Although all teratogens increase the *risk* of harm, none *always* cause damage. The ultimate impact depends

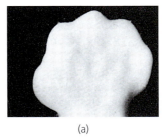
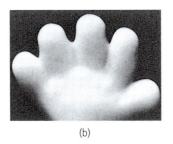

(a)   (b)

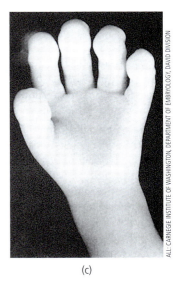

A Week for Fingers The impact of a potential teratogen partially depends on when the developing organism is exposed to it. This is because there is a critical period in the formation of every body part during which the part is especially vulnerable. Shown here are three stages in finger development that define the critical period: *(a)* Notches appear in the hand at day 44; *(b)* fingers are separated and lengthened by day 50; *(c)* fingers are completely formed by day 55, and the critical period for hand development is over. Other parts of the body, including the eyes, heart, and central nervous system, take much longer to complete development, so the critical period during which they are vulnerable to teratogens lasts for months rather than days.

(c)

ALL: CARNEGIE INSTITUTE OF WASHINGTON, DEPARTMENT OF EMBRYOLOGY, DAVID DIVISION

!*Answer to Observational Quiz* (from page 96): Both parents appear to provide excellent care without anxiety or stress. The father seems used to carrying the 2-year-old, and the mother holds the older child's wrist to make sure she doesn't go astray. Moreover, the woman appears to take pregnancy in stride, wearing comfortable shoes and strolling at this Labor Day festival, just as her doctor would recommend.

critical period In prenatal development, the time when a particular organ or other body part is most susceptible to teratogenic damage.

Response for Fathers-to-Be (from page 97): Before conception, through his influence on the mother's attitudes and health.

threshold effect The condition whereby a teratogen is relatively harmless in small doses but becomes harmful once exposure reaches a certain level (the threshold).

interaction effect The condition whereby the risk of a teratogen causing harm increases when it occurs at the same time as another teratogen or risk.

on the complex interplay of many factors, both destructive and protective. (Several of these factors—such as timing, dosage, and genetic vulnerability—are described below; others—such as early care, attachment, and education—are discussed later in Chapter 5.) Understanding risk is crucial for understanding human development; every period of life entails certain risks, and much harm can be avoided.

Timing of Exposure

One crucial factor in risk is timing—the age of the developing organism. Some teratogens cause damage only during specific days early in prenatal development, when a particular part of the body is forming. Others can be harmful at any time, but the severity and site of the insult depend on when exposure occurred.

The time of greatest susceptibility is called the **critical period.** As you can see in Figure 4.3, each body structure has its own critical period. The entire six weeks of the embryonic stage can be called a critical period for physical structure and form, with the specifics varying somewhat week by week (Moore & Persaud, 1998). Because the early days are critical, most obstetricians today recommend that *before* pregnancy, all couples get counseling, start taking multivitamins, stop taking psychoactive drugs, and update their immunizations (Kuller et al., 2001). Note that the brain and nervous system can be harmed throughout prenatal development and infancy. When it comes to behavioral teratogens, there is no safe period.

Amount of Exposure

A second important factor is the dose and/or frequency of exposure. Some teratogens have a **threshold effect;** that is, they are virtually harmless until exposure reaches a certain level, at which point they "cross the threshold" and become damaging (O'Rahilly & Muller, 2000). Indeed, a few substances are actually beneficial in small amounts but fiercely teratogenic in large quantities (Kraft & Willhite, 1997). For example, vitamin A is an essential part of a good prenatal diet and is in most multivitamins for pregnant women, but more than 10,000 units per day may be too much and 50,000 units can cause abnormalities in the fetus's body structures.

For most teratogens, experts are reluctant to specify a threshold below which the substance is safe. One reason is the **interaction effect,** when one substance

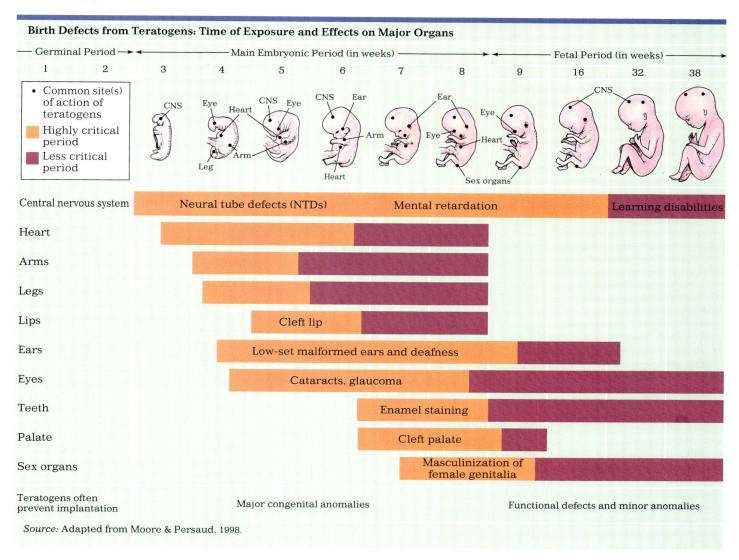

Birth Defects from Teratogens: Time of Exposure and Effects on Major Organs

FIGURE 4.3 Critical Periods in Human Development The most serious damage from teratogens is likely to occur in the first eight weeks after conception (orange bars). However, significant damage to many vital parts of the body, includ-ing the brain, eyes, and genitals, can occur during the last months of pregnancy as well (purple bars).

intensifies the effects of another. Alcohol, tobacco, and marijuana are among the substances that interact, doing more harm in combination than any one of them would do alone.

Genetic Vulnerability

A third factor that determines whether a specific teratogen will be harmful, and to what extent, is the developing organism's genes (O'Rahilly & Muller, 2000). When a woman carrying dizygotic twins drinks alcohol, for example, the twins' blood alcohol levels are exactly equal; yet one twin may be more severely af-fected than the other (Maier et al., 1996). This difference probably involves a gene affecting a specific enzyme (alcohol dehydrogenase) that is crucial to the break-down of alcohol.

Similar genetic susceptibilities are suspected in other birth disorders—includ-ing cleft lip, cleft palate, and club foot—which seem to be the product of genes

Especially for the Friend of a Pregnant Woman Suppose that your friend is frightened of having an abnormal child. She refuses to read about prenatal development because she is afraid to learn about what could go wrong. What could you tell her?

combined with stress (Hartl & Jones, 1999). Because of epigenetic variability, even monozygotic twins may be affected differently. For example, all four of the monozygotic Genain quadruplets (born in 1930) developed schizophrenia, but the severity and type of each woman's condition varied (Plomin et al., 2001). Given that they were born so long ago, it is not known what variations could have occurred, but inadequate prenatal nutrition (which affected their birthweights) is a likely suspect.

Genes are also implicated in the teratogenic effect of a deficiency of folic acid (a B-complex vitamin) in the mother-to-be's diet. Folic-acid deficiency can pro-

TABLE 4.4 Teratogens: Effects of Exposure and Prevention of Damage

Teratogens	Effects on Child of Exposure	Measures for Preventing Damage
Diseases		
Rubella (German measles)	In embryonic period, causes blindness and deafness; in first and second trimesters, causes brain damage.	Get immunized before getting pregnant.
Toxoplasmosis	Brain damage, loss of vision, mental retardation.	Avoid eating undercooked meat and handling cat feces, garden dirt.
Measles, chicken pox, influenza	May impair brain functioning.	Get immunized before getting pregnant; avoid infected people during pregnancy.
Syphilis	Baby is born with syphilis, which, untreated, leads to brain and bone damage and eventual death.	Early prenatal diagnosis and treatment with antibiotics.
AIDS	See the Changing Policy feature (p. 102) for a full discussion.	
Other STDs, including gonorrhea and chlamydia	Not usually harmful during pregnancy but may cause blindness and infections if transmitted during birth.	Early diagnosis and treatment. If necessary, cesarean section, treatment of newborn.
Infections, including infections of urinary tract, gums, and teeth	May cause premature labor, which increases vulnerability to brain damage.	Get infection treated, preferably before getting pregnant.
Pollutants		
Lead, mercury, PCBs (polychlorinated biphenyls), dioxin, and some pesticides, herbicides, and cleaning compounds	May cause spontaneous abortion, preterm labor, and brain damage.	Most common substances are harmless in small doses, but pregnant women should still avoid regular and direct exposure, such as drinking well water, eating unwashed fruits or vegetables, using chemical compounds, eating fish from polluted waters.
Radiation		
Massive or repeated exposure to radiation, as in medical X-rays	In the embryonic period, may cause abnormally small head (microcephaly) and mental retardation; in the fetal period, suspected but not proven to cause brain damage. Exposure to background radiation, as from power plants, is usually too low to have an effect.	Get sonograms, which have replaced X-rays during pregnancy. Pregnant women who work directly with radiation need special protection or temporary assignment to another job.
Social and Behavioral Factors		
Very high stress	Early in pregnancy, may cause cleft lip or cleft palate, spontaneous abortion, or preterm labor.	Get adequate relaxation, rest, and sleep; reduce hours of employment; get more help with housework and child care.
Malnutrition	When severe, may interfere with conception, implantation, normal fetal development, and full-term birth.	Eat a balanced diet (with adequate vitamins and minerals, including, especially, folic acid, iron, and vitamin A). Achieve normal weight before getting pregnant, then gain 25–35 lbs. (10–15 kg) during pregnancy.
Excessive, exhausting exercise	Can affect fetal development when it interferes with pregnant woman's sleep or digestion.	Get regular, moderate exercise.

duce *neural-tube defects*—either *spina bifida,* in which the spine does not close properly, or *anencephaly,* in which part of the brain does not form. Neural-tube defects occur more commonly in certain ethnic groups (specifically, Irish, English, and Egyptian) and less often in others (most Asian and African groups). That variability led researchers to identify a defective gene, one which produces an enzyme that prevents the normal utilization of folic acid (Mills et al., 1995). In 1996 the United States government mandated that all breakfast cereals be fortified with folic acid. This law has been credited with a 26 percent reduction in the rate of neural-tube defects (*MMWR,* September 13, 2002).

Response for the Friend of a Pregnant Woman (from page 99): Reassure her that almost all pregnancies turn out fine, partly because most defective fetuses are spontaneously aborted and partly because protective factors are active throughout pregnancy. Equally important, the more she learns about teratogens, the more she will learn about protecting her fetus. Many birth defects and complications can be prevented with good prenatal care.

Teratogens	Effects on Child of Exposure	Measures for Preventing Damage
Medicinal Drugs		
Lithium	Can cause heart abnormalities.	Avoid all medicines, whether prescription or over-the-counter, during pregnancy unless they are approved by a medical professional who knows about the pregnancy and is aware of the most recent research.
Tetracycline	Can harm the teeth.	
Retinoic acid	Can cause limb deformities.	
Streptomycin	Can cause deafness.	
ACE inhibitors	Can harm digestive organs.	
Phenobarbital	Can affect brain development.	
Thalidomide	Can stop ear and limb formation.	
Psychoactive Drugs		
Caffeine	Normal use poses no problem.	Avoid excessive use: Drink no more than three cups a day of beverages containing caffeine (coffee, tea, cola drinks, hot chocolate).
Alcohol	May cause fetal alcohol syndrome (FAS) or fetal alcohol effects (FAE) (see text).	Stop or severely limit alcohol consumption during pregnancy. Especially dangerous are three or more drinks a day or five or more drinks on one occasion.
Tobacco	Increases risk of malformations of limbs and urinary tract, and may affect the baby's lungs.	Stop smoking before and during pregnancy.
Marijuana	Heavy exposure may affect the central nervous system. When smoked, may also hinder fetal growth.	Avoid or strictly limit marijuana consumption.
Heroin	Slows fetal growth and may cause premature labor. Newborns with heroin in their bloodstream require medical treatment to prevent the pain and convulsions of sudden withdrawal.	Get treated for heroin addiction before getting pregnant. If already pregnant, gradual withdrawal on methadone is better than continued use of heroin.
Cocaine	May cause slow fetal growth, premature labor, and learning problems in the first years of life.	Stop using cocaine before getting pregnant. Babies of cocaine-using mothers need special medical and educational attention in their first years of life.
Inhaled solvents (glue or aerosol)	May cause abnormally small head, crossed eyes, and other indications of brain damage.	Stop sniffing inhalants before getting pregnant; be aware that serious damage can occur before a woman knows she is pregnant.

Note: This table summarizes some relatively common teratogenic effects. As the text makes clear, many individual factors in each pregnancy affect whether a given teratogen will actually cause damage and what that damage might be. This is a general summary of what is known; new evidence is reported almost daily, so some of these generalities will change. Pregnant women or women who want to become pregnant should consult with their physicians.

Sources: Brown, 1997; Larsen, 1998; Lyons & Rittner, 1998; Singer, 1999; O'Rahilly & Muller, 2000; Singer et al., 2002.

In some cases, genetic vulnerability is related to the sex of the developing organism. Generally, males (XY) are at greater risk than females (XX). This greater vulnerability is one explanation for a well-known fact—namely, that male fetuses are more often aborted spontaneously. In addition, newborn boys have more birth defects, and older males have more learning disabilities and other problems caused by behavioral teratogens.

Specific Teratogens

Because of the many variables involved, risk analysis cannot precisely predict the results of teratogenic exposure in individual cases (Jacobson & Jacobson, 1996). However, decades of research have revealed the possible effects of some of the most common and damaging teratogens. More important, much has been learned about how individuals and society can reduce the risks. Table 4.4 lists some teratogens and their possible effects, as well as preventive measures that can be taken. Remember that the effects vary a great deal: Some pregnant women are exposed to these with no evident harm to their fetuses; other women's fetuses suffer in ways not listed in the table. Women are advised to avoid all possible teratogens and consult their doctors *before* becoming pregnant, because damage can occur in the critical first weeks.

The role that the larger community can play in preventing prenatal damage is complex, as the Changing Policy feature reveals.

Changing Policy

AIDS and Alcohol as Teratogens

Sixty years ago, it was believed that a pregnant woman's placenta screened out all harmful substances, preventing them from reaching and damaging the fetus. Then two sudden, tragic episodes showed otherwise: an increase in babies born blind, which was traced to a rubella epidemic on an Australian military base (Gregg, 1941, reprinted in Persaud et al., 1985), and an increase in newborns with deformed limbs, which was traced to maternal use of thalidomide, a new drug widely prescribed in Europe (but not in the United States) in the late 1950s (Schardein, 1976). It was now sadly apparent that diseases and drugs could cross the placenta and that policies that assumed this wasn't the case had inadvertently allowed both tragedies—and others besides.

In the past few decades scientists have identified hundreds of teratogens that *might* harm an embryo or fetus. Almost every common disease, almost every food additive, most prescription and nonprescription drugs (even caffeine and aspirin), trace minerals in the air and water, emotional stress, exhaustion, and even hunger impair prenatal development, but only at some times, in some doses, in some mammals. Preventing possible, but uncertain, harm raises many dilemmas for those who formulate public health policies.

The most devastating viral teratogen is the **human immunodeficiency virus (HIV)**, which gradually overwhelms the body's natural immune response and eventually leads to *AIDS (acquired immune deficiency syndrome)* when the immune system can no longer defend against deadly illnesses. Pregnant women who have the virus transmit it to their newborns in about 25 percent of cases (precise percentages vary, depending on factors such as maternal health), and those infected babies usually die by age 5 (Parker, 2002). In medically advanced nations, early and ongoing medical treatment allows HIV-positive children to survive long enough to attend school, make friends, and understand their illness (Brown et al., 2000). Their survival is a victory, but their ongoing suffering makes the prevention of mother-to-child transmission of HIV even more urgent.

Fortunately, prevention is possible. A pregnant woman who knows she is HIV-positive, takes antiretroviral drugs (such as ZDV and AZT) from 14 weeks after conception until birth, gives birth by cesarean section, does not breast-feed, and provides antiretroviral drugs for her newborn is much less likely to transmit the virus to her baby. For example, in the state of Michigan, comprehensive counseling and free

Hope for the Future Marilis and Anol, of the Dominican Republic, are especially delighted with their 18-month-old daughter, Yolanda, because their first child died of AIDS at age 2. Both parents are HIV-positive, but Yolanda is not. To avoid transmitting the virus to her baby, Marilis took the anti-AIDS drug AZT during her pregnancy, delivered Yolanda by cesarean section, and gives the baby formula rather than breast milk. Yolanda, too, received AZT for the first six weeks of her life. Marilis and Anol hope that their story will inspire other people to do all they can to reduce the transmission of HIV.

treatment cut prenatal transmission of HIV from 19 to 3 percent in just seven years (CDC, February 8, 2002). As a result of such measures, the incidence of pediatric AIDS has plummeted in some nations. The declining number of cases in the United States is diagrammed in Figure 4.4. Even minimal intervention (e.g., only one or two crucial doses of antiretroviral drugs) cuts the rate of mother-to-child transmission in half (Gallo & Montagnier, 2002).

Still, almost a million HIV-positive children are born each year, half of them in sub-Saharan Africa. Most pregnant women with the virus receive no treatment (Leroy et al., 2002). One reason is that the women and their medical providers may not be aware that the woman has the virus. Another reason is that the drugs are expensive: Even in nations such as Brazil, where the drugs are free, and India, where inexpensive combination drugs are used, medicine does not reach most women. And a third reason is that women may refuse or be denied treatment because their sociocultural context is hostile to persons with AIDS. This situation raises public policy questions, such as: *Should HIV-positive women be allowed to refuse prenatal testing and treatment? And in these circumstances, should governments and drug manufacturers intervene? If so, how?*

Similar questions can be asked about the most common teratogen in developed nations, alcohol. High doses of alcohol cause **fetal alcohol syndrome (FAS),** and less intense drinking causes *fetal alcohol effects (FAE)*. FAS and FAE are the leading teratogenic causes of birth defects and mental retardation (National Task Forces on Fetal Alcohol Syndrome and Fetal Alcohol Effects, 2002). Sometimes alcohol ingested during pregnancy affects the features of the face (especially the eyes, ears, and upper lip), but even if the newborn looks unharmed, alcohol may affect the brain, causing hyperactivity, reducing concentration, impairing spatial reasoning, and impeding learning (Streissguth & Conner, 2001).

The damage is increased when alcohol is combined with other *psychoactive drugs,* which are any mood-altering substances, including cigarettes, smokeless tobacco, heroin, methadone, cocaine, crack, LSD, inhalants, and antidepressants. All psychoactive drugs affect the developing brain, as is evidenced in a newborn's fitful crying, erratic sleeping, and impaired sucking and evidenced later in a child's impulsiveness, irritability, and slowness to talk. Given such wide-

New AIDS Cases Diagnosed in U.S. Children Under Age 5

Number of cases diagnosed (y-axis: 0, 100, 200, 300, 400, 500, 600, 700)

Year (x-axis: 1991, 1993, 1995, 1997, 1999, 2001)

Source: Statistical Abstract of the United States, various years.

human immunodeficiency virus (HIV) A virus that gradually overwhelms the body's immune responses, causing AIDS, which makes the individual vulnerable to opportunistic infections.

fetal alcohol syndrome (FAS) A cluster of birth defects, including abnormal facial characteristics, slow physical growth, and retarded mental development, caused by the mother's drinking alcohol when pregnant.

FIGURE 4.4 **Down to 100 a Year** The number of young children diagnosed with AIDS has fallen dramatically over the past 10 years in the United States. The rate of decline is much greater than that for older children and adults. The reason is the reduction in mother-to-child transmission—thanks to better drugs as well as better understanding of the process of infection. In less developed nations, the incidence of pediatric AIDS continues to increase.

Differences and Similarities The differences between these two children are obvious at a glance: One is an African-American teenager, the other a Swedish toddler. One similarity is obvious, too: Both are girls. However, the most important similarity—fetal alcohol syndrome—is apparent only on closer observation. Among the visible characteristics of FAS are abnormally spaced eyes and thin upper lip.

spread deficits and interaction effects, many experts advise women to abstain from alcohol (as well as from other psychoactive drugs) completely. Total abstinence requires pregnant and potentially pregnant women to avoid a legal substance that many people use routinely. Again, some difficult public policy questions arise: *Should pregnant women be allowed to drink if they choose? If not, to what extent should governments intervene—fining pregnant women who drink? Jailing them?*

The dilemmas for public policy are compounded by problems of interpreting the research data. For example, even when a child with apparent problems is born to a woman who is an alcoholic or drug addict, the correlation is often confounded by the presence of other factors. These factors may include some combination of the following: additional psychoactive drugs; unstable eating and sleeping patterns; bouts of anxiety, stress, or depression; accidental injuries; domestic violence; sexual promiscuity; malnutrition; infections; illnesses; lack of family support; and inadequate medical care. If such problems continue after the child's birth,

the increased risk of learning problems in children, which has been proven in many studies, may not be caused solely by the mother's prenatal consumption of alcohol.

Doubts about all the psychoactive drugs are raised by revelations about the drug most studied, cocaine. Virtually every fetus exposed to cocaine is also exposed to alcohol, other drugs, and various deprivations (Singer, 1999). Although many teachers and school psychologists blame children's learning difficulties on mothers' use of crack cocaine, even experienced assessors often guess wrong about which preschool children with learning problems were prenatally exposed to cocaine and which were not (Rose-Jacobs et al., 2002).

As this discussion has shown, high-dose and multiple-drug use are very risky, and even small, occasional doses of any psychoactive drug may harm a fetus (Singer, 1999). But it has also been shown that targeting only one teratogen, such as alcohol, would be simplistic. The issue of what policies are needed to protect future children is clearly a complex one.

Low Birthweight

One final complication of prenatal development is insufficient body weight. Sometimes a fetus is growing too slowly or a newborn weighs less than normal. **Low birthweight (LBW)** is defined by the World Health Organization as a weight of less than 5½ pounds (2,500 grams) at birth. LBW babies are further grouped into *very-low-birthweight (VLBW)* babies, weighing less than 3 pounds (1,500 grams), and *extremely-low-birthweight (ELBW)* babies, weighing less than about 2 pounds (1,000 grams).

The rate of LBW varies enormously from nation to nation (see Figure 4.5); the U.S. rate of 7.6 percent in 2000 was twice that of some other developed nations, and it is not improving (see Figure 4.6). In fact, more low-birthweight infants were born in the United States in 2001 than 10 years earlier, and low birthweight remains the second most common cause of neonatal death (see Figure 4.7).

low birthweight (LBW) A birthweight of less than 5½ pounds (2,500 grams).

Especially for Social Workers When is it most important to convince women to be tested for HIV—a month before pregnancy, a month after conception, or immediately after birth?

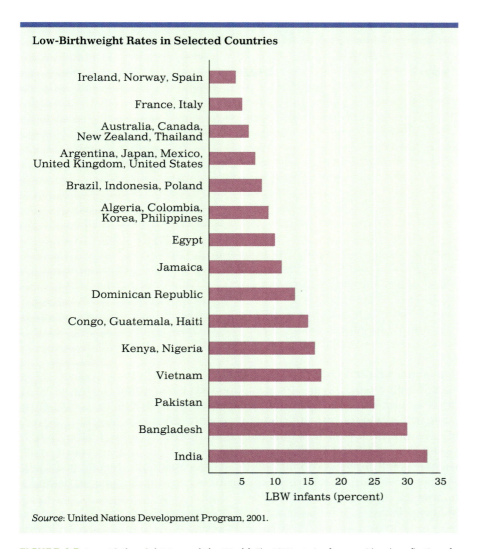

Low-Birthweight Rates in Selected Countries

Source: United Nations Development Program, 2001.

FIGURE 4.5 **Low Birthweight Around the World** The LBW rate is often considered a reflection of a country's commitment to its children as well as of its economic resources.

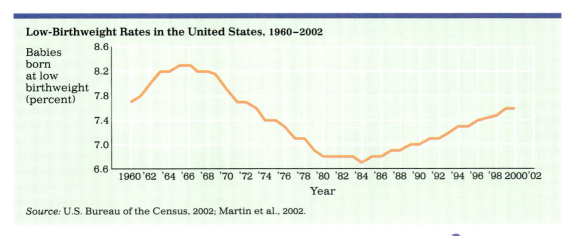

Low-Birthweight Rates in the United States, 1960–2002

Source: U.S. Bureau of the Census, 2002; Martin et al., 2002.

FIGURE 4.6 **Not Improving** The LBW rate is often taken to be a measure of a nation's overall health. In the United States, the rise and fall of this rate are related to many factors, among them prenatal care, maternal use of drugs, overall nutrition, and number of multiple births.

?*Observational Quiz* (see answer, page 107): In what year was one out of every 13 U.S. babies (7.5 percent) born weighing less than 5 ½ pounds?

FIGURE 4.7 **Why Babies Die** Three causes of infant mortality have taken a marked downturn over the past 15 years. For two of them (congenital abnormalities and respiratory distress), intense research and medical technology have made a difference, including advanced genetic testing and counseling, neonatal intensive care, and new drugs given to newborns. Deaths caused by low birthweight are increasing, however.

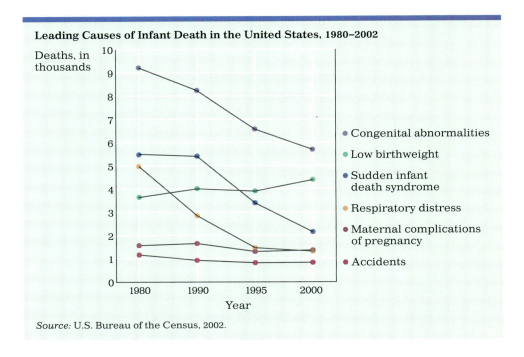

Leading Causes of Infant Death in the United States, 1980–2002

Deaths, in thousands (y-axis, 0 to 10)

- Congenital abnormalities
- Low birthweight
- Sudden infant death syndrome
- Respiratory distress
- Maternal complications of pregnancy
- Accidents

Year (x-axis: 1980, 1990, 1995, 2000)

Source: U.S. Bureau of the Census, 2002.

preterm birth Birth that occurs 3 weeks or more before the full term of pregnancy has elapsed—that is, at 35 or fewer weeks after conception.

small for gestational age (SGA) A birthweight that is significantly lower than expected, given the time since conception. For example, a 5-pound newborn is SGA if born on time, but not SGA if born two months early. (Also called *small-for-dates.*)

Remember that fetal body weight normally doubles in the last trimester of pregnancy, with a typical gain of almost 2 pounds (900 grams) occurring in the final three weeks. Thus, a baby born **preterm**, defined as 3 or more weeks before the standard 38 weeks, usually (though not always) has a low birthweight. Conversely, not all low-birthweight babies are preterm. Some fetuses simply gain weight too slowly throughout prenatal development. They are called *small-for-dates* or **small for gestational age (SGA).** As a sign of prenatal problems, SGA is far more serious than preterm birth, because it signifies impairment throughout the pregnancy.

Maternal illness is one reason for SGA. Remember Pearl, the newborn who weighed only 10 ounces? She was so small because her mother had an illness that affected blood circulation throughout her body, especially to her fetus. That was why she had an elective cesarean section at 27 weeks: Continuing the pregnancy would have put the mother's life in danger.

Maternal behavior is a far more common cause of SGA than illness. Every psychoactive drug slows fetal growth, but tobacco is the worst as well as the most prevalent. Cigarette smoking is implicated in 25 percent of all low-birthweight births worldwide. Ironically, although smoking among women of childbearing age is declining in the United States, it is rising in many other nations. Thus, many of the LBW rates shown in Figure 4.5 are likely to increase in the near future (Satcher, 2001).

Which Baby is Oldest? The baby at the left is the oldest, at almost one month; the baby at the right is the youngest, at just 2 days. Are you surprised? The explanation is that the 1-month-old was born 9 weeks early and now, at 7½ weeks, weighs less than 5½ pounds; the 2-day-old was full-term and weighs almost 8 pounds. The baby in the middle, born full-term but weighing only 2 pounds, is the most worrisome. Her ears and hands are larger than the preterm baby's, but her skull is small; malnutrition may have deprived her brain as well as her body.

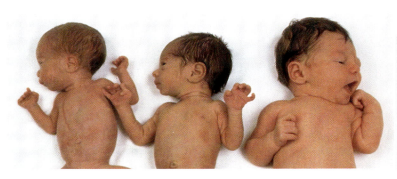

RON SUTHERLAND / SCIENCE PHOTO LIBRARY / PHOTO RESEARCHERS, INC.

Another common reason for slow fetal growth is maternal malnutrition. Women who begin pregnancy underweight, eat poorly during pregnancy, or do not gain at least 3 pounds (1½ kilograms) per month in the last six months run a much higher risk than others of having a low-birthweight infant. Malnutrition (not age) is the primary reason young teenagers tend to have small babies: They tend to eat sporadically and poorly, and their diet is inadequate to support the growth of their own bodies, much less that of another developing person (Buschman et al., 2001). Unfortunately, three of the risk factors mentioned here—underweight, undereating, and smoking—tend to occur together.

The many factors that impede or interrupt normal prenatal growth are not inevitable. Quality of medical care, education, culture, and social support affect every developing person before birth, via their impact on the pregnant woman.

> Before reading about the normal birth, let us summarize the major complications that may arise during prenatal development. Risk analysis is complex but necessary, because the fetus cannot be protected from all hazards, including diseases, drugs, and pollutants. Many factors reduce risk, including the mother's health and nourishment before pregnancy and early prenatal care (to diagnose and treat problems and then guide the woman to protect the fetus). Risk is also affected by the dose and frequency of teratogens, as well as the fetus's own genes and stage of development. Another hazard is low birthweight, when a fetus is born too soon (preterm, before 34 weeks) or gains weight too slowly (small for gestational age). Maternal illness, malnutrition, and drug use are major factors in low birthweight. Unfortunately, low birthweight, very low birthweight, and extremely low birthweight seem to be increasing in some developed nations (including the United States) and may soon increase in developing nations as well.

The Birth Process

For a full-term fetus and a healthy mother, birth can be simple and quick. At some time during the last month of pregnancy, most fetuses change position for the final time, turning upside down so that the head is low in the mother's pelvic cavity. They are now in position to be born in the usual way, head first. (About 1 in 20 do not turn and are in position to be born "breech," that is, buttocks, feet, or knees first.)

At about the 266th day after conception, the fetal brain signals the release of certain hormones that pass into the mother's bloodstream (Lye & Challis, 2001). These hormones trigger her uterine muscles to contract and relax, starting the process that becomes active labor. The triggering process is not yet fully understood. It is "an extremely complex system involving various hormones and tissues," and irregular contractions typically occur hours, days, or even weeks before active labor begins (Chow & Yancey, 2001).

Contractions eventually become strong and regular, less than 10 minutes apart. The baby is born, on average, after eight hours of active labor for first births and three hours for subsequent births (Chow & Yancey, 2001). The sequence is shown in Figure 4.8.

The Newborn's First Minutes

Do you picture just-delivered babies as being held upside down and spanked so that they will start crying and breathing? Wrong image. Newborns usually start to breathe and cry on their own. As the first spontaneous cries occur, the first

Especially for Women of Childbearing Age If you have decided to become pregnant soon, you obviously cannot change your genes, your age, or your economic status. But you can do three things in the next month or two that can markedly reduce the chance of having a low-birthweight baby a year from now. What are they?

Response for Social Workers (from page 104): Voluntary testing and then treatment can be useful at any time, because women who learn that they are HIV-positive are more likely to get treatment, in order to reduce the likelihood of transmission, and to avoid pregnancy. If pregnancy does occur, diagnosis early in pregnancy is best, because abortion is one option and taking antiretroviral drugs such as AZT is another—one that prevents many cases of pediatric AIDS.

!Answer to Observational Quiz (from page 105): In both 1972 and 2002. The LBW rate was falling in 1972, but began to climb again in the mid-1980s.

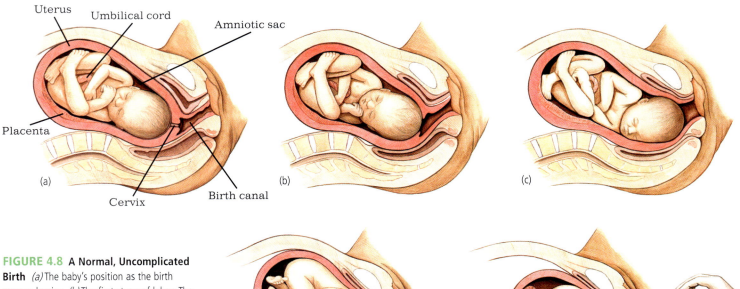

FIGURE 4.8 A Normal, Uncomplicated Birth *(a)* The baby's position as the birth process begins. *(b)* The first stage of labor: The cervix dilates to allow passage of the baby's head. *(c)* Transition: The baby's head moves into the "birth canal," the vagina. *(d)* The second stage of labor: The baby's head moves through the opening of the vagina ("crowns") and *(e)* emerges completely.

? Observational Quiz (see answer, page 110): In drawing (e), what is the birth attendant doing as the baby's head emerges?

Apgar scale A means of quickly assessing a newborn's body functioning. The baby's color, heart rate, reflexes, muscle tone, and respiratory effort are scored (from 0 to 2) at one minute and five minutes after birth, and compared with an ideal for healthy babies (a perfect 10).

Response for Women of Childbearing Age (from page 107): Avoid all drugs, check your weight (gain some if you are under the norm), and receive diagnosis and treatment for any infections—not just sexual ones but infections anywhere in your body, including your teeth and gums.

breaths of air cause the infant's color to change from a bluish tinge to pinkish as oxygen begins to circulate throughout the system. The eyes open wide; the tiny fingers grab anything they can; the even tinier toes stretch and retract. The newborn is instantly, zestfully, ready for life.

Nevertheless, there is much for those attending the birth to do. Any mucus that might be in the baby's throat is removed, especially if the first breaths seem shallow or strained. The umbilical cord is cut to detach the placenta, leaving the "belly button." The infant is weighed and wrapped to preserve body heat. If the birth is assisted by a trained health worker—as are 99 percent of the births in industrialized nations and about half of all births worldwide (Rutstein, 2000)—the newborn is immediately checked for body functioning.

One assessment is the **Apgar scale** (see Table 4.5). The examiner checks five vital signs—heart rate, breathing, muscle tone, color, and reflexes—at one minute after birth and again at five minutes, and assigns each a score of 0, 1, or 2 (Moster et al., 2001). If the five-minute total score is 7 or better, there is no danger. If the five-minute total score is below 7, the infant needs help establishing normal breathing. If the score is below 4, the baby needs urgent critical care. Most newborns are just fine, which reassures the new mother and father, who can then hold their baby and congratulate each other.

Variations

How closely any given birth matches the foregoing depends on the parents' preparation for birth, the physical and emotional support provided by birth attendants, the position and size of the fetus, and the practices of the mother's culture.

TABLE 4.5 Criteria and Scoring of the Apgar Scale

Score	Color	Heartbeat	Reflex Irritability	Muscle Tone	Respiratory Effort
0	Blue, pale	Absent	No response	Flaccid, limp	Absent
1	Body pink, extremities blue	Slow (below 100)	Grimace	Weak, inactive	Irregular, slow
2	Entirely pink	Rapid (over 100)	Coughing, sneezing, crying	Strong, active	Good; baby is crying

Source: Apgar, 1953.

Almost every birth in every developed nation now occurs amid some medical activity, typically including drugs to dull pain or speed contractions; sterile procedures that involve special gowns, gloves, and washing; and electronic monitoring of both the mother and the fetus. In about 22 percent of births in the United States, a **cesarean section** is performed to remove the fetus through incisions in the mother's abdomen and uterus (Martin et al., 2002). The rate of surgical birth varies markedly from place to place, with many developed nations having far fewer cesareans than the United States but others having more (see Figure 4.9).

Worldwide, the actions of doctors, midwives, and nurses save millions of lives each year—the lives of mothers as well as of infants. Indeed, a lack of medical attention during childbirth and the hazards of illegal abortions are the major reasons why motherhood is still hazardous in the least developed nations; about one in 20 African women die of complications of pregnancy and childbirth (Daulaire et al., 2002).

At the same time, many aspects of hospital births have been criticized as being rooted more in medical tradition than in medical necessity. Even worse, financial considerations or fear of lawsuits may affect medical decisions. For example, one careful study in the Midwest found that the rate of cesarean deliveries was 17 percent among women with private insurance, 14 percent for those with Medicaid, and only 10 percent for those who had no insurance (Aron et al., 2000).

In response to these criticisms, alternatives to the conventional hospital birth have become more widespread. By the 1990s only 41 percent of all U.S. hospital births occurred in delivery rooms with high-tech equipment, whereas 53 percent occurred in a *labor room*—typically a smaller, more homelike room where a woman

cesarean section A surgical childbirth, in which incisions through the mother's abdomen and uterus allow the fetus to be removed quickly, instead of being delivered through the vagina.

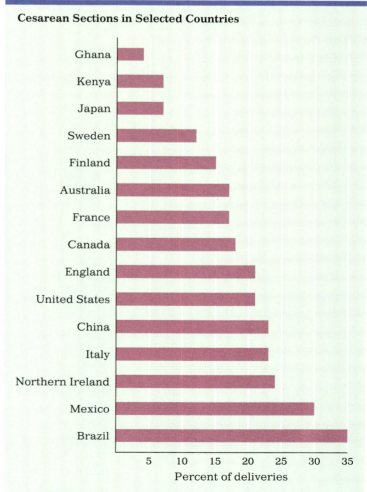

Cesarean Sections in Selected Countries

Percent of deliveries

Sources: Belizan et al., 1999; Gomes et al., 1999; Royal College of Obstetricians and Gynecologists, 2001; Buekens et al., 2003.

FIGURE 4.9 Too Many Cesareans or Too Few? Rates of cesarean deliveries vary widely from nation to nation. In general, cesarean births are declining in North America and increasing in Africa. Latin American countries have the highest rates in the world (51 percent of all births in the state of Sao Paulo in Brazil are by cesarean), and sub-Saharan Africa has the lowest. The underlying issue is whether some women who should have cesareans do not get them, while other women have unnecessary cesareans.

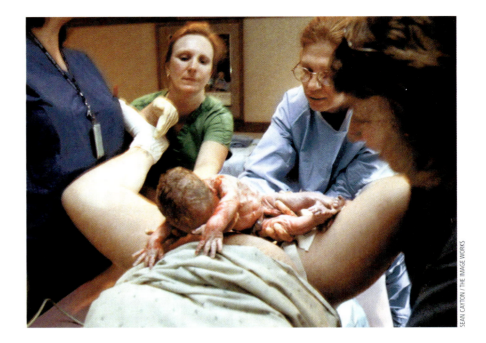

No Doctor Needed In this Colorado Springs birthing center, most babies are delivered with the help of nurse-midwives. This newborn's bloody appearance and bluish fingers are completely normal; an Apgar test at five minutes revealed that the baby's heart was beating steadily and that the body was "entirely pink."

stays, with her husband or other familiar person, from the time she enters the hospital until she and her baby have recovered from the birth. In this setting, doctors and nurses intervene when needed, but the woman has much more control over what happens and when. It is *her* room and she is with *her* partner, so it is *her* birth—and that itself reduces anxiety, pain, stress, and complications.

Another 5 percent of U.S. births occur in freestanding *birthing centers,* which are even more family oriented. As one woman recounts:

> When we arrived at the Birthing Center to have the baby, we were told to go right to the room we had chosen ahead of time. There weren't any strong hospital odors, no people rushing around, no papers for Gary to fill out while I was wheeled off down a long hall without him. We just walked together to our room.
>
> There is always some amount of anxiety in starting labor; but the atmosphere at the Birthing Center was so relaxing that it had a calming effect on me. . . .
>
> Several hours later, our third daughter was born. She never left us to go to the nursery with harsh lights and lots of other crying babies. She remained in our quiet room with us. We could hold her when she wanted to be held and feed her when she wanted to be fed. Gary and I both were there when the pediatrician checked her.
>
> Even though it was my most difficult labor and delivery, it was our happiest.
>
> *[quoted in La Leche, 1997]*

Only 1 percent of U.S. births take place at home—about half of these by choice, attended by a midwife, and half due to unexpectedly rapid birth. Such births are usually quite normal and healthy, but any complications can become serious problems before medical help can be obtained (Pang et al., 2002).

In many regions of the world, as modern medical practices are introduced, a clash has developed between traditional home births attended by a midwife and modern hospital births attended by an obstetrician. Unfortunately, all too often, women need to choose one or the other, rather than deriving the benefits of both. An example comes from the Inuit, native people of northern Canada:

> Until thirty or forty years ago every woman, and most men, learned midwifery skills and knew what to do to help at a birth if they were needed. . . . They helped the woman kneel or squat on caribou skins, and tied the cord with caribou

!Answer to Observational Quiz (from page 108): The birth attendant is turning the baby's head after it has emerged; doing this helps the shoulders come out more easily.

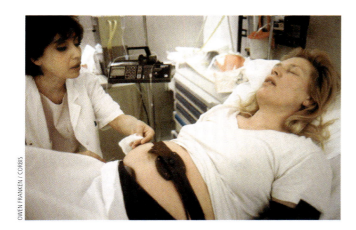

OWEN FRANKEN / CORBIS

VIVIANE MOOS

sinews. . . . Since the 1950s, as the medical system took control in the belief that hospital birth was safer, more and more pregnant women were evacuated by air to deliver in large hospitals in Winnipeg and other cities. . . . Around three weeks before her due date a woman is flown south to wait in bed and breakfast accommodation for labor to start, and to have it induced if the baby does not arrive when expected. Anxious about their children left at home, mothers became bored and depressed. . . . Women . . . deliver in a supine [on their back] position instead of an upright one, which was part of their tradition, and also describe being tied up while giving birth. Many women say that children who have been born in a hospital are different and no longer fit into the Inuit lifestyle. . . . Several new birth centres have now been created [in the Inuit homeland] and nurse-midwives are bringing in traditional midwives as assistants during childbirth, training some Inuit midwives to work alongside them, and at the same time learning some of the old Inuit ways themselves.

[Kitzinger, 2001, pp. 160–161]

Same Event, Thousands of Miles Apart Both these midwives—one in New York City and the other in Rajasthan, India—are assessing the size, position, and heartbeat of a developing fetus. Which pregnancy is more likely to result in a healthy baby? If it is a high-risk birth, high-tech medical equipment might be critical. However, if the pregnancy is a normal one, as most pregnancies are, the experience and empathy of the trained attendant are more important than the diagnostic tools used.

Another example of a traditional custom incorporated into a hospital birth is the *doula*; long a tradition in many Latin American countries, a doula helps women in labor, delivery, breast-feeding, and newborn care. Many women in North America now hire a professional doula to perform these functions (Douglas, 2002).

From a developmental perspective, such combinations of traditional and modern birthing practices are excellent, for neither is necessarily better than the other.

Birth Complications

When a fetus is already at risk because of low birthweight, preterm birth, genetic abnormality, or teratogenic exposure, or because the mother is unusually young, old, small, or ill, birth complications are more likely. The crucial point to emphasize is that such complications are part of a sequence of events and conditions that begin long before the first contractions and continue in the months and years thereafter. This means, of course, that prevention and treatment are ongoing.

As an example, **cerebral palsy** (difficulties with movement control resulting from brain damage) was once thought to be caused solely by birth procedures: excessive pain medication, slow breech birth, or delivery by forceps (which are sometimes used to pull the fetal head through the birth canal). In fact, however, cerebral palsy often results from genetic vulnerability and may be worsened by teratogens and a birth that includes **anoxia**—a temporary lack of oxygen that

cerebral palsy A disorder that results from damage to the brain's motor centers. People with cerebral palsy have difficulty with muscle control, which can affect speech or other body movements.

anoxia A lack of oxygen that, if prolonged, can cause brain damage or death.

can cause brain damage. Anoxia has many causes and is always risky—that's why the fetal heart rate is monitored during labor and why the newborn's color is one of the five criteria on the Apgar scale. How long a fetus can experience anoxia without suffering brain damage depends on genes, weight, drugs in the bloodstream, and a host of other factors. Thus, cerebral palsy caused by anoxia is not solely the result of the birth process.

Another example of a birth complication is an infection called Group B streptococcus (GBS), which is often fatal to newborns if not recognized and treated with antibiotics in the first days after birth (Schrag et al., 2000). The infection is transmitted to the fetus by the pregnant woman, who may not know she has GBS unless she has a laboratory test. Proper prenatal diagnosis and prompt treatment of the newborn can prevent any damage (*MMWR,* August 16, 2002).

Similarly, low-birthweight infants are at risk for many problems before, during, and immediately after birth, especially when they are born very early or very small. As we have seen, these problems have their origins in factors that exist even before conception, such as a woman's being underweight, smoking cigarettes, or taking other drugs. The problems sometimes persist throughout life, but here, too, their impact depends on many influences. Let us now look at the sequence of these influences shortly after the birth of high-risk infants.

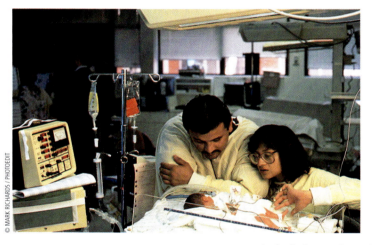

Getting to Know You If these new parents were kept at a distance, they might be troubled by the intravenous drips, the beeping monitor, and the protective plastic of the intensive-care nursery. Through the intimacy of closeness and touch, the LBW patient becomes, to the parents, simply "our baby."

kangaroo care Care that occurs when the mother of a low-birthweight infant spends at least an hour a day holding the infant between her breasts, like a kangaroo who carries her immature newborn in her pouch. If the infant is capable, he or she can easily breast-feed.

First, Intensive Care . . .

Vulnerable infants are typically placed in intensive-care nurseries, where they are hooked up to one machine or another and surrounded by bright lights and noise. Although these measures are often medically warranted, they deprive neonates of the gentle rocking they would have experienced if they still were in the womb and of the regular handling involved in feeding and bathing if they were at low risk. To overcome this deprivation, many hospitals provide high-risk infants with regular massage and soothing stimulation, which aid weight gain and increase overall alertness (Field, 2001).

Ideally, parents share in this early caregiving, in recognition of the fact that they, too, are deprived and stressed. They must not only cope with uncertainty about their baby's future but also struggle with feelings of inadequacy and perhaps sorrow, guilt, and anger. Such emotions are relieved somewhat if they can cradle and care for their vulnerable newborn.

One way to achieve this parental involvement is through **kangaroo care,** in which the mother of a low-birthweight infant spends at least an hour a day holding the infant between her breasts, skin-to-skin, allowing the tiny baby to hear her heart beat and feel her body heat. A comparison study (Feldman, Weller, Sirota, & Eidelman, 2002) found that kangaroo-care newborns slept more deeply and spent more time alert than infants who received standard care. By 6 months, infants who had received kangaroo care were more responsive to their mothers. These findings could be the outcome of either improved infant maturation or increased maternal sensitivity.

. . . Then Home

For high-risk infants who survive, complications await, including minor medical crises and slow development. Preterm infants are often late to smile, to hold a bottle, and to communicate. As the months go by, short- and long-term cognitive difficulties may emerge. Cerebral palsy affects 20 percent of those who were ELBW (see Table 4.3) and 7 percent of those who weighed between 3½ and 5½ pounds (1,500 and 2,500 grams) (Hack et al., 1995). High-risk infants who escape such obvious impairments are nevertheless more distractible, less obedient, and slower to talk (Girouard et al., 1998; Taylor et al., 2000). Even in young adulthood, some risks persist (Hack et al., 2002).

Fortunately, long-term handicaps are not inevitable. Some newborns who had heart defects or other serious abnormalities, or were extremely low birthweight, can and do develop quite normally, although most do not (Miller et al., 2001; Taylor et al., 2000). Thus, parents should assume neither that a high-risk birth was the child's last major challenge nor that severe intellectual and medical problems will follow. Often, ongoing medical care, family support, and special educational services are needed for many years (Petrou et al., 2001). By early childhood, the best predictors of a preterm infant's cognitive development are not complications at birth but social support in infancy.

Mothers, Fathers, and a Good Start

Humans are social creatures from the beginning to the end of life, always affected by, and affecting, their families and their societies. Accordingly, prenatal development and birth involve not only the fetus but also the mother, father, and many others. As you have already read, a woman's chance of avoiding risks during pregnancy depends partly on her family, her ethnic background, and the nation where she lives.

The experiences of women born in Mexico and now living in the United States illustrate this statement. As Figure 4.10 shows, their rate of LBW births is lower than those of other Spanish-speaking groups, as well as those of Americans of European and African descent. This is especially remarkable because fewer Mexican-Americans obtain early prenatal care, and more live in poverty, than these other groups. Chicanas who emigrate from Mexico have even better birth outcomes than those Mexican-Americans from the same neighborhoods and circumstances who were born in the United States. Obviously, social practices, not genes, are the reason (Aguirre-Molina et al., 2001).

The credit probably belongs to *familia,* strong family support. Almost all Mexican-American new mothers are married, and almost all their husbands, grandparents, and other relatives consider it their duty to make sure the infant is healthy. The same is true for Chinese-Americans, the other American group with

FIGURE 4.10 Low Birthweight and Mother's Country of Origin Overall, and for almost every ethnic group, mothers born in the United States have a higher rate of underweight newborns than do mothers born elsewhere who have immigrated to the United States. This benefit for immigrant women occurs despite three risks: They tend to be poorer, less educated, and less likely to obtain prenatal care. They also tend to have three advantages, however: They are less often teenagers, unmarried, and users of drugs and alcohol.

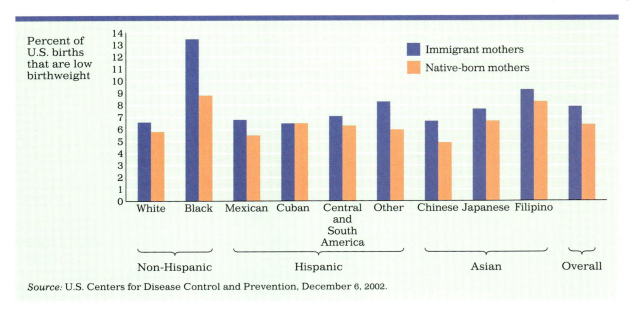

Source: U.S. Centers for Disease Control and Prevention, December 6, 2002.

FIGURE 4.11 Wisdom Doesn't Cut It Logically, one might think that older women and women with job experience and education would never drink to the point of endangering their fetus, but this isn't so. The only factor that seems to make a powerful difference is marriage.

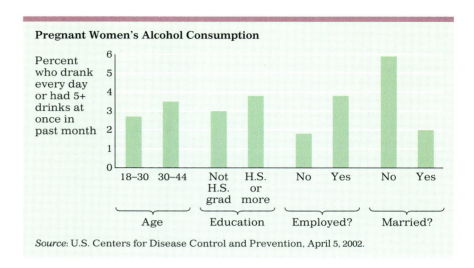

Pregnant Women's Alcohol Consumption

Percent who drank every day or had 5+ drinks at once in past month

Source: U.S. Centers for Disease Control and Prevention, April 5, 2002.

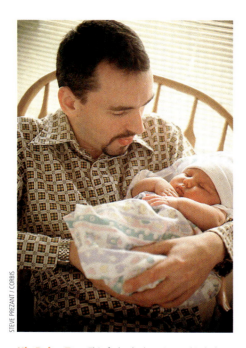

His Baby, Too This father's devotion to his baby illustrates a truism that developmental research has only recently reflected: Fathers contribute much more than half their child's genes. They also contribute to their offspring's physical, cognitive, and psychosocial health from the early prenatal period through adulthood. Some of that contribution is direct, as in this photograph; some is indirect, through the father's influence on the mother; and some of it becomes apparent only when the father is absent from the child's life.

remarkably good birth outcomes despite a high rate of poverty. The family concern is protective: Most pregnant Chicanas and Chinese-Americans gain ample weight and avoid all psychoactive drugs, and comparatively few have a first child as teenagers.

This example makes an important point: The father plays a crucial role. A supportive father-to-be is often the reason a future mother is healthy, well nourished, and drug free. One example involves alcohol, as Figure 4.11 shows. Most educated women know that alcohol is not good for a fetus, but neither education nor employment correlates with decreased alcohol consumption during pregnancy. Marriage does. For alcohol at least, husbands may help their wives abstain.

Fathers also can reduce maternal stress, which can affect the fetus if it reaches the point that the mother's circulation is impaired or her digestion is disrupted. Of course, prospective fathers can become as stressed as mothers, and both partners need to help each other in order to help their future child. Levels of the stress hormone cortisol are correlated between expectant fathers and mothers (Berg & Wynne-Edwards, 2002). Remember John and Martha, the young couple you met in Chapter 3, whose amniocentesis revealed trisomy-21? One night at 3:00 A.M., after about seven months of pregnancy, Martha was crying uncontrollably. She told John she was scared.

> "Scared of what?" he said, "Of a little baby who's not as perfect as you think he ought to be?" . . .
>
> "I didn't say I wanted him to be perfect," I said. "I just want him to be normal. That's all I want. Just normal."
>
> "That is total bullshit. . . . You don't want this baby to be normal. You'd throw him in a dumpster if he just turned out to be normal. What you really want is for him to be superhuman."
>
> "For your information," I said in my most acid tone, "I was the one who decided to keep this baby, even though he's got Down's. You were the one who wanted to throw him in a dumpster."
>
> "How would you know?" John's voice was still gaining volume. "You never asked me what I wanted, did you? No. You never even asked me. . . ."
>
> [Beck, 1999, p. 255]

This episode ended well, with a long, warm, and honest conversation between the two prospective parents. Both parents now understood better what their Down syndrome fetus meant to them. Adam, their future son, became an impor-

STEVE PREZANT / CORBIS

tant part of their relationship. Such honest discussions between parents are crucial throughout pregnancy and throughout child rearing to form a **parental alliance,** a commitment by both parents to cooperate in raising the child.

A strong parental alliance was particularly crucial for John and Martha, because their fetus had disabilities that required extra dedication. However, even when all seems normal with the pregnancy and birth, the mother of the newborn may need extra support from the father and from others. In the days and weeks after the birth, between 10 and 20 percent of women experience **postpartum depression,** a sense of inadequacy and sadness (called *baby blues* in the mild version and *postpartum psychosis* in the most severe form). Postpartum depression lasting more than a few weeks can have a long-term impact on the child, so it should be diagnosed and alleviated as soon as possible (Goodman & Gotlib, 2002; Hay et al., 2001).

A developmental perspective notes that some causes of postpartum depression predate the pregnancy (such as preexisting depression, financial stress, or marital problems); others occur during pregnancy (for example, women are more likely to be depressed two months before birth than two months after); and still others are specific to the particular infant (health, feeding, or sleeping problems) (Ashman & Dawson, 2002; Evans et al., 2001). In every case, the father's support can greatly benefit the mother, and his attachment to the baby can overcome any negative impact on the developing child (National Institutes of Health, 2001).

One cause of postpartum depression is directly related to the first hours after birth: the mother's perception that she is incompetent (O'Hara, 1997). For mothers who are vulnerable to depression, or for first-time low-income mothers, observation and discussion with a nurse or doctor of their newborn's reflexes and motor skills improve their mothering skills and attentiveness to their babies in the next weeks (Brazelton & Cramer, 1991; Hart et al., 1999; Wendland-Carro et al., 1999). They benefit from seeing their newborn grasp a finger so tightly that the baby's body weight can be supported or watching the newborn stare directly at a person's eyes or suck and swallow in rhythm (reflexes are further described on pages 132–133).

To what extent are the first hours and days crucial to the formation of the **parent–infant bond,** a strong, loving connection that forms as parents hold, examine, and feed their newborn? It has been claimed that this bond develops in the first hours after birth as mothers touch their naked newborns, just as sheep and goats must smell and nuzzle their newborns in order to nurture their offspring (Klaus & Kennell, 1976).

Although the concept of bonding has been used to argue against the impersonal medicalization of birth, research does not find that early skin-to-skin contact is essential for family bonding (Eyer, 1992; Lamb, 1982). Unlike sheep and goats, most mammals do not need immediate contact for parents to nurture their offspring. In fact, substantial research on monkeys begins with *cross-fostering,* a strategy in which newborns are removed from their biological mothers in the first days of life and raised by another female or even a male. A strong and beneficial relationship sometimes develops (Suomi, 2002).

Developmentalists are wary of taking extreme positions for and against bonding. A new mother must not be instructed to experience a cultural ideal of "active love right after birth . . . that many women find impossible to meet" (Eyer, 1992). Her failure to live up to this ideal might trigger postpartum depression. However, a woman's hormonal and physiological condition immediately after birth "is clearly a state of intense effect" (Corter & Fleming, 1995). In this emotional period, she should be able to cherish her infant's touch, smell, and appearance, and the father should be an integral part of the new family formation.

parental alliance Cooperation between mother and father because of their mutual commitment to their children. In a parental alliance, both parents agree to support each other in their shared parental roles.

postpartum depression A mother's feelings of sadness, inadequacy, and hopelessness in the days and weeks after giving birth. These feelings are partly physiological (especially hormonal) and partly cultural, particularly if the woman does not receive adequate assistance and encouragement from the baby's father and other helpers.

parent–infant bond A strong, loving connection that forms as parents hold, examine, and feed their newborn.

To summarize what is and is not known about birth: Labor usually lasts less than eight hours and results in a newborn who weighs about 7 pounds (3,000 grams), who scores at least 7 on the Apgar scale, and who is ready to thrive without medical assistance. If necessary, neonatal surgery and intensive care can save lives and prevent long-term complications. However, prenatal care and ongoing assistance after birth are at least as important in fostering optimal development as is medical intervention during the birth process. Although modern medicine has made death and serious impairment less common in advanced nations, many critics fear that some hospitals treat birth as a medical crisis instead of a natural event, which may increase postpartum depression and impede family bonding.

The concept of bonding is controversial. Human parents and infants seem to benefit from contact in the hours and days following the birth, but they also seem able to fare quite well without it. The family relationship begins before conception, may be strengthened by the birth process, and continues lifelong.

SUMMARY

From Zygote to Newborn

1. The first two weeks of prenatal growth are called the germinal period. During this period, the single-celled zygote develops into an organism of more than 100 cells, travels down the fallopian tube, and implants itself in the lining of the uterus. Most zygotes do not develop and never implant.

2. The period from the third through the eighth week after conception is called the embryonic period. The heart begins to beat, and the eyes, ears, nose, and mouth begin to form. By the 8th week, the embryo has the basic organs and features of a human, with the exception of the sex organs.

3. The fetal period extends from the 9th week until birth. By the 12th week all the organs and body structures have formed. The fetus attains viability when the brain is sufficiently mature to regulate basic body functions, around the 22nd week after conception.

4. The average fetus weighs approximately 3 pounds at the beginning of the last three months of pregnancy and 7½ pounds at birth. Maturation of brain, lungs, and heart ensures survival for more than 99 percent of all full-term babies. Toward the end of prenatal development, the fetus can hear and respond to movement.

Risk Reduction

5. Diseases, drugs, and pollutants can all cause birth defects. Some teratogens cause explicit physical impairment. Others, called behavioral teratogens, harm the brain and therefore impair cognitive abilities and personality tendencies.

6. Whether a particular teratogen harms a particular embryo or fetus depends on timing, amount of exposure, and genetic vulnerability. To protect against prenatal complications, good public and personal health practices are strongly recommended. There are no guarantees, for good or ill, however.

7. Low birthweight (under 2,500 grams, or 5½ pounds) may arise from some combination of the mother's poor health, malnutrition, smoking, drinking, drug use, and age, as well as the fetus's genes and whether twins or other multiples are developing. Both preterm and small-for-gestational-age babies are more likely than full-term babies to suffer from stress during birth and to experience medical difficulties, especially breathing problems and brain damage.

The Birth Process

8. Birth typically begins with contractions that push the fetus, head first, out from the uterus and then through the vagina. The Apgar scale, which rates the neonate's vital signs at one minute and again at five minutes after birth, provides a quick evaluation of the infant's health.

9. Medical intervention in the birth process can speed contractions, dull pain, and save lives. However, many aspects of the medicalized birth have been faulted. Contemporary birthing practices are aimed at finding a balance, protecting the baby but also allowing the mother and father more involvement and control.

10. Birth complications, such as unusually long and stressful labor that includes anoxia (a lack of oxygen to the fetus), have many causes. Vulnerable newborns are placed in an intensive-care unit for monitoring and treatment. These babies benefit from parental as well as medical care. Long-term handicaps are not inevitable for such children, but careful nurturing is required once they are taken home.

11. Many women feel unhappy, incompetent, or uninterested in the days immediately after giving birth. In its mild form, called *baby blues,* this postpartum depression lifts if the baby's father and others are supportive. Mother–infant interaction should be encouraged, although the benefits of forming an early parent–infant bond have been exaggerated.

KEY TERMS

germinal period (p. 91)
embryonic period (p. 91)
fetal period (p. 91)
implantation (p. 92)
embryo (p. 93)
fetus (p. 94)
age of viability (p. 95)
teratogens (p. 97)

behavioral teratogens
  (p. 97)
risk analysis (p. 97)
critical period (p. 98)
threshold effect (p. 98)
interaction effect (p. 98)
human immunodeficiency
  virus (HIV) (p. 102)

fetal alcohol syndrome (FAS)
  (p. 103)
low birthweight (LBW) (p. 104)
preterm birth (p. 106)
small for gestational age
  (SGA) (p. 106)
Apgar scale (p. 108)
cesarean section (p. 109)

cerebral palsy (p. 111)
anoxia (p. 111)
kangaroo care (p. 112)
parental alliance (p. 115)
postpartum depression
  (p. 115)
parent–infant bond (p. 115)

APPLICATIONS

1. Go to a nearby greeting-card store and analyze the cards regarding pregnancy and birth. Do you see any cultural attitudes (e.g., variations depending on sex of the newborn or of the parent)? If possible, compare cards with those from a store that caters to another economic or cultural group.

2. Interview three mothers about their birth experiences. Make your interviews open ended—let them choose what to tell you, as long as they give at least 10 minutes of description. Then compare and contrast the three accounts. Discuss whether differences were the result of culture, personality, circumstance, cohort, or other factors.

3. People who have never been pregnant sometimes wonder how any pregnant woman could jeopardize the health of her fetus. To gain some insight, consider your own health-related behavior in the past month—your patterns of exercise, sleep, nutrition, drug use, medical and dental care, disease avoidance, and so on. Could you easily follow the health recommendations for women before, during, and after pregnancy? Would it be more difficult to follow these recommendations if your family, your partner, and you yourself did not want a baby?

Part II

Adults don't change much in a year or two. Sometimes their hair gets longer or grows thinner, or they gain or lose a few pounds, or they become a little wiser. But if you were reunited with friends you haven't seen for several years, you would recognize them immediately.

If, in contrast, you cared for a newborn 24 hours a day for the first month and then did not see the baby until two years later, you probably would not recognize him or her. After all, would you recognize a best friend who had quadrupled in weight, grown 14 inches (35 cm), and sprouted a new head of hair? Behavior changes, too. A hungry newborn just cries; a hungry toddler says "more food" or climbs up on the kitchen counter to reach the cookies.

A year or two is not much time compared to the 80 years of the average life span. However, children in their first two years reach half their adult height, develop cognitive abilities that have surprised researchers, and express almost every emotion—not just joy and fear but also many others, including jealousy and shame. And two of the most important human abilities, talking and loving, are already apparent. The next three chapters describe these radical and wonderful changes.

The First Two Years: Infants and Toddlers

Chapter Five

The First Two Years: Biosocial Development

In the first two years of life, rapid growth is obvious in all three domains—body, mind, and social relationships. Picture biosocial development, from birth to age 2: Roll over . . . sit . . . stand . . . walk . . . run! Reach . . . touch . . . grab . . . throw! Listen . . . stare . . . see! Each object, each person, each place becomes something to explore with every sense, every limb, every organ, while clothes are outgrown before they become too stained or torn to wear. Invisible developments are even more striking. Small infant brains become larger, with neurons connecting to one another at a dizzying, yet programmed, pace. Tiny stomachs digest food and more food, dispatching nourishment to brain and body to enable the phenomenally rapid growth.

Parents and cultures are pivotal to this process, which makes this bio*social*—not merely biological—development. Even here, then, nurture interacts with nature. Adults provide the nurture that enables infant growth, with specifics that must change daily because infants change daily. As one expert explains, "Parenting an infant is akin to trying to hit a moving target" (Bornstein, 2002, p. 14).

In this chapter we will describe that target as it moves, including weight, height, and motor skills at key ages. Throughout, we emphasize the brain growth that provides the foundation. We will also explain what parents and cultures must provide—stimulation, encouragement, vaccinations, and nutrition. Ignorance contributes to the neglect and death of an estimated 10 million of the world's infants each year (Rice et al., 2000). The knowledge that you will gain from this chapter will help the infants you know, and some whom you will never meet, make it safely to age 2 and beyond.

Body Changes

In infancy, growth is so fast and the consequences of neglect so severe that gains need to be closely monitored. Medical checkups, including measurement of height, weight, and head circumference, should occur every few weeks or months. Any slowdown in these areas is a cause for immediate concern, because sensation, perception, and cognition all depend on early growth.

Body Size

Exactly how rapidly does normal growth occur? At birth the average North American weighs a little more than 7 pounds (3.2 kilograms) and measures about 20 inches (51 centimeters). This means that the typical newborn weighs less than a gallon of milk and is about as long as the distance from a man's elbow to the tips of his fingers.

Infants typically double their birthweight by the fourth month and triple it by the end of the first year. Physical growth slows in the second year, but it is still rapid. By 24 months most children weigh almost 30 pounds (13 kilograms) and measure between 32 and 36 inches (81–91 centimeters). This means that typical 2-year-olds are already astonishingly tall, half of their adult height. They are also about 15 to 20 percent of their adult weight, four times as heavy as at birth. (See Appendix pages A-6, A-7.)

Much of the weight increase in the early months is fat, to provide insulation for warmth and a store of nourishment. This stored nutrition keeps the brain growing if teething or the sniffles interfere with eating. Thus, if nutrition is temporarily inadequate, the body stops growing but not the brain, a phenomenon called **head-sparing** (Georgieff & Rao, 2001). (Chronic malnutrition is discussed on pages 142–143.)

Each of these numbers is a **norm,** an average or standard for a particular population. Norms need to be carefully interpreted. The "particular population" for the norms above is a representative sample of North American infants, who may not be comparable to infants from other continents. To understand norms, you also need to understand percentiles. An average child is at the 50th **percentile,** a number that would represent the midpoint between 1 and 99, with 49 percent of the children above it and 49 percent below it.

A child's growth is not only compared to that of other children but also looked at in the context of the parents, siblings, and, especially, that child's past growth. Pediatricians and nurses pay special heed to children whose growth is far from the average, but the critical factor for height and weight is not the absolute number but the rank: A drop in a child's percentile ranking alerts parents and professionals that something might be wrong. Consider the following report.

head-sparing The biological protection of the brain when malnutrition temporarily affects body growth.

norm A standard, or average, measurement, calculated from many individuals within a specific group or population.

percentile Any point on a ranking scale of 1 to 99. For example, the 50th percentile is at the midpoint, with half the subjects ranking higher and half ranking lower.

A Case to Study

Toni's Well-Child Visit

Toni is a 17-month-old girl who has been brought to the doctor for a well-child visit. She was last seen at 11 months and is behind in immunizations. Toni was born at term to an 18-year-old mother and weighed 3,850 grams (75th percentile) and measured 50 centimeters in length (50th percentile). Prenatal history was negative for problems, and her health has been good, according to her mother. At Toni's last visit, her height and weight were at the 50th percentile.

Today Toni weighs 9,400 grams (20th percentile) and is 79 centimeters tall (40th percentile). Development, according to her mother, is normal, although her language skills are delayed—she has only a five-word vocabulary. Toni's mother describes Toni as busy, always on the go. The family history for medical problems is negative. Toni's mother is 5 feet 5 inches tall and weighs 130 pounds. Her father is reported to be about 6 feet tall. He is not in the household.

There have been no significant illnesses since the 11-month visit. The physical exam, as well as screening laboratory tests, are essentially negative except for mild anemia.

Toni's mother has recently (within the past 4 months) returned to work as a waitress. She has pieced together a patchwork of child care. The child is cared for by a variety of family members. She [the mother] has indicated that she is afraid of using strangers. She has a difficult time giving a feeding history because multiple providers feed Toni, who apparently do not communicate with each other about her intake. Mealtimes vary from household to household as do other routines, such as naps and bedtime. Toni's mother's meals are also erratic, and the two rarely eat a meal together. Toni falls asleep in front of the television every night and generally awakens too late for breakfast at home, prior to [being rushed] out in order to accommodate her mother's work schedule.

[Yoos et al., 1999, pp. 380, 381, 383]

Toni's case will be referred to throughout our three chapters on infancy. From Chapter 4, you can recognize several aspects of Toni's development that represent strengths. A full-term, 8½-pound infant, born to an 18-year-old mother, is beginning life very well. (A birthweight below 5½ pounds or a mother younger than 16 would be a risk.) In addition, since many teenage parents use various health care providers—which makes accurate records regarding immunizations, birth complications, and weight gain unavailable—the facts that Toni's mother brought her for a well-child checkup only a few months late and that Toni's medical history is available are both positive signs, not to be taken for granted.

Records are particularly useful in this case. Toni's 17-month measurements, by themselves, are not seriously low, but her weight has dropped from the 75th to the 50th to the 20th percentile. Furthermore, Toni is mildly anemic; her mother had difficulty giving a feeding history; caregivers do not communicate with one another about Toni's eating; household routines vary; Toni's height percentiles are also decreasing; and Toni doesn't eat breakfast. No single one of these facts means that Toni is malnourished, but the combination points toward that conclusion.

Be assured that because of head-sparing, Toni's malnutrition had not yet damaged her brain. Typically, reduced weight is the first sign of malnutrition, stunted height is the next, and finally comes slow head growth (Rao & Georgieff, 2000). There is no indication that Toni's head circumference was too small, and her weight and height were still in the normal range. In fact, this case was published partly to show when intervention was needed. Toni soon gained weight. Further discussion and follow-up recommendations for Toni are presented in Chapter 7.

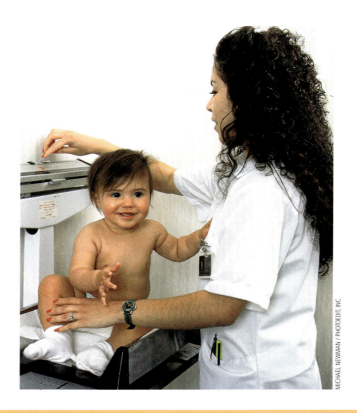

The Weigh-In At her one-year well-baby checkup, Blair sits up steadily, weighs more than 20 pounds, and would scramble off the table if she could. Both Blair's development and the nurse's protective arm are quite appropriate.

MICHAEL NEWMAN / PHOTOEDIT, INC.

Sleep

New babies spend most of their time sleeping and eating. It is obvious why they eat so much: They must double their weight in four months! However, it is not obvious why they sleep 17 hours or more a day. What *is* known is that, throughout childhood, regular and ample sleep correlates with brain maturation, learning, emotional regulation, and psychological adjustment in school and within the family (Bates et al., 2002; Sadah et al., 2000). In addition, more growth hormones are released during sleep than during wakefulness, another possible reason that rapidly growing infants sleep as much as they do (see Figure 5.1).

Over the first months, the relative amount of time spent in the different stages of sleep changes. **REM sleep** (rapid eye movement sleep, characterized by dreaming and rapid brain waves) declines, as does "transitional sleep," the dozing stage when a person is half awake. At about 3 or 4 months, quiet sleep (also called slow-wave sleep) increases markedly (Salzarulo & Fagioli, 1999).

Many new parents are troubled not by how much but *when* their infants sleep. Parents want infants to sleep through the night, but infants are too immature—in their brain, digestion, and circadian rhythm—to do so. To some extent, this mismatch between infant wakefulness and parents' wishes is created by the time pressures and schedule urgency of modern life. In many more traditional cultures, by contrast, family harmony is not disturbed if an infant wakes several times each night, because the mother is sleeping within reach.

REM sleep Rapid eye movement sleep, a stage of sleep characterized by flickering eyes behind closed lids, dreaming, and rapid brain waves.

FIGURE 5.1 **Sweet Dreams** On average, the older we are, the less sleep we get, probably because older people dream less. At age 60, we spend only about one hour per night dreaming. The mystery is, What can newborns be dreaming about?

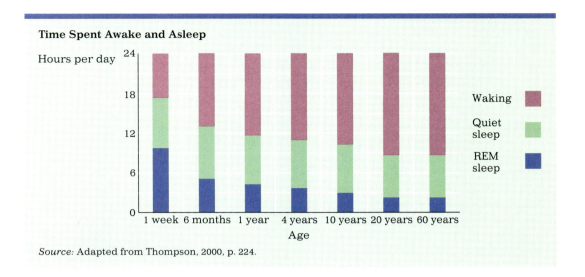

Time Spent Awake and Asleep

Hours per day

Waking

Quiet sleep

REM sleep

1 week 6 months 1 year 4 years 10 years 20 years 60 years

Age

Source: Adapted from Thompson, 2000, p. 224.

Between birth and age 1, infant sleep gradually comes closer to matching the day–night activities of the family. No newborns but 80 percent of all 1-year-olds in North America "sleep through the night," although many preschoolers still wake up while their parents are still asleep (Weissbluth, 1999).

Both nature and nurture are influential in every aspect of physiological development, including sleep. By nature, infants sleep a great deal and wake up often. However, sleep cycles are influenced not only by brain maturation but also by child-rearing practices. For example, if parents respond to predawn cries with food and playtime, children are likely to wake up night after night. First-born infants typically "receive more attention and better care" (Bornstein, 2002, p. 28), which may be why they exhibit more sleep problems than later-borns. This report from one mother tells what can happen when this greater attention combines with a focus on the parents' schedule:

Dreaming, Dozing, or Sound Asleep? Babies spend most of their time sleeping.

? *Observational Quiz* (see answer, page 126): Can you tell which kind of sleep this infant is experiencing?

I . . . raised my first taking him wherever I went, whenever I went, confident he would adapt. While he was always happy, he was never a good sleeper and his first 4 years were very hard on me (I claim he didn't sleep through the night until he was 4, but I could be wrong, I was so sleep-deprived). . . . [When my third child] came along . . . , I was determined to give her a schedule. . . . She is a GREAT sleeper, happy to go to bed. I am convinced, anecdotally, that schedules are the most important part of this. When I talk to new mothers, I give them this advice: Let the baby determine the schedule, then let nothing interfere with it.

[Freda, personal communication, 1997]

That is good advice. Developmentalists agree that insisting that an infant conform to the parents' schedule can be frustrating to the parents and, in some cases, harmful to the infant, but letting a child continually interrupt the adults' sleep can be harmful to the parents.

Now, before describing the brain, let us review the remarkable growth of the body in a mere two years. Birthweight doubles, triples, and quadruples by 4 months, 12 months, and 24 months, respectively; height increases by about a foot (about 30 centimeters). Such maturation norms are useful as general guidelines, but percentiles over time are more significant, to indicate whether a particular infant is growing as expected. Sleep becomes regular, and distinct

> sleep–wake patterns develop, usually including a long night's sleep; time spent dreaming decreases to about what it is for an older child. Cultural and caregiving practices influence norms, schedules, and expectations.

Early Brain Development

No aspect of biosocial growth is more critical than the rapid growth of the brain, "by far the most complex structure in the known universe" (Thompson, 2000, p. 1). Recall that the newborn's skull is disproportionately large. That's because it must be big enough to hold the brain, which at birth has already attained 25 percent of its adult weight. The neonate's body weight, by comparison, is typically only 5 percent of the adult weight. By age 2, the brain is about 75 percent of adult weight, while the body is only about 20 percent (see Figure 5.2).

Connections in the Brain

Head circumference provides a rough idea of how much growth goes on within the skull. The distance around the head typically increases from 34 to 46 centimeters (about 35 percent) within the first year. Much more significant (although harder to measure) are changes in the brain's communication systems. Early brain development has many implications for early child rearing—for example, pointing to the importance of avoiding neglect and overstimulation. To understand this requires some familiarity with brain structure and functioning (see Figure 5.3).

Basic Brain Structures

The brain's communication system begins with nerve cells, called **neurons.** Most neurons are created before birth, at a peak production rate of 250,000 new brain cells per minute at mid-pregnancy (Bloom et al., 2001). In infancy, the human brain has billions of neurons, about 70 percent of which are in the **cortex,** the brain's outer layer (also called the neocortex and sometimes called the gray matter). Only mammals have a cortex, which is the location of most thinking, feeling, and sensing. (Other parts of the brain participate in these functions, but the cortex is the crucial, and conscious, part.)

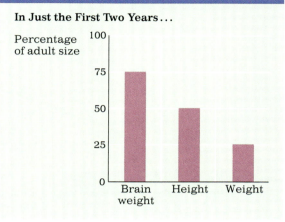

In Just the First Two Years…

FIGURE 5.2 Growing Up Two-year-olds are barely talking and are totally dependent on adults, but they have already reached half their adult height and three-fourths of their adult brain size. This is dramatic evidence that biosocial growth is the foundation for cognitive and social maturity.

neuron A nerve cell of the central nervous system. Most neurons are in the brain.

cortex The outer layer of the brain in humans and other mammals; it is the location of most thinking, feeling, and sensing.

Frontal cortex The front part of the cortex assists in planning, self-control, and self-regulation. It is very immature in the newborn.

Cortex The crinkled outer layer of the brain (colored here in pink, tan, purple, and blue) is the cortex

Auditory cortex Hearing is quite acute at birth, the result of months of eavesdropping during the fetal period.

Visual cortex Vision is the least mature sense at birth because the fetus has nothing to see.

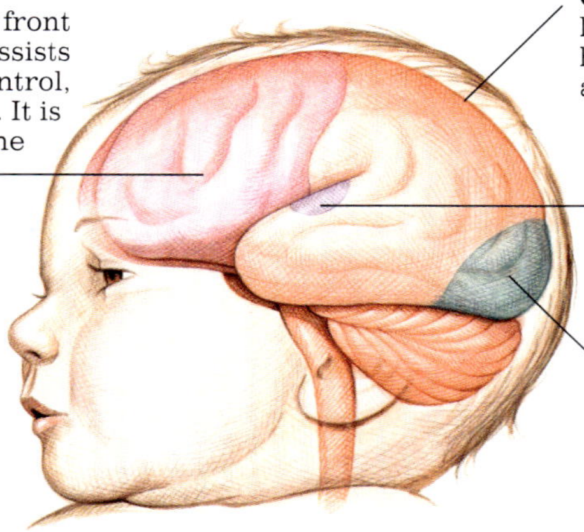

FIGURE 5.3 The Developing Cortex The cortex consists of six thin layers of tissue that cover the brain. It contains virtually all the neurons that make conscious thought possible. Some areas of the cortex, such as those devoted to the basic senses, mature relatively early. Others, such as the frontal cortex, mature quite late.

!*Answer to Observational Quiz* (from page 124): The baby's outstretched right arm suggests dreaming, which occupies about six hours of every day's sleep at this age. Direct observation or a video, not a photograph, could demonstrate whether this is REM (dreaming) sleep. Quiet sleep is characterized by shallow breathing, still eyes, and relaxed muscle tone.

axon A nerve fiber that extends from a neuron and transmits electrical impulses from that neuron to the dendrites of other neurons.

dendrite A nerve fiber that extends from a neuron and receives electrical impulses transmitted from other neurons via their axons.

synapse The intersection between the axon of one neuron and the dendrites of other neurons.

Various areas of the cortex specialize in particular functions. For instance, there are a visual cortex, an auditory cortex, and an area dedicated to the sense of touch for each body part—for each finger of a person or, in rats, for each whisker (Bloom et al., 2001). A word of caution: Definitive research linking brain areas to brain functions is easier to conduct for motor skills than for cognitive processes and is easier with lower animals than with humans. However, it seems likely that areas of the human cortex specialize in very particular aspects of cognition, such as memory, parts of speech, and recognition of patterns. As one science reporter explains:

> It's a complicated world out there, visually, full of things that look a lot alike. Yet people rarely identify a TV remote control as a cell phone or confuse a pencil with a swizzle stick. . . . In the past few years, brain imaging studies have identified one region [of the area of the brain called the *ventral temporal cortex*] that specializes in recognizing faces and another that processes places. More recently, researchers have found that even mundane objects such as shoes, chairs, and plastic bottles also light up distinct areas in part of the brain.
>
> [Helmuth, 2001, pp. 196, 198]

Within and between brain areas, neurons are connected to other neurons by intricate networks of nerve fibers called **axons** and **dendrites** (see Figure 5.4). Each neuron has a single axon and numerous dendrites, with the latter spreading out like the branches of a tree. The axon of one neuron meets the dendrites of other neurons at intersections called **synapses,** which are critical communication links within the brain. To be more specific, a neuron communicates by sending an electrical impulse through its axon to the synapse, where it is picked up by the dendrites of other neurons. The dendrites bring the message to the cell bodies of those neurons, which, in turn, convey the message to still other neurons.

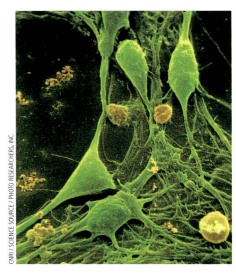

CNRI / SCIENCE SOURCE / PHOTO RESEARCHERS, INC.

FIGURE 5.4 How Two Neurons Communicate The link between one neuron and another is shown in this simplified diagram. The infant brain actually contains billions of neurons, each with one axon and many dendrites. Every electrochemical message to or from the brain causes thousands of neurons to fire simultaneously, each transmitting the message across the synapse to neighboring neurons. The electron micrograph above shows several neurons, greatly magnified, with their tangled but highly organized and well-coordinated sets of dendrites and axons.

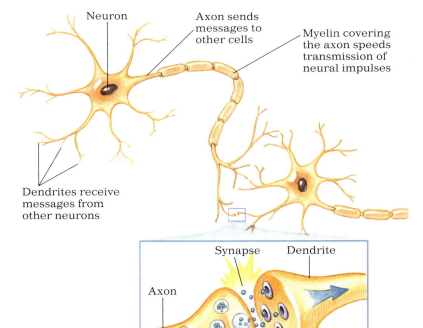

Neuron

Axon sends messages to other cells

Myelin covering the axon speeds transmission of neural impulses

Dendrites receive messages from other neurons

Synapse   Dendrite

Axon

Neurotransmitters

In the synapse, or intersection between an axon and dendrite, neurotransmitters carry information from one neuron to another.

Axons and dendrites do not touch at synapses. Instead, the electrical impulse excites brain chemicals, called *neurotransmitters,* which carry information from the axon of the sending neuron, across the *synaptic gap,* to the dendrites of the receiving neuron.

Exuberance

At birth, the brain contains more than 100 billion neurons, far more than any person will ever need, and far fewer dendrites and synapses than the person will eventually possess. During the first months and years, major spurts of growth and refinement in axons, dendrites, and synapses occur, especially in the cortex. Dendrite growth is probably the major reason that brain weight triples in the first two years.

Indeed, an estimated fivefold increase in dendrites in the cortex occurs in the 24 months after birth, a process called **transient exuberance.** As many as 15,000 new connections may be established *per neuron* (Thompson, 2000). This exuberant proliferation enables neurons to become connected to, and communicate with, a greatly expanding number of other neurons within the brain. Synapses, dendrites, and even neurons continue to form throughout life, though much less rapidly than in infancy.

These connections are necessary because thinking and learning require making connections between many parts of the brain. For example, to understand the import of any word in this text, you need to understand the surrounding words, the ideas they convey, and even how they relate to your other thoughts and experiences. Baby brains have the same requirement, although at first they have few experiences to build on.

Experience Enhances the Brain

The specifics of brain structure and growth depend partly on experience, as is illustrated by the pruning process that closely follows the dendrite growth of transient exuberance (see Figure 5.5). Exuberance is *transient*—a transitional stage between the immaturity of the newborn brain and the maturity of the brain of the older child or adult. Soon after the exuberant expansion, some neurons wither because they are underused—that is, because experiences have not caused their dendrites to connect with other neurons' axons at the synapses. Underused neurons are inactivated (Bloom et al., 2001). This process is called *pruning* because it resembles the way a gardener prunes a rose bush by cutting away some stems to enable more, or more beautiful, roses to bloom. It has also been called "sculpting" because it resembles the way a sculptor takes a block of stone or wood and chisels it into a work of art, discarding the useless chips. Both these analogies illustrate the point that cell death benefits the developing person's thinking ability. Indeed, one form of mental retardation (fragile-X syndrome) occurs when too many neurons survive (Comery et al., 1997). Experience shapes the brain, for good or ill.

An example of the importance of experience comes from reactions to stress. The production of stress hormones by the brain is lifelong, but the amount produced relates partly to early experiences (Gunnar & Vasquez, 2001). If too many stress hormones are required early on (for instance, if an infant is terrified or anticipates pain much of the time), then the developing brain loses the capacity to

Electric Excitement This infant's delight at his mother's facial expressions is visible, not just in his eyes and mouth but also in the neurons of the outer layer of his cortex. Electrodes map his brain activation region by region and moment by moment. Every month of life up to age 2 shows increased electrical excitement.

transient exuberance The great increase in the number of dendrites that occurs in an infant's brain over the first two years of life.

FIGURE 5.5 Brain Growth in Response to Experience These curves show the rapid rate of experience-dependent synapse formation for three functions of the brain (senses, language, and analysis). After the initial increase, the underused neurons are gradually pruned, or inactivated, as no functioning dendrites are formed from them.

? Observational Quiz (see answer, page 128): Why do both "12 months" and "1 year" appear on the "Age" line?

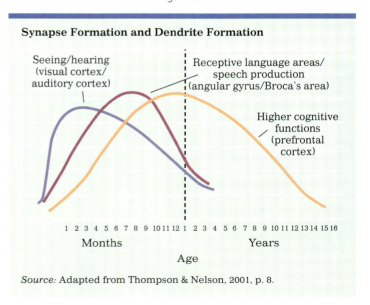

Source: Adapted from Thompson & Nelson, 2001, p. 8.

! *Answer to Observational Quiz* (from page 127): "One year" signifies the entire year, from day 365 to day 729, and that is indicated by its location between "12 months" and "2 years."

experience-expectant Refers to brain functions that require basic common experiences (which the infant can be expected to have) in order to develop normally.

experience-dependent Refers to brain functions that depend on particular, and variable, experiences and that therefore may or may not develop in a particular infant.

Let's Talk Infants evoke facial expressions and baby talk, no matter where they are or which adults they are with. Communication is thus experience-expectant: Young human brains expect it and need it.

? *Observational Quiz* (see answer, page 130): Are these two father and daughter? Where are they?

EASTCOTT / MOMATIUK / THE IMAGE WORKS

react normally to stress; the reason may be that the normal neuronal reactions have been pruned to allow rapid responses. Later the child may be hypervigilant (always on the alert) or seemingly indifferent (not happy, sad, or angry). For instance, a kindergarten teacher might notice that a certain child too readily becomes angry or afraid, or that another child seems indifferent to everything; the cause for the child's behavior could be the excessive production of stress hormones in infancy. If an adult loves or hates too quickly, extremely, and irrationally, again the cause could be abnormal brain growth resulting from early abuse that triggered excessive stress hormones (Teicher, 2002).

A scientist named William Greenough has identified two experience-related aspects of brain development. **Experience-expectant** brain functions require basic common experiences in order to develop—experiences that almost every infant will have (and will need for normal brain development). **Experience-dependent** functions depend on particular, and variable, events that occur in some families and cultures but not in others (Greenough et al., 1987). Expected experiences *must* happen for normal brain maturation to occur, and they almost always do happen: The brain is designed to expect them and use them for growth. By contrast, dependent experiences *might* happen; because of them, one brain differs from another.

Human brains are designed for the *expected* experiences that virtually all normal infants have, no matter where they are raised. In deserts and the Arctic, on isolated farms and in crowded cities, all babies have things to see and people to feed and carry them. As a result, their brains develop normally. Some particular experiences, such as which language the baby hears or how the mother reacts to frustration, vary. *Depending* on those various experiences, infant brains will be structured and connected one way or another. Consequently, each person not only is a unique product of a particular family and culture but also is similar to every other member of the human race.

The brain expects certain experiences at a particular age. This is generally not a problem, as the expected experiences are precisely those that infants normally have. However, in unusual situations, knowledge of this fact and of the particular ages at which certain developmental events occur can help us overcome problems that might destroy a part of the infant's brain. For example, proliferation and pruning occur first in those parts of the cortex that are connected to the eyes and ears, at about 4 months. Consequently, diagnosis of blind or deaf newborns, and treatment with surgery or visual or auditory aids, should occur in the first weeks of life, to prevent premature atrophy of neurons that are primed to expect visual or auditory input. (If early visual or auditory neuronal connections are not made, those areas of the brain may become dedicated to other senses, such as touch. Braille, for that reason, is easier for a blind person to read than for a seeing person, because blind people often have more brain cells dedicated to the sense of touch.) Similarly, the language areas of the brain develop most rapidly from 6 to 24 months, which means that infants need to hear a lot of speech during that period.

Overall, our understanding of the brain implies that caressing a newborn, talking to a preverbal infant, and showing affection toward a small person may be essential for developing full human potential. If such experiences are missing from the early weeks and months, that is tragic. But remember that human brains are designed to be adaptable, and some plasticity is retained throughout life. New connections and pathways can develop, as long as new experiences continue (Greenough, 1993). It is never too late, but earlier is better, as the following discussion reveals.

Thinking Like a Scientist

Plasticity and Young Orphans

Neuroscientists once thought that brains were formed solely by genes and prenatal influences. By contrast, many social scientists once thought that childhood environment was crucial, that cultures (according to anthropologists) or society (according to sociologists) or parents (according to psychologists) could be credited or blamed for a child's emotions and actions.

Now most scientists, especially life-span developmentalists, are multidisciplinary, believing in *plasticity* (first described on page 15)—that is, the concept that personality, intellect, habits, and emotions change throughout life for a combination of reasons, not just one (Wachs, 2000). How much, and when, does experience affect the brain? Two research projects—one with caged rats and the other with adopted babies—shed some light.

William Greenough and his colleagues raised some rats together in large cages filled with interesting rat toys, and others alone in small, barren cages. On autopsy, the brains of the rats in the first group were far better developed, with more dendrite branching, than the brains of the rats in the second group (Greenough & Volkmar, 1973).

A chilling natural experiment on humans began with the Romanian dictator Nicolae Ceausesçu. In the 1980s, his government forbade all birth control and paid parents a bonus for every baby born—but did not provide the economic infrastructure that made child rearing financially reasonable. More than 100,000 children were abandoned to the streets or to crowded, understaffed, state-run orphanages (D. E. Johnson, 2000). These children were not isolated or deprived of stimulation. If anything, their experience was worse: They were overburdened with stress without any social reassurance and love to buffer it. In 1989, after Ceausesçu was ousted and killed, thousands of these children were adopted by North American or Western European families who believed that "lots of love and good food would change the skinny, floppy waif they found in the orphanage into the child of their dreams" (D. E. Johnson, 2000, p. 154).

All the children grew and gained weight quickly (O'Connor et al., 2000). However, during early childhood many still showed signs of emotional damage: They were too friendly to strangers, or too angry without reason, or too frightened of normal events (Chisolm, 1998). If scientists expected dire consequences, the news is good: "The human infant has built-in 'buffers' against early adversity" (O'Connor et al., 2000). If they expected complete recovery, the news is bad: The identifica-

A Fortunate Pair Elaine Himelfarb *(shown in the background),* of San Diego, California, is in Bucharest to adopt 22-month-old Maria. This adoption was an exception to the Romanian government's current ban on international adoptions. Adopted children like Maria, who have been well fed and who are less than 2 years old, are especially likely to develop well.

tion of "persistent deficits in post-institutionalized children is repeated in all longitudinal studies of Romanian orphans" (D. E. Johnson, 2000, p. 152).

In the years to come, more research on these children will reveal how much recovery, under what circumstances, is possible for children who are severely deprived in infancy. We already know that the particulars of the early years have a greater effect than the particulars of the adoptive homes, almost all of which are highly nurturing. The Romanian adoptees who have fared best were adopted before age 2 and were cared for by their birth parents before being turned over to the orphanage. For those other, less fortunate orphans, now approaching adolescence, further research is needed. Thinking like a scientist, in this case, means condemning every government, culture, or family that allows young children to be raised without the experiences they need, and praising the brain growth and buffers that mitigate deprivation, while also admitting that the answers to many questions about early brain development and later experiences are still unknown.

Especially for Social Workers An infertile couple in their late 30s asks for your help in adopting a child from Eastern Europe. They particularly want an older child. How do you respond?

Response for Social Workers (from page 129): You would advise them that such a child requires more time and commitment than most children do, and you would assess their readiness to cope with that. You might ask whether both are prepared to cut down on their working hours in order to have time to meet with other parents of international adoptees, to schedule weekly professional help (for speech, nutrition, physical development, and/or family therapy), and so on. In addition, you would explain that adoptees who adjust well are typically under age 2 and that older adoptees need as much attention as babies. You might encourage them instead to adopt a special-needs child from their own area, to become foster parents, or to volunteer at least 10 hours a week at a day-care center. One reason for making these recommendations is to assess their willingness to help a real—not imagined—child. If they are willing to do all this, and understand why it may be necessary, you might help them adopt the child they want.

sensation The response of a sensory system (eyes, ears, skin, tongue, nose) when it detects a stimulus.

perception The mental processing of sensory information, when the brain interprets a sensation.

!Answer to Observational Quiz (from page 128): The man's straight black hair, high cheekbones, and weather-beaten face indicate that he could be an Indian from North or South America. Other clues pinpoint the location more closely. Note his lined, hooded jacket and the low, heat-conserving ceiling of the house—he is an Inuit in northern Canada. A father's attention makes a baby laugh and vocalize, not look away, so this man is not the 6-month-old baby's father. She is being held by a family friend whom she is visiting with her parents.

To summarize: We know many specifics of early brain growth. Dendrites and the synapses within the cortex increase exponentially, so that by age 2 the brain already weighs three-fourths of what it will weigh in adulthood and has begun rapid growth (transient exuberance) and notable pruning. The shrinkage of underused and unconnected neurons begins in the sensory and motor areas and then occurs in other areas, including those dedicated to language. Although some brain development is maturational, experience is also essential—both the universal experiences that almost every infant has (experience-expectant brain development) and the particular experiences that vary depending on the family or culture (experience-dependent brain development).

The Senses and Motor Skills

You learned in Chapter 2 that Piaget called the first period of intelligence the *sensorimotor* stage, thus emphasizing that cognition develops from the senses and motor skills. The same concept—that infant brain development depends partly on the sensory experiences and early movements of the baby—underlies the discussion you have just read. Now we will look explicitly at those early sensory and motor abilities.

Sensation and Perception

All the senses function at birth. Newborns have eyes open, ears sensitive to noise, and responsive smell, taste, and touch. Throughout their first year, infants use their senses to sort and classify their many experiences. Indeed, "infants spend the better part of their first year merely looking around" (Rovee-Collier, 2001, p. 35). You may have noticed that very young babies have their eyes wide open when they are awake, and you have probably also noticed that they seem to look at everything, without focusing on anything in particular.

Since a newborn's senses all function, why don't newborns seem to perceive much? To understand this, you need to grasp the distinction between sensation and perception. **Sensation** occurs when a sensory system detects a stimulus, as when the inner ear reverberates with sound or the pupil and retina of the eye intercept light. Thus, sensations begin when an outer organ (eye, ear, skin, tongue, or nose) meets anything in the external world that can be seen, heard, touched, tasted, or smelled.

Perception occurs when the brain notices and processes a sensation. Perception occurs in the cortex, usually as the result of a message from one of the sensing organs—a message that experience suggests might be worth interpreting. Some sensations are beyond comprehension at first: A newborn has no way to know that the letters on a page might have significance, that mother's face needs to be distinguished from father's face, or that the smell of roses and the smell of garlic might need to be differentiated. Perceptions require experience.

Cognition is one step beyond perception. It occurs when a person actually thinks about what he or she has perceived. (Indeed, cognition can occur without either sensation or perception; a person can imagine something.) Thus, there is a sequence, from sensation to perception to cognition. A baby's sense organs must function if this chain of comprehension is to begin. No wonder the parts of the cortex dedicated to the senses develop rapidly: This is what allows all the other developments to occur.

Listening

The sense of hearing is already quite acute at birth. Certain sounds seem to trigger reflexes, even without conscious perception, probably because the fetus heard those sounds during the last trimester in the womb. Sudden noises startle newborns, making them cry; rhythmic sounds, such as a lullaby or a heartbeat, soothe them and put them to sleep. Even in the first days of life, infants turn their heads toward the source of a sound, and they soon begin to adapt that response to connect sight and sound, with increasing accuracy (Morrongiello et al., 1998).

Young infants are particularly attentive to the human voice, a striking example of genetic programming for social interaction. One overview of hearing in childhood explains:

> Infants are exposed to a variety of different sounds in their native environments. Some of these are produced with great frequency by other active, non-human creatures, such as family pets, and others by electromechanical devices, such as alarm clocks. Yet, the sounds that infants choose to imitate, the ones which seem to attract their attention most, are the ones produced by other human beings.
>
> [Aslin et al., 1998, p. 158]

As time goes on, sensitive hearing combines with the developing brain to distinguish patterns of sounds and syllables. Infants become accustomed to the rules of language, such as which syllable is usually stressed (various English dialects have different rules), whether changing voice tone is significant (as it is in Chinese), whether certain sound combinations are often or never repeated, and so on. All this is based on very careful listening to human speech, even speech not directed to them and uttered in a language they do not yet understand (Jusczyk, 1997; Marcus, 2000).

Looking

Vision is the least mature sense at birth, partly because the fetus has nothing to see and thus the connection between the eyes and the visual cortex cannot form before birth. Newborns focus on objects between 4 and 30 inches (10 and 75 centimeters) away and merely stare at whatever they see (most often the faces of their caregivers) as if trying to figure out who or what that might be. Visual experience combines with maturation of the visual cortex to improve visual ability. By 6 weeks, infants look more intently, recognizing the human face and smiling—somewhat tentatively and fleetingly, but smiling nonetheless. Over time, scanning becomes more organized, more efficient, and centered on important aspects of a visual stimulus. Thus, 3-month-olds look more closely at the eyes and mouth, which contain the most information.

Binocular vision is the ability to focus the two eyes in a coordinated manner in order to see one image. Because using both eyes together is not possible until the baby is outside the womb, many newborns seem to use one eye or the other to focus or momentarily to use the two eyes independently, seeming temporarily wall-eyed or cross-eyed. At about 14 weeks, binocular vision appears quite suddenly (Held, 1995).

Tasting, Smelling, and Touching

As with vision and hearing, the senses of taste, smell, and touch function at birth and rapidly adapt to the social world. For example, one study found that a taste of sugar calmed 2-week-olds but had no effect on 4-week-olds—unless accompanied by a human face looking reassuringly at the baby (Zeifman et al., 1996).

JAMES KING-HOLMES / SCIENCE PHOTO LIBRARY / PHOTO RESEARCHERS, INC.

Before Leaving the Hospital Even as he sleeps, this newborn has his hearing tested via vibrations of the inner ear in response to various tones. The computer interprets the data and signals any need for more tests—as is the case for about 1 baby in 100. Normal newborns hear quite well.

binocular vision The ability to focus the two eyes in a coordinated manner in order to see one image.

Especially for Grandparents Suppose that you realize that you seldom talked to your children until they talked to you and that you never used a stroller or a walker but put them in cribs and playpens. Did you limit their brain growth and their sensory capacity?

What Next? This 8-month-old obviously finds the lemon very sour—evidence of the refined sense of taste among infants. Even stronger than the sour taste may be the passion for exploration: The baby may soon take another bite.

Another study found that sugar was a good anesthetic for newborns (Gradin et al., 2002). Older babies learn that sugar does not always soothe and may start crying when they go to the doctor's office, anticipating the pain of a shot rather than the comfort of sugar.

Similar adaptation occurs for the senses of smell and touch. As babies learn to recognize their caregiver's smell and handling, they relax only when cradled by their caregiver, even when their eyes are closed. The ability to be comforted by the human touch is one of the important "skills" tested in the Brazelton Neonatal Behavioral Assessment Scale (26 items of newborn behavior, as well as several reflexes, used to measure normal newborn functions). Although almost all newborns respond to cuddling, over time the response becomes more specific to the particulars of touch.

The entire package of early sensation seems organized for two goals: social interaction (to respond to familiar caregivers) and comfort (to be soothed amid the disturbances of infant life). Even the sense of pain and the sense of motion, not among the five basic senses because no body part is dedicated to them, are attuned in infants to aid both socialization and comfort. Early breast milk, for instance, seems to have a mild anesthetic quality, so the newborn literally feels happier at the mother's breast, connecting taste, touch, and smell with that experience, and sight as well (a breast-feeding woman's face is exactly within the limited focusing range of a newborn's eyes). Similarly, crying infants often appreciate the sense of motion as well as touch, so many a new parent finds that rocking, carrying, or even driving around the neighborhood with the baby in the car helps the baby sleep—thus again connecting infant comfort with social interaction. In sum, infants seem genetically programmed with senses that help them happily join the human family.

Motor Skills

We now come to the most visible and dramatic body changes of infancy, those that ultimately allow the child to "stand tall and walk proud." Thanks to their ongoing changes in size and proportion and their increasing brain maturation, infants markedly improve their motor skills, which are the abilities needed to move and control the body.

Reflexes

reflex A responsive movement that seems automatic, because it almost always occurs in reaction to a particular stimulus.

Newborns are quite able to move their bodies—curl their toes, grasp with the hands, screw up their faces—but these movements do not seem to be under voluntary control. There is a reason for this. Strictly speaking, the infant's first motor skills are not skills but reflexes. A **reflex** is an involuntary response to a particular stimulus. Newborns have dozens of them. Three sets of reflexes are critical for survival and become stronger as the baby matures:

Response for Grandparents (from page 131): Probably not. Experience-expectant brain development is programmed to occur for all infants, requiring only the stimulation that virtually all families provide—warmth, reassuring touch, overheard conversation, facial expressions, movement. Extras such as baby talk, music, exercise, mobiles, and massage may be beneficial, but they are not needed for normal development.

- *Reflexes that maintain oxygen supply.* The *breathing reflex* begins in normal newborns even before the umbilical cord, with its supply of oxygen, is cut. Additional reflexes that maintain oxygen are reflexive *hiccups* and *sneezes,* as well as *thrashing* (moving the arms and legs about) to escape something that covers the face.
- *Reflexes that maintain constant body temperature.* When infants are cold, they *cry, shiver,* and *tuck in their legs* close to their bodies, thereby helping to keep themselves warm. When they are hot, they try to *push away* blankets and then stay still.
- *Reflexes that manage feeding.* The *sucking reflex* causes newborns to suck anything that touches their lips—fingers, toes, blankets, and rattles, as well as natural and artificial nipples of various textures and shapes. The *rooting*

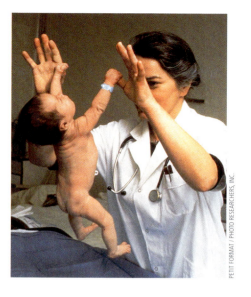

Never Underestimate the Power of a Reflex
For developmentalists, newborn reflexes are mechanisms for survival, indicators of brain maturation, and vestiges of evolutionary history. For parents, they are mostly delightful and sometimes amazing. Both of these view-points are demonstrated by three star performers: A 1-day-old girl stepping eagerly forward on legs too tiny to support her body; a newborn grasping so tightly that his legs dangle in space; and a newborn boy sucking peacefully on the doctor's finger.

reflex causes babies to turn their mouths toward anything that brushes against their cheeks—a reflexive search for a nipple—and start to suck. *Swallowing* is another important reflex that aids feeding, as are *crying* when the stomach is empty and *spitting up* when too much has been swallowed too quickly.

Gross Motor Skills

Gross motor skills, which involve large body movements, emerge directly from reflexes. Newborns placed on their stomachs reflexively move their arms and legs as if they were swimming and attempt to lift their heads to look around. As they gain muscle strength, they start to wiggle, attempting to move forward by pushing their arms, shoulders, and upper bodies against the surface they are lying on. Usually by the age of 5 months or so, they become able to use their arms, and then legs, to inch forward on their bellies.

Between 8 and 10 months after birth, most infants can lift their midsections and crawl (or *creep*) on "all fours," coordinating the movements of their hands and knees in a smooth, balanced manner (Adolph et al., 1998). Within the next couple of months, infants also learn to climb up onto couches and chairs—as well as up onto ledges and windowsills, and down into other dangerous places, including pools and lakes.

Walking shows a similar progression: from reflexive, hesitant, adult-supported stepping to a smooth, speedy, coordinated gait (Bertenthal & Clifton, 1998). On average, a child can walk while holding a hand at 9 months, can stand alone momentarily at 10 months, and can walk well, unassisted, at 12 months. Walking (and running, six months later) can lead to danger; each new skill requires caregivers to be ever more vigilant.

gross motor skills Physical abilities involving large body movements, such as walking and jumping.

Now a Toddler As this very young lady begins to walk, she demonstrates why such children are called toddlers: They move unsteadily from side to side as well as forward.

?Observational Quiz (see answer, page 134): What emotions and fine motor skills usually accompany early walking, as shown here?

Fine Motor Skills

fine motor skills Physical abilities involving small body movements, especially of the hands and fingers, such as drawing or picking up a coin.

Fine motor skills involve small body movements, usually of the fingers. Newborns have a strong reflexive grasp but seem to have no hand control. During their first two months, babies excitedly stare and wave their arms at an object dangling within reach; by 3 months of age they can usually touch it. But they cannot yet grab and hold on unless the object is placed in their hands, partly because their eye–hand coordination is too limited.

By 4 months, infants sometimes grab, but their timing is off: They close their hands too early or too late, and their grasp tends to be of short duration. Finally, by 6 months, with a concentrated stare and deliberation, most babies can reach for, grab at, and hold onto almost any object that is of the right size. They can hold a bottle, shake a rattle, and yank a sister's braids. Moreover, they no longer need to see their hands in order to grab; they can grasp a moving object that is illuminated in an otherwise dark room (Robin et al., 1996), although when the lights are on, they use vision to help them carefully reach for objects (McCarty & Ashmead, 1999).

Also by 6 months, most infants can transfer objects from one hand to the other. By 8 or 9 months, they can adjust their reach in an effort to catch an object. And by 11 or 12 months, they can coordinate both hands to enclose an object that is too big for one hand alone (de Róiste & Bushnell, 1996). They can also point at objects and figure out what someone else is pointing at, an accomplishment that other primates never attain. Before 1 year, those who will speak sign language are already forming appropriate gestures—although in a baby-talk version, without the grammatical nuances of adult sign language.

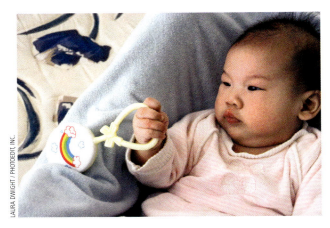

Mind in the Making Pull, grab, look, and listen. Using every sense at once is a baby's favorite way to experience life, generating brain connections as well as commotion.

Variations and Ethnic Differences

Although all healthy infants develop motor skills in the same sequence, the age at which these skills are acquired varies greatly. Table 5.1 shows age norms for mastery of each major motor skill. These percentiles are based on a large representative sample of infants from many ethnic groups in the United States.

!*Answer to Observational Quiz* (from page 133): Walking is thrilling to most toddlers, a source of pride and joy (see infant's face)—and perhaps disobedience, if the seated woman is unwilling to follow along and so asks her to stop. Finger skills take a leap forward, too: Notice the dirt in the baby's right hand and the extended finger pointing on the left.

TABLE 5.1 Age Norms (in Months) for Gross Motor Skills

Skill	When 50% of All Babies Master the Skill	When 90% of All Babies Master the Skill
Lifts head 90° when lying on stomach	2.2 months	3.2 months
Rolls over	2.8	4.7
Sits propped up (head steady)	2.9	4.2
Sits without support	5.5	7.8
Stands holding on	5.8	10.0
Walks holding on	9.2	12.7
Stands momentarily	9.8	13.0
Stands alone well	11.5	13.9
Walks well	12.1	14.3
Walks backward	14.3	21.5
Walks up steps (with help)	17.0	22.0
Kicks ball forward	20.0	24.0

Note: These norms came from a large cross section of infants in 1960 in the western half of the United States. Infants born more recently or babies from other nations may have different norms.

Source: The Denver Developmental Screening Test (Frankenburg et al., 1981).

?*Observational Quiz* (see answer, page 136): Is a 6-month-old developing normally if he or she can sit propped up but cannot stand up, even while holding on?

Throughout infancy, African-Americans are more advanced in motor skills than Americans of European ancestry (Rosser & Randolph, 1989). Internationally, the earliest walkers in the world seem to be in Uganda, where well-nourished and healthy babies walk at 10 months. Some of the latest walkers are in France, where taking one's first unaided steps at 15 months is not unusual.

What accounts for this variation? The power of genes is suggested by the fact that identical twins are far more likely to sit up or to walk on the same day than are fraternal twins. Striking individual differences, probably genetic, are apparent in the strategies, effort, and concentration that infants apply to the mastering of motor actions; these differences affect the timing of motor-skill achievements (Thelen et al., 1993).

Patterns of infant care are also influential. For example, in Uganda, infants are held next to an adult's body, usually in the upright position, virtually all day long; they are cradled and rocked as the adult works. Continually feeling the rhythm and changes of an adult's gait stimulates the infant to practice movement, unlike infants who spend much of each day in a crib or playpen.

Although some North American parents believe crawling helps later cognitive development by patterning the brain, and most delight in their baby's first steps, certain cultures discourage or even prevent infants from developing one or another motor skill. The people of Bali, Indonesia, never let their infants crawl, for babies are considered divine and crawling is for animals (Diener, 2000). By contrast, the Beng people of the Ivory Coast are proud when their babies start to crawl but do not let them walk until 1 year. Although the Beng do not recognize the connection, one reason for this prohibition may be birth control, because Beng mothers do not resume sexual relations until their baby begins walking (Gottlieb, 2000).

Although variation in the timing of the development of motor skills is normal, a pattern of slow development suggests that the infant needs careful examination. Slow infants may be mentally retarded, physically ill, seriously neglected—or perfectly fine, as I know from experience.

MIKE GREENLAR / THE IMAGE WORKS

Safe and Secure Like this Algonquin baby in Quebec, many American Indian infants still spend hours each day on a cradle board, to the distress of some non-Native adults, until they see that most of the babies are quite happy that way. The discovery in the 1950s that Native American children walked at about the same age as European-American children suggested that maturation, not practice, led to motor skills. Later research found that most Native American infants also received special exercise sessions each day, implying that practice plays a larger role than most psychologists once thought.

In Person

The Normal Berger Daughters

Cultural beliefs affect every parent and baby. When I had our first child, Bethany, I was a graduate student. I had already memorized such norms as "sitting by 6 months, walking by 12." During her first year, Bethany reached all the developmental milestones pretty much on time. However, at 14 months, she was still not walking.

I became a little anxious. I read about developmental norms with a sharper eye and learned three comforting facts:

▪ Variation in timing is normal.
▪ When late walking is a sign of a problem, it is accompanied by other signs of delayed development: Bethany was already talking—no problem there.

▪ Norms for motor-skill development vary from nation to nation. I took comfort in knowing that my grandmother came from France, where babies tend to walk late.

Two months later, Bethany was walking. I began marshaling evidence that motor skills follow a genetic timetable. My students provided additional testimony as to the power of genes. Those from Jamaica, Cuba, and Barbados expected babies to walk earlier than those from Russia, China, and Korea. Many of my African-American students proudly cited their sons, daughters, or younger siblings who walked at 10 months, or even 8 months, to the chagrin of their European-American classmates.

Believing now in a genetic timetable for walking, I was not surprised when our second child, Rachel, took her first steps at 15 months. Our third child, Elissa, also walked "late"—though on schedule for a Berger child with some French ancestry. I was not worried about her late motor-skill development, partly because Bethany had become the fastest runner in her kindergarten.

By the time our fourth child, Sarah, was born, I was an established professor and author, able to afford a full-time caregiver, Mrs. Todd, who was from Jamaica. Mrs. Todd thought Sarah was the brightest, most advanced baby she had ever seen, except, perhaps, her own daughter Gillian. I agreed, of course, but I cautioned Mrs. Todd that Berger children walk late.

"She'll be walking by a year," Mrs. Todd told me. "Maybe sooner. Gillian walked at 10 months."

"We'll see," I replied, confident in my genetic interpretation.

However, I underestimated Mrs. Todd. She bounced baby Sarah on her lap, day after day. By the time Sarah was 8 months old, Mrs. Todd was already spending a good deal of time bent over, holding Sarah by both hands and practicing walking—to Sarah's great delight. Lo and behold, with Mrs. Todd's urging and guidance, Sarah took her first step at exactly 1 year—late for a Todd baby, but amazingly early for a Berger.

As a scientist, I know that a single case proves nothing. It could be that the genetic influences on Sarah's walking were different from those on her sisters. She is only one-eighth French, after all, a fraction I had ignored when I was explaining Bethany's late walking to myself. But in my heart I think it much more likely that practice, fostered by a caregiver with a cultural tradition different from mine, made the difference. Now, as I teach, I always emphasize both nature and nurture in describing motor-skill development.

My Youngest at 8 Months When I look at this photo of Sarah, I see evidence of Mrs. Todd's devotion. Sarah's hair is washed and carefully brushed, her dress and blouse are cleaned and pressed, and the carpet and footstool are perfect equipment for standing practice. Sarah's legs—chubby and far apart—indicate that she is not about to walk early, but given all these signs of Mrs. Todd's attention to caregiving, it is not surprising, in hindsight, that my fourth daughter was my earliest walker.

HAZEL HANKIN

!*Answer to Observational Quiz* (from page 134): Yes—somewhat slow, but still quite normal. By age 6 months, the average baby can stand up while holding on, but 40 percent master this skill later, between 6 and 10 months.

To summarize the development of the senses and motor skills in infants: The five senses (seeing, hearing, tasting, touching, smelling) function quite well at birth, although hearing is far superior to vision, probably because of experience—that is, the fetus has much more to hear than to see. After birth, vision develops rapidly, leading to binocular vision at about the 14th week. Quite sensitive perception by all sense organs is evident by 1 year.

Motor skills begin with reflexes for survival but quickly expand to include various body movements that the infant masters. Infants lift their heads, then sit, then stand, then walk and run. All the sensory and motor skills follow a genetic and maturational timetable, but all are also powerfully influenced by experiences, which result from specific actions of the caregiver and are influenced by the culture.

Public Health Measures

Although we don't have precise worldwide statistics, we can say that more than 6 billion children were born between 1950 and 2000. Probably about 1 billion died before age 5. As high as this figure is, it would have been at least double without various advances in newborn care, childhood immunization, oral rehydration therapy (giving restorative liquids to children who are sick and have diarrhea;

this alone saves 3 million young children *per year*), nutrition, and other public health measures (Rutstein, 2000; Victora et al., 2000).

According to reliable current statistics, in the healthiest nations (such as Japan, the Netherlands, and France), fewer than 1 in 200 babies who survive the first days after birth will die before age 6. Even in the nations with the most childhood deaths (Malawi, Niger, and Ethiopia), fewer than 20 percent of newborn survivors die before age 6 (McDevitt, 1998). In 1900, by contrast, no matter where they were born, about 1 in 3 children died that young (Bogin, 1996).

Immunization

Measles, whooping cough, pneumonia, and other illnesses were once common childhood killers. Although these diseases can still be fatal, especially for malnourished children, they are no longer common. Most children are protected because of **immunization** (which primes the body's innate immune system to defend against a specific contagious disease), a scientific development said to have had "a greater impact on human mortality reduction and population growth than any other public health intervention besides clean water" (Baker, 2000).

If someone contracts a contagious disease, that person's immune system produces antibodies that protect against contracting the disease again in the future. In a healthy person, a vaccine—a small dose of inactive virus (often via a "shot" in the arm)—stimulates the production of antibodies to protect against the disease. Some details about various vaccines are given in Table 5.2. Stunning successes in immunization include the following:

- Smallpox, the most lethal disease for all children in past centuries, has been eradicated worldwide. Since 1971, routine vaccination against smallpox has not been recommended. Stockpiles of the virus and the vaccine, and immunization of emergency workers, are precautions only against bioterrorism, not against a normal outbreak.
- Polio, a crippling and sometimes fatal disease, is very rare. Widespread vaccination, begun in 1955, has led to elimination of polio in most nations (including the United States).
- Measles (rubella), which can cause fatal dehydration, is disappearing, thanks to a vaccine developed in 1963. In all of the Americas, only about 100 cases of measles occurred in 2002, down from 53,683 just five years earlier (*MMWR*, 2003).

immunization A process that stimulates the body's immune system to defend against attack by a particular contagious disease.

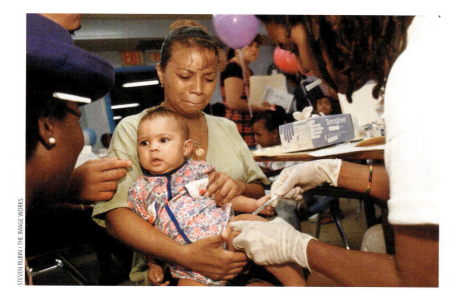

STEVEN RUBIN / THE IMAGE WORKS

Look Away! The benefits of immunization justify the baby's brief discomfort, but many parents still do not appreciate the importance of following the recommended schedule of immunizations.

TABLE 5.2 Details About Vaccinations

Vaccine	Year of Introduction	Peak Annual Disease Total	1999 Total	Consequences of Natural Disease	Percent of Children Vaccinated	Known Vaccine Side Effects
Chicken pox (varicella)	1995	4 million*	N/A	Encephalitis (2 in 10,000 cases), bacterial skin infections, shingles (300,000 per year)	59.4	Mild rash (1 in 20 doses)
DTaP					83.3	Prolonged crying, fever of 105 °F or higher
Diphtheria	1923	206,939	1	Death (5 to 10 in 100 cases), muscle paralysis, heart failure		
Tetanus	1927	1,560*	40	Death (30 in 100 cases), fractured bones, pneumonia		Peripheral neuritis, Guillain-Barré syndrome (temporary paralysis—rare)
Pertussis	1926 (whole cell) 1991 (acellular)	265,269	7,288	Death (2 in 1,000 cases), pneumonia (10 in 100 cases), seizures (1 to 2 in 100 cases)		Brain disease (0 to 10 in 1 million doses—whole-cell vaccine only)
H influenzae B (childhood)	1985	20,000*	71	Death (2 to 3 in 100 cases), meningitis, pneumonia, blood poisoning, inflammation of epiglottis, skin or bone infections	93.5	
Hepatitis B	1981	300,000*	7,694	Death from cirrhosis or liver cancer (4,000 to 5,500 per year)	88.1	
MMR					91.5	Fever of 103 °F or higher (5 to 15 in 100 doses)
Measles	1963	894,134	100	Encephalitis (1 in 1,000 cases), pneumonia (6 in 100 cases), death (1 to 2 in 1,000 cases), seizure (6 to 7 in 1,000 cases)		
Mumps	1967	152,209	387	Deafness (1 in 20,000 cases), inflamed testicles (20 to 50 in 100 postpubertal males)		
Rubella	1969	56,686	267	Blindness, deafness, heart defects and/or retardation in 85 percent of children born to mothers infected in early pregnancy		Temporary joint pain (25 in 100 adult doses in women)
Pneumoccal** (childhood)	2000	93,000*	New vaccine	Meningitis (800 cases per year), pneumonia (77,000 cases), blood poisoning (15,000 cases)	New vaccine	Fever over 100.3 °F (22 in 100 doses)
Polio (paralytic)	1955	21,269	0	Death (2 to 5 in 100 cases in children), respiratory failure, paralysis, postpolio syndrome	89.6	Vaccine-induced polio (oral vaccine only—1 in 2.4 million doses)

*Estimated.
**Lieu et al., 2000.
Source: Centers for Disease Control and Prevention, in *Consumer Reports,* August 2001, p. 19.

In protecting children against common childhood diseases, immunization protects them against serious complications that sometimes occur, among them deafness, blindness, sterility, meningitis, and even death. Less obviously, immunization of each child protects many other people. Infants too young for their first vaccinations may die if they catch a disease from an older child; a fetus whose mother contracts rubella may be born blind, deaf, and brain-damaged; adults suffer much more from mumps or measles than children do; and vulnerable adults (the elderly, those who are HIV-positive, or chemotherapy patients whose immune systems are impaired) can be killed by any number of "childhood" diseases. Fortunately, a 90 percent immunization rate is sufficient to halt any outbreak.

Many parents are concerned about the potential side effects of vaccinations. However, the risks of the diseases that once were common are far greater than the risks of unintended hazards from immunization. A review of all the published research concludes: "Immunizations are not without their problems and critics, but the data demonstrate consistently that the overall benefit of vaccinations ranks among the foremost achievements in modern public health" (Dershewitz, 2003). The biggest problem is that more than a million children in developing nations die each year because there are not yet approved, effective vaccines against AIDS, malaria, cholera, typhoid, and shigellosis (Russell, 2002). (Current childhood immunization schedules for the United States are given on Appendix page A-4.)

Sudden Infant Death Syndrome

Infant mortality worldwide has plummeted in recent years (see Figure 5.6). Several reasons have already been mentioned: advances in newborn care, better nutrition, better access to clean water, and widespread immunization. Another reason is fewer sudden deaths of seemingly healthy babies, known as **sudden infant death syndrome (SIDS)**.

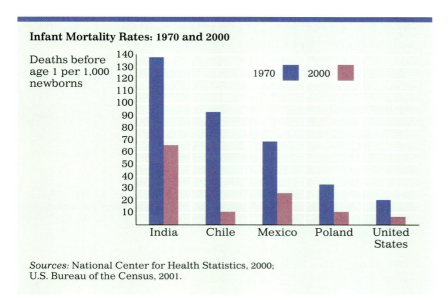

Infant Mortality Rates: 1970 and 2000

Deaths before age 1 per 1,000 newborns

1970   2000

India   Chile   Mexico   Poland   United States

Sources: National Center for Health Statistics, 2000;
U.S. Bureau of the Census, 2001.

FIGURE 5.6 More Babies Are Surviving Improvements in public health—better nutrition, cleaner water, more widespread immunization—over the past three decades have meant millions of survivors.

? *Critical Thinking Question* (see answer, page 140): The United States seems to be doing very well on reducing infant deaths. Can you suggest another way to present the U.S. data that would lead to another impression?

Especially for Nurses and Pediatricians A mother refuses to have her baby immunized because she says she wants to prevent side effects. She wants your signature to apply for a religious exemption. What should you do?

sudden infant death syndrome (SIDS) A situation in which a seemingly healthy infant, at least 2 months of age, dies unexpectedly in his or her sleep.

Response for Nurses and Pediatricians (from page 139): It is very difficult to convince people that their traditional child-rearing methods are wrong, although, given what you know, it is your obligation to try. In this case, you might listen respectfully and then cite cases you know of when a child got seriously ill or an adult died from a childhood disease. Ask the mother to ask her parents and grandparents whether they have known anyone who was seriously ill from polio, tuberculosis, or tetanus. If you cannot convince this mother, do not despair—vaccination of 95 percent of toddlers is usually sufficient to protect the 5 percent whose parents reject vaccination. If the mother is refusing vaccination for religious reasons, you could discuss the risks with her pastor and then sign the form, perhaps adding a warning letter. Keep the relationship open, as she may change her mind later.

In sudden infant death syndrome, infants who are at least 2 months old and appear healthy—already gaining weight, learning to shake a rattle, starting to roll over, and smiling at their caregivers—die unexpectedly in their sleep. In 1990 in the United States, 5,000 babies died of SIDS, about 1 infant in 800, with similar rates in Canada, England, Australia, and virtually every other European and South American nation. That rate has been cut in half, primarily because fewer infants are put to sleep on their stomachs and because fewer parents smoke cigarettes around the baby. The first of these preventive measures has arisen from a deeper respect for cultural differences.

Ethnicity and SIDS

Within ethnically diverse nations such as the United States, Canada, Great Britain, Australia, and New Zealand, babies of Asian descent are less likely (and babies of African descent are more likely) to succumb to SIDS than are babies of European descent. For example, Bangladeshi infants in England tend to be low in both birthweight and socioeconomic status, yet they have *lower* rates of SIDS than white British infants, who are more often of normal birthweight and middle-class. For decades, pediatricians thought the reasons for this difference were either genetic (racial) or related to ethnicity (such as the rate of teenage pregnancy).

Fortunately, new attention to culture led to a closer look at specific infant-care routines. For example, Bangladeshi infants, even when they sleep, are usually surrounded by many family members in a rich sensory environment, continually hearing noises and feeling the touch of their caregivers. Therefore, they do not sleep deeply for very long. By contrast, their white British age-mates tend to sleep in their own private spaces in an environment of enforced quiet, and these "long periods of lone sleep may contribute to the higher rates of SIDS among white infants" (Gantley et al., 1993).

Similarly, Chinese infants, born either in China or elsewhere, have a low rate of SIDS (Beal & Porter, 1991). Why? First, Chinese parents tend to their babies periodically as the infants sleep, caressing a cheek or repositioning a limb. Second, most Chinese infants are breast-fed, which makes them sleep less soundly (cow's milk is harder to digest, so it causes more tiredness and thus a deeper sleep). Therefore, Chinese infants rarely fall into a deep, nonbreathing sleep.

When pediatricians, nurses, and anthropologists compared the specifics of infant care among Asians and Europeans, they noticed one other factor: sleeping position. In all the ethnic groups with a low incidence of SIDS, babies were put to sleep on their backs; in all those with high rates, babies slept on their stomachs. The expressed reasons varied. For example, until recently, Benjamin Spock's (1976) book of advice for parents, which has sold more than 30 million copies, recommended stomach sleeping:

¡ Answer to Critical Thinking Question (from page 139): The same data could be presented in terms of rate of reduction in infant mortality. Chile's rate in 2000 was only 10 percent of what it had been in 1970—much better than the U.S. rate, which in 2000 was 35 percent of what it had been in 1970. At the same time, India's reduction is even less impressive: only about 50 percent. (Other data show that about 25 developed nations have lower infant mortality rates than the United States.)

> A majority of babies seem, from the beginning, to be a little more comfortable going to sleep on their stomachs. . . . There are two disadvantages to babies sleeping on their back. If they vomit, they're more likely to choke. Also, they tend to keep the head turned toward the same side, usually toward the center of the room. This may flatten that side of the head. It won't hurt the brain, and the head will gradually straighten out, but it may take a couple of years.
>
> *[Spock, 1976, p. 199]*

In Turkey, meanwhile, mothers were advised to swaddle their newborns

> for several months until the baby seems strong and healthy . . . [and] never put a swaddled baby to sleep on its stomach, for it would not be able to breathe. Instead, put the baby down to sleep on its back.
>
> *[Delaney, 2000, p. 131]*

Both these experts were mistaken: Babies sleeping on their stomachs can breathe, and babies sleeping on their backs do not choke. Neither "expert" realized the connection between SIDS and sleeping position. In fact, Spock wrote:

> Every once in a while, a baby between the ages of 3 weeks and 7 months is found dead in bed. There is never an adequate explanation, even when a postmortem examination is done. . . . Though crib death has been studied extensively, there is no satisfactory, scientific explanation.
>
> *[Spock, 1976, pp. 576–577]*

These are chilling, and sobering, words, since millions of babies died because conventional wisdom was mistaken. In this example, Asian advice was best, but every culture promotes some practices that are harmful and some that are beneficial.

Finally, researchers advised a group of non-Asian mothers to put their infants to sleep on their backs. The results were dramatic: Far fewer infants died. For example, one comparison study found that the risk of SIDS was only one-fourth as high when infants slept supine (on their backs) instead of prone (Ponsoby et al., 1993).

It is now accepted that "back to sleep" (as the public-awareness slogan puts it) is safest. Most caregivers heed this advice, although some still lay babies on their sides—better than on their stomachs, but not as safe as on their backs. In the United States, in the four years between 1992 and 1996, the stomach-sleeping rate decreased from 70 to 24 percent, and the SIDS rate dropped from 1.2 to 0.7 per 1,000, a "remarkable success" (Pollack & Frohna, 2001). Note from these data that changing sleeping position is not a magic cure: Reducing cigarette smoking before and after birth, preventing low birthweight, and encouraging breast-feeding are among the other protective practices.

Nutrition

Nutrition has been mentioned indirectly throughout this chapter. You have learned that pediatricians closely monitor early weight gain, that head-sparing protects the brain from temporary undernourishment, and that oral rehydration therapy prevents childhood diseases from being fatal. Now, we focus directly on how infants are fed.

Breast Is Best

For most newborns, good nutrition starts with mother's milk. First comes *colostrum,* a thick, high-calorie fluid secreted by the woman's breasts at the birth of her child. After three days, the breasts produce less-concentrated milk, which is the ideal infant food, partly because it helps prevent almost every infant illness and allergy (Isolauri et al., 1998). Breast milk is always sterile and at body temperature; it contains more iron, vitamins C and A, and many other nourishing substances than cow's or goat's milk; it provides antibodies against any disease that the mother has been immunized against. The specific fats and sugars in breast milk make it more digestible, and probably better for the infant brain, than any prepared formula (Talukder, 2000).

Formula may be better than breast milk only when the mother is HIV-positive, uses toxic drugs, or has some other condition that makes her milk unhealthy. The World Health Organization (WHO) recommends that infants be fed exclusively with breast milk for the first four to six months. At that point, other foods can be added—especially cereals and fruits, which are relatively easy to digest and provide the vitamins and minerals an older infant needs. Breast-feeding should continue until the infant is 2 years old or so, although it may be stopped sooner if the woman is in poor health and if formula prepared with clean water is available (Savage & Lhotska, 2000).

Especially for Police Officers and Social Workers If an infant died suddenly, what would you look for to distinguish SIDS from homicide?

Relaxation—and Sound Nutrition Breast-feeding is ideal, if not always as idyllic as it appears in this scene, set in Palm Beach Gardens, Florida.

AMY ETRA / PHOTOEDIT, INC.

In developed nations, where formula is convenient and inexpensive, many women choose breast-feeding because it is best for their infants. Infants can nonetheless be adequately nourished by formula, and many are. In fact, in many developed nations, only half of all babies are breast-fed even for a month; one reason is that bottle-feeding is more convenient for working parents (See Appendix page A-5 for variations within the United States.) In poor nations, however, breast milk can be crucial protection against severe malnutrition. In such countries, formula is not only expensive, but is often prepared with non-sterile water or bottles, thereby causing illness.

Malnutrition

protein-calorie malnutrition A condition in which a person does not consume sufficient food of any kind.

The most serious nourishment problem is **protein-calorie malnutrition,** which occurs when someone does not consume sufficient food of any kind. Roughly 8 percent of the world's children are severely malnourished because they do not get adequate calories and protein (Rutstein, 2000).

Severe malnutrition can be detected by comparing an infant's weight and height with the detailed norms presented on Appendix pages A-6 and A-7. As you remember, a small child may simply be genetically small, but weight loss during the first two years is an ominous sign. Birthweight should triple by age 1, and the 1-year-old's legs and cheeks should be chubby with baby fat. Chronic malnutrition is apparent in children who are far too short for their age—as are about a third of the world's children (de Onis et al., 2000) (see Figure 5.7). Chronically malnourished infants and children suffer in three ways:

1. Their brains may not develop normally. If malnutrition has continued long enough to affect the baby's height, it may also affect the brain (Grantham-McGregor & Ani, 2001).
2. Malnourished children have no body reserves to protect them if disease strikes. About half of all infant deaths occur because malnutrition makes a childhood disease much more lethal than it normally would be (Rice et al., 2000).

marasmus A disease of severe protein-calorie malnutrition during early infancy, in which growth stops, body tissues waste away, and the infant eventually dies.

3. Some diseases—notably, two serious conditions called marasmus and kwashiorkor—are the direct result of malnutrition. In **marasmus,** early

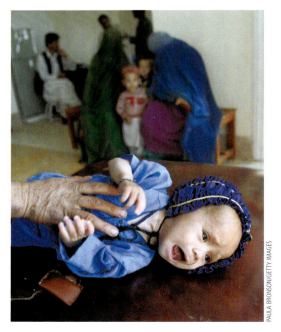

Two Starving Children Two thousand miles apart, these children from the Congo and Afghanistan share a common fate—severe malnutrition caused by civil war. The baby at right is more likely to die, but the 8-year-old above faces an uncertain future. His mother has been killed, his village has been burned, and he looks angry as well as hungry.

growth stops, body tissues waste away, and an infant eventually dies. Prevention of marasmus begins with good nutrition for the pregnant woman and continues with breast-feeding on demand and frequent check-ups to monitor weight gain. If malnutrition begins after age 1, it may take the form of **kwashiorkor,** a condition caused by a deficiency of protein in which the child's face, legs, and abdomen swell with water. In children with kwashiorkor, the essential organs claim whatever nutrients are available, so other parts of the body become degraded. This includes the children's hair, which usually becomes thin, brittle, and colorless—a telltale sign of chronic malnutrition.

Many public health practices save millions of infants each year. Widespread immunization, putting infants to sleep on their backs, and breast-feeding are all simple yet life-saving steps. Note, however, that these are called "public health" measures rather than parental practices because they go beyond the private decisions made by caregivers. Young lives are saved through national policies and cultural practices; they are the responsibility of everyone.

An underlying theme throughout this chapter is that healthy biological growth is the result not simply of genes and nutrition but also of a social environment that provides opportunities for growth, such as lullabies and mobiles for stimulating the infant's senses, encouragement for developing the first motor skills, and protection against disease. Each aspect of development is linked to every other aspect, and each developing person is linked to family, community, and world, as will become even more apparent in the next two chapters on infancy.

kwashiorkor A disease of chronic malnutrition during childhood, in which a deficiency of protein causes the child's face, legs, and abdomen to bloat, or swell with water, and makes the child more vulnerable to other diseases, such as measles, diarrhea, and influenza.

Response for Police Officers and Social Workers (from page 141): An autopsy, or at least a speedy examination, by a medical pathologist, is needed, because any suspicions of foul play need to be substantiated with evidence or firmly rejected so that the parents can grieve. However, your careful notes about the immediate circumstances—such as the position of the infant when he or she was discovered, the state of the mattress and nearby blankets, the warmth and humidity of the room, and the baby's health (any evidence of a cold)—can be informative. Further, while SIDS victims sometimes turn blue overall and thus might seem bruised, they rarely display signs of specific injury or neglect, such as a broken limb, a scarred face, an angry rash, or a skinny body. Especially if maltreatment is evident and the dead baby is not between 2 and 4 months of age, something other than SIDS may have occurred.

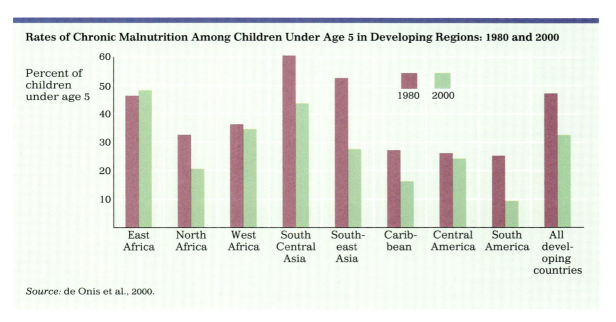

Rates of Chronic Malnutrition Among Children Under Age 5 in Developing Regions: 1980 and 2000

Source: de Onis et al., 2000.

FIGURE 5.7 Except in Africa Children in every region of the world are being fed better than they were 20 years ago, although children in all the poorer nations far exceed the 3 percent expected from normal height variation. Among chronically malnourished children, the body uses calories not for growth but for basic survival. Civil war and AIDS have reduced child nourishment in one area of the world, sub-Saharan Africa.

SUMMARY

Body Changes

1. In the first two years of life, infants grow taller, gain weight, and increase in head circumference—all indicative of development. The norm at birth is slightly more than 7 pounds, 20 inches (about 3⅓ kilograms, 51 centimeters).

2. Infants typically double their birthweight by 4 months, triple it by 1 year, and more than quadruple it by 2 years, when they weigh about 30 pounds (14 kilograms). Norms for height and head circumference show steady, though less dramatic, increases.

3. Percentiles indicate how a child compares to others the same age, which is useful over time to see whether a child's growth is proceeding as it should. Some normal children are consistently smaller or larger than others.

4. Sleep gradually decreases over the first two years (from almost 18 hours a day to 11), with less REM sleep, less night waking, and more slow-wave sleep over time. As with all areas of development, variations in sleep patterns are normal, caused by both nature and nurture.

Early Brain Development

5. The brain increases dramatically in size, from 25 percent to 75 percent of its adult weight in the first two years. Complexity increases as well, and transient exuberance of cell growth, dendrite development, and synapse connections occur.

6. Experience is vital for brain formation, particularly for linkages between neurons. In the first year, parts of the cortex dedicated to the senses and motor skills mature. If neurons are unused, they atrophy, and the brain regions are rededicated to other sensations. Normal stimulation allows experience-expectant maturation.

7. Most experience-dependent brain growth reflects the varied, culture-specific experiences of the infant. Therefore, one person's brain differs from another's. However, all normal infants are equally capable in the basic ways—emotional, linguistic, and sensual—that all humans share.

8. The precise harm to the networks and growth of the brain caused by early deprivation is not yet known. However, research on lower animals and neglected human infants suggests that the early years are critical for later brain functioning.

The Senses and Motor Skills

9. At birth, all the senses are able to respond to stimuli, with hearing the most mature and vision the least mature because of prenatal experience. Vision improves quickly; binocular vision emerges at about 14 weeks. Infants use all their senses to strengthen their early social interactions.

10. The only motor skills apparent at birth are reflexes, including the survival reflexes of sucking and breathing. Reflexes indicate brain maturation and provide a foundation for later skills.

11. Gross motor skills involve movement of the entire body, from rolling over to sitting up (at about 6 months), from standing to walking (at about 1 year), from climbing to running (before age 2). Variations in these norms depend on both genes and culture.

12. Fine motor skills are difficult for infants, but babies gradually develop the hand and finger control needed to grab, aim, and manipulate almost anything within reach.

Public Health Measures

13. About a billion infant deaths have been prevented in the past half-century because of improved medical care and public health measures. One major innovation is immunization, which has eradicated smallpox and virtually eliminated polio and measles.

14. Sudden infant death syndrome (SIDS) once killed about 5,000 infants per year in the United States, but this number has been reduced by half since 1990. The major reason is that researchers compared cultural habits regarding infant care and discovered that putting infants to sleep on their backs makes SIDS less likely.

15. Breast-feeding is best for infants, partly because breast milk reduces disease and promotes growth of every kind. The World Health Organization advocates breast-feeding exclusively for six months and some breast-feeding until age 2. However, many families—some by choice, but others by necessity—use formula in bottles instead of breast milk.

16. Severe malnutrition stunts growth and can even cause death, typically through marasmus or kwashiorkor.

KEY TERMS

head-sparing (p. 122)
norm (p. 122)
percentile (p. 122)
REM sleep (p. 123)
neuron (p. 125)
cortex (p. 125)
axon (p. 126)

dendrite (p. 126)
synapse (p. 126)
transient exuberance (p. 127)
experience-expectant (p. 128)
experience-dependent (p. 128)
sensation (p. 130)
perception (p. 130)

binocular vision (p. 131)
reflex (p. 132)
gross motor skills (p. 133)
fine motor skills (p. 134)
immunization (p. 137)
sudden infant death syndrome (SIDS) (p. 139)

protein-calorie malnutrition (p. 142)
marasmus (p. 142)
kwashiorkor (p. 143)

APPLICATIONS

1. Immunization regulations and practices vary, partly for social and political reasons. Ask at least two faculty or administrative staff what immunizations students at your college must have and why. Don't stop asking if you hear "it's a law"; ask why that law is in place.

2. Observe three infants whom you do not know in public places such as a store, playground, or bus. Look closely at body size and motor skills, especially how much control each baby has over legs and hands. From that, estimate the age in months, and then ask the caregiver how old the infant is. (Most caregivers know the infant's exact age and are happy to tell you.)

3. *This project can be done alone, but it is more informative if several students or an entire class pool the responses they receive.* Ask 3 to 10 adults whether they were bottle-fed or breast-fed and, if breast-fed, for how long. If anyone does not know, or if anyone expresses embarrassment about how long they were breast-fed, that itself is worth noting. Do you find any correlation between adult body size and mode of infant feeding?

Chapter Six

The First Two Years: Cognitive Development

adaptation The cognitive processes by which new information is taken in and responded to. Both assimilation and accommodation are kinds of adaptation.

This chapter is about infant *cognition,* a word that means "thinking" in a very broad sense, including intelligence, learning, memory, and language. Intelligence in babies? Yes, indeed.

New and constantly changing images, sounds, smells, and body sensations bombard a newborn's limited consciousness. All these sensations are fascinating but disconnected, and that is where intelligence is needed. Newborns strive to organize perceptions and to put them all together: sensations, sequences, objects, people, events, permanent and transient features, causes and effects. This is the beginning of cognition.

By the end of the first year—and often much sooner—babies organize their perceptions, have goals and know how to reach them, understand what to do with various objects and people, and begin to talk. By the end of the second year, they speak in sentences, think before acting, and pretend to be someone or something (a mother, an airplane) that they know they are not.

We begin with the framework provided by Jean Piaget for observing this amazing intellectual progression, from newborns who know nothing to toddlers who are able to make a wish and blow out their birthday candles. Indeed, cognitive development is even faster than Piaget realized, as this chapter describes.

Sensorimotor Intelligence

It is impossible to understand early intelligence without referring to Piaget, a Swiss scientist born in 1896, whose ideas "continue to be an important source of inspiration for contemporary infant research" (Rochat, 2001, p. 7). Piaget concluded that humans of every age and circumstance are active learners and that their understanding occurs in four specific, age-related periods.

At every period, people adapt their thinking to their experiences. **Adaptation** occurs in two complementary ways: by assimilation and by accommodation (as you learned in Chapter 2). *Assimilation* means taking new information into the mind by incorporating it into previously developed mental categories, or action patterns—in Piaget's terminology, "schemas." *Accommodation* means taking new information into the mind in such a way as to readjust, refine, or expand previous schemas.

These adaptive processes occur throughout life. Indeed, for Piaget, adaptation is the essence of intelligence. There are numerous definitions of *intelligence,* but for Piaget, an unintelligent person is rigid, stuck, unable or unwilling to adapt his or her cognitive processes.

TABLE 6.1 The Six Stages of Sensorimotor Intelligence

For an overview of the stages of sensorimotor thought, it helps to group the six stages into pairs. The first two stages involve the infant's responses to its own body (*primary circular reactions*):

Stage One (birth to 1 month)	*Reflexes*—sucking, grasping, staring, listening.
Stage Two (1–4 months)	*The first acquired adaptation* (assimilation and coordination of reflexes)—sucking a pacifier differently from a nipple; grabbing a bottle to suck it.

The next two stages involve the infant's responses to objects and people (*secondary circular reactions*):

Stage Three (4–8 months)	*An awareness of things*—responding to people and objects.
Stage Four (8–12 months)	*New adaptation and anticipation*—becoming more deliberate and purposeful in responding to people and objects.

The last two stages are the most creative, first with action and then with ideas (*tertiary circular reactions*):

Stage Five (12–18 months)	*New means through active experimentation*—experimentation and creativity in the actions of the "little scientist."
Stage Six (18–24 months)	*New means through mental combinations*—considering before doing provides the child with new ways of achieving a goal without resorting to trial-and-error experiments.

The first period of cognitive development begins at birth. Piaget called it **sensorimotor intelligence** because infants learn through their senses and motor skills. This two-year period of rapid change is subdivided into six stages (see Table 6.1).

sensorimotor intelligence Piaget's term for the intelligence of infants during the first period of cognitive development, when babies think by using their senses and motor skills.

Stages One and Two: Primary Circular Reactions

In every aspect of intelligence, there is an active interaction between the brain and the senses, as sensation, perception, and cognition cycle back and forth (circling round and round) in what Piaget calls a circular reaction. The first two stages of sensorimotor intelligence are examples of **primary circular reactions,** which are reactions that involve the infant's own body. Stage one, called the *stage of reflexes,* lasts only for a month. It includes reflexes (described on pages 132–133), such as sucking and grasping, and also senses, which are so responsive at birth that they seem like reflexes. Simple inborn actions and reactions are all that newborns can use for sensorimotor intelligence, but these simple reflexes soon begin to help infants think as well as react. Sensation becomes perception, which becomes cognition; reflexes become deliberate.

primary circular reactions The first of three types of feedback loops, this one involving the infant's own body. The infant senses motion, sucking, noise, and so on, and tries to understand them.

At this point, the baby enters stage two, *first acquired adaptations* (also called the stage of first habits). This change from reflexes to deliberate action occurs because repeated use

Time for Adaptation Sucking is a reflex at first, but adaptation begins as soon as an infant differentiates a pacifier from her mother's breast or realizes that her hand has grown too big to fit into her mouth. This infant's expression of concentration suggests that she is about to make that adaptation and suck just her thumb from now on.

of reflexive responses provides information about what the body does and how that action feels. This ushers in *adaptation* of reflexes and senses to the specifics of the context.

As an example, newborns suck anything that touches their lips; sucking is one of the strongest and most apparent reflexes. At about the age of 1 month, infants start to adapt sucking. Adaptation, remember, comes in two forms, assimilation and accommodation. Some items, such as the nipple of a bottle (for a breast-fed infant), merely require assimilation: The same old sucking reflex brings nourishment. Others require more accommodation: Pacifiers do not provide food, so they need to be sucked without the tongue-pushing and swallowing reflexes. This adaptation is a sign that infants have begun to organize their perceptions; they are "thinking."

In other words, adaptation in the early weeks relies primarily on reflexive assimilation—everything suckable is assimilated as worthy of being sucked until accommodation occurs. After several months, new responses are established: Suck some things to soothe hunger, suck others to bring comfort, and suck still others (fuzzy blankets, large balls) not at all. If the baby is hungry, only familiar nourishing nipples will do—all other objects are rejected. Similarly, when babies are not hungry but want the reassurance of rhythmic sucking, they will suck a pacifier. If no pacifier has been offered in the stage of reflexes, infants begin sucking their thumbs, fingers, or knuckles (a choice that depends on whatever the baby first assimilates).

Especially for Parents When should parents decide whether to feed their baby only by breast, only by bottle, or using some combination? When should they decide whether or not to offer a pacifier?

Stages Three and Four: Secondary Circular Reactions

In stages three and four, development switches from primary circular reactions, involving the baby's own body (stages one and two), to **secondary circular reactions,** involving the baby with an object or with another person.

During stage three (age 4 to 8 months), infants interact diligently with people and objects to produce exciting experiences, to *make interesting events last.* Realizing that rattles make noise, for example, they shake their arms and laugh whenever someone puts a rattle in their hand. Even the sight of something that normally delights an infant—a favorite toy, a favorite food, a smiling parent—can trigger an active attempt at interaction.

Stage four, which occurs from about 8 months to 1 year, is called *new adaptation and anticipation,* or "the means to the end," because babies now think about a goal and begin to understand how to reach it. This is a much more

secondary circular reactions The second of three types of feedback loops, this one involving people and objects. The infant is responsive to other people and to toys and other objects that can be manipulated.

ESBIN-ANDERSON / THE IMAGE WORKS

Talk to Me This 4-month-old is learning how to make interesting sights last: The best way to get Daddy to respond is to vocalize, stare, smile, and pat his cheek.

LAURA DWIGHT

Where's Rosa? At 18 months, Rosa knows all about object permanence and hiding. Her only problem here is distinguishing between "self" and "other."

object permanence The realization that objects (including people) still exist even when they cannot be seen, touched, or heard.

sophisticated kind of thinking than occurs in stage three, when babies merely understand how to continue an experience once it is under way.

In stage four, babies adapt in new, more deliberate ways. They anticipate events that will fulfill their needs and wishes, and they try to make such events occur. A 10-month-old girl who enjoys playing in the tub might see a bar of soap, crawl over to her mother with it as a signal to start her bath, and then remove all her clothes to make her wishes crystal clear—finally squealing with delight when she hears the bath water being turned on. Similarly, if a 10-month-old boy sees his mother putting on her coat to leave without him, he might begin tugging at it to stop her or he might drag over his own jacket to signal that he is coming along.

All these examples reveal *goal-directed behavior*—that is, purposeful action. The baby's obvious goal-directedness at this age stems from the development of an enhanced awareness of cause and effect as well as better memory for actions already completed (Willatts, 1999). That cognitive awareness coincides with the emergence of the motor skills infants need to achieve their goals.

Piaget thought that the concept of **object permanence** begins to emerge during stage four. Object permanence refers to the awareness that objects or people continue to exist when they are no longer in sight. The *goal-directed* search for toys that have fallen from the baby's crib, rolled under a couch, or disappeared under a blanket does not begin to emerge until about 8 months, just as Piaget indicated. Many current scientists question Piaget's conclusions, as the following discussion explains.

Thinking Like a Scientist

Object Permanence Revisited

Although it no doubt seems obvious to you that an object, an animal, and your mother continue to exist when you cannot see them, Piaget discovered that this is not at all obvious to very young infants. If a 5-month-old sees a ring of keys, for instance, and reaches for it, making it "disappear" behind your back, or even in your closed hand, produces only a fleeting expression of disappointment. No further crying or reaching transpires, because out of sight is literally out of mind. When an infant does demonstrate object permanence (in this case by trying to pry open your hand to get the keys), that is considered evidence that the infant finally understands that objects exist permanently, even when they are not visible. Object permanence has been the subject of intense developmental research. The design and implications of that research continue to be controversial (Baillargeon, 1999; Butler et al., 2002).

To understand that controversy, we begin with an appreciation of Piaget. Before Piaget, it was assumed that infants understood objects just as adults do. Piaget developed a simple experiment that has been replicated with thousands of infants in dozens of nations and that proved that assump-

tion wrong. An adult shows a very young infant an interesting toy and then covers it up with an easy-to-remove blanket or cloth. The results:

- Infants younger than 8 months do not search for hidden objects.
- At about 8 months, infants search if they can do so immediately but lose interest or forget if they have to wait a few seconds.
- By 2 years, the concept of object permanence is quite well understood. However, even 3-year-olds playing hide-and-seek may become fearful that someone has really disappeared, or they may hide themselves in obvious places (such as behind a coat rack with their feet still visible or as a big lump under a sheet on a bed).

As you learned in Chapter 1, scientists realize that observations, even when replicated many times, are always subject to reinterpretation. Does the fact that infants fail to search mean infants have no concept of object permanence? Could other immaturities, such as imperfect motor skills or fragile memory, mask an understanding that objects still exist when they are not seen? A series of clever experiments, tracing infant eye movements and brain activity when objects seem to disappear behind a screen reveal some inkling of object permanence at 4½ months (Spelke, 1993). Apparently, then, Piaget was mistaken.

Most developmentalists still respect Piaget's work on infancy, particularly two basic ideas: (1) Infants do not understand everything that adults assume they understand, and (2) young infants are smarter than many people realize. Piaget did not realize just how rapidly infant intelligence develops, but he demonstrated that babies are intelligent in many ways.

Peek-a-Boo The best hidden object is Mom under an easily moved blanket, as 7-month-old Elias has discovered. Peek-a-boo is fun from about 7 to 12 months. In another month, Elias will search for more conventionally hidden objects. In a year or two, his surprise and delight at finding Mom will fade.

Stages Five and Six: Tertiary Circular Reactions

In their second year, infants begin experimenting in thought and deed. Actually, they experiment first in deed and then in thought, because toddlers typically act first and think later. **Tertiary circular reactions** occur when, rather than simply responding to their own bodies (primary reactions) or to other people or objects (secondary reactions), 1-year-olds take independent and varied actions to actively discover the properties of people and objects.

Especially for Parents One parent wants to put all the breakable or dangerous objects away because their toddler is now able to move around independently. The other parent says that the baby should learn not to touch certain things. Who is right?

tertiary circular reactions The third of three types of feedback loops, this one involving active exploration and experimentation. The infant explores a range of new activities, varying responses as a way of learning about the world.

Response for Parents (from page 149): Within the first month, the stage of reflexes. If parents wait until the infant is 4 months or older, they may discover that they are too late. It is difficult to introduce a bottle to a 4-month-old who has been exclusively breast-fed, or a pacifier to a baby who has already adapted the sucking reflex to a thumb.

A Boy with a Purpose At 10 months, this little boy is goal-oriented, stuffing the bread into his mouth with his left hand. In a few months, he will also experiment, probably by dropping crumbs on the floor, dipping the bread in gravy, or conducting many other creative experiments.

CHAD EHLERS / INDEX STOCK IMAGERY / PICTUREQUEST

Can You Hear Me Now? How does this baby know about a cellular phone? Months of watching adults have led to this moment of deferred imitation.

little scientist Piaget's term for the stage-five toddler (age 12 to 18 months), who actively experiments without anticipating the results.

deferred imitation A sequence in which an infant first perceives something that someone else does and then performs the same action a few hours or even days later.

habituation The process of getting used to an object or event through repeated exposure to it.

fMRI Functional magnetic resonance imaging, a measuring technique in which the brain's magnetic properties indicate activation anywhere in the brain; fMRI helps locate neurological responses.

Stage five (age 12 to 18 months), called *new means through active experimentation,* builds directly on the accomplishments of stage four: Infants' goal-directed and purposeful activities become more expansive and creative. Toddlerhood is a time of active exploration and experimentation, a time when babies "get into everything," as though trying to discover all the possibilities their world has to offer.

Because of the experimentation that characterizes this stage, Piaget referred to the stage-five toddler as a **little scientist** who "experiments in order to see." Having discovered some action or set of actions that is possible with a given object, stage-five infants seem to ask, "What else can I do with this?" Their scientific method is one of trial and error, but their devotion to discovery sounds familiar to every adult researcher—and to every parent.

In the final stage of sensorimotor intelligence (age 18 to 24 months), toddlers begin to anticipate and solve simple problems by using *mental combinations,* a kind of intellectual experimentation that supersedes the active experimentation of stage five. They try out various actions mentally before actually performing them; and they think about the consequences their actions might bring, hesitating a moment before yanking the cat's tail or dropping a raw egg on the floor.

Being able to use mental combinations also makes it possible for the child to pretend. A toddler might sing to a doll before tucking it into bed. This is in marked contrast to the younger infant, who might treat a doll like any other toy, throwing or biting it.

Piaget describes another stage-six intellectual accomplishment, involving both thought and memory. **Deferred imitation** occurs when infants copy behavior they noticed hours or days earlier (Piaget, 1962).

Piaget and Modern Research

Infants sometimes reach the various stages of sensorimotor intelligence before Piaget predicted they would. For example, pretending and deferred imitation are evident before 18 months. One reason Piaget underestimated infant cognition is that he was limited by direct observation of his own three infants, lacking more recent research tools, particularly habituation studies and fMRI.

Habituation (from the word *habit*) refers to getting used to an experience after repeated exposure to it, as when infants hear the same sound or see the same picture again and again until they seem to lose interest. In a habituation study, babies become habituated to one stimulus and then are presented with another, slightly different sound or sight or other sensation. Any of several indicators—a longer or more focused gaze; a faster or slower heart rate; more or less muscle tension around the lips; a change in the rate, rhythm, or pressure of suction on a nipple—might indicate that the baby detects a difference between the two stimuli.

By using habituation followed by a new stimulus, scientists have learned that even 1-month-olds can detect the difference between a *pah* sound and a *bah* sound, between a circle with two dots inside it and a circle without any dots, and much more. These are secondary circular reactions that Piaget did not expect until about 4 months.

More recent techniques involve measurement of brain activity (see Table 6.2). For example, **fMRI** (functional magnetic resonance imaging) and other techniques indicate that preverbal infants have memories, goals, and even mental combinations in advance of Piaget's stages.

TABLE 6.2 Some Techniques Used by Neuroscientists to Understand Brain Function

Technique	Use
EEG (electroencephalogram)	Measures electrical activity in the top layers of the brain, where the cortex is.
ERP (event-related potential)	Notes the amplitude and frequency of electrical activity (as shown by brain waves) in specific parts of the cortex in reaction to various stimuli.
fMRI (functional magnetic resonance imaging)	Measures changes in activity anywhere in the brain (not just the outer layers).
PET (positron emission tomography)	Also (like fMRI) reveals activity in various parts of the brain. Locations can be pinpointed with precision, but PET requires injection of radioactive dye to light up the active parts of the brain.

Because of practical and ethical concerns, none of these techniques have been used with large, representative samples of normal infants.

Developmentalists worry that, as the first three years of life, once thought to be intellectually empty, are shown to be prime time for cognitive development, the public might hastily conclude that these years are the *only* ones that provide a foundation for brain growth and learning. Not so. As a report from 20 leading developmentalists summarizes:

> Early experiences clearly affect the development of the brain. Yet the recent focus on "zero to three" as a critical or particularly sensitive period is highly problematic, not because this isn't an important period for the developing brain, but simply because the disproportional attention to the period from birth to 3 years begins too late and ends too soon.
>
> *[National Research Council and Institute of Medicine, 2000]*

It is possible that all the recent research, especially the sophisticated technology and analyses that are now available, distracts observers from noticing the entire sweep of the developmental process. Thus, in collecting detailed data about the moment-by-moment, neuron-by-neuron processes, we may lose sight of the brain building and mental reorganization that characterize human intelligence from prenatal days through adulthood. Piaget was limited by his simple methodology, which allowed him access only to the general trends of infant cognition; yet his overall observations remain relevant.

To summarize Piaget's contributions, we emphasize again his discovery that infants are active learners. They use their senses and motor skills to gain an understanding of their world, using reflexes for the first month but then using adaptation, including assimilation and accommodation, in a total of six sensorimotor stages. Object permanence, goal pursuit, and deferred imitation all develop during infancy. Crucial in all six stages of sensorimotor intelligence is the idea of circular reactions: Babies use basic sensory experiences to build cognitive structures. In the first two stages, infants use their bodies (primary circular reactions); in the next two stages, they use their immediate experiences (secondary circular reactions); and in the final two stages, they use creative experimentation with anything at hand (tertiary circular reactions). Although modern research finds that Piaget underestimated infant cognition, his basic concepts still inspire researchers.

Response for Parents (from page 151): It is easier and safer to babyproof the house, because toddlers, being little scientists, want to explore. However, it is also important for both parents to encourage and guide the baby, so it is preferable to leave out a few untouchable items if that will help prevent a divorce.

Information Processing

information-processing theory A perspective that compares human thinking processes, by analogy, to computer analysis of data, including sensory input, connections, stored memories, and output.

Piaget was a "grand" theorist of cognition throughout the life span, with an appreciation of shifts in the nature of cognition that occur at about years 2, 6, and 12. His sweeping overview contrasts with **information-processing theory**, a perspective modeled on computer functioning.

Information-processing theorists suggest that a step-by-step description of the mechanisms of human thought aids our understanding of the development of cognition at every age. Human information processing begins with input in the form of sensory messages picked up by the five senses; proceeds to brain reactions, connections, and stored memories; and concludes with some form of output. For infants, the output might consist of moving a hand to uncover a hidden toy (object permanence), or saying a word (e.g., *mama*) to signify recognition of a person, or staring to demonstrate that a stimulus is noticed.

The information-processing perspective helps tie together the various aspects of infant cognition that are the topic of extensive study and exciting discoveries. We review two of these now: affordances and memory. Affordances concern perception, or, by analogy, input. Memory concerns brain organization and output—in other words, storage and retrieval.

Look at Me These 1-year-olds are just learning about the affordances of objects. Thus, a rattle may be pushed against a friend's face to gain the friend's attention. This little scientist has not yet discovered that doing so may not be a good idea.

? *Observational Quiz* (see answer, page 156): Are these two toddlers boys or girls?

Affordances

Perception, remember, is the mental processing of information that arrives at the brain from the sensory organs. It is the first step of information processing—the input to the brain. One of the puzzles of life is that two people can have discrepant perceptions of the same situation, not only interpreting it differently but actually observing it differently.

A lifetime of thought and research led Eleanor and James Gibson to conclude that perception is far from automatic (E. Gibson, 1969; J. Gibson, 1979). Perception—for infants, as for the rest of us—is a cognitive accomplishment that requires selection from a vast array of possibilities: "Perceiving is active, a process of obtaining information about the world. . . . We don't simply see, we look" (E. Gibson, 1988, p. 5).

affordance An opportunity for perception and interaction that is offered by people, places, and objects in the environment.

The Gibsons contend that the environment (people, places, and objects) *affords*, or offers, many opportunities for perception and interaction (E. Gibson, 1997). Each of these opportunities is called an **affordance.** Which particular affordances are perceived and acted on depends on four factors: sensory awareness, immediate motivation, current development, and past experience.

As a simple example, a lemon may be perceived as something that affords smelling, tasting, touching, viewing, throwing, squeezing, and biting (among other things). Each of these affordances is further perceived as offering pleasure, pain, or some other emotion. Which of the many affordances a particular person perceives and acts on depends on the four factors just mentioned. Consequently, a lemon might elicit quite different perceptions from an artist about to paint a still life, a thirsty adult in need of a refreshing drink, and a teething baby wanting something to gnaw on.

Clearly, infants and adults perceive quite different affordances. A toddler's idea of what affords running might be any unobstructed surface—a meadow, a long hallway in an apartment building, or an empty road. To an adult eye, the degree to which these places afford running may be restricted by such factors as a bull grazing in the meadow, neighbors in the hallway, or traffic on the road. Moreover, young children love to run and therefore notice affordances for running; some adults may be less inclined to move and therefore not perceive whether running is afforded or not.

Sudden Drops

The affordances that an infant perceives evolve as the infant gains experience. An example is provided by the **visual cliff,** an apparatus designed to provide the illusion of a sudden dropoff between one horizontal surface and another (see the accompanying photograph).

Researchers once thought that perception of a visual cliff was purely a matter of visual maturity: Young babies, because of their inadequate depth perception, could not see the sudden drop, but by about 8 months, maturation of the visual cortex allowed such awareness. "Proof" came when 6-month-olds could be enticed to wiggle forward over the supposed edge of the visual cliff, in contrast to 10-month-olds, who fearfully refused to budge, even when their mothers called them (E. Gibson & Walk, 1960).

Later research found, however, that this interpretation of the data was wrong. Even 3-month-olds can notice the difference between a solid surface and an apparent cliff, as evidenced by their slowed heart rate and wide-open eyes when they are placed over the "edge." But they do not realize that one affordance of the cliff is falling. That realization comes after they start crawling. Their memory of a caregiver's fear (or perhaps their own tumble off a bed) teaches them that the edge of a precipice (as in stairs that go down) affords danger (Campos et al., 1978).

Blocks Are for . . . To adults, blocks afford learning about letters and numbers. To young children, blocks are for stacking. Can you see an affordance that no adult could discover? Blocks are also for sitting.

visual cliff An experimental apparatus designed to provide the illusion of a sudden dropoff between one horizontal surface and another.

Depth Perception Like thousands of crawling babies before him, this infant refuses to crawl to his mother because the visual-cliff apparatus makes him think there is a dropoff between himself and her.

? *Observational Quiz* (see answer, page 157): What does he see when he looks down?

dynamic perception Perception that is primed to focus on movement and change.

ULLI SEER / IMAGE BANK

One Constant, Multisensual Perception
From the angle of her arm and the bend of her hand, it appears that this infant recognizes the constancy of the furry mass, perceiving it as a single entity whether it is standing still, rolling in the sand, or walking along the beach.

❗*Answer to Observational Quiz* (from page 154): Surprise! Both babies are girls, named Anne and Sarah. Illustrating the power of stereotyping, many observers would have guessed that they are boys because their blue garments afford masculinity.

Especially for Parents This research on early affordances suggests a crucial lesson about how many babysitters an infant should have. What is it?

Movement and People

Despite all the variations from one infant to another in the particular affordances they perceive, two general principles of perception are shared by all infants. One is **dynamic perception**, which is perception primed to focus on movement and change. Infants love motion. As soon as they can, they move their own bodies—grabbing, scooting, crawling, walking. To their delight, these movements change what the world affords them. Other creatures that move, especially their own caregivers, are among the first and best sources of pleasure. That is one reason it's almost impossible to teach a baby not to chase and grab a dog, a cat, or even a cockroach.

The second universal principle of infant perception is fascination with people. This characteristic may have evolved over the centuries, because humans of all ages survived by learning to attend to, and rely on, one another. Even in the first days of life, babies listen to voices, stare at faces, and are soothed by human touch. Soon they prefer the particular voice, face, and touch of their primary caregiver and connect sound with sight, and so on (Aslin et al., 1998; Kellman & Banks, 1998).

It is remarkable that, very early in life, humans are most interested in the emotional affordances of their caregivers, using their limited perceptual abilities to focus on the social world. One example is an infant's ability to connect facial expressions with vocal tone long before being able to understand language. This ability has led to a hypothesis:

> Given that infants are frequently exposed to their caregivers' emotional displays and further presented with opportunities to view the affordances (Gibson, 1959, 1979) of those emotional expressions, we propose that the expressions of familiar persons are meaningful to infants very early in life.
>
> [Kahana-Kalman & Walker-Andrews, 2001, p. 366]

As with the earlier research, these researchers presented infants with two moving images on a video screen. Both images were of a woman visibly expressing joy or sorrow, accompanied by an audiotape of that woman's happy or sad talk. The infants were only 3½ months old. Not surprisingly, given their immaturity, when the infants did not know the woman, they failed to match the verbal emotion with the face, a task that 7-month-olds can master. That is, when the face was that of a stranger, 3½-month-olds did not tend to look more at the face whose expression fit the talk they heard.

However, when the infants saw two images (happy and sad) of their own mothers, with an audio that was either their mother's happy words or her sad ones, they correctly matched visual and vocal emotions. They looked longest of all at their happy mothers talking in a happy way, but they also looked at their sad mothers when the audio they heard was their mother's sad voice—an amazing display of the very young infant's ability to connect the tone of speech with facial expressions.

These experimenters noticed something else. When infants saw and heard their happy mothers, as opposed to the happy strangers, they smiled twice as quickly, seven times as long, and much more brightly (with cheeks raised as well as mouth upturned) (Kahana-Kalman & Walker-Andrews, 2001). Obviously, experience had taught these babies that a smiling mother affords joy, especially if you smile back. The affordances of a smiling stranger are more difficult to judge.

Memory

A certain amount of experience and maturation is required in order to process and remember experiences. Infants have great difficulty storing new memories in their first year, and older children are often unable to describe events that occurred when they were younger. But on the basis of a series of experiments, developmentalists now agree that very young infants *can* remember IF:

- Experimental conditions are similar to real life.
- Motivation is high.
- Special measures aid memory retrieval.

The most dramatic evidence for infant memory comes from a series of innovative experiments in which 3-month-old infants were taught to make a mobile move by kicking their legs (Rovee-Collier, 1987, 1990). The infants lay on their backs, in their own cribs, connected to a brightly colored mobile by means of a ribbon tied to one foot.

Virtually all the infants began making some occasional kicks (as well as random arm movements and noises) and realized after a while that kicking made the mobile move. They then kicked more vigorously and frequently, sometimes laughing at their accomplishment. So far, this is no surprise—self-activated movement is highly reinforcing to infants.

When some infants had the mobile-and-ribbon apparatus reinstalled in their cribs *one week later,* most started to kick immediately— indicating that they did remember. But when other infants were retested *two weeks later,* they began with only random kicks. Apparently they had forgotten what they had learned—evidence for fragile memory processing early in life.

MICHAEL NEWMAN / PHOTOEDIT

He Remembers! In this demonstration of Rovee-Collier's experiment, a young infant immediately remembers how to make the familiar mobile move. (Unfamiliar mobiles do not provoke the same reaction.) He kicks his right leg and flails both arms, just as he learned to do several weeks ago.

Reminders and Repetition

However, the lead researcher, Carolyn Rovee-Collier, developed another experiment that demonstrated that 3-month-old infants *could* remember after two weeks *if* they had a brief reminder session prior to the retesting (Rovee-Collier & Hayne, 1987). A **reminder session** is any perceptual experience that might make a person recollect an idea or thing. In this particular reminder session, two weeks after the initial training, the infants watched the mobile move but were *not* tied to the ribbon and were positioned so that they could *not* kick. The next day, when they were again connected to the mobile and positioned so that they *could* move their legs, they kicked as they had learned to do two weeks earlier. In effect, their faded memory had been reactivated by watching the mobile move on the previous day.

Overall, some early memories can be "highly enduring, and become even more so after repeated encounters with reminders" (Rovee-Collier & Gerhardstein, 1997). Repetition and reminders are key: Infants under 6 months do not remember meeting their grandparents when they see them again a year later, nor do they remember a sudden trauma, such as emergency surgery. Early in life, under the best conditions, long-term storage and retrieval of memories appear to be fragile and uncertain. Memory is facilitated by repetition, reminders, and active involvement of the infant, although even then memories fade much more quickly than in childhood.

reminder session A perceptual experience that helps a person recollect an idea or experience, without testing whether the person remembers it at the moment.

A Little Older, a Little More Memory

After about six months, infants become capable of retaining information for longer periods of time with less training or reminding. Toward the end of the first year, even deferred imitation is apparent. For example, suppose a 9-month-old watches someone playing with a toy the baby has never seen before. The next day, if given the toy, the 9-month-old is likely to play with it in the same way as the person he or she observed had played. (Younger infants do not usually do this.) Over the next few months, deferred imitation becomes more elaborate.

!Answer to Observational Quiz (from page 155): He sees a visual cliff. It has the same attractive pattern as the surface on which he rests, but he perceives a 1-meter (3-foot) drop (that's why he hesitates).

Memory Aid Personal motivation and action are crucial to early memory, and that is why Noel has no trouble remembering which shape covers the photograph of herself as a baby.

Response for Parents (from page 156): It is important that infants have time for repeated exposure to each caregiver, because infants adjust their behavior to maximize whatever each particular caregiver affords in the way of play, emotions, and vocalization. Parents should find one steady babysitter rather than several.

Infants are particularly likely to imitate other children (Heimann & Meltzoff, 1996; Oliver Ryalls et al., 2000).

By the middle of the second year, toddlers are capable of remembering and reenacting more complex sequences. In one experiment, 16- and 20-month-olds first watched an experimenter perform various activities, such as putting a doll to bed, making a party hat, and cleaning a table (Bauer & Dow, 1994). For each activity, the experimenter used particular props and gave a brief "instruction" for performing each step. For instance, to clean the table, the experimenter wet it with water from a white spray bottle, saying "Put on the water"; wiped it with a paper towel, saying "Wipe it"; and placed the towel in a wooden trash basket, saying "Toss it." A week later, most toddlers remembered how to carry out the sequence just from hearing "Put on the water. Wipe it. Toss it." They did this not only when given the same props the experimenter had used but also when given quite different props (for instance, a clear spray bottle, a sponge, and a plastic lidded garbage can).

Memory is not one thing, "not a unitary or monolithic entity" (Schacter & Badgaiyan, 2001, p. 1). People are inaccurate when they say, "I have a good memory" or "My memory is failing," because fMRI research finds many distinct brain regions devoted to particular aspects of memory. Thus, humans have a memory for words, for images, for actions, for smells, for experiences, for "memorized" facts, for "forgotten" faces, and so on. Each type of memory is encoded by neurons in a particular part of the cortex. At least for adult verbal memories, separate networks become dedicated to names of vegetables, of animals, of tools, of people, and so on (Gabrieli, 1998; Rolls, 2000). (For the basics about the brain's structure and function, see Chapter 5.)

Because there are many types of memory, it is not surprising that infants remember some things better than others: That's the way human brains are constructed. Thus, early memories are *both* fragile and enduring, depending on which type of memory is described. Infants probably store within their brains many emotions and sensations that they cannot readily retrieve, whereas memories of motion (dynamic perception) are remembered once the context cues that particular action (as when the infants remembered how to kick to make the mobile move). Until language is established, motor skills are remembered in a nonverbal part of the brain. This explains why most adults remember how to crawl but few can describe it verbally. (First one side and then the other? Knees and elbows? No and no.)

Language: What Develops in Two Years?

Language, with thousands of basic vocabulary words, hundreds of idiomatic phrases, dozens of grammar rules, and many exceptions to those rules, is the most impressive intellectual achievement of the young child. In fact, language is the most impressive accomplishment of all humans: It differentiates our species from all others and is probably the reason human brains are more complex than those of any other animal.

For instance, humans and gorillas are close relatives, with about 99 percent of their genes in common. Gorillas are bigger than people, but an adult gorilla's brain is only one-fourth as big as a human's, which also has far more dendrites, synapses, and so on (Thompson, 2000). This means that a 2-year-old human has three times as much brainpower as a full-grown gorilla. The size of the cortex is the key difference. Other animals communicate, but none have anything approaching the neurons and networks that support one or more of the 6,000 human languages.

The Universal Sequence of Language Development

Children around the world follow the same sequence of early language development (see Table 6.3). Timing and depth of linguistic ability vary; the most advanced 10 percent of 2-year-olds know more than 550 words, and the least advanced 10 percent speak fewer than 100 words—a fivefold difference (Merriman, 1998). (Some explanations are discussed at the end of this chapter.) But the sequence of language learning is the same for almost all, with every human surpassing even the smartest ape many times over. We now describe this sequence.

First Noises and Gestures

Infants are equipped to learn language even before birth, partly due to brain readiness and partly due to their auditory experiences during the final prenatal months (Aslin et al., 1998). Newborns prefer to hear speech over other sounds; they prefer to listen to **baby talk**—high-pitched, simplified, and repetitive adult speech that is quite distinct from normal speech. As scientists use the term, *baby talk* is not the way babies talk but the way adults talk to babies (and thus it is sometimes called *child-directed speech*). The sound of a human voice—whether it comes from mother or father, another child, a stranger, or even someone speaking a foreign language—is always fascinating to babies.

Newborns do much more than listen. They are noisy creatures—crying, cooing, and making a variety of other sounds even in the first weeks of life. These noises gradually become more varied until, by the age of 4 months, most babies have verbal repertoires that include squeals, growls, gurgles, grunts, croons, and yells, as well as some speechlike sounds (Hsu et al., 2000).

Too Young for Language? No. The early stages of language are communication through noise, gestures, and facial expressions, very evident here between this !Kung grandmother and granddaughter.

baby talk The high-pitched, simplified, and repetitive way adults speak to infants; also called *child-directed speech.*

TABLE 6.3 The Development of Spoken Language: The First Two Years

Age*	Means of Communication
Newborn	Reflexive communication—cries, movements, facial expressions.
2 months	A range of meaningful noises—cooing, fussing, crying, laughing.
3–6 months	New sounds, including squeals, growls, croons, trills, vowel sounds.
6–10 months	Babbling, including both consonant and vowel sounds repeated in syllables.
10–12 months	Comprehension of simple words; simple intonations; specific vocalizations that have meaning to those who know the infant well. Deaf babies express their first signs; hearing babies use specific gestures (e.g., pointing) to communicate.
12 months	First spoken words that are recognizably part of the native language.
13–18 months	Slow growth of vocabulary, up to about 50 words.
18 months	Vocabulary spurt—three or more words learned per day.
21 months	First two-word sentence.
24 months	Multiword sentences. Half the infant's utterances are two or more words long.

*The ages of accomplishment in this table reflect norms. Many healthy and intelligent children attain these steps in language development earlier or later than indicated here.
Sources: Bloom, 1993, 1998; Lenneberg, 1967.

babbling The extended repetition of certain sylla-bles, such as *ba-ba-ba*, that begins at about 6 or 7 months of age.

Baby Talk Infants' verbal understanding advances well ahead of their abilities at verbal production. *Fishee* is probably one of dozens of words that this child readily recognizes even though he has yet to say them himself.

naming explosion A sudden increase in an infant's vocabulary, especially in the number of nouns, that begins at about 18 months of age.

Especially for Educators An infant day-care center has a new child whose parents speak a language other than the one the teachers speak. Should the teachers learn basic words in the new language, or should they expect the baby to learn the majority language?

Babbling

By 6 or 7 months, babies begin to repeat certain syllables (*ma-ma-ma, da-da-da, ba-ba-ba*), a phenomenon referred to as **babbling** because of the way it sounds. Babbling is experience-expectant learning; all babies do it if given half a chance. Moreover, the sounds they make are similar no matter what language their parents speak.

Over the next few months, babbling incorporates more sounds from the native language, perhaps as infants imitate the sounds they hear (Boysson-Bardies et al., 1989; Masataka, 1992). Many cultures assign important meanings to the sounds that babies babble, with *ma-ma-ma, da-da-da,* and *pa-pa-pa* usually taken to apply to significant people in the infant's life (Bloom, 1998). (See Appendix A, page A-4.)

Deaf babies make babbling sounds later and less frequently than hearing infants do. However, many deaf infants are advanced in their use of gestures and begin babbling manually at about the same time hearing infants begin babbling orally (Petitto & Marentette, 1991). Analysis of videotapes of deaf children whose parents communicate via sign language reveals that 10-month-old deaf infants use about a dozen distinct hand gestures—which resemble the signs used by their parents—in a rhythmic, repetitive manner analogous to oral babbling.

First Words

Finally, at about 1 year of age, the average baby speaks (or signs) a few words. Usually, caregivers understand the first word before strangers do, which makes it hard for researchers to pinpoint exactly what a 12-month-old can say (Bloom, 1998). For example, at 13 months, Kyle knew standard words such as *mama,* but he also knew *da, ba, tam, opma,* and *daes,* which his parents knew to be, respectively, "downstairs," "bottle," "tummy," "oatmeal," and "starfish" (yes, that's what *daes* meant) (Lewis et al., 1999).

The Language Explosion and Early Grammar

Once vocabulary reaches about 50 words, it begins to build rapidly, at a rate of 50 to 100 words per month (Fenson et al., 1994). This language spurt is some-times called the **naming explosion,** because the first words include a dispropor-tionate number of nouns, or naming words (Gentner & Boroditsky, 2001). Almost universally, labels for each significant caregiver (often *dada, mama, nana, papa, baba, tata*), sibling, and sometimes pet appear between 12 and 18 months. Other frequently uttered words refer to the child's favorite foods and, if toilet training is an issue, elimination (*pee-pee, wee-wee, poo-poo, doo-doo*).

No doubt you have noticed that all these words have a similar structure: two identical syllables, each a consonant followed by a vowel. Variations follow that pattern—not just *baba* but also *bobo, bebe, bibi*—or are slightly more compli-cated, not just *mama* but also *ma-me, ama,* and so on.

Short, two-syllable words with *m, n, t, d, b,* or *p* are easiest for the child to say because they follow directly from babbling, and, as mentioned earlier, all cul-tures use those spontaneous babbles to form words. This facilitates early com-munication for both the child and the listener. Facilitation of communication is likely important to young children's rapid acquisition of words (see Figure 6.1).

Although all new talkers say many names at first, the ratio of nouns to verbs shows cultural influences. For example, by 18 months, English-speaking infants say more nouns but fewer verbs than Chinese or Korean infants do. One expla-nation is directly linguistic: Chinese and Korean are "verb-friendly" languages, in that adults use more verbs and place them at the beginning or end of sentences. In English, verbs are more difficult to learn because they occur in various positions within sentences, and they change in illogical ways (think of *go, gone, will go, went*). This makes English verbs harder for novice learners (Gentner & Boroditsky, 2001).

An alternative explanation considers the entire social context: Playing with a variety of toys and learning about dozens of objects are crucial in North American culture, whereas East Asian cultures emphasize human interactions—specifically, how one person responds to another. Accordingly, North American infants need to name many inanimate things, whereas Asian infants need to encode social interactions into language.

To figure out your own bias here: What would you do if a 1-year-old was fussing in her crib? Give her a toy, turn on a mobile, find a pacifier, offer a bottle, pick her up, rub her back, hum a lullaby, speak to her, or close the door? The first four are object-centered; the next four are interaction-centered; the last one suggests that you are too tired to cope.

As toddlers' vocabulary builds, adults tend to notice their misuses of words, failing to notice their linguistic progress. In fact, their overall speed and efficiency in acquiring both vocabulary and grammar are impressive.

Toddlers seem to "experiment in order to see" with words, just as the little scientist that Piaget described (stages five and six) experiments with objects. Little scientists become little linguists. It is not unusual for 18-month-olds to walk down the street pointing to every vehicle, asking "Car?" "Truck?" and even "Fire engine?" "Motorcycle?" Or, again and again, "Wha' dat?"—perhaps to confirm their hypothesis about which words go with which things, or perhaps simply because they enjoy conversation and "What's that?" keeps the talk coming.

The first words soon take on nuances of tone, loudness, and cadence that are precursors for the first grammar, in that a single word—called a **holophrase**—conveys a particular message in the way that it is spoken. You can imagine meaningful sentences encapsulated in "Dada!" "Dada?" and "Dada." Each is a *holophrase,* a single word that expresses an entire thought.

Grammar includes all the methods that languages use to communicate meaning. Word order, prefixes, suffixes, intonation, loudness, verb forms, pronouns and negations, prepositions and articles—all of these are aspects of grammar. Infants begin using grammar even in holophrases, but grammar is

BETTY PRESS / WOODFIN CAMP & ASSOCIATES

A Family in Nairobi This baby's intellectual development is well nourished.

?*Observational Quiz* (see answer, page 163): Can you spot four signs of this?

holophrase A single word that is used to express a complete, meaningful thought.

grammar All the methods—word order, verb forms, and so on—that languages use to communicate meaning, apart from the words themselves.

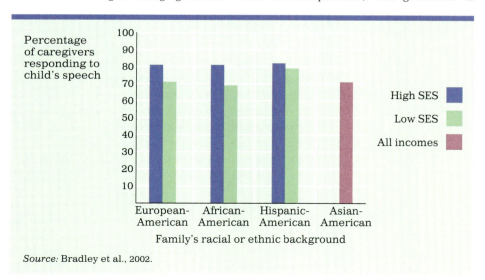

Source: Bradley et al., 2002.

FIGURE 6.1 When Young Children Talk, Caregivers Usually Respond More than 5,000 pairs of caregivers and children under age 3 were observed and interviewed at home. Most of the caregivers, regardless of racial or ethnic background or socioeconomic status, responded to the infant's speech. This may be one reason language development progresses so rapidly.

especially obvious in their first sentences. At about 21 months of age, infants manage their first two-word sentences, with some normal infants achieving this milestone at 15 months and others not reaching it until 24 months. These sentences take the form of "Baby cry" or "More juice," rather than the reverse order of words, and soon "Mommy read book," rather than any of the eight other possible combinations of those three words.

Theories of Language Learning

Worldwide, people who weigh less than 33 pounds (15 kilograms) and are not yet 2 years old can already use language quite well. Bilingual infants even know which listeners understand which languages and choose the correct words to get their meaning across. The process of language learning continues throughout childhood, with some teenagers able to compose lyrics or deliver orations that move thousands of their co-linguists. How does this happen?

Answers to this question have come from three schools of thought, each with its own history, body of research, and committed scholars, and each connected to one of the major theories (behaviorism, epigenetic theory, and sociocultural theory) described in Chapter 2. The first says that infants are directly taught, the second that infants naturally understand language, and the third that social impulses propel infants to communicate. Each of these has implications for caregivers and early-childhood educators, all of whom want their young charges to speak fluently and well but none of whom want to waste their time teaching something that 1-year-olds cannot learn, or would learn just as well without any instruction. Which theory should guide them?

Theory One: Infants Are Taught

The seeds of the first perspective were planted more than 50 years ago, when the dominant theory in North American psychology was behaviorism, or learning theory. The essential idea was that all learning is acquired, step by step, through associations and reinforcements. Just as Pavlov's dogs learned to associate the sound of a bell with the smell of food (see Chapter 2), infants associate objects with words they have heard often, especially if reinforcement occurs.

B. F. Skinner (1957) noticed that spontaneous babbling at 6 to 8 months is usually reinforced. Typically, every time the baby says "ma-ma-ma-ma," a grinning mother appears, repeating the sound as well as showering the baby with attention, praise, and perhaps food. These affordances of mothers are exactly what the infant wants, and the baby will make those sounds again to get them.

Most parents are excellent intuitive instructors. For instance, parents who talk to their young infants typically name each object: "Here is your *bottle*," "There is your *foot*," "You want your *juice*?" and so on, often touching and moving the named object at the same time as they speak the target word loudly, clearly, and slowly (Gogate et al., 2000). They also use *baby talk*, which captures the baby's interest with higher pitch, shorter sentences, elongated words, stressed nouns, and simpler grammar. All these features help infants associate words with things (L. Smith, 1995). The core ideas of this theory are: Parents are the first teachers, frequent repetition is instructive, and well-taught infants become well-spoken children, perpetuating the accents, gestures, and phrases of their first role models.

Support for the view that children must be taught language begins with an undeniable fact: Wide variations are apparent in language fluency, especially when children from various cultures are compared. Some 3-year-olds converse in elaborate sentences; others just barely put one simple word together with another. Such wide variations correlate with teaching and learning practices. For example, parents of the most verbal children teach language throughout in-

Response for Educators (from page 160): Probably both. Infants love to communicate, and they seek every possible way to do so. Therefore, the teachers should try to understand the baby, and the baby's parents, but should also start teaching the baby the majority language of the school.

Cultural Values If his infancy is like that of most babies raised in the relatively taciturn Ottavado culture of Ecuador, this 2-month-old will hear significantly less conversation than infants from most other regions of the world. According to many learning theorists, a lack of reinforcement will result in a child who is insufficiently verbal. In most Western cultures, that might be called maltreatment. However, each culture tends to encourage the qualities it most needs and values, and verbal fluency is not a priority in this community. In fact, people who talk too much are ostracized, and those who keep secrets are valued, so encouragement of language may be maltreatment here.

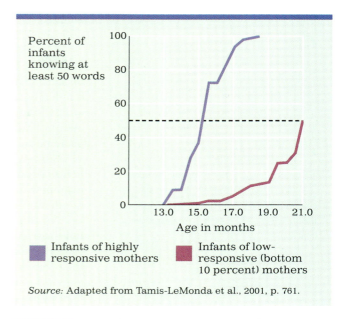

Source: Adapted from Tamis-LeMonda et al., 2001, p. 761.

FIGURE 6.2 **Maternal Responsiveness and Infants' Language Acquisition** Learning the first 50 words is a milestone in early language acquisition, as it predicts the arrival of the naming explosion and the multi-word sentence a few weeks later. Researchers found that half the infants of highly responsive mothers (top 10 percent) reached this milestone as early as 15 months of age and the other half reached it by 17 months. The infants of nonresponsive mothers (bottom 10 percent) lagged significantly behind.

fancy, singing, explaining, listening, and responding; parents of the least verbal children rarely talk to their babies and don't even realize that their children's language delays are connected to parental practices (Law, 2000).

The importance of parental input has been confirmed by thousands of studies. One recent study of infants from 9 to 17 months (Tamis-LeMonda et al., 2001) analyzed the language used by mothers before the infants could talk. One mother never responded by imitating her infant's vocalization; another mother imitated 21 times in 10 minutes. Overall, mothers were more likely to respond with descriptions than anything else (e.g., "That is a spoon you are holding—spoon"). Again, the range was vast: One mother used description only 4 times in 10 minutes; another used it 33 times.

The frequency of maternal responsiveness predicted the rate of language acquisition many months later, as Figure 6.2 dramatically illustrates. Cause, not correlation, is suggested, because some mothers of quiet infants were quite verbal, suggesting play activities, describing things, and asking questions. Nonverbal infants with that kind of mother usually became talkative later on. This is in keeping with the behaviorist theory that adults teach language and then infants learn it. This theory holds that the main linguistic difference between one child and another originates with their caregivers' behavior.

Theory Two: Infants Teach Themselves

The seeds of the second perspective were planted soon after Skinner first proposed his theory of verbal learning. Noam Chomsky (1968, 1980) and his followers believe that language is too complex to be mastered so early and so easily merely through step-by-step conditioning. Although behaviorists focus on variations

!Answer to Observational Quiz (from page 161): The delight on both parents' faces, the mother's "breast is best" shirt, the variety of surrounding objects that stimulate exploration and conceptualization, and the language of gesture that obviously communicates to all three.

among children in vocabulary size and the like, Chomsky noted that all young children worldwide learn the rudiments of grammar at approximately the same age.

Chomsky hypothesized that the human brain is uniquely equipped to learn language. That is, acquiring a language is an experience-expectant function, because centuries of evolution made it adaptive for humans to use words to communicate—a theory accepted by many psychologists (e.g., Irwin, 2002). Chomsky writes about *universal grammar,* which includes some generally understood elements of human language, such as a higher tone at the end of a question. Universal grammar is evidence for brain structure, according to Chomsky.

Somewhat boldly, Chomsky labeled this neurological structure the **language acquisition device,** or **LAD.** The LAD enables children to derive the rules of grammar quickly and effectively from the speech they hear every day, regardless of whether their native language is English, Thai, or Urdu.

No reputable researcher argues that language emerges without some input, but most agree with Chomsky that infants are innately ready to use their minds to understand and speak whatever language is offered (Gopnik, 2001). Further, the various languages of the world, as different as they are, are all logical, coherent, and systematic. Infants, who are also logical, are primed to grasp the particular language they are exposed to, making caregiver speech "not a 'trigger' but a 'nutrient'" (Slobin, 2001, p. 438).

There is no need for a language trigger, according to theory two, because words are "expected" by a LAD in the developing brain, which quickly and efficiently connects neurons and synapses to support whichever of the thousands of possible languages the infant hears. As part of universal grammar, all languages have names for people, objects, and actions, have adjectives, ask questions using the same basic intonation, and use add-ons of some sort to indicate tense and other aspects of grammar. This is experience-expectant, embedded in LAD. The particular pronunciation, vocabulary, and grammar of each language is experience-dependent, but language itself is not.

Research supports this perspective as well. As you remember, all infants babble a *mama* and *dada* sound (not yet referring to mother or father) by 6 months (Goldman, 2001). No reinforcement or teaching is needed; all they need is for dendrites to grow, mouth muscles to strengthen, synapses to connect, and speech to be overheard.

More generally, in infancy, "developing cognition provides the foundational grammatical abilities" (Langer, 2001, p. 38). In other words, thought (not instruction) leads to both vocabulary and grammar. Toddlers learn by overhearing, as many parents discover—occasionally to their dismay (Akhtar et al., 2001).

language acquisition device (LAD) Chomsky's term for a hypothesized brain structure that enables humans to learn language, including the basic aspects of grammar, vocabulary, and intonation.

Show Me Where Pointing is one of the earliest forms of communication, emerging at about 10 months. As Carlos demonstrates, accurate pointing requires a basic understanding of social interaction, because the pointer needs to take the observer's angle of vision into account.

MICHELLE D. BRIDWELL / PHOTOEDIT, INC.

Theory Three: Social Impulses Foster Infant Language

The third theory is called *social-pragmatic,* because it perceives the crucial starting point to be neither vocabulary reinforcement (behaviorism) nor the innate thought–language connection (epigenetic), but the social reason for language: communication. According to this perspective, infants communicate in every way they can because humans are social beings, dependent on one another for survival and joy.

Newborns look searchingly at human faces and listen intently to human voices, because they seek to respond to emotional tone, not because they want to know content. Before 1 year, infants vocalize, babble, gesture, listen, and point—with an outstretched little index finger that is soon accompanied by a very sophisticated glance to see if the other person is looking in the right spot. These and many other examples show how humans are compelled to be social from the very start.

If a 1-year-old is playing intently with an unnamed new toy, and an adult utters a word that might be that toy's name, would the child learn that word as the name of the mystery toy? From a purely behaviorist, learning-by-association perspective, the answer might be "yes," but the actual answer is "no." In an experiment, toddlers in such a situation interrupt their activity, look up, analyze the direction of the adult's gaze, and figure out what object the adult was looking at when the word was said. Babies then assign the new word to that object, not to the fascinating toy in front of them (Baldwin, 1993). This study supports theory three by suggesting that infants are socially focused and that they consider language a useful social tool.

Social compulsion (theory three), not explicit teaching or brain maturation (the first two perspectives), makes infants learn language, "as part of the package of being a human social animal" (Hollich et al., 2000). They seek to understand what others want and intend, and therefore "children acquire linguistic symbols as a kind of by-product of social action with adults" (Tomasello, 2001).

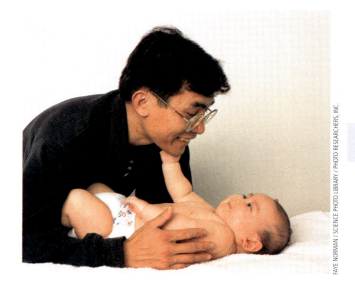

Not Talking? No words yet, but this infant communicates well with Dad, using eyes, mouth, and hands. What are they telling each other?

A Hybrid Theory

Which of these three perspectives is correct? There is research to support each position, which makes finding one true perspective impossible. Many scientists seek to reconcile all the research and theories, acknowledging the merits of each (e.g., Bowerman & Levinson, 2001; Boysson-Bardies, 1999; Gelman & Williams, 1998; K. Nelson, 1996).

One attempt at integration was published in a monograph written by three scholars, which was based on twelve experiments designed by eight researchers (Hollich et al., 2000). The authors developed a hybrid (which literally means a new creature, formed by combining two other living things) of previous theories. They called their model an *emergentist coalition,* because it combines valid aspects of several theories about the emergence of language during infancy.

Given that children learn language to do numerous things—indicate intention, call objects by name, put words together, talk to their family, sing to themselves, express their wishes, remember the past, and much more—it seems to these researchers that some aspects of language are best learned in one way at one age, others in another way at another age. For example, the name of the family dog may be learned by association (e.g., behaviorist), but the distinctions among "cat," "dog," and "horse" may reflect a neurological predilection (epigenetic), which means that the human brain may be genetically wired to differentiate those species. Just as neuroscientists have recently discovered that memories

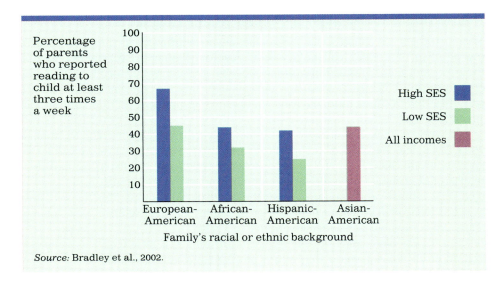

High SES

Low SES

All incomes

FIGURE 6.3 Not Even a Bedtime Story? To build vocabulary, most psychologists and educators recommend reading to a child several times a week. This graph reflects the fact that in the United States, caregivers of children under 3 usually don't follow this advice, especially if they are poor and have a non-European background. Some language-learning theorists contend that these variations are not problematic, but behaviorists are troubled by them.

arise from many parts of the brain and that each memory is retrieved under different conditions, language may also be learned and expressed by many parts of the brain, in many ways.

In fact, fMRI research finds that the cortex contains not one language center, but many. Similarly, decades of cross-cultural studies have found that cultures vary tremendously in language acquisition practices. For example, caregivers in some cultures seldom or never read to their infants, and others often do so (see Figure 6.3). Yet all normal infants learn to talk.

Because communication is crucial for humans, nature provides several paths toward language learning. Each path may be preferred, or may be more efficient, in some stages, cultures, and families, but every child (except those who are severely brain-damaged) will learn language. That is how humans are designed. This perspective returns the child to center stage, because children themselves have many ways to learn and they do so actively, not passively. As one expert concludes:

> Word learning theories will have to come to terms with the fact that children in the typical, everyday word learning scenario are more than perceivers, receivers, or possessors of external supports. Instead, the word learning child is a child with feelings and thoughts about other persons, a child engaged in dynamic real-life events, a child learning to think about a world of changing physical and psychological relationships—in short, a child poised to act, to influence, to gain control, a child reaching out to embrace the learning of language for the power of expression it provides.
>
> [Bloom, 2000, p. 133]

To review early language learning: From the first days of life, babies attend to words and expressions, responding as well as their limited abilities allow—crying, cooing, and, by 6 months, responsive babbling. Even before age 1, they understand simple words and communicate with gestures. By a year, most infants start to speak; deaf children begin signing. Vocabulary accumulates slowly at first, but then the holophrase, the naming explosion, and the two-word sentence are evidence that toddlers are rapid language learners, mastering grammar as well as vocabulary.

The impressive language learning that babies do in the first two years can be explained in many ways. One theory of language development contends that caregivers should reinforce every vocal expression and should use words to describe the many objects and experiences in the infant's life. Another theory relies on an inborn "language acquisition device," which means that, given a normal environment and exposure to language, infants will talk. A third theory stresses social interaction and thus implies that all will be well with language as long as the infant's social context, including culture and family, is supportive. The final model is a hybrid that combines the first three. Because infants themselves vary in culture, learning styles, and families, each theory might be best suited to a particular aspect of language.

A Note for Caregivers

Obviously, there are many ways to foster an infant's language development, or, for that matter, cognition. All three theories can be applied: The infant can be deliberately taught and encouraged, the brain and curiosity can be nourished and supported, and the social drive of the young human can be appreciated and even celebrated.

As you can see from Figure 6.1, about three-fourths of all caregivers respond to the infant's early talking, as theory three recommends; but, as Figure 6.3 shows, many parents do not expand their infants' language learning by regularly reading to them, as behaviorists would recommend. Perhaps reading to young children is not necessary. However, if a 1-year-old is not progressing in language, something may be seriously wrong.

Remember 17-month-old Toni, whom you met in Chapter 5? She had an expressive vocabulary of only 5 words, which is about average at 13 months. Many infants Toni's age already speak 50 words. The hybrid model would notice problems with Toni's situation from all three theoretical perspectives. Toni's language delay may be caused by a combination of (1) inadequate teaching from her patchwork of caregivers and from TV, which Toni spends a lot of time watching (behaviorist); (2) abnormal brain development, perhaps related to poor nutrition or disorganized, erratic experiences (epigenetic); and (3) a lack of social incentive because her mother had suddenly returned to work and there was no steady caregiver (social-pragmatic).

Given what we know about early infant cognition and brain development, Toni's limited vocabulary, which signals that her intellectual growth is slow, may be more worrisome than is her percentile decline in weight, which signals undernutrition. Worrisome, yes; cause for panic, no. Remember that no particular norm is universal; everything must be considered in context.

Language delay indicates that it is time to check Toni's hearing and other aspects of communication. The published case study does not mention whether Toni uses gestures or whether her mother provides encouraging touch and facial expressions. This information is crucial to assess Toni's language-learning context. Thus, we cannot say whether Toni is on the verge of her language explosion or whether special intervention is needed now.

All the research and norms presented in this chapter alert caregivers and professionals to the importance of the intellect in these first two years. If the next generation of children are to become bright, verbal, high achievers in a society that values knowledge, then providing infants with objects, words, and social play may be essential. Or maybe not. But since all infants enjoy discovery, accomplishment, and social responses, there is surely no harm in providing opportunities for learning from the very start. The next chapter, on psychosocial development, continues our examination of caregivers' role in infant development.

SUMMARY

Sensorimotor Intelligence

1. Piaget realized that very young infants are active learners, seeking to understand their complex observations and experiences. Adaptation in infancy is characterized by sensorimotor intelligence, the first of Piaget's four stages of cognitive development. At every stage of intelligence, people adapt their thoughts to the experiences they have.

2. Reflexes provide the foundation for the beginning of intelligence. The continual process of assimilation and accommodation is evident even in the first acquired adaptations, from about 1 to 4 months. The sucking reflex accommodates the particular nipples and other objects that the baby learns to suck.

3. Sensorimotor intelligence develops in six stages—three pairs of two stages each—beginning with reflexes and ending with the toddler's active exploration and use of mental combinations. In each pair of stages, development occurs in one of three types of circular reactions, or feedback loops, in which the infant takes in experiences and tries to make sense of them. Primary circular reactions involve the infant's own body; secondary circular reactions involve other people and objects; and tertiary circular reactions involve active exploration and experimentation.

4. Infants gradually develop an understanding of objects over the first two years of life. As shown in Piaget's classic experiment, infants understand object permanence and begin to search for hidden objects at about 8 months. Other research finds that Piaget underestimated the cognition of young infants.

Information Processing

5. Another approach to understanding infant cognition is information-processing theory, which looks at each step of the thinking process, from input to output. The perceptions of a young infant are attuned to the particular affordances, or opportunities for action, that are present in the infant's world.

6. Objects that move are particularly interesting to infants, as are other humans. Objects as well as people afford many possibilities for interaction and perception, and therefore they enhance early cognition as early affordances.

7. Infant memory is fragile, but not completely absent. Reminder sessions help trigger memories, and young brains learn motor sequences long before they can remember verbally.

Language: What Develops in Two Years?

8. Communication is apparent throughout the first year. Infants babble at about 6 months and speak their first words at about 1 year.

9. Vocabulary builds very slowly at first until about 18 months, when a naming explosion begins. Toward the end of the first year, toddlers begin putting two words together, showing by their word order that they understand the rudiments of grammar.

10. Various theories attempt to explain how infants learn to talk as quickly as they do. The three main theories emphasize different aspects of early language learning: that infants must be taught, that their brains are genetically attuned to language, and that their social impulses foster language learning.

11. Each of these theories seems partly true. The challenge for developmental scientists has been to formulate a hybrid theory that uses all the insights and research on early language learning. The challenge for caregivers is to respond appropriately to the infant's early attempts to communicate.

KEY TERMS

adaptation (p. 147)
sensorimotor intelligence (p. 148)
primary circular reactions (p. 148)
secondary circular reactions (p. 149)

object permanence (p. 150)
tertiary circular reactions (p. 151)
little scientist (p. 152)
deferred imitation (p. 152)
habituation (p. 152)
fMRI (p. 152)

information-processing theory (p. 154)
affordance (p. 154)
visual cliff (p. 155)
dynamic perception (p. 156)
reminder session (p. 157)
baby talk (p. 159)

babbling (p. 160)
naming explosion (p. 160)
holophrase (p. 161)
grammar (p. 161)
language acquisition device (LAD) (p. 164)

APPLICATIONS

1. Try to elicit verbal behavior from a baby under age 2—noises if the baby is under age 1, words if older. Write down all the baby says for 10 minutes. Then ask the primary caregiver to elicit noises (or words) for a 10-minute period, and write these down. Is there a difference between the two attempts? If so, what and why? Finally, compare what you have found with the norms described in the chapter. What discrepancies, if any, did you notice?

2. Piaget's definition of intelligence is adaptation. Others consider a good memory or an extensive vocabulary, for example, to be signs of intelligence. How would you define intelligence? Give an example of something you did that was intelligent according to your definition, and explain why you consider that behavior smart.

3. Some educators suggest that parents read to babies even before the babies begin talking. How do you feel about this advice? What theory of language development does it reflect? How does reading affect the language use of people you know?

4. Test an infant's ability to search for a hidden object. Ideally, use an infant at the cusp of learning, about 8 months, and check this ability over a period of weeks. If the infant already searches for a hidden object, try pausing a few moments between the hiding and searching, or try moving the object from one hidden place to another (in an obvious way) and see what the baby does.

5. Developmentalists are concerned that too much emphasis on cognitive development in the early years might supplant ongoing efforts to improve education at every stage of life. Find one to three recent newspaper or magazine articles, or several Internet sources, on learning during the first three years. Is the information accurate according to what you've learned in this text so far? Does an article or source exaggerate the importance of the first three years of life?

Chapter Seven

The First Two Years: Psychosocial Development

Psychosocial development includes both emotional (*psycho-*) and social development, both the individual psyche and the social context, and the dynamic interaction between the two. In the first two years, psychosocial development is extremely varied and rich. There are far more potential topics than we can even introduce here, let alone discuss adequately.

You have undoubtedly witnessed countless scenes of infant psychosocial development: Tiny babies break into smiles when they stare at an engaging face; 1-year-olds cling to their parents when something frightens them; toddlers flop to the floor, kicking and screaming, after being told "no." Almost every minute of a baby's waking life is a psychosocial minute, because babies depend on other people for minute-to-minute survival.

The chapter opens with discussions of two infants, Jacob and Toni (you met Toni in Chapter 5). These discussions are instructive, for they demonstrate that infants do not always develop normally and parents do not always respond appropriately. Human interactions, in other words, are not always instinctual, predictable, or beneficial.

Following the case study about Jacob and the brief review of Toni's situation, we revisit the five theories that were first described in Chapter 2, exploring how each theory organizes and explains infant emotions and interactions. This discussion will lead us into an examination of the development of infant emotions—from a mere two to a wide range of feelings that reflect an awareness of self and others. We will then describe some aspects of caregiver–infant interaction—synchrony, attachment, and social referencing—that are at the center of infant psychosocial development.

An increasing number of infants are cared for outside the home for a substantial part of each day, so we take a brief look at the effects of infant day care. Finally, we return to Toni and Jacob to see how the knowledge we have gained can be applied to help these two infants—as well as many others.

A Case to Study

Parents on Autopilot

Here is a father's description of his reaction to the early development of his third child, Jacob:

> We were convinced that we were set. We had surpassed our quota of 2.6 children and were ready to engage parental auto-pilot. I had just begun a prestigious job and was working 10–11 hours a day. The children would be fine. We hired a nanny to watch Jacob during the day.
>
> As each of Jacob's early milestones passed, we felt that we had taken another step toward our goal of having three normal children. We were on our way to the perfect American family. Yet, somewhere back in our minds we had some doubts. Jacob seemed different than the girls. He had some unusual attributes. There were times when we would be holding him and he would arch his back and scream so loud that it was painful for us.

> *[Jacob's father, 1997]*

Jacob was unable to relate to his parents (or to anyone else) for the first two years of his life, although his parents paid little attention to the problem, focusing instead on physical "milestones" such as sitting up and walking. When they noticed that something was odd, they told themselves "boys are different"; they blamed Jacob's inability to talk on a nanny who did not speak English well. His father continues:

Jacob had become increasingly isolated [by age 2]. I'm not a psychologist, but I believe that he just stopped trying. It was too hard, perhaps too scary. He couldn't figure out what was expected of him. The world had become too confusing, and so he withdrew from it. He would seek out the comfort of quiet, dark places and sit by himself. He would lose himself in the bright, colorful images of cartoons and animated movies.

Jacob was finally diagnosed with a "pervasive development disorder" at age 3. This is a catchall diagnosis that can include autistic reactions (discussed in detail in Chapter 11). At the moment, you need to know only that the psychosocial possibilities for Jacob were unappreciated. His despairing parents were advised to consider residential placement, because he would never be normal and, with such a placement, they at least would no longer be constantly reminded of their "failure." This recommendation ignored the commitment that Jacob's parents, like most, felt toward their child.

Despite their commitment, as you just read, Jacob's parents, in their satisfaction that he had successfully passed the biosocial "milestones," had paid little heed to his psychosocial growth. Thus, they overlooked Jacob's early social problems even though some evidence—such as his reaction to being held; his failure to talk; and the absence of smiling, social play, and imitation—should have raised an alarm.

Toni's situation is another example of insufficient focus on psychosocial difficulties. The case manager's report on Toni (on pages 122–123) does mention some worrisome social factors—the mother went back to work when Toni was about 1 year old, Toni's father is "not in the household," many relatives provide "patchwork care," the mother does not trust strangers to care for Toni. But these factors were not properly evaluated. For example, if Toni's father is financially supportive and actively involved in her care, it may not matter much where he lives, but all we are told is that he does not live in the household. Thus, no evaluation is possible of his role in Toni's development.

In this chapter we focus on that too-often-underexamined piece: the infant's emotional and social development. In fact, early emotional development follows age norms, which are related to the norms for physical and cognitive development, and can be assessed. Before describing these norms, we turn to theories of psychosocial growth.

© 1998 BORIS DRUCKER FROM CARTOONBANK.COM. ALL RIGHTS RESERVED.

"I get along fine with people my age and I get along fine with people your age—it's the ones in the middle who give me all kinds of problems."

Parents Are the Problem According to psycho-analytic theory, the inevitable conflicts between parents and young children create the need for personality quirks and defensive measures.

Theories About Early Psychosocial Development

The infant's psychosocial development reflects, above all, the powerful, enduring bond between parents and their infants. The grand theories (see Chapter 2) emphasize the crucial role of parents, particularly mothers, in shaping emotions and personality. The two emerging theories emphasize factors beyond the parents' control: Epigenetic theory stresses biology, and sociocultural theory highlights culture.

Psychoanalytic Theory

Psychoanalytic theories connect biosocial and psychosocial development, emphasizing the need for responsive maternal care. Both major psychoanalytic theorists, Sigmund Freud and Erik Erikson, describe two distinct stages of infancy. Freud (1940/1964) called his the *oral stage* and the *anal stage*. Erikson (1963) called his stages of infancy *trust versus mistrust* and *autonomy versus shame and doubt.*

Freud: The Oral and Anal Stages

Psychological development begins in the first year of life with the *oral stage,* so named because the mouth is the young infant's prime source of gratification. In the second year, with the *anal stage,* the infant's prime source of gratification shifts to the anus—particularly to the sensual pleasure of bowel movements and, eventually, the psychological pleasure of controlling them.

According to Freud (1935), both the oral and anal stages are fraught with potential conflicts that can have long-term consequences. If a mother frustrates her infant's urge to suck—by, say, weaning the infant from the nipple too early or preventing the child from sucking on fingers or toes—the child may become distressed and anxious and eventually become an adult with an *oral fixation.* Such a person is stuck (fixated) at the oral stage and therefore eats, drinks, chews, bites, or talks excessively, in quest of mouth-related pleasures that were denied in infancy.

Similarly, if toilet training is overly strict or if it begins before the infant is mature enough, interaction between parents and child may become locked into a conflict over the toddler's refusal or inability to comply. The child becomes fixated and develops an *anal personality;* as an adult, he or she may seek control of self and others and may demonstrate an unusual need for regularity in all aspects of life. When is a child sufficiently mature? Even experts are not sure, but a recent study has shown that toilet training can take a year or more if it is started before 27 months, compared with 5 months if started when the child is 33 to 36 months old (Blum et al., 2003).

A Moment of Bliss Freud thought that oral gratification through breast-feeding was an erotic experience as well as, in his day, a nutritional necessity. Modern psychologists question the power and even the existence of Freud's stages, but his emphasis on the universality of unconscious, primitive urges may not be as far-fetched as some believe.

Erikson: Trust and Autonomy

In the first crisis of life, **trust versus mistrust,** the infant learns whether the world is essentially a secure place where basic needs will be readily satisfied or an unpredictable arena where needs are met only after much crying—and sometimes not even then. Babies begin to develop a sense of security when their mothers provide food and comfort with "consistency, continuity, and sameness of experience." When interaction with the mother inspires trust and security, the child (and later the adult) experiences confidence in engaging with and exploring the world (Erikson, 1963).

The next crisis, which occurs in toddlerhood, is **autonomy versus shame and doubt.** Toddlers want autonomy, or self-rule, over their own actions and bodies. If they fail in their effort to gain it, either because they are incapable or because their caregivers are too restrictive, they feel ashamed of their actions and doubtful of their abilities. According to Erikson, the key to meeting this crisis and gaining a sense of autonomy is parental guidance and protection.

trust versus mistrust Erikson's term for the first crisis of psychosocial development, in which the infant learns whether the world is essentially a secure place where basic needs are always met or an unpredictable arena where needs (for food, comfort, etc.) are sometimes unmet.

autonomy versus shame and doubt Erikson's term for the second crisis of psychosocial development, in which toddlers either succeed or fail in gaining a sense of self-rule over their own actions and bodies.

A Mother's Dilemma Infants are wonderfully curious, as this little boy demonstrates. Parents, however, must guide as well as encourage the drive toward autonomy. Notice this mother's expression as she makes sure her son does not crush or eat the flower.

Like Freud, Erikson believed that problems that begin in early infancy can last a lifetime. He maintained that the adult who is suspicious and pessimistic, or who always seems burdened by shame, may have been an infant who did not develop sufficient trust, or a toddler who did not achieve sufficient autonomy.

Behaviorism

From the perspective of behaviorism, an infant's emotions and personality are molded as parents reinforce or punish the child's spontaneous behaviors. If parents smile and pick up their baby at every glimmer of an infant grin, the baby will become a child—and later an adult—with a sunny disposition. Such parental responses teach an infant some very important lessons about communicating.

The strongest statements on this issue were made by early behaviorists—for example, John Watson:

> Failure to bring up a happy child, a well-adjusted child—assuming bodily health—falls squarely upon the parents' shoulders. [By the time the child is 3] parents have already determined . . . whether . . . [the child] is to grow into a happy person, wholesome and good-natured, whether he is to be a whining, complaining neurotic, an anger-driven, vindictive, over-bearing slave driver, or one whose every move in life is definitely controlled by fear.
>
> *[Watson, 1928]*

Later behaviorists noted that infants also learn through social learning—that they observe and then imitate personality traits of their parents. A child might develop a hot temper, for instance, if a parent regularly displays anger and in return gets respect—or at least obedience—from other family members.

Cognitive Theory

Cognitive theory holds that thoughts and values determine a person's perspective on the world. Cognitive theorists believe that early family experiences are important primarily because our thoughts, perceptions, and memories make them so, not because they are buried in the unconscious (as psychoanalytic theory maintains) or burned into the brain patterns (according to behaviorism). Cognitive theory suggests that early psychosocial development is shaped by infants' attempts to form a general concept of what to expect from other people.

working model In cognitive theory, a set of assumptions that are used to organize perceptions and experiences.

Infants use their early relationships to develop a **working model,** a useful set of assumptions that become a frame of reference that can be called upon later in life (Bretherton & Munholland, 1999). It is called a "model" because these early relationships are seen as a prototype or blueprint; it is called "working" because, while usable, it is not necessarily fixed or final.

For example, if a 1-year-old girl develops a working model, based on how her mother responds to her, that people are not to be trusted, then she will use that assumption whenever she meets a new person. Her childhood relationships will be insecure, and as an adult she will be suspicious of people, always on guard against further disappointment. To use Piaget's terminology, people develop a cognitive schema to organize their perceptions of all humans. It is the child's interpretation of early experiences that is crucial, not necessarily the experiences themselves (Schaffer, 2000).

Epigenetic Theory

temperament According to Rothbart and Bates (1998), "constitutionally based individual differences in emotion, motor, and attentional reactivity and self-regulation."

Epigenetic theory holds that psychosocial development is influenced by traits that a person is genetically predisposed to develop. Among these are traits of temperament. **Temperament** is defined as "constitutionally based individual differences" in emotions, activity, and self-control (Rothbart & Bates, 1998, p. 109).

These differences give rise to behavioral tendencies, so that, for example, one person tends to be *cautious* whereas another tends to be a *risk taker*. In terms introduced in Chapter 3, one person tends to be *inhibited*, another *uninhibited*.

Temperament is based in the person's "constitution," or fundamental genetic structure, and then is expressed in actions and attitudes. As you might imagine, temperament is similar to personality; they differ in that personality includes traits that are primarily learned (e.g., honesty and humility). Although temperamental traits are not learned, the fact that they are epigenetic means that the environment—from prenatal nurturance to ongoing social context and experiences—influences their expression. Early environmental influences are particularly important, because genetic tendencies are most vulnerable to nurture at that point.

Twins They were born on the same day and now are experiencing a wading pool for the first time.

? *Observational Quiz* (see answer, page 177): Are these monozygotic or dizygotic twins?

Research on Temperament

Although no one doubts that infants have inborn traits, measuring those traits has proven difficult. Many attempts to quantify temperamental differences begin with brain research: Scientists record brain activity, measure various parts of the cortex, assess various biochemical reactions to stress, and so on. This research is exciting but frustrating: The correlations found thus far between neurological measurements and childhood behavior are small and sometimes contradictory (Gunnar, 2000; National Research Council & Institute of Medicine, 2000; Thompson & Nelson, 2001).

Accordingly, most research on temperament still relies on checklists and assessments reported by parents (Rothbart & Bates, 1998). The most famous, comprehensive, and long-term study of children's temperament is the classic New York Longitudinal Study (NYLS), begun more than four decades ago and based on rigorous interviews of parents of young infants (Thomas & Chess, 1977; Thomas et al., 1963). According to the researchers' initial findings, in the first days and months of life babies differ in nine characteristics:

■ *Activity level*. Some babies move around a great deal in their bassinets; others tend to stay in one place.
■ *Rhythmicity*. Some babies eat, sleep, and defecate on schedule almost from birth; others are unpredictable.
■ *Approach–withdrawal*. Some babies delight in everything new; others withdraw from every new situation.
■ *Adaptability*. Some babies adjust quickly and happily to new experiences; others do not.
■ *Intensity of reaction*. Some babies chortle when they laugh and howl when they cry; others merely smile or whimper.
■ *Threshold of responsiveness*. Some babies sense every sight, sound, and touch and react to it, usually with distress; others seem oblivious.
■ *Quality of mood*. Some babies seem constantly happy, smiling at almost everything; others are always irritable.
■ *Distractibility*. Some babies can easily be distracted from a fascinating but dangerous object or a distressful experience; others cannot be sidetracked.
■ *Attention span*. Some babies play happily with one toy for a long time; others flit from one thing to another.

The lead NYLS researchers, Alexander Thomas and Stella Chess (1977), believed that "temperamental individuality is well established by the time the infant

LEONG KA TAI / MATERIAL WORLD

Which Sister Has a Personality Problem? Culture always affects the expression of temperament. In Mongolia and many other Asian countries, females are expected to display shyness as a sign of respect to elders and strangers. Consequently, if the younger of these sisters is truly as shy as she seems, her parents are less likely to be distressed about her withdrawn behavior than the typical North American parent would be. Conversely, they may consider the relative boldness of her older sister to be a serious problem.

is two to three months old." They found that almost half the infants were easy, about 15 percent were timid but then warmed up to a new person or situation, and about 10 percent were difficult—irregular, intense, disturbed by every noise, unhappy, and hard to distract for very long. The remaining 25 percent were hard to classify.

Temperament and Caregiving

Even though they do not determine temperament, culture and child-rearing practices can have an effect on temperament. In one longitudinal study, infants were placed in three categories of temperament—positive, inhibited, and negative—on the basis of brain patterns as well as observable behavior (Fox et al., 2001). (These categories are similar to the NYLS "easy," "slow to warm up," and "difficult.") At re-examinations, which occurred periodically up to 4 years, many of the children were consistently positive, inhibited, or negative. However, not every child showed consistency. The inhibited children were most likely to change, especially if they were in a day-care setting where they could learn to control their fear; the exuberant children were least likely to change (see Figure 7.1). This makes sense: An exuberant temperament already fits well with the expectations of most families and preschools, but a fearful one can (and should) be encouraged to shift over time. Other research also finds that inhibited toddlers usually become less inhibited children *if* their mothers are responsive and encouraging (Rubin, Burgess, & Hastings, 2002; Colder, Mott, & Berman, 2002; Pfeifer, Goldsmith, Davidson, & Rickman, 2002).

FIGURE 7.1 Do Babies' Temperaments Change? The temperamental patterns of the 4-month-olds in this study tended to continue, especially if they were already happy and out-going.

?Observational Quiz (see answer, page 179): Which category of infant was most likely to keep changing after the assessment at 4 months?

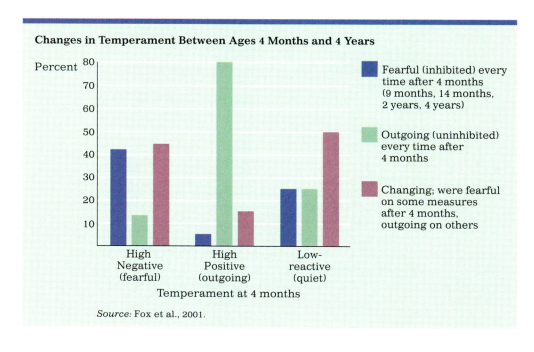

Changes in Temperament Between Ages 4 Months and 4 Years

Percent

Temperament at 4 months: High Negative (fearful), High Positive (outgoing), Low-reactive (quiet)

Legend:
- Fearful (inhibited) every time after 4 months (9 months, 14 months, 2 years, 4 years)
- Outgoing (uninhibited) every time after 4 months
- Changing; were fearful on some measures after 4 months, outgoing on others

Source: Fox et al., 2001.

The need for parental adjustment for infant temperament is captured by a concept called *goodness of fit*. Development proceeds well if all participants adapt to each other, that is, if there is a good match between infant and the social context. More specifically, **goodness of fit** among caregiver, caregiving context, and infant allows a smooth interaction between family and baby, thus enabling development to proceed well. When there is goodness of fit, parents of slow-to-warm-up children give them time to adjust to new situations; parents of exuberant, happy, curious children make sure that they do not hurt themselves while exploring their surroundings; parents of difficult children patiently guide them and build a positive interaction with them. It can be comforting for parents to realize that, even with difficult young children, patient and responsive caregiving usually results in a socially adjusted child. This has been demonstrated in longitudinal studies from infancy to adulthood conducted around the globe, from Sweden (Stattin & Trost, 2000) to New Zealand (Caspi et al., 2002).

goodness of fit A pattern of smooth interaction between the individual and the social milieu, including family, school, and community.

Sociocultural Theory

According to sociocultural theory, the entire social context can have a major impact on infant–caregiver relationships and thus on the infant's development. For example, low socioeconomic status correlates with low child intelligence. However, closer examination reveals that poverty does not directly affect infants but often puts the parents under so much stress that the infants are neglected. Then, and only then, does poverty impair later behavior and achievement (Linver et al., 2002; McLoyd, 1998).

Sociocultural theory also emphasizes that culture has an impact on the parents and on how they raise their infants. For their part, infants are primed to be shaped by their culture as expressed by all their caregivers. We have already seen many examples of this in these three infancy chapters. There is no doubt that culture influences caregivers' attitudes and behaviors in many areas—from breast-feeding to language learning, from immunization to object play—and that these attitudes and behaviors affect infant development. The only question is *how much* influence culture has.

Goodness of Fit Attachment to the father can be very strong, especially for boys. If the mother is unavailable for any reason, a secure attachment to the father or another caregiver can make the difference in the child's emotional health.

In summarizing the five theories, we could highlight the differences or similarities among them. Psychoanalytic theory stresses the crucial role of mothers as they respond to infants' needs for food and elimination (Freud) or for security and independence (Erikson). Behaviorism also stresses caregiving—not as a mother responds to an infant's urges, but as any caregiver reinforces desired learning in a baby. Learning is also crucial for cognitive theory—not the moment-by-moment learning highlighted by behaviorism, but rather the infant's overall concept, or model, of the world. Epigenetic theory begins with the genetic imprint and then shows that environment can shape the expression of those genes. Sociocultural theory, too, sees an interaction between nature and nurture but emphasizes that nurture is varied and powerful.

As you can see, each of the five theories differs from the others, but all consider infancy crucial, with basic biological forces interacting with caregiving practices. We now look in detail at the gradual development of infant emotions. You can judge for yourself the roles played by biology, parenting, and culture in that development.

!Answer to Observational Quiz (from page 175): True tests of zygosity involve analysis of blood type, although physical appearance often provides some clues. Here such clues are minimal: We cannot see differences in sex, coloring, or hand formation—although the shapes of the skulls seem different. The best clue from this photo is personality. Confronting their first experience in a wading pool, these twins are showing such a difference on the approach–withdrawal dimension of temperament that one would have to guess they are dizygotic.

TABLE 7.1

Ages When Emotions Emerge

Age	Emotional Expression
Birth	Crying Contentment
6 weeks	Social smile
3 months	Laughter Curiosity
4 months	Full, responsive smiles
4–8 months	Anger
9–14 months	Fear of social events (strangers, separation from caregiver)
18 months	Self-awareness Pride Shame Embarrassment

stranger wariness Fear of unfamiliar people, exhibited fleetingly at 6 months and at full force by 10 to 14 months.

separation anxiety Fear of abandonment, exhibited at the departure of a beloved caregiver; usually strongest at 9 to14 months.

Stranger Wariness Becomes Santa Terror
For toddlers, even a friendly stranger is cause for alarm, especially if Mom's protective arms are withdrawn. Ironically, the most frightening strangers are men who are unusually dressed and who act as if they might take the child away. Santa Claus remains terrifying until children are about 3 years old.

Emotional Development

Within the first two years, infants progress remarkably in emotional expression, from simple reactions of pain and pleasure to complex patterns of social awareness (see Table 7.1). We now describe that unfolding.

The First Year

Newborns seem to have only two identifiable emotions: distress and contentment. They cry when they are hungry or in pain, when they are tired or frightened (as of a loud noise or a sudden loss of support), and sometimes for no apparent reason. Newborns look happy and relaxed when they are recently fed and drifting off to sleep.

After the first few weeks, additional emotions become recognizable. Curiosity, or at least interest, is shown when infants stare at something new, or hear a melodic voice, or watch a mobile. Interest in people becomes pleasure, evidenced first by the social smile at about 6 weeks and then, at 3 or 4 months, by laughter, especially when a caregiver makes faces and noises that offer the right combination of familiarity and novelty.

Anger emerges a little later. Anger is usually triggered by frustration, which occurs when a person has a goal and something or someone interferes with attainment of that goal. According to Piaget, goal seeking begins at 8 months, although, as you remember from Chapter 6, many infants reach Piaget's stages earlier than he predicted. This may explain why some infants seem angry as early as 4 months.

Fully formed fear of something (not just distress at a sudden noise or sensation) emerges at about 9 months. Then it builds rapidly, becoming more frequent as well as more apparent to an onlooker. The two kinds of fear most clearly expressed are stranger wariness and separation anxiety:

- **Stranger wariness** is evident when an infant no longer smiles at any friendly face and cries if an unfamiliar person moves too close, too quickly.
- **Separation anxiety** is expressed in tears or anger when a beloved caregiver leaves. Separation anxiety is most obvious at 9 to 14 months. This is one sign of attachment to a caregiver, discussed later in this chapter.

The Second Year

Throughout the second year and beyond, anger and fear typically decrease and become targeted toward things that are really infuriating or terrifying. Similarly, both laughing and crying tend to be more discriminating, so that the experiences that once reliably triggered shrieks of joy or pain no longer do so. For example, 1-year-olds who are learning to run often tumble; between falling down and reacting, they seem to pause to decide whether the fall was fun or hurtful. Then, and only then, do they burst into laughter or tears.

New emotions appear toward the end of the second year: pride, shame, embarrassment, and even guilt. Because these emotions require an awareness of what other people might be thinking, they emerge from the family setting, which is itself influenced by the culture. In fact, throughout the first two years, the social context elicits, guides, and identifies the various emotions of the child, so that a 2-year-old not only experiences and expresses a wide range of emotions but also knows which emotions are welcomed and which ones are discouraged by the particular family and culture (Rothbart & Bates, 1998). For example, in some families anger is almost never expressed; but in other families anger is a common reaction, even to minor transgressions. All emotions, particularly pride and shame, show some cultural as well as familial variation (Eid & Diener, 2001).

Self-Awareness

Another foundation for emotional growth is **self-awareness,** which is a person's realization that he or she is a distinct individual whose body, mind, and actions are separate from those of other people. This emerging sense of "me" and "mine" fosters the growth of many self-conscious emotions, from pride and confidence to guilt, shame, and embarrassment. Self-awareness leads to new consciousness of others. That consciousness fosters other-directed emotions, including defiance and jealousy as well as empathy and affection. As one developmentalist explains:

> With the emergence of consciousness in the second year of life, we see vast changes in both children's emotional life and the nature of their social relationships. . . . With consciousness the child can feel what I have called self-conscious emotions, like pride at a job well done or shame over a failure.

[Lewis, 1997, p. 132]

The onset of self-awareness is strikingly evident when infants of various ages are compared. Very young infants have no sense of self. In fact, a prominent psychoanalyst, Margaret Mahler, theorized that for the first 4 months of life infants see themselves as part of their mothers. They "hatch" at about 5 months and spend the next several months developing a sense of themselves as separate from their mothers (Mahler et al., 1975).

Whether or not Mahler is correct, there is no doubt that the infant becomes a self-aware individual. The period from 15 to 18 months "is noteworthy for the emergence of the Me-self, the sense of self as the object of one's knowledge" (Harter, 1998).

In a classic experiment (Lewis & Brooks, 1978), babies looked into a mirror after a dot of rouge had been surreptitiously put on their noses. If the babies reacted to the mirror image by touching their own noses, that meant they knew they were seeing their own faces. With 96 babies between the ages of 9 and 24 months, the experimenters found a distinct developmental shift. None of the babies under 12 months reacted to the mark as if it were on their own faces (they sometimes smiled at and touched the dot on the baby in the mirror). However, most of those between ages 15 and 24 months did react with self-awareness, sometimes touching their own faces with an expression of curiosity and puzzlement.

Pride and Shame

Self-awareness soon becomes linked with self-concept, as toddlers figure out the extent of their abilities. Toddlers' self-evaluations become significant at this point. If someone else tells them "You're very smart," they may smile, but usually they already feel quite smart, pleased, and proud about what they have done.

Self-evaluation is key. In fact, one study found that toddler-age boys who receive *less* parental praise become *more* proud of themselves, perhaps because they are better able to form their own positive self-evaluations (Belsky et al., 1997). Another longitudinal study found that positive comments from a mother to a 2-year-old did *not* lead to more pride or less shame by age 3 (Kelley et al., 2000). However, certain negative comments (such as "You're doing it all wrong") diminished effort and increased shame. Neutral suggestions, in addition to

self-awareness A person's realization that he or she is a distinct individual whose body, mind, and actions are separate from those of other people.

LAURA DWIGHT

A Beautiful Bonnet At 18 months, Austin recognizes himself, obviously delighted by his colander hat. Once self-recognition begins at about this age, many children spend hours admiring themselves with various hats, makeup, and other accessories. Almost every view of themselves is a joy; children are not yet worried about looking stupid or ugly.

!Answer to Observational Quiz (from page 176): The quiet babies changed the most, perhaps because they were neither distinctly fearful nor distinctly outgoing at 4 months.

guiding toddlers to complete activities on their own, fostered the willingness to try new challenges later on (Kelley et al., 2000). It seems that building self-esteem is not a matter of simple praise but of enabling young children to accomplish things that make them feel proud.

How can a toddler's own pride be more compelling than parental approval? Look, for example, at Ricky, the grandson of a noted psychologist. Shortly before his second birthday, Ricky teased his mother by deliberately pouring a cup of juice onto a rug. Evidence that Ricky knew he was being naughty was his reaction to his mother's scolding: He was unsurprised and unfazed by her angry words and was quite willing to help her clean up the mess. Only when his mother sent him to his room did he protest angrily, apparently not having anticipated such punishment.

Later that day he told his grandmother, "Juice on a floor." Her response was "Juice doesn't go on the floor," delivered somewhat sternly. "Yes, juice on a floor, juice on a floor," Ricky laughingly repeated several times, pretending to turn an imaginary cup upside down. As Ricky's grandmother comments:

> The boy's pleasure at watching the juice spill and anger at being sent to his room are emotions that are typical at all periods of infancy, but his obvious pride at his ability to act counter to convention or his mother's wishes is possible only when self-awareness is firmly established.
>
> *[Shatz, 1994]*

Now we review the emotional expansion of the first two years. Newborns seem to have only two simple emotions, distress and contentment, expressed by crying or looking happy. Very soon more emotions appear, including pleasure, expressed in social smiles and laughter, and curiosity. By the second half of the first year, anger and fear are increasingly evident, especially in reaction to social experiences, such as encountering a stranger.

In the second year, as infants become self-aware, they express emotions that are connected to themselves, including pride, shame, and embarrassment as well as other-directed emotions, such as defiance and affection. Although these emotions are universal, they show cultural and familial variations, and family setting is crucial to the emergence of emotions.

The Development of Social Bonds

Social connections are pivotal for understanding not only infant psychosocial development but also human emotions throughout the entire life span. As you have already seen, social interaction is crucial in infancy; the specifics change as the child grows older.

Synchrony

Although any face elicits a social smile at about 6 weeks, by the time an infant is 3 months old, familiar caregivers are more likely to provoke grins, arm waving, and other reactions that signify that the infant "knows" them (Rochat, 2001).

At this point, **synchrony** begins. Synchrony is a coordinated interaction between caregiver and infant, who respond to each other with split-second timing. Synchrony has been variously described by researchers as the meshing of a finely tuned machine (Snow, 1984), an emotional "attunement" of an improvised musical duet (Stern, 1985), and a smoothly flowing "waltz" that is mutually adap-

synchrony A coordinated interaction between caregiver and infant, who respond to each other's faces, sounds, and movements very rapidly and smoothly.

tive (Barnard & Martell, 1995). The critical factor is the timing of the interaction, such that each partner responds to the other almost instantly, in a chain of mutual communication. Synchrony helps infants learn to read other people's emotions and to develop some of the basic skills of social interaction, such as taking turns and paying attention, that they will use throughout life.

Synchrony also helps infants learn to express their own feelings. A sensitive parent responds to every hint ("Ooh, are you hungry?" "Aahaaa, you're tired," "Uuumm, you see the rattle?"). The adult reacts to each expression with exaggerated facial movements and a solicitous tone of voice as well as with action, such as getting food, putting the baby's head to the shoulder, or handing over the rattle (Gergely & Watson, 1999).

Imitation is pivotal. Infants sometimes imitate caregivers: Even newborns can imitate mouth movements, and as their imitation improves over the first year, they begin to feel the emotions that go with the expressions their faces make (just as adults who laugh begin to feel better). But parents' imitation of infants, not infants' imitation of parents, is the major force that drives the synchronous activity.

If an emotion is visible from an infant's expression (and infants all over the world make the same facial expressions in response to the same stimuli) and the infant sees a familiar face mirroring that emotion, then the infant begins to connect his or her internal state with the external expression (Rochat, 2001). Emotional understanding begins.

Although synchrony is evident early in life, it becomes more frequent and more elaborate as time goes on; a 6-month-old is a much more responsive social partner than a 3-month-old. Parents and infants spend about an hour a day in face-to-face play, although wide variations are apparent from baby to baby, time to time, culture to culture (Baildam et al., 2000; Lee, 2000).

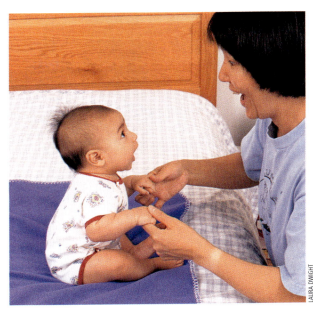

Emotion Shared Three-month-old Mathias and his mother experience synchrony, with eyes wide and staring, mouths open, and hands touching. What would you call the emotion they are sharing—excitement, pride, exhilaration? The experience may be too powerful for any ordinary word to describe.

Especially for College Men Who Are Not Yet Fathers Imagine you have a male friend who has an infant niece. He says he is afraid he might look silly if he tried to play with her. What do you tell him?

Attachment

Toward the end of the first year, face-to-face play almost disappears; once infants can move around and explore on their own, they are no longer content to stay in one spot and mirror an adult's facial expressions. A new connection replaces the early synchrony, a connection called *attachment*. **Attachment**, according to Mary Ainsworth (1973), is an emotional bond that one person forms with a specific other person. Attachments form in infancy and usually remain lifelong.

When people are attached to each other, they try to be near each other and they interact in many ways. Infants show their attachment through *proximity-seeking behaviors,* such as approaching and following the caregiver and climbing onto the caregiver's lap, and through *contact-maintaining behaviors,* such as clinging, resisting being put down, and looking back at their caregiver as they explore.

Caregivers show their attachment as well. They keep a watchful eye on the baby, even when there is no danger, and respond affectionately and sensitively to the baby's vocalizations, expressions, and gestures. Many a mother or father, awakening at 3:00 A.M. to go to the bathroom, tiptoes to the crib to gaze fondly at their sleeping infant. During the day, many like to smooth the toddler's hair or pat a hand or a cheek. These are just a few of many obvious examples of proximity-seeking and contact-maintaining behaviors. Attachment not only deepens the parent–child relationship but, over our long evolutionary history, may have contributed to human survival by keeping infants near their caregivers and keeping caregivers vigilant.

attachment According to Ainsworth (1973), "an affectional tie that one person or animal forms between himself and another specific one—a tie that binds them together in space and endures over time."

(a)

(b)

Personality of Caregiver Both nature and nurture may be in evidence here, in that the mother's personality obviously affects the quality of interaction with her offspring. Adults typically use special social behaviors *(a)* with their young infants—leaning in close, opening their eyes and mouths wide in exaggerated expressions of surprise or delight, maintaining eye contact—because those behaviors elicit the baby's attention and pleasure. But such behaviors are subdued or absent when the adult is depressed or stressed *(b)*, and this makes social interaction much less enjoyable for each partner.

secure attachment A relationship of trust and confidence; during infancy, a relationship that provides enough comfort and reassurance to enable independent exploration of the environment.

base for exploration The caregiver's role in a relationship of secure attachment, in which the child freely ventures forth and returns.

insecure attachment A relationship that is unstable or unpredictable; in infancy such relationships are characterized by the child's fear, anxiety, anger, clinging, or seeming indifference toward the caregiver.

insecure-avoidant Referring to a pattern of attachment in which one person tries to avoid any connection with another, as an infant who is uninterested in the caregiver's presence or departure and ignores the caregiver on reunion.

insecure-resistant/ambivalent Referring to a pattern of attachment in which anxiety and uncertainty keep one person clinging to another, as an infant who resists active exploration, is very upset at separation, and both resists and seeks contact on reunion.

Strange Situation A laboratory procedure developed by Mary Ainsworth to measure attachment by evoking an infant's reactions to stress, specifically episodes of a caregiver's or stranger's arrival at and departure from a playroom where the infants can play with many toys.

Secure and Insecure Attachment

The concept of attachment was originally developed by John Bowlby (1969, 1973, 1988), a British developmentalist who was inspired both by psychoanalytic theory and by ethology, particularly by observation of the interactions of monkeys. His ideas inspired Mary Ainsworth, then a young American graduate student, to devote her career to defining and measuring attachment. Ainsworth discovered that virtually all normal infants develop special attachments to the people who care for them. Some infants are more secure in their attachments than others—an observation later confirmed by hundreds of other researchers (Cassidy & Shaver, 1999).

Secure attachment (called type B) provides comfort and confidence, as evidenced first by the infant's attempt to be close to the caregiver and then by the infant's readiness to explore. In such a relationship the caregiver acts as a **base for exploration**, which gives the child the confidence to venture forth. The child might, for example, scramble down from the caregiver's lap to play with a toy but periodically look back, vocalize a few syllables, and perhaps return for a hug.

By contrast, **insecure attachment** is characterized by an infant's fear, anxiety, anger, or seeming indifference toward a caregiver. The insecurely attached child has much less confidence, perhaps playing without trying to maintain contact with the caregiver or, the opposite, being unwilling to leave the caregiver's arms. Both these extremes are signs of insecure attachment; the first is called **insecure-avoidant** (type A) and the second **insecure-resistant/ambivalent** (type C) (see Table 7.2).

Measuring Attachment

Ainsworth developed a now-classic laboratory procedure, called the **Strange Situation,** to measure an infant's attachment. In a well-equipped playroom, the infant is closely observed in eight three-minute-long episodes. In a given episode, the infant is with the caregiver, with a stranger, with both, or alone. The first episode has caregiver and child together, and then every three minutes the stranger or the caregiver enters or leaves the playroom. The infant's response to these potentially stressful comings and goings is observed.

The infant's reactions indicate motivation to be near the caregiver (proximity-seeking and contact-maintaining) and ability to use the caregiver's presence as a

TABLE 7.2 Patterns of Attachment in Infancy

Pattern of Attachment	Characteristics
Secure (type B) (between half and two-thirds of all normal infants)	Explores freely when the caregiver is present, using the caregiver as a "secure base." May be distressed at separation; always greets the caregiver on reunion. If distressed during separation, seeks contact and comfort during reunion, then settles down to continue play.
Insecure-avoidant (type A) (about one infant in six)	Explores freely, seems uninterested in the caregiver's presence or departure. On reunion, ignores or actively avoids caregiver.
Insecure-resistant/ambivalent (type C) (about one infant in six)	Resists active exploration. Preoccupied with caregiver. Upset at separation. On reunion, both resists and seeks contact, showing anger, passivity, or clinging. Does not easily return to play.
Disorganized (type D) (about one infant in ten)	Neither plays freely nor responds to the caregiver in any one coherent mode. May cry and then hit; may "freeze"; trancelike; may move in slow motion or other stereotyped manner; may show fear of parent.

Sources: Adapted from Braungart-Rieker et al., 2001; Goldberg et al., 1995; Vondra & Barnett, 1999.

? *Critical Thinking Question* (see answer, page 185): Why are the proportions of attachment patterns A, B, C, and D given as "about" a fraction, rather than as percentages that add up to 100?

Response for College Men (from page 181): Go ahead and play. Infants need adults who are willing to look silly, because making odd noises and facial expressions is part of synchrony and play—both important for infant development. This is not only how infants learn; it is also what fathers throughout the world do, bringing great joy to their babies.

secure base (having confidence to venture forth). The key observational aspects of the Strange Situation are the following:

■ *Exploration of the toys.* A securely attached toddler plays happily when the caregiver is present.
■ *Reaction to the caregiver's departure.* A securely attached toddler usually shows some sign of missing the caregiver.
■ *Reaction to the caregiver's return.* A securely attached toddler exhibits a welcoming response when the caregiver returns to the room—especially when the caregiver has left and come back twice.

Almost two-thirds of all normal infants tested in the Strange Situation demonstrate secure attachment (type B). The mother's presence in the playroom is enough to give them courage to explore the room and investigate the toys. (The father's presence makes some infants even more confident.) The caregiver's

The Attachment Experiment In this episode of the Strange Situation, Brian shows every sign of secure attachment. *(a)* He explores the playroom happily when his mother is present; *(b)* he cries when she leaves; and *(c)* he is readily comforted when she returns.

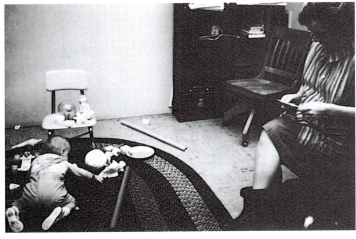
(a)

(b)

(c)

ALL: COURTESY OF MARY AINSWORTH

disorganized A category of attachment that is neither secure nor insecure but is marked by the child's and caregiver's inconsistent behavior toward each other.

departure may cause some distress (usually expressed through verbal protest and a pause in playing); the caregiver's return is a signal to reestablish positive social contact (by smiling or climbing into his or her arms) and then resume playing. This balanced reaction—being concerned about the caregiver's departure but not overwhelmed by it—reflects secure attachment.

About a third of all infants show insecure attachment, appearing either indifferent (type A) or unduly anxious (type C). Some extremely insecure infants fit into none of these categories; such infants are classified as **disorganized**, or type D. Their reactions are hard to classify because they may shift from hitting the mother to kissing her, staring blankly, crying hysterically, or pinching themselves.

The percentages of children classified as type A, B, C, and D vary across studies, partly because groups of infants differ in their family and cultural experiences and therefore in their attachment patterns. For example, some studies find that insecure Japanese infants are more often type C than type A, but the opposite is true for insecure German infants (Grossman & Grossman, 1990). In Mali, West Africa, infants who are not securely attached are often type D (True et al., 2001).

Insecure Attachment as a Warning Sign

Attachment status does not necessarily determine future emotional development, but insecure attachment can indicate that something is amiss. For this reason, it is important to better understand insecure attachment.

It is estimated that 10 percent of mothers (and 20 percent of low-income mothers) of young infants are clinically depressed. Insecure attachment is much more common in such cases (National Research Council & Institute of Medicine, 2000; Thompson, 1998). However, attachment status appears to be determined not by the mother's poverty or even the degree of her depression but, rather, by her overt responses to the infant's attempts at synchrony and attachment (does she smile and play or express rejection or indifference?). Thus, we cannot draw conclusions about attachment from knowing that a mother is depressed; we must look at the mother–infant interaction. Intervention can make a difference. A mother can be shown how to interact responsively, even before her underlying problems of income and mood are addressed.

One reason infant attachment status does not determine later emotional development is that attachment status can change. Insecure attachments can be repaired. At least in the early years of life, children sometimes recover from periods of maternal depression, responding more to their mother's current behavior

Nobody's Children These orphans in Kabul, Afghanistan, are living casualties of years of civil war. They appear well nourished, but, with their parents dead and with no adult to develop an attachment to, they are emotionally deprived. Also, this Spartan orphanage gives them physical shelter but inadequate mental stimulation. These conditions lessen their chances of developing normally.

TABLE 7.3 **How Disturbed Mothers Develop Type D (Disorganized) Attachment in Their Infants**

Mothers of type D infants are at least three times more likely than mothers of types A, B, and C infants to exhibit these behaviors:

Laugh when infant is crying	Pull infant by the wrist
Invite approach and then distance	Mock and tease the infant
Use friendly tone while maintaining threatening posture	Tell a crying infant to hush
	Ignore an infant who falls down
Direct infant to do something and then say not to do it	Use a loud or sharp voice
Display a sudden change of mood, not elicited by the context	Remove a toy with which the infant is engaged
Handle the infant as though the infant were not alive	Hold infant away from body with stiff arms
Display a frightened expression	Speak in hushed, intimate, sexy tones to the infant
Withhold a toy from the infant	Talk in "haunted" or frightened voice
Neglect to soothe a distressed infant	

Source: Adapted from Lyons-Ruth et al., 1999.

than to her behavior months earlier (National Research Council & Institute of Medicine, 2000). Unfortunately, attachment status can change in the other direction as well. Factors that disrupt a family, such as abuse or divorce, can shake loose a secure attachment, as happened to a majority (61 percent) of a group of 18-year-olds who had been secure at age 1 but had experienced disruptive family events before age 12 (Beckwith et al., 1999).

One of the remarkable discoveries regarding attachment is that infants are active partners, trying to find an adaptive response to the care they receive. Essentially, type A infants ignore the mother who is already ignoring them, exploring the environment instead. Often, as part of this exploration, they seek another attachment figure. If these infants succeed in their search—that is, if a father, grandparent, or day-care provider offers secure attachment—they often develop normally (Goodman & Gotlib, 1999).

Similarly, type C (insecure-resistant/ambivalent) infants sometimes manage, through their clinging and protesting, to induce change in their caregivers. A more secure, less manipulative relationship may develop.

Type D (disorganized) infants experience the greatest difficulties in responding and have the most serious problems in later childhood. They are disorganized because their mother's inconsistent behavior makes it impossible to devise an effective attachment strategy, even one of the insecure types. Their mothers give conflicting messages—love/hate, sad/glad—that are beyond the ability of a 1-year-old to decipher and respond to coherently (see Table 7.3). Not surprisingly, if infants are unable to learn any effective strategy for dealing with other people, even an avoidant or resistant strategy, they lash out in pain and confusion. They become hostile and aggressive for no apparent reason in preschool and later (Lyons-Ruth et al., 1999).

Social Referencing

As you have seen, infants seek to understand caregivers' emotions. This search for information about another person's feelings is called **social referencing.** Essentially, the infant consults a person for clarification or information, much

!Answer to Critical Thinking Question (from page 183): Each study in each nation with each sample finds different values. For example, insecure German infants tend to be type A; Japanese, type C; and West African, type D. Throughout the world, however, type B is more common than any other type.

social referencing Seeking information about an unfamiliar or ambiguous object or event by observing someone else's expressions and reactions. That other person becomes a reference, consulted when the infant wants to know how to react.

like we might consult a dictionary or other reference work. A mother's glance of calm reassurance or words of caution, a father's expression of alarm, pleasure, or dismay—each can become a guide to action, telling an infant how to react to an unfamiliar or ambiguous event.

After age 1, as infants move into the stage of active exploration (Piaget) and autonomy (Erikson), their need and desire to understand a caregiver's emotions become more pressing. Toddlers search for emotional cues in gaze and facial expressions, pay close attention to outbursts of pleasure or disgust, and watch carefully to detect the intentions behind the actions of others (Baldwin, 2000).

Social referencing is particularly noticeable at mealtime, when infants look to caregivers for cues about new foods. This explains why caregivers the world over smack their lips, pretend to taste, and say "yum-yum" (or the equivalent) as they feed toddlers their first beets, liver, spinach, or whatever. They are trying to lead the infants to like whatever is offered. For their part, toddlers become quite astute at reading expressions, insisting on the foods that the adults *really* like. Through this process, children develop a taste for cranberries or raw fish or curried goat or refried beans or smelly cheese—foods that children in other cultures never learn to eat.

CORBIS / MICHAEL S. YAMASHITA

Social Referencing Is it dangerous or joyous to ride in a bicycle basket through the streets of Osaka, Japan? Check with Mom to find out.

Referencing Mom

Most everyday examples of social referencing occur with mothers, who in most cases are the primary caregivers for infants and who particularly communicate emotion—happiness, fear, disgust, and so on. One example of social referencing is toddlers' willingness to respond to their mother's requests. In cultures that value independence, toddlers often refuse to do as they are told. In an experiment, about three toddlers in four would not obey their mother's request to pick up dozens of toys that they had not spilled (Kochanska et al., 2001). Their refusal actually indicates some emotional maturity: Self-awareness had led to pride and autonomy and to shame elicited by their *own* actions, not by someone else's spilled toys.

However, the same toddlers were much more likely to comply when their mothers told them not to touch some very attractive toys within easy reach. The mothers used tone and expression as well as words to make this prohibition clear and to point out the forbidden toys. To be specific, about half of the 14-month-olds and virtually all of the 22-month-olds obeyed even when their mother was out of sight. Indeed, 80 percent of the older toddlers not only acquiesced but seemed to accept the mother's judgment (which the researchers called *committed compliance*). One even said "no-no touch" as a reminder (Kochanska et al., 2001).

Referencing Dad

Early research on the psychosocial context of development usually studied mother–infant relationships, partly because it was assumed that mothers were the main caregivers. It is now apparent, however, that a range of relatives and unrelated people (including fathers, siblings, grandparents, neighbors, and other children's parents) have always been crucial to development, especially for children growing up outside middle-class North America.

Within North America, various changes in recent decades may have expanded the sources infants may use as references. For example, in the United States, by age 1 (although not before 6 months) even the television is often a source for social referencing (Mumme & Fernald, 2003). More important, in the United States and elsewhere, fathers are spending more time with their children.

Worldwide, the one person whose role is increasingly recognized and increasingly significant is the father, who, through social referencing and in other ways, is often crucial to infant personality and learning. This is not always the case as children grow older. A study in Africa found that when fathers stayed with their families rather than traveling to earn more money, the children were not as healthy as those whose fathers sent home money. The mothers' brothers may have helped in fathering, or the mothers who were financially secure may have been better able to care for their children. The same study found that the children of fathers who left the family to find employment did better academically than children whose fathers continued to live at home. This finding indicates not only that fathers make a difference but also that there may be a trade-off between spending more time on child care and earning more money (Bock & Johnson, 2002).

Infants use Dad as a social reference as much as they do Mom, if both parents are present. In fact, fathers tend to be more encouraging than mothers, who are more protective. As a result, when toddlers are about to begin exploring, they often seek a man's approval to spur their curiosity (Parke, 1995).

As researchers looked closely at parents and infants, they discovered a significant gender difference: Although fathers tend to provide less basic care, they play more. In general, infants look to fathers for fun and to mothers for comfort (Lamb, 2000; Parke, 1996). Compared to mothers' play, fathers' play is more noisy, emotional, boisterous, physical, and idiosyncratic (as fathers tend to make up active and exciting games on the spur of the moment); sons are particularly likely to elicit such roughhousing.

In the first year of a baby's life, fathers are more likely to move the baby's legs and arms in imitation of walking, kicking, or climbing; to zoom the baby through the air (playing "airplane"); or to tap and tickle the baby's stomach. Mothers tend to caress, murmur, or sing soothingly; to combine play with caretaking routines such as diapering and bathing; or to use standard sequences that involve only one part of the body, such as peek-a-boo and patty-cake. Not surprisingly, young infants typically laugh more—and cry more—when playing with Dad.

In all probability, physically active play helps children master motor skills and develop muscle control (Pellegrini & Smith, 2001). In addition, play with Dad may contribute to the growth of social skills and emotional expression. In one study, one or the other parent sat passively nearby while their 18-month-old met a stranger. The toddlers were more likely to smile and play with the new person when the father was present than when the mother was, a difference especially apparent among the boys. The authors of the study speculated that previous boisterous, idiosyncratic interactions with Dad made his presence a signal to be bold and playful (Kromelow et al., 1990).

Cultural Differences

The fact that fathers are good playmates does not mean they are limited to that role. Fathers are quite capable of forming secure relationships with their babies and providing all necessary emotional and cognitive nurturing (Geiger, 1996; Lamb, 1997). Single mothers can do the same, as can grandparents or married mothers in cultures where fathers rarely see their babies.

Diversity of roles is obvious; as each set of parents cooperate to raise their children, they develop their own roles. Such diversity is more evident for fathers' involvement than mothers' involvement (Marsiglio et al., 2000). This greater diversity reflects cultural differences: Some cultures encourage fathers to be directly involved with their infants; others do not.

In general, the father's involvement in infant care benefits not only the child's later development but also the mother's self-confidence and the emotional strength of the father himself (Aldous et al., 1998; Eggebeen & Knoester, 2001; Vandell et al., 1997). Apparently, throughout today's changing world, mothers and fathers together are better able to meet all their infant's needs—biological, cognitive, and psychosocial—than is either parent alone (Cabrera et al., 2000).

Up, Up, and Away! The vigorous play typical of fathers is likely to help in the infant's mastery of motor skills and the development of muscle control.

Especially for Grandmothers A grandmother of an infant boy is troubled that the baby's father stays with him whenever the mother is away. She says that men don't know how to care for infants, and she notes that he sometimes plays a game in which he tosses his son in the air and then catches him.

infant day care Regular care provided for babies by trained and paid nonrelatives.

Response for Grandmothers (from page 187): Fathers can be great caregivers, and most mothers prefer that the father provide care. It's good for the baby and the marriage. Being tossed in the air is great fun (and no harm, as long as the father is a good catcher!). A generation ago, mothers didn't let fathers care for infants, so today's grandmothers may not know how good fathers can be.

Especially for Day-Care Teachers A mother who brings her child to your care says that she knows she is harming her baby but must work out of economic necessity. What do you say?

Infant Day Care

You have seen that the development of social bonds is crucial to infants. What, then, is the effect of **infant day care,** in which infants are regularly cared for by trained and paid nonrelatives? This kind of day care is distinct from nonmaternal care, which simply means care by someone other than the mother (usually a relative) and is typical in the early months.

As the child's age and family income increase, nonmaternal care more often takes the form of an organized and structured program conducted outside the baby's home. The program may be *family day care,* with fewer than 6 children cared for in someone's home, or *center care,* usually with 15 children or more in a place set aside for early child care. More than half of all 1-year-olds in the United States are in "regularly scheduled" nonmaternal care, and the percentage has been rising every year (National Research Council & Institute of Medicine, 2000). Other nations have even higher percentages of infants in day care.

The effects of infant day care are controversial for reasons of culture and ideology, so every research finding is vulnerable to dispute. Nonetheless, most developmental scientists agree that children are not harmed by, and sometimes benefit from, professional day care (Lamb, 1998). In fact, the evidence is overwhelming that good preschool education (from age 3 to age 5) is beneficial, helping children learn more language, think with more perspective, develop better social skills, and achieve more in the long term, as Chapter 9 describes in detail. What about under age 3? Opinions vary, perhaps in part because the grand theories emphasized the mother. A massive (1,300 children), multistate (10 regions), longitudinal study (from birth to age 3) is seeking more concrete answers (NICHD Early Child Care Research Network, 1996, 1998, 1999, 2000, 2001, 2002).

Clearly, the quality of a program makes a difference (see Table 7.4 for characteristics of high-quality day care). According to the Early Child Care Research Network, the *only* condition in which early day care seems detrimental is when the mother is insensitive *and* the infant spends more than 20 hours each week in a poor-quality program (too few caregivers, with too little training). The detrimental effects of poor care have also been found in a study in Israel of 758 infants. Those cared for at home by a father or grandmother seemed to do very well; those cared for in a day-care center with untrained caregivers and six or more infants per adult fared poorly (Sagi, Koren-Karie, Gini, Ziu, & Joels, 2002).

TABLE 7.4 High-Quality Day Care

High-quality day care has four essential characteristics:

1. *Adequate attention to each infant.* This means a low caregiver-to-infant ratio and a small group of infants. The ideal situation might be two reliable caregivers for five infants. Infants need to be able to rely on one or two adults, so continuity of care from the same caregivers is very important.

2. *Encouragement of sensorimotor exploration and language development.* Infants should be provided with a variety of easily manipulated toys and should have a great deal of language exposure through games, songs, and conversations.

3. *Attention to health and safety.* Cleanliness routines (such as handwashing before meals), accident prevention (such as the absence of small objects that could be swallowed), and safe areas for exploration (such as a clean, padded area for crawling and climbing) are all good signs.

4. *Well-trained and professional caregivers.* Ideally, every caregiver should have a degree or certificate in early-childhood education and should have worked in this field for several years. Turnover should be low, morale high, and enthusiasm evident. Good caregivers love their children and their work.

Out-of-home day care is sometimes better than in-home care, especially when the infant needs special stimulation and care that the home is unlikely to provide (Ramey et al., 2002). Among the benefits of day care is the opportunity to express emotions. When a toddler is temperamentally very shy or aggressive, he or she is less likely to remain so if other caregivers and children are used as social references (Fox et al., 2001; Zigler & Styfco, 2001). Exclusive maternal care cannot offer such a variety of emotional experiences.

Infants seek to develop social bonds, and they can do so with one or more people, as long as the caregivers are responsive and familiar. In the early months, synchrony begins: Infants and caregivers interact face to face, making split-second adjustments to their emotional responses to each other.

Early responsiveness evolves into attachment, an emotional bond between adult and child that encourages the toddler to, for example, explore a new play area. Secure emotional attachment thus allows learning to progress; insecure infants are less confident and may develop emotional impairments. As infants become more curious and as they encounter new toys, people, and events, they use social referencing to learn whether such new things are fearsome, fun, or disgusting.

Although mothers are infants' usual, and most studied, social partners, the emotional connections evident in synchrony, attachment, and social referencing can also occur with fathers, other relatives, and day-care providers. Instead of harming infants, as was once feared, nonmaternal care can enhance infants' psychosocial development.

Conclusions in Theory and Practice

You have seen in this chapter that the first two years are filled with psychosocial developments, all of which result from genes, maturation, culture, and caregivers. Each of the five major theories seems plausible, yet they differ in assessing the significance of the experiences of the first two years of life.

What conclusions can be drawn from theory and research? No single theory stands out as the best interpretation. The first two years are important, but early emotional and social development is influenced by the mother's behavior, the father's support, the quality of day care, cultural patterns, and inborn traits. We do not know the extent to which one influence, such as a good day-care center, can compensate for another, such as a depressed mother (although it does seem as if maternal influence is always significant).

On the basis of what you have learned, you could safely advise parents to play with their infants, respond to their physical and emotional needs, let them explore, maintain a relationship, pay attention to them, and expect every toddler to be sometimes angry, sometimes proud, sometimes uncertain. These parental actions and attitudes may or may not have a powerful impact on later development, but they certainly make infants happier. Parental attentiveness is crucial to synchrony, attachment, and social referencing, which are, in turn, crucial to infant and toddler development.

Such generalities are not good enough for our two toddlers, Toni and Jacob, or for all the other infants who show signs of undernutrition, delayed language development, poor social skills, abnormal emotional development, disorganized attachment, and other deficits. In dealing with individual children with problems, we need to be specific.

A Practical Approach for Toni

The health workers who reported on Toni's development (see Chapter 5) used her as an example of the need for good nutrition. That certainly is a valid concern, but let us now interpret Toni's experiences from the standpoint of her psychosocial development.

Toni's social world was turned upside down when her mother went back to work. Having lived exclusively with her mother, Toni suddenly was cared for outside her home by a variety of family members. The mother's mistrust of strangers may keep Toni and her mother from getting the support they need. That Toni is not gaining weight and not talking much may be the result of feelings of anger, depression, or fearfulness.

Like all toddlers, Toni needs stability of care, but she has none. The ideal solution is a day-care center that is near her home and has all four characteristics of high-quality day care described in Table 7.4. However, such care is very expensive in the United States and is not always supported by public funds. Inadequate care, with frequent turnover of caregivers, may be all that is available for Toni. Could that be good enough? Perhaps, but the research suggests that it is risky.

Ideally, one person is the alternative caregiver. This can be a day-care teacher, the father, a grandmother, or a neighbor who stays home with a toddler of her own. Toni needs a steady attachment figure who will provide good care. The author of the case study reported that a social worker had been assigned to help Toni's mother find a day-care center in her neighborhood. We hope she found one with an adequate number of professional teachers who will provide continuity and support for Toni and her mother.

A Practical Approach for Jacob

Jacob was in more critical condition, psychosocially, than Toni. He may have been understimulated by the nanny who did not speak English; he may have been suffering from a lack of parental attention. All infants need one or two people who are emotionally invested in them from the first days of life, and it is not clear that Jacob had anyone. He did not seem attached at all. Even worse, he was diagnosed as having a pervasive developmental disorder, which sometimes indicates autism or brain damage.

Something had to be done, as his parents eventually realized. Jacob was evaluated at a major teaching hospital and seen by at least 10 experts, none of whom had anything encouraging to say.

Fortunately, Jacob's parents consulted a psychologist who was skilled in helping infants who have emotional problems. Saying "Now I am going to teach you how to play with your son," the psychologist showed them a way to build a relationship with Jacob. They learned about "floor time," four hours a day set aside for them to get on their son's level and interact with him: Imitate him, act as if they are part of the game, put their faces and bodies in front of his, create synchrony even though Jacob did nothing to initiate it.

The father reports:

> We rebuilt Jacob's connection to us and to the world—but on his terms. We were drilled to always follow his lead, to always build on his initiative. In a sense, we could only ask Jacob to join our world if we were willing to enter his. . . . He would drop rocks and we would catch them. He would want to put pennies in a bank and we would block the slot. He would want to run in a circle and we would get in his way. I remember a cold fall day when I was putting lime on our lawn. He dipped his hand in the powder and let it slip through his fingers. He loved the way it felt. I took the lawn spreader and ran to the other part of our yard. He ran after me. I let him have one dip and ran across the yard again. He dipped, I ran, he dipped, I ran. We did this until I could no longer move my arms.

[Jacob's father, 1997]

Response for Day-Care Teachers (from page 188): Reassure her that you will keep her baby safe and will develop the baby's mind and social skills through synchrony and attachment. More important, tell her that the *quality* of mother–infant interaction at home is more essential than anything else for psychosocial development; mothers who are employed full time usually have wonderful, secure relationships with their infant. If need be, you can teach her ways of being a responsive mother.

Jacob's case is obviously extreme, but many infants and parents have difficulty establishing synchrony. From the perspective of early psychosocial development, nothing could be more important than a connection like the one Jacob and his parents established.

> In Jacob's case it worked. He said his first word at age 3, and by age 5, . . . he speaks for days at a time. He talks from the moment he wakes up to the moment he falls asleep, as if he is making up for lost time. He wants to know everything. "How does a live chicken become an eating chicken? Why are microbes so small? Why do policemen wear badges? Why are dinosaurs extinct? What is French? [A question I often ask myself.] Why do ghosts glow in the dark?" He is not satisfied with answers that do not ring true or that do not satisfy his standards of clarity. He will keep on asking until he gets it. Rebecca and I have become expert definition providers. Just last week, we were faced with the ultimate challenge: "Dad," he asked: "Is God real or not?" And then, just to make it a bit more challenging, he added: "How do miracles happen?"
>
> *[Jacob's father, 1997]*

Miracles do not always happen; in fact, infants diagnosed with a pervasive developmental disorder usually require special care from parents and teachers throughout childhood. Nevertheless, the amazing fact is that almost all infants, almost all the time, develop relationships with their close family members. The significance of early psychosocial development is now obvious to every developmentalist and, it is hoped, to every reader of this text.

SUMMARY

Theories About Early Psychosocial Development

1. According to all five major theories, caregiver behavior is especially influential in the first two years of life. Freud stressed the mother's impact on early oral and anal pleasure; Erikson emphasized early trust and autonomy.

2. Behaviorists emphasize learning, with parents serving as their baby's first teachers about various emotions—when to be fearful or joyful, for instance. Cognitive theory holds that infants develop working models based on early experiences.

3. Epigenetic theory recognizes the importance of traits of temperament, genetic traits whose expression is influenced by the environment. Parents can either inhibit or guide a child's temperament.

4. The sociocultural approach notes the impact of both social and cultural factors on parents and the parent–infant relationship.

Emotional Development

5. Two emotions, contentment and distress, appear as soon as an infant is born. Anger emerges when efforts are frustrated, at between 4 to 8 months of age. Although reflexive fear is apparent in very young infants, fear of something specific, including fear of strangers and fear of separation, does not appear until toward the end of the first year.

6. The increasing self-awareness of toddlerhood allows further development of the more social emotions, such as pride and shame.

7. In the second year, increasing social awareness leads to more selective fear, anger, joy, and distress. At that point, toddlers begin to express new emotions that are social in nature, such as jealousy and shame.

The Development of Social Bonds

8. In infancy the social bond between parents and children is expressed in synchrony and attachment.

9. By age 3 months, infants become more responsive and social, and synchrony begins. Synchrony involves moment-by-moment interaction between a baby and an adult. The caregiver needs to be responsive and sensitive, interpreting the infant's signals for play or rest.

10. Attachment is measured by the baby's reaction to the caregiver's presence in or departure from a strange playroom. Some infants seem indifferent (type A—insecure-avoidant) or overly dependent (type C—insecure-resistant/ambivalent), instead of secure (type B). The most worrisome form of attachment is disorganized (type D). Infants with disorganized attachment are likely to develop serious psychological problems later in life.

11. Infants look at other people's facial expressions to detect whether a particular object or experience is frightening or enjoyable, a process called social referencing.

12. Fathers are wonderful playmates for infants, who frequently consult them as social references. Each family is different, but generally mothers are more nurturing and fathers more exciting and more likely to encourage exploration.

13. Day care for infants seems, on the whole, to be a positive experience, especially for cognitive development. Psychosocial characteristics, including secure attachment, are more influenced by the quality of home care than by the number of hours spent in nonmaternal care. Quality of care is crucial, no matter who provides that care.

Conclusions in Theory and Practice

14. Exactly how critical early psychosocial development might be is still debated by experts. However, it is obvious that all infants need caregivers who are committed to them, available for and responsive in play, and dedicated to encouraging each aspect of early development.

KEY TERMS

trust versus mistrust (p. 173)
autonomy versus shame and doubt (p. 173)
working model (p. 174)
temperament (p. 174)
goodness of fit (p. 177)
stranger wariness (p. 178)

separation anxiety (p. 178)
self-awareness (p. 179)
synchrony (p. 180)
attachment (p. 181)
secure (type B) attachment (p. 182)
base for exploration (p. 182)

insecure attachment (p. 182)
insecure-avoidant (type A) attachment (p. 182)
insecure-resistant/ambivalent (type C) attachment (p. 182)
Strange Situation (p. 182)

disorganized (type D) attachment (p. 184)
social referencing (p. 185)
infant day care (p. 188)

APPLICATIONS

1. One cultural factor influencing infant development is the mode in which infants are carried from place to place. Ask four mothers whose infants were born in each of the past four decades how they transported them—front or back carriers, facing out or in, strollers or carriages, car seats or on mother's laps, and so on. Why did they choose the mode(s) they chose? What are their opinions and yours on how that cultural practice might affect infants?

2. Observe synchrony for three minutes. Ideally, ask a parent of an infant under 8 months of age to play with the infant. If small in-

fants are not available, observe a pair of lovers. Note the sequence and timing of every facial expression, noise, or gesture of both partners.

3. Telephone several day-care centers to try to assess the quality of care they provide. Ask about such factors as adult–child ratio, group size, and training for caregivers of children of various ages. Is there a minimum age for acceptance into the program? If so, why was that age chosen? After hearing the answers, analyze them, using Table 7.4 as a guide.

Part II

The First Two Years: Infants and Toddlers

Body, Brain, and Nervous System

Over the first two years, the body quadruples in weight and the brain triples in weight. Connections between brain cells grow into increasingly dense and complex neural networks of dendrites and axons. As neurons become coated with an insulating layer of myelin, they send messages faster and more efficiently. The infant's experiences are essential in "fine-tuning" the brain's ability to respond to stimulation.

Motor Abilities

Brain maturation allows the development of motor skills from reflexes to coordinated voluntary actions, including grasping and walking. At birth, the infant's senses of smell and hearing are quite acute. Vision at first is sharp only for objects that are about 10 inches away; visual acuity approaches 20/20 by age 1.

Health

The health of the infant depends on nutrition (ideally, breast milk), immunization, and parental practices. Survival rates are much higher today than they were even a few decades ago.

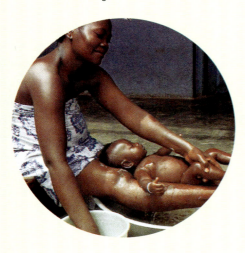

COGNITIVE

Cognition

As Piaget describes it, in sensorimotor intelligence the infant progresses from knowing his or her world through immediate sensorimotor experiences to being able to "experiment" on that world through the use of mental images. Concepts, such as object permanence and deferred imitation, are evident. The infant is most interested in affordances, that is, in what various experiences and events offer him or her. Movement and personal sensory experiences contribute to the perception of affordances as well as to early memory. Active curiosity and inborn abilities interact with various experiences to develop early cognition.

Language

Babies' cries are their first communication; they then progress through cooing and babbling. Interaction with adults through "baby talk" exposes them to the structure of language. By age 1, an infant can usually speak a word or two; by age 2, a toddler is talking in short sentences, displaying an ability that distinguishes humans from all other animals and probably develops through many pathways.

PSYCHOSOCIAL

Emotions and Personality Development

Emotions change from quite basic reactions to complex, self-conscious responses. Infants become increasingly independent, a transition explained by Freud's oral and anal stages, by Erikson's crises of trust versus mistrust and autonomy versus shame and doubt, and by cognitive theory's working models. While these theories emphasize the parents' role, research finds that much of basic temperament—and therefore personality—is inborn and apparent throughout life, as epigenetic theory explains. Sociocultural theory stresses cultural norms, which affect what parents do with their babies.

Parent–Infant Interaction

Early on, parents and infants respond to each other by synchronizing their behavior in social play. Toward the end of the first year, secure attachment between child and parent sets the stage for the child's increasingly independent exploration of the world. The infant becomes an active participant in this social interaction, first in directly reacting to others and then in seeking out opinions through social referencing. Fathers, other relatives, and day-care providers, in addition to mothers, give infants more social confidence.

Part III

The period from age 2 to age 6 is usually called *early childhood,* or the *preschool period.* Here we shall call it the *play years* as well. Play occurs at every age, of course, but the years of early childhood are the most playful of all. It is then that young children spend most of their waking hours at play—creating, laughing, and imagining as they acquire the skills, ideas, and values that are crucial for growing up. They chase each other and attempt new challenges (developing their bodies); they play with sounds, words, and ideas (developing their minds); they invent games and dramatize fantasies (learning social skills and moral rules).

The playfulness of young children can cause them to be delightful, exasperating, or both at once. To them, growing up is a game, and their enthusiasm for it seems unlimited—whether they are quietly tracking a beetle through the grass or riotously turning their bedroom into a shambles. Their minds seem playful, too, for the immaturity of their thinking enables them to explain that "a bald man has a barefoot head" or that "the sun shines so children can go outside to play."

If you expect them to sit quietly, think logically, or act realistically, you are bound to be disappointed. But if you enjoy playfulness, you will enjoy caring for, listening to, and even reading about children between ages 2 and 6.

The Play Years

Chapter Eight

The Play Years:
Biosocial Development

Between ages 2 and 6, significant development occurs on several fronts. The most obvious changes are in size and shape, as chubby toddlers seem to stretch upward, becoming thinner as well as taller. Less obvious but more crucial changes occur in the brain. Maturation turns a clumsy, impulsive 2-year-old into a deft, deliberate 6-year-old.

Rapid growth and active play make young children vulnerable to many biosocial hazards, including injury and abuse. That aspect of early childhood is covered in this chapter as well, to aid not only in the recognition of maltreatment but also in its prevention. There is much that can be done to ensure a happy, pain-free childhood for everyone.

Body and Brain

As in infancy, the young child's body and brain develop according to powerful epigenetic forces—biologically driven and socially guided, both experience-expectant and experience-dependent (see Chapter 5). Nevertheless, early childhood differs markedly from infancy.

Body Shape and Growth Rates

Just looking at a toddling 1-year-old and a cartwheeling 6-year-old makes some of the many changes obvious. During the play years, children generally become slimmer as the lower body lengthens and some baby fat melts away. Gone are the protruding belly, round face, short limbs, and large head that characterize the toddler. By age 6, body proportions are similar to those of an adult.

Steady increases in height and weight accompany these changes in proportions. Each year from ages 2 through 6, well-nourished children add almost 3 inches (about 7 centimeters) in height and gain about 4½ pounds (2 kilograms) in weight. By age 6, the average child in a developed nation weighs about 46 pounds (21 kilograms) and measures 46 inches (117 centimeters). As my nephew said at that point, "In numbers I am square now." These are averages; children vary a great deal, especially in weight. As noted in Chapter 5, percentiles are more useful than norms in monitoring the growth of a particular child (see Appendix A).

Ethnic and Cultural Differences

When many ethnic groups live together in one developed nation (such as England, France, Canada, Australia, or the United States), children of African descent tend to be tallest, followed by Europeans, then Asians, and then Latinos. These are very broad generalities; many individual families exhibit quite different inherited height patterns (Eveleth & Tanner, 1991). Height is particularly variable among children of

African descent, because various groups living on that large continent have developed substantial genetic diversity.

Cultural patterns also have an impact on growth rates. In many South Asian families, males are better fed and cared for. Consequently, girls are not only much shorter and smaller than boys but also more likely to die (their death rate in India is almost twice as high) between ages 1 and 4 (Costello & Manandhar, 2000). By contrast, in many North American families with ample food, mealtimes are family rituals in which children who are polite and quiet earn extra helpings of dessert; in those families, the girls may be too fat.

Many factors influence growth. The three most influential factors, each accounting for several inches of height by the end of childhood, are genes, health, and nutrition. In fact, nutrition is largely responsible for the dramatic differences in height between children in developed and underdeveloped nations. Several other factors also make a difference, including birth order, sex, and geography. Moreover, first-borns, males, and those living in cities at sea level tend to be taller than their opposites.

Genes, health, and malnutrition were covered in Chapter 5. Although under-nutrition continues to be a concern in early childhood, especially in developing nations, we need not repeat the discussion of inadequate protein or calories here. However, when food is abundant, new concerns arise regarding a balanced diet for young children.

Eating Habits

Compared to infants, young children—especially modern children, who play outdoors less than their parents or grandparents did—need far fewer calories per pound of body weight. Appetite decreases between ages 2 and 6, causing many parents to fret, threaten, and cajole ("Eat all your dinner, and you can have ice cream"). However, reduced appetite in early childhood is not a medical problem, unless a child is unusually thin or gains no weight at all. Percentiles indicate whether children are losing or gaining weight compared with their peers; these measures are certainly a better guide to under- or overnourishment than are the leftovers on the dinner plate (Wardley, Puntis, & Taitz, 1997).

Although most children in developed nations consume enough, or more than enough, calories for energy, they do not always obtain adequate minerals or vitamins (Wardley et al., 1997). The major nutritional problem in early childhood is an insufficient intake of iron, zinc, and calcium. Foods containing these crucial minerals get crowded out by other foods. For example, the past 20 years have seen a decline in calcium consumption because at snacktime, milk has been replaced by soda pop or fruit juice (Jahns et al., 2001).

To Each His Own Lifelong food preferences are formed during early childhood, which may be one reason why the two children on the right seem dubious about the contents of the pink lunchbox, broccoli and all. Nevertheless, each of these children appears to be a model of healthful eating.

Sweetened cereals and drinks, advertised as containing 100 percent of a day's vitamin requirements, are a poor substitute for a balanced diet, for two reasons. First, some essential nutrients have not yet been identified. Second, it is easy for a child to consume too much of one nutrient and not enough of another if fortified cereals and juice drinks rather than fresh fruits and vegetables are the mainstays of the diet (Wardley et al., 1997). Indeed, high-calorie foods can cause vitamin or mineral deficiencies if they reduce an already small appetite.

Too much sugar is the leading cause of early tooth decay, the most prevalent disease of young children in developed nations (Lewit & Kerrebrock, 1998). Many cultures promote children's eating of sweets, in the form of birthday cake, holiday candy, Halloween treats, and such. The details (e.g., chocolate Easter bunnies or Hanukkah gelt) depend on family ethnicity and religion, but the general trend is pervasive and hard to resist.

The best tactic parents can use is to offer ample healthy foods when the child is hungry and to cut down on high-calorie snacks. This approach, however, is all too infrequent in the United States, where children typically consume several snacks each day (Jahns et al., 2001).

Brain Development

Brain development begins very early in life, as we described in Chapters 4 and 5. Indeed, by age 2, most pruning, or sculpting, of dendrites has already occurred, as has major brain growth: The 2-year-old brain weighs 75 percent as much as the adult brain.

If most of the brain is already present and functioning by age 2, what remains to develop? The most important parts! Brain weight continues to increase faster than the child's body weight, reaching 90 percent of adult weight by age 5 and almost 100 percent by age 7—when the rest of the child's body still has about 100 pounds (45 kilograms) to gain. More important, those functions of the brain that make us most human are the ones that develop after infancy, enabling quicker, more coordinated, and more reflective thought. Human brain growth after infancy is one crucial difference between humans and other animals.

Speed of Thought

After infancy, continued proliferation of the communication pathways results in some brain growth, but the more life-changing transformations occur because of **myelination,** a process that continues through early adulthood (Sampaio & Truwit, 2001). All the brain's networks become coated with *myelin,* a fatty substance that speeds transmission of nerve impulses between neurons. The added insulation of myelin enables children to think and react much more quickly than toddlers can. This greater speed is apparent with single thoughts—as when children quickly recognize familiar faces or respond to their own names—but becomes pivotal when several thoughts must occur in rapid succession.

With increasing myelination, thoughts follow each other fast enough that children can perform one task and then immediately remember to do the next. They can hear and then speak, catch and then throw a ball, and so on.

Of course, parents of young children must still be patient when listening to them talk, when helping them get dressed, or when watching them try to write their names—all these tasks are completed much more slowly by 3-year-olds than by 13-year-olds. However, young children are certainly quicker than toddlers, who take so long with even the simplest task that they may forget what they were doing before they finish.

Myelination is not essential for basic communication between neurons, but it *is* essential for fast and complex communication. Experience affects the rate of myelination: Practice makes thoughts come more quickly (Merzenich, 2001). Because young infants spend almost all their waking hours looking and listening, the visual and auditory cortexes are among the earliest to become myelinated. During the play years, myelination proceeds most rapidly in the areas of the brain dedicated to memory and reflection.

A 5-year-old, for example, can remember last year, can stop and think, and can act after some contemplation—all of which are impossible for a 1-year-old, who acts on an impulse immediately. Inadequate myelination early in life means

myelination The process by which axons and dendrites become insulated with a coating of myelin, a fatty substance that speeds transmission of nerve impulses from neuron to neuron in the brain.

that a message to one part of the brain is not immediately sent to another part, so that coordinated reflection is impossible.

Connecting the Brain's Hemispheres

One particular part of the brain that grows and myelinates rapidly during the play years is the **corpus callosum**, a band of nerve fibers that connect the left and right sides of the brain (see Figure 8.1). The corpus callosum is "250–800 million fibers that do nothing other than keep the hemispheres coordinated in their processing" (Banich & Heller, 1998, p. 1). As a result of growth in the corpus callosum, communication between the two brain hemispheres becomes markedly more efficient, allowing children to coordinate functions that involve both halves of the brain or body (Banich, 1998).

To understand the significance of this, you need to realize that, although it looks as if the two sides of the body and brain are identical, in many crucial ways they are not. The two sides of the body or brain specialize, so that one side is dominant for a certain function—a process called **lateralization.** You already know that almost everyone is either right-handed or left-handed. But you may not realize that lateralization is also apparent in arms, legs, feet, eyes, ears, and brain. The entire body is divided into two hemispheres, which are not identical.

Such specialization begins before birth and is epigenetic, prompted by genes or prenatal hormones and by early experiences. Sleeping newborns usually turn their heads rightward (or leftward, for those who will be left-handed) and bend their limbs toward one side. As infants lie in their cribs, they face toward one hand, moving it as they watch, gaining dexterity, making that hand more dominant. Thus, experience influences hand preference. Later experience can also make a difference, altering a genetic preference, as happened to millions of children once forced (sometimes with physical punishment) to be right-handed.

Why would anyone force a child to change hand preference? Actually, all societies favor right-handed people. This bias is apparent in language (in Latin, *dexter* [the root for *dexterity*] means "right" and *sinister* [also meaning "evil"] means "left"), in customs, in tools, and in taboos. In many Asian and African nations today, the left hand's only exclusive function is wiping after defecation; it is a major insult to give someone anything or to perform any other observable action with that "dirty" hand. In every nation, tools—scissors, steam irons, faucets, screws—are designed for right-handed people. Thus, well-meaning adults might force children to avoid the social stigma of being left-handed.

Any training of one side of the body or the other is easier in the young, before patterns of lateralization are firmly established (Merzenich, 2001). For this reason, damage to the left side of the brain, where in most people language functions are located, is more serious in adults than in children. When the left side of the brain is entirely gone (as may happen when a major brain tumor is surgically removed), young children often switch language functions to the right side, learning to talk, listen, and read quite well. Interestingly, although such children score in the normal

corpus callosum A long, narrow strip of nerve fibers that connect the left and right hemispheres of the brain.

lateralization Literally, "sidedness," here referring to the differentiation of the two sides of the body so that one side specializes in certain functions. Brain lateralization allows the left side of the brain to control the right side of the body, and vice versa.

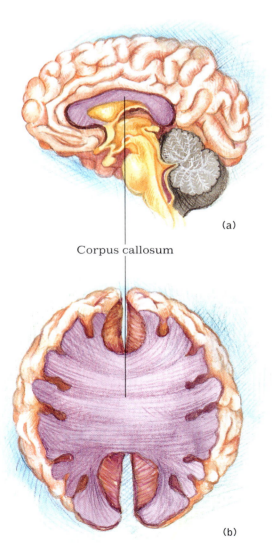

(a)

Corpus callosum

(b)

FIGURE 8.1 Connections Two views of the corpus callosum, a band of nerve fibers (axons) that convey information between the two hemispheres of the brain. When developed, this "connector" allows the person to coordinate functions that are performed mainly by one hemisphere or the other. *(a)* A view from between the hemispheres, looking toward the right side of the brain. *(b)* A view from above, with the gray matter not shown in order to expose the corpus callosum.

range on various tests of language abilities, some subtle deficiencies in fluency indicate that the whole brain is needed for most complex tasks (Stiles, 1998).

Through studies of people with brain damage, neurologists have determined how the brain's hemispheres specialize: The left half of the brain controls the right side of the body and contains the areas dedicated to specific logic, detailed analysis, and the basics of language; the right half controls the left side of the body and generalized emotional and creative impulses, including appreciation of most music, art, and poetry. Thus, the left side notices details and the right side grasps the big picture—a distinction that should provide a clue in interpreting Figure 8.2.

No one (except severely brain-damaged people) is either left-brained or right-brained. Every cognitive skill requires both sides of the brain, just as every important motor skill requires both sides of the body (Efron, 1990; Springer & Deutsch, 1997). Because they do not have a mature corpus callosum, "the hemispheres of young children are more functionally disconnected than those of adults" (Banich, 1998, p. 36), and some behaviors are clumsy, wobbly, and slow. Because older children and adults have myelinated fibers in the corpus callosum that carry faster signals between the two hemispheres, better thinking and quicker action are possible.

FIGURE 8.2 Copy What You See Brain-damaged adults were asked to copy the figure at the left in each row. One person drew the middle set, another the set at the far right.

? *Observational Quiz* (see answer, page 202): Which set was drawn by someone with left-side damage and which set by someone with right-side damage?

Planning and Analyzing

The **prefrontal cortex** is the last part of the human brain to reach maturity. Sometimes called the *frontal cortex* or *frontal lobe,* it is an area in the very front part of the brain's outer layer (the cortex). The prefrontal cortex is crucial for humans, undeveloped in nonhuman primates, and completely absent in rats and other lower animals.

Maturation of the prefrontal cortex occurs gradually and is not complete until mid-adolescence (Bloom et al., 2001). This long process explains many of the changes of early childhood. For example, sleep becomes more regular. Emotions become more nuanced and responsive to particulars of the external world (think of shrieks of joy at a father's tickling but cries of anger when a sibling does the same thing). Temper tantrums subside; uncontrollable tears or laughter are common in toddlers, still apparent by age 5, but rare in adulthood. The frontal lobe "shows the most prolonged period of postnatal development of any region of the human brain" (Johnson, 1998, p. 33), with dendrite density increasing throughout adolescence.

Of course, what the child is able to learn depends on brain maturation. Just imagine a 3-year-old who jumps from task to task, unable to sit still for long, even in church or other settings that require quiet. Impulsiveness is also obvious in a day-care center with many children and toys, where some younger children want to play immediately with whatever toy another child has but are no longer interested by the time that toy becomes available. Advances in prefrontal cortex development occur at about age 3 or 4 (Posner & Rothbart, 2000), making control of impulses more likely and formal education more possible.

Perhaps the example of the jumpy 3-year-old reminded you of a 3-year-old you know who stays in one spot and plays with the same toy for hours. **Perseveration** is the tendency to persevere in, or stick to, one thought or action long after it is time to move on. Some 2-year-olds sing the same song again and again, or scribble the same drawing, or throw a tantrum when their favorite TV show is interrupted. That temper tantrum itself may perseverate, with the child's crying becoming uncontrollable, unstoppable, as if the child is stuck in that emotion until exhaustion sets in. This is one reason the toddler stage is called the "terrible twos": Brain patterns lead children to lose control and to be too impulsive or too perseverative in their emotional expression (Denham, 1998).

prefrontal cortex The area at the front of the cortex of the brain that specializes in the "executive function"—planning, selecting, and coordinating thoughts. (Also called the *frontal lobe* or *frontal cortex*.)

perseveration The tendency to persevere in, or stick to, one thought or action even when it has become useless or inappropriate.

Although impulsiveness and perseveration seem opposites, they are actually two manifestations of the same deficiency—a lack of self-control, appropriate focus, and emotional balance. In other words, they are signs of an undeveloped prefrontal cortex, which characterizes all 2-year-olds and far fewer 5-year-olds. Gradually, children become less likely to bump into walls or each other as they learn to "look before they leap." Both impulsiveness and perseveration are quite normal before the prefrontal cortex has matured, although they are signs of brain damage in older children.

Educational Implications of Brain Development

Most 6-year-olds (and a few 4- and 5-year-olds) are ready to do the following:

- Sit in one place for an hour or so
- Scan a page of print, moving the eyes systematically from left to right (or, for some languages, from top to bottom or right to left), not allowing the eyes to dart around the page
- Balance the sides of the body, enabling skipping, galloping, and kicking or catching balls
- Draw and write with one hand, accurately copying shapes or letters
- Listen and think before talking
- Remember important facts and instructions for more than a few seconds
- Control emotions, with tears, temper, or laughter seldom erupting at the wrong time

!Answer to Observational Quiz (from page 201): The middle set, with its careful details, reflects damage to the right half of the brain, where overall impressions are found. The person with left-brain damage produced the drawings that were just an M or a Δ, without the details of the tiny z's and squares. With a whole functioning brain, people can see both "the forest and the trees."

As you can imagine, experience as well as maturation is crucial to these abilities (Merzenich, 2001). For this reason, children whose family life is extremely stressful or whose emotions are inadequately channeled are severely handicapped in their brains as well as their actions (De Bellis, 2001).

Even for normally developing children, brain development is not smooth and linear; brain functions do not improve at exactly the same age for every child (Fisher, 1997; Haier, 2001). Some 6-year-olds have not yet acquired the neurological maturity expected after years of experience-expectant brain growth, particularly of the corpus callosum and prefrontal cortex. First-grade teachers generally assume normal brain functioning, which allows them to teach children to read, write, add, and so on.

Brain immaturity explains why it is frustrating to try to teach 4-year-olds to read a book, because their eyes and thoughts move around too erratically. Most 3-year-olds can "read" the *M* of a McDonald's sign from a hundred feet away, but the child's brain is not ready to follow a line of print. Running around, not sitting at a desk, is more appropriate for the 3-year-old's body and brain.

Ideally, every section of both sides of the brain develops in proper proportion, and the communication networks throughout allow smooth and rapid coordination among the various parts. Many deficiencies in cognition, peer relationships, emotional control, and classroom learning are directly tied to inadequate lateralization of the brain and to immaturity and asymmetry (an uneven balance) of the frontal cortex.

The signs and consequences of brain abnormalities are discussed in later chapters. The main point to remember here is that the brain provides the foundation for thinking and learning. Any impediment to normal growth of the brain puts all other accomplishments, including academic achievement, on shaky ground, because many connections between neurons and hemispheres are involved in attaining them.

Consider the significance of all the biological changes just described. During the play years, appetite seems to decrease even as children grow taller and proportionately thinner. The brain continues to mature, particularly in the corpus callosum, which connects the left and right sides of the brain and therefore the right and left sides of the body, including the hands, feet, eyes, and ears. Increasing myelination also speeds up actions and reactions.

One part of the brain, the prefrontal cortex, enables impulse control, allowing children to think before they act as well as to stop one action in order to begin another. As impulsiveness and perseveration decrease, and emotional control and concentrated attention increase, children become much better able to learn in school, as shown in the next trio of chapters. Now, in the play years, children use their new size and neurological maturation to practice their motor skills.

Motor Skills and Avoidable Injuries

As bodies grow slimmer, stronger, and less top-heavy, maturation of the prefrontal cortex permits greater impulse control, and the increased myelination of the corpus callosum permits coordination of arms and legs. These developments allow children between 2 and 6 years to move with greater speed and grace. They become more capable of directing and refining their own activity. Physical maturation also makes them more vulnerable to injury, but let's begin by celebrating their new skills.

Gross Motor Skills

Gross motor skills—which, as we saw in Chapter 5, involve large body movements such as running, climbing, jumping, and throwing—improve dramatically. When you watch children play, you see clumsy 2-year-olds who fall down and sometimes bump into stationary objects. But you also see 5-year-olds who are both skilled and graceful. To be specific, most North American 5-year-olds can ride a tricycle; climb a ladder; pump a swing; and throw, catch, and kick a ball. Some can skate, ski, dive, and ride a bicycle—activities that demand balance as well as coordination. In some nations, 5-year-olds swim in ocean waves or climb cliffs that, in other nations, few people of any age would attempt. A combination of brain maturation, motivation, and guided practice makes each of these skills possible.

Generally, children learn motor skills from other children, rather than through adult instruction. According to sociocultural theory, learning from peers is the best way for children to master skills they will need. As long as children have ample time, adequate space, and suitable playmates, their gross motor skills develop as rapidly as their maturation, body size, and innate ability allow. Unfortunately, space, playmates, and free time cannot be taken for granted, especially in large cities. Ideally, every urban block should have a spacious, safe playground designed for young children, but, in reality, buildings predominate.

More Curiosity Than Caution As they master their gross motor skills, children of every social group seem to obey a universal command: "If it can be climbed, climb it." That command is usually heard louder than any words of caution—one reason direct supervision is needed during the play years.

Fine Motor Skills

Fine motor skills, which involve small body movements (especially those of the hands and fingers), are much harder to master than gross motor skills. Pouring juice from a pitcher into a glass, cutting food with a knife and fork, and achieving anything more artful than a scribble with a pencil are difficult for young children, even with great concentration and effort.

The chief difficulty with fine motor skills is simply that young children do not have the necessary muscular control, patience, and judgment—in part because

Especially for Immigrant Parents You and your family eat with chopsticks at home, but you want your children to feel comfortable in Western culture. Should you change your family eating customs?

ROYCE BAIR / MONKMEYER

What Is She Accomplishing? The papier-mâché animals produced by this girl and her preschool classmates are more likely to be mushy and misshapen than artistic. However, the real product is development of eye–hand coordination. With intensive, dedicated practice, fine motor skills are mastered by the school years, when children's artwork is sometimes truly remarkable.

their central nervous system is not yet sufficiently myelinated. Many fine motor skills involve two hands and thus two sides of the brain: The fork stabs the meat while the knife cuts it, one hand steadies the paper while the other writes, and tying shoes, buttoning shirts, pulling on socks, and zipping zippers require two coordinated hands. If "one hand knows not what the other hand does" because of an immature corpus callosum and prefrontal cortex, shoelaces get knotted, paper gets ripped, zippers get stuck, and so on. For many young children, neurological immaturity is compounded by short, stubby fingers; tools (e.g., scissors, pencils, hammers) designed for adults; and some confusion about which hand is dominant. Unless caregivers keep these limitations in mind when selecting utensils, toys, and clothes, frustration and destruction may result.

Artistic Expression

During the play years, children are imaginative, creative, and not yet very self-critical. They love to express themselves, especially if their parents applaud, display their artwork, and otherwise communicate approval. This makes all forms of artistic expression a joy—dancing around the room, building an elaborate block tower, making music by pounding in rhythm, and putting bright marks on shiny paper.

Children's artwork reflects their unique perception and cognition. For that reason, it is better to ask "What is it?" than to guess. For example, researchers asked young children to draw a balloon and, later, a lollipop. Even though the actual drawings were indistinguishable, children were quite insistent as to which was which (Bloom, 2000) (see Figure 8.3).

In every artistic area, gradual maturation of brain and body is apparent. For example, when drawing the human figure, 2- to 3-year-olds usually draw a "tadpole"—a circle for a head with eyes and sometimes a smiling mouth, and then a line or two beneath to indicate the rest of the body. Tadpoles are "strikingly characteristic" of children's art (Cox, 1993); they are drawn univer-

(a)

(b)

(c)

ALL: LAURA DWIGHT

No Ears? Strategically connected circles, lines, and dots are the mainstays of 1- to 6-year-olds' drawings of human figures. However, continuous development of fine motor skills is apparent as time goes on. *(a)* Like 2-year-old Peter, most very young children connect legs to the head, making a "tadpole person." *(b)* The family members that 4-year-old Elizabeth draws are hairless, armless, and unisex—but they all have belly buttons, feet, noses, and big smiles that reach their foreheads. *(c)* By age 5, this boy draws his mother with eyelashes, arms, and fingers.

sally, in all cultures. With time, the dangling lines become legs, and a circle is placed between them to indicate a stomach. By age 5, a torso is added and, after 5, arms and hands (Cox, 1997). Preschoolers enjoy drawing the same picture again and again, just as they repeatedly practice their other motor skills.

Serious Injuries

Except in times of famine, more of the world's children die of accidents than any other cause. Detailed statistics are compiled in the United States, where newborns have about 1 chance in 700 of dying from an unintended injury before age 15—three times the odds of dying of cancer, which is the leading lethal childhood disease (National Center for Health Statistics, 2002). The rate for boys is almost twice that for girls: A boy's odds of dying accidentally before age 15 are about 1 in 500 and a girl's, about 1 in 900.

Worldwide, unintended injuries cause millions of premature deaths each year: Not until age 40 does any disease overtake accidents as a cause of mortality. Accidents occur at every age, but 1- to 4-year-olds have higher rates of serious injuries than do slightly older children, aged 5 to 15.

Age-related trends are also apparent in the particular kinds of accidents. Teenagers and young adults are most often killed in traffic accidents, but this is not true of young children, especially now that car seats are legally required. For children, death is more likely to be caused by some other type of accident: a deadly poison that is gulped down, a fire that burns more than 80 percent of a small body, a fall that shatters a skull, a small object or an amount of water that stops all breath. Drowning, in fact, is the leading cause of death for young children in the dozen or so American states where home swimming pools are common.

For small children, the rate of nonlethal injuries reported by hospitals and doctors is about 400 times the rate of injury-caused deaths. As an example, in the United States in 2001, for every child who choked to death, 110 were treated in hospitals because they swallowed something that obstructed their breathing (*MMWR*, October 25, 2002). At least twice that number choked (usually on a piece of candy or a coin), but the object was coughed out or swallowed without a trip to the emergency room.

Why such high accident rates for such small children? As you read earlier in this chapter, neurological immaturity makes young children unlikely to think things through, so they plunge into dangerous places and activities. Unlike infants, their motor skills allow them to run, leap, scramble, grab, and squeeze in a flash, and their curiosity is boundless. They need protection, but they do not always get it. As one team of experts explains, "Injuries are not unpredictable, unavoidable events. To a large extent, society chooses the injury rates it has" (Christoffel & Gallagher, 1999, p. 10).

How could a society *choose* injury, pain, and lifelong damage for any of its children? Injury prevention is no accident; it is a choice made by parents, by manufacturers, by legislators, and by society as a whole.

To understand this, consider the implications of some commonly used terminology. The word *accident* implies that an injury is a random, unpredictable event, an "act of God." If anyone is to be blamed, the guilty one is a careless parent and an accident-prone child. Using the word *accident* thus allows the general public to feel blameless.

In response, public health experts now refer to **injury control** (or **harm reduction**) not "accident prevention." *Injury control* implies that harm can be minimized if appropriate social controls are in place. Minor "accidents" may occur,

A lollipop

A balloon

The experimenter

The child

FIGURE 8.3 Which Is Which? The child who made these drawings insisted that the one at top left was a lollipop and the one at top right was a balloon (not vice versa), and that the drawing at bottom left was the experimenter and the one at bottom right was the child (not vice versa).

Response for Immigrant Parents (from page 203): Children develop the fine motor skills that they see and practice, so you might want to make sure they get practice using forks, spoons, and knives, whether at home, at preschool, or with friends. Do not abandon chopsticks, however; young children can readily learn several ways of doing things.

injury control/harm reduction The idea that accidents are not random and can be made less harmful with proper control. In practice, this means anticipating, controlling, and preventing dangerous activities.

but the harm can be reduced. Putting controls in place and reducing harm are choices that the general public makes.

Three Levels of Prevention

Prevention and control begin long before any particular child or parent does something foolish or careless. In **primary prevention**, the overall background situation is changed to make injuries less likely. Primary prevention fosters conditions that reduce everyone's chance of injury. **Secondary prevention** is more specific, averting harm in high-risk situations in the minutes before it could occur. **Tertiary prevention** occurs after an injury, reducing damage from any particular trauma, saving lives, and preventing permanent disabilities. Let us look at an example incorporating all three levels of prevention.

An Example: Pedestrian Deaths More than 100,000 pedestrians were killed by motor vehicles in the United States between 1980 and 2000, most of them under age 15 or over age 65. *Primary prevention* to reduce pedestrian deaths and injuries would include better sidewalks, fewer cars, slower speeds, pedestrian bridges, wider roads, longer traffic signals, brighter street lights, vision tests before driver's license renewal, fewer drunk drivers, rigorous annual auto inspections, and strengthened law enforcement—in short, any step that would make traffic conditions safer overall.

Secondary prevention reduces the danger of high-risk situations and people. Requiring flashing lights on stopped school buses, employing school-crossing guards, refusing alcohol to teenagers, providing better visibility on curving roads, insisting that children walk with adults—all these are secondary prevention measures because they decrease the chance that a particular child will be killed by a particular driver at a particular spot. As you can see, the distinction between primary prevention and secondary prevention is not clear-cut. In general, secondary prevention is more targeted, focusing on specific risk groups (e.g., young children) and proven dangers (e.g., walking to school) rather than on the overall culture, politics, or economy.

Finally, *tertiary prevention* reduces damage after impact. For pedestrians, tertiary prevention includes laws against hit-and-run driving, speedy and well-trained ambulance drivers, emergency room procedures that reduce brain swelling, and effective rehabilitation techniques. If an injured person gets to an emergency room within the "golden hour" after a crash, the chances of recovery are much better. Yet too often inefficiency, along with shock and guilt, uses up that hour (Christoffel & Gallagher, 1999).

Many measures at all three levels have been instituted in the United States in the past 20 years, with very good results. The number of pedestrian deaths decreased from more than 8,000 in 1980 to about 5,000 in 2002 (U.S. Bureau of the Census, 2002). Similar trends are apparent in almost every nation, although the specifics differ.

Parents, Education, and Protection

Consider the relationship between income and injury. The poorest countries have the highest childhood mortality, not only from disease but also from "accidents" (Mohan, 2000). Within nations, the same differences are apparent. A fatal home fire is six times more likely to occur in low-income neighborhoods than in high-income communities in the United States (Christoffel & Gallagher, 1999), and in Canada the poorest children are six times more likely to be injured than the richest (Macpherson et al., 1998).

Both prevention and protection are needed. On the societal level, public health advocates believe that laws that apply to everyone are more effective than educational efforts that assume that people are ready to learn and willing to change. "Too often, we design our physical environment for smart people

primary prevention Actions that change overall background conditions to prevent some unwanted event or circumstance, such as injury, disease, or abuse.

secondary prevention Actions that avert harm in the immediate situation, such as stopping a car before it hits a pedestrian.

tertiary prevention Actions that are taken after an adverse event occurs, aimed at reducing the harm or preventing disability. Immediate and effective medical treatment of illness or injury is tertiary prevention.

Especially for Urban Planners Describe a neighborhood park that would benefit a community, including its young children.

Protective Settings In order for parents to safeguard their children from injury, they need to become aware of hazards and then take whatever action is necessary to prevent accidents. In two of these photos, the parents are to be commended: The mother in *(b)* probably has been securing her child in a safety seat from infancy. The parents of the child in *(c)* not only put a helmet on their skater but protected his knees, wrists, elbows, and hands as well. However, the boy in *(a)* may be in danger, depending on the kind of surface that is under him.

who are highly motivated" (Baker, 2000), whereas in real life, everyone has moments of foolish indifference. At those moments, automatic safety measures save lives. On the familial level, parents need to anticipate problems and supervise adequately.

The data make it obvious that even the middle-class preschooler in the wealthiest nation is at risk. I know this from personal experience. Our first child, Bethany, at age 2 found, opened, and swallowed most of a bottle of baby aspirin. Where was I? Nursing our second child and watching television a few feet away (foolish indifference). What prevented serious injury? Laws limiting the number of baby aspirin per container (primary prevention) and my earlier purchase of syrup of ipecac, which makes children throw up swallowed poison (tertiary prevention).

Changing Policy

Fences All Around the Pool

Only half as many 1- to 5-year-olds in the United States were fatally injured in 2000 compared with 20 years earlier, thanks to laws about poisons, fires, and cars. However, safety laws are difficult to write, pass, and enforce. Consider the experience of one Australian city, Brisbane, that had no law requiring private swimming pools to be fenced in: Brisbane had nine times as many child drownings as Canberra, another Australian city that did have such a law. The need for

Safe and Happy? The type of pool fence shown here—with a locked gate and bars that are too high to climb and too closely spaced to be squeezed through—should be legally required everywhere to prevent accidental drownings.

? *Observational Quiz* (see answer, page 208): Can you identify at least three dangers that could lurk in this apparently safe situation?

legislation seemed obvious (Baker, 2000). A law was written in 1978, requiring that every swimming pool in Brisbane be surrounded on all four sides by a high fence whose gate had a self-locking latch. Objections involving fencing costs, private property, parental responsibility, and community aesthetics stalled the bill until 1990 and led to poor enforcement. Then a 3-year-old drowned in a motel pool that had no self-locking gate. That death finally brought community outrage and police action (Nixon, 2000).

Even when laws are passed, faulty assumptions can thwart prevention. In southern California, a pool-fencing ordinance passed with one small modification: The fourth side of the pool enclosure could be the wall of a house, with a door that could lock. Child drownings did not decline, partly because children could enter their families' swimming pools through that door (Morgenstern et al., 2000). Parents and legislators protected trespassing children but evidently did not realize that the family's own children might drown.

!Answer to Observational Quiz (from page 207): (1) The fence may not surround all four sides of the pool area. (2) The child's sunglasses may not be shatterproof. (3) The sunglasses may not provide effective protection from the sun's ultraviolet rays. (4) The toy car tempts the young driver to venture onto the street.

Response for Urban Planners (from page 206): The adult idea of a park—a large, grassy open place—is not best for young children, and they are the ones who need parks most. For them, you would design an enclosed area, small enough and with adequate seating to allow caregivers to socialize while watching their children. The playground surface would need to be protective (because young children are clumsy), and equipment that encourages both gross motor skills (such as climbing) and fine motor skills (such as a large sandbox) would be useful. Swings are not very beneficial, because they do not develop many motor skills. Teenagers and dogs should play elsewhere.

Preschool children practice all their motor skills with diligence and enthusiasm, not only gross motor skills such as running and climbing but also the fine motor skills needed for getting dressed or drawing pictures. As they move with more speed and agility, they also encounter new dangers, becoming seriously injured more often than slightly older children. Three levels of prevention are needed: primary, secondary, and tertiary. For example, laws and practices should protect everyone (primary prevention), adult supervision should guard against each mishap (secondary prevention), and medical treatment should be quick and effective when injury occurs (tertiary prevention). With a little encouragement and guidance, children develop almost every motor skill; with a little care and protection, they can do so with only minor scrapes and bruises.

Child Maltreatment

Throughout this chapter and elsewhere in this text, we have assumed that parents naturally want to foster their children's development and protect them from every danger. Yet daily, it seems, reporters describe shocking incidents of parents who harm their offspring. Tragic though these incidents are, they distract attention from other, far more typical incidents, and our emotional reaction to the extremes obscures the lessons we need to learn (Larner et al., 1998). Such lessons begin with an understanding of what abuse is.

Changing Definitions of Maltreatment

Until about 1960, child maltreatment was thought of as obvious physical assault resulting from a rare outburst of a mentally disturbed person, typically someone the family did not know. Today we know that maltreatment is neither rare nor sudden, and almost all the perpetrators are the child's own parents or immediate relatives (U.S. Department of Health and Human Services, 2001).

child maltreatment All intentional harm to, or avoidable endangerment of, anyone under 18 years of age.

child abuse Deliberate action that is harmful to a child's physical, emotional, or sexual well-being.

child neglect Failure to meet a child's basic physical, educational, or emotional needs.

With this recognition came a broader definition: **Child maltreatment** includes all intentional harm to, or avoidable endangerment of, anyone under 18 years of age. Thus, child maltreatment includes both **child abuse**—deliberate action that is harmful to the child's physical, emotional, or sexual well-being—and **child neglect**—failure to appropriately meet a child's basic physical or emotional needs. Note that abuse is deliberate, inflicted with the intention of doing harm, which is one reason it is so hurtful. When the abuser is a parent, the young child realizes that harm comes from a person who should provide protection and love. When one parent is abusive, the other parent is neglectful if he or she does not intervene to protect the child. (Sexual abuse is discussed in Chapter 14.)

Compared to physical abuse, neglect is twice as common and can be even more damaging (Garbarino & Collins, 1999). The first sign of neglect is typically a lack of normal growth, such as lack of language, play, or laughter at age 1. One specific sign of neglect is called **failure to thrive**; it becomes apparent when an otherwise healthy infant or young child gains no weight. Typically, the mother explains that the child refuses to eat, but if hospitalization produces rapid weight gain, nonorganic failure to thrive is confirmed.

Another sign of maltreatment is *hypervigilance,* or excessive watchfulness: A child seems unable to concentrate on anything because he or she is always nervously looking around. Hypervigilance can signify abuse if children are routinely hit for no reason, but it is also a sign of neglect if children often witness frightening events (Dutton, 2000; Kerig et al., 2002). The event most often witnessed is their father beating up their mother.

A comparison has been made between children who grow up in abusive homes and soldiers thrust into unpredictable battle. Many maltreated children are hyperactive and hypervigilant, startled at any noise, quick to counterattack for an imagined insult, confused between fantasy and reality. These are all symptoms of **post-traumatic stress disorder (PTSD)**, a syndrome that was first described in combat veterans but is also apparent in some abused children (De Bellis, 2001; Dutton, 2000). Children can also suffer from *medical neglect,* when a life-threatening illness is not treated (Dubowitz, 1999), or from *educational neglect,* when an older child receives no schooling (Gelles, 1999).

Reported maltreatment cases are those about which the authorities have been informed; **substantiated maltreatment** cases are those that have been investigated and verified (see Figures 8.4 and 8.5). Since 1993, the number of *reported* cases of maltreatment in the United States has been about 3 million a year, and the number of *substantiated* cases has been not quite 1 million, an annual

MISHAWAKA POLICE DEPARTMENT / GETTY IMAGES

Nobody Watching? Madelyn Gorman Toogood looks around to make sure no one is watching before she slaps and shakes her 4-year-old daughter, Martha, who is in a car seat inside the vehicle. A security camera recorded this incident in an Indiana department store parking lot. A week later, after the videotape was repeatedly broadcast nationwide, Toogood was recognized and arrested. The haunting question is: How much child abuse takes place that is not witnessed?

failure to thrive A situation in which an infant or young child gains little or no weight, despite apparently normal health.

post-traumatic stress disorder (PTSD) A syndrome in which a victim or witness of a trauma or shock has lingering symptoms, which may include hyperactivity and hypervigilance, displaced anger, sleeplessness, sudden terror or anxiety, and confusion between fantasy and reality.

reported maltreatment Maltreatment about which the police, child welfare agency, or other authorities have been officially notified.

substantiated maltreatment Maltreatment that has been reported, investigated, and verified.

INGE KING

Cultural Differences This baby waits outside alone while his mother eats sweets in the café.

? *Observational Quiz* (see answer, page 210): What signs indicate that this is maltreatment?

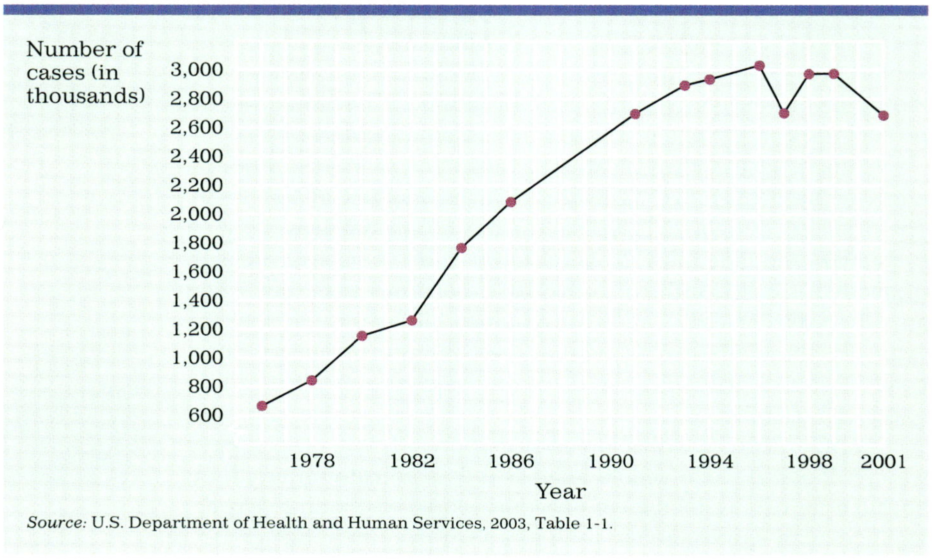

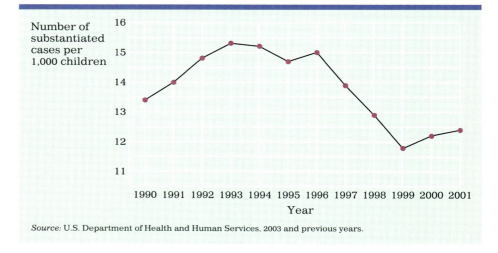

FIGURE 8.4 **Reported Cases of Child Maltreatment, United States, 1976–2001**
After doubling in the 1970s and doubling again in the 1980s, the number of children reported as maltreated has declined somewhat. What explanations are possible for this pattern?

FIGURE 8.5 **Rates of Substantiated Child Maltreatment, United States, 1990–2001**
The number of substantiated cases of child maltreatment in the United States is too high, but there is some good news: The rate has declined significantly from the peak in 1993.

? *Observational Quiz* (see answer, page 212): The dot for 1999 is close to the bottom of the graph. Does that mean it is close to zero?

! *Answer to Observational Quiz* (from page 209): None! The baby is obviously well cared for, with a hat to protect him from the sun, warm and colorful socks, and a chance to experience the fresh air and the view. If you thought this was neglect, you need to note from the sign that this café is in Germany, where toddlers are often parked in carriages or strollers outside restaurants without injury, kidnapping, or any other distress. (A Danish mother did the same thing in New York City in 1997. She was arrested and jailed, and her baby was put in temporary foster care—a response that could itself be considered maltreatment.)

rate of 1 child in every 70. This 3-to-1 ratio of reported to substantiated cases is attributable to three factors:

- A particular case may be reported many times but will be tallied as only one substantiated case because it involves just one child.
- For a case to be substantiated, investigators must find some proof—usually visible, unmistakable injuries; malnutrition; or credible witnesses.
- The report may be mistaken or even deliberately misleading.

In many nations, any professional who comes in contact with a child who may be maltreated is legally required to report it to the authorities. These laws (passed in the United States in the early 1980s) may be the reason why reports of maltreatment have increased while the number of substantiated cases has leveled off.

It is just as important for those who care about children to spot and report the signs of neglect as it is to spot evidence of physical abuse. Most children who experience one form of maltreatment suffer others as well, over a long period of time. Noticing and halting one episode will stop many more, not only for that child but probably for brothers and sisters as well. Many hospital workers and police officers are now trained to distinguish forms of maltreatment and to respond appropriately.

A Case to Study

The Neglect of Neglect: A 2-Year-Old Boy

Three million reported cases of maltreatment per year are a lot. However, many more cases, especially of neglect, are not reported. Consider the following case involving a small child in a low-income family:

> B. V., a 2-year-old male, was found lying face down in the bathtub by an 8-year-old sent to check on him. He had been placed in the bathtub by his mother, who then went to the kitchen and was absent for approximately 10 minutes. B. V. was transported by ambulance to a local hospital. He was unresponsive and had a rectal temperature of 90 degrees Fahrenheit. After medical treatment, the child's breathing resumed, and he was transported to a tertiary care hospital. B. V. remained in the pediatric intensive care unit for 9 days with minimal brain function and no response to any stimuli. He was then transferred to a standard hospital room where he died 2 days later. The mother refused to have an autopsy performed. Subsequently, the death certificate was signed by an attending physician, and cause of death was pneumonia with anoxic brain injury as a result of near-drowning.
>
> The CPS [Child Protective Services] worker advised B. V.'s mother that 10 minutes was too long to leave a 2-year-old in the bathtub unsupervised. B. V.'s mother replied that she had done it many times before and that nothing had happened. Further examination of the medical chart revealed that prior to B. V.'s death, he had a sibling who had experienced an apparent life-threatening event (previously termed a "near miss" sudden infant death syndrome). The sibling was placed on cardiac and apnea (breathing) monitors for 7 to 8 months. In addition, B. V. had been to the children's hospital approximately 2 weeks prior for a major injury to his big toe. B. V.'s toe had been severed and required numerous stitches. The mother stated that this incident was a result of the 4-year-old brother slamming the door on B. V.'s foot. Furthermore, B. V. had been seen in a different local hospital for a finger fracture the month before his death. None of the available reports indicate the mother's history of how the finger fracture occurred.
>
> [Bonner et al., 1999, pp. 165–166]

No charges were filed in the death of B. V. The team who reported this case explain:

> This case illustrates chronic supervisory neglect but also shows that a child's death can occur in a short period of time. The mother's self-reported practice of leaving the child in the bathtub unsupervised is an example of a pattern of chronic failure to supervise in a manner appropriate for the age and development of the child. Also note that the series of suspicious events that preceded the death did not result in protective or preventive services for the family.
>
> [Bonner et al., 1999, p. 166]

Who Is to Blame? This note was left at a makeshift memorial outside the Texas home where Andrea Yates drowned her five children. It attests to the possibility that some parents, overwhelmed by their children's needs and demands, will become negligent or abusive; sometimes the child's death is the outcome. In the Yates case, the pressures of caring for five young children were increased by the mother's long-standing mental illness. Vigilance by and support from family, friends, and the community at large (members of the clergy, health care providers, and others) might help to prevent some of these tragedies.

This case is chilling. Signs that something was awry in this family—the near-miss SIDS, the fractured finger, the severed toe—were ignored. Not even B. V.'s death resulted in charges against the mother or caused her to acknowledge that she had been neglectful.

There is no mention of the possible emotional trauma suffered by the 8-year-old who found his dying brother or by the 4-year-old who reportedly severed the toddler's toe. These children are also at high risk of maltreatment. Indeed, the most serious injury to a child's mental health is caused not by abuse itself but by chronic feelings of helplessness and danger (De Bellis, 2001). This family is typical of many who are high-risk.

To be specific, physical abuse and all forms of neglect fall most heavily on children under age 6 who face the following circumstances:

- Three or more siblings
- An unemployed or absent father
- A mother who did not complete high school
- A home in a poor, high-crime neighborhood

All these factors signify poverty and lead to greater poverty, and all were present in B. V.'s case. Further, B. V.'s medical care is typical for low-income children, who are taken to various hospital emergency rooms and

DAVID J. PHILLIP / AP / WIDE WORLD PHOTOS

treated by overworked staff who know nothing about the family. If B. V. had had a private pediatrician, the maltreatment would probably have been noticed and addressed. If he were the much-wanted, only child of two devoted parents, it is more likely that someone would have been watching him in the tub and would have rescued him as soon as his face was submerged. Instead, he died.

Consequences of Maltreatment

What if maltreatment is not spotted early in a child's life, reported, and stopped? Every aspect of a maltreated child's development is impaired, especially education and social skills.

Brain Damage and Consequences for Learning

Maltreated children have difficulty learning not only because they are less likely to be taught, guided, encouraged, or even talked to but also because they may develop brain patterns that make learning difficult. The most serious pattern is **shaken baby syndrome,** which results when infants are held by the shoulders and shaken back and forth, sharply and quickly, to stop their crying. Sometimes the neck breaks, but even if not, ruptured blood vessels in the brain and broken neural connections lead to severe damage.

shaken baby syndrome A serious condition caused by maltreatment involving shaking a crying infant back and forth, sharply and quickly. Severe brain damage results from internal hemorrhaging and broken neural connections.

Another form of brain damage can occur in a child who is often terrorized or despondent. As one team of authors explains:

> Exceptionally large quantities of stress hormones and neurotransmitters may be released during the trauma, which lead to high levels of activation of the sympathetic nervous system. This may cause the brain to enter a very different biochemical state than is usually the case when ordinary experiences are encoded into memory.

[Macfie et al., 2001, p. 234]

As a result of such abnormal brain development, memory may be impaired and logical thinking delayed until long past 6 years, the age at which the prefrontal cortex should mature (Teicher, 2002).

Another brain disorder occurs in children who are neglected because their mothers are clinically depressed, unable to provide the encouragement and emotional guidance that young children need. In these children the right side of the prefrontal cortex develops more than the left. As a result, negative emotions (fear, sadness, anxiety) dominate and depression becomes more likely (Dawson & Ashman, 2000). Depressed children, like stressed children, have difficulty learning. Of course, there are genetic explanations for the link between depressed mothers and depressed children, but early-childhood neglect seems a potent influence as well.

Even without damage to blood vessels or nerve connections in the brain, abuse disrupts learning in other ways. At the simplest level is nourishment: As you remember from Chapter 5, long-term malnutrition impedes brain growth. Many neglected infants are underfed; many neglected preschoolers eat few healthy foods (Wachs, 2000).

Impaired Social Skills

! *Answer to Observational Quiz* (from page 210): No. The number is actually 11.8. Note the little squiggle on the graph's vertical axis below the number 11. This means that many numbers between zero and 11 are not shown.

Although intellectual and academic handicaps are substantial, deficits are even more apparent in maltreated children's social skills. They tend to regard other people as hostile and exploitative, and hence they are less friendly, more aggressive, and more isolated than other children. The longer their abuse continues and the earlier it started, the worse are their relationships with peers (Bolger et al., 1998).

A maltreated child is likely to be a difficult member of any group, often a bully or a victim or both. As adolescents and adults, people who were severely maltreated in childhood (either physically or emotionally) often use drugs or alcohol to numb their emotions, choose unsupportive relationships, become victims or aggressors, sabotage their own careers, eat too much or too little, and generally engage in self-destructive behavior (Crittenden et al., 1994; Wolfe et al., 1998).

Three Levels of Prevention, Again

Just as with injury control, there are three levels of prevention of child maltreatment. The ultimate goal of child-care policy is to keep all maltreatment from ever beginning. This is called *primary prevention* because it must occur before the problem starts. Stable neighborhoods, family cohesion, income equality, and measures that decrease financial instability, family isolation, and teenage parenthood are all examples of primary prevention; their nature and impact are described in every chapter of this book.

Secondary prevention involves spotting warning signs and intervening to keep a problematic situation from getting worse. For example, insecure attachment, especially of the disorganized type, is a sign of a disrupted parent–child relationship. Slow weight gain, late language development, poor emotional regulation, and unusual play patterns are some other troubling signs. Secondary prevention includes measures such as home visits by a social worker, high-quality day care, and preventive medical treatment—all designed to help high-risk families.

Obviously, secondary prevention is tricky. Efforts to identify problem families might increase the risks, not reduce them. A systems approach (first described in Chapter 1) is needed, because "many of the most effective solutions to social problems are not readily apparent and may even be counterintuitive. . . . Any single action may reverberate and produce . . . unintended consequences" (Garbarino & Collins, 1999, p. 4).

Reformers must consider the overall context and specific conditions, and then must use scientific methods to evaluate the results of any program (Thompson & Nelson, 2001). For instance, one program providing social support to depressed mothers was found to be worse than no intervention at all, perhaps because the intervention made the mothers feel even more inadequate (National Research Council and Institute of Medicine, 2000). Clearly, secondary prevention should adhere to the following guidelines:

- It must not stigmatize certain families as inadequate.
- It must not undermine atypical family or cultural patterns that actually nurture children.
- It must not create a sense of helplessness in the family, leading them to rely on outsiders rather than strengthening their confidence, skills, and resources.

Even more complex than secondary prevention is *tertiary prevention*— intervention to reduce the harm done by actual abuse—which sometimes comes too late. If a case of maltreatment has been substantiated, the first priority is to protect the child by planning for long-term care. Such permanency planning may mean setting goals and a timetable for improvement that the parents must meet or finding a foster or adoptive home that will nurture the child until adulthood.

In contemporary society, **foster care** generally means a legally sanctioned, publicly supported arrangement in which children are officially removed from their parents' custody and entrusted to another adult or family who is paid to nurture them. About 600,000 children in the United States are in foster care, a number that has risen over the past decade (U.S. Department of Health and Human Services, 2001). About half are from minority groups, almost all of them are from low-income families, and many of them have multiple physical, intellectual, and

JOAN LEBOLD COHEN / PHOTO RESEARCHERS, INC.

Intergenerational Bonding Devoted grandfathers, such as this one in Su Zhou, China, prevent the social isolation that is a prerequisite for serious abuse. Can you imagine this man's response if he thought his granddaughter was underfed, overdisciplined, or unloved?

Especially for the General Public You are asked to give a donation to support a billboard campaign against child abuse. You plan to make $100 in charitable contributions this year. How much of this total should you contribute to the billboard campaign?

foster care A legally sanctioned, publicly supported plan that transfers care of maltreated children from parents to someone else.

STEPHANIE MAZE/CORBIS

Tertiary Prevention Particularly for 9-year-old Leah, clinging to her mother, adoption has been her salvation. The mother, Joan, has five adopted children. Adoption is generally better than foster care for maltreated children, because it is a permanent, stable arrangement.

kinship care A form of foster care in which a relative of the maltreated child becomes the approved caregiver.

Response for the General Public (from page 213): Maybe nothing. Educational campaigns rarely change people's habits and thoughts, unless they have never thought about an issue at all. If you want to help prevent child abuse and neglect, you might offer free babysitting to parents you know who seem overwhelmed by their child-care responsibilities but who have little money for babysitters.

emotional problems—partly because intervention came too late. At present, about 200,000 new placements are needed each year (Curtis et al., 1999). **Kinship care,** in which a relative of the maltreated child becomes the approved caregiver, is used for about one-fourth of all foster children in the United States (U.S. Department of Health and Human Services, 2001). Generally, children fare as well in kinship care as in the homes of strangers if the kin receive the same screening, supervision, and support as other foster parents (Berrick, 1998).

Adoption is the final choice. It is the preferred option when parents are incompetent and children are young. This solution is a permanent commitment and therefore is usually better for the child. However, judges and biological parents must release children for legal adoption, and often they are reluctant to do so.

Theory and research in human development suggest that abuse-prevention programs should be broad enough to involve the entire social context. We know that poverty, youth, drug abuse, isolation, and ignorance tend to correlate with unwanted births, inadequate parenting, and injury and maltreatment of children. Primary prevention may be the most cost-effective approach after all.

Although every culture seeks to protect children, and we need to differentiate between what is destructive and what is merely culturally different, serious maltreatment occurs in every nation. About a million children a year in the United States are substantiated as victims of abuse or neglect. Most abusers are the child's own parents, which makes the psychic consequences worse. Children who have been mistreated are often unusually quiet and withdrawn or unusually aggressive. Neglect is more common than abuse and potentially even more harmful to development. Stopping maltreatment of all kinds is urgent but complex, because the source is often the family system, not a deranged stranger. Ideally, abuse and neglect should be reported as soon as they occur, and families should receive immediate help and guidance. Sometimes foster care, either with a relative or with an unrelated family, is better for the child. Primary prevention includes changing the social context so all parents protect and love their children. This is expensive but may be cost-effective over the long term. Secondary prevention focuses on families at high risk—the poor, the drug-addicted, the overwhelmed. In tertiary prevention, the abused child is rescued before further damage occurs.

SUMMARY

Body and Brain

1. Children continue to gain weight and height during early childhood. Generally, they become thinner and more active.

2. Height and weight variations are caused primarily by genes in developed nations and by nutrition when children from various parts of the world are compared. Many children have unbalanced diets, eating more fat and sugar and less iron and calcium than they need.

3. The brain reaches adult size by age 7. Myelination speeds messages from one part of the brain to another. This enables more reflective, coordinated thought and memory, as well as quicker responses.

4. With better myelination, various parts of the brain can specialize. Some functions occur more on the left side of the brain, with the right hemisphere specializing in other functions. The corpus callosum connects the two sides of the brain; about 500 million nerve fibers carry messages back and forth.

5. Maturation of the prefrontal cortex, the executive area of the brain, is the final neurological development. The ability to plan ahead and control impulses makes formal education possible and enables children to regulate their emotions.

Motor Skills and Avoidable Injuries

6. Gross motor skills continue to develop, so that clumsy 2-year-olds become 5-year-olds able to move their bodies in whatever ways their culture values and they themselves have practiced. Muscular control, practice, and brain maturation are also involved in the development of fine motor skills.

7. Accidents are by far the leading cause of death for children and young adults, with 1- to 4-year-olds, boys, and low-income children more likely to suffer a serious injury or premature death. Biology, culture, and community conditions combine to make these children more vulnerable.

8. Accident prevention and injury control must occur on many levels, including long before and immediately after each harmful incident, with primary, secondary, and tertiary prevention. Laws seem more effective than educational campaigns. Close supervision is required to protect young children from their own eager, impulsive curiosity.

Child Maltreatment

9. Child maltreatment occurs far too often, usually in the form of ongoing abuse and neglect by a child's own parents. Each year about 3 million cases of child maltreatment are reported in the United States, about 1 million of which are substantiated.

10. Brain development, school learning, and social skills are all impeded by ongoing child abuse and neglect. Physical abuse is the most obvious form of maltreatment, but neglect is more common and perhaps more harmful in the long term.

11. Foster care, adoption, and kinship care are necessary and beneficial alternatives to parental care for some mistreated children. Primary and secondary prevention of maltreatment help parents provide adequate care for their children, avoiding the need for tertiary measures.

KEY TERMS

myelination (p. 199)
corpus callosum (p. 200)
lateralization (p. 200)
prefrontal cortex (p. 201)
perseveration (p. 201)
injury control/harm reduction
 (p. 205)

primary prevention (p. 206)
secondary prevention (p. 206)
tertiary prevention (p. 206)
child maltreatment (p. 208)
child abuse (p. 208)
child neglect (p. 208)
failure to thrive (p. 209)

post-traumatic stress disorder
 (PTSD) (p. 209)
reported maltreatment
 (p. 209)
substantiated maltreatment
 (p. 209)

shaken baby syndrome
 (p. 212)
foster care (p. 213)
kinship care (p. 214)

APPLICATIONS

1. Keep a food diary for 24 hours, writing down what you eat, how much, when, how, and why. Then think about nutrition and eating habits in early childhood. Do you see any evidence in yourself of imbalance (e.g., not enough fruits and vegetables, too much sugar or fat, not eating when you are hungry)? Did your food habits originate in early childhood, in adolescence, or at some other time?

2. Go to a playground or other place where young children play. Note the motor skills that the children demonstrate, including abilities and inabilities, and keep track of age and sex. What differences do you see among the children? Does anything surprise you?

3. Ask several parents whether their children were ever injured accidentally. Ask the parent to describe each injury, particularly how it happened. Then analyze whether any primary, secondary, or tertiary preventive laws or practices would have made a difference (e.g., better surfaces in playgrounds, better traffic regulations). What was the response of the parents and the medical community? What percent of the injuries were truly "accidents"—that is, unforeseeable events that could not have been prevented or treated differently?

4. Describe the injuries you yourself have sustained, including injuries that resulted in stitches, broken bones, or scars. Could any of these injuries have been prevented? If so, would the preventive measures have impeded some other aspect of your growth (e.g., self-confidence, peer acceptance, physical skills)?

Chapter Nine

The Play Years:
Cognitive Development

W here do dreams come from? Most 3-year-olds place the source somewhere outside your head (maybe God, or the sky, or your pillow), but 5-year-olds almost always know better (in your mind, inside you) (Woolley & Boerger, 2002).

This is one of hundreds of scientific discoveries about the many aspects of cognition from ages 2 to 6, some of which are described in this chapter. The examples lead to the conclusion that much learning occurs during early childhood. For instance, sometime between ages 3 and 5 children develop a "theory of mind," an understanding of how minds work (as in knowing that dreams do not come from your pillow or knowing how to fool your little brother into letting you play with his toy). One result of these discoveries is a completely new understanding of early schooling. No longer merely "day care," early education is now considered a vital learning experience. As one developmental psychologist explains:

> People often call this the "preschool period," but that's not only a mundane name for a magic time, it's also a misnomer. These three-ish and five-ish years are not a waiting time before school or even a time of preparation for school, but an age stage properly called "early childhood" that has a developmental agenda of its own.
>
> *[Leach, 1997, p. 431]*

The goal of this chapter is to convey that "developmental agenda" by explaining some of the theories and findings on the language explosion, early education, and other aspects of cognitive development. For instance, with proper adult encouragement, the halting, simple sentences of the typical 2-year-old become the nonstop, complex outpourings of a talkative 6-year-old. This chapter describes how such verbal mastery develops. For learning two or more languages, or for understanding that life includes numbers, points of view, and many sequences of simple tasks, the years from 2 to 6 are prime time, perhaps even the best time.

How Children Think: Piaget and Vygotsky

Undeniably, young children's thinking is often magical and self-absorbed. For many years, this aspect of cognition dominated developmentalists' descriptions of early childhood. In this they followed the lead of Jean Piaget, the Swiss developmentalist whose theory was introduced in Chapter 2. Piaget thought young children were severely and inevitably limited by their own perspective. He called their thinking **egocentric** (literally, "self-centered"). The label stuck.

More recent research has highlighted another side of early childhood cognition. Sometimes children *are* attuned to the wishes and emotions of other people. Exactly how children are guided by the social and cultural context that surrounds

egocentrism Piaget's term for a type of centration in which the young child contemplates the world exclusively from his or her personal perspective.

them was stressed by another great developmental theorist, Lev Vygotsky, who was also introduced in Chapter 2. To understand both the egocentrism and the social awareness of early cognition, we consider both Piaget and Vygotsky.

Piaget: Preoperational Thought

Piaget's term for cognitive development between the ages of about 2 and 6 is **preoperational thought.** Until about age 6 or 7, according to Piaget, children cannot yet think *operationally;* that is, they cannot figure out logical ideas because their thinking is limited by what they see at the moment. For instance, they know that their mother is their mother, but they cannot grasp that their mother was once their grandma's baby girl.

In each of Piaget's stages of cognition, children are active learners who develop a mental *structure,* or connected set of assumptions, that aids thought. The structure of sensorimotor thought is built exclusively by senses and motor skills. The preoperational structure is more advanced than the sensorimotor one because it includes language and other aspects of symbolic thought. However, it also includes magical, self-centered imagination and thus has no room for the structures (or operations) of logic.

Obstacles to Logical Operations

Piaget discovered and explained four characteristics of preoperational thought.

Centration is the tendency to focus on one aspect of a situation to the exclusion of all others. Young children may, for example, insist that lions and tigers are not cats because they "center" on the house-pet aspect of the cats they know. Or they may insist that Daddy is a *father,* not a brother, because they center on the role that each family member fills for them.

This second example also illustrates a particular type of centration, called ego-centration, which is better known as egocentrism. The egocentric child contemplates the world exclusively from his or her personal perspective. Thus, children center on their father's relationship to them. As Piaget described it, young children are not necessarily selfish; they would, for example, rush to comfort a tearful parent. But the comfort would come in a decidedly egocentric form, such as a teddy bear or a lollipop. Children offer the lollipop not only because they do not know what comforts adults but also because it hasn't occurred to them that someone else's response might differ from their own. That is egocentrism.

A second characteristic of preoperational thought is its **focus on appearance** to the exclusion of other attributes. A girl given a short haircut might worry that she has turned into a boy. Or upon meeting, say, a tall 4-year-old and a shorter 5-year-old, a child might mistakenly insist that "bigger is older."

Third, preoperational children use **static reasoning,** assuming that the world is unchanging, always in the state in which they currently encounter it. A child might be shocked to see his preschool teacher buying groceries, because the assumption is that the teacher is always a teacher and nothing else. If anything does change, it changes totally and suddenly. When she awakened on her fifth birthday, my daughter Rachel asked, "Am I 5 yet?" Told "yes," she grinned, stretched out her arms, and said, "Look at my 5-year-old hands."

Finally, **irreversibility** means that preoperational thinkers fail to recognize that reversing a process can sometimes restore whatever existed before the process occurred. A 3-year-old who cries because his mother put lettuce on his hamburger might not think to suggest removing the lettuce. Indeed, he might refuse to eat the hamburger even after the lettuce is removed, because he believes that what is done cannot be undone. If his mother takes the "contaminated" hamburger away, secretly removes the lettuce, and then brings back the "new" hamburger, the child might happily eat it.

preoperational thought Piaget's term for cognitive development between the ages of about 2 and 6; characterized by centration (including egocentrism), focus on appearance, static reasoning, and irreversibility.

centration A characteristic of preoperational thought in which the young child focuses on one aspect of a situation to the exclusion of all others.

Four Aspects of Preoperational Thought

1. Centration
2. Focus on appearance
3. Static reasoning
4. Irreversibility

focus on appearance A characteristic of preoperational thought in which the young child ignores all attributes except appearance.

static reasoning A characteristic of preoperational thought in which the young child assumes that the world is unchanging.

irreversibility A characteristic of preoperational thought in which the young child fails to recognize that reversing a process can sometimes restore whatever existed before the transformation occurred.

Tests of Various Types of Conservation

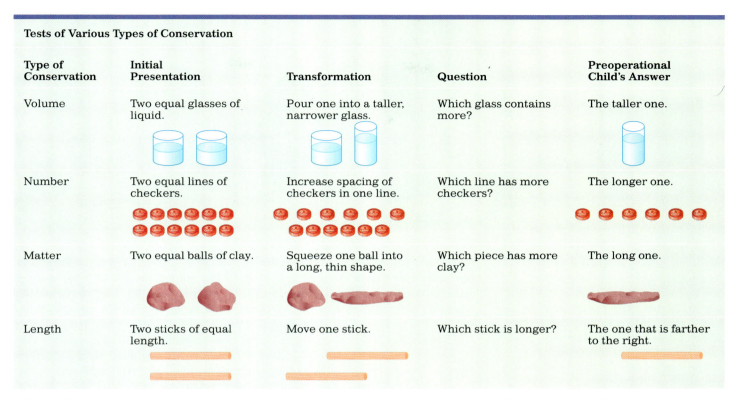

Type of Conservation	Initial Presentation	Transformation	Question	Preoperational Child's Answer
Volume	Two equal glasses of liquid.	Pour one into a taller, narrower glass.	Which glass contains more?	The taller one.
Number	Two equal lines of checkers.	Increase spacing of checkers in one line.	Which line has more checkers?	The longer one.
Matter	Two equal balls of clay.	Squeeze one ball into a long, thin shape.	Which piece has more clay?	The long one.
Length	Two sticks of equal length.	Move one stick.	Which stick is longer?	The one that is farther to the right.

FIGURE 9.1 **Conservation, Please** According to Piaget, until children grasp the concept of conservation at (he believed) about age 6 or 7, they cannot understand that the transformations shown here do not change the total amount of liquid, checkers, clay, and wood.

Conservation and Logic

Piaget devised many experiments to test and illustrate the ways in which these four preoperational characteristics—centration, focus on appearance, static reasoning, and irreversibility—limit young children's ability to reason logically. In several experiments, he studied **conservation,** the principle that the amount of a substance is not affected by changes in its appearance. Piaget found that because of their preoperational thinking, conservation is not at all obvious to young children.

As an example, suppose two identical glasses contain the same amount of liquid. Then the liquid from one of the glasses is poured into a taller, narrower glass. If young children are asked whether one glass contains more liquid than the other, they will insist that the narrower glass, with the higher liquid level, contains more. They make that mistake because they *center* on the liquid's *appearance,* noticing only the immediate *(static)* condition and assuming that it is unchangeable. They seem unaware that they could *reverse* the process and recreate the liquid level they had seen a moment earlier.

Similarly, if an experimenter lines up seven pairs of checkers in two rows of equal length and asks a 4-year-old whether the rows have the same number of checkers, the child will say "yes." But suppose that, as the child watches, the experimenter elongates one of the rows by spacing its checkers farther apart. If the experimenter asks again whether the rows have the same number of checkers, most children will reply "no." Other conservation tasks, shown in Figure 9.1, produce similar results. Children are not logical, at least about conservation, until about age 7.

Notice, however, that Piaget's tests of preoperational cognition depend on the child's words, not actions. Other research finds that even 3-year-olds can distinguish appearance from reality if the test is nonverbal, as when children reach

conservation The principle that the amount of a substance is unaffected by changes in its appearance.

COURTESY OF KATHLEEN BERGER

Demonstration of Conservation

My youngest daughter, Sarah, here at age 5¾, demonstrates Piaget's conservation-of-volume experiment. First, she examines both short glasses to be sure they contain the same amount of milk. Then, after the contents of one are poured into the tall glass and she is asked "Which has more?", she points to the tall glass, just as Piaget would have expected. Later she added, "It looks like it has more because it's taller," indicating that some direct instruction might change her mind.

theory-theory Gopnik's term for the idea that children attempt to construct a theory to explain everything they see and hear.

for objects rather than talk about them (Sapp et al., 2000). Children can remember and report transformations in a gamelike setting, as when a toy puppet, rather than the adult experimenter, does the rearranging. For example, if a "naughty bear" rearranges the checkers, children know that the elongated line still has the same number as before.

Researchers now believe that Piaget underestimated conceptual ability during early childhood, just as he underestimated it during infancy. He designed his experiments to reveal what young children seemed *not* to understand, rather than to identify what they *could* understand. According to Vygotsky (1978), many adults make a similar error: They notice what children cannot do rather than helping them learn what they can.

Vygotsky: Children as Apprentices

Every developmentalist, every preschool teacher, and every parent knows that young children strive to understand the world that fascinates and sometimes confuses them. People naturally want explanations. Thus, one theory of human cognitive development is that people develop theories. One researcher even coined the term **theory-theory,** stressing that children attempt to construct a theory to explain everything they see and hear:

> More than any animal, we search for causal regularities in the world around us. We are perpetually driven to look for deeper explanations of our experience, and broader and more reliable predictions about it. . . . Children seem, quite literally, to be born with . . . the desire to understand the world and the desire to discover how to behave in it.
>
> *[Gopnik, 2001, p. 66]*

Thus, according to theory-theory, the best conceptualization of, and explanation for, mental processes is that humans always seek reasons, causes, and underlying principles. Although theory-theory is not universally accepted, no one doubts that children are active thinkers, not passive ones; they are agents reacting to perceptions, not passive recipients of sensations (Bloom & Tinker, 2001; Brandtstädter, 1998).

Vygotsky was the first leading developmentalist to emphasize a related point: Children do not strive alone; their efforts are embedded in a social context. They ask questions—about how machines work, why weather changes, where the sky ends—assuming that others know the answers. In response, those who care about children do more than just answer. They actively guide a young child's cognitive growth in numerous ways:

- Presenting challenges for new learning
- Offering assistance with tasks that may be too difficult
- Providing instruction
- Encouraging the child's interest and motivation

In many ways, then, a young child is an **apprentice in thinking** whose intellectual growth is stimulated and directed by older and more skilled members of society. In the most developed nations, with families of one or two children, parents and child-care providers are the most common teachers; in less developed nations, older siblings often play a particularly important educational role (Maynard, 2002; Rogoff, 1990). With the help of these mentors, children learn to think by means of their **guided participation** in social experiences and in explorations of their universe.

The reality that children are curious about everything, and that they then learn and remember as much as they do, is evidence of their cognitive ability. Ability to learn indicates intelligence. In fact, "What children can do with the assistance of others might be in some sense even more indicative of their mental development than what they can do alone" (Vygotsky, 1978, p. 5).

Guided Participation Through shared social activity, adults in every culture guide the development of their children's cognition, values, and skills. Typically, the child's curiosity and interests, rather than the adult's planning for some sort of future need, motivate the process. That seems to be the case as this Guatemalan girl eagerly tries to learn her mother's sewing skills.

How to Solve a Puzzle

To see how Vygotsky's approach works in practical terms, let's look at an example. Suppose a child tries to assemble a jigsaw puzzle, fails, and stops trying. Does that mean the task is beyond the child's ability? Not necessarily. What would happen if the child had help?

An adult or older child might begin by praising the child for choosing a hard puzzle and then might encourage the child to look for a particular missing piece ("Does it need to be a big piece or a little piece?" "Do you see any blue pieces with a line of red?"). Suppose the child finds some pieces of the right size that are blue with a red line but still seems stymied. The tutor might become more directive, selecting a piece to be tried next, or rotating a piece so that its proper location is obvious, or actually putting a piece in place with a smile of satisfaction. Throughout, the tutor would praise successes, maintain enthusiasm, and help the child recognize that together they are progressing toward the goal of finishing the puzzle.

The crucial element in guided participation is that the two partners interact to accomplish the task, with the tutor sensitive and responsive to the precise needs of the child. Eventually, as a result of such mutuality, the child will be able to succeed independently—the ultimate goal of Vygotsky's "apprenticeship in thinking."

apprentice in thinking Vygotsky's term for the young child whose intellectual growth is stimulated and directed by older and more skilled members of society.

guided participation The process by which young children, with the help of mentors, learn to think by having social experiences and by exploring their universe.

Scaffolding

As you saw in Chapter 2, Vygotsky believed that for each developing individual, there is a **zone of proximal development (ZPD)**, that is, a range of skills that the person can perform with assistance but cannot quite perform independently. How and when children master their potential skills depends, in part, on the willingness of others to provide **scaffolding**, or sensitive structuring, of children's participation in learning encounters. Most caregivers do this, at least to some extent (Conner et al., 1997; Rogoff, 1998). For example, a study of adults reading to 3-year-olds found very sensitive scaffolding—explaining, pointing, listening—toward the zone of proximal development in response to the child's needs at the moment (Danis et al., 2000).

zone of proximal development (ZPD) Vygotsky's term for a range of skills that a person can exercise with assistance but is not quite able to perform independently.

scaffolding A sensitive structuring of the young child's participation in learning encounters.

Another study, this one of siblings, found 8-year-old Tonik teaching 2-year-old Katal to wash a doll by demonstrating, encouraging, and ending the lesson. After several minutes of demonstrating and describing, Tonik continues the lesson:

> **Tonik:** Pour it like this. *(Demonstrates)*
> **Tonik:** Sister, pour it. *(Hands glass)*
> **Tonik:** Look! Pour it.
> **Katal:** *(Pours, with some difficulty)*
> **Tonik:** Like that. *(Approval)*
> **Katal:** *(Looks away)*
> **Tonik:** It's finished now.
>
> *[Maynard, 2002, p. 977]*

private speech Vygotsky's term for the internal dialogue that occurs when people talk to themselves and through which new ideas are developed and reinforced.

Vygotsky believed that words are part of this scaffold. When people talk, they are using a cognitive tool that is essential to intellectual growth in two ways. First, internal dialogue, or **private speech,** occurs when people talk to themselves, and this helps them develop new ideas (Vygotsky, 1987).

Young children use private speech often, usually out loud. They review what they know, decide what to do, and explain events to themselves and, incidentally, to anyone else within earshot. Older preschoolers use private speech more selectively and effectively than younger ones, and they sometimes do so in a whisper or even without any speech (Winsler et al., 2000).

social mediation A function of speech by which a person's cognitive skills are refined and extended.

The second way in which language advances thinking, according to Vygotsky, is as the *mediator of the social interaction* that is vital to learning. This **social mediation** function of speech occurs both during explicit instruction and during casual conversation, as a tool of verbal interaction that refines and extends a person's skills. Language allows a person to enter and traverse the zone of proximal development, because words provide a bridge from the child's current understanding to what is almost understood. This concept that language becomes a conceptual tool is now accepted by many developmentalists (e.g., Gelman, 2003).

Social mediation is particularly apparent in the development of an understanding of numbers, memories, and routines. Among the major differences between younger children and 5-year-olds is that the latter can count (accurately, up to 20 or 100 or more), can remember (again accurately, although they sometimes get confused when false memories are planted in their minds), and can verbalize sequences (such as the usual scenario for a birthday party, a restaurant meal, and so on).

Researchers have concluded that the social context of all these cognitive accomplishments, particularly parental instruction and encouragement, is crucial (e.g., Hubbs-Tait et al., 2002; Mix et al., 2002). Although all children reach sufficient neurological maturity to comprehend the concepts underlying such intellectual achievements by age 3 or 4, whether or not a child actually demonstrates them depends on family, school, and culture, with language a key mediator in what they understand and remember (Haden et al., 2001; Schneider & Pressley, 1997).

The theories of Piaget and Vygotsky are "compatible in many ways" (Rogoff, 1998, p. 681). However, each perspective supplements the other (see Table 9.1).

Theory of Mind

theory of mind An understanding of human mental processes.

Human mental processes—thoughts, emotions, beliefs, motives, and intentions—are among the most complicated and thought-provoking phenomena in a young person's world. Whether trying to understand a playmate's unexpected anger, determine when a sibling will be generous, or avoid an aunt's too-wet kiss, children want to understand and predict what goes on in another person's mind. To do so, they develop a kind of "folk psychology," an understanding of human mental processes called **theory of mind.**

TABLE 9.1 **Comparing Piaget and Vygotsky**

Piaget	Vygotsky
Learning Process	
Active Learning	**Guided Participation**
The child's own search for understanding, motivated by the child's inborn curiosity.	The adult or other mentor's aid in guiding the next step of learning, motivated by the learner's need for social interaction.
Nature of Child	
Egocentric	**Apprentice**
The preschooler's tendency to perceive everything from his or her own perspective and to be limited by that viewpoint.	The preschooler's tendency to look to others for insight and guidance, particularly in the cognitive realm.
Components	
Structure	**Scaffold**
The mental assumptions and scenarios the child creates to help him or her organize an understanding of the world. Structures are torn down and rebuilt when disequilibrium makes new structures necessary.	The building blocks for learning put in place by a "teacher" (a more knowledgeable child or adult) or a culture. Learners use scaffolds and then discard them when they are no longer needed.

Similarities and Differences Piaget and Vygotsky are similar in many ways. However, there are differences as well: in the learning process (active learning versus guided participation), in the nature of the child (egocentrism versus apprenticeship), and in the source of the basic components of cognition (structure versus scaffold).

Emergence at Age 4

Theory of mind might be seen as an example of theory-theory (which, as we noted earlier, refers to the view that young children tend to devise theories about everything). However, theory-theory is a new idea, not universally accepted, but virtually every developmentalist agrees that preschoolers develop a theory of mind. There is no doubt that children experience "an important intellectual change at about 4 years" (Perner, 2000, p. 396)—or earlier in some societies, later in others (see Table 9.2). Young children suddenly grasp something about how other people think that they did not understand before (Wellman et al., 2001). As you will see, both maturation and social experience are factors in this development, so theory of mind can be seen as evidence for the theories of both Piaget and Vygotsky.

What is it that children suddenly understand? Between the ages of 3 and 6, children come to realize that mental phenomena may not reflect reality. This idea leads to the theory-of-mind concept that individuals can believe untrue things and, therefore, that people can be deliberately deceived or fooled—an idea that is beyond most younger children, even when they have themselves been deceived. Consider an experiment in which an adult shows a 3-year-old a candy box and asks, "What is inside?" The child says, naturally, "Candy." But, in fact, the child has been tricked:

> **Adult:** Let's open it and look inside.
> **Child:** Oh . . . holy moly . . . pencils!
> **Adult:** Now I'm going to put them back and close it up again. *(Does so)* Now . . . when you first saw the box, before we opened it, what did you think was inside it?
> **Child:** Pencils.
> **Adult:** Nicky *(friend of the child)* hasn't seen inside this box. When Nicky comes in and sees it . . . when Nicky sees the box, what will he think is inside it?
> **Child:** Pencils.
>
> *[Adapted from Astington & Gopnik, 1988, p. 195]*

TABLE 9.2 **Age at Which Theory of Mind Emerges**

Age (years)	Place
3	None
3½	Baka (Cameroon)
	Canada
4	Australia
	Korea
	United States
4½	Austria
	United Kingdom
5	Japan
6	None
7	Quechua (Peru)

Source: Adapted from Wellman et al., 2001.

Understanding How Others Think This table shows the average age at which theory of mind appears in children of various cultures. A child was said to have developed theory of mind when he or she correctly answered half the theory-of-mind questions asked. These findings are based on a detailed meta-analysis of 143 studies. Children from every society studied (except those in rural Peru) showed rapid growth in theory of mind from age 4 to age 5½ .

Especially for Social Scientists Can you think of any connection between Piaget's theory of preoperational thought and 3-year-olds' errors in this theory-of-mind task?

Brotherly Love In addition to their shared joy, these brothers, aged 5 years and 11 months, are both learning the intricacies of social interaction. Such sharing is one reason that children with siblings usually develop a theory of mind more quickly than "only children" do.

This experiment has become a classic, performed with thousands of children from many cultures. When it is replicated exactly, 3-year-olds almost always make the same mistake. They seem to confuse belief and reality, and this "realist bias" makes it difficult for them to remember ever having believed something that contradicts what they now see (Mitchell & Kikuno, 2000). Another way of describing this is to say that they are "cursed" by their own prior knowledge (Birch & Bloom, 2003) and are too egocentric to grasp other perspectives.

As a result, until about age 4, children are notoriously bad at fooling other people. They play hide-and-seek by hiding in the same place time after time, or they signify the truth when they try to tell a lie. Their understanding of what other people are likely to think or believe is very limited, although some research finds that they can figure out strategies to trick someone else by age 3, a year younger than they can realize that they themselves have been tricked (Hala & Chandler, 1996).

Contextual Influences on Theory of Mind

Recently, developmentalists have asked what, precisely, strengthens theory of mind at about age 4. Is it nature or nurture, brain maturation or experience?

Consider one study, in which 68 children aged 2½ to 5½ were presented with four standard theory-of-mind situations, including a Band-Aid box that really contained pencils (similar to the candy-box experiment described earlier) (Jenkins & Astington, 1996). More than one-third of the children succeeded at all four tasks (for example, they understood that someone else might initially believe, as they had, that the Band-Aid box would contain Band-Aids); more than one-third succeeded on just one or none of the tasks. The remaining 26 percent were in between, succeeding at two or three tasks. Age had a powerful effect: The 5-year-olds were most likely to succeed on all four tasks, while the 3-year-olds were most likely to fail every time. This age-related advance suggests that maturation of the prefrontal cortex (which usually reaches a new level at about age 4) is the underlying factor (Perner et al., 2002).

General language ability also appears to be significant: The greater a child's verbal proficiency (at any age), the more likely he or she is to have a theory of mind (Astington & Jenkins, 1999; de Villiers & de Villiers, 2000). Language ability may be partly the result of maturation of particular areas of the brain, but it is also the result of language experience, especially mother–child conversations that involve thoughts and wishes, not just facts (Ruffman et al., 2002).

Now the Green One This 14-month-old is, for the moment, following his 4-year-old sister's instructions to stack the plastic rings the "right" way, something no toddler normally does. Both are content now, but what if he wanted to put the blue one next? Both siblings would advance in theory of mind.

When the effects of both age and language ability are accounted for, a third important factor emerges: having at least one older brother or sister (Jenkins & Astington, 1996). One researcher estimates that, in theory-of-mind development, "two older siblings are worth about a year of chronological age" (Perner, 2000, p. 383).

Before concluding that maturation, with a little help from language and siblings, produces theory of mind at age 4, consider one more study (Vinden, 1996). All the 4- to 8-year-olds in a village in Peru were tested on a culturally appropriate version of the candy-box situation, in this case a sugar bowl that contained tiny potatoes. Of course, the children at first thought the bowl contained sugar, as anyone from that village would. But surprisingly, even up to age 8, many of these children answered theory-of-mind questions incorrectly: They could not explain why someone would initially expect sugar to be in a sugar bowl and then be surprised to discover potatoes instead.

Culture is probably the key difference between the Peruvian children and those Westernized children who had usually been studied. In the Peruvians' mountainous, isolated village, "there is no reason or time for elaborate deception . . . where subsistence farmers, working from dawn to dusk just to survive, . . . live mostly on the landscape of action, and not on the landscape of consciousness" (Vinden, 1996, p. 1715). Neither their language nor their culture describes false belief or "how people's thoughts might affect their actions." Thus, culture is a fourth crucial factor in the development of theory of mind (Lillard, 1998; Vinden, 1996).

> To summarize, cognition develops rapidly from ages 2 to 6. Children's active search for understanding was first recognized by Piaget, who realized that few children are logical (which is why he called this period *preoperational*) because their egocentrism limits their understanding of the social context. By contrast, Vygotsky believed that children can understand the social context if they are properly guided within their zones of proximal development. According to Vygotsky, parents, siblings, and other mentors use language to aid young children's apprenticeship in learning.
>
> Recent scholars have focused particularly on theory of mind, an understanding that other people can have thoughts and ideas that are unlike one's own. Neurological maturation, linguistic competence, family context, and culture all affect the attainment of theory of mind at about age 4.

Theory of Mind Is Advanced by . . .

1. Maturation of prefrontal cortex
2. Language: *believe, think*
3. An older sibling
4. A culture that anticipates the future

Response for Social Scientists (from page 223): Children who focus on appearance and on static conditions, who cannot mentally reverse a process, and who egocentrically believe that everyone else thinks as they do would naturally believe that they had always known that the candy box held pencils and that their friend would know that, too.

Language

Language learning, particularly of extensive vocabulary and complex grammatical structure, provides a crucial foundation for **emergent literacy,** as the skills needed to learn to read are called. Both by talking to their young children (without too many commands) and by reading to them, parents can prepare children for fluent reading during primary school (Senechal & LeFevre, 2002).

To be specific, maturation and myelination in the language areas of the brain, as well as the centrality of words for most young children at home, at play, and in school, make ages 2 to 6 the prime time for learning language. Indeed, some scientists once thought that these years were a *critical period* for language learning—that is, the only time when a first language could be mastered and by far the best time for learning a second or third language.

Many scholars believed that if language structure and pronunciation were not learned in early childhood, then the necessary brain neurons and synapses would no longer be available and language could never be mastered (Lenneberg, 1967; Scovel, 1988). This turns out to be an exaggeration: Humans can and do master their native language after early childhood and can learn second languages even after puberty (Bialystok, 2001).

These scholars were not completely mistaken, however. Although not a critical period, early childhood does seem to be a *sensitive period* for emergent literacy. This means that ages 2 to 6 are a time when vocabulary, grammar, and pronunciation can be rapidly and easily learned, not only because of the neurological characteristics of the developing brain but also because most young children have a powerful social motivation (they want to communicate) and an absence of self-criticism (they are not embarrassed to be wrong). Consider some of the basics of acquiring vocabulary, grammar, and a second language.

emergent literacy The skills needed to learn to read.

Vocabulary

In early childhood, vocabulary increases exponentially, from about 500 words at age 2 to more than 10,000 at age 6. One scholar says that 2- to 6-year-olds learn an average of 10 words a day (Clark, 1995); another estimates one new word for every two waking hours from about age 2 to age 20 (Pinker, 1994). Estimates vary, partly because children and their exposure to language vary, but all agree that the most rapid vocabulary expansion usually occurs before age 7.

How does this happen? As discussed in Chapter 6, one explanation is that after a year or so of painstakingly learning one word at a time, the human mind develops an interconnected set of categories for vocabulary, a kind of grid or mental map on which to chart the meanings of various words. This speedy and not very precise process of acquiring vocabulary by "charting" new words is called **fast mapping** (Woodward & Markman, 1998). Children quickly learn new animal names, for instance, because they can be mapped in the brain close to already-known animal names. Thus, "animals" is one category, and "big cats" falls into it, making *tiger* easier to map if you already know *lion*. Similarly, children learn new color names by connecting them with those they already know.

The process is called fast mapping because, rather than stopping to figure out an exact definition and waiting until a word has been understood in several contexts, the child simply hears a word once or twice and sticks it on a mental language map. In its imprecision, it is not unlike our mental map of the world. When asked, for instance, where Nepal is, most people can locate it approximately ("near India"), but few can locate it precisely, citing each border.

Closely related to fast mapping is logical extension: After learning a word, children apply it to other, unnamed objects in the same category. One child told her father she had seen some Dalmatian cows, which made him remember that she had petted a Dalmatian dog the weekend before her school trip to a farm. It is as if children use their available vocabulary to cover all the territory they want to talk about (Behrend et al., 2001).

Of course, even the fastest language learner must hear each new word at least once, in a context that allows the child to map it. For this reason, parents

fast mapping The speedy and not very precise process of acquiring vocabulary by mentally "charting" new words into interconnected categories.

MICHAEL WICKES / THE IMAGE WORKS

What's That? By far the best way for a parent to teach a young child new vocabulary is by reading aloud. Ideally, the interaction should be a very social one, with much pointing and talking, as this Idaho pair demonstrate. If such experiences are part of her daily routine, this little girl not only will develop language but also will be among the first of her classmates to learn how to read.

Show and Tell—and Remember Vocabulary builds rapidly during early childhood. Young children need to be exposed just once to a new object in order to learn and remember its name. All these children probably knew *bird* already, and some of them knew *parrot* or *chicken*, but after today, they will all know *dove* as well.

LISETTE LE BON / SUPERSTOCK

should have frequent and elaborate conversations with their children (Hoff & Naigles, 2002). Even so, preschoolers sometimes map words wrong, as I learned the hard way.

In Person

Fast Mapping: Mommy the Brat

Fast mapping has an obvious advantage in that it fosters quick vocabulary acquisition. However, it also means that children *seem* to know words merely because they use them when, in actuality, their understanding of the words is quite limited. One common example is the word *big,* a word even 2-year-olds use and apparently understand. In fact, however, young children often use *big* when they mean *tall* or *old* or *great* ("My love is so big!") and only gradually come to use *big* correctly (Sena & Smith, 1990).

When adults realize that children often do not fully comprehend the meanings of words they use, it becomes easier to understand—and forgive—the mistakes children make. I still vividly recall an incident that stemmed from fast mapping when my youngest daughter, then 4, was furious at me.

Sarah had apparently fast-mapped several insulting words into her vocabulary. However, her fast mapping did not provide precise definitions or reflect nuances. In her anger, she called me first a "mean witch" and then a "brat." I smiled at her innocent imprecision, knowing the first was fast-mapped from fairy tales and the second from comments she got from her older sisters. Neither label bothered me, as I don't believe in witches and my brother is the only person who can appropriately call me a brat.

But then Sarah let loose an X-rated epithet that sent me reeling. Struggling to contain my anger, I tried to convince myself that fast mapping had probably left her with no real idea of what she had just said. "That word is never to be used in this family!" I sputtered. My appreciation of the speed of fast mapping was deepened by her response: "Then how come Rachel [her older sister] called me that this morning?"

The vocabulary-building process occurs so quickly that, by age 5, some children seem to understand and use almost any term they hear. In fact, 5-year-olds can learn any word or phrase if it is explained to them with specific examples and used in context or if they themselves can figure out what the word means. A teacher (who had been my student) asked her preschoolers what they had done over the weekend. Among standard answers—watched television, went to church, bought groceries—one child answered:

"I went to a protest."

"What is a protest?" another child asked.

"A lot of people get together, walk around, and yell," the first child replied, revealing her concept of what had occurred.

The second child nodded, mapping the word *protest* into her vocabulary.

Young children cannot accurately comprehend *every* word they hear, although, as this example shows, they try to do so. Abstract nouns and metaphors are difficult because there is no referent in their experience and because the fast-mapping process is quite literal, allowing only one meaning per word or phrase. For example, the phrase *live with* is taken literally, as meaning "reside in the same home as." One mother warned her child, who was jumping on the bed:

Mother: Stop. You'll hurt yourself.
Child: No I won't. *(Still jumping)*
Mother: You'll break the bed.
Child: No I won't. *(Still jumping)*
Mother: OK. You'll just have to live with the consequences.
Child: *(Stops jumping)* I'm not going to live with the consequences. I don't even know them.

[*Adapted from* The New York Times, *November 2, 1998]*

Talk to Me A cellular phone is a convenient size for a young child to carry around and use for a conversation with Grandmother, Dad, or anyone else who is willing to do without the usual verbal responses. Many 2-year-olds, when asked a question on the phone, simply nod or shake their heads.

overregularization The young child's tendency to apply the rules of grammar even when doing so is not necessary or appropriate.

Young children also have difficulty with words that implicitly express comparisons—such as *tall* and *short, near* and *far, high* and *low, deep* and *shallow*—because they do not understand the *relative* nature of these words (Oliver Ryalls, 2000). Once young children know which end of the swimming pool is the deep end, for instance, its depth becomes their definition of *deep*. They might obey parental instructions to stay out of deep puddles by splashing through every puddle they see, insisting that none of those is *deep*.

Words expressing relationships of place and time—such as *here, there, yesterday,* and *tomorrow*—are difficult as well. More than one pajama-clad child has awakened on Christmas morning and asked, "Is it tomorrow yet?" As with toddlers, however, it is easy to focus on children's vocabulary mistakes, forgetting that the language explosion between ages 2 and 6 adds thousands of new words each year. The play years could appropriately be called the language years, except that so much else develops as well.

Grammar

The *grammar* of a language includes the structures, techniques, and rules that are used to communicate meaning. Word order and word repetition, prefixes and suffixes, intonation and pronunciation—all are part of this element of language.

By the time children are 3 years old, their grammar is quite impressive: English-speaking children not only place the subject before the verb but also put the verb before the object and the adjective before the noun. They say "I eat red apple," not any of the 23 other possible combinations of those four words. They can form the plurals of nouns; the past, present, and future tenses of verbs; and the nominative, objective, and possessive forms of pronouns.

Parental input and encouragement lead directly to faster and more correct language use (Barrett, 1999). In a study of twins (who are often delayed in language development because they experience less individualized conversation), researchers found that the speed and depth of language learning depended on how much the parents spoke to each twin (Rutter et al., 2003).

Young children learn their grammar lessons so well that they tend to apply the rules of grammar even when they should not. This tendency, called **overregularization**, creates trouble when a child's language includes many exceptions to the rules. As an example, one of the first rules that English-speaking children apply is to add *-s* to form the plural. Overregularization leads many young children to talk about foots, tooths, sheeps, and mouses. They may even put the *-s* on adjectives when the adjectives are acting as nouns, as in this dinner-table exchange between my 3-year-old and her father:

> **Sarah:** I want somes.
> **Father:** You want some what?
> **Sarah:** I want some mores.
> **Father:** Some more what?
> **Sarah:** I want some more chickens.

Although technically wrong, overregularization is actually a sign of verbal sophistication; it shows that children are applying the rules. Indeed, as young children become more conscious of grammatical usages, they exhibit increasingly sophisticated misapplications of them. A child who at age 2 correctly says she "broke" a glass may at age 4 say she "braked" it and then at age 5 say she "did broked" it.

Learning Two Languages

In today's world, bilingualism is an asset, even a necessity. But should infants and young children be addressed in two distinct languages—for instance, if one parent or caregiver speaks another language? Some argue that the primary task of young children is to become proficient in one and only one language and that good monolingual ability will help them master a second language later on. Others argue that everyone should learn at least two languages and that the language-sensitive years of early childhood are the best time to do it.

The second argument seems more valid. Remarkably, very young children can master two distinct grammars quite well, using not only the proper word order but even the characteristic pauses and gestures soon after the vocabulary explosion (Bates et al., 2001; Mayberry & Nicoladis, 2000). These are also the best years to learn native pronunciation—more evidence for early childhood as a sensitive period for language learning.

This is not to say that most 6-year-olds can "speak like a native." In fact, many monolingual 6-year-olds have difficulty pronouncing certain sounds. Rather, it means that, during the early years, neurons and dendrites adjust to the languages a child hears. This auditory sensitivity enables children to master pronunciation with time, unlike those who learned a language after puberty.

Tiene Identificación Lista Are you pleased or angered by this bilingual sign at a school in Chelsea, Massachusetts, that serves as a polling place on election day? In this election, voters were deciding whether or not to eliminate government funding for bilingual education. Those who favored immersion argued that signs like this one would soon become unnecessary if children were taught only in English. Those who favored bilingual education held that without it, children from minority-language families would be likely to drop out of school before mastering any language.

Especially because language is an integral part of culture, bilingualism can be a deeply emotional topic. One group of researchers explains:

> A question of concern to many is whether early schooling in English for language minority children harms the development and/or maintenance of their mother tongue and possibly children's language competence in general. . . . Such debate quickly and unfortunately becomes highly politicized, and productive scholarly discussion of the issues is hampered by extreme and emotional political positions.

> [Winsler et al., 1999, p. 350]

Evidence regarding cognitive development points to both advantages and disadvantages of bilingualism. Supporters of bilingualism point out, correctly, that children who speak two languages by age 5 are less egocentric in their understanding of language and more advanced in their theory of mind. Opponents point out, also correctly, that bilingual proficiency comes at the expense of vocabulary development in one or both languages, slowing down emergent literacy (Bialystok, 2001).

Many immigrant parents find to their sorrow that their children make a *language shift,* becoming more fluent in their new language than in their home language (Min, 2000; Wong & Lopez, 2000).

Parents are reluctant to choose between one language and another if they believe one choice deprives children of their roots, heritage, and identity and the other deprives them of success in a new country (Suarez-Orozco & Suarez-Orozco, 2001). Many monolingual citizens are critical of anyone who does not speak the new language fluently.

The best solution seems to be to allow children to become "balanced bilinguals," fluent in two languages. Is that possible? Yes. Developmental research

SUSAN KUKLIN / PHOTO RESEARCHERS, INC.

One Family's Multiculturalism One of the first cultural preferences to travel successfully is food, and Italian cuisine is one of the world's most popular. This family lives in New York, the parents were born in Taiwan, their children are learning to speak both Chinese and English—and they all love pepperoni pizza.

confirms that, in these sensitive play years, children *can* become equally fluent in two or more languages, although they seldom do so (Romaine, 1999).

Balanced bilingualism is easiest to attain if the parents themselves speak two languages. Ideally, one family member uses one language, explaining vocabulary, correcting grammar, reading books, singing songs, and so on, and another family member spends as many hours each day teaching the other language. The principles of language learning—the language explosion, fast mapping, overregularization, parental encouragement—apply to two languages as well as to one. However, learning two languages requires twice as much language exposure.

Another possibility is to send the child to a preschool where the second language is taught. This strategy works not only in nations where everyone is expected to become bilingual (such as Canada, Switzerland, and the Netherlands) but even in countries where one language dominates (such as the United States). One cluster of bilingual preschools in California taught English and Spanish. The children, who were from Spanish-speaking families, became proficient in both languages. Indeed, the children's mastery of Spanish exceeded that of Spanish-speaking children who stayed home (Winsler et al., 1999). Preschool education itself seems to advance children in many other aspects of cognition as well, as we will discuss next.

First, however, let us pause to admire as well as summarize the linguistic talents of 2- to 6-year-olds. They explode into speech, from a hundred or so words to many thousands, from halting baby talk to fluency in one or even several of the world's languages. Fast mapping and application of grammatical rules are among the sophisticated strategies that young children use, even though these strategies sometimes backfire: Children may use words too literally or apply rules too rigidly. Early childhood is not a critical period for language learning, but no other time in the entire life span is as sensitive to language. Preschool children should be immersed in words, to sponge up whatever they hear, in one or more languages.

Early-Childhood Education

Parents are the first teachers, and they continue to influence learning, partly by deciding whether, when, and where to send their young children to school. All young children benefit from high-quality, regularly scheduled educational experiences, but such experiences can take many forms. Moreover, these forms can be hard to sort out, because the labels are deceptive.

Many Types of Programs

The distinctions among "day care," "preschool," "nursery school," and "pre-K" have more to do with history and local terminology than with a school's philosophy or the quality of its education program. All the same, some distinct educational curricula have been developed.

Montessori Schools

A hundred years ago, Maria Montessori opened nursery schools for poor children in Rome. She believed that children need structured, individualized projects that would give them a sense of accomplishment, such as completing particular puzzles, using a sponge and water to clean a table (even if it was not dirty), and drawing shapes. Today's Montessori schools still emphasize individual pride and accomplishment, although many tasks are different.

Child-Centered and Readiness Programs

Many newer programs are "developmental," or "child-centered," stressing child development and growth. Such programs often use a Piaget-inspired model that allows children to discover ideas at their own pace. Therefore, materials and the physical space are organized in such a way that children are encouraged to play with dress-up materials, art supplies, puzzles, blocks of many sizes, and other toys that lend themselves to self-paced social interaction.

An alternative is a program that stresses "readiness" or "academics." The basic idea is that children need to prepare for school, so they need to learn letters, numbers, shapes, and colors, as well as how to listen to the teacher, sit quietly, and work in groups. Praise and other reinforcement are given for good behavior, and time-outs (not being able to play with the other children) are used as punishment. Readiness programs are quite structured, more teacher-directed than child-centered, but they also take into account the abilities of the child.

Some readiness programs explicitly teach basic school skills, including reading, writing, and arithmetic, typically using "direct instruction" by a teacher. For example, young children are given practice in forming letters, sounding out words, counting objects, and writing their names. Homework may be assigned for practice in basic skills, and listening to the teacher is key. If a 4-year-old learns to read, that is considered a success, whereas in a developmental program, it would arouse suspicion that the child was not being allowed to play creatively. Many of these readiness programs were obviously inspired by behaviorism.

Reggio-Emilia and Kindergarten

An impressive new form of early-childhood education is called *Reggio Emilia,* inspired by a program pioneered in the Italian city of that name. Every young child is encouraged to master skills not usually seen until age 7 or so. The Reggio Emilia curriculum also encourages artistic expression, exploration of the environment, and collaboration between parents and teachers (Edwards et al., 1998).

Seventy years ago, the world's children stayed home until first grade—which is why it was called "first" and why young children were called "preschoolers." Even kindergarten (German for "children garden") was optional and innovative. Today, kindergarten thrives everywhere (Wollons, 2000), and almost every 5-year-old is in school (see Figure 9.2 for U.S. trends). Not only do many mothers participate in the labor force (see Figure 9.3 for U.S. data), but research has shown that young children have amazing cognitive potential, which is best actualized by specific teaching and learning practices.

Another Place for Children High ceilings, uncrowded play space, varied options for art and music, a glass wall revealing trees and flowers—all these features reflect the Reggio Emilia approach to individualized, creative learning for young children. Such places are rare in other nations of the world besides Italy.

ATELIER—FROM "OPEN WINDOWS." © MUNICIPALITY OF REGGIO EMILIA—INFANT-TODDLER CENTERS AND PRESCHOOLS, PUBLISHED BY REGGIO CHILDREN 1994.

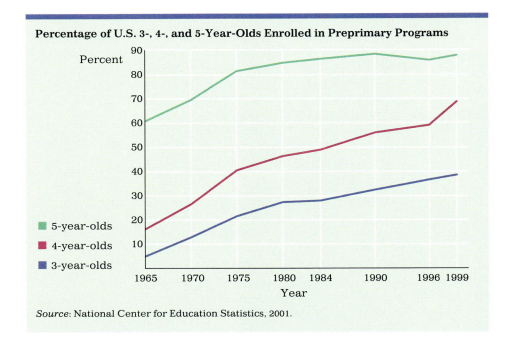

Percentage of U.S. 3-, 4-, and 5-Year-Olds Enrolled in Preprimary Programs

- 5-year-olds
- 4-year-olds
- 3-year-olds

Source: National Center for Education Statistics, 2001.

FIGURE 9.2 **Changing Times** As research increasingly finds that preschool education provides a foundation for later learning, more and more young children are in educational programs. Currently, almost half of all 3- and 4-year-olds in the United States are in school. That proportion is expected to increase even more in the twenty-first century.

Learning Is Fun The original purpose of the Head Start program was to boost disadvantaged children's academic skills. The most enduring benefits, however, turned out to be improved self-esteem and social skills, as is evident in these happy Head Start participants, all crowded together.

? *Observational Quiz* (see answer, page 234): How many of these children are in close physical contact without discomfort or disagreement?

Research and Applications

Developmental researchers always seek to link research findings and practical applications. They have discovered that early childhood is a prime learning period for every child but that some children learn several times as much as others. To be specific, the achievement gap between the most and least accomplished is narrow in infancy—almost all children begin to walk and talk at about 12 months—but it widens with every year of early childhood.

As a result, kindergartners differ a great deal in their ability to learn, talk, or even listen (Morrison et al., 1997). Then this divergence in achievement stabilizes—maintaining a wide gap—throughout the school years. This led to one conclusion: Nations should provide quality early education. Some nations (e.g., China, France, Italy, Sweden) do this for all children.

Head Start

In the United States, the focus has been on children living in poverty. Project Head Start is a federal program, launched in 1965, designed for low-income or minority children who, at least in theory, needed a "head start" on their education. The quality and results of Head Start vary, and some of the long-term consequences are unknown because scientific evaluation is not built into the program. However, Head Start has provided half-day education for literally millions of 3- to 5-year-olds, boosting their abilities and skills at least temporarily, and has probably provided long-term benefits as well (Zigler, 1996).

Longitudinal Research

The same research that led to Head Start also led to more intensive, well-evaluated programs with longitudinal follow-up to adulthood. Three projects in particular have excellent data: one in Michigan, called Perry or High/Scope (Schweinhart & Weikart, 1997); one in North Carolina, called Abecedarian (Campbell et al., 2001); and one in Chicago, called Child–Parent Centers (Reynolds, 2000). All three programs enrolled children for several years before kindergarten, all compared experimental groups of children with matched control groups of children, and all reached the same conclusions: Early education has substantial long-term benefits, which become especially apparent when the children are in the third grade or later.

Children in these three programs scored higher on math and reading achievement tests than other children from the same backgrounds, schools, and neighborhoods. They were significantly less likely to be placed in special classes for slow or disruptive children or to repeat a year of school. In adolescence, they had higher aspirations and a greater sense of achievement as well as being less likely to be mistreated. As young adults, they were more likely to attend college and less likely to go to jail.

Quality Learning

All three research projects found that direct cognitive training, with specific instruction in various readiness skills, was useful. Although the programs cost several thousand dollars per child per year (perhaps as much as $12,000 annually per child in 2003 dollars), in the long run the decreased need for special education saved more than the initial cost (Karoly et al., 1998). By comparison, full-day care in an accredited program costs about $8,000 per child per year in 2003 dollars; Head Start is cheaper, about $5,000 per child per year, primarily because it usually provides only half-day care for only 34 weeks (National Research Council and Institute of Medicine, 2000).

A key finding from all the research is that quality matters. As a review of all aspects of early-childhood development by 22 experts concludes:

> In sum, the positive relation between child care quality and virtually every facet of children's development that has been studied is one of the most consistent findings in developmental science. While child care of poor quality is associated with

Mothers in the Labor Force

Source: U.S. Bureau of the Census, 2000.

FIGURE 9.3 **Most U.S. Mothers Now Work Outside the Home**

?Observational Quiz (see answer, page 234): Which group experienced the biggest change— mothers of children under age 3 or mothers overall?

Especially for Parents In finding a preschool program, what should a parent look for?

Learning from One Another Every nation creates its own version of early education. In this scene at a nursery school in Kuala Lumpur, Malaysia, note the head coverings, uniforms, bare feet, and absence of boys. None of these elements would be found in most early-childhood education classrooms in North America or Europe.

?Observational Quiz (see answer, page 234): What seemingly universal aspects of childhood are visible in this photograph?

PAUL CHESLEY / STONE / GETTY IMAGES

❗*Answer to Observational Quiz* (from page 232): All five—not four (look again at the right-hand side of the photograph)!

❗*Answer to Observational Quiz* (from page 233): Mothers of young children. The rate of increase was about 30 percent for mothers in general (the percentage of all mothers participating in the labor force increased from about 45 percent to 70 percent), but the rate of increase almost doubled (a jump from 32 percent to 60 percent) for mothers of children under age 3.

Response for Parents (from page 233): There is much variation, and there is no right answer that fits every parent's values. However, children should be engaged in learning, not allowed to sit passively or to squabble with each other. Before deciding, parents should look at several programs, staying long enough to see the children in action.

❗*Answer to Observational Quiz* (from page 233): Three aspects are readily apparent: These girls enjoy their friendships; they are playing a hand-clapping game, some version of which is found in every culture; and, most important, they have begun the formal education that their families want for them.

poorer developmental outcomes, high-quality care is associated with outcomes that all parents want to see in their children, ranging from cooperation with adults to the ability to initiate and sustain positive exchanges with peers, to early competence in math and reading.

[National Research Council and Institute of Medicine, 2000]

What constitutes high-quality care? Some basics seem obvious and have been described in Chapter 6: safety, adequate space and equipment, a low adult–child ratio, positive social interactions among children and adults, and trained staff (or educated parents) who are unlikely to leave the program. Continuity helps. (One of the best questions that parents comparing options can ask is, "How long has each staff member worked at this center?") Beyond that, curriculum may be important, especially during the play years. Worst seem to be programs that have no philosophy or direction. Best may be programs with an emphasis on learning, reflected in a curriculum that includes extensive practice in language, fine and gross motor skills, and basic number skills.

Considering all the research about cognitive development between the ages of 2 and 6, the benefits of a high-quality educational program for young children come as no surprise. However, history teaches that new research will find additional abilities in the brains of 2- to 6-year-olds and additional strategies to develop that potential. Evaluation studies (longitudinal comparisons of similar groups of children with varied experiences) are still too rare. Some readers of this book will be among those who undertake the research, parent the children, and staff the schools that will again cause us to revise our view of the thinking of the very young.

> Until a few decades ago, it was widely assumed that young children were *always* better off with their mothers at home. Then research, particularly studies of Head Start and other programs for low-income children, proved that early education benefits mothers entering the labor force and that good day care benefits children, who improve in language, in social skills, and in prospects for the future. The crucial factors are quality of care, staff training, and the specifics of learning opportunities, as well as curriculum and adult–child ratios. Each nation, each region, and sometimes each preschool differs on these factors, but all children can learn valuable skills by playing together in an educational setting.

SUMMARY

How Children Think: Piaget and Vygotsky

1. Piaget stressed the egocentric and illogical aspects of thought during the play years. He called this stage preoperational thought, because young children cannot yet use logical operations to think about their observations and experiences.

2. Piaget noted many characteristics of preoperational thinking. Young children's thinking is largely prelogical. They sometimes focus on only one thing (centration) and use only their own viewpoint (egocentrism), remaining stuck on appearances and on current reality. They cannot understand that things change, actions can be reversed, and other people have other perspectives.

3. Vygotsky stressed the social aspects of childhood cognition, noting that children learn by participating in various experiences, guided by more knowledgeable adults or peers. That guidance assists learning within the zone of proximal development, which includes the knowledge and skills that the child has the potential to learn.

4. According to Vygotsky, the best mentors use various clues, guidelines, and other tools to provide the child with a scaffold for new learning. He believed that learning occurs in social interaction, not in isolation. Language is a bridge of social mediation between the knowledge that the child already has and the learning that the society hopes to impart. For Vygotsky, words are a tool for learning that both mentor and child use.

5. Children develop a theory of mind—an understanding of what others might think—throughout early childhood. Notable advances in theory of mind occur at around age 4. At that point, children become less egocentric and better able to understand the differences among perception, emotion, and fact.

Language

6. Language develops rapidly during early childhood, which is probably a sensitive period but not a critical one for language learning. Vocabulary increases dramatically, with thousands of words added between ages 2 and 6. In addition, basic grammar is mastered, and many children learn to speak more than one language.

7. Bilingualism is controversial, largely because language use is intimately connected to culture and heritage. Ideally, children become balanced bilinguals, equally proficient in two languages, by age 6. This ideal, however, is not easily attained.

Early-Childhood Education

8. Organized educational programs during early childhood advance cognitive and social skills.

9. Quality matters: Education works best if there is a clear curriculum and if the adult–child ratio is low. The training and continuity of early-childhood teachers are also important.

10. According to longitudinal research on comprehensive childhood education programs, early intervention works. Graduates of these programs are less likely to need special education or to repeat a grade and are more likely to attend college and to become law-abiding adults.

KEY TERMS

egocentrism (p. 217)
preoperational thought (p. 218)
centration (p. 218)
focus on appearance (p. 218)

static reasoning (p. 218)
irreversibility (p. 218)
conservation (p. 219)
theory-theory (p. 220)
apprentice in thinking (p. 221)

guided participation (p. 221)
zone of proximal development (ZPD) (p. 221)
scaffolding (p. 221)
private speech (p. 222)

social mediation (p. 222)
theory of mind (p. 222)
emergent literacy (p. 225)
fast mapping (p. 226)
overregularization (p. 228)

APPLICATIONS

By far the best way to understand the mind of the young child is to talk to a child directly. For that reason, the first two applications require an actual child. Children may be scarce on some campuses, though, so the last two applications do not require them.

1. Until you replicate Piaget's conservation experiment, you may find it hard to believe that young children are preoperational. The easiest experiment is conservation of liquids (pictured in Figure 9.1). Find a child under age 5, and make sure the child himself or herself tells you that two identically shaped glasses contain the same amount of liquid. Then carefully pour one glass of liquid into a narrow, taller glass. Ask the child which glass contains more now, or if the glasses contain the same amount.

2. To demonstrate how rapidly language is learned, show a preschool child several objects and label one with a nonsense word the child has never heard. (*Toma* is often used; so is *wug*.) Then shuffle the objects and ask the child to name them. (This can also be done with objects the child does not know the name of, such as

a wrench, a spatula, or a coin from another nation.) The problem with using the actual names is that, if the child learns the name quickly, you may think the child already knew it. If you ask, most children will say they knew it all along.

3. Theory of mind emerges at about age 4, but many adults still have trouble understanding other people's thoughts and motives. Ask several people why someone in the news did whatever they did (e.g., a scandal, a crime, a heroic act). Then ask your informants how sure they are of their explanation. Compare and analyze the reasons as well as the degrees of certainty. One person will probably be quite sure of an explanation that someone else thinks impossible.

4. Think about an experience in which you learned something that was initially difficult. To what extent do Vygotsky's concepts (guidance, motivation, apprenticeship, zone of proximal development) explain the experience? Write a detailed, step-by-step description of your learning process, using theory to explain when relevant.

Chapter Ten

The Play Years: Psychosocial Development

Picture a 2-year-old and a 6-year-old. Consider how emotionally and socially different they are. Chances are the 2-year-old still has many moments of clinging, of tantrums, and of stubbornness, vacillating between dependence and self-assertion. Such a young child cannot be left alone, even for a few moments, wherever curiosity might lead to danger or destruction. If a parent takes that child to the playground and then gets absorbed in reading the newspaper, after five minutes the child may be at the top of a very high slide or tasting a pretend cake in the sandbox.

A 6-year-old is quite safe as long as adults are somewhere nearby. The 6-year-old might say goodbye to Mom or Dad at the door of the first-grade classroom and then take care of business: following classroom routines, befriending certain classmates and ignoring others, respecting and learning from teachers.

This chapter details that 2-to-6 transformation. You will see that parents and peers are pivotal socializing agents in this process, but the child's own maturation and motivation are important, too.

Emotional Development

As you remember from the chapters on infancy, by age 2 children have a sense of themselves and their goals, and they have developed a range of emotions. During the play years all three of these—self, goals, and emotions—come together, with emotions as the linchpin that enables the self to reach the goals.

Initiative Versus Guilt

Positive enthusiasm, effort, and self-evaluation characterize ages 3 to 6, according to Erik Erikson's psychosocial theory (first discussed in Chapter 2). During the third developmental stage described by Erikson, called **initiative versus guilt**, self-esteem emerges from the skills and competencies that demonstrate independence and initiative. This forms the **self-concept**, or understanding of the self.

The typical young child has an immodest and quite positive self-concept, believing that he or she is strong, smart, and good-looking, and thus that any goal is quite achievable. As one group of researchers explained:

> Young children seem to be irrepressibly optimistic about themselves. . . . Consider, for example, the shortest, most uncoordinated boy in a kindergarten class who proclaims that he will be the next Michael Jordan.
>
> [Lockhart et al., 2002, pp. 1408–1409]

initiative versus guilt The third of Erikson's eight stages of psychosocial development, in which the young child eagerly begins new projects and activities and feels guilt when his or her efforts result in failure or criticism.

self-concept People's understanding of who they are. Self-concept usually includes appearance, personality, and abilities.

Most young children leap at almost any opportunity to show that "I can do it!" Spontaneous play becomes goal-directed. Children are not merely active, as they were at younger ages in Piaget's sensorimotor period and in Erikson's autonomy-versus-shame stage. Now, in the initiative stage, they want to *begin and complete something* and take pride in their accomplishment. Accordingly, their attention span becomes much longer, because their activity is goal-directed. Many 3- or 4-year-olds can spend up to an hour in one episode of pretend play, practicing one new motor skill, or creating one work of art—something no normal toddler does.

Pride leads not only to concentration and persistence but also to a willingness to try new experiences, such as to climb a taller ladder, speak a new language, pet a strange animal, and so on. Typical 2- to 6-year-olds enjoy undertaking various tasks, and they expect all others—grandparents, playmates, stuffed animals—to be a patient, admiring audience. Self-confidence is the foundation for practice and then mastery. Preschoolers predict that they can solve impossible puzzles, remember long lists of words, and control the dreams that come when they are asleep (Stipek et al., 1995; Woolley & Berger, 2002), and such naive predictions help them learn.

Notice that the negative consequence of this stage is guilt, not shame. Erikson believed that children develop a new awareness of themselves, and they feel guilt when their efforts fail. Many psychologists and philosophers believe that guilt is a more mature emotion than is shame. Guilt comes from within the child; shame comes from knowing that someone else might see and criticize what the child has done (Tangney, 2001). Both shame and guilt originate from social standards, but guilt indicates that the child has become self-motivated and self-regulated.

Emotional Regulation

The preeminent accomplishment between ages 2 and 6 is the ability to inhibit, enhance, direct, and modulate emotions (Eisenberg et al., 1997). Children who master this task become more competent in every aspect of their lives (Denham et al., 2003). Pride is tempered by guilt (and vice versa); joy, by sadness; anger, by fear; and all the negative emotions (guilt, anger, and fear), by routines that would be considered irrational and obsessive in an older person (as explained in Chapter 8). All emotions are regulated and controlled by the 4-year-old in ways unknown to the exuberant, expressive, and often overwhelmed toddler.

This ability, called **emotional regulation,** is developed as children learn to meet society's expectations that they "manage frustration" and "modulate emo-

emotional regulation The ability, beginning in early childhood, to direct or modify one's feelings, particularly feelings of fear, frustration, and anger.

Close Connection Unfamiliar events often bring developmental tendencies to the surface, as with the curious boy and his worried brother, who are attending Colorado's Pikes Peak or Bust Rodeo breakfast. Their attentive mother keeps the livelier boy calm and reassures the shy one.

?*Observational Quiz* (see answer, page 240): Mother is obviously a secure base for both boys, who share the same family and half the same genes, but are different ages: One is 2 and the other is 4. Can you tell which boy is younger?

SEAN CAYTON / THE IMAGE WORKS

tional expression" (Sroufe, 1996). By age 5, most children accomplish this difficult task quite successfully: They are friendly to new acquaintances but not too friendly, angry but not explosive, frightened by a clown but not terrified.

Emotional regulation begins with impulse control. The impulse most in need of control is anger, because "dysregulated anger may trigger aggressive, oppositional behavior" (Gilliom et al., 2002, p. 222). A frustrated 2-year-old might flail at another person or lie down screaming and kicking, but a 5-year-old should have much more self-control.

Without adequate control, emotions can overpower a child. This occurs in two, seemingly opposite, ways. Some children have **externalizing problems:** They lash out in impulsive anger, attacking other people or things. They are sometimes called "undercontrolled." Other children have **internalizing problems:** They are fearful and withdrawn, turning emotional distress inward. They are sometimes called "overcontrolled."

Both externalizing and internalizing children are unable to regulate their emotions properly or, more precisely, to regulate the *expression* of their emotions, exercising some control but not too much (Cole et al., 1996; Eisenberg et al., 2001). Why would a child have internalizing or externalizing problems?

Neurons and Nurture

Emotional regulation is in part neurological, a matter of brain functioning. It is also learned, a matter of social awareness, fostered by parents who are able to regulate their own emotions. Cultures and parents differ as to which particular emotions need expression, suppression, or control and when in a child's life such control is expected (Garner & Spears, 2000; Olson et al., 2001). The actual development of young children depends on a combination of neurological maturation (true for all children), sociocultural practices (dependent on family), and individual differences (temperament).

We begin with the brain. As we saw in Chapter 8, the ability to regulate emotions, to think before acting, to decide whether and how to display joy or anger or fear is directly connected to the maturation of the prefrontal cortex. Normally, advances occur at about age 4 or 5, as the child becomes less likely to throw a temper tantrum, provoke a physical attack, or burst into uncontrollable giggles. Throughout the period from age 2 to 5, violent temper tantrums, uncontrollable crying, and terrifying phobias diminish, and the capacity for self-control—such as not opening a wrapped present immediately if asked to wait—becomes more evident (Kochanska et al., 2001). By school age, children tend to like other children best if they are neither overcontrolled nor undercontrolled in their emotions.

Not every child develops the ability to regulate emotions at the same age. A particular child might be neurologically slow because of genes or certain early care experiences.

Genetic Variations First, temperament comes into play: Some people are naturally expressive and others more inhibited, a range found in infants as well as adults. A longitudinal study of children aged 4 months to 4 years found considerable stability, not only in emotional reactions (laughing or crying when a strange clown appeared, for instance) but also in electrical activity in the prefrontal cortex. Just as with adults, young children who were more fearful had greater activity in their right prefrontal cortex, while those who were more exuberant showed more activity in their left prefrontal cortex (Fox et al., 2001).

This continuity from infancy through childhood indicates that some of the variation in emotional expression is genetic. Consequently, certain children need to work to regulate their exuberance, others must try to overcome their anxiety, and still others have neither problem, finding it quite easy to control their emotions. Emotional regulation seems to

externalizing problems Difficulties that arise from a child's tendency to externalize emotions, or experience emotions outside the self, lashing out in impulsive anger and attacking other people or things.

internalizing problems Difficulties that arise from a child's tendency to internalize emotions, or inhibit their expression, being fearful and withdrawn.

Who's Chicken? Genes and good parenting have made this boy neither too fearful nor too bold. Appropriate caution is probably the best approach to meeting a chicken.

FRANK SIMONETTI / STOCK CONNECTION / PICTUREQUEST

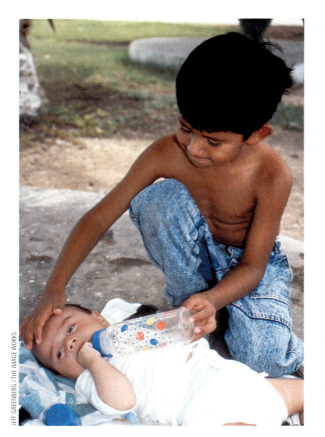

JEFF GREENBERG / THE IMAGE WORKS

Emotional Regulation Older brothers are not famous for being loving caregivers. However, in the Mayan culture, older children learn to regulate their jealousy and provide major care for younger siblings while their parents work.

?Observational Quiz (see answer, page 242): What do you see that suggests that this boy is paying careful attention to his brother?

!Answer to Observational Quiz (from page 238): Size is not much help, since children grow slowly during these years and the heads of these two boys appear about the same size. However, emotional development is apparent. Most 2-year-olds, like the one at the right, still cling to their mothers; most 4-year-olds are sufficiently mature, secure, and curious to watch the excitement as they drink their juice.

be attained more readily by girls than boys, perhaps for genetic reasons connected to the XX or XY chromosomes (Colder et al., 2002).

Early Stress Brain-related differences in emotional regulation can also result from neurological damage during development, either prenatally (if the pregnant woman was stressed, ill, or a heavy drug user) or postnatally (if the infant was chronically malnourished, injured, or frightened) (McEwen, 2000). Repeated exposure to extreme stress kills some neurons and stops others from developing properly (Sanchez et al., 2001). For children whose brains no longer respond normally to stress, even an ordinary stressor—such as an unexpected loud noise or a critical remark—could release a flood of hormones, particularly the hormone *cortisol*. A 4- or 5-year-old might overreact, experiencing terror or fury at something that another child would experience as only mildly upsetting (De Bellis, 2001).

A direct link from excessive stress in infancy to abnormal emotional outbursts is not always found. Some research finds lower, not higher, levels of cortisol in abused children (Gunnar & Vasquez, 2001). Their blunted stress response indicates that their emotions are dampened and distorted instead of regulated, and this may be a sign of depression. In any case, researchers agree that early stresses can change the electrical activity, dendrite growth, and production of various hormones in the brain.

The child's early care experiences may either relieve or aggravate stress. If rat pups are raised by highly nurturing mothers and are exposed to repeated stress, their brains are not affected, because their mothers lick, nuzzle, groom, and feed them more than an average rat mother would (Kaufman & Charney, 2001). In humans, children who have been well nurtured tend to form secure attachments, and securely attached children can control their emotional outbursts better than insecure children can (Gilliom et al., 2002; Kochanska, 2001).

The effects of a child's past care are revealed in many ways, including reactions to another child's cry of pain. Normally, children express empathy, comforting, reassuring, getting help if need be. By contrast, children with insecure attachments respond abnormally. Some do whatever

> . . . would precisely further distress the child (e.g., scaring a child with the very mask that had been frightening, taunting a crying child and calling him or her a "cry baby," or punching a child with a stomach ache in the stomach). . . . [Others] would often become upset themselves when another was distressed (e.g., holding their own lip and seeking a teacher's lap when another child had fallen).
>
> [Sroufe, 1996, p. 227]

The effects of early care are particularly evident in 4- to 6-year-olds who have been mistreated. One study found that 80 percent of such children were "emotionally disregulated," either strangely indifferent or extremely angry when a stranger criticized their mothers (Maughan & Cicchetti, 2002). Neglect or abuse in the first years of life is likely to cause later internalizing or externalizing problems, even more so than mistreatment later on. Brain circuits are formed especially during infancy and toddlerhood, which is the probable explanation for the damage caused by early mistreatment (Keiley et al., 2001; Manly et al., 2001).

A leading team of developmental researchers concluded:

> In sum, then, there are multiple converging pathways—including not only the neural circuits that are activated by physical, psychological, and immunological stressors, but also the influence of genetics, early experience, and ongoing life events that determine the neural response to different stressors.
>
> [Cicchetti & Walker, 2001, p. 414]

Cognition and Emotions

A first step toward emotional regulation is the recognition of one's own emotions and of the emotional responses of others, which, as you remember, emerges as part of a child's "theory of mind." Both maturation and experience are needed for emotional regulation, just as they are for theory of mind. Yet both have cognitive roots as well.

Daniel Goleman (1998) contends that the ability to modulate and direct emotions is crucial to **emotional intelligence,** an understanding of how to interpret and express emotions. Emotional intelligence develops throughout life but is crucial in early childhood. During these formative years, the reflective and intellectual areas of the cortex, especially the prefrontal cortex, gradually come to govern the rush of fear, anger, and other passion from the *amygdala,* an emotional hotspot deep within the brain.

Goleman is convinced that parents use children's natural attachment to teach them how and when to express feelings—in other words, to govern the amygdala. If the children learn these lessons during early childhood, they will become balanced and empathetic human beings, neither overwhelmed by nor unresponsive to their own emotions.

All other learning, according to Goleman, builds on emotional intelligence or, more broadly, on emotional regulation. For example, one study found that securely attached infants were better able to control their frustrations and impatience at age 3 (primarily by distracting themselves) and were more likely to become cooperative kindergartners without externalizing problems at age 5 (Gilliom et al., 2002).

emotional intelligence Goleman's term for the understanding of how to interpret and express emotions.

Empathy and Antipathy

We have just described one dimension of children's emotions: the degree of emotional regulation. Children can have appropriate, too much, or too little self-control. Too much or too little self-control may lead to internalizing or externalizing problems, respectively. There is another dimension: Children may feel either **empathy** for another person, truly understanding that person's emotions, or **antipathy,** disliking or even hating someone else.

Empathy often leads to **prosocial** actions, in which the child helps another person without gaining any obvious benefit for himself or herself. Expressing sympathy, offering to share food or a toy, and including a shy child in a game or conversation are examples of prosocial behavior.

empathy A person's true understanding of the emotions of another, including the ability to figure out what would make that person feel better.

antipathy A person's feelings of anger, distrust, dislike, or even hatred toward another.

prosocial Behaving in ways that help other people without obvious benefit to oneself.

LAURA DWIGHT

What Will She Do? By age 3 or 4, children can respond with empathy to another child's distress, as the girl on the left is doing. Such emotions usually lead to prosocial actions: She is likely to ask the distressed boy at the right to play with her at the sand table.

antisocial Behaving in ways that are deliberately hurtful or destructive.

!*Answer to Observational Quiz* (from page 240): Look at his hands, legs, and face. He is holding the bottle and touching the baby's forehead with delicacy and care; he is positioning his legs in a way that is uncomfortable but suited to the task; and his eyes and mouth suggest he is giving the baby his full concentration.

In contrast, antipathy may lead to **antisocial** behavior, in which a child injures another person or destroys something that belongs to another person (Caprara et al., 2001). Examples of antisocial actions include verbal insults, social exclusion, and physical assaults. By age 4 or 5—as a result of brain maturation, theory of mind, emotional regulation, and caregiving interactions—most children can and do act in a deliberately prosocial or antisocial manner (Eisenberg, 2000).

Sharing

It is easy to tell whether sharing is a prosocial act or not. The young child who is commanded to share may scowl, purse his or her lips, and hand over the cherished toy or half a cookie with evident reluctance. The prosocial child spontaneously gives over the object, smilingly anticipating the playmate's happiness and shared pleasure. As you can see, empathy involves much more than simply following a parent's or teacher's moral prescription to share a toy or comfort another child. Empathy requires a person's true understanding of the emotions of another, including the ability to figure out what would make that person feel better.

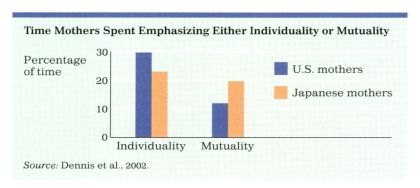

Time Mothers Spent Emphasizing Either Individuality or Mutuality

Source: Dennis et al., 2002.

FIGURE 10.1 How Empathy Is Taught During free play with their 4-year-olds, Japanese mothers were more likely than U.S. mothers to emphasize mutuality, or interdependence. U.S. mothers tended to stress individuality, or self-reliance. This study demonstrates the role of culture in children's development of empathy.

Empathy is encouraged by parents who, in turn, are guided by their culture. For example, a study that compared mothers and 4-year-olds from Japan and the United States found that the Japanese mothers were much more likely to emphasize mutuality (e.g., "This puzzle is hard for us") during a play session and U.S. mothers were more likely to emphasize individuality (e.g., "You are having a hard time with this puzzle") (Dennis et al., 2002) (see Figure 10.1).

Aggression

The gradual regulation of emotions is nowhere more apparent than in the most antisocial behavior of all, *active aggression*. Infants are aggressive whenever they are frustrated. In Richard Tremblay's dramatic words, "The only reason babies do not kill each other is that we do not give them knives or guns" (quoted in Holden, 2000, p. 580).

If aggression is not properly regulated during early childhood, it can become a serious social problem (Coie & Dodge, 1998). As one group of researchers reports:

> Children with [emotional] control problems observed by home visitors at ages 3 and 4 years were seen by teachers as more hostile and hyperactive in the classroom at age 5 years. . . . Early onset aggression, in particular, is likely to become entrenched and linked to multiple problems late in development.
>
> *[Zahn-Waxler, Schmitz, et al., 1996, pp. 118, 103]*

In other words, although almost all 2-year-olds are aggressive, a child who is more antisocial at ages 3 and 4 than other children may be headed for trouble at age 5, 10, or even 15 or 25 (Loeber & Farrington, 2000).

Emotions need to be regulated, not repressed; some assertion and self-protection are probably beneficial (Hawley, 1999). Accordingly, the implications of aggression in early childhood are not necessarily dire: Every normal child sometimes deliberately hits, kicks, bites, pinches, pulls hair, calls names, or twists an arm. Such aggressive

Me First! An increase in aggression by about age 4 is typically accompanied by an increase in self-control. This struggle will not escalate to instrumental aggression if both children have learned some emotional regulation and if neither has been misguided by racism or by a false image of maleness.

TABLE 10.1 The Four Forms of Aggression

Type of Aggression	Definition	Comments
Instrumental aggression	Forceful behavior that is aimed at getting or keeping something (such as a toy, a place in line, or a turn on the playground swing) that is also desired by another person.	The form of aggression that is most likely to increase from age 2 to age 6; involves objects more than people, is quite normal, so is not of serious concern; not so much antisocial as egocentric.
Reactive aggression	Forceful behavior that is an angry retaliation for another person's intentional or accidental act.	An impulsive reaction to a real or imagined hurt; indicates a lack of emotional regulation, which is characteristic of 2-year-olds. A 5-year-old should be able to stop and think, figuring out whether the hurt was intentional and whether reactive aggression will make the situation better or worse.
Relational aggression	Forceful behavior that takes the form of insults or social rejection and is aimed at harming the social connection between the aggressor and another person.	Involves a personal attack and thus is directly antisocial.
Bullying aggression	Forceful behavior that takes the form of an unprovoked physical or verbal attack on another person, especially one who is unlikely to defend himself or herself.	Both bullies and victims are characterized by inadequate emotional regulation. Bullying in early childhood is an urgent sign that bully and victim should be guided by adults to understand and control their emotions before entering the school years; discussed in detail in Chapter 13.

behavior normally increases between ages 1 and 4 because, as the self-concept builds and children play more with peers, they are likely to defend their interests. In fact, an internalizing 4-year-old who cries and retreats from every threat is likely to become overwhelmed by anxiety or depression later on and may be victimized by bullies. But normal 4-year-olds are aggressive only in certain instances, choosing issues and targets.

Researchers recognize four forms of aggression (see Table 10.1). *Instrumental aggression* is very common, *bullying aggression* is most ominous, and *relational aggression* is most hurtful. Victims of relational aggression are lonely and unhappy. For example, if a 3-year-old has a toy snatched by another child, he might cry and try to get it back; but if another child calls him dirty, dumb, or bad (examples of relational aggression), there is no obvious remedy. Perhaps not surprisingly, friendships are severed by relational aggression but not usually by instrumental aggression (Crick et al., 1999).

Learning Social Skills Through Play

Thus far, we have emphasized the role of adults in children's psychosocial development. However, **peers**, who are other people of about the same age and status, not only are the best playmates but also provide opportunities to practice social skills. Developmentalists believe that play is the most productive and adaptive activity that children can undertake. Play is both universal and variable by culture, gender, and age, and thus is an ideal forum for learning specific social skills (Sutton-Smith, 1997). Although children play when they are alone or with adults, they are much more likely to play with other children.

Think of how play develops from age 2 to 6. The younger child's social play consists mainly of simple games (such as bouncing and trying to catch a ball and becoming upset if another child does not cooperate). By contrast, the 5-year-old

instrumental aggression Forceful behavior that is aimed at getting or keeping an object or privilege that is also desired by another person.

reactive aggression Forceful behavior that is an angry retaliation for some intentional or accidental act.

relational aggression Forceful behavior that takes the form of insults or social rejection, aimed at harming social connections.

bullying aggression Forceful behavior that takes the form of an unprovoked physical or verbal attack on another person, especially one who is unlikely to defend himself or herself.

peers People who are about the same age and status as oneself.

Male Bonding Sometimes the only way to distinguish aggression from rough-and-tumble play is to look at the faces. The hitter is not scowling, the hittee is laughing, and the hugger is just joining in the fun. Another clue that this is rough-and-tumble play comes from gender and context. These boys are in a Head Start program, where they are learning social skills, such as how to avoid fighting.

rough-and-tumble play Play that mimics aggression through wrestling, chasing, or hitting but that actually occurs in fun, with no intent to harm.

sociodramatic play Pretend play in which children act out various roles and themes in stories that they create themselves.

knows how to gain entry to a play group, to manage conflict through the use of humor, and to select and keep friends and playmates—all signs of a sophisticated theory of mind. How does play teach those skills? Let us look at two forms of play that develop during early childhood.

Active Play

Children need to be active in order to develop muscle strength and control. It is much easier for a young child to be active with someone else than alone. Active play is usually social play during these years.

One beneficial form of such play is called **rough-and-tumble play,** because it looks quite rough and the children seem to tumble over each other. The term was actually coined by scientists who studied baby monkeys in East Africa (Jones, 1976). They noticed that the monkeys chased, attacked, rolled over in the dirt, and wrestled, quite roughly, but without hurting each other. If another monkey wanted to play, all it had to do was to come close, catch the eye of a peer, and then run away as if being chased. This was an invitation, which the other monkey almost always accepted.

When the scientists returned to their families, they realized that their children acted like the baby monkeys—that human youngsters also engage in rough-and-tumble-play! Unlike aggression, rough-and-tumble play is fun and constructive: It teaches children how to enter a relationship, assert themselves, and respond to the actions of someone else while exercising gross motor skills, all without hurting the other person (Pellegrini & Smith, 1998). (Adults who are unsure whether they are observing a fight that should be broken up or a social activity that should continue should look for a "play face." Children almost always smile, and often laugh, in rough-and-tumble play, whereas they frown and scowl in real fighting.)

Rough-and-tumble play is universal. It has been observed in Japan, Kenya, and Mexico as well as in every income and ethnic group in North America, Europe, and Australia (Boulton & Smith, 1989). Situational factors influence its occurrence, however. Two of the most important are space and supervision: Children are much more likely to engage in rough-and-tumble play when they have room to run and when adults are not directly nearby. This is one reason the ideal physical environment for children includes ample safe space for gross motor activities, with adults within earshot but not underfoot (Bradley, 1995).

Rough-and-tumble play requires both provocation and self-control and is carefully regulated and moderated by the children. It usually occurs among children who have had considerable social experience, often with one another. Not surprisingly, then, older children are more likely to engage in rough-and-tumble play than younger ones. In fact, the incidence of rough-and-tumble play increases with age, peaking at about age 8 to 10 and then decreasing (Pellegrini & Smith, 1998).

Imaginative Play

Children can and do use their imaginations by themselves. But they are most likely to develop a strong self-concept through interaction with others. In another type of social play, called **sociodramatic play,** children act out various roles and themes in stories they themselves have created, taking on "any identity, role, or activity that they choose. They can be mothers, babies, Cinderella, or Captain Hook. They can make tea or fly to the moon. Or they can fight, hurt others, or kill or imprison someone" (Dunn & Hughes, 2001, p. 491). Sociodramatic play provides a way for children to learn from each other as they do the following:

- Explore and rehearse the social roles they see being enacted around them
- Test their own ability to explain and convince others of their ideas
- Regulate their emotions through imagination, as they pretend to be afraid, angry, and so on
- Develop a self-concept in a nonthreatening context, taking the part of a brave soldier, a happy mother, and so on

The beginnings of sociodramatic play can be seen when a toddler "feeds" or "cuddles" or "punishes" a doll or stuffed animal. Sociodramatic play becomes more interactive and greatly increases in frequency and complexity between the ages of 2 and 6. Although both sexes engage in sociodramatic play, girls do it more, and they are less likely than boys to use violent themes. Boys playing together are more likely than girls to engage in rough-and-tumble play. Despite these differences, both sexes apparently learn important prosocial skills as they play.

The best setting for children to practice social skills with peers is a high-quality educational program with ample play space, playmates, and play materials, where teachers can help them master fear and anger. Children learn to modify their emotional expressions in response to the reaction of their playmates: For instance, if a child gets hurt in rough-and-tumble play or gets confused in sociodramatic play, the play partner learns how to be more careful and clear.

To summarize this section, we begin with a quote from a report by 22 leading researchers on early childhood:

> The developmental tasks of this period range from the mastery of essential building blocks for learning and the motivation to succeed in school, to the ability to get along with other children, to make friends, and become engaged in a social group, as well as the capacity to manage powerful emotions.
>
> [National Research Council and Institute of Medicine, 2000, p. 386]

As you can see, in listing six tasks of early childhood, they begin with one cognitive task, then cite four emotional tasks, and conclude with emotional regulation. From Erikson's stage of initiative versus guilt to Goleman's notion of emotional intelligence, every observer realizes that emotional development is crucial in early childhood. Excessive stress or maltreatment can disrupt such regulation, causing externalizing or internalizing problems.

Gradually, all 2- to 6-year-olds get better at controlling their emotions. Negative emotions, such as anger and fear, are particularly likely to become regulated. The self-concept develops: Pride, purpose, and initiative are typical of young children's optimism, as Erikson describes. Those children who, because of genetic patterns or early mistreatment, do not regulate their emotions (perhaps at age 6 still bursting into tears when they are frightened or exploding in temper when they are angry) are likely to have social difficulties during the school years, because their emotions are overcontrolled or undercontrolled. Many researchers believe that emotional regulation is the foundation for later social skills and cognitive growth. Such growth is evident when children become more prosocial and less antisocial, expressing empathy more than anger. All forms of social play, including rough-and-tumble and sociodramatic play, help develop such regulation as children teach one another the limits of both emotional expression and fantasy.

LAURA DWIGHT

Sociodramatic Play Just like the boys in the previous photograph, these girls are developing their social skills—in this case, as store owner and grocery shopper.

? *Observational Quiz* (see answer, page 246): Which specifics of the girls' fantasy play are similar to the real thing, and which are not?

Parenting Patterns

We have seen that young children's emotions and actions are affected by many things, including brain maturation, peers, gender, and culture. Parenting patterns are also influential (Maccoby, 2000; Patterson, 1998). Many observers, however, have exaggerated the role of parents:

> Contemporary students of socialization largely agree that early researchers often overstated conclusions from correlational findings; relied excessively on singular, deterministic views of parental influence; and failed to attend to the potentially confounding effects of heredity. Contemporary researchers have taken steps to remedy many of these shortcomings. Unfortunately, the weaknesses of old studies still permeate presentations of socialization research in introductory textbooks and the mass media, partly because they appeal to preferences for simple generalizations.
>
> *[Collins et al., 2000, p. 218]*

It is equally false to *deny* the impact of parents. Particularly in early childhood, parents are pivotal not only in direct interaction but also indirectly, in choosing whether and where children go to school, which friendships are encouraged, and how much children can play. Detailed research, such as that just reviewed on emotional regulation, finds that particulars of parental behavior have a decided influence—as do many other factors.

That said, another conclusion of recent research must be emphasized: There is no single "best" way to parent a young child. Ideally, every young child has both a mother and a father figure (not necessarily the biological parents) who are warm and encouraging. Specifics of good parenting vary (Dishion & Bullock, 2002). This becomes apparent when families from many cohorts and cultures are compared (Hulbert, 2003).

Baumrind's Three Styles of Parenting

The study of parenting patterns has been greatly influenced by the early work of Diana Baumrind (1967, 1971). Baumrind began with 100 preschool children, all from California and almost all European-American and middle class. (The limitations of this sample were not obvious at the time.)

As a careful researcher, Baumrind used many measures of behavior, several of them involving naturalistic observation. First, she observed the children's activities in preschool and, on the basis of their actions, rated their self-control, independence, self-confidence, and other attributes. She then interviewed both parents of each child and observed parent–child interaction in two settings, at home and in the laboratory.

Baumrind found that parents differed on four important dimensions:

- *Expressions of warmth,* or nurturance, which ranged from very affectionate to quite cold parental behavior
- *Strategies for discipline,* which might involve parental explanation, criticism, persuasion, and/or physical punishment
- *The quality of communication* between parents and children; some parents listened patiently, while others demanded silence
- *Expectations for maturity,* evident in how much responsibility and self-control was demanded by parents

On the basis of these four dimensions, Baumrind identified three basic styles of parenting:

1. **Authoritarian parenting.** The parents' word is law, not to be questioned. Misconduct brings strict punishment, usually physical (although authoritarian parents do not cross the line into physical abuse). Demands for maturity

! *Answer to Observational Quiz* (from page 245): The girls' hats, necklaces, and shoes are all quite different from those their mothers would likely wear to the store, and the stock, the money holder, and the grocery bag are not typical. However, the essence of shopping is here: Money is exchanged for goods, and both participants politely play their roles.

authoritarian parenting Baumrind's term for a style of child rearing in which standards for proper behavior are high, misconduct is strictly punished, and parent–child communication is low.

are high. Authoritarian parents communicate their rules and standards, but communication is not interactive; discussion about emotions is especially rare. One adult from such a family said that there were only two acceptable responses to "How do you feel?": "Good" or "Tired." Although they love and care about their children, authoritarian parents seem aloof, showing little affection or nurturance.

2. **Permissive parenting.** Some parents make few demands, hiding any impatience they feel. Discipline is lax because expectations for maturity are low. Permissive parents are nurturant and accepting. They listen to whatever their offspring say, and they share their own emotions without restrictions. They view themselves as available to help their children but not as responsible for shaping how their children turn out. They hope to be friends, not authorities, to their children.

3. **Authoritative parenting.** Authoritative parents set limits and enforce rules. However, they also listen to their children's requests and questions and discuss feelings and problems. The parents demand maturity of their offspring, but they are also nurturant and understanding, forgiving (rather than punishing) a child when demands for maturity are not met. They bend the rules in some circumstances. They seek to be guides and mentors, neither authorities nor friends.

The characteristics of these three styles are summarized in Table 10.2.

All three styles of parenting reflect underlying love and concern. This is crucial for every child's well-being. Children from every ethnic group and every continent benefit if they believe that their parents love and appreciate them. Children suffer if they feel rejected and unwanted, according to a detailed summary of dozens of studies (Khaleque & Rohner, 2002). Several other styles of parenting have been identified, two of which are especially harmful: *neglectful parenting* (also called *uninvolved*), in which the parents do not seem to care at all, and *indulgent parenting,* in which the parents accommodate the child's every whim.

Baumrind and many others have continued to study parenting styles, following the original 100 children as they grew and studying thousands of other children of various backgrounds and ages. They have come to the following conclusions:

- *Authoritarian* parents raise children who are likely to be conscientious, obedient, and quiet; however, the children are not especially happy. They are more likely to feel guilty or depressed. They internalize their frustrations, blaming themselves when things don't go their way. As adolescents, they sometimes rebel.
- *Permissive* parents raise children who are likely to be even less happy and to lack self-control, especially within the give-and-take of peer friendships. Their inadequate emotional regulation makes them immature and impedes friendship formation.
- *Authoritative* parents raise children who are likely to be successful, articulate, intelligent, happy with themselves, and generous with others. These children tend to be liked by teachers and peers.

Follow-up research has found that, at least for middle-class families of European ancestry, the initial advantages of the authoritative approach grow stronger over time, helping children to achieve in school, adolescents to avoid drug abuse, and young adults to have high self-esteem. Other research finds that the best way to promote prosocial behavior and to limit aggression is to induce children to think about and then verbalize the human consequences of cultural differences. This is easier for children raised in authoritative homes, where thought and expression are encouraged.

permissive parenting Baumrind's term for a style of child rearing in which the parents seldom punish, guide, or control the child but are nurturant and communicate well with the child.

authoritative parenting Baumrind's term for a style of child rearing in which the parents set limits and provide guidance for their child but are willing to listen to the child's ideas and to make compromises.

Parenting Style This woman is disciplining her son, who does not look happy about it.

? *Observational Quiz* (see answer, page 248): Which parenting style is shown here?

TABLE 10.2 Characteristics of Parenting Styles Identified by Baumrind

| | | | Characteristics | | |
| | | | | Communication | |
Style	Warmth	Discipline	Expectations of Maturity	Parent to Child	Child to Parent
Authoritarian	Low	Strict, often physical	High	High	Low
Permissive	High	Rare	Low	Low	High
Authoritative	High	Moderate, with much discussion	Moderate	High	High

Baumrind named two of her three parenting styles with almost the same word; only the last syllables differ. How will you remember them? One student said that "authoritarian" *Is Awfully Negative (-ian),* but "authoritative" *Is Very Excellent (-ive).* Maybe this memory trick will work for you, too.

!Answer to Observational Quiz (from page 247): The authoritative style. Note the firm hold this woman has on her defiant son; he must listen (evidence that she is not permissive). Also note that she is talking to him, not hitting or yelling, and that her expression is warm (evidence that she is not authoritarian).

Many recent studies have found the link between parenting styles and the child's behavior to be less direct than in Baumrind's original research (Galambos et al., 2003). First, the child's temperament interacts with the parent's style. A fearful child needs gentle parenting, and a bolder child needs more restrictive (but still warm) parenting (Bates et al., 1998; Kochanska et al., 1997). Second, community and cultural differences influence the child's perception of the quality of parenting. Perception is crucial: The same remark may be interpreted by the child as either kind or critical. Effective Asian-American and African-American parents are often stricter, at least as measured by Baumrind's typology, than effective European-American parents (Chao, 2001; Wachs, 1999).

This last finding surprised developmentalists. The first hypothesis to explain the success of strict nonwhite parents was that more authoritarian parenting is required when families live in stressful, violent neighborhoods. However, even in "good" neighborhoods in the United States, minority parents tend to impose strict guidelines and to use some physical punishment, and these strategies tend to produce high-achieving, emotionally regulated children; the same strategies are less successful in European-American families (Darling & Steinberg, 1997). The crucial factors seem to be parental warmth, support, and concern for the child, which are expressed in ways that vary with the family's cultural background and current circumstances.

Among the indicators of parental warmth are caressing or hugging the child, answering the child's questions, and inviting the child to participate in a conversation between adults. Such warmth buffers the potentially harmful effects of strict standards of behavior (McLoyd & Smith, 2002). The reason may be that children within each culture have specific perceptions about good parenting, and they interpret whatever their parents do in light of their culture and their emotional attachment to their parents. This is true whether children are evaluating fathers or mothers (Townsend, 2002).

Punishment

How a parent disciplines a child is an integral part of parenting style. Given what researchers have learned about cognition, it is apparent that proactive and preventive discipline is preferable to punishment. Four specific recommendations are listed in Table 10.3.

Techniques of Discipline

No disciplinary technique works quickly and automatically. Instead, over the years from 2 to 6, children gradually learn to reflect on the consequences of their actions, and their actions become more in line with expectations.

Culture is a strong influence on disciplinary techniques. Japanese mothers, for example, use reasoning, empathy, and expressions of disappointment to control their children's social behavior more than North American mothers do.

TABLE 10.3 **Relating Discipline to Developmental Characteristics During Early Childhood**

1. *Remember theory of mind.* Young children gradually understand things from other viewpoints. Hence involving empathy ("How would *you* feel if . . .?") will increase prosocial and decrease antisocial behavior.

2. *Remember emerging self-concept.* Young children are developing a sense of who they are and what they want, sometimes egocentrically. Adults should protect that emerging self: They should not force 3-year-olds to share their favorite toys, nor should they tell them, "Words can never hurt." Relational aggression is painful, as young children know.

3. *Remember the language explosion and fast mapping.* Young children are eager to talk and think, but they are not always accurate in their verbal understanding. Hence, a child who doesn't "listen" should not necessarily be punished, because a command might be heard but not understood. Conversation before and after an event helps the child learn.

4. *Remember that young children are not yet logical.* The connection between the misdeed and the punishment needs to be immediate and transparent. A child might not learn from waiting several hours to be spanked for deliberately breaking a dish but might learn from picking up the pieces, mopping the floor, and perhaps contributing some saved pennies toward a replacement.

These techniques work quite well, partly because the mother–child relationship is much stronger in Japan (where it is referred to as *amae,* a very close interpersonal bond) than in North America (Rothbaum et al., 2000).

Each culture has its own expectations, offenses, and punishments. What is "rude" or "nasty" or "undisciplined" behavior in one community is perfectly OK, even encouraged, in another. For example, unlike Japanese parents, parents in the United States allow and even encourage emotional expression of all sorts, including anger. Perhaps as a result, in a series of experimental situations designed to elicit distress and conflict, American 4- to 5-year-olds were more aggressive than their Japanese counterparts (Zahn-Waxler, Friedman, et al., 1996).

One disciplinary technique often used in North America is the **time-out,** which involves requiring the child to stop all activity and sit in a corner or to stay indoors for a few minutes. Other punishment practices are *withdrawal of a privilege,* such as television watching, and *withdrawal of affection,* as when the parent expresses disappointment or gives the child a stern "look."

Each of these techniques may have unintended consequences. Developmentalists stress the need for parents to choose punishments carefully, noting the effect on the child. Once again, the child's temperament, age, and perceptions are crucial. For example, time-out is severe punishment for a child who seeks social approval and fears public shame, but time-out may be welcomed by a child who is a defiant loner. In fact, for such a child, time-out may be a reinforcement instead of a punishment.

As mentioned, talking with a child is often effective because it helps the child understand and learn. This may explain why parents and preschoolers are three times as likely to talk about the reasons for negative emotions (e.g., fear, sadness, anger, worry) than about the reasons for positive emotions (e.g., joy, pleasure, pride) (Lagattuta & Wellman, 2002). Once again, however, the effectiveness of talking depends partly on the child's temperament (Fowles & Kochanska, 2000) as well as age. Few 3-year-olds have any answer to an angry parent's question: "Why did you do that?"

What About Spanking?

Many developmentalists wonder whether punishment in any form might boomerang. Do children who are criticized develop low self-esteem? Do those

time-out A disciplinary technique in which the child is required to stop all activity and sit in a corner or stay indoors for a few minutes.

DAVID STRICKLER / MONKMEYER

Angela at Play Research suggests that being spanked is a salient and memorable experience for young children, not because of the pain but because of the emotions. Children seek to do what they have learned; they know not only how to place their hands but also that an angry person does the hitting. The only part of the lesson they usually forget is what particular misdeed precipitated the punishment. Asked why she is spanking her doll, Angela will likely explain, "She was bad."

Especially for Parents Suppose you agree that spanking is destructive, but you sometimes get so angry at your child's behavior that you hit him or her. Is your reaction appropriate?

who are shamed feel that they are not loved? Do those who are physically punished learn to be more aggressive?

Many cultural issues are involved in questions about punishment. In Sweden, for instance, physical punishment of children is against the law for parents as well as for teachers. By contrast, in some Caribbean nations, all parents are expected to physically punish their children and to be very sparing of praise (Durbrow, 1999). In the United States, physical punishment is more commonly accepted in the Deep South than in the states along the Canadian border.

Ninety percent of North American adults were spanked as children, and most consider themselves none the worse for it. Indeed, not only in North America but also throughout Asia, Africa, and South America, parents usually believe that spanking is acceptable, legitimate, and necessary at times (Durrant, 1996; Levinson, 1989). They are especially likely to spank 2- to 6-year-olds, because young children are considered "old enough to know better" but "not old enough to listen to reason." Spanking is so common that parents of all types resort to it: permissive parents in exasperation, authoritative parents as a last resort after a series of warnings, and authoritarian parents as a direct consequence of breaking a rule.

Many developmentalists fear that children who are physically punished will learn to be more aggressive. Domestic violence of any type—from spanking a child to letting siblings "fight it out" to exposing children to mutual insults or hitting between the parents—seems to increase aggression between peers and within families (Straus, 1994).

Spanking is only one factor in later peer violence and domestic abuse. It is not always destructive of later prosocial actions (McLoyd & Smith, 2002). The question developmentalists ask is "Why take the risk?" when physical punishment tends to increase antisocial behavior and only temporarily increases obedience (Gershoff, 2002). If punishment is harsh, with frequent spanking and yelling, it is likely to produce an angry, disobedient child, no matter what the parenting style or family background (Amato & Fowler, 2002).

The Challenge of Video

Some people who are not parents imagine that parenting is a straightforward task. They may believe that they will raise their own children as they were raised or that they will provide clear rules and their children will obey. It is never that simple: Preschoolers are emotionally immature, sometimes angry or fearful or defiant in ways that not only distress the parents but also may harm the child. Normal children want to talk when they should be quiet, run when they should walk, show off when they should be modest.

One particular dilemma for parents revolves around allowing children to watch television and play video games—as almost every North American child does for several hours each day. Parents find that video is a good babysitter and can sometimes be an educational tool, and they find it very difficult to follow the advice of some nonparents and many experts.

For example, six major organizations concerned with the psychological and physical well-being of children (the American Psychological Association, the

American Academy of Pediatrics, the American Medical Association, the American Academy of Child and Adolescent Psychiatry, the American Academy of Family Physicians, and the American Psychiatric Association) suggest that parents turn off the TV and avoid exposing their children to video violence—whether in cartoons, situation comedies, video games, or the evening news (Anderson & Bushman, 2002).

The Evidence on Aggression

Film and TV executives say the media are merely reflecting reality, but critic Michael Medved (1995) asks, if TV violence is part of everyday life,

> . . . then why do so few people witness murders in real life but everybody sees them on TV and in the movies? The most violent ghetto isn't in South Central L.A. or Southeast Washington, D.C.; it's on television. About 350 characters appear each night on prime-time TV, but studies show an average of seven of these people are murdered every night. If this rate applied in reality, then in just 50 days everyone in the United States would be killed and the last one left could turn off the TV.

At 10 A.M. on Saturday mornings, more than half of all young North American children are watching TV (Comstock & Scharrer, 1999). What do they see and learn? The "good guys," whether in cartoons or police dramas, do as much hitting, shooting, and kicking as the bad guys, yet the consequences of their violence are sanitized, justified, or made comic. All the good guys are male, even on educational television (Big Bird, Barney), and no matter how nonhuman (e.g., SpongeBob SquarePants), no hero is nonwhite, although villains sometimes are. Women are portrayed as victims or adoring girlfriends, almost never as leaders—except in a very few sex-stereotyped programs that boys never watch.

Video games are worse than broadcast television in every respect—more violent, more sexist, more racist. Almost all the characters in 33 popular Nintendo and Sega Genesis video games are male and Anglo, and 80 percent of the games include violence or aggression as an essential strategy the child must use to score points (Dietz, 1998). Children of all ages who watch violent television become more violent themselves (Huesmann et al., 2003; Johnson et al., 2002; Singer et al., 1999).

The Evidence on Content

Parents like me who cannot forbid *all* television can at least monitor the content of the TV programs and video games their children see. The messages conveyed on the screen are influential, as confirmed by a longitudinal study that surveyed children at about age 5 and again at about age 16. Young children who watched educational television (mostly *Sesame Street* and *Mr. Rogers' Neighborhood*) became teenagers who earned higher grades and did more reading than other high school students, especially if they were boys. By contrast, those who watched violent TV programs had lower grades, especially if they were girls (Anderson et al., 2001). Using a variety of statistical safeguards, the researchers found causation, not merely correlation. In other words, although parents who encouraged their children to watch *Mr. Rogers' Neighborhood* might also be parents who encouraged their children to get good grades (correlation), this research found that educational television in and of itself had a positive impact (causation).

The fact that content is crucial is one reason video games are of great concern to many developmental researchers. Remember that good science is

Dangerous Video Game? It is easy to understand and justify a preschooler's fascination with video games. This 4-year-old in Sweden is developing computer skills, learning to read, and unlikely to get into trouble as he sits quietly and stares at the screen. However, developmentalists would point out that neurological pathways developed while children play video games, especially violent ones, may lead to antisocial, aggressive behavior later in life.

ALEX FARNSWORTH / THE IMAGE WORKS

Response for Parents (from page 250): The worst time to spank a child is when you are angry, because you might seriously hurt the child and because the child will associate anger with violence and may follow your example. Better to learn to control your anger and develop other strategies for disciplining your child or for preventing him or her from misbehaving in the first place.

accumulated in a deliberate fashion, with various methods and diverse populations and samples, over a period of years. Scientists are reluctant to state flatly that violent video games are worse than violent TV programs because few controlled, longitudinal studies have compared the actual impact of the two. Ideally, a third comparison group, of children from the same types of families and cultures but who *never* watched TV or played video games, would be studied—but in reality, such groups of children do not exist anywhere in the world.

The research that we do have has confirmed that violent TV and video games are destructive, pushing children to be more violent than they would otherwise be (Bushman & Anderson, 2001). Computer games are probably worse, because "It seems likely that the impact of watching characters being killed on television will be exceeded for a child playing a computer game who is doing the virtual killing" (Larson, 2001, p. 150).

From a developmental perspective, early childhood may be the most vulnerable period for the impact of video images for two reasons. First, young children spend more time in front of the TV and other video screens than do people of any other age group. Second, young children are just beginning to learn about society, culture, and emotions. One popular solution among religious parents is to show their children Veggie Tales, videotapes in which vegetables depict Bible stories; these parents believe that content matters.

Developmentalists focus on more than the overt topics of video content:

■ Perpetuation of sexist, ageist, and racist stereotypes
■ Depiction of violent solutions for every problem, with no expression of empathy
■ Encouragement of quick, reactive emotions, not thoughtful regulation

From what you already know about child development, you can understand why those six leading organizations hope that children never watch television or play video games. What you know about parenting probably helps you understand why this is a difficult challenge. (When you read the In Person feature on page 227, did you wonder why my daughter Sarah was so frustrated that she called me names? It was because I had unplugged the TV.)

Parent–child interaction is not the only influence on children's psychosocial development, but parenting practices do have a significant impact. Over the past 40 years, Diana Baumrind and most other developmentalists have found that authoritative parenting (warm, with guidance) is more effective than either authoritarian (very strict) or permissive (very lenient) parenting.

It is also true that, worldwide, children see their parents through the lens of their culture. In any culture, children thrive when their parents appreciate them and care about their accomplishments. The children of parents who are uninvolved or uncaring are seldom happy, well-adjusted, or high-achieving.

Cultures differ in their views of appropriate methods of punishment. Spanking can be a quick way to make children stop whatever they are doing, but most developmentalists believe that nonphysical techniques of discipline, such as time-outs, are more effective over the long term. Children who are frequently spanked do not necessarily become more obedient, and they are more likely to become angry and hostile.

Good parenting is not achieved by following any one simple rule; children's temperaments vary, and cultural dictates diverge. Violent television programs and video games pose a particular challenge to parents, because children who watch them tend to become more aggressive and because all children are attracted to the moving images on the video screen. Parental monitoring of the content of TV programs and video games—the underlying messages as well as the overt themes—is crucial.

Boy or Girl: So What?

Male or female identity is an important feature of self-concept as well as a particular concern of many parents. Indeed, from the moment a baby is born, others ask "Boy or girl?" and parents select gender-distinct clothes, blankets, and even pacifiers. By age 2, children already know their own sex and become more aware of gender with every year of childhood (Maccoby, 1998).

Social scientists distinguish between **sex differences,** which are the biological differences between males and females, and **gender differences,** which are culturally imposed differences in the roles and behaviors of males and females. Curiously, although true *sex* differences are far less apparent in childhood (when boys and girls are about the same size and shape) than in adulthood (when physical differences become more visible and anatomy becomes critical in sexual intercourse, pregnancy, and birth), *gender* differentiation seems more significant to children than to adults.

sex differences Biological differences between males and females.

gender differences Culturally imposed differences in the roles and behavior of males and females.

The Development of Gender Awareness

Even at age 2, gender-related preferences and play patterns are apparent. Children already know whether they are boys or girls, can identify adult strangers as mommies or daddies, and can apply gender labels (*Mrs., Mr., lady, man*) consistently. That simple cognitive awareness becomes, by age 3, a rudimentary understanding that sex distinctions are lifelong (although some pretend, hope, or imagine otherwise). By age 4, children are convinced that certain toys (such as dolls or trucks) and certain roles (such as nurse or soldier) are appropriate for one gender but not the other (Bauer et al., 1998; Ruble & Martin, 1998).

When given a choice, children play with children of their own gender, a tendency that is apparent at age 2 and is clear-cut by age 4, with children becoming more selective and exclusive as they mature (Martin & Fabes, 2001). By school age, a few children still have a friend of the other sex, but they rarely play with that friend when other children are around (Kovacs et al., 1996).

Throughout the play years, children confuse gender and sex. Awareness that a person's sex is a biological characteristic, not determined by words, opinions, or clothing, develops gradually, becoming firm at age 8 or so (Szkrybalo & Ruble, 1999). This uncertainty about the biological determination of sex was demonstrated by a 3-year-old who went with his father to see a neighbor's newborn kittens. Returning home, the child reported to his mother that there were three girl kittens and two boy kittens. "How do you know?" she asked. "Daddy picked them up and read what was written on their tummies," he answered.

Two Sets of Cousins Same day, same trampoline, and similar genes and culture, because these eight children are cousins. But sex or gender differences are quite apparent in the later preschool years. This group, like any group of preschoolers, offers suggestive evidence of boy–girl differences, here including one specific aspect of their apparel.

?*Observational Quiz* (see answer, page 254): What sex or gender differences can you see?

(a)

(b)

! *Answer to Observational Quiz* (from page 253): The most obvious gender differences are in appearance. The girls have longer hair, and the colors and styles of their clothes are different. Did you notice the wearing-apparel difference—that the soles of all four boys' shoes are black, whereas the girls' are white or pink? Now let's get more speculative. The girl on the left, who may need to establish her alliance with the group since she is the only one in colors a boy might wear, is looking at and talking with her cousins—a very female thing to do. In addition, the girls' facial and body expressions suggest they are much more comfortable with this close contact. In fact, the two boys on the left seem about to be relieving their tension with a bout of rough-and-tumble play.

phallic stage Freud's term for the third stage of psychosexual development, which occurs in early childhood and in which the penis becomes the focus of psychological concern as well as physiological pleasure.

Oedipus complex In the phallic stage of psychosexual development, the sexual desire that boys have for their mothers and the hostility that they have toward their fathers.

identification A defense mechanism that lets a person symbolically take on the behaviors and attitudes of someone more powerful than him- or herself.

superego In psychoanalytic theory, the part of the personality that is self-critical and judgmental and that internalizes the moral standards set by parents and society.

Electra complex In the phallic stage of psychosexual development, the female version of the Oedipus complex: Girls have sexual feelings for their fathers and accompanying hostility toward their mothers.

Theories of Gender Differences

Experts as well as parents disagree about what proportion of observed gender differences is biological (perhaps a matter of hormones, of brain structure, or of body size and musculature) and what proportion is environmental (perhaps embedded in centuries of cultural history or in the immediate, explicit home training each child receives) (Beal, 1994; Leaper, 2002). For example, you may remember a mention in the first section of this chapter that girls seem to be more advanced in emotional regulation than boys. This difference may be genetic, tied to the chromosomal differences between XX and XY that affect prenatal brain development. An alternative explanation is that mothers treat their sons and daughters differently in this regard, encouraging girls to control their emotions and boys to "let it all hang out" (Colder et al., 2002).

Explanations of gender differences are many and varied because the topic is so vast, individual experiences so disparate, and the research so wide-ranging that firm conclusions are elusive. To develop a framework for analyzing the conflicting evidence, we need a theory. Fortunately, we have five major theories, which were first described in Chapter 2.

Psychoanalytic Theory

Freud (1938) called the period from about age 3 to 6 the **phallic stage,** because he believed its central focus is the *phallus,* or penis. At about 3 or 4 years of age, said Freud, the process of maturation makes a boy aware of his male sexual organ. He begins to masturbate, to fear castration, and to develop sexual feelings toward his mother.

These feelings make every young boy jealous of his father—so jealous, according to Freud, that every son secretly wants to replace his dad. Freud called this the **Oedipus complex,** after Oedipus, son of a king in Greek mythology. Abandoned as an infant and raised in a distant kingdom, Oedipus later returned to his birthplace and, not realizing who they were, killed his own father and married his mother. When he discovered what he had done, he blinded himself in a spasm of guilt.

Freud believed that this ancient story still echoes throughout history because every man feels horribly guilty for the incestuous and murderous impulses that are buried in his unconscious. Boys fear that their fathers will inflict terrible punishment if their secret impulses are discovered. Therefore, they hide their feelings, even from themselves. Specifically, boys cope with their guilt and fear through **identification,** a defense mechanism that allows a person to ally him- or herself with another person by symbolically taking on that person's behavior and attitudes. Because they cannot replace their fathers, young boys strive to become them, copying their fathers' masculine mannerisms, opinions, and actions.

Boys also develop, again in self-defense, a powerful conscience, called the **superego,** that is quick to judge and punish "the bad guys." According to Freud's theory, a young boy's fascination with superheroes, guns, kung fu, and the like comes directly from his unconscious urges to kill his father. An adult man's obsession with crime and punishment might be explained by an imperfectly resolved phallic stage. In this perspective, a poorly resolved phallic stage is a likely explanation for homosexuality, either overt or latent, and for homophobia.

Freud offered two overlapping descriptions of the phallic stage in girls. One centers on the **Electra complex** (also named after a figure in classical mythology), which is similar to the Oedipus complex: The little girl wants to eliminate her mother and become intimate with her father. In the other description, the little girl becomes jealous of boys because they have penises, an emotion Freud called *penis envy.* The girl blames her mother for this "incompleteness" and decides that the next best thing to having a penis is to become sexually attractive so that someone who does have a penis—preferably her father—will love her (Freud, 1933/1965). Her *identification* is with women her father finds attractive; her superego strives to avoid his disapproval. Thus, the origins and consequences of the phallic stage are similar for girls and for boys.

As a woman, and as the mother of four daughters, I have regarded Freud's theory of sexual development as ridiculous, not to mention antifemale. I am not alone. Psychologists generally agree that Freud's explanation of sexual and moral development is one of the weaker parts of his theory, reflecting the values of middle-class Victorian society at the end of the nineteenth century more than any universal developmental pattern. In fact, most developmental researchers over the past 50 years have been very critical of psychoanalytic theory; only recently have they come to recognize the validity of some of Freud's ideas. I myself have softened my criticism of Freud, as the following In Person feature explains.

In Person

Berger and Freud

My family's first "Electra episode" occurred in a conversation with my eldest daughter, Bethany, when she was about 4 years old:

> **Bethany:** When I grow up, I'm going to marry Daddy.
> **Mother:** But Daddy's married to me.
> **Bethany:** That's all right. When I grow up, you'll probably be dead.
> **Mother:** *(Determined to stick up for myself)* Daddy's older than me, so when I'm dead, he'll probably be dead, too.
> **Bethany:** That's OK. I'll marry him when he gets born again.

At this point, I couldn't think of a good reply, especially since I had no idea where she had gotten the concept of reincarnation. Bethany saw my face fall, and she took pity on me:

> **Bethany:** Don't worry, Mommy. After you get born again, you can be our baby.

The second episode was a conversation I had with my daughter Rachel when she was about 5:

> **Rachel:** When I get married, I'm going to marry Daddy.
> **Mother:** Daddy's already married to me.
> **Rachel:** *(With the joy of having discovered a wonderful solution)* Then we can have a double wedding!

The third episode was considerably more graphic. It took the form of a "valentine" left on my husband's pillow by my daughter Elissa, who was about 8 years old at the time. It is reproduced here.

Finally, when my youngest daughter, Sarah, turned 5, she also expressed the desire to marry my husband. When I told

her she couldn't, because he was married to me, her response revealed one more reason why TV can be pernicious: "Oh yes, a man can have two wives. I saw it on television."

I am not the only feminist developmentalist to be taken aback by her own children's words. Nancy Datan (1986) wrote about the Oedipal conflict: "I have a son who was once five years old. From that day to this, I have never thought Freud mistaken." Obviously, these bits of "evidence" do not prove that Freud was correct. I still think he was wrong on many counts. But Freud's description of the phallic stage now seems less bizarre to me than it once did.

Pillow Talk Elissa placed this artwork on my husband's pillow. My pillow, beside it, had a less colorful, less elaborate note—an afterthought. It read "Dear Mom, I love you too."

Behaviorism

In contrast with psychoanalytic theorists, behaviorists believe that virtually all roles are learned and hence are the result of nurture, not nature. To behaviorists, gender distinctions are the product of years of ongoing reinforcement and punishment rather than of any specific stage.

What evidence supports this theory? Parents, peers, and teachers all reward behavior that is "gender-appropriate" more than "gender-inappropriate" (Ruble & Martin, 1998). Parents praise their sons for not crying ("He took it like a man"), for example, but caution their daughters about the hazards of rough play ("Act like a lady"). This male–female distinction seems to be more significant to fathers and to young boys than to older boys or to females of any age (Banerjee & Linstern, 2000). Boys are criticized for being "sissies" more than girls are criticized for being "tomboys." Fathers, more than mothers, expect their daughters to be feminine and their sons to be tough. Behaviorists attribute this discrepancy to culture: Society punishes "weak" men more than "strong" women.

Behaviorists stress that children learn about proper behavior not only through direct reinforcement (such as a gift or a word of praise) but also by observation in social learning. They model their behavior particularly after that of people they perceive to be nurturing, powerful, and yet similar to themselves. For young children, those people are usually their parents. And parental attitudes about gender differences become increasingly influential as children grow older (Tenenbaum & Leaper, 2002).

Ironically, fathers and mothers of young children follow sex-stereotyped roles more than do people of any other life stage, because the care of very young children is still considered primarily a woman's job. This means that if boys and girls model their behavior after that of their parents, they will follow examples that are quite sex-specific. The importance of modeling is also shown in the fact that young children of either sex who have older brothers become more masculine and those who have older sisters become more feminine, just as behaviorism would predict (Rust et al., 2000).

Thus, conformity to gender expectations is still rewarded, punished, and modeled, especially for young children and especially for boys. This may explain why girls can aspire to traditionally male occupations but boys cannot aspire to traditionally female occupations without experiencing disapproval, especially from other males.

Note again that gender prejudice is strongest during the play years. If a college man wants to be a nurse or a preschool teacher, most of his classmates respect his choice. If a 4-year-old boy wants the same thing, his peers probably tell him he is wrong. As one professor reports:

> My son came home after 2 days of preschool to announce that he could not grow up to teach seminars (previously his lifelong ambition, because he knew from personal observation that everyone at seminars got to eat cookies) because only women could be teachers.

> [Fagot, 1995, p. 173]

Cognitive Theory

In explaining gender identity and gender differences, cognitive theorists focus on children's understanding—on the way a child intellectually grasps a specific issue or value (Martin, 2000). Young children, they point out, have many gender-related experiences but not much cognitive depth. They tend to see the world in intellectually simple terms. For this reason, male and female are categorized as opposites, even when some evidence (such as the father whom they saw cleaning the living room) contradicts such a sexist assumption. Nuances, complexities, exceptions, and gradations are beyond the intellect of the preoperational child.

RONNIE KAUFMAN / CORBIS

Rehearsal for Future Motherhood This preschooler is demonstrating three behaviors that are considered appropriate for girls and are almost never seen in boys: She is wearing a skirt, tucking her crossed legs back, and cradling a doll.

Remember that the basic tenet of cognitive theory is that a person's thinking determines how the world is perceived and how that perception is acted on. When personal experience is ambiguous or puzzling, young children search for the categories they have formed describing appropriate gender behavior. For example, when researchers gave young children unfamiliar, gender-neutral toys, the children first tried to figure out whether the toys were for boys or for girls and then decided whether or not they personally would like to play with them (Martin et al., 1995).

Similarly, when older children were shown drawings of people engaging in unfamiliar (actually nonexistent) occupations, they judged the status of the occupation according to whether the workers were men or women, ranking the supposedly female occupations lower than the male ones. The point is that children develop a mental set, a cognitive perception, which biases their views of whatever experiences they have.

Sociocultural Theory

Proponents of the sociocultural perspective point out that many traditional cultures emphasize gender distinctions. In societies where adult activities and dress are strictly separated by gender, girls and boys attend sex-segregated schools and virtually never play together (Beal, 1994). In such cultures, children quickly adopt the patterns of talking, behaving, and even thinking that are prescribed for their sex.

The particulars of gender education—such as which activities are promoted for which sex—vary by region, socioeconomic status, and historical period. For example, women in many regions of the world are responsible for growing the vegetables and grains; but on North American farms, men are in charge of growing all the crops. Yet every society has powerful values and attitudes regarding preferred behavior for men and women, and every culture teaches these to the young, even though the particular tasks assigned to males and to females vary from one society to another. To sociocultural theorists, this proves that society, not biology, determines where the sexual divide is drawn.

After 30 years of feminist campaigns for gender equity, one might imagine that any remaining sex differences in developed nations would be biological, not cultural. This is not the case: Gender stereotypes are still omnipresent for young children in every country. Consider Halloween dress-up, a North American custom. (Most nations have no Halloween.) Only 10 percent of children's costumes in a recent study of 469 different costumes were gender-neutral, and those neutral ones were designed for babies. Girls trick-or-treated as pumpkin princesses, blushing brides, and beauty queens; boys dressed as warriors and villains of all sorts, including Hercules, Dracula, and the serial killer Jack the Ripper. Even animal costumes were sex-specific, with girls dressed as black cats and pink dragons, boys as lions and T-Rex dinosaurs (Nelson, 2000).

To break through the restrictiveness of culture and to encourage individuals to define themselves primarily as human beings, rather than as males or females, many parents and teachers embrace the idea of androgyny. As developmentalists use the term, **androgyny** means a balance, within a person, of traditionally male and female psychological characteristics. To achieve androgyny, boys should be encouraged to be nurturant and girls to

Especially for Gender Idealists Suppose you want to raise an androgynous child. What would happen if you told no one your newborn's sex, dressed it in yellow and white, not pink or blue, and gave it a gender-neutral name, such as Chris or Lee?

androgyny A balance, within a person, of traditionally male and female psychological characteristics.

Trick or Treat? Any doubt about which of these children are girls and which are boys? No. Any question about whether such strict gender distinctions are appropriate at age 4? Maybe.

be assertive, so that they will develop less restrictive, not gender-bound, self-concepts (Bem, 1993).

Sociocultural theory stresses, however, that androgyny (or any other gender concept) cannot be taught to children simply through cognition or parental reinforcement. The only way children will be truly androgynous is if their entire culture promotes such ideas and practices—something no culture has yet done. Why not? The reasons may lie buried far deeper in human nature than the political forces or social values of the moment, as epigenetic theory suggests.

Epigenetic Theory

We saw in Chapter 2 that epigenetic theory contends that every aspect of human behavior is the result of interaction between genes and early experience—not just for the individual but also for all humans. The idea that many gender differences are genetically based is supported by recent research in neurobiology, which finds biological differences between male and female brains. Sex hormones produced by XX (female) or XY (male) chromosomes begin to circulate in the fetal stage, affecting the development of the brain throughout life (Cameron, 2001).

Although epigenetic theory stresses the biological and genetic origins of behavior, it also stresses that the environment shapes, enhances, or halts those genetic impulses. Here is one example: Infant girls seem to be genetically inclined to talk earlier than boys, perhaps because in prehistoric times, when women stayed home together to care for the children while men hunted, women had to become more adept at social interaction. Consequently, female brains favored language.

Today, while females no longer need a linguistic advantage, girls genetically tend to be more responsive to language than boys, and mothers are usually more verbal than fathers. Mother–daughter pairs typically talk more than father–son pairs do (Leaper, 2002). Thus, a baby girl's slight linguistic advantage in inherited brain circuitry will become a notably higher level of language proficiency as she grows up (Leaper et al., 1998). By school age, the average girl is better at language arts than the average boy, for epigenetic, not merely genetic, reasons.

Epigenetic theorists note that the language areas of an infant's brain develop as the infant is regularly spoken to. Suppose a boy is an only child, raised in a household with several nurturant women. He may be talked to, sung to, and read to by all his devoted caregivers. His linguistic environment (which is much richer than that of most infants), interacting with his genetic potential (which might be slightly less than that of the typical girl), will cause him to develop superior verbal ability. In this way, environmental factors will greatly enhance his genetic capabilities, perhaps allowing him to be tops in all the language arts in the first grade. In the same way, all sex and gender differences may have genetic roots, for reasons that originated thousands of years ago, but modern society can enhance or redirect those differences.

Conclusion: Gender and Destiny

The first and last of our five major theories—psychoanalytic theory and epigenetic theory—emphasize the power of biology. A reader who is quick to form opinions might seize on those theories to decide that the gender-based behavior and sexual stereotypes exhibited by young children are impossible to change. This conclusion might be reinforced by the fact that gender awareness emerges early, by age 2. But the other three theories—behaviorism, cognitive theory, and sociocultural theory—all present persuasive evidence for the influence of family and culture.

Response for Gender Idealists (from page 257): Because babies are raised by a society and community as well as by the parents, and because at least some gender differences are biological, this attempt at androgyny would not succeed. First, other interested parties would decide for themselves that the child was male or female. Second, the child would sooner or later develop gender-specific play patterns, guided by the other boys or girls.

Thus, our five major theories, collectively, lead in two directions:

- Gender differences are rooted in biology, not merely culture.
- Biology is not destiny: Children are shaped by their experiences.

With these conclusions in mind, consider the question: What gender patterns *should* children learn, ideally? Answers vary among developmentalists as well as among mothers, fathers, and cultures. If all children responded only to their own inclinations, they might choose behaviors, express emotions, and develop talents that are taboo—even punished—in cultures that adhere to strict gender norms. In Western cultures, little boys might put on makeup, little girls might wear pants, and both sexes might go naked outside in hot weather. Whether these practices should be permitted is a question for the adults to answer, not the children.

How can we summarize all the evidence on sex and gender? To begin with, young boys and young girls are seen as quite different, not only by parents and other adults but even more forcefully by the children themselves. Each of the five major theories has an explanation for this phenomenon: Freud describes unconscious incestuous urges; behaviorists note social reinforcement; cognitive theorists describe immature categorization of sexual opposites; sociocultural explanations focus on the gender patterns that appear throughout every culture; and epigenetic theory begins with the hereditary aspects of brain and body development. Both nature and nurture influence gender, and during the play years, children become very conscious of male–female differences. Although each theory offers an explanation, theories don't answer questions about moral and social values. Perhaps that is why cultures and individuals draw such different conclusions about sex as well as gender.

SUMMARY

Emotional Development

1. In Erikson's theory, the play years include the crisis of initiative versus guilt. Children normally feel pride and self-esteem, sometimes mixed with feelings of guilt and shame, as the self-concept develops.

2. Regulation of emotions is crucial during the play years, when children learn emotional control. Both externalizing and internalizing problems can be seen as indications of inadequate self-control. Emotional regulation is made possible by brain maturation, particularly of the prefrontal cortex. Too many stressful experiences in infancy affect the production of stress hormones, impeding normal development.

3. Both empathy, which leads to prosocial behavior, and antipathy, which leads to aggression, develop during early childhood. Instrumental aggression occurs when children fight over toys and privileges, and reactive aggression occurs when children react to

being hurt. More worrisome are relational and bullying aggression, which can become very damaging to both aggressor and victim if the pattern persists.

4. Children learn to control their emotions, particularly their antisocial ones, through play with peers. Cooperation gradually develops through rough-and-tumble and sociodramatic play, both of which require adjustment to the needs and imaginations of one's playmates.

Parenting Patterns

5. Three classic styles of parenting have been identified: authoritarian, permissive, and authoritative. Generally, children are more successful and happy when their parents express warmth and set guidelines. Parenting that is rejecting and uninvolved is harmful to child development.

6. Punishment should fit not only the age and temperament of the child but also the culture. Generally, developmentalists are concerned that any physical punishment increases reactive and bullying aggression. Time-outs and parental conversations with the child about misbehavior tend to promote prosocial behavior.

7. The themes and characters of many television programs and video games reflect sexism and racism. Television tends to increase aggression later on. Video games are probably even worse, although longitudinal, controlled research is not complete. Parents find it difficult to ban television, but monitoring of content can be an effective alternative.

Boy or Girl: So What?

8. Even 2-year-olds correctly use sex-specific labels, such as *boy* and *girl, mommy* and *daddy.* During early childhood, children become more aware of gender differences in clothes, toys, future careers, and playmates, becoming quite sex-stereotyped by age 6.

9. Each major theory has a perspective on sex and gender distinctions. Freud emphasized that children are attracted to the opposite-sex parent and eventually seek to identify, or align themselves, with the same-sex parent.

10. Behaviorists hold that gender-related behaviors are learned through reinforcement and punishment (especially for males) and social modeling. Cognitive theorists note that simplistic preoperational thinking leads to gender stereotypes. Sociocultural theorists point to the many male–female distinctions apparent in every society.

11. An epigenetic explanation makes it clear that gender differences are not determined by either biology or culture but are affected by both. Specifically, gender differences are partly the result of hormones affecting brain formation in the months before and after birth, but experiences enhance or halt those neurological patterns.

KEY TERMS

initiative versus guilt (p. 237)
self-concept (p. 237)
emotional regulation (p. 238)
externalizing problems (p. 239)
internalizing problems (p. 239)
emotional intelligence (p. 241)
empathy (p. 241)

antipathy (p. 241)
prosocial (p. 241)
antisocial (p. 242)
instrumental aggression (p. 243)
reactive aggression (p. 243)
relational aggression (p. 243)
bullying aggression (p. 243)
peers (p. 243)

rough-and-tumble play (p. 244)
sociodramatic play (p. 244)
authoritarian parenting (p. 246)
permissive parenting (p. 247)
authoritative parenting (p. 247)
time-out (p. 249)

sex differences (p. 253)
gender differences (p. 253)
phallic stage (p. 254)
Oedipus complex (p. 254)
identification (p. 254)
superego (p. 254)
Electra complex (p. 254)
androgyny (p. 257)

APPLICATIONS

1. Observe a young child's interaction with other children. Present your observation in four columns headed, respectively, Emotion, Reasons, Results, and Emotional Regulation. Note every display of emotion (laughter, tears, etc.), the reason for it, the consequences, and, considering the context, which emotions showed signs of emotional regulation and which did not. For example: "Anger; Another child took toy; Child suggested sharing; Emotional regulation apparent."

2. Ask three people about punishment of children. What kinds of punishment does each person think proper? Do they believe that punishment should differ by a child's age, sex, misdeed, and/or the punisher's relationship to the child? (Should only parents punish?) Then ask your informants how they were punished as children and how that affected them. Write a report on your findings.

Describe your own opinions in this report, explaining how and why your opinions differ from those expressed by your informants, your parents, and the chapter text. If all your sources agree, and you agree with them, try to find someone from another culture or cohort who has a different view.

3. Because we are so accustomed to our social context, gender indicators often go unnoticed. Go to a public place (park, restaurant, busy street) and spend at least 10 minutes recording examples of gender differentiation, such as articles of clothing, mannerisms, interaction patterns, activities. Quantify what you see, such as baseball hats on eight males and two females or (better but more difficult) four male–female conversations, with the number of seconds each man and woman talked and with gender differences in interruptions, sentence length, word choice, and so on.

Part III

The Play Years

Brain and Nervous System The brain continues to develop, attaining 90 percent of its adult weight by the time the child is 5 years old. Both the proliferation of neural pathways and myelination continue. Coordination between the two halves and the various areas of the brain increases, allowing the child to settle down and concentrate when necessary and to use various parts of the body in harmony. Gross motor skills, such as running and jumping, improve dramatically. Fine motor skills, such as writing and drawing, develop more slowly.

Maltreatment Child abuse and neglect, potential problems at every age, are particularly likely in homes with many children and few personal or community resources. Recognition of the problem has improved, but treatment is still uneven. Distinguishing the ongoing problems of a family that needs support from the immediate danger for a child who needs to be removed and placed in foster care is critical for long-term development. Planning a permanent solution for a maltreated child is much better than repeatedly moving the child from one house to another.

Cognitive Skills Children think in magical ways, self-centered yet aware of others. Many cognitive abilities become more mature if the social context is supportive. Children begin to develop a theory of mind, in which they take into account the ideas and emotions of others. Social interaction, particularly in the form of guided participation, is of help in this cognitive advancement. At the same time, however, children's thinking can be quite illogical and egocentric.

Language Language abilities develop rapidly; by the age of 6, the average child knows 10,000 words and demonstrates extensive grammatical knowledge. Children also learn to adjust their communication to their audience, and they use language to help themselves learn. Preschool education helps children develop language and express themselves as well as preparing them for later education and adult life. Long-term benefits of preschool are apparent, especially for children with stressful home lives.

Emotions and Personality Development Self-concept emerges, as does the ability to regulate emotions. Externalizing problems may be the result of too little emotional regulation; internalizing problems may result from too much control. Empathy produces prosocial behavior; antipathy leads to antisocial actions, including aggression.

Play Children engage in play that helps them master physical and intellectual skills and that teaches or enhances social roles. As their social and cognitive skills develop, children engage in ever more complex and imaginative types of play, sometimes by themselves and, increasingly, with others.

Parent–Child Interaction Parenting styles that are most responsive to the child, with much communication, seem to be most effective in encouraging the child to develop autonomy and self-control.

Gender Roles Increasingly, children develop stereotypic concepts of sex differences in appearance and gender differences in behavior. The precise roles of nature and nurture in this process are unclear, but both of these forces are obviously involved.

SHARON SCHOOL DISTRICT

Part IV

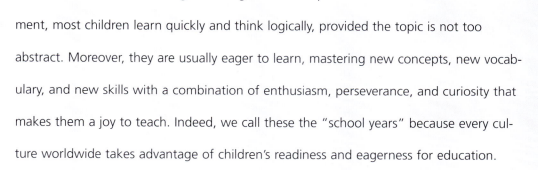

|f someone asked you to pick the best years of the entire life span, you might choose the years from about 7 to 11 and defend your choice persuasively. Physical development is almost problem-free (unless puberty begins), making it easy to master dozens of new skills. With regard to cognitive development, most children learn quickly and think logically, provided the topic is not too abstract. Moreover, they are usually eager to learn, mastering new concepts, new vocabulary, and new skills with a combination of enthusiasm, perseverance, and curiosity that makes them a joy to teach. Indeed, we call these the "school years" because every culture worldwide takes advantage of children's readiness and eagerness for education.

Finally, the social world of middle childhood seems perfect: Most school-age children think their parents are helpful, their teachers fair, and their friends loyal. Moral reasoning and behavior have reached that state where right seems clearly distinguished from wrong, without the ambiguities and conflicts that complicate morality during adolescence. As you will see, however, the years of middle childhood are not the best time for all children. Some must cope with special educational needs, the challenges of learning a new language, a nontraditional family structure, and other complexities.

The next three chapters celebrate the joys and acknowledge the occasional difficulties of middle childhood.

The School Years

Chapter Eleven

The School Years: Biosocial Development

Context changes. The biggest influence on development during the school years is the changing social context, as children enter wider educational and cultural communities. No longer do children depend on their families to dress, feed, and wash them or to send them to a preschool. By age 6 or 7, self-care (dressing, eating, bathing) is taken for granted and school attendance is mandated, with a state-approved curriculum. Both the independence from parents and the entry to school affect biosocial development. This chapter describes similarities among all school-age children but also significant differences—in size, in health, in ability to learn in school.

Underlying such similarities and differences are the neurons and networks of the brain. Ongoing maturation and myelination make all kinds of motor skills and behaviors much easier for some children than others. This chapter describes brain growth in detail.

As you learn more about differences later in the chapter, bear in mind that children who are designated "special" are not so different from those designated "normal" or average in every aspect of growth—and no child is completely normal. Once we look closely at real children, it becomes obvious that every child has unique strengths and liabilities.

Diversity splinters into further diversities; multiculturalism becomes multi-multi-multi-cultural. To highlight this point, we begin with two children of Mexican heritage who are living in southern California. The differences between them, and between any two children who may superficially seem similar because of their age and background, will become apparent.

In Person

Two Children of Mexican Heritage in California

In the following accounts, Yolanda Piedra and Paul Chavez (not their real names) reflect on their school years.

Yolanda:

When I got here [from Mexico at age 7], I didn't want to stay here, 'cause I didn't like the school. And after a little while, in third grade, I started getting the hint of it and everything and I tried real hard in it. I really got along with the teachers. . . . They would start talking to me, or they kinda like pulled me up some grades, or moved me to other classes, or took me somewhere. And they were always congratulating me.

Actually, there's one friend of mine. . . . She's been with me since first grade until eighth grade, right now. And she's always been with me, in bad or good things, all the time. She's always telling me, "Keep on going and your dreams are gonna come true." . . .

I see some other kids that they say, like, they'd say they're Colombian or something. They try to make themselves look cool in front of everybody. I just say what I am and I feel proud of myself. . . . It's okay for me being born over there 'cause I feel proud of myself. I feel proud of my culture.

[quoted in Nieto, 2000, pp. 220–221]

Paul:

I grew up . . . ditching school, just getting in trouble, trying to make a dollar, that's it, you know? Just go to school, steal from the store, and go sell candies at school. And that's what I was doing in the third or fourth grade. . . . I was always getting in the principal's office, suspended, kicked out, everything starting from the third grade.

My fifth grade teacher, Ms. Nelson . . . she put me in a play and that like tripped me out. Like why do you want me in a play? Me, I'm just a mess-up. Still, you know, she put me in a play. And in the fifth grade, I think that was the best year out of the whole six years. I learned a lot about the Revolutionary War. . . . Had good friends. . . . We had a project we were involved

in. Ms. Nelson . . . just involved everyone. We made books, this and that. And I used to write, and wrote two, three books. Was in a book fair. . . . She got real deep into you. Just, you know, "Come on now, you can do it." That was a good year for me, fifth grade.

I think right now about going Christian, right? Just going Christian, trying to do good, you know? Stay away from drugs, everything. And every time it seems like I think about that, I think about the homeboys. And it's a trip because a lot of the homeboys are my family, too, you know? . . .

Let's say I'm Chicano and dress like a gang member. They're gonna look at you like one of these crazy kids, you know, Mexican kid. . . . I don't really know if it's 'cause I'm Brown or it's 'cause of my gang tattoo, so I can't really pinpoint. But for me, as far as me being a Chicano, it's prideful, it's pride of your race, of what you are.

[quoted in Nieto, 2000, pp. 249–251]

Surely you have noticed differences between these two children. In the third grade Paul considered himself "just a mess-up," whereas Yolanda was beginning to get "the hint of it." Yolanda's friend encouraged her to "keep on going," whereas Paul's friends prevented him from "going Christian."

There are similarities, too. Both children were strongly influenced by teachers and friends, and both children were proud of their heritage (as most school-age children of every background are). Taken together, these children illustrate development from ages 7 to 11: For all children, learning is important, and these school years are the foundation for adolescence and adulthood. Yet each child is different and should be recognized as such.

Yolanda's Favorite Holiday This Cinco de Mayo (Fifth of May) fiesta at a Los Angeles school is part of an effort to celebrate Mexican traditions. At the same time that the Mexican students' native culture is recognized, they need to be taught the English language and U.S. traditions.

?Observational Quiz (see answer, page 268): Why are some of the children wearing green, white, and red?

FELICIA MARTINEZ/PHOTOEDIT, INC.

A Healthy Time

In general, genetic and developmental factors are protective of biological growth. For thousands of years, infants who survived their early years were quite hardy, protected by nature from serious illness so they could reach their reproductive years. Certainly, for physical ailments, such as cancer and heart disease, children age 7 to 11 are the healthiest group of humans (see Figure 11.1). Even unintended injuries and serious abuse, which are the leading causes of morbidity and mortality during childhood, occur less often from age 7 to 11 than before or after those years. (These topics were first discussed in Chapter 8.)

    Therefore, during **middle childhood** (so called because it is after early childhood and before early adolescence), most parents can relax a little. School-age children not only stay healthy but also care for their basic needs with competence and caution. Most prefer playing apart from adults, especially when they are with their friends, and most manage both play and friendship quite well. Middle childhood is usually a happy, easy time.

middle childhood The period from age 7 to 11.

Typical Size and Shape

One reason middle childhood is easy is that growth slows down. Children grow more slowly from age 7 to 11 than they did a few years earlier or than they will a few years later. Partly as a result, many become quite skilled at controlling their own bodies. School-age children can master almost any basic skill, sometimes with impressive grace and precision, as long as it doesn't require too much strength or split-second judgment of speed and distance.

    "Growing more slowly" refers to the *rate of increase;* children actually gain at least as much weight each year as they did at age 3 or 4, but the proportional

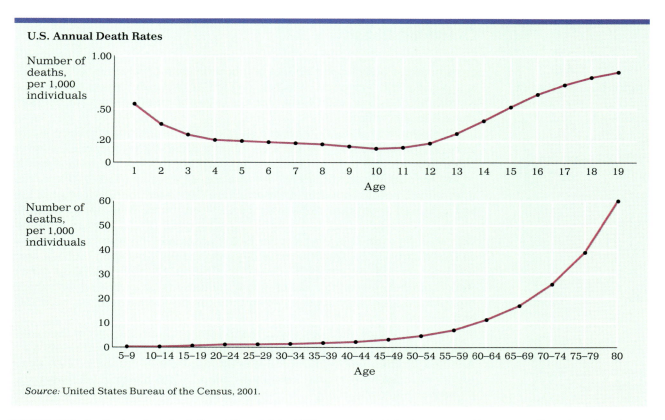

Source: United States Bureau of the Census, 2001.

FIGURE 11.1 **Death at an Early Age? Almost Never!** Schoolchildren are remarkably hardy, as measured in many ways. These charts show that death rates for 7- to 11-year-olds are lower than those for children under 7 or over 11 and about a hundred times lower than for adults.

LAURA DWIGHT

All The Same These boys are all friends in the third grade, clowning in response to the camera— as school-age boys like to do. Outsiders might notice the varied growth rates and genetic differences, but the boys themselves are more aware of what they have in common.

overweight A body weight that is 20–29 percent above the weight that is considered ideal for the person's age and height.

obesity A body weight that is 30 percent or more above the weight that is considered ideal for the person's age and height.

!Answer to Observational Quiz (from page 266): Green, white, and red are the colors of the Mexican flag. These colors are not often worn in Mexico but are highly symbolic for Mexicans living in the United States.

gain is less, and that makes all the difference. For example, a typical 8-year-old already weighs 55 pounds (25 kilograms), so a gain of 5 pounds is taken in stride.

Generally, each year from age 7 to 11, well-nourished children gain 5 to 7 pounds (about 3 kilograms) and at least 2 inches (almost 6 centimeters). By age 10, they weigh about 70 pounds (32 kilograms) and are 4½ feet (1.37 meters) tall. (See Appendix A, pages A–6 and A–7, for specifics.) Growth varies, depending not only on genes and gender but also on nutrition.

Obviously, children who are malnourished or undernourished gain less weight, as we saw in Chapter 8. Undernutrition does not disappear with age or a nation's wealth. For instance, a study of low-income schoolchildren in Philadelphia and Baltimore found that 8 percent were often hungry, a condition that correlated not only with less growth and more illness but also with poor functioning in school—including excessive absences, inattention, and emotional outbursts (Murphy et al., 2001).

Typically, however, school-age children in developed nations eat enough food. They seem to become slimmer as their height increases, their limbs lengthen, and their body proportions change. Muscles become stronger as well. Thus, the average 10-year-old throws a ball twice as far as the average 6-year-old does. Lung capacity expands, so with each passing year children can run faster and exercise longer.

Childhood Obesity

There is one major exception to this generally placid picture of children's growth: excess body fat sufficient to put the individual's health at risk. The problem is not just **overweight**, which is defined as being 20 percent above ideal weight for one's age and height, but also **obesity**, being 30 percent or more above this benchmark.

Almost a third of North American children are obese, a rate that has doubled since 1980 (Dietz, 1999). For children, obesity reduces exercise and increases blood pressure. Both these developments increase the risk for serious health problems in adulthood, including heart disease, stroke, and diabetes. Obese children who do not slim down in adolescence are more likely to experience psychological as well as physical problems, especially depression (Mustillo et al., 2003).

However, adults need to be careful in getting children to slim down. Children who respond to adult pressure by becoming obsessed with body size may have eating disorders as adolescents and young adults, including bulimia and anorexia nervosa, as will be discussed in Chapter 17 (Fisher & Birch, 2001). Adults can help overweight children and adolescents by exercising with them, especially in activities that people of any size can do, such as walking, bicycling, and swimming.

Why might one child be heavier than another? Genes are part of the explanation, affecting activity level, taste preferences, body type, and metabolism. Adopted children whose biological parents were obese are more often overweight (no matter what the weight of their adoptive parents) than other adoptees (Grilo & Pogue-Geile, 1991).

However, genes never act in isolation, and genes change very little from one generation to the next. Environmental factors are the major reasons for the re-

MICHAEL NEWMAN / PHOTO EDIT

Will She Drink Her Milk? The first word many American children read is *McDonald's*, and they all recognize the golden arches. Fast food is part of almost every family's diet, and that is one reason the rate of obesity has doubled in every age group in the United States since 1980. Even if the young girl stops playing with her straw and drinks the milk, she is learning that soda and French fries are desirable food choices.

cent increase in childhood obesity (Robinson & Killen, 2001), with lack of exercise crucial. Fifty years ago, most children played outside until dark; now they typically watch television until their parents send them to bed.

In most developing nations (and in developed nations before the twentieth century), starvation has long been a common threat to survival. A layer of body fat to protect against famine signified health, wealth, and high status. Good fathers were "breadwinners" who "brought home the bacon"; good mothers prepared abundant "home cooking" for the family; and good children were fat and happy, rewarded for cleaning their plates, punished by not getting dessert.

It is not surprising, then, that people from nations where starvation was prevalent continue customs that once protected against early death but now encourage children to gain weight. For example, the most recent immigrants from Mexico have the highest rate of obesity of any ethnic group in the United States. In many other ways, immigrant children born in Mexico are healthier than their U.S.-born peers, but not in diet (Flores & Zambrana, 2001). Overall, immigrant children are more often overweight than their native-born peers, not only because they exercise too little but also because their family heritage is unprepared for the onslaught of junk food, videos, and inactivity that they encounter in the United States and other developed countries.

Especially for Teachers A child in your class is overweight, but you are hesitant to say anything to the parents, who are also overweight, because you do not want to insult them. What should you do?

Chronic Illness: The Case of Asthma

We noted earlier that middle childhood is generally a healthy time. In fact, it is healthier now in every nation of the world than it was just 30 years ago. Immunization worldwide has reduced the death rate dramatically. Even accidents, infections, and chronic sore throats are less common. In the United States, the improved health of school-age children is apparent in many ways. Tonsillectomy—a type of surgery "practically every child" experienced as recently as 1980 (Larson, 1990, p. 698)—is relatively rare today. Hearing impairments and anemia are only half as common as they were, and blood levels of lead are much lower.

Children during the school years become more aware of one another's, and their own, minor physical imperfections. This means that walking with a limp, wearing glasses, or blowing one's nose makes children very self-conscious. In addition, some conditions become more noticeable during the school years, including Tourette's syndrome (uncontrollable noises or movements), stuttering, and some allergies. Health conditions and anything else that prevents normal play or school attendance strongly correlate with all the emotional and social problems of childhood, from low achievement to loneliness, from being left back to breaking the law. A recent report found that 12 percent of all school-age children had physical problems that limited their performance in school. The most common cause of school absence in many developed nations, and especially in cities, is now asthma (Msall et al., 2003).

Causes of Asthma

asthma A chronic inflammatory disorder of the airways.

Asthma is a chronic inflammatory disorder of the airways. It affects between 10 and 20 percent of school-age children in North America, about half of whom are repeatedly absent from school because of it. Asthma is three times as common as it was only 20 years ago, and its incidence is expected to double again by 2020 (Pew Environmental Health Commission, 2000).

Many researchers are studying the possible causes of asthma. Genetic contributors to the diseases may appear on chromosomes 2, 11, 12, 13, and 21. Some infections that once protected against asthma by strengthening the immune system now seldom occur. As a result, ironically, the same medical advances that limit childhood diseases may make asthma more likely. For those who are vulnerable, several aspects of modern life—carpeted floors, dogs and cats living inside the house, airtight windows, less outdoor play, and urbanization (which crowds people together in buildings where cockroaches multiply)—increase the risk of asthma attacks (Carpenter, 1999). (Strictly speaking, allergens such as pet hair, dust mites, cockroaches, and air pollution are triggers, not causes, of asthma.)

Some international variations in the incidence of asthma are the result of imprecise definitions of asthma, wheezing, and bronchitis. Nevertheless, in Africa, Latin America, and Eastern and Western Europe, asthma seems to be increasing and is known to be related to crowded urban living conditions (Crane et al., MacIntyre et al., 2001; Stewart et al., 2001; Strachen, 1999).

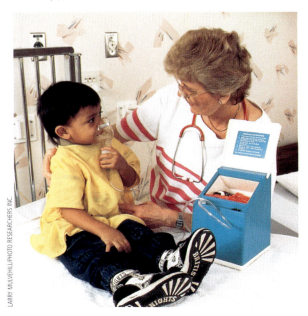

Already Too Late A nurse uses an inhaler to open a young asthma patient's airways. Such hospital care is tertiary prevention, which will avoid death, but it represents a failure of primary and secondary prevention.

LARRY MULVEHILL/PHOTO RESEARCHERS, INC.

Prevention of Asthma

Let us apply to asthma our understanding of the three levels of prevention discussed in Chapter 8. *Primary prevention* is the best approach of all, although the hardest to achieve by individuals. Proper ventilation of schools and homes, decreased pollution, eradication of cockroaches, and safe outdoor play spaces would make life and health better for school-age children, especially those who might become asthmatic.

The benefit of primary prevention was demonstrated by a natural experiment during the Summer Olympics in Atlanta, Georgia. The city imposed traffic restrictions, encouraged carpooling, and offered free mass transit for 17 days in order to ease the movement of athletes and spectators. An unexpected consequence was a sudden dip in the incidence of acute asthma. Compared to four weeks earlier and four weeks later, Medicare asthma treatments decreased by 42 percent and HMO asthma claims were down 44 percent (Friedman et al., 2001). Visits to hospital emergency rooms for asthma treatment also declined. Could the reason for this improvement have been something other than pollution? Perhaps all the children were more carefully tended by their parents during this special time. However, hospitals and insurance agencies reported no change in the frequency of other acute-care incidents involving children (injuries, heart ailments, accidental poisoning, etc.). This research makes it clear that urban car pollution makes asthma worse.

Secondary prevention depends on families and thus might be easier to achieve. If there is a genetic history of allergies, ridding the house of allergens *before* the disease appears and breast-feeding newborns can cut the rate of asthma in half (Gdalevich et al., 2001). New parents may be reluctant to change their habits and lifestyles (by, for example, giving away their pets) just because their baby *might* develop asthma.

Finally, *tertiary prevention,* which is the prevention of serious consequences once an ailment is recognized, occurs every day in physicians' offices and hospital emergency rooms. For asthma, prompt use of injections, inhalers, and pills that are prescribed and monitored by specialists markedly reduces the rate of acute wheezing and overnight hospitalizations. A "clinical pathways" approach (following a standard procedure for testing and treating in the hospital) reduces hospital stays for acute asthma attacks, but not every hospital takes this approach (Glauber et al., 2001).

Less than half the asthmatic children in the United States receive adequate tertiary prevention; those from Spanish-speaking homes are particularly likely to get inadequate care (Halterman et al., 2000). Why? One-third of school-age children, including more than half of African-American and Hispanic children, have no health insurance (U.S. Department of Health and Human Services, 2000). Further, some mistrust arises between the doctors (mostly white, high-income older men) and the parents (often nonwhite, low-income younger women). Among one group of Hispanic immigrant mothers of asthmatic children, 88 percent thought drugs were overused in the United States, and 72 percent did not give their children the asthma medication their doctors had prescribed (Bearison et al., 2002).

> Overall, as you have just read, school-age children are healthy, strong, and capable. Immunizations protect them against childhood diseases, and developmental advances give them the strength and coordination to take care of their own basic needs (eating, dressing, bathing).
>
> However, their growing awareness of themselves and of one another, as well as their increasing independence from parents, makes every physical impairment a potential problem, particularly if it interferes with school attendance. Obesity and asthma are two notable examples. Both have genetic and early-childhood origins but become more serious during middle childhood, when they may interfere with self-esteem, friendship, and learning. Prevention is very important, because ongoing obesity may cause many health problems and chronic asthma may affect school achievement.

Response for Teachers (from page 269): Speak to the parents—not accusingly (because you know that genes and culture have a major influence on body weight), but helpfully—to alert them to a potential social and health problem. Most parents are very concerned about their child's well-being and will be glad to work with you to improve the child's snacks and exercise. If they are overweight themselves, they will probably understand and appreciate your concern about their child.

Brain Development

Remember that the brain, proportionally large at birth, continues to grow more quickly than the rest of the child's body, reaching adult size at about age 7. By then, not only are the basic areas of the sensory and motor cortexes functioning but so, too, are the more complex language, logic, memory, and spatial areas, each with many dendrites reaching out to other neurons as experiences accumulate.

Also recall that, in early childhood, emotional regulation, theory of mind, and left–right coordination begin to emerge as the maturing corpus callosum connects the two hemispheres of the brain and as the prefrontal cortex—the executive part of the brain—plans, monitors, and evaluates all the impulses from the various sectors of the brain. Hemispheric specialization makes the brain more efficient overall.

Advances in Middle Childhood

In middle childhood, ongoing maturation of those parts of the brain as well as of the cerebellum becomes apparent in both motor and cognitive development, which are neurologically connected to each other (Diamond, 2000). For example, the child can now control several behaviors common in early childhood—emotional outbursts, perseveration, inattention, and the insistence on routines. The prefrontal cortex allows the child to analyze consequences before lashing out in anger or dissolving in tears, knowing when a curse word seems advisable (on the playground to a bully, perhaps) and when it doesn't (during math class or in church).

Attention and Automatization

Two other advances in brain function become increasingly evident in middle childhood. The first is the ability to attend to information from many areas of the brain at once and to pay special heed to the most important elements—an ability called *selective attention*. In the classroom, children must listen to the teacher, write down what is important, and ignore another child's whispering. In the cafeteria, children must understand another child's gestures and facial expressions and respond quickly and appropriately. On the ball field, children must not only calculate the trajectory of a batted ball but also start running in the right direction while noting where other teammates are positioned and whether anyone besides the batter is trying to reach base.

Three-year-olds do not have the thinking capacity to process these multiple demands for action and inaction from various parts of the brain. The thoughtful and competent older child must select and coordinate the simultaneous impulses from all neurological regions, developing "large-scale cortical networks" that link the various parts together. Thus, the child can think in a coordinated manner and is not confused by myriad signals from the millions of scattered neurons in various parts (Bressler, 2002). This coordination requires extensive myelination and increased production of neurotransmitters, which are among the advances of middle childhood.

The second advance in brain function that becomes apparent in middle childhood is in **automatization,** a process by which thoughts and actions are repeated in sequence until they become automatic, or routine, and no longer need much conscious thought. Almost all behaviors that originate in the cortex require careful, slow, and focused concentration the first few times they are performed. After many repetitions, with neurons firing together in a particular sequence, behavior becomes more automatic and more patterned. Less neuronal effort is required, because firing one neuron leads to a chain reaction that fires an entire sequence.

Automatization becomes easier and quicker as myelination enables the signals between one part of the brain and another to travel more rapidly. For a clear example of automatization, consider reading. It begins with the child using the eyes (sometimes aided by a finger and the lips) to sound out letters and guess at words; this series of fine motor skills leads to perception in the brain. At first, reading is slow and painstaking. Then it gradually becomes so automatic that, finally, a person can glance at billboards or cereal boxes and read, even when not intending to do so.

Motor Skills

The most obvious evidence (apart from fMRI) of brain maturation occurs in the school-age child's motor skills. Every motor skill involves several abilities, which

JOHNATHAN KIM / STOCK CONNECTION / PICTUREQUEST

Brain Music If this boy is to become a competent violinist, the brain must coordinate arms, hands, fingers, ears, and memory. All this is possible only after practice has made some of it automatic. Automatization frees the brain's cortex for more emotional and coordinated expression in response to the conductor.

automatization A process by which thoughts and actions are repeated in sequence so often that they become automatic, or routine, and no longer require much conscious thought.

improve during childhood. One key element is **reaction time** (the length of time it takes a person to respond to a particular stimulus), a consequence of brain maturation, especially ongoing myelination. Reaction time shortens with each year until about age 16; then it stabilizes and, beginning at about age 20, slows down again, so that older adults (aged 60–81) are about as quick as 8-year-olds (Williams et al., 1999). Further, because of neurological development, hand–eye coordination, balance, and judgment of movement (including time, distance, and trajectory) continue to develop during the school years, and thus 12-year-olds are better in all of these abilities than 9-year-olds, who in turn are better than 6-year-olds.

reaction time The length of time it takes a person to respond to a particular stimulus.

In many other ways, a child's motor habits, especially in coordinating both sides of the body and performing complex tasks, benefit from connections formed in the brain. The corpus callosum between the brain's hemispheres continues to mature. Because neurons that fire together are strengthened together, practicing any particular skill—from moving a pencil on paper to kicking a ball toward a goal post—gradually makes processing in the brain faster and more efficient (Merzenich, 2001). Hours of practicing penmanship, throwing a softball, or cutting one's meat with knife and fork develop neurological pathways, so that automatization becomes possible.

According to research on lower animals, brain development is advanced through play, especially the active, erratic, rough-and-tumble frolicking that many children love. As we saw in Chapter 10, children learn to regulate and express their emotions through play with peers. Indeed, one expert believes that such play particularly helps boys overcome a tendency toward hyperactivity and learning disabilities, to which male hormones predispose them. Rough-and-tumble play may help regulate and coordinate the frontal lobes of the brain (Panksepp, 1998). Whether or not this is true, it is apparent that children's impulses toward active play need to be guided but not repressed. Rough-and-tumble play aids not only motor skills but probably emotional regulation and interpretation as well (Pellegrini & Smith, 2001).

Keep It Rolling This boy in Orissa, India, is using an old bicycle tire as a hoop. Although they use different objects, children everywhere have the impulse to play, and many of their games are the same.

? *Observational Quiz* (see answer, page 276): Is this boy malnourished?

It is the brain more than the muscles that throws the ball toward the catcher's mitt instead of into the dugout. If a particular communication network is flawed, as seems to be the case in some forms of childhood psychopathology, then the person will be unable to produce the coordinated responses that the activity requires. The problem may not be in a specific part of the brain but rather in "inattention to the whole" (Fisher, 1998).

Of course, the brain does not develop in isolation. Culture and practice are crucial, as illustrated by the proper use of chopsticks, a fine motor skill attained in chopstick-using cultures by half the 4-year-olds, by virtually all the 6-year-olds (Wong et al., 2002), and by almost no children elsewhere, even if they go to a restaurant where eating with chopsticks is encouraged.

Hereditary differences also affect the development of motor skills. As children grow and play school sports, it is increasingly obvious that some children will become star athletes and others seem uncoordinated, unable to throw or kick a ball with as much strength and accuracy as their peers. The same is true for fine motor skills. Some children naturally write more neatly than others, and those children usually practice their penmanship, refining the curve of the s and the slant of the t, for instance. Here, as with every other brain advance, practice accentuates neurological or cultural differences. Because of both nature and nurture, about 6 percent of all children are considered to have a motor coordination disability serious enough to interfere with school achievement (American Psychiatric Association, 2000).

Brain and Intelligence

The maturation of the brain affects not only movement of the body but also movement within the mind, as one idea leads to another. If children become quicker, more automatic thinkers, they become more able to learn and, as a result, they learn more. This increase is apparent, among many other ways, on standardized tests of aptitude and achievement.

Tests of Ability

In theory, **aptitude** is the potential to learn, or master, a particular skill or body of knowledge. The most important aptitude for school-age children is intellectual aptitude, or the ability to learn in school. This aptitude is measured by **IQ tests.** "IQ" is an abbreviation for "intelligence quotient," reflecting the fact that originally an IQ score was actually a quotient—the answer to a division problem. IQ was once found by dividing the child's mental age, measured by an intelligence test, by chronological age and then multiplying the result by 100. Note that age is emphasized in both the numerator and the denominator of the fraction, because maturation has always been considered related to learning. Today, IQ tests use a more complicated formula to make sure the overall distribution of scores follows the normal curve (see Figure 11.2), but the underlying concept is the same. Chronological comparisons remain crucial until adulthood, when the brain is considered full-grown.

In theory, achievement, or what a person has already accomplished, is quite different from aptitude. **Achievement tests** measure reading proficiency, math knowledge, science facts, writing skills, and whatever else has actually been mastered. Achievement tests are given routinely in school, but aptitude tests are given only when a child's achievement is unexpectedly high or low and adults want to find out if the child is a gifted, normal, or retarded learner.

Two highly regarded IQ tests are the *Stanford-Binet* and the *Wechsler* intelligence tests. There are Wechsler tests for preschoolers (the Wechsler Preschool and Primary Scale of Intelligence, or WPPSI), adults (the Wechsler Adult Intelligence Scale, or WAIS), and school-age children—the **Wechsler Intelligence Scale for Children (WISC).** Like the other IQ tests, the WISC is given by a trained examiner to one child at a time; the test items are varied to assess many abilities, including vocabulary, general knowledge, memory, and spatial comprehension. The examiner reads the questions out loud to avoid measuring the child's reading achievement. Some items are timed, but the child is not rushed and is allowed to finish a puzzle after time is up (although no points are given for doing so) (Kaufman & Lichtenberger, 2000).

IQ tests are quite reliable in predicting school achievement and somewhat reliable in predicting adult career attainment. In other words, children of above-

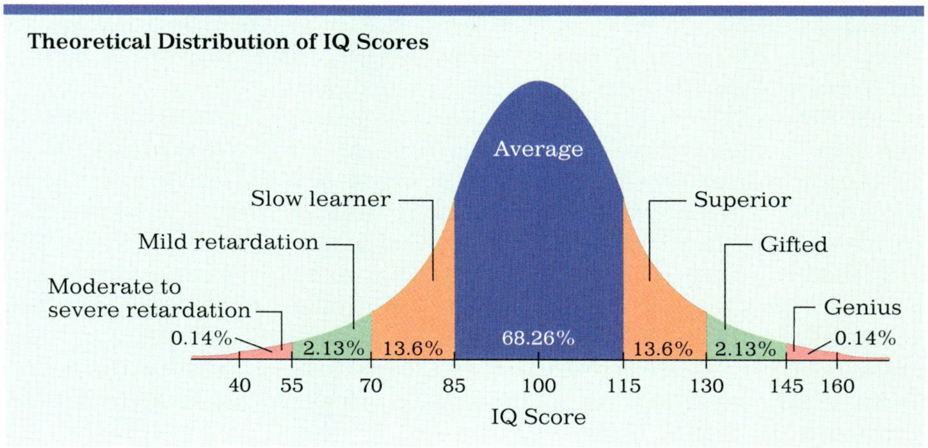

---

aptitude The potential to learn, or master, a particular skill or body of knowledge.

IQ tests Aptitude tests designed to measure a person's intellectual aptitude, or ability to learn in school. This aptitude was originally defined as mental age divided by chronological age, times 100—hence, intelligence quotient, or IQ. An example:
Actual age of three children: 12, 12, 12
Mental ages of the three: 15, 12, 8
IQ of each of these three:
$^{15}/_{12} = 1.25 \times 100 = 125$ (superior)
$^{12}/_{12} = 1 \times 100 = 100$ (average)
$^{8}/_{12} = 0.75 \times 100 = 75$ (slow learner)

achievement tests Measures of reading ability, math knowledge, science facts, writing skills, or any other subject matter that has actually been mastered.

Wechsler Intelligence Scale for Children (WISC) An IQ test designed for school-age children; it is administered by a trained examiner to one child at a time, and the questions are varied to hold the child's interest and to assess many abilities, including vocabulary, general knowledge, memory, and spatial comprehension.

FIGURE 11.2 In Theory, Most People Are Average Almost 70 percent of IQ scores fall within the normal range. Note, however, that this is a norm-referenced test. In fact, actual IQ scores have risen in many nations; 100 is no longer exactly the midpoint. Further, in practice, scores below 50 are slightly more frequent than indicated by the normal curve shown here, because severe retardation is the result, not of the normal distribution, but of genetic and prenatal factors.

?*Observational Quiz* (see answer, page 276): If a person's IQ is 110, what category is he or she in?

Theoretical Distribution of IQ Scores

Average

Slow learner — Superior

Mild retardation — Gifted

Moderate to severe retardation — Genius

0.14%   2.13%   13.6%   68.26%   13.6%   2.13%   0.14%

40   55   70   85   100   115   130   145   160

IQ Score

average IQ earn above-average grades in school and are likely to attain above-average amounts of higher education; as adults, more of them earn an above-average income, secure a professional or managerial job, and even marry and own homes (Sternberg et al., 2001).

Criticisms of IQ Testing

Many developmentalists criticize the use of IQ tests to measure intelligence. They argue that only in theory, not in fact, can any test measure potential without also measuring achievement or do so without reflecting the culture. Further, each person's intellectual potential changes over time, so a score that is tied to chronological age applies to a moment in time, not to a developing person.

Moreover, humans may have many intelligences, not just one, which would mean that the very idea of using one test to measure intelligence is based on a false and narrow assumption. Indeed, just as there are many discrete functions within the brain, there may be many abilities and many ways to demonstrate potential. Robert Sternberg (1996), for example, describes three distinct types of intelligence:

- *Academic* (measured by IQ and achievement tests)
- *Creative* (evidenced by imaginative endeavors)
- *Practical* (seen in everyday interactions)

Similarly, Howard Gardner described eight distinct intelligences: linguistic, logical-mathematical, musical, spatial, bodily-kinesthetic (movement), interpersonal (social understanding), intrapersonal (self-understanding), and naturalistic (understanding of nature, as in biology, zoology, or farming) (Gardner, 1983; Torff & Gardner, 1999).

According to this perspective, standard IQ tests measure only linguistic and logical-mathematical ability, not all that brains contain. The fact that most schools emphasize language and math explains why traditional IQ tests predict school success. However, if intelligence is the multifaceted jewel that Gardner (1993) believes it to be, schools need to develop a broader curriculum so that every child can shine. Moreover, if IQ tests, as currently used, predict college and occupational success, low scores may mean that schools should change.

Every developmentalist realizes that children of various cultural or linguistic backgrounds may not demonstrate their true potential on IQ tests designed for children of another background. For this reason, intelligence tests are not usually given to children unless there is some special concern about a child's aptitude. Even then, the test score is only one of many measures of a dynamic assessment. A child who is truly a slow learner is delayed in every aspect of development, not only those measured by IQ. All told, the brain is a much more complex organ that any one means of assessment can reveal.

Performance IQ This puzzle, part of a performance subtest on the Wechsler IQ test, seems simple until you try to do it. Actually, the limbs are difficult to align correctly and time is of the essence, with a bonus for speed and failure after a minute and a half. However, this boy has at least one advantage over most African-American boys who are tested. Especially during middle childhood, boys tend to do better when their examiner is of the same sex and race.

Demonstration of High IQ? If North American intelligence tests truly reflected all the aspects of the mind, children would be considered mentally slow if they could not replicate the proper hand, arm, torso, and facial positions of a traditional dance, as this young Indonesian girl does brilliantly. She is obviously adept in kinesthetic and interpersonal intelligence. Given her culture, it would not be surprising if she were deficient in the logical-mathematical intelligence required to use the Internet effectively or to surpass an American peer on a video game.

! *Answer to Observational Quiz* (from page 273): Although malnutrition is common in India, school-age children worldwide are more often too fat than too thin. This boy has healthy hair; his ribs do not show; and, most important, he seems to have adequate energy and coordination for active play. Although a definitive answer would depend on his age and his height and weight percentiles, he is probably just fine.

! *Answer to Observational Quiz* (from page 274): He or she is average. Anyone with a score between 85 and 115 is of average IQ.

During middle childhood the brain functions faster, more automatically, and with better coordination, particularly as the prefrontal cortex continues to mature. This is apparent in quick reaction time. The abilities to stop before acting, to screen out distractions, and to wait for a turn are crucial for learning in school and for developing gross and fine motor skills.

Increasing brain maturation is evident in many school-related abilities, as measured on aptitude tests, particularly intelligence tests. IQ (intelligence quotient) tests are scored as if children become smarter as they grow older (mental age divided by chronological age equals IQ). The underlying assumption is that children who are intellectually gifted or mentally retarded have an unusually high or low basic aptitude, and this means that they will always be fast or slow learners for every skill. This assumption is challenged by many modern theorists, such as Gardner and Sternberg, who believe that the brain contains not just one aptitude but many and that culture and experience are pivotal in turning potential into achievement.

Children with Special Needs

All parents watch with pride and satisfaction as their offspring become smarter, taller, and more skilled. For many parents, however, these feelings mingle with worry and uncertainty when their children unexpectedly encounter difficulties in one area of development or another. Often delay, overactivity, or clumsiness in motor skills is the first problem to be noticed; other problems become apparent once formal education begins (Lerner, 2000).

Although developmental problems usually originate in the brain, the observable symptoms and the many factors that inhibit or amplify those tendencies are social and cognitive (Rutter & Sroufe, 2000). That is, the symptoms of disability become more apparent on the playground or in the classroom than at home or in the pediatrician's office. Adults may respond by focusing on those disabilities instead of on the child's abilities. Here we try to keep both abilities and disabilities in mind. Consider Billy, a third-grader with a problem at school.

A Case to Study

Billy: Dynamo or Dynamite?

In many ways, Billy was a typical 8-year-old with a history of healthy development. He was born full term after an uncomplicated pregnancy; he sat up, walked, and talked at the expected ages. His parents were proud of his energy and curiosity: "Little Dynamo," they called him affectionately. They did not consider him handicapped—he began to read on schedule, and he looked quite normal. But Billy's third-grade teacher, Mrs. Pease, referred him to a psychiatrist because his behavior in class was "intolerably disruptive" (Gorenstein & Comer, 2002, p. 250), as the following episode illustrated:

Mrs. Pease had called the class to attention to begin an oral exercise: reciting a multiplication table on the blackboard.

The first child had just begun her recitation when, suddenly, Billy exclaimed, "Look!" The class turned to see Billy running to the window.

"Look," he exclaimed again, "an airplane!"

A couple of children ran to the window with Billy to see the airplane, but Mrs. Pease called them back, and they returned to their seats. Billy, however, remained at the window, pointing at the sky. Mrs. Pease called him back, too.

"Billy, please return to your desk," Mrs. Pease said firmly. But Billy acted as though he didn't even hear her.

"Look, Mrs. Pease," he exclaimed, "the airplane is blowing smoke!" A couple of other children started from their desks.

"Billy," Mrs. Pease tried once more, "if you don't return to your desk this instant, I'm going to send you to Miss Warren's office."

Mrs. Pease tried again. "Who knows 3 times 7?" This time Billy raised his hand, but he still couldn't resist creating a disruption.

"I know, I know," Billy pleaded, jumping up and down in his seat with his hand raised high.

"That will do, Billy," Mrs. Pease admonished him. She deliberately called on another child. The child responded with the correct answer.

"*I* knew that!" Billy exclaimed.

"Billy," Mrs. Pease told him, "I don't want you to say one more word this class period."

Billy looked down at his desk, sulkily, ignoring the rest of the lesson. He began to fiddle with a couple of rubber bands, trying to see how far they would stretch before they broke. He looped the rubber bands around his index fingers and pulled his hands farther and farther apart. This kept him quiet for a while; by this point, Mrs. Pease didn't care what he did, as long as he was quiet. She continued conducting the multiplication lesson while Billy stretched the rubber bands until finally they snapped, flying off and hitting two children, on each side of him. Billy let out a yelp of surprise, and the class turned to him.

"That's it, Billy," Mrs. Pease told him, "You're going to sit outside the classroom until the period is over."

"No!" Billy protested. "I'm not going. I didn't do anything!"

"You shot those rubber bands at Bonnie and Julian," Mrs. Pease said.

"But it was an accident."

"I don't care. Out you go!"

Billy stalked out of the classroom to sit on a chair in the hall. Before exiting, however, he turned to Mrs. Pease. "I'll sue you for this," he yelled, not really knowing what it meant.

[Gorenstein & Comer, 2002, pp. 250–251]

You will soon read more about Billy's diagnosis and treatment. The psychiatrist found him to be a **child with special needs**, one who requires extra help in order to learn. The specific diagnosis that gives rise to "special needs" might be any of dozens of conditions, including aggression, anxiety, Asperger syndrome, attachment disorder, attention-deficit disorder, autism, bipolar disorder, conduct disorder, depression, developmental delay, Down syndrome, and many more. All of these begin with a biological anomaly, which might be the extra chromosome of Down syndrome or simply an inherited tendency.

A special need is sometimes the direct consequence of an obvious physical handicap, such as blindness, deafness, or paralysis, but this is the case for less than 10 percent of the children with special needs (Msall et al., 2003). Although a specific brain or genetic abnormality may be connected to a particular disability, often the problem is simply a number of minor problems that combine to produce a major difficulty (Plomin, 2002).

In 2000, about 13 percent of all schoolchildren in the United States received special educational services, up from 8 percent in 1975 (National Center for Education Statistics, 2001) (see Table 11.1). Most educators believe that this increase is the result of better diagnosis and recognition, not that more children are impaired. Special-needs children who have not been identified as such probably amount to another 13 percent.

A special-needs child who has been identified has usually first been noticed by a teacher (not a parent or pediatrician), who makes a *referral*, a special request for evaluation based on specific behaviors. According to U.S. law, after a referral other professionals must observe and test the child to determine whether the child has special needs. The parents then meet with the professionals to discuss the diagnosis and to agree on an **individual education plan (IEP)** (see Table 11.2).

Developmental Psychopathology

Psychologists and psychiatrists who study childhood disorders have joined with those who study normal development to create the field of **developmental psychopathology.** In developmental psychopathology, knowledge about normal development contributes to the study and treatment of various disorders, and vice versa. The emphasis is on all the "biological, psychological, social and cultural

child with special needs A child who, because of a physical or mental disability, requires extra help in order to learn.

individual education plan (IEP) A legally required document specifying a series of educational goals for a child with special needs.

developmental psychopathology A field in which knowledge about normal development is applied to the study and treatment of various disorders.

TABLE 11.1 Prevalence of Some Categories of Childhood Psychopathology: United States

Categories	American Psychiatric Association DSM-IV-R	Students Receiving Special Education (as percent of all students)	
	2000	1975	1999
Mental Retardation (MR)*	1%	2%	1%
Significantly delayed adaptation to life, often measured by a score of less than 70 on an IQ test			
Specific Learning Disorder or Disability (LD)	6%	2%	6%
Academic achievement substantially below expected in a basic academic skill			
Communicative Disorders	11%	3%	2%
DSM-IV-R includes several types, including:			
Expressive—Understanding but poor expression (5% at school age; 12% under age 3)			
Receptive-expressive—Deficits in understanding and expression (3% of school-age children)			
Phonological—Child's speech cannot be understood (2%)			
Stuttering—Severe disturbance in fluency (1%) (rare before age 5)			
Pervasive Developmental Disorder (PDD)	0.1%	0.01%†	0.14%
(Includes autism and Asperger syndrome)			
Attention-deficit/hyperactivity disorder (AD/HD, ADD)	5%	**	**
Inattentiveness, impulsivity, and/or overactivity (see text for clarification of definitions and symptoms)			
Conduct Disorder (CD)	5%	**	**
Bullying, threatening, cruelty to people or animals, lying			
Oppositional Defiant Disorder (ODD)	8%	**	**
Negativity, disobedience, hostility toward authorities			
Serious Emotional Disturbance (ED)	††	0.6%	1%
Totals: §	25%	8%	13%

* Specialists often refer to categories using only abbreviations. To help with interpretation, the common abbreviations are given in parentheses.

† Autism data compare 1990 and 1999, because autism was not a recognized category in 1975.

** These categories are not qualified for special education, according to U.S. law.

†† The American Psychiatric Association uses more specific categories for serious emotional problems and has no general estimate of prevalence.

§ Totals include additional children not listed in specific categories. For DSM-IV-R, these include uncommon psychological disturbances, such as feeding disorders, tic disorders, and attachment disorders. Some children have several disabilities, so the total of 25 percent is less than the sum of all categories; but special-education children are given only one primary diagnosis. The current educational total includes only those referred, diagnosed, and accepted for special education. Disorders of speech are not often diagnosed, and three common problems—attention-deficit disorder, conduct disorders, and oppositional behavior— are not recognized as educational categories. A few children with those problems receive special services because they are learning-disabled or emotionally disturbed, but most simply go without any special help.

Sources: American Psychiatric Association, 2000; National Center for Education Statistics, 2001.

processes" that produce "multiple risks and protective factors" (Cicchetti & Sroufe, 2000, p. 256). The "core identity" of developmental psychopathology is dynamic, not static. It involves "discovering processes of development [in order to comprehend] the emergence, progressive unfolding, and transformation of patterns of adaptation and maladaptation over time" (Cicchetti & Sroufe, 2000, pp. 258–259).

Given this emphasis, it is not surprising that research in developmental psychopathology has provided four lessons that apply to all children:

1. *Abnormality is normal.* Most children sometimes act in ways that are decidedly unusual, and most children with serious disorders are, in many respects, quite normal. Children with psychological disorders should be viewed primarily as children—with the many developmental needs that all children share—and only secondarily as children with special challenges.

2. *Disability changes over time.* The behaviors associated with almost any special problem change as the person grows older. A child who seems severely handicapped at one stage of development may seem quite capable at the

TABLE 11.2 Laws Regarding Special Education in the United States*

PL (Public Law) 91-230: Children with Specific Learning Disabilities Act, 1969

Recognized learning disabilities as a category within special education. Before 1969, learning-disabled children received no special education or services.

PL 94-142: Education of All Handicapped Children Act, 1975

Mandated education of all school-age children, no matter what disability they might have, in the *least restrictive environment (LRE)*—which meant with other children in a regular classroom, if possible. Fewer children were placed in special, self-contained classes, and even fewer in special schools. This law required an *individual education plan (IEP)* for each child, specifying exactly what educational goals are next to be reached, and periodic reassessment to evaluate progress.

PL 105-17: Individuals with Disabilities Education Act (IDEA), 1990; updated 1997

Refers to "individuals," not children (to include education of infants, toddlers, adults), and to "disabilities," not handicaps. Emphasizes parents' rights to be consulted and to agree to or refuse referral, testing, placement, and IEP. Parents may invite interpreters and advocates, and may appeal any decision.

*Other nations have quite different laws and practices, and states and school districts within the United States interpret these laws in various ways. Parents and teachers should consult local support groups and authorities, including legal experts, if necessary.

next stage, or vice versa. In fact, "discontinuity in disorders from childhood to adulthood" is typical (Silk et al., 2000, p. 728). Such changes are not simply due to the passage of time; they result from the interplay of maturation, treatment, and contextual change.

3. *Adolescence and adulthood may be better or worse.* Many children with seemingly serious disabilities, even blindness or mental retardation, become happy and productive adults once they find a vocational setting in which they can perform well. Indeed, they sometimes display unusual gifts once they find their niche. Conversely, any disability that makes a child unusually aggressive and socially inept becomes more serious during adolescence and adulthood, when physical maturity and social demands make self-control and appropriate social interaction particularly important.

4. *Diagnosis depends on the social context.* The official fourth edition (revised) of the diagnostic guide of the American Psychiatric Association, the **Diagnostic and Statistical Manual of Mental Disorders,** or **DSM-IV-R,** recognizes that the "nuances of an individual's cultural frame of reference" need to be understood before any disorder can be accurately diagnosed (American Psychiatric Association, 2000, p. xxxiv). Nonetheless, many researchers believe that DSM-IV-R does not go far enough in this direction, because disorders may not reside "inside the skin of an individual" but "between the individual and the environment" (Jensen & Hoagwood, 1997, p. 238).

We have space here to examine only two of the many categories of disorders that developmental psychopathologists study: pervasive developmental disorders and attention-deficit disorders. Understanding these two will help us understand the development of all children.

Diagnostic and Statistical Manual of Mental Disorders **(DSM-IV-R)** The American Psychiatric Association's official guide to the diagnosis of mental disorders. The fifth edition will soon be published.

Pervasive Developmental Disorders

Pervasive developmental disorders are severe problems that affect many aspects of psychological growth. Jacob, the withdrawn, nonspeaking 3-year-old whom you met in Chapter 7, had a pervasive developmental disorder. The diagnosis involves applying developmental norms, such as the ones you have already learned about—for example, walking and talking by age 1, and engaging in rough-and-tumble play and sociodramatic play in early childhood.

pervasive developmental disorders Severe problems, such as autism, that affect many aspects of a young child's psychological growth.

Hope for Autism The prime prerequisite in breaking through the language barrier in a nonverbal autistic child, such as this 4-year-old, is to get the child to pay attention to another person's speech. Note that this teacher is sitting in a low chair to facilitate eye contact and is getting the child to focus on her mouth movements—a matter of little interest to most children but intriguing to many autistic ones. Sadly, even such efforts were not enough: At age 13 this child was still mute.

autism A pervasive developmental disorder marked by an inability to relate to other people in an ordinary way, by extreme self-absorption, and by an inability to learn normal speech.

Asperger syndrome A set of less severe symptoms of autism, in which the individual has fairly normal speech and intelligence but severely impaired social interaction.

Incidence

The most severe type of such disorders is **autism,** which is marked by an "inability to relate in an ordinary way to people . . . an extreme aloneness that, whenever possible, disregards, ignores, shuts out anything that comes to the child from the outside" (Kanner, 1943). Autism is quite rare; it occurs in about 1 of every 2,000 children, according to DSM-IV-R (American Psychiatric Association, 2000).

When the entire spectrum of pervasive developmental disorders is taken into account, about 1 child in 300 (and four times as many boys as girls) shows autistic traits (Szatmari, 2001). Fewer than 1 child in 1,000 develops one of the other severe developmental disorders (including Rett syndrome, a genetic disorder that affects only girls). The number of children with pervasive developmental disorders is climbing in the United States, particularly in California, where five times more children were diagnosed as autistic in 1994 than in 1990.

Possible Causes

Particular genes probably make some embryos more vulnerable than others. Teratogens that harm the embryonic brain stem about three weeks after conception probably increase the genetic weakness that leads to autism (Rodier, 2000).

The belief that pervasive developmental disorders are caused by childhood immunization has been disproved. It originated in the fact that problems with social interaction and language become evident at about the same time that the MMR (measles-mumps-rubella) injections are given in the first year (Dales et al., 2001). The research that definitively refuted this hypothesis was a longitudinal study of all the children (half a million of them) born in Denmark from 1991 to 1998 (Madsen et al., 2002). Of the 18 percent who were not vaccinated, 53 children developed autism and 77 had other pervasive developmental disorders. These conditions occurred at the same rates among the children who did get vaccinated.

Other theories, such as increased diagnosis in children who would previously have been diagnosed as mentally retarded or the influence of some new teratogen (perhaps a pesticide commonly used in California), are still under investigation.

Changes over Time

The first of the four lessons from developmental psychopathology (listed on pages 278–279)—"abnormality is normal"—makes us seek similarities between people diagnosed as "abnormal" and people considered "normal." Many children and adults seem autistic, but their speech and social awareness are not so impaired that normal interaction is impossible; in fact, although they are extremely self-absorbed, they are quite intelligent and verbally adept. Their pervasive developmental disorder may be **Asperger syndrome** (Barnhill et al., 2000; Green et al., 2000), also called *high-functioning autism.*

These are truly *developmental* disorders (as is emphasized by lesson 2 in our list: "Disability changes over time"). As babies, many developmentally disordered children seem quite normal and sometimes unusually "good" (that is, undemanding), although autistic infants are often hypersensitive to noise or other stimulation, and the way they roll over, sit up, crawl, and walk may be less coordinated than the norm (Teitelbaum et al., 1998). If a child is affected with a pervasive developmental disorder, deficits soon appear in three areas:

- Ability to communicate
- Social skills
- Imaginative play

Some children with pervasive developmental disorders seem almost normal until age 2 or 3, but most lack spoken language or typical responses to others (Osterling et al., 2002). During the play years, many such children continue to be mute, not talking at all, while others engage exclusively in a type of speech called *echolalia,* in which they repeat, word for word, television jingles or phrases said to them ("Good morning, John" is echoed with "Good morning, John"). They avoid spontaneous interaction with peers. Instead, they typically engage in repetitive movements (spinning a top over and over) or compulsive play (assembling a puzzle in a particular order time after time).

As children with pervasive developmental disorders grow older, their symptoms vary widely (lesson 3: "Adolescence and adulthood may be better or worse"). Most score in the mentally retarded range on intelligence tests, but a closer look at their intellectual performance shows isolated areas of remarkable skill (such as memory for numbers or ability to put puzzles together). In general, their strongest cognitive skills are in abstract reasoning; their weakest, in social cognition (Scheuffgen et al., 2000). For example, on a trip to the grocery store, a child might quickly calculate that each apple in a bag of a dozen costs exactly 10½ cents and then blurt out to strangers that they must buy apples at this bargain price. Some never speak or have only minimal verbal ability, but many learn to express themselves in language by age 6, becoming quite fluent by adulthood if given intensive behavioral training (Shreibman, 2000). In light of the importance of social context (lesson 4: "Diagnosis depends on the social context"),

> people with Asperger syndrome or high-functioning autism might not necessarily be disabled in an environment in which an exact mind, attracted to detecting small details, is an advantage. In the social world there is no great benefit to such a precise eye for detail, but in the world of math, computing, cataloging, music, linguistics, craft, engineering, or science, such an eye for detail can lead to success rather than disability. In the world of business, for example, a mathematical bent for estimating risk and profit, together with a relative lack of awareness of the emotional states of one's employees or rivals, can mean unbounded opportunities.
>
> *[Baron-Cohen, 2000, pp. 497–498]*

In other words, in some contexts, a child with a pervasive developmental disorder might become an adult who functions reasonably well. This should not be taken as a reason to do nothing but hope for the best. In fact, most experts in behavioral genetics hope for early "preventive intervention rather than waiting to intervene when language and learning problems begin to cast a long and wide shadow over children's development" (Plomin, 2002, p. 59).

Attention-Deficit Disorders

ADD and AD/HD

One of the most puzzling and exasperating of childhood problems is **ADD (attention-deficit disorder),** in which the child has great difficulty concentrating for more than a few moments at a time. The most common type is **AD/HD (attention-deficit/hyperactivity disorder).** Children with AD/HD can have three problems: They can be inattentive, impulsive, and overactive. After sitting down to do homework, for instance, an AD/HD child might repeatedly look up, ask irrelevant questions, think about playing outside, get a drink of water, sit down, fidget, squirm, tap the table, jiggle his or her legs, and then get up again for a snack or to go to the bathroom. Often this need for distraction and diversion is accompanied by excitability and impulsivity.

ADD (attention-deficit disorder) A condition in which a child has great difficulty concentrating (but, unlike a hyperactive child, is not impulsive and overactive); the child may be prone to anxiety and depression and may seem lost in thought, spaced out, or distracted.

AD/HD (attention-deficit/hyperactivity disorder) A condition in which a child has great difficulty concentrating for more than a few moments at a time and, as a result, is inattentive, impulsive, and overactive.

The origin of ADD or AD/HD may be neurological (Aman et al., 1998; Casey, 2001): a brain deficit that results in great difficulty in "paying attention" and in *not* reacting to irrelevant stimuli. The underlying problem may be an abnormality in some part of the brain, but more often it is that the neurotransmitters (particularly dopamine and norepinephrine) do not transmit signals quickly enough to enable the child to avoid distraction (Fisher, 1998).

Genetic vulnerability, prenatal teratogens, postnatal damage such as lead poisoning (Oosterlaan et al., 1998), and simply the extreme end of a normal distribution have all been shown to disrupt expected attention abilities. Billy, the 8-year-old in the Case to Study feature, was diagnosed with AD/HD. His attention problems were evident in that he looked at the airplane when he was supposed to stay in his chair, and his poor impulse control meant he could not wait to say his math answer.

Teachers notice such disruptive children, but a formal diagnosis may never be made. A checklist of the DSM-IV-R criteria for AD/HD was given to all teachers in every elementary school in one Tennessee county. Although fewer than 5 percent (the typical proportion) of the children had already been diagnosed as having AD/HD, 16 percent of the children met the criteria (Wolraich et al., 1998). In this study, as happens generally, about four times as many boys met the criteria for AD/HD as girls.

Learning Disabilities

About half of all children with AD/HD also have a specific learning disability. In fact, some experts believe that a deficit in attention is itself a kind of learning disability, although it is not classified as such in DSM-IV-R.

In general, **learning-disabled** children fall markedly behind in a particular aspect of learning but have no obvious physical handicap, no overall mental retardation, and no unusually stressful home environment that could cause their learning difficulty. Thus, the crucial factor in the diagnosis of a learning disability is a *measured discrepancy* between expected learning and actual accomplishment in a particular academic area.

The most common learning disability is **dyslexia,** which is unusual difficulty with reading. Most dyslexic children seem bright and happy in the early years of school, volunteering answers to difficult questions, diligently completing their worksheets, and quietly looking at their books in class. If a child is advanced in comprehension through the use of contextual clues but is behind in ability to match letters to sounds, that is a sign of dyslexia (Nation & Snowling, 1998) (see Figure 11.3). However, no single test successfully diagnoses any learning disability (Sofie & Riccio, 2002).

Many learning-disabled children score normally on intelligence tests, although sometimes the scores on particular subtests are scattered around the norm—some unusually high and others unusually low (Kaplan et al., 2000). According to the guidelines of many states, a discrepancy between aptitude and achievement scores indicates a learning disability. The specifics vary, with a one-year discrepancy usually considered sufficient to signal disability at age 7 and a two-year discrepancy at age 11 (Lerner, 2000).

Other specific academic subjects that may reveal a learning disability are math, spelling, and handwriting. A child might be mystified by simple subtraction that requires "borrowing" (e. g., 12 – 4), might read at the fifth-grade level but repeatedly make simple spelling mistakes ("kum accros the rode"), or might take three times as long as any classmate to copy something from the chalkboard—and then produce only a large, illegible scrawl. Although the neurological patterns that underlie dyslexia (and probably other disabilities as well) are universal, the severity of a child's disability depends on whether or not early, targeted instruction was provided and on what language the child has learned

learning-disabled Having a marked delay in a particular area of learning that is not associated with any obvious physical handicap, overall mental retardation, or unusually stressful home environment.

dyslexia Unusual difficulty with reading.

Is She Dyslexic? No. Some young readers have difficulty "tracking" a line of print with their eyes alone. Using a finger to stay on track can be a useful temporary aid.

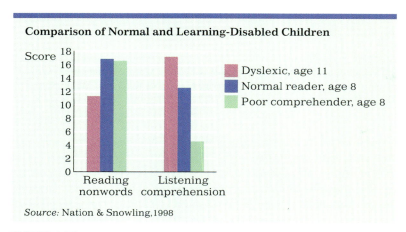

Comparison of Normal and Learning-Disabled Children

Legend:
- Dyslexic, age 11
- Normal reader, age 8
- Poor comprehender, age 8

Source: Nation & Snowling, 1998

FIGURE 11.3 **Reading and Comprehension** In this study, three groups of children were compared, all reading at the third-grade level. The children in one group were dyslexic, and they were age 11, on average. The children in the other two groups were 8 years old, but half of them were normal readers and the other half had problems with reading comprehension. As this graph shows, the groups differed markedly in their ability to read and pronounce a nonword (letters combined to make a possible word that does not mean anything, such as *wug* or *tedork*) or to comprehend a passage read to them. Each group would require a different pattern of reading instruction.

Culture Clash This Tibetan boy attends a Chinese school. Chinese is very difficult to learn to read, especially if it is not one's native language. He may indeed have learned to decode the printed symbols—or he may have learned to fake it.

(Italian dyslexics fare better than French or English ones) (Paulesu et al., 2001). Of course, patient, individualized instruction is much easier to deliver if the child is not overactive, which is one reason treatment for AD/HD is crucial whenever it is also present. A milder form of ADD almost always accompanies a learning disability, because it is hard to pay attention to a task that is impossible to perform. Learning-disabled students need help, whether or not they have AD/HD.

Treatment of Attention-Deficit Disorders

Not surprisingly, children with ADD develop academic difficulties, and those with AD/HD are usually troublesome to adults and rejected by their peers. Medication, psychotherapy, and changes in the family and school environments can help some children, especially when all three approaches are combined. In general, the family and the school need to be very precise in delivering the consequences of behaviors, making sure the child is rewarded for the correct, appropriate actions.

For reasons not yet determined, certain drugs that stimulate adults have the reverse effect on many—but not all—children with attention-deficit problems. Among these psychoactive drugs are certain amphetamines (e.g., Adderall) and methylphenidate, known as *Ritalin,* widely prescribed for adults as a stimulant. In many cases, the effects of these drugs are remarkable: The child can sit still and concentrate for the first time. Ritalin was prescribed for Billy, and his parents and teacher were taught how to help him. He "improved considerably" within two months, not only staying in his seat and completing his schoolwork but also making some friends (Gorenstein & Comer, 2002).

A reported 11 million prescriptions were written for Ritalin in the United States in 1999 (Shute et al., 2000). At least 20 other psychoactive drugs, including Prozac, Zoloft, and Paxil, are now prescribed for children, some of them as young as age 2 (Fisher, 1998). Prescribing medication for such young children

Not a Cure-All Ritalin has been found to calm many children with AD/HD—but it does not necessarily make them models of good behavior. Like this 5-year-old boy with multiple handicaps, including AD/HD (for which he is given Ritalin), they are still capable of having a tantrum when frustrated.

Especially for Health Workers Parents ask that some medication be prescribed for their kindergarten child, who is much too active for them to handle. How do you respond?

mainstreaming A policy (mandated by the Education of All Handicapped Children Act in 1975) under which children with special needs must be taught in "the least restrictive environment" available, which usually means that they are taught with other children in the general classroom.

least restrictive environment (LRE) A legally required school setting that offers children with special needs as much freedom as possible to benefit from the instruction available to other children; often, in practice, the general classroom.

resource room A room set aside in some schools for special-needs children to spend part of each day with a teacher who is trained and equipped to work with their disabilities.

inclusion A policy under which learning-disabled children are included in the regular class, as in mainstreaming, but are supervised by a specially trained teacher or paraprofessional for all or part of the day.

Every Child Is Special One reason for a school policy of inclusion is to teach children to accept and appreciate children who have special needs. The girl with Down syndrome (in yellow) benefits from learning alongside her classmates, as they learn from her. An effective teacher treats every child as a special individual.

LAURA DWIGHT

raises serious concerns, because medication alone does not resolve learning difficulties (Gorski, 2002). One expert contends:

> Squirming in a seat and talking out of turn are not "symptoms" and do not reflect a syndrome. [Such behaviors may be] caused by anything from normal childhood energy to boring classrooms or overstressed parents and teachers. We should not suppress these behaviors with drugs. . . .
>
> *[Breggin, 2001, p. 595]*

This is one opinion; many others suggest trying drugs to see if they help, just as one would try aspirin to see if it relieves a splitting headache. All agree that ongoing changes at home and at school are essential. Drugs can, at best, control behavior; moreover, they are often underprescribed or overprescribed (Angold et al., 2000). The critical question is whether or not the child is learning as much in school as other children of the same overall ability.

Educating Children with Special Needs

Once a child is referred for evaluation and parents and professionals agree that the child has special needs, where should that child be educated? In many cases before 1960, most children with special needs simply left school. Public policy did not sanction the use of public money to educate such children, and specialized private schools focused only on children with obvious physical handicaps, such as blindness. If retarded, disturbed, or otherwise disabled students were educated in schools, they were often placed in a separate classroom. This segregation from regular students impaired the development of normal social skills and slowed advancement in areas in which a child was not disabled. Many parents resisted their children's assignment to "Special Ed," and instead the children struggled in regular classrooms.

In response to the obvious problems of educating children in segregated classrooms or not at all, **mainstreaming** emerged about 35 years ago. The Education of All Handicapped Children Act of 1975 mandated that children with special needs be taught in the **least restrictive environment (LRE)** possible. The thinking behind this law was that children should not be restricted to a special classroom if a less restrictive environment could be made available. In practice, that often meant they were taught with children in the general (main) classroom. The regular teacher was asked to be particularly sensitive to the special-needs children, perhaps using alternative methods to teach them or allowing them extra time to complete assignments and tests. The presumption was that they belonged *with* their peers, not apart from them.

Mainstreaming did not meet all children's educational needs. Consequently, many schools set aside a **resource room**, where special-needs children would spend part of each day with a teacher who was trained and equipped to work with their disabilities. But pulling the child out of regular class undermined classroom social relationships and left the regular teacher unaccountable for the progress of the child. Further, scheduling resource-room time meant that the child missed out on vital parts of the regular school day, either play periods or practice in academic skills.

The most recent approach to placement is called **inclusion:** Children with special needs are "included" in the regular class, as in mainstreaming. However, a specially trained teacher or paraprofessional assists with the special-needs children, for all or part of the day, in the regular classroom. This solution is expensive,

© ROBIN L. SACHS / PHOTOEDIT

What Are These Children Learning? This deaf boy is fortunate—he is with his hearing peers and his teacher knows how to sign to him. Are the other children doing their work? One hopes, over the course of the year, they will learn more from the inclusion of the special child than they miss from the teacher's targeted attention.

and it requires adjustment on the part of both teachers, who are not used to working side by side. Nonetheless, children who need both social interaction with their schoolmates and special treatment for their learning difficulties may learn more than if they were to be pulled out of the regular class to be taught in a resource room (Swenson, 2000; Waldron & McLeskey, 1998).

Unfortunately for children with special needs, no placement always solves their academic and social problems (Siperstein et al., 1997). For example, hyperactive and learning-disabled children tend to have fewer friends than other children, no matter what their classroom placement (Wiener & Schneider, 2002). From a developmental perspective, this is not surprising: All manner of disabilities, from severe physical impairment to subtle learning disabilities, are real, and long-standing. They may be improved by the proper educational context, but, as a study of inclusion in eight nations made clear (Booth & Ainscow, 1998), they are unlikely to disappear completely.

Once parents, teachers, and children understand that disabilities do not stem from laziness, stupidity, or stubbornness, but from a brain pattern that needs to be restructured, then advances in the child's development can occur. This happened with the late Ennis Cosby (1997), son of comedian Bill Cosby, who wrote, "The happiest day of my life occurred when I found out I was dyslexic. I believe that life is finding solutions, and the worst feeling to me is confusion."

Some children do not learn as readily as others, and therefore they have special learning needs. The field of developmental psychopathology emphasizes that no child is completely average or normal and that children who have specific disabilities may improve or become less capable as they grow older. Education and social context influence psychopathology.

The dozens of possible disorders vary in cause, treatment, and prognosis, although many share certain characteristics. This is illustrated by pervasive developmental disorders and attention-deficit disorders. These can lead to adequate adult functioning or to lifelong problems, depending not only on the severity of the initial disability but also on family, school, and culture. In 2000, about 13 percent of all children in the United States were receiving special education services in school, and perhaps another 13 percent might benefit from such services. Specifics of diagnosis, placement, medication, and teaching strategies are controversial, but there is no doubt that many children need special help to learn.

Response for Health Workers (from page 284):
On this topic, ideology far outdistances information. Medication helps some hyperactive children, but not all; it might be useful at age 4, but other forms of intervention should probably be tried first. Therefore, you should compliment the parents on their concern about their child but refer them to an expert in early childhood. The expert can evaluate the child and the family and then make recommendations, which may include medication but definitely will include behavior-management techniques geared to the particular situation.

Conclusion

Suggestions for teachers and parents of children with special needs can be gleaned from the next two chapters, for everything that helps cognition (Chapter 12) and psychosocial development (Chapter 13) will help all children. A few particular suggestions arise from the research. Simply telling parents to be patient, or responsive, or strict does *not* work, but teaching them specific ways to encourage appropriate behavior in their child does (Scott et al., 2001). Simply offering teachers general instructions (e.g., give him easy books and spend more time on reading) is not effective, but providing learning strategies for each aspect of school instruction is useful (Swanson, 1999).

What if a developmental problem is not recognized, diagnosed, or treated? This often happens, as was shown by the Tennessee study mentioned earlier. Many health and learning problems become evident in childhood but often are not diagnosed soon enough for effective early intervention.

Life-span developmental research finds that childhood problems rarely disappear, although the specifics of home and school affect the lifelong impact. Ideally, special needs are spotted by age 5 and teachers and parents provide the necessary educational and emotional support. If not, older children may still find ways to compensate for, overcome, or limit their difficulties; many adults realize, in retrospect, that some aspect of their school learning was unusually hard for them (Rutter & Sroufe, 2000).

We continue this theme in the next two chapters, which focus specifically on what school-age children learn (a prodigious amount) and how they cope with their problems (quite well, for the most part), as well as on the many ways schools and families can foster pride and success for every child. As we stressed at the beginning of this chapter with Yolanda and Paul, and as you can see with Billy as well, each child is unique, but all have common needs and concerns and all benefit from teachers, parents, and peers who care about them.

SUMMARY

A Healthy Time

1. Middle childhood is generally a healthy time of steady growth and few serious illnesses. Because of their increasing independence and ability to care for themselves, school-age children join the wider social world, comparing themselves with others the same age.

2. Children perceive almost any physical difference between one child and another as a deficit, a reason to feel ashamed and lonely. The most common of these observable differences is childhood obesity, which is becoming an epidemic.

3. Asthma is an increasingly common ailment among school-age children in developed nations. Although the origins are genetic and the triggers are specific allergens, primary prevention includes longer breast-feeding, more outdoor play, and reduced air pollution, which would benefit all children.

Brain Development

4. Brain development continues during middle childhood, enhancing every other aspect of development. Particularly important are increased myelination and greater production of neurotransmitters, which speed communication between neurons. In addition, the prefrontal cortex and the corpus callosum continue to mature, allowing not only analysis and planning but also automatization and simultaneous use of the entire cortex.

5. Both gross and fine motor skills continue to develop during middle childhood, as neurological maturation continues. As with every other aspect of maturation, neurological advances are aided by practice and culture.

6. IQ tests are designed to quantify intellectual aptitude. Such tests assess language and logical ability and predict school achievement. Critics contend that intelligence is actually manifested in multiple ways, which conventional IQ tests are too limited to measure.

Children with Special Needs

7. The field of developmental psychopathology uses an understanding of normal development to inform the study of unusual development. Four general lessons have emerged from the field: Abnormality is normal; disability changes over time; adolescence and adulthood may be better or worse; and diagnosis depends on the social context.

8. Some children with obvious educational or psychological disabilities are recognized, referred, evaluated, diagnosed, and treated in early childhood. For the most part, however, behavioral or learning problems are not spotted until the children enter elementary school and are compared with other children in a setting that demands maturity and learning.

9. About 13 percent of all school-age children in the United States receive special education services. These services begin with an IEP (individual education plan) and assignment to the least restrictive environment—all with the parents' approval.

10. Children with pervasive developmental disorders typically have odd and delayed language; lack of social awareness, with impaired interpersonal skills; and play that is repetitive and unimaginative. The most severe of such disorders is autism; a less severe manifestation is called Asperger syndrome.

11. Children with attention-deficit/hyperactivity disorder (AD/HD) have potential problems in three areas: inattention, impulsiveness, and overactivity. Children who are not especially overactive but who have trouble concentrating and who seem anxious, depressed, and distracted may be diagnosed with attention-deficit disorder (ADD). Many ADD and AD/HD children also have learning disabilities, measured by a discrepancy of a year or two between aptitude and achievement.

12. The best treatment for attention deficits is probably a combination of medication, home management, and education. Stimulant medication often helps AD/HD children focus, but it requires targeted teaching and careful management at home.

13. Decisions about the educational placement of special-needs children are complicated by conflicts between ideological concerns and practical needs, and sometimes between educational professionals and parents. The inclusion approach is controversial, although it is generally considered better than mainstreaming.

KEY TERMS

middle childhood (p. 267)
overweight (p. 268)
obesity (p. 268)
asthma (p. 270)
automatization (p. 272)
reaction time (p. 273)
aptitude (p. 274)
IQ tests (p. 274)
achievement tests (p. 274)
Wechsler Intelligence Scale
  for Children (WISC) (p. 274)

child with special needs
  (p. 277)
individual education plan
  (IEP) (p. 277)
developmental
  psychopathology (p. 277)
*Diagnostic and Statistical
  Manual of Mental Disorders*
  (DSM-IV-R) (p. 279)
pervasive developmental
  disorders (p. 279)

autism (p. 280)
Asperger syndrome (p. 280)
ADD (attention-deficit
  disorder) (p. 281)
AD/HD (attention-deficit/
  hyperactivity disorder)
  (p. 281)
learning-disabled (p. 282)
dyslexia (p. 282)
mainstreaming (p. 284)

least restrictive environment
  (LRE) (p. 284)
resource room (p. 284)
inclusion (p. 284)

APPLICATIONS

1. Compare play spaces for children in different neighborhoods in your vicinity—ideally, in an urban, a suburban, and a rural area. Note differences in size, safety, and population of available playgrounds. Discuss how the differences might affect the weight and motor skills of children.

2. Special education teachers are in great demand in many nations, particularly the United States. Find out from your state or city board of education the ratio of regular to special education teachers and how many were trained to teach special education. Then find out the ratio of regular and special-needs children in self-contained classrooms, resource rooms, and inclusion classrooms. How do your results compare with the material in the chapter?

3. Developmental psychologists believe that every teacher should be skilled at teaching children with a wide variety of needs. Investigate the curriculum at your college or at the nearest university that educates future teachers. Are there distinct requirements for special education teachers? Do you think all teachers should take the same courses or that some teachers need particular training? Give reasons for your opinion.

4. Web sites vary in quality, no matter what the topic, but this may be particularly true of Web sites designed for parents of children with special needs. Pick one childhood disability or disease and find several Web sites about that condition. How might parents evaluate the information provided?

Chapter Twelve

The School Years: Cognitive Development

concrete operational thought Piaget's term for the ability to reason logically about the things and events that one perceives.

Especially for Teachers How might Piaget and Vygotsky help in teaching geography to a class of third-graders?

School-age children are learners. They can learn almost anything that is not too abstract, including how to multiply and divide fractions, how to prepare a nutritious, delicious dinner, how to surf the Web to uncover an obscure fact, how to medicate and tend a sick donkey. Every such skill takes time to master—and for 7- to 11-year-olds, each day advances knowledge a tiny bit.

The speed, depth, and content of learning reflect motivation more than maturation—motivation that is guided by cultural priorities and channeled by intricate connections in the brain. Nurture and nature interact to allow each child to learn in his or her own way. Nonetheless, all school-age children are primed to learn, and adults in every culture are eager to teach them.

We begin this chapter by describing the universals of cognitive development. Jean Piaget and Lev Vygotsky describe these universals in different ways, as we will illustrate by describing their views on moral development. Next, we look at how information-processing theory helps us understand the child's mind. Then we turn to schooling during middle childhood, including facts and controversies regarding reading, math, class size, and bilingual education. Parents as well as teachers affect each of these issues, with cultural values sometimes obvious, sometimes hidden.

Building on Piaget and Vygotsky

Both Piaget and Vygotsky, as you remember from Chapter 9, emphasize the structures, or scaffolding, that children develop in preparation for learning during middle childhood (Rogoff, 1998). In Piaget's view, the most important cognitive achievement of middle childhood is the attainment of **concrete operational thought,** which is characterized by a collection of logical concepts that enable children to reason logically.

Sometime between ages 5 and 7, children begin to understand certain logical principles. Soon after grasping them, they apply them in *concrete* situations—that is, situations that deal with visible, tangible, real things. Children thereby become more systematic, objective, scientific—and educable—thinkers.

Vygotsky (1934/1994) agreed with Piaget's attention to the actual thinking of the child. He considered this approach a marked improvement over the dull "meaningless acquisition" approach favored by the schools of his time. Such schools rendered the child "helpless in the face of any sensible attempt to apply any of this acquired knowledge" (pp. 356–357). Unlike Piaget, Vygotsky regarded instruction by others as crucial, with peers and teachers providing the bridge to connect the child's innate developmental potential with the skills and knowledge that education should bring.

Logical Principles

To understand concrete operational thought, consider four logical principles: classification, identity, reversibility, and reciprocity. The concepts, from which these four principles arise, are almost impossible for younger children to comprehend but are gradually grasped during middle childhood.

Classification is the process of organizing things into groups (or *categories* or *classes)* according to some property they have in common. For example, a child's parents and siblings belong to the class called "family"; toys, animals, people, and food are other common classes. Each class includes some elements and excludes others, and each is part of a hierarchy. Food, for instance, is a broad class, which contains the subclasses of meat, grains, fruits, and so on. Most subclasses can be further divided: Meat includes poultry, beef, and pork, which again can be further subdivided. It is apparent to adults, but not always to children, that items at the bottom of the class hierarchy belong to every higher category (bacon is always pork, meat, and food) but that the process does not work in reverse—most foods are not bacon.

Piaget developed many experiments that reveal children's understanding of classification. For example, an examiner shows a child a bunch of nine flowers— seven yellow daisies and two white roses (revised and published in Piaget et al., 2001). The examiner makes sure the child knows that all are called "flowers," and that some are called "daisies" and others are called "roses." Then comes the crucial question: "Are there more daisies or more flowers?" Until about age 7, most children say "more daisies." Pushed to justify their answer, some say that there are more yellow ones than white ones or that, because the daisies are daisies, they can't be called flowers. Such conflicting answers usually come from 6- and 7-year-olds. By age 8, most children have a solid understanding of the classification of objects they can see (not yet of hypothetical objects), and they answer confidently that there are more flowers than daisies.

Identity is the principle that certain characteristics of an object can remain the same even if other characteristics appear to shift. Children who understand identity realize that superficial changes in an object's appearance do not alter that object's underlying substance or quantity. In conservation tests, for example

classification The logical principle by which things are organized into groups (or categories or classes) according to some property they have in common.

Response for Teachers (from page 289): Here are two of the most obvious ways. First, use logic. Once children can grasp classification and class inclusion, they can understand cities within states, states within nations, and nations within continents. Organize your instruction to make logical categorization easier. Second, make use of children's need for concrete and personal involvement: You might have children learn first about their own location, then about the places where friends and family live, and finally about places beyond their personal experience via books, photos, guest speakers, and films.

identity The logical principle that certain characteristics of an object remain the same even if other characteristics change.

Learning by Doing Active learning—the hands-on experience of, in this case, connecting wires with positive and negative charges—is a valuable supplement to book learning and rote learning.

(see pages 219–220), identity means that pouring a liquid from one container into a different container does not change the amount of liquid present. "It's still the same milk," a 9-year-old might say. "You haven't changed that."

School-age children also come to understand **reversibility,** the idea that sometimes a thing that has been changed can be returned to its original state by reversing the process by which it was changed. A school-age child might prove that the amount of liquid has not changed by pouring it back into the first container, thus reversing the process.

Finally, children begin to understand the logical principle of **reciprocity.** Reciprocity (also called *inversion*) occurs when two things change in opposite ways in order to balance each other out. A child might explain, in the conservation experiment, that the amount of

liquid remains the same—because the new container is both wider and shorter, the liquid's decreased height is balanced out by its increased width.

Identity, reversibility, and reciprocity are all relevant to mathematical understanding, and they all take time to develop. Thus, a first-grader might understand identity in that 6 is always 6, whether it is the result of 2 + 4 or 3 + 3. Reversibility is a little harder: If 2 + 4 = 6, then 6 – 4 = 2. Finally, reciprocity allows children to understand that 4 × 6 is the same as 2 × 12, because if the 4 is divided by 2, then the 6 has to be multiplied by 2. Such logic is beyond almost all children in the early years of primary school, which is why multiplication and division are difficult at first (Piaget & Moreau, 2001).

The same logical ideas apply to other aspects of learning during middle childhood. For example, a tadpole can become a frog (identity), steam from boiling water can become water again (reversibility), being kind to a classmate might reduce that classmate's aggression (reciprocity). Note, however, that understanding such concepts does not mean that they are always applied, either in school or in social situations. For that, children learn best if adults guide them, as Vygotsky emphasized.

Logic and Culture

Piaget's basic idea about concrete operational thought—that children during middle childhood gradually come to comprehend and to apply logical ideas that they did not understand well before—remains valid. In math, in physics, in explaining how people can or cannot catch physical or mental illnesses from someone else, and in many other ways children become more logical and less egocentric as they mature, just as Piaget described (Howe, 1998; Keil & Lockhart, 1999; Siegler & Jenkins, 1989).

Vygotsky's emphasis on the influence of the sociocultural context of learning adds to Piaget's ideas, illuminating why children learn and think as they do. According to Vygotsky, children are powerfully influenced by the people around them, who guide them in one direction or another, and by the cultural context. Whether school-age children grasp certain concepts depends a great deal on the particulars of instruction and on the influence of their peers. In short, developmentalists' understanding of how children learn depends largely on "a framework that was laid down by Piaget and embellished by Vygotsky" (Howe, 1998, p. 207).

Measuring Soil Absorbency This science lesson in the fourth grade of a public school in New York City seems well designed for concrete operational thinking. The children analyze, investigate, and classify samples of soil by putting them in water, not by reading a textbook. Note also that each does his or her own work within a social setting—another sign of effective elementary education.

reversibility The logical principle that sometimes a thing that has been changed can be returned to its original state by reversing the process by which it was changed.

reciprocity The logical principle that two things may change in opposite ways in order to balance each other out. Also called *inversion*.

Street Smarts Javier Garcias sells candy and cigarettes on the streets of San Salvador, the capital of El Salvador, from 5 A.M. until 1 P.M. and from 5 P.M. to 8 P.M. In between, he goes to school. That combination of work experience and formal education may add up to excellent math skills—if Javier is awake enough to learn.

Most of the research on children's cognition has been done in North America and England, but the same principles are apparent worldwide. In Zimbabwe, for example, children's understanding of the logical principle of classification was found to be influenced not only by their age but also by the particulars of their schooling and their family's socioeconomic status (Mpofu & van de Vijver, 2000). Japanese 4- to 11-year-olds' understanding of time, speed, and distance, as Piaget would predict, improved with age: Although younger children sometimes grasped the relationship between two of these three, they could not put all three together, as some of the oldest children could. However, comprehension of the three-way reciprocity of time, speed, and distance varied much more than a straightforward stage theory of development would predict, suggesting that sociocultural factors were influential as well (Matsuda, 2001). Another study of Japanese children found that *some* mathematical skills closely followed Piaget's theory but that others were definitely the result of specific school instruction, as Vygotsky would have expected (Naito & Miura, 2001).

The most detailed international example of the importance of culture and experience comes from 6- to 15-year-old street children in Brazil, who sell fruit, candy, and other products to earn their living. Many have never attended school and consequently score poorly on standard math achievement tests. However, most become quite adept at pricing their wares, making change, and giving discounts for large quantities—a set of operations that must be recalibrated almost every day to adjust to changes in the rate of inflation, wholesale prices, and customer demand. These children calculate "complex markup computations and adjust for inflation in these computations by using procedures that were widespread in their practice but not known to children in school" (Saxe, 1999, p. 255). Thus, advances in these children's cognitive performance came from the demands of the situation, the social learning attained from other sellers, and their daily experience. Education was not completely irrelevant, however. Children who had some schooling and some street experience performed best of all (Saxe, 1991).

Further research on Brazilian 4- to 14-year-olds confirms the special relationship between cognitive development and experience. The cognitive advantage of actually having dealt with money was greatest for children age 6 to 11, in middle childhood. Younger children were less able to understand the arithmetic problems as presented to them, even with experience, and older ones could do just as well whether or not they had sold items on the street (Guberman, 1996). In short, learning is both developmental and sociocultural; both Piagetian and Vygotskyan.

Overall, Piaget constructed a valid sketch of cognitive development, but he underestimated the influence of context, culture, and particular instructional practices. His basic ideas—that concrete operational thought is characteristic of children during middle childhood and that logical principles, including conservation, classification, identity, reversibility, and reciprocity, are grasped first between ages 5 and 7, and then more securely between ages 7 and 11—can still be demonstrated with children throughout the world today. However, Piaget underestimated the variability from one child to another. Research inspired by Vygotsky and the sociocultural perspective fills in Piaget's outline with details of the actual learning situation.

Moral Development

Moral development is discussed many times throughout this text, because morals and ethics belong to many ages and domains. Here we focus on the theories of Lawrence Kohlberg, who built on Piaget's stages of cognition to describe stages of moral development.

Kohlberg's Stages

Kohlberg analyzed the responses of children and adolescents (and eventually adults) to a set of ethical dilemmas. The most famous dilemma involves the conflict between private property and human life as experienced by Heinz, a poor man whose wife is dying of cancer. A local pharmacist has developed the only cure, a drug sold for thousands of dollars—far more than Heinz can pay and 10 times what the drug costs to make.

> Heinz went to everyone he knew to borrow the money, but he could only get together about half of what it cost. He told the druggist that his wife was dying and asked him to sell it cheaper or let him pay later. But the druggist said "no." The husband got desperate and broke into the man's store to steal the drug for his wife. Should the husband have done that? Why?

[Kohlberg, 1963]

In people's responses to such dilemmas, Kohlberg found three levels of moral reasoning—*preconventional, conventional,* and *postconventional*—with two stages at each level (see Table 12.1). In theory, each level of moral reasoning matches one of Piaget's stages of cognitive development. **Preconventional moral reasoning** is similar to preoperational thought, in that it is egocentric. **Conventional moral reasoning** is related to concrete operational thought in that it relates to current, observable practices within the community. And **postconventional moral reasoning** is similar to formal or postformal thought, which includes logical ideas and ideals, which go beyond what can be concretely observed.

COURTESY OF THE HARVARD UNIVERSITY ARCHIVES

Lawrence Kohlberg Kohlberg was a scholar, researcher, and philosopher who described the logical structures that underlie specific moral decisions.

preconventional moral reasoning Kohlberg's first level of moral reasoning, in which emphasis is placed on getting rewards and avoiding punishments.

conventional moral reasoning Kohlberg's second level of moral reasoning, in which emphasis is placed on social rules.

postconventional moral reasoning Kohlberg's third level of moral reasoning, in which emphasis is placed on moral principles.

TABLE 12.1 Kohlberg's Three Levels and Six Stages of Moral Reasoning

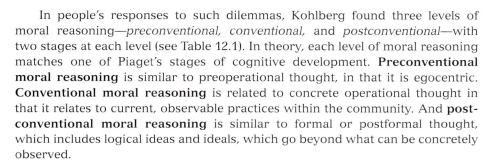

Level I: Preconventional Moral Reasoning
Emphasis is placed on getting rewards and avoiding punishments; this is a self-centered level.

- *Stage One: Might makes right* (a punishment and obedience orientation). The most important value is obedience to authority, so as to avoid punishment while still advancing self-interest.

- *Stage Two: Look out for number one* (an instrumental and relativist orientation). Each person tries to take care of his or her own needs. The reason to be nice to other people is so that they will be nice to you.

Level II: Conventional Moral Reasoning
Emphasis is placed on social rules; this is a community-centered level.

- *Stage Three: "Good girl" and "nice boy."* Proper behavior is behavior that pleases other people. Social approval is more important than any specific reward.

- *Stage Four: "Law and order."* Proper behavior means being a dutiful citizen and obeying the laws set down by society.

Level III: Postconventional Moral Reasoning
Emphasis is placed on moral principles; this level is centered on ideals.

- *Stage Five: Social contract.* One should obey social rules because they benefit everyone and are established by mutual agreement. If the rules become destructive, however, or if one party doesn't live up to the agreement, the contract is no longer binding.

- *Stage Six: Universal ethical principles.* General universal principles, not individual situations or community practices, determine right and wrong. Ethical values (such as "life is sacred") are established by individual reflection and may contradict the egocentric or legal values of earlier stages.

According to Kohlberg, *how* people reason, rather than what specific moral conclusions they reach, determines their stage of moral development. For example, reasoning that seeks social approval (stage 3) might produce opposite conclusions: Either Heinz *should* steal the drug (because people would blame him for not saving his wife) or he *should not* steal it (because people would call him a thief). In both cases, the underlying moral principle (and stage) is the same—that people should behave in ways that earn the approval of others.

Children, adolescents, and adults gradually move up Kohlberg's hierarchy, reasoning at a more advanced stage as time goes on. During middle childhood, children's answers are generally at the first two levels—primarily preconventional before age 8 and conventional for 9- to 11-year-olds—although much depends on the specific context and on the child's opportunity to discuss moral issues. This shift in middle childhood is what might be expected as children leave egocentric preoperational thinking and advance to concrete operational logic.

Remember Vygotsky's stress on cultural variations and social guidance? Kohlberg reflected some awareness of social forces in that he believed that school-age children should discuss moral dilemmas with each other and that doing so would advance their thinking from simple self-interest to a higher level.

Kohlberg's Critics

Although the basic scheme proposed by Kohlberg has been replicated (Boom et al., 2001; Walker et al., 2001), his ideas have also been widely criticized, particularly with regard to culture and gender. It is now well established that every culture has distinctive values and morals, which are sometimes connected to a particular religion, sometimes not. For example, children may hold the belief that eating beef (or pork, whale, or dog) is immoral; such a value is not universal but culture-specific. Kohlberg was from a Western intellectual background. Did this influence his hierarchy?

Some critics of Kohlberg believe that his level III (stages 5 and 6) reflects only liberal, Western intellectual values. In many non-Western nations and among some ethnic groups within Western cultures, the good of the family, the well-being of the community, or adherence to religious tradition takes moral precedence over all other considerations (Wainryb & Turiel, 1995). Members of such cultures and groups may not move up Kohlberg's hierarchy as fast as others.

For example, in a study of teenagers in the Netherlands, Moroccan and Turkish students were significantly behind Dutch and Surinamese adolescents in Kohlberg's hierarchy (De Mey et al., 1999). The Moroccan and Turkish emphasis on family and community, taken as a handicap in Kohlberg's scheme, may be considered a higher form of moral thinking than the individualism and rationality enshrined by Kohlberg. Indeed, many people believe that abstract reasoning about the justice of hypothetical situations is not the only, or necessarily the best, way to measure moral judgment (Emler, 1998).

In contrast, Kohlberg's hierarchy may underestimate the reasoning capacity of some school-age children in some cultures. In one study, Canadian 6- to 10-year-olds judged whether laws were just and condoned disobedience when a law was unjust—a stage-five reaction. These issues are not discussed in elementary school, presumably because they are thought to be beyond young children (Helwig & Jasiobedzka, 2001); but in this belief Kohlberg and his followers may underestimate children's capacity if their culture provides the guided participation that Vygotsky advocates.

Carol Gilligan (1982) raised another criticism—that Kohlberg overlooked significant gender differences. Gilligan explains that females develop a **morality of care** more than a **morality of justice.** The morality of care makes girls and women reluctant to judge right and wrong in absolute terms (justice) because

morality of care In Gilligan's view, the tendency of females to be reluctant to judge right and wrong in absolute terms because they are socialized to be nurturant, compassionate, and nonjudgmental.

morality of justice In Gilligan's view, the tendency of males to emphasize justice over compassion, judging right and wrong in absolute terms.

they are socialized to be nurturant, compassionate, and nonjudgmental (caring).

As an example, Gilligan (1982) cited the responses of two bright 11-year-olds, Jake and Amy, to the Heinz story. Jake considered the dilemma "sort of like a math problem with humans," and he set up an equation that showed that life is more important than property. Amy, in contrast, seemed to sidestep the issue, arguing that Heinz "really shouldn't steal the drug—but his wife shouldn't die either." She tried to find an alternative solution (a bank loan, perhaps) and then explained that stealing wouldn't be right because Heinz "might have to go to jail, and then his wife might get sicker again, and he couldn't get more of the drug."

Amy's response may seem just as ethical as Jake's, but Kohlberg would score it lower. Gilligan argues that this is unfair, because what appears to be females' moral weakness—their hesitancy to take a definitive position based on abstract moral premises—is, in fact,

Give Peace a Chance The setting is Israel; the sheep washers include Jews and Muslims. In all probability, these boys are aware that their cooperative efforts are in accord with moral values but are contrary to the social customs prevailing around them. The school years are a good time to teach children about other races and cultures, a lesson best learned through personal experience.

> inseparable from women's moral strength, an overriding concern with relationships and responsibilities. The reluctance to judge may itself be indicative of the care and concern that infuse the psychology of women's development.
>
> *[Gilligan, 1982]*

Many researchers have tested Gilligan's ideas with children, by looking for a morality of care or a morality of justice. The evidence does not support Gilligan's provocative theory of a gender divide in people's thinking about morals (Walker, 1988). Boys and girls, men and women seem to be more affected by cultural differences than by biological ones where social issues are concerned, just as Vygotsky would predict.

As this discussion indicates, trying to understand how children advance in their thinking about moral issues reveals both the insights and limitations of Piaget's and Vygotsky's theories. However, both Piaget and Vygotsky, as well as all those who study children's moral thinking, recognize that ages 7 to 11 are

Especially for Parents Suppose you and your school-age children move to a new community that is 50 miles from the nearest location that offers instruction in your religious faith or secular value system. Your neighbor says, "Don't worry, they don't have to make any moral decisions until they are teenagers." What do you do?

> years of eager, lively searching on the part of children, whose parents and teachers are often hard put to keep up with them as they try to understand things, to figure them out, but also to weigh the rights and wrongs of this life. This is the time for growth of the moral imagination, fueled constantly by the willingness, the eagerness of children to put themselves in the shoes of others.
>
> *[Coles, 1997]*

Piaget and Vygotsky both recognized that school-age children are avid learners, actively building on the knowledge that they already have. Piaget emphasized the child's own logical thinking, as the principles of classification, identity, reversibility, and reciprocity come to be understood during the stage he called concrete operational thought.

Vygotsky was much more aware that children need guidance from their culture, from adults, and from other children. The advancement of moral cognition is an example of school-age cognition: Children are eager to develop moral values, either in stages (as Kohlberg, inspired by Piaget, described) or in response to cultural norms (as Vygotsky and Gilligan emphasize).

Information Processing

An alternative approach to understanding cognition arises from *information-processing theory*. This approach takes its name from the way computers operate. Computers receive and store vast quantities of information (numbers, letters, pixels, or other coded symbols) and then use preset programs to process that information. People, too, take in and remember large amounts of information. They use mental processes (preset programs) to perform three functions: to search for specific units of information when needed (a search engine), to analyze situations, and to express the analysis in a format that another person (or a networked computer) can understand.

Information-processing theory is useful precisely because people "can learn anything, sense or nonsense" (Simon, 2001, p. 205), and this theory helps scientists understand the mechanisms of such learning, even when the content seems irrelevant or foolish. Learning seems particularly rapid in childhood. Many 7- to 11-year-olds not only soak up knowledge in school but also outscore their elders on computer games, memorize the lyrics of their favorite rap songs, and recognize out-of-towners by the clothes they wear. Some children, by age 11, beat their elders at chess, play a musical instrument so well that adults pay to hear them, or write poems that get published. Other children that age live by their wits on the street or become soldiers in civil wars—having learned lessons that few adults ever want to know.

This enormous and impressive range of knowledge makes it clear that older school-age children are very different kinds of learners from, say, 4- or 5-year-olds. Not only do they know more, they also use their minds much more effectively, and that means their information processing has advanced. As with a computer, greater efficiency means not simply having more information stored somewhere but also having better access strategies and quicker analysis. That's what makes 11-year-olds better thinkers than 7-year-olds.

Memory

The **sensory memory** (also called the *sensory register*) is the first component of the information-processing system. It stores incoming stimuli for a split second after it is received, to allow it to be processed. To use terms first explained in Chapter 5, *sensations* are retained for a moment while the person selects some sensations to become *perceptions*.

This first step of information processing is quite good in early childhood, continues to improve slightly until about age 10, and remains adequate until middle or late adulthood. (For most people, hearing and vision decline noticeably in middle age.) Once sensations become perceptions, the brain selects meaningful ones to transfer to working memory for further analysis.

It is in **working memory** (sometimes called *short-term memory*) that current, conscious mental activity occurs. Your working memory includes, at this moment, your understanding of this paragraph, any previous knowledge you recall that is related to it, and perhaps distracting thoughts about the weekend or the interesting person sitting beside you. Working memory is constantly replenished with new information, so thoughts are not retained for very long. Working memory improves significantly in middle childhood (Gathercole, 1998).

Finally, information may be transferred to **long-term memory**, which stores information for minutes, hours, days, months, or years. The capacity of long-term memory—how much information can be crammed into one brain—is virtually limitless by the end of middle childhood. Together with the sensory memory and working memory, long-term memory assists in organizing ideas and reactions. Crucial here is not merely *storage* (how much material has been deposited in long-term memory) but also *retrieval* (how readily the material can be brought

Response for Parents (from page 295): Your neighbor is mistaken: These are prime years for moral education. You might travel those 50 miles once or twice a week or recruit other parents to organize a local program. Whatever you do, don't skip moral instruction. Discuss and demonstrate your moral and religious values, and help your children meet other children who share those values.

sensory memory The component of the information-processing system in which incoming stimulus information is stored for a split second to allow it to be processed. Also called the *sensory register.*

working memory The component of the information-processing system in which current conscious mental activity occurs. Also called *short-term memory.*

long-term memory The component of the information-processing system in which virtually limitless amounts of information can be stored indefinitely.

to the conscious mind to be used). Certain information is more readily retrievable (you remember your birth date more easily than your childhood phone number), but all the information in long-term memory is stored somehow, unless something (such as a stroke) destroys it.

Especially for Teachers How might your understanding of memory help you teach 2,000 new words to a class of fourth-graders?

Speed of Processing

Older children are much quicker thinkers than younger children, and this greater speed benefits memory and a host of other cognitive skills (Williams et al., 1999). Speed directly increases mental capacity, because faster thinking allows more thoughts to be processed in the conscious mind (working memory) at once. A sixth-grader can listen to the dinner-table conversation of her parents, respond to the interruptions of her younger siblings, think about her best friend, and still remember to ask for her allowance. In school, increased processing capacity means that she can answer a teacher's question with several relevant ideas rather than just one and, at the same time, monitor her words for grammar and pronunciation while noting her classmates' reactions.

Speed of thinking continues to increase throughout childhood and adolescence (Kail, 2000). Neurological maturation, especially the ongoing myelination of neural axons and the development of the frontal cortex, partly accounts for these changes (Benes, 2001). But the advances seem more directly a matter of learning from experience than of simple maturation.

Speed and capacity increase because as children use their brains more efficiently, myelination increases and dendrites become more dense (Schneider & Pressley, 1997). As this happens, repetition makes many neurons fire in a coordinated and seemingly instantaneous way (Merzenich, 2001). When people use their intellectual skills, processes that first required hard mental labor become automatic. This increases processing speed, frees up capacity, allows more information to be remembered, and advances thinking in every way (Demetriou et al., 2002).

Progress from initial effort to automatization (see Chapter 11) often takes years, which is why repetition and practice during the school years are crucial. Many children lose cognitive skills over the summer because the halt in daily schooling erases earlier learning (Huttenlocher et al., 1998). Not until something is overlearned does it become automatic.

Eye on the Ball This boy's concentration while heading the ball and simultaneously preparing to fall is a sign that he has practiced this maneuver enough times that he can perform it automatically. Not having to think about what to do on the way down, he can think about what to do when he gets up, such as pursuing the ball or getting back to cover his position.

Knowledge Base

Children have absorbed much more knowledge by the school years. The more they know, the more they can learn. That is, having an extensive **knowledge base,** a broad body of knowledge in any particular subject area, makes it easier to master new learning in that area.

Knowledge also depends on opportunity and motivation. This has been illustrated by millions of school-age children whose knowledge base is far greater in some domains, and far smaller in others, than their parents or teachers would like it to be. In one recent research example, British schoolchildren were asked to identify 10 of a random sample of 100 Pokémon creatures and 10 of 100 types of wildlife common in the United Kingdom. As you can see in Figure 12.1, the 4- to 6-year-olds knew only about a third of the 20 items, but they could identify more living things than imaginary ones. From ages 8 to 11, however, knowledge of Pokémon creatures far exceeded knowledge of living creatures. A peak occurred at age 8 and was higher for boys than girls (not shown). It is easy to understand why: Third-grade boys were often intensely engaged in collecting Pokémon cards (Balmford et al., 2002).

The connections between bits of information improve as the knowledge base expands. When people learn more about a particular topic, they find it easier to remember how the new knowledge relates to the previous knowledge, and this connection helps them remember both the new and the old. This explains why

knowledge base A broad body of knowledge in a particular subject area that makes it easier to master new learning in that area.

FIGURE 12.1 **Knowledge of the Real and the Imaginary** Every child's knowledge base expands with age, but the areas of special interest tend to shift as the child grows older. At about 8 years of age, British schoolchildren's ability to identify Pokémon characters on flashcards began to surpass their ability to identify real-life animals and plants.

? *Observational Quiz* (see answer, page 300): What does this graph suggest about the state of wildlife conservation in the United Kingdom in the year 2020?

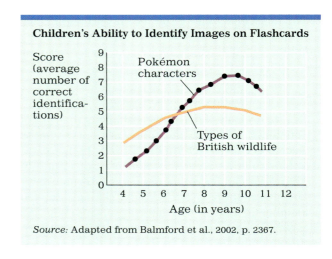

Children's Ability to Identify Images on Flashcards

Source: Adapted from Balmford et al., 2002, p. 2367.

Response for Teachers (from page 297): Children can be taught strategies for remembering at this age, making links between working memory and long-term memory. Accordingly, you might break down the vocabulary list into word clusters—looking for root words, making connections to the children's existing knowledge, applications, or (as a last resort) grouping them by first letters or rhymes. Active, social learning is useful; perhaps in groups the students could write a story each day that incorporates 15 new words. Each group could read its story aloud to the class. Four days a week, 15 new words a day, would be appropriate for this activity.

control processes The mechanism—consisting of selective attention, metacognition, and emotional regulation—that puts memory, processing speed, and knowledge together in order to regulate the analysis and flow of information within the information-processing system.

selective attention The ability to screen out distractions and to focus on the details that will help in later recall of information.

learning by rote is fragile, while learning by comprehension endures. Such connections increase in middle childhood and beyond; the older a person is, the worse "sheer memory" (unprocessed and disconnected) becomes.

Control Processes

The mechanisms that put memory, processing speed, and knowledge together are the **control processes,** which regulate the analysis and flow of information within the system. Control processes include selective attention, metacognition, and emotional regulation. When someone wants to concentrate on only one part of all the material in the sensory memory or summon a rule of thumb from long-term memory to working memory in order to solve a problem, control processes assume an executive role in the information-processing system. That is, they organize, decide, and direct as a chief executive officer is supposed to do.

If this sounds familiar, that's because you read in Chapter 8 about the maturation of the prefrontal cortex, where the brain regulates and coordinates emotions and thoughts. This part of the brain (actually several parts, including the medial prefrontal cortex, the orbital prefrontal cortex, the anterior cingulate, and the hypothalamus) is sometimes called the *executive function* precisely because it controls the other parts.

Selective Attention

In the play years, impulse control is crucial to learning. In middle childhood, as you saw in Chapter 11, a common sign of psychopathology is attention-deficit disorder. For all school-age children, a developing control process is the ability to concentrate on what is important. This is a process called **selective attention.**

If you were to compare children learning in a kindergarten classroom with those in a fifth-grade classroom anywhere in the world, you would see many differences in attention. Younger children are easily distracted, whether they are listening to a story or printing letters of the alphabet. While they are working, they chatter with each other, look around, fidget, call out to the teacher, and sometimes get up to visit friends or just wander around. Their curriculum is designed to be highly varied, with plenty of changes of activity, because the teachers know the nature of their 5-year-old charges.

By contrast, fifth-graders can work independently at desks or in groups around a table, reading, writing, discussing, and seeking assistance without distracting, or being distracted by, other students. They can all quietly follow a demonstration at the chalkboard, raising their hands to be called on rather than shouting out. Do you remember Billy from Chapter 11? He was the boy with

AD/HD. His problem was not that he didn't know the right answer (he did), but that he could not raise his hand and wait quietly to be called on; that difficulty was what made his teacher send him out of the room. As Billy's experience demonstrates, toward the end of middle childhood, teachers expect students to persist in difficult academic challenges, waiting and thinking.

Metacognition

During the school years, children develop a higher form of thinking called **meta-cognition**, which is sometimes called "thinking about thinking." Metacognition is the ability to evaluate a cognitive task to determine how best to accomplish it, and then to monitor and adjust performance on that task. Marked advances in metacognition occur over the school years (Case, 1998; Ferrari & Sternberg, 1998). For example, preschool children find it difficult to judge whether a problem is easy or hard, or whether or not they remember a particular fact. Thus, when they study, they wastefully devote as much effort to the easy as to the hard, and as much to what they already know as to what they don't yet know. They might remember something adults consider irrelevant (the color of the teacher's shirt, for instance) but forget the most important part of the lesson (that 2 + 2 = 4). Some children at the start of middle childhood still lack metacognition (Schneider, 1998).

By around age 8 or 9, however, metacognition is evident. Children become much more accurate about what they already know and thus more efficient when they study. They can evaluate their learning progress, judging whether they have learned the spelling of words or the science principles, rather than simply asserting (as many younger children do) that they know it all (Harter, 1999).

In short, older children approach cognitive tasks in a more strategic and analytical manner. Storage and retrieval strategies improve as they learn when something is worth learning, how to pluck something from memory, when to use mnemonic devices (memory aids, such as "*i* before *e* except after *c*"), and how to concentrate. All these abilities are parts of metacognition, and they are all products of maturation and experience.

metacognition "Thinking about thinking," or the ability to evaluate a cognitive task to determine how best to accomplish it, and then to monitor and adjust one's performance on that task.

They've Read the Book Acting in a play based on *The Lion, the Witch, and the Wardrobe* suggests that these children have metacognitive abilities beyond those of almost any preschooler. Indeed, the book itself requires a grasp of the boundary between reality (the wardrobe) and fantasy (the witch). "Thinking about thinking" is needed in order to appreciate the allegory.

? Observational Quiz (see answer, page 301): Beyond the book, what are three examples of metacognition implied here? Specifically, how does the ability to memorize lines, play a part, and focus on the play illustrate metacognition?

The Pragmatics of Language

The information-processing perspective illuminates the advances in spoken language that are common in middle childhood. Mastering a language involves far more than learning the vocabulary and grammar that most 5-year-olds know. It means using the language fluently in many types of situations. This practical application of linguistic knowledge is called the *pragmatics* of language, and it improves noticeably in middle childhood. Children learn to speak one way on the playground, another way in the classroom, and a third way at home.

The pragmatics of language include vocabulary and grammar. Indeed, some school-age children learn as many as 20 new words a day and become skilled at applying grammar rules, definitions, and metaphors. However, these "new" words and applications are not like the language explosion of the play years. Logic, memory, and the ability to make connections between one bit of knowledge and another—these three distinguish language learning during the school years from the play years. For example, every 2-year-old knows what an egg is, but 10-year-olds are likely to know egg salad, egg-drop soup, eggplant, egghead, and even metaphors such as "walking on eggshells," "egg on my face," and

! *Answer to Observational Quiz* (from page 298): As the authors of this study observe, "People care about what they know." As their knowledge about their country's animal and plant life declines with age, these British children's concern for wildlife conservation is likely to decline, too.

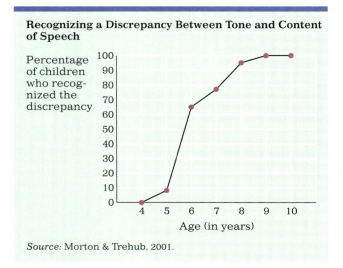

Recognizing a Discrepancy Between Tone and Content of Speech

Percentage of children who recognized the discrepancy

Source: Morton & Trehub, 2001.

FIGURE 12.2 Do You Mean What You Say?
A sudden leap of understanding occurs at the beginning of concrete operational thinking, when children can realize that a speaker is using a sad tone to describe a happy event, or vice versa. By age 9 or 10, all children are aware of this phenomenon.

"last one in is a rotten egg." They understand that each of these expressions is logically connected to *egg* and can use them all appropriately. Appropriate use also includes picking the audience carefully: 10-year-olds do not call their parents rotten eggs, even when the parents are the last to sit down at dinner. In this case, selective attention includes selective use of language.

A schoolchild's more comprehensive understanding of language was illustrated by a study in which children heard someone saying 20 sentences in a tone that contradicted the content (Morton & Trehub, 2001). For example, a voice reported, sadly, "My mommy gave me a treat" or, joyfully, "I lost my sticker collection." The children were asked whether the speaker was actually happy or sad and whether there was anything silly or tricky in what they heard. None of the 4-year-olds correctly realized the discrepancy between tone and content, but all the older children did (see Figure 12.2).

Notice the sudden leap in recognition at the start of middle childhood: That is when most children realize that many elements, including tone of voice, word choice, and context, override the surface content of speech. This is also when teachers and parents, by breaking down language learning into information-processing components, can help children most effectively. Partly because of the child's learning process, speech teachers usually focus on school-age children, classroom teachers explain grammar rules, and parents expect children to listen and remember everything from a grocery list to the time a playdate is scheduled.

As a result of a new level of language skills, school-age children enjoy the sounds and the meanings of words. Consider the poems children write, the secret languages they develop, the slang they use, and the jokes they tell. Joke-telling, for instance, requires intellectual flexibility and sophistication, including memory for sequence and punch line and an appreciation of puns. One classic school-age joke is, "What is black and white and red all over?" The answer, "a newspaper," is funny to children who are newly aware that *red* and *read* are homophones. Once children remember the *red/read* riddle (which they tell their parents, certain that the joke is new), they begin to enjoy the alternative answers (an embarrassed skunk, a sunburned zebra), which are funny only because the original answer is known and the joke-teller enjoys trapping the unsuspecting listener.

Connections Basic vocabulary is learned by age 4 or so, but the school years are best for acquiring expanded, derivative, and specialized vocabulary, especially if the child is actively connecting one word with another. With his father's encouragement, this boy in San Jose, California, will remember *Jupiter, Mars,* and the names of the other planets and maybe even *orbit, light-years,* and *solar system.*

RACHEL EPSTEIN / THE IMAGE WORKS

An understanding of the processes of metacognition is one of the advantages of the information-processing approach, for it enables teachers and parents to help children master the underlying strategies and skills of learning. As you know from your current college work, a precise understanding of study skills is useful at every stage.

> To summarize, information-processing theory alerts us to the many components of thinking that advance during middle childhood. Although sensory memory and long-term memory do not change much, the speed and efficiency of working memory can improve dramatically. Better working memory makes these children much better thinkers than they were at younger ages. In addition, children become more selective and strategic in what they attend to and how they process perceptions. This is evident in their advances in language. Control processes such as selective attention and metacognition enable them to direct their minds to learn whatever they are motivated to learn and whatever adults are motivated to teach them.

Teaching and Learning

Experts agree that children aged 7 to 11 are great learners. They can develop strategies, accumulate knowledge, apply logic, and think quickly. All that makes them more teachable with every passing year. They leave behind the magical and often egocentric thinking of younger children, but they have not yet reached the suspicion and rebellion that sometimes emerge in adolescence.

During these years children are willing to learn anything if it is presented properly, but they cannot learn everything at once. Instruction at this age is most effective if it is concrete and straightforward, neither abstract nor circuitous (Simon, 2001). When new learning builds on an established knowledge base, when it connects to other material, when it is taught deliberately and sequentially, then school-age children remember and master complex ideas quite well.

Internationally and across the decades, school-age children learn reading, writing, and arithmetic, and 95 percent of the world's children now spend at least some time in school. Nations and schools choose what should be taught, for how many years, by and to whom, and with what type of funding. For example, oral expression and reasoned argument are taught in Russia and France but not in India or the United States (Alexander, 2000). Memorization is important in India; less so in England. Variations are apparent not only in basic subjects and teaching methods but also in such matters as curriculum (e.g., the arts and physical education are sometimes not taught at all), social expectations (e.g., respect for the teacher), and makeup of the student body (e.g., some schools are segregated by gender).

In all these variations, developmentalists who suggest that one curriculum is best may be caught in a tangle of ideology, politics, and culture, disconnected from educational research (Rayner et al., 2001). Even political and educational leaders say one thing and do another, in a discrepancy between "expressed aim and observed reality" (Alexander, 2000, p. 176).

Which Curriculum?

The problems posed by vast international differences in educational goals and structures have been explicitly recognized by experts who have developed assessments of student learning in various countries. In one series of assessments, called TIMSS (Trends in Math and Science Study), the researchers differentiate among *intended, implemented,* and *attained* curricula (Robitaille & Beaton, 2002). *Intended* refers to the content the political and educational leaders

!Answer to Observational Quiz (from page 299): (1) Memorizing extensive passages requires an understanding of advanced memory strategies that combine meaning with form. (2) Understanding how to play a part so that other actors and the audience respond well requires a sophisticated theory of mind. (3) Staying focused on the moment in the play despite distractions from the audience requires selective attention.

decide to endorse; *implemented* means what the teachers and school adminis-trators actually offer; and *attained* refers to what the students learn. For exam-ple, many nations have added the concept of mathematical probability to their primary school curriculum (intended curriculum). The outcome has been low student understanding (attained curriculum), mainly because teacher training and student maturation make probability difficult to teach before middle school (implemented curriculum) (Howson, 2002).

In practice, every aspect of the curriculum is ideological as well as practical, so every specific recommendation about education is likely to provoke debate. In the context of such disagreement, it is helpful to recognize the existence of the *hidden curriculum.*

hidden curriculum The unofficial, unstated, or implicit rules and priorities that influence the academic curriculum and every other aspect of learning in school.

The **hidden curriculum** is the unspoken and often unrecognized lessons that children learn in school (Holme, 2001). Covert lessons are taught by having a security guard at the door; by educating children with special needs in a separate room on the top floor; by interrupting classes with fire drills, trip permissions, or disruptive students; by recognizing sports, drama, music, or art; by the composi-tion of the student body; by the education, training, and compassion of the teachers; and by the age, race, sex, and perhaps sexual orientation of all the school staff. Even the physical condition of the school (spacious classrooms with modern technology and large, grassy playgrounds or small, poorly equipped classrooms with cement yards) teaches the children how much the adults value their education.

School organization and schedule also arise from the hidden curriculum. For example, most schools in the United States begin at 8 A.M. and finish before 3 P.M., five days a week, nine months a year. In many other nations, schools do not finish until late afternoon, six days a week, eleven months a year. What is the hidden message here?

Another aspect of the hidden curriculum is the number of students per teacher, which varies internationally from an average of 11 in Austria to 31 in Turkey (National Center for Education Statistics, 2000). Crowded classrooms are a common complaint against public schools in the United States, even though the U.S. average (17 pupils) is relatively low. As the following Thinking Like a Scientist report reveals, the data are not nearly as clear as the public sentiment, which suggests again that ideology is part of the decision-making process.

Thinking Like a Scientist

How Does Class Size Affect Learning?

It seems obvious to most parents, teachers, and politicians that children learn better when there are fewer children in each class. This aspect of the school environment has become so important that it is no longer hidden: Class size is one reason parents send their children to private schools.

Surprisingly, research support for this popular assump-tion is weak (Betts, 1995; Hanushek, 1999). The pupil/teacher ratio is lower in the United States than in many other nations, having declined from 25-to-1 to 18-to-1 between 1969 and 1997 (Alexander, 2000), but no comparable advance in student attainment has accompanied this change in policy. The lack of improvement may be because, over the past 30 years, schools in the United States have had more low-income, special-needs, and immigrant children and

fewer qualified teachers. Could the lack of correlation between learning and class size be caused by changes in the student body or teacher quality? Could the private school advantage result from selectivity at the outset, not from more learning in smaller classes (Ehrenberg et al., 2001)?

For answers, we need experimental (not correlational) evidence. In Tennessee, 12,000 kindergarten children and teachers were randomly assigned to one of three classroom conditions: regular (22–26 children); regular with aide (22–26 children with a full-time teacher's assistant), or small (13–17 children). Children (especially nonwhite children) in the small classes learned more (those in the regular classes with an aide did no better than those in regular classes without an aide). Follow-up research showed that even after the children had been in regular classes for years, those formerly in small classes still outperformed their peers (Finn et al., 2001).

Experts disagree about how substantial the small-class benefits were, why they occurred, and whether the gains were worth the expense (Rayner et al., 2001). The state of California, inspired by Tennessee, reduced class sizes in the early grades—but, unlike Tennessee, California had neither enough qualified teachers nor suitable classrooms for this expansion, and the average class was reduced only to 20 pupils (from 30). The California results were "disappointing"—statistically significant, but very small (Stecher & Bohrnstedt, 2000).

A review of all the research leaves many questions unanswered. The early grades may be the crucial time for small classes, but other years may be equally important—perhaps sixth grade, when puberty hits, or twelfth grade, when high school graduation should occur. Other reforms—raising

teacher salaries; improving professional education; extending school hours; expanding the school year; or including more sports, music, or reading—might be more effective than reducing class size.

Until evaluative research is done, the connection between developmental research and educational policy will remain problematic (Thompson & Nelson, 2001). As one review explains:

> . . . reductions in class size are but one of the policy options that can be pursued to improve student learning. Careful evaluations of the impacts of other options, preferably through the use of more true experiments, along with an analysis of the costs of each option, need to be undertaken. However, to date there are relatively few studies that even compute the true costs of large class-size reduction programs, let alone ask whether the benefits . . . merit incurring the costs.
>
> *[Ehrenberg et al., 2001]*

The Reading Wars

There are two distinct methods of teaching children to read: phonics and whole language (Rayner et al., 2001). (A third method, called "look–say," based on sight recognition of a whole word, has been discarded. It doesn't work even for Chinese children, who are used to looking at a whole word rather than individual letters [McBride-Chang & Treman, 2003]).

Clashes over the two approaches have been called "the reading wars." These battles have sometimes been waged without concern for scientific evidence, developmental changes, or children's needs (Adams et al., 1998).

Phonics Versus Whole Language

Traditionally, the **phonics approach** (from the root word for "sound") meant requiring children to learn the sounds of each letter before they began to decipher simple words. The phonics approach works well in learning to read languages such as Italian, where the sound–letter connections are clear and children move quickly from sounding out words to reading, but not as well in English, where there are many exceptions. In the first half of the twentieth century, schools in the United States were characterized by:

> drill and more drill . . . instruction in letter–sound relationships and pronunciation rules. . . . Children had to learn so much abstract material by rote before doing any significant amount of reading.
>
> *[Diederich, 1973, p. 7]*

By contrast, the **whole-language approach** considers language as an entire set of skills—talking and listening, reading and writing—all with the goal of communication. With this concept, children are encouraged to write on their own, inventing the spelling. For example, one 4-year-old boy tried to keep others out of his room with this sign on his door: GNYS AT WRK (Bissex, 1980); a schoolgirl named Karla wrote a stern note to her mother (see Figure 12.3). These demonstrate the whole-language idea that children can communicate their emotions in writing long before they have mastered standard spelling. They are powerfully motivated to read and write, and they eventually learn standard spelling as a result.

phonics approach The teaching of reading by requiring children to learn the sounds of each letter before they begin to decipher simple words.

whole-language approach The teaching of reading by encouraging children to develop all their language skills—talking and listening, reading and writing—all with the goal of communication.

> From karla to My mom
>
> It's No fare
> that you mad
> me Lat my Lade
> bug Go Wat
> If I was your
> mom and I mad
> you tack your
> Lade bug tam
> Shh you wud
> be sad like me
> that lade bug
> mat of bar a orfan
> So you sod ov latme
> hav it ane wae

Source: Lerner, 2000, p. 462.

FIGURE 12.3 "You Wud Be Sad Like Me"
Although Karla, a first-grader, uses invented
spelling, her arguments show that she is reasoning
quite logically; her school-age mind is working quite
well. (If you have trouble deciphering Karla's note,
turn the book upside down for a translation.)

"From Karla to my mom. It's no fair that you made
me let my lady bug go. What if I was your mom and
I made you take your lady bug. I am sure you would
be sad like me. That lady bug might have been an
orphan. So you should have let me have it anyway."

Both these approaches make sense. Children are motivated to learn when they can use their knowledge quickly, as in the whole-language approach. For concrete operational thinkers, abstract, decontextualized memorization is difficult—no wonder traditional phonics did not always succeed. However, unlike talking, which is experience-expectant, reading is experience-dependent. Few children figure out reading and spelling on their own without explicit instruction in the relationship among sounds, letters, and words. Beginning readers often need to be taught how to translate spoken words into printed ones, and vice versa. Instruction and practice with phonics enable children to decipher words. According to the phonics perspective, without practice, automatization in reading will not occur, because brain patterns are established only through extensive repetition (Rayner et al., 2001; Stanovich, 2000).

Research arising from the information-processing perspective emphasizes that each step of development, each component of language learning, and each child's learning style and maturation level are unique in crucial ways. In practical terms, this means that phonics may be particularly useful for children who are just beginning to read and for those who need help with learning to decipher new words. Some children have additional needs. If children speak another language or do not have strong listening and speaking skills, they need explicit vocabulary-building and pronunciation practice.

Most developmentalists, and many reading specialists, now believe that teachers should use many methods and strategies, for there are "alternate pathways in learning to read" (Berninger et al., 2002, p. 295). Phonics should be part of instruction, but other aspects of literacy, taught in other ways, are important as well (Adams & Bruck, 1995; Rayner et al., 2001).

The Socioeconomic Divide

Language development and reading attainment correlate with socioeconomic status, as research over the past 40 years has shown again and again (Plank & MacIver, 2003). For young children, the lower the family income, the less developed a child's vocabulary and grammar. By the beginning of elementary school, differences between low-SES and high-SES children are vast. For example, some 6-year-olds know 5,000 words and others know 20,000 words, a 400 percent difference that usually reflects the educational attainment of the parents (Moats, 2001). Not only do children from low-income families have smaller vocabularies, but their grammar is simpler (fewer compound sentences, dependent clauses, conditional verbs) and their sentences are shorter (Hart & Risley, 1995). Once reading begins, children of low SES fall farther behind in reading with each year, particularly in the United States.

Why this correlation? Remember that correlation is not causation. In fact, some children from impoverished backgrounds speak, read, and write well (MacWhinney & Bornstein, 2003). The crucial factor seems to be the child's actual exposure to language. Although many low-income families do not use elaborate and extensive speech with the children, this disadvantage is not inevitable. Children from impoverished families learn well if given extensive and direct opportunity to learn in their homes, neighborhoods, and schools (Duncan & Brooks-Gunn, 1997; McLoyd, 1998; Yeung et al., 2002).

A pair of researchers studied the conversations of 53 low-income mothers and their 5-year-olds during meals, play, and reading (Weizman & Snow, 2001). Although all the families were quite poor, analysis of more than 2,500 minutes of interaction revealed that some mothers provided much less linguistic encourage-

TABLE 12.2 Variability in Maternal Talking During Mealtime Interactions

	Average	Least	Most
Time spent by mother in interaction with child	20 minutes	1 minute	47 minutes
Number of different words used by mother	259 words	3 words	595 words
Percentage of words not in child's basic vocabulary	3.5%	None	More than 8%

Source: Weizman & Snow, 2001.

ment and language exposure than others (see Table 12.2). At mealtime, some mothers just told their children "eat," but others offered informal language instruction. Here is one example:

> **Child:** *(Makes gulping noise in throat)*
> **Mother:** Please stop.
> **Child:** Okay.
> **Mother:** Were you planning to eat more?
> **Child:** No.
> **Mother:** We kinda wasted some of that first piece of chicken there. Don't you think?
> **Child:** No. *(Makes noise again)*
> **Mother:** Stop it now.
> **Child:** Okay.
> **Mother:** Now you're gonna have to roll up your sleeves and wash your hands and your face. Try not to get your pajama top wet. See how you do. You can wash your face with the face cloth.
> **Child:** Okay.
> **Mother:** Don't you make that gulping noise.
> **Child:** *(Laughs for a while)*

> [adapted from Weizman & Snow, 2001, p. 269]

This child said only two words, "okay" and "no," but the mother employed a fairly extensive vocabulary, including *planning, wasted, gulping, roll up,* and *face cloth,* using each term in the immediate context so that it had concrete meaning for the child. Poverty put all the children in this study "at risk," but those 5-year-olds with mothers like this one became school-age children with large vocabularies, as measured on standardized tests.

Vocabulary size is the best predictor of school achievement and overall intelligence. As these authors summarize, there is a "powerful linkage" between adult linguistic input and child output (Weizman & Snow, 2001, p. 276). Given school-age children's logical minds and strategic use of their knowledge base, one goal of instruction should be to ensure—using phonics, whole language, and every other method that works—that all children acquire the scaffolding that makes new learning possible.

How to ensure that all children enter school with extensive vocabularies and that all children become fluent readers gives rise to controversial, ideological questions that cannot be answered here. Developmentalists are convinced that high-quality preschool programs (described in Chapter 9) are helpful and that low income does not necessarily mean low achievement. Beyond that, disagreements over governmental and educational policy ensure that uncertainty reigns.

Talk to Me! In a detailed study of low-income mothers in the Boston area and their 5-year-old children, five interactions were recorded for each pair: two reading, two playing, and one mealtime. Despite their similar economic and geographic status, the mothers varied enormously in how much time they spent interacting with their child (by a factor of 3), how much they said (by a factor of 5), and, especially, how many words they used that were not part of a child's expected basic vocabulary (by a factor of 12). Note that the percentage of new words used by the mothers at mealtime—the only one of these five interactions that is always part of each child's day—was greater than the average (mean) percentage for all five interactions. By the time they reached second grade, the children who had heard the most varied maternal talk were ahead of their peers in vocabulary acquisition.

The Math Wars

Most nations are doing a pretty good job of teaching children to read and write in at least one language. Worldwide, literacy has increased dramatically over the past 50 years, with almost every child attending some school. The United States

TABLE 12.3 Rankings on Math Achievement Scores, Selected Countries and Regions

| Country | Rankings | | |
	8th-Graders (1998)	4th-Graders (1994)	8th-Graders (1994)
Singapore	1	2	1
Korea	2	1	3
Hong Kong	3	4	4
Japan	4	3	2
Netherlands	5	5	7
Hungary	6	7	6
Canada	7	10	8
Australia	8	8	9
Czech Republic	9	6	5
United States	10	9	11
England	11	11	12
New Zealand	12	12	10

North America Lags Behind Although 41 nations participate in TIMSS (the Trends in Math and Science Study), only a dozen countries reported valid average scores for all three math assessments: fourth- and eighth-graders in 1994 and eighth-graders in 1998. Among those who did report, the top four always were Japan, Korea, Hong Kong, and Singapore, while the average scores for the United States, England, and New Zealand were always relatively low.

?Observational Quiz (see answer, page 308): Which nation seems to have done best overall at teaching math between 1994 and 1998?

compares well with other nations; only six (New Zealand, Finland, Australia, Canada, the United Kingdom, and Ireland) have a higher percentage of 15-year-olds who can read very well (National Center for Education Statistics, 2002).

However, many nations have decided that math and science are the key areas in which children should learn so as to be ready for the challenges of the future. Economic advancement seems closely connected to advances in science and technology, and these, in turn, seem related to understanding mathematics. For that reason, TIMSS, the international assessment mentioned earlier, focuses on math and science. Like every other international comparison, TIMSS finds that children from East Asian nations score highest in math achievement and that children from the United States rank relatively low (see Table 12.3).

Data from the United States over the past decade are not encouraging. Although younger children may have been learning more math, by twelfth grade these early gains have faded. The National Assessment of Educational Progress found that math achievement scores for twelfth-graders in 2000 were no better than they had been for twelfth-graders in 1992 (see Figure 12.4). For obvious reasons, North American educators have battled over how best to teach math, not always to the benefit of children. One researcher noted that in some areas "the math wars have taken hold and done enormous damage in schools" (Boaler, 2002, p. xvi). She was writing specifically about California, but she noted that the same battle was being waged in her native England and elsewhere in the world.

Historically, math was taught through rote learning; children memorized number facts, such as the multiplication tables, and filled page after page of workbooks. As a result, many children came to hate math and did poorly in it. In response, many governments supported research devoted to improving the math curriculum, and experts, inspired by Vygotsky, found ways to make math a more active, engaging subject (Ginsburg et al., 1998).

One notable set of standards and practices in the United States came from the National Council of Teachers of Mathematics (1989), which developed a new curriculum emphasizing concepts and problem solving, estimating and probability. Recommended pedagogical techniques included social involvement, with student interaction in problem solving: "Students are obligated to explain and

FIGURE 12.4 Not Much Improvement The scores of U.S. high school seniors on math achievement tests improved a bit from 1990 to 1992, perhaps because the nationwide math curriculum had been reformed in 1989. However, the results for 2000 show no improvement over those for 1992. This means that one-third of all twelfth-graders cannot do basic math, such as fractions and percentages.

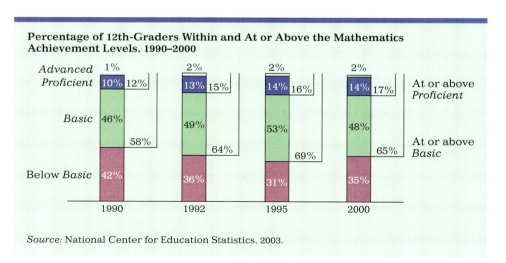

Percentage of 12th-Graders Within and At or Above the Mathematics Achievement Levels, 1990–2000

	1990	1992	1995	2000
Advanced	1%	2%	2%	2%
Proficient	10% / 12%	13% / 15%	14% / 16%	14% / 17%
Basic	46% / 58%	49% / 64%	53% / 69%	48% / 65%
Below Basic	42%	36%	31%	35%

At or above *Proficient*
At or above *Basic*

Source: National Center for Education Statistics, 2003.

justify solutions, to attempt to make sense of solutions given by others . . . and to ask clarifying questions or challenge alternatives" (Cobb, 2000, pp. 464–465). The focus is on the process, not on the product—that is, on learning how to do math, not on getting the right answer quickly. One teacher asked the class how many runners were in a race that had two teams of six runners each. The children had already worked in pairs to come up with the process for answering, called the "answer solution."

Teacher: Jack, what answer solution did you come up with?
    Jack: Fourteen.
Teacher: Fourteen. How did you get that answer?
    Jack: Because 6 plus 6 is 12. Two runners on two teams . . .

(Jack stops talking, puts his hands to the side of his face and looks down at the floor. Then he looks at the teacher and at his partner, Ann. He turns and faces the front of the room with his back to the teacher and mumbles inaudibly.)

Teacher: Would you please say that again. I didn't quite get the whole thing. You had—say it again, please.
    Jack: *(Softly, still facing the front of the room)* It's six runners on each team.
Teacher: Right.
    Jack: *(Turns to look at the teacher)* I made a mistake. It's wrong. It should be twelve. *(He turns and faces the front of the room again.)*

(Jack's acute embarrassment . . . confounded the teacher's intention that the children should publicly express their thinking and, more generally, engage in mathematical practice characterized by conjecture, argument, and justification.)

Teacher: *(Softly)* Oh, okay. Is it okay to make a mistake?
Andrew: Yes.
Teacher: Is it okay to make a mistake, Jack?
    Jack: Yeah.
Teacher: You bet it is. As long as you're in my class, it is okay to make a mistake. Because I make them all the time, and we learn from our mistakes— a lot. Jack already figured out, "Ooops, I didn't have the right answer the first time" *(Jack turns and looks at the teacher and smiles),* but he kept working at it and he got it.

[Cobb et al., 1993]

This approach may be working. The National Assessment of Educational Progress (the same assessment that found no change in twelfth-graders' math achievement) found that, in the decade from 1990 to 2000, the proportion of fourth-graders who performed at the level called "proficient" increased from 13 percent to 26 percent, while the proportion who could not do basic math decreased from 50 percent to 31 percent (National Center for Educational Statistics, 2003).

However, this approach is controversial. Many parents as well as educators believe that children need to know number facts (such as, in the above example, $2 \times 6 = 12$) before they can analyze alternative solutions. As with phonics in reading, it seems that math involves a particular set of rules, symbols, and processes that must be explicitly taught rather than discovered (Smith, 2002).

In a research effort to understand math learning, the TIMSS experts videotaped 231 math classes in three nations— Japan, Germany, and the United States (Stigler & Hiebert, 1999). Striking national differences were found. The North American teachers presented math at a lower level, with more definitions but less coherence and connection to other learning, because the "teachers seem to believe that learning terms

Especially for Parents You are tired but are setting out to buy groceries. Your 7-year-old son wants to go with you. Should you explain that you are too tired to take him?

Collaborative Learning Japanese children are learning mathematics in a more structured and socially interactive way than are their North American counterparts.

RUSSELL D. CURTIS / PHOTO RESEARCHERS, INC.

Response for Parents (from page 307): Your son would understand your explanation, but you should take him along. Any excursion is a learning opportunity. You wouldn't ignore his need for food or medicine; don't ignore his need for learning. While shopping, you can teach vocabulary (does he know *pimientos, pepperoni, polenta?*), categories ("root vegetables," "freshwater fish"), and math (which size is cheaper?). Explain in advance that you need him to help you find things and carry them, and that he can choose only one item that you wouldn't normally buy. Seven-year-olds can understand rules, and they enjoy being helpful.

! *Answer to Observational Quiz* (from page 306): Canada.

Friendly Immersion The poster is in English, because this Toronto teacher is explaining a sign in the city, but all the instruction occurs in French, even though none of these children are native French speakers. Their parents chose this program not only because French immersion works successfully in Canada but also because such programs have a reputation for academic rigor, including high standards for conduct and achievement. Attitudes, not just instruction, facilitate learning a second language.

JOHN O'BRIAN / CANADA IN STOCK, INC.

and practicing skills is not very exciting" (p. 89). In contrast, the Japanese teachers worked collaboratively and professionally to build the children's knowledge, structuring it so that the children developed proofs and alternative solutions, alone and in groups. Teachers used social interaction (among groups of children and groups of teachers) and sequential curricula (each day, week, and year builds on mathematical knowledge that was learned before). In Japan, students from all ability levels are in every math classroom, which fosters collaborative learning, according to a British study (Boaler, 2002). The less able students in Japan tend to receive after-school tutoring, which may advance their learning.

Another area of controversy is in technology, specifically the use of computers in education. In the United States, many observers lament the *digital divide,* the gap between the rich and the poor in computer access. In 1997, of school-age children whose annual family income was under $20,000, only 16 percent had a computer at home, compared to 78 percent of those whose family income was above $75,000 (National Center for Education Statistics, 2000). Consequently, political leaders and private industry have teamed up to equip and wire every school with computers and access to the Internet, a goal that 95 percent of all schools had reached by 2003.

Recent data show that U.S. students are more than twice as likely to use computers in their math and science classes as are students in other nations (12 and 21 percent versus 5 and 8 percent). Indeed, twice as many U.S. schools are networked compared with other nations. Nonetheless, math and science achievement scores of U.S. students remain relatively low, and students who never use computers score almost as high as students who often use computers (Robitaille & Beaton, 2002). Here again, experimental rather than correlational evidence is needed.

Bilingual Education

Bilingual education is another educational issue that has political and economic implications. Almost every nation has a sizable minority whose members speak a nonmajority language; for them, learning the majority language is a necessity. In fact, most of the estimated 6,000 languages of the world are never used in formal educational settings. Consequently, many of the world's children are educated in a language other than their mother tongue (Tucker, 1998).

While the best time to *learn* a second language by listening and talking is early childhood, the best time to be *taught* a second language seems to be during middle childhood. Because of their eagerness to communicate, their wish to be good students, their grasp of logic, and their ear for nuances of pronunciation, children aged 7 to 11 are at their prime for being taught a second language.

The rapid rise of globalization has made the need for bilingual education more urgent. Globalization has meant a surge in immigrants in every nation of the world, including the United States, where about 20 percent of all students are children of immigrants (Suarez-Orozco, 2001).

Ideally, every child should be fluent in a second language by age 11. In the United States, however, bilingual education programs are often designed only to teach the majority language, English, to non-native speakers, while the native speakers remain monolingual. Thus, bilingual education has become part of the political debate about citizenship, patriotism, and immigration.

Various Approaches

No single approach to teaching a second language has yet been recognized as best for all children in all contexts (Bialystok, 2001). Strategies include both extremes—from **total immersion,** in which instruction occurs entirely in the second (majority) language, to *reverse immersion,* in which the child is taught in his or her first (native) language for several years, until the second language can be taught as a "foreign" language. This approach traditionally has been used to teach English-speaking Americans a second language, without much success.

Variations that fall between these extremes include presenting some topics of instruction in one language and other topics in the other; presenting every topic in both languages; or conducting separate after-school classes in a "heritage language" to allow children to connect with their culture while learning academic subjects in the dominant tongue (see Table 12.4).

Which teaching strategy is best? In Canada, immersion seems to have succeeded with more than 300,000 English-speaking children who were initially placed in French-only classrooms. These children showed no decline in the English skills they had learned at home or in other academic achievement (Edwards, 1994; Lambert et al., 1993). Indeed, even when Canadian children whose native language is English were immersed in two other languages—French and Hebrew—from the first to the sixth grade, they did well on achievement tests in all three languages (Genesee, 1998).

However, immersion tends to fail if children are made to feel shy, stupid, or socially isolated because of their language difference, as some teachers do (Midobuche, 2001). In such cases, this educational approach might more aptly be called *submersion,* because children are more likely to sink than swim (Edwards, 1994). Immersion that occurs after puberty, even if the children already have some knowledge of the second language, is not as successful (Marsh et al., 2000).

In the United States, submersion may be the most apt description of policy for Native American children who, for most of the twentieth century, were sent to boarding schools to learn white ways. Many of them became sick, ran away, or became alienated from their families, victims of an attempt at cultural obliteration that has only recently been recognized (Coontz, 1998).

Attitudes and Achievement

Success or failure in second-language learning seems to lie in the attitudes of the parents, the teachers, and the larger community. If both languages are valued as well as used extensively, then *additive bilingualism* occurs, with fluency in the second language added to fluency in the first. Sometimes, however, neither language is learned well, and the child ends up *semilingual,* not even monolingual—literally possessing only part of one language (Swain & Johnson, 1997). As one review regarding the need for well-trained language teachers explained, "Whether policies are overtly articulated, covertly implied, or invisible in the making, the central concern in multilingual education appears to be how much status and recognition within the educational system should be given to the languages of the minority group" (Nunan &

TABLE 12.4 Two Strategies for Teaching English

English as a Second Language (ESL)
Requires all non-English-speaking students to undergo an intensive instructional period together, with the goal of mastering the basics of English in six months or so. In classes using ESL, the teacher neither speaks in the child's native language nor allows the children to talk to each other in any language except English.

Bilingual Education
Requires that the teacher instruct the children in school subjects using their native language as well as English. In the early years, children are greeted, instructed, and (when necessary) disciplined in the two languages, in the hope that they will progress in both. Informal talk between one child and another is almost always in the native language, as is much of the teacher's informal conversation.

total immersion An approach to teaching a second language in which instruction occurs entirely in that language and the learner's native language is not used at all.

Maintaining Tradition Some would say that these Vietnamese children in Texas are fortunate. They are instructed in two languages by a teacher who knows their culture, including the use of red pens for self-correction as well as teacher correction. Others would say that these children would be better off in an English-only classroom.

BOB DAEMMRICH / THE IMAGE WORKS

Lam, 1998). This is a political question more than a developmental one—a matter of the hidden curriculum, not just the intended one. Disagreements about the role and purpose of school occasionally become overt, not hidden. Here are excerpts from three letters to the editor of a local newspaper in British Columbia (quoted in Mitchell, 2001, pp. 64–65). One mother wrote in favor of a traditional school:

> Our children's performances are much lower both in academic and moral areas. I noticed the children have learnt very little academically. They learned to have self-confidence instead of being self-disciplined; learned to speak up instead of being humbled; learned to be creative instead of self-motivated; and learned to simplify things instead of organizing. All of these characteristics were not balanced, and will be the source of disadvantage and difficulties in children in this competitive society.

Two other parents were in favor of a more progressive school:

> These characteristics she disapproves of are the very characteristics I encourage in my children, as do their teachers and the public schools. Self-confidence, creativity, and individuality are wonderful qualities, which in no way detract from a child being respectful and pleasant, and achieving academic success.

> She wants her children to be self-disciplined, humble, self-motivated and organized, instead of being self-confident, assertive, creative and analytic. . . . These repressive, authoritarian, "traditional" parents who hanker for the days of yore, when fresh-faced school kids arrived all neatly decked out in drab-grey uniforms and shiny lace-up leather shoes, are a menace to society.

Societies throughout the world recognize that school-age children are avid learners and that educated citizens are essential to economic development. However, the nature and content of education bring up ideological and political concerns, which have given rise to the reading wars, the math wars, and the various forms of bilingual education.

It does seem that some direct instruction (in phonics; in mathematical symbols and procedures; or in the vocabulary, grammar, and syntax of a second language) is useful. It also seems that some concern for children's motivation, pride, and social interaction is essential. Balancing these needs is not easy (as the three quotations above demonstrate), and no culture has yet been successful in ways that can be proven—and then imitated by other nations.

SUMMARY

Building on Piaget and Vygotsky

1. According to Piaget, children enter the stage of concrete operational thought at about age 6 or 7. Egocentrism diminishes, and logical ideas, including identity and irreversibility, are applied to every aspect of experience. School-age children's new logical abilities enable them to understand classification, conservation, and many other concepts.

2. Vygotsky stressed the social context of learning, including the role of teachers and peers in guiding each child's education. International research finds that maturation is one factor in the cognitive development of school-age children (as Piaget predicted) and that cultural and economic forces are also influential (as Vygotsky predicted).

3. School-age children are passionately concerned about moral questions. Kohlberg described three levels of moral reasoning, from preconventional (self-concerned) to conventional (community-centered) to postconventional (overarching principles). Kohlberg urged discussion of moral issues among children to help with value clarification, which would advance their moral thinking.

Information Processing

4. An information-processing approach examines each step of the thinking process, from input to output, using the computer as a model. Humans are more creative than computers, but this approach is useful for understanding memory, perception, and expression.

5. Memory begins with sensory memory, which briefly stores information that reaches the brain from the sense organs. Then information proceeds to working memory, where perceptions are processed for a short time in active consciousness. Some images and ideas are stored indefinitely in long-term memory.

6. Advances in memory during middle childhood occur primarily because of improvement in working memory, aided by selective attention and logical retrieval. Long-term memory increases as well, as more material in the knowledge base makes more learning possible.

7. Speed of thought accelerates with continued brain myelination. Faster processing advances every aspect of cognition, including working memory. Repeated practice makes thought patterns and skill sets almost automatic, requiring little time or conscious effort.

8. Children become better at controlling and directing their thinking as the prefrontal cortex matures. Consequently, metacognition advances and children learn better, as advances in language demonstrate.

Teaching and Learning

9. Adults from all over the world agree that children should learn to read, and 95 percent of the world's children now attend at least some years of primary school. Nations and experts disagree about exactly how that education should occur. Not only do schools teach academic subjects; they also express a hidden curriculum—values that are embedded in school routines, structures, and processes, as well as in the overall selection of students and teachers.

10. Smaller class size does not necessarily advance achievement, although a massive experiment in Tennessee that reduced class size to about 15 in kindergarten through the third grade resulted in higher achievement. It is not clear whether the Tennessee experiment is generalizable and cost-effective.

11. The "reading wars" pit advocates of phonics against advocates of the whole-language approach. Low socioeconomic status correlates with low reading achievement but does not cause it.

12. The "math wars" contrast math learned by memory with math learned by social interaction. Math and science achievement are higher in East Asian nations than elsewhere, perhaps because in those countries math lessons are better prepared to be sequential, challenging, and interactive. In the United States, most schools now have computers, but this narrowing of the digital divide has not dramatically improved learning.

13. During the school years, children are particularly open to learning a second language. The specifics of second-language instruction remain controversial, with marked variations from nation to nation.

KEY TERMS

concrete operational thought (p. 289)
classification (p. 290)
identity (p. 290)
reversibility (p. 291)
reciprocity (p. 291)
preconventional moral reasoning (p. 293)
conventional moral reasoning (p. 293)

postconventional moral reasoning (p. 293)
morality of care (p. 294)
morality of justice (p. 294)
sensory memory (p. 296)
working memory (p. 296)
long-term memory (p. 296)
knowledge base (p. 297)

control processes (p. 298)
selective attention (p. 298)
metacognition (p. 299)
hidden curriculum (p. 302)
phonics approach (p. 303)
whole-language approach (p. 303)
total immersion (p. 309)

APPLICATIONS

1. Visit a local elementary school and look for signs of the hidden curriculum, the values implicit in the way the school is structured. For example, do the children ever line up? If so, when and how? If not, why not? Are there differences based on gender, age, ability, or talent among the groups of children or in the selection of staff? What is on the walls of the school? What nonteaching staff are present (nurse, cook, janitor)? Are parents involved within the classrooms or kept outside the building? For everything you observe, imagine how it might be different and speculate on what the underlying assumptions are.

2. Interview a 7- to 11-year-old child to find out what he or she knows *and understands* about mathematics. Relate both correct and incorrect responses to the logic of concrete operational thought.

3. What do you remember about how you learned to read? Compare your memories with those of two other people, one at least ten years older and the other at least five years younger than you. Can you draw any conclusions about effective reading instruction? If so, what are they? If not, why not?

4. The text notes socioeconomic disparities in education. If you are adept at finding public information, you can discover how much various schools in your state spend per student. Compare the richest and the poorest schools. (Try to get data for all the costs that relate to each child's education, including the estimated costs of building and maintaining the school, of transportation, of special education programs, and so on.)

Chapter Thirteen

The School Years: Psychosocial Development

latency Freud's term for middle childhood, during which children's emotional drives are quieter, their psychosexual needs are repressed, and their unconscious conflicts are submerged.

industry versus inferiority The fourth of Erikson's eight crises of psychosexual development, in which school-age children attempt to master many skills and develop a sense of themselves as either industrious and competent or incompetent and inferior.

In middle childhood, children break free from the closely supervised and limited arena of the younger child. Usually with their parents' blessing but sometimes breaking the rules, school-age children explore the wider world of neighborhood, community, and school. They experience new vulnerability, increasing competence, ongoing friendships, troubling rivalries, and deeper social understanding.

Our goal in this chapter is to examine the interplay between expanding freedom and guiding forces. We will look first at emotional growth, then at peer and family influences that direct and propel that growth, and, finally, at strategies and strengths that enable most children to move forward, ready for adolescence. To anchor our analysis, we begin with the perspectives on development in middle childhood that have been offered by the five major theories that were introduced in Chapter 2.

The Child's Emotions and Concerns

As we have seen in the previous two chapters, school-age children are noticeably more independent, more responsible, and more capable than younger children (Collins et al., 2002). This increased competence is recognized by parents and schools, in every nation, and in every developmental theory.

Theories of Development During Middle Childhood

The first set of theories to describe middle childhood were psychoanalytic theories, all of which noted that children are eager to learn about their expanding social universe. For example, Sigmund Freud described middle childhood as the period of **latency**, during which children's emotional drives are quieter, their psychosexual needs are repressed, and their unconscious conflicts are submerged. This makes latency "a time for acquiring cognitive skills and assimilating cultural values as children expand their world to include teachers, neighbors, peers, club leaders, and coaches. Sexual energy continues to flow, but it is channeled into social concerns" (Miller, 2002, p. 131).

Erik Erikson agreed with Freud that middle childhood is a quiet period emotionally. The child "must forget past hopes and wishes, while his exuberant imagination is tamed and harnessed to the laws of impersonal things," becoming "ready to apply himself to given skills and tasks" (Erikson, 1963, pp. 258, 259). During Erikson's crisis of **industry versus inferiority**, children busily try to master whatever abilities their culture values. They judge themselves as either *industrious* or *inferior*—that is, competent or incompetent, productive or failing, winners or losers.

KOJI SASAHARA / AP PHOTO

Industry on Display One characteristic of school-age children is their obsession with collecting, whether their interest is stamps or insects, Harry Potter paraphernalia, or, as shown here, Yu-Gi-Oh cards, which are the latest collecting fad in Japan. Children are much more industrious than adult collectors, busily counting, organizing, and trading their treasures.

social cognitive theory A perspective that highlights how the school-age child advances in learning, cognition, and culture, building on maturation and experience to become more articulate, insightful, and competent.

Developmentalists influenced by the two other grand theories—behaviorism and cognitive theory—are concerned with the acquisition of new skills and self-understanding, respectively. One offshoot of behaviorism, **social cognitive theory**, is particularly relevant to middle childhood because it highlights how the school-age child advances in learning, cognition, and culture (Bandura, 2001). Social cognitive theory recognizes that maturation and experience combine to allow school-age children to be articulate, reflective, and active, able to understand themselves and to be effective and competent. They think logically, as we saw in Chapter 12, and they apply their new learning ability to their expanding social world.

In practical terms, 10-year-olds can explain their emotions to their parents, or decide to wake up early to study for a test, or choose which friend to phone for the homework assignment. All these actions make the older child more active than passive in the social world, displaying "social efficacy" (Bandura, 1997). The proud smile of any 10-year-old who has just won a race, earned a perfect grade, or finished a work of art conveys this efficacy.

The two emergent theories, sociocultural and epigenetic, also acknowledge the new independence of school-age children. Sociocultural theory looks not only at children from widely separated parts of the world—for instance, rural China versus urban Canada—but also at various subcultures within one nation or even on one city block. In every case, each child's particular sociocultural context affects development. Consider the two children in A Case to Study at the beginning of Chapter 11, Yolanda and Paul, who are from the same nation (United States), state (California), region (Los Angeles area), and ethnic heritage (Mexican-American). Here is what they say:

> *Yolanda:* I feel proud of myself when I see a [good] grade. And like I see a C, I'm going to have to pull this grade up. . . . I like learning. I like really getting my mind working. . . . [Education] is good for you. . . .

> *Paul:* I try not to get influenced too much, pulled into what I don't want to be into. But mostly, it's hard. You don't want people to be saying you're stupid. "Why do you want to go to school and get a job? . . . Drop out."

> *[quoted in Nieto, 2000, pp. 220, 221, 252]*

These opposite feelings about school are not surprising, given that each child lives in "a culture within a culture" (Stewart & Bond, 2002). Research inspired by the sociocultural perspective has found that immigrants from Mexico (like Yolanda) are much more motivated to achieve academically than are native-born children of the same ethnicity; studies have also found that schools themselves are cultural institutions that discourage Latino children, especially boys (like Paul) (Conchas, 2001; Suarez-Orozco & Suarez-Orozco, 2001).

Epigenetic influences are apparent as well: Not only are all schoolchildren genetically driven to master the skills they will need in adulthood, but girls and boys have different visions and role models for adulthood. Thus, Yolanda has been influenced by her female teachers and friends; Paul has been affected by his father (who is in prison) and by older boys (all gang members). Each of these children, influenced by culture, has chosen his or her own path in a gender-specific way.

Notice that all five major theories describe the child from ages 7 to 11 in similar ways—as competent, eager, and increasingly influenced by school and community norms. Worldwide, cultures recognize the wonderful characteristics of this stage by selecting these years as the time to give the child more inde-

Celebrating Spring No matter where they live, 7- to 11-year-olds seek to understand and develop whatever skills are valued by their culture. They do so in active, industrious ways, as described in behaviorism as well as cognitive, sociocultural, psychoanalytic, and epigenetic theories. This universal truth is illustrated here, as four friends in Assam, northeastern India, usher in spring with a Bihu celebration. Soon they will be given sweets and tea, which is the sociocultural validation of their energy, independence, and skill.

pendence and responsibility, from attending first grade to making one's First Communion, from doing significant chores at home to facing major challenges at school (Collins et al., 2002).

Understanding Self and Others

All theories depict school-age children as developing a sense of themselves as individuals connected to school, religion, and neighborhood. Indeed, human development can be depicted as a progression from total dependence in infancy to self-determination in adulthood. Middle childhood is the time when children learn the skills they will need as adults, concretely (Piaget's word) or industriously (Erikson's word) going their own, self-centered way, shedding their dependence on parents during latency (Freud's word). Although children may be going their own way, their development occurs with parents and peers, no less in middle childhood than earlier or later. The following self-description could have been written by many 10-year-olds:

> I'm in the fourth grade this year, and I'm pretty popular, at least with the girls. That's because I'm nice to people and can keep secrets. Mostly I am nice to my friends, although if I get in a bad mood I sometimes say something that can be a little mean. I try to control my temper, but when I don't, I'm ashamed of myself. I'm usually happy when I'm with my friends, but I get sad if there is no one to do things with. At school, I'm feeling pretty smart in certain subjects like Language Arts and Social Studies. I got A's in these subjects on my last report card and was really proud of myself. But I'm feeling pretty dumb in Math and Science, especially when I see how well a lot of the other kids are doing. Even though I'm not doing well in those subjects, I still like myself as a person, because Math and Science just aren't that important to me. How I look and how popular I am are more important. I also like myself because I know my parents like me and so do other kids. That helps you like yourself.
>
> *[quoted in Harter, 1999, p. 48]*

In this statement, and in many research studies, it is apparent that school-age children have a much more elaborate and nuanced understanding of abilities and traits, as "children in middle childhood contrast sharply with younger children in their abilities for greater social understanding" (Collins et al., 2002, p. 75). A person could be better than others in language arts but worse in math, sometimes nice and sometimes mean, or shy instead of outgoing (Heyman & Gelman, 2000).

Push and Pull During middle childhood, children become aware of their unique traits—for example, whether they are bold or cautious—by comparing themselves with others.

? *Observational Quiz* (see answer, page 318): What do you see that suggests that these children are friends?

social comparison The tendency to assess one's abilities, achievements, social status, and other attributes by measuring them against those of other people, especially one's peers.

Nonacademic skills are also compared. A boy might, for example, realize that he is weak at playing the piano, OK at basketball, and a whiz at Nintendo.

Increased self-understanding comes at a price. Self-criticism and self-consciousness rise and self-esteem dips (Merrell & Gimpel, 1998). Older children usually accept the standards set by their parents, teachers, and peers. They use **social comparison**, their ability to compare themselves with other people, even when no one else explicitly makes the comparison. They value those abilities they really have, abandoning the imaginary, rosy self-evaluation of preschoolers (Grolnick et al., 1997; Jacobs et al., 2002). This may indicate that they are more realistic and therefore able to work on the skills they lack (recall the discussion of metacognition in Chapter 12) or it may foreshadow the emotional uncertainty and psychic stress that many adolescents feel. In any case, families are now only one of the significant influences used for social comparison; other children are another (Berndt & Murphy, 2002; Wigfield et al., 1997).

Cultural influences are also reflected. Many social groups teach children not to be *too* outstanding; for example, Australians have a saying that "tall poppies" are cut down, and in Japan, social comparison is not supposed to be used to make oneself feel superior (Toyama, 2001). Although Chinese children tend to excel at mathematics, only 1 percent said that they were "very satisfied" with their performance in that subject (Stevenson et al., 2000; see Figure 13.1). An overview of research on self-esteem found that academic and social competence is aided by objective evaluation of achievement, not by artificially high self-esteem (Baumeister et al., 2003). Nonetheless, in every nation, school-age children become much more aware of social standards and comparisons than they were as preschoolers, and this awareness probably makes them more eager to learn.

> Every theory of development recognizes that school-age children differ from their younger selves: They are more independent, capable, and self-aware. Moreover, they can assess their own strengths and weaknesses (with some loss of self-esteem) and work on their shortcomings, newly aware of how they compare with others.

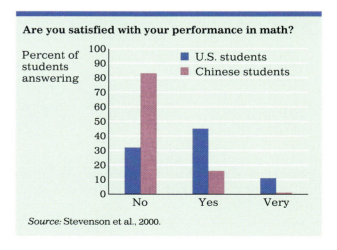

Are you satisfied with your performance in math?

Percent of students answering

- U.S. students
- Chinese students

No   Yes   Very

Source: Stevenson et al., 2000.

FIGURE 13.1 Not Satisfied Yet? They do far better in math than do their peers in the United States, but Chinese children are seldom satisfied with their math performance. The relatively high satisfaction of the Americans may be cultural, may reflect more adult encouragement, or may be associated with low effort and low accomplishment.

The Peer Group

The **peer group** is a group of individuals of roughly the same age and social status who play, work, or learn together. Most developmentalists consider getting along with peers to be crucial during middle childhood, "central to living a full life and feeling good" (Borland et al., 1998, p. 28). "Ample evidence exists that difficulties with peers place a child at risk for developing subsequent problems of a psychological nature" (Rubin et al., 1998, p. 674). Conversely, being well-liked by peers is protective, even for children from stressful, conflictful, or punitive homes (Criss et al., 2002).

There is an important developmental progression here. Younger children have friends and learn from playmates, of course, but they are more egocentric and therefore less affected by another child's acceptance or rejection. In middle childhood, however, children care about the opinions and judgments of their classmates. They become more dependent on each other, not only for companionship but also for self-validation and advice. An additional reason for this dependence is that peer relationships, unlike adult–child relationships, involve partners who must learn to negotiate, compromise, share, and defend themselves as equals (Hartup, 1996). Children need peers so they can learn lessons that adults cannot teach, not only because adults are from a different generation but also because adults are not equals: They can be too authoritarian or too indulgent.

Because peers are so important to children, developmentalists are troubled if children have no free time to spend with each other. Friends are crucial for social growth and for school adjustment (Berndt, 1999).

Throughout the world, many of the norms and rules of the peer group implicitly encourage independence from adults, and some go even further, demanding distance from adult society. By age 10, if not before, the peer group pities children (especially boys) whose parents kiss them in public ("momma's boy"), teases children whose teachers favor them ("teacher's pet"), and despises those who betray other children to adults ("tattletale," "snitch," "rat"), especially adults in authority such as teachers or the police.

Not surprisingly, adults do not always approve of peer influence (Hartup & Stevens, 1999). Children tend to take on the characteristics and values of those in their group, so parents might try to encourage their children to associate with peers whom they approve of (Dishion & Bullock, 2002). For example, peers are one of the best sources of language learning—which is essential if a child needs to learn a second language but less benign if the new code includes a marked regional accent and unacceptable slang and cursing. By age 9, Paul, the California boy you met in Chapter 11, believed that "I got in just to be in a gang, be somewhere, be known from somewhere," whereas Yolanda was always encouraged by her best girlfriend (Nieto, 2000).

peer group An aggregate of individuals of roughly the same age and social status who play, work, or learn together.

The Rules of the Game These young monks in Burma are playing a board game that adults also play, but the children have some of their own refinements of the general rules. Children's peer groups often modify the norms of dominant culture, as is evident in everything from superstitions to stickball.

Friendship

While acceptance by the entire peer group is valued, personal friendship is even more important to children (Erwin, 1998). Indeed, if they had to choose between being popular but friendless or having close friends but being unpopular, most children would take the friends. Such a choice is consistent with developmentalists' view of the close relationship between friendship and psychosocial development (Hartup & Stevens, 1999; Ladd, 1999).

Friends and Culture Like children everywhere, these children—two 7-year-olds and one 10-year-old, of the Surma people in southern Ethiopia—model their appearance after that of slightly older children, in this case adolescents who apply elaborate body paint for courtship and stick-fighting rituals.

?Observational Quiz (see answer, page 320): Are these boys or girls, and which two are best friends?

For example, one study found that children from violent and nonviolent homes said they had similar numbers of acquaintances, but the children from violent homes were less likely to have close friends and more likely to be lonely. The authors explained, "Skill at recruiting surface acquaintances or playmates is different . . . from the skill required to sustain close relationships," and the latter is needed if the child is to avoid loneliness, isolation, and rejection (McCloskey & Stuewig, 2001, p. 93). A 12-year longitudinal study of peer acceptance (popularity) and close friendship (mutual loyalty) among fifth-graders found that both peers and friends affected social interactions and emotional health many years later but that the friends were more important than the acquaintances (Bagwell et al., 2001).

Friendships become more intense and intimate for older children. They demand more of their friends, change friends less often, become more upset when a friendship breaks up, and find it harder to make new friends (Erwin, 1998). Older children are also pickier: They tend to choose best friends whose interests, values, and backgrounds are similar to their own. In fact, from ages 3 to 13, close friendships increasingly involve children of the same sex, age, ethnicity, and socioeconomic status (Aboud & Mendelson, 1996). By age 10, most children often have one "best" friend to whom they are quite loyal. This trend toward fewer but closer friends is especially apparent among girls (Borland et al., 1998; Buhrmester, 1996; Erwin, 1998).

All children occasionally feel left out or unwelcomed by their peers, but only a small minority are spurned *most* of the time. In one study, researchers asked 299 children which classmates they wanted or did not want as playmates. For each of six years, the rankings were tabulated and clustered into three groups: popular, or often chosen; average, or sometimes chosen; and unpopular, or often rejected. These clusters changed from year to year, but overall 36 percent of the children were popular, 47 percent were average, and only 17 percent were rejected. The crucial finding was that most of the children (89 percent) changed from one category to another over the six years. Only 2 percent were consistently unpopular (Brendgen et al., 2001).

Other researchers have identified three distinct types of unpopular children. One group is *neglected,* not really rejected: No classmate picks them as friends, but nobody avoids them, either. This is far from ideal, but it may not be harmful to long-term psychosocial development, especially if these children have good family relationships or outstanding talent (in music or the arts or some other area). Many adults who are quite successful had few friends as children.

!Answer to Observational Quiz (from page 316): The children's age and sex provide the clues. Pulling a reluctant playmate toward the end of the diving board might seem mean (and probably would be mean if these children were girls or preschoolers), but physical play is part of close friendships among boys this age. Not only are both boys smiling, but the one at left would not have gotten on the board if his friend had not encouraged him, and the boy at right would pull arms, not feet, or would simply push sideways if he were not just playing with his buddy.

Can I Play? If she dares to ask, she is likely to be rejected, because the rules of bonding at this age tend to exclude as well as include.

TABLE 13.1 Examples of the Perceptions and Reactions of Popular and Unpopular Children

Situation	Child B's Type	Typical Interpretation	Typical Response
Child A spills a glass of milk on child B during lunch.	Aggressive-rejected	It was on purpose.	Pour milk on child A, or say something mean.
	Withdrawn-rejected	It was on purpose, or it was accidental.	Ignore it, or leave the table.
	Well-liked	It was accidental.	Get a towel, or ask how it happened.

The other two types of unpopular children are actively rejected, not just neglected. They may be either **aggressive-rejected**—that is, disliked because of their antagonistic, confrontational behavior—or **withdrawn-rejected**—disliked because of their timid, anxious behavior. These seemingly opposite types of rejected children are similar in certain ways: Both have problems regulating their emotions, and both are likely to come from homes where they have been mistreated (Pollak et al., 2000).

Children who are well-liked are typically helpful toward and willing to assume the best about other children (Ladd, 1999). In particular, well-liked children assume that social slights, from a push to an unkind remark, are accidental and not intended to harm; therefore, they do not react with fear (as withdrawn children do) or anger (as aggressive children do) (see Table 13.1). In ambiguous situations, well-liked children try to solve the problem, perhaps by first asking the other child for an explanation (Erdley & Asher, 1996). Given a direct conflict between themselves and another child, they seek not revenge but rather a compromise that maintains the friendship (Rose & Asher, 1999).

These prosocial skills—benign social perceptions, insight into human relationships, and the tendency to help rather than to attack others—are rare in rejected children of any type (Ladd, 1999). Both aggressive-rejected and withdrawn-rejected children misinterpret other people's words and behavior, are poor listeners, and avoid social situations. They tend to be clumsy, awkward, and inept around other children.

Unless the problems are spotted and overcome by first grade, the situation of rejected children becomes progressively worse. Their behavior soon becomes not only a cause but also a consequence of their social rejection. Other children tend to make unfavorable social comparisons, expecting a particular child to behave in an unacceptable way. This is known from several studies, including longitudinal research on AD/HD children, who have increasingly poor relationships with peers, even if treatment eventually helps them concentrate in school (Mrug et al., 2001). One solution is for the rejected child to convince a popular child to become his or her buddy or protector.

aggressive-rejected Referring to children who are actively rejected by their peer group because of their aggressive, confrontational behavior.

withdrawn-rejected Referring to children who are actively rejected by their peer group because of their withdrawn, anxious behavior.

BOB DAEMMRICH / THE IMAGE WORKS

Following Social Rules This argument in a schoolyard is not just a fight between two boys—it is a sociocultural event.

?Observational Quiz (see answer, page 321): What can you see in the behavior of these four boys that suggests that they are aware of the rules of such confrontations?

Bullies and Their Victims

Any discussion of aggressive and withdrawn children is likely to bring to mind bullies and their victims. Bullying occurs in every nation and in every type of school—rural and urban, large and small, multiethnic public and homogeneous church-related. Contrary to some common assumptions, bullies are not necessarily rejected and victims are not necessarily odd in appearance or background, although they are always rejected. Some definitions are thus in order.

bullying A child's repeated, systematic efforts to inflict harm on another, particular child through physical, verbal, or social attacks.

!Answer to Observational Quiz (from page 318): They are girls. The short hair and necklaces give conflicting signals, from a Western perspective, but the unmistakable sign is that two of them have outlined their future breasts, in imitation of their older sisters. They are all friends, but the two younger girls are especially close: The photographer reports that they decorated their bodies in similar ways to show their affection for each other.

bully-victim A bully who is or has been a victim of bullying. Also called *provocative victim.*

Especially for Former Victims of Bullying How can you overcome the psychic scars of having been a victim?

Types of Bullying

Researchers define **bullying** as repeated, systematic efforts to inflict harm through physical attack (such as hitting, pinching, or kicking), verbal attack (such as teasing, taunting, or name-calling), or social attack (such as deliberate shunning or public mocking). A key word in this definition is *repeated*. Most children experience isolated attacks or social slights from other children and come through unscathed. For example, when the social play described in Chapter 10 turns hurtful, the conflict soon ends and the aggressor and the injured party usually repair their friendship. Best friends sometimes fight and make up. But when a child endures shameful experiences again and again—being forced to hand over lunch money, or to drink milk mixed with detergent, or to lick someone's boots, or to be the butt of insults and practical jokes, with everyone watching and no one defending—the effects can be deep and long-lasting. Not only are bullied children anxious, depressed, and underachieving during the months and years of their torment, but longitudinal studies suggest that self-esteem drops and loneliness increases even when the child is no longer being actively bullied (Hanish & Guerra, 2002; Kochenderfer-Ladd & Wardrop, 2001).

Victims of bullying are usually "cautious, sensitive, quiet, . . . lonely and abandoned at school. As a rule, they do not have a single good friend in their class" (Olweus, 1999, p. 15). Withdrawn-rejected children are thus likely to become victims. Surprisingly, aggressive-rejected children may also become victims—victims of a special kind, called **bully-victims** (or *provocative victims*) (Schwartz et al., 2001). Bully-victims are the minority; most bullies are neither victims nor rejected. In fact, bullies usually have a few admiring friends (henchmen) and are socially perceptive—but without the empathy that characterizes prosocial children. They are adept at being aggressive without getting into immediate trouble with peers, parents, or teachers.

Bullies and their victims are usually of the same gender. Boys who are bullies are often above average in size, whereas girls who are bullies are often above average in verbal assertiveness. Boy victims are often physically weaker, whereas girl victims are more shy.

These gender differences are reflected in bullying tactics: Boys typically use force or the threat of force; girls often mock or ridicule their victims, making fun of their clothes, behavior, or appearance, revealing their most embarrassing secrets, or spreading destructive rumors about them. In other words, boys typically use *physical* aggression and girls use *relational* aggression. Physical aggression, as you remember from Chapter 10, involves punching, kicking, and otherwise causing the victim physical pain; relational aggression involves undercutting the victim's friendships and self-esteem. Bullying may also be categorized as *direct* (obvious, as a physical or verbal attack) and *indirect* (spreading a rumor or social shunning, which begins with a ringleader whom the victim cannot confront directly).

Bullying in Many Nations

Following the suicides of three victims, the government of Norway asked Dan Olweus to determine the extent and severity of bullying in that country. After concluding a confidential survey of direct bullying among Norway's 90,000 school-age children, Olweus reported that bullying was widespread and serious (see Figure 13.2); that teachers and parents were "relatively unaware" of specific incidents; and that even when adults noticed, they rarely intervened. Of all the children Olweus surveyed, 9 percent said that they were bullied "now and then" and 3 percent that they were victims once a week or more; 7 percent admitted that they themselves sometimes deliberately hurt other children, verbally or physically (Olweus, 1993b).

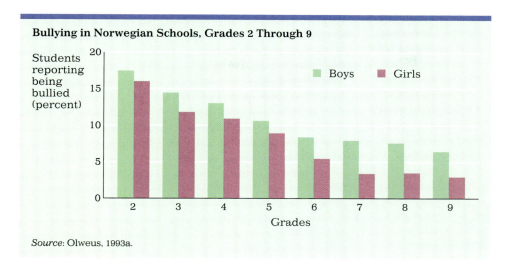

Bullying in Norwegian Schools, Grades 2 Through 9

Source: Olweus, 1993a.

FIGURE 13.2 Every Country Has Bullies
The rates of being bullied in the various grades as reported by Norwegian schoolchildren are typical of the rates in many other countries. This chart shows physical bullying only; relational bullying may increase with age. Although physical bullying is less common among older children, relational bullying becomes more devastating, because older children depend much more on peers for self-esteem.

Olweus's work inspired social scientists all over the world, who discovered that the numbers for Norway are equaled or exceeded in many other countries (Smith et al., 1999). For instance, confidential surveys found that 10 percent of British children bullied another child at least once a week (Smith et al., 1999), as did 18 percent of Italian and Australian children and 13 percent of Japanese children (Fonzi et al., 1999; Morita et al., 1999; Rigby & Slee, 1999). The sex differences are universal, with boys bullying other boys more than girls bully other girls—except in Japan, where social shunning is the primary tactic of both sexes and girls use it more than boys (Morita et al., 1999; Tanaka, 2001).

When older children and adults are queried about past bullying, most remember it well. In one survey in the midwestern United States, 80 percent of respondents said they had done some bullying (although few considered themselves bullies) (Bosworth et al., 1999). In a retrospective study, 65 percent of American adults remembered being victims (Eslea & Rees, 2001).

International research has revealed other patterns in bullying. A child's social status and behavior often change from year to year and from place to place. For example, in the United States, when children from kindergarten through third grade were asked every year whether they had been the target of physical or relational aggression, only 4 percent answered "yes" for all four years, but 60 percent answered yes for at least one year (Kochenderfer-Ladd & Wardrop, 2001).

Changes in the extent and type of bullying are especially common in transitional grades. The first years of elementary school are the time of greatest shift, as some children learn to act in prosocial rather than antisocial ways and thus attain more social acceptance (Haselager et al., 2002). Typically there is a sudden increase in bullying at about age 11, as children enter middle school (Pellegrini & Long, 2002).

Culture is always a factor in the incidence of bullying. For example, among girls in Israel, those from Orthodox, non-European backgrounds are *most* likely to be bullies at age 11 but *least* likely to be bullies at age 15 (Landau et al., 2002). Although cross-national comparisons are tricky, Australia, Poland, and Italy seem to have a higher incidence of bullying than do the respective nearby countries of New Zealand, Finland, and Spain (Smith et al., 1999).

Everywhere, bullies are difficult to change. The origins of all kinds of antisocial behavior, including bullying, predate middle childhood. Brain abnormalities or genetic impulses may be strengthened by insecure attachment, poor emotional regulation, and other deficits (Cairns & Cairns, 2001; Holden, 2000). In fact, bullying may come naturally to all young humans, who instinctively use

❗Answer to Observational Quiz (from page 319): The boy on the left, by his facial expression, knows he must stand his ground or risk losing status among his peers. The boy in the middle, angry as he is, keeps his hands down because to start hitting would be unacceptable. And the two boys at the right watch intently as judge, jury, and police, standing close enough to hold back or egg on the antagonist if the argument escalates and they decide intervention is appropriate. If the disagreement does escalate into a physical fight, other children will join the onlookers, not only to observe but also to monitor and moderate—making sure that neither boy unfairly pummels the other.

Response for Former Victims of Bullying (from page 320): Realize that it was not your fault; the bully was in the wrong and should have been stopped by adults at home and at school. Make sure your self-esteem is not still damaged. Write about the situation, see a psychotherapist, or talk it over with a supportive friend.

force to try to get their way (Hawley, 1999). As one researcher quipped, "Babies do not kill each other because we do not give them access to guns" (Tremblay, 2000, p. 581). Yet the impulse to dominate others must be redirected during childhood, for the sake of the bullies' healthy development as well as that of the victims.

Fortunately, overt victimization can be reduced over the school years. Although adult intervention can backfire during the teen years, some young bullies become much less antisocial by adolescence (Aguilar et al., 2000; Reid et al., 2002). Some schools manage to reduce bullying, as the following Thinking Like a Scientist feature explains.

Thinking Like a Scientist

Intervention to Stop Bullying: Impossible?

Bullies and victims share one firm cognitive assumption: Adults will not intervene. Robert Coles (1997) describes a 9-year-old boy who reported to the teacher that one of his classmates, a girl, was cheating. The boy was then bullied—not only by his classmates but also by the teacher and the principal, who made excuses for the girl. Coles believes that the overall moral climate teaches many children to ignore the actions of bullies and to downplay the feelings and needs of victims of bullying.

Researchers in Ontario, Canada, unobtrusively recorded playground bullying (verbal and physical) and reported several disturbing findings. Girls were as involved as boys (though indirectly); teachers intervened only 4 percent of the time; and other children stopped only 12 percent of the incidents. The principal of the school with the most bullying denied that his school had any bullying at all (Pepler et al., 1999). In general, children are sympathetic to victims, fear bullies, and believe that teachers could stop the bullies but, in one child's words, are "too soft. . . . The most she'll do is, like, go 'Don't do it again'" (quoted in Borland et al., 1998). As the years go by, students become indifferent.

Developmentalists believe that intervention must change the social climate of the entire school, not merely protect the victims and punish (or ignore) the bullies. A "whole-school" approach was first demonstrated in Norway. Dan Olweus had been studying bullying for many years when the Norwegian government asked him to design an intervention effort. Olweus collected data from all the children (summarized in Figure 13.2) and then, using an ecological approach, began to change the culture of many schools.

In the first phase of intervention, all parents received pamphlets that described signs of victimization (such as a child's having bad dreams, no real friends, damaged clothes, torn books, or unexplained bruises). All students saw videotapes intended to evoke sympathy for victims. All teachers were given special training in intervention.

The second phase was more direct. In every classroom, students discussed why and how to stop bullying, to medi-

Shake Hands or Yell "Uncle" Many schools, such as this one in Alaska, have trained peer mediators who intervene in disputes, hear both sides, take notes, and seek a resolution. Without such efforts, antagonists usually fight until one gives up, giving bullies free rein. Despite Alaska's higher rate of alcohol abuse, the state's adolescent homicide rate is lower than the national average.

? *Observational Quiz* (see answer, page 324): Could this be one reason?

ate peer conflicts, and to befriend lonely children. The last action is particularly crucial: Having at least one protective peer "watching your back" not only prevents the escalation of bullying but reduces its emotional sting (Hodges et al., 1999). For this reason, teachers organized cooperative learning groups within classes so that no child could be isolated and then bullied, and teachers halted each incident of name-calling or minor assault because they now recognized the undercurrent beneath the bully's excuses and the terror behind the victim's silence or nervous laughter. Principals learned that adult supervision in the lunchroom, restrooms, and playground was pivotal, and they redeployed staff to keep watch and intervene.

In the Norwegian schools, if bullying occurred despite these preventive steps, counselors used very direct measures: They conducted intensive family therapy with the bully and parents; they removed the bully to a different class, grade, or even school; and they helped the victim strengthen social and academic skills. (Note that bullies and their families bore the major burden. If the victim were to change schools and the bully were to stay, the wrong child would be punished.)

Twenty months after this campaign began, Olweus surveyed the children again. He found that bullying had been reduced overall by more than 50 percent, with dramatic improvement for both boys and girls at every grade level (Olweus, 1992). These results are thrilling to developmentalists, because they show that research can lead to an inexpensive, widespread intervention that effectively reduces a serious problem.

Similar efforts are underway in a dozen nations, notably Canada, Australia, Sweden, and Great Britain. Some programs in certain schools in the United States also seem to make a difference, although the effects are less dramatic than in the Norwegian example (e.g., Aber et al., 1998; Flannery et al., 2003; Shapiro et al., 2002).

In designing and implementing programs to prevent bullying, research has made three things clear:

- The target should be the entire school, not just the identified bullies.
- Early intervention is more effective than later. (High school may be too late.)
- Evaluation is critical. Programs that look good on paper may not be effective in practice.

This final point merits special emphasis. Efforts that are well intentioned, such as letting children work out all their own disputes or having guards in the school, may actually make the situation worse. The scientific method is useful precisely because human assumptions can be mistaken. Bullying is a prime example.

All 6- to 11-year-olds want peer acceptance and close, mutual friendships. These two social supports buffer against loneliness and depression, not only during childhood but also for years beyond. Most children experience some peer rejection as well as social acceptance. However, children who are repeatedly rejected and friendless become victims, harassed directly and indirectly.

Bullying occurs in every school in every nation, although its frequency and type depend on the school climate, the culture, and the child's age and gender. Fortunately, bullying can be reduced and contained, if not eliminated. Parents and teachers can help children develop cooperative and constructive relationships with friends and with peers, as protection against the personal and social problems of middle childhood, and they can change the culture of a school to make bullying less likely.

Especially for the Parents of a Bully
Another parent has told you that your child is bullying his or her child, but your child denies it and explains that the other child doesn't mind being teased. What do you do?

Families and Children

No one doubts that both peers and friends are vital during middle childhood or that schools can make a marked difference in what, and how much, children learn. Almost everyone believes that families are important as well, but parents and the general public are more convinced than are developmental researchers that parental practices play a primary role (Ladd & Pettit, 2002; Reiss, 2000). In fact, a debate rages between those who believe that parenting styles and processes are very influential and those who believe that a child's genes and peers are much more powerful than anything the parents might do (Maccoby, 2000). Those who argue that parenting is crucial say:

> The vulnerabilities of older children may differ substantially in kind from those of young ones, but the potential consequences of risks remain equally great throughout the developmental period. The extent to which parents provide healthy and supportive environments for their developing children is a critical component in their lifelong well-being.
>
> [Ramey, 2002, p. 48]

And those who believe that heredity predominates contend:

> Children somewhat resemble their biological parents and siblings in personality, but the genes they have in common can account for almost all of the resemblance. These results indicate that being reared by conscientious parents does not, on average, make children more (or less) sociable, and that being reared by open-minded parents does not, on average, make children more (or less) open-minded.
>
> [Harris, 2002, p. 5]

Children Need Families

All developmentalists agree that families are crucial for healthy development at every point of the life span. The few children who have no families (not even foster parents or caregiving grandparents) are seriously troubled in every way. They are much more likely than their peers to become drug addicts, school dropouts, criminals, and suicides (Miller et al., 2000).

Children themselves recognize the importance of families. Consider, for example, a study of 1,000 8- to 12-year-olds that included children of various races who lived in single-parent households, stepfamilies, and foster families (Brannen et al., 2000). Regardless of their circumstances, "Children considered parents to be very important to them and their expectations of them were high." Their definition of parents—"people who never ever don't care about you" (p. 93)—emphasized caregiving, not legalities. More broadly,

> Children's criteria for family life included: the presence of children; living with at least one parent; a sense of security and a place to belong, and, most important of all, . . . unconditional love and care.
>
> [Brannen et al., 2000, p. 205]

The debate, then, is not about families versus no families, but about the particulars of family practice: whether bedtime is regular, whether honesty is explained, how children are disciplined, and so on. How can scientists measure the impact of such child-rearing particulars? One approach is to compare children of varying degrees of genetic similarity (twins, full siblings, stepsiblings, adopted children) from various families (Reiss, 2000). The varying extents to which children share genes (100 percent for monozygotic twins, 50 percent for full siblings, 25 percent for half-siblings, and so on) can be used to calculate how much of the variation in a trait is inherited. The remaining variations presumably arise from the environment.

Scientists further distinguish *shared* environmental influences, such as those that occur because children are raised by the same parents in the same home, from *nonshared* ones, which may result from contact with different teachers, peer groups, and so on (Turkheimer & Waldron, 2000). Environmental influences are presumed to be shared by stepsiblings, adoptive siblings, and biological siblings who grow up in the same household.

Surprisingly, nonshared influences on almost every trait are far greater than shared ones (Plomin et al., 2001; Reiss & Neiderheiser, 2000). Could it be that,

Response for the Parents of a Bully (from page 323): The future is ominous if the charges are true and your child's denial is a symptom of a problem. (If your child were not a bully, he or she would be worried about the other child's misperception instead of categorically denying that any problem exists.) You might ask the teacher and guidance counselor what they are doing about bullying in the school. Since bullies often learn behavior at home, perhaps family counseling would help you to become less punitive and your child to become less aggressive. Because bullies often have friends who encourage them, you may need to monitor your child's friendships and perhaps even befriend the victim. Talk matters over with your child, as often as necessary. Ignoring the situation may lead to heartache later on.

! Answer to Observational Quiz (from page 322): Yes. Children learn their conflict-resolution patterns in elementary school and then tend to use them in adolescence.

apart from their genetic contribution at the time of conception, parents have little impact on their children's characteristics? That is one possible explanation for the relative insignificance of a shared environment.

Some researchers think that this conclusion is too hasty. Perhaps, contrary to the usual assumption, nonshared factors can originate in the same household. If so, large nonshared, nongenetic differences among siblings might nevertheless be the result of parenting practices. For example, suppose that a husband and wife spend years squabbling but, when they move to another neighborhood, find that they are happier with each other. The impact of the move on their children will depend partly on how old the children are. A 7-month-old and a 7-year-old will not share the same reaction, though they live in the same household.

The maturity level of the children is not the only factor that makes a difference. Parents themselves change over the years, perhaps becoming less strict or more stressed or wealthier, and the effect of those changes will vary, depending on a child's age, gender, and temperament. Indeed, temperament may be particularly important, for a child who is genetically predisposed to be difficult may experience a very different upbringing than does an easygoing sibling (Putnam et al., 2002). Because parents respond differently to each child's temperament, siblings do not experience the same parenting. Home is thus nonshared.

Families may be analyzed in two ways: by function and by structure.

Family Function

Family function refers to how a family works to meet the needs of its members, which vary with age. Schoolchildren need their families to do five things:

1. *Provide food, clothing, and shelter.* In middle childhood, children can eat, dress, wash, and go to bed by themselves, but they cannot obtain the basic necessities of life without their families' help.
2. *Encourage learning.* A critical task during middle childhood is to master academic skills. Families must get their children to school and then guide and motivate their education.
3. *Develop self-esteem.* As they become more cognitively mature, children become more self-critical. Families help their children feel competent, loved, and appreciated.
4. *Nurture friendships with peers.* Families provide time, space, opportunity, and social skills to develop peer relationships.
5. *Provide harmony and stability.* Children need to feel safe and secure, with protective and predictable family routines.

Thus, a family provides material and cognitive resources as well as emotional security, so that the children grow in body and mind. Families can be evaluated on each of these five factors, with some doing quite well and others functioning poorly. However, no family always functions perfectly. For example, recurrent conflict, such as constant arguing, is common but harmful, whether or not the child is directly involved (Cox & Brooks-Gunn, 1999; Cummings et al., 2002).

family function The ways in which a family works to meet the needs of its members. Children need their families to provide them with food, clothing, and shelter; to encourage them to learn; to develop their self-esteem; to nurture their friendships with peers; and to provide harmony and stability at home.

Mom Urges Fit over Fashion One function of families is to provide children with basic necessities, such as clothing. When middle-class school-age children are involved, this is more difficult than it seems. The peer group is often quite specific about the most desirable brand, color, and design of every item of clothing, especially shoes.

JOHN BOYKIN / PHOTOEDIT

Family Structure

family structure The legal and genetic relationships among the members of a particular family.

Family structure refers to how a family is legally constructed and how its members are genetically connected. A family's structure changes over time only when marriage, divorce, or other such transitions occur. When social scientists (or the U.S. Census) define family structure, they consider only relatives who live together in the same household. Since this chapter is about children, the statistics in Table 13.2 refer only to families with children younger than 18.

TABLE 13.2 Common Family Structures

The family structures listed here are present in every nation, but the estimated percentages refer only to the United States (and are based on data from U.S. Bureau of the Census, 2002). Excluded are family types (e.g., polygamous families) that are very rare in North America, even if they are common elsewhere in the world.

Two-parent families

At any given moment, there are far more two-parent than one-parent families (73 percent to 27 percent) in the United States (see Figure 13.3). Two-parent households can be further subdivided according to the biological relationship of the adults and children.

1. **Nuclear family**   Named after the nucleus (the tightly connected core particles of an atom), the nuclear family consists of a husband and wife and their biological offspring. This family structure was idealized a few decades ago as the only acceptable type, but now more structures are accepted (Coontz, 1992). Nonetheless, half of all families with children are nuclear. About 58 percent of all school-age children live in nuclear families.

2. **Stepparent family**   Many parents who split up begin new partnerships, particularly if they are fathers (Stewart et al., 2003). Mothers are less likely to remarry, but when they do, the children usually live with her and their stepfather. At any given moment, about 10 percent of school-age children live with one biological parent and a stepparent.

3. **Blended family**   If a household includes children born to several families, such as the biological children from the spouses' previous marriages, and the biological children of the new couple, that is a blended family. Such families are home to about 5 percent of school-age children.

4. **Adoptive family**   About one-third of the estimated 15 percent of all married couples who are infertile decide to adopt. Fewer adoptable children are available than in earlier decades. About 2 percent of school-age children are in adoptive families in which neither parent is their biological relative.

One-parent families

A **one-parent family** consists of a child living with only one parent, who has never been married, is divorced, or (in less than 1 percent of families with school-age children) is widowed. The proportion of one-parent families (now 27 percent) is increasing.

1. **Single mother, never married**   In 2000, 33 percent of all babies in the United States were born to unmarried mothers, who were usually under age 22 and intended to marry someday (Musick, 2002). Although having a child decreases a woman's chance of marriage, many unmarried mothers

eventually do get married, often to their baby's father. By school age, about 10 percent of children live with never-married mothers.

2. **Single mother, divorced**   Although almost half of all marriages end in divorce, many of those couples had no children, and many divorced people remarry. Consequently, only about 10 percent of school-age children live with a single, divorced mother.

3. **Single father, divorced or never married**   Divorced or unmarried fathers assume physical custody (i.e., they live with their children) about 20 percent of the time (either by court order or by informal agreement). About 5 percent of school-age children live in households headed by a single father. This is the most rapidly increasing family type.

Other Family Types

Although 100 percent of children live in one or another of the seven family structures described above, some live in less common variations of these.

1. **Grandparent family**   About 9 percent of school-age children live in their grandparents' homes. (This does not include families in which a frail, elderly grandparent moves in with an adult child.) Such homes may be further classified by whether the child's biological parents are also in the household (extended family) or not (grandparents alone).

2. **Extended family**   In the United States, about 7 percent of school-age children live with their grandparents and at least one of their parents (and often with other relatives as well). Extended families are the norm in some nations and are common among Asian and Latino immigrants in the United States.

3. **Grandparents alone**   For about 2 percent of school-age children, their one or two "parents" are actually grandparents, acting as surrogates because both biological parents are dead, imprisoned, or otherwise unable to live with their children.

4. **Homosexual family**   About 1 percent of school-age children live in a homosexual family. This living arrangement typically occurs when, after a divorce, the custodial parent takes a homosexual partner. Less often, children are adopted by a homosexual couple or an unmarried lesbian has a biological child (Patterson, 2002).

5. **Foster family**   As discussed in Chapter 8, many children spend some time in a foster family, either kinship care or stranger care. Such arrangements are considered temporary; some agencies discourage foster parents from becoming too attached to their foster children (Haugaard & Hazan, 2002). At any given time, about 1 percent of school-age children are living in foster families.

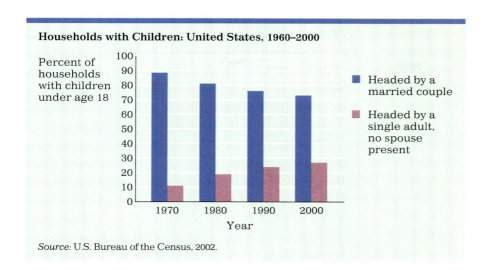

Households with Children: United States, 1960–2000

Percent of households with children under age 18

- ■ Headed by a married couple
- ■ Headed by a single adult, no spouse present

Source: U.S. Bureau of the Census, 2002.

FIGURE 13.3 And Baby Makes Two In more than one-fourth of all families raising children in the United States today, only one parent is present. In actuality, however, only about 20 percent of all children live in single-parent homes. That is because married couples tend to have more children in the household than single parents do, and some of these single parents, while not legally married, are living with long-term partners.

Family structures involving children may be two-parent or one-parent, with *parent* meaning any resident adult who acts in a caregiving capacity (and who may or may not be a biological parent). (In households with more than two caregiving adults, the child is still said to have only one or two parents.) As you can see from Table 13.2, four types of two-parent families and three types of one-parent families are common; five variations on these types are less common. The percentages given in the table represent a snapshot of just one moment in time, and only in the United States. Although about two-thirds of the children born in the United States in the past few years will spend at least some time in a one-parent family, the two-parent structure called the *nuclear family* (a married couple and their dependent offspring) is still the most common type overall.

Connecting Structure and Function

Although families may be looked at in terms of either structure or function, in practice structure influences function, which muddies any conclusions one might draw about the impact of families on children. For example, if one merely compares children growing up in various family structures, it is obvious that children raised in nuclear families are more successful. They usually finish school, obey the law, have happy marriages, and pursue fulfilling careers (McLanahan & Sandefur, 1994). By contrast, children in never-married, single-mother families "are at greatest risk," faring worst on every measure (Carlson & Corcoran, 2001, p. 789). The other family structures rank somewhere between these extremes. For instance, children in extended families typically do quite well, and those in divorced single-mother families quite poorly, although the particulars vary.

When these "varied particulars" are taken into account, the legal bonds, or the specifics of who lives with whom, make almost no difference (Carlson & Corcoran, 2001). For example, parents in a nuclear family tend to be wealthier, better educated, psychologically and physically healthier, more willing to compromise, and less hostile than parents in any other family structure. Those characteristics make a person more likely to marry—and more likely to *stay* married and have children. Furthermore, their genetic connection to their children and the fact that they share a home with the child's other biological parent increase their emotional involvement and time commitment, and this benefits the children as well.

nuclear family A family that consists of a father, a mother, and the biological children they have together.

stepparent family A family that consists of a parent, his or her biological children, and his or her spouse, who is not biologically related to the children.

blended family A family that consists of two adults, the biological children from a previous union of one or both adults, and any children the adults have together.

adoptive family A family that consists of one or more nonbiological children whom an adult individual or couple have voluntarily, legally, and permanently taken to raise as their own.

one-parent family A family that consists of one parent and his or her biological children.

grandparent family A family that consists of children living in their grandparents' home, either with their parents (extended family) or without them (grandparents alone).

extended family A family that consists of three or more generations of biologically related individuals.

grandparents alone A family that consists of one or two grandparents and their grandchildren.

homosexual family A family that consists of a homosexual couple and the biological or adopted children of one or both partners.

foster family A family in which one or more orphaned, neglected, abused, or delinquent children are temporarily cared for by an adult individual or couple to whom they are not biologically related.

When researchers control for all these factors and compare children from nuclear families with children from other family structures whose parents are equal in wealth, education, health, and so on, the differences between the children disappear. This is particularly true in non-European families in the United States, where children in extended families or single-parent families often thrive (García-Coll et al., 2001; Dunifon & Kowaleski-Jones, 2002). Does a long-lasting marriage with offspring cause, or at least enhance, parental assets? If so, family structure is not irrelevant, because the structure increases the income, the commitment, and so on. Nonetheless, function seems much more critical than structure. Children in every type of family structure sometimes grow up very well and sometimes run into serious trouble, so it is "not enough to know that an individual lives in a particular family structure without also knowing what takes place within that structure" (Lansford et al., 2001, p. 850).

The importance of analyzing what actually happens within a home, rather than just looking at family structure, is evident in the two underlying family circumstances that affect school-age children most powerfully: income and conflict.

Family Income

Family income strongly correlates with optimal child development, according to every study (McLoyd, 1998). The only question for researchers is whether income is the predominant factor or is only one of several powerful influences (Hetherington et al., 1998). In any case, household wealth makes it easier for families to fulfill all five of the basic functions listed earlier. They can readily provide the child with food, clothing, and shelter (function 1). The children attend better schools (which advances learning—item 2); own whatever possessions help them to feel accepted (which protects self-esteem—item 3); live in bigger homes in safer neighborhoods (making it easier to bring friends over—function 4); and parents need not argue about money (which provides harmony and stability—function 5). Thus, either directly or indirectly, all of the family functions are enhanced by adequate family income (Yeung et al., 2002), especially for children aged 6 to 9 (Gennetian & Miller, 2002).

Further evidence for the importance of sufficient income emerges when children within the same structures are compared. For example, extended families with several well-educated wage earners raise more successful children than do equally large, multigenerational families that are receiving public assistance (Rumbaut & Portes, 2001). Likewise, children in single-mother households achieve much more in school if their father regularly pays adequate child support (Graham & Beller, 2002) or if the nation subsidizes single parents (as Austria and Iceland do) (Pong et al., 2003). Finally, the risks to optimal development that children of teenage mothers encounter are more clearly related to the mother's SES than to her age (Jaffee et al., 2001; Turley, 2003).

Harmony at Home

The second factor that has a crucial impact on school-age children is the warmth or conflict that characterizes family interaction (Buehler & Gerard, 2002; Khaleque & Rohner, 2002). Children are handicapped if family members fight, especially if parents physically or verbally abuse each other (Cummings & Davies, 1994). Indeed, about a third of all divorces that involve children end marriages in which the parents were openly hostile to each other, and children benefit from the separation. By contrast, parents who divorce because they are merely dissatisfied with or distant from each other are more likely to harm than to help their children by ending the marriage (Booth & Amato, 2001). Ideally, parents not only avoid open fighting but also form a *parental alliance*—that is, a cooperative relationship that allows them to support each other's parenting.

Especially for Readers Who Are Not Yet Parents Should children call their parents by their first names, participate freely in the adults' discussions, and wear whatever clothes, hairstyles, and accessories they choose? Or should children be expected to be seen and not heard, to do their household chores regularly and well, and to excel in school?

The importance of family harmony explains why blended families are problematic for children (Hetherington & Kelly, 2002). In general, blended families include many people, and typically children feel jealous and adults disagree about child rearing. The more members a family has, the greater the stress, particularly when change occurs. Stress produces conflict, in the adults as well as the children, which is one reason that children usually achieve less in school and lose some friendship support during a divorce, a remarriage, or other family transition (Emery & Forehand, 1994). Children particularly are affected by multiple transitions, suffering more from a series of separations than from living in a stable, single-mother household.

The "single mother, unmarried" household has potential for continuity, yet it often involves disruptions. Some unmarried mothers are stable and devoted to their children, providing dependable warmth and guidance that strongly enhance child development. Most unmarried mothers, however, are young and poor, frequently change jobs and homes, and are involved in a series of romances, which may include repeated cohabitation, marriage, and divorce (Bumpass & Lu, 2000). If many emotional changes and intimate relationships occur in a mother's life, her stress is transmitted to her children, who may rebel when their mother diverts her attention to a new adult and who resent a stepparent and stepsiblings. Consequently, in families with many transitions, children are more likely to quit school, leave home, use drugs, become delinquent, and have children of their own before age 20.

The importance of warmth and stability helps explain an ethnic difference in the effectiveness of parenting styles. As you remember from Chapter 10, authoritative parenting—marked by loving guidance and consistent discipline—is generally more likely than authoritarian or permissive parenting to produce outgoing, self-confident, and accomplished children. This is as true for older children as it is for preschoolers, and this type of parenting is found among families of every structure, income, cultural background, and ethnicity (Amato & Fowler, 2002).

However, especially in middle childhood, a subgroup of families do not fit this generalization. Parents who use harsh discipline are usually categorized as authoritarian, but their children sometimes become happy and successful. In the United States, such families are not usually European-American, but are more likely to be Asian-, African-, and Mexican-American (Chao, 2001; Hill et al., 2003; McLoyd & Smith, 2002). The probable explanation is that many of these families are also very warm and accepting of their children. They delight in the child's actions, appreciate what the child says, and believe in the child's potential. Because of this warmth, the harsh discipline is perceived by the child as a sign of caring. In non-Western nations, similar patterns are apparent. The child's perception and interpretation of parenting practices is crucial: Feelings of encouragement and caring are beneficial; feelings of rejection and neglect are harmful (Stewart & Bond, 2002).

An important factor in this pattern is how isolated or supported the family itself is. Immigrant and African-American communities tend not to isolate single mothers, and many people help in child rearing (Roschelle, 1997). For example, often a man other than the biological father (sometimes the mother's brother or grandfather) becomes a "social father"; he is particularly likely to help a child with school learning (Jayakody & Kalil, 2002). In addition, grandmothers often live nearby, providing guidance, warmth, and practical help. Such socially embedded families produce a strong sense of family honor and ethnic pride. The children try to make their parents and community proud and hence try to stay out of trouble (Hill et al., 2003).

VALICA BOUDRY / AP PHOTO

The One-Parent Family Single parents are of two types: never married and formerly married. This divorcée is a pediatrician, so she and her daughter have a higher income than many other one-parent families. To combat the other hazards faced by single parents—including loneliness, low self-esteem, and ongoing disputes with the former spouse—she has established a divorce resource center in her hometown in Michigan.

Especially for Readers Whose Parents Are Middle-Aged Suppose your mother tells you she misses taking care of young children and she wants to become a foster parent. How do you advise her?

Families may be analyzed by structure or by function. Structures are becoming increasingly diverse. In the United States, 27 percent of all families with children are headed by a single parent. The nuclear family is still the most common family type. Nuclear families seem generally better for children than one-parent families, but the reason may be factors that correlate with two-parent homes (e.g., higher income), not the structure itself. Extended families, grandparent families, one-parent families, blended families, and adoptive families can raise successful, happy children. No structure automatically causes poor child development or guarantees a well-functioning family.

For school-age children, the family serves five crucial functions: to provide food, clothing, and shelter; to encourage learning; to develop self-esteem; to nurture friendships with peers; and to provide harmony and stability. Low income, conflict, and parental coldness, as well as the stresses of adjusting to new schools, new siblings, or new parents, interfere with these functions, no matter what the family structure.

Response for Readers Who Are Not Yet Parents (from page 328): Each set of practices is typical in some families, and both sets can result in happy, successful children. If you judged one style or the other to be categorically wrong, think again.

Coping with Problems

As you have seen throughout our discussion of middle childhood, the expansion of a child's social world may bring disturbing problems. The beginning of formal education forces learning disabilities to the surface. Speaking a minority language may hinder academic learning and provoke prejudice. The peer group may attack rather than support, and lack of close friends may lead to rejection. Living in a family that is hostile, stressful, or unstable is destructive in every domain.

These problems of middle childhood are often made worse by long-standing problems that harm children of every age, such as having a parent who is emotionally disturbed, drug-addicted, or in prison, or growing up in a community that is crumbling, violent, and crime-filled or in a household that is chronically poor. Because of a combination of problems, some children fail at school, fight with their friends, fear the future, or cry themselves to sleep.

Almost every child experiences some of the stresses and hassles of middle childhood. Surprisingly, many children who experience extensive and severe problems seem unscathed by their family troubles. Such children have been called "resilient" or even "invincible"—although developmentalists now use these terms cautiously, if at all (see Table 13.3). They acknowledge that every stress has an impact, but at the same time some children protect themselves so well that the impact is not apparent.

Resilience and the Assessment of Stress

Resilience has been defined as "a dynamic process encompassing positive adaptation within the context of significant adversity" (Luthar et al., 2000). There are three important parts to this definition:

- Resilience is a *dynamic process,* not a stable trait. Thus, a given child is not resilient in all situations. For example a child may become a good reader in a crowded classroom with an ineffective teacher, but that same child's self-esteem may suffer if he or she is rejected by peers. Another child in the same situation may be resilient socially but not academically, perhaps finding a close friend to buffer the rejection but not being able to concentrate on schoolwork.

TABLE 13.3 Dominant Ideas About Challenges and Coping in Children, 1965–Present

1965	All children are the same, with the same needs for healthy development.
1970	Some conditions or circumstances—such as "absent father," "teenage mother," "working mom," and "day care"—inevitably harm any child.
1975	All children are *not* the same. Some children are resilient, coping easily with stressors that cause harm in other children.
1980	Nothing inevitably causes harm. Indeed, some nonnuclear families function very well, and both maternal employment and preschool education usually benefit children.
1985	Factors beyond the family, both in the child (low birthweight, prenatal alcohol exposure, aggressive temperament) and in the community (poverty, violence), are potentially very risky for the child.
1990	Risk–benefit analysis finds that some children seem to be "invulnerable" to, or even to benefit from, circumstances that destroy others. (Some do well in school despite extreme poverty, for example.)
1995	No child is invincibly resilient. Risk factors always harm children—if not academically, then psychosocially.
Today	Risk–benefit analysis involves the interplay among all three domains (biosocial, cognitive, and psychosocial), in many systems, and it includes factors within the child (genes, intelligence, temperament), the family (function as well as structure), and the community (including neighborhood, school, church, and culture). Over the long term, most people overcome problems.

Sources: Luthar et al., 2000; Walsh, 2002; Werner & Smith, 2001.

This table simplifies the progression of the dominant ideas about the challenges that children face and about their ability to cope. Certainly the 1960s idea that all children are the same still seems true to some extent, and today's idea that risk–benefit analysis involves many factors is not a brand-new discovery. Nonetheless, the emphasis within the research has shifted over the past 40 years, as discovery, oversimplification, and criticism have yielded greater understanding of the complexity of the concept of resilience.

■ Resilience is not the absence of pathology but rather a *positive adaptation* to stress, resulting in some new strength or insight. For example, a socially isolated child would not be considered resilient merely because she is not depressed but might be considered resilient if her isolation prompts her to find other sources of social support—perhaps a grandparent, a younger child, a Sunday school teacher.

■ The adversity must be *significant.* Research informs us which stresses are not adverse at all (maternal employment, single parenthood), which ones are minor (large class size, poor vision), and which ones are major (victimization by peers, neglect by parents).

The Impact of Stress

To determine whether a particular stress is significant for a particular child, three questions must be answered: (1) How many stresses is the child experiencing? (2) Is the child's daily life affected? (3) How does the child interpret the stress?

No stressor inevitably causes harm. However, if it is added to other burdens—even mild ones that might be called "daily hassles" rather than "stressful events"—the child can suffer evident damage (Durlak, 1998; Shaw et al., 1994).

As question 2 implies, daily routines are crucial. For example, having a depressed mother may affect a child very little if the father compensates for, and

Response for Readers Whose Parents Are Middle-Aged (from page 329): Foster parenthood is probably the most difficult type of parenthood, yet it can be very rewarding if all needed support is available and a permanent arrangement is likely. Advise your mother to make sure that doctors and psychotherapists are available, that the biological parents are unlikely to reclaim the child, and that the placement agency truly cares about children's well-being.

protects the child from, the dysfunctional parent. However, the situation may become overwhelming if the child himself must do the following:

■ Manage his own daily care and school attendance
■ Contend directly with the mother's confused, depressed, or irrational thinking
■ Supervise and discipline younger siblings
■ Keep friends away from the house

Such a situation is especially likely to cause harm if the child is living in poverty, in a crime-ridden and violent neighborhood, and in an unsafe or unstable home with an unreliable supply of food and clothes. Poverty then becomes shameful, not simply a burden, and school signifies failure instead of escape. That child may develop a lifelong tendency to feel inferior rather than industrious, as Erikson would put it.

The importance of daily routines explains why homelessness is so hard on children. Each year, about 20 percent of all children move from one residence to another, a rate three times that of adults over age 50 (U.S. Bureau of the Census, 2000). Even if the move is to a wealthier neighborhood, school-age children are particularly disrupted because they have stronger local networks than younger or older people do. Unfortunately, the frequency of moves increases as income falls, with the poorest children moving, on average, two to three times *a year* before becoming homeless and moving into a shelter (Buckner et al., 1999).

Shelter life produces many stresses and few paths of recovery for a child. Typically, children change schools, have no place to bring friends, and carry the stigma of being a shelter kid. These factors reduce self-esteem and thus reduce the ability to cope.

A longitudinal study of babies in Hawaii born at high risk—in poverty, with birth complications, to parents who were alcoholic or mentally ill—found that two-thirds were unable to cope (they had internalizing or externalizing problems, as explained in Chapter 10). The other one-third did well if they avoided further stresses by achieving in school and having good friends and adult mentors who helped them (Werner & Smith, 1992). As adults, many escaped their childhood stressors by leaving their family problems behind and establishing healthy families of their own (Werner & Smith, 2001). Similar longitudinal results were found in another sample (Vaillant, 2002). In general, school success, creativity, religion, and supportive marriages promote coping with stress.

Attitude is crucial. An intriguing study of 8- to 11-year-olds measured three factors: conflict between the parents, problems in the children, and the children's feelings of self-blame and threat. By far the most important correlate with the children's problems was whether the children blamed themselves for or felt threatened by their parents' marital discord: "Children who do not perceive that marital conflict is threatening to them and do not blame themselves for the conflict may be better able to [reduce] the negative impact of the stressor" (El-Sheikh & Harger, 2001, p. 883). The impact of self-blame is shown in Figure 13.4.

Another study also found that children's coping depended more on their appraisal of the events than on the objective nature of the events themselves (Jackson & Warren, 2000). Finally, in the Hawaii longitudinal study, even for children with learning disabilities, "a realistic goal orientation, persistence, and

FIGURE 13.4 **When Parents Fight and Children Blame Themselves** Husbands and wives who almost never disagree are below the first standard deviation (−1 SD) in verbal marital conflict. By contrast, couples who frequently have loud, screaming, cursing arguments are in the highest 15 percent (+1 SD). In such high-conflict households, children are not much affected—*if* they do not blame themselves for the situation. However, if children do blame themselves, they are likely to have internalizing problems, such as nightmares, stomach aches, panic attacks, and feelings of loneliness.

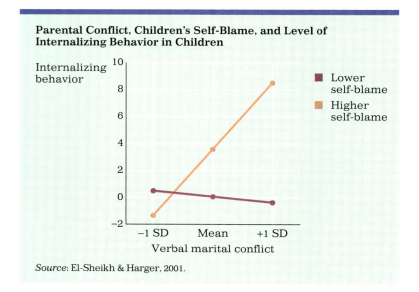

Parental Conflict, Children's Self-Blame, and Level of Internalizing Behavior in Children

Source: El-Sheikh & Harger, 2001.

'learned creativity' enabled . . . a remarkable degree of personal, social, and occupational success" (Werner & Smith, 2001, p. 140).

Social Support and Coping

A major factor that helps children deal with problems—one we have already touched on—is the social support they receive. A strong bond with a loving and firm parent can see a child through many difficulties. Even in war-torn or deeply impoverished neighborhoods, secure attachment to a parent who has been consistently present since infancy tends to allow children to be resilient (Masten & Coatsworth, 1998). Many immigrant children do surprisingly well, academically and emotionally, despite all their stresses, if their families and schools are supportive (Fuligni, 2001). Similarly, parenting practices can buffer stress even for impoverished children living in very adverse conditions (Wyman et al., 1999).

When the specifics of social support are considered, cultural differences must be respected. Although every school-age child tries to make friends, honor parents and other adults, and master the various skills that each culture values, some turn more readily to siblings or grandparents than others, some cope by confronting their problems, others by turning to creative outlets. These variations were apparent in a study of East Asian immigrants, most of whom entered the United States during middle childhood. They were asked what problems they encountered and how they coped. As you can see from Figure 13.5, social support was by far the dominant coping measure, but other specifics varied (Yeh & Inose, 2002).

For all school-age children, their expanding social world allows additional sources of social support, people who stand by the child despite adversity.

Grandmother Knows Best About 20,000 grandmothers in Connecticut are caregivers for their grandchildren. This 15-year-old boy and his 17-year-old sister came to live with their grandmother in New Haven after their mother died several years ago. This type of family works best when the grandmother is relatively young and has her own house, as is the case here.

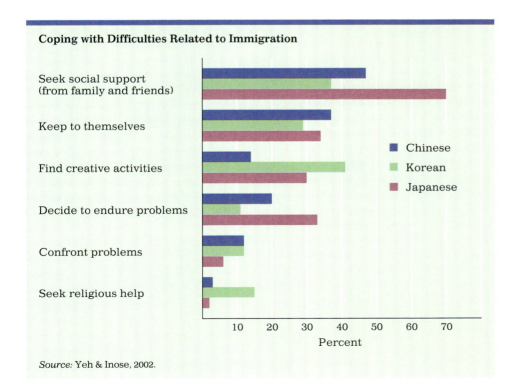

Coping with Difficulties Related to Immigration

- Seek social support (from family and friends)
- Keep to themselves
- Find creative activities
- Decide to endure problems
- Confront problems
- Seek religious help

■ Chinese
■ Korean
■ Japanese

Percent: 10 20 30 40 50 60 70

Source: Yeh & Inose, 2002.

FIGURE 13.5 Similar Cultures, Different Styles of Coping Unlike children who emigrate from Europe or Africa to the United States, immigrant Asian children are more likely to keep to themselves and endure their difficulties than to confront them. As this graph shows, immigrant children from China, Korea, and Japan, though all are from East Asian cultures, have unique patterns of coping.

Having a network of supportive family and friends is a much better buffer than having only one close person (Jackson & Warren, 2000). For example, a child whose parents are fighting bitterly on their way to divorce may spend hours on the phone with a friend whose parents have successfully separated, may often be invited to dinner at a neighbor's house where family harmony prevails, or may devote himself or herself to helping a teacher or a coach or to working with a community group. Grandparents, unrelated adults, peers, and even pets are often very helpful to children under stress in middle childhood (Borland et al., 1998).

Religious Faith and Coping

Religion can be a powerful aid to coping (Johnson et al., 2000), even though the religious convictions of children are very diverse (Richards et al., 2003). Especially for children in difficult circumstances, religious faith itself can be psychologically protective. Church involvement is particularly beneficial in African-American communities, where social stresses abound (Akiba & García-Coll, 2003). As one boy, living in one of the worst neighborhoods in the United States, wrote:

> No violence will there be in heaven. There will be no guns or drugs or IRS. You won't have to pay taxes. You'll recognize all the children who have died when they were little. Jesus will be good to them and play with them. At night he'll come and visit at your house. God will be fond of you.
>
> *[quoted in Kozol, 1991]*

School-age children develop their own theology, influenced by whatever formal religious education they receive and by cultural values. This personalized set of beliefs helps them structure life and deal with worldly problems (Hyde, 1990; Richards et al., 2003). An 8-year-old African-American girl who, in the 1960s, was one of the first to enter a previously all-white school remembers walking past a mob of adults yelling insults:

> I was alone, and those people were screaming, and suddenly I saw God smiling, and I smiled. A woman was standing there, and she shouted at me, "Hey you little nigger, what are you smiling at?" I looked right up at her face, and I said "At God." Then she looked up at the sky, and then she looked at me, and she didn't call me any more names.
>
> *[quoted in Coles, 1990]*

In a way, this example illustrates many aspects of children's coping abilities, for it was not only faith but also a measure of self-confidence, social understanding, and skill at deflecting her own emotional reactions that enabled this child to deal with a very real threat.

> Research on coping in middle childhood clearly suggests that as they grow older, most children develop ways to deal with all varieties of stress, from minor hassles to major traumatic events. We can summarize this section of the chapter with a quotation from two experts on resilience in childhood:
>
>> Successful children remind us that children grow up in multiple contexts— in families, schools, peer groups, baseball teams, religious organizations, and many other groups—and each context is a potential source of protective factors as well as risks. These children demonstrate that children are protected not only by the self-righting nature of development, but also by the actions of adults, by their own actions, by the nurturing of their assets, by opportunities to succeed, and by the experience of success. The behavior of adults often plays a critical role in children's risks, resources, opportunities, and resilience.
>>
>> *[Masten & Coatsworth, 1998, p. 216]*

As you will see in the next three chapters, adolescence is a continuation of middle childhood as well as a radical departure from it. Stresses and strains continue to accumulate, and "known risk factors," including drug availability and sexual urges, become more prevalent. Fortunately, for many young people protective resources and constructive coping also increase (Masten, 2001). Personal competencies, family support, and close friends get most children through childhood and adolescence undamaged. Indeed, the same factors help each of us throughout the life span, as we overcome the problems, and build on the strengths, that characterized the first decade of our lives.

SUMMARY

The Child's Emotions and Concerns

1. All theories of development acknowledge that school-age children become more independent and capable in many ways. In psychoanalytic theory, Freud described latency, when psychosexual needs are quiet; Erikson emphasized industry, when children are busy mastering various tasks. Behaviorism and cognitive theory stress the new skills that maturation and wider social opportunities afford.

2. Social cognitive theory combines these theories to describe how children begin to think more deeply about their social context and to act effectively within it. The sociocultural and epigenetic theories also describe an increase in independence in middle childhood.

3. The interplay of self-understanding and social perception is increasingly evident during the school years. Children figure out who they are partly by comparing themselves to others. Self-esteem tends to become more closely connected to specific competence.

The Peer Group

4. Peers are crucial. Social learning and social interaction are an important part of middle childhood. Friendships become increasingly close and influential. Usually friends provide needed companionship and allow development of social skills.

5. Rejected children may be neglected, aggressive, or withdrawn. All three types have difficulty interpreting the normal give-and-take of childhood. Rejection is usually temporary.

6. Bullies do obvious damage over the years to themselves and to their victims. In most nations, boys are often bullies and tend to use physical attacks. Girls are more likely to use relational aggression, involving social exclusion and rumor spreading, which can be very destructive.

Families and Children

7. Families influence children in many ways, as do genes and peers. The five functions of a supportive family are to satisfy children's physical needs; to encourage them to learn; to help them develop friends; to protect their self-esteem; and to provide them with a safe, stable, and harmonious home. Impoverished families find all five functions difficult to fulfill; poor children are at greater risk for emotional and behavioral problems. Parental warmth seems very helpful.

8. Family structures that are common today include nuclear, stepparent, blended, adoptive, one-parent, grandparent (either extended or grandparents alone), homosexual, and foster families. Generally, it seems better for children to have two parents rather than one, because a parental alliance can form.

9. No particular family structure guarantees good—or bad— child development. Any change in family structure, including divorce and remarriage, is likely to impede child development, at least for a few years, particularly reducing school achievement.

Coping with Problems

10. Although most experiece some stresses, school-age children tend to be resilient. Many cope well with major problems—learning disabilities, immigration, social rejection, families that are not supportive, poverty, violence.

11. In general, children benefit from social support (perhaps a best friend or a grandparent), from natural assets (intelligence, a winning personality, a special skill), and from personal strengths (religious faith, a stable early childhood). The innate drive toward competence and independence keeps most school-age children from being overwhelmed by problems.

KEY TERMS

latency (p. 313)
industry versus inferiority
  (p. 313)
social cognitive theory (p. 314)
social comparison (p. 316)
peer group (p. 317)

aggressive-rejected (p. 319)
withdrawn-rejected (p. 319)
bullying (p. 320)
bully-victim (p. 320)
family function (p. 325)
family structure (p. 326)

nuclear family (p. 327)
stepparent family (p. 327)
blended family (p. 327)
adoptive family (p. 327)
one-parent family (p. 327)
grandparent family (p. 327)

extended family (p. 327)
grandparents alone (p. 327)
homosexual family (p. 327)
foster family (p. 327)

APPLICATIONS

1. Go to a place where school-age children congregate, such as a schoolyard, a park, or a community center. Do naturalistic observation for at least half an hour. On the basis of your observations of their interactions, can you describe behavior that characterizes popular, average, withdrawn, and rejected children?

2. Some surveys of adults suggest that almost everyone remembers being bullied and doing some bullying when they were children. Focusing on verbal bullying, describe at least two times when someone said a hurtful thing to you and two times when you said something hurtful to someone else. Are there any differences between the two types of situations? If so, why do such differences occur?

3. It is a normal human tendency to think that one's childhood was pretty good; only about 20 percent of people remember their childhood as pretty bad. What would your childhood have been like if your family had been different in structure—for example, if you had (or had not) lived with your grandparents, if your parents had (or had not) gotten divorced, if you had (or had not) lived in a foster family. Describe how that structure would have been better *and worse* for your development than the family structure in which you actually grew up.

4. The chapter suggests that school-age children develop their own theology, distinct from the one their parents teach them. Interview a child, aged 6 to 12, asking what he or she thinks about God, sin, heaven, death, and any other religious topics you think relevant. Compare the child's responses with the formal doctrines of the religion to which his or her family belongs.

BIOSOCIAL

Growth and Skills During middle childhood, children grow more slowly than they did during infancy and toddlerhood or than they will during adolescence. Increased strength and lung capacity give children the endurance to improve their performance in skills such as swimming and running. Slower growth contributes to children's increasing bodily control, and children enjoy exercising their developing skills of coordination and balance. Which specific skills they master depends largely on culture, gender, and inherited ability.

Special Needs Many children have special learning needs that may originate in brain patterns but that express themselves in educational problems. Early recognition, targeted education, and psychological support help all children, from those with autism to the much milder instance of a specific learning disability or AD/HD.

COGNITIVE

Thinking During middle childhood, children become better able to understand and learn, in part because of growth in their processing capacity, knowledge base, and memory capacity. At the same time, metacognition techniques enable children to organize their learning. Beginning at about age 7 or 8, children also develop the ability to understand logical principles, including the concepts of identity, reciprocity, and reversibility.

Language Children's increasing ability to understand the structures and possibilities of language enables them to extend the range of their cognitive powers and to become more analytical in their use of vocabulary. Some children become bilingual.

Education Formal schooling begins worldwide, with the specifics of the curriculum depending on economic and societal factors. An individual child's learning success depends on the time allotted to each task, specific guided instruction from teachers and parents, and the overall values of the culture. Curricula and goals vary, and some variations are more crucial than others.

PSYCHOSOCIAL

Emotions and Personality Development School-age children come to understand themselves, as well as what is right in their relations with others. The peer group becomes increasingly important as children become less dependent on their parents and more dependent on friends for help, loyalty, and sharing of mutual interests. Rejection and bullying become serious problems.

Parents Parents continue to influence children, especially as they exacerbate or buffer problems in school and the community. During these years, families need to meet basic needs, encourage learning, develop self-esteem, nurture friendship, and—most important—provide harmony and stability. Most one-parent, foster, or grandparent families are better than families in open conflict, but a family with two biological parents, both of whom are cooperative with each other and loving to the child, is generally best. Fortunately, school-age children often develop competencies and attitudes to defend against the stress that most experience. Friends, family, school, and community can all be helpful.

Part V

Adolescence is the transition from childhood to adulthood. It is probably the most challenging and complicated period of life to describe, to study, or to experience. The biological changes that begin adolescence are universal, but their expression and timing show enormous variety, depending on gender, genes, and nutrition. Cognitive development varies as well: Many adolescents are egocentric, while others think logically, hypothetically, and theoretically. The third domain, psychosocial development, shows the greatest diversity of all. Adolescents seek their own identities—choosing from a vast number of sexual, moral, political, and educational paths. Most of this diversity simply reflects social and cultural contexts, with adolescents finding acceptable, albeit divergent, identities. But some adolescents—about one in four—make choices that put them on an ominous trajectory, handicapping and sometimes destroying their future.

Despite all the variations, there are some universals of the adolescent experience. All adolescents must adjust to their changing body size and shape, to their sexual awakening, and to new ways of thinking. They all strive for the emotional maturity and economic independence that characterize adulthood. As we will see in the next three chapters, efforts to come to grips with these challenges are often touched with confusion and poignancy—and, eventually, success.

Adolescence

Chapter Fourteen

Adolescence: Biosocial Development

During **adolescence,** humans everywhere cross a great divide between childhood and adulthood—biosocially, cognitively, and psychosocially. In this chapter, we outline the normative biological changes of adolescence—the rise in hormone levels, the new body shapes and sizes, the sexual maturation, and the timing and sequence of puberty. We then discuss variations, particularly in reactions to all these biological changes. One adolescent is adult size at age 12, another anxiously awaits the first signs of puberty at age 15; one is thrilled by the appearance of facial hair, another is horrified; one wolfs down a whole pizza, another slowly munches half a cracker. Some flaunt their sexuality, some hide it under baggy clothes. Some deal with their emotions and impulses by using alcohol and drugs.

These responses to puberty, including health hazards such as sex and drugs, are part of this chapter. We start at the beginning, when the body shifts away from childhood.

Puberty Begins

Puberty is the period of rapid physical growth and sexual maturation that ends childhood and begins adolescence, producing a person of adult size, shape, and sexual potential. The forces of puberty are unleashed by a cascade of hormones that bring on the numerous visible changes.

Although the age at which puberty begins varies by several years, the sequence is almost always the same (see Table 14.1). For girls, the visible changes include, in sequence, the onset of breast growth, initial pubic hair, peak growth spurt, widening of the hips, the first menstrual period (menarche), completion of pubic-hair growth, and final breast development. For boys, the visible physical changes of puberty include, in approximate order, growth of the testes, initial pubic hair, growth of the penis, the first ejaculation of seminal fluid (spermarche), peak growth spurt, voice deepening, beard development, and completion of pubic-hair growth (Biro et al., 2001; Herman-Giddens et al., 2001; Malina, 1990).

Typically, growth and maturation are complete three or four years after the first visible signs of puberty. Some individuals (more often late developers) gain an additional inch or two of height, and most (especially early developers) gain additional fat and muscle over the next decade. What starts the process?

adolescence The period of biological, cognitive, and psychosocial transition from childhood to adulthood, usually lasting a decade or so.

puberty A period of rapid growth and sexual change that occurs in early adolescence and produces a person of adult size, shape, and sexual potential.

TABLE 14.1 The Sequence of Puberty

Girls	Approximate Average Age*	Boys
Ovaries increase production of estrogen and progesterone†	9	
Uterus and vagina begin to grow larger	9½	Testes increase production of testosterone†
Breast "bud" stage	10	Testes and scrotum grow larger
Pubic hair begins to appear; weight spurt begins	11	
Peak height spurt	11½	Pubic hair begins to appear
Peak muscle and organ growth (also, hips become noticeably wider)	12	Penis growth begins
Menarche (first menstrual period)	12½	Spermarche (first ejaculation); weight spurt begins
First ovulation	13	Peak height spurt
Voice lowers	14	Peak muscle and organ growth (also, shoulders become noticeably broader)
Final pubic-hair pattern	15	Voice lowers; visible facial hair
Full breast growth	16	
	18	Final pubic-hair pattern

*Average ages are rough approximations, with many perfectly normal, healthy adolescents as much as three years ahead of or behind these ages.

†Estrogen, progesterone, and testosterone are hormones that influence sexual characteristics, including reproductive function. All three are also provided, in small amounts, by the adrenal glands in both sexes. Major production, however, occurs in the gonads, with marked male–female differences.

hypothalamus An area at the base of the brain that, in addition to regulating several maintenance activities (eating, drinking, and body temperature), directs the production of hormones via the pituitary gland.

pituitary gland A gland that, in response to a biochemical signal from the hypothalamus, produces hormones that regulate growth and control other glands, including the adrenal glands.

adrenal glands A pair of glands located above the kidneys that secrete the hormones epinephrine (adrenaline) and norepinephrine (noradrenaline), which help to arouse the body in time of stress.

HPA axis The hypothalamus/pituitary/adrenal axis, a route followed by many kinds of hormones to trigger the changes of puberty and to regulate stress, growth, sleep, appetite, sexual excitement, and various other bodily changes.

gonads The pair of sex glands in humans. In females, they are called the ovaries; in males, they are called testes or testicles.

estrogen A sex hormone, secreted in greater amounts by females than by males.

testosterone A sex hormone, secreted in greater amounts by males than by females.

Hormones

Hormones—dozens of them—affect every aspect of growth and development. The production of many hormones begins deep in the base of the brain, in an area called the **hypothalamus**. A biochemical signal from the hypothalamus is sent to the **pituitary gland**, located next to the hypothalamus. The pituitary produces hormones that stimulate the **adrenal glands** (two small glands located above the kidneys at either side of the torso), and the adrenal glands then produce more hormones. This route, which is called the **HPA axis** (hypothalamus/pituitary/adrenal axis), is taken by the many hormones that regulate stress, growth, sleep, appetite, sexual excitement, and various other changes. The HPA axis also leads to puberty, not only the growth spurt but also the development of sexual characteristics (see Figure 14.1).

In addition to stimulating the adrenal glands, the pituitary activates the **gonads**, or sex glands (the ovaries in females and the testes, or testicles, in males). The gonads are the first parts of the body to enlarge at puberty, in part because they must produce hormones as well as gametes (sperm and ova). In girls, the changes in the ovaries are invisible; in boys, the scrotum (the pouch that encases the testicles) increases in size and changes in color from red to pink.

One hormone in particular, GnRH (*gonadotropin-releasing hormone*), causes the gonads to dramatically increase their production of sex hormones, chiefly **estrogen** in girls and **testosterone** in boys. Although testosterone is considered the male hormone and estrogen the female hormone, both boys and girls produce increased amounts of estrogen and testosterone at puberty. However, the

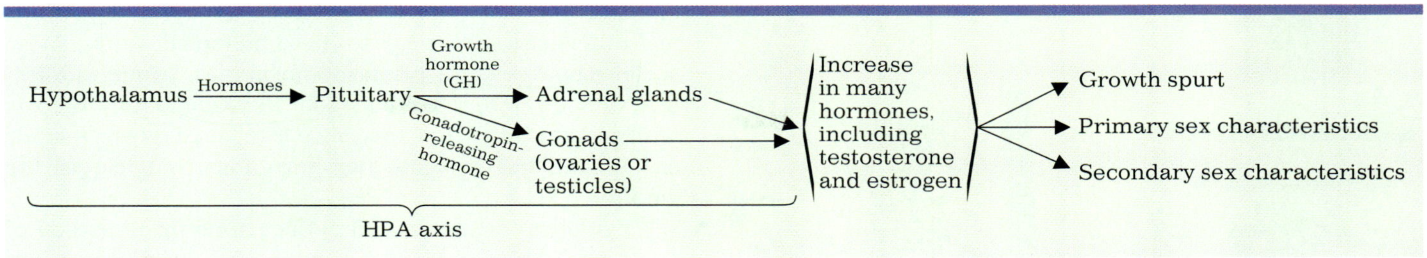

FIGURE 14.1 **Biological Sequence of Puberty** Puberty begins with a hormonal signal from the hypothalamus to the pituitary gland. The pituitary, in turn, signals the adrenal glands and the ovaries or testes to produce more of their hormones.

rate of increase is sex-specific: Testosterone production skyrockets in boys, up to 18 times the level in childhood, but increases much less in girls. Estrogen production increases up to 8 times in girls but not nearly as much in boys (Malina & Bouchard, 1991).

Direct Effects on Emotions

The connection between hormones and emotions is complex. Evidence suggests that conflict, moodiness, and sexual urges rise during adolescence (Arnett, 1999a). Hormones are part of the explanation (Susman, 1997; Weisfeld, 1999). To be specific:

- Rapidly increasing hormone levels, especially of testosterone, precede rapid arousal of emotions.
- Hormone levels correlate with quick shifts in emotional extremes—from feeling great to feeling awful.
- For boys, hormonal increases precipitate thoughts about sex, as well as masturbation. (Such thoughts seem more loosely tied to hormone levels in adolescent girls.)
- For girls, changes in hormone levels during the menstrual cycle produce mood changes, from happiness at mid-cycle to sadness or anger a day or two before the menstrual period starts.

Although these hormonal effects are lifelong, they are more erratic and powerful, and less familiar and controllable, in the years right after puberty begins (Susman, 1997).

Indirect Effects on Emotions

Detailed studies suggest that hormone levels make a relatively small *direct* contribution to the daily emotional outbursts of puberty—that is, to the conflicts, moods, and sexual urges. Hormonal influence on the overall emotional tone of adolescence (both positive and negative) is primarily *indirect*, via the psychological impact of the visible changes. That is, emotions accompany the obvious body changes, and yet "by the time physical characteristics indicate the beginning of this transitional period, puberty, as assessed by hormonal measurements . . . is well under way" (Reiter & Lee, 2001).

In other words, it *is* true that hormones *directly* cause moods and emotions to change more quickly than in childhood or adulthood. Hormones *directly* make adolescents seek sexual activity, which also makes them emotional, aroused, and frustrated. However, hormones have their greatest impact *indirectly*, by producing visible signs of sexual maturation, such as breasts and beards and the adult shape

Especially for Parents of Teenagers Why would parents blame adolescent moods on hormones?

MIKE KING / AP PHOTO

That's What Friends Are For Jennifer's preparations for her prom include pedicure and hairstyle courtesy of her good friends Khushbu and Meredith. In every generation and society the world over, teenagers help their same-sex friends prepare for the display rituals involved in coming of age, but a senior prom in Florida in 2002 would have been unimaginable to the grandmothers of these three girls.

and size that make onlookers expect new maturity. Adults and other teenagers react to these biological signs. These social responses, not primarily hormones, trigger adolescent moods and reactions. The 13-year-old girl who is whistled at is likely to experience a surge of anger, fear, or excitement, but it is not her hormones that trigger the emotion.

Evidence for this indirect effect came from a study of adolescents who showed no signs of puberty two years after the usual age of onset (Schwab et al., 2001). Doctors prescribed 24 months of treatment, alternating 3 months of testosterone or estrogen with 3 months of a placebo (a look-alike pill that the participants did not know was chemically inert). The researchers found few psychological effects that could be attributed to the relatively high or low levels of hormones in the bloodstream—although the increased physical development that had occurred by the end of the study had a positive effect on the teenage participants' moods.

An understanding that the role of hormones is primarily an indirect one makes it apparent that the effects of the sociocultural context are dramatic. Even the one change that is most directly linked to hormone levels—thinking about sex—is powerfully affected by culture, which shapes sexual thoughts into enjoyable fantasies, shameful preoccupations, frightening impulses, or goads to action.

Reactions to sexual urges are different for boys and girls, but this difference is primarily cultural, not biological, in origin (Martin, 1996). In the United States, sexual activity levels are quite similar for boys and girls at various ages, with about one-fourth of both sexes having had sexual intercourse by about age 14, half by age 17, and 90 percent by age 21 (Hogan et al., 2000; Santelli et al., 2000). The same is true in the Netherlands. Other nations have a discrepancy between the sexes: In Finland and Norway, girls tend to become sexually experienced earlier than boys do; in Greece and Portugal, the average age at first intercourse is 17 for girls and 19 for boys (Teitler, 2002).

The Timing of Puberty

Hormones cascading into the bloodstream via the HPA axis always begin puberty, and the sequence of changes is the same, but the age of puberty is highly variable. Normal children begin to notice body changes between the ages of 8 and 14. This range adds to the difficulties of puberty: It is hard to prepare properly without knowing what will occur and when. Fortunately, some prediction is possible, through the assessment of four factors: sex, genes, body fat, and stress.

Sex, Genes, and Weight

Sex differences in timing are easy to notice. Girls begin puberty ahead of boys; many seventh-grade girls are several inches taller than their male classmates. By age 10, one or two girls in a class have already developed visible breasts and begun to grow to woman-height; not until about age 17 has the last boy in the class sprouted facial hair and attained man-height. These are the extremes, but even the average girl seems to be about two years ahead of the average boy.

However, look closely at Table 14.1. Sex differences are not as great as they might seem at first glance, because height is deceptive. The maximum height spurt occurs about midway in a girl's pubescence but is one of the later events for boys (Reiter & Lee, 2001). One-third of all boys in the United States already show some genital changes at age 9 (Herman-Giddens et al., 2001); hormonally, boys are only half a year behind the girls.

As for genes, most of the research on the genetics of puberty looks at girls, not boys. That is primarily because **menarche**, the first menstrual period, is easier to date than **spermarche**, when a boy first produces live sperm. Menarche normally occurs between ages 9 and 15, with age 12 the average (Biro et al., 2001). Genes are a powerful reason for that variation. A daughter's age of menarche is related to her mother's age of menarche, which occurred under quite different historical and familial circumstances (Golub, 1992). Other pubertal changes, for boys as well as for girls, also follow genetic patterns (Brooks-Gunn, 1991).

A third major influence on the age of puberty is body fat. In general, stocky individuals experience puberty earlier than do those with taller, thinner builds. The onset of puberty correlates with weight in both sexes, although this correlation is more obvious in girls (Vizmanos & Marti-Henneberg, 2000). Menarche does not usually occur until a girl weighs about 100 pounds (45–48 kilograms) (Berkley et al., 2000). Females who have little body fat (either because they are severely malnourished or because they are serious athletes) menstruate later and less regularly than the average girl.

For both sexes, chronic malnutrition limits fat and therefore delays puberty by several years. For this reason, in many nations, puberty often begins years earlier now than it once did. Reliable historical data on many populations are not available, but it is certain that puberty occurred as late as age 17 in Europe from about the sixteenth to the eighteenth century (Tanner, 1978).

Stress in Families

The fourth, recently recognized, influence on the age of puberty is family stress. For some years biochemists have noticed that, throughout life, stress levels affect the production of hormones (Sanchez et al., 2001), the most obvious effects being on the sexual-reproductive system. Stress causes irregular menstruation in some young women when they go away to college or travel to distant lands, stress decreases viable sperm and mature ova in adults, and stress can trigger spontaneous abortions or premature births (Veldhuis et al., 1997).

Logically, stress probably affects the hormones that cause puberty (Belsky et al., 1991; Ellis & Garber, 2000; Kim & Smith, 1998; Wierson et al., 1993). Suggestive evidence comes from many nations: Girls in New Zealand whose parents are divorced experience puberty earlier than do girls of married parents (Moffitt et al., 1992); girls from India adopted by Swedish parents reach menarche earlier than girls in India or than Swedish girls raised by their biological parents (Proos et al., 1991); Polish teenagers of both sexes who live in crowded cities mature earlier than their rural contemporaries (Hulanicka, 1999); boys in the United States in 2000 began puberty about a year earlier than boys did in the 1960s (Herman-Giddens et al., 2001). Stress could be the common cause of all these differences.

The stress hypothesis gathered further support from a study that, controlling for nutrition, ethnicity, and genes, found two factors that influenced early puberty: (1) conflicted relationships within the family and (2) an unrelated man (stepfather or mother's boyfriend) living in the home (Ellis & Garber, 2000). The longer a woman had lived with a man who was not her daughter's father, the earlier the girl's puberty tended to be.

Research on lower animals also implicates stress. Stressed mice, rats, and opossums experience puberty, pregnancy, and death earlier than their genetic relatives who are less stressed (Warshofsky, 1999), and infant female mice reach puberty earlier if they are exposed to unrelated adult male mice (Caretta et al., 1995).

menarche A female's first menstrual period.

spermarche A male's first ejaculation of live sperm, whether through masturbation, a wet dream, or sexual contact with another person.

Response for Parents of Teenagers (from page 343): If something causes adolescents to shout "I hate you," to slam the door, or to cry uncontrollably, parents may decide that hormones are the problem. This makes it easy to disclaim personal responsibility for the anger. However, evidence on stress and hormones suggests that this comforting attribution is too simplistic.

Why would stress trigger the hormones that start puberty?

> Over the course of our natural selective history, ancestral females growing up in adverse family environments may have reliably increased their reproductive success by accelerating physical maturation and beginning sexual activity and reproduction at a relatively early age.
>
> *[Ellis & Garber, 2000, p. 486]*

(As already noted, research on age of male puberty is less precise; presumably, however, the same stress factors affect males.) In other words, by becoming mature and having babies before age 18, teenagers in stressful times were likely to replace themselves before they died. Although from the perspective of society today, it might be better if puberty did not occur until later, a combination of improved nutrition and ancient genetic factors connected to increased stress may result in the hypothalamus triggering puberty earlier.

Too Early or Too Late

Few adolescents care if they reach puberty earlier than their parents or remote ancestors did. However, every adolescent wants to experience puberty "on time," not much earlier or later than their friends. Off-time puberty may be a particular problem for early girls and late boys, who are off schedule compared to the other sex as well as their own (Downs, 1990; Graber et al., 1994).

Think about the early-maturing girl. If she has visible breasts in the fifth grade, boys tease her; they are awed by the sexual creature in their midst. She must fit her womanly body into a school chair designed for younger children, and she may try to disguise her breasts in large T-shirts. Early-maturing girls tend to have lower self-esteem, more depression, and poorer body image than other girls (Siegel et al., 1999).

As a remedy for their low self-esteem, many early-maturing girls turn to romantic involvement. Older boys and young men find these girls, with their combination of innocence and physical development, attractive. Girls in these relationships may drink alcohol, smoke cigarettes, and become sexually active before girls typically do (Brooks-Gunn, 1991). They are "isolated from their on-time-maturing peers (and) tend to associate with older adolescents. This increases their emotional distress" (Ge et al., 2003, p. 437).

In general, late-maturing boys are not as troubled as early-maturing girls. Although the tenth-grade boy who is still short and skinny may be shunned by the girls, the timing of puberty is not so crucial for boys as for girls (Ge et al., 2003). If late-maturing boys are in a school and culture that value intellectual accomplishments, and they themselves are academically inclined, they may be especially likely to excel at schoolwork, go on to college, and eventually succeed at careers that suit their talents (Downs, 1990).

Now we look specifically at what adolescent growth and maturation entail.

BOB DAEMMRICH / STOCK, BOSTON

An Awkward Age The normal variation in age of puberty is readily apparent in this junior high gym class in Texas.

? *Observational Quiz* (see answer, page 348): What three signs can you see that the boy in the foreground wants to be taller and the girl beside him wishes she were less conspicuous?

The Growth Spurt

Hormones trigger growth as well as sexual changes. In late childhood and early adolescence, a major **growth spurt** occurs—a sudden, uneven, and somewhat unpredictable jump in the size of almost every part of the body.

growth spurt The period of relatively sudden and rapid physical growth of every part of the body that occurs during puberty.

Growth proceeds from the extremities to the core (the opposite of the prenatal and infant growth spurts): The fingers and toes lengthen before the hands and feet, the hands and feet before the arms and legs, and the arms and legs before the torso. Because the torso is the last part of the body to grow, many pubescent children are temporarily big-footed, long-legged, and short-waisted, appearing to be "all legs and arms" (Hofmann, 1997).

Wider, Taller, Then Stronger

While the bones lengthen, the child eats more and gains weight, to provide energy for the many changes taking place. As a result, fat accumulates. In fact, parents typically notice that their children are cleaning their plates, emptying the refrigerator, and straining the seams of their clothes even before they notice that their children are growing taller.

By the end of middle childhood, usually between the ages of 10 and 12, all children become noticeably heavier. Exactly when, where, and how much fat accumulates depends partly on heredity, partly on diet and exercise, and partly on sex. Females gain more fat overall, so that eventually about one-fourth of their body weight is fat, almost double the average for males (Daniluk, 1998). Sex differences in body fat are especially notable on the legs and hips, because evolution favored young adult females who had extra body fat to sustain pregnancy and lactation and favored young adult males who moved swiftly in the hunt.

A height spurt follows, burning up some of the stored fat and redistributing some of the rest. About a year or two after that, a period of muscle increase occurs (Hofmann, 1997). As a consequence, the pudginess and clumsiness typical of early puberty generally disappear a few years later. Overall, boys increase in muscle strength by at least 150 percent (Armstrong & Welsman, 1997). This is particularly noticeable in their upper bodies. Between ages 13 and 18, male arm strength more than doubles (Beunen et al., 1988).

Other Body Changes

While the torso grows, internal organs also grow. Over the course of adolescence, the lungs increase in size and capacity, actually tripling in weight. Consequently, the adolescent breathes more deeply and slowly than a child (a 10-year-old breathes about 22 times a minute, while an 18-year-old breathes about 18 times). The heart doubles in size and the heart rate decreases, slowing from an average of 92 beats per minute at age 10 to 82 at age 18. In addition, the total volume of blood increases (Malina & Bouchard, 1991). One organ system, the *lymphoid system*, which includes the tonsils and adenoids, *decreases* in size at adolescence, making teenagers less susceptible to respiratory ailments. Mild asthma, for example, often switches off at puberty (Clark & Rees, 1996).

These changes in the lungs and the heart increase physical endurance. Many teenagers can run for miles or dance for hours without stopping to rest. Note, however, that the more visible spurts of weight and height occur before the less visible spurts of muscles and internal organs. This means that athletic training and weight lifting for an adolescent should be designed to match the young person's size of a year or so earlier (Murphy, 1999). Sports injuries are the most common school accidents, resulting from poor judgment on the part of coaches and parents and from the aspirations and actions of the young people themselves (Patel & Luckstead, 2000).

The hormones that trigger puberty also affect the circadian rhythm, the diurnal (daily) cycles whereby the body responds

Does He Like What He Sees? During adolescence, all the facial features do not develop at the same rate, and the hair often becomes less manageable. If B. T. here is typical, he is not pleased with the appearance of his nose, lips, ears, or hair.

!Answer to Observational Quiz (from page 346): He is on his tip-toes, his arms stretch their longest, and even his hairstyle adds an inch or two. The girl beside him has her feet flat and wide apart, her T-shirt big and loose, and her hair as short and unfeminine as she can make it. If you noticed that his No. 23 Bulls shirt is Michael Jordan's number, give yourself extra credit.

to day and night. Because of hormonal shifts and increases (especially in the growth hormones), many teenagers crave sleep in the mornings and are wide awake at night, when their parents are conveniently asleep (Greydanus, 1997b; Wolfson & Carskadon, 1998).

Unfortunately, today's school schedules are holdovers from earlier times: In 1900, 90 percent of North American children lived on farms and many woke up at dawn to milk the cows, got home in time to feed the animals before dark, and spent their summers as field laborers. As a result, millions of teenagers today are challenged by calculus and chemistry at 8:00 A.M. and are bored by three months of summer vacation (Barber et al., 1998).

Finally, the hormones of puberty cause many relatively minor physical changes that, while insignificant in the grand scheme, have substantial psychic impact. For instance, the oil, sweat, and odor glands of the skin become much more active. One result is acne, which occurs to some degree in about 90 percent of boys and 80 percent of girls (Greydanus, 1997a). Another result is oilier hair and smellier bodies, which is one reason adolescents spend more money on shampoo and deodorants than does any other age group. The eyes also undergo a change: The eyeballs elongate, making many teenagers sufficiently nearsighted to require corrective lenses. All told, no part of the older adolescent's body functions or appears quite the same as it once did.

Sexual Maturation

Even more revolutionary than the growth spurt is a set of changes that transform boys into men and girls into women. Not only do young people look sexually mature, but they become capable of reproduction.

Primary Sex Characteristics

primary sex characteristics The sex organs—those parts of the body that are directly involved in reproduction, including the vagina, uterus, ovaries, testicles, and penis.

The **primary sex characteristics** are those parts of the body that are directly involved in conception and pregnancy. During puberty, every primary sex organ becomes much larger. In girls, the ovaries and the uterus grow and the vaginal lining thickens even before any outward signs of puberty appear. In boys, the testes grow and, about a year later, the penis lengthens and the scrotum enlarges and becomes pendulous.

A Woman at 15 Dulce Giovanna Mendez dances at her Quinceañera, the traditional fifteenth-birthday celebration of a Hispanic girl's sexual maturity. Dulce lives in Ures, Mexico, where many older teenagers marry and have children. This was the expected outcome of puberty in earlier decades in the United States as well.

JOANNA B. PINNEO / AURORA PHOTOS

Menarche is usually taken to indicate sexual maturity and fertility in girls, although the first ovulation usually does not occur until several months later. For boys, the comparable indicator is spermarche, which may occur during sleep in a nocturnal emission (a "wet dream"), through self-stimulation with masturbation, or through sexual touch by another person, with or without intercourse. Neither menarche nor spermarche indicates that a person is biologically ready for parenthood, but both signify that reproductive maturity is only a few months away. (Psychic readiness ususally comes many years in the future.)

Secondary Sex Characteristics

Along with maturation of the reproductive organs (primary sex characteristics) come changes in **secondary sex characteristics**, which are bodily characteristics that signify sexual development although they do not directly affect fertility. One obvious example is body shape, which is virtually unisex in childhood but differentiates at puberty. Males grow taller than females (by 5 inches, on average) and become wider at the shoulders (because prehistorically they needed to do the heavy lifting, carrying, and throwing). Girls become wider below the waist, to prepare for pregnancy, and develop breasts, to prepare for lactation. Breasts and hips are often considered badges of sexuality, but neither affects fertility and thus neither is a primary sex characteristic.

For most girls, the first sign of puberty is the "bud" stage of breast growth, when a small accumulation of fat causes a slight rise around the nipples. From then on, breasts develop gradually, with full breast growth reached when almost all the other changes of puberty are completed (Malina, 1990). In boys as well as girls the diameter of the areola (the dark area around the nipple) increases during puberty. To their consternation, about 65 percent of all adolescent boys experience some breast enlargement (typically in mid-puberty) (Behrman, 1992). However, their worry is usually short-lived, because this enlargement normally disappears by age 16.

Another secondary sex characteristic is the voice, which becomes lower as the lungs and larynx grow. This change occurs in both sexes but is most noticeable in boys. (Even more noticeable, to the chagrin of the young adolescent male, is an occasional loss of voice control that throws his newly acquired baritone into a high squeak.) The "Adam's apple," the visible lump in the throat, also becomes more prominent in boys, which is why it is named for Adam, not Eve. Although few people are conscious of the connection between sexual maturity and voice, many consider a low voice "manly" and a throaty female voice "sexy."

During puberty, girls and boys both notice that existing hair on the head, arms, and legs becomes coarser and darker, and new hair grows under the arms, on the face, and in the groin area. Visible facial hair and body hair are sometimes considered signs of manliness. This notion is mistaken; how often a man needs to shave, or how hairy his chest is, is a matter of genes, not virility. The variation in the prominence of girls' facial and body hair similarly reflects genes, not femininity.

> To review, the process of puberty usually begins between the ages of 8 and 14 with a hormonal trigger deep within the brain, from the hypothalamus to the pituitary to the adrenal glands and the gonads. Various factors, including genes, body fat, and probably family stress, interact to determine when that hormonal cascade begins. Hormones affect the emotions as well as the physique, but most effects on the emotions are indirect: People notice developing breasts or increasing girth and respond to those changes; teenagers then react in kind.
>
> Once the process begins, the sequence is almost always the same. For girls, it begins with primary sex characteristics (growth of internal sex organs)

CLEVE BRYANT / PHOTOEDIT

Male Pride Teenage boys typically feel serious pride when they first need to shave. Although facial hair is taken as a sign of masculinity, a person's hairiness is actually genetic as well as hormonal. Further evidence that the Western world's traditional racial categories have no genetic basis comes from East Asia: Many Chinese men cannot grow beards or mustaches, but most Japanese men can.

secondary sex characteristics Body characteristics that are not directly involved in reproduction but that indicate sexual maturity, such as a man's beard or a woman's breasts.

and then secondary sex characteristics (pubic hair, breast buds). The growth spurt and, finally, menarche complete puberty in girls. For boys, primary sex characteristics (including growth of the testes and penis and then spermarche) precede the growth spurt. Although the two sexes obviously diverge at puberty, for both boys and girls, puberty is quite rapid and unsettling. The entire body is transformed from boy to man or girl to woman.

Hazards to Health

Twisted Memorial This wreck was once a Volvo, driven by a Colorado teenager who ignored an oncoming train's whistle at a rural crossing. The car was hurled 167 feet and burst into flames. The impact instantly killed the driver and five teenage passengers. They are among the statistics indicating that accidents (many of which result from unwise risk taking) kill 10 times more adolescents than diseases do.

Adolescence is a healthy time. The minor illnesses of childhood (including flu, colds, earaches, and childhood diseases of all sorts) become much less common, because inoculations, bouts of illness, and years of exposure have increased immunity. The major diseases of adulthood are rare.

Although diseases generally do not attack teenagers, and the many biological changes of puberty are life-enhancing, not life-threatening, injury and even death sometimes result from teenagers' own actions. The average annual death rate for teenagers aged 15 to 19 is five times that of children aged 5 to 9, a disproportion found in almost every cohort and culture. Rates of violent death and serious injury escalate from about age 10 until a peak at age 25. The peak in young adulthood is foreshadowed by destructive health habits that begin in adolescence. To be specific, few teenagers eat as well as they should, many take sexual risks, and almost all experiment with drugs that interfere with healthy development and that can handicap their future. We now discuss these three hazards in detail.

Poor Nutrition

The rapid bodily changes of puberty require fuel in the form of additional calories as well as additional vitamins and minerals. In fact, the recommended daily intake of calories is higher for an active adolescent than for anyone else; the greatest calorie requirement occurs at about age 14 for girls and 17 for boys (Malina & Bouchard, 1991). During the growth spurt, the need for calcium, iron, and zinc (for both bone and muscle development) is about 50 percent greater than it was only two years earlier.

These requirements are physiological; every adolescent needs more calories, vitamins, and minerals than a child does. In recent years, many adolescents have become fat and flabby, not because they are eating too much (they are consuming the same totals as before) but because they are exercising too little (Sutherland, 2003) and eating the wrong foods. Most teenagers snack on their own, eat fast food with peers, and rarely have breakfast, lunch, and dinner at home. As a result, they consume too much salt, sugar, and fat and not enough calcium or iron.

A Thousand Hamburgers per Person per Year Some teenagers easily reach the thousand mark, wolfing down three burgers a day in after-school or midnight snacks—or even breakfast at noon. This Charlotte, North Carolina, basketball star knows that he should avoid high-fat foods and fill up on whole grains, fresh fruits, and various vegetables. However, for him and for most other teenagers, knowledge does not change habits.

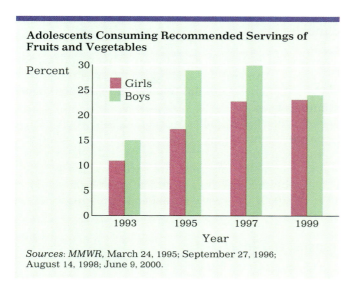

Adolescents Consuming Recommended Servings of Fruits and Vegetables

Sources: *MMWR*, March 24, 1995; September 27, 1996; August 14, 1998; June 9, 2000.

FIGURE 14.2 Five or More a Day Nutritionists recommend that everyone eat at least five portions of fruits and vegetables a day—and more would be better. Less than one-third of high school seniors reach this minimum. Perhaps surprisingly, younger adolescents do better on this measure than high school seniors do.

Only one in five U.S. high school seniors consumes the recommended five servings of fruits and vegetables a day (see Figure 14.2). This bodes ill for the future, since an adequate diet protects against the two leading killers of adults—heart disease and cancer. Even fewer high school seniors (9 percent of girls and 19 percent of boys) drink three glasses of milk a day, a dramatic decline from several decades ago, when most adolescents drank a quart or more of milk a day. This is even a cutback from the usual consumption in ninth grade, when 13 percent of girls and 25 percent of boys drink at least three glasses of milk each day (CDC, June 28, 2002).

Inadequate milk consumption is particularly troubling because calcium, which milk provides, is a major contributor to bone growth and about half of adult bone mass is acquired during adolescence. Insufficient bone mass increases the risk of osteoporosis, a leading cause of disability, injury, and even death among older women. By choosing carbonated soft drinks over milk, today's teens endanger their bones, their teeth, and the rest of their bodies (Harnack et al., 1999).

Fewer than half of all teenagers consume the recommended daily dose of 15 milligrams of iron, a nutrient that is present mainly in green vegetables, eggs, and meat. Because each menstrual period depletes the body of some iron, females between the ages of 15 and 17 are more likely to suffer from iron-deficiency anemia (low blood hemoglobin) than any other subgroup of the population (Baynes & Bothwell, 1990). This means, for example, that if a teenage girl seems apathetic and lazy, she should have her hemoglobin checked before her behavior is attributed to a poor attitude or psychological difficulties.

Nutritional deficits sometimes arise from distorted self-perception. Problems with *body image*—that is, a person's idea of how his or her body looks—are common in adolescence. Almost never is a teenage girl satisfied with her body (Ohring et al., 2002), and many boys think they look too weak. For girls especially, problems with body image can lead to nutritional deprivation and even to life-threatening diseases, such as anorexia and bulimia nervosa, both described in Chapter 17. For boys, problems with body image can be a factor leading to drug use, which we'll discuss soon. First, however, consider how sexual maturation itself can jeopardize health.

Sexual Messages This teen couple is aware that everyone who lifts weights should have a spotter, to prevent accidents. They also seem to be acutely body-conscious and to be using the occasion to exchange messages through their eye contact, facial expressions, and clothing.

MICHAEL NEWMAN / PHOTOEDIT

Sex Too Soon

Adolescents, like every other sexually mature creature, have a genetic urge to mate and reproduce. Over the millennia, this urge has made possible the survival of the human species. Although for humans in the twenty-first century population explosion is a bigger threat than population extinction, genes continue to make adolescents seek sex.

In the United States today, puberty occurs considerably earlier than it used to and marriage considerably later. There is thus a long period of time between adolescents' first sexual urges and their first formal relationship. Significantly, more than one-fourth of all adolescents are sexually active by age 14, and about one-half are active by the time they graduate from high school (Hogan et al., 2000; Santelli et al., 2000). This early sexual activity increases the risk of several hazards to health.

Sexually Transmitted Infections

sexually transmitted infection (STI) An infection spread by sexual contact, including syphilis, gonorrhea, herpes, chlamydia, and HIV.

Sexually active teenagers have higher rates of *gonorrhea, genital herpes, syphilis,* and *chlamydia*—the most common **sexually transmitted infections (STIs)**—than any other age group (CDC, 2000). Because a smaller portion of teens are sexually active, the absolute rates of these STIs are actually higher among 20- to 24-year-olds (Panchaud et al., 2000). Nevertheless, STIs are dangerous in adolescence, because many teens do not get adequate medical care. Few STIs are serious if promptly treated, but untreated STIs can cause lifelong sterility and life-threatening complications. Sexually active adolescents also risk exposure to the HIV virus, a risk that increases if a person:

- Is already infected with other STIs
- Has more than one partner within a year
- Does not use condoms during intercourse

All three of these conditions are common among teenagers and their sex partners (who are often unmarried young adults), making them the most likely to catch the virus, which causes the deadly disease AIDS.

Especially for Young Adults Suppose your parents never talked to you about sex or puberty. Was that a mistake?

To be specific, recent data from thousands of students throughout the United States reveal that, by their senior year of high school, 22 percent have already had four or more sexual partners and only half (more younger than older teens) used a condom at last intercourse (CDC, June 28, 2002). Similar results emerged from an intensive longitudinal study, which found that sexually transmitted infections are most likely in high school and yet condom use drops with every year of sexual experience among adolescents (Capaldi et al., 2002).

The younger people are when they contract an STI, the more reluctant they are to seek treatment and to alert their sexual partners. Not only do they feel ashamed and afraid, but also many young adolescents do not recognize the symptoms or know where to find inexpensive, confidential, and respectful medical treatment. As a result, their reinfection rate is higher than that of older people (Xu et al., 2000).

Teenage Pregnancy

Another developmental risk for sexually active adolescents is pregnancy. Unintentional pregnancy causes two distinct sets of problems, one for teens under age 16 and the other for all teens.

If a girl becomes pregnant within a year or two of menarche, she is at increased risk of almost every complication of pregnancy and birth—including spontaneous abortion, high blood pressure, stillbirth, cesarean section, and a low-birthweight baby—all because her uterus and overall body functioning are not yet mature (Phipps & Sowers, 2002).

Moreover, throughout puberty, the body must adjust to new hormones, add bone density, redistribute weight, and grow taller. Pregnancy interferes with this, because the girl's body must respond to another set of hormones and to the nutritional needs of another developing person. Women who have given birth under age 16 tend to be shorter and sicker as adults, and to die at younger ages, than other women. Part of the explanation is actually socioeconomic, not biological: Pregnancy occurs more often among low-income teenagers, who tend to have health problems even if they do not become pregnant. However, the sheer biological burden of pregnancy, imposed on the body before it is ready, adds to the toll poverty takes.

Because older teenagers are fully grown, pregnancy and birth complications are no more common from ages 16 to 19 than they are from age 20 up (Phipps & Sowers, 2002); nor are there direct physiological consequences in adulthood. However, other problems still abound. One reason is that 80 percent of teenage mothers in the United States are not married. The biological father is less likely to be supportive, making the pregnancy itself a greater strain.

In addition, teenage motherhood slows educational achievement and restricts personal growth. No matter what a teenager's family situation, personal income, or intellectual capacity is, becoming a mother reduces academic achievement by three years on average (Klepinger et al., 1995). It also reduces her chances of employment and marriage. To make matters worse, if a pregnant teenager marries, she is more likely to be abused, abandoned, or divorced by her husband than a nonpregnant teenage bride is.

These conclusions are based on the experiences of women in the United States, but a recent study of all women born in Sweden between 1941 and 1970 found the same long-term consequences. This study included 140,000 teen mothers. Lifetime income and employment figures for teenage mothers were worse than those for older mothers, with the youngest mothers faring the worst of all (Olausson et al., 2001). Other research finds that health hazards from pregnancy increase as education, employment, and income fall (Adler & Snibbe, 2003), so even among older teens motherhood is, indirectly, a health hazard.

The likely consequences for the child are even more troublesome. Babies of young teenagers have more prenatal and birth complications, including brain damage as well as low birthweight. As they develop, children who were born to adolescents experience more mistreatment of all kinds and less educational success of any kind. They are more likely to become drug abusers, delinquents, dropouts, and—against their mothers' advice—parents themselves (Borkowski et al., 2002; Fergusson & Woodward, 1999; Jaffee et al., 2001). Some of these problems are related to low socioeconomic status, as both a cause and a consequence of teen pregnancy (Turley, 2003). But adolescent pregnancy itself creates problems, especially if the mother is not married.

These problems of pregnancy among older teens are linked to culture and cohort, not biology. In the past, to be 17 years old and having a baby was ideal not only for the society but also for the young woman, who usually had a husband a few years older with a steady job and no need for college. Even today in some nations—Burma, Bangladesh, and Yemen among them—virtually no young women and only about 5 percent of all young men are enrolled in higher education of any kind, so early marriage and parenthood are desirable. The teen birth rate in those nations is more than four times that of Japan, Canada, or Western Europe, where staying in school until at least age 21 is the norm. In these latter nations, first-time parenthood at age 30 is not considered too late, but motherhood at age 17 is a lifetime handicap. Remember, however, that the social context, not the physiological strain, creates this handicap. To blame the 17-year-old mother for having unprotected sex or for not choosing to terminate the pregnancy is to blame the victim, not the true cause.

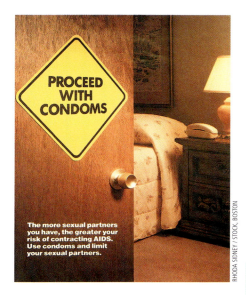

Better Protection For decades, sex educators have bemoaned the fact that teenage girls have been considered solely responsible for practicing birth control. However, as this poster suggests, the AIDS epidemic has changed advertising and individual practice, with clear results. Almost half of all sexually active boys use condoms regularly, and the rate of teen pregnancy—though still relatively high in the United States—has been decreasing since 1990.

Perhaps as a result of wider recognition of the difficulties associated with teen pregnancies, the teen birth rate has fallen in every nation of the world since 1990. Even so, the U.S. rate (about one birth per twenty 15- to 19-year-old women per year) is still five times higher than that of Japan or any European nation and more than twice that of Great Britain, Canada, Australia, or New Zealand (Teitler, 2002; U.S. Bureau of the Census, 2002).

Sexual Abuse

sexual abuse The use of an unconsenting person for one's own sexual pleasure. Sexual activity is abusive whenever it is not mutual, whenever consent is not freely given, or whenever a person does not understand or feels obligated to agree to a sexual encounter.

child sexual abuse Any activity in which an adult uses a child for his or her own sexual stimulation or pleasure—even if the use does not involve physical contact. Child pornography, fondling, and lewd comments by strangers are all examples of child sexual abuse.

Sexual abuse is defined as the use of an unconsenting person for one's own sexual pleasure. Accordingly, sexual activity is abusive whenever it is not mutual or whenever consent is not freely given.

Free consent is considered impossible for children or young adolescents to give. They have little understanding of the implications of sexual activity, and they are physically weaker than their elders and psychologically dependent on them. Accordingly, **child sexual abuse** is defined as any erotic activity that arouses an adult and excites, shames, or confuses a person under age 16, whether or not the victim protests and whether or not genital contact is involved. Thus, sexual abuse may consist of sexualized teasing, taking erotic photographs, asking intrusive questions about the child's body, or—especially once puberty begins—invading the privacy of the child's bathing, dressing, or sleeping routines.

As with other forms of maltreatment (see Chapter 8), the harm done by sexual abuse increases if it is repeated, if it distorts the adult–child relationship, if it is coercive, or if it impairs the child's relationships with peers (Haugaard, 2000; Stevenson, 1999). Ongoing sexual abuse by a parent is particularly harmful, damaging a person's lifelong ability to establish a trusting, comfortable, and intimate relationship. Parents are the perpetrators in more than half of all cases of child sexual abuse. Fathers or stepfathers are the likely abusers; mothers contribute by ignoring, allowing, or even encouraging the abuse (Sheinberg & Fraenkel, 2001).

Sexual victimization often begins in childhood, with parental fondling, explicit nudity, or suggestive comments, but overt sexual abuse typically begins in puberty (Stewart, 1997). How common this problem is depends on one's definition of sexual abuse. Prevalence reports range from more than 50 percent to less than 5 percent of children (Haugaard, 2000). Broad definitions of abuse (such as "any sexual involvement") are preferred by developmentalists, who seek to prevent all possible harm; narrow definitions ("forced genital activity") are used by legal authorities, who prosecute offenders.

Adolescent girls are prime targets for victimization by fathers, other male relatives, family friends, and young men they know. In a U.S. survey of young women of four ethnic groups (African-, Native, Mexican-, and European-Americans), about one-third of each group reported sexual abuse; in one-fifth of these cases, the abuse had involved rape (Roosa et al., 1999). Young Canadian women report similarly high rates (DeKeseredy & Schwartz, 1998). Involuntary sexual intercourse, without any protection against pregnancy or infection, is particularly common among adolescents under age 16 (Kalmuss et al., 2003).

Response for Young Adults (from page 352): Yes, but maybe you should forgive them. Ideally, parents should talk to their children about sex, presenting honest information and listening to the child's concerns. However, many parents find this very difficult because they feel embarrassed and ignorant. Silence was a mistake—but no parent is perfect.

Adolescent boys can also be victims of sexual abuse, and they may suffer even more than girls. A molested boy is likely to feel shame at being weak and unable to defend himself—all contrary to the macho image that many young adolescent boys strive to attain. A male perpetrator does not necessarily consider himself homosexual, nor is a boy's involvement an indication of his sexual orientation. However, when the abused boy is gay, shame escalates. And if his own father or stepfather is the sexual abuser, the problems of vulnerability and loss of self-esteem are multiplied (Finkelhor, 1994). Boys often turn their anger outward. An estimated 30 to 50 percent of child molesters are adolescent boys who had been abused themselves (Jones et al., 1999).

Indeed, every problem of adolescence—unintended pregnancy, drug abuse, suicide, delinquency, eating disorders, and so on—is more common in victims of past sexual abuse than in other teenagers (Friedrich, 1998). For example, in a survey of more than 6,000 Minnesota high school students, boys who were sexually abused were 10 times more likely than their peers, and girls twice as likely, to have an eating disorder (Hernandez, 1995). Whenever an adolescent seems troubled, past sexual abuse is a possibility that should be explored in confidence, with effective help at the ready.

Drug Use and Abuse

The topic of drugs is a lightning rod for distorted statistics, latent prejudices, and murky thinking. Let's seek clarity, beginning with definitions. **Drug use** is simply the ingestion of a drug, regardless of the amount or effect. **Drug abuse** is the ingestion of a drug to the extent that it impairs the user's biological or psychological well-being. **Drug addiction** occurs when a person craves more of a drug in order to feel physically or psychologically at ease. Addiction is obvious when absence of the drug arouses symptoms of withdrawal, such as restlessness, depression, or physical disturbance (dizziness, nausea, and the like). (If an addict uses a drug continually, withdrawal symptoms do not occur.) Drug *abuse* is always harmful. Drug use may or may not be harmful, depending on the reasons for, and the effects of, that use.

When it comes to drug use, nations differ considerably, in both laws and cultural norms. Some nations, including the United States, legally prohibit almost any nonmedicinal drug use by persons under age 18. Indeed, some jurisdictions within the United States forbid the sale of alcohol to anyone, of any age, or outlaw cigarette smoking except in a private home or outdoors. Other nations, including most European ones, allow children to drink alcohol. In still other countries, including most of those in Asia, young men are expected to smoke cigarettes, but smoking by young women is frowned upon.

Religions also differ. Some religions forbid any drug use, while others include drugs or alcohol as an essential part of their ceremonies. Such variations suggest that, although the problems of excess are obvious, the solutions are not.

The Gateway Drugs

In the United States, research on adolescent drug use has focused especially on the **gateway drugs**: tobacco, alcohol, and marijuana. These three are called gateway drugs because their use is often the initial step toward drug abuse and addiction, although the relationship is complicated (see Figure 14.3).

A link between the occasional use of gateway drugs and later drug abuse and addiction as well as social problems—violence, early sexual activity, and school failure—has been found again and again. Drug use is both a cause and a symptom of adolescent problems (Cairns & Cairns, 1994; Kandel & Davies, 1996; Raskin-White et al., 1999).

This finding is contrary to the belief of many adolescents and even some parents. It is easy to justify use of gateway drugs as a way to help teens cope with the stresses of puberty or with the need for social interaction or with worry about the future. Certainly, most people who use gateway drugs avoid lifelong addiction. However, most developmentalists believe that these "justifications" are merely excuses and that parents should discourage drug

drug use The ingestion of a drug, regardless of the amount or effect.

drug abuse The ingestion of a drug to the extent that it impairs the user's biological or psychological well-being.

drug addiction A situation in which a person craves more of a drug in order to feel physically or psychologically at ease.

gateway drugs Drugs—usually tobacco, alcohol, and marijuana—whose use increases the risk that a person will later use harder drugs, such as cocaine and heroin.

FIGURE 14.3 Why Stop at the Gate? Adolescents sneer at scare tactics suggesting that use of gateway drugs will make them lifetime addicts or serious drug abusers. This happens only sometimes: It is not inevitable. However, avoiding any use of gateway drugs is one way to make drug addiction very unlikely.

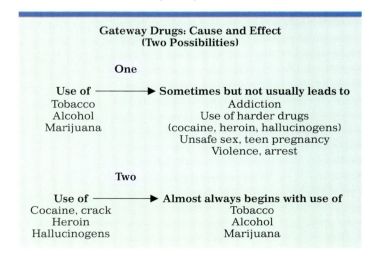

**Gateway Drugs: Cause and Effect
(Two Possibilities)**

One

Use of ──────▶ Sometimes but not usually leads to
Tobacco   Addiction
Alcohol   Use of harder drugs
Marijuana   (cocaine, heroin, hallucinogens)
                       Unsafe sex, teen pregnancy
                            Violence, arrest

Two

Use of ──────▶ Almost always begins with use of
Cocaine, crack   Tobacco
Heroin   Alcohol
Hallucinogens   Marijuana

use of all kinds. Consider the research on the use of the gateway drugs during adolescence.

Tobacco The use of tobacco decreases food consumption and interferes with the absorption of nutrients, a problem that has especially serious consequences at puberty. Young people who are habitual smokers are significantly shorter and smaller than they would have been if they did not smoke or had not started to smoke until they were fully grown. Smoking at an early age can shorten the life span, as every year of smoking increases the risk of cancer, heart disease, and stroke. In addition, many studies find that smoking markedly reduces fertility in both sexes, which suggests that the entire reproductive system is probably affected (Fiscella et al., 1998).

Most adolescents who become steady smokers are quickly hooked, because the nicotine in cigarettes is one of the most addictive substances known. Yet, just as with other addictions (such as extreme dieting or gambling), teenagers seem blithely unaware that they are at risk (Orford, 2001). For example, one study of teenage smokers found that 95 percent thought they would quit within five years, even though only 25 percent of all adolescent smokers actually do quit by early adulthood. In this study, almost all participants had tried to quit smoking and failed, but they nonetheless believed that they would not still be smoking as young adults (Siqueira et al., 2001).

Alcohol Drinking alcohol is also more harmful in adolescence than in adulthood. One reason is that, even in small doses, alcohol loosens inhibitions and impairs judgment—dangerous in young persons who are already coping with major physical, sexual, and emotional changes. Another reason is that drinking in adolescence correlates with abnormal brain development; alcohol impairs memory and self-control by damaging the hippocampus and the prefrontal cortex (Brown et al., 2000; De Bellis et al., 2000).

Remembering that correlation is not necessarily causation, you may wonder whether these brain abnormalities predated the alcohol use. Maybe young people become drinkers if they are brain-damaged, unable to think as clearly as normal adolescents. Neurologists tested this possibility by giving alcohol to lower animals. The results were clear: Alcohol does not merely correlate with the abnormalities; it causes them (White et al., 2000).

Marijuana The third gateway drug, marijuana, seriously slows down thinking processes, particularly those related to memory and abstract reasoning. As you will learn in detail in the next chapter, abstract reasoning is exactly the cognitive advance that can be expected to begin at about age 12. Impairment of memory and reasoning is especially problematic in early adolescence, when academic learning requires better recall and a higher level of abstract thinking.

In addition, over time, repeated marijuana "mellowness" may encourage a general lack of motivation and indifference toward the future. The result is apathy at the very time when young people should be focusing their energy on meeting the challenges of growing up. This may explain the results of a longitudinal study in which children who became marijuana users experienced a developmental slowdown in adulthood: They were later than their peers to graduate from college, to obtain steady employment, and to marry (Brook et al., 1999).

Patterns of Adolescent Drug Use

Almost every teenager in the United States tries one or more of the gateway drugs; by high school graduation, most have tried all three. This is also true in many other nations, although in some regions, alcohol use is far more common

Especially for Older Brothers and Sisters A friend said she saw your 13-year-old sister smoking. Should you tell your parents?

LAUREN GREENFIELD

Looking Cool Their tight clothing, heavy makeup, multiple rings, and cigarettes are meant to convey to the world that Sheena, 15, and Jessica, 16, are mature, sophisticated women. Tobacco is the one gateway drug that girls use as much as boys, perhaps because boys have other ways of communicating their readiness to take on the world.

❓**Observational Quiz** (see answer, page 359): Did these girls buy their own cigarettes?

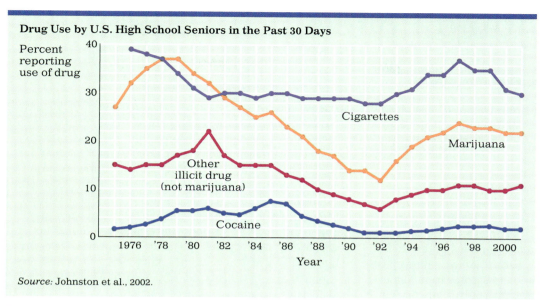

Drug Use by U.S. High School Seniors in the Past 30 Days

Source: Johnston et al., 2002.

FIGURE 14.4 Rise and Fall By asking the same questions year after year, the *Monitoring the Future* study shows notable historical effects. It is encouraging that something in the society, not something in the adolescent, makes drug use increase and decrease. However, as Chapter 1 emphasized, survey research cannot prove what causes change.

than is use of other drugs—and in still other regions, smoking is more common than drinking (Eisner, 2002).

Variations occur by cohort as well as by culture. One of the most notable and reliable surveys is an annual, detailed, confidential survey of nearly 50,000 eighth-, tenth-, and twelfth-grade students from more than 400 high schools in the United States. Since its inception in 1975, this survey (called *Monitoring the Future*) has shown that more than 8 out of 10 high school seniors have drunk alcohol (more than a few sips), 2 out of 3 have smoked at least one cigarette, and about half have tried at least one illegal drug, usually marijuana (Johnston et al., 2002). The numbers vary from year to year, with an overall high in the 1970s and low in the 1980s; but the most recent survey still reports that 80 percent have tried alcohol and 54 percent have tried at least one illegal drug. It appears that drug use now begins earlier than it once did, with usage rates increasing among 13-year-olds.

At least in theory, one taste or puff is merely an experiment. To exclude the curious experimenters, it is informative to survey teens on their drug use in the past 30 days. More than half of all high school seniors admit to using at least one drug in the past month (see Figure 14.4). Actual use in the late teen years is higher than the percentages on the chart indicate, not only because teenagers underreport their serious drug use but also because high school absentees and dropouts do not receive this questionnaire.

The *Monitoring the Future* survey finds that daily drug use and drug abuse increase every year throughout late adolescence (Johnston et al., 2002). Drug problems in adults often trace back to increasing use during adolescence. It is important to keep this in mind because, for example, in one recent year in Los Angeles, no teenager died of a drug overdose, but 562 adults did (Males, 1999).

It seems that, worldwide, drug-abuse problems tend to begin in adolescence, to become more serious in early adulthood, and then to decrease in the late 20s (Eisner, 2002). This suggests that one way to prevent the worst consequences of abuse and addiction is to postpone the first use of drugs. This is a complex strategy, however, as is explained in the following Changing Policy feature.

Changing Policy

Postponing Teenage Drug Experimentation

If experimental use of gateway drugs cannot be completely prevented (and in some cohorts and cultures, this may be the case), it should at least be postponed until a young person is fully grown and mature enough to monitor the risks and recognize the early signs of possible addiction. How can this postponement be accomplished?

Some adults believe that any antidrug effort is a step in the right direction. This is not true; even well-intentioned efforts can boomerang. The best example is one of the most popular and costly drug education programs in the United States. In Project D.A.R.E. (Drug Abuse Resistance Education), police officers go into classrooms from kindergarten through high school to present a curriculum that emphasizes the harmfulness of drugs, showing videos of the frightening consequences of illegal drug abuse. Parents, politicians, and police departments like the program, funding it generously, but longitudinal research has found that the program leads only to an increase in knowledge about specific drugs, not to a rejection of drug use.

Students who experience D.A.R.E. are no more likely to abstain from drugs over the high school years than those who do not experience it (Clayton et al., 1996; Ennett et al., 1994; Wysong et al., 1994). Is there some long-term "sleeper" effect, protecting D.A.R.E. recipients in young adulthood? No. In fact, 10 years later, drug use was similar between one group of high school students who had experienced D.A.R.E. and another group who had not. The only difference was that the D.A.R.E. group had lower self-esteem than the non-D.A.R.E. group. Drug use by the two groups was similar, but the D.A.R.E group felt worse about themselves, perhaps because they were more fearful or guilty (Lynam et al., 1999).

Another research project used group discussions among delinquent youth in an intense summer-camp experience as a way of guiding teenagers toward constructive behavior. Again, longitudinal research found that they fared worse: They were more likely to use drugs and to be arrested than those without such group training (Dishion et al., 1999). Finally, research evaluating antimarijuana advertisements found that some actually make smoking marijuana seem more attractive (Fishbein et al., 2002). Messages warning against other drugs can similarly backfire (Block et al., 2002).

Obviously, drug education programs must be carefully developed, with teen involvement, adult example, and accurate research findings and evaluation procedures. A recent decline in cigarette smoking among adolescents followed headline news about the addictiveness of nicotine, unethical business practices by tobacco companies, and the hazards of secondhand smoke. State legislatures imposed higher taxes on cigarettes and greater penalties for tobacco sales to minors. All this may have made a difference.

Some states have used the settlement money from successful lawsuits against tobacco companies to fund youth antismoking campaigns with various strategies to prevent smoking among students. Florida was one. In that state, smoking declined by 40 percent among middle school students from 1998 to 2000 (Bauer et al., 2000).

Researchers are finding factors that protect against drug use (Benson et al., 1998). One is an active, problem-solving style of coping (Wills et al., 2001); another is a sense of competence and well-being (Griffin et al., 2001); a third is cognitive maturity (Ammerman et al., 2001). Family and school can enhance these cognitive skills, while keeping drugs out of reach. Parent–child conversations (not necessarily about drugs), religious and community organizations, and after-school sports, drama, and music—even midnight basketball—may be drug prevention in disguise.

Experimenting with Alcohol These young people in a Florida motel room, rejoicing in their beer, have temporarily—and artificially—overcome the awkwardness and unease that most teenagers feel with each other.

CHRISTOPHER BROWN / STOCK, BOSTON

Cultural Differences in Drug Use

Whether a particular teenager uses drugs, and which drugs he or she uses, depends largely on his or her peers as well as on the wider community. For instance, in one survey of ninth- to twelfth-graders, only 40 percent of those in the heavily Mormon state of Utah had ever puffed on a cigarette even once, but 75 percent of those in West Virginia had done so; in fact, many of the latter group were already heavy smokers (CDC, June 9, 2000). Whereas Mormon youth would not impress their friends by smoking, West Virginia teens who smoked might be considered mature by their peers.

As these findings suggest, among many adolescent peer groups, drug experimentation, as well as other kinds of rebellion against adults, is admired as a sign of maturity (Bukowski et al., 2000; Leaper & Anderson, 1997). Thus, "in young adolescence, use of substances . . . provides a form of commerce with the social world" (Dishion & Owen, 2002, p. 489). In other words, the socially awkward, pubescent child may use drugs to establish friendships, a strategy that is as logical as it is foolish. Similar examples of foolish logic are in evidence among girls who smoke to stay thin (smoking does decrease appetite, but it also reduces height, eventually making the body less slender) or boys who take steroids to get strong (steroids do help build muscle, but they also increase injury rates).

Variations are apparent at the national level as well. Adolescents in European nations have shown increases in use of drugs (particularly heroin) since 1980, at the same time that overall drug use among North American adolescents has decreased. In Australia, drug use has increased, and the preferred drugs are different from those most often used in either Europe or North America (Maxwell, 2000).

Gender patterns of drug use vary across and within nations. For example, the United States is almost the only nation in which adolescent girls are as likely to smoke as adolescent boys, and most teen girls who smoke are of European extraction. In most Asian and African countries, very few women smoke. For example, in Indonesia, 53 percent of men but only 4 percent of women smoke; the corresponding percentages are 61 and 7 in China and 24 and 7 in Nigeria (U.S. Department of Health and Human Services, 2001).

Just as music, clothes, and hairstyles change from one year to the next, so does drug use, not only in frequency (for lifetime use, 1978 saw an all-time high and 1992 saw an all-time low in the United States) but also in composition (marijuana is now stronger than it used to be), in mode of delivery (heroin need not be injected), and in form (smokeless tobacco is much more common). New drugs come into fashion. For example, "ice" and "ecstasy" were unknown before 1990, and GBH, ketamine, and bidis were almost never used before 1995, yet all five have become popular among high school seniors in recent years—and all five are considered quite harmful by medical researchers. These variations mean that drug use is not part of the universal experience of puberty but rather part of the peer culture at one place and time.

Adolescence can be a dangerous and hazardous time as well as a glorious and healthy time. The physical changes of adolescence require increased nourishment to sustain the adolescent's growth and also result in new sexual urges. Unfortunately, neither good nutrition nor healthy sexuality is routine. Many teens do not eat a balanced diet and thus do not get the calcium and iron they need for strong bones and ample energy. Their sexuality makes them vulnerable to sexually transmitted infections, unwanted parenthood, and even sexual abuse.

Most teenagers in the United States experiment with gateway drugs (alcohol, cigarettes, and marijuana). The dangers of abuse and addiction are

Response for Older Brothers and Sisters (from page 356): Smoking is very addictive; your sister needs to stop now. Most adolescents care more about immediate concerns than the distant possibility of cancer or heart disease, so tell her about a smoker you know whose teeth are yellow, who smells of smoke, and who is shorter than the rest of his or her family. Then tell your parents; they are your best allies in helping your sister have a healthy adolescence.

! Answer to Observational Quiz (from page 356): No, they bummed them from a stranger at this San Jose, California, shopping mall. If you answered no, you probably had in mind the fact that most states, including California, are strictly enforcing their laws against selling cigarettes to minors. You may also have noticed the awkward way the girls are holding their cigarettes and realized that they have not yet been smoking long enough to become addicted to nicotine.

not usually apparent to teenagers; nor do they realize that the use of gateway drugs in early adolescence may affect body and brain growth. Cultures vary widely in the specifics and legalities of drug use during adolescence, which suggests that social factors are more influential than biological ones.

Centuries ago puberty did not begin until age 16 or so, and marriage and employment followed soon after. Today, however, when puberty begins at age 11 or 12, young people may not be cognitively or socially capable of the autonomy their bodies seek. Fortunately, the social context can make a difference in how teenagers respond to their biological growth. Education and social pressures still guide young people in positive and healthy directions. For example, we no longer have courtship rituals and apprenticeship programs, but schools and colleges can provide informal socializing and job preparation. Obviously, some adults and some communities do a much better job of this than others. Cognitive and psychosocial guidance are explored in the next two chapters.

SUMMARY

Puberty Begins

1. Puberty refers to the various changes that transform a child's body into an adult one. Biochemical signals from the hypothalamus to the pituitary gland to the adrenal glands (the HPA axis) increase levels of testosterone, estrogen, and various other hormones. These hormones cause the body to grow and change.

2. Puberty is accompanied by many emotions. Some, such as quick mood shifts and thoughts about sex, are directly caused by hormones, but most are only indirectly hormonal. Instead, they are caused by other people's reactions to the adolescent body changes; hence, they are more a matter of nurture than nature.

3. The visible changes of puberty normally occur any time from about ages 8 to 14; the child's sex, genetic background, body fat, and level of family stress all contribute to this variation. Girls generally begin and end the process before boys do. Boys who mature late and girls who mature early are stressed by the sociocultural consequences of not being "on time."

4. The growth spurt is an acceleration of growth in every part of the body. The peak weight increase usually comes before the peak height and then peak muscle increase. The lungs and the heart also increase in size and capacity. The entire process is usually completed about three to four years after it begins.

5. Sexual characteristics emerge at puberty. The maturation of primary sexual characteristics means that by age 13 or so, menarche and spermarche have occurred, and the young person is soon able to reproduce.

6. Secondary sexual characteristics are not directly involved in reproduction but signify that the person is a man or a woman. Body shape, breasts, voice, body hair, and numerous other features differentiate males and females.

Hazards to Health

7. Adolescents tend to be healthy. Diseases, both mild (such as colds and flu) and serious (such as cancer and heart disease), are rare. However, adolescents take risks that can lead to injury and accidental death at a rate five times that of younger children.

8. To sustain body growth, most adolescents consume large quantities of food, although they do not always make healthy choices. Many adolescents are deficient in calcium and iron, which affect bones, teeth, and energy.

9. The biological impulse to become sexually active in adolescence is strong, for genetic reasons. Whether or not a teenager acts on that impulse depends largely on culture and context, with about half of all 18-year-olds in the United States sexually active. Two common hazards are sexually transmitted infections and unwanted pregnancies.

10. Child sexual abuse does not necessarily involve force or genital contact. Although immediate consequences may be shame and guilt, the worst effects are lifelong difficulties for the victim in establishing normal intimate relationships. Puberty is a particularly vulnerable time because young teens are attractive to adults but are not yet able to protect themselves.

11. The use of drugs (including the gateway drugs—tobacco, alcohol, and marijuana) is even more harmful in adolescence than at later ages because of the physiological and psychological immaturity of the young person.

12. Each culture and cohort has its own patterns of drug use and abuse during adolescence. Lessons learned from the research may help adolescents postpone drug use until they are better able to make wise decisions.

KEY TERMS

adolescence (p. 341)
puberty (p. 341)
hypothalamus (p. 342)
pituitary gland (p. 342)
adrenal glands (p. 342)
HPA axis (p. 342)

gonads (p. 342)
estrogen (p. 342)
testosterone (p. 342)
menarche (p. 345)
spermarche (p. 345)
growth spurt (p. 346)

primary sex characteristics
   (p. 348)
secondary sex characteristics
   (p. 349)
sexually transmitted infection
   (STI) (p. 352)

sexual abuse (p. 354)
child sexual abuse (p. 354)
drug use (p. 355)
drug abuse (p. 355)
drug addiction (p. 355)
gateway drugs (p. 355)

APPLICATIONS

1. Visit a fifth-, sixth-, or seventh-grade class. Note variations in the size and maturity of the students. Do you see any patterns related to gender, ethnicity, body fat, or self-confidence?

2. Interview two to four of your friends who are in their teens or early 20s about their memories of menarche or spermarche, including their memories of others' reactions. Do their comments indicate that these events are emotionally troubling for young people?

3. Talk with someone who became a parent before the age of 20. Were there any problems with the pregnancy, the birth, or the first years of parenthood? Would the person recommend young parenthood to another person? What would have been different if the baby had been born either three years earlier or three years later?

4. Adults disagree about the dangers of drugs. Find two people with very different opinions (e.g., a parent who would be horrified if his or her child used any drug and a parent who believes that young people should be allowed to drink or smoke at home). Ask them to explain their reasons, and write these down without criticism or disagreement. Later, present each with the arguments from the other person. What is their response? How open, flexible, and rational does it seem to be? Why are attitudes about drugs so deeply held?

Chapter Fifteen

Adolescence: Cognitive Development

Talking with a 16-year-old about international politics, about hot new music, or about the meaning of life is obviously quite different from conversing on the same topics with an 8-year-old. Adolescents are increasingly aware, both of world concerns and of personal needs—other people's as well as their own. They are more adult in their use of analysis, logic, and reason.

Adolescents, with their frequent sarcasm, cynicism, and arrogance, may appear tough-minded. But the opposite is more likely true. Adolescents can be naive, idealistic, troubled by their own introspections, and supersensitive to criticism, real or imagined.

We begin by exploring adolescent thought processes, which are characterized by advanced logical powers (sometimes called analytic, or formal, thinking) as well as by greater emotional force (sometimes called intuitive, or egocentric, thinking). Then the chapter describes the schools where adolescents study and the decisions they make, guided by their developing cognition.

Intellectual Advances

Adolescent thinking advances in three ways: Basic cognitive skills continue to develop, logic emerges, and intuitive thinking becomes quicker and more compelling. Let's look at each of these three changes in turn.

More and Better Cognition

First, every basic skill of information processing—memory, knowledge base, speed, control, and attention, as described in Chapter 12—continues to develop during adolescence. Selective attention becomes more skillfully deployed, enabling students to do homework when they are surrounded by peers or blaring music (or both) *if* motivation is high. Expanded memory skills and a growing knowledge base allow adolescents to connect new ideas and concepts to old ones. Metacognition helps them become better students.

Brain maturation continues, and this may be the underlying reason for improved cognitive skills. Myelination (see Chapter 8) is ongoing, making reaction time even shorter, not only on the athletic field but also in the classroom. Adolescents are able to grasp, connect, and refute ideas much faster than younger children can (Sampaio & Truwit, 2001).

The prefrontal cortex, in particular, becomes more densely packed and more efficient, enabling adolescents to plan their lives, to analyze possibilities, and to pursue goals much more effectively than children can. In fact, the executive functions of the brain, which originate primarily in the prefrontal cortex, improve markedly throughout adolescence (Cepeda et al., 2001).

Language mastery improves. The nuances of grammar and vocabulary choice are better understood. This makes code-switching more sophisticated: Most adolescents have several speech codes, using different ones for parents and teachers, for same-sex and other-sex friends, and so on. Many adolescents develop a personal style in their writing and speech, combining advanced linguistic skills with deeper emotional expression. As a result, impassioned poets, diarists, and debaters emerge in every high school classroom.

Abstraction Way Beyond Counting on Fingers and Toes This high school student explains an algebra problem, a behavior that requires a level of hypothetical and abstract thought beyond that of any concrete operational child—and of many adults. At the beginning of concrete operational thought, children need blocks, coins, and other tangible objects to help them understand math. By later adolescence, in the full flower of formal operational thought, such practical and concrete illustrations are irrelevant.

WILL McINTYRE / PHOTO RESEARCHERS, INC.

formal operational thought In Piaget's theory, the fourth and final stage of cognitive development; arises from a combination of maturation and experience.

New Logical Abilities

A second type of cognitive advance in adolescence is the development of new logical abilities. Jean Piaget was the first to notice that adolescents can reason more abstractly than younger children, which is the hallmark of **formal operational thought,** the fourth and final stage of Piaget's sequence of cognitive development. Formal operational thinking is characterized by the ability to think logically about abstract ideas, not just about personal experiences, as in concrete operational thought. The adolescent can consider concepts and possibilities that exist only in the mind, not in remembered reality. Formal operational thought arises from a combination of maturation and experience (Inhelder & Piaget, 1958).

Most developmentalists agree with Piaget that adolescent thought is *qualitatively* different from children's thought (Fischer & Bidell, 1998; Flavell et al., 2001; Moshman, 2000). They disagree about whether this change is quite sudden (Piaget) or gradual (information-processing theory) and about whether change results from new context (sociocultural theory) or advanced biology (epigenetic theory).

Thinking Like a Scientist

Piaget's Balance Experiment

Scientists not only develop theories but also develop experiments that refute or support their theories. To study the reasoning of children of various ages, Piaget and his colleagues devised a number of now-famous tasks designed to reveal the onset of formal operational thought (Inhelder & Piaget, 1958). They sought to demonstrate that, "in contrast to concrete operational children, formal operational adolescents imagine all possible determinants, . . . systematically vary the factors one by one, observe the results correctly, keep track of the results, and draw the appropriate conclusions" (Miller, 2001, p. 57).

In one experiment (diagrammed in Figure 15.1), children are asked to balance a scale with weights that can be hooked onto the scale's arms. To master this task, children must realize that the heaviness of the weights and their distance from the center interact reciprocally, so that a heavier weight close to the middle can be counter-balanced with a lighter weight far from the center on the other side. This means that something half as far from the center must be twice as heavy (e.g., something weighing 6 grams and placed 4 centimeters to the left of the center will balance something weighing 12 grams and placed 2 centimeters to the right of the center).

This understanding, and a method to discover it, was completely beyond the ability of 3- to 5-year-olds. In Piaget's experiments, they randomly hung different weights on different hooks. By age 7, children realized that the scale could be balanced by putting the same amount of weight on both arms, but they didn't realize that the distance of the weights from the center of the scale is also important.

By age 10, near the end of the concrete operational stage, children often realized the importance of the weights' locations on the arms, but their efforts to coordinate weight and distance from the center to balance the scale were based on trial-and-error experimentation, not logical deduction.

Finally, by about age 13 or 14, some children hypothesized that there is a relationship between a weight's distance from the center of the scale and the effect it has on a balance. By systematically testing this hypothesis, they correctly formulated the mathematical relation between weight and distance from the center and could solve the balance problem accurately and efficiently.

Piaget attributed each of these advances to the children's attainment of the next-higher cognitive stage, proof of his theory of cognitive development, with adolescents and adults attaining formal operational thought. Other scientists are not convinced that the stages are as Piaget described them or that progress is stagelike.

Recent research finds much more variation among adolescents than Piaget originally proposed. Specifically, many adolescents (and adults) perform quite poorly on standard tests of formal reasoning, such as the balance-scale task. In fact, research with various international populations finds that only about half of all adolescents and young adults perform at the formal operational level on Piaget's measures (Larivee et al., 2000).

Moreover, a teenager who can easily use deductive reasoning to figure out a mathematics problem may have great difficulty in deducing the solution to a problem in biology, or in assessing the ethics of various approaches to national health insurance, or in determining the most effective way to deal with a complex human dilemma. In other words, adolescents apply formal logic to some situations but not to others. Further experimentation and correlations indicate that each individual's intellect, experiences, talents, and interests affect the ability to rea-

son formally and that application of that ability is affected by emotional as well as maturational factors (Fischer & Bidell, 1998).

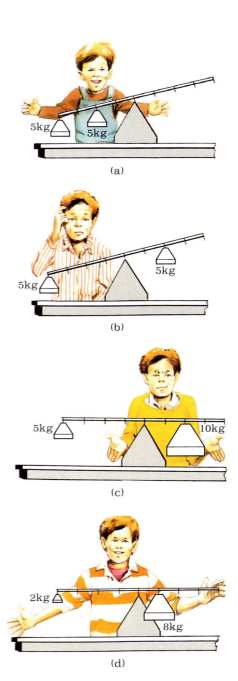

FIGURE 15.1 How to Balance a Beam Piaget's balance-scale test of formal reasoning, as it is attempted by *(a)* a 4-year-old, *(b)* a 7-year-old, *(c)* a 10-year-old, and *(d)* a 14-year-old. The key to balancing the scale is to make weight times distance from the center equal on both sides of the center; the realization of that principle requires formal operational thought.

Hypothetical-Deductive Thought

One of the most prominent aspects of adolescent thought is the capacity to think of *possibility,* not just reality. Adolescents "start with possible solutions and progress to determine which is the real solution" (Lutz & Sternberg, 1999). Adolescents realize with joy that some things are merely more possible than other, less probable, things. Nothing is inevitable, and even the impossible can be considered (Falk & Wilkening, 1998). "Here and now" is only one of many alternatives that include "there and then," "long, long ago," "nowhere," "not yet," and "never." In Piaget's words:

> . . . there is a reversal of the direction of thinking between *reality* and *possibility* in the subject's method of approach. *Possibility* no longer appears merely as an extension of an empirical situation or of action actually performed. Instead, it is *reality* that is now secondary to *possibility.*

[Inhelder & Piaget, 1958, p. 251; emphasis in original]

hypothetical thought Thought that includes propositions and possibilities that may or may not reflect reality.

deductive reasoning Reasoning from a general statement or principle, through logical steps, to a specific conclusion.

inductive reasoning Reasoning from one or more specific experiences or facts to a general conclusion.

Adolescents are therefore primed to engage in **hypothetical thought,** reasoning about propositions that may or may not reflect reality.

Hypothetical thought transforms the way teenagers perceive their world. Reflection about serious issues becomes a complicated process, because many hypothetical ideas are considered, sometimes sidetracking conclusions about the immediate issues at hand. The complications were illustrated on a personal level by one high school student who wanted to keep a friend from making a life-threatening decision but did not want to judge her, because

> to . . . judge [someone] means that whatever you are saying is right and you know what's right. You know it's right for them and you know it's right in every situation. [But] you can't know if you are right. Maybe you are right. But then, right in what way?

[quoted in Gilligan et al., 1990]

Deductive Reasoning High school chemistry classes first teach students the general principles and then ask them to test the principles with specific substances. There is no way a student could simply be given these materials and told to figure out some generalities, as a teacher of 8-year-olds, with much simpler and safer substances, might do. Younger children think inductively; these students think deductively as well.

Although adolescents are not always sure what is "right in what way," they can be quick to see what is "wrong." Unlike children, they do not accept current conditions because "that's how things are." They criticize what is, precisely because of their hypothetical thinking. They can imagine how things could be, would be, and should be in a world where justice is realized, people are always sincere, and the sanctity of human life is truly recognized. This may be hypothetical thinking at its best.

In developing the capacity to think hypothetically, adolescents also become more capable of **deductive reasoning,** which begins with a logical idea or premise and then uses logic to draw specific conclusions. By contrast, as you remember from Chapter 12, during the school years, children increasingly use their accumulated knowledge of facts, as well as their personal experience, to reach inductive conclusions. In essence, their reasoning goes like this: "This is a duck; it waddles and quacks. This other duck also waddles and quacks. Therefore, if a creature waddles like a duck and quacks like a duck, then it must be a duck." Such reasoning from particulars ("waddles like" and "quacks like") to a general conclusion ("it's a duck") is called **inductive reasoning.** By contrast, deductive reasoning is reasoning from the general to the specific: "If it's a duck, it will waddle and quack" (see Figure 15.2).

An Example: Religious Freedom Versus Economic Justice The power of deductive thought is most evident when moral issues are involved, because then rationality is tested by competing principles.

DOUG MARTIN / PHOTO RESEARCHERS, INC.

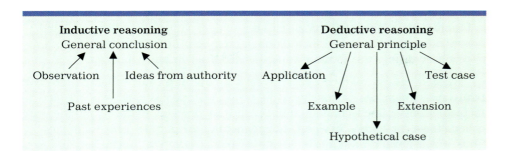

FIGURE 15.2 Bottom Up or Top Down? Children, as concrete operational thinkers, are likely to draw conclusions on the basis of their own experiences and what they have been told. This is called inductive, or bottom-up, reasoning. Adolescents can think deductively, from the top down.

When asked, three groups of adolescents—seventh-graders, eleventh-graders, and college students—in northern California all endorsed the abstract principle of free exercise of religion, as upheld by the United Nations as well as the United States Constitution. Then their easy endorsement was put to the test, with questions such as "What if a particular religion refused to allow low-income people to become priests?" This hypothetical *what-if* question would be rejected as impossible by most concrete operational thinkers, who have a very difficult time following any logical argument that begins with a false premise (Moshman, 2000).

Unlike the probable rejection or confusion of younger children, all three age groups of adolescents attempted to answer—and their answers varied by age, as Figure 15.3 shows. Almost all members of the youngest group (94 percent) abandoned freedom of religion if a religion excluded low-income priests. In contrast, 81 percent of those in mid-adolescence (the eleventh-graders) stuck to the principle. They used deductive reasoning to go from the premise of religious freedom to the conclusion that religious freedom should prevail even when a particular religious practice seemed unfair.

If you are thinking that such cold logic is not always desirable, you may be reassured to learn that many psychologists hypothesize a fifth stage of reasoning that follows formal operational thought. This stage, sometimes called *postformal thought,* involves a struggle to reconcile logic and experience. In this experiment, the college students engaged in such a struggle: 38 percent decided that economic justice was a more important principle than religious freedom, while 62 percent felt that religious freedom was more important. Postformal thought is discussed in Chapter 18.

More Intuitive, Emotional Thought

The fact that adolescents and adults *can* use hypothetical-deductive reasoning does not necessarily mean that they *will* use it. This advanced reasoning is counterbalanced by the increasing importance of intuitive thinking, the third cognitive change that occurs in adolescence.

Apparently, humans have "two parallel, interacting modes of information-processing" (Epstein, 1994, p. 709), and both modes advance during adolescence (Moshman, 2000):

■ The first mode is the formal, logical, hypothetical-deductive thinking described by Piaget. This is called *analytic thought,* because it involves rational analysis of many factors whose interactions must be separately calculated, as in the problem of balancing the scale. Analytic thinking requires a certain level of intellectual maturity, brain capacity, motivation, and practice.

■ The second mode begins with a prior belief or an assumption, rather than with a logical premise or objective method. This second type is called *intuitive* (or *heuristic* or *experiential*) *thought,* in that thoughts spring forth from memories and feelings that are then applied, instead of hypothesized and then analyzed one by one. Intuitive cognition is quick and powerful; it feels

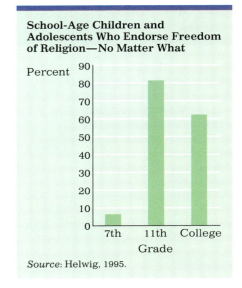

School-Age Children and Adolescents Who Endorse Freedom of Religion—No Matter What

Source: Helwig, 1995.

FIGURE 15.3 Adherence to Principle High school students are more capable of deductive reasoning than are middle schoolers, as shown by the fact that a much higher percentage of eleventh-graders were able to perceive religious freedom as a basic principle and to cling to it no matter what conflicting circumstances were proposed by the researcher. (College students were more aware that one of those conflicting circumstances might in itself represent a basic principle, so they were more likely than the eleventh-graders to temper their adherence to religious freedom.)

Especially for High School Guidance Counselors Given what you know about adolescent thinking, should you spend more time helping students with college applications, with summer jobs, with family problems, or with high school course selection?

"right," even when analysis might lead in a different direction. Brain maturation may aid this type as well, as ongoing myelination and accumulated memory speed thought. In addition, increased production of hormones at puberty brings an emotional quickness to bear on every thought.

Many research methods now reveal that the brain has at least these two pathways, which are variously called conscious/unconscious, explicit/implicit, factual/creative, intellectual/emotional, and so on. No matter what they are called, these pathways develop independently, on parallel processing tracks. Thus, on each track, thoughts build and develop, leading to conclusions and generalizations that might conflict with conclusions reached in the other mode (Epstein, 1994; Macrae & Bodenhausen, 2000; Stanovich, 1999). One track is not necessarily better than the other, and thoughts along each track can coexist or conflict. This two-track thinking is demonstrated by adolescents as they think about themselves and as they respond to logical problems.

Adolescent Egocentrism

Adolescents frequently think about themselves. When they do so, they tend to think intuitively, not logically. They worry about how others perceive them; they try to sort out their conflicting feelings about parents, school, and close friends; they think deeply (but not always realistically) about their future possibilities; they reflect, at length, on each day's experiences.

New ventures in introspection are part of the expanding self-awareness that is part of the maturation process. However, introspection can be distorted by **adolescent egocentrism** (remember from Chapter 9 that *egocentric* means "self at the center"), a self-view in which adolescents regard themselves as much more socially significant (noticed by everyone) than they actually are (Elkind, 1967, 1984; Lapsley, 1993). Younger adolescents tend to hypothesize about what others might be thinking (especially about them) and then egocentrically take their hypotheses to be fact—a kind of inductive and then deductive reasoning that can lead to very false conclusions. For example, a frown from a stranger or an offhand critique from a teacher could be used to induce the general idea that "no one likes me," which can lead to the deduction that "I am hateful" or even "I do not deserve to live." Opposite but equally vague responses from others could lead to the idea that "everyone loves me," with equally distorted deductions.

Several aspects of adolescent egocentrism have special names. One is the **invincibility fable,** adolescents' idea that they cannot be conquered or even harmed by anything that might vanquish a normal mortal. Because they falsely believe in their invincibility, some young people are convinced that, unlike other people, they will not suffer the consequences of dangerous behavior, such as using drugs, driving drunk, or having unprotected sex.

A second logical lapse resulting from adolescent egocentrism is the **personal fable:** Adolescents imagine their own lives as unique, heroic, or even legendary. Justin, one of my teenage students, complained that it was patently unfair that millions mourned the Tejano singer Selena's tragic death. Using hypothetical thinking, he imagined that he might die but few would mourn him or even care. I told him I would care; he dismissed that as unimportant. I also pointed out that Selena was extraordinarily talented and accomplished, that she brought joy to millions. He replied, "But I am very talented, too; if I died, millions would never experience the joy I would bring them." When I looked quizzical, he was annoyed at me: "How do you know I'm not just as talented as she was?" In the personal fable, the young person perceives him- or herself as exceptional, distinguished by unusual experiences, talents, perspectives, and values, and then becomes upset if others do not share those perceptions.

A third false conclusion is the **imaginary audience.** Adolescents tend to think of themselves as being at center stage, with all eyes on them, because they

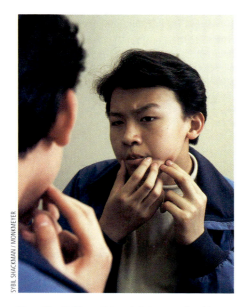

Boys Do It, Too Although it is generally girls who are considered to be overly aware of minor flaws in their complexion or attire, the truth is that adolescent boys also pay exaggerated attention to their appearance. The cognitive capacity to think about oneself in egocentric terms makes many young people of both sexes spend hours combing their hair, adjusting their clothing, and searching for blemishes.

adolescent egocentrism A characteristic of adolescent thinking that sometimes leads young people to focus on themselves to the exclusion of others and to believe, for example, that their thoughts, feelings, and experiences are unique.

invincibility fable A teenager's false belief, stemming from adolescent egocentrism, that he or she cannot be conquered or even harmed by anything that might vanquish a normal mortal, such as unprotected sex, drug abuse, or high-speed driving.

personal fable A teenager's false belief, stemming from adolescent egocentrism, that he or she is destined to have a unique, heroic, or even legendary life.

imaginary audience A teenager's false belief, stemming from adolescent egocentrism, that others are intensely interested in his or her appearance and behavior.

SYBIL SHACKMAN / MONKMEYER

assume that other people are as intensely interested in them as they themselves are. As a result, they tend to fantasize about how others react to their appearance and behavior. The imaginary audience can cause teenagers to enter a crowded room as if they believe themselves to be the most attractive human beings alive, or (the reverse) to avoid any attention because everyone will notice their slight facial blemish or a spot on their shirt.

As this acute self-consciousness reveals, young people are not yet comfortable in the broader social world. This is one reason many seem obsessed with their hair, clothing, and so on, before going out in public. It also explains their concern about the audience of their peers, who presumably judge every visible nuance of their appearance and behavior. No wonder, then, that one adolescent remarked, "I would like to be able to fly if everyone else did; otherwise it would be rather conspicuous" (quoted in Steinberg, 1993).

The various forms that adolescent egocentrism can take are the most obvious forms of intuitive, emotional thought. At every age, humans have a "self-serving bias." They take credit for good things that happen to them and avoid blaming themselves for bad things; they evaluate themselves more favorably than their friends and their friends more favorably than their other peers (Duval & Silvia, 2002; Suls et al., 2002). Such illogic is used by everyone; it is just more obvious to adults (especially parents and researchers) when adolescents do it.

As researchers become more aware of the links between adolescent and adult thought, they realize that adolescent egocentrism is not necessarily destructive, "not distorted, egocentric, and somewhat paranoid thinking" (Vartanian, 2001, p. 378). Instead, the imaginary audience and other aspects of intuitive thinking "may signal growth toward cognitive maturity" and personal adaptation (Vartanian, 2001, p. 378). At least adolescents try to imagine the opinions of others and attempt to reflect on their own existence. Their distorted conclusions may be an advance over the child who does not even contemplate such ideas.

Reality and Fantasy Because teenagers can think analytically and hypothetically, they can use computers not only to obtain factual information and to keep in touch with friends but also to leave the reality of daily life and escape into the realm of imagination and fantasy. This temporary reprieve may be particularly important for adolescents like 17-year-old Julisa (*right*). She is a student in a high school in Brownsville, Texas, that offers computer labs and other programs to help children of migrant laborers keep up with their peers.

Intuitive Conclusions

The advantage of intuitive thinking is that it is quick and emotional; the disadvantage is that it is often wrong (Moshman, 2000). To see this, think about the following problem. Every card in a pack has a letter on one side and a number on the other. Prove or disprove this proposition: *If a card has a vowel on one side, then it always has an even number on the other side.* Of the following four cards, turn over *only those cards* that will confirm or disconfirm the statement:

E   7   K   4

Which cards must be turned over?

While you are pondering (the answer will be presented soon), consider the research of Paul Klaczynski on the thought processes of hundreds of adolescents, half younger (average age 13) and half older (average age 16). In one study (Klaczynski, 2001), adolescents were presented with 19 problems of logic, including the following one:

> Timothy is very good looking, strong, and does not smoke. He likes hanging around with his male friends, watching sports on TV, and driving his Ford Mustang convertible. He's very concerned with how he looks and with being in good shape. He is a high school senior now and is trying to get a college scholarship.

Response for High School Guidance Counselors (from page 367): It depends on what your particular students need; schools vary a great deal. However, all students need to talk and think about their choices and options so that they will not act impulsively. Therefore, providing information and a listening ear might be the most important thing you can do. You will also want to keep all students in challenging and interesting classes until they graduate.

Based on this [description], rank each statement in terms of how likely it is to be true. . . . The most likely statement should get a 1. The least likely statement should get a 6.

_____ Timothy has a girlfriend.
_____ Timothy is an athlete.
_____ Timothy is popular and an athlete.
_____ Timothy is a teacher's pet and has a girlfriend.
_____ Timothy is a teacher's pet.
_____ Timothy is popular.

In ranking these statements, 71 percent of the older adolescents made at least one analytic error. They ranked a double statement (e.g., athlete *and* popular) as more likely than either of the single statements included in it (athlete *or* popular). A double statement cannot be more likely than either of its parts; therefore, those 71 percent were illogical and wrong. This is an example of intuitive thought because the adolescents jumped ahead to the more inclusive statement, taking a quick, experiential leap rather than sticking to the narrow, logical task at hand.

Almost all adolescents (even the younger ones) were analytical and logical on some problems and illogical on others. Generally, logic improved with age, although not necessarily with intelligence. Klaczynski (2001) is convinced that most adolescents are sufficiently mature to solve logical problems, but "most adolescents do not demonstrate a level of performance commensurate with their abilities" (p. 854).

What would motivate adolescents to use—or fail to use—their newly acquired analytic mode of information processing? In another series of experiments, Klaczynski (2000) asked adolescents to judge the strength and persuasiveness of a bogus research report. When the conclusion was *unfavorable to their own religion,* most adolescents noticed and articulated the logical fallacies. Some even rejected the premise as implausible. One said, "I don't see why they did this research," oblivious to the fact that research is needed to disprove as well as to prove hypotheses. However, when the conclusion was *favorable to their own religion,* fewer adolescents found fault with either the logic or the research hypothesis.

The older adolescents were more analytic than the younger group, and they identified weaknesses even in the research that favored their own religion. But they were also *more* biased. They saw greater weaknesses in the research that was unfavorable to their religion, and they were more likely to dismiss such research as implausible, impossible, and flat-out wrong (Klaczynski, 2000).

Interestingly, after reading the bogus research, the adolescents tended to value their faith more than they had before. In other words, analyzing research did not detract from religious beliefs already held; just the opposite. It seems that reaching adolescence improves both kinds of thought—the ability to analyze logically and the ability to justify intuitive conclusions. Klaczynski (2000) wrote:

> Analytic reasoning competence . . . has long been considered the pinnacle of adolescent cognitive development [but] . . . biased use of judgmental heuristics [rules of thumb] . . . increases with age in some social arenas. One possible explanation for this unexpected finding is that . . . older adolescents are more flexible and are more geared toward cognitive economy.

[pp. 1347, 1361]

Cognitive economy means the most efficient and effective use of mental resources. As the knowledge base increases, as thinking processes accelerate, and as both analysis and intuition become more forceful, adolescents use their minds better. It is efficient to use formal, analytic thinking in science class and to use emotional, experiential thinking (which is quicker and more satisfying) for personal issues. For example, if an adolescent meets a possible romantic partner, an

JACKSONVILLE JOURNAL COURIER / THE IMAGE WORKS

Thinking Many Moves Ahead Unlike simple games of chance, which younger children enjoy, chess requires some deductive thinking, which involves general principles, such as protecting your king, focusing on the center, and changing strategies as the game progresses. These students are among 20 who played simultaneous chess games against an adult champion.

? *Observational Quiz* (see answer, page 372): Beyond the intellectual challenge of chess, what other type of problem do these adolescents seem to be solving?

analytic response would include assessing that person's background, personality, habits, and values and measuring those traits according to one's personal history and preferences. Intuitive thinking, by contrast, would respond to sparks of interest and perhaps voice tone, body shape, and smile. In this case, intuition would be quicker, and analysis might come later—before marriage, not before the first date. Adolescents are quick to "fall in love" and quick to "break up," partly because of their cognitive approach.

As you can see, both analytic and intuitive thought are useful, each in its own way. As one scientist explains:

> How we do think, I believe, is with two minds, experiential and rational. Our hope lies in learning . . . how to use them in a harmonious manner.
>
> *[Epstein, 1994, p. 721]*

For adolescents, learning how to use both modes of thought usually results from social thinking. For example, the task in the E–7–K–4 example is "notoriously difficult." The first thought is to turn over the even-numbered card. Almost everyone wants to turn over the E and the 4, and almost everyone is wrong (Moshman, 2000). However, when college students who guessed wrong on their own are given a chance to discuss the problem as a group, 75 percent get it right, avoiding the 4 card (even if the 4 card has a consonant on the other side, that doesn't disprove the statement) and selecting the E and the 7 cards (if the 7 had a vowel on the other side, the proposition would be false) (Moshman & Geil, 1998). This example demonstrates a very important idea: Quick, intuitive thinking can, with discussion and guidance, become analytic and logical. Adolescents can, and do, change their minds when a logical argument is presented to them.

Any overview of adolescent thought must begin by describing the impressive advances of this stage. In part because of brain maturation, adolescents improve their existing cognitive skills, deductive logic is added to their cognitive repertoire, and intuitive thinking becomes faster and more intense. Consequently, adolescents know more, think faster, and realize hypothetical

!Answer to Observational Quiz (from page 371): The photo shows partners who must collaborate in order to produce the desired outcome. How to work with another adolescent is the most urgent curriculum of all during the secondary school years, requiring speculation, strategy, and study of each individual case.

possibilities, using systematic analysis and abstract logic beyond the ability of most younger children. Piaget called this stage *formal operational thought,* and he developed many experiments to demonstrate its occurrence.

Contemporary researchers find that formal operational thought is much more variable, from person to person and from domain to domain, than Piaget imagined. Intuitive thought is evident, especially at the younger ages, in adolescent egocentrism, when self-centered young people are notably illogical and self-conscious. Adolescents sometimes use intuitive or heuristic reasoning, especially when their emotions are involved. Although formal operational thought is not universally used, it may be universally possible after age 11. When encouraged by adults or peers, adolescents can analyze a situation's various possibilities.

Adolescent Decision Making

An understanding that adolescent thinking is both analytic and intuitive is important for a practical reason: to help students choose wisely. For the first time in their lives, teenagers make independent decisions that have far-reaching consequences. They decide how diligently to study, whether to stay in school, what courses to take, whether and where to go to college, whom to befriend, which career to pursue, for whom to vote, how to express their religious beliefs, what to do about sex, which drugs and foods to consume or avoid, whether to get a job, how to spend their money.

Because they think about possibilities more than practicalities, however, adolescents seldom actually decide such matters by rationally exploring all the options and choosing the best one. Peers can help, but their advice is often ill-informed. Adult guidance may help—or it may backfire.

Weighing Risks and Benefits

Adults are not necessarily wiser than teenagers in calculating the risks and benefits of various decisions (Gruber, 2001). In fact, adults do not necessarily decide wisely for themselves: In almost every nation in the world, the worst outcomes (drug addiction, homicide, accidental death) are far more common after age 20 than before (Heuveline, 2002). Adult decision making is often based on mistaken assumptions, damaging ignorance, and questionable priorities, just as adolescent thought is (Allwood & Selart, 2001; Byrnes, 1998; Ranyard et al., 1997).

Nevertheless, teenagers need special protection from poor judgment, for several reasons (O'Donoghue & Rabin, 2001):

- The younger a person is, the more serious are the consequences of risk taking. A year in prison, for example, is much more damaging at age 16 than at age 46.
- Adolescent choices are long-lasting. "A significant determinant of the well-being of many older persons will be the risky decisions that they made in their youth," such as dropping out of school, having a baby, or joining a gang (Gruber, 2001, p. 25).
- Adolescents are particularly likely to overrate the joys of the moment and disregard the risks of a mind-altering drug, a sexually arousing situation, a disrespectful police officer, a dangerous dare, and the like. They discount consequences, miscalculate probabilities, and risk their futures (O'Donoghue & Rabin, 2001).

Every decision requires the weighing of risk against opportunity. How should risk itself be weighed? Some people are "risk-averse"—they never do anything that might end in disaster. Others "throw caution to the wind"; they enjoy the thrill of spontaneity, of impulse, of being close to danger. Good decision making avoids both extremes, rejecting both overly risky and overly cautious choices. Personality, culture, and situation are all factors in risk assessment, but age is probably the strongest influence of all. The allure of risky behavior increases from age 11 to age 18.

There are also interesting sex differences. Boys are more inclined than girls to seek thrills, such as parachuting or roller coasting, and to rebel against adult authority, as by engaging in secret drinking or illicit sex (Gullone et al., 2000). But adolescent girls admire risk-taking boys, which encourages the boys to be even more daring. For both sexes, behaviors that adults consider foolhardy (skipping school, using drugs, breaking the law, having unprotected sex, driving too fast, and so on) are ways to gain status and respect, to become sexually attractive, to strengthen friendship bonds, and to demonstrate freedom from parental restraints (Lightfoot, 1997). In adolescent culture, risk taking is viewed as brave, while caution is considered "goody-goody" or wimpish.

MICHELLE AGINS / NYT PICTURES

Which College, Where? As a 17-year-old basketball star, high school senior Niesha Butler had a critical decision to make—which of hundreds of colleges to choose. Her top list included Harvard, Virginia, Notre Dame, and Georgia Tech—although she thought of skipping college and turning pro because "if the money is there, why not?" That was a possibility her parents—who had banned television from their home years before—would not let her consider. She chose Georgia Tech, where she was awarded a full scholarship and received living expenses.

Good decision-making skills take time to develop. This was shown by a study in which life dilemmas were posed to 204 subjects aged 14 to 37. Among the adolescents, wiser, more mature analysis was evident with each passing year. This gradual improvement suggests that "adolescents are acquiring reasoning capacities that may support both the acquisition and expression of wisdom-related knowledge and judgment" (Pasupathi et al., 2001, p. 358).

Making Decisions About School, Jobs, and Sex

Now let's explore adolescent decision making in three key areas: school, employment, and sex.

School: The Volatile Mismatch

Graduation from high school confers many benefits. In every nation, high school graduates stay healthier, live longer, are richer, and are more likely to marry, vote, stay out of jail, and buy homes than their less educated contemporaries. U.S. statistics illustrate the point: Yearly income of heads of household (that is, the principal breadwinner, male or female) averages $16,154 for those who never attended high school, twice that ($34,373) for those with a high school diploma, and almost twice that again ($66,474) for those with at least a bachelor's degree (U.S. Bureau of the Census, 2000). High school graduates are more likely to be employed, not only immediately but for the next 40 years (U.S. Department of Education, 2001). Other variables (family background and IQ among them) affect these statistical correlations, but even when they are equalized, education is a significant predictor of success.

Worldwide statistics show that, even in the poorest nations, more children are attending high school. Similarly, the graduation rate has improved for all ethnic groups in the United States over the past 30 years, with the African-American dropout rate cut in half (see Figure 15.4). Nonetheless, too many youth, especially Hispanics, still leave school without a diploma. As you can see from Figure 15.5 (on page 375), almost every nation has some high school dropouts.

Why would any adolescent jeopardize his or her future by deciding to drop out of school? Many critics blame a **volatile mismatch** (Carnegie Council on Adolescent Development, 1989) between the current needs of adolescents and the traditional structures of their schools (Bruner, 1996).

volatile mismatch A lack of fit between a person and his or her environment that causes the person to become angry, hostile, or depressed. Such a situation is said to be typical of teenagers and schools.

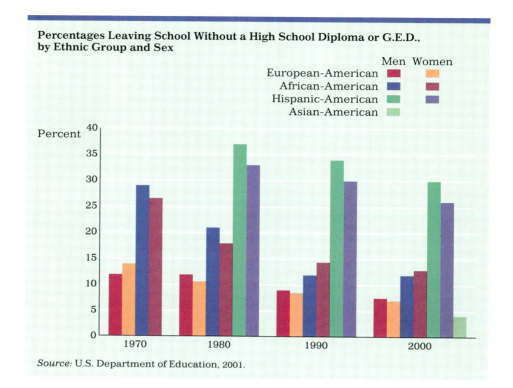

Percentages Leaving School Without a High School Diploma or G.E.D., by Ethnic Group and Sex

	Men	Women
European-American	■ (red)	■ (orange)
African-American	■ (blue)	■ (dark red)
Hispanic-American	■ (green)	■ (purple)
Asian-American	■ (light green)	

Source: U.S. Department of Education, 2001.

FIGURE 15.4 No Diploma Shown here are the percentages of U.S. adolescents and young adults, ages 16–24, who are not in high school and do not have a high school diploma or its equivalent. The percentage has decreased for some groups, but the dropout rate remains high among Hispanics.

? *Critical Thinking Question* (see answer, page 376): Why are no Hispanic rates shown for 1970?

To begin with, supportive interaction among students and, especially, between teachers and students is crucial for helping adolescents find the harmonious balance between analytic and intuitive thought. However, compared to primary schools (which were designed for the cognitive abilities of younger children), most secondary schools still seem focused on the elite, in that they feature intensified competition, rigid behavioral demands, and academic standards that do not reflect adolescents' needs. This structure was established in 1900, when few students in any nation (only 8 percent in the United States) completed high school, and it persists today in many nations.

Lessons Their Ancestors Never Studied
Education today prepares students to think for themselves, not just memorize facts. This photo shows a class in prehistory, in contrast to traditional history classes, which began with the first written texts. Note also the "hidden" curriculum—the way learning occurs. The teacher is acting as a guide rather than as an authority figure. The students are encouraged to draw their own conclusions about the evidence before them. Moreover, this interracial school is in Johannesburg, South Africa. All these features impart lessons that, presumably, will serve these young people well in the twenty-first century.

AP / WIDE WORLD PHOTOS

Grades on report cards almost always decline as students move to secondary schools; the first year after primary school is usually a "low ebb" of learning (Covington & Dray, 2002). That decline sets in place the mismatch between student learning and school structure.

One problem is the systemic lack of adult guidance. For example, teacher–student conversations are almost impossible in large high schools, because the two groups have separate lunchrooms, bathrooms, and even parking lots. Hallways are designed to keep people moving, not to encourage social interaction. Yet all the research suggests that adolescents learn best with guided participation.

Even school schedules undercut education. In the United States, the first bell typically rings before 8:00 A.M., when adolescent minds are not yet awake. The curriculum is divided into disciplines (originally delineated centuries ago, distinguishing biology from chemistry, history from literature, psychology from health) and is often taught in 40-minute blocks by a variety of teachers, who instruct about 200 students each week. All this makes it more difficult for students to make the logical connections between disciplines and thus to achieve formal operational thought. Schools let out for the summer, an echo of the days when most children had to help out on the family farm. Taken as a whole, these factors hinder the wide-ranging curiosity and personal involvement that are central to adolescent cognitive development.

A related problem is school size. In large schools only a few juniors and seniors can be involved in extracurricular activities, such as sports, theater, music, art, science fairs, and chess clubs. All these activities encourage student commitment to their schools and foster constructive relationships with teachers and with other students, thereby enhancing school attendance and academic performance (Eccles & Barber, 1999). Yet most students (60 percent) in the United States attend high schools with enrollments of more than 1,000. Only 3 percent attend high schools, either public or private, with fewer than 200 students (U.S. Department of Education, 2001). The larger the school, the less involved and motivated the individual students are.

Ironically, to save money, over the last decade schools have grown in size and cut back on extracurricular activities, including sports. This affects all adolescents, but Hispanic students, who are most likely to drop out, are also least likely to be on high school sports teams (CDC, June 28, 2002). The lack of such involvement not only makes adolescents more likely to leave school but also makes them less likely to learn overall (Hansen et al., 2003).

Internationally, education systems vary in expectations (virtually everyone graduates from high school in Japan and Norway, but only a third do in Brazil, Indonesia, and Mexico), in curriculum (language arts are stressed in France, math in China), in average class size (23 in Canadian high schools, 8 in Norwegian ones), in teacher training, in pedagogical methods, and in legal requirements (Alexander, 2000; U.S. Department of Education, 2001). It is not obvious which particular features are best for students, but high teacher expectations tend to increase student interest and aspirations (Wentzel, 2002). Contrary to what many teachers intuitively believe, motivation is not innate (Torff & Sternberg, 2001), and self-esteem by itself does not promote success (Baumeister et al., 2003).

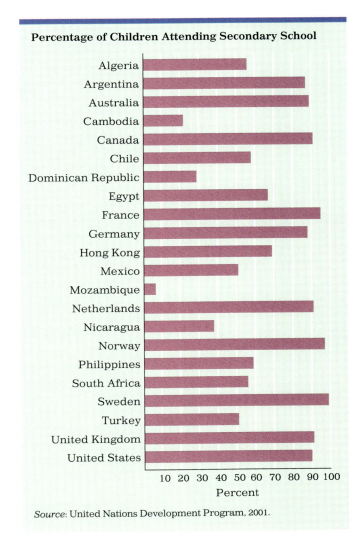

Percentage of Children Attending Secondary School

Algeria, Argentina, Australia, Cambodia, Canada, Chile, Dominican Republic, Egypt, France, Germany, Hong Kong, Mexico, Mozambique, Netherlands, Nicaragua, Norway, Philippines, South Africa, Sweden, Turkey, United Kingdom, United States

10 20 30 40 50 60 70 80 90 100
Percent

Source: United Nations Development Program, 2001.

FIGURE 15.5 Growing Recognition of Secondary Education's Importance These percentages were calculated by dividing the number of children in secondary school (grades 7–12) by the total number of children in the corresponding age group. Every nation has a certain proportion of children of the appropriate age who are not in school.

A study of 300 tenth-grade students found that the best teachers "take pupils seriously," "have confidence in them," "push them to do well," and "make it easier for them to understand" (Tatar, 1998). A critical factor seems to be the belief, on the part of students and teachers, that learning is the result of effort, not an inborn trait. Learning enhances self-esteem more than the other way around. Students who believed that they could learn more if they put forth more effort

> told us they felt smart, not only when they were striving to master new tasks, but also when they put their knowledge to work to help their peers learn. Thus within this framework, rather than being rivals for self-esteem, peers can gain self-esteem by cooperating and by facilitating each other's learning.
>
> *[Dweck, 1999]*

All this suggests that the problem of poor motivation during secondary education can be overcome once families and schools understand what adolescent cognitive development requires and take the needed steps: "Motivation is not just a characteristic of the individual but also a result of the home and school environmental contexts" (Wigfield & Eccles, 2002, p. 5). Students decide what to study and how much to work, as well as whether to stay in school, but all these decisions are powerfully affected by teachers and parents.

Working Outside of School

Few adolescents can, or should, decide their future careers. Nonetheless, in keeping with the concept of the personal fable, unrealistic career expectations are typical during high school. For example, in one large study 37 percent expected (and 45 percent wanted) careers that only 1 percent of the employed population actually have. Most of the other 63 percent also had unrealistic goals (Csikszentmihalyi & Schneider, 2000).

One aspect of adolescent life that has surprised researchers is the extent of employment outside of school. In some nations, part-time jobs prepare students for adult employment. This is not true in the United States, where most adolescents work at boring, dead-end positions. The decision to seek work is not carefully thought out. Instead of analysis and rational planning, adolescents use easier heuristic thinking ("jobs bring money"), and so do their parents ("work teaches responsibility"). Not coincidentally, one study found that seniors in high school who were employed, no matter how few hours per week they worked, had lower grades and poorer relationships with parents and friends. They also were more likely to smoke cigarettes—a gateway drug that indicates poor decision making in other areas as well (Largie et al., 2001). Similarly, teenage girls who are employed are more likely to be sexually active than those who are not working (Rich & Kim, 2002).

Attitudes and practices regarding jobs and school vary a great deal from country to country (Hamilton & Lempert, 1996). In some nations, such as Japan, almost no adolescent is employed or even does significant chores at home, because the family and culture agree that the adolescent's obligation is to study. In other nations, including several in Europe, some older adolescents have jobs that are an integral part of their school curriculum. For example, in Germany most students pursue a dual-track curriculum—academic training coupled with on-the-job experience. Adolescents choose a particular vocation from the 360 that are offered, and then they are chosen by a particular employer, who trains them in conjunction with their schoolwork. The hope of the students is that training will lead to a paying job. However, even in Germany the job–school connection is breaking down, because employers want flexible, independent employees, not newly trained 18-year-olds, and adolescents prefer to be among the 20 percent who study for college and a profession (Cook & Furstenburg, 2002).

Especially for Junior High Teachers You think your class is interesting and you know you care about your students, yet many of them cut class, come late, or seem to sleep through it. What do you do?

!*Answer to Critical Thinking Question* (from page 374): Before 1980, the U.S. government did not collect separate data on Hispanics. People with Latin American ancestors were categorized as either black or white.

Worldwide, meaningful jobs for teens are scarce. Sixty years ago, work kept adolescents out of trouble, enabled them to help the family meet its expenses, and taught them money-management skills, but none of that is true today. Especially when adolescents are employed more than 20 hours a week, having a job means less study, lower grades, and more risk taking. The money earned usually goes for clothes, entertainment, cars, alcohol, and drugs—not the basic household necessities or into a savings account (Bachman & Schulenberg, 1993; Mortimer et al., 1996; Steinberg & Dornbusch, 1991).

Provocative data comparing North American and European nations show a negative correlation between hours of after-school employment and learning in school (Kelly, 1998). Even from one year to the next, having a job pulls down the grade point average (Steinberg, 1993). Thus, from a life-span perspective, adolescence should be a time for academic learning, not vocational experience. Most U.S. teenagers have part-time jobs before they graduate from high school, but the demands of the economy and of employers do not mesh with the intellectual and educational needs of adolescents.

What Teenagers Decide About Sex

As you saw in Chapter 14, sex is a biological drive, and the decisions adolescents make about sex can have biological consequences, including sexually transmitted infections (STIs) and teen pregnancy. However, decisions about sex are far from biologically inevitable. An adolescent's culture and cohort have a strong influence, as the following facts suggest:

■ *International differences in teen birth rates are dramatic* (Teitler, 2002). Teenagers in the United States have far more babies than do their peers in any other developed nation, both because U.S. teens are more sexually active and because they use less contraception and have fewer abortions. The birth rate among unmarried adolescent girls is more than 10 times higher in the United States than in Japan.

■ *Cultural differences in onset of sexual intercourse are vast.* In Mali, by age 18, 72 percent of the girls but only 26 percent of the boys are sexually experienced. In Brazil, the genders are reversed: 29 percent of the girls and 63 percent of the boys are sexually active by age 18. In other nations, the sexes are equal in rate of sexual experience, but the rates vary. For example, in the Philippines, only 6 percent of 17-year-old girls and 7 percent of the boys are sexually experienced; in Canada, 50 percent of both boys and girls are sexually active by age 17 (Singh et al., 2000).

■ *The teen birth rate worldwide is decreasing.* This trend began in the early 1980s and has continued steadily ever since. In the United States, while the overall rate of teen births is still high relative to rates in other countries, every ethnic group (especially African-Americans) and every age group (especially 15- to 17-year-olds) shows a decrease (National Center for Health Statistics, 2001) (see Figure 15.6).

■ *The use of contraceptives has increased.* Contraception, particularly condom use among adolescent boys, has at least doubled in most nations since 1990. Usage rates of specific contraceptive methods vary enormously. For example, oral contraceptives (the Pill) are very rare in Japan and the recently legalized "morning-after" pill is seldom used in the United States, but both methods are quite popular in France.

All these facts point to the same conclusion: Although biology has not changed, today's adolescents are making different decisions about sex than their

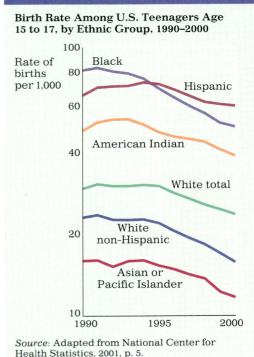

Birth Rate Among U.S. Teenagers Age 15 to 17, by Ethnic Group, 1990–2000

Source: Adapted from National Center for Health Statistics, 2001, p. 5.

FIGURE 15.6 Fewer Children Having Children The recent across-the-board drop in the rate of births to adolescents aged 15 to 17 is especially remarkable for two reasons: The abortion rate among teenage girls has dropped slightly, and the rate of sexual activity among 15- to 17-year-old girls has not changed significantly.

sexually active Traditionally, a euphemism for "having had sexual intercourse"; still in use, even though today many adolescents engage in many sexual activities other than intercourse.

Response for Junior High Teachers (from page 376): Students need both challenge and involvement. Make sure your lessons are not too easy and that all students participate. For example, structure discussions by small groups that must report to the whole class, assign oral reports that must bring new information to the class, create debates and role-plays that require some rehearsing and practice, and so on. As a teacher, you probably value abstract ideas; remember that adolescents value each other's opinions and their own voices.

predecessors did a mere 10 years ago, and those decisions are influenced by culture more than by biology. In most nations, today's adolescents decide to have less sex, with fewer partners, using better contraception than a generation ago. What changed their thinking? Scientists have many hypotheses, but political disagreements make solid sex research difficult. For example, federal law forbids researchers to ask teenagers confidential questions unless their parents have given written permission, and even large surveys are hindered by uncertainties over terminology and sample makeup.

Indeed, researchers are not even sure what the term **sexually active** means to teenagers. Ten years ago, when adolescents were said to be sexually active, that meant they had had sexual intercourse (penile-vaginal penetration). Consequently, almost all research on adolescent sex today asks whether the person has had intercourse; if the answer is no, the person is assumed to be sexually inactive.

However, adolescent sexual behavior is far more diverse than the "Did they or didn't they?" question about intercourse reveals (Whitaker et al., 2000). It often includes mutual masturbation, oral sex, and shared bathing. Yet many young people who have oral sex do not consider themselves to be having sex (Horan et al., 1998; Remez, 2000; Sanders & Reinisch, 1999) and therefore do not think they need any information about their sexual decisions, about STIs, or about contraception. An adolescent's notion that oral sex is "safe" is an uninformed, and dangerously egocentric, belief (Kalmuss et al., 2003).

Sex Education in School

Almost all secondary schools worldwide provide sex education, often beginning at age 11 or earlier (Landry et al., 2000). Beyond providing the facts about sexually transmitted infections, reproduction, and puberty, most high school programs teach students how to say "no" to unwanted sexual activity (*MMWR*, 2000). From a developmental perspective, this is to be commended: Teenagers need not only experience with formal operational thinking (the facts of biological

A Public Kiss The specific ways in which physical affection is expressed depend on cultural context and cohort, not just on biological processes—as Mike knew when he presented Tiffany with a white carnation for Valentine's Day.

? *Observational Quiz* (see answer, page 380): In what year and in which country did this kiss occur?

sex and the likelihood of pregnancy) but also practice with the emotional expression and social interaction that reflect their intuitive thinking.

In the United States, almost all schools (93 percent) teach students about sex and health (a marked increase since 1980, and even since 1990), emphasizing how to avoid drugs, AIDS, and pregnancy. Most focus on the dangers of sex and the benefits of abstinence, sometimes exclusively. There are declines here, as well: Only 43 percent of U.S. schools teach the correct use of condoms, a decline over the past decade (CDC, August 18, 2000). Teachers today are less likely to explain methods of contraception (only 40 percent mention mifepristone, the drug that halts pregnancy in the first few weeks), less likely to provide referrals for medical treatment (35 percent, down from 48 percent in 1988), less likely to discuss sexual orientation (51 percent, down from 68 percent) (Darroch et al., 2000). In 2000, about 35 percent of all school districts in the United States (especially in the South) required that sexual abstinence be taught as the only acceptable alternative to marriage and forbade mention of contraception, but few teachers are actually that inflexible in the classroom (Gold & Nash, 2001).

Most adolescents get additional information by talking with friends, older siblings, and parents once sex education begins. That may explain why today's 15- to 17-year-olds have fewer pregnancies than did their predecessors. However, the students who are most vulnerable to STIs and unwanted pregnancy are under age 16 and cognitively immature—unlikely to postpone sex until they have sex education in school, where they might learn to say "no" (Kalmuss et al., 2003).

Some adults worry that if teenagers know too much about sex and contraception, they will be encouraged to experiment. Given the nature of adolescent cognition, this worry seems needless. Adolescents are eager to learn what is possible, and they enjoy disputing conventional wisdom, but possibility does not necessarily become reality and discussion does not necessarily lead to action. A review of more than 100 sex-education programs by the Surgeon General of the United States found that teaching adolescents about contraception

> does not increase adolescent sexual activity, either by hastening the onset of sexual intercourse, increasing the frequency of sexual intercourse, or increasing the number of sexual partners. . . . Some evaluated programs increased condom use or contraception use for adolescents who were sexually active.
>
> *[Satcher, 2001]*

From what we know about adolescent thinking—hypothetical, questioning, deductive—it makes sense that adolescents do not necessarily try out whatever they learn. Possibility does not mean actuality (see Appendix A, p. A-16). A Boston survey of high school students, some sexually active and some not, found that the two groups agreed that schools should provide more factual information about sex, and they resented the moral instruction that was often presented along with it (Hacker et al., 2000).

Cultures are dynamic, not static. They can work to decrease the birth rate as well as to foster it, and every nation has witnessed shifts in rates of adolescent sex, STIs, and pregnancy. One notable example comes from France, where nurses in all the public and church-sponsored schools were authorized, as of January 2000, to provide emergency contraception to any girl who requested it. They were also told to encourage sexually active girls to talk to their parents. France's teen pregnancy rate is only a third as high as that of the United States, but the French want to reduce it further. One government official explained:

> Young people, we assume, are going to be interested in sexual relationships. You can't forbid sex, but you can ask young people to be responsible. That's what this campaign is about—protecting young people.
>
> *[quoted in Boonstra, 2000]*

Especially for Religious Leaders Suppose you believe very strongly in some tenet of your faith, but the youth group includes teenagers who act contrary to your belief. What do you do?

Risk Taking, Decision Making, and Cultures

When it comes to assumptions about adolescent decision making, cultures vary widely. In the United States, for instance, adolescents are expected to chart their own educational, vocational, and sexual courses about a decade younger than in Italy, where most single young adults continue to live with their parents (Cook & Furstenburg, 2002).

Culture and national trends are very influential. For example, research on specific programs of sex education for adolescents in Africa found wide differences in program impact, which resulted partly from the cultural context. The most dramatic decreases in STIs and unwanted pregnancies have occurred in Cameroon, where youth leaders facilitated sex discussion groups in which low-cost condoms were sold and where condom use was demonstrated at soccer games (Agha, 2002). The approach was well suited to that culture, in which youths are highly likely to listen to other youths and where soccer is the focus of adolescent gatherings and conversations.

There are many similarities as well as differences in cultural approaches to adolescent decisions regarding sex. No culture wants overpopulation, sick mothers, or dying children. Consequently, every nation seeks health education for its young people that may differ in its specifics but includes instruction in responsible sexual decision making. "Reproductive decisions and behavior are products of interaction of individuals in their cultural context" (David & Russo, 2003, pp. 195–196), so sex education for, and decision making by, adolescents may reflect both the individual culture and the universal goal: a young person whose future is not jeopardized by uninformed choices.

No one is a helpless product of his or her age, sex, culture, or cohort. The final decisions about sex, drugs, school, careers, and other matters are made by individuals, in consultation with their families and peers and guided by their communities. A review of family planning across the globe notes that people of all ages make responsible, healthy decisions about sex if the facts—and confidential services—are available (Townsend, 2003).

This point was forcefully made by researchers who analyzed the data from Ad Health, a comprehensive, longitudinal study of U.S. teenagers (Blum et al., 2000). Each ethnic group had somewhat different patterns of teenager risks (see Table 15.1), yet family factors outweighed ethnic differences. No matter what their ethnicity, adolescents who lived with both their parents took fewer risks than did adolescents in single-parent homes; adolescents from high-income families were more cautious with sex and weapons and more adventurous with alcohol and cigarettes. Yet, as these researchers report, influences beyond these family characteristics must be taken into account:

> Knowing race/ethnicity, income, and family structure provides little predictive power at the individual level. . . . Rather we must look at neighborhood, family,

!Answer to Observational Quiz (from page 378): The contemporary United States is one of the few countries where large, comprehensive high schools are common and rules against public displays of affection by students had been lifted by 1990. In fact, this high school is in Syracuse, New York, and the photograph was taken in 1999.

Risky Business This table, which uses the U.S. census ethnic categories for responses in the Ad Health study, shows the comparative risk taking of the three largest ethnic groups of adolescents. Not tallied are Asian-Americans, who are lowest on all five indicators, and Native Americans, who are relatively high. Knowing people's ethnicity, or even knowing their income or family structure, does not make it possible to predict how likely an individual is to take any particular risk. Much more relevant is knowing thought processes and immediate social context—family and peers.

TABLE 15.1 Adolescent Risk Taking by U.S. Ethnic Group

Risky Behavior	Whites	Hispanics	Blacks
Smoking cigarettes: frequency and amount	Highest	Medium	Lowest
Drinking alcohol: frequency and amount	Highest	Medium	Lowest
Carrying a weapon or being involved in an incident where a weapon was used	Lowest	Quite high	Highest
Sex: ever had intercourse	Lowest	Quite low	Highest
Suicidal thoughts, attempts	Highest	Quite high	Lowest

Source: Blum et al., 2000.

Not Me! A young woman jumps into the Pacific Ocean near Santa Cruz, California, while at a friend's birthday party. The jump is illegal, yet since 1975, 52 people have died on these cliffs. Hundreds of young people each year decide that the thrill is worth the risk, aided by the invincibility fable and by what they think are sensible precautions. (Note that she is wearing shoes. Also note that the dog has apparently decided against risking a jump.)

school, peer and individual characteristics and how those characteristics interact within various demographic groups to truly understand the dynamics that contribute to specific risk behaviors.

[Blum et al., 2000]

Gaining a true understanding of the dynamics of adolescent decision making is a challenge. It is apparent that many adolescents make faulty choices and that many families, schools, and cultures do not provide teenagers with adequate instruction and support. It is not obvious how adolescent thinking might be matched with twenty-first-century realities. What is known is that to learn how adolescents make their choices—what facts, thoughts, and values they use—one must ask detailed and personal questions of hundreds of them, from every region and group, and listen to the answers carefully, without judging. Such research is currently impossible on a large scale, but every reader of this book knows teenagers who could explain their thoughts and practices regarding schools, sex, and the future. Embarrassing, perhaps—but think about the consequences of not asking.

Response for Religious Leaders (from page 379): This is not the time for dogma; teenagers intuitively rebel against authority. Nor is it the time to be quiet about your beliefs, because teenagers need some structures to help them think. Instead of going to either extreme, begin a dialogue. Listen respectfully to their concerns and emotions, and encourage them to think more deeply about the implications of their actions.

A major adult concern in regard to adolescent cognition is that adolescents often take foolish risks and make destructive decisions. Although adolescent egocentrism is one factor, people of all ages sometimes think illogically. Moreover, adolescents gain status among their peers by taking risks, so their risk taking is not as thoughtless as adults may think.

Educational practices and social values may contribute to poor choices, and many adolescents are more interested in their momentary impulses and the advice of peers than in the wise counsel of their elders. The young person who quits school, who works more than 20 hours a week, or who is naive about sex may choose actions with long-lasting repercussions. Schools, curricula, and teachers have influence in all these areas. So can the specifics of sex education, as shown by international variations and by the recent downturn in the rate of adolescent pregnancy.

Adolescent thought processes may seem egocentric, intuitive, and reckless, but teenagers become more logical with every passing year. How does cognitive development actually affect the decisions that teenagers make? Adolescents take risks and follow their intuitions and emotions, but they also ask questions and analyze logical alternatives.

A few statistics will serve as a thought-provoking conclusion: Almost half of all U.S. high school seniors are virgins, and 96 percent of all teenage girls have never given birth. Most adolescents plan to go to college and expect to become workers and taxpayers, husbands and wives, fathers and mothers. Most graduate from high school, including 70 percent of Hispanic boys, the U.S. ethnic and gender group with the highest dropout rate. More than 99 percent of all teenagers in the world reach age 20 alive and in good health, primarily because they have learned to think about all the possibilities that life in the twenty-first century might hold for them.

SUMMARY

Intellectual Advances

1. All the aspects of cognition that have been developing since infancy continue to advance during adolescence. Underlying all these advances is brain maturation. As myelination continues and coordination between various parts of the brain becomes more elaborate, adolescents become quicker and deeper thinkers.

2. *Formal operational thought* is Piaget's term for adolescent and adult cognition, the fourth of his four periods of cognitive development. He tested and demonstrated formal operational thought with various problems that might be encountered by students in a high school science or math class, such as adjusting weights and their distance from the center to make a scale balance.

3. Adolescents are no longer earthbound and concrete in their thinking; they prefer to imagine the possible, the probable, and even the impossible, instead of focusing on what is real. They develop hypotheses and explore, using deductive reasoning.

4. Intuitive thinking, also known as experiential or heuristic thinking, becomes more forceful during adolescence. One manifestation, called adolescent egocentrism, is highly self-centered and emotional, in contrast to the objective, abstract thinking of formal operational thought. Adolescent egocentrism gives rise to the invincibility fable, the personal fable, and the imaginary audience.

5. Adolescents sometimes use illogical, intuitive ways to solve problems, even though they are capable of logical thought. Ideally, adolescents as well as adults combine analytic and intuitive thinking, using the two modes harmoniously to find the best solutions.

Adolescent Decision Making

6. Adolescents have different priorities from those of adults, so they often make choices adults do not condone. Some of these decisions involve taking risks, partly because emotional thinking and impulses will hold sway unless the adolescent takes time to discuss and reflect.

7. Adolescents must decide whether to stay in school and, if they do so, what to study. Many take less challenging courses than they should. Others drop out, even though education correlates with later success in every arena.

8. As students move from primary to secondary education, their grades usually fall and their level of involvement decreases. The reasons include the competitiveness of secondary schools, inappropriate school schedules, and large school size.

9. Given the complexity and discontinuity of career paths in today's world, the teen years are probably too early to settle on a career. Employment during high school is likely to undermine academic achievement instead of teaching useful adult skills.

10. Worldwide, the teen birth rate is declining. Within the United States, specific information about contraception, sexual orientation, and medical services is often not included in sex education.

11. Although education, national policies, and cultural norms affect risk taking, much of the variation in personal risk taking depends on more immediate factors, such as the individual's personality, cognitive maturity, conversations with parents, and peer groups.

KEY TERMS

formal operational thought (p. 364)
hypothetical thought (p. 366)
deductive reasoning (p. 366)

inductive reasoning (p. 366)
adolescent egocentrism (p. 368)

invincibility fable (p. 368)
personal fable (p. 368)
imaginary audience (p. 368)

volatile mismatch (p. 373)
sexually active (p. 378)

APPLICATIONS

1. Ask three people of varied ages or academic experiences to tackle the four-cards problem on page 369. Ask each respondent to express his or her reasoning out loud, as you write it down. Then describe any signs of analytic or heuristic thinking, relating what your respondents said to what you know about adolescent thought.

2. Think of life-changing decisions you have made. In what ways was each decision based on logic and in what ways on emotion? Can you think of a decision you would have made differently if you had known more or analyzed the situation differently?

3. Try to get a copy of the curriculum for sex education at your local high school (if doing so is difficult, analyze why). Comment on which aspects seem helpful and which harmful, noting topics that are omitted as well as those that are included.

4. Talk to a teenager, keeping these questions in mind: How does he or she think? What factors influence his or her decisions? Does he or she seem overly adventurous or overly cautious? Write a paragraph summarizing the answer to each question.

Chapter Sixteen

Adolescence: Psychosocial Development

identity A consistent definition of one's self as a unique individual, in terms of roles, attitudes, beliefs, and aspirations.

possible selves Various ideas of who one might be or might become, each of which is typically acted out and considered as possible identity.

You saw in Chapter 14 that adolescence starts when the physical changes of puberty begin transforming a childish body into an adult one. Then Chapter 15 described how the cognitive changes of adolescence enable the young person to move beyond concrete thought, to think hypothetically. However, as you'll see in this chapter, the psychosocial changes—relating to parents with new independence, to friends with new intimacy, to society with new commitment, and to oneself with new understanding—are the critical ones that bring the young person to adulthood. Becoming an adult is not a matter of size or intellect; it requires social maturity (Grotevant, 1998).

Think of your fellow students in college, specifically of one or two whom you consider "immature." Obviously, that adjective does not refer to physical immaturity or cognitive deficits. Instead, it refers to the psychosocial aspects of maturity—the abilities to regulate emotions, to listen to others, and to assert one's own identity. All these psychosocial developments are included in this chapter.

The Self and Identity

Psychosocial development during adolescence is best understood as a quest for self-understanding, for answering the question "Who am I?" Momentous changes—growth spurt, sexual awakening, schools that are less personal, friendships that are more intimate, and risks that are truly hazardous—challenge each adolescent to find **identity,** a unique and consistent self-definition.

The search for identity is universal. Adolescents worldwide seek to discover who they are and then to determine how their newly identified self relates to past experiences and future goals.

The first step in the identity process is to establish the integrity of personality—that is, to align emotions, thinking, and behavior to be consistent no matter what the place, time, circumstances, or social relationship. "Two-faced," "wishy-washy," and "hypocritical" are among the worst accusations one adolescent can throw at another, because integrity is fervently sought but is frustratingly elusive. Indeed, without some sense of continuity and consistency amidst biological and social change, adolescents feel adrift and depressed.

Multiple Selves

Particularly in early adolescence, teenagers have not one identity but many, some with the potential to become the final identity, or self, and others false and temporary. To be specific, in the process of trying to find their true selves, many adolescents try out **possible selves**—that is, various

TONY FREEMAN / PHOTOEDIT

I'm a Big Girl Now Young teenagers are likely to use their musical taste, their clothing and hairstyles, and sometimes their facial expression to make it very obvious to parents that they are no longer the obedient, predictable children they once were.

false self A set of behaviors that is adopted by a person to combat rejection, to please others, or to try out as a possible self.

identity versus role confusion Erikson's term for the fifth stage of development, in which the person tries to figure out "Who am I?" but is confused as to which of many possible roles to adopt.

identity achievement Erikson's term for the attainment of identity, or the point at which a person understands who he or she is as a unique individual, in accord with past experiences and future plans.

images of who they really are, who they are in different groups or settings, and who they might become (Markus & Nurius, 1986; Markus et al., 1990). Like possible ideas (discussed in Chapter 15), possible selves are explored more imaginatively than realistically.

Many teenagers are keenly aware of how much they are affected by changing settings and circumstances: Their behavior switches from reserved to rowdy, from cooperative to antagonistic, from loving to manipulative. Aware of the inconsistencies among these multiple selves, they ask which one, if any, is the "real me," changing their self-perceptions day by day. One developmentalist noted, "The tortuous search for the self involves a concern with who or what I am, a task made more difficult given the multiple me's that crowd the landscape" (Harter, 1999, p. 68).

As they try to sort through their possible selves, adolescents fear taking on a **false self**, acting in ways that they know are contrary to their core being—even if they are not sure what that core being is. According to one group of researchers (Harter et al., 1996), adolescents display three distinct types of false selves:

- *The acceptable false self.* This false self arises from the adolescent's perception that the real self is rejected by parents and peers—a perception often shaped by the adolescent's own feelings of self-hate. Adolescents who adopt a false self in order to be accepted tend to feel worthless, depressed, and hopeless; they engage in self-betrayal to hide their true nature. They also report low levels of real self-understanding.
- *The pleasing false self.* This second type of false self arises from a wish to impress or please others. It is quite common among adolescents. Those who adopt it appear to be less debilitated psychologically, and to have greater self-understanding, than those whose false selves arise from rejection.
- *The experimental false self.* This false self is one that adolescents try out "just to see how it feels." Compared with adolescents who engage in the first two types of false behavior, these experimenting adolescents report higher self-esteem and self-knowledge. Although they acknowledge that their experimentation is not their usual, expected behavior, they do not feel it is totally fake. In this case, the false self is also a possible self.

This same group of researchers found a developmental pattern: False and contradictory selves are less common at the end of adolescence than in early or mid-adolescence (Harter et al., 1997). One 17-year-old looked back at her possible selves in these words: "In high school, I've explored being an intellectual . . . a class clown . . . a rebellious delinquent. And I've found advantages and disadvantages to all these . . . and this was the beginning of my own self-identity" (quoted in Kroger, 2000, p. 59). By adulthood, false selves have usually been left behind and one of the possible selves is chosen as an identity; the choice is made easier in some cultures and contexts than in others.

Identity Status

Adolescents must decide their unique values and lifestyle. Worldwide, they consider identity one of their top four concerns (see Figure 16.1). They ponder their career options, political identification, religious commitment, and gender identity, questioning how these fit with their expectations for the future and with the beliefs they acquired in the past. These are the four aspects of identity—vocation, politics, religion, and sex—first highlighted by Erik Erikson (1968).

FIGURE 16.1 Who Am I? In one of the most ambitious international studies of adolescents ever done, teams of researchers asked thousands of teenagers—male and female, older and younger, advantaged and disadvantaged, rich and poor—on four continents to "name one concern or problem that causes you to feel worried or pressured; please describe this concern in more detail." Of the fourteen possible categories, ten were rarely mentioned, including war, sexuality, and extreme poverty. The four categories most often mentioned were material desires (such as the need to earn money), schooling (such as worry about school failure), interpersonal (such as friendship), and identity (including self-concept). Answers varied by gender, age, socioeconomic status, and nationality.

?Observational Quiz (see answer, page 389): On each of the four concerns, which nation ranks highest and which ranks lowest?

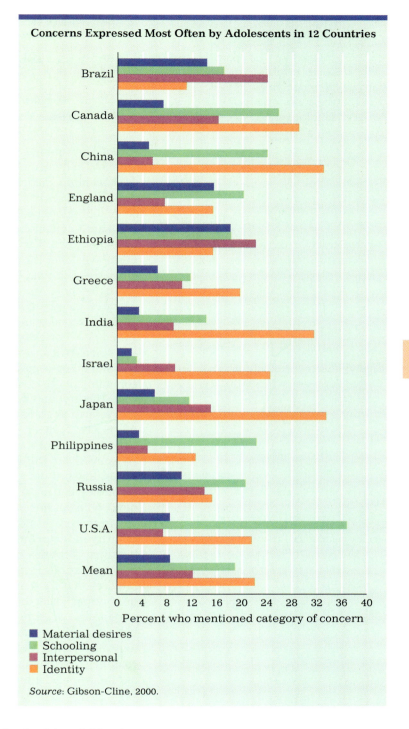

Concerns Expressed Most Often by Adolescents in 12 Countries

Percent who mentioned category of concern

- ■ Material desires
- ■ Schooling
- ■ Interpersonal
- ■ Identity

Source: Gibson-Cline, 2000.

Identity Achievement

As they deal with these increasingly diverse and complex aspects of selfhood, adolescents confront the fifth psychosocial challenge, referred to by Erikson as **identity versus role confusion.** For developmentalists like Erikson, the search for identity leads to the primary crisis of adolescence—a crisis in which the young person struggles to reconcile a quest for "a conscious sense of individual uniqueness" with "an unconscious striving for a continuity of experience . . . and a solidarity with a group's ideals" (Erikson, 1968).

The ultimate goal, called **identity achievement,** is reached through "selective repudiation and mutual assimilation of childhood identifications" (Erikson, 1968). That is, adolescents establish their own identities by reconsidering the goals and values set by their parents and culture, then accepting some and rejecting others.

Adolescents who "achieve" identity know who they are; they remain connected to all the morals and attitudes they have learned, but they are not inescapably bound to any of them. As a group of Canadian researchers explain it, amid all the biosocial changes of adolescence, people seek to maintain a sense of continuity with their past in order to move toward their future (Chandler et al., 2003).

Alternative Statuses

Identity achievement is difficult. Many young people first choose one of several other identity statuses, which Erikson recognized but considered less than the ideal of achieved identity. Erikson first described the identity crisis 40 years ago (Erikson, 1963, 1968). Shortly after that, James Marcia (1966; Marcia et al., 1993) developed a series of questions to measure alternative identity statuses. Marcia distinguished foreclosure, diffusion, moratorium, and achievement (see Table 16.1 on the next page).

Some young people short-circuit their quest by never examining traditional values. The result is **foreclosure,** closing out a process before it is complete. In identity foreclosure, an adolescent adopts parents' or society's roles and values wholesale, rather than exploring alternatives and forging a personal identity.

foreclosure Erikson's term for premature identity formation, which occurs when an adolescent adopts parents' or society's roles and values wholesale, without questioning and analysis.

Is Identity Achievement Always Best? Each of Erikson's four identity statuses is characterized by how much questioning and how much commitment the status includes. For Erikson, the ideal was identity achievement, with the adolescent ranking high on both questioning and commitment; the least satisfactory was identity diffusion. Might it be better to avoid commitment, staying in moratorium for years, or to choose foreclosure, avoiding the hard questions?

TABLE 16.1 Identity Status and Commitment

	No Commitment	Commitment
Not questioning	Diffusion	Foreclosure
Questioning	Moratorium	Achievement

A typical example is a young man who has always wanted (or been pressured) to follow in his father's footsteps and does so. If his father was a doctor, the adolescent might diligently study chemistry and biology in high school and take premed courses in college.

Other adolescents decide that the roles their parents and society expect them to fill are unattainable or unappealing, yet they cannot find alternatives that are truly their own. The reaction may be a **negative identity**, that is, an identity opposite whatever is expected. The teacher's child refuses to go to college, the religious leader's child becomes a prostitute—the crucial factor in negative identity is not the choice itself but the rebellious defiance that underlies it. One version of negative identity is *oppositional identity* (Ogbu, 1993), which occurs when the adolescent rejects the dominant culture by adopting and exaggerating a negative stereotype. For example, some gay young men proudly call themselves "queer," and some African-Americans take pride in being the "baddest."

Still other young people experience **identity diffusion,** typically having few commitments to goals or values and often being apathetic about taking on any role. These young people have difficulty meeting the usual demands of adolescence, such as completing school assignments, finding a job, and thinking about the future. Instead, they sleep too much, waste time watching television and hanging out, and claim not to care about anything because "nothing matters" or "whatever. . . ." Diffusion is not exactly an identity status as much as a lack of any status, any self-definition, any commitment. For example, if diffusion continues, an adolescent may move from one sexual or platonic relationship to another, never with passion and commitment.

In the process of finding a mature identity, many young people declare an **identity moratorium,** a kind of time-out during which they experiment with alternative identities (possible selves). The culture provides formal moratoriums through various institutions. The most obvious example is college, which usually requires that students sample a variety of academic areas before concentrating on any particular one. Being a full-time student also forestalls pressure from parents and peers to settle down, choose a career, and find a mate. Other institutions that permit a moratorium are the military, religious mission work, and various internships. Unlike diffusion, adolescents in moratorium attempt to fill the role they are in (student, soldier, or whatever), but they consider it temporary, not their final identity.

negative identity An identity that is taken on with rebellious defiance, simply because it is the opposite of whatever parents or society expect.

identity diffusion A situation in which an adolescent does not seem to know or care what his or her identity is.

identity moratorium Erikson's term for a pause in identity formation that allows young people to explore alternatives without making final identity choices.

Status Versus Process

To better understand the distinctions among the four major identity statuses, consider religious identity. If a teenager self-identifies as a committed Christian, Jew, Muslim, Buddhist, or so on, specifies a subcategory such as Pentecostal or Orthodox, and worships and prays regularly, then such commitment, which includes beliefs and practices, means that the person has a religious identity. This identity is either foreclosed or achieved, depending on whether or not the person has asked the hard questions (e.g., why God allows suffering, why some people in that faith are immoral). Foreclosed members of a religious group have never really doubted; achieved members have questioned, struggled, and then developed their own answers, but both, at least, have established a particular religious identity. Teenagers without a religious identity include both those in moratorium, who are questioning but who have not found answers, and those in diffusion, who are indifferent and alienated—claiming, for instance, that "all religions are meaningless."

Developmentalists are more interested in ongoing processes than in status outcomes (Grotevant, 1998). This concern has led to two additional questions about the process of achieving identity—and the answers found:

1. *Can a person achieve identity in one domain but still be searching in another? For example, could a person have foreclosed on religious identity, be diffused politically, be in moratorium on vocational identity, and have achieved sexual identity?*

   Yes. In fact, in the twenty-first century, such a combination is not unusual. Vocational identity is particularly complex, because the choices are in the tens of thousands and because virtually no teens simply take up their parents' occupation, as many once did (Csikszentmihalyi & Schneider, 2000). And political identity seems unimportant to most adolescents, so it can be diffused for years (Torney-Purta et al., 2001).

2. *Is identity formed from within, when a person recognizes his or her true nature, or from without, after family and social forces push a teenager to adopt a particular identity?*

   The answer is both: Identity is considered to be constructed, neither merely discovered nor blindly accepted (Muuss, 1996). In achieving a sexual identity (Moshman, 1999), for example, teenagers identify as homosexual or heterosexual not entirely for biological or sociological reasons. Nature and nurture both contribute to the complex process of developing one's sexual orientation.

Gender and Ethnic Identity

Sexual identity refers to the person's self-identification as either male or female. Originally, many experts in the psychoanalytic tradition, including Erikson, thought of the two sexes as opposites (Miller & Simon, 1980). Following some sexual confusion at puberty (caused by embarrassed, secretive adults), people identified as a heterosexual male or female, taking on appropriate roles, unless something was developmentally abnormal (Erikson, 1968; Freud, 1958/2000). The concept of androgyny (see Chapter 13) had not yet been described. Sexual identity was closely tied to biology.

Later research, an outgrowth of multicultural perspectives and historical change, revealed that sexual identity is much more varied than a simple male–female division. We now speak of **gender identity**, to include the roles and behaviors that society associates with the biological category of male or female. Each adolescent makes a multitude of decisions about sexual behavior and selects from many gender roles. Teenagers decide how and with whom to become sexually active, choosing abstinence or promiscuity or anything in between. Further, teenagers decide what jewelry and clothing to wear, what occupations to prepare for, how and when to talk, move, laugh, and so on. All these are reflections of gender identity.

Gender identity is often connected to ethnic identity because male and female roles are defined differently by different cultures. This connection, and its

!*Answer to Observational Quiz* (from page 387):
Material desires: Highest, Ethiopia; lowest, Israel
Schooling: Highest, USA; lowest, Israel
Interpersonal: Highest, Brazil; lowest, Philippines
Identity: Highest, Japan; lowest, Brazil
Which of these is most surprising to you? Why?

gender identity A person's acceptance of the roles and behaviors that society associates with the biological category of male or female.

complexity, may be seen in a decision one Indian-American 15-year-old made in defiance of her heritage:

> I wanted to feel free and independent. . . . I wanted a haircut. But I couldn't make myself do it. A haircut was a big decision. My hair was more than just a bunch of dead cells. It was a symbol of control. For my parents and relatives, long hair is considered an essential part of being a woman. Especially for "good Indian girls."
>
> *[Chikkatur, 1997]*

Torn by these conflicts, one day this young woman decided and—before she told her family or changed her mind––had her hair cut. For the next month, as all her relatives criticized her, she alternated between thinking she had made a "huge mistake" and being "glad I cut my hair." She considered her short hair a symbol of her independence, not only from her family and from Indian traditions but also from what she perceived as the dominant American culture regarding gender expectations about beauty, marriage, and sexual orientation.

She is not alone in questioning both her ethnic identity and the dominant American identity: Many adolescents in multiethnic nations experience the same struggle. In the United States, this is particularly acute for the 40 percent of all teenagers who are not native-born of European descent (U.S. Bureau of the Census, 2002). Many were raised in neighborhoods with others of similar ethnic and economic backgrounds. This general similarity within a multiethnic nation allows them to follow detailed ethnic patterns, not only in matters of diet, gender roles, and language but even in ways of feeding a baby or greeting a stranger—and to do so without much thought until adulthood approaches.

As they grow older, the need for a distinct, regionalized ethnic identity becomes less pressing for young Americans of African or Hispanic or Asian descent, while the need to be proud of their general heritage becomes more important. Many North American youth no longer identify primarily as descendants of a particular place but, more generally, as members of broad ethnic categories (Falcon et al., 2001). Young people of every background tend to connect to their peers, taking on generational attitudes toward drugs, parents, sex, or school as soon as they are able (Hamm, 2000). As one 18-year-old explains:

> Our parents separated us from the majority culture. . . . Our mother strictly forbade us girls to ever date a "European boy" and with us living at home, she was easily able to do this. But last year I left home . . . [for] a year full of experimentation and exploration.
>
> *[quoted in Kroger, 2000, p. 126]*

The Same but Different Traditionally, minority identity in the United States focused on race, with young people of color needing to find their place in a white world. Currently, however, the issue has broadened to be seen as ethnic, not racial. These California high school students look physically similar but are from very different backgrounds: The one in the foreground of the left-hand photo is from Cambodia and the one in the right-hand photo is from Mexico. Each is finding her own bicultural identity. Their backgrounds differ, but the search is universal; many adolescents of European descent also struggle with issues of heritage and self.

The psychosocial task of every adolescent is to figure out his or her identity, exploring possible selves and discarding false selves. Many adolescents take years to achieve a solid identity, the product of exploration and commitment. During those years, some seem to care about nothing (identity diffusion), some make premature choices (foreclosure), some take a socially sanctioned pause (moratorium), and some simply react against social norms (negative identity).

It is quite possible for an adolescent to be at various identity statuses simultaneously, because vocational, sexual, religious, and political identities follow their own distinct paths—paths that differ for every person, depending on family and social context. For contemporary adolescents, achieving gender and ethnic identity can be particularly complex. Life choices and patterns are no longer simple dichotomies, such as male/female, majority/minority, black/white, because multicultural, multiethnic, and androgynous possibilities are also evident.

Sadness and Anger

As you learned in Chapter 14, puberty brings intense and rapid changes of mood, from happy to sad (or even from ecstatic to despondent) and back again. Happier feelings can lead to activity and joy, and, as described in Chapter 15, perhaps to fantasies of invincibility and grandeur. However, for some adolescents, mood changes veer out of bounds. Sadness becomes depression, which is closely tied to anger, which sometimes becomes reckless or antisocial aggression. Psychologists categorize emotional problems in two broad ways, as either internalizing or externalizing. **Internalizing problems** are manifested inward, when troubled individuals inflict harm on themselves. **Externalizing problems** are, at least superficially, the opposite: People "act out," injuring others, destroying property, or defying authority.

Internalizing problems include eating disorders, self-mutilation, overuse of sedative drugs, and clinical depression (defined as marked feelings of sadness and worthlessness leading to lack of interest in and isolation from normal activity for two weeks or more). Suicide is usually considered internalizing, because completed suicides are the ultimate example of self-harm. However, some individuals, especially adolescents, use suicide as a strategy to "get back at" someone—and this would make suicide externalizing. One example is called "suicide by cop," a situation in which a teenager deliberately provokes an armed police officer. Many violent adolescent deaths, provoked homicides, or deliberate accidents may be an externalizing outgrowth of depression, a desperate attempt to establish an identity.

Both internalizing and externalizing problems increase markedly at adolescence, with a dramatic gender difference: Externalizing problems are more common among boys and internalizing problems are more common among girls. Distinguishing normal adolescent emotions from serious problems is crucial, and can even be life-saving, as we will now see.

The Usual Dip

The general emotional trend in adolescence is more downward than upward. For example, a cross-sequential study showed that children from ages 6 to 18 feel less competent, on average, each year in most areas of their lives (see Figure 16.2 on the next page) (Jacobs et al., 2002).

internalizing problems Emotional problems that are manifested inward, when troubled individuals inflict harm on themselves.

externalizing problems Emotional problems that are manifested outward, when people "act out" by injuring others, destroying property, or defying authority.

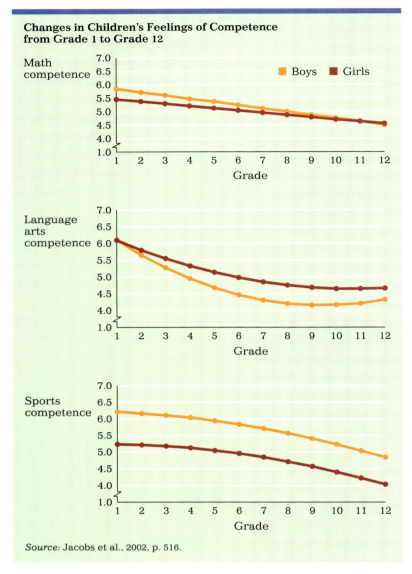

Changes in Children's Feelings of Competence from Grade 1 to Grade 12

Math competence

■ Boys ■ Girls

Language arts competence

Sports competence

Source: Jacobs et al., 2002, p. 516.

FIGURE 16.2 All the Children Are Above Average U.S. children, both boys and girls, feel less and less competent in math, language arts, and sports as they move through grades 1–12. Their scores on tests of feelings of competence could range from 1 to 7, and the fact that the twelfth-grade average was between 4 and 5 indicates that, overall, teenagers still consider themselves above average.

Other research, in various places and nations, also finds a drop in self-esteem beginning at about age 12 (e.g., Eccles et al., 1998; Fredricks & Eccles, 2002; Harter, 1999; Marsh, 1989). Some research shows more dramatic declines than those in Figure 16.2 but then a small rise—though never to as high a level as the childhood peak (e.g., Cole et al., 2001). Day by day, hour by hour, assessments suggest peaks and valleys in adolescence, not stable moods (Arnett, 1999a; Larson & Richards, 1994). The specifics depend on cohort, culture, and the particular domain of life or academics being measured, but the overall trend is similar among groups of adolescents everywhere.

A particular risk occurs for those who were raised to believe they are innately intelligent, skilled, and protected. All this is challenged at adolescence, when almost everyone's grades fall and when friendships shift, coaches become more critical, and so on. Unless they understand the need for realistic goals, adolescents may quit school or feel hopeless (Dweck, 1999). Realism is key, as extremes of either self-doubt or self-confidence may have undesirable effects (Sniezek, 1999).

Does a drop in self-esteem prepare teenagers to compete realistically for jobs, colleges, and sexual partners, or does it make them vulnerable to self-destructive and defiant behaviors, such as drug use, sexual risk taking, and suicide? It depends. Some adolescents are more vulnerable because they lack support and guidance from family, friends, or school and lose faith in their culture. A loss of self-esteem pushes them not toward realism but toward serious depression. An overwhelming feeling of sadness and hopelessness can disrupt all normal, regular activities, signaling an emotional crisis.

Depression

At puberty the rate of clinical depression more than doubles, to about 15 percent, affecting about 1 in 5 teenage girls and 1 in 10 teenage boys. Causes and signs predate adolescence, including genetic vulnerability and a depressed mother who was the adolescent's primary caregiver in infancy (Cicchetti & Toth, 1998). Contextual factors, such as the school setting, also have an impact, as does puberty itself.

Many researchers wonder why individuals, especially females, suddenly experience more depression when they reach adolescence (Ge et al., 2001; Hankin & Abramson, 2001; A.C. Peterson et al., 1993). The hormonal changes of puberty are one explanation, coupled with the psychic stresses of school, friends, sexual drives, and identity crises. No doubt depression arises from a combination of factors: Genes make a person vulnerable to mood disorders, and stress increases the risk (Caspi et al., 2003). Social and cultural factors can either push people over the edge of despair or protect them from the consequences of adolescent mood shifts—even the most lethal consequence, suicide.

Adolescent Suicide

Teenagers are just beginning to explore life's possibilities. Even if they experience troubling events—failing a class, ending a romance, fighting with a parent—don't they realize that better days lie ahead? Not always. One-third of all U.S. adolescent girls say they have felt hopeless in the past year, and one-fourth have seriously thought about suicide (CDC, June 28, 2002). **Suicidal ideation**—that is, thinking about committing suicide—is so common among high school students that it might be considered normal (Diekstra, 1995).

Suicidal ideation is common, but completed suicides are not. Before delving deeper, we need to correct a misconception. Adolescents under age 20 are *less* likely to kill themselves than adults are. Why, then, do many people think suicide is common in adolescence? Four reasons account for it:

- The rate, low as it is, is much higher today than in 1962 (see Figure 16.3).
- Statistics often lump adolescents and young adults together, and 20- to 24-year-olds typically have a much higher suicide rate than teenagers do.
- Most adolescent suicides capture media attention; most adult suicides don't.
- Suicide *attempts* are more common in adolescence than in adulthood.

Parasuicide

Let us focus on suicide attempts. **Parasuicide** (any attempt that does not result in death) is common in adolescence, with an international rate between 6 and 20 percent. The results of one U.S. survey of suicidal ideation and parasuicide among adolescents are summarized in Table 16.2 on the next page.

Experts prefer the word *parasuicide* over *attempted suicide* or *failed suicide* because this term does not assume intention (Diekstra et al., 1995). Particularly in adolescence, most self-destructive acts are accompanied by extreme emotional agitation and confusion. Intent may not be clear, even to the individuals themselves, who perform the act in the role of a possible self, not as a person with an

suicidal ideation Thinking about suicide, usually with some serious emotional and intellectual or cognitive overtones.

parasuicide A deliberate act of self-destruction that does not end in death. Parasuicide may be a fleeting gesture, such as a small knife mark on the wrist, or potentially lethal, as when a person swallows an entire bottle of sleeping pills.

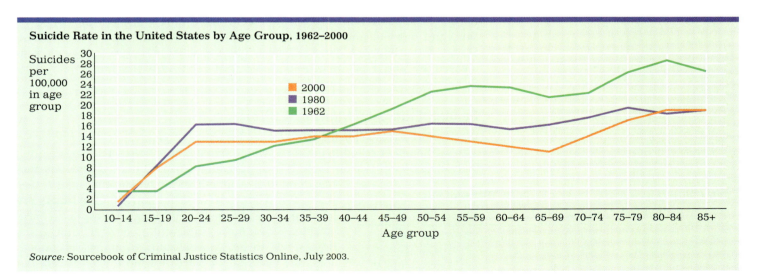

Suicide Rate in the United States by Age Group, 1962–2000

Suicides per 100,000 in age group

Legend: 2000, 1980, 1962

Age group: 10–14, 15–19, 20–24, 25–29, 30–34, 35–39, 40–44, 45–49, 50–54, 55–59, 60–64, 65–69, 70–74, 75–79, 80–84, 85+

Source: Sourcebook of Criminal Justice Statistics Online, July 2003.

FIGURE 16.3 So Much to Live For A historical look at U.S. suicide statistics reveals two trends. First, teenagers are twice as likely to take their own lives as they once were. Second, today young adults are more suicidal and older adults less so. Have increased family and school pressures made adolescence more problematic, while better health care and improved retirement benefits have made the later years of life easier today than they were in 1962?

? *Observational Quiz* (see answer, page 394): In a typical cross-section of 1,000 U.S. 15- to 19-year-olds, how many committed suicide in 2000?

TABLE 16.2 Suicidal Ideation and Parasuicide, U.S., 2001

		Felt Sad or Hopeless	Seriously Considered Attempting Suicide	Planned Suicide	Parasuicide (Attempted Suicide)	Actual Suicide (Ages 14–18)
Overall		28%	19%	15%	9%	Less than 0.01% (about 7 per 100,000)
Girls:	9th grade	36	26	19	13	
	10th grade	35	24	19	12	Girls: About 2
	11th grade	34	24	19	12	per 100,000
	12th grade	33	19	13	7	
Boys:	9th grade	22	15	13	8	
	10th grade	20	14	11	7	Boys: About 11
	11th grade	23	14	12	5	per 100,000
	12th grade	21	14	11	4	

Sources: CDC, June 28, 2002, based on a survey of 13,627 students from 38 states. Actual suicide rates estimated from U.S. Bureau of the Census, 2002.

!*Answer to Observational Quiz* (from page 393): None. The rates are given per 100,000 in each age group. This means that fewer than one in 10,000 teens commit suicide in a year.

?*Critical Thinking Question* (see answer, page 396): What might account for the ethnic differences in adolescent suicide rates?

TABLE 16.3 U.S. Suicide Rates of 15- to 19-Year-Olds by Ethnic Group, 2000

	Males (Rate per 100,000)	Females (Rate per 100,000)	Females as Percent of Total
American Indian and Alaskan Native	28	9.1	25%
European-American	15	2.9	16%
Hispanic-American	10	2.5	20%
African-American	10	1.5	13%
Asian-American	9	3.6	29%

Source: National Vital Statistics Report, 49(11), October 12, 2001.

established identity. Many who make a potentially lethal attempt soon feel relieved that they did not die and wonder what they were thinking; yet if a particular parasuicide is dismissed as not serious, adolescents usually try again.

Whether or not adolescent suicidal ideation eventually leads to a plan, a parasuicide, or death depends on many factors:

- Availability of lethal means, especially guns
- Lack of parental supervision
- Use of alcohol and other drugs
- Being male
- Cultural attitudes

The first three factors suggest why youth suicide in North America and Europe has doubled since 1960: Adolescents have more guns, less adult supervision, and more alcohol and drugs than they did 40 years ago. In the United States, accessibility of guns is a major culprit; adolescent gunshot suicide increased by about 50 percent between 1980 and 1995 (Kachur et al., 1995; Sickmund et al., 1997).

Gender, Ethnic, and National Differences

Worldwide, parasuicide is higher for females but completed suicide is higher for males. The only exception is China, where females complete suicide more often than males. One reason for the usual predominance of male suicides is that men tend to use immediately lethal means—guns rather than pills. Another reason is that depressed boys are less likely to ask for help or to signal distress (as in parasuicide), which makes intervention difficult. Suicide for boys tends to be externalizing, an angry reaction to someone else's anger. Girls are more likely to act out of self-hatred. Suicide rates vary dramatically among countries and among ethnic groups within countries (see Table 16.3).

When continents are compared, Africa and South America have low rates and Europe (especially Eastern Europe) high rates; Hungary's is among the highest worldwide, and Japan's is among the lowest. Canada and the United States have very similar rates, midway between the extremes (Schmidtke et al., 1998). In Australia, Aboriginal youth are particularly vulnerable, in part because of cultural romanticism regarding suicide (Tatz, 2001).

Romanticism also underlies **cluster suicides**, several suicides committed within the same group in a brief period of time. When a particular town or school sentimentalizes a "tragic end," such publicity can trigger suicidal thoughts, talk, and attempts in other adolescents (Joiner, 1999). Cluster suicides are particularly common among Native Americans (Beauvais, 2000).

Adolescent Rebellion

Are rebellion and defiance normal, particularly for adolescent boys? Most psychologists influenced by the psychoanalytic perspective answer "yes," since expression of anger is expected. A leading advocate of this view was Anna Freud, who believed that adolescent resistance to parental authority was "welcome . . . beneficial . . . inevitable." Indeed, a lack of defiance was troubling to her. She explained:

> We all know individual children who, as late as the ages of fourteen, fifteen or sixteen, show no such outer evidence of inner unrest. They remain, as they have been during the latency period, "good" children, wrapped up in their family relationships, considerate sons of their mothers, submissive to their fathers, in accord with the atmosphere, idea and ideal of their childhood background. Convenient as this may be, it signifies a delay of their normal development and is, as such, a sign to be taken seriously.
>
> [A. Freud, 1958/2000, p. 263]

Of course, many psychologists, most teachers, and almost all parents are quite happy with well-behaved, thoughtful teenagers.

Breaking the Law

The most dramatic example of rebellion is breaking the law in such a way as to bring arrest and conviction. Worldwide, arrests are most likely in the second decade of life; they rise rapidly at about age 12, peak at about age 16, and then decline slowly with every passing year (Rutter, 1998). In the United States, 44 percent of all arrests for crimes categorized as serious (crimes of violence, arson, or theft involving thousands of dollars) are of persons between the ages of 10 and 20 (Maguire & Pastore, 1998). These are **incidence** data; they are obtained by determining the age distribution of all arrested persons. They tell us that incidence is high during adolescence, but they do not tell us **prevalence**—that is, how widespread adolescent lawbreaking is.

To explain this distinction, suppose that, as some contend, a small minority of repeat offenders commit almost all the crimes. In this case, the prevalence of adolescent lawbreaking would be low even though the incidence was high. *If* this were true, and *if* adolescents on the path to a criminal career could be spotted early and then imprisoned, the *incidence* of adolescent crime would plummet, because those few offenders could no longer commit their many crimes. This supposition and strategy have led to attempts to "crack down" and "put away" young criminals.

Developmentalists over the past decades have proven this supposition to be false (except for a small group discussed below). Juveniles are mostly experimenters; they have not settled on any career yet, let alone a criminal one. Most have no more than one serious brush with the law, and even chronic offenders typically are convicted of a mix of offenses—some minor, some serious, and usually only one violent crime. In fact, 99 of every 100 youths who are arrested have committed only one violent offense. In other words, serious crimes are committed

cluster suicides Several suicides committed within the same group in a brief period of time.

LELAND BOBBE / STONE / GETTY IMAGES

If You Were His Father or Mother . . . Would you agree with Anna Freud that teenage rebellion is welcome and beneficial?

incidence How often a particular behavior or circumstance occurs.

prevalence How widespread within a population a particular behavior or circumstance is.

Especially for Police Officers You see a group of young teenagers knocking over garbage cans. What do you do?

JOHN MCCUTCHEN, POOL / AP PHOTO

Do You Know This Boy? His name is Andy Williams. Is he a 15-year-old freshman lost in a large California high school and ignored by his parents? Or is he a crazed killer, who brought his father's revolver to school one day, murdered two schoolmates, and wounded 13 more? In fact, he is both, and that was the reason for this court hearing, where the judge decided that Williams should be tried as an adult. Later, Williams pleaded guilty.

❓Observational Quiz (see answer, page 398): Who are the adults with Andy?

adolescence-limited offender A person whose criminal activity stops by age 21.

life-course-persistent offender A person whose criminal activity typically begins in early adolescence and continues throughout life; a career criminal.

❗Answer to Critical Thinking Question (from page 394): In every ethnic group, U.S. teenagers born in another nation use guns less often, drink less alcohol, and kill themselves less often than do their U.S.-born peers. This may explain why rates are low among Hispanic- and Asian-Americans: Many of them are immigrants. It does not explain the low rates among African-Americans, however.

by many one-time offenders rather than by a few multiple offenders. The high incidence of adolescent crime is caused by its high prevalence, not by a few very active delinquents (Snyder, 1997).

Both the prevalence and the incidence are far greater than police records indicate. Many acts of "juvenile delinquency" (lawbreaking under age 18) never come to the attention of the police, and few officers arrest a young first-time offender. In a confidential longitudinal study (Fergusson & Horwood, 2002), the average boy admitted to three serious offenses between ages 10 and 20 and the average girl to one—although virtually none of the subjects had been arrested.

Similarly, although U.S. statistics show that adolescent males are three times as likely as females to be arrested, that African-Americans are three times as likely as European-Americans to be arrested, and that European-Americans are three times as likely as Asian-Americans to be arrested (U.S. Department of Justice, 2001), confidential self-reports find much smaller gender and ethnic differences (Rutter et al., 1998). When all illegal acts—including underage drinking, disorderly conduct, breaking a community curfew, playing hooky, sneaking into a movie or onto a bus without paying, and buying cigarettes or beer—are taken into account, virtually every adolescent is a repeat offender.

Let us make no mistake here. The fact that rebellion is expected or that lawbreaking is common does not mean juvenile crime is inevitable or insignificant; quite the contrary. Communities need to limit such rebellion to relatively harmless actions.

Beyond halting young criminals, there is another reason everyone who cares about adolescents should pay attention to crime: protecting young victims. The overall victimization rate of adolescents is two to three times that of adults, with an even greater imbalance for victims of violent crimes (assault, rape, murder) (Hashima & Finkelhor, 1999). (See Appendix A, p. A-18.) Victims of violence often become perpetrators, and vice versa—yet another reason to protect adolescents (Bjarnason et al., 1999).

Limiting the Damage

A useful distinction has been made between the many **adolescence-limited offenders**, whose criminal activity stops by age 21, and the few who are **life-course-persistent offenders**, who become career criminals (Moffitt, 1997a). Life-course-persistent offenders are recognizable long before adulthood. They are antisocial in preschool and elementary school. They show signs of brain damage—perhaps being slow to express ideas in language, or being hyperactive, or having poor emotional control. They are the first of their cohort to have sex and use gateway drugs; even by age 14, they are least involved in school activities and most involved in "hanging out" with older, lawbreaking youths (Farrington, 1994; Rutter et al., 1998; Sampson et al., 1997). Without intervention, they are likely to end up in prison, or worse.

Almost all career criminals have this childhood history. However, only about half of the children with these characteristics become career criminals. In early adolescence, a particularly cohesive neighborhood, an especially effective school, a supportive peer group, a stable family, or a best friend who discourages crime can halt the progression toward serious crime (Yoshikawa, 1994). If neighborhood, school, family, and peers fail, then intensive intervention that teaches life-course-persistent teenagers new ways of coping with their long-standing biological, cognitive, and psychosocial problems may help, especially if parents and teachers are taught as well (Rutter et al., 1998). In fact, longitudinal research finds parental retraining to be an effective preventive strategy if it begins early in an angry, antisocial child's life (Reid et. al., 2002). Reseach also shows that, although ineffective parenting may not immediately seem harmful, children from such families may explode at adolescence (Compton et al., 2003).

Residential incarceration in a prison or reform school is needed for very few youthful offenders. Special programs backfire when young lawbreakers become friends with other externalizing, deviant youth (Dishion, Bullock, & Granic, 2002; Mahoney et al., 2001). If a young adolescent offender is taken from family, school, and friends and placed in a context where toughness and defiance are required for survival, then temporary externalizing is likely to become habitual. Although younger children learn externalizing behavior at home from punitive, unresponsive parents, adolescents learn such actions from cultural context and peers (McCabe et al., 2001). Placement of high-risk youth with foster parents who are trained to provide effective discipline is much more successful than reform school (Chamberlain et al., 2002).

In summary, adolescent hopelessness and rebellion are both potentially serious, requiring intervention but not overreaction. Compared to people of other ages, many adolescents experience sudden and extreme emotions that lead to temporary, powerful feelings of sadness and anger. These feelings are usually expressed within supportive families, friendships, neighborhoods, and cultures that contain and channel various outbursts. For some teenagers, however, profound emotions are unchecked or even exacerbated by their social surroundings. This can lead to suicide attempts (especially for girls), to minor lawbreaking (for both sexes), and, more rarely, to actual suicide and serious lawbreaking (especially for boys).

Adults need to be alert to internalizing and externalizing actions as warning signs. Depression and rebellion can be moderated, making such behavior adolescent-limited rather than life-course-persistent.

Especially for Parents of Teenagers Your 13-year-old comes home after a sleepover at a friend's house with a new, weird hairstyle—perhaps cut or colored in an ugly or bizarre manner. What do you say and do?

Response for Police Officers (from page 395): Neither ignore the behavior nor arrest the teens. Some rebellion is normal, but it escalates if social guidelines are not in place. A strong warning is likely to help them stop at minor lawbreaking.

Family and Friends

The changing seas of development are never sailed alone. At every turn, a voyager's family, friends, and community provide sustenance, provisions, directions, ballast for stability, and a safe harbor or at least an anchor when it is time to rest. Through example or insistence, societal forces also provide a reason to move ahead. In adolescence, when the winds of change blow particularly strong, parents and peers are powerful. The self-destruction of internalizing problems and the social destruction of externalizing problems can be averted with the support of family and friends. Fortunately, social approval "is a high priority, often even higher than the pursuit of academic goals" (Covington, 2000). Adolescents seek out the companionship they need.

Parents

Adolescence is often characterized as a time of waning adult influence, a period when the values and behaviors of young people become increasingly detached from those of their parents and other adults. According to all reports, however, the **generation gap,** as the distance between the younger generation and the older one has been called, is not necessarily wide. In fact, younger and older generations have very similar values and aspirations, especially when adolescents are compared not with adults in general but with their own parents (Elder &

generation gap The distance between generations in values, behaviors, and knowledge, marked by a mutual lack of understanding.

NANCY RICHMOND / THE IMAGE WORKS

Not in My Kitchen Both parents and teenagers are invested in their relationship, but each generation has its own stake, or perspective, on their interactions. The generational stake may result in bickering, often over minor issues.

? *Observational Quiz* (see answer, page 400): What do you see in the body positions of these two that suggests generational stake?

generational stake The need of each generation to view family interactions from its own perspective because each has a different investment in the family scenario.

bickering Petty, peevish arguing, usually repeated and ongoing.

! *Answer to Observational Quiz* (from page 396): They are not Andy's parents, who were not present at this hearing. Andy is flanked by his court-appointed defense attorneys.

? *Critical Thinking Question* (see answer, page 400): Why would young adolescent daughters and their mothers be most likely to bicker?

Conger, 2000). (An exception occurs when the parents were raised in a very different place, as when parents grew up in a rural region of a developing nation and their teenager is growing up in a big city in a developed nation [Harris, 1998].) For example, religion was thought to be an area in which adolescents rebelled. At best, parents could hope to provide a "channel" to a congregation or a youth group where their child's faith would be nurtured. However, research finds that contemporary parents have a strong and direct influence on their children's religious beliefs (Martin et al., 2003).

Although the generation gap is typically narrow, this does not mean that all is harmonious. Each generation has its own distinct **generational stake** (Bengtson, 1975). That is, each generation has a natural tendency to interpret interactions between the generations from the viewpoint of its own position in the family. Consider a conflict about a curfew. A parent may see it merely as a problem of management, the latest version of trying to get the child to bed on time, but a teenager may consider it evidence of the parents' outmoded values or lack of trust. On a deeper level, what parents see as an attempt to love and protect, teenagers may see as an attempt to control and dominate. No wonder they disagree.

Overall, parents have a stake in believing that all is well and that their children are basically loyal to the family despite a superficial show of rebellion caused by factors outside the family, such as hormones or peer pressure. Adolescents have a stake in believing that their parents are limited, old-fashioned, and out of touch. This attitude emerges for good reason, because human evolution requires that adolescents break free from parental restraints to find their own mates and peers (Weisfeld, 1999). Thus, biological maturation leads to a strong, innate drive for independence.

Parent–Adolescent Conflict

As long as parents and adolescents live under the same roof, a certain amount of conflict arises when the young person's drive for independence clashes with the parents' tradition of control. The depth and specifics of the disagreement depend on many factors, including the child's age, gender, and the cultural context.

Parent–adolescent conflict typically emerges in early adolescence, particularly with daughters who mature early and with mothers more than fathers (Arnett, 1999a; Caspi et al., 1993). Typically, it takes the form of **bickering** (repeated, petty arguments, more like nagging than fighting) about habits of daily life—hair, neatness, and clothing. Relatively young adolescents often feel compelled to make a statement—with bare midriff or blaring music—to establish that a new stage has arrived. Bickering follows.

Few parents can resist making a critical comment about the dirty socks on the floor or about the ring on the eyebrow, and few adolescents can calmly listen to "expressions of concern" without feeling they are being unfairly judged (Smetana & Asquith, 1994). In general, bickering peaks in early and mid-adolescence; family life becomes less conflicted as the parents grant more autonomy (Steinberg & Morris, 2001). Normally, adjustment occurs on both sides; with the child's physical maturity and emotional independence come mutual appreciation and respect, but this process takes time.

An ethnic variation may be found in the *timing* of parent–child conflict. For Chinese-, Korean-, and Mexican-American teens, stormy relations with parents may not surface until late in adolescence. Perhaps because these cultures encourage dependency in children and emphasize family closeness, the typical teenager's quest for autonomy is delayed (Greenberger & Chen, 1996; Molina & Chassin, 1996). Variations within each ethnic group and each family affect this pattern, with some adolescents experiencing more conflict at age 12, others at age 22, others somewhere in between.

Most research on families finds that conflict is part of growing up but that parent–child relationships that are very high in conflict and low in support impair normal adolescent development (Demo & Acock, 1996). Adolescents have *never* been found to benefit from families that are permissive to the point of laxness *or* strict to the point of abuse (Maccoby, 2000).

Avoiding these extremes can be particularly difficult for single mothers who were teenagers when their children were born. When their children become adolescents, these mothers tend to be too lax or too harsh, unable to find the proper balance in dealing with a young person who is as tall, and seems almost as mature, as the young mothers themselves (Borkowski et al., 2002; Loeber et al., 2000).

The dangers of laxness are magnified in deteriorating communities. The worse a neighborhood is, the stronger the pull of deviant peers and externalizing actions, and the greater the need for parental guidelines, monitoring, and support (Walker-Barnes & Mason, 2001). However, in any type of family or neighborhood, if conflict reaches the point where the adolescent becomes a runaway or a throwaway—kicked out of the house—disaster is likely to follow, with indiscriminate sex, drug abuse, violence, or even suicide (Yoder et al., 1998).

Other Family Characteristics

Conflict is only one aspect of the parent–teen relationship that has been studied. Other aspects include:

- Communication (Do parents and teens talk openly with one another?)
- Support (Do they rely on one another?)
- Connectedness (How close are they?)
- Control (Do parents encourage or limit adolescent autonomy?)

Each of these is much more evident in some families than in others. No researcher doubts that the first two aspects, communication and support, are beneficial, if not essential. However, it is not easy to specify the effects of connectedness and control, because in some contexts, extreme family closeness and parental control are destructive, and in others, they seem constructive. One example is the extent to which parents know where their children are.

On the one hand, a powerful deterrent of delinquency, risky sex, and drug abuse is **parental monitoring**—that is, parental vigilance regarding where one's child is, what he or she is doing, and with whom (Fletcher et al., 1995; Rogers, 1999; Sampson & Laub, 1993). Monitoring helps limit alcohol, drugs, and weapons by keeping the adolescent in places the parent considers acceptable.

On the other hand, too much parental interference and control predict adolescent depression. A tactic called *psychological control* (threatening withdrawal of love and support) is particularly harmful (Barber, 2002; Pettit et al., 2001). Apparently, adolescents need some freedom to feel competent, trusted, and loved (Barber, 2002). It is not easy for parents to show involvement without interference, concern without suspicion. Communication is beneficial, but intrusiveness

Response for Parents of Teenagers (from page 397): Remember: Communicate, do not control. Say something—neutral, if possible—and let your child talk about the meaning of the hairstyle. Remind yourself that it is not your hair, and a hairstyle in itself is harmless. Don't say "What will people think?" or "Does this mean you are using drugs?" or express any other thought that might give a rebellious young adolescent a reason to break off the communication with you.

Especially for Police Officers You see some 15-year-olds drinking beer in a local park when they belong in school. What do you do?

parental monitoring Parents' awareness of what their children are doing, where, and with whom.

A Guiding Hand Organized extracurricular activities, with appropriate adult supervision, supplement parental monitoring as a way of helping adolescents stay out of trouble.

! *Answer to Observational Quiz* (from page 398): The mother's folded arms show her determination to keep her son in line. The young man sits on the kitchen counter and wears his cap in the house to stress his independence.

! *Answer to Critical Thinking Question* (from page 398): Conflicts typically occur about habits of dress and cleanliness. Mothers are most directly involved with daily enforcement and daughters traditionally are more docile—and therefore their rebellion brings maternal surprise and resistance.

makes the child feel guilty and anxious and leads to distress and sometimes rebellion (Larson & Gillman, 1999). In fact, parental monitoring itself may be harmful when, instead of indicating a close connection with the adolescent, it derives from harsh, suspicious parenting (Stattin & Kerr, 2000).

The importance of a trusting relationship may be most obvious when the topic is sex. The Ad Health longitudinal study (see Chapter 15) found that parent–child communication, trust, and closeness are predictors of less sexual activity as well as safer sex. Yet, if parents stress only ways to avoid pregnancy and disease, teenagers may infer that their parents approve of sexual activity. That "mixed message" makes intercourse (albeit with a condom) more likely. The best parental strategy apparently is to include information about "the social, emotional, familial, and moral consequences" of sexual activity when they discuss the biological aspects of sex with their children (Jaccard & Dittus, 2000). Finding the right balance, once again, is not simple, as the following In Person suggests.

In Person

Talking to My Children About Marriage and Parenthood

When our first daughter, Bethany, was newborn, toothless, and perfect, my husband worried about how we would pay for her teenage orthodonture. I knew he was being ridiculous (neither he nor I ever wore braces). I thought my own worry was more sensible, arising as it did from my experience teaching high school students and from the mistakes my own parents had made. My worry was that I would not be able to talk to my baby girl about sex when the time came.

Fortunately, my ongoing understanding of developmental science helped me to answer the questions all my children asked about sex and to clarify mistaken ideas they had heard from their friends. For example, Rachel invited a classmate to her birthday party at a roller rink, but the child was forbidden to come because her parents thought she might catch AIDS in any place that was open to the public. I promptly explained how HIV is actually transmitted.

Especially when puberty drew near, I tried to make sure that my children trusted me, that communication channels were open, that I met their friends, that I knew where they were going and how they were getting there, that they knew I cared. No need to rush into marriage or parenthood, I taught them.

When Bethany was about 16, she showed us a friendship ring her boyfriend had given her. We were worried, until we met him—a polite, shy kid. By the time we gave our approval, it was already too late: Bethany and he had broken up, partly because they didn't agree about their favorite music. That was the only time we felt any concern about

our teenage daughters' boyfriends; all their relationships seemed quite innocent. The fears I had when Bethany was born—drugs, diseases, pregnancy—were unfounded, at least as far as I know. (One of my college students has called me naive about this.) My husband was actually wiser than I was: Bethany did wear braces on her teeth for two years.

Three of my daughters are now older than I was when Bethany was born, and none have ever been married or pregnant. Once Bethany met a wonderful man—brilliant, witty, interested in her. She said they had a lot of fun together, but "no sparks"! Another time I arranged a blind date for her. She telephoned me, laughing: "Mom, you are crazy. You're lucky you found Dad, because you have horrible judgment in men." I think she is wrong, but I know my values are a product of my context and cohort, and that has made me reassess myself.

Today's young adults have children years later than my generation did, and most of them are better parents because of it. I am very proud of the women my daughters have become. But recently I have another fear. My epigenetic clock makes me want grandchildren.

My own grandmother married before she was 20 and gave birth to 14 children; I would not want my children to have done the same. However, I wonder whether the message of my generation—be careful about sex and become self-supporting, independent people—was incomplete. Did my grandmother teach me something I forgot to communicate to my children?

Peers

Friendships, already prominent in middle childhood, become even more crucial during early adolescence. From hanging out with a large group to having whispered phone conversations with a trusted confidant or romantic partner, relations with peers are vital for the transition from childhood to adulthood. Friendships become very personal and, once trust and intimacy have been established, are not easily replaced. Most adolescent friendships are quite durable, with more stability from year to year than at younger ages (Degirmencioglu et al., 1998; Erwin, 1998). Many adults still rely on friends made during their teenage years.

Peer Pressure Unmasked

The constructive role of peers is contrary to the stereotype of **peer pressure**— that is, of the social pressure from peers that makes adolescents do things that they otherwise would not do. The notion of negative peer pressure is not completely false, but it is unbalanced and misses three important points:

- The pressure to conform to peers is short-lived. It rises dramatically in early adolescence, until about age 14, but then declines.

- Peers "serve to bridge the gap between childhood and adulthood" (Bagwell et al., 2002, p. 26), easing the transition between childish modes of behavior and full independence.

- Peer standards are not always negative. Indeed, "friends generally encourage socially desirable behaviors" (Berndt & Murphy, 2002, p. 281), such as joining sports teams, studying for exams, avoiding smoking, and applying to colleges.

The reality of positive peer influence does not negate another reality: Young people can lead one another into trouble. Collectively, peers sometimes become involved in escapades that none of them would engage in alone, effectively providing "deviancy training" for one another (Dishion et al., 2001, p. 82).

Peer pressure is particularly likely to be negative in periods of uncertainty. For example, young people are more likely to admire aggressive boys when they themselves are new to a school, are experiencing the physical changes of puberty, and are uncomfortable with heterosexual attraction—as they might be in the first months of middle school (Bukowski et al., 2000).

To understand why peer pressure is not usually the negative, mesmerizing influence that corrupts good adolescents, we need to understand its dynamics. Peers choose one another; teenagers associate with other teenagers whose values and interests they share, particularly in regard to behavior such as drug use and involvement in academics (Hamm, 2000). Once peers have chosen one another, it becomes easy for them to act the same way. Thus, there is both a selection process and a facilitation effect (Lacourse et al., 2003). This facilitation effect is indirect and pervasive, a group phenomenon rather than one individual leading another astray. As one adolescent described it:

> The idea of peer pressure is a lot of bunk. What I heard about peer pressure all the way through school is that someone is going to walk up to me and say "Here, drink this and you'll be cool." It wasn't like that at all. You go somewhere and everyone else would be doing it and you'd think, "Hey, everyone else is doing it and they seem to be having a good time—now why wouldn't I do this?" In that sense, the preparation of the powers that be, the lessons that they tried to drill into me, they were completely off. They had no idea what we are up against.

[quoted in Lightfoot, 1997]

peer pressure Social pressure to conform with one's friends or contemporaries in behavior, dress, and attitude; usually considered a negative force, as when adolescent peers encourage each other to defy adult authority.

Response for Police Officers (from page 399): Avoid both extremes: Don't let them think this situation is either harmless or serious. You might bring them to the police station and call their parents in. However, these adolescents are not life-course-persistent offenders; jailing or grouping them with other lawbreakers might encourage more serious acts of rebellion.

Fortunately, most peer-inspired misbehavior is a short-lived experiment rather than a foreshadowing of long-term delinquency; that is, it is adolescence-limited rather than life-course-persistent.

One other aspect of the role of peers needs to be mentioned, because it shows why peers are sometimes valued by teenagers and devalued by parents. Peers allow the adolescent to experiment with possible selves and in this way help with identity formation. Thus, teenagers who argue that they *must* engage in a particular activity, dress a certain way, or hang out in certain parts of town because "everyone else does it" are trying to lighten their responsibility for some demeanor, style, or philosophy that they wish to try (Ungar, 2000). Peers, in other words, are used by adolescents to deflect, and defend against, adult criticism.

The Peer Group for Immigrants

Peers play a special role for adolescents whose parents are immigrants. Such adolescents comprise an increasing proportion in almost every nation of the world, especially in cities, accounting for one-third of all adolescents in Frankfort, one-half in Amsterdam, and two-thirds in Los Angeles and New York.

Some of these young people are obedient to their parents, respectful to their elders, and hardworking at home and school. They earn higher grades and seem better-adjusted than their peers of the same ethnicity whose families are not recent immigrants (Fuligni, 1997; 1998; Liebkind & Jasinskaja-Lahti, 2000; Salazar et al., 2001).

Other adolescents and families face more complex demands, especially if the parents are from regions where undernutrition delayed puberty and high mortality rates encouraged early marriage and childbearing. Customs and expectations in such places dictate that adolescents marry when and whom the parents choose. Obedient, respectful adolescents are quite different from the typical Westernized teen who has an identity crisis, complete with bickering, experimentation, and rebellion. Thus, some immigrant offspring are caught between their strict family traditions and their generational push for autonomy. In such situations, peers are crucial. They help each adolescent negotiate conflicting cultures as well as conflicting maturity demands.

This is illustrated by tens of thousands of individuals, including Layla, whose family lives near Detroit, Michigan (Sarroub, 2001). Layla's parents were raised in Yemen, and at age 15 Layla was sent back to Yemen to marry her father's nephew. She returned to the Michigan public high school that was "both liberating and a sociocultural threat," trying to keep her marriage secret (she wore no ring). Layla respected her parents and adhered to her religion (Islam), but she resisted many aspects of her family's heritage. For example, she was troubled that her father smoked qat (a legal narcotic in Yemen), that he wanted her to wear a long Arab dress (she wore jeans instead), that he did not want her to get a divorce and go to college, and that tradition gave more freedom to boys than to girls.

> At times Layla was confused and unhappy at home. She . . . preferred going to school where she could be with her Yemeni friends who understood her problems and with whom she could talk. "They make me feel like really happy. I have friends that have to deal with the same issues." . . . Layla was often angry that girls in Yemen were taken out of school. . . . She thought that the boys had been given too much freedom, much more than the girls.
>
> *[Sarroub, 2001, pp. 408–409]*

Peers are important for all adolescents, even though some (especially girls) give in to parental control—perhaps living at home until an early marriage—and others (usually boys) rebel completely—perhaps joining peers in a delinquent group of the same ethnicity, who provide codes of behavior, standards of dress (e.g., gang colors), and social bonding. Ethnic gangs are common in immigrant communities living in multiethnic cities (Johnson-Powell & Yamamoto, 1997; Wong, 1999), which makes psychological sense. For example, one researcher found that Latinos chose to join gangs to "satisfy their desire for self-identity," especially if their parents did not provide much affection or supervision (Arfániarromo, 2001).

Which path a particular adolescent takes—studious obedience, conflicted uncertainty, or defiant rebellion—depends on many factors within the particular family, including communication, support, connectedness, control, and cultural assimilation (Fuligni, 1998). A wide discrepancy between family background and future demands pushes many adolescents in immigrant families toward the extremes, the obedient or rebellious (Suarez-Orozco & Suarez-Orozco, 2001).

In any case, most adolescents have a cluster of friends who follow the same trajectory. At every step of the maturation process, peer support—by siblings and cousins if the family is large and extended, or by other youth who have similar stresses between heritage and future—aids in the formation of identity.

Romantic Attraction

During most of childhood, voluntary segregation of the sexes is common (Maccoby, 1998). Then, as puberty begins, boys and girls notice one another in a new way. Most feel stirrings of heterosexual attraction, although developing a sexual identity and then expressing it with a partner takes many years.

The sequence of heterosexual attraction, first described 40 years ago (Dunphy, 1963), follows this general pattern:

- Groups of friends, exclusively one sex or the other
- A loose association of a girls' group and a boys' group, with all interactions very public
- A smaller, mixed-sex group, formed from the more advanced members of the larger association
- A final peeling off of heterosexual couples, with private intimacies

Cultural factors affect the timing and manifestation of these stages, and homosexual couples are slower to connect, but the basic sequence seems biologically based and hence consistent across the centuries, cultures, and even species (Weisfeld, 1999). In modern developed nations, where puberty begins at about age 11 and marriage does not occur until a decade or two later, each of these stages typically lasts several years, with exclusive same-sex groups dominant in elementary school and heterosexual couples in later high school or college.

Look at Figure 16.4. In the fifth and sixth grades, when they were on the edge of adolescence, children in a multiethnic public school outside of Chicago spent about 1 percent of their waking time (less than an hour a week) with the other sex. (Classroom time was not counted.) By the eleventh grade, however, boys were spending 5 hours a week with girls, and girls about 10 hours with boys. (The numbers are not equal because

Young Lovers Young lovers spend as much time together as possible. The affection evident in their smiles and physical closeness might alarm their parents, but any attempt to break up young lovers is likely to backfire, risking early pregnancy and elopement. Parental support and good communication are crucial when adolescents become romantically involved.

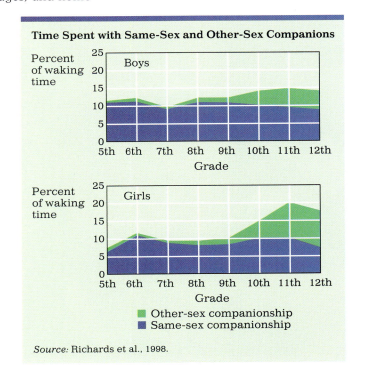

Time Spent with Same-Sex and Other-Sex Companions

FIGURE 16.4 **We'll Still Be Friends** Through adolescence, young people spend increasing amounts of time with peers of the other sex, while maintaining almost the same amount of time spent with same-sex friends. The focus of happiness also shifts: Adolescents reported greater happiness with same-sex peers at age 13 but with other-sex peers at age 17.

Source: Richards et al., 1998.

TABLE 16.4 Typical Adolescent Responses to the Opposite Sex*

	From Girls	From Boys
Age 11	"Boys are a sort of disease."	"Girls are a pin prick in the side."
Age 13	"Boys are stupid although important to us."	"Girls are great enemies."
Age 15	"Boys are strange—they hate you if you're ugly and brainy but love you if you are pretty but dumb."	"Girls are the main objective."
Age 16	"Boys are a pleasant change from the girls."	"Girls have their good and bad points—fortunately, the good outnumber the bad."

*The quotations come from a study of adolescents in New Zealand.
Source: Kroger, 1989.

most mixed-sex time was in groups that included more girls than boys; also, girls tended to spend time with older boys.) Related research found that adolescents spend about as much time thinking about the other sex as actually interacting (Richards et al., 1998). Obviously, relationships with the other sex are time-consuming and thought-provoking—something parents do not seem to understand and same-sex peers love to discuss.

Another indication of the move toward romantic attraction is a change in attitudes. Usually, the first sign of heterosexual attraction is not an overt, positive interest but a seeming dislike (see Table 16.4). The pace of the change depends on several factors. One factor is the biology of puberty, with early maturers likely to be first to reach out to the other sex. Another factor is peer culture, which may push a given teenager to date, dance, or whatever, or may encourage a delay in forming other-sex relationships. Parents are also a strong influence through supervision and example. Families in which the parents are fighting, separated, or divorced tend to have adolescents who pair off at younger ages (Collins, 2003). The final factor is availability, which hinges on the adolescent's appearance and boldness, both of which are partly genetic. For all these reasons, some 12-year-olds are much more advanced romantically than their classmates—or even than some 20-year-olds.

Some Gay, Some Straight These adolescents were among the 6,000 people who marched in the Gay/Straight Youth Pride parade in Boston in May 2001. This annual march has the goal of fostering self-esteem in teens, regardless of their sexual orientation.

MARILYN HUMPHRIES / THE IMAGE WORKS

Homosexual Youth

For those adolescents who are gay or lesbian, complications usually slow down the formation of romantic attachments. To begin with, many are reluctant to acknowledge that they are homosexual. For example, a confidential study of more than 3,000 ninth- to twelfth-grade teenagers found that only 0.5 percent identified themselves as gay or lesbian (Garofalo et al., 1999), far fewer than the estimated proportion of adult homosexuals (from 2 to 10 percent, depending on definitions).

Perhaps even in a confidential survey, some adolescents did not want to acknowledge their orientation. A retrospective study of homosexual adults reported that they first became aware of their sexual interests at age 11, on average, but they did not tell anyone until age 17 (Maguen et al., 2002).

Especially in homophobic cultures, many young men with homosexual feelings deny these feelings altogether or try to change or conceal them by becoming heterosexually involved. Similarly, many young women who will later identify themselves as lesbian spend their teenage years relatively oblivious to, or in denial of, their sexual urges. This may have social consequences: Depression and suicide are much higher among homosexual than heterosexual youth.

Overall, adults tend to underestimate the significance of romantic pairing (heterosexual or homosexual) during adolescence. Typically, between ages 15 and 17, relationships become less superficial and more meaningful. About half of the older adolescents in one large survey had been involved in a romance that had lasted a year or more (Collins, 2003). Teachers, parents, and peers should all realize that close friendship and intimate partnership are likely to bring happiness and further the search for identity, as well as create conflict.

Before you turn to the final section of this chapter, read the following Case to Study, remembering what you have just read about parents and peers.

Especially for an Adult Friend of a Teenager If your 14-year-old friend asks you where to get "the Pill," what do you say?

A Case to Study

Julia, the Conscientious Student

Julia is the high-achieving elder daughter of married parents, part of a nuclear family who all lived together in their suburban home until Julia went to college. Her background indicates that she is not at risk for drug abuse, delinquency, or unintended pregnancy. We might expect her adolescence to be easy, and by her own report, at age 17, it seems to have been:

In high school, I took advanced-level classes and earned good grades. I also got along quite well with my teachers, and ended up graduating in the top 10% of my class. I know this made my mother really proud, especially since she works at the school. She would get worried that I might not be doing my best and "working to my full potential." All through high school, she tried to keep on top of my homework assignments and test schedules. She liked to look over my work before I turned it in, and would make sure that I left myself plenty of time to study for tests.

In addition to schoolwork, the track and cross-country teams were a big part of high school for me. I started running in junior high school because my parents wanted me to do something athletic and I was never coordinated enough to be good at sports like soccer. I was always a little bit chubby when I was a kid. I don't know if I was exactly overweight, but everyone used to tease me about my baby fat. Running seemed like a good way to lose that extra weight. . . .

My parents didn't like me hanging out with boys unless it was in a group. Besides, the boys I had crushes on were never the ones who asked me out. So any free time was mostly spent with my close girlfriends. We would go shopping or to the movies and we frequently spent the night at each other's houses. I was annoyed that although I never did anything wrong, I had the earliest curfew of my friends. Also I was the only one whose parents would page me throughout the night just to check in. . . . I guess they were just worried and wanted to be sure that I was safe.

[quoted in Gorenstein & Comer, 2002, pp. 274–275]

On the surface, everything seems fine with Julia. She was a hardworking high school student, with parents who cared about her and girlfriends to talk to. She was active on two sports teams, and athletic participation is usually good for health, self-confidence, and social skills (Murphy, 1999). She attended a well-respected college, close to home but far enough away that she lived in a dorm, on a full athletic and academic scholarship.

However, as you just read, conflict with parents, solidarity with peers, and romantic involvement are typical during adolescence. Julia had none of these. Too much parental control can lead to depression. Even Julia's time with her girlfriends was interrupted by her early curfew and parental phone calls "throughout the night." Note that she writes of getting along well with her teachers (not a sign of peer approval) and that her chosen athletic involvement was cross-country and track (the least social of the high school sports). We will meet Julia again in the next chapter, but this first encounter suggests that all is not well, even though Julia herself sees no problems.

Response for an Adult Friend of a Teenager
(from page 405): Practical advice is important: Steer your friend to a reputable medical center that provides counseling for adolescents about various methods of avoiding pregnancy (including abstinence). You don't want your friend using ineffective or harmful contraception, or becoming sexually active before he or she is ready. Try to respond to the emotions behind the question, perhaps addressing the ethics and values involved in sexual activity. Remember that adolescents do not always do the things they talk about, nor are they always logical; but they can analyze alternatives and assess consequences if you lead them in that direction.

Most adolescents experience mutual respect with their parents and supportive intimacy with their friends. Although each generation has a distinct "stake" in their interaction, and although bickering between parents and children is common, the generation gap on major issues is usually narrow. Communication is more typical than alienation. Successful parents monitor and control their children to some degree, but not too strictly; they find a balance between closeness and autonomy, between intrusiveness and independence.

Peers generally help adolescents become more mature and more socially confident. It is true that friends sometimes engage together in rebellion and adventure, but, for the most part, peer pressure is more likely to be constructive, not destructive. Friends encourage each other to achieve in school, stay healthy, and relate well to people of both sexes and all ages. Romances often begin during high school, with both sexes gradually spending more enjoyable time in heterosexual groups and relationships, but neither sex abandons peer friendships once romantic involvement begins.

Conclusion

Let us look again at all of adolescence. Except perhaps for the very first months of life, no other developmental period is characterized by such multifaceted and compelling biological changes. Nor are developing persons at any other age likely to experience a more fascinating, unnerving, and potentially confusing sequence of intellectual and social transitions. The adolescent's developmental tasks—to reach adult size and sexuality, to adjust to changed educational expectations and intellectual patterns, to develop autonomy from parents and intimacy with friends, to achieve a sense of identity and purpose—are too complex to be accomplished without surprises.

As you have seen, most adolescents and most families survive this transition fairly well. Teenagers skip school, eat unwisely, drink too much, experiment with drugs, break laws, feel depressed, rush into sexual activity, conform to peer pressure, disregard their parents' wishes—but all these behaviors typically stay within limits. Parents and children bicker and fight, but they still respect and love each other. For most young people, the teenage years overall are happy ones, during which they escape potentially serious problems and discover the rewards of maturity.

All adolescents have some difficulties, but those with one major problem often have several other serious problems as well (Galambos & Leadbeater, 2000). For instance, girls who become mothers by age 16 are also likely to be from troubled families, to leave school, and to experiment with hard drugs. Boys who become chronic criminals also tend to have learning disabilities, to be alienated from their families, to fail in school, and to abuse drugs (Rutter et al., 1998). Many adolescents who commit suicide have been heartbreakingly lonely and seriously depressed for years, receiving inadequate social support from family and friends (Davila & Daley, 2000).

In almost every case, these problems stem from earlier developmental events. They began with genetic vulnerability and prenatal injuries and continued with family disruptions and discord as well as with learning disabilities and lack of emotional regulation in elementary school—all within a community and culture that did not provide adequate intervention. With the inevitable stresses of puberty, problems become worse, more obvious, more pervasive, and more resistant to change.

An encouraging theme emerges, however: No developmental path is set in stone by previous events; adolescents are, by nature, innovators, idealists, and risk takers, open to new patterns, goals, and lifestyles. Some break free from destructive or ominous beginnings (Belsky et al., 2001). Plasticity throughout the life span means that early experiences can be overcome. Research on effective schools, on teenage sex, on the positive role of friendship, and on identity achievement shows that every problem can be adolescence-limited. Young people can find a path that leads them away from the restrictions and burdens of their past.

For some, adulthood is the time when they can distance themselves from their origins, never completely escaping their legacy but no longer imprisoned by it. For many, adulthood is not that different from earlier life, a time of new challenges to be met with help from mind and spirit, from friends and family.

SUMMARY

The Self and Identity

1. Adolescence is a time for self-discovery, which begins as adolescents try out various roles and personalities. A period of multiple selves may include some selves that the person considers false—perhaps developed as a means of exploration or in reaction to parental criticism or peer perceptions.

2. According to Erikson, as adolescents seek to resolve their identity crisis, they must overcome role confusion, particularly in four areas—vocation, politics, religion, and sex. None of these issues are easy to resolve: Many adolescents opt for a hasty foreclosure or for postponement via moratorium. Some may react against parental and social pressure by taking on a negative, or oppositional, identity.

3. During the identity crisis, which can last 10 years or more, almost every adolescent experiences a period of identity diffusion. Values and goals shift, and the individual seems adrift, without direction. Identity is often achieved in one domain before another.

4. Adolescents achieve a sexual, or gender, identity not only by figuring out their sexual orientation but also by choosing specifics of male or female behavior. Finding ethnic identity is also complex, especially in a multiethnic society.

Sadness and Anger

5. Almost all adolescents lose some of the confidence and self-esteem they had when they were children. According to psychoanalytic theory, emotional turbulence is normal during these years. A few individuals become chronically sad and depressed, intensifying problems they have had since childhood.

6. Most adolescents think about suicide, and parasuicides (suicide attempts) are not rare, especially among adolescent girls. Few adolescents actually kill themselves; most who do are boys. Not only gender but also ethnic differences are apparent in completed suicide, with Native American males having the highest

rates and Asian-American females the lowest. Drug and alcohol use, gun availability, alienation from parents, and lifelong depression are risk factors.

7. Almost all adolescents become more independent and rebellious as part of growing up. Often this rebelliousness manifests itself in lawbreaking, especially by adolescent boys.

8. Adolescence-limited delinquents stop breaking the law when they reach adulthood. They should be redirected and prevented from hurting themselves or others. Life-course-persistent offenders are more difficult to treat, because their problems typically start in early childhood and extend into adulthood.

Family and Friends

9. Parents continue to influence children during adolescence, despite bickering over minor issues. Ideally, communication and warmth remain high within the family, while parental control decreases and adolescents are allowed to develop autonomy. Cultural differences are apparent in autonomy as well as in the timing of rebellion. Parental neglect or hostility is always destructive.

10. Friends help the developing adolescent cope with the conflicting demands of school, family, peers, and physical growth. Peer pressure is both beneficial and harmful, depending on the adolescent's choice of friends.

11. Peers can be crucial for immigrant adolescents. Those who have a strong commitment to family values tend to be successful in school and unlikely to rebel by using drugs or in other ways. Some, however, rebel completely, with the support of other immigrant teens.

12. Heterosexual friendships and romances begin in early adolescence and become increasingly important for self-concept and maturation. Whether or not a particular adolescent is romantically attached depends on many factors, both personal and cultural.

KEY TERMS

identity (p. 385)
possible selves (p. 385)
false self (p. 386)
identity versus role confusion
 (p. 387)
identity achievement (p. 387)
foreclosure (p. 387)

negative identity (p. 388)
identity diffusion (p. 388)
identity moratorium (p. 388)
gender identity (p. 389)
internalizing problems (p. 391)
externalizing problems
 (p. 391)

suicidal ideation (p. 393)
parasuicide (p. 393)
cluster suicides (p. 395)
incidence (p. 395)
prevalence (p. 395)
adolescence-limited offender
 (p. 396)

life-course-persistent offender
 (p. 396)
generation gap (p. 397)
generational stake (p. 398)
bickering (p. 398)
parental monitoring (p. 399)
peer pressure (p. 401)

APPLICATIONS

1. Is it more difficult to achieve vocational identity today than it used to be? Interview two or three adults over age 40. What career goal did they have as adolescents? Did their aspirations change over the years? If so, how and why?

2. Locate a story in your local newspaper about a teenager who committed suicide. Does the article indicate that there were warning signs that were ignored? Does the news report glorify the adolescent's life and death in a way that might encourage cluster suicides?

3. The data suggest that most adolescents have broken the law, but few have been arrested or incarcerated. Is this less true for

people you know, especially those in college? Ask 10 of your fellow students whether they broke the law when they were under 18. Assure them of confidentiality and ask specific questions (e.g., Did you ever drink alcohol, buy cigarettes, take something that was not yours?). Do your results suggest any hypothesis about teenage lawbreaking?

4. As a follow-up to question 3, ask your fellow students about the circumstances. What lawbreaking was done with peers or alone? What response came from police, parents, judges, and peers? Discuss the effect of peers and families.

Part V

Adolescence

BIOSOCIAL

Physical Growth Sometime between the ages of 8 and 14, puberty begins, with increases in various hormones that trigger a host of changes. Within a year of the hormonal increases, the first perceptible physical changes appear—enlargement of the girl's breasts and the boy's testes. About a year later, a growth spurt begins, when boys and girls gain in height, weight, and musculature.

Sexual Maturation Toward the end of puberty, primary sexual development includes menarche in girls and ejaculation in boys. Secondary sexual characteristics also develop. Males become taller than females and develop deeper voices and characteristic patterns of facial and body hair. Females become wider at the hips; breast development continues for several years. Some teenagers become vulnerable to sexual abuse and/or unhealthy dieting. Others use drugs at an age or dose that is harmful to healthy growth, particularly the gateway drugs—tobacco, alcohol, and marijuana. Both sexes risk diseases and premature parenthood.

COGNITIVE

Adolescent Thinking Adolescent thought can deal with the possible as well as the actual, thanks to a newly emerging ability to think hypothetically, to reason deductively, and to explain theoretically. At the same time, adolescent egocentrism, along with feelings of uniqueness and invincibility, can make adolescents extraordinarily self-absorbed, thinking intuitively rather than rationally.

Both logic and intuition advance during adolescence, although few teenagers combine them successfully.

Decision Making For some adolescents, risk taking is more attractive than rational planning. This is apparent regarding vocational choices, studying in school, and sex education. Culture and cohort are powerful in an adolescent's every thought, emotion, and choice. Adults who criticize adolescent thinking should examine the structures, assumptions, and messages they have given to teenagers.

PSYCHOSOCIAL

Identity One goal of adolescence is self-understanding and identity achievement. Achieving identity can be affected by personal factors—including relationships with family and peers. Sexual and ethnic identity are especially complex.

Sadness and Anger Depression and thoughts about suicide are common in adolescence, especially among girls, although boys are more likely to actually complete a suicide. While most adolescents break the law in some way, the minority who commit serious crimes often come from a troubled family and a debilitating social context. More supportive communities can moderate these problems, as can constructive peer pressure and authoritative parenting.

Parents and Peers The peer group becomes increasingly important in fostering independence and interaction, particularly with members of the other sex. Parents and young adolescents are often at odds over issues centering on the child's increased assertiveness or lack of self-discipline.

22409

Part VI

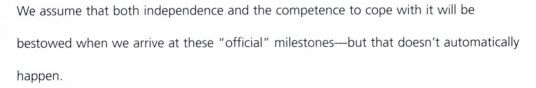

As younger children, we look forward to the day when we will be "all grown up," imagining that adult size will automatically bring mastery of roles, privileges, and responsibilities. Young teenagers likewise impatiently await their high school graduation or their 18th or 21st birthday. We assume that both independence and the competence to cope with it will be bestowed when we arrive at these "official" milestones—but that doesn't automatically happen.

Young adults, who must make their own decisions about career goals, intimate relationships, social commitments, and moral conduct, find these aspects of independence, though exciting, far from easy. This is especially true today, because the array of lifestyle choices is vast and varied. No matter which roles young adults choose or how thoughtfully and eagerly they strive to play them, they are confronted with stresses, setbacks, and second thoughts. Yet for most young adults, problems faced and solved, and limitations accepted or overcome, make the years from ages 20 to 35 exhilarating. Young adults often feel they are living to the fullest. The next three chapters describe how people cope with the engrossing, multidimensional realities of early adulthood.

Early Adulthood

Early Adulthood: Biosocial Development

In terms of biosocial development, early adulthood, from roughly age 20 to age 35, can be considered the prime of life. Bodies are stronger, taller, and healthier than during any other period. The beginning of young adulthood is the best time for hard physical work, for problem-free reproduction, and for peak athletic performance. Although some physiological declines are evident by age 30 or so, during young adulthood most real declines in health and strength are caused not by normal aging but by poor choices. Typical development and problems in young adulthood are both discussed in this chapter.

Growth, Strength, and Health

The overall status of physical development in young adulthood can be summed up as follows: Young adults are strong, healthy, and almost disease-free. We begin with some specifics that justify that statement.

Norms and Peaks

Girls usually reach their maximum height by age 16 and boys by age 18, with the exception of a few late-maturing boys who undergo final skeletal growth in their early 20s (Behrman, 1992). Muscle growth and fat accumulation continue into the early 20s, when women attain their full breast and hip size and men reach full shoulder and upper-arm size. Because the proportion of muscle in body mass is greater in males than in females, men are typically stronger than women of the same age. For both sexes, however, physical strength generally increases during the 20s, reaches a peak at about age 30, and then decreases. Young adults are better than any other age group at, say, running up a flight of stairs, lifting a heavy load, or gripping an object with maximum force. The decrease in strength occurs more rapidly in the back and leg muscles than in the arm muscles, so the young adult who loses at arm-wrestling to someone older might propose a stair-climbing race and win (Masuro, 1999).

All the body systems, including the digestive, respiratory, circulatory, and sexual-reproductive systems, function at an optimum level in young adulthood. Consequently, visits to the doctor between ages 15 and 44 are less than half what they will be between ages 45 and 75, and a third what they will be after age 75 (U.S. Bureau of the Census, 2002). Those young-adult visits are usually because of injuries (often drug- or sports-related) or pregnancy, not because of sickness or for preventive care. Even the common cold is less frequent in early adulthood than in any other part of the life span.

TABLE 17.1 Annual U.S. Death Rates from Five Leading Diseases*

Age Range	Deaths per 100,000
15–24	9
25–34	21
35–44	75
45–54	251
55–64	751
65–74	2,068
75–84	2,961
85+	10,110

*In order of overall frequency: heart disease, cancer, stroke, obstructive pulmonary disease, and pneumonia. (Under age 75, cancer is the leading cause of disease death. This list does not include accidents, suicides, and homicides, which are the leading causes of death from age 1 to 40.)

Source: National Center for Health Statistics. *Vital Statistics of the United States,* 2002.

senescence The state of physical decline, in which the body gradually becomes less strong and efficient with age.

These findings are for the United States, where young adults are the age group least likely to have health insurance (U.S. Bureau of the Census, 2002). Out-of-pocket cost is not the principal reason for the age difference in visits to the doctor, however. Young adults generally feel strong and healthy. In a mammoth survey, 96 percent of young adults rated their health as good, very good, or excellent, and only 4 percent rated it as fair or poor (National Center for Health Statistics, 2000).

Death from disease is exceedingly rare during early adulthood. This is true worldwide (Heuveline, 2002). Detailed data come from the United States, where, for example, the annual death rate from cancer, the leading killer of adults under age 75, is less than 1 in 10,000 for adults between ages 20 and 34, compared with more than 1 per 1,000 for those between ages 35 and 65 and more than 1 per 100 for those over age 65 (U.S. Bureau of the Census, 2002). The data in Table 17.1 make especially clear the relatively low mortality rate among young adults for disease overall.

There is one major dark spot in this rosy view: violent death. The specifics vary internationally, but overall, as the disease deaths have decreased, the proportion of violent deaths during young adulthood has risen: Homicide, suicide, and motor-vehicle deaths—the deadly trio—now account for 43 percent of the total (see Figure 17.1). Males are particularly vulnerable; indeed, worldwide more men in their 20s die violently than die of all the diseases combined. More homicides occur in the early 20s than at any other time of the entire life span; the overall incidence of suicides and accidents is typically U-shaped—high in early adulthood, lower in middle adulthood, and then peaking again at the end of adulthood.

Signs of Senescence

When overall growth stops, **senescence,** defined as a gradual physical decline related to age, begins. Senescence is ongoing throughout adulthood: We are all aging, each at our own rate. Childhood's tight connection between physical change and chronological age loosens in adulthood. A 50-year-old could have the body of a typical 30-year-old, or vice versa. Variation in rate of senescence is also apparent in every organ. For example, your liver may be aging much faster than your heart. The rate of senescence is influenced by genes, the environment, and personal choices.

Although most young adults are strong and healthy, signs of senescence are present long before middle age. The first visible age-related changes are seen in the skin. At about age 20, collagen, the connective tissue of the body, begins to decrease in total quantity by about 1 percent per year (Timiras, M., 2003). As a result, the skin becomes thinner and less flexible, and wrinkles become visible, particularly around the eyes, by age 30. Skin all over the body, especially on the face (because it is almost never covered against sun, rain, heat, cold, wind, or pollution), shows "creases, discoloration, furrows, sagging, and loss of resiliency" (Whitbourne, 2002).

Graying hair, another visible sign of aging, also appears around age 30, because of a reduction in the number of pigment-producing cells. Hereditary baldness in men typically begins in the 30s, and both sexes have fewer hairs as a result of hormonal changes and a reduced blood supply to the skin, which stops some hair follicles from production.

Signs of decline appear in every body system. For example, lung efficiency is reduced beginning in the 20s, with vital capacity (the total amount of air that can be expired after a deep breath) dropping about 5 percent per decade (faster for people who smoke) (De Martinis & Timiras, 2003); and the kidneys become less

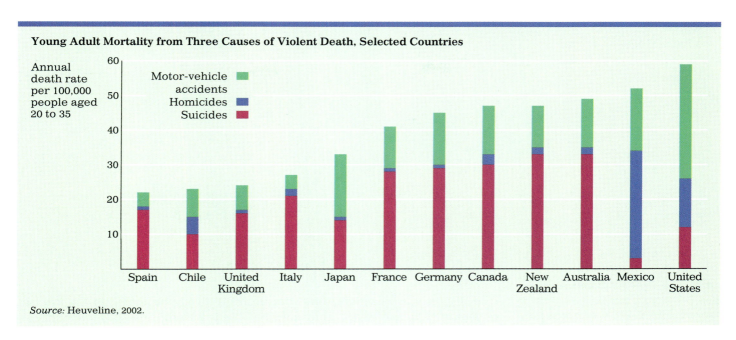

Young Adult Mortality from Three Causes of Violent Death, Selected Countries

Annual death rate per 100,000 people aged 20 to 35

- Motor-vehicle accidents
- Homicides
- Suicides

Spain, Chile, United Kingdom, Italy, Japan, France, Germany, Canada, New Zealand, Australia, Mexico, United States

Source: Heuveline, 2002.

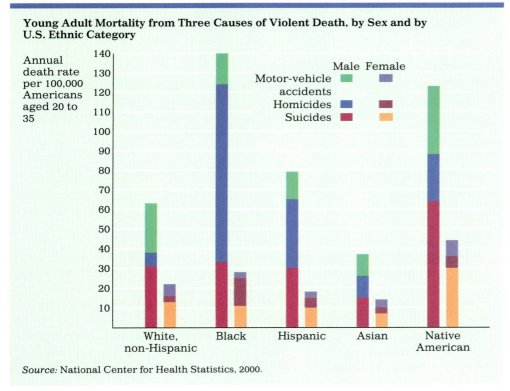

Young Adult Mortality from Three Causes of Violent Death, by Sex and by U.S. Ethnic Category

Annual death rate per 100,000 Americans aged 20 to 35

Male Female
- Motor-vehicle accidents
- Homicides
- Suicides

White, non-Hispanic; Black; Hispanic; Asian; Native American

Source: National Center for Health Statistics, 2000.

FIGURE 17.1 A Dangerous Time of Life
These graphs show the rates of violent death among young adults in selected countries worldwide *(top)* and by U.S. ethnic category *(bottom)* at the end of the 1990s. Although these rates are high, other data show that they have decreased since 1990. Early adulthood is the peak period for all forms of violent death except suicide, which has higher rates among older white males and older Asian females than in young adults.

? *Observational Quiz* (see answer, page 416): In the United States, which two groups have the lowest rates of motor-vehicle death?

efficient around age 30, with a slow reduction in functioning (about 4 percent per decade) unless alcohol or disease speeds up kidney senescence (Masuro, 1999).

Not only do organs vary in their rate of senescence but so do the particular functions of each organ, as is especially apparent in the sense organs (Meisami et al., 2003). Consider visual acuity (the ability to see objects a distance) and accommodation (the ability to focus on objects that are close). Difficulty with objects at

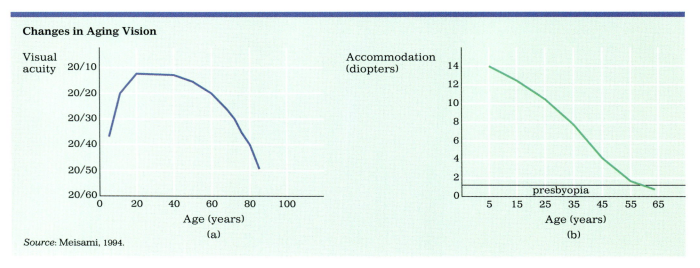

Changes in Aging Vision

(a)

Source: Meisami, 1994.

FIGURE 17.2 **Age-Related Declines in Vision** Every aspect of bodily functioning follows its own rate of senescence. Vision is a prime example. *(a)* Sharpness of distance vision, as measured by the ability to see an object at 20 feet, reaches a peak at about age 20 and declines gradually until old age. *(b)* By contrast, ability to focus on a small point about 12 inches in front of the eyes declines from childhood on; at about age 60 the typical person becomes officially farsighted.

a distance, or nearsightedness, increases gradually beginning in the 20s (see Figure 17.2). In contrast, difficulty with objects that are close, or farsightedness, begins even earlier, as the aging lens loses its ability to change shape to adjust to close-up focusing; it increases more rapidly in the 30s. This explains why 40-year-olds tend to hold reading matter almost twice as far away from their eyes as 20-year-olds do (Meisami et al., 2003). By about age 60, farsightedness reaches the point where it is labeled *presbyopia* (literally, "aging vision") and reading glasses are needed.

Similar losses occur in hearing. People have more acute hearing at age 10 than at any later age, but not until about age 60 does *presbycusis* (literally, "aging hearing") occur, when loss becomes apparent. Thus, although senescence begins in early adulthood, its effects are negligible until much later.

Gender Differences in Health and Senescence

Rates of aging vary, but they are not random (Austad, 2001). Sex, genes, ethnicity, income, education, location, lifestyle, and culture all speed up some aspects of senescence and slow others down. People who are male, of low socioeconomic status, and from ethnic minorities tend to age more quickly. Many of the particulars will be discussed throughout the nine chapters on adulthood: Ethnic differences are described in detail in Chapter 20. Here we focus on gender differences.

Young adulthood is defined here as occurring from age 20 to 35 for everyone. In a certain sense, however, women might be said to have fewer years of young adulthood and more years of middle adulthood. The reason is that appearance seems more important for women than for men: Women spend more money combating wrinkled skin and covering gray hair, and they are considered old sooner by marriageable men, by employers, and by themselves. Thus, although both sexes experience similar superficial signs of aging in early adulthood, women tend to be more troubled by them and consider themselves middle-aged earlier.

In some ways, however, women are slower to become old. Females are generally healthier than men overall, with better health habits in early adulthood, fewer fatal diseases in middle age, and longer life spans—five years longer, on average. They take better care of themselves in hundreds of ways—eating lots of vegetables, using seat belts, avoiding illegal drugs, getting preventive care, even brushing their teeth more. Women outlive men in all but one (Namibia) of the 170 nations for which the United Nations has data.

!Answer to Observational Quiz (from page 415): Black or Hispanic females.

In only two ways are females at a health disadvantage compared with males: undernourishment and reproductive-system problems. Men are more vulnerable to almost every other health problem. It is often noted that among the very old there are twice as many women as men; however, the imbalance occurs not primarily because old men die at higher rates than old women (they do not), but because more younger males die. The effect is cumulative, so that at age 80, women outnumber men 2 to 1 (U.S. Bureau of the Census, 2002). Three explanations have been proposed:

- *Biological*: Because of the evolutionary need for females to reproduce and care for young children, something about their biology (perhaps the second X chromosome or the higher levels of estrogen) protects them until their childbearing years are over.
- *Cognitive*: Because men are taught to be independent and tough, they take risks and avoid precautions, and this gets them into dangerous situations. In addition, many men consider preventive health care unmanly (Williams, 2003).
- *Psychosocial:* Marriage, family life, friendship, and help-seeking are all protective of health; women are more likely to engage in all of these.

As you know, all three domains—biological, cognitive, and psychosocial—interact at every point of life. Thus, all three of these explanations are probably partly true. What can men do to change the odds against them? Of course, men cannot change their biology, nor should they marry just to be healthier. But cognitions and culture can change. One observer notes:

> Men are socialized to project strength, individuality, autonomy, dominance, stoicism, and physical aggression, and to avoid demonstrations of emotion or vulnerability that could be construed as weakness. These . . . combine to increase health risks.
>
> *[Williams, 2003, p. 726]*

A man certainly could, and should, overcome his self-destructive reluctance and get preventive health care. Everyone who is concerned about men's health could be part of a cultural shift that makes maleness less risky (Williams, 2003).

Homeostasis

Many body functions seek **homeostasis;** that is, they attempt to maintain physiological functioning in a state of balance, or equilibrium. When people exercise and therefore use oxygen more rapidly, breathing and heart rate automatically increase to deliver more oxygen to the cells. That is homeostasis. When their body gets too hot, people sweat to give off body heat and their movements slow down so less heat is generated. When their body gets too cold, people shiver to raise body temperature. These thermoregulatory mechanisms, too, are for homeostasis. As the body's overall salt, glucose, water, and acid levels fluctuate, an ongoing homeostatic process, which involves a complex interaction among many internal organs and systems, returns the body to equilibrium by making people hungry, thirsty, and so on (Holliday, 1995).

For weight there also is a homeostatic **set point,** or settling point, affected by genes, diet, age, hormones, and exercise, that makes people eat when they are hungry and stop when they are full to keep their body weight stable (Bouchard & Bray, 1996; Woods et al., 2000). A person's genes and cultural pressures can disrupt that mechanism, but homeostasis naturally works to keep every bodily system, including the food–energy–weight system, balanced.

As you can see from these examples, homeostasis involves many physiological functions, which adjust to each other as well as to the whole. This means that

homeostasis The adjustment of the body's systems to keep physiological functions in a state of equilibrium. As the body ages, it takes longer for these homeostatic adjustments to occur, so it becomes harder for older bodies to adapt to stresses.

set point A particular body weight that an individual's homeostatic processes strive to maintain.

an age-related decline, say, in the efficiency of the lungs, can be compensated for, say, by the breathing rate, when need be. Many of the mechanisms of homeostasis are regulated by the pituitary, sometimes called "the master gland," which robustly defends the body through various hormonal shifts, as well as by more obvious mechanisms, to maintain homeostasis (Timiras, 2003a).

The older a person is, however, the longer it takes for the entire set of homeostatic adjustments to occur, so the harder it is for older bodies to adapt to, and recover from, physical stress. If a younger and an older athlete, both equally fit, compete at the same intensity for the same duration, the older adult's heart rate, breathing, blood pH (acidity), and blood glucose (sugar) will take longer to reach peak levels and longer still to return to normal when the game is over. Similarly, older adults have more difficulty adjusting to work that is physiologically stressful.

These changes might mean that, in contrast to an adolescent, the average 35-year-old can no longer skip a night's sleep or spend a day in hard physical activity and then bounce back the next day and that a 30-year-old woman is more fatigued by pregnancy than a 20-year-old. As this slowdown continues throughout adulthood, less efficient homeostasis affects each organ as well as overall functioning; by late adulthood, overheating, a chill, or exertion is a potentially lethal event (Masuro, 1999).

Reserve Capacity

Senescence might seem frightening to college students just at the start of early adulthood. Fortunately, the subjective experience of senescence is much less daunting than one might imagine from the data on the body's decline. In normal day-to-day life, most adults of all ages feel that their bodies are quite strong and capable, not much less efficient than they were 10 years earlier. And for the most part, this perception is correct, not simply wishful thinking: Homeostasis adjusts to whatever demands there are, keeping overall functioning adequate.

In fact, if they maintain their bodies, most adults can function quite well until at least age 70. The reason is that the declines of aging affect **organ reserve**, the extra capacity that each organ has for responding to unusually stressful events or conditions that demand intense or prolonged effort (Fries & Crapo, 1981; Holliday, 1995). People seldom need this capacity, so gradual declines in organ reserve go unnoticed. Thus, although 60-year-olds take 50 percent longer than 20-year-olds to run 5,000 meters (Austad, 2001) because the reserve capacity of their hearts and lungs is not as great as it once was, adults of both ages walk from place to place with nearly equal ease. Similarly, while a pregnant woman in her late 30s might find her kidneys, blood pressure, and lung capacity more affected than when she was pregnant 15 years earlier, she also finds that when she is not pregnant, these organs function very well.

Bodies have a muscle reserve as well. Few adults today develop, or ever need to use, all the muscle capacity that they could attain during their years of peak strength. Maximum strength *potential* typically begins to decline at about age 30, with leg muscles affected more than those of the arms and hands. However, this occurs gradually. At age 50, adults retain 90 percent of the strength they had at age 20; the 10 percent that is lost is rarely missed (Rice & Cunningham, 2002). Consequently, in developed countries, where hard physical labor is not a daily necessity for most people, a healthy 50-year-old can perform virtually all the tasks of everyday living as well as a 20-year-old can. Moreover, because few adults today develop their full muscle capacity, 50-year-olds who begin working out may become stronger than ever.

organ reserve The extra capacity of the heart, lungs, and other organs that makes it possible for the body to withstand moments of intense or prolonged stress. With age, organ reserve is gradually depleted, but the rate of depletion depends on the individual's general state of health.

Man of Steel Declines in physical strength are irrelevant in modern-day occupations, even in the steel industry, where brute strength and unflagging endurance were once essential. Today's hard-hatted steel workers can perform most of their jobs with their fingertips.

TOM CARROLL / INTERNATIONAL STOCK

The most important muscle of all, the heart, shows a similar pattern. The average maximum heart rate—the number of times the heart can beat per minute under extreme stress—declines steadily as the heart's reserve capacity is reduced with age. But the resting heart rate remains very stable. Once again, although peak performance declines, normal functioning is not affected by aging until late adulthood. Most people, at age 70, do *not* have coronary artery disease (Timiras, 2003b).

Even in the smaller changes of aging, such as the wearing down of the teeth or loss of cartilage in the knees, serious reductions are not normally reached until late adulthood. As one expert explains, "A remarkable feature of aging is that various organs and structures have evolved to 'last a lifetime'" (Holliday, 1995). Thus, age-related biological changes during the first decades of adulthood are normally of little consequence. There are two notable exceptions to this generalization: athletic performance and reproduction.

Sports Stars and the Rest of Us

Minor differences in strength, reaction time, and lung efficiency have a significant impact on professional athletes—and on serious weekend players as well. Athletic performance peaks somewhere between ages 15 and 35, with variations not only from person to person and sport to sport but also from skill to skill within a sport.

In almost all sports, because of the preparation required, "peak performance is attained many years after peak physical maturity is reached" (Ericsson, 1996). Performance peaks earlier in sports that depend more on strength and gross motor skills than in those that depend more on fine motor skills. The variation within a sport by skill can be considerable: In baseball, for example, a comprehensive study of professional players found that the number of stolen bases peaked at age 27, earned run average at 29, and fielding percentage at 30 (Schulz et al., 1994).

On most skills, elite players, particularly Hall of Famers, peak somewhat later than other team members and sustain their high level of performance longer. Other research finds that superior performance in any group of professional athletes does not correlate with the small differences in reaction time or in specific skills (Shea & Powell, 1996). Instead, something more cerebral—and less likely to decline—probably makes the final, crucial difference once skills are already high.

What about the rest of us? There is a consolation for those of us who are on "the downward slope of the performance curve": Since few people are so fit that they achieve their peak levels in their 20s, our best performance could still lie ahead (Schulz et al., 1994).

There is another consolation, as well as an ongoing challenge. The impact of aging depends on lifestyle, including decisions made each day about consumption and exertion. Maintaining good health habits, avoiding drugs, and sticking to a rigorous training schedule extend the years of high-level performance. Conditioned older athletes perform so much better than most unconditioned younger persons that they are an inspiration. Practiced marathoners in their 60s have run 26 miles at under 8 minutes a mile. If some 20- and 30-year-olds who can't even run around the block begin walking briskly for a few hours a week, running a few miles will eventually be no problem.

Sexual Responsiveness

At every age, both male and female bodies follow a similar sequence of sexual activation: arousal, peak excitement, release through orgasm, refraction (during which arousal is impossible), and recovery. These similarities are apparent

The Great Michael Jordan at 39 Professional athletes are one of the few groups for whom the bodily declines of early adulthood may have significant consequences. However, depending on the sport and the particular skills involved, the benefits of experience and vigorous conditioning may permit superior athletes to perform at the top of their game well into their 30s.

Together Again Although biologists and psychologists describe the differences between the sexes, the reality is that young adult men and women are similar in many ways. Both seek one special other person and are thrilled to be together.

Especially for Marriage Counselors A young wife complains that her husband is "oversexed," and he says she is "frigid." What do you advise?

despite much individual variation in both stimuli and response, and despite some major sex differences and some age-related differences.

First, we describe the typical male responses. During the early years of manhood, sexual arousal and excitement (which includes both a faster heartbeat and penile erection) can occur very quickly in response not only to an exciting partner but also to many other stimuli—even an idea, a photograph, or a passing remark. Typically, orgasm during sexual activity also occurs fairly quickly. For some young men, the refractory period may be very brief—a matter of minutes. Arousal and excitement are slower in older men, often requiring explicit or prolonged stimulation; more time elapses between excitement and full erection, between erection and ejaculation, and between orgasm and recovery (Everaerd et al., 2000).

That these changes are in part physiological, not merely psychological or social, is suggested by research on lower animals such as rats and monkeys. When caged with a receptive female, young male rats are twice as sexually active as middle-aged rats, which, in turn, are more active than older rats, some of whom fail to mate at all (Hokado et al., 1993).

As with all age-related biological patterns, the overall slowing down is universal, but the rate of decline varies a great deal, depending on the person, the culture, and the context. Specific events (such as a new sex partner) can temporarily speed up responses, in rats as well as in humans.

Age-related trends in sexual responsiveness are not as clear-cut for women (or female rats) as they are for men (Masters et al., 1994). In general, however, it seems that arousal, excitement, and orgasm take longer for women than for men (Renshaw, 1998). As women move from early adolescence toward middle adulthood, arousal and orgasm become more likely, rather than less likely as for men (Rutter & Rutter, 1993).

Why do women's responses seem to pick up just when men are sexually slowing down? Several explanations have been suggested. The age-related slowing of the man's responses makes the sex act last longer, which means the woman's response has time to build. A related possible explanation is that, with experience, both partners have learned which aspects of their lovemaking prolong the man's excitement and intensify the woman's sexual responses.

Another set of explanations are cultural. In most nations, young men are expected to be lustful, sex driven, and uncontrolled, so their sexual expression at first is rapid and self-centered, only gradually accommodating the emotional aspects of a relationship. They see having repeated orgasms as "great sex," because they have been conditioned to believe that "more is better."

Young women, by contrast, are conditioned to see sex as "violent" and "victimizing" (Lear, 1997) and thus to resist, repressing their own desire and overemphasizing control of the experience. As a result, it may take years for women to acknowledge and appreciate their sexuality, and consequently to experience orgasm on a regular basis (Daniluk, 1998). This means that healthy sexuality emerges later in a woman's life, preceded by much "unlearning" (Johnston, 1997).

A final possible explanation comes from evolutionary psychology (Badcock, 2000): Sexually promiscuous males with insistent sexual urges produce more offspring and hence pass on their genes more often (an evolutionary goal). In contrast, women need to restrain their sexual urges during their prime reproductive years in order to concentrate on successful pregnancy, birth, breast-feeding, and child care, spacing their births every three years or so for maximum child welfare. Therefore, when aging makes reproduction less likely for women, they can express their sexual passions without jeopardizing their children.

Despite their differences, these explanations are consistent with a generality that applies to every aspect of physiological aging during young adulthood: How people think is as important as the biological changes. When it comes to sex, how old you are matters less than where you have been, what you value, and who your partner is.

Fertility

Young adulthood is the most common time for men and women to have a baby. In fact, of the newborns in the United States in 2000, 85 percent had a mother younger than 35 and a father younger than 45, even though female fertility normally continues to about age 50 and male fertility continues until death.

Most young adults worry more about having children too soon than about waiting too long. There is good reason for this; with maturation, adults are wealthier, more patient, and more stable—all of which may make them better parents. However, advanced age is a disadvantage when it comes to fertility.

Overall, between 2 and 30 percent of all couples experience **infertility,** usually defined as the failure to conceive a child after a year or more of intercourse without contraception. The range of these estimates is wide because "infertility varies from country to country and from cohort to cohort" (Bentley & Mascie-Taylor, 2000, p. 1) as a result of differences in cultural norms and medical care.

The United States estimate is about 15 percent because cultural practices postpone reproduction until after the most fertile ages. The older a couple is, the more likely they are to be infertile. For example, of those who try to conceive when the woman is in her 40s, about half fail and a higher proportion of the pregnancies that do occur end in miscarriage, stillbirth, or other reproductive problems (Barbieri, 1999). Prospective fathers and prospective mothers are about equally likely to be the source of infertility (Diamond et al., 1999).

At any given moment, billions of sperm are in the process of development. Anything that impairs a man's normal body functioning (such as a high fever, radiation, prescription drugs, environmental toxins, unusual stress, drug abuse, alcoholism, or cigarette smoking) adversely affects the number, shape, and motility (activity) of the sperm for several months. These adverse effects also occur as men grow older. As a result, men over age 40 take three times longer (measured by months of sexual activity before conception occurs) to produce a pregnancy than men under age 25 (Seibel, 1993).

Women can be infertile for many reasons. The most common is failure to ovulate—that is, to release an egg from the ovary. This failure may result from drug use (including use of alcohol and tobacco) and from anything that impairs a woman's normal bodily functioning, including being underweight and being obese (Seibel, 1993). As middle age approaches, ovulation gradually becomes more erratic. By age 40 women experience some menstrual cycles with no ovulation and other cycles in which several eggs are released, thus taking longer to conceive but having higher rates of twins.

Another common reason for female infertility is blockage of the fallopian tubes, which is usually caused by **pelvic inflammatory disease (PID).** PID may occur when an infection of the female organs is not treated promptly. Blocked fallopian tubes are not caused by aging (even in late adulthood, most women's fallopian tubes are still open). But over the years, sexual activity with different partners can increase the risk of a sexually transmitted infection, such as gonorrhea or chlamydia, and thus of PID.

As you can see, for both sexes, successful conception gradually becomes more difficult with the passing years. Most physicians recommend that would-be mothers start trying to conceive before age 30 and would-be fathers, before age 40, to increase the likelihood of conception and to reduce the incidence of problems with pregnancy and birth. Not only does the incidence of spontaneous abortion and stillbirth increase with age, but so does that of chromosomal problems: With mothers over age 45, about 1 newborn in 10 has an abnormal chromosomal count.

infertility The lack of a successful pregnancy after one year of regular intercourse without contraception.

MONIKA GRAFF / THE IMAGE WORKS

A Mature Commitment Today the promise "to have and to hold" is one that is often not made until after age 30. Although this postponement of marriage may increase the chances of marital success, for many couples it may also increase the chances of infertility.

pelvic inflammatory disease (PID) A common result of recurring pelvic infections in women. Pelvic inflammatory disease often leads to blocked fallopian tubes, which, in turn, can lead to infertility.

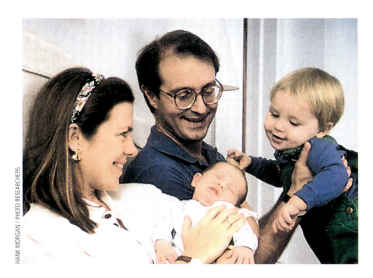

HANK MORGAN / PHOTO RESEARCHERS

Medical Miracles Although they obviously differ in age, brothers David and Nicholas might be called "twins," since they were conceived at the same time. Because their mother had a blocked fallopian tube that prevented normal conception, the boys' parents turned to IVF. One of the embryos that resulted from the procedure (David) was used immediately; another embryo (Nicholas) was kept frozen and then used about a year later.

in vitro fertilization (IVF) A technique in which ova (egg cells) are surgically removed from a woman and fertilized with sperm in the laboratory. After the original fertilized cells (the zygotes) have divided several times, they are inserted into a woman's uterus.

assisted reproductive technology (ART) The collective name for the various methods of medical intervention that can help infertile couples have children.

Especially for Couples What can be done, without seeing a doctor, to enhance fertility?

Nevertheless, the relationship between age and fertility should not be exaggerated. Certainly in young adulthood age is rarely the primary cause of complications with conception, pregnancy, or birth. Adults who wait until their 30s and then find conception difficult might have had the same problem if they had started trying 10 years earlier. Moreover, many fertility problems can be solved by modern medical techniques. Minor physical abnormalities that cause infertility in men (such as varicoceles, or varicose veins, in the testes and partially blocked genital ducts) are often correctable through surgery. In women, drugs can stimulate ovulation and blocked fallopian tubes can often be opened surgically.

Another possibility is **in vitro fertilization (IVF)**, in which ova are surgically removed, fertilized by sperm in the laboratory, and allowed to divide until the zygote reaches the eight- or sixteen-cell stage. In vitro fertilization sidesteps problems not only with ovulation but also with low sperm count: In the laboratory, a technician can insert one sperm into one ovum, thus avoiding the need for millions of sperm per ejaculate. The resulting zygotes are then placed directly into the uterus (avoiding the journey through the fallopian tubes) with the hope that one or more will become implanted—a hope fulfilled about 30 percent of the time (American Society for Reproductive Medicine, 2002). Since 1978, when the first "test-tube" baby was born, a million children in at least 40 nations have been born using IVF (IFFS Surveillance 01, 2001).

These and other methods are collectively called **assisted reproductive technology (ART)**. Most infertile couples can be helped by medical intervention to give birth to a baby *if* they are under age 35 and *if* they can afford it (the cost per baby is about $32,000 if the woman is under 35, about $90,000 if she is older) (Hughes & Giacomi, 2001). Unfortunately, many infertile couples do not recognize their problem until they are over age 35 or do not have the money or medical care to solve it. The highest rate of infertility is in Africa, primarily because of inadequate and expensive medical care and high rates of untreated sexually transmitted infections (Caldwell & Caldwell, 2000).

The overall prognosis for health in early adulthood is excellent, although the rate of violent death, especially among young males, is disturbingly high. As growth stops, every body system is stronger and more resistant to disease than at any later time. Senescence begins during these years, but at such a slow rate as to be largely imperceptible.

Many bodily functions work to maintain a physiological balance, called homeostasis. And because breathing, heart rate, blood flow, and various hormones interact to maintain body temperature, oxygen, nutrition, and so on, the various strains and stresses of daily life do not tax a person too much. Furthermore, each organ has a certain extra reserve, to be called on when unusual demands arise. Thus, only in extraordinary circumstances, as in professional athletics, are the declines of aging apparent.

The sexual-reproductive system performs well throughout early adulthood. At the beginning of adulthood women's sexual arousal, excitement, and release often seem slow and men's fast, but this imbalance tends to be corrected over time. Although about 15 percent of all U.S. couples are infertile and rates of infertility increase after age 40, almost every couple can conceive a baby if they begin trying before age 35. In vitro fertilization and medical treatment sometimes help couples conceive.

Emotional Problems in Early Adulthood

Although early adulthood is generally a healthy time, it also seems that young adults are particularly troubled by several sets of problems whose basis is at least partly emotional. Young adults are more likely than older adults to use drugs; they are also more likely to suffer from psychopathologies. There is an overlap between these two problems. For example, many young adults of both sexes use drugs to deal with depression. Other problems are more common in one sex or the other: eating disorders in females and violence in males.

Dieting as a Disease

Nutrition is a lifelong concern. It is an oversimplification to say, "You are what you eat," but at every stage of life, diet affects development. Fortunately, most humans eat well enough. A fascinating aspect of culture is that, despite substantial diversity in schedules (some human groups "graze," i.e., eat small amounts all day long, while others eat just one big meal per day), in body size, and in energy requirements, most humans eat enough to survive yet not so much that they are dangerously overweight (Woods et al., 2000). Unfortunately, there are many exceptions.

We have already discussed the devastating effects on the brain of malnutrition in infancy. Obesity was discussed in Chapter 11 and will be taken up again in Chapter 20, because its life-threatening consequences typically emerge in middle or late adulthood (Engeland et. al., 2003). Of course, people at every age can suffer from an inadequate food supply or from overeating. Here we focus on another problem—that of voluntary undereating, which begins in adolescence and reaches full force in early adulthood.

Most teenagers eat too little or too much, or they eat the wrong foods at the wrong times, choosing, for example, to eat only fruits and vegetables just when their bodies need increased iron and calcium (Belamarich & Ayoob, 2001). Girls are especially likely to worry that they are getting too fat, when they are actually just gaining the weight needed for their bodies to become womanly. Many girls undereat, reaching age 20 still underweight. About a fourth of all teenage girls in the United States have used diet pills, which are addictive (Johnston et al., 2001).

As young adults, they continue to strive for a "girlish figure," a foolish and frustrating attempt. Such attempts are encouraged by cultural and especially diet industry messages that losing weight is not difficult and will lead to success and happiness (Polivy & Herman, 2002).

Actually, almost half of North American women who diet to lose weight have a **body mass index (BMI)** under 25 and thus are not at all overweight. (BMI is a ratio between weight and height that clinicians use to assess whether a person is too thin or too fat; see Table 17.2.) In the United States, the average 17- to 28-year-old woman would like to be eight pounds lighter. Few young adults are satisfied with their present weight; the average man would like to be five pounds heavier (Mintz & Kashubeck, 1999).

Many young women continue to connect self-concept with body image and to have distorted ideas about food and food consumption. Such ideas are especially common among women of European descent, and not only in the United States. An anthropologist in Australia reports that almost all Australian women of British descent, unlike Aboriginal women or women of Asian descent, have distorted ideas about food consumption (Park, 2001).

In extreme cases, excessive dieting can lead to serious illness and even death. So, too, can anorexia and bulimia nervosa, which also usually begin in adolescence, affecting about 1 young adult woman in 20.

AFP / CORBIS

Queen of the World Agbani Darego of Nigeria is crowned Miss World for 2002—a testament to her stunning beauty. She is also unusually thin, especially for an African women. This is visible evidence that the Western vulnerability to eating disorders has spread worldwide.

body mass index (BMI) The ratio of a person's weight in kilograms divided by his or her height in meters squared.

Response for Marriage Counselors (from page 420): Male and female bodies differ, so neither is to blame. You might tell them to be more respectful of each other's needs and assure them that time will probably bring them closer together. If they insist that this is a problem, probe for what else is amiss; sex is a cognitive and social event, not just a biological one.

TABLE 17.2 Body Mass Index (BMI)

To find your BMI, locate your height in the first column, then look across that row. Your BMI appears at the top of the column that contains your weight.

BMI	19	20	21	22	23	24	25	26	27	28	29	30	35	40
Height							**Weight (pounds)**							
4'10"	91	96	100	105	110	115	119	124	129	134	138	143	167	191
4'11"	94	99	104	109	114	119	124	128	133	138	143	148	173	198
5'0"	97	102	107	112	118	123	128	133	138	143	148	153	179	204
5'1"	100	106	111	116	122	127	132	137	143	148	153	158	185	211
5'2"	104	109	115	120	126	131	136	142	147	153	158	164	191	218
5'3"	107	113	118	124	130	135	141	146	152	158	163	169	197	225
5'4"	110	116	122	128	134	140	145	151	157	163	169	174	204	232
5'5"	114	120	126	132	138	144	150	156	162	168	174	180	210	240
5'6"	118	124	130	136	142	148	155	161	167	173	179	186	216	247
5'7"	121	127	134	140	146	153	159	166	172	178	185	191	223	255
5'8"	125	131	138	144	151	158	164	171	177	184	190	197	230	262
5'9"	128	135	142	149	155	162	169	176	182	189	196	203	236	270
5'10"	132	139	146	153	160	167	174	181	188	195	202	207	243	278
5'11"	136	143	150	157	165	172	179	186	193	200	208	215	250	286
6'0"	140	147	154	162	169	177	184	191	199	206	213	221	258	294
6'1"	144	151	159	166	174	182	189	197	204	212	219	227	265	302
6'2"	148	155	163	171	179	186	194	202	210	218	225	233	272	311
6'3"	152	160	168	176	184	192	200	208	216	224	232	240	279	319
6'4"	156	164	172	180	189	197	205	213	221	230	238	246	287	328
			Normal					**Overweight**					**Obese**	

Source: National Heart, Lung and Blood Institute.

Adult BMI One objective assessment of appropriate weight is the body mass index (BMI), which is calculated by dividing weight (in kilograms) by height (in meters) squared. A healthy BMI is somewhere between 19 and 25, a range that allows for considerable individual variation in body type and composition, although sometimes a tall, muscular person can be healthy at 26 or even 27, because muscle and bone weigh more than fat. Unfortunately, many young adults within this range want to be thinner (mostly women) or heavier. The wish to be thin may be pathological.

Anorexia Nervosa

anorexia nervosa A serious eating disorder in which a person restricts eating to the point of emaciation and possible starvation. Most victims are high-achieving females in early puberty or early adulthood.

Anorexia nervosa is characterized by self-starvation; individuals voluntarily eat so little and exercise so much that they risk dying because their vital organs are deprived of the nourishment they need to function. Between 5 and 20 percent of the victims of anorexia nervosa die of this disease (Mitchell & McCarthy, 2000). One was Karen Carpenter, a gifted singer who reached the top of the charts with "Rainy Days and Sundays" and who died at age 32.

According to DSM-IV-R, anorexia nervosa is diagnosed on the basis of four symptoms:

■ Refusal to maintain body weight at least 85 percent of normal for age and height
■ Intense fear of gaining weight
■ Disturbed body perception and denial of the problem
■ In adolescent and adult females, lack of menstruation

If someone's BMI is 18 or lower, or if she (or, less often, he) loses more than 10 percent of body weight within a month or two, anorexia is suspected (American Psychiatric Association, 2000).

Anorexia is a disease of the social context; in other words, the culture supports it (Mitchell & McCarthy, 2000). The disease was virtually unknown before 1950, when it was first diagnosed in some high-achieving, upper-class young American women. Within a few decades, it became prevalent among young

Response for Couples (from page 422): Good health practices make a big difference. Avoid drugs, eat a balanced diet, don't get sick, and relax. These solve about half of all fertility problems. However, timing is crucial—especially if a couple is over age 30—so don't wait too long to seek medical help.

women in developed nations, and it is currently on the rise in developing nations, especially in urban areas (Gordon, 2000; Walcott et al., 2003). It has thus spread to groups that were once unaffected—African-Americans and Hispanic-Americans as well as Asians, Africans, and Latin Americans. As a result, "it is critical that the possibility of eating and body image concerns are considered for all individuals, regardless of ethnic background" (Dounchis et al., 2001, p. 82). About 1 percent of women in developed nations suffer from anorexia at some point in their lives, with rates much higher among athletes, particularly runners, gymnasts, and dancers (Perriello, 2001; Thompson & Sherman, 1993).

A Case to Study

Julia Again: "Too Thin, As If That's Possible"

We return to Julia, whom you first met in Chapter 16. Julia writes of her college experience:

I have never before felt so much pressure. Because my scholarship depends both on my running and on my maintaining a 3.6 grade point average, I've been stressed out much of the time. Academic work was never a problem for me in the past, but there's just so much more expected of you in college.

It was pressure from my coach, my teammates, and myself that first led me to dieting. . . . I know that my coach was really disappointed in me. He called me aside about a month into the season. He wanted to know what I was eating, and he told me the weight I had gained was undoubtedly hurting my performance. He said that I should cut out snacks and sweets of any kind, and stick to things like salad to help me lose the extra pounds, and get back into shape. He also recommended some additional workouts. I was all for a diet—I hated that my clothes were getting snug. . . . At that point, I was 5 feet, 6 inches and weighed 145 pounds. When I started college I had weighed 130 pounds. . . .

Once I started dieting, the incentives to continue were everywhere. My race time improved, so my coach was pleased. I felt more a part of the team and less like an outsider. My clothes were no longer snug, and when they saw me at my meets my parents said I looked great. I even received an invitation to a party given by a fraternity that only invited the most attractive . . . women. After about a month, I was back to my normal weight of 130 pounds.

. . . I set a new weight goal of 115 pounds. I figured if I hit the gym more often and skipped breakfast altogether, it wouldn't be hard to reach that weight in another month or so. Of course, this made me even hungrier by lunchtime, but I didn't want to increase my lunch size. I found it easier to pace myself with something like crackers. I would break them into several pieces and only allow myself to eat one piece every 15 minutes. The few times I did this with friends in the dining hall I got weird looks and comments. I finally started eating lunch alone in my room. . . . I couldn't believe it when the scale said I was down to 115 pounds. I still felt that I had excess weight to lose. Some of my friends were begin-

ning to mention that I was actually looking too thin, as if that's possible.

. . . All of which brings me to the present time. Even though I'm running great and I'm finally able to stick to a diet, everyone thinks I'm not taking good enough care of myself. . . . I'm doing my best to keep in control of my life, and I wish that I could be trusted to take care of myself.

Julia's roommate writes:

There were no more parties or hanging out at meals for her. . . . We were all worried, but none of us knew what to do. . . . I looked in the back of Julia's closet. A few months ago I had asked to borrow a tampon. She opened a new box and gave me one. The same box was still there with only that one missing. For the first time, I realized how serious Julia's condition could be.

A few days later, Julia approached me. Apparently she just met with one of the deans, who told her that she'd need to undergo an evaluation at the health center before she could continue practicing with the team. She asked me point blank if I had been talking about her to anyone. I told her how her mother had asked me if I had noticed any changes in her over the past several months, and how I honestly told her yes. She stormed out of the room and I haven't seen her since. I know how important the team is to Julia, so I am assuming that she'll be going to the health center soon. I hope that they'll be able to convince her that she's taken things too far, and that they can help her to get better.

[quoted in Gorenstein & Comer, 2002, pp. 275-280]

Julia, with her rapid weight loss that she does not see as a problem, is a classic case of anorexia nervosa. Denial and lack of menstruation are typical. Julia thinks she is finally able to stick to a diet and is in control of her life, when in fact she is not at all in control but is addicted to exercise and weight loss. Serious depression is linked to anorexia, and suicide is a danger for Julia.

Undoubtedly you wonder why her coach, her parents, and her friends did not notice her problem sooner and insist that she get help. This time lag is common: "By the time the anorexic reaches the point at which the disorder is clinically identified, she has already become entrapped in a complex web of psychological attitudes" (Gordon, 2000). Before that point, many people encourage rapid weight loss instead of welcoming the normal weight gain of a healthy developing woman. Actually, just at the time that her coach suggested she diet, Julia's weight after a month of college (145 for an athlete who is five feet, six inches tall) was within the normal BMI. She was not even marginally overweight, much less obese. Yet everyone seemed pleased when she lost 15 pounds in the next month. Although Julia was in evident danger, her parents and the fraternity boys continued to give her emotional incentives to continue dieting.

Bulimia Nervosa

bulimia nervosa An eating disorder in which the person, usually female, engages repeatedly in episodes of binge eating followed by purging through induced vomiting or use of laxatives.

About three times as common as anorexia, especially among young female adults, is the other major eating disorder of our time, **bulimia nervosa.** This condition involves compulsive binge eating, in which thousands of calories may be consumed within an hour or two, followed by purging through either vomiting or inducing diarrhea by taking massive doses of laxatives. Such behaviors are performed on occasion by many young adult women; some studies find that half of all college women have binged and purged at least once (Fairburn & Wilson, 1993), while other research finds bulimia present in virtually every city (but not every rural area) of the world (Walcott et al., 2003).

To warrant a clinical diagnosis of bulimia, bingeing and purging must occur at least once a week for three months, with uncontrollable urges to overeat and a distorted self-judgment based on misperceived body size. Between 1 and 3 percent of women in the United States are clinically bulimic during early adulthood (American Psychiatric Association, 2000). People who suffer from bulimia are usually close to normal in weight and therefore unlikely to starve to death. However, they can experience serious health problems, including severe damage to the gastrointestinal system and cardiac arrest from the strain of electrolyte imbalance (Gordon, 2000).

Theories of Eating Disorders

Although bulimia typically emerges in early adulthood and anorexia often worsens at that time, the origins of both conditions lie in puberty or even earlier. According to longitudinal research, 12-year-olds who overeat to the point that they feel painfully stuffed are more likely to be bulimic by age 19 than are 12-year-olds who have never overeaten to that degree (Calam & Waller, 1998). Other research suggests that even in infancy and childhood,

> parental control in child feeding may have unintended effects on the development of eating patterns; emphasis on "external" cues in eating and decreased opportunities for the child to experience *self*-control in each . . . parental pressure to eat may result in food dislike and refusal, and restriction may enhance children's liking and consumption of restricted foods.
>
> [Fisher & Birch, 2001, p. 35]

In all eating disorders, consumption is disconnected from the internal cue of hunger, serving some psychological or social rather than bodily need. The stresses, weight gain, and changing body shape of puberty, in a culture obsessed with thinness, make every contemporary teenage and young adult woman vulnerable (Gordon, 2000). Most do not develop a disorder; genes and habits may help explain who does and who does not. But almost every female wishes to be a little thinner and thus risks ignoring the early signs of disease, in herself and her friends.

From a developmental perspective, it is not surprising that eating disorders are rooted in childhood. But it is not obvious why females are so much more likely than males to be caught up in such destructive self-sabotage. Each theory of development offers an explanation:

- A *psychoanalytic* hypothesis is that women develop eating disorders because of a conflict with their mothers, who provided their first nourishment and from whom the daughters cannot psychically separate.
- *Behaviorism* notes that for some people with low self-esteem (more often women than men), fasting, bingeing, and purging "have powerful effects as immediate reinforcers—that is, [as means of] relieving states of emotional distress and tension" (Gordon, 1990), thus setting up a destructive stimulus–response chain.
- One *cognitive* explanation is that as young adult women compete with men in jobs and careers, they want to project a strong, self-controlled, masculine image antithetical to the buxom, fleshy body of the ideal woman of the past.
- *Sociocultural* explanations include the contemporary cultural pressure to be "slim and trim" and model-like—a pressure that seems to be felt particularly by unmarried young women seeking autonomy from their parents, especially when the parents espouse traditional values (Walcott et al., 2003).
- The *epigenetic* perspective emphasizes the genetic roots of disorders and the impact they may have on the evolutionary mandate to reproduce. Because girls with eating disorders sometimes stop developing and do not ovulate, they avoid pregnancy. In addition, their bony appearance and their obsession prevent romance. For girls who are frightened by the sexual impulses of womanhood, eating disorders are a powerful defense.

No matter what the explanation, for many young women, fear and a distorted body image can undercut health and even threaten survival.

Drug Abuse and Addiction

Older adolescents and young adults are the "chief initiators and heaviest users" of drugs (Robins, 1995) and therefore those most at risk for serious drug problems (Bachman et al., 2002). Remember from Chapter 14 that *drug abuse* is defined as using a drug in a quantity or a manner that is harmful to physical, cognitive, or psychosocial well-being. Even one-time or occasional use can constitute abuse if there are consequences, as when a person drinks several beers and wrecks a car. More often, however, abuse entails frequent use (such as a regular pattern of marijuana smoking) and high doses (for instance, consuming four or more drinks on one occasion) that impair the body, the mind, and/or social interaction.

Drug addiction, also discussed in Chapter 14, is measured by the need for more of a drug. When the absence of a drug causes a craving to satisfy a physiological need (to stop the shakes, to settle one's stomach, to get to sleep) or a psychological need (to quiet fears, to lift depression), those withdrawal symptoms are the telltale sign of addiction. *Use* typically begins in adolescence; *abuse* and *addiction* are more common in early adulthood.

The early 20s are the peak time for use of marijuana and other illicit drugs, heavy drinking, and chain smoking (see Figure 17.3). Abuse often eases before age 30, as is apparent in most nations that collect data (Eisner, 2002). A U.S. survey found that 69 percent of the marijuana smokers and 67 percent of the cocaine users had quit by that age, as had 11 percent of the drinkers (Chen & Kendal, 1995).

There is one exception to this young-adult quit rate: Most cigarette smokers do not quit at age 30, and some (especially African-American women) actually

drug addiction A condition of drug dependence in which the absence of the given drug in the individual's system produces a drive—physiological, psychological, or both—to ingest more of the drug.

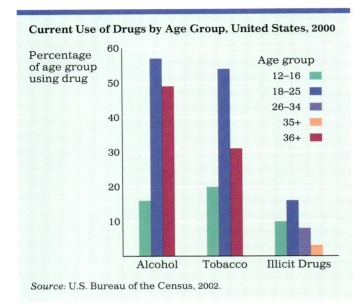

Current Use of Drugs by Age Group, United States, 2000

Percentage of age group using drug

Age group
12–16
18–25
26–34
35+
36+

Alcohol   Tobacco   Illicit Drugs

Source: U.S. Bureau of the Census, 2002.

FIGURE 17.3 Drug Users This chart shows age-related trends in reported current use (within the past 30 days) of various drugs. Not all drug users are abusers or addicts, but the incidence of drug problems correlates with patterns of use. Most drug-related injuries and deaths occur in early adulthood.

start smoking at about that age (Moon-Howard, 2003). Not until age 60 do the rates of smoking in the United States fall dramatically overall (U.S. Bureau of the Census, 2002).

There are marked gender, ethnic, and national variations in rates of drug abuse: Men use and abuse most drugs at a higher rate than women do; European- and Hispanic-Americans are more likely to use drugs than are African- or Asian-Americans; and internationally, English-speaking countries have the highest rates of drug use (Eisner, 2002).

Why the high rates in early adulthood? All these variations are intriguing, but here we focus on the developmental aspects. The genes that predispose to drug abuse include those for attraction to excitement, intolerance of frustration, and vulnerability to depression—all traits that increase in everyone in adolescence and young adulthood. These traits, in young adulthood, push those who are genetically vulnerable over the edge to abuse and addiction.

In addition, many young adults, no longer supervised by their parents, are free to make their own choices but are pressured to complete an education, establish a career, and find a mate. Wanting to quiet the resulting anxieties and to feel sophisticated and socially at ease, they are tempted to use drugs (Bachman et al., 2001).

Also encouraging drug use are the settings where young adults congregate—for example, college dorms, large parties, rock concerts, and sports events. Enlisting in the U.S. military also put young adults at risk until a change of policy began to discourage drug use: In 1990, drug use was higher among soldiers than among civilians; by 1997, it was only half as high (Ammerman et al., 1999).

Not only do legal restrictions slow down drug use, but so can conveying the fact that most adults do not smoke, do not use illegal drugs, and do not drink to excess. This "social norms" approach can be particularly helpful with college students, whose age and setting (around age 20, living in a dorm) put them at high risk for drug abuse (Bachman et al., 2002; Perkins, 2003). Social norms, specifically peer norms, may also help to explain why drug use decreases during young adulthood. As Figure 17.4 shows, far lower percentages of 30-year-olds than 18-year-olds believe their friends regularly get drunk.

FIGURE 17.4 Perception and Reality Over the years of early adulthood, most people of both sexes believe that their friends cut down dramatically on the use of alcohol and marijuana. According to the social norms theory, this perception leads to a reduction in drinking and marijuana use. Other data suggest that 18-year-olds overestimate their friends' use of alcohol and marijuana, while 30-year-olds' estimates are more accurate.

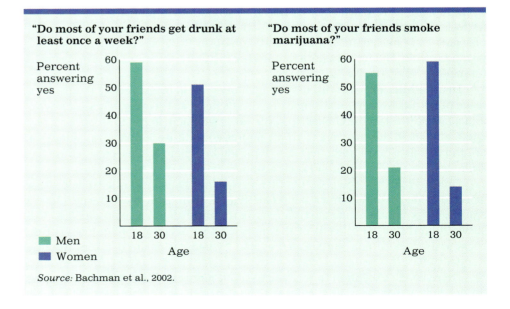

Source: Bachman et al., 2002.

ANDREW LICHTENSTEIN / THE IMAGE WORKS

"Eggs and Kegs" Alcohol serves as a social lubricant for many young adults. In this regular ritual, college students ("eggheads") in the Albany, New York, area gather to drink beer until the last keg runs out, toward dawn. By then, most of them have made new friends and are tired but happy. Others, however, are sick, angry, and tearful.

Medical advice, marriage, and, particularly for women, religious involvement also discourage drug use. Here again, young adults may be especially vulnerable. As a group, they are least likely to see a doctor or to attend religious services (Gallup, 1996), and young adults are increasingly postponing marriage and parenthood (Bachman et al., 2002).

The consequences of drug use and abuse in young adulthood are often serious. Compared with others their age, young adult drug users are more likely to avoid, flunk out of, or drop out of college; to work below their potential and then lose or quit those jobs; to be involved in transitory, uncommitted sexual relationships; to die violently (accidents, homicides, suicides); and to experience serious psychological difficulties of all kinds.

Psychopathology

Many young adults struggle with serious emotional difficulties. About 12 percent experience at least one episode of major depression, schizophrenia, or pathological rage, often made worse if the person turns to alcohol and other drugs to "self-medicate." Some of the difficulties originate in childhood, particularly if the parents were severely abusive, neglectful, or erratic. The death of a mother, for instance, or raging alcoholism in a father, causes almost every child to internalize or externalize emotional problems (Werner & Smith, 1982).

Other problems emerge in adolescence. Depression among girls and delinquency among boys at least triples from age 10 to 16 (Angold & Costello, 1995). Often adolescent psychopathology improves by early adulthood, but not always, because "early adult life is a demanding period," likely to trigger psychological problems of many kinds (Champion, 2000). Causes are therefore complex; as Table 17.3 shows, biological factors may also be involved.

TABLE 17.3 Causes of Emotional Disturbance

The Past: Childhood Trauma	Ongoing: Biological Problems	Current: Environmental Stress
Severe abuse and neglect	Genetic tendencies	Family disruption
Disorganized attachment	Neurotransmitter deficiency	Extreme poverty
Loss of family members	Brain damage from injury	Unemployment
Lead or other toxins	Hormonal imbalance	Homelessness

It is a truism in developmental psychopathology that the relationship between causes and problems is complex. For example, the fact that one monozygotic twin can become schizophrenic while the other, with the same genes, does not become schizophrenic means that a cause—a genetic tendency—does not always have the same effect—schizophrenia. Similarly, a single problem, such as depression, may be caused by many factors: a mother's death, a hormonal imbalance, prolonged unemployment. In addition to being multifactorial (having many causes), psychopathologies are often comorbid; that is, they occur together, which further complicates the picture (Gottlieb & Halpern, 2002).

Thus, childhood disturbances, biological problems, and environmental stress can each cause disturbances, but typically all three are involved. To simplify, we emphasize biology here, but remember that cognitive and cultural influences, related to childhood experiences and environmental stress, are always involved.

Depression

Between ages 20 and 35, about 15 percent of women and 8 percent of men suffer from at least one episode of major depression that results in a "loss of interest or pleasure in nearly all activities" for two weeks or more. Other difficulties (e.g., in sleeping, concentrating, eating, carrying on friendships, and experiencing hope and meaning in life) are also present (American Psychiatric Association, 2000, p. 249).

Major depression is fueled biochemically, through neurotransmitters and hormones, although external events may trigger a depressive episode. More activity in the right prefrontal lobe of the cortex than in the left indicates a vulnerability to depression, as does greater activation of the amygdala (an emotional hotspot, deep within the brain) (Kosslyn et al., 2002). Among the neurotransmitters involved are dopamine, norepinephrine, and serotonin.

Regulating those neurotransmitters is a goal of most new antidepressant drugs, including Prozac, an SSRI (selective serotonin reuptake inhibitor), and many tricyclic antidepressants. Other drugs are used to regulate stress hormones or to promote cell growth (Holden, 2003). Sleep disorders are a symptom of depression, but studies of brain waves suggest that impaired sleep may also be a cause (American Psychiatric Association, 2000).

Because the causes are complex, it is difficult to predict who will experience a depressive episode and when, although familial and personal past depression make an episode more likely. However, within the past 20 years, as the biochemistry of depression has become better understood, more effective treatment of the symptoms has become possible.

Remission is particularly likely with treatment that includes both cognitive therapy and medication. Unfortunately, depression often goes untreated or is inappropriately treated. Because of individual variation, therapy and drugs that help one person may not work for another; many sufferers, family members, and physicians lack the hope and patience to persist with treatment until they find the right combination. These problems make depression one of the leading causes of impairment and premature death worldwide (World Health Organization, 2001).

Schizophrenia

About 1 percent of all adults experience at least one episode of schizophrenia, when disorganized and bizarre thoughts, delusions, hallucinations, emotions, and language overtake them (American Psychiatric Association, 2000). Symptoms typically begin in adolescence and come to full force in early adulthood. In fact, if people have no symptoms by age 35, they almost never become schizophrenic later on.

It appears that the causes are usually genes (not one gene, but many) and severe early trauma, particularly anoxia at birth (Cannon et al., 2000), with later stresses of various sorts making the problem worse (Lavender, 2000). The risk of becoming schizophrenic increases if one's relatives have the disease, but sometimes one monozygotic twin is schizophrenic and the other is not, so obviously genes are not the only cause (Lavender, 2000). In fact, most schizophrenics have no close relatives with the disease.

Medication seems to be most effective if the person gains some understanding of the disease. Such understanding, along with taking medication on schedule, also makes recovery more likely. The odds of recovery are further increased if the onset of the illness was sudden and if the person is female, without schizophrenic parents.

Violence

In the United States, between the ages of 15 and 25, almost 1 male in every 100 dies violently, through suicide, homicide, or a motor-vehicle accident (U.S. Bureau of the Census, 2002). Violent death rates among young men in Canada, Mexico, and Australia are almost as high as in the United States (see Figure 17.1, p. 415). The specific combination of suicides, homicides, and accidents varies from country to country: Canada, for example, has far more suicides than homicides, and most European and Asian nations have far lower homicide rates than the United States.

Despite these variations, every nation that tallies such statistics finds that young men in their early 20s are at least twice as likely to die violently as from disease or famine and are far more likely to die violently than women of the same age (Heuveline, 2002): Four times as many young men as young women commit suicide or die in motor-vehicle accidents, and six times as many are murdered, almost always by another young man. Broken down more specifically (by nation, ethnic groups, etc.), the male-to-female ratio for violent deaths varies from 3:1 to 10:1.

Developmentalists have suggested two sets of reasons for this sex difference, each set based on plausible theory and scientific evidence (Brennan & Raine, 1997; Moffitt et al., 2001). The first is biological, particularly hormonal. In lower animals as well as in people, higher levels of testosterone correlate with impulsive, angry reactions to many events (Booth & Osgood, 1993). The second is in the socialization of males. As one expert explains:

> Few people would consider male gender socialization to be a public health issue . . . yet there is considerable evidence that links sexual abuse and a vast array of interpersonally abusive and violent behavior to the process by which male children, male adolescents, and young men are socialized into masculinity.
>
> *[Lisak, 1997]*

Psychological factors are involved as well. One analysis finds aggression to be the result of an "explosive combination" of high self-esteem and dashed expectations, a combination that is more likely to result in violence when it coincides with the presence of alcohol, a weapon, and a lack of self-restraint (Baumeister & Boden, 1998). Women are likely to blame themselves for their problems, so they diet, they cry, and so on. Men are less likely to blame themselves, so their frustration erupts against others.

AP / WIDE WORLD PHOTOS

Who, Where, and When? The sad reality is that this could be young men in almost any place or time. In fact, this photo was taken in southern France on June 14, 1998, the night before the World Cup soccer match between England and Tunisia. Street fighting—such as this between supporters of the two teams, which led to 80 arrests, hundreds of wounded, but, fortunately, no deaths—is common among teenage boys in blue jeans, no matter what their ethnicity. The only comforting truth is that most of those rioting young men are adolescent-limited criminals, unlikely to persist in violent crime after age 25 or so.

Young women are at risk for eating disorders, the most alarming example of which is anorexia, when a person voluntarily risks death by starvation. First apparent among well-educated young women in developed nations, anorexia is now emerging among young women worldwide. Other eating disorders, especially bulimia, are also increasingly common in early adulthood, suggesting that the current culture somehow works against healthy nutrition.

Young adults are particularly vulnerable to many types of drug abuse and addiction, although drug use often diminishes by age 30. The problems arise in part because young adults, who are often on their own, need to confront new challenges, to cope with new stresses and strains. These stresses, along with childhood trauma and biological factors, contribute to the relatively high incidence of psychopathologies in early adulthood, including depression and schizophrenia.

In early adulthood, the rates of violent death for men—from suicides, homicides, and accidents—are disturbingly high. Explanations center on hormones and on male socialization.

This chapter leads to two obvious conclusions for young adults reading this text. The first is that, although these years are the prime of health in a purely biological way, they also are stressful times. Many problems, including drug use and various forms of psychopathology, occur. Everyone needs to be aware of the symptoms that may appear in any young adult, including classmates, friends, and romantic partners.

Second, before jumping to conclusions about drugs or moods in early adulthood (or before demanding a prescription from the doctor), you need to understand cognitive and psychosocial factors. As you will learn in the next two chapters, cognition and the social context can be part of the problem as well as part of the solution.

SUMMARY

Growth, Strength, and Health

1. While young adults do not grow significantly taller in their 20s, they typically grow stronger and healthier as their bodies reach adult size. In terms of overall health as well as peak physical condition, early adulthood is the prime of life.

2. With each year, signs of senescence become more apparent. All the body systems gradually become less efficient (though at different rates), and homeostasis takes increasingly longer to reach.

3. However, because of organ reserve, none of these changes are particularly troublesome or even noticeable for most young adults most of the time. Even athletic performance, while slowed somewhat, can remain at a high level.

4. One common reason for fertility problems is that the man's sperm are insufficient in quantity or motility. The woman may be infertile for reasons including failure to ovulate and blocked fal-

lopian tubes (often caused by pelvic inflammatory disease). The normal aging process is rarely the primary cause of infertility in early adulthood, but age can be a contributing factor.

5. A number of procedures, ranging from drugs that stimulate ovulation to surgery that unblocks fallopian tubes to IVF (in vitro fertilization), offer potential answers to infertility. In the laboratory, a technician can insert a single sperm into an ovum, thus avoiding the problem of low sperm count.

Emotional Problems in Early Adulthood

6. Eating disorders are more common during young adulthood than at other ages, as some young women feel a compulsion to be thinner than their bodies naturally tend to be. Both anorexia and bulimia nervosa can be life-threatening.

7. Young adults are more likely to abuse alcohol and illicit drugs than are people of any other age, often doing themselves or others serious harm. Many young adults stop such abuse before middle age, partly because their social context changes and partly because they themselves become more mature.

8. Many forms of psychopathology are more prevalent in early adulthood than at other ages. Depression is relatively common and occurs at an increasing rate among current cohorts, partly because they are less likely to be married and more likely to experience stress over financial and vocational issues.

9. All forms of psychopathology, including eating disorders, drug abuse, depression, and schizophrenia, are treatable once they are recognized as problems. In general, all become less severe as adults become more mature.

10. Suicide, homicide, and fatal accidents are serious problems for young adults, especially for young men. The reasons are at least as much cultural as biological, as revealed by national and historical differences in the rates of homicide, suicide, and motor-vehicle deaths.

KEY TERMS

senescence (p. 414)
homeostasis (p. 417)
set point (p. 417)
organ reserve (p. 418)

infertility (p. 421)
pelvic inflammatory disease (PID) (p. 421)
in vitro fertilization (IVF) (p. 422)

assisted reproductive technology (ART) (p. 422)
body mass index (BMI) (p. 423)

anorexia nervosa (p. 424)
bulimia nervosa (p. 426)
drug addiction (p. 427)

APPLICATIONS

1. Some experts believe that the discrepancies in male and female sexual responses in their 20s are primarily biological; others believe that they are primarily social. Which idea makes more sense to you? Ideally, use experiences of several people, including your own, to support your conclusions.

2. Compare yourself to your parents and grandparents in terms of health and strength. For each difference, do you think health habits or senescence is the primary explanation?

3. Survey at least 10 people of various ages regarding current and past drug use, including the frequency of smoking and drinking. Do you see age-related shifts in use, abuse, and addiction, as described in the chapter?

4. Some people say that doctors and other medical personnel do not encourage preventive care, particularly for young men. From your own experience, what changes could be made in the practice of medicine to help young adults be healthier?

Chapter Eighteen

Early Adulthood: Cognitive Development

During adulthood, thinking changes from the omnivorous learning and questioning of childhood and adolescence to a more mature cognition. It continues to change over many years in quality, quantity, speed, topics, efficiency, depth, values, skills. In contrast to the relatively linear cognitive achievements of childhood, adulthood changes are *multidirectional*: Some abilities improve, others wane, and some remain stable.

Adult thinking is also more *multicontextual*. Instead of originating primarily in the classroom, it is fostered by many contexts and challenges. The tasks that adults are expected to accomplish at least once include finding a career and a mate; supervising other workers and helping run a political, religious, or community group; protecting and guiding a child or a friend. Adults need to make many decisions, some major—such as whether or not to have a child—and others less significant—such as whether or not to buy a new coat.

Obviously, the life-span perspective, first explained in Chapter 1, is needed here. The study of adult cognition must be multidisciplinary and only loosely connected to chronological age. Researchers take many approaches to explain adult cognitive development:

- The *postformal approach* picks up where Piaget left off, exploring possible new stages of thinking and reasoning that build on earlier cognitive skills.
- The *psychometric approach* analyzes components of intelligence as measured by IQ tests, describing which skills and what types of knowledge improve or decline during adulthood.
- The *information-processing approach* studies the encoding, storage, and retrieval of information, including the adaptation that takes place as the individual grows older and sensory abilities change.

All three approaches provide valuable insights. However, to examine all three in each of the chapters (18, 21, and 24) about adult cognition would be repetitive and confusing. Therefore, in this chapter, the primary focus is on the postformal approach; in Chapter 21, the psychometric approach will be emphasized; and Chapter 24 will consider information-processing theory. Each of these chapters will also look at some age-related influences on cognitive abilities. This chapter examines the effects that college education has on development.

Postformal Thought

Adult thinking differs from adolescent thinking in three major ways: It is more practical, more flexible, and more dialectical. In all three areas, it combines emotions with logic. Taken together, these characteristics are considered the **postformal stage** of cognitive development, combining a new "ordering of formal operations" with a "necessary subjectivity" (Sinnott, 1998, p. 24).

A Fifth Stage of Cognitive Development?

postformal stage A proposed adult stage of cognitive development, following Piaget's four stages, that is characterized by postformal thought, which is more practical, more flexible, and more dialectical—capable of combining contradictory elements into a comprehensive whole—than is adolescent thinking.

Postformal thought is sometimes considered a fifth stage of thinking, following Piaget's four stages (Arlin, 1984, 1989). It is characterized by "problem finding," not "problem solving." Adults do not wait until someone else presents an issue and then seek the solution. Instead, adults consider all aspects of a situation, noting difficulties and finding problems, but not being stopped by them.

Compare that to the thinking of adolescents, who try to distill universal truths, develop arguments, and resolve the world's problems in terms of absolutes. When formal logical reasoning is too cumbersome, teenagers use quick, intuitive thought, acting without exploring the consequences, engaging in "the game of thinking."

In adulthood, intellectual skills are harnessed to real occupational and interpersonal demands, and conclusions and consequences matter. This makes adults less playful and more practical. They don't want to stay up all night to argue, winning points in debate. They want to figure out what their options are, and then act. Adults learn to accept, and adapt to, the contradictions and inconsistencies of everyday experience. They realize that most of life's answers are provisional, not necessarily permanent, and that irrational and emotional factors need to be considered. Does that outlook constitute a new stage of cognitive development?

You know that scholars disagree about whether or not cognitive development in childhood occurs in stages. This dispute is even stronger where adult cognition is concerned. If "stage" is taken to mean attaining a new set of cognitive skills (as from sensorimotor to preoperational), then adulthood has no stages. However, some thinking processes appear in adulthood that are rarely found earlier and that represent "qualitative and quantitative change in cognitive functioning through the adult life span" (Schaie & Willis, 2000, pp. 175–178); these processes can be considered stages (see Figure 18.1).

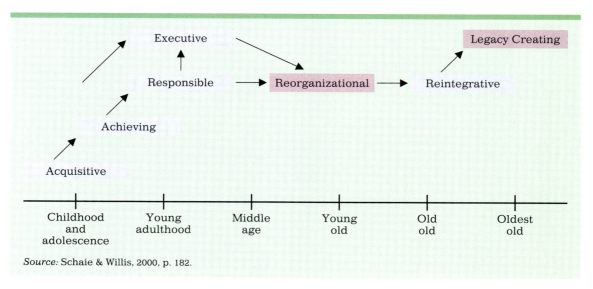

Source: Schaie & Willis, 2000, p. 182.

FIGURE 18.1 A Model for Cognitive Stages in Adulthood K. Warner Schaie and Sherry Willis, two researchers who have studied adult cognition for more than 30 years, believe that there are several stages of adult cognition, all of which use the knowledge acquired in childhood and adolescence.

The Practical and the Personal

Adult stages are not about acquiring new cognitive skills but about applying those skills in ways that are practical, flexible, and dialectical.

Subjectivity and Objectivity

A distinction can be made between subjective and objective thinking. **Subjective thought** arises from the personal experiences and perceptions of an individual; **objective thought** follows abstract, impersonal logic. Traditional models of formal thought devalue subjective feelings, personal faith, and emotional experience and value (or overvalue) objective, logical thinking. This outlook is seen in Piaget's description of the logical reasoning of the advanced adolescent and in Kohlberg's description of a postconventional level of morality (see pp. 292–294).

Objectivity is valuable as a corrective to subjective thinking, especially when the latter is prejudiced, narrow, and highly emotional. As you read in Chapter 1, the scientific method was designed to overcome the biases of traditional, culture-bound perspectives, encouraging scientists to seek objective data that can be verified through replication. Appendix B, at the back of this book, further explains some techniques that scientists use to maintain their objectivity. Every social scientist is expected to understand how to analyze statistics in order to reflect data, not personal preferences.

However, purely objective, logical thinking becomes maladaptive when adults seek to understand and deal with the complexities and commitments of their personal lives (Labouvie-Vief, 1992). Subjective feelings and personal experiences must be taken into account, or the result will be objective reasoning that is too limited, rigid, and impractical to be useful for everyday experience (Sinnott, 1998). Truly mature thought involves the interaction between the abstract, objective forms of processing and the expressive, subjective forms that arise from sensitivity to context. Note that adult thought does not abandon objectivity; instead, "postformal logic combines subjectivity and objectivity" (Sinnott, 1998, p. 55) so as to include both the personal and the practical.

Emotions and Logic

Combining emotions and logic is a particular challenge when issues are hotly emotional. In Chapter 15, you read that an adolescent's cognition suffered when his or her own religion was the target of bogus research or when adolescent egocentrism and intuitive thinking overwhelmed the ability to use formal operational thought. Adults are less likely to have these problems.

In one study of the effect of emotions on reasoning ability (Blanchard-Fields, 1986), adolescents, young adults, and middle-aged adults were presented with several reasoning tasks, each of which involved two accounts of a fictional event presented from conflicting points of view. For example, a war between "North Livia" and "South Livia" was described by opposing historians. The North Livian historian said that a particular battle had turned the tide "heavily in favor of the North," while the historian for South Livia described the same battle as a "minor" setback. This particular cognitive dilemma was designed to be emotionally neutral.

Other dilemmas were intended to be arousing. For example, a teenage boy's visit to his grandparents was described by the boy's parents (who said that they had reasoned with their son and convinced him to go) and by the boy himself (who said that his parents had lectured him on his duty and had forced him to go). The boy's parents said he had a good time at his grandparents and enjoyed "the family closeness," but the boy said he was as polite as possible but bored and forced into everything he did.

The study participants were asked what each conflict was about, who was to blame, how the conflict was resolved, who emerged the winner, and why the

subjective thought A kind of thinking that arises from the personal experiences and perceptions of an individual.

objective thought A kind of thinking that follows abstract, impersonal logic.

versions differed. The researchers developed a rubric of six levels of reasoning, ranging from level 1, an absolutist approach in which only one narrow perspective was taken, to level 6, a multiple-perspectives stance that weighed conflicting reports and considered the validity of various sources. Overall, only 16 percent of the adolescent responses were above level 3, compared with 36 percent of the young adult responses and 61 percent of the middle-aged adult responses.

Particularly striking was the difference in adolescents' and young adults' reasoning on emotional questions, such as those about the visit to the grandparents (see Figure 18.2). The adolescent participants' reasoning was worse on that topic than on the Livia story, which they interpreted almost as well as the young adults did. According to Fredda Blanchard-Fields (1986), the author of this study,

> An emotionally salient context may be more disruptive for the younger than for older thinkers, thus affecting performance. . . . Cognition is pitted against emotion.
>
> [p. 331]

Blanchard-Fields (1999) has undertaken many studies of cognitive development from adolescence throughout adulthood. In general, she finds that teenagers strongly believe in either objective *or* subjective reasoning, but that adults are able to combine both. This balance becomes more evident with every decade of adulthood until old age, when either/or reasoning again becomes prevalent.

How does this combination of emotions and intellect work in practice? If people cannot achieve the combination, they tend to swing to the extremes, as many older adolescents do. Extreme behaviors—such as bingeing, anorexia, obesity, addiction, and violence (all reviewed in previous chapters)—are outgrowths of absolutist thought. By contrast, adults are more balanced, combining personal experience with knowledge. This is evident in what Laura, one of my students, wrote:

> Unfortunately, alcoholism runs in my family. . . . I have seen it tear apart not only my uncle but my family also. . . . I have gotten sick from drinking, and it was the most horrifying night of my life. I know that I didn't have alcohol poisoning or anything, but I drank too quickly and was getting sick. All of these images flooded my head about how I didn't want to ever end up the way my uncle was. From that point on, whenever I have touched alcohol, it has been with extreme caution. . . . When I am old and gray, the last thing I want to be thinking about is where my next beer will come from or how I'll need a liver transplant.

Laura's experiences have combined with her knowledge (e.g., of alcohol poisoning) to enable her to think about drinking using postformal thought. Few other college students have reached that point. In the United States and elsewhere, students are more likely to abuse alcohol in college than in high school (Bachman et al., 2002; Eisner, 2002). As explained in Chapter 17, most young adults generally moderate their drinking by age 25 or 30, when their cognitive maturity combines with their personal experience—as happened for Laura by age 20.

Cognitive Flexibility

A second hallmark of postformal cognition is the awareness that each person's perspective is only one of many, that each problem has many potential solutions, and that knowledge is dynamic, not static (Sinnott, 1998). In general, living life to the fullest often requires a flexible perspective, or a realization that "there are multiple views of the same phenomenon" (Baltes et al., 1998, p. 1093).

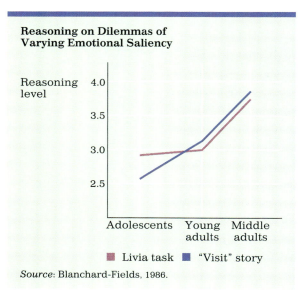

Reasoning on Dilemmas of Varying Emotional Saliency

Source: Blanchard-Fields, 1986.

FIGURE 18.2 Cognition and Emotion In the Blanchard-Fields study of age-related reasoning on social dilemmas, older, more mature thinkers scored higher because they were better able to take into account the interpretive biases of each party's version of events. As you can see, this was especially true when the social dilemma was emotionally charged.

Flexible Problem Solving

Predicting and planning are useful, but life does not always proceed as expected. In fact, because challenges are inevitable, adult thinking requires flexible adaptation (Wethington, 2000). Thus, corporate restructuring might mean losing a job, a child's entry into school might reveal a learning disability, a teenager might abuse drugs, or a doctor might diagnose a serious illness. Cognitive flexibility allows us to cope with any such unanticipated event. Although life experiences may make some people retreat, blindly following only emotions or intellect, most adults realize that they need to combine the two and that they must imagine and analyze various options (Lutz & Sternberg, 1999).

In one study (Artistico et al., 2003), adults suggested several solutions to real-life problems. In this research, the experimenters selected fifteen situations, five of which are common in early adulthood, five in late adulthood, and five throughout adulthood. Adults were asked to suggest solutions to all fifteen. Most found several possible solutions for each problem, as postformal thinkers (but not concrete or formal thinkers) usually do.

As a decided contrast to adolescent single-mindedness regarding personal experiences, for these adults familiarity led to flexibility, yielding more solutions, not fewer. For example, one problem typical of young adults (loss of motivation to finish a college degree) evoked an average of four solutions from younger adults but only one or two from older adults. By contrast, a problem familiar to older adults (wanting relatives to visit more frequently) evoked an average of four solutions from older adults but only two from younger adults. Adults of all ages suggested an equal number of solutions for life problems that occur throughout adulthood, such as being lonely over the weekend or being unable to visit a sick relative in a faraway town (Artistico et al., 2003).

The ability to come up with many solutions for a problem is a hallmark of postformal thought (Sinnott, 1998). Of course, individuals differ in their cognitive flexibility, just as Laura's comments show that individuals differ in their ability to combine personal experience and logic. Evidence for this variability comes from another study, in which older adults were asked what a man should do if his lawn needs mowing but his doctor has told him to take it easy (Marsiske & Willis, 1995, 1998). Four people's responses are given in Table 18.1; before you look at the table, think of as many solutions as you can to the lawn-mowing problem.

You may have noticed that the respondents were older adults, even though this chapter is one of the three on early adulthood. Remember that all three approaches to adult cognition are relevant throughout adulthood. Postformal thinking, including flexibility, can occur at any point of adult life. Once adolescence is over, cognitive advancement depends more on experience, training, and personal traits than on age. This is also true for the pinnacle of flexible thinking, creative works of art. Although the peak of creativity usually occurs before age 40, people can continue to produce high-quality creative works well into old age (Simonton, 1998).

Stereotype Threat

Flexibility, particularly the ability to put aside an automatic reaction, is needed to counter stereotypes. This is obvious when you hold a stereotype about someone else, but flexibility is also needed to counter the highly emotional thought that someone is stereotyping you—is assuming that you are stupid (or worse) because of some innate characteristic, such as your ethnicity, gender, or age. The mere *possibility* of being negatively stereotyped arouses emotions that can disrupt cognition. It is called **stereotype threat**; it may be defined as the possibility that one's appearance or behavior will be misused to confirm another person's oversimplified, prejudiced attitude (Steele, 1997).

stereotype threat The possibility that one's appearance or behavior will be misused to confirm another person's oversimplified, prejudiced attitude.

TABLE 18.1 Four Adults' Solutions to an Everyday Problem: Examples of Practical Creativity

Problem: Let's say that a 67-year-old man's doctor has told him to take it easy because of a heart condition. It's summertime and the man's yard needs to be mowed, but the man cannot afford to pay someone to mow the lawn. What should he do?

Subject A
- Do not mow the yard.
- Pray that someone will do it for me . . . Let my church know I have a need . . . Tell any help agency.
- If I have children . . . let them know of my need.

Subject B
- If the man has a yard, he must be living in a house. The best thing he could do would be to sell the house and move into an apartment with no yard or upkeep.
- He could trade services with a younger neighbor. The neighbor would mow his lawn in return for the man walking the neighbor's dog, watching his children, etc.
- He could call his city or county human services department . . . and ask if there are volunteers.
- He could ask a grandson to mow it without pay.

Subject C
- Immediately start planning to live in a situation that is suitable to his condition. Plan ahead.
- In the meanwhile, he should see if relative or friend could help him until he changes abode.
- Possibly he could exchange the mowing for some service he can do, like babysitting or tutoring.
- Be sure to get a second medical opinion.
- Talk to his church or organization people. Trade services.
- Check civic organizations.
- Possibly [borrowing] a riding mower might be suitable—until he changes abode.
- Get a part-time job, and earn enough to pay for help.

Subject D
- Move to quarters not having a yard to maintain.
- Cover lawn with black plastic sheeting . . . remove plastic in fall and sow rye grass.
- Rent a room to a man who will care for yard as part payment of room.
- Marry a young physical training teacher who loves yard work.
- Tether sheep in yard.
- Buy a reconditioned remote-controlled power mower, shrubbery, and flowers.
- Plant shade trees.
- Cover yard with river rock and/or concrete and apply weed killer when necessary.
- Plant a vegetable garden in yard.
- Plant a grain seed and sell harvest.

Sources: Marsiske & Willis, 1995, 1998, in Adams-Price, 1998, pp. 100–101.
The problem comes from Denney and Pearce, 1989.

Not everyone experiences stereotype threat, and not every context evokes it. It is particularly strong in adolescence, when ethnic and/or gender identity is being developed. Usually, young people who become aware of prejudice against them because of their minority status—as a black person or a homosexual, for example—identify strongly with their minority group, explicitly denying that the prejudice contains any truth. Psychologically, such strong identification is healthier than *disidentification,* which is deliberately refusing to identify with their group, and is much healthier than counteridentification, which is identifying with the majority and thereby believing the stereotype. None of these responses—identification, disidentification, or counteridentification—requires flexibility, however.

Some circumstances are more likely to evoke stereotype threat than others. In one study, young adults were asked to solve 20 difficult math problems taken from the Graduate Record Exam. Half the students simply took the test, but the other half were told beforehand that the results would be used to discover differences between males and females in math ability. On average, men and women scored similarly except for one subgroup: women who were told that sex differences would be assessed *and* who identified strongly as women. When those factors were present, the women's average math scores were lower than the men's (Schmader, 2002).

Feeling threatened by a stereotype usually evokes two emotions: first anxiety and then a particular form of disidentification in which self-esteem is disconnected from the trait in question. To use myself as an example, I am a poor speller (as my students and editors can attest to). Since my parents and my older brother won spelling bees, and since I always enjoyed reading and writing, my poor spelling is puzzling. Disidentification provides an explanation. When we were children, my brother let it be known that his superior spelling skills meant that I was stupid, a stereotype often held by older siblings and believed by younger ones. I protected my self-concept by disidentifying with my family of champion spellers, not only devaluing spelling but also taking pride in my ineptness. I refused to study spelling, telling myself that accurate spelling had nothing to do with being smart and that I could prove it by misspelling.

Young African-American men have lower grade point averages and higher dropout rates than do young African-American women, or European- or Asian-Americans of either gender. There are many possible explanations (Cokley, 2003) for this disturbing fact. Stereotype threat is one of them, although it is not the entire explanation (Sackett et al., 2004). Reacting to the stereotype of themselves as scholastically inferior, African-American boys discount academic achievement. They conclude not only that grades are overrated but also that success in school is for females and whites, not for black males (Fordham & Ogbu, 1986). This response is self-protective and preserves self-esteem, but it is ultimately harmful.

BILL ARON / PHOTO EDIT

The Threat of Bias If students fear that others expect them to do poorly in school because of their ethnicity or gender, they may disidentify with academic achievement and do worse on exams than they otherwise would have.

Similar examples of stereotype threat are apparent among many groups in addition to women, younger sisters, and young African-American men. It affects "caste-like minorities in industrial and nonindustrial nations throughout the world (e.g., the Maoris of New Zealand, the Baraku of Japan, the Harijans of India, the Oriental Jews of Israel, and the West Indians of Great Britain)" (Steele, 1997, p. 623).

How does stereotype threat relate to postformal thinking? Obviously, stereotypes are limiting, and adults need to be flexible to overcome them, abandoning any prejudices learned in childhood or adolescence. Is this possible? Yes, as the following feature explains.

Thinking Like a Scientist

Reducing Stereotype Threat

One indication of the power of stereotype threat, as just explained, is that it can make women and minorities doubt their intellectual ability. They may become anxious in academic contexts and disidentify with intellectual achievement.

Changes in the overall historical context have had an effect here. According to various polls regarding racial integration and sexual equality, adults have fewer sexist or racist stereotypes than they did a few decades ago. Stereotype threat has diminished, too. As a result, higher education is now less threatening for women and minorities. In the United States, almost twice as many women and minorities earned college degrees in 2000 as in 1980. The increase is particularly noticeable for advanced degrees, which, presumably, are earned by adults who identify with academic accomplishments.

Many programs have been developed to improve the academic achievement of groups whose potential might otherwise go unfulfilled. Notably successful are colleges whose students are predominantly women or minorities. Apparently, students who have gender or race in common study harder, learn more, and are less likely to drop out, perhaps because stereotype threat is not present.

Beyond the general cultural shift, and beyond specific programs to bolster the self-esteem or achievement of groups who might experience stereotype threat, scientists have used their knowledge to help individuals. Remember that thinking like a scientist requires using theory, past research, and the scientific method.

In theory, people will be less threatened by any stereotype regarding their intellectual potential if they believe that intelligence depends on effort and is not entirely genetic (Steele, 1997). In other words, if adults accept the self-protective idea that IQ can be improved through hard work, they may be flexible enough to overcome handicaps caused by stereotypes.

This possibility led to a hypothesis: Intellectual performance will increase if people *internalize* (believe wholeheartedly, not just intellectually) the concept that intelligence is plastic and can be changed. One group of scientists tested this hypothesis, building on two findings from prior research: (1) Stereotype threat regarding intellectual ability is powerful among African-Americans, and (2) people are more likely to accept and internalize ideas when they express those ideas, a phenomenon called "saying is believing" (Aronson et al., 2002).

In an experiment to test this hypothesis, researchers never mentioned race to the African-American and European-American undergraduates who participated in the study, in order to avoid direct evocation of stereotypes. The students were arbitrarily divided into three groups consisting of both blacks and whites. Students in Group I were measured before and after the experimental period, with no intervention, to see if the mere passage of time had any effect. Students in Groups II and III experienced almost identical interventions, in three sessions. First, they were asked to write an encouraging response, incorporating current research on intelligence, to a letter said to be written by a younger, low-income student. In the second session, they read a thank-you note from the student and were asked to prepare a speech to encourage other young students. The speech was videotaped as a first draft and then, at the third session, it was taped again in a "final" version. All three sessions were designed to help them internalize the message that intelligence can be improved.

The only difference between the two experimental groups was in the particular IQ research they were asked to incorporate into their letters and speeches. Group II was told to emphasize that there are multiple intelligences (see Chapter 11). Group III was asked to explain that intelligence expands with effort and that new neurons may grow (e.g., Segalowitz & Schmidt, 2003). This later research undercuts the notion that racial differences in IQ are genetic, thus deflecting stereotype threat.

The intervention succeeded. Student participants' ideas about intelligence changed, as did their attitudes about academic achievement, and their grades improved. Table 18.2 shows some of the data. This experiment and other research suggest that stereotype threat is powerful, but that emotions about cognition can be affected by belief and context and that adults have the potential to be flexible in what they think and feel. Ideally, postformal thinkers flexibly combine emotional reasoning and logic.

TABLE 18.2 Attitudes and Grades in Academic Term Following Stereotype-Threat Experiment

	Group I (no intervention)		Group II (IQ is multiple)		Group III (IQ is malleable)	
	Blacks	Whites	Blacks	Whites	Blacks	Whites
Value placed on academics, from 1 (lowest) to 7 (highest)	3.5	5.7	3.9	5.7	4.8	5.6
Average grade	B	B+	B	B+	B+	A–

Source: Aronson et al., 2002.

Dialectical Thought

Postformal thought, at its best, becomes **dialectical thought,** said to be the most advanced cognitive process (Basseches, 1984, 1989; Riegel, 1975). The word *dialectic* refers to a philosophical concept (first developed by the German philosopher Georg Hegel in the early nineteenth century) that every idea or truth bears within itself the opposite idea or truth.

To use the words of philosophers, each idea, or **thesis,** implies an opposing idea, or **antithesis.** Dialectical thought involves considering both these poles of an idea simultaneously and then forging them into a **synthesis**—that is, a new idea that integrates both the original and its opposite. Because ideas always initiate their opposites, change is inevitable and the dialectical process never ends. Each new synthesis deepens and refines the thesis and antithesis that initiated it: Dialectical change results in developmental growth (Sinnott, 1998).

In daily life, dialectical thinking involves the constant integration of beliefs and experiences with all the contradictions and inconsistencies that are encountered. This process is particularly potent for life-span researchers, who believe that "the occurrence and effective mastery of crises and conflicts represent not only risks, but also opportunities for new development" (Baltes et al., 1998, p. 1041). The result of dialectical thinking is dynamic, because few, if any, of life's most important questions have single, definitive, correct answers. Change, as emphasized in Chapter 1, is multidirectional, ongoing, and often surprising.

Do Love Affairs Fail?

Let us look at dialectical thought as it applies to an experience familiar to many: the fading of a love affair (Basseches, 1984). A nondialectical thinker is likely to believe that each of the partners in a relationship has stable, independent traits. Faced with a troubled romance, then, the nondialectical thinker concludes that one partner (or the other) is at fault or that the relationship was a mistake from the beginning because the two partners were a "bad match."

dialectical thought The most advanced cognitive process, characterized by the ability to consider a thesis and its antithesis simultaneously and thus to arrive at a synthesis. Dialectical thought makes possible an ongoing awareness of pros and cons, advantages and disadvantages, possibilities and limitations.

thesis A proposition or statement of belief; the first stage of the process of dialectical thinking.

antithesis A proposition or statement of belief that opposes the thesis; the second stage of the process of dialectical thinking.

synthesis A new idea that integrates the thesis and its antithesis, thus representing a new and more comprehensive level of truth; the third stage of the process of dialectical thinking.

AP / WIDE WORLD PHOTOS

One Woman's Dialectical Journey In dialectical thinking, an individual develops new thoughts that seem opposed to his or her original thinking. Eventually, a new cognitive pattern incorporates both the original idea and the opposing one. In 1994, Carolyn McCarthy thought of herself primarily as a wife, mother, nurse (thesis)—until her husband was senselessly murdered, and her son seriously wounded, by a gunman who went on a shooting rampage with an assault rifle on a Long Island commuter train. She then began questioning many of the basic assumptions of her life and of the social order (antithesis). In particular, she opposed her congressman—whom she, as a lifelong Republican, had previously supported—because he was against gun control. This led to a synthesis in which she herself ran for Congress, as a Democrat, winning the seat to become a public advocate for a much wider community.

?*Observational Quiz* (see answer, page 446): What event is Rep. McCarthy promoting?

By contrast, the dialectical thinker sees people and relationships as constantly evolving; partners are changed by time as well as by their interaction. Adjustment is necessary and inevitable. Therefore, a romance does not become troubled because the partners are fundamentally incompatible or because one partner or the other is at fault, but because both have changed without adapting their relationship accordingly. Marriages do not "break" or "fail"; they either continue to develop over time (dialectically) or become stagnant. Ideally, adults move beyond the thesis ("I love you because you are perfect") but do not get stuck in antithesis ("I hate you"). Instead, they achieve synthesis ("Neither of us is perfect, but we can work things out").

Recognition of the continual evolution of human relationships gives the dialectical thinker a broader and more flexible perspective, making him or her better able to adapt to the flux of life. New demands, roles, responsibilities, and even conflicts themselves become opportunities for growth and synthesis rather than sources of stress and dysfunction (Wethington, 2002). When emotions clash with the intellect, the risk-taking, egocentric adolescent is likely to abandon logic, but the dialectical thinker has the wisdom to combine them to form a new synthesis.

Culture and Cognition

Does cultural background affect cognitive processes? Do some cultures encourage flexible, dialectical reasoning more than others? Several researchers hold that the answer is "yes." They believe that ancient Greek philosophy has led Europeans to use analytic logic—to take sides in a battle between right and wrong, good and evil—whereas Confucianism and Taoism have led the Chinese and other Asians to seek compromise, the "Middle Way." Asians think holistically, about the whole rather than the part, and dialectically, seeking the synthesis, because "in place of logic, the Chinese developed a dialectic" (Nisbett et al., 2001, p. 305).

According to a team of scientists who designed experiments to explore the thought of adults of many cultures. "East Asians and the Americans responded in qualitatively different ways in study after study" (Nisbett et al., 2001, p. 305). For example, Asians and North Americans were shown a series of pictures and asked to describe them. Asians were likely to begin by describing the background and North Americans to describe the object in the middle. Later, when shown the objects without the background, Asians were less able to remember them than the North Americans. This suggests that the selective perception of people from the two continents tends to differ, depending on what their culture has taught them to focus on.

In another series of experiments, investigators found that Asians were more likely to seek compromise between extremes, whereas Americans were more polarized. Asian and European-American students were asked to respond to questions like the following:

> Mary, Phoebe, and Julie all have daughters. Each mother has held a set of values that has guided her efforts to raise her daughter. Now the daughters have grown up, and each of them is rejecting many of her mother's values. How did it happen and what should they do?
>
> *[Peng & Nisbett, 1999]*

Observers who did not know the ethnic backgrounds of the respondents judged whether answers sought some middle ground (a dialectical response) or took sides. For example, a response like "Both mothers and daughters have failed to understand each other" was a dialectical statement, whereas "Mothers have to recognize daughters' rights to their own values" was not (Peng & Nisbett, 1999). Asians were more often dialectical.

A third series of studies compared students in Seoul, Korea; Korean-Americans who had lived most of their lives in the United States; and native-born European-Americans. Participants were asked:

> Suppose you are the police officer in charge of a case involving a graduate student who murdered a professor. . . . As a police officer, you must establish motive.
>
> *[Choi et al., 2003]*

Participants indicated which of 97 possible items of information they would *not* want to know. Some of the 97 items were clearly relevant (e.g., whether the professor had publicly ridiculed the graduate student), and virtually every student wanted to know them. Some were clearly irrelevant (e.g., the graduate student's favorite color), and almost everyone left them out. Other items were questionable (e.g., what the professor was doing that fateful night; how the professor was dressed). Compared with both groups of Americans, the Korean students asked for 15 more items, on average. The authors believe that students in Seoul wanted to know more items because of a cultural bias in favor of including the entire context, of finding a holistic, balanced synthesis (Choi et al., 2003).

All these researchers agree that notable differences between Eastern and Western thought are the result of nurture, not nature—that "cognitive differences have ecological, historical and sociological origins" (Choi et al., 2003, p. 47), not genetic ones. None insist that one way of thinking is better than the other. (The idea that there is a "best way" is not dialectical.)

Developmentalists agree with these researchers that culture shapes thought. Because the life-span perspective is multicontextual and multicultural, developmentalists extend the evidence on the power of culture by stressing that adults change with maturation and life experiences. Thus, although not every adult thinks in a postformal or dialectical manner, life experiences throughout adulthood (involving greater personal responsibility and more direct job and family decision making) can move a person's thinking past the adolescent, formal-operational stage.

Adult thinking advances as well as declines over many decades, not following a strict chronological timetable or reaching stages that are universally recognized. Some researchers believe that a fifth stage of cognition follows Piaget's fourth stage of formal-operational thought. This postformal stage is characterized by more subjective, practical, flexible, and dialectical thinking. The real-life responsibilities that are typically experienced by adults propel thinking forward, because the logical solutions of the formal thinker are no longer adequate. Adults combine emotions with logic for practical, postformal thought. Ideally, adults think dialectically, with thesis leading to antithesis and then synthesis. This ever-changing, dynamic cognition is characteristic of intellectually advanced adults, although it is more evident in some contexts and cultures than others.

Adult Moral Reasoning

According to many researchers, the responsibilities, experiences, and concerns of adulthood affect moral reasoning as well as intellectual analysis. The process by which they do so begins in early adulthood and continues through middle age (Pratt & Norris, 1999). Indeed, according to James Rest (1993):

Dramatic and extensive changes occur in young adulthood (the 20s and 30s) in the basic problem-solving strategies used to deal with ethical issues. . . . These changes are linked to fundamental reconceptualizations in how the person understands society and his or her stake in it.

[p. 201]

!*Answer to Observational Quiz* (from page 444): Reading the letters on the sign helps with the answer, if you are not only good at guessing the missing words but also politically astute about gun control. She is promoting the Million Mom March that was held in May 2000 to demand stronger gun-control laws.

Rest's research indicates that one stimulus for shifts in moral reasoning is college education, especially if the student's coursework includes extensive discussion of moral issues or if the student's future profession (such as law or medicine) requires subtle ethical decisions.

Other researchers agree that academic debate can start the process, but they add that in order to be capable of "truly ethical" reasoning, a person must have "the experience of sustained responsibility for the welfare of others and the experiences of irreversible moral choice which are the marks of adult personal experience" (Kohlberg, 1973, p. 196). Young adults of all ethnic groups agree that taking responsibility for one's own actions is the marker of adulthood, over and above reaching a certain age, completing college, or having a job (Arnett, 2003).

The challenges and dilemmas of adulthood, combined with postformal thinking processes, lead to new forms of moral reasoning. As one scholar explains it, "The evolved human brain has provided humans with cognitive capacity that is so flexible and creative that every conceivable moral principle generates opposition and counterprinciples" (Kendler, 2002, p. 503). In other words, just by living daily life while thinking in an advanced, flexible, dialectical manner, the adult encounters moral dilemmas and devises new responses.

Addressing Specific Dilemmas

One researcher asked adults how their thought had changed over time. Among the answers were: "I learned . . . how to love and relax . . . what was important in life . . . that there is more than one right way to do things." And they learned it "by having a family . . . by almost losing my job." This scholar concludes:

> Spurred by everyday social encounters, fresh from the everyday problem-solving tasks of creating a marriage, a long-term friendship, a parent–child relationship, an organization, a social role, a self . . . [the adult develops] ways of filtering life with a new postformal logic that combines subjectivity and objectivity.

[Sinnott, 1998, p. 55]

Parenthood is a prime example. From the birth of a first child, which tends to make both parents feel more adult—thinking about themselves and their responsibilities differently—through the unexpected issues raised by adolescent children, parenthood is undoubtedly an impetus for cognitive growth (McAdams et al., 1998).

Of course, nonparents also confront moral issues. Life events force almost all adults to think more deeply about the nature and meaning of their lives and their relationships with others. The beginning or end of an intimate relationship, a job promotion or dismissal, victimization by or escape from a violent crime, exposure to a radically different lifestyle, an intense religious experience or in-depth psychotherapy, the serious illness or death of a loved one—all these experiences may give rise to cognitive disequilibrium and reflection. This experience, in turn, can lead to deeper convictions about self and life.

Evidence for this type of cognitive growth abounds in biographical and autobiographical literature, where it is difficult for scientists to measure objectively. Nonetheless, most readers of this book probably know someone (or may actually be that someone) who seemed to have a narrow, shallow outlook on the world in early adulthood but who developed a broader, deeper perspective in response to subjective experiences combined with insight. In other words, adulthood brings

Mothers and Morals The Million Mom March in Washington, D.C., in May 2000 brought together mothers from all over the United States. The premise was that mothers would probably advocate gun control, sex education, and children's health care, among other issues, but this was not always the case.

moral issues to the forefront of everyone's thinking, but only some adults are able to master such issues and refine their ethical principles.

Moral dilemmas are particularly likely to occur in early adulthood. Every young adult must make choices about sexuality, reproduction, marriage, and child rearing. Carol Gilligan believes that such decisions particularly advance moral thinking (Gilligan, 1981; Gilligan et al., 1990). According to Gilligan, women have been raised to develop a *morality of care,* so that they regard human needs and relationships as the most important moral value; in contrast, men have been raised to develop a *morality of justice,* so that they seek the right and wrong of every issue. This distinction between male and female moral priorities has not been verified by research. Gilligan herself believes that the two sexes can, and should, develop both perspectives.

Other moral issues that contemporary adults are likely to confront arise from increasing globalization and immigration (Arnett, 2002). Young adults are particularly likely to move from place to place in search of work. As they do so, they find coworkers and neighbors whose values and religion differ radically from their own. If the adult thinks in a postformal manner, "insights about the diversity of subjective responses" (Ross & Ward, 1996, p. 131) are likely to aid in their understanding of moral conflicts, as they seek a common ground.

Moral dilemmas for young adults also arise from television, popular music, and the Internet, all of which present alternative values at the touch of a button. For some young adults, the result is freedom and joy, but others develop "an acute sense of alienation and impermanence as they grow up with a lack of cultural certainty and a lack of clear guidelines for how life is to be lived" (Arnett, 2001, p. 776).

Measuring Moral Growth

How can we assess whether a person's moral thinking has arrived at a postformal level? You read about Kohlberg's stages of moral development in Chapter 12. Another approach was taken by a group of scientists led by James Rest, who developed a series of questions about moral dilemmas called the **Defining Issues Test (DIT).** As an example, in one of the DIT's dilemmas, a reporter who must

Defining Issues Test (DIT) A series of questions developed by James Rest and designed to assess respondents' level of moral development by having them rank possible solutions to moral dilemmas.

An Expression of Faith In any group of worshippers, be they in a mosque, temple, or church (including a mega-church like the Crystal Cathedral, shown here), some will be at Fowler's first stages of faith and some will be in the final one, depending on their experiences and maturation, not on their devotion to particular items of creed or ritual.

decide whether or not to publish some old personal information that will damage a political candidate.

Instead of simply answering open-ended questions (as in Kohlberg's dilemmas), respondents to the DIT must rank their priorities, from personal benefits ("credit for investigative reporting") to higher goals ("serving society"). Ranking items leads to a number score, which makes it easier to correlate moral development with other aspects of adult cognition, experience, and life satisfaction (Schiller, 1998). In general, scores rise with age and with education, because adults gradually become less doctrinaire and more flexible as they get older or acquire more education (Rest et al., 1999).

This growth over the course of adulthood may be true of faith as well. This is the contention of James Fowler (1981, 1986), who developed a sequence of six stages of faith, building on the stages of Piaget and Kohlberg:

- *Stage 1: Intuitive-projective faith* Faith is magical, illogical, imaginative, and filled with fantasy, especially about the power of God and the mysteries of birth and death. It is typical of children ages 3 to 7.
- *Stage 2: Mythic-literal faith* Individuals take the myths and stories of religion literally and believe simplistically in the power of symbols. God is seen as rewarding those who follow His laws and punishing others. Stage 2 is typical from ages 7 to 11, but it also characterizes some adults. Fowler cites a woman who says extra prayers at every opportunity, to put them "in the bank."
- *Stage 3: Synthetic-conventional faith* This is a conformist stage. Faith is conventional, reflecting concern about other people and favoring "what feels right" over what makes intellectual sense. Fowler quotes a man whose personal rules include "being truthful with my family. Not trying to cheat them out of anything. . . . I'm not saying that God or anybody else set my rules. I really don't know. It's what I feel is right."
- *Stage 4: Individual-reflective faith* Faith is characterized by intellectual detachment from the values of the culture and from the approval of other people. College may be a springboard to stage 4, as the young person learns to question the authority of parents, teachers, and other powerful figures and to rely instead on his or her own understanding of the world. Faith becomes an active commitment.
- *Stage 5: Conjunctive faith* Faith incorporates both powerful unconscious ideas (such as the power of prayer and the love of God) and rational, conscious values (such as the worth of life compared with that of property). People are willing to accept contradictions, obviously a postformal manner of thinking. Fowler says that this cosmic perspective is seldom achieved before middle age.
- *Stage 6: Universalizing faith* People at this stage have a powerful vision of universal compassion, justice, and love that compels them to live their lives in a way that many people think either saintly or foolish. A transforming experience is often the gateway to stage 6, as happened to Moses, Muhammad, the Buddha, and St. Paul, or, more recently, Mohandas Gandhi, Martin Luther King Jr., and Mother Teresa. Stage 6 is rarely achieved.

If Fowler is correct, faith, like other aspects of cognition, progresses from a simple, self-centered, one-sided perspective to a more complex, altruistic (unselfish), and multisided view. Although not everyone agrees with Fowler's particular stages, the role of religion in human development is now widely accepted, especially when people are confronted with "unsettling life situations" (Day & Naedts, 1999; Miller & Thoresen, 2003). Faith, apparently, is one way people combat stress, overcome adversity, and analyze challenges.

Like almost all forms of thinking and analyzing, faith is not static but changes as life does, with values shifting as experience accumulates (Rest et al., 1999). My own experience with faith is one example.

In Person

Faith and Tolerance

When I was in college, I had a discussion about religion with a young woman whose beliefs seemed simplistic and naive to me. She hadn't really given her faith much thought, I concluded. Wanting to help her without being too harsh, I asked, "How can you be so sure of what you believe?"

Instead of recognizing the immaturity of her thought, she stunned me by saying, "I hope that someday you reach the certainty that I have."

In the years since then, I have encountered many other people whose religious beliefs seem too pat, too unquestioning. Yet when they have told me that they are praying for me and my family, or have asked for my prayers, I have been grateful, even when I know that the person's concept of God is quite different from mine.

Does this mean that I have become more flexible than I once was? Has my faith moved up the hierarchy that James Fowler (1981, 1986) described? I hope so. But from my college days until now, never has anyone told me that my faith is more advanced than theirs. This is humbling.

I agree with Hunter Lewis's (2000) observation that "people need to consider their own values, consider them seriously, consider them for themselves" (p. 248), and I think Fowler's description of six stages of faith can aid such consideration. There is one problem, however: I wonder if religious beliefs do indeed advance up Fowler's hierarchy. So few people are at the upper stages that there is an implied criticism of most of us as being immature when it comes to religious belief. It is still galling to learn about stages of faith that are beyond the level that most adults reach, just as it was when I was in college many years ago.

Moral issues challenge cognitive processes, as adults move beyond acceptance of authority in childhood and rebellion in adolescence. Some people become more open and reflective in their moral judgments and in their religious faith as they mature and as personal experiences (especially those related to parenthood) deepen their ethical understanding. However, as globalism advances, young adults encounter conflicting value systems and divergent religious faiths; this exposure presents potential challenges and practical difficulties. It is not obvious that some people are more advanced in moral judgment and faith than others, although some developmentalists suggest that this is the case.

Cognitive Growth and Higher Education

Of particular interest to many developmental researchers and to readers of this text is the relationship between college education and adult development. The evidence is positive: It seems that college graduates are not only healthier and wealthier than other people but also deeper and more flexible thinkers. These conclusions are so favorable that they should be considered with some suspicion; perhaps selection effects or cohort effects lead to exaggeration of the benefits of a college education. Before considering such possibilities, however, let us review the data.

The Effects of College on Cognition

Most students attend college primarily to secure better jobs and to learn specific skills (especially to prepare for careers in the new knowledge and service industries, such as Internet businesses and health care) and secondarily to gain a good general education. These motives may apply especially to young adults in the

LOUISE GUBB / CORBIS

Thumbs Up! These graduates in Long Beach, California, are joyful that they have reached a benchmark. Ideally, their diplomas will earn them not only better jobs but also an intellectual perspective that will help them all their lives.

United States (see Figure 18.3), but it seems to be the trend elsewhere as well (Jongbloed et al., 1999).

A student of mine named Erin acknowledged both goals:

A higher education provides me with the ability to make adequate money so I can provide for my future. An education also provides me with the ability to be a mature thinker and to attain a better understanding of myself. . . . With a higher rate of health problems and payments to doctors' offices, an education provides the means for a better job after college, which will support me and allow me to have a stable, comfortable retirement.

Erin's concern, at age 18, about her future medical costs and retirement income may seem premature, but she is not unusual. Many students in the United States today are concerned about their economic future, and they are aware that a college degree is likely to increase their income. Every set of statistics from every nation confirms the economic value of college. For example, in the year 2000 in the United States, the average income of householders who had earned a master's degree was $78,000, more than twice the $37,000 average income of householders with only a high school diploma (U.S. Bureau of the Census, 2002). College also correlates with better health practices: College graduates everywhere are less likely to smoke, to overeat, to avoid exercise, and to die young.

These figures are encouraging to every student of human development, but this chapter focuses on cognition. Does higher education lead to postformal thinking? Does college make people more likely to combine the subjective and objective in a flexible, dialectical way? Probably yes. Every year of college seems to improve verbal and quantitative abilities, knowledge of specific subject areas, skills in various professions, reasoning, and reflection. According to one comprehensive review:

Compared to freshmen, seniors have better oral and written communication skills, are better abstract reasoners or critical thinkers, are more skilled at using reason and evidence to address ill-structured problems for which there are no verifiably correct answers, have greater intellectual flexibility in that they are better able to understand more than one side of a complex issue, and can develop more sophisticated abstract frameworks to deal with complexity.

[Pascarella & Terenzini, 1991, p. 155]

Some research finds that students' thinking changes with each year of college (Clinchy, 1993; King & Kitchener, 1994; Perry, 1981/1998). According to many observers, first-year students believe that clear and perfect truths exist, and they are disturbed if their professors do not explain these truths. Freshmen tend to gather knowledge as if facts were nuggets of gold, each one separate from other bits of knowledge and each one pure and true. One first-year student said he was like a squirrel, "gleaning little acorns of knowledge and burying them for later use" (in Bozik, 2002, p. 145).

This initial phase is followed by a wholesale questioning of personal and social values, including doubts about the idea of truth itself. No fact is taken at face value, much less stored intact for future use.

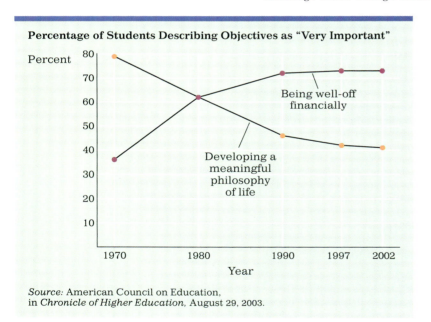

Percentage of Students Describing Objectives as "Very Important"

Being well-off financially

Developing a meaningful philosophy of life

Source: American Council on Education, in *Chronicle of Higher Education,* August 29, 2003.

FIGURE 18.3 Primary Reason for Going to College: Wealth Versus Wisdom The American Council on Education surveys college freshman every year. Cohort shifts are particularly significant regarding income. Does a generation gap exist between current professors and their students?

Finally, as graduation approaches, after considering many opposing ideas, students become committed to certain values, even as they realize they need to remain open-minded (Pascarella & Terenzini, 1991; Rest et al., 1999). Facts are neither gold nor dross but are useful steps toward a greater understanding. According to one classic study (Perry, 1981/1998), thinking progresses through nine levels of complexity over the four years of college, moving from a simplistic either/or dualism (right or wrong, success or failure) to a relativism that recognizes a multiplicity of perspectives (see Table 18.3). Perry found that the college experience itself causes this progression: Peers, professors, books, and class discussion all stimulate new questions and thoughts, as students advance through their college years.

In general, the more years of higher education and of life experience a person has, the deeper and more dialectical that person's reasoning is likely to become (Pascarella & Terenzini, 1991). Which aspect of college is the primary catalyst for such growth? Is it the challenging academic work, professors' lectures, peer discussions, the new setting, the experience of living away from home? All of these are possible. Every scientist who has studied cognition from infancy to late adulthood has found that social interaction and intellectual challenge advance

TABLE 18.3 **Scheme of Cognitive and Ethical Development**

Dualism modified	Position 1	Authorities know, and if we work hard, read every word, and learn Right Answers, all will be well.
	Transition	But what about those Others I hear about? And different opinions? And Uncertainties? Some of our own Authorities disagree with each other or don't seem to know, and some give us problems instead of Answers.
	Position 2	True Authorities must be Right, the others are frauds. We remain Right. Others must be different and Wrong. Good Authorities give us problems so we can learn to find the Right Answer by our own independent thought.
	Transition	But even Good Authorities admit they don't know all the answers *yet!*
	Position 3	Then some uncertainties and different opinions are real and legitimate *temporarily,* even for Authorities. They're working on them to get to the Truth.
	Transition	But there are *so many* things they don't know the Answers to! And they won't for a long time.
Relativism discovered	*Position 4a*	Where Authorities don't know the Right Answers, everyone has a right to his own opinion; no one is wrong!
	Transition	Then what right have They to grade us? About what?
	Position 4b	In certain courses Authorities are not asking for the Right Answer. They want us to *think* about things in a certain way, *supporting* opinion with data. That's what they grade us on.
	Position 5	Then *all* thinking must be like this, even for Them. Everything is relative but not equally valid. You have to understand how each context works. Theories are not Truth but metaphors to interpret data with. You have to think about your thinking.
	Transition	But if everything is relative, am I relative too? How can I know I'm making the Right Choice?
	Position 6	I see I'm going to have to make my own decisions in an uncertain world with no one to tell me I'm Right.
	Transition	I'm lost if I don't. When I decide on my career (or marriage or values), everything will straighten out.
Commitments in relativism developed	Position 7	Well, I've made my first Commitment!
	Transition	Why didn't that settle everything?
	Position 8	I've made several commitments. I've got to balance them—how many, how deep? How certain, how tentative?
	Transition	Things are getting contradictory. I can't make logical sense out of life's dilemmas.
	Position 9	This is how life will be. I must be wholehearted while tentative, fight for my values yet respect others, believe my deepest values right yet be ready to learn. I see that I shall be retracing this whole journey over and over—but, I hope, more wisely.

Source: Perry, 1981/1998.

thinking. Further, development is "a dialectical process" between individuals and social structures (Giele, 2000, p. 78), and college is a social structure that for centuries has been dedicated to fostering cognitive growth.

Possible Factors in Cognitive Growth During College

You probably noticed that Perry's study was first published in 1981. Because cohort effects are powerful, conclusions based on information about college students of 30 years ago may no longer apply, especially because both sides of the dialectic—students and social structures—have changed. Further, the fact that an institution is designed to foster cognitive growth does not necessarily mean it actually does so. We have seen several times in this text that intentions do not always produce the desired results. Let's look at the various factors we have mentioned to see if college education does, in fact, produce deeper thinkers.

Changes in the Students

The sheer number of students receiving higher education has multiplied in virtually every country worldwide. In the developed nations of Western Europe, Japan, and North America, fewer than one in every twenty young adults in the first half of the twentieth century earned a college degree, but in 2000 almost one in three did (Rhodes, 2001). Although the proportions are lower, more dramatic increases have occurred in Africa and Asia. For example, when India gained its independence in 1948, only 100,000 students were in college. By the end of the twentieth century, there were 4 million Indian college students, a 4,000 percent increase (Altbach, 1998).

SPENCER GRANT / PHOTOEDIT, INC.

United States? Canada? Guess Again!
These students attend the University of Capetown in South Africa, where previous cohorts of blacks and whites would never have been allowed to socialize so freely.

The characteristics of the student body have also changed, with more women, more older students, more international students, and more minority students. Worldwide, campuses are more diverse, although there are differences in the specifics. For instance, although women are still the minority in most colleges in developing nations, only one developed nation (Germany) has more men students than women (Bulmahn, 1999).

Most of this demographic change has occurred very recently, as the data for the United States show. About twice as many minority students, and twice as many women, are now earning bachelor's degrees in U.S. colleges as in the early 1980s (see Table 18.4 and Figure 18.4). The life experiences of students are also more diverse. More students are low-income, have children, attend college part time and live at home, are employed during their college years, and choose career-based programs (computer programming, health services, engineering, accounting, business) rather than liberal arts curricula.

The values and attitudes of today's college students are quite different from those of students 30 years ago (see Figure 18.5). Thus, not only are there many more students today, but today's students are unlike previous cohorts of students in dozens of ways.

Changes in the Institutions

As students are changing, so is the structure of higher education. In the United States, there are almost twice as

TABLE 18.4 High School Graduates and Women in College

Year	High School Graduates Who Enroll in College (%)	College Students Who Are Female (%)
1960	45	41
1970	52	48
1980	49	51
1990	60	53
1997	67	55
2000	63	55

Source: U.S. Bureau of the Census, 2002.

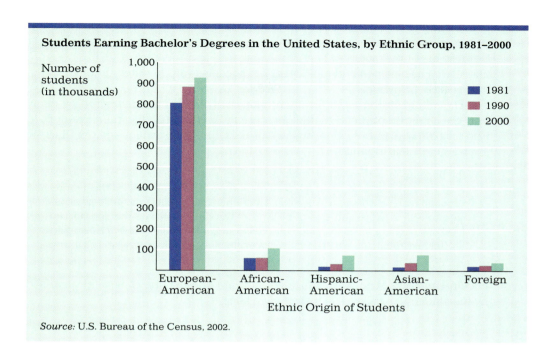

Students Earning Bachelor's Degrees in the United States, by Ethnic Group, 1981–2000

Source: U.S. Bureau of the Census, 2002.

FIGURE 18.4 Increases Across the Board At least twice as many students in each category are earning bachelor's degrees today compared to a decade ago. Less encouraging is the fact that European-Americans still make up the vast majority of college students, and minorities are underrepresented.

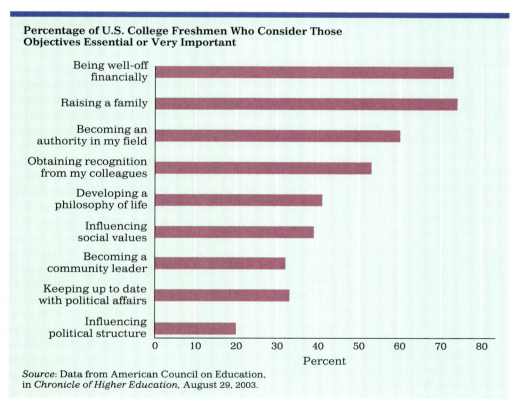

Percentage of U.S. College Freshmen Who Consider Those Objectives Essential or Very Important

Source: Data from American Council on Education, in *Chronicle of Higher Education,* August 29, 2003.

FIGURE 18.5 Personal Aspirations The American Council on Education began surveying college freshmen in 1966. Over the decades, students have gradually become more interested in their personal success and less concerned about larger issues of developing a philosophy and acting on it. For example, keeping up to date on politics was important to 58 percent in 1966 but to fewer than half as many (27 percent) in 1998. Whether the college experience will change the perspective of entering students, as it did in the past, remains to be seen.

many institutions of higher learning today as there were in 1970; enrollment at community colleges is up 144 percent. More career programs are offered, taught by more part-time faculty (43 percent, compared to 22 percent in 1970), and more instructors are women and minorites. The specifics vary in other nations, but the trends are worldwide.

The administrators and faculty of many universities are distressed by many of these changes, particularly the decrease in liberal arts education. Frank H. T. Rhodes (2001), president emeritus of Cornell University, argues against "narrow job training," fearing that

> the nagging questions of our common humanity, once confronted by the liberal arts, are now hushed or ignored, even though we have never needed them more. A young man or woman will become a more humane physician after some exposure to Shakespeare and Dostoyevsky. . . . The time to debate the appropriate level of a patient's bill is not in the hospital examination room; it is in the economics seminar room. . . . We need specialist professionals with generalist views.
>
> *[p. 35]*

Faculty members who were educated 30 years ago may be especially surprised by the students of today, as I myself have been.

In Person

A Dialectical View of Cheating

CHEATING IS REACHING EPIDEMIC PROPORTIONS WORLDWIDE, RESEARCHERS SAY, reported a headline in the *Chronicle of Higher Education* (Desruisseaux, 1998). A recent review called cheating "endemic" to all colleges (Whitley & Keith-Spiegel, 2002). It appears that:

- Almost every student knows of instances of cheating.
- Almost no student who witnesses cheating reports it to college authorities.
- About 1 student in 12 believes that cheating is sometimes necessary to get better grades.

This last statistic is the most disturbing to professors, who usually see cheating as an insult to the learning process, an assault on academic integrity. Another study found that few students approve of cheating, but 20 percent had cheated at least three times and almost 80 percent are aware of incidents when other students have cheated (McCabe & Trevino, 1996). Students who are more closely connected to their academic institutions because they attend full time or live on campus are more likely to accept cheating than are students who attend part time or commute (see Table 18.5). Other research shows that fraternity and sorority members, who may be most closely connected to college life, cheat more than do non-Greeks (Storch & Storch, 2002).

Professors and students often have quite different concepts of cheating (Whitley & Keith-Spiegel, 2002). As a result, students sometimes cheat when even they do not realize that they are doing so.

Although almost all my students realize that copying someone else's paper or sneaking a page of facts into a final exam is cheating, many students seem oblivious to plagiarism, to the guilt of those who allow others to copy from

TABLE 18.5 "Some Forms of Cheating Are Necessary to Get the Grades I Want": College Students Who Agree

Student Characteristics	Percentage Agreeing
All students	8%
Type of institution	
Two-year colleges	5
Four-year institutions	9
Universities	11
Attendance	
Full-time	9
Part-time	3
Gender	
Men	10
Women	5
Resident status	
Residence hall or fraternity	11
Commuter	6
Age	
25 or younger	10
Over 25	3

Source: Data cited in McCabe & Trevino, 1996.

them, and to the limits of cooperation in doing homework. The reality of this gap was forcefully brought home to me when I noticed that three students had given identical answers on the essay portion of a test. Instead of simply failing the offenders and stating the college's policy, I passed out an anonymous questionnaire to the entire class. The results:

- 35 percent were certain cheating was going on in the class.
- 52 percent strongly suspected it.
- 13 percent thought there was no cheating.

Why had none of the 87 percent who were aware of cheating told me about it? In the next class, I reported the data, divided the students into groups, told each group to figure out what I should do and appoint a spokesperson to report to me, and I left the room. When I came back, I learned that my students did not share my distress. Some noncheaters felt superior (cheaters are "only hurting themselves"). Some expressed ethnic prejudice (foreign students "whisper things in their language"). Some thought cheating was necessary ("Your tests are too hard") and even beneficial (we should "help our friends"). Some thought I did not care, and one told me later that she hadn't reported any cheating because she thought I must have been aware of it and decided not to act!

Using postformal thinking, I realized that my culture (in this case, the academic system) considers cheating an attack on education, but the students' culture values cooperation and mutual support. My thesis is that cheating is evil; their antithesis is that cheating may help someone get a diploma and a better job. Indeed, research finds that cheaters are more likely to believe that the purpose of attending school is to get good grades, not to learn (Anderman et al., 1998). From that perspective, copying someone else's work seems permissible.

Dialectical theory suggests that, once both sides understand each other's perspective, a new synthesis can be found. My students taught me to be much more explicit about my requirements and to stress my values, in words and actions. I now ask students to sit far apart during tests; I use alternate versions of exams; and I require creative, current homework. If cheating occurs, I talk to all the offenders in my office. The direct consequence is usually an F on the assignment or test, but an opportunity to pass the course by submitting their own work for the rest of the semester.

The academic value system is one among many. I have chosen to uphold the values, customs, and practices of that system, but I no longer assume that my students share my perspective. Research suggests that confusion about the academic system is common among students (Deil-Amen & Rosenbaum, 2003). Part of my role as a teacher is to clarify it for them, and I do so, using more practical and flexible thinking than I once did.

Evaluating the Research

Three factors may keep a college education today from being as powerful a force in producing cognitive growth as it might have been:

- Cohort effects
- Selection effects
- Dropout rates

Cohort effects are obvious, in that students and colleges have changed, as you saw earlier. However, these changes may be just as likely to work in favor of cognitive advancement as against it. Among the factors that enhance cognitive development are interactions with people of different backgrounds and various views. Certainly the increased diversity of today's students works in that direction. Further, the very fact that more students are parents and employed today than previously should enhance their ability to combine emotions and logic, to the benefit of all.

Selection effects raise the possibility that more advanced cognition, as well as better jobs, higher incomes, and better health, do not result directly from a college education but from factors that correlate with college attendance. Remember that correlation is not causation, and students who are already intellectually inclined and relatively well-off are more likely to enroll in college as well as more likely to earn degrees. Perhaps the benefits connected with college are not really the result of college attendance itself but of having been selected (by admissions offices, parents, or oneself) to enroll in the first place. This hypothesis has been explored, and has been only partly supported. In addition to selection effects, careful research has found that college itself aids development (Pacarella & Terenzini, 1991). When 18-year-olds of similar backgrounds and abilities have been compared, those who go straight into the job market after high school eventually achieve less than those who earn a college degree.

The third factor, the dropout rate, is substantial, and this may dilute the beneficial effect of college. Only half of the students who enroll as freshmen go on to earn a bachelor's degree. The dropout rate is particularly high among community college students, 80 percent of whom believe it is likely that they will earn a bachelor's degree, but less than 20 percent of whom actually do so (Brint, 2003). It is not necessarily the less intellectually able who drop out, but those for whom the costs of education become too high. Postformal thinking—the ability to cope with the complexities of personal emotions and logical decision making—may be the goal and the eventual result of higher education, but many students may not be able to stay around long enough to attain that goal. Students

> may be able to adapt to complexities better as they proceed through college, after acquiring social know-how and academic successes. An individual's capacity to adapt to . . . [bureaucratic and curricular impediments of college] may depend on the attainment of basic skills or increased maturity.
>
> *[Deil-Amen & Rosenbaum, 2003, p. 141]*

Certainly a college education does not guarantee a leap ahead in cognitive development. However, the weight of the evidence suggests that college advances income, promotes health, deepens thinking, and increases tolerance of differing political, social, and religious views. Meeting fellow students and professors from backgrounds that are not familiar, as well as learning about new ideas and reading books never known before, are bound to broaden a person's perspective. College classes that are career-based, as well as courses in the liberal arts, raise ethical questions and promote moral thinking (Rest et al., 1999). All the evidence suggests that higher education can still be "a transforming element in human development" (Benjamin, 2003, p. 11).

For many readers, this will come as no surprise. College is a stimulus for mature thought, no matter how young the student is. From orientation week to graduation day, college students learn not only information and issues pertaining to their majors but also how to think and reason more deeply, reflectively, and broadly.

> Many life experiences advance thinking processes. College is one of them, as years of classroom discussion and guided reading can lead students to more openness of thought and more dynamic and dialectical reasoning. Most young adults in developed nations now register for some college coursework, although many leave before earning a degree. Cognitive advancement seems to be correlated with degree attainment, liberal arts education, and full-time, residential academic enrollment. Even though the context differs from that of a few decades ago, college education still promotes cognitive development.

SUMMARY

Postformal Thought

1. Adult cognition can be studied in any of several ways: from a postformal perspective, from a psychometric perspective, or from an information-processing perspective. This chapter focuses on the postformal perspective.

2. Many researchers believe that, in adulthood, the complex and often ambiguous or conflicting demands of daily life produce a new type of thinking called postformal thought. It is well suited to addressing problems that may have no single correct solution. Postformal thought is practical, flexible, and dialectical, integrating emotions and logic.

3. One hallmark of adult thought is the ability to combine emotions and rational analysis. This ability is particularly useful in responding to emotionally arousing situations, as when one is being stereotyped.

4. Dialectical thinking recognizes and synthesizes complexities and contradictions. Instead of seeking absolute, immutable truths, dialectical thought is flexible and ever-changing.

Adult Moral Reasoning

5. Thinking about questions of morality, faith, and ethics may also progress in adulthood, along the same lines as postformal thought. James Rest describes stages of morality, and James Fowler describes stages of faith—both plausible ideas, but not universally accepted.

6. Adults of both sexes come to recognize the limitations of basing moral reasoning solely on abstract principles or personal concerns and try to integrate the two. As people mature, life confronts them with ethical decisions, including many related to parenthood and, for young adults particularly, to globalization.

Cognitive Growth and Higher Education

7. Research over the past several decades indicates that college education not only increases wealth and health but also tends to advance cognitive processes. Students gradually become less inclined to seek absolute truths from authorities and more inclined to make their own decisions.

8. Today's college students are different from earlier cohorts in many ways. In almost every nation of the world, not only has the sheer number of students increased, but more students are female, from ethnic minorities, part time, commuter, older, and low-income.

9. Colleges as institutions have also changed. It is likely, though not certain, that the effect of cohort changes is to advance cognitive development.

KEY TERMS

postformal stage (p. 436)
subjective thought (p. 437)
objective thought (p. 437)

stereotype threat (p. 439)
dialectical thought (p. 443)
thesis (p. 443)

antithesis (p. 443)
synthesis (p. 443)

Defining Issues Test (DIT)
(p. 447)

APPLICATIONS

1. Read a biography or autobiography that includes information about the person's thinking from age 18 to 35. Cite evidence of cognitive advancement (or lack of it) in postformal thought, in moral development, and in religious faith. What is the effect of personal experiences and intellectual ideas?

2. Statistics on changes in students and in colleges are fascinating, but only a few from the United States are reported here. Find data from another nation, or other statistics within the United States (a reference librarian can help you find many data sources). Report the data and discuss the reasons for and the implications of cohort changes.

3. The best way to try to verify that cognitive development changes over the years of college is to study cases. (Remember that, as explained in Chapter 1, case studies are provocative but not definitive.) If you are a senior, look back at work that you did, diary entries that you wrote, or decisions that you made in your first year, and compare them with current equivalents. If you are new to college, find another student close to graduation, and do the same. On the basis of your intensive study of one person, what hypotheses would you like to test, and what do you think would be the best way to do so?

Chapter Nineteen

Early Adulthood: Psychosocial Development

In terms of psychosocial development, the hallmark of contemporary adult life is diversity. No longer limited by the pace of biological maturation or bound by parental restrictions, young adults choose their own paths—and the array of choices for career, marriage, parenthood, lifestyle, and friendship is mind-boggling. Between ages 20 and 35, the average adult in the United States changes jobs nine times, spends five to ten years unmarried, and then marries, has a 50/50 chance of divorce, and conceives one or two children. (Adults in other nations approach these numbers, although variations exist. For example, Italians have fewer job changes, fewer divorces, and fewer children.) Almost every adult everywhere has close friends who follow other paths—including marrying and divorcing several times, adopting children, avoiding parenthood, entering a homosexual partnership, or living happily alone.

Just looking at averages is deceptive. My two closest women friends in early adulthood (both roommates of mine for a year) and I are now middle-aged women. The three of us have had three husbands and five children—exactly average. But one never married or had children. Another married, divorced, remarried, and had her only child at age 40. I often felt like the odd one, with lots of children (four) and only one husband.

How does any adult make choices? One way they do so is by trying to figure out, within all the options presented by their culture, genes, and cohort, how to meet their basic needs. Thus, to sort out these various paths, we first describe two psychosocial needs that underlie and organize the complexity and diversity of adulthood.

Theories of Adulthood

Given the diversity of paths through adult life, it is not surprising that there are many theories that describe, analyze, and predict the transformations that occur during adult life. However, when the different theories describe psychological needs, they reach surprisingly similar conclusions.

Love and Work

Descriptive terms for the two basic psychosocial needs vary: affiliation and achievement, or affection and instrumentality, or interdependence and independence, or communion and agency (Bakan, 1966). Sigmund Freud (1935) simply said that a healthy adult is one who can "love and work."

FIGURE 19.1 Maslow's Hierarchy of Human Needs Abraham Maslow was a major proponent of a psychosocial theory called *humanism*. He believed that, rather than focusing on people with problems, psychologists should study those who are happy and productive. Once the basic needs are satisfied, people strive for self-actualization, when they feel in tune with nature, God, and their fellow human beings.

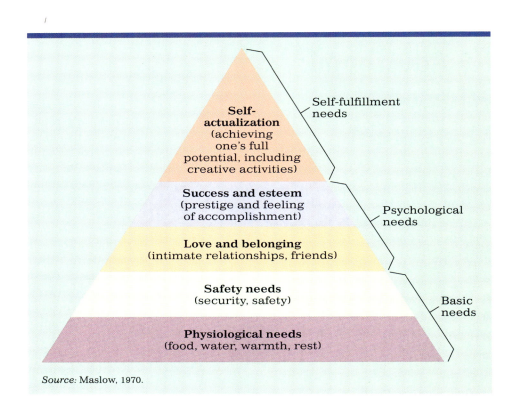

Source: Maslow, 1970.

Many Words for Two Concepts	
Affiliation	**Achievement**
Affection	Instrumentality
Interdependence	Independence
Communion	Agency
Love	Work
Love and belonging	Success and esteem
Intimacy	Generativity

intimacy versus isolation The sixth of Erikson's eight stages of development. Adults seek someone with whom to share their lives in an enduring and self-sacrificing commitment. Without such commitment, they risk profound aloneness and isolation.

generativity versus stagnation Erikson's seventh stage of development, in which adults seek to be productive through vocation, avocation, or child rearing. Without such productive work, adults stop developing and growing.

These two needs are also elements of Abraham Maslow's (1968) hierarchy (see Figure 19.1). Maslow thought that people strive for a higher level only after their lower-level needs are satisfied. Thus, a person who is starving may be too focused on food (a physiological need) to seek love or success; but a person whose basic needs for survival and safety are met can focus on "love and belonging" and then "success and esteem" (psychological needs). Although these two levels are not identical to Freud's "love and work" or to the other formulations, all theories recognize two basic psychological needs: the need to connect with other people in mutually nurturing relationships and the need to accomplish something.

Perhaps the clearest developmental formulation of adulthood, age 20 to 60, came from Erik Erikson. Erikson maintained that, after resolving the identity crisis of adolescence, young adults confront the crisis of **intimacy versus isolation.** This crisis arises from the powerful desire to share one's personal life with someone else. Without intimacy, an adult suffers from loneliness and isolation. As Erikson (1963) explains:

> The young adult, emerging from the search for and the insistence on identity, is eager and willing to fuse his identity with others. He is ready for intimacy, that is, the capacity to commit himself to concrete affiliations and partnerships and to develop the ethical strength to abide by such commitments, even though they call for significant sacrifices and compromises.
>
> *[p. 263]*

Erikson's next stage is **generativity versus stagnation,** when people need to be productive in some meaningful way, usually through work or parenthood. Without a sense of generativity, says Erikson, life is empty and purposeless and adults are filled with "a pervading sense of stagnation and personal impoverishment" (Erikson, 1963, p. 267).

Remember that, according to Erikson, each stage builds on the previous stages, and difficulties at one stage carry over into the next. This is seen in the case of Linda, reported by James Marcia (2002).

A Case to Study

Linda: "Her Major Issues Were Relationships and Career"

At age 34, Linda became a patient of therapist James Marcia. Her identity crisis had never been resolved, intimacy was difficult for her, and, without intimacy, generative work and parenthood were unattainable. Marcia (2002) described her situation as follows:

> Linda was the middle of three siblings in a blended family. Redheaded and slight of stature, Linda was exceptionally well-dressed. . . . She said that she was the best-dressed person in her high school class and that the one thing her father had done for her was to give her money to buy good clothes. Although she had grown up Roman Catholic, she had not been at all religious and had never felt this to be an important issue to her. She said that she had been somewhat sexually promiscuous in high school—as a way of gaining attention and affection.
>
> She made several attempts at postsecondary education. The first was a brief stay in nursing school. This had been her mother's plan for her, but Linda found herself uninterested in school as well as unwelcome there. She then made several brief forays into courses in fashion design at two other institutions. . . .
>
> After she defaulted on her higher education, Linda went back to her small hometown and found a job waiting tables. She met and fell in love with Jacqueline, a French Canadian woman. . . . The relationship began to go increasingly sour as Jacqueline became more and more involved with drugs and alcohol, coming in at early morning hours to an anxious and frantic Linda. After about 5 years of this, Linda met Greg, who took it on himself to "rescue" her. . . .
>
> . . . Although she could have moved in with Greg after leaving Jacqueline, Linda decided to leave the whole area and move 3,000 miles away to the Pacific Northwest, to a strange city, and began to make a new life on her own, . . . independent from her mother's designs, Jacqueline's demands, and Greg's directions. She had never before lived alone for a lengthy period of time and had a difficult year getting settled in a new city and beginning a new job. She found her employment as an office receptionist considerably more fulfilling than waiting tables, and the office staff and professionals began to constitute a new community for her. . . .
>
> Her major issues were relationships and career, both of which had at their base questions of self-esteem. . . . Linda was still emotionally attached to Jacqueline and Greg, neither of whom provided her with any support. Jacqueline had cut off communication, and Greg was unreliable in contacting her and was emotionally unavailable when he did.

[Marcia, 2002]

We will read about Linda's progress at the end of this chapter.

Ages and Stages

Erikson and the other grand theorists working in the mid-twentieth century based their stages of adulthood on financially secure men from Western Europe or North America. According to their formulations, the typical man chose his lifetime occupation and finished his education by his early 20s (identity); married, bought a house, and had children by age 30 (intimacy); and then devoted himself to climbing the career ladder in order to be "a good provider" (generativity). Similarly, his wife married in her early 20s (intimacy) and had children by age 30, achieving generativity (as well as identity and intimacy) through her work as wife, mother, and homemaker.

Following in this tradition of dividing adulthood into age stages and using middle-class men as the norm, several American developmentalists attempted to subdivide the periods of adulthood. The most famous of these was Daniel Levinson, who studied a small group of men in the 1960s and noticed that they

TABLE 19.1 Levinson's Stages of Adulthood

Stage	Age	Change or Challenge Involved
Early adult transition	17 to 22	Leave adolescence, make preliminary choices for adult life.
Entering the adult world	22 to 28	Make initial choices in love, occupation, friendship, values, lifestyle.
Age 30 transition	28 to 33	Changes occur in life structure, either a moderate change or, more often, a severe and stressful crisis.
Settling down	33 to 40	Establish a niche in society, progress on a timetable, in both family and career accomplishments.
Midlife transition	40 to 45	Life structure comes into question, usually a time of crisis in the meaning, direction, and value of each person's life. Neglected parts of the self (talents, desires, aspirations) seek expression.
Entering middle adulthood	45 to 50	Choices must be made, a new life structure formed. Person must commit to new tasks.

Source: Levinson, 1978.

Anyone You Know? Daniel Levinson proposed that all men go through the stages and transitions listed here. Other researchers find that relatively few men have a midlife transition.

had major life changes at approximately ages 20, 30, and 40 and that further transitions occurred every five years or so (Levinson, 1978) (see Table 19.1).

However, in the twenty-first century, matching particular ages with particular stages of development appears to be a somewhat limited approach. These theories now appear narrow, insensitive, and perhaps even racist and sexist. Researchers now recognize that adult lives "are less orderly and predictable than stage models suggest" (McAdams & de St. Aubin, 1998) and that "adulthood is less definable and less easily attained than it was" (Furstenberg et al., 2002, p. 13).

The Social Clock

As research has moved beyond stage models, it has become clear that even the biological clock that measures physical aging is influenced by medical care, lifestyle, and perceptions, both personal and cultural, as well as by the passage of time (Hartup, 2002; Staudinger & Bluck, 2001).

Even more variable is the **social clock,** a timetable for various events and endeavors that is based on social norms (Neugarten & Neugarten, 1986). These norms establish "best" ages for such milestones as becoming independent of one's parents, finishing school, establishing a career, and having children (Keith, 1990; Settersten & Hagestad, 1996).

Cross-culturally, social-clock norms vary both in scope and in rigidity. In many nations, there are legal ages for driving, drinking, voting, getting married, and signing a mortgage. There are also expected ages for marriage, first baby, completion of childbearing, grandparenthood, and so on. The specific ages vary by cohort, culture, region, and gender. For example, in some South American countries, marriage is legal at age 12 for women and 14 for men; more than half of all brides in Brazil, Ecuador, Paraguay, and Venezuela are under age 22. By contrast, men and women in Germany cannot legally marry until they are at least 18; most wait much longer, the median age of marriage being 27 for women and 31 for men (EuroStat, 2002). In the United States in the 1950s, a woman was expected to begin having children at about age 19. In the late twentieth and early twenty-first century, first births after age 30 are not unusual. Indeed, the number

social clock Refers to the idea that the stages of life, and the behaviors "appropriate" to them, are set by social standards rather than by biological maturation. For instance, "middle age" begins when the culture believes it does, rather than at a particular age in all cultures.

ROGER DOLLARHIDE
SALLY CASSIDY

? *Observational Quiz* (see answer, page 464): Although these pairs are separated by 6,000 miles and at least 30 years, they display two similarities that are universal to close relationships of every kind. What are they?

Resetting the Social Clock Social-clock settings in developed nations tend to be notably different from those in developing nations. In developed countries, for example, the social clock now permits grandmothers to be college graduates *(left)* and discourages teenagers from becoming mothers. This is in marked contrast to developing nations such as Indonesia, where grandmothers never go to college and many young teenagers, like this Javanese girl *(right)* become mothers.

of women having their first baby at age 30 or older doubled between 1980 and 2000 (U.S. Bureau of the Census, 2002).

Beyond national norms, a primary influence on the social clock is socioeconomic status (SES): The lower the SES, the sooner people are expected to reach life's major milestones. Women from low-SES families are pressured to finish childbearing by age 30, while high-SES women are allowed another decade or so (see Table 19.2).

The variation in the speed of the social clock should not obscure a larger truth: Although cultures, cohorts, and individuals differ as to exactly when various events of adulthood are expected to occur, the needs for intimacy and generativity are universal. Generally, sometime between ages 20 and 35, adults establish lifelong friendships, commit to a partner (both intimacy examples), become a parent, and begin a career (both generativity examples).

TABLE 19.2 Expected Age for a Woman to . . .

	Low SES	High SES
Finish school	18 (high school)	30 (graduate degree)
Marry	18	32
Have first baby	19	34
Have last baby before	30 (3–4 children)	40 (2 children)
Be employed full time	20–50	30–60
Become grandmother	40	65
Be an old lady	55	75

Isn't It Time? Like all social-clock norms, these are approximate, based on expectations for women in North America through much of the twentieth century.

A Woman Now Two young girls participate in the traditional coming-of-age ceremony in Japan. Their kimonos and hairstyles are elaborate and traditional, as is the sake (rice wine) they drink. This is part of the ceremony signifying passage from girlhood to womanhood.

? *Observational Quiz* (see answer, page 466): At what age do you think this event occurs in Japan—15, 16, 18, or 20?

AP / WIDE WORLD PHOTOS

! *Answer to Observational Quiz* (from page 463): Physical touching (note their hands) and physical synchrony (note their bodies leaning toward each other).

Throughout the world, adult psychosocial development progresses along divergent paths. Theories of adult development vary as well. One cluster of theories attempted to describe stages of development, focusing primarily on a homogeneous elite society in the United States in the 1950s. However, as more age groups, populations, and cultures are studied by researchers of various backgrounds, variations lead today's developmentalists to emphasize the social clock rather than the chronological one. Every culture expects life's milestones—marriage, childbirth, career advancement, retirement—to occur by a particular age, but the specific ages depend more on cohort, gender, subgroup, and SES than on birthdays.

Some human needs are universal, including the need to love and to work or, using Erikson's terminology, to achieve intimacy and generativity. Although universal, these goals are accomplished in many ways throughout adulthood, as we will now begin to describe.

Intimacy

To meet the need for intimacy (a sense of affiliation, affection, interdependence, communion, belonging, love), an adult may become a friend, lover, spouse, or all three. These various intimate relationships have much in common—not only the psychic needs they satisfy, but also the behavior they require. They all involve a progression, from initial attraction to close connection and then ongoing commitment. Each role demands some personal sacrifice, an openness and vulnerability that bring deeper self-understanding and shatter the isolation caused by too much self-protection. Each role has the potential for giving and receiving care; adults learn to depend on their intimates for social support, for "true friendship." As Erikson explains, to establish intimacy, the young adult must

> face the fear of ego loss in situations which call for self-abandon: in the solidarity of close affiliations [and] sexual unions, in close friendship and in physical combat, in experiences of inspiration by teachers and of intuition from the recesses of the self. The avoidance of such experiences . . . may lead to a deep sense of isolation and consequent self-absorption.
>
> *[Erikson, 1963, pp. 163–164]*

Two primary sources of intimacy are discussed here: close friendship and romantic partnership. (A third source, family ties across the generations, is discussed in Chapter 22.)

Friendship

Throughout life, friends are even better than family members to buffer against stress, to guide toward self-awareness, and to provide joy (Bukowski et al., 1996; Pahl & Spencer, 1997). Personal choice is one reason. Siblings, cousins, parents, and children are ours by accident of birth, but we choose our friends for the very qualities (understanding, tolerance, loyalty, affection, humor) that make them good companions, trustworthy confidants, and reliable sources of support.

The fact that friendship ties are voluntary (in contrast to family obligations) makes having friends a sign of personal worthiness. We earn our friends, and they choose us; no wonder having close friends is positively correlated with happiness and self-esteem.

Choosing Young-Adult Friends

Although family is always important, friendships, new and old, are particularly crucial for contemporary young adults. Today's young adults postpone marriage and parenthood and rarely provide extensive care for older relatives (who are usually quite independent until age 80 or so), so that young adults are free to enter many social arenas. In college, work, and neighborhood, each young adult can find acquaintances who provide companionship, information, advice, and sympathy. But what moves acquaintanceship forward to become friendship? For establishing any intimate relationship, four factors act as **gateways to attraction** (Fehr, 1996):

- Physical attractiveness (even in platonic same-sex relationships)
- Apparent availability (willingness to chat, to do things together)
- Absence of "exclusion criteria" (no unacceptable characteristics)
- Frequent exposure

> **gateways to attraction** The various qualities, such as appearance and proximity, that are prerequisites for the formation of close friendships and intimate relationships.

The first two factors on this list are straightforward. People throughout the centuries have been attracted to others who are good-looking and seem interested in them. That is, worldwide, perhaps for evolutionary reasons, people look for friends and partners who appear healthy and strong, and people choose companions who have time for them.

The third factor, **exclusion criteria**, is noteworthy for its variability, in that one person's reason for shunning another is insignificant to someone else. For example, religion or politics does not matter to some people, whereas other people would never befriend someone who was not, say, a fundamentalist Christian or a devout Muslim or a political liberal. Some people exclude anyone who, say, smokes cigarettes or is homosexual or whom they feel is stupid, fat, or old; others do not care about these characteristics. Exclusion criteria do not necessarily indicate intolerance. In fact, most young people appreciate diversity, value tolerance, and accept a wide variety of human choices. However, when it comes to close confidants, most people have two or three filters that screen out certain people.

> **exclusion criteria** A person's reasons for omitting certain people from consideration as close friends or partners. Exclusion criteria vary from one individual to another, but they are strong filters.

Finally, the fourth factor, exposure, is surprisingly powerful. Lifelong friends from college are more likely to be those who chanced to sit next to each other in class rather than a few seats away or who lived on the same dorm floor rather than one floor above. Work acquaintances more often become friends if they happen to ride the same bus home day after day.

Gender Differences in Friendships

In friendships, men and women tend to differ in what they do, say, and feel (Fehr, 1996). Men friends share activities and interests; women friends are more intimate and emotional, providing shared confidences and practical assistance. Female friends engage in self-disclosing talk, revealing secrets from their past,

Such Good Friends Friendship patterns vary from person to person, and gender stereotypes regarding these patterns are often wide of the mark. Nonetheless, friendships between men tend to take a different direction from that taken by friendships between women. Men typically do things together—with outdoor activities frequently preferred, especially if they lend themselves to showing off and friendly bragging. Women, in contrast, tend to spend more time in intimate conversation, perhaps commiserating about their problems rather than calling attention to their accomplishments.

?Observational Quiz (see answer, page 468): What have the young men at right just accomplished?

Especially for Young Men Why would you want at least one close friend who is a woman?

!Answer to Observational Quiz (from page 464): The most obvious clue—that the girls look like teenagers—is misleading. Remembering that the social clock is slower in developed nations and that Asian adolescents mature relatively late, you might accurately guess age 20, five years after Quinzeaña, the similar Latina occasion, and four years after the European-American "Sweet Sixteen."

health problems, and difficulties with their romances or relatives. Male friends talk more about external matters—sports, work, politics, cars—and conversation is typically peripheral to some shared activity.

As a result of these gender differences, men and women have different expectations (Fehr, 1996). Women expect to reveal their weaknesses and problems to friends and to receive an attentive and sympathetic ear and, if necessary, a shoulder to cry on. Men are less likely to talk about their weaknesses and problems, but, when they do discuss them, they expect practical advice rather than sympathy (Tannen, 1990).

Ironically, the most open expressions of affection between men tend to occur in situations where they are banded together in the name of aggression, such as competitive athletics or military combat—perhaps because these are situations in which few people would question a man's masculinity. The butt-slapping or body-slamming that follows a sports victory, or the sobbing in a buddy's arms that follows a battlefield loss, rarely occur in everyday male friendships.

Of course, friendships are not always between people of the same sex. In part because of the differences discussed above, cross-sex friendships pose special problems. For example, a woman might be genuinely upset by good-natured teasing (the kind her male friend exchanges with his male friends), while a man might be frustrated that his female friend continues to talk about her problems rather than taking his advice on how to solve them. An additional complicating factor is that cross-sex friendships, especially in young adulthood, are both "enriched and plagued by fluctuating and unclear sexual boundaries" (Swain, 1992).

Which pattern of friendship is best for meeting intimacy needs? The typical female–female friendship pattern may be better in reducing loneliness and self-absorption, and the male–male pattern of keeping emotional distance may be the most effective and efficient, especially at work (Rawlins, 1992). Perhaps the best solution is close friendships of various kinds, each meeting different needs, as most young adults have.

The Development of Love

The effort to find one partner, one "significant other," one person with whom to bond throughout life is a highly complex undertaking. People sometimes talk and act as though love between two adults were a simple, universally understood experience—as though the Beatles lyric "All you need is love" said it all. In fact, however, personal preferences, mutual interactions, developmental stages, gender differences, socioeconomic forces, and historical and cultural context all make love complex and often confusing.

TABLE 19.3 Qualities Preferred in a Romantic Partner

		European-American	African-American	Jamaican	Japanese
Men	1.	Trust	Honesty	Love	Beauty
	2.	Friendship	Patience	Trust	Cooking ability
	3.	Love	Trust	Caring	Kindness
	4.	Honesty	Understanding	Communication	Youth
Women	1.	Trust	Communication	Truth	Love
	2.	Friendship	Love	Love	Wealth
	3.	Love	Honesty	Honesty	Fun
	4.	Honesty	Trust	Respect	Honesty

Source: Nicotera, 1997.

This complexity is seen in a study of the qualities young adults seek from a partner in a romantic relationship (Nicotera, 1997). College students from four ethnic groups ranked their preferences as shown in Table 19.3. Obviously, men and women from another culture or at an older age might give rankings different from those shown in the table. However, the differences make it clear why, for example, a young Jamaican woman might be furious if her Japanese boyfriend lied to her, but he might accuse her of making too much of that—especially if he adores and appreciates her in many other ways.

Clearly, culture profoundly influences our expectations and perceptions. Some young adults might see themselves as exemplary romantic partners and be dumbfounded if conflicts arise (Nicotera, 1997) between them and their mate of another ethnic group.

The Dimensions of Love

Robert Sternberg (1988) describes three distinct aspects of love—passion, intimacy, and commitment—that often occur in a developmental progression. Passion is strong at the beginning of a relationship, joined by intimacy and then by commitment if the relationship endures. Sternberg believes that the relative presence or absence of these three components gives rise to seven different forms of love (see Table 19.4).

Early in a relationship, passion is evident in "falling in love," an intense physical, cognitive, and emotional onslaught characterized by excitement, ecstasy, and euphoria. Such moonstruck joy is often bittersweet, because passion and intimacy are not the same. As one observer explains, "Falling in love is absolutely

TABLE 19.4 Sternberg's Seven Forms of Love

	Present in the Relationship?		
Form of Love	**Passion**	**Intimacy**	**Commitment**
Liking	No	Yes	No
Infatuation	Yes	No	No
Empty love	No	No	Yes
Romantic love	Yes	Yes	No
Fatuous love	Yes	No	Yes
Companionate love	No	Yes	Yes
Consummate love	Yes	Yes	Yes

Source: Sternberg, 1988.

SONDA DAWES / THE IMAGE WORKS

Intimacy Shared laughter and overlapping legs, at midday in a public place, are universal indications of a couple who know each other well and enjoy their relationship. This couple is in San Sebastian, Spain, but they could be in any European or North American country.

Response for Young Men (from page 466): Not for sex! Women friends are particularly responsive to deep conversations about family relationships, personal weaknesses, and emotional confusion. But women friends might be offended by sexual advances, bragging, or advice-giving. Save these for a potential romance.

! *Answer to Observational Quiz* (from page 466): A day-long bike trek up and down a mountain. Among the clues are backpacks, long shorts, sunglasses, smiles, and setting sun. The setting— Aspen Mountain, Colorado—is harder to guess.

no way of getting to know someone. With good fortune that will come later, but in its early iridescent days love is a blind bewitchment which may or may not turn out for the best" (Sullivan, 1999, p. 225).

Commitment takes even longer. It grows through a series of day-to-day decisions to spend time together, to care for each other, to share possessions, and to overcome problems even when that involves some personal sacrifice. Devotion and mutual dependence are traits of commitment (Aron & Westbay, 1996).

The Western ideal is consummate love, which is characterized by the presence of all three components: passion, intimacy, and commitment. This ideal combines "the view of love promulgated in the movies . . . [and the] more prosaic conceptions of love rooted in daily and long-lived experience" (Gerstel, 2002, p. 555).

For developmental reasons, this ideal is difficult to achieve. Passion is fueled by unfamiliarity, unexpectedness, uncertainty, and risk, all of which are diminished by the growing familiarity and security that contribute to intimacy and by the time needed to demonstrate commitment.

As lovers get used to their physical relationship, maintaining the same level of arousal requires increasing degrees of physical, psychological, and fantasy stimulation. In the same way, early in a relationship, the simplest shared confidence can trigger a rush of feelings of trust, but once a certain level of intimacy is taken for granted, deeper sharing is required to promote similarly intense feelings of togetherness. In other words, with time, passion tends to fade and intimacy tends to grow and then stabilize, while commitment develops. This developmental pattern is true over the years for all types of couples—married, unmarried, and remarried; heterosexual and homosexual; young and old (Ganong & Coleman, 1994; Kurdek, 1992).

Contact and Courtship

Worldwide throughout history, marriages were commonly arranged by the parents of the bride and groom. Sometimes the future spouses had no contact until the wedding day; sometimes the future partners met a few times to undertake a formal courtship (during which it was possible, but unlikely, for either one to void the agreement); sometimes a prospective groom would present himself to the bride's father (often with a "bride price" of goods and animals), asking for the bride. When "romantic love" appeared, it was not considered an appropriate prelude to a marriage commitment or even to an intimate relationship, except by naive teenagers, as memorialized in Shakespeare's *Romeo and Juliet.*

Arranged marriages are still common today in many nations and among certain cultures in North America. Young adults sometimes prefer parental arrangements over finding, courting, and wooing their own spouse. The groom "popping the question," the contrasting bridal shower and bachelor party, and the father "giving away" the bride are all enduring traditions from an earlier era when marriages were arranged. Because passionate love is unpredictable, excited by novelty and danger, it may never arise in an arranged marriage. But arranged marriages are high in commitment and seldom end in divorce. In other words, in such situations, commitment is a given; passion and intimacy are not.

For most readers of this book, the pattern of contact and courtship is initiated and sustained by the two people most directly involved. The process usually begins in adolescence and often involves an intimate sexual partnership (Teitler, 2002). Most of these early relationships soon end and new relationships form. Their duration and seriousness increase until couples marry, typically about 10 years after their first love affair.

The four gateways to attraction, explained earlier in the context of friendship, are even more important in romance. This explains why unattached young people strive to be physically attractive (perhaps spending hours exercising at the gym and shopping for clothes, cosmetics, and various other products), attempt to signal their availability, and rely on a network of friends who understand their exclusion criteria.

Once contact is made and a relationship begins, courtship follows a predictable pattern, designed to move from passion to intimacy. The couple spends more time together, sharing experiences, secrets, and emotional interactions. Sexual attraction is generally a crucial part of the process but is seldom the reason for marriage (or divorce). As one author explains, "Sex and love drift in and out of each other's territories and their foggy frontiers cannot be rigidly staked out. . . . Although lust does not contain love, love contains lust" (Sullivan, 1999, pp. 95–96).

Living Together

Many couples live together without being formally married; such an arrangement is called **cohabitation.** (Seltzer, 2000). Cohabitation is not just for the young who are exploring the possibility of marriage. In some places, including Sweden, Jamaica, and Puerto Rico, cohabitation is the norm throughout adulthood. In others, including Japan, Ireland, and Italy, less than 10 percent of all adults have *ever* cohabited (Batalova & Cohen, 2002).

Slightly more than half of all women aged 25 to 40 in the United States have cohabited, as have many young adults in Canada, Northern Europe, England, and Australia. Cohabitation is less common in Southern Europe, where young people typically live with their parents until they are ready for marriage and parenthood (Iacovou, 2002).

In North America, middle-aged and older adults who are divorced or widowed sometimes cohabit, not as a prelude to marriage but as an alternative to it. However, in this chapter we explore cohabitation among young adults who hope to marry (Smock, 2000). Compared with couples who are involved in a steady romantic relationship but not living together, cohabiters are more likely to anticipate getting married and less likely to consider marriage a major change. They do not think marriage will markedly change the quality of their lives, emotionally or financially (McGinnis, 2003), partly because cohabitation prepares them for it. They are mistaken.

Despite its popularity, researchers find that cohabitation does not necessarily benefit the participants, either while they are cohabiting or after they get married. A study of 18,000 adults in 17 nations found that cohabitants were much less happy, less healthy, and less satisfied with their financial status than married people were. In this research, cohabitants were slightly happier than single, never-married adults (Stack & Eshleman, 1998).

Two other studies, each using a specific longitudinal sample, suggest that cohabitation increases stress. One, which focused on 25- to 31-year-olds in New Jersey, found that compared with single adults, cohabitants were much more likely to have serious problems with alcohol, especially if they were young men who felt pressure to marry but were financially unable to do so (Horwitz & White, 1998). The other study, which looked at a cohort of 21-year-olds in New Zealand, found that physical abuse was three times more common among cohabitants than among either dating or married peers (Maydol et al., 1998). This contrast with the dating couples held true even when a dozen possibly confounding background or demographic factors (such as income and education) were taken into account.

Contrary to widespread belief, cohabitation is not like marriage, which is a social institution. Living together before marriage does not seem to solve the problems that might arise after marriage—quite the opposite (Cohen & Kleinbaum, 2002; Kamp Dush et al., 2003).

AP / WIDE WORLD PHOTOS

Mail-Order Bride He was looking for a woman with green eyes and reddish hair, and without strong religious convictions—his particular exclusion criteria, which he posted on the World Wide Web. That led to an email courtship and eventually marriage to "the girl of my dreams."

cohabitation An arrangement in which a man and a woman live together in a committed sexual relationship but are not formally married.

Marriage

Marriage is not what it once was—a legal and religious arrangement sought as the *exclusive* avenue for sexual expression, the *only* legitimate prelude for child-bearing, and a *lifelong* source of intimacy and support. Here are some U.S. statistics that make this point:

- The proportion of adults who are unmarried is higher than at any time in the past century.
- Only 10 percent of brides are virgins.
- Nearly one-half of all first births are to single mothers, who are increasingly unlikely to marry the fathers of their babies.
- At least another 20 percent of all first births are conceived before marriage.
- The divorce rate is 49 percent of the marriage rate.
- The rate of first marriages in young adulthood is the lowest in 50 years (Bachu, 1999; Zavodny, 1999). Most adults aged 20 to 30 are not yet married (62 percent) (U.S. Bureau of the Census, 2002).

Low marriage rates in young adulthood are by no means limited to the United States: Adults in many developed countries now spend, on average, half of the years between ages 20 and 40 unmarried, with men less likely to marry before age 30 than women (Iacovou, 2002).

Nevertheless, marriage remains a personal as well as public commitment, celebrated in every culture of the world by a ceremony with special words, clothes, blessings, food, drink, and often many guests and great expense. The hoped-for outcome is a love that deepens over the years as the couple's bond is cemented by bearing and raising children, weathering economic and emotional turbulence, surviving serious illness or other setbacks, and sharing social and financial commitments.

Research from all over the world finds that married people are happier, healthier, and richer (Stack & Eshleman, 1998). Although gender roles have changed over the years, U.S. couples in 2000 rated their marriages as satisfying as did couples in 1980 (Amato et al., 2003). Let's look at some ingredients of that satisfaction.

What Makes Marriages Work

From a developmental perspective, marriage is a useful institution: Children generally thrive when two parents are directly committed to their well-being, and adults thrive if one other person satisfies their need for intimacy and for generativity. Yet, clearly, not all marriages accomplish these goals. Why do some marriages work well, while others do not? Some specific sources of marital difficulty are listed in Table 19.5 (on page 472).

One developmental factor that influences the success of a marriage is the maturity of the partners. In general, the younger the bride and groom, the less likely their marriage is to succeed (Amato et al., 2003). That may be because, as Erikson pointed out, intimacy is hard to establish until identity is secure. Thus, in a series of studies, college students who were less advanced on Erikson's identity and intimacy stages tended to define love in terms of passion, not intimacy or commitment—butterflies and excitement, not openness, trust, and loyalty (Aron & Westbay, 1996).

A second influence on marital success is the degree of similarity between husband and wife. Anthropologists distinguish between **homogamy**, or marriage within the same tribe or ethnic group, and **heterogamy**, or marriage outside the group. Traditionally, homogamy meant marriage between people of the same cohort, religion, socioeconomic status, ethnicity, and education. For contemporary marriages, homogamy and heterogamy refer to similarity in interests, attitudes, and goals (Cramer, 1998).

Especially for Social Scientists Suppose your 30-year-old Canadian friend, never married, says, "Look at the statistics. If I marry now, there is a 50/50 chance I will get divorced." What three statistical facts, found in the next few pages, allow you to insist, "Your odds of divorce are much lower"?

homogamy Defined by developmentalists as marriage between individuals who tend to be similar with respect to such variables as attitudes, interests, goals, socioeconomic status, religion, ethnic background, and local origin.

heterogamy Defined by developmentalists as marriage between individuals who tend to be dissimilar with respect to such variables as attitudes, interests, goals, socioeconomic status, religion, ethnic background, and local origin.

One study of 168 young couples found that **social homogamy,** defined as similarity in leisure interests and role preferences, is particularly important to marital success (Houts et al., 1996). For instance, if both spouses enjoyed (or hated) picnicking, dancing, swimming, going to the movies, listening to music, eating out, or entertaining friends, the partners tended to be more "in love" and more committed to the relationship. Similarly, if the two agreed on who should make meals, pay bills, shop for groceries, and so on, then ambivalence and conflict were reduced.

The authors of this study do not believe that "finding a mate compatible on many dimensions is an achievable goal." In reality, "individuals who are seeking a compatible mate must make many compromises if they are to marry at all" (Houts et al., 1996). They found that, for any young adult, fewer than 1 in 100 potential mates provides minimal social homogamy, defined as sharing three favorite leisure activities and three role preferences. Most successful couples learn to compromise, adjust, or agree to disagree about many things.

A third factor affecting the success of a marriage is *marital equity,* the extent to which the two partners perceive a rough equality in the partnership. According to **social exchange theory,** marriage is an arrangement in which each person contributes something useful to the other (Edwards, 1969). Historically, the two sexes traded gender-specific commodities: Men provided social status and financial security, while women provided homemaking, sex, and children (Townsend, 1998).

In many modern marriages, the equity that is sought is not an exchange but rather shared contributions of a similar kind: Instead of husbands earning all the money and wives doing all the domestic work, both are now expected to do both. Similarly, both partners expect equality and sensitivity to their needs regarding dependence, sexual desire, shared confidences, and so on, and happier marriages are those in which both partners are adept at emotional perception and expression (Fitness, 2001). Evidence for the new form of exchanges is that over the past few decades wives have begun earning more money and husbands have begun doing more housework—with the result that overall marital satisfaction has improved (Amato et al., 2003) What matters most, however, is the perception of fairness, not absolute equality (Sanchez, 1994; Wilkie et al., 1998).

social homogamy The similarity of a couple's leisure interests and role preferences.

social exchange theory The view that social behavior is a process of exchange aimed at maximizing the benefits one receives and minimizing the costs one pays.

Sorting Things Out The kind of gender equality shown here makes wars between the sexes less likely in the future. Note that the girl is showing the boy something on the computer—an example of twenty-first-century androgyny.

BLAIR SEITZ / PHOTO RESEARCHERS

TABLE 19.5 Factors That Make Divorce More Likely

Before marriage

Parents were divorced

Either partner is under age 21

Family is opposed

Cohabitation before marriage

Previous divorce of either partner

Large discrepancy in age, background, interests, values (heterogamy)

During marriage

Divergent plans and practices regarding childbearing and child rearing

Financial stress, unemployment

Communication difficulties

Lack of time together

Emotional or physical abuse

In the culture

High divorce rate of others in cohort

Lack of strong religious values

Laws that make divorce easier

Response for Social Scientists (from page 470): First, no other nation has a divorce rate as high as the United States. Second, even the 50/50 divorce rate in the United States comes from dividing the number of divorces by the number of marriages. Because some people get married and divorced many times, that minority provides data that drives up the ratio and skews the average. (Actually, even in the United States, only one *first* marriage in three—not one in two—ends in divorce.) Finally, because you have read that teenage marriages are especially likely to end, you can deduce that older brides and grooms are less likely to divorce. The odds of your friend getting divorced are only one in five, as long as the couple has established a fair degree of social homogamy.

Same-Sex Partners

Long-term gay or lesbian partnerships, once hidden, are now more open and visible. An estimated 2 to 5 percent of all adults in the United States are involved in such a relationship at some point (Laumann et al., 1994). Recent court decisions in the United States have confirmed that sexual behavior between adults is a private matter. However, most governments still do not legally recognize same-sex marriages or the less official arrangements known as civil unions. Among the exceptions are Belgium, the Netherlands, Canada, and several states in the United States.

In general, homosexual couples have the same relationship issues as heterosexual couples. Passion is no guarantee of intimacy, and relationship quality and acceptance by friends and families affect their satisfaction and commitment over the years (Kurdek, 1998). More and more gay and lesbian couples are becoming parents, with emotional complications for some of the parents but with no negative effects on the children (Allen & Burrell, 2002; Glazer & Drescher, 2001; Shanley, 2001).

Divorce

Throughout this text, we have recognized that many developmental events that seem isolated, personal, and transitory are actually interconnected, socially mediated, and enduring in their consequences. Divorce is a prime example. Marriages do not end in a social vacuum but rather are influenced by factors in the overall social and political context, and the end of a marriage affects the lives of many people for years (Cott, 2000). Indeed, recent research suggests that older adults—and their grandchildren—can still be affected by a breakup decades earlier (King, 2003).

The power of the social context is evident in international variations in divorce rates. In the United States, almost one out of every two first marriages ends in divorce, the highest rate in the world. Many other industrialized countries (including Canada, Sweden, Great Britain, and Australia) have a divorce rate of about one in three, while in others (including Japan, Italy, Israel, and Spain) fewer than one in five marriages end in divorce.

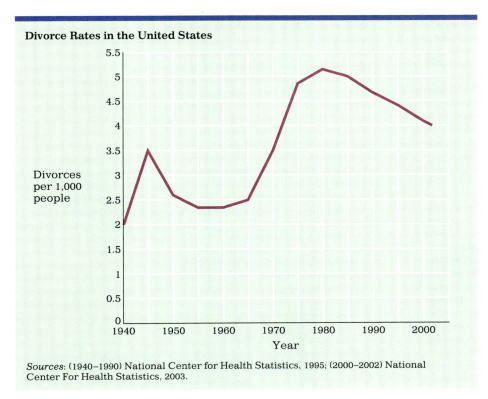

Divorce Rates in the United States

Sources: (1940–1990) National Center for Health Statistics, 1995; (2000–2002) National Center For Health Statistics, 2003.

FIGURE 19.2 Divorce Rates Still High The divorce rate has been declining in recent years in the United States. Still, almost 50 percent of first marriages that take place today will end in divorce. One reason for the lower divorce rate is a lower marriage rate.

Historical variations are even more marked than national ones. In many countries, divorce rates increased over most of the past 50 years but have stabilized recently. In England, for example, the divorce rate more than doubled between 1970 and 1980 but has increased by less than 10 percent over the last 25 years. In the Netherlands, the rate of divorce tripled between 1970 and 1992 and then leveled off. In the United States, a rapid increase that began in the 1970s reached a high of 5.2 divorces per 1,000 people in 1980 and has declined slightly since then (see Figure 19.2).

The Role of Expectations

Social scientists of various backgrounds have divergent explanations for the high divorce rate in the United States (Thompson & Wyatt, 1999). One set of explanations comes from economists, who point to low income for young men (reducing the marriage rate) and higher employment for women (increasing the divorce rate).

Many developmentalists believe that an underlying explanation is a cognitive shift that has led people to expect more from their marriage partner than they did in the past (Glenn, 1999). In earlier decades, women had to cook, clean, and raise children, while men had to provide the income; in this exchange, each depended on the other. Today, expectations are much broader—and not always as well defined; marriage partners expect each other to be friends, lovers, and confidants as well as wage earners and caregivers (Cramer, 1998). Ironically, although couples today expect more from a relationship than couples once did, and more equity is apparent, they spend less time together and interact less than couples once did (Amato et al., 2003). Expectations are one reason young adults are marrying later than they once did, as I have learned from my own experience.

In Person

Romance and Reality: Changing Expectations

Cohort changes in patterns of intimacy reassure me. I married late (age 25) for my cohort, and had children even later (two by age 30, another two by age 40). Now I have three daughters older than 25, all wonderful women who are not yet wives or mothers. I listen very carefully to what my students have to say about love and marriage. I note that their expectations usually change over time. One student, Kerri, wrote:

> All young girls have their perfect guy in mind, their Prince Charming. For me he will be tall, dark, and handsome. He will be well-educated and have a career with a strong future, . . . a great personality, and the same sense of humor as I do. I'm not sure I can do much to ensure that I meet my soul mate. I believe that is what is implied by the term *soul mate;* you will meet them no matter what you do. Part of me is hoping this is true, but another part tells me the idea of soul mates is just a fable.

Her classmate, Chelsey, of a similar age and background, wrote:

> I dreamt of being married. The husband didn't matter specifically, as long as he was rich and famous and I had a long, off-the-shoulder wedding dress. Thankfully, my views since

then have changed. . . . I have a fantastic boyfriend of almost two years who I could see myself marrying, as we are extremely compatible. Although we are different, we have mastered . . . communication and compromise. . . . I think I will be able to cope with the trials and tribulations life brings.

Kerri is already becoming more mature in her thinking about romantic relationships. She uses *Prince Charming* and *fable* to express her awareness that these ideas may be childish. I am glad she is not already married; her youthful expectations might lead to disillusionment and divorce.

Chelsey seems wiser than Kerri. Why? One obvious reason is that Chelsey is involved in a long-term relationship, which usually teaches both partners about intimacy and commitment. Chelsey may have another advantage: Her parents had a bitter divorce. Divorce often impairs children's development, but a divorce that ends years of hostility may be beneficial to the children, not only making their day-to-day lives easier but also giving them wisdom. This is speculation when it comes to individuals, of course. In any case, maturation dramatically affects people's expectations about love and marriage and about their ability to form supportive intimate relationships.

The Developmental Impact of Divorce

Initially, divorce is usually worse than anticipated for all family members in almost every way—health, happiness, self-esteem, financial stability, social interaction, and achievement (Hetherington & Kelly, 2002). The stress of a breakup is greater the longer a couple was together, the more intimate they once were, and the more commitments they shared (such as joint property, mutual friends, and, most important, children).

There are three reasons why problems are worse than anticipated, all of which are related to intimacy. First, unhappy spouses focus on what is missing from their marriage and are "hardly aware of needs currently being well served" (Glenn, 1991). Thus, when they do separate, they lose benefits they didn't realize they had. Second, emotional entanglement is almost inevitable: Feuding as well as friendly ex-partners experience ongoing currents of emotion (hate, love, resentment, jealousy) after the breakup (Madden-Derdich & Arditti, 1999). Third, friends, relatives, and the couple's children often behave unpredictably and badly, creating new problems instead of providing the social support that ex-spouses need.

Indeed, the social circle usually shrinks: The couple's friends and in-laws find it difficult to remain on good terms with them after they divorce; neighborhood friends are lost when one or both spouses move away; casual friends and coworkers distance themselves if a colleague becomes emotionally needy. Given all this, it is not surprising that newly divorced people are prone to loneliness, disequilibrium, promiscuous sexual behavior, drug and alcohol abuse, and erratic eating, sleeping, and working behavior. Surveys from many nations find that single divorced adults are less happy with their lives, not only compared to married people but also compared to never-married or widowed adults of the same age (Stack & Eshleman, 1998).

These statements are true for some divorced people but not all of them. As one expert has observed:

> The increase in marital instability has not brought society to the brink of chaos, but neither has it led to a golden age of freedom and self-actualization. Divorce benefits some individuals, leads others to experience temporary decrements in well-being, . . . and forces others on a downward cycle.
>
> *[Amato, 2000]*

Domestic Violence

Violence in intimate relationships is quite common. Surveys in the United States and Canada find that each year, about 12 percent of all spouses push, grab, shove, or slap their partner at least once and that between 1 and 3 percent use more extreme measures: hitting, kicking, beating up, or threatening with a knife or a gun (Dutton, 1992; Straus & Gelles, 1995). Abuse is especially common among cohabiting young couples, whether heterosexual, gay, or lesbian. Most studies show that women are as likely as men to abuse their partners, but men are more likely to cause physical injury. (Anderson, 2002; Archer, 2000).

Why do people who love each other also hurt each other? Many contributing factors have been identified, including social pressures that create stress, cultural values that condone violence, personality pathologies (such as poor impulse control), and drug and alcohol addiction. From a developmental perspective, one critical factor is a history of maltreatment in childhood. Children who are harshly punished, who are sexually abused, or who witness regular spousal assault are at risk for both becoming an abuser and becoming a victim (Heyman & Slep, 2002).

Spouse abuse occurs in two forms: common couple violence and intimate terrorism. Each form has its own distinct causes and patterns of development (Johnson & Ferraro, 2000).

Common Couple Violence

Common couple violence is characterized by mutual outbursts of yelling, insults, and attack. Often, both partners suffer from depression, abuse substances, and punish their children. In many cultural groups, some interspousal violence is acceptable, or at least not rare. For example, one cross-sectional survey of Canadian women found that 11 percent experienced occasional interpersonal conflict—the intermittent outbursts characteristic of common violence—but not systematic abuse (MacMillan & Gartner, 1999).

common couple violence A form of abuse in which one or both partners of a couple engage in outbursts of verbal and physical attack.

Intimate Terrorism

Intimate terrorism (Johnson & Ferraro, 2000) occurs when one partner, almost always the man, systematically isolates, degrades, and punishes the other. Intimate terrorism leads to the *battered-wife syndrome,* with the woman not only beaten but also psychologically and socially broken, increasingly vulnerable to permanent injury and death. This cycle of violence and submission feeds on itself, because each act that renders the wife helpless adds to the man's feeling of control and the woman's feeling that she cannot, must not, fight back.

intimate terrorism Spouse abuse in which, most often, the husband uses violent methods of accelerating intensity to isolate, degrade, and punish the wife.

This type of abusive pattern is less prevalent than common couple violence, and the perpetrator is usually antisocial and violent in many ways (Johnson & Ferraro, 2000). In the Canadian study mentioned earlier, less than 2 percent of the women experienced this "qualitatively different" type of systematic abuse. These women were also more likely to experience coercive control, agreeing to statements such as the following (MacMillan & Gartner, 1999):

■ Partner is jealous and doesn't want you to talk to other men.
■ Partner tries to limit your contact with family and friends.
■ Partner insists on knowing who you are with and where you are at all times.

It is the violent control of one partner by the other that is the key difference between common couple violence and intimate terrorism.

> Particularly in early adulthood, people seek friends and romantic partners. The initial gateways to attraction are appearance, availability, acceptability of basic traits, and exposure. Young adults typically have many friends, mostly of their own sex but also some of the other sex, and they spend time talking and sharing secrets (especially women) and doing things together (especially men).
>
> Love includes three aspects: passion, intimacy, and commitment. Commitment is expressed publicly in marriage, an institution that exists in every culture.
>
> Marriage is less common and occurs later in adulthood than it once did: In many developed nations, half the young adults are not married. Living together before marriage does not necessarily make a marriage stronger. Contemporary marriages seem to benefit from social homogamy, from equity in roles and tasks, and from the maturity of the partners. Divorce is never easy, particularly because marriage meets intimacy needs, although some relationships are clearly destructive.

Generativity

The motivation to achieve—or the drive to be generative—is a powerful theme of adulthood. The expression of generativity varies with personality, culture, gender, and cohort.

Generativity is achieved primarily through employment and parenthood. The crucial factor is the adult's feeling that he or she is accomplishing something; that the day-by-day repetition of punching a clock, washing a child's dirty face, sending completed work to a boss, or folding the laundry is part of a bigger plan. Then evidence of accomplishment leads not only to pride in work well done but also to self-esteem and mental health.

The Importance of Work

From a developmental perspective, a paycheck is only one of many possible benefits of employment. Work provides a structure for daily life, a setting for human interaction, a source of status and fulfillment (Wethington, 2002). Work can satisfy generativity needs by allowing people to do the following:

■ Develop and use their personal skills
■ Express their creative energy
■ Aid and advise coworkers, as a mentor or friend
■ Contribute to the community by providing goods or services

STEVEN RUBIN / THE IMAGE WORKS

Tomorrow's Fresh-Cut Bouquet For guests to bring imported fresh flowers to their hostess was impossible until relatively recently. This gardener in Chile takes satisfaction from growing and carefully tending flowers to be cut and flown overnight to the United States.

The pleasure of "a job well done" is universal. Research from many cultures confirms that job satisfaction correlates more strongly with challenge, creativity, and productivity than with high pay and easy work (Myers, 1993; Wicker & August, 1995).

New Patterns of Employment

All over the world in the past 20 years, new patterns have become apparent in every aspect of employment—the work, the workers, the employers, the schedule, the teamwork, and the typical career sequence (Kompier & Cooper, 1999). Much of this change is a consequence of globalization and an altered world economy. In the poorest regions of the world, the shift is from agriculture to industry, as multinational corporations seek cheap labor. Developed nations, meanwhile, are shifting from industry-based economies to information and service economies (Sicker, 2002).

Indicative of this restructuring is the fact that between 1995 and 2005 the manufacturing and mining components of the U.S. economy were expected to shrink by a third from their already reduced levels. Rapid growth is occurring in jobs that require the worker to provide information, a treatment, or a service rather than a product. The seven fastest-growing occupations are all related to computers, and other occupations on the fastest-growing list include physical or occupational therapists and aides, human service workers, home health aides, medical assistants, fitness trainers, and special education teachers (U.S. Bureau of Labor Statistics, 2001).

The workplace itself is characterized by ongoing reorganization and growing automation. Significantly, 57 percent of all workers in the United States use computers on the job and almost always use programs that have been invented or updated in the past three years (U.S. Bureau of the Census, 2002). Companies pursue greater efficiency, using such strategies as downsizing, leveling, outsourcing, and mergers—many of which mean losses of, and changes in, workers' jobs.

The timing and pace of jobs are also changing. Most people once worked from 9:00 to 5:00 on weekdays only, but now work is expanding and shifting as

Just Like Homemade Mixing, kneading, rising, kneading, rising, and finally baking—making bread was once a time-consuming household chore. It was also central to family life, which is why slang terms for money include *bread* and *dough*. Now most homemaking tasks are more efficiently done elsewhere, and women are employees as well as homemakers, collectively changing the work of women.

companies seek to meet customers' demands for services "24/7." In the United States today, 29 percent of all workers have flexible schedules, including many of the 15 percent who work from home. Although flexible hours can benefit some workers, they also often mean reduced job security and increased stress, and disrupted family life (Geurts & Gründemann, 1999; Ryan, 1998). The income gap between those with knowledge and expertise and those without is becoming wider (Sicker, 2002).

The burden of these new work patterns falls particularly on young adults, who do not yet have the seniority that provides some continuity in finances, scheduling, and employment. Instead, even in wealthy nations, only about two-thirds of all young men and half of all young women are able to support themselves solely on their earnings (Smeeding & Phillips, 2002). (Among Western European nations, wages for young adults are highest in the Netherlands and lowest in Italy.)

Automation and reorganization mean that every few years workers in various industries must learn specific new skills that build on general abilities, such as decision making, memory, cooperation, and problem solving (Chmiel, 1998). Both higher education and specific job training make workers more effective as times change.

Diversity in the Workplace

A major social change in work and family life in the past few decades is that most adult women are employed. In many developed nations, almost half the civilian labor force is female: 40 percent in Japan and the United Kingdom; 45 percent in Canada, Australia, and the United States (U.S. Bureau of Labor Statistics, 2002).

Especially for Employers Suppose you want to keep a particular new trainee working for you. What incentives should you offer?

The Global Market These women sorting cashews *(left)* and these men working on an offshore oil rig *(right)* are participants in globalization—a phenomenon that has changed the economies of every nation and every family in the world. Radical changes coexist with traditional inequities. For instance, the women are said to have easy, unskilled work, which is the reason they are paid less than 10 percent of the men's wages.

Some occupations in some nations continue to be sex-segregated, but less so than before: Today, 7 percent of nurses are men and 3 percent of firefighters are women—double the proportions in 1980 (U.S. Bureau of the Census, 2002).

Motherhood is no longer considered an impediment to employment. In fact, in the United States today, most married mothers are in the labor force, including 78 percent of those whose youngest child is in school and 62 percent of those who have a child under age 6 (U.S. Bureau of the Census, 2002). Almost all (97 percent) of their husbands are in the labor force as well, but most also share domestic tasks with their wives, sometimes providing a major portion of child care.

Furthermore, in the happiest couples, neither spouse works either very long hours (more than 60 hours a week) or very few hours. This balance allows both partners to contribute to the household finances and to the unpaid work needed to maintain a home (Moen & Yu, 1999).

Gender and ethnic diversity in the workplace is increasing in every developed nation, although many women and members of ethnic minorities still encounter the obstacle known as the **glass ceiling.** This invisible barrier to career advancement is constructed from cultural assumptions and biases. The existence of the glass ceiling is easy to demonstrate with statistics. For example, of the 800,000 managers of marketing, advertising, and public relations in the United States, only 4 percent are African-Americans, only 4 percent are Hispanic-Americans, and only 39 percent are women (these three groups make up, respectively, 12, 11, and 50 percent of the total population) (U.S. Bureau of the Census, 2002).

Work teams function best when they are diverse—when members have a variety of talents and backgrounds—although both stereotypes and stereotype

glass ceiling An invisible barrier experienced by many women in male-dominated occupations—and by many minority workers in majority-dominated occupations—that halts their advancement and undercuts their power at a level of the organization below that of top management.

Response for Employers (from page 478): Money alone won't do it. Although everyone would like more money, employees are also concerned with obtaining recognition and respect for their personal contributions and understanding of family pressures. Women and minorities are particularly wary of discrimination and are fearful that their jobs might disappear. Employers can best hold onto their employees by fostering a work culture in which each employee is needed and valued and workers are able to adjust their work situation (hours, location, and benefits) to meet family obligations.

threat (see Chapter 18) can keep diverse teams from making their members happy and relaxed (Chmiel, 1998; Senior, 1997). The problem is that people's bias in favor of their own values and assumptions and their prejudices against other groups are "mainly involuntary and unconscious" (Dasen & Mishra, 2002, p. 266).

Functioning effectively and happily in a diverse workplace requires a mature generativity, which may take time, experience, and postformal thinking to develop. Today more than ever, success at work requires the same human relations skills needed in successful friendships and marriages. According to one survey of employers, only 9 percent of all new employees who got fired lost their jobs because they were unable to do the work. The other 91 percent were fired because of attitude, absenteeism, or inability to adapt to the work environment (Cascio, 1995).

As emphasized throughout this text, almost everyone can learn at least average skills if they are well taught, but marked variation is apparent in psychosocial development, partly because those skills tend to be neglected. This theme is evident yet again in employment performance, where emotional intelligence, all too often neglected in our formal education, seems more crucial than aptitude (Caruso & Wolfe, 2001).

Parenthood

When one stranger asks another "What do you do?" the answer is rarely "Raise children." Yet adults are as likely to be parents as to be employed, and many of them consider successful child rearing their most important goal. As Erikson points out, while generativity can take many forms, its chief form is "establishing and guiding the next generation," usually through parenthood (Erikson, 1963, p. 267).

Caring for children fulfills an important adult need, although "the fashionable insistence on dramatizing the dependence of children on adults often blinds us to the dependence of the older generation on the younger one" (Erikson, 1963, p. 266). The mature adult "needs to be needed," and the interdependence of parents and children is a lifelong process that begins at conception and continues throughout late adulthood. Four specific aspects of this interdependence merit mention here: that the parent–child bond is reciprocal, that parental employment is complex, that divorce may change the parental role, and that biological parenthood is not the only way to "guide the next generation."

Children Affect Their Parents

Because the parental role is thoroughly explored in the first half of this book, here we need only reiterate that children affect their parents at least as much as parents affect them. Parenthood—having offspring, nurturing them, and finally launching them into the adult world—has a major impact (McAdams & de St. Aubin, 1998).

Each stage of a child's development brings not only satisfactions but also different challenges. During infancy, for example, the parents experience the joy of getting to know a new human being who is just beginning to take shape as an individual—and they also experience the overwhelming task of providing that infant with constant care. During the preschool years, the primary challenge involves authority over the child and the division of that authority between the spouses. Direct conflict between husband and wife is greatest at this period because of increasing financial burdens, multiplying household tasks, and shifting parental roles. Parents of young children also find that their hours of work increase and their leisure decreases (Kluwer et al., 2002). Having school-age children requires the adults to interact with the larger community of teachers, coaches, and other parents. Adolescence presents new parenting issues, as volatile teenagers demand the privileges of adulthood and question parental values, assumptions, and competence As one wit put it, "Raising adolescents is like nailing Jell-o to the wall." In short, every parent is tested and transformed by ongoing challenges. Just when adults think that they have mastered the art of parenting, their child's advancement to the next stage requires major adjustment.

Few young adults anticipate the time required for parenting. As one woman lamented: "The costs are that I have absolutely no free time. I don't do cross-stitch. I don't read. You know, as far as having a lot of time to myself, I don't have it anymore" (Hattery, 2001, p. 63). Although the intimacy and satisfaction of marriage often decrease with parenthood, the level of commitment increases (Bradbury et al., 2000). Ideally, a *parental alliance* forms as the parents cooperate in child rearing.

Employed Parents

A woman who is simultaneously wife, mother, and employee does not necessarily experience **role overload,** as the stress of multiple obligations is called; nor, for that matter, does a man who has several roles to fulfill. Of course, adults of either sex can become overloaded, as when several small children insist on undivided attention and one spouse wants home-cooked meals, a picture-perfect house, and romantic evenings during the same week that the other spouse's employer requires extensive overtime. Work stress leads to family stress, and vice versa, especially among men (Crouter et al., 1999; Larson & Almeida, 1999).

Role buffering in families where both spouses are employed is more prevalent than role overload. For both sexes, achievement in one role—spouse, parent, or employee—provides a buffer or cushion that reduces the impact of disappointment in the other roles. Moreover, the fact that two people share obligations cushions the inevitable troubles, such as a seriously sick child or a period of unemployment, that virtually every parent and worker encounters (Barnett & Hyde, 2001).

Generally those adults who, over the years, manage to balance their marital, parental, and vocational roles are healthier, happier, and more successful than those who function in only one or two of them (Hertz et al., 2001; Milkie & Peltola, 1999). In fact, men and women are mentally healthier if they manage to combine all roles in a satisfying way. If an adult cannot perform all three roles, two are usually better than one (Frone, 2003; Grzywacz & Bass, 2003).

Family logistics—coordinating births, job changes, further training, relocations, housework, child care, work schedules, medical leave, vacations, and such specifics as who will dress Mary, mop up Johnny's spilled milk, and feed the baby just as the phone is ringing and the carpool driver is honking—require a level of mutual agreement and planning that was unnecessary in earlier generations. In many families, the father is expected to do a major portion of child care, and about one-third of all working couples schedule their hours so the father can provide child care while the mother works (Presser, 2000).

This logical solution succeeds only for day or evening work, not when either parent works a night shift. Although couples without young children do not suffer from a night schedule, those with small children and nighttime jobs are at high risk of divorce (see Figure 19.3). One reason is that the marital relationship, like the parental relationship, requires time. As one woman explained:

Not Happy with Mommy Working at home sounds like an ideal way to combine motherhood and a career—until one tries it. Letting a child chew on a cord is risky, but so is asking your client to call you back at naptime.

role overload The stress of multiple obligations that may occur for an adult who is simultaneously a spouse, a parent, and an employee.

role buffering A situation in which achievement in one role that an adult plays—spouse, parent, or employee—reduces the impact of disappointments that may occur in other roles.

Off to Work We Go Even from the back, this European mother and daughter seem to be thriving. Note that the mother is carrying a laptop computer, the daughter is well dressed, and the two are in step, literally as well as figuratively.

Right now I feel torn between a rock and a hard place—my husband and I work opposite shifts, so we do not have to put our children in day care. Now, however, my husband claims opposite shifts [are] putting a strain on our marriage. . . . It is very stressful.

[quoted in Glass, 1998]

Another reason is more practical: A sleep-deprived parent who tries to work, babysit, or doze while the children are awake is often cranky and impatient.

There is no simple solution to this problem. Some families follow traditional gender roles; others practice equity in all aspects; others switch traditional roles, with the wife acting as the primary wage earner and the husband becoming a stay-at-home dad; and still others follow each of these patterns in sequence, changing as employment and parenthood demands change (Gorman, 1999). Over the decades in any family, new babies arrive and older children grow up, job opportunities emerge or disappear, financial burdens increase or decrease, income is almost never adequate, and seldom are all the children thriving. Throughout, many couples remain amazingly resilient—evidence that marriage and family life can benefit all concerned (Ganong & Coleman, 2002).

Children and Divorce

Children make divorce more complicated. Many divorcing parents are surprised by "the discovery that, although they seek to end a marital relationship with a spouse, they must nonetheless maintain a future relationship with the parent of their children" (Thompson & Wyatt, 1999, p. 225). Following a divorce, children often become more demanding, disrespectful, or depressed (Morrison & Coiro, 1999). Moreover, the presence of children adds financial pressure, requires ex-spouses to compromise about visitation, and makes remarriage less likely.

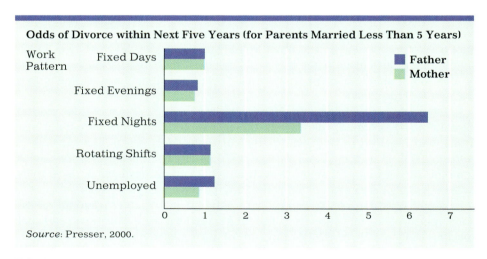

Source: Presser, 2000.

FIGURE 19.3 Parents' Work Schedules and the Risk of Divorce Both the wife's and the husband's work schedules affect their chances of getting divorced. To interpret this graph, you need to know that the odds of divorce are set at a baseline of 1.0 for those who are working "fixed days" (that is, most work hours occur between 8 A.M. and 4 P.M.). The odds of divorce for other couples are higher or lower than 1, depending on whether the risk is greater or less than that of the fixed-days group.

This study was longitudinal, measuring work schedules of 3,476 married couples over five years. Of those who initially had been married less than five years, 21 percent had divorced; of those who had been married more than five years, 8 percent had divorced.

?*Observational Quiz* (see answer, page 484): Looking closely at the graph, can you say what effect parental unemployment has on a marriage with small children?

The financial burden of child rearing usually falls more heavily on the custodial parent, who is most often the mother. Only half of all fathers pay full child support (Meyer, 1999)—a rate that is half as high in some states as in others (see Appendix A, p. A-20). In fairness, those men who are most delinquent have the least money themselves. However, even if both parents contribute as much to child rearing as they did before the divorce, it is not enough to maintain the same lifestyle, because two residences are costly and they no longer save money through joint shopping, meal preparation, and child care.

Noncustodial parents suffer, too: They lose the intimate bonds formed through daily and nightly interactions. This physical and psychic distance is particularly distressing for many contemporary fathers who had been active parents since their children were born. Few maintain intimate relationships with their noncustodial children, partly because of legal restrictions on visitation. For about 10 percent of couples, children are is better off not visiting the noncustodial parent. The other 90 percent would benefit from ongoing relationships with both parents, including regular overnight visits. Yet only one-third of all custody agreements require such interaction (Lamb, 1999).

Children's interests and emotional needs change as they mature, and parents need frequent, ongoing interaction with the child to maintain a parental relationship. Children do best with an involved, authoritative father who helps with homework, pays expenses, provides guidance and discipline consistent with those of the mother, and spends substantial time with his children. Mere father contact, especially when limited to fun and food, does not help either the adults or the children (Amato & Rivera, 1999). Ongoing involvement is more important than biological parenthood, as the following discussion explains.

Alternative Routes to Parenthood

As described in Chapter 13, children can thrive in any family structure, whether nuclear or extended, heterosexual or homosexual, single mother or single father. Here we focus on what nonbiological parenthood—that is, being a step-, adoptive, or foster parent—means for the adults. As you will see, the challenges for adults in such families are greater than for biological parenthood, which means that the feeling of generativity from a job well done is potentially greater as well.

Roughly one-third of all North American adults become stepparents, adoptive parents, or foster parents at some point in their lives. The core problem facing them concerns the strength of the parent–child attachment. Strong bonds between parent and child are particularly hard to create if a child has strong attachments to other caregivers who are still available. This is usually the case with stepchildren, because the average new dependent stepchild is about 9 years old. Stepmothers may enter the marriage with visions of healing a broken family through love and understanding, while stepfathers may believe that their new children will welcome a benevolent disciplinarian. Not so (Coleman et al., 2000).

If all goes well, the stepparent usually becomes a close friend, an "intimate outsider," who nonetheless remains much more distant from the child's personal life than he or she initially imagined (Hetherington & Kelly, 2002). Many stepchildren are fiercely loyal to the absent parent, sabotaging any newcomer's effort to fill the traditional parental role, perhaps by directly challenging authority ("You're not my father, so don't tell me what to do") or by continually intruding on the couple's privacy (interrupting any close moment) or by evoking guilt by getting hurt, sick, lost, or (if the child is a teenager) pregnant, drunk, or arrested. Such childish reactions, often unconscious, may cause adult overreaction or anger, further alienating the child (Coleman et al., 2000).

Some foster and older adopted children are strongly attached to their birth parents, an attachment that can be especially volatile because of the difficult situations that led to their separation. Other children may never have been attached

RICHARD LORD / THE IMAGE WORKS

What's Wrong with This Picture? The beaming man is obviously a proud and responsive father, old enough (age 33) to take his responsibilities seriously. A close look at his 22-month-old daughter suggests that he is doing a good job: She is delighted at the game he is playing with the ball, and he has moved his tall body way down, to be exactly at face level with her. Another fact also makes bonding easier: She is the biological child of these two young adults. So in terms of child and adult development, everything is right with this family picture—but some people might be troubled by one detail: Neither parent has a wedding ring. They have never married.

to anyone and may thus be suspicious of the new parents' attempts to win them over. Attachment between foster parents and children is further hampered because both realize that their bond can be suddenly severed for reasons that have nothing to do with the quality of care.

Stepparents face different but equally significant threats to their relationship with their spouse's children (Papernow, 1993). One potential problem is another divorce, which occurs (typically within five years) in about half of all marriages involving stepchildren and severs the children's relationship with their ex-stepparent. The child's other biological parent may resent the stepparent and undermine the relationship. For these and other reasons, stepparents and foster parents are less likely to invest themselves in the parent–child relationship, and children respond in kind.

Adoptive families have an advantage here: They are legally connected for life. Nevertheless, during the child's adolescence, emotional bonds may abruptly stretch and loosen, for adoptive children sometimes become intensely rebellious and rejecting of family control, even as they insist on information about, or reunification with, their birth parents (Kohler et al., 2002). The children's reasons— whether to test their parents' devotion or to discover their roots or to establish an identity independent from their adoptive family—are understandable. But the result is often a painful demonstration that the parent–child relationship is more fragile than the law pretends (Rosenberg, 1992).

One sign of the difficulties with parent–child attachments in all three situations is that stepchildren, foster children, and adoptive children tend to leave home. They run away, marry, join the military, go away to school, or move out on their own—earlier than adolescents living with both biological parents (Aquilino, 1991; Goldscheider & Goldscheider, 1998).

We must not exaggerate the difficulties of nonbiological parenting. Most adoptive and foster parents cherish their parenting experiences, typically seeking a second child within a few years of the arrival of the first. Similarly, stepparents usually find satisfaction in their role. For their part, children usually reciprocate—if not immediately, then later on (Keshet, 1988; Rosenberg, 1992).

Perhaps even more than biological parenthood, alternative routes to parenthood tend to make adults more humble, less self-absorbed, and more aware of the problems facing children everywhere. When this occurs, adults become true exemplars of generativity as Erikson and others (1986) described it, characterized by the virtue that is perhaps the most important of all—caring for others.

❗*Answer to Observational Quiz* (from page 482): The effect of unemployment is not large, but it is significant. If the father is unemployed, the marriage is more likely to break apart; if the mother is unemployed, the marriage is more likely to stay together. Reasons for this gender difference are many—but that is a matter of interpretation, not observation.

The traditional sources of generativity were a steady job and biological children. Today, however, work is less secure and young adults need to prepare for job shifts. The workforce has become more diverse in gender and ethnicity, but women and members of ethnic minorities must still contend with stereotype threat and the glass ceiling.

Similarly, the joys of parenthood are elusive, even for married parents who raise their biological children together, but especially for the many single parents or the adults who are adoptive, step-, or foster parents. A crucial factor here seems to be the strength of the attachment between parents and children. This reciprocity advances adult generativity as well as child development.

A Case to Study

Linda: "A Much Sturdier Self"

Remember Linda, the case to study at the beginning of this chapter? Her therapist reports on her progress:

Even though she was extremely lonely, she successively negotiated herself away from a romantic involvement with a convict who had some connection with her in her duties as an office receptionist. She converted that potentially disastrous relationship into a casual friendship.

Linda decided that she wanted to apply to university to try again in an arena where she felt she had failed so badly. This move was not easy, particularly for someone haunted by shame. It would be difficult to describe the fear, ambivalence, and procrastination with which she approached this challenge. However, after much equivocation, Linda did send off her application and she was accepted for university admission. . . .

She lost her job as an office receptionist because of the company's downsizing. Previously this would have been such a blow to her self-esteem that she would have given up on her plans to go to university. However, Linda picked herself up, got a job with another firm, finally let go emotionally of Jacqueline, gave Greg his ultimatum (on which he defaulted), began a relationship with an eligible partner in the new company, and made plans to move back east to begin university. . . .

Linda's story is not over by any means. I do not know whether she will be the criminology major and psychological counselor she aims to be. I do not know what will become of her current relationship. However, I do know that she takes a much sturdier self and a much stronger identity into her new world.

[Marcia, 2002, pp. 24–25]

Linda found constructive ways to build intimacy through friendship and romance, and she is developing skills that will be generative. However, even as a single woman, her life is not straightforward, and she shares this complexity with those young adults who are parents, workers, and spouses by age 35. Every young adult probably has the potential to become "a much sturdier self," but such psychosocial growth is not guaranteed.

It seems as if adults can achieve intimacy as well as generativity, but each form of friendship has advantages and disadvantages; intimacy and commitment do not necessarily follow passion; divorce often follows marriage; taking many jobs in sequence is more likely than having one fulfilling career; children create new problems. The overall conclusion of this chapter is that young people can manage to combine work and family, finding many sources of intimacy and generativity that help to buffer their development against the inevitable stresses of life. Creative dependence on friends and partners, as well as living in a way that meets both affiliation and achievement needs, seems crucial. The next three chapters continue these themes into middle adulthood, when both stresses and buffers become more evident in all domains.

SUMMARY

Theories of Adulthood

1. Adult development is remarkably diverse, yet it appears to be characterized by two basic needs. The first need is for intimacy, which is achieved through friendships and love relationships. The second need is for generativity, which is usually achieved through satisfying work and/or parenthood.

2. Traditional patterns of development that followed specific age-related stages have been replaced to a large extent by more varied and flexible patterns. The culturally set social clock still influences behavior but less profoundly than it used to.

Intimacy

3. During early adulthood, a primary source of intimacy is friendship, with notably different needs being served by men's and women's same-sex friendships. Cross-sex friendships present unique challenges and benefits.

4. For most people, the deepest source of intimacy is found through sexual bonding with a mate, a bonding that frequently involves cohabitation and marriage. High expectations are sometimes fulfilled by marriage, but about half the time the outcome is divorce.

5. Of the many factors that can affect the success or failure of a marriage, three are particularly notable: the age of the partners at marriage; the similarity of their background, values, and interests; and the couple's perception of the degree of equity in the marriage.

6. The divorce rate has risen dramatically over the past 50 years. Divorce is emotionally draining for both partners and particularly difficult for those who have children.

Generativity

7. For most adults, work is an important source of satisfaction and esteem, as the pleasure of a job well done helps meet the need to be generative.

8. Significant new patterns are emerging in today's world of work. A shift from a manufacturing- to a service-based economy means workers must acquire flexible skills that will enable them to perform a variety of different jobs over their careers. Increased diversity in the workplace also creates a need for cultural sensitivity on the part of both employer and employee. Globalization adds new challenges.

9. Parenthood is the other common expression of generativity. The specific challenges and satisfactions that parents experience depend in part on the child's stage of development. While some divorced parents manage to maintain good relationships with each other and with their children, more typically mothers have more work and less money than before and fathers become estranged from their children.

10. Nonbiological parents experience the same challenges and satisfactions as biological parents, but they also are likely to face special problems. Attachment issues are common, although most nonbiological parents are happy with their rules.

KEY TERMS

intimacy versus isolation (p. 460)
generativity versus stagnation (p. 460)
social clock (p. 462)
gateways to attraction (p. 465)
exclusion criteria (p. 465)

cohabitation (p. 469)
homogamy (p. 470)
heterogamy (p. 470)
social homogamy (p. 471)
social exchange theory (p. 471)

common couple violence (p. 475)
intimate terrorism (p. 475)
glass ceiling (p. 479)
role overload (p. 481)
role buffering (p. 481)

APPLICATIONS

1. Trace the changing social clock in your own family. At what age did your parents, grandparents, and other relatives complete their education, marry, have children, retire? Include you and your siblings if you have already begun this journey, and include your parents' and grandparents' siblings, if you know their life history. Report and discuss what you find.

2. Friends are especially needed at certain times of life. One way to note this is simply in number of friends. Ask 10 adults of various ages to name their close friends, and chart the relationship between the person's age and the number of friends. Do you find an age-related trend of more friends in early and late adulthood and fewer in middle age?

3. Reread the In Person feature, "Romance and Reality: Changing

Expectations," on page 474. Then ask at least three people to describe their concept of marriage. At least one person should be under 15, one should be age 18–25, and one should be over age 35. Analyze the effects of maturation, cohort, and culture.

4. Visit the career-planning office at your college. What kinds of tests and interviews does it offer? Would you benefit more from a test of your interests and aptitudes, your personality, or your skills? Sign up for at least one assessment, and report how helpful or useless it was.

5. The idea that children affect their parents as much as the parents affect them may come as a surprise. Talk to at least three parents whose children are grown. Ask them how different their lives would have been if they had not had children.

BIOSOCIAL

Growth, Strength, and Health Noticeable increases in height have stopped by age 20, but increases in muscle strength continue until about age 30. All body systems and senses function at optimal levels as the individual enters adulthood. Declines in organ reserve and sensory acuity are so gradual that the onset of senescence is rarely noticed.

Sex and Gender Differences For both sexes, sexual responsiveness remains high in early adulthood: The only notable changes are that men experience some slowing of their responses with age and women become more likely to experience orgasm. In both sexes, problems with fertility increase with age. While disease is rare, the years of early adulthood are peak times for hazards that are chosen by individuals and encouraged by the culture, specifically drug abuse, violent death (particularly for men), and destructive dieting (particularly for women).

COGNITIVE

Adult Thinking As an individual takes on the responsibilities and commitments of adult life, thinking may become more adaptive, practical, and dialectical to take into account the inconsistencies and complexities encountered in daily experiences. Partly as a result, moral thinking becomes deeper and religious faith becomes more reflective, with more appreciation of diverse viewpoints and also more commitment to one's own convictions.

The Effects of College College students today are more often part time and older than they were 40 years ago, when the first research on higher education was reported. The majority of college students are now female, and a higher proportion are from minority groups. Moreover, most college students are more concerned about their current financial status and their future careers. Nevertheless, college education still seems to foster openness to new ideas as well as higher lifetime earnings.

Life experiences—marriage, childbirth, promotion, job loss, and dramatic events of every kind—can also foster cognitive growth.

PSYCHOSOCIAL

Intimacy The need for affiliation is fulfilled by friends and, often, by a romantic commitment to a partner. Friendships are important throughout adulthood but are particularly so for individuals who are single. The developmental course of marriage depends on several factors, including the presence and age of children and whether the interests and needs of the partners converge or diverge over time. Divorce is powerfully affected by cultural pressures.

Generativity The need for achievement can be met both by finding satisfying work and by parenthood, including several types of nonbiological parenthood. The labor market is changing radically, and individuals should expect to experience several job changes and an increasing need for knowledge and flexibility within a diverse group of coworkers.

Traditional parenthood is one way adults achieve generativity. An increasing number become nonbiological parents, with similar rewards but additional stresses, compared with raising one's biological offspring.

487

Part VII

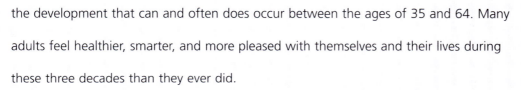

Popular conceptions of middle adulthood are riddled with clichés—like "midlife crisis," "middle-aged spread," and "autumn years"—that conjure up a sense of dullness, resignation, and perhaps a touch of despair. Yet the tone of these clichés is far from reflecting the truth of the development that can and often does occur between the ages of 35 and 64. Many adults feel healthier, smarter, and more pleased with themselves and their lives during these three decades than they ever did.

Of course, such a rosy picture does not apply to everyone. Some middle-aged adults are burdened by health problems, by a decline in intellectual powers, or by unexpected responsibilities for aged parents or adult children. Some feel trapped by choices made in early adulthood. But the underlying theme of the next three chapters is that in middle age, the quality of life is directly related to perceptions and decisions, sometimes new ones, about how to live. There are still many turning points ahead that allow new directions to be set, new doors to be opened, and a healthier and happier life story to be written.

Middle Adulthood

Chapter Twenty

Middle Adulthood: Biosocial Development

primary aging The age-related changes that inevitably take place in a person as time goes by.

secondary aging The age-related changes that take place as a consequence of a person's behavior or a society's failure to eliminate unhealthy conditions.

How old are you? More important, do you feel your age? Will you feel middle-aged, not old, when you are in your 60s, as most people in developed countries do (Lachman & Betrand, 2001)? Chronological age seems increasingly irrelevant as the years go by, yet day-by-day biological aging is described in all three of this book's chapters on adult biosocial development. That's because the passage of time does relate to aging and development, although precise chronological age does not (Staudinger & Block, 2001).

In early adulthood (Chapter 17), the effects of aging are barely perceptible—a first wrinkle, a slightly slower reaction time. In late adulthood (Chapter 23), senescence becomes unavoidably apparent. In this chapter, we describe biosocial development halfway between the beginning and end of adulthood, changes that are obvious but not necessarily disabling. We focus particularly on variations in aging, influenced not only by genes but also by income, ethnicity, and lifestyle. No one is exactly as old as they feel, but past habits and current behaviors make people act older or younger than their years. Moreover, other people's illnesses and one's own changing appearance may lead to improved habits and perceptions. As one middle-aged woman wrote:

> These days I'm into the truth and the truth is I'm not crazy about my looks but I can live with them. . . . After the third funeral [of a friend], . . . I vowed to set my priorities straight before some fatal illness did it for me. Since then I have been trying to focus on the things that really matter. And I can assure you that being able to wear a bikini isn't one of them.
>
> [Pogrebin, 1996]

Primary and Secondary Aging

Although aging happens to all of us, many researchers divide it up into two types first described in 1969: primary and secondary (Busse, 1969). Inevitable age-related changes are called **primary aging.** Everyone experiences this as time goes by, although genetic differences vary its timing.

Secondary aging involves all the age-related changes that are the consequence of years of a person's behavior or a society's failure to eliminate unhealthy conditions. Secondary aging includes many diseases and chronic conditions—from skin cancer to arthritis to diabetes to heart disease—that are more common as we grow old but are influenced by habits such as drinking, smoking, eating, and exercising. Fortunately, most aspects of secondary aging can be slowed or even reversed by a change in behavior before the first signs appear or by the drugs and surgical interventions of modern medicine. Although this distinction between primary and secondary aging is useful and clear in theory, most actual manifestations of aging reflect both types. For example, most cancers are more common with age (primary aging) but are also affected by pollutants (secondary aging). Now let us examine how aging affects appearance, the senses, vital organs, and menopause.

Looking Old

As people advance toward late adulthood, visible signs of aging abound. Hair usually turns gray and gets thinner; skin becomes drier and more wrinkled; middle-age spread appears as stomach muscles weaken; pockets of fat settle on various parts of the body—most noticeably around the abdomen, but also on the upper arms, the buttocks, the eyelids, and the "infamous 'double chin'" (Whitbourne, 2001). People even get shorter! Back muscles, connective tissue, and bones lose strength, making the vertebrae in the spine collapse somewhat. This causes notable height loss (about an inch, or 2 to 3 centimeters) by age 65 (Merrill & Verbrugge, 1999).

These changes are inevitable results of primary aging. But they can be made worse by lack of exercise, poor nutrition, smoking, heavy drinking, and exposure to sun and cold. It has been said that, under age 30, your face is the one you were born with, and over age 30, your face is the one you have made. Appearance is one of those aspects of life that we can accept or change as we grow older. Some people spare no pain or expense in trying to reverse the signs of aging, while others are untroubled by the "pox of time" (de Beauvoir, 1964).

"Old is Ugly"? The message of these adds is clear: Old is considered ugly. American women are bombarded daily with similar messages from all the media, instilling in them the idea that they have two choices, to fight age or be unattractive—a lose-lose proposition.

The Senses

Sometime during middle age, virtually all adults notice that their sense organs are duller than they were. Vision was discussed in some detail in Chapter 17. Suffice it to say that, between roughly ages 35 and 65, the lens of the eye becomes less elastic and the cornea becomes flatter. As a result, almost everyone needs reading glasses by the end of middle age, and many find bifocals helpful. The senses of taste, smell, and touch also become less sharp.

Now we describe hearing in some detail. The auditory sense is a good example of the distinction between those losses that are the inevitable result of primary aging and avoidable losses that reflect secondary aging.

Some middle-aged people hear much better than others, but none hear perfectly. "Perfect" hearing is impossible to define, because hearing is always a matter of degree. Even the profoundly deaf sense the vibration of very loud noises. One fairly accurate measure of hearing loss is the "whisper test": A person who can understand a whisper, unseen, 3 feet away is not considered hard of hearing (Pirozzo et al., 2003). Most young adults pass this test, but only about half of all adults over age 65 do—which makes it obvious that hearing loss often occurs during middle adulthood.

As part of primary aging, genes on our sex chromosomes (the X and Y, or the 23rd pair) interact with genes on other chromosomes in a way that causes men's hearing to decline twice as fast as women's (Pearson et al., 1995). Sensitive laboratory tests reveal that an average 30-year-old man already has as much hearing loss as does the average 50-year-old woman. By age 65, most men are hard of hearing; their losses are apparent not only in the whisper test but also in daily life—they frequently ask others to repeat themselves or turn the TV up too loud for those unfortunate enough to be sharing the couch.

VAUGHN YOUTZ / LIAISON

Hard Rocking, Hard of Hearing Les Claypool is an example of the dangers posed by prolonged exposure to loud noise. Night after night of high-decibel rocking with his band, Primus, has damaged his hearing. When this photo was taken in 1999, Claypool was not only performing but also protecting his remaining hearing. He is active with H.E.A.R—Hearing Education and Awareness for Rockers.

With hearing, as with almost all the physiological declines of middle age, secondary aging makes a decided difference (Meisami et al., 2003). Every loud noise—traffic, music, construction—does a tiny bit of damage to the eardrums. Some of that noise can be avoided, but many young adults (especially men) work on loud machines without protection or listen to music at ear-splitting levels, developing hearing deficits that will later become apparent.

Because the ability to distinguish pure tones declines faster than the ability to hear conversation (see Table 20.1), the first sign of loss may be the inability to hear a doorbell or a telephone ringing in the next room. Speech deficits begin with high-frequency tones, as when a woman or small child talks excitedly, and with attending to one voice despite background noises, as in a crowded restaurant.

As you can see, some age-related hearing loss is genetic (primary) and some is the consequence of ear damage (secondary). In middle age, most is mild enough that compensation—like finding a quieter restaurant or looking at people when they whisper—is quite easy. More notable sensory losses and more complex compensation—hearing aids and the like—are discussed in Chapter 23.

TABLE 20.1 Hearing Loss at Age 50

	Men	Women
Can understand even a whisper	65%	75%
Can understand soft conversation but cannot understand a whisper	28%	22%
Can understand loud conversation but cannot understand soft conversation	5%	2%
Cannot understand even loud conversation	2%	1%

Vital Body Systems

Similar generalities apply to vital organs (Masaro, 1999; Whitbourne, 2001). Some decline is inevitable, some is caused by lifestyle, and most can be minimized until late adulthood. The systemic declines noted in Chapter 17 continue in middle age, reducing organ reserve in the lungs, heart, digestive system, and so forth. As this organ reserve is depleted, people gradually become more vulnerable to chronic disease and even death if a major stress occurs (see Table 20.2).

Decline is also evident in the immune system, as will be discussed in Chapter 23. Middle-aged people are actually less likely to catch diseases, such as flu and the common cold, because their immunity has developed over the years through exposure to similar viruses. However, systemic declines as a result of primary aging are such that, if an invader overcomes the initial immunity, with every year recovery (from everything from chickenpox to major surgery) takes longer.

TABLE 20.2 The Increments of Chronic Disease

Age	Stage	Atherosclerosis (hardening of arteries)	Cancer	Arthritis	Diabetes	Emphysema	Cirrhosis
20	Start	Elevated cholesterol	Carcinogen exposure	Abnormal cartilage staining	Obesity, genetic susceptibility	Smoker	Drinker
30	Discernible	Small lesions on arteriogram	Cellular metaplasia*	Slight joint space narrowing	Abnormal glucose tolerance	Mild airway obstruction	Fatty liver on biopsy
40	Subclinical	Larger lesions on arteriogram	Increasing metaplasia	Bone spurs	Elevated blood glucose	Decrease in surface area and elasticity of lung tissue	Enlarged liver
50	Threshold	Leg pain on exercise	Carcinoma in situ	Mild articular pain	Sugar in urine	Shortness of breath	Upper GI hemorrhage
60	Severe	Angina pectoris	Clinical cancer	Moderate articular pain	Drugs required to lower blood glucose	Recurrent hospitalization	Fluid in the abdomen
70	End	Stroke, heart attack	Cancer spreads from site of origin	Disabled	Blindness; nerve and kidney damage	Intractable oxygen debt	Jaundice; hepatic coma
Prevention or postponement		No cigarettes; normal weight; exercise	No cigarettes; limit pollution; diet; early detection	Normal weight; exercise; minimize stress on joints	Normal weight; exercise; diet	No cigarettes; exercise; limit pollution	No heavy drinking; diet

*Abnormal replacement of one type of cell by another.
Source: Adapted from Fries & Crapo, 1981.

Potential Stages of Disease The ages shown in this table for the stages of chronic diseases are only averages. A person could follow the progressions of each disease from start to finish more rapidly and die by age 40, or the progress could be more gradual, with a 70-year-old still in the early stages.

The costs and benefits of flu shots for healthy adults are debatable, but for middle-aged people who already have diabetes, asthma, heart disease, or some other illness that depletes organ reserve, a flu shot is recommended. This is not because flu is more likely (actually, college students are most likely to catch it) but because reduced immunity and depleted reserves may make the disease more serious, even fatal (Nichol, 2001). Autoimmune diseases, including rheumatoid arthritis and lupus, when the immune system attacks the body itself, become more destructive.

For most middle-aged people who receive advanced medical care, these systemic changes are not critical because modern medicine is usually able to detect, and halt, the first signs of serious illness and chronic disease. Deaths and serious illnesses before age 70 have declined dramatically throughout the developed world, especially from the two leading killers, heart disease and cancer. About half the improvements occur because of medical advances, and half result from improved health practices by individuals (Michaud et al., 2001).

Specifically, since 1940, despite the advent of AIDS (the most common deadly disease among people aged 25 to 44), the U.S. death rate during middle age has been cut in half. About 90 percent of all U.S. adults now age 35 will still be alive when they are 60 (U.S Bureau of the Census, 2002). In other nations (including Japan, Canada, and Western European countries), middle-aged people are even less likely to die. But in countries where citizens have limited access to expensive and life-saving medical treatments and are vulnerable to infectious diseases because of poor sanitation and crowded living conditions—Afghanistan, Cambodia, Kenya, and Nigeria among them—less than half the population survives past middle age.

The Sexual-Reproductive System

For both sexes, throughout adulthood, the levels of sex hormones gradually diminish. As a result, sexual responses become slower and reproduction becomes less likely (see Chapter 17). We focus now on the aspects of change in the sexual-reproductive system that are distinct to middle age.

Menopause

Sometime between ages 42 and 58 (the average age is 51), ovulation and menstruation stop because of a marked decrease in the production of several hormones, especially estrogen, progesterone, and testosterone (Wise, 2003). This process is called menopause. Strictly speaking, **menopause** is dated one year after a woman's last menstrual period. The exact age at which menopause occurs is primarily related to genes and to chance factors before birth (Finch & Kirkwood, 2000). However, health habits, particularly cigarette smoking and malnutrition, increase the chances that menopause will occur earlier. A hysterectomy (surgical removal of the uterus, experienced by one in nine 35- to 45-year-old U.S. women) often also includes removal of the ovaries, resulting in sudden, premature menopause (*MMWR*, July 12, 2002).

The term *menopause* is also sometimes loosely used to refer to the *climacteric*, or *perimenopause*, which extends from three years before to three years after cessation of the menstrual cycle. Typically, the first symptom of the climacteric is shorter menstrual cycles. Then, usually toward the end of her 40s, the timing of a woman's periods becomes erratic, the duration variable, and ovulation unpredictable. Instead of occurring mid-cycle as in earlier years, ovulation sometimes occurs early or late in a cycle; sometimes several ova are released, sometimes none. This explains why some women who thought they knew their body's rhythm well enough to avoid both pregnancy and contraception find themselves with a "change of life" baby.

The reduction in estrogen production during and after menopause causes two serious health risks. One is loss of bone calcium, which can eventually lead to **osteoporosis,** a porosity and brittleness of the bones that makes them break easily. The other is an increase of fat deposits in the arteries, which sets the stage for *coronary heart disease,* in which the heart becomes less efficient and blood circulation is impaired. Osteoporosis and coronary heart disease are each experienced by about half of all women in late adulthood. Both conditions are influenced by multiple causes, genetic and behavioral, not simply by primary aging—that is, by menopause.

Other symptoms of the climacteric are *hot flashes* (suddenly feeling hot), *hot flushes* (suddenly looking hot), and *cold sweats* (feeling cold and clammy). These symptoms are caused by *vasomotor instability,* a temporary disruption in the body's homeostatic mechanism (see Chapter 17) that constricts or dilates the blood vessels to maintain body temperature (Wise, 2003). Vasomotor instability varies widely in severity: Of every five menopausal women, one is very troubled by these symptoms, three notice them but are not particularly bothered, and one doesn't even notice (Avis, 1999).

Lower estrogen levels produce many other changes in a woman's body, including drier skin, less vaginal lubrication during sexual arousal, and loss of some breast tissue, again with substantial variation. Sudden menopause caused by surgery is likely to produce marked symptoms, for both biological and psychosocial reasons.

Some women also find that during the climacteric, their moods change inexplicably from day to day. This is commonly thought to be a direct result of hormonal changes, but it may be caused indirectly, like other types of moodiness, by exhaustion (if hot flashes interrupt sleep night after night). Clinical depression is

menopause The time in middle age, usually around age 50, when a woman's menstrual periods cease completely and the production of estrogen, progesterone, and testosterone drops considerably. Strictly speaking, menopause is dated one year after a woman's last menstrual period.

osteoporosis A loss of calcium that makes bone more porous and brittle. It occurs to some degree in everyone with aging, but serious osteoporosis is more common in elderly women than men. Osteoporosis is the main reason the elderly suffer broken hip bones much more often than do the young.

JENS LUCKING / STONE / GETTY IMAGES

Could This Be Your Grandmother? Probably. Most middle-aged women are strong and competent, like this grandmother cutting wood in rural Italy.

hormone replacement therapy (HRT) Treatment to compensate for hormone reduction at menopause or following surgical removal of the ovaries. Such treatment, which usually involves estrogen and progesterone, minimizes menopausal symptoms and diminishes the risk of osteoporosis in later adulthood.

rare during menopause, except in women who already have a history of depression (Avis, 1999).

In fact, the psychic consequences of menopause are extremely variable (Wise, 2003). European and North American cultures' perceptions of this aspect of menopause have changed dramatically over time (Daniluk, 1998). Once doctors described menopausal women as "diseased, sexless, irritable, and depressed" (Golub, 1992). Such negative views may have created a self-fulfilling prophecy, leading some North American women to focus on the symptoms of menopause, fearing the worst and having their fears confirmed by their physicians. A stark contrast to the historical Western notion that menopausal women temporarily lose their minds (Neugarten & Neugarten, 1986) is the view among Hindi women in India that menopause brings liberation (Menon, 2001).

Hormone Replacement Therapy

Over the past 20 or 30 years, it was common for women who experienced disabling perimenopausal symptoms or just the discomfort of hot flashes—or even (in some cases) who believed they would retain their youth longer—to use **hormone replacement therapy (HRT)** to alleviate their distress. They took estrogen pills to replace the main hormone that their bodies were no longer producing. They also usually took another hormone, progesterone, which allowed their bodies to maintain periodic bleeding and was associated with a lower risk of uterine cancer.

Initial correlational studies found that HRT reduced the risk of heart disease and senility. Researchers now believe that those studies were invalid, because most women who used HRT were also higher in SES than average. The key to their long-term health may have been their income and education rather than HRT.

In fact, the Women's Health Initiative, in controlled longitudinal studies of thousands of women, has discovered that long-term use of HRT (for 10 years or more) *increases* the risk of heart disease, stroke, and breast cancer, and has no proven effects on senility (U.S. Preventive Task Force, 2002). On the plus side, it reduces hot flashes and decreases the risk of osteoporosis. For most women, the benefits of HRT do not outweigh the risks.

These findings point to the need for specific risk analysis in place of generalities, because each woman has her own risks and benefits from any drug. Much depends on the woman's likelihood of contracting whatever disease the drug is designed to prevent. Osteoporosis, for example, is most prevalent in small-framed women of European descent. These women need to have their bone density checked to see if their primary aging puts them at risk. If so, they need to strengthen their bones through weight-bearing exercise, a diet high in calcium, and perhaps hormones or drugs to reduce the risk of fractures. Women at risk should also avoid cigarettes and alcohol, both of which reduce bone strength.

Thus primary aging—in this case menopause—puts some women at greater risk for osteoporosis, but secondary aging—the fractures and immobility that come as a result of osteoporosis—is not inevitable. In fact, as we will soon describe in detail, most measures taken by high-risk women to avoid broken bones, including avoiding cigarettes and getting plenty of exercise, are advisable for everyone, male and female. Through good health practices, secondary aging can be largely controlled or prevented.

Male Menopause?

Do men also undergo a form of menopause? There is no sudden drop in male reproductive ability or hormonal levels, as there is with women. Most men continue to produce sperm indefinitely, and their testosterone levels do not suddenly plummet, as women's estrogen levels do (Gould et al., 2000). However, there are important age-related declines in the levels of testosterone and in the number and motility of sperm (see Chapter 17). Older men are less likely to be fertile (Hassan & Killick, 2003). The average levels of testosterone and other androgens (male hormones) decline with age.

Strictly speaking, there is no dramatic andropause, or "male menopause" (Gould et al., 2000). However, this phrase may have been coined because of another phenomenon characteristic of middle adulthood: men's anxiety about impotence. Men do suffer from sudden, stress-related shifts in hormone levels. In part, this is caused by a circular relationship between testosterone levels and anxiety: Testosterone dips markedly if a man becomes sexually inactive or unusually worried, as might happen if he were faced with unemployment, marital problems, serious illness, or unwanted retirement. Levels of testosterone correlate with levels of sexual desire and speed of sexual responses, so a man with low testosterone may be unable to have an erection when he wishes. This experience, especially when added to age-related reduction in desire, may make a man anxious about his sexual virility; anxiety reduces testosterone. The result seems like menopause, that is, a sudden drop in reproductive potential and hormones (Rossi, 1994).

The opposite can also occur: A man of any age who lands a new, ego-enhancing job or who adds some novelty to his sex life may experience a rise in self-esteem and, consequently, rising testosterone, renewed desire, and a reliable erection. The new woman gets the credit, until she becomes familiar.

Underlying such situational peaks and valleys, however, is the steady, gradual decline brought on by primary aging as well as lower levels of androgens (Veldhuis et al., 2003). Even with the help of new drugs, most recently Viagra and Levitra, most men will experience a decline in sexual desire and speed of intercourse as they age. And underlying some men's need for a novel sexual partner or an expensive drug is their unhappiness with the sexual consequences of primary aging.

Some men have turned directly to hormone replacement, in this case testosterone—a hormone for which almost 2 million prescriptions were written in 2002. Research has not yet demonstrated long-term hazards and benefits, but many men (and some women) hope to reverse the sexual slowdown of primary aging with this drug (Institute of Medicine, 2003), although general use is not recommended.

As we've seen, secondary aging—including worries about aging bodies and life changes—magnifies the sexual consequences of primary aging for both sexes. A cross-sectional study of British adults (age 18–75) found that 30 percent were unhappy with their sexual functioning; loss of desire was the most common complaint (Nazareth et al., 2003).

The key seems to be to relax and appreciate what you have; with this attitude, many older couples can have an enjoyable sexual relationship. The Greek philosopher Socrates, more than 2,000 years ago, welcomed this part of aging. Longitudinal data show that important parts of the sexual experience—affection, caressing, and pleasure—continue throughout life for men *and* women; reproduction and the frequency of intercourse are the only parts that inevitably decline (Rossi, 1994).

So Happy Together This long-married couple still demonstrate great affection for each other after years of familiarity.

CLEO PHOTOGRAPHY / PHOTOEDIT, INC.

> Aging may be either primary or secondary, depending on whether the particular manifestation of aging is the result of the ongoing march of time (primary) or the diverse actions of people (secondary). Some age changes are universal and inevitable, including changes in appearance (gray hair, thin skin, pockets of fat), in organ reserve (slower heart rate, less efficient breathing), and in the sexual-reproductive system (infertility, less frequent intercourse). Other changes are secondary, the outcome of long-term neglect of health and abuse of the body (such as reduced lung capacity because of smoking). Some effects of aging can be halted, reversed, or reinterpreted. For example, some hearing losses can be prevented, and sexual pleasure can continue though old age, although primary aging affects its expression.

Measuring Health

Being healthy means much more than merely being alive. There are at least four distinct ways to measure health: mortality, morbidity, disability, and vitality. Each can be assessed separately; each is useful.

Mortality and Morbidity

mortality Death. As a measure of health, mortality usually refers to the number of deaths each year per 1,000 members of a given population.

At the farthest extreme, death is the ultimate sign of poor health. This basic indicator, **mortality,** is usually expressed as the number of deaths each year per 1,000 individuals in a particular population. For example, the mortality rate of people in the United States in 2000 was 8.7. The figure for various age groups ranged from just 0.12 for 10-year-olds to 156 for those aged 85 and older (U.S. Bureau of the Census, 2002). In middle age, death is uncommon; only 1 in 2,000 U.S. residents aged 35–65 dies per year.

Mortality statistics are compiled from legally required death certificates, which indicate age, sex, and immediate cause of death. This procedure makes valid international and historical comparisons possible, because deaths have been counted and recorded in almost every nation for the past 50 years—and sometimes for several centuries. Mortality rates are often *age-adjusted* so as to take into account the higher death rate among the very old. By that measure, Japan has the lowest mortality (about 5 per 1,000) and Sierra Leone the highest (about 35 per 1,000).

morbidity Disease. As a measure of health, morbidity refers to the rate of diseases of all kinds in a given population—physical and emotional, acute (sudden) and chronic (ongoing).

Although mortality rates are an important indicator of the health populations, some people are alive but not at all healthy. A more comprehensive measure of health is **morbidity,** or the incidence of illness. Morbidity refers to illnesses and diseases of all kinds—fatal, contagious, chronic, and emotional. Morbidity statistics reveal important information that mortality statistics cannot, especially about illnesses that are chronic but not usually fatal. For example, worms and parasites are common causes of illness in some nations, and arthritis affects almost half of all women after age 50; thus, these are significant sources of morbidity worldwide, even though they seldom directly cause death (Michaud et al., 2001).

Disability and Vitality

disability Long-term difficulty in performing normal activities of daily life. As a measure of health, disability refers to the portion of the population who cannot perform activities that most others can.

To truly portray overall health, we must broaden the picture further to include not only death and disease (mortality and morbidity) but also how fulfilling and satisfying life is. For this, we need two additional measures: disability and vitality.

Disability refers to a person's long-term difficulty performing normal activities of daily life because of a "physical, mental, or emotional condition" (U.S.

Bureau of the Census, 2002). Limitation in normal functioning, not the diagnosis or severity of disease, is the measure of disability (Merrill & Verbrugge, 1999). Morbidity and disability do not necessarily coincide. For example, heart disease is an illness that might make it impossible for a person to walk 200 feet without having to rest. This would be a serious disability for a person who usually walks several miles a day for work or leisure but not for someone who always drives, never walking more than a few steps at a time. Similarly, mental illnesses are instances of morbidity, but how disabling they are depends a great deal on the social context. Schizophrenia is usually very disabling for someone who lives alone in a modern city, but much less disabling for someone in a stable rural family. Beyond social context, treatment can make a disease less disabling (as medication sometimes does for schizophrenia). It is also possible for someone to be disabled without having a disease; for instance, a healthy person might become so afraid of falling that he or she always uses a wheelchair. The point is that disease does not always lead to disability.

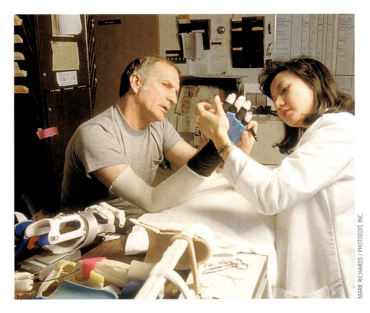

Overcoming Disability This man is discovering that the loss of a hand need not mean permanent disability, thanks to recent advances in prosthetic and reconstructive surgery and physical therapy.

Disability is more costly to society than either mortality or morbidity, because when a person cannot perform the tasks of daily life, society not only may lose an active contributor but also may need to provide special care. In the United States about one in five middle-aged persons is disabled; half of all people over age 75 are disabled in some way (U.S. Bureau of the Census, 2002). Thus, disability is common in middle age, and the rate increases as late adulthood approaches.

Levels of disability can be reduced by medical care and by increased exercise, improved diet, and other health-related behaviors. As an example, in the United States in 1984, one in six people aged 50 to 65 had difficulty walking three city blocks, but 10 years later, this was true of only one in eight in this age group, at least partly because regular exercise became more prevalent during the 1980s (Freedman & Martin, 1998).

The fourth measure of health, **vitality**, refers to how healthy and energetic—physically, intellectually, and socially—an individual actually feels. Vitality is *joie de vivre*, the zest for living, the love of life. Vitality is a subjective measure, based on the individual's own appraisal of his or her life. Some people say their health is excellent even though they have several chronic diseases and obvious disabilities. Precisely because it is subjective, vitality is probably more important to quality of life than any other measure of health (Stewart & King, 1994).

vitality A measure of health that refers to how healthy and energetic—physically, intellectually, and socially—an individual actually feels.

Most experts, as well as the general public, now agree that the goal of medicine should be extending and improving vitality rather than simply postponing mortality, preventing morbidity, or remediating disability. Indeed, the motto of those who study aging is to "add life to years" not just to "add years to life" (Timiras, 2003, p. 6).

The Burden of Poor Health

Recognizing the validity and importance of all four measures of health, researchers and public health experts have sought a way to combine measurements of all kinds of poor health or well-being. Two measures they have found are known as *QALYs* and *DALYs*.

Calculating **quality-adjusted life years**, or **QALYs**, is a way of evaluating just how healthy people are—of determining whether they are merely surviving or whether they are enjoying perfect vitality. If a person is completely well, the

quality-adjusted life years (QALYs) A way of comparing mere survival without vitality to survival with health. QALYs indicate how many years of full vitality are lost to a particular physical disease or disability. They are expressed in terms of life expectancy as adjusted for quality of life.

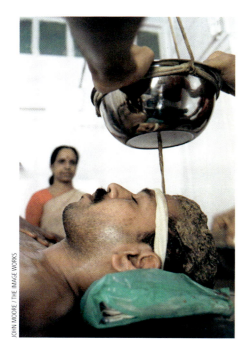

JOHN MOORE / THE IMAGE WORKS

Feeling Better Quality of life self-assessment and attitude. This principle was known thousands of years ago in India. At this Ayurvedic clinic in New Delhi, a patient is treated with oils and massage prescribed for his particular needs. The desired results are lower blood pressure and increased vitality.

disability-adjusted life years (DALYs) A measure of the impact that disability has on quality of life. DALYs are the reciprocal of quality-adjusted life years: A reduction in QALYs means an increase in DALYs.

quality of life is said to be 100 percent, which means that a year of that person's life equals 1 full QALY. If a person has a disease or disability, the quality of a year of that person's life is expressed in terms of less than 1 calendar year.

The first part of calculating QALYs is fairly simple: If a person dies prematurely, before reaching the end of his or her expected life span, then those years are completely lost. For example, if a man is statistically expected to live to be 70 but is shot and killed at age 30, then 40 quality-of-life years are lost.

The second part of the calculation is more difficult, because it measures how much reduction in life's fullness is caused by a particular condition. If a 30-year-old is shot and disabled—perhaps severely brain-injured—then each remaining year of that person's life might be considered to provide only half the usual quality of life, and thus 20 QALYs would be lost by age 70. Or if a 30-year-old is shot, undergoes 4 years of recovery that are so painful and disabling that he experiences only one-fourth of full vitality, and then recovers completely to live a healthy life until age 70, he would lose only 3 years—meaning that he would have 37 QALYS during the 40 years between ages 30 and 70.

Disability-adjusted life years, or **DALYs,** are the reciprocal of QALYs. A person who enjoys a year of full quality of life, with no disability, incurs no DALY score. Each year that is lost due to premature death and each fraction of full quality of life that is lost due to disability reduces a person's QALYs and increases DALYs.

The picture is further clouded by the fact that, while doctors and social scientists agree that vitality should be measured because it is a useful public health assessment, they disagree about how to calculate it (Anan & Hanson, 1997; Johannson & Johansson, 1997). For example, in the World Health Organization's calculations of worldwide DALYs, each year of life lost by a 1-year-old who dies counts as fewer DALYs than does each year lost by a 30-year-old who dies. Many agencies assign a lower value to each year of life lost after age 70 than to a year lost in young adulthood (Kaiser, 2003).

Subjective experience and personal evaluations also make it difficult to agree on how quality of life should be calculated. For some people, visibly growing older reduces quality of life. They may temporarily lower their QALYs even further by undergoing the expense, risk, and pain of plastic surgery. Others would never consider such surgery, because their level of vitality is not reduced by looking older and thus their QALYs are not affected. In general, appearance and even obesity are *not* considered in QALYs calculations, although some of the consequences (such as diabetes) are.

Despite the difficulties involved, the calculation of QALYs is very useful in evaluating the costs and benefits of various medical interventions. For example, clean water, immunizations, and adequate nutrition all improve the quality as well as the length of life for billions of people, and therefore the return in QALYs makes them well worth the expense of providing them.

Some other public health measures seem less effective, including many early-diagnosis procedures used in developed nations (Kaplan, 2000). For example, self-examinations for breast tumors and the common PSA blood test for prostate cancer may extend life by a few days on average in a large population (Brawley, 2001; Chan et al., 2003; Harris & Kinsinger, 2002). While they may detect the first signs of cancer in a few people, the incidence of false positives, which cause needless surgery and anxiety, reduces the overall quality of life by months or even years. In that light, some screening procedures reduce morbidity by enabling some cases of disease to be cured; but when QALYs are calculated for the broad population, they could be more harmful than helpful (Kaplan, 2000). The same dilemma applies to various disease screens throughout the life span, including tests for genetic disorders in newborns and for risk factors for Alzheimer's disease in the elderly (Holtzman, 2003).

JOHN BERRY / THE IMAGE WORKS

Looking for Signs of Trouble A technician examines mammograms for breast abnormalities, such as tiny lumps that cannot be felt but may be malignant. The National Cancer Institute recommends a screening mammogram every one to two years for women who are 40 or older or who have certain risk factors for breast cancer.

Such screening tests, when properly interpreted, remain useful for high-risk individuals. For populations as a whole, worldwide calculations help to establish priorities; for example, preventing the spread of HIV is much more effective in boosting QALYs and reducing DALYs than is the prevention of prostate cancer; some public health campaigns are far more beneficial than others; and some treatments (such as antipollution programs) should be weighed against targeted interventions (such as surgery).

If those concerned with public health focus only on mortality and morbidity, their efforts at prevention are likely to be tertiary (saving only the seriously ill from dying) or secondary (spotting early stages of ill health). If the goal is less disability and more vitality, then priority must be given to primary prevention (promoting better diet, more exercise, and less smoking) to increase overall quality-of-life years as well as to prevent death and disease. The latter viewpoint has led health officials to think in terms of the **burden of disease,** the total reduction in vitality that is caused by disease-induced disability in a given population (see Table 20.3).

burden of disease The total reduction in vitality that is caused by disease-induced disability in a given population.

TABLE 20.3　The 10 Leading Causes of DALYs Worldwide

Rank	Cause	DALYs (thousands)	Percent of Total DALYs	Deaths (thousands)
1.	Lower respiratory tract infections	96,682	7	3,963
2.	HIV/AIDS	89,819	6	2,673
3.	Birth complications and defects	89,508	6	2,356
4.	Diarrhea	72,063	5	2,213
5.	Unipolar depression	59,030	4	1
6.	Heart disease	58,961	4	7,089
7.	Vaccine-preventable diseases (e.g., measles)	54,638	4	1,554
8.	Cerebrovascular diseases (e.g., stroke)	49,856	3	5,544
9.	Malaria	44,998	3	1,086
10.	Malnutrition	44,539	3	493

Source: Adapted from World Health Organization, 2000.

The Global Burden of Disease Calculating the global burden of disease reveals that the top four health problems are treatable by modern medicine, which has not yet reached many of the world's people. Note that the statistics for disability (expressed in DALYs) and for mortality (deaths) follow different patterns. Cancer, which is the second leading cause of death in North America, does not even appear; worldwide, cancer is not a major cause of disability.

Assessing quality of life, rather than mortality, morbidity, or disability, is particularly important in middle age, for two reasons. First, self-assessed health is the best predictor of future illness in late adulthood. Second, vitality is lower between ages 45 and 65 than earlier or later. That was the finding of a large survey of U.S. adults, in which the average middle-aged person reported experiencing reduced quality of life on eight days out of the preceding 30 (*MMWR,* November 21, 2003), more than younger or older adults (about six days).

> Mortality statistics reveal that, in developed nations, death is rare in middle age. However, three other measures of health—morbidity, disability, and vitality—show widespread health problems before age 65. Developmentalists attend to all four measures, which can affect the quality of life throughout the life span.

Health Habits Through the Years

From a life-span perspective, prevention or reduction of illness through changes in health behaviors is possible at any stage of life. Improvements undertaken early add more QALYs than do treatments begun after illness has been recognized. Indeed, inadequate nutrition during pregnancy affects the likelihood that a woman's fetus will develop heart disease 50 years later (Finch & Kirkwood, 2000). As one physician explained, "Healthy aging begins with the fetus, not the adult" (Rabin, 2003, p. 1202). At the other end of the life span, even the very elderly can enhance their quality of life by improving their habits. Overall, health habits affect physical well-being as much as or more than medical care does (Johnson, 2003).

Although health habits are relevant throughout life, the three decades from 35 to 65 are a crucial time for reassessment and improvement. Signs from their bodies, advice from their doctors, birthdays that end with a zero, and the death of a parent (in one large survey, 41 percent of people enter middle age with both parents alive but 71 percent leave it with both parents dead) drive home the reality of aging. As a result, many middle-aged adults change their health habits and reshape their lives during these years (Lachman, 2001; Siegler et al., 1999).

Although, as you will soon see, individual biological and environmental variations can affect who gets healthier, choices are crucial. As one review of health in midlife concludes: "For most conditions and diseases, it's the way we live our lives that has the greatest influence on delaying and preventing physiological decline" (Merrill & Verbrugge, 1999). Four habits are critical: smoking, drinking, overeating, and exercising.

Tobacco

In North America, at least, the news about cigarette smoking in middle age is good. Among the middle-aged in the United States, about one-fourth of all adults are currently smokers, but at least that many are former smokers. In 1970, half of all adult men and a third of all adult women smoked. Currently, almost everyone who still smokes in middle age quits by late adulthood (*MMWR,* October 10, 2003). Canadian rates of smoking—and quitting—in middle age are similar to those in the United States (Pechmann et al., 1998).

For some smokers, quitting by age 65 is too late. Death rates for lung cancer (by far the leading cause of cancer deaths) reflect smoking patterns of several

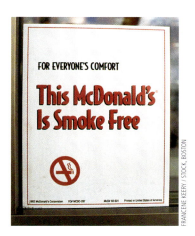

Times Change—for the Better Health, as much as any aspect of life, is affected by social norms. At mid-century, smoking was the "thing to do," and the dancing Old Gold cigarette packs shown here were typical of cigarette advertising that dominated every medium, including television, in the 1950s. An immediate result of such promotion was the highest rate of cigarette smoking in U.S. history, followed 30 years later by the highest rates of lung cancer. Today, "smoke-free" is in, and the rate of smoking among U.S. adults has dropped by half.

decades earlier. Because fewer North American men now smoke than did 50 years ago, the lung cancer death rate for 35- to 65-year-old males is down 20 percent from the 1980 peak (see Appendix A, p. A-15). During the same period, more women took up smoking, so the lung cancer death rate for women rose, increasing in the United States by 20 percent between 1980 and 1995. It has stabilized since then (U.S. Bureau of the Census, 2002), but female lung cancer deaths are twice that of deaths from breast, uterine, and ovarian cancers combined. Fifty years ago, breast cancer killed twice as many women as lung cancer (U.S. Bureau of the Census, 2002).

In addition to dramatically raising the risk of lung cancer, smoking increases the rate of most other serious diseases, including cancer of the bladder, kidney, mouth, and stomach, as well as heart disease, stroke, pneumonia, and emphysema. Worldwide, the incidence of tobacco-related illnesses is increasing (Mascie-Taylor & Karim, 2003). The causal agent seems to be more than just nicotine, as marijuana, low-nicotine cigarettes, cigars, bidis (flavored cigarettes), and chewing tobacco all increase the incidence of disease, although researchers are uncertain whether they are equally, more, or less harmful than regular cigarettes.

Smoking also reduces lung capacity, which increases disability and reduces vitality (Eisner et al., 2002). Even the brain is affected: A prospective longitudinal study measured cognition in many adults, and then compared *declines* over time in both groups, smokers and nonsmokers. It found that smoking hastens cognitive decline throughout adulthood, especially affecting memory loss between ages 43 and 53 (Richards et al., 2003).

All smoking diseases are dose- and duration-sensitive: A middle-aged man who has smoked two packs a day for 40 years is three times as likely to die of lung cancer than is a contemporary who has smoked one pack a day for 30 years (Pechmann et al., 1998). Throughout adulthood, quitting at any time adds years to life (Taylor et al., 2002) (see Figure 20.1).

Secondhand smoke is also dangerous, as hundreds of studies in many nations have found. For example, according to an Australian study of people middle-aged and older, people married to smokers are twice as likely to suffer a stroke (You et al., 1999). Another study, of thousands of nonsmoking adults from 16 countries, found that exposure to passive smoke at work increased respiratory disabilities of all kinds (Janson et al., 2001).

Worldwide, tobacco use is expected to cause more deaths in the year 2020 than any other single condition (Michaud, 1999). Smoking rates in most European nations have not dropped as dramatically as they have in North America.

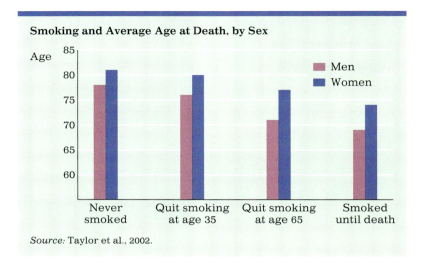

Smoking and Average Age at Death, by Sex

Source: Taylor et al., 2002.

FIGURE 20.1 **Quit Smoking Now** Smoking is dose- and duration-sensitive, so every cigarette smoked can be said to shorten life by a small amount.

Indeed, about 50 percent of men and 30 percent of women in Germany, Denmark, Poland, Holland, Switzerland, and Spain are smokers (United Nations, 1991). In Asian and Latin American nations, rates are even higher: Among men, 55 percent smoke in China, 58 percent in Argentina, and 75 percent in Indonesia. Traditionally, less than 10 percent of Asian and Latina women smoked, but rates among these women are rising rapidly. (Perhaps surprisingly, in the United States, smoking rates are lowest among adults of Asian or Hispanic heritage [*MMWR,* October 10, 2003].)

The wide variations from nation to nation, cohort to cohort, and group to group show that this particular habit is not merely a personal choice or a genetic compulsion but is a response to social norms. As those norms change, smoking can decrease and health can improve, or the opposite. The success of efforts in North America over the past 40 years to discourage smoking offers hope that other unhealthy habits can be discouraged.

Alcohol

Contrary to traditional assumptions, adults who drink wine, beer, spirits, or other alcohol *in moderation*—no more than two servings a day—tend to live longer than those who never drink (Berger et al., 1999). The major benefit is a reduction in coronary heart disease. One possible reason is that alcohol increases the blood's supply of HDL (high-density lipoprotein), often referred to as "good cholesterol." HDL is instrumental in reducing LDL (low-density lipoprotein), which is the "bad" cholesterol that causes clogged arteries and blood clots (Wannametheen & Shaper, 1999). Small amounts of alcohol, taken with food, may also reduce tension and aid digestion.

Whatever the potential health benefits, however, alcohol comes with notable risks. Many people do not (perhaps cannot) drink in moderation, and middle-aged people are particularly vulnerable to chronic alcohol abuse. Heavy daily drinking over the years is the main cause of cirrhosis of the liver, which kills 14,000 middle-aged adults and 12,000 older adults in the United States each year (U.S. Bureau of the Census, 2002).

Alcohol is a major cause of injury and disease worldwide (Michaud et al., 2001). Excessive alcohol use stresses the heart and stomach, destroys brain cells, hastens the calcium loss that causes osteoporosis, decreases fertility, and increases the incidence of many forms of cancer, including breast, stomach, and throat cancer. Even moderate alcohol consumption poses a health risk if it is associated with cigarette smoking or overeating. More immediately, drinking accompanies almost half of all fatal accidents, suicides, and homicides.

In Russia, increased vodka consumption during the 1990s was one reason homicides of men skyrocketed and death from other causes rose as well. Precise morbidity is difficult to prove, because so many changes occurred in the former Soviet Union in the 1990s and no prospective longitudinal studies were undertaken of individuals; but most experts point to vodka consumption as a major contributor to recent disability and death in Russia (Pridemore, 2002; Walberg, et al., 1998).

A longitudinal study involving 6,000 men has been conducted in Scotland. Over a 21-year period, men who initially said they consumed five drinks a day died at a rate twice that of other men. Those who had two or three drinks a day were one-third more likely to die; this group had lower rates of heart disease but higher mortality from almost all other causes (Hart et al., 1999).

The fact that moderate drinking has health benefits should not delude anyone. For many people, alcohol is a major health risk.

Obesity and Overweight

The World Health Organization has declared that there is a worldwide epidemic of obesity and overweight. Ironically, although a substantial minority of the world's population is still undernourished, a rising number are overweight and obese to the point that their health is affected.

Excess pounds bring poorer health on every measure; overweight 40-year-olds lose three years of life, on average, and obese 40-year-olds lose seven years (Peeters et al., 2003). A recent editorial in the *Journal of the American Medical Association* warned, "Obesity is a worldwide epidemic and will be followed by a worldwide epidemic of diabetes" (Bray, 2003, p. 1853).

The Impact of the Epidemic

Detailed, longitudinal statistics are available for the United States, which is in the forefront of the obesity epidemic. In 2000, 65 percent of adults in the United States were overweight (defined as having a body mass index above 25), 30 percent were obese (a BMI of 30 or more), and 5 percent were morbidly obese (a BMI of 40 or more) (Flegal et al., 2002). (The calculation of BMI was explained in Chapter 17; see Table 17.2.) There is no developmental bright spot in these statistics: Obesity has increased significantly for both sexes, in every decade, in every cohort, and in every ethnic group. Although rates of overweight and obesity are high throughout childhood and adulthood, the worst years are from age 45 to 65, when three of every four adults are overweight.

If the BMI guidelines seem abstract, picture a person who is 5 feet, 8 inches tall. If that person weighs about 150 pounds, the BMI is about 24, a normal weight. If he or she weighs 200 pounds or more, the BMI is 30 or higher; the person is obese. If he or she weighs more than 300 pounds, the BMI is over 40 and that person is morbidly obese and is likely to suffer from poor physical and psychological health—to be disabled, with low vitality—and to die prematurely. Note that 5 percent of adults in the United States are in this extremely obese group. You may not have been aware of how common this problem is because the morbidly obese are less likely than normal-weight people to walk down the street, to enroll in college, or to attend public events of any kind—a reflection of obesity's often-disabling nature.

In almost every nation, people weigh more than they weighed a few decades ago and weigh considerably more than earlier cohorts. For example, in the United Kingdom, the rate of obesity has tripled since 1980 (Mascie-Taylor & Karim, 2003). People are putting on excess weight at a rate of about 2 pounds a year throughout middle adulthood—more than their parents and grandparents did when they were middle-aged. Similar trends are apparent in Central and South America, Europe, and Asia. Even when it does not reach the level of obesity, overweight increases the risk of heart disease, diabetes, and stroke, and it contributes to arthritis, the most common disability among adults.

Multicultural analysis suggests some caution here. Europeans and European-Americans have been the primary participants in most large-scale studies of the effects of weight on health, yet non-Europeans in developed nations are more often overweight. Some experts suggest that people who are African-, Asian-American, or Latino are unharmed by a BMI of 25–30. However, everyone agrees that obesity (BMI over 30) is always harmful, no matter what the person's ethnic background (Strawbridge et al., 2000).

Just to maintain the same weight, people need to eat less as they grow older. The reason is that between ages 20 and 50, metabolism normally slows down by a third, which means that eating the same quantity of food would cause weight to balloon over the decades. As the rate of metabolism decreases, so does the efficiency of oxygen consumption and the speed of recuperation after stress and exercise. Compensating for all these age-related slowdowns is another reason to slim down and relieve the stress that excess weight places on the organs (Merrill & Verbrugge, 1999).

Losing Weight

What accounts for the trends in overweight and obesity? "Slim down" is simple advice, but obviously many people find this very difficult despite many diets and good intentions. Various explanations focus on environmental factors (people eat much more fast food than they once did, and portions of food at restaurants have doubled in size in the past 30 years), on evolution (homeostasis makes people who lose weight crave food to protect against starvation), and on genes (which regulate hunger and satiation, as well as metabolism and fat accumulation). Habits of infancy and childhood and parental attitudes are also major developmental factors, as described in earlier chapters.

The environmental explanations are particularly useful in explaining trends over the decades. They are also important to pinpoint, because environmental causes of overweight and obesity can be altered much more readily than evolutionary or genetic causes. Individuals can change their own behavior, and groups of individuals can change the cultural context (as has occurred in the United States with smoking). School lunches, television ads, and restaurant serving sizes are prime cultural targets. For example, only one-fourth as many French adults are obese as in the United States; this may be because the French take longer to eat but take smaller portions and thus consume less (Rozin et al., 2003).

Developmentalists advocate cultural and lifestyle changes to combat overweight, because those changes are more likely to last a lifetime (Walden & Skunkard, 2002). However, many overweight individuals turn to drugs that reduce appetite or speed digestion and, increasingly, to surgery that reduces the stomach or the intestines. In the United States, the number of operations to halt obesity doubled in only two years, from 47,000 in 2001 to almost 100,000 in 2003 (Mitka, 2003). The results have generally been positive, but long-term analysis of QALYs has not yet been possible.

Lettuce Eat Healthy If this couple regularly eats a well-balanced diet, with lots of vegetables, statistics predict that they are likely to enjoy each other's company into their 80s.

ARIEL SKELLEY / CORBIS

Exercise

The best way to lose weight is to get more exercise: In fact, though, one-fourth of all middle-aged adults and about one-third of all older adults never exercise (see Figure 20.2).

Physical activity burns calories, decreases appetite, and increases metabolism. Even if weight remains the same, vigorous exercise reduces the ratio of body fat to body weight. This is only the beginning of the health benefits: Exercise causes (is not merely correlated with) a decline in the risk of almost every serious illness; the benefits are apparent even if a person is overweight or a smoker (Carnethon et al., 2003; Manson et al., 1999).

By contrast, sitting for long hours in one spot, especially watching television, correlates with obesity and diabetes, both of which pose additional serious health risks (Hu et al., 2003). Even a little movement—gardening, light housework, walking to the bus stop—helps. Walking briskly for 30 minutes a day is better, and more intense exercise (swimming, jogging, bicycling, and the like) is ideal, significantly increasing heart and lung capacity, HDL levels, and metabolism and decreasing the risk of diabetes, LDL levels, and—of course—weight gain (Carnethon et al., 2003; Lemaitre et al., 1999; Tuomilehto et al., 2001). Exercise can reduce blood pressure, allowing people to avoid hypertension (dangerously high blood pressure) (Chobanian et al., 2003).

An additional advantage of both vigorous and modest exercise, especially for middle-aged and older people, is enhanced cognitive functioning, probably because of improved blood circulation to the brain (Stones & Kozma, 1996).

Working Out at Work Regular exercise enhances health on all four measures. Companies that provide gyms at the workplace usually see declines in employee absenteeism and health-related expenses.

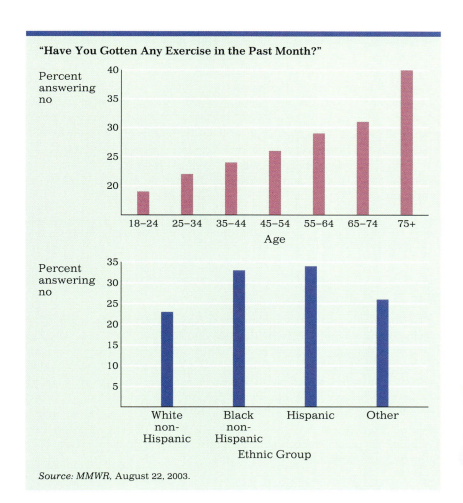

"Have You Gotten Any Exercise in the Past Month?"

Source: MMWR, August 22, 2003.

FIGURE 20.2 **American Adults Are Sedentary**
The proportion of people who exercise declines throughout adulthood, although even the very elderly can benefit from regular exercise.

? *Observational Quiz* (see answer, page 508): Who is less likely to exercise: the typical 80-year-old or the typical Hispanic of any age?

Especially for Doctors and Nurses If you had to choose between recommending various screening tests and recommending various lifestyle changes in a 35-year-old, which would you do? (See answer, page 511.)

Perhaps for this reason, exercise decreases depression and hostility, making a person psychologically healthier as well as physically more fit.

Despite the proven benefits of exercise, many people choose to remain sedentary. This self-defeating paradox takes various forms and, in one version or another, applies to all of us, as the following feature explains.

Thinking Like a Scientist

World Health and the Tragedy of the Commons

Cultural variation in health habits, and the reality that behavior affects health at least as much as medical technology, raises many ethical issues (Johnson, 2002). It is obvious that behavior change would benefit individuals and society; it is not at all obvious how this can be accomplished.

On a global level, scientists from every discipline bemoan the fact that individuals tend to seek their own immediate pleasure even when doing so harms the well-being of society and will eventually harm the individuals themselves. This is called the *tragedy of the commons*. The grazing field that every New England community once made available to its farmers was called a *common*. All too often, some farmers, reasoning that it would cost them nothing to feed additional cows or sheep, began increasing the size of their herds until overgrazing eventually made the commons useless for themselves as well as all the other farmers. Modern examples of such shortsightedness include the refusal of drivers to form carpools, the readiness of manufacturers to pollute the air or water, and the refusal of some parents to have their children immunized.

The tragedy of the commons may take the form of the inability to sustain life on earth if trends such as global warm-

ing, the burning of fossil fuels, and population expansion (from 2 billion in 1950 to 6 billion in 2000) continue (Ostrom et al., 2002; Smil, 2003). One review explains:

> Humankind is jeopardizing its own longer-term interests by living beyond Earth's means, thereby changing atmosphere composition and depleting biodiversity, soil fertility, ocean fisheries, and freshwater supplies.
>
> [McMichael et al., 2003, p. 1919]

Particularly relevant to this chapter is health-related shortsightedness. Three intestinal parasites afflict one-third of the world's population, and 115 million of the world's children are malnourished; yet there is an "unabated pandemic of childhood and adult obesity" (Mascie-Taylor & Karim, 2003, p. 1921; Rosegrant & Cline, 2003).

Every one of us knows that smoking, drinking, overeating, and lack of exercise are harmful and that the luxuries of daily life in some nations could save millions of lives elsewhere. Yet knowledge does not change behavior very much. This dilemma is personal as well as political. If this sounds like preaching, at least it is directed as much to myself as to you—and I do not always follow my own advice.

! *Answer to Observational Quiz* (from page 507): The typical 80-year-old, but not by much. About 40 percent of 80-year-olds and about 35 percent of Hispanics report that they never exercise.

During middle age, health habits are crucial. If every 40-year-old did not smoke, drank alcohol only in moderation, ate less, and exercised more, the majority of this age group would live to at least 80 and would improve the quality of their lives in middle age and beyond. For example, 65 percent of all cancer deaths are attributable to lifestyle behaviors—specifically, smoking (30 percent), poor diet and obesity (30 percent), and lack of exercise (5 percent) (Willett & Trichopoulos, 1996). Cigarette smoking is decreasing among middle-aged people in the United States, but overweight and obesity are increasing to epidemic levels. Regular exercise—even at moderate levels—can avert many diseases and increases vitality.

Ethnic Variations in Health

Thus far we have been describing the "average" or "typical" middle-aged adult, but statistics about the average person's health in midlife conceal many variations. For instance, women outlive men in every nation of the world, as already discussed in Chapter 17. Other variations are connected to income and education: Well-educated, financially secure individuals tend to live longer, to avoid chronic illness and disability, and to feel healthier than do people of the same age, sex, and ethnicity who have less education and money. In part because of income, education, and access to services, people who live in metropolitan areas generally are healthier than are those who live in the countryside. However, people in any of the world's crowded urban slums have the highest rates of mortality and morbidity.

Explaining Variations

Income and education are tied to two important determinants of variations in health: community support and quality of health care. Personal factors—both genetic and cultural—also affect the variations. Thus, medical, socioeconomic, genetic, dietary, religious, cognitive, and additional cultural patterns may explain, for example, why fatal heart attacks are more than twice as common in Mississippi and West Virginia as in Utah and Colorado and why some particular individuals in Mississippi, unlike their neighbors, are at very low risk for heart failure (U.S. Bureau of the Census, 2002). Variations are evident not just by region, but also by neighborhood; almost every state in the United States has some counties where the premature death rate is four times as high as that of another county less than 100 miles away (Mansfield et al., 1999). As one expert put it, "The way you age depends on where you live" (Cruikshank, 2003).

Midway between sweeping generalizations and specific cases are vital details: Thus, for example, the risk of any random person in the United States dying sometime between ages 35 and 65 is about one in five; but for some specific clusters of people, it is as high as 50 percent (e.g., Indian men in South Dakota) or as low as 2 percent (e.g., Asian women in New Jersey).

The Influence of Ethnicity on Health

Many of these "vital details" are linked to ethnic heritage. Ethnicity, with its attendant genetic and cultural factors, is a powerful influence on all four measures

MICHAEL KELLER / CORBIS

Healthy Eyes Annual examinations of the lens and retina are crucial for all middle-aged adults, especially those who are of African heritage.

of health. Mortality data on the five ethnic groups tracked by the U.S. Bureau of the Census make the point clearly: Between the ages of 45 and 54, African-Americans die at twice the rate of European-Americans, who themselves die at twice the rate of Asian-Americans. Native Americans have about a 20 percent higher death rate, and Hispanic-Americans a 20 percent lower rate, than the overall average (see Figure 20.3).

In general, morbidity and disability follow the same ethnic patterns in middle age as does mortality, with African-Americans most likely to be sick and disabled. These patterns are further reflected in self-reports of health status (see Figure 20.4).

FIGURE 20.3 **Death Rates in Middle Age**
Racial differences in death rates are probably caused more by environmental factors than by heredity. (Note the rates for Native Americans and Asian-Americans, who are quite similar genetically.) Sex differences are more marked than racial differences. Some believe that a biological explanation (the second X chromosome or female hormones) underlies women's lower death rates. Others favor social and psychological factors.

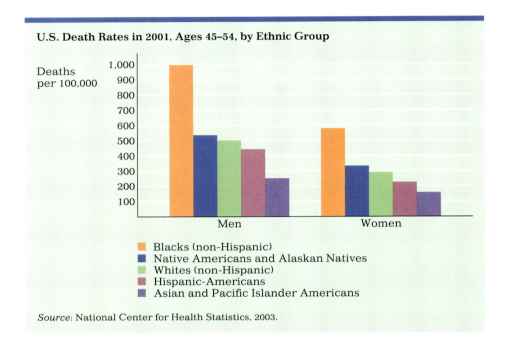

U.S. Death Rates in 2001, Ages 45–54, by Ethnic Group

Deaths per 100,000

- Blacks (non-Hispanic)
- Native Americans and Alaskan Natives
- Whites (non-Hispanic)
- Hispanic-Americans
- Asian and Pacific Islander Americans

Source: National Center for Health Statistics, 2003.

FIGURE 20.4 **Reports of Fair or Poor Health**
Asking people about their health reveals that ethnic groups differ significantly. Other data show that new immigrants generally report better health than native-born adults. This may explain why Asians are the only group not improving: Far more of this group were recent immigrants in 1991 than in 2001.

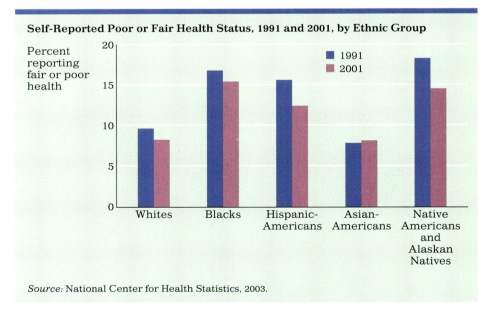

Self-Reported Poor or Fair Health Status, 1991 and 2001, by Ethnic Group

Percent reporting fair or poor health

- 1991
- 2001

Whites, Blacks, Hispanic-Americans, Asian-Americans, Native Americans and Alaskan Natives

Source: National Center for Health Statistics, 2003.

Each subgroup within each of these five broad ethnic categories has its own pattern. Among middle-aged Hispanics, for instance, the death rate of Cuban-Americans is quite low, while that of Puerto Ricans is relatively high. Among Asians, Japanese-Americans tend to live longer than Filipino-Americans. Morbidity statistics also vary for each disease: African-Americans have much higher rates of diabetes but lower rates of osteoporosis than do European-Americans, for instance.

Across ethnic groups and within many nations, immigrants are healthier than long-time residents of the same age and ethnicity (Abraido-Lanza et al., 1999; Scribner, 1996; Singh & Yu, 1996). Factors that may explain this difference include the following:

- Self-selection; only the hardiest individuals emigrate
- Health habits, particularly with regard to alcohol, other drugs, exercise, and diet
- Optimism, because a hopeful attitude can add years to life
- Family communication and support

These explanations suggest that culture may be the underlying reason for ethnic variations in health. Direct examples involving U.S. ethnic groups include a higher incidence of skin cancer among European-Americans, which is attributable not only to a genetic makeup that provides less melanin but also to a cultural approval of the "healthy" look of a suntan. Similarly, the relatively high incidence of lung cancer deaths among African-American smokers may be explained by a preference among black smokers for menthol cigarettes, which deliver more nicotine than do regular cigarettes (McCarthy et al., 1995). Other factors here may be the erroneous belief that lung surgery can cause cancer to spread (Margolis et al., 2003) or the presence of other diseases—including hypertension and diabetes—that make surgery and radiation treatment more risky. Of course, factors beyond individual genes, choices, diseases, and attitudes are also at work.

Three Causes of Ethnic Variations in Health

It is crucial to recognize three levels of causes of ethnic differences in health:

1. Genetic risks, such as the inherited vulnerability of a particular person to a particular illness
2. Specific health care behaviors in the individual as a patient, in health care personnel, or in medical routines
3. Social context factors, including stress, prejudice, and poverty

Genetic Risks

The first of these three factors is now obvious to every developmentalist (Finch & Kirkwood, 2000). Each individual has particular genetic risks of which he or she needs to be aware. Many middle-aged people become acutely conscious of their own vulnerabilities as they watch their parents and other older relatives age and die. Family history can make some risks apparent, and medical tests sometimes provide confirmation of genetic influences. However, as we have emphasized many times, most genes act epigenetically; genes and lifestyle interact. For instance, someone who is Native American or Latino is particularly likely to have a familial risk of type II diabetes and therefore needs to avoid excess weight. The combination of genetic risk and overweight is what actually triggers the onset of diabetes. Likewise, almost every genetic risk factor can be made better or worse by behavior.

Response for Doctors and Nurses (from page 508): Obviously, much depends on the specific patient. Overall, however, far more people develop disease or die because of years of poor health habits than because of various illnesses not spotted early. With some exceptions, age 35 is too early to detect incipient cancers or circulatory problems, but it's prime time for stopping cigarette smoking, curbing alcohol abuse, and improving exercise and diet.

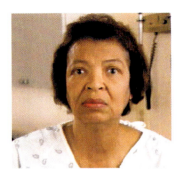   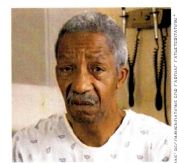

   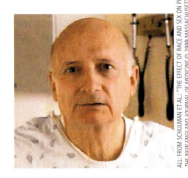

ALL: FROM SCHULMAN ET AL., "THE EFFECT OF RACE AND SEX ON PHYSICIANS' RECOMMENDATIONS FOR CARDIAC CATHETERIZATION," *THE NEW ENGLAND JOURNAL OF MEDICINE* © 1999 MASSACHUSETTS MEDICAL SOCIETY. PHOTOS COURTESY OF DR. KEVIN A. SCHULMAN

All Equally Sick? These photographs were used in a study that assessed physicians' biases in recommending treatment (Schulman et al., 1999). These supposed "heart patients" were described as identical in occupation, symptoms, and every other respect except age, race, and sex. However, the physician subjects who looked at the photos and the fictitious medical charts that accompanied them did not make identical recommendations. The appropriate treatment for the supposed symptoms would be catheterization; but for the younger, white, or male patients, catheterization was recommended 90, 91, and 91 percent of the time; for the older, female, or black patients, 86, 85, and 85 percent of the time. Are you surprised that the bias differences were less than 10 percent? Or are you surprised that physician bias existed at all?

Doctors and Patients

The second causal factor in health variations is more difficult to sort out. There is no doubt that the U.S. health care system works less well for ethnic minorities and for the poor. Individuals in these groups are much less likely than others to have health insurance or to seek medical care. When they do get care, it is less than it might be.

Doctors, like other Americans, do not believe that their behavior reflects sexism, racism, or other forms of prejudice, and patients believe that they do their best to maintain their health. However, health disparities arise partly because no human is completely free of bias (Davidio & Gaertner, 1999). In one study, researchers asked more than 700 physicians to recommend treatment for one or another of eight heart patients. Each doctor was shown a photograph of one of the patients (see above)—either male or female, black or white—and given information on that patient's symptoms, background, and insurance policies. Actually, all eight "patients" were actors, and, with the exception of age, which was said to be either 55 or 70, the information given was identical for all. Cardiac catheterization is the medically preferred treatment; it was recommended most often if the "patient" was a middle-aged white male and somewhat less often if the "patient" was older, black, or female (Schulman et al., 1999). Similar results are apparent in real life; one study found that black coronary patients at veterans' hospitals were only half as likely as white patients to have bypass or angioplasty surgery (Ibrahim et al., 2003).

As for consumers of health care, African-Americans, Native Americans, and Hispanic-Americans are less likely to seek preventive care, to know their blood pressure, or to have tests for various types of cancer (Cornelius et al., 2002; *MMWR,* August 22, 2003). Men, especially members of ethnic minorities, rarely see doctors (Williams, 2002). Middle-aged African-Americans with chronic diseases are less likely to be vaccinated against influenza (Egede & Zheng, 2003). Middle-aged Asian- and Hispanic-Americans are less satisfied with their medical care than are European-Americans (Saha et al., 2003).

All of these findings could be blamed on patients, on doctors, or on both. No matter who is to blame, good health cannot be attained unless a smoother fit between the health care system and the population it serves is reached.

The Social Context

The most difficult factor to assess is the third one on the list, the social context. One important aspect of an individual's social context is income.

Compared to people in rich nations, people in poor nations experience higher rates of almost every disease, injury, and cause of death. Thus, for example, babies born between 2000 and 2005 in the more developed nations are expected to live to age 77; in less developed nations, to 65; and in the least developed nations, to 52 (United Nations, 1998). Within nations and across ethnic subgroups, economic disparities are evident (Michaud et al., 2001). That Cuban-Americans live longer than Puerto Ricans and Japanese-Americans live longer than Filipino-Americans correlates with the average income levels of the subgroups, as well as with prejudice. Among Native Americans, the wealthier tribes have longer life expectancies and higher social status.

Some conditions once seemed more common in richer people and nations. These **diseases of affluence** might appear to be exceptions to the rule about socioeconomic status (SES) and health. For example, lung cancer was once more common among the affluent than the poor, among the more educated than the less educated, and among European-Americans than Americans of minority groups. However, once smoking became cheaper, rates of lung cancer among the poor began to rise. Today, educated people are less likely to smoke than less educated people are, and lung cancer deaths are higher among the poor.

diseases of affluence Illnesses, such as lung cancer and breast cancer, that are—or once were—more common in richer people and nations than in poorer ones.

Blue Skies Ahead Turkey is one of the nations where children still die at high rates, but some adults live long, happy, and active lives. The social context, illustrated by this man riding a donkey, is the reason.

Similarly, breast cancer was once considered a disease of affluence because wealthier nations, and wealthier women within nations, seemed to have higher rates of the disease. However, this may have been a discrepancy in diagnosis, not incidence. For instance, in the United States, although African-American women have lower rates of diagnosed breast cancer, they also have lower rates of mammograms and are more likely to die once they are diagnosed. This suggests later detection, not less cancer. (Especially among elderly women, breast cancer grows slowly, so many minority women may have died before early-stage cancer was diagnosed.) The rates of diagnosed breast cancer among African-Americans, and among women in less developed nations, are "catching up" to the rates for more affluent women (Krieger, 2002).

Income may also help to explain an interesting pattern mentioned earlier: The health of immigrants on almost every measure is better than that of native-born members of the same ethnic group. The key to solving this puzzle may be childhood SES, which affects illness in adulthood (Kuh & Ben-Shlomo, 1997). Immigrants often were raised in families that were relatively wealthy, at least wealthy enough within their country that as young adults they had the education, drive, and income to emigrate. Thus, immigrants are healthy as adults partly because of their early SES, which conferred health benefits that they retained in their new country, even though their SES declined. Remember that health depends at least as much on habits—diet, drug use, attitudes, and exercise—as on medical intervention, and immigrants further benefit from this aspect of behavior. Unfortunately, children of immigrants are often at the bottom of the economic heap, and their average health is worse than that of people the same age and ethnicity who were raised elsewhere.

Income does not inevitably mean that wealthier people always have better health habits, good medical care, and so on. A study comparing adults in England and France found that, as expected, the wealthier were healthier, but that at least when it came to habits, the specifics differed: In England, but not in France, the wealthy ate more fruits and vegetables and smoked fewer cigarettes than the poor; in France, but not in England, the wealthy drank less alcohol than the poor. According to these researchers, the SES differences in health are the result not so much of specific health habits as of factors such as employment stresses and housing access. Poor people have less control over their routines and schedules (Fuhrer et al., 2002), and stress can lead to poor health habits.

How does the connection between income and social context explain ethnic differences in health? First, it is apparent that the social context of poverty includes more pollution, more crowding, and more health hazards of every kind and that ethnic minorities often average lower income than majorities. Beyond that, stress in daily life may be the key factor. For example, black Americans have relatively high rates of poverty and of stress. It is well established that high blood pressure (a stress-related condition) is more common among African-Americans, and this underlies the high rates of death from heart attacks and strokes among African-Americans. Similarly, hypertension among American women reveals patterns of both race and income, as one might expect (see Table 20.4).

However, among African-American adult males, those of higher SES have higher—not lower—rates of hypertension (Williams, 2003). The likely explanation has to do with work stress. Those relatively few African-American men who earn high incomes are usually surrounded by members of other ethnic groups and therefore are especially likely to feel the brunt of discrimination, stress, and prejudice, either real

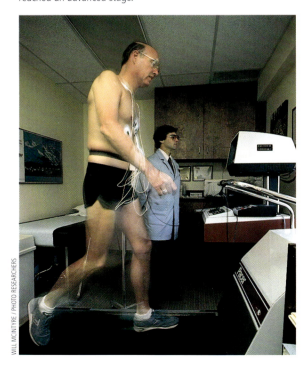

Diagnostic Differences Until recently, heart disease was regarded by most doctors as a man's disease, and diagnostic procedures such as the stress test shown here were performed almost exclusively on men. As a result, heart disease tended not to be recognized in women until it had reached an advanced stage.

WILL McINTYRE / PHOTO RESEARCHERS

TABLE 20.4 Rates of Adult Female Hypertension, U.S., 1988–1994

Income Level	Rate of Hypertension (Percent)	
	White	Black
Poor	30	40
Near-poor	24	36
Middle or high income	20	30

Source: Williams, 2002.

or in the form of stereotype threat (see Chapter 18). For such men, race and (high) income combine to raise blood pressure. An added problem for African-American men is that, even more than men in general, they try to be strong and self-sufficient and are therefore less likely to seek medical care, particularly for something that is not immediately disabling, such as hypertension (Addis & Mahalik, 2003; Williams, 2003).

All in all, factors such as gender, ethnicity, income, and birthplace affect almost every indicator of health. As one group of researchers has put it:

> There is a complex causal web involving socioeconomic determinants such as income, education, employment, . . . environmental factors such as tobacco use, physical activity, diet . . . [and] physiological factors such as cholesterol levels, blood pressure, and genes that influence mortality and disability.
>
> *[Michaud et al., 2001, p. 537]*

This complex web cannot be disentangled, but it is obvious that health messages and practices need to be tailored for each group and individual. For example, African-American women especially need to be screened for diabetes and European-American women to be screened for bone density. Similarly, Asian-American women are unlikely to get breast cancer but are more likely than women of other ethnicities to get other cancers; for example, Chinese women have more stomach cancer, and cervical cancer is four times more common among immigrants from Vietnam than among European-Americans (Ro, 2002). These differences affect the particulars of effective gynelogical care: A wise health worker would not skip the Pap smear for a Vietnamese woman in order to counsel her about breast self-examination.

Marked variations are apparent in the risk of poor health between one person and another and in the quality of each day of each person's life. Income is the most obvious reason for these differences; low-income people are much more likely to report poor health, to get sick, and to die. This is particularly true in nations where the best health care depends on private payment and private insurance. Health disparities are also evident between ethnic groups, but the reasons are more elusive, in part because immigrants often have better health than native-born individuals of the same ethnic background and income level. Genetic risks, cultural norms, stress, caregiver prejudices, attitudes about preventive care, and social bias are all parts of the explanation.

Ethnic differences in health risks lead to a final point. As you remember from Chapter 1, each of us is powerfully affected by all the contexts and cultures that surround us, but none of us are just like everyone else in our group. It is true that men tend to avoid doctors and preventive care, women tend to worry about their appearance, people of lower SES tend to exercise too little and eat too many unhealthy foods, and so on, in part because of group norms.

However, no individual is bound to certain behaviors by belonging to a particular group, and no doctor should assume that a person is somehow just like others from that group. An African-American man born in 1970 has a statistical life expectancy of 60 years (National Center for Health Statistics, 2000), but he can be screened for hypertension, glaucoma, and prostate cancer (all more common among middle-aged black men than among other men), he can avoid cigarettes and maintain a healthy diet, he can walk or run an hour a day to stay healthy and decrease stress—and he can live to a healthy age 100, as many African-American men do. Everyone can follow his example.

In other words, each of us can live in such a way throughout middle age that our health is likely to be excellent—no matter how it is measured and no matter what our background is—for decades to come.

SUMMARY

Primary and Secondary Aging

1. Both primary and secondary aging are evident in middle age, from 35 to 65. A person's appearance undergoes gradual but notable changes as middle age progresses, including more wrinkles, less hair, and new fat, particularly on the abdomen. With the exception of excessive weight gain, changes in appearance have little impact on health.

2. Hearing gradually becomes less acute, with noticeable losses being more likely for high-frequency sounds, particularly in men. Vision also becomes less sharp with age. One particular difficulty for many middle-aged people is reading small print. For the most part, these sensory changes are minor; blindness and deafness are rare in middle age.

3. During middle age, declines in all the body's systems become apparent, but generally they are not sufficient to impair normal functioning. The death rate for today's middle-aged adults is significantly lower than for earlier cohorts, although notable problems are apparent for some groups and in some indicators.

4. At menopause, as a woman's menstrual cycle stops, ovulation ceases, and levels of estrogen are markedly reduced. This hormonal change produces various symptoms and possible problems, although most women find the experience of menopause much less troubling than they had expected.

5. Hormone production declines in males as well as in females, although not as suddenly. Reproduction is possible for men, much more than for women, past age 50. For both sexes, hormone replacement therapy should be used cautiously, if at all.

Measuring Health

6. Variations in health—which can be measured in terms of mortality, morbidity, disability, and vitality—arise from a combination of many factors. Quality-adjusted life years are more important than mere survival. Particular screening measures may be less beneficial than better personal health habits and public health measures, especially worldwide.

Health Habits Through the Years

7. There is evidence that the middle-aged in the United States are more conscious of good health habits. However, many people still put their health at risk by smoking cigarettes, drinking alcohol excessively, eating poorly, gaining weight, and maintaining a sedentary lifestyle.

8. Health habits vary by age and ethnicity, as well as by nationality, but all middle-aged people could be healthier. Obesity is the most recent global epidemic.

Ethnic Variations in Health

9. Both genetic and cultural factors affect the overall health of various ethnic groups to a large extent, but social and psychological factors may be even more influential. Members of certain ethnic groups in certain settings are much more prone to health risks, and inadequate medical care and neighborhood characteristics affect minorities adversely.

10. To improve the health of the total population, individuals, medical personnel, and cultures need to change.

KEY TERMS

primary aging (p. 491)
secondary aging (p. 491)
menopause (p. 495)
osteoporosis (p. 495)

hormone replacement therapy
  (HRT) (p. 496)
mortality (p. 498)
morbidity (p. 498)

disability (p. 498)
vitality (p. 499)
QALYs (quality-adjusted life
  years) (p. 499)

disability-adjusted life years
  (DALYs) (p. 500)
burden of disease (p. 501)
diseases of affluence (p. 513)

APPLICATIONS

1. Younger adults typically make fun of older adults who attempt to look younger, especially when they fail—with gray roots visible under dyed hair, for instance. To gain sympathy and perspective, make a list of the attempts you have made to change your appearance through drugstore purchases, clothes, exercise, diet, and so on. Why does appearance matter so much?

2. Using the United Nations (see, e.g., www.un.org) or another international source, compare mortality and morbidity statistics in several nations for one specific aspect of health or disease.

What are the causes and consequences of the differences you find?

3. During middle age, virtually everyone adjusts to at least one chronic condition (consider mobility, sexuality, the senses, diseases) and seeks to prevent several others. Interview two or more people age 50 or above about their current and potential diseases and disabilities. How do you explain any differences, in QALYs or attitude, between your interviewees?

Chapter Twenty-One

Middle Adulthood: Cognitive Development

I once asked my class if people get smarter or dumber as they grow older. Opinions were divided until one student, himself over age 30, said, "Both." Exactly. This chapter explains how we get smarter in some ways and dumber in others.

Specifically, this chapter describes adult cognitive development as measured by various tests. The focus is on middle age, but test results from ages 18 to 80 are reported. Remember that Chapter 18 discussed adult thinking as a postformal stage. Chapter 24 will take an information-processing perspective. This chapter uses the psychometric approach, as psychologists have done for more than a century. (*Metric* means "measure"; *psychometric* refers to the measurement of psychological characteristics, especially intelligence.)

Surprisingly, conclusions drawn from various tests have changed every few decades, although the raw data have always been the same. This paradox is possible because, while the data remain consistent and valid, new answers have been found to the crucial question: How should intelligence be measured and interpreted over adulthood? Different answers result in different strategies for measurement and theories about what is found, and that changes the conclusions (Perfect & Maylor, 2000).

As you will see, intelligence was once thought to decline from age 20 on; now it is thought to rise until very late in life. Biology, especially genes, was once thought to be the primary determinant of IQ; now contexts, cultures, and even personal choices seem equally influential.

What Is Intelligence?

For most of the twentieth century, almost everyone, scientists and the general public alike, assumed that there was such a thing as intelligence. It seemed obvious that some people are smarter than others because they have more intelligence than others. One leading theoretician who expressed this idea was Charles Spearman (1927), who proposed that there is a single entity, **general intelligence**, which he called **g**.

Spearman contended that, although it cannot be measured directly, *g* can be inferred from various abilities, such as vocabulary, memory, and reasoning. A person could be assigned one overall IQ score, based on carefully standardized tests of intelligence, and that score would indicate whether the person was a genius, average, or retarded.

The idea that there is a single quality called intelligence continues to influence thinking on this subject (Jensen, 1998; Sternberg & Grigorenko, 2002). Many scientists are trying to find the common factor that undergirds IQ. Is it genetic

general intelligence *(g)* The idea that intelligence is one basic trait, underlying all cognitive abilities. According to this concept, people have varying levels of this general ability.

inheritance, prenatal brain development, experiences in infancy, or physical health? Some psychologists have an "unwavering hope" that some neurological construct will be found that explains how the intellect works (Frensch & Buchner, 1999). Most who study adulthood no longer have this hope.

Studying Intelligence During the Twentieth Century

Even though psychometricians believed that intelligence could be measured and quantified with a single IQ score, they disagreed about whether general intelligence rises or falls after age 20 or so. As you will see, methodology was one reason for that disagreement.

Cross-Sectional Research

For the first half of the twentieth century, psychologists were convinced that intelligence gradually declines during adulthood, after rising in childhood and peaking in adolescence. This belief was based on solid evidence. For instance, the U.S. Army tested the aptitude of all literate draftees in World War I. When the test scores of men of various ages were compared, one conclusion seemed obvious: The intellectual ability of the average male reached its peak at about age 18, stayed at that level until his mid-20s, and then began to decline (Yerkes, 1923).

Similar results came from a classic study of 1,191 individuals, aged 10 to 60, from 19 carefully selected New England villages. Most of those studied had lived in these villages all their lives, as had their parents and grandparents. This insular tradition was ideal for the researchers, who wanted to test the intelligence of people who differed in age but not very much in ethnicity, genes, or life experience. The IQ scores of these men and women revealed that intellectual ability peaked between ages 18 and 21 and then gradually fell, with the average 55-year-old scoring the same as the average 14-year-old (Jones & Conrad, 1933).

Hundreds of other cross-sectional studies, in many nations, also found that younger adults outscored older adults on measures of intelligence. The case for an age-related decline in IQ was considered proven.

Smart Enough for the Trenches? These young men were drafted to fight in World War I. Younger men (about age 17 or 18) did better on the military's intelligence tests than slightly older ones.

? *Observational Quiz* (see answer, page 522): Beyond the test itself, what conditions of the testing favored the teenage men?

Longitudinal Research

Shortly after mid-century, two psychologists, Nancy Bayley and Melita Oden (1955), analyzed the adult intelligence of the children originally selected by Lewis Terman in 1921 for his study of child geniuses (a group studied by a succession of researchers over the past 80 years). Bayley was an expert in intelligence testing. She knew that "the invariable findings had indicated that most intellectual functions decrease after about 21 years of age" (Bayley, 1966, p. 117). But in her longitudinal analysis she found, instead, that the IQ scores of these gifted individuals *increased* between ages 20 and 50.

Bayley wondered whether their high intelligence in childhood had protected this group against the usual age-related declines. To find out, she retested adults who had been selected in infancy as representative of the population of Berkeley, California. Past IQ testing and current retesting indicated that, far from peaking at age 21, the ability of most 36-year-olds was still improving on vocabulary, comprehension, and information (key subtests of adult intelligence scales). Bayley concluded that the "intellectual potential for continued learning is unimpaired through 36 years" and probably beyond (Bayley, 1966, p. 136).

Why did Bayley's finding contradict previous conclusions? Recall that her studies used a *longitudinal* design (the same people were tested repeatedly as they grew older), whereas earlier studies were *cross-sectional* (groups of people who were similar in every way except age were tested).

As you remember from Chapter 1, cross-sectional research can yield a misleading picture of adult development because each cohort has unique life experiences. Because of their early history, adults who grew up during the Great Depression, for example, developed different cognitive skills than cohorts born at the turn of the twentieth century or cohorts who grew up later. Over time, improvements in the quality and extent of public education, the variety of cultural opportunities, and expanded sources of information from newspapers, radio, and, later, television and the Internet resulted in intellectual growth.

Even more significant, elderly adults who grew up early in the twentieth century, when most children left school before eighth grade, were less likely to have developed their full academic intelligence. Those who grew up later, when high school was normative, or even later, when many people went to college, were able to develop their intellect. On IQ tests, at least, each generation is smarter than the previous one, because each generation is better educated.

The Flynn Effect

Powerful evidence for the rise in average IQ over the generations has come from research that has compared test scores in many nations over time. In every country where accumulated data allow a valid comparison, more recent cohorts outscore older ones. This trend toward increasing average IQ is called the **Flynn effect**, after James Flynn, the researcher who first reported it (Flynn, 1984, 1987). He found "massive gains" in IQ scores over the twentieth century in every developed nation, both longitudinally and cross-sectionally.

Flynn effect A trend toward increasing average IQ, found in all developed nations during the twentieth century.

Because of the Flynn effect, widely used IQ tests are now renormed (that is, new levels are set to convert raw scores into IQ numbers) every 15 years or so. A person must answer more questions correctly just to maintain the same score (Kanaya et al., 2003). There are many possible reasons for the overall rise in IQ, including not only wider education and experience, as mentioned earlier, but also more direct effects on the brain, such as better nutrition, fewer toxins (e.g., lower lead levels), and smaller family size (allowing more intellectual stimulation for each child) (Neisser, 1998).

No matter what the reasons for the rise, it is unfair—and scientifically invalid—to compare IQ scores of a cross section of adults of various ages. Older adults will score lower, but that does not mean that they have lost any of their intellectual power. Adults should be studied longitudinally, that is, compared with themselves at younger ages; such research shows most adults gaining over time.

Cross-Sequential Research

Longitudinal research is better than cross-sectional research, but it is not perfect. The same individuals are tested repeatedly, which allows them to get practice on whatever test items are used. Practice may produce learning, and thus a longitudinal rise in IQ scores may show learning, not increased intelligence.

Further, test subjects who do not return for retesting may be those who believe they are not performing well or those who move away, get sick, or have serious disruptions in their lives. This is not speculation: Dropouts do tend to be those who did poorly on previous tests, and most of the reasons people do not get retested are also the reasons for lower scores (Sliwinski et al., 2003).

Thus, longitudinal research finds IQ scores increasing partly because the people who return for retesting are those who continue to improve. In addition, to study adult intelligence longitudinally requires many decades of diligence and patience. The results then reflect only one cohort, who might have experienced

! *Answer to Observational Quiz* (from page 520): Sitting on the floor with no back support, with a test paper at a distance on your lap, and with someone standing over you holding a stopwatch—all are enough to rattle anyone, especially people over 18.

Seattle Longitudinal Study The first cross-sequential study of adult intelligence. This study began in 1956; the next testing is scheduled for 2005.

an unusual historical event (e.g., a war or an advance in public health) that makes their data less applicable to other cohorts. Such drawbacks of longitudinal methods led many researchers to cross-sectional research.

K. Warner Schaie found a way to diminish problems with both strategies. In 1956, as part of his doctoral research, Schaie tested a cross section of 500 adults at particular ages between 20 to 50 on five standard *primary mental abilities* that are widely considered to be the foundation of intelligence. These five are: (1) verbal meaning (vocabulary comprehension), (2) spatial orientation, (3) inductive reasoning, (4) number ability, and (5) word fluency (rapid verbal associations).

Schaie's initial results showed a gradual decline in each ability with age, as others had found with cross-sectional comparisons. However, seven years later, he retested his initial sample *and* tested new groups of adults at each age interval. He continued in this way, every seven years, retesting each group and adding new groups. By comparing the scores of the retested individuals with their own earlier scores and with the scores of a new group at that age, he obtained a more accurate view of development than was possible from either cross-sectional or longitudinal research alone.

Schaie's new design, called *cross-sequential research,* was illustrated in Chapter 1. Cross-age comparisons made possible by both longitudinal and cross-sectional data over many years allow analysis of potential influences, including retesting, cohort differences, experience, and gender. The results of Schaie's ongoing project, known as the **Seattle Longitudinal Study,** confirm and extend what others had found: People improve in most mental abilities during adulthood. As Figure 21.1 shows, each particular ability at each age has a distinct pattern. We will discuss this later; at the moment, note the gradual rise and the eventual decline of all abilities and the narrowness of the range.

Schaie concludes: "It is not until the 80s are reached that the average older adult will fall below the middle range of performance for young adults" (Schaie, 1996, p. 353). Confirmation of this general conclusion comes from research in many nations. For example, Paul Baltes (2003) tested hundreds of older Germans

FIGURE 21.1 Age Differences in Intellectual Abilities Cross-sectional data on intellectual abilities at various ages would show much steeper declines. Longitudinal research, in contrast, would show more notable rises. Because Schaie's research is cross-sequential, the trajectories it depicts are more revealing: None of the average scores for the five abilities at any age is above 60 or below 35. Because the methodology takes into account the cohort and historical effects, the age-related differences from age 25 to 60 are very small.

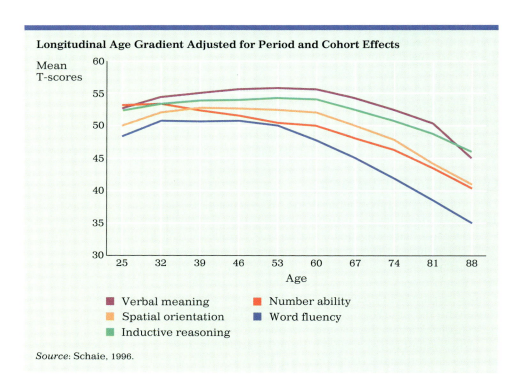

Longitudinal Age Gradient Adjusted for Period and Cohort Effects

Legend:
- Verbal meaning
- Spatial orientation
- Inductive reasoning
- Number ability
- Word fluency

Source: Schaie, 1996.

in Berlin and found that only at age 80 did every cognitive ability show age-related declines. Thus, middle age is usually a time of increasing, or at least maintaining, IQ.

Another crucial finding from cross-sequential research is that "virtually every possible permutation of individual profiles has been observed in our study" (Schaie, 1996, p. 351). One replication occurred in Sweden, with monozygotic and dizygotic twins aged 41 to 84 (Finkel et al., 1998). The results, markedly similar to those in Schaie's reports, reveal "vast individual differences in the aging process," even for monozygotic twins. Intellectual abilities sometimes rise, fall, stay the same, or fall and then rise higher than before. In short, IQ is multidirectional (Fischer et al., 2003; Neisser, 1998).

Components of Intelligence: Many and Varied

Responding to all these data, developmentalists are now looking closely at patterns of gains and losses in the intellect over the adult years. Because virtually every pattern is possible, it is misleading to ask whether intelligence either increases or decreases; it often zigzags. It is, however, possible to ask how many distinct abilities there might be and why a particular person or a specific ability might increase or decrease.

Different Forms of Intelligence This scientist investigating the genetics of breast cancer *(left)* and this camera operator shooting video for a public-access TV station *(right)* demonstrate highly specialized intellectual abilities. Imagine the difficulty of trying to create a single IQ test that would allow both individuals to demonstrate their intelligence equally.

Most psychologists have given up the search for one simple general intelligence. Instead, they envision several intellectual abilities, each of which might show an independent pattern of rise and fall.The current question is how many such abilities there are, and how and why each is affected by age. We now consider proposals that there are two, three, five, or eight such abilities.

Two Clusters: Fluid and Crystallized

In the 1960s a leading personality researcher, Raymond Cattell, teamed up with a PhD student, John Horn, to study the results of various intelligence tests given to adults. They concluded that intelligence is best understood if it is clustered into two categories, which they called fluid and crystallized intelligence.

As its name implies, **fluid intelligence** is like water, flowing to its own level no matter where it happens to be. Fluid intelligence is quick and flexible, enabling a person to learn anything, even things that are unfamiliar and unconnected to what is already known. Fluid intelligence allows people to draw inferences, to understand relations between concepts, to readily process new ideas

fluid intelligence Those types of basic intelligence that make learning of all sorts quick and thorough. Abilities such as short-term memory, abstract thought, and speed of thinking are all usually considered part of fluid intelligence.

and facts. Underlying fluid intelligence are basic mental abilities, such as inductive reasoning, abstract thinking, analysis, and short-term memory. Someone high in fluid intelligence is quick and creative with words and numbers and enjoys intellectual puzzles. The kinds of questions that test fluid intelligence include:

What comes next in each of these two series?*
4 5 6 3 4 5 2 3 4 5 6
B D A C Z B Y A

Puzzles are often used to measure fluid intelligence, such as those on IQ tests that award the test-taker bonus points for quick completion and no credit at all if the solution comes too slowly. Immediate recall—of nonsense words, of numbers, of a sentence just read—is one indicator of fluid intelligence, because working memory helps a person process new thinking.

Crystallized intelligence is the accumulation of facts, information, and knowledge as a result of education and experience within a particular culture. The size of vocabulary, the knowledge of chemical formulas, and long-term memory for dates in history all indicate crystallized intelligence. Tests designed to measure this intelligence might include questions like these:

What is the meaning of the word *philanthropy*?
Who would hold a harpoon?
Explain πr^2.
What are the boundaries of Sri Lanka, and what was it called in 1950?

Although such questions may seem to measure achievement, not aptitude, intelligent people have a large base of general knowledge, in part because intelligent people learn quickly and remember what they learn. Vocabulary, for example, is learned but is also a critical component of almost every IQ test, including the Wechsler and Binet tests. Because the more people know, the more they can learn, high crystallized intelligence at one point predicts a high IQ later on. Thus, it is not surprising that 4-year-olds with extensive vocabularies almost always become 40-year-olds with above-average IQs.

To reflect the total picture of a person's intellectual potential, both fluid and crystallized intelligence must be measured. Age complicates these calculations. In general, scores on items measuring fluid intelligence decrease with age and scores on items measuring crystallized intelligence increase. Subtests follow one or the other of these patterns (Horn & Masunaga, 2000). These two aspects changing in opposite directions cancel each other out on IQ tests, which is why IQ scores remain fairly steady from ages 30 to 70, even though many particular abilities change.

Age impairs fluid intelligence, especially processing speed and short-term memory, in the same way that a 30-year-old is slower than a younger person to react to a speeding baseball or a verbal slur. For this reason, fluid intelligence is called aging-sensitive and crystallized intelligence is called aging-resistant. However, although brain slowdown (resulting from slower blood circulation and fewer new neurons and dendrites, among other things) begins before middle age, it is rarely apparent then (Horn & Hofer, 1992). Not until late adulthood, when declines in fluid intelligence become so massive that crystallized intelligence is also affected, does IQ overall start to fall (Lindenberger, 2001).

Horn and Cattell (1967) wrote that they had

shown intelligence to both increase and decrease with age—depending upon the definition of intelligence adopted, fluid or crystallized! Our results illustrate an essential fallacy implicit in the construction of omnibus measures of intelligence.

[p. 124]

crystallized intelligence Those types of intellectual ability that reflect accumulated learning. Vocabulary and general information are examples. Some developmental psychologists think crystallized intelligence increases with age, while fluid intelligence declines.

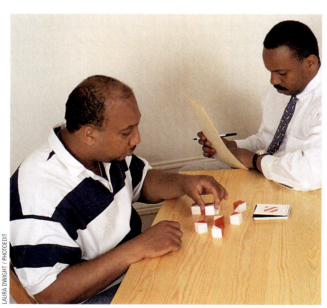

The Wechsler Adult Intelligence Test This is a timed, one-on-one exam that involves 10 separate subtests, including the spatial-design item shown here.

? *Observational Quiz* (see answer, page 526): Can you see three reasons why this middle-aged test-taker might be made anxious by the testing context and thus score lower than he otherwise might?

In other words, it is useless to try to construct a single overall measure of intelligence, because two underlying components need to be measured. These two diverge with age, which makes searching for one general intelligence particularly misleading over the life span.

Three Forms of Intelligence: Sternberg

Robert Sternberg (1988, 2003; Sternberg et al., 2000) agrees that one intelligence score is misleading. He has proposed that there are three fundamental forms of intelligence: *analytic, creative,* and *practical.*

Analytic intelligence includes all the mental processes that foster academic proficiency by making efficient learning, remembering, and thinking possible. Thus, it draws on abstract planning, strategy selection, focused attention, and information processing, as well as on verbal and logical skills. Strengths in those areas are particularly valuable at the beginning of adulthood—that is, in college, in graduate school, and in job training. Multiple-choice tests and brief essays that require analysis of remembered information (especially if there is one and only one right answer) reward analytic intelligence.

> **analytic intelligence** A form of intelligence that involves such mental processes as abstract planning, strategy selection, focused attention, and information processing, as well as verbal and logical skills.

Creative intelligence involves the capacity to be intellectually flexible and innovative. Creative intelligence is prized whenever life circumstances change or new challenges arise. Over the long run, creativity is a better predictor of accomplishment than are traditional measures of IQ (Csikszentmihalyi, 1996). However, at first some manifestations of creativity are so innovative and out of touch with the culture that the creator can be the object of scorn, legal action, or—worst of all—complete indifference (Sternberg et al., 2004).

> **creative intelligence** A form of intelligence that involves the capacity to be intellectually flexible and innovative.

Creative thinking is *divergent* rather than *convergent;* that is, approaches to problems are diverse, innovative, and unusual, rather than standard and conventional. Curiously, creativity is evident not only in great works of art but also when adults solve the dilemmas of daily life. For example, when figuring out how to save money while buying groceries to feed a family, how to choose a health insurance policy, or how to get several people from one place to another (determining, for example, who should take which car or bus along which route at what time of day), some adults use calculations that are quite advanced and innovative, unlike any they learned in school (Sternberg, 1999).

Practical intelligence involves the capacity to adapt one's behavior to the demands of a given situation. This capacity includes an accurate grasp of the expectations and needs of the people involved and an awareness of the particular skills that are called for, along with the ability to use these insights effectively. Practical intelligence is sometimes described as the product of "the school of hard knocks," or as "street smarts," not "book smarts." Emotional intelligence (discussed in Chapter 10) can be considered a kind of practical intelligence.

> **practical intelligence** The intellectual skills used in everyday problem solving.

Practical intelligence is useful for managing the conflicting personalities in a family or for convincing members of an organization (e.g., business, social group, school) to do something. Without practical intelligence, a solution that is ideal according to analytic intelligence, or one that is a stunning demonstration of creative intelligence, is doomed to failure. The reason is that, when not coupled with practical intelligence, people resist academic brilliance because it is unrealistic and they fear creative thinking because it is weird. For example, imagine a manager without practical intelligence trying to introduce policies that are incompatible with an organization's culture. The organization's members will refuse to endorse them, predict that they will fail, and balk at attempts to implement them (Beach et al., 1997).

It can be argued that practical intelligence is most useful in middle adulthood, when all the demands of daily life require it (Berg & Klazynski, 2002). Interestingly, practical intelligence is unrelated to traditional intelligence as measured by IQ tests (Sternberg et al., 2000). Certainly, few middle-aged adults

*The correct answers are: 1 and X.

TONY FREEMAN / PHOTOEDIT, INC.

Listening Quietly This elementary school teacher appears to be explaining academic work to one of her students, a boy who seems attentive and quiet.

? *Observational Quiz* (see answer, page 528): If this situation is typical in this classroom, what kind of intelligence is valued?

! *Answer to Observational Quiz* (from page 524): The pressure is on him, as is made clear by the test-giver's timekeeping (he is looking at his watch), clothing (his white shirt and tie are signs of formal high status), and sex (men often feel more pressure when performing in front of other men). In addition, the test item, block design, is an abstract, out-of-context measure of performance IQ, which usually declines with age.

need to define obscure words or deduce the next element in a number sequence (analytic intelligence); nor do they need to imagine new ways to play music, structure local government, or write a poem (creative intelligence). Instead they try to solve real-world challenges: maintaining a home; advancing a career; managing family finances; analyzing information from media, mail, and the Internet; addressing the emotional needs of family members, neighbors, and colleagues.

To assess practical intelligence, no abstract IQ test will do, because of the "centrality of context for understanding practical problem-solving" (Sternberg et al., 2001, p. 226). Adults must be observed dealing with their lives, not taking tests, to assess their practical intelligence.

Sternberg is careful to explain that each of these three forms of intelligence is useful and that adults should deploy the strengths and guard against the limitations of each:

> People attain success, in part, by finding out how to exploit their own patterns of strengths and weaknesses. . . . Analytic ability involves critical thinking; it is the ability to analyze and evaluate ideas, solve problems, and make decisions. Creative ability involves going beyond what is given to generate novel and interesting ideas. Practical ability involves implementing ideas; it is the ability involved when intelligence is applied to real world contexts.
>
> *[Sternberg et al., 2000, p. 31]*

Think about this cross-culturally. In rural Kenya, a smart child is one who knows which herbal medicines cure which diseases, not one who excels in school. As Sternberg reported:

> Knowledge of these natural herbal medicines was negatively correlated both with school achievement in English and with scores on conventional tests of crystallized abilities. . . . [In rural Kenya,] children who spend a great deal of time on school-based learning may be viewed as rather foolish because they are taking away from the time they might be using to learn a trade and become economically self-sufficient. These results suggest that scores on ability or achievement tests always have to be understood in the cultural context in which they are obtained.
>
> *[Sternberg et al., 2000, p. 19]*

This example highlights a universal problem: If a school curriculum is only analytic, and if that form of intelligence is useless in adulthood, those children who are high in practical intelligence will opt out of academic achievement because they know it is irrelevant. Because IQ tests are designed to measure potential for school learning, in Western cultures those who are high in IQ are also those who learn well in school, earn various degrees, and secure high-paying jobs. However, this may not be true in other places.

Five Primary Abilities

As you remember, K. Warner Schaie traced five primary abilities over the years of adulthood. Each of the five follows a somewhat different path, which can be explained by context. Take a closer look at Figure 21.1. In general, four of the five primary cognitive abilities increase from age 20 until the late 50s. The fifth, number ability, begins to shift downward earlier, by age 40. After age 60, decreases for all five abilities are small but statistically significant.

Each successive cohort (born at seven-year intervals from 1889 to 1966) tended to score higher than the previous generations in verbal memory and inductive reasoning, and lower in number ability, until late adulthood, when scores of all cohorts on all abilities fell. These cohort effects (recent generations up in reasoning and down in math) may be the result of younger cohorts completing more education, taught by teachers who encouraged logic and self-expression more than teachers once did. The overall impact of these trends in education is reflected in IQ scores (the Flynn effect). Changes in teaching strategy may also explain the inferior arithmetic skills in the cohorts who attended primary school after 1940. When they were children, older adults were drilled in number facts; no wonder they score high on number skills, as described in the following.

Thinking Like a Scientist

Case by Case

The portrayal of adult intelligence may seem abstract when it is based on group averages, but individual profiles of intellectual change can be separated out from group trends, allowing growth, decline, and stable functioning to be examined case by case. Using data from his Seattle Longitudinal Study, Schaie (1989) portrayed individual changes in verbal meaning. Examine the four patterns in Figure 21.2 and then read Schaie's explanations.

The first two profiles represent two . . . women who throughout life functioned at very different levels. Subject 155510 is a high school graduate who has been a homemaker all of

her adult life and whose husband is still alive and well-functioning. She started our testing program at a rather low level, but her performance has had a clear upward trend. The comparison participant subject (154503) had been professionally active as a teacher. Her performance remained fairly level and above the population average until her early sixties. Since that time she has been divorced and retired from her teaching job; her performance in 1984 dropped to an extremely low level, which may reflect her experiential losses but could also be a function of increasing health problems.

The second pair of profiles shows the 28-year performance of two . . . men . . . in their eighties. Subject 153003,

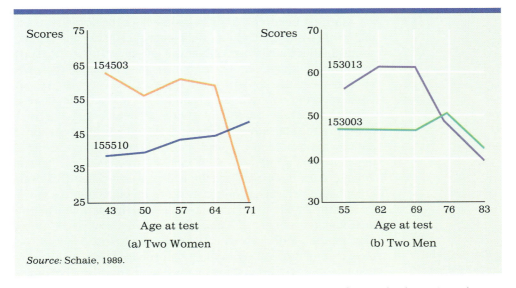

Source: Schaie, 1989.

FIGURE 21.2 Two Pairs of Profiles of Word Recognition Ability These figures index changes in word recognition scores (which are used as a measure of crystallized intelligence) for two pairs of comparable adults over time. Notice how distinctly different the profiles of individual change for each person are—even though each is the same age and part of the same birth cohort. These differences underscore how much intellectual change in adulthood is affected by occupational, marital, health, and other experiences that vary from one person to another.

who started out somewhat below the population average, completed only grade school and worked as a purchasing agent prior to his retirement. He showed virtually stable performance until the late sixties; his performance actually increased after he retired, but he is beginning to experience health problems and has recently become a widower, and his latest assessment was below the earlier stable level. By contrast, subject 153013, a high school graduate who held mostly clerical types of jobs, showed gain until the early sixties and stability over the next assessment interval. By age 76, however, he showed substantial decrement that continued through the last assessment, which occurred less than a year prior to his death.

Accurate predictions about adult cognition are elusive. No one could predict, precisely, the later-life intellectual performance of these participants by looking at the scores at their first testing and knowing the trends in intelligence.

Education, occupation, and health contribute to unique profiles of intellectual change. The lesson: Intellectual changes are woven into the changing life circumstances of each adult life. Nonetheless, old age and poor health eventually pull the intellect down.

Some other researchers would downplay the importance of education, vocation, and health, all of which Schaie stresses. Instead they would ask about the living situation, economic background, and ethnicity of each of these four people.

Thinking like a scientist, what do you think the important factors are? Do you think it would be possible to find an individual whose scores kept rising, even after age 80? Schaie found none, but he does report "rare individuals who function exceedingly well even in the mid-eighties" (Schaie, 2002, p. 316).

!*Answer to Observational Quiz* (from page 526): Solely academic learning. Neither practical nor creative intelligence is fostered by a student working quietly at her desk (the girl at right) or the boy coming up to the teacher for private instruction. Fortunately, there are signs that this is not typical for this teacher; notice her sweater, earrings, lipstick, and, especially, the apple on her desk.

Eight Intelligences: Gardner

As noted in Chapter 11, Howard Gardner (1983, 1998) believes that there are at least eight distinct intelligences: linguistic, logical-mathematical, musical, spatial, bodily-kinesthetic, naturalistic, social-understanding, and self-understanding. According to Gardner, each of these intelligences has its own neurological network in a particular section of the brain, which explains why brain-damaged people can be amazingly skilled in some intelligences (able to draw, play music, or calculate) despite enormous deficits in others (such as social interaction or language).

Gardner believes that most people have the capacity to achieve at least minimal proficiency in all eight intelligences but that each person is more gifted in some abilities than in others. Natural giftedness helps, but social contexts also affect proficiency. Families, communities, and life situations prize some intellectual abilities more than others, leading parents to encourage the prized abilities and children to develop, schools to emphasize, and adults to maintain them.

Consider high school. In schools that value athletics, the most popular students are the star athletes, and sports contests are occasions for rallies, cheers, dances, awards, and parental involvement. In effect, bodily-kinesthetic intelligence is valued highly in such schools, so students are encouraged to practice athletic skills more than academic or musical skills. This example makes a general point: Each social context evokes some intelligences more than others.

Cultural and historical contexts reveal this as well. The role of culture was illustrated in Chapter 18. Asian cultures in general, and Chinese culture in particular, may be more dialectical and inclusive, less likely to seek a single correct answer, and more likely to find compromises for various problems. Asians may emphasize interpersonal intelligence over some other types. The role of historical context is starkly illustrated with an example from colonial America 300 years ago. The Puritans condemned dance and the visual arts as the work of the devil. In that repressive context, those intelligences were never developed; whatever talent a child might have had in those areas faded by adulthood. In the same way, context and cohort affect all eight of Gardner's intelligences.

Gardner's ideas make it apparent that every way to measure intelligence reflects assumptions about the construct being measured and that cultures and families value different intelligences. Psychometricians are increasingly aware that most tests of intelligence originated in Western Europe (France and England) and have been refined and standardized by the academic elite in the United States. They are valid measures of the verbal and logical skills of North American, native-born, English-speaking children (who have always been the basis for setting the norms), but they may not be valid for other people or other skills.

Culture and Abilities

Cultural assumptions about aging probably affect concepts of intelligence and the development of intelligence tests. U.S. culture has been described as one that, unlike some Asian and African cultures, values youth and devalues age (Makoni & Stroeken, 2002; Menon, 2001). This might explain why the very abilities that favor the young (quick reaction time, capacious short-term memory) are central to psychometric intelligence tests, whereas the strengths of older adults, such as recognizing and upholding traditional values, are not.

It now seems obvious that psychometric evaluation of adult intelligence must consider the cultural background of the person and the assumptions held by the tests' authors. If intelligence is essentially the power to adapt to life's demands (as many psychologists believe it is), then tests should measure adaptation to specific cultures and to the demands of particular phases of the life span.

This point may be particularly relevant as people grow older. Paul Baltes (2003) believes that biology is significant during childhood but that culture becomes increasingly important as adults grow older. For instance, the medical innovations that allow survival into late adulthood are the result of cultural change. Equally, the way older adults do, or do not, use their minds depends on their social milieu.

Education is a manifestation of culture: Cognitive abilities are enhanced by years of schooling and can be deliberately altered through training. Most educational institutions are designed for young adults, but numerous studies of middle-aged and older adults find that training in a specific area—such as techniques of memory improvement or mathematical problem solving—improve proficiency (Schaie, 1996; Verhaeghen et al., 1992). Adults of all ages can be successful students, especially if what they are taught is relevant to their daily lives.

Older adults can even learn the specific skills valued by psychometricians if their particular cultural setting encourages it. In the Seattle Longitudinal Study, Schaie provided special training for a group of 60-year-olds who had declined markedly in spatial or reasoning skills. After five one-hour sessions of personalized training, 40 percent of them improved so much that they reached the level they had been at 14 years earlier (Schaie, 1996). At least under these circumstances, time didn't just stop—it moved backward.

Schaie's emphasis on education and vocation, and Sternberg's and Gardner's stress on context and culture, may overlook the realities of physical aging. Remember that fluid intelligence declines throughout adulthood because of slower blood circulation, fewer new neurons and dendrites, and other changes in the brain. Every researcher has noted these losses of late adulthood; many have considered the possibility of a common biological factor (perhaps slower reaction time, or reduced visual acuity, or decreased short-term memory because of a shrinking hippocampus) that powerfully influences intelligence after age 70 or so. All these factors are aspects of primary aging; as you learned in Chapter 20, culture and education cannot stop them. They will be discussed in detail in Chapter 24; now, be assured that most people aged 35 to 65 are as intelligent as they ever were. What happens later, and why, remain open questions.

Especially for Prospective Parents In terms of the intellectual challenge, what type of intelligence is most needed for effective parenthood?

Response for Prospective Parents (from page 529): Because parenthood demands flexibility and patience, Sternberg's practical intelligence or Gardner's social-understanding is probably most needed. Anything that involves finding a single correct answer, such as analytic intelligence or number ability, would not be much help.

Although psychometricians once believed that intelligence decreased beginning at about age 20, it has been demonstrated that many abilities actually increase throughout adulthood. Crystallized abilities such as vocabulary and general knowledge improve throughout middle age, although some aspects of fluid intelligence, particularly speed, decrease. Intelligence is now believed to be not a single entity but rather a combination of various abilities (which have been categorized as fluid and crystallized; analytic, creative, and practical; five primary mental abilities; and eight intelligences). These abilities rise and fall partly because of events in each person's life, partly because of culture and cohort, and partly because of age. The overall picture of adult intelligence, as measured by various tests, is complex.

Selective Gains and Losses

Thus far we have discussed intellectual changes over adulthood as if factors beyond individual control affected the patterns of change. In many ways, this assumption is valid. Aging neurons, cultural pressures, past education, and current life events all affect intelligence. None of these are under direct individual control, although, as Chapter 20 emphasized, some health habits are chosen.

Beyond that, many researchers believe that adults make deliberate choices about their intellectual development, quite separate from their culture or education. For example, the fact that number skills declined more for recent cohorts than for earlier ones may be the result not of past math curricula (as was suggested), but of modern adults' tendency to use calculators instead of paper-and-pencil (or mental) calculations.

Optimization with Compensation

selective optimization with compensation The theory, developed by Paul and Margaret Baltes, that people try to maintain a balance in their lives by looking for the best way to compensate for physical and cognitive losses and to become more proficient at activities they can do well.

Paul and Margaret Baltes (1990) developed a theory, called **selective optimization with compensation,** to describe the "general process of systematic function" (Baltes, 2003, p. 25), the way that people attempt to maintain a balance in their lives as they grow older. The idea is that people always seek to optimize their development, looking for the best ways to compensate for physical and cognitive losses and to become more proficient at activities they can do well. For example, a 55-year-old man who is an aircraft mechanic might be slower to talk and move than he was when he was younger, but he might carefully maintain his ability with spatial and sequential configuration, and thus do his job very well. One father tried to explain this concept to his son as follows:

> I told my son: triage
> Is the main art of aging.
> At midlife, everything
> Sings of it. In law
> Or healing, learning or play,
> Buying or selling—above all
> In remembering—the rule is
> Cut losses, let profits ring.
> Specifics rise and fall
> By selection.
>
> *[Hamil, 1991]*

expertise The acquisition of knowledge in a specific field. As individuals grow older, they concentrate their learning in certain areas that are of the most importance to them, becoming selective experts in these areas while remaining relative novices in most fields.

Selective optimization applies to every aspect of life, from choosing friendships to playing baseball. When applied to cognition, it assumes that cognitive skills and achievements can be broken down into discrete components, sometimes much smaller than the particular aspects of intelligence already described. Each person seeks to maximize gains and minimize losses, and therefore chooses to practice some abilities and ignore others (Wellman, 2003).

All abilities can be enhanced or diminished, depending on how, when, and why a person uses them. As Baltes and Baltes (1990) explain, selective optimization means that each person selects certain aspects of intelligence to emphasize and optimize and neglects the rest. If those aspects that are not selected, and that are therefore ignored, happen to be the ones measured by IQ tests, then intelligence scores will fall, even if a person's selection results in improvement (optimization) elsewhere.

Another way to express this idea is that everyone develops **expertise.** Each person becomes a selective expert, specializing in activities that are personally meaningful, whether they involve car repair, gourmet cooking, diagnosis of illness, or fly-fishing. As people develop expertise in one or a few areas, they pay less attention to others. For example, each adult skips over certain sections of the newspaper, ignores some realms of human experience, and has no interest in attending particular events that other people would give anything to go to. The wide variety of expertise is one of the most important lessons being a mother has taught me, as the following feature explains.

What Adults Need to Learn Many adults rely on their teenage children for expertise with computer programs, cell-phone setup, and VCR recording. However, these members of an adult education class realize that many jobs now require computer proficiency, and they have decided to compensate for the limits of their earlier education.

In Person

An Experienced Parent

A mother I know joked "I wish children were like pancakes, and I could throw out the first batch if they didn't turn out right." Her comment reflected the widespread belief that first-born children are more difficult to raise than later-borns, although eventually they may be the most obedient because of all the effort their parents expend on them (Sputa & Paulson, 1995; Sulloway, 1997).

It is also recognized that children raise their parents while their parents raise them, which explains why new parents often seem bewildered and experienced parents seem more relaxed. I was much more worried about fevers, rashes, and laundry soap for my first-born than for my last-born, because I became more expert about babies.

When they were teenagers, Bethany, my eldest daughter, told Rachel: "You have it easy, because I broke them in." I see the truth in that. Of course, Rachel did not appreciate that Bethany had laid the groundwork. In fact, she complained, "It's not fair, Mommy. You like Bethany best because you've known her longer." As an experienced parent, I smiled, because I had learned to take comments from adolescents "not too seriously, not too personally." With each teenager, adolescence has become easier for me.

Bethany was not completely wrong. Research on parents of adolescents has found that parenting skills improve with experience. Specifically, mothers and fathers know more about the daily lives of their second teenager than their first, and such parental awareness, or *monitoring,* is thought to be pivotal in raising children well (Whiteman et al., 2003). Similarly, grandparents are believed to be more patient and playful (both qualities that benefit children) than they were when they were parents.

I do not doubt that. I have learned about parenthood from my years of practice, and I am more confident and skilled because of it. For example, I readily pick up other people's children who reach out to me, something I was afraid to do before I had experience with my own. Many of my students ask me questions about their children, instead of asking my colleagues who are equally knowledgeable about the research on child rearing but who have less personal experience. My students believe that some skills are best learned on the job.

One powerful lesson my four children taught me is that each human is unique, different from me and from every other person in appearance, behavior, the kind of intelligence they value, and the expertise they develop. Each person reflects the values of his or her cohort, especially when it comes to crystallized knowledge.

Like other parents, I am astonished at aspects of human experience that my children know but I do not (current music being the most blatant example). They are amazed at things I do not know (Elissa at age 10 once asked me how could I teach American history when I didn't know how George Washington died), and I am troubled that there are things they have not learned (Bible stories, Shakespearean quotes, and, of course, psychology). The impact of culture, cohort, and context becomes very obvious to all parents.

An enormous challenge of family life is to know when to advise, guide, or outright insist on certain actions from people you love—and when to bite your tongue, realizing that children need to make their own choices and learn their own lessons. This becomes easier with experience. I now know more, but I say less.

Even harder is to know when to *take* advice. I sometimes heed my daughters' suggestions about my clothes and hair, because I know their expertise outshines mine in those areas; but I resist their suggestions about most other areas of my life. By the time I reach late adulthood, I may be wise enough to listen to them on this score as well. Not yet.

Culture and context guide all of us in selecting which areas of expertise we develop. Many adults 50 years ago were much better than today's adults at writing letters with distinctive but legible penmanship. Unlike today, however, a substantial minority could not read at all.

What Is Expert Cognition?

In these examples, you can see that an expert is not necessarily someone who has attained rare and outstanding proficiency. Although sometimes developmentalists use the term *expert* to mean someone who is extraordinarily gifted, a genius recognized by everyone, often they mean more—and less—than that (Ericsson, 1996; Ericsson & Charness, 1994; Masunaga & Horn, 2001; Sternberg & Horvath, 1999). Many researchers use a broader, more inclusive definition of an **expert:** someone who is notably more skilled, proficient, and knowledgeable at a particular task than the average person. Expertise is not innate; it is the product of training and practice over time.

Although experts are not necessarily extraordinary, what distinguishes them is not simply more knowledge about a subject (Wellman, 2003). At a certain point, the accumulation of knowledge, practice, and experience becomes transformative, putting the expert in a different league from the less adept person. What distinctive characteristics create this advanced quality, as well as quantity, of cognition? Expert thought is *intuitive, automatic, strategic,* and *flexible.*

expert Someone who is notably more skilled and knowledgeable about a specific intellectual topic or practical ability than is the average person.

Intuitive

Novices are guided by formal procedures and rules. Experts rely more on their past experience and on the immediate context. Their actions are therefore more intuitive and less stereotypic. For example, when they look at X-rays, expert physicians interpret them more accurately than do young doctors, though often they cannot verbalize exactly how they arrived at their diagnosis. As one team of researchers explains:

> The expert physician, with many years of experience, has so "compiled" his knowledge that a long chain of inference is likely to be reduced to a single association. This feature can make it difficult for an expert to verbalize information that he actually uses in solving a problem. Faced with a difficult problem, the apprentice fails to solve it at all, the journeyman solves it after long effort, and the master sees the answer immediately.
>
> *[Rybash et al., 1986]*

An astonishing example of expert intuition is chicken sexing, the ability to tell if a newborn chicken is male or female. As David Myers (2002) tells it:

> Poultry owners once had to wait five to six weeks before the appearance of adult feathers enabled them to separate cockerels (males) from pullets (hens). Egg producers wanted to buy and feed only pullets, so they were intrigued to hear that some Japanese had developed an uncanny ability to sex day-old chicks. . . . Hatcheries elsewhere then gave some of their workers apprenticeships under the Japanese. . . . After months of training and experience, the best Americans and Australians could almost match the Japanese, by sexing 800 to 1,000 chicks per hour with 99 percent accuracy. But don't ask them how they do it. The sex difference, as any chicken sexer can tell you, is too subtle to explain.
>
> *[p. 55]*

Especially for Nurses If someone seems sick but might be okay, and no equipment (not even a watch to check for a pulse) is available, what would a medical expert do to determine whether this is an emergency?

Automatic

Many elements of expert performance are automatic; that is, the complex action and thought they involve have become routine, making it appear that most aspects of the task are performed instinctively. Experts process incoming information more quickly and analyze it more efficiently than nonexperts, and then they act in well-rehearsed ways that make their efforts appear nonconscious.

This is no doubt apparent if you are an experienced driver and have attempted to teach someone else to drive. Excellent drivers who are not experienced driving instructors find it hard to recognize or verbalize things that have become automatic, such as noticing pedestrians and cyclists on the far side of the road, or feeling the car shift gears as it heads up an incline or the tires lose traction on a bit of sand. Yet such factors differentiate the expert from the novice.

This explains why, despite powerful motivation, quicker reactions, and better vision, teenagers have far more car accidents than middle-aged drivers. Sometimes teenage drivers deliberately take risks, of course, but more often they simply misjudge and misperceive conditions that a more experienced driver would automatically take into account.

Strategic

Experts have more and better strategies for accomplishing a particular task. Strategy may be the crucial difference between a skilled person and an unskilled one. For example, expert team leaders use the strategy of ongoing communication, especially during slow times, so that when stress builds, no team member misinterprets plans, commands, and requirements. This strategy is used by effective military commanders as well as by civilian leaders (Sternberg et al., 2000).

Of course, strategies themselves need to be updated as situations change and people gain knowledge. The monthly fire drill required by some schools, the standard lecture given by some professors, and the pat safety instructions read by airline attendants before each flight may be less effective than they once were. I recently heard a flight attendant precede his standard talk with, "For those of you who have not ridden in an automobile since 1960, this is how you buckle a seat belt." That was one of the few times I actually listened to the words.

The superior strategies of the expert permit selective optimization with compensation. Many developmentalists regard the capacity to accommodate to changes over time (compensation) as essential to successful aging (Baltes & Carstensen, 2003; Rowe & Kahn, 1998). People need to compensate for any slippage in their fluid abilities.

Such compensation was evident in a study of airplane pilots, who were allowed to take notes on directions given by air traffic controllers in a flight simulation (Morrow et al., 2003). Experienced pilots took notes that were more accurate and complete. They used better graphic symbols (such as arrows) than did pilots who were trained to understand air traffic instructions but who did not have much flight experience. In other words, even though nonexperts were trained and had the proper tools (paper, pencil, and a suggestion that they might take notes), they did not use them as well as the experts did.

In actual flights, too, older pilots take more notes than younger ones do, because they have mastered this strategy, perhaps to compensate for their slower working memory. Probably as a result, these researchers found no differences in the read-back proficiency among experienced pilots of three age groups: 22–40, 50–59, and 60–76 (Morrow et al., 2003). People who are not experts show age-related deficits in many studies (including this one), but experts of all ages maintain their proficiency at work in many occupations.

Flexible

Finally, perhaps because they are intuitive, automatic, and strategic, experts are also more flexible. The expert artist, musician, or scientist is creative and curious, deliberately experimenting and even enjoying the challenge when things do not go according to plan (Csikszentmihalyi, 1996; John-Steiner, 1986).

Consider the expert surgeon, who takes the most complex cases and prefers unusual patients over typical ones because operating on them might bring sudden, unexpected complications. Compared to the novice, the expert surgeon is not only more likely to notice telltale signs (an unexpected lesion, an oddly shaped organ, a rise or drop in a vital sign) that may signal a problem but is also more flexible, more willing to deviate from standard textbook procedures if they prove ineffective (Patel et al., 1999).

In the same way, experts in all walks of life adapt to individual cases and exceptions—somewhat like an expert chef who adjusts ingredients, temperature, technique, and timing as a dish develops and seldom follows a recipe exactly. Expert checkers and chess players, auto mechanics, and violinists do the same (Myers, 2002).

Expertise and Age

Not everyone becomes an expert as they grow older, but everyone needs time in order to develop expertise. Practice is crucial. According to some researchers, practice must be extensive, at least 10 years and several hours a day (Charness et al., 1996; Ericsson, 1996). Motivation is crucial as well. As the authors of a study

Response for Nurses (from page 533): Clinical judgment is based on experience more than on technology. Feeling the forehead, looking at skin color and eye brightness, listening to breathing and to the answers to simple questions, and taking the pulse would yield more than enough information to know if an emergency exists.

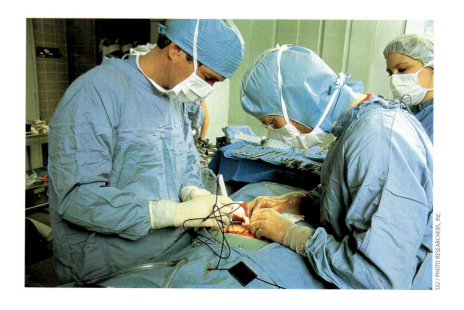

Expertise Takes Practice The importance of experience is obvious for a surgeon. Almost anyone would agree that the more practice the surgeon has had with a particular operation, the better. Less obvious, but equally valuable, is expertise in other areas. For example, for the auto mechanic, the airplane pilot, the cook, and the parent, years of practice produce a combination of intuition, creativity, and wisdom that makes the job easier and the results better.

SIU / PHOTO RESEARCHERS, INC.

PHILIPPE GONTIER / THE IMAGE WORKS

Voila! This chemist is thinking intensely and watching carefully for a result that will merit an excited "Voila!" He is in France, so we can guess his linguistic expertise; but unless we are also experienced chemists, we would not recognize an important result if it happened. Expertise is astonishingly selective.

of figure skaters explain, "Everyone has the will to win, but there are only a few who have the will to prepare to win" (Starkes et al., 1996). Circumstances, training, talent, ability, practice, and age all affect the development of expertise.

Age and expertise also interact in another way: Expertise sometimes—but not always—overcomes the effects of age. In one study, participants aged 17 to 79 were asked to identify nine common tunes (such as "Happy Birthday" and "Old MacDonald Had a Farm") when notes from midsong were first played very slowly and then gradually faster until the listener identified the tune. The listeners were grouped according to their musical experience, from virtually none to 10 or more years of training and performing.

In this slow-to-fast phase of the experiment, responses correlated with expertise but not with age. Those individuals who had played more music themselves were quicker to recognize songs played very slowly (Andrews et al., 1998). In other words, with this unusual task (for which practice was not likely), no matter what their age, novices were similar to one another and were slower than the experts, who were equally proficient at all ages.

In another phase of this study, the songs were played very fast and then gradually slowed down. In this condition, the older people took longer to recognize the tunes. Although the experts of every age did better than the novices, the older adults (novice or expert) were slower than the younger adults to decode the fast music when novices were compared with novices and experts with experts (Andrews et al., 1998). Thus, the benefits of expertise are specific, overcoming some effects of age but not others. (Note that pace made the difference here; speed is one part of fluid intelligence.)

Expertise on the Job

Research on cognitive plasticity confirms that experienced adults often use *selective optimization with compensation*. This is particularly apparent in the everyday workplace (Sterns & Huyck, 2001). In fact, the best employees are often the older ones—if they are motivated to do their best.

Complicated work requires more cognitive practice and expertise than routine work and may, as a result, have intellectual benefits for the workers themselves. In the Seattle Longitudinal Study, the cognitive complexity of the occupations of more than 500 workers was measured, including the complexities involved in the workers' interactions with other people, with things, and with data. All three kinds of occupational challenges maintained the workers' intellectual prowess.

In another longitudinal study of adults, the authors found that

... the level of complexity of their paid work continued to affect the level of their intellectual functioning as it had when they were 20 and 30 years younger. Doing paid work that is substantially complex appears to raise the level of participants' intellectual functioning; doing paid work that is not intellectually challenging appears to decrease their level of intellectual functioning. Furthermore, the positive effect ... appears even greater for older than for somewhat younger workers.

[Schooler et al., 1999, p. 491]

Waiting on Tables

Waiting on tables in a restaurant is a job that demands a wide range of cognitive skills, including knowledge of menu items; memory for orders; delivery procedures; simultaneous management of several tables, each at a different stage of the meal; the ability to combine, organize, and prioritize various tasks; and the monitoring of social relations with customers and coworkers—as well as physical stamina! Adolescents and young adults in these roles have an advantage over older adults in their strength as well as in their speed and memory. But, are older employees necessarily less efficient or can they compensate?

Marion Perlmutter and her colleagues sought to answer this question. They identified the skills required for successful performance in restaurant work and then assessing those skills in 64 restaurant and cafeteria employees who varied in age (from 19 to 60) and work experience (from 2 months to 31 years) (Perlmutter et al., 1990).

The workers were assessed on tests of memory ability, physical strength, dexterity, knowledge of the technical and organizational requirements of the job, and social capacities. They were also observed during different times of the workday, including rush and slack periods, to determine their effectiveness. Perlmutter and her colleagues wanted to know if younger and older employees differed in their overall job performance—and if so, whether the cause was physical and cognitive skills, work experience, or both.

They were surprised to discover that experience had little impact on work performance or on work-related physical or cognitive skills. Apparently, expertise at waiting on tables takes far less than 10 years to attain. As others have also found, after one has learned the basic requirements of some jobs, additional experience does not necessarily yield better performance (Ceci & Cornelius, 1990).

However, in the restaurant study, the employees' age (independent of their experience) made a significant difference (Perlmutter et al., 1990). Younger workers, as expected, had better physical skills and memory abilities, and they were quicker in calculating customers' checks. Nevertheless, older employees outperformed their younger counterparts in the number of customers served even during rush periods. One owner learned this the hard way. He said:

A pretty girl is an asset to any business, but we tried them and they fell apart on us. . . . They could not keep up the pace of our fast and furious lunch hours. . . . Our clients want good service; if they want sex-appeal they go elsewhere.

[quoted in Perlmutter et al., 1990, p. 189]

The researchers noted that many restaurant managers

consistently reported that older workers chunk tasks to save steps by combining orders for several customers at several tables and/or by employing time management strategies such as preparing checks while waiting for food delivery. . . . Although younger experienced food servers may have the knowledge and skills necessary for such organization and chunking, they do not seem to use the skills as often, perhaps because they do not believe they need to.

[Perlmutter et al., 1990, pp. 189–190]

Thus, older waitresses developed strategies to compensate for their declining job-related abilities. The researchers concluded that "adaptive competence in adulthood represents functional improvements that probably are common, particularly in the workplace" (Perlmutter et al., 1990, p. 196).

Working in an Office

Researchers have found similar results for office workers. Timothy Salthouse (1984) reported that skilled older typists perform at speeds comparable to those of younger typists, but they use different strategies to attain the same result. Specifically, they read ahead and develop a longer mental span of letters to be typed in order to compensate for age-related declines in their perceptual and motor skills. The workers in the waitress and typist studies were all women, but similar interactions between employment and age have been found to occur for both sexes (Schooler et al., 1999).

Among bank employees aged 24 to 58, the older workers who were most successful (measured by authority, salary, and ratings) were not necessarily the ones who scored highest on standard measures of intelligence. Instead, they scored well on a measure of practical intelligence of bank management.

The author of this study cautions against making judgments about the expertise of middle-aged workers based on either age or psychometric tests. Practical, everyday assessment is more pertinent (Colonia-Willner, 1998). Through selective optimization with compensation, older adults can maintain their performance levels. They find strategies to perform their work that accommodate cognitive changes.

Expertise in Daily Life

Thus far we have discussed expertise primarily as it relates to various occupations. Earlier in this chapter we touched on practical intelligence, and in Chapter 20 we explained how years of caring for one's own body and watching infirmities, illnesses, and addictions in others often lead to better health habits. In parenthood, too, as evident throughout this text, experience and time lead to a kind of practical expertise. Here we discuss only one more example: developing expertise to cope with stress.

The Stresses of Life

Life is stressful in thousands of ways, perhaps even more for adults than for younger people. Remember from Chapter 18 (Figure 18.1) that middle-aged adults are in the "responsible," "executive," and even "reorganization" stages of life, and each of these stages places new demands on cognitive ability (Schaie & Willis, 2000).

Middle-aged adults are often in the thick of life as parents of teenagers, children of aging parents, homeowners, employees, and leaders of religious, political, or neighborhood groups. These roles entail numerous conflicts and daily hassles, requiring adults to deal with the stresses of noise, traffic, demanding family members, difficult colleagues, money problems, and illnesses, as well as occasional major disruptions. Furthermore, no one lives from age 35 to 65 without at least one trauma: the death of an immediate family member, a divorce, unemployment, major surgery, an unwelcome encounter with the police.

Thus, stress is everywhere. Moreover, each stress has the potential to become a *stressor*—that is, a circumstance or event that damages a person's physical or psychological well-being (Horan et al., 2000). Stressors contribute to heart attacks and strokes, to overeating and alcohol abuse, to severe depression and explosive anger. It is crucial, then, especially as their organ reserves are diminishing, that adults cope with stress in such a way that they remain unscathed. Are adults able to do this, and if they are, do they get better at it as the years go by? The data are mixed, but the answer seems to be "yes" (Aldwin & Levenson, 2001).

Ways of Coping with Stress

Research suggests that, for humans, cognitive appraisal of a stressful event is critical in determining whether or not that event becomes a stressor (Cassidy, 1999). In other words, what people think and how they think affects how much stress they feel.

A stress may be ignored or perceived as a challenge, not a threat. If the challenge is successfully met, the body's potentially damaging response to stress—increased heart and breathing rates, hormonal changes, and so on—is averted. Effective coping may produce other physiological changes, especially with the immune system, that promote health, not sickness. Similar benefits can occur with personality, as when a person turns a stress into a challenge and then a victory, becoming stronger as a result (Ryff et al., 1998). In middle age, potential stressors can become positive turning points (Aldwin & Levenson, 2001).

Psychologists have differentiated two major ways of coping with stress. In **problem-focused coping**, people try to solve their problems by attacking them in some way (as through confrontation or negotiation). In **emotion-focused coping**, people try to change their emotions (for instance, from anger to acceptance or from frustration to denial). In general, younger adults are more likely to attack a problem and older adults to accept it, coping by changing their feelings about it (Aldwin, 1994).

problem-focused coping Dealing with a stressor by solving the problem—e.g., confronting an annoying person, getting the rules changed at work, or changing the habits of a family member.

emotion-focused coping Dealing with a stressor by changing one's feelings about it. For example, anger can turn into sympathy; frustration can be used to spot a defect in one's own character.

FIGURE 21.3 Not So Fast One expert depicts a person's response to major stress as a camera, with various lenses, reflectors, and intensifiers that can turn some stresses (e.g., a change in work) into high blood pressure and even a stroke. Note, however, that perception is a crucial first step and that several coping mechanisms must fail before a stressful event can cause illness.

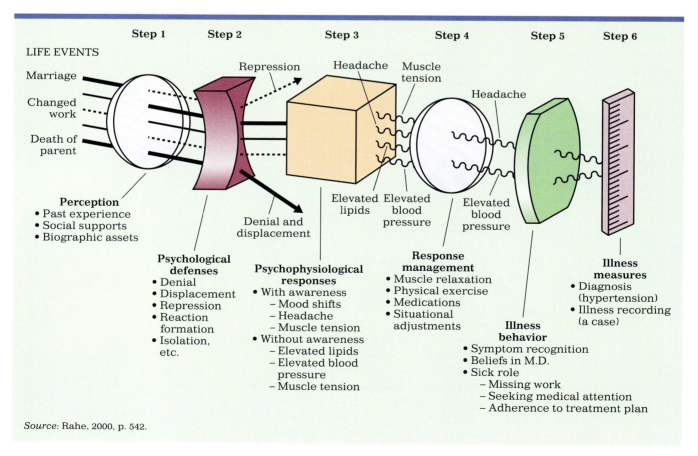

Source: Rahe, 2000, p. 542.

Many psychologists favor problem-focused coping, reasoning that "psychological defenses are extremely helpful in the short term but prove to be maladaptive over the long run" (Rahe, 2000, p. 543). If emotion-focused coping prevents a person from tackling problems head-on, then the older adult's preferred coping strategy may backfire. The consequences of ongoing stress can be quite serious—and even lethal. If organ reserves are depleted, the physiological toll can lower immunity, increase blood pressure, speed up the heart, reduce sleep, and produce many other reactions that can lead to serious illness (Horan et al., 2000).

In actuality, however, there are many steps between experiencing an external source of stress and developing an illness (see Figure 21.3). Many older adults seem able to cope well. In fact, research (reviewed in more detail in later chapters) finds that older adults have a more positive attitude toward life than younger adults do and that they take care to select their confidants. This kind of emotional coping fosters better health and longer life (Charles & Carstensen, 1999). Generally,

> Older individuals have had the opportunity to learn how to cope with stressful experiences and how to adjust their expectations. . . . On the basis of age and experience, older persons have developed more effective skills with which to manage stressful life events and to reduce emotional stress.
>
> *[Penninx & Deeg, 2000).*

One skill for managing a stressful life event is talking about it with someone, as Jenny did with me.

A Case to Study

"Men Come and Go"

My students sometimes seem surrounded by crushing stresses. I have learned, from years of parenthood, teaching, and friendship, that often I need to listen quietly when people talk about their problems. I ask questions and even make suggestions, but I try not to recommend only one solution.

Consider Jenny, who was an A student in my child development class. I knew from that class that she was divorced, raising her own two children and two nephews of her former husband. The boys' parents had died—one of AIDS and one of a bullet. I remember her telling the class about all the free activities for children she had found—parks, museums, the zoo, Fresh Air camps, and so on. I was awed by her ability to cope.

After that course ended, I didn't see Jenny again for two years, when I chanced to meet her in the hall.

"God must have put you in my path," she said. "I need to talk with you."

As soon as she mentioned God, I knew she was in trouble and so was I. This would not be a routine teacher–student conversation.

When she came to my office, I learned what the trouble was: She was four weeks pregnant. She thought she should get an abortion. This was not against her religious beliefs, but by asking questions, I learned why she was distressed.

Billy, the father of Jenny's embryo, was married, and he refused to leave his wife and son. He did not promise to stay with Jenny if she had the baby but said he would pay for an abortion. Jenny was on welfare, and her four children were living with her in a small apartment in the projects in the South Bronx. She was about to graduate with honors, and she planned to get a job and move out of her dangerous neighborhood. She worried that the baby would have sickle-cell anemia (she was a carrier; Billy had not been tested for the trait). She also thought she was too old to have another baby.

As I listened, the answer became obvious to me, as it did to her.

"Thank you, I know what I am going to do," she said.

Then she stunned me by saying, "I'll have the baby. Men come and go, but children are always with you."

Instead of attacking the problem, by having the abortion and getting rid of the man, she coped by changing her feelings about the situation. Emotion-focused coping led her to reinterpret this unwelcome stress as a positive opportunity, another child to love. I kept my advice to myself.

It turned out to be a smart choice. Billy's wife hired a detective, who found out about Jenny. The wife told her husband he must never see Jenny again or she would sue for divorce. Two years later, the divorce came through, and Billy and Jenny got married. They moved to Florida, got good jobs, bought a house with a pool, and raised their child well—she is now in college.

None of this means that everyone, or even anyone, should follow Jenny's path. It does mean, however, that "we know more than we can tell" (Polanyi, quoted in Myers, 2002, p. 57); that is, experience sometimes leads to expert intuition that cannot be easily expressed. Jenny knew more about her baby's father than his words to her conveyed, and she knew more about her own values than she verbalized to me. She made a wise choice, even an expert choice—quite different from the choice other experts might make if they had only the facts, not the intuitive understanding.

People choose to become adept at some aspects of cognition, charting their course by using selective optimization with compensation. Choices and practice produce expertise, which is intuitive, automatic, strategic, and flexible. Expertise allows people to continue performing well throughout adulthood. This is evident in many occupations: Experienced workers can continue to hold their own even when some intellectual abilities start to slip. Expertise also plays a role in more personal aspects of midlife, including the ability to cope with stress. Emotion-focused coping and problem-focused coping are both useful, depending on the situation and the individuals involved.

SUMMARY

What Is Intelligence?

1. It was traditionally assumed that there is one general entity called intelligence that individuals have in greater or lesser quantity. It was also assumed that IQ decreases across the decades of adulthood; cross-sectional evidence confirmed this view.

2. Longitudinal research has found that each person tends to increase in IQ, particularly in vocabulary and general knowledge, until age 60 or so. In addition, James Flynn found that average IQ scores increased over the twentieth century, perhaps because later cohorts had more education.

3. Cross-sequential research has confirmed that IQ increases in individuals and in generations over time. It has also found that some abilities (e.g., math) are not as high in current cohorts as in earlier ones, while other abilities (e.g., reasoning) are higher in more recent cohorts. Although almost everyone's IQ begins to decline in late adulthood, individual variations are evident.

4. Intelligence can be divided into several types or clusters. Raymond Cattell and John Horn concluded that crystallized intelligence, which is based on accumulated knowledge, increases with time, and that fluid intelligence, which includes quick and flexible reasoning skills, inevitably declines with age.

5. Robert Sternberg proposed three fundamental forms of intelligence: analytic, creative, and practical. Analytic intelligence is most useful in academic settings. Creative intelligence helps people cope with new challenges. Practical intelligence improves throughout adulthood.

6. K. Warner Schaie found that some primary abilities decline with age, while others (such as vocabulary) increase. Education, vocation, and family, as well as age, seem to affect these abilities.

7. Howard Gardner identified eight intelligences: linguistic, logical-mathematical, musical, spatial, bodily-kinesthetic, naturalistic, social-understanding, and self-understanding. The individual's genes, culture, and context affect which among these eight are prized and developed.

Selective Gains and Losses

8. As people grow older, they select certain aspects of their lives to focus on. They optimize development in those areas, compensating for declines, if need be, and ignoring other aspects. Applied to cognition, this means that people become expert in whatever intellectual skills they choose to develop. Meanwhile, abilities that are not exercised may fade.

9. In addition to being more experienced, experts are better thinkers than novices because they are more intuitive. Their cognitive processes are automatic, often seeming to require little conscious thought; they use more and better strategies to perform whatever task is required; and they are more flexible.

10. Expertise during middle age is particularly apparent at the workplace. Middle-aged workers often surpass younger workers because of their ability to specialize and harness their efforts, compensating for any deficits that appear.

11. Middle-aged adults usually cope with the stresses of their lives in ways that keep those stressors from becoming harmful. Both problem-focused and emotion-focused coping are useful, because all coping begins with interpretation of the problem. Ongoing stressors endanger health.

KEY TERMS

general intelligence (*g*) (p. 519)
Flynn effect (p. 521)
Seattle Longitudinal Study (p. 522)

fluid intelligence (p. 523)
crystallized intelligence (p. 524)
analytic intelligence (p. 525)
creative intelligence (p. 525)

practical intelligence (p. 525)
selective optimization with compensation (p. 530)
expertise (p. 531)
expert (p. 532)

problem-focused coping (p. 538)
emotion-focused coping (p. 538)

APPLICATIONS

1. The importance of context and culture is illustrated by the things that people think are basic knowledge. Write four questions that you think are hard but fair as measures of general intelligence. Then give your test to someone else, and answer the four questions that person has prepared for you. What did you learn from the results?

2. Skill at video games is sometimes thought to reflect intelligence. Go to a public place where people play such games, and interview three or four people who play them. What abilities do they think video games require? What do you think these games reflect in terms of experience, age, and motivation?

3. People choose to develop their expertise. Which of Gardner's eight intelligences are you least proficient at? Why is that? (Consider genes, family influences, culture, and personal choice.)

Chapter Twenty-Two

Middle Adulthood: Psychosocial Development

Myths abound concerning psychosocial development in middle age. Some of these myths have been given catchy names—midlife crisis, sandwich generation, role overload. Such myths have endured because, until recently, midlife was "unstudied territory in human development . . . [an] unexplored part of the life span" (Brim, 2001, p. xi).

These myths are now being discredited. For instance, many people do reassess their priorities in middle age, but this introspection rarely leads to a crisis. Moreover, although middle-aged adults are midway up the family ladder, they are neither squeezed nor sandwiched; instead, they are the link that keeps the family connected. And, although middle-aged adults do have many roles—workers, spouses, parents, leaders, managers, mentors, and more—this load is more likely to protect mental health than to damage it.

This chapter begins with the foundation for development, specifically personality as affected by genes, family background, and culture. It then explores two specific contexts: family and work. Sometimes conflicts arise among an individual's personality traits, social expectations, family demands, and work requirements, causing severe stress. Often, however, all these responsibilities and contexts make adults happy and productive, or, in Erik Erikson's words, generative, not stagnant.

Personality Throughout Adulthood

Personality is a major source of continuity, providing coherence and identity, allowing people to know themselves and allowing others to know them (Caspi & Roberts, 1999; Cloninger, 2003). Paradoxically, when discontinuity in life experiences occurs, the stability of personality becomes apparent. People seek, interpret, and react to life events in ways that reflect their distinctive traits. As two researchers explain:

> People undoubtedly do change across the life span. Marriages end in divorce, professional careers are started in mid-life, fashions and attitudes change with the times. Yet often the same traits can be seen in new guises: Intellectual curiosity merely shifts from one field to another, avid gardening replaces avid tennis, one abusive relationship is followed by another. Many of these changes are best regarded as variations on the "uniform tune" played by individuals' enduring dispositions.
>
> *[McCrae & Costa, 1994, p. 174]*

To better understand this pattern, we need to distinguish between basic personality traits and their expression.

Stable Traits: The Big Five

Big Five The five basic clusters of personality traits that remain quite stable throughout adulthood: extroversion, agreeableness, conscientiousness, neuroticism, and openness.

Extensive longitudinal, cross-sectional, and multicultural research has discovered five basic clusters of personality traits—referred to as the **Big Five**—that remain quite stable throughout adulthood (Digman, 1990; McCrae & Costa, 2003). Although various experts use somewhat different terms to describe these clusters, the consensus among them is that the Big Five can be summarized as follows:

- Neuroticism—anxious, moody, self-punishing, critical
- Extroversion—outgoing, assertive, active
- Openness—imaginative, curious, artistic, open to new experiences
- Agreeableness—kind, helpful, easygoing, generous
- Conscientiousness—organized, deliberate, conforming, self-disciplined

Whether a given individual ranks high or low in each of the Big Five is determined primarily by the interaction of genes, culture, and early-childhood experiences. Also influential are decisions made between ages 15 and 30 because, once free of parental restrictions, many young adults follow genetic impulses rather than parental wishes. By middle adulthood, continuity of the Big Five is the rule, although the general trend is for everyone to become a little less neurotic and open, and a little more agreeable and conscientious (Roberts & Caspi, 2003).

ecological niche The particular lifestyle and social context adults settle into that are compatible with their individual personality needs and interests.

Personality has great power in people's lives, especially because each person finds an **ecological niche** of his or her own. This niche is a chosen lifestyle and social context, including the person's vocation, neighborhood, mate, and routines. People make choices that fit their personalities. We should "ask not how life's experiences change personality; ask instead how personality shapes lives" (McCrae & Costa, 2003, p. 235).

A hypothetical example involving extroversion can help clarify the ecological niche. A person high in extroversion might well marry someone who was also an extrovert. The couple would likely have a social life that included a wide circle of friends and acquaintances, have jobs that required interaction with many people (perhaps in sales, politics, or public relations), live in a busy neighborhood close to, say, their amateur sports league, political club, and religious organization. (The particulars would depend on the couple's culture, income, and other personality traits.) Moreover, after 20 years of marriage, the basics would likely be

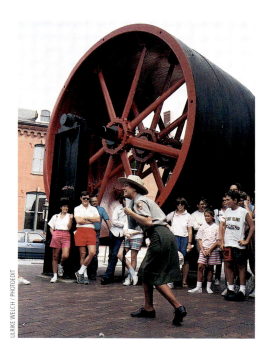

Niche-Picking The Marine sergeant in the righthand photo and the park ranger on the left have much in common. Both are middle-aged women, serving their country in uniform. However, if their expressions here are at all indicative, they have quite different personality traits, and each has picked a vocational niche that is compatible with those traits and reinforces them—a niche in which the other would probably feel quite out of place.

the same, except that the couple might have even more friends and connections and several children, who would probably also be extroverts (inheriting both the genes and the habits from their parents).

Developmental Changes in Personality

Personality traits are not rigid. In the course of the life span some change may occur (Lachman & Bertrand, 2001). However, personality change is more common before age 30; by midlife most traits are quite stable.

In large-scale cross-cultural research, the stability of the Big Five is impressive. Occasionally, "quite dramatic interindividual differences" occur, although there is an "underlying pattern" for most traits (Jones & Meredith, 1996, p. 63). Warmth toward others and confidence about oneself (both related to extroversion) are influenced by friendships and jobs and thus may be modified if the context changes.

If life circumstances are dramatically altered—perhaps by divorce or the death of a spouse, a new marriage or career, recovery from a long-standing addiction, a move to a nation with a different culture, a religious conversion, a treated mental illness (such as depression)—people sometimes act in ways they had not before. Often, however, as we have seen, new events simply bring out old personality patterns (McCrae & Costa, 2003; Roberts & Caspi, 2003).

When asked whether their personalities had changed since young adulthood, middle-aged adults usually say yes, believing they have improved over time (Lachman & Bertrand, 2001). To some degree, the general trends bear them out: The MacArthur study of personality throughout middle age (a massive research endeavor called MIDUS, Midlife in the United States) found that, of the Big Five, agreeableness and conscientiousness increased slightly with age, and openness and neuroticism decreased. Extroversion was the only trait that, on average, did not change much (Lachman & Bertrand, 2001). However, although each person notices small changes in himself or herself, and although middle-aged adults are generally a little more agreeable and a little less neurotic than they were in their early 20s, these are minor shifts, not dramatic reversals.

Similar life-span trends appear in many other countries that have national histories very different from that of the United States. Figure 22.1 shows data from four nations on only one of the Big Five traits (conscientiousness), but data from many nations confirm the stability of the five-factor analysis, with slight age-related trends similar to those found in North America (McCrae et al., 1999; McCrae & Allik, 2002).

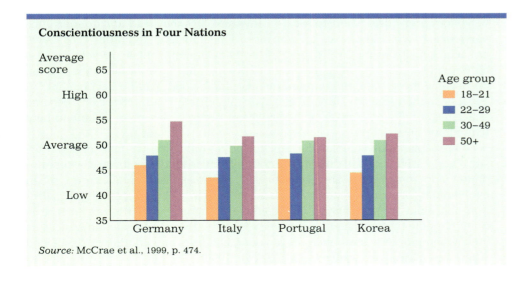

Conscientiousness in Four Nations

Source: McCrae et al., 1999, p. 474.

FIGURE 22.1 Better over Time? In every nation surveyed, older adults rated themselves higher in the Big Five trait of conscientiousness than when they were younger. They tend to value self-discipline and attention to duty. Younger adults, who tend to be higher in openness (imaginativeness, curiosity), may not agree.

TABLE 22.1 Trait Descriptions Reflecting Cultural Values in the United States and Italy

	English Descriptors	Italian Descriptors
High on openness	Creative, intellectual, imaginative, philosophical, artistic, inventive, intelligent, innovative	Nonconformist, rebellious, progressive, innovative, original, revolutionary, extravagant, ironical
Low on openness	Uncreative, unimaginative, unintellectual, simple, unintelligent, imperceptive, shallow, unsophisticated	Traditional, devoted, conservative, conventional, obedient, servile, religious, Puritan

Source: McCrae et al., 1999.

Is It "Creativity" or "Rebellion"? The Big Five personality structure is apparent in humans of many cultures. However, the particular terms used to describe each trait vary, depending on the values of the society. The most divergent descriptions are for "openness," which is regarded more highly in the United States than in Italy. Accordingly, a person high in openness is described in more positive terms in English, while a low degree of openness is referred to more favorably in Italian. (Italian descriptors are back-translated from a version of the personality test developed and validated within Italy by native Italians.)

Following Erikson's view, another developmental change in personality involves increasing generativity. Generativity was described by Erikson before the Big Five were defined, but the caring for others that is part of generativity is part of agreeableness and conscientiousness. Adults of all ages vary in how generative they are—some are much more likely to guide and support other people, while others are markedly self-absorbed—but there is a trend toward increasing generativity from about age 30 to age 65 (Jones & Meredith, 1996; McAdams, 2001). This is evident in behavior: Middle-aged people often coach the team, host the family celebration, teach the Sunday school class, mentor younger coworkers.

In considering developmental changes, remember that cultures differ in the traits they value (see Table 22.1). For instance, conscientiousness is particularly valued in China, extroversion in Australia, openness in the United States, and agreeableness in the Philippines. Despite such cultural differences, the similarities of all humans in all cultures seem more apparent than the differences (McCrae & Allik, 2002).

Gender Convergence

One developmental change may occur in many cultures: Gender restrictions loosen during middle age, allowing both men and women to explore feelings and behaviors previously reserved for the other sex. This may lead to a **gender convergence**, in which the sexes become more similar, or even a **gender crossover**, an actual switching of roles and of traits (Gutmann, 1994; Huyck, 1999)—although few cohorts or clusters seem to go that far. Many middle-aged women do become more self-confident and many middle-aged men do become able to express tenderness or sadness more openly. Some young warriors become peacemakers; some obedient housewives become assertive grandmothers (Gutmann, 1994). Why?

One explanation is biological. Sex hormones influence the male tendency toward aggressiveness and dominance and the female tendency toward accommodation and nurturance. These hormonal influences developed as part of an evolutionary process, as these tendencies in the early adult years of mate selection and child rearing proved important to human survival (Rossi, 1994). It is quite possible that one set of personality traits, with male–female differences, is ideal when mothers and fathers have young children, and another set is needed when the children are grown (McCrae et al., 1999).

gender convergence A tendency for men and women to become more similar as they move through middle age.

gender crossover The idea that each sex takes on the other sex's roles and traits in later life. This idea is disputed, but there is no doubt that maleness and femaleness become less salient in middle age.

This pattern is the basis of the traditional arrangement in which young mothers stay at home with small children (who need every ounce of nurturance an adult can muster) and fathers go out to earn the family's living (with self-assertion critical to how much he earns). In a sense, the "parental imperative" involves a "chronic state of emergency" that pushes parents into traditional gender roles (Gutmann, 1994).

In middle age, hormone levels decrease, and the parental imperative becomes less of a factor. At this point, cultural norms become less restrictive, even encouraging convergence or crossover. In Asia, for example, whereas young women are expected to be submissive and shy, older women are expected to be dominant and assertive. Men are expected to be more meditative and spiritual as they approach their later years (Menon, 2001).

Although it is logical that hormonal changes are the origin of this shift, it is also possible that changing life situations *cause* (not merely reflect) the biological shift. In any case, both nature and nurture allow the personalities of men and women to become more similar in middle age. Remember, however, the larger picture that includes stability of the Big Five for both sexes. Gender convergence may occur, but it does not change a person's overall personality—just the manifestation of some traits.

The psychoanalyst Carl Jung theorized that everyone has both a masculine and a feminine side but that, because of social pressure, young adults develop only those traits that "belong" to their own gender (1933). Thus, young women strive to be more tender and deferential than they might naturally be, while young men try to be brave and assertive even when they feel afraid. According to Jung (1933), in middle age adults finally realize that

> . . . the achievements which society rewards are won at the cost of a diminution of personality. Many—far too many—aspects of life which should have been experienced lie in the lumber-room among dusty memories.
>
> *[p. 104]*

Kiss It, Daddy In the magical thinking of preschoolers, pain will disappear with a kiss or a bandage. Children today are as likely to seek such a cure from Daddy as from Mommy.

Thus, middle-aged adults of both sexes choose to explore the *shadow side* of their personality—women, their repressed masculine traits and men, their repressed feminine traits.

Although all these biosocial, cultural, and psychoanalytic explanations are intriguing, longitudinal survey research suggests yet another explanation, a historical one. Perhaps many middle-aged and older individuals become less tightly bound by gender restrictions because times have changed (Barnett & Hyde, 2001). It is not that adults themselves mature but that each decade of the past century witnessed expansion of gender roles for everyone of every age. Older adults who vividly remember more rigid gender divisions may be more conscious of the shift (Stewart & Ostrove, 1998).

Historical change might explain an interesting finding from longitudinal research: Current middle-aged adults are less likely to converge in sex roles than the previous cohort did (Helson et al., 1995; Moen, 1996). Perhaps because male–female differences in personality are less apparent today, middle-aged adults do not need to demonstrate their "liberation" from gender restrictions (Brody, 1999).

We do not know if gender crossover actually occurs or if it is another myth about middle age, reflecting a historical circumstance rather than an enduring middle-aged shift. Eleanor Maccoby (2002), a leading expert on sex differences and similarities, calls for more research. She suggests that the research agenda needs to include epigenetic and psychobiological perspectives, so that we can better understand which differences are basic to human development and which are cultural or cognitive.

midlife crisis A period of unusual anxiety, radical reexamination, and sudden transformation that is widely associated with middle age but which actually has more to do with developmental history than with chronological age.

The "Midlife Crisis"

If personality throughout adulthood is increasingly stable, with small shifts for the better as each culture defines it, then why do people speak of a **midlife crisis**, a period of unusual anxiety, radical reexamination, and sudden transformation around the 40th birthday? The idea of a midlife crisis was popularized by Gail Sheehy (1976), who referred to the "age 40 crucible" and by Daniel Levinson (1978), who studied a small group of midlife men, many of whom experienced

> . . . tumultuous struggles within the self and with the external world. . . . Every aspect of their lives comes into question, and they are horrified by much that is revealed. They are full of recriminations against themselves and others.
>
> *[p. 199]*

Contrary to Levinson's assertion, no large study of midlife men has found anything like a midlife crisis. Moreover, researchers have found that midlife women are more likely to experience a rebirth, if anything (Heckhausen, 2001); for women, it is a time for midcourse corrections that lead to happier times (Stewart & Ostrove, 1998). One woman expressed the dominant view of her cohort when she was asked how she felt about turning 50: "Great! I'm a better 50-year-old than I was at other ages. I've been waiting for it" (quoted in Stewart & Ostrove, 1998, p. 1189). If a midlife crisis ever did exist, it was the norm only for middle-class men who reached age 40 in about 1960.

How could this myth have seemed plausible? A number of potentially troubling personal changes cluster in the 40s. The most obvious is simply that the biological clock signals that one is growing old, as the mirror reflects the signs of aging, the gray hairs and wrinkles. Beginning with the "Big Four-O," birthdays are seen in a new perspective—not years since birth, but years left to live. Those who thought that they had ample time to accomplish their life goals suddenly see the door to the future closing. This perceptual shift may be highlighted by the death or serious illness of an older relative or friend. Within the immediate family at midlife, teenage children challenge one's authority, young adults distance themselves from their home, and some realize that middle age is the last chance for divorce and remarriage—or an extramarital fling.

As you will soon read, such changes do not necessarily cluster at age 40, and they are usually taken in stride. How people react to the challenges and changes of middle adulthood has more to do with their personality than with calendar milestones. Chronological age, as a predictor of development, is like "an initially appealing false lover who tells you everything and nothing" (Birren & Schroots, 1996, p. 17).

Returning to our original question, if the midlife crisis has been exposed as a myth, why do many people still talk about it as if it were real?

> Scholars have been puzzled by the resilience of the myth about the midlife crisis despite numerous studies showing no common pattern indicative of a crisis in the middle years (e.g., Chiriboga, 1989; Hunter & Sundel, 1989; Whitbourne, 1986). It may be that part of this resilience of the midlife crisis lies in its benefit: to anticipate the worst at midlife and be pleasantly surprised by one's own comparatively smooth sail.
>
> *[Heckhausen, 2001, p. 378]*

In other words, the myth may enable adults to cope with the disappointment, frustration, and sorrow caused by all the factors we have mentioned, and still consider themselves fairly fortunate.

Personality is usually quite stable over the years. Enduring traits become especially evident in the individual's reaction to unexpected or disrupted life events. Personality characteristics have been clustered into the Big Five:

neuroticism, extroversion, openness, agreeableness, and conscientiousness. Although each person is relatively high or low on each of these traits, some developmental changes occur over time: Neuroticism and openness decrease slightly, and agreeableness and conscientiousness increase. Some theorists describe gender convergence or even crossover, attributing it to biology, culture, or a combination of the two. Gender convergence may or may not occur. However, except in one cohort of North American men, midlife crises are unlikely.

Family Relationships in Midlife

It is hard to overestimate the importance of the family. It is "our most important individual support system" (Schaie, 2002, p. 318). It is a "problem-solving system" (Wilson et al., 1995, p. 85) that "persists over time . . . as households wax and wane" (Troll, 1996, p. 246). Although made up of individuals, a family is much more than the individuals that belong to it. Families raise children, care for the sick, provide resources for all members, and create a family culture that gives meaning to, and provides models for, personal aspirations and decisions.

No other group system has replaced the family in any nation or century, although the form taken by "family," as a connection among relatives, varies among different cultures. Families do not always do their job or always do it well. Some adults wisely keep their distance from their blood relatives. Some become "fictive kin" in another family; that is, they are accepted and treated like family even though they are not legally or biologically related. Fictive kin arise in any culture, but they are particularly likely to be found in African and African-American families (Stack & Burton, 1993).

Where do middle-aged adults fit into this picture? Right in the center, often as the linchpin that holds it all together. They are the cohort bridge, the "generation in the middle," between aging parents and adult children. As they sometimes also have grandparents and/or grandchildren, they may actually be in the middle of four or five generations.

For the middle-aged, members of the same generation (typically spouses and cousins) are important fellow travelers on the **social convoy**, a group of people who "provide a protective layer of social relations to guide, encourage, and socialize individuals as they go through life" (Antonucci et al., 2001, p. 572). Now we look at the key source of family support: the chosen partner.

social convoy A group of people who form relationships with an individual through which they guide and socialize that person as he or she moves through life.

Partners

Having an intimate relationship is a source of happiness, comfort, and self-respect. For most (70 percent) middle-aged adults in the United States, and even more (75 to 90 percent) in some other nations, this intimate relationship is with a spouse.

For some divorced, widowed, or never-married middle-aged adults, intimacy is achieved through cohabitation. The 2000 U.S. Census revealed that about 5 percent of 35- to 65-year-olds live in households with an unrelated adult of the other sex and less than 1 percent in households with a same-sex partner. Many of the remaining 25 percent of unmarried middle-aged adults find intimacy in a romantic relationship that does not include declaring a shared household.

Friendship, reviewed in Chapter 19, is particularly important for single adults, most of whom see friends and acquaintances often. Many also have strong ties with siblings, parents, cousins, and others. Churches, neighborhoods, schools, and organizations also provide fulfilling roles, with the happiest adults typically having five roles, not just one or two (Thoits, 1992).

Especially for Young Couples Suppose you are one half of a turbulent relationship, in which moments of intimacy alternate with episodes of abuse. Should you break up?

In fact, *role overload* (discussed in Chapter 19) is another myth. Most middle-aged adults have a partner or best friend as well as many roles, and they are quite happy with all of them. Research on the impact of most of these relationships in middle age is sparse. However, much is known about marriage.

Marital Happiness

As detailed in Chapter 19, marriage is linked to personal happiness, health, wealth, and other advantages in every nation. The general trend in marriage seems to be happiness at first (the honeymoon period), then a dip for a decade or so, and then a gradual rise over the years of middle adulthood (Glenn, 1991). Surprisingly, the presence of children tends to reduce satisfaction within a marriage, especially for mothers when the children are young (Twenge et al., 2003).

Chapter 19 also described common couple violence and intimate terrorism. These destructive relationships arise from personality patterns (high in neuroticism, low in agreeableness), cultural contexts, and childhood experiences that precede marriage, which make them particularly difficult to change (DeMaris et al., 2003). Fortunately, some improvement is possible. Worldwide, spouse abuse is far more common among younger spouses than among middle-aged spouses. For example, a study that compared couples in Korea and the United States found that in both cultures, with maturity, couples were much less likely to verbally or physically abuse each other (Felson et al., 2003).

Among the reasons middle-aged marriages seem better than young adult marriages are that most couples have less stress from the children, higher incomes, and more time together. Many couples adjust their work lives to have adequate—but not too much—time for the marriage relationship, and this balance improves satisfaction (Becker & Moen, 1999; Werner & Smith, 2001). In many other ways, the passage of time benefits the relationship. As one person said: "Our love for each other for 26 years keeps us together. You don't just give that up" (quoted in Previti & Amato, 2003). With every year of marriage, divorce becomes less likely.

Some people stay married for the wrong reasons, fearing, for example, the expense of divorce or the resulting loneliness. But such barriers to divorce often simply postpone a breakup rather than preventing it: Many people who divorce in middle age have been waiting for the right time to quit the relationship. However, a survey of long-married people found that most of them stayed married because of the love, trust, and joy in their relationship, not primarily because it was difficult to break up (Previti & Amato, 2003).

Enjoying the Empty Nest During the empty-nest period, many middle-aged parents regain their freedom to frolic, invigorating their marriage with renewed closeness and the sharing of activities that the earlier demands of work and family life may have curtailed. All couples, whether they live in Spain *(left)* or the Arctic *(right),* seek this renewed closeness in ways that suit their personalities and culture.

It is sometimes said that marriages are not as satisfying as they once were, but the evidence does not support this claim. Although the divorce rate in the United States has remained high (almost 50 percent), it has not increased in the past 20 years and has even begun to decrease. Fewer people are getting married. More directly to the point, studies of marriages in recent decades suggest that long-term marriages provide as much satisfaction today as they did in the past (Amato et al., 2003).

The specifics of marriage have shifted: Couples are more likely to share domestic tasks (which makes the wives more happy but the husbands less so), and wives are more often employed (which means more money but less time together). Overall, despite significant economic and social changes, marriage relationships seem to have adjusted (Amato et al., 2003). College students of both sexes still hope for one enduring, committed, relationship (Pedersen et al. 2002).

That marriage remains satisfying, especially in midlife, is supported by studies in various cultures. One specific example is a recently published midlife report from a longitudinal study of all the babies born in 1955 in Kauai, Hawaii. These babies were of five distinct ethnicities. This cohort experienced a positive shift in their development by age 40, with an intact marriage being one of the best sources of resilience and satisfaction (Werner & Smith, 2001).

Some unhappy marriages end before they become long-term; thus, they are not reflected in surveys of middle-aged marriages. Further, generalities obscure individual realities: Some long-term marriages are blissful; others are horrible. Economic stress creates marital friction, no matter how many years a couple has been together (Conger et al., 1999). Nevertheless, marriage relationships are likely to get better over time, especially when compared with the divorce-prone first five years after the wedding.

Divorce and Remarriage

Causes and consequences of divorce are similar throughout adulthood (see Chapter 19). Divorce is less common after years of marriage and children. It also has more impact when it does happen. Specifically, for middle-aged husbands as well as wives, divorce reduces income and weakens family ties at a stage of life when long-term social bonds are especially needed (Amato, 1999).

Not only does divorce usually halt supportive relationships with former in-laws, but the parent–child relationship is often curtailed (especially for non-custodial parents). Even the relationships between the children and their grandparents on both sides are affected (unless the grandparents become surrogate caregivers, in which case the parent–child attachment weakens). Simply put, divorce weakens family bonds (Hofferth & Anderson, 2003; King, 2003; Lamb, 1999).

Almost half (46 percent) of all U.S. marriages are actually remarriages for at least one of the spouses, with the average age at remarriage being about 35. Most divorced men remarry—on average, within five years of being divorced. Thus, many middle-aged adults—far more men than women—are in a second marriage. Remarriage is more likely if the divorced person is a relatively young man, in part because there are more potential partners still available. For the same reason, many divorced women do not remarry, especially if they have custody of the children.

Remarriage often brings initial happiness and other benefits: Men usually become healthier and more sociable, and women become more financially secure (Hetherington & Kelly, 2002). For remarried fathers, bonds with a new wife's custodial children or with a new baby may replace strained relationships with their children from the previous marriage (Hofferth & Anderson, 2003). For both men and women, having a child with a new spouse typically strengthens the second

Response for Young Couples (from page 550): There is no simple answer, but you should bear in mind that, while abuse usually decreases with age, breakups become more difficult with every year, especially if children are involved.

marriage and improves relationships with parents, while loosening the remaining emotional bonds of the first marriage (Ganong & Coleman, 1999).

Despite popular wisdom to the contrary, there is no guarantee that love is better the second time around. Second marriages end in divorce more often than first marriages, and children suffer more each time a parent changes marital status (Coleman et al., 2000; Hetherington & Kelly, 2002).

Developmentalists hesitate to interpret these findings as a warning against divorce. Correlation is not causation, and these correlations may be caused by other factors, such as personality. For example, if someone's Big Five traits include high neuroticism, high openness, low conscientiousness, and low agreeableness, sustaining a marriage might be more difficult than seeking a divorce. Children of divorced parents might be troubled because of their parents' personalities or because of the personality traits they inherited. Further, because economic stress is one reason for divorce as well as one reason some children are low achievers, the financial circumstances that preceded the divorce might be more problematic for the children than marital disruptions are. For whatever reason, the more times a person has been married, the more likely it is that a current marriage will end in divorce and that children will suffer academically and socially.

The Marriage Market for Middle-Aged Adults

Marriage is likely to benefit middle-aged adults. However, middle-aged women are at a disadvantage for marrying or remarrying, for two reasons. First, men die at younger ages. Beginning at about age 45, there are more women than men. Second, men tend to marry younger women. For example, in 1998, of all married men in the United States aged 35 to 44, 25 percent had a wife under age 35 and only 2 percent had a wife over age 44 (U.S. Bureau of the Census, 1999). If all divorced and never-married men married women in their own age group or a decade younger, then men would have three times as many possible partners as midlife women would. This imbalance works to the advantage of young women but to the disadvantage of older women (see Figure 22.2).

The extent of the disadvantage varies from group to group. For example, partly because men are more likely to immigrate than women, 54 percent of all never-married or divorced Hispanic, but only 44 percent of African-American, adults living in the United States are men.

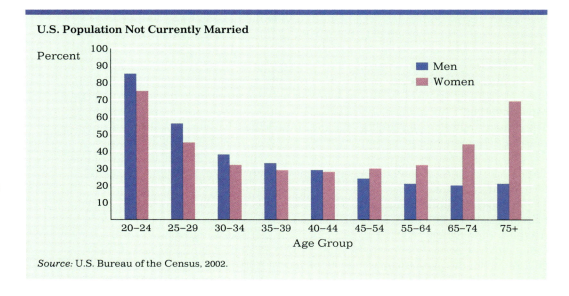

FIGURE 22.2 Advantage: Older Men, Younger Women Male partners are even scarcer for women than this chart shows, because men typically choose younger women as marriage partners. There is a woman for every man, but there is not a man for every woman.

Source: U.S. Bureau of the Census, 2002.

The marriage odds are stacked against African-American women for other reasons as well. For one thing, 6 percent of African-American men marry outside their ethnic group, compared with only 2 percent of African-American women (U.S. Bureau of the Census, 2002). Further, twice as many African-American women as men obtain a BA degree, and marriages are more likely between people of equal education; if unequal, the man is usually the one with higher education.

What should an unmarried middle-aged woman do? Once the answer was to live with, and care for, aging parents. But social norms have changed: An increasing number of women have careers, and an increasing number raise children—without being married (see Table 22.2).

TABLE 22.2 Women as Sole Heads of Households with Children

Year	Female-Headed Households (Percent)			
	White	Black	Asian	Hispanic
1960	8.7	22	—	—
1980	12	40	11	20
2000	19	55	13	28

Source: U.S. Bureau of the Census, 2002.

Other Relatives

It is easy to underestimate the critical role of family dynamics for the middle generation in modern Western cultures, because people less often live with relatives other than a spouse and young children. However, the word *family* should not be confused with **household**—that is, people who live in the same dwelling; increasingly, families live in several small households, not all together in a single big one. The decrease in the size of U.S. households is dramatic. As Figure 22.3 shows, more than a third of the U.S. population today live alone or with one other person, usually a spouse.

The fact that several generations no longer sleep under the same roof does not mean that family ties have weakened. In every nation that has been studied, most relatives frequently call, write, and visit one another, even when they live at a distance. They provide each other with substantial help, ranging from advice and emotional support to gifts, loans, babysitting, home repair, and health care (Connidis, 2001; Farkas & Hogan, 1995). Although it is tempting to idealize the traditional large household, contemporary family members may be more supportive of one another, with less tension and discord, when they live apart than when they live together (Coward et al., 1992; Fry, 1995; Umberson, 1992). They need one another, but they do not need to share a household.

The generation most capable of providing family support is the middle-aged, because they are physically healthy, cognitively practical, psychosocially generative, and, usually, without small children of their own. Often, someone in the middle generation becomes the family's **kinkeeper,** the one who ensures that relatives maintain contact, who plans and hosts family get-togethers, who provides help in times of illness or other crisis.

Most kinkeepers are women, although middle-aged men sometimes take on this role (Rossi, 2001). Today's families tend to have fewer siblings, so, because many middle-aged women are employed, it is less likely that a family will have a female member with both the time and temperament to be a natural kinkeeper.

If no natural kinkeeper is available when an elderly person needs ongoing care from an adult child, a daughter may feel that she must quit her job, a daughter-in-law may be recruited to provide care, a son may be the only adult child available to step in, or a granddaughter may put her own life on hold. In these cases, care of the elderly person may be resented as an interruption, a burden, a developmental halt. Daughters-in-law are particularly

household A group of people who live together in one dwelling and share its common spaces, such as kitchen and living room.

kinkeeper The person who takes primary responsibility for celebrating family achievements, gathering the family together, and keeping in touch with family members who do not live nearby.

FIGURE 22.3 The Shrinking U.S. Household
As the U.S. population has become less rural, with fewer people needed to work on family farms, the average household has gotten smaller.

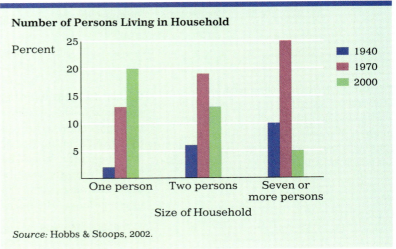

Number of Persons Living in Household

Source: Hobbs & Stoops, 2002.

likely to feel unfairly burdened with elder care (Ingersol-Dayton, Starrels, & Dowler, 1996). This situation is *not* typical in middle age, as we will soon see.

Aging Parents

The relationship between middle-aged adults and their parents often improves with time (Connidis, 2001). One reason is that, as adult children mature, they develop a more balanced view of their relationship with their parents, especially when they look back at their years of growing up. The perspective of time can lead to a measure of forgiveness, as both generations acknowledge past mistakes in their relationships. This is especially true when young adults gain a firsthand understanding of the pressures of parenthood.

Current cohorts are particularly likely to experience closer relationships, because most of the elderly today are healthy, active, and independent. They typically prefer *not* to live with their adult children, and most of them can afford to live on their own. The resulting freedom and privacy enhance the relationship between the two generations.

Positive relationships between the middle and older generations are also apparent in subcultures in which co-residence is still the custom. For example, Hispanic- and Asian-Americans are likely to live in three-generation families, for the most part harmoniously, in part because cultural values strongly endorse family solidarity. When a conflict does arise, the source is usually either a very dependent and demanding elderly person or a rebellious teenager, not the generation in the middle (Johnson, 1995; Mindel et al., 1998).

familism The idea that family members should support one another because family unity is more important than individual freedom and success.

Whether or not middle-aged adults and their parents live together depends mostly on the basic value called **familism**, the belief that family members should be close and supportive of one another, even if that means sacrificing some individual freedom and success. Practical considerations, such as poor health and inadequate finances, make three-generation households more likely; but when familism is weak, ways are sought to avoid co-residence (Burr & Mutchler, 1999). For example, in California, where husbands and wives are both heavily committed to their jobs, young Chinese-American families often hire a Chinese caretaker when an elderly parent needs ongoing assistance (Lan, 2002). Generally, familism and co-residence are more common among ethnic minorities than among the majority (see Figure 22.4) (Burr & Mutchler, 1999).

Strong family ties can be either supportive or destructive, depending not only on the values of the culture but also on the specifics of the situation. A strong marriage bond between the elderly parents benefits the middle-aged children, and this is currently the norm in the United States. Indeed, today's elderly adults are the most married of any cohort in the past 100 years. As one result, about half the time, a spouse is available to provide help with daily care. If both partners are somewhat disabled, often they collaborate; together they manage to cope (Dixon, 1999). If they themselves have parents who are still alive (the grandparents of the middle-aged generation), they usually either provide any care needed or arrange for paid care.

The middle-aged keep in touch with their parents, especially on issues related to their parents' well-being. When disagreements arise, the older generation does not necessarily heed their children's advice, preferring to maintain their independence. Here are one father and daughter:

Father: My daughter called up my wife and said, "You must sell your house." I have this heart condition, and my daughter doesn't want me to walk up a flight

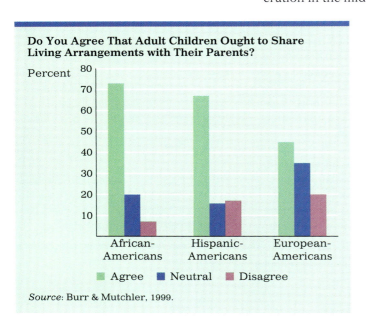

Do You Agree That Adult Children Ought to Share Living Arrangements with Their Parents?

Source: Burr & Mutchler, 1999.

FIGURE 22.4 No Place Like Home Members of ethnic minorities tend to place a higher value on family cohesiveness than on individual achievement. As a result, they are less likely than white adults to move out of their parents' home and set up separate households of their own.

of stairs to go up to the bedroom. . . . So my wife says, "No. I'm never going to sell it. . . . I love the place we live in."

Daughter: I've always been close to my mother, but it's only this last, well, maybe the last 2 years that I'm beginning to resent the fact that she lives in this big house and that I have to keep worrying about her and going there and making sure that they're all right. My dad is too ill to live in a big house, but she just doesn't want to give it up. . . . My mother refuses to leave the house, and I'm beginning to resent her selfishness; I really am.

[quoted in Pyke, 1999, p. 666]

In such cases in North America, the marriage relationship usually outweighs the parent–child one, so this house will probably not be sold unless the mother agrees. The middle generation cannot take over decision making unless the older generation is frail. Even then, the elderly may resist suggestions to stop driving, to move, or to have surgery. If the older generation really requires help, relationships between elders and their adult children, and among siblings, may be disrupted (Pyke, 1999).

Siblings

One of the seldom-studied yet vital aspects of adulthood is the relationship between siblings, who often become closer in the second half of life than they were in young adulthood (Cicirelli, 1995). They help one another with problems involving their teenage children, stressful marriages, and family contacts. One researcher described the usual pattern between siblings as an "hourglass effect": close during childhood, increasingly distant until middle adulthood, then gradually closer again as late adulthood progresses (Bedford, 1995). Siblings who respected and liked each other but never spent much time together before often become confidants and may even live together again if a spouse dies or a marriage dissolves. Relationships between sisters are particularly likely to become close.

Childhood Echoes The specifics of sibling relationships in middle and late adulthood are strongly influenced by family values instilled in childhood. If the family encouraged a child to "protect your sister" or "stick up for your brother," this value is likely to reemerge when problems arise (Cicirelli, 1995).

I observed this with my own parents. When they were middle-aged, they lived in Pennsylvania, far from their Minnesota birthplace, where 12 of their siblings still lived. Despite the geographical distance, they kept in frequent phone contact with their brothers and sisters, and they even found a nearby job for one of my unemployed uncles so that he and my aunt could move near them. When my parents thought about retirement, they rejected Arizona, where some of their friends had gone, and moved back to snowy Minnesota to be near their siblings, some of whom were widowed, frail, or sick.

My phone conversations with my parents in Minnesota revealed more about sibling rivalry than I expected. I heard that two of my mother's sisters, Harriet and Laura, were so angry at each other that they had stopped speaking. Dumbfounded that siblings in their 80s could hold a grudge, I asked my mother what the argument was about. "It began long ago," she explained. "Papa favored Laura. She is the pretty one." The only difference I could see between the two was that Laura's eyes were blue and Harriet's brown, but neither could accurately be called "the pretty one"—both were overweight and wore thick glasses. Outside intervention can help resolve family conflict at any age: Thanks to my father, Harriet and Laura resumed daily phone conversations several months before Laura died of cancer.

As in this example, closeness between siblings can be affected by rivalries rooted in childhood (Cicirelli, 1995). During midlife, such rivalries are often put aside, because the brothers and sisters have their own mates, careers, and homes.

New Challenges Problems can reemerge (or emerge for the first time) when a parent needs special care and there is no spouse to provide it. As we have seen, one adult child usually becomes the major caregiver. This burden traditionally falls on a daughter who lives nearby and is not working; but in today's smaller families, such a daughter may not exist. Then another daughter (in the United States) or a son (in Asia) is considered primarily responsible. The inequity of one child becoming the primary caregiver is often resented on all sides. Instead of finding a way to distribute the responsibility, siblings often maintain emotions that originated when they were younger. For example, one caregiving sister complained that another sister, who lived out of state, flew in once a year to help out and then left "for the beach." The caregiver was trying not to cross

> a real thin line between just taking her head off some day. . . . It just pisses me off royally, and now that it's summer and I want to do weekends with my family, she feels imposed on during the summer to go one day a weekend.
>
> *[quoted in Ingersoll-Dayton et al., 2003, p. 205]*

In another family, the sister who was providing most of the care quelled her resentment of her two siblings by describing one as "real immature . . . a little slow" and the other as "very irresponsible," adding, "When it came right down to having to bathe and having to take care of physical [tasks], neither of them would be able to handle it" (quoted in Ingersoll-Dayton et al., 2003, p. 209).

In both of these examples, the caregiver is struggling emotionally. Siblings who do not provide care struggle, too. One brother explained why his sister-in-law was caring for his parents by saying that she "doesn't work, you know, outside the home, and so she was there and able to follow up a lot." A brother in another family felt that his sister exaggerated her caregiving responsibilities: "My sister reminds me all the time that she's taking care of them. They're actually pretty self-sufficient" (Ingersoll-Dayton et al., 2003, pp. 208–209).

In some cases, the death of the parents, rather than freeing siblings from a life-long rivalry, actually increases it, especially if there are disagreements about the funeral, the personal effects, and the inheritance. Even the death of a sibling does not necessarily release the survivor from resentment or jealousy (Cicirelli, 1995).

The death of parents may bring siblings closer together—at least, some siblings think so. One man, the youngest of six, explained:

> When our mother died, a big shift happened in our family. Instead of counting on Mom to arrange family gatherings or parties, we all realized we would have to do that ourselves. It's true that Emily [the oldest sibling] has become a "surrogate Mom" and takes responsibility for remembering all the birthdays and who would bring what for Thanksgiving dinner. But all of us feel closer.
>
> *[quoted in Gold, 1996, pp. 238–239]*

In general, siblings are a potential resource for middle-aged adults, sometimes welcomed, sometimes spurned, whether the issue is aging parents, family harmony, or their own growing children.

Adult Children

Parents generally maintain close relationships with their children, even when the latter are fully grown, independent, and living away from the family home. One in-depth, longitudinal study of four generations found that "most mothers and daughters had stormy relationships during the daughters' adolescence but close and friendly ones once the daughters left home, whether or not the daughters married" (Troll, 1996, p. 253).

A seven-nation survey of thousands of middle-aged adults found that the majority (75 percent) communicated with their adult children several times a

Like Parent, Like Child Even when a child becomes bigger than a parent, as is evident with this Mexican son and California daughter, parents enjoy not only the company but also the flattery through imitation (note the similar clothing and positions) provided by their adult children.

week; only a tiny minority (less than 5 percent) got in touch only once a year or less. Most adults of both sexes and both generations said that they would turn to each other for help of every kind, from emotional support to furniture arranging (Farkas & Hogan, 1995).

Typically, money and a variety of services (from home repair to laundry) flow more freely from middle-aged parents to young adults than in the other direction. Parents benefit from their adult children's generosity in less tangible ways. They usually take great pride in their accomplishments, and their self-esteem is enhanced when their offspring are well-functioning adults (Keyes & Ruff, 1999).

Middle-aged adults are often surprised by the ongoing dependency of their young adult children. Instead of flying away, leaving an empty nest, many young adults stay on or return. This phenomenon has prompted one observer to describe the "swollen nest" phase of life, an uncomfortable period that often follows the child-rearing phase (Ginn & Arber, 1994).

In the United States, at any given moment, almost half of all middle-aged parents have at least one child still living with them, sometimes a teenager but often a young adult. How long adult children live with their parents differs significantly across countries, as Table 22.3 shows for some European countries. Italian and Japanese young adults (especially men) are likely to stay on, whereas Scandinavian young adults (especially women) are likely to leave (Iacovou, 2002; Raymo, 2003).

Young adult children are especially likely to stay on at home when their parents are in good health and when they themselves are financially needy, perhaps because they are unemployed or single parents (Nilsson & Strandh, 1999; Whittington & Peters, 1996). In Japan, 65 percent of unmarried children older than 30 are still living with their parents, a rate that has been increasing (Raymo, 2003). No matter where in the world such overfull households exist, the middle-aged parents pay most of the bills and do most of the housework (Ward & Spitze,

TABLE 22.3 Average Age at Which European Men No Longer Live with Their Parents

Country	Age
Denmark	22
Netherlands	23
England	24
France	24
Germany	26
Austria	27
Greece	28
Spain	28
Italy	30

Source: Iacovou, 2002.

1996). In North America, neither generation is particularly happy living in a swollen nest. Parents, especially, regard independent living as the natural order of things, and both generations feel the loss of privacy and the increase in conflict that sharing a household entails (Alwin, 1996; White & Rogers, 1997).

Grandchildren

Grandparenthood often begins in middle age, although its timing and prevalence vary from culture to culture, cohort to cohort, and person to person. In the United States, more than two-thirds of those between ages 40 and 65 become grandparents. A smaller group become grandparents "off-time," typically before age 40 (about 10 percent overall) and occasionally after age 65. The rest (about 15 percent) never become grandparents, usually because they themselves have no children.

When the first grandchild arrives, almost every grandparent reacts with pride and wonderment. As one grandfather exulted, "Now I'm immortal!" The actual experience of being a grandparent is highly variable, ranging from fulfilling to frustrating, from pivotal to peripheral.

Personality, ethnicity, national background, and past parent–child relationships all influence the nature of the grandparent–grandchild relationship, as do the age and the personality of the child (Mueller & Elder, 2003). The grandparent–grandchild bond tends to be closer if the following are the case:

- The grandchild is relatively young.
- The parent is the first sibling to have children.
- The grandparent is neither too young nor too old—retired but not frail.

Types of Grandparents

Generally, ongoing grandparent–grandchild relationships take one of three forms: remote, involved, or companionate (Cherlin & Furstenberg, 1986; Gratton & Haber, 1996).

remote grandparents Grandparents who are distant but who are honored, respected, and obeyed by the younger generations in their families.

involved grandparents Grandparents who actively participate in the lives of their grandchildren, seeing them daily.

companionate grandparents Grandparents whose relationships with their children and grandchildren are characterized by independence and friendship, with visits occurring by the grandparents' choice.

- **Remote grandparents** are emotionally distant but esteemed elders who are honored, respected, and obeyed by children, grandchildren, and great-grandchildren. Often, remote grandparents control the family land, business, or other wealth. Even when they do not, they may see themselves as the patriarch or matriarch of the family, responsible for maintaining traditional values. Remote grandparents were typical a century ago in the United States and are still prevalent in some traditional cultures.
- **Involved grandparents** are active in the day-to-day life of the grandchildren. They live in or near the grandchildren's household, and see them daily, and provide substantial care. In the United States, this pattern was prevalent for most of the twentieth century but is relatively rare today, except among immigrant and ethnic-minority families.
- **Companionate grandparents** are independent and autonomous, maintaining a separate household and their own lifestyle. They decide how generational interaction occurs, which grandchildren get the most attention, and whether to babysit. They entertain and "spoil" their grandchildren, but they do not discipline them—especially in ways, or for reasons, that the parents would not.

Most grandparents in developed nations "strive for love and friendship rather than demand respect and obedience" (Gratton & Haber, 1996), choosing to be companions rather than authorities. A major reason is that grandparents now are independent, living in their own households with their own values, social lives, and jobs (middle-aged grandmothers as well as grandfathers are usually employed these days).

Most grandparents are pleased to be companions. They boast about their grandchildren, display their photographs, and provide fun, treats, and laughter—and leave the responsibilities to the parents (Erikson et al., 1986). Many grandparents confess that they are "glad to see them come and glad to see them go." In fact, among contemporary adults, companionate grandparents generally enjoy grandparenting more than do remote grandparents, who are frustrated when they cannot maintain family rules and traditions. Companionate grandparents are especially glad they do not need to be intensely involved (Hayslip & Patrick, 2003).

Immigrant Grandparents

Many immigrant grandparents happily become involved with their grandchildren, especially when all the family members speak a common language (Toledo et al., 2000). Often they live in the same household. Of all U.S. households, only 4 percent of those with a native-born head of household include grandchildren. By contrast, 25 percent of those households with a Mexican-born head, 18 percent of those headed by an Asian refugee, and 15 percent of those headed by someone born in the Caribbean region include three or four generations (Glick et al., 1997). Especially in such extended families, grandparents are often very involved with the youngest generation.

Among the native-born in the United States, this involved pattern is most common in minority families. For example, grandparents whose heritage is non-European are three times more likely than European-Americans to provide full-time care, year after year, for their young grandchildren (Vandell et al., 2003).

Children seem to develop better when they are cherished and guided by a large family (Keller & Stricker, 2003). Adults may not benefit, however. In the United States the involved grandparenting role is often undertaken not only for cultural reasons but for practical reasons as well:

■ Many immigrant and minority families do not trust the majority culture to transmit "the values, beliefs, language, and customs" that allow each new generation to understand its cultural heritage (Silverstein & Chen, 1999). Grandparents are the best source of cultural continuity, especially in a majority culture that ignores or disparages the traditions and values of the ethnic group.

DAVID YOUNG-WOLFF / PHOTOEDIT, INC.

Can You Make Rice Cakes? If you can, it's probably because you, like these Japanese-American girls, were fortunate enough to have a grandmother nearby to teach you. Note how intently and carefully all three are working to prepare the food for a large family gathering.

- Many immigrant and minority grandparents are not well positioned in the labor market, and thus they can be caregivers without giving up satisfying employment.
- Most immigrant and minority parents are poor, and grandparent care is often free, unlike a good day-care center that may cost hundreds of dollars a month.

Thus, whatever the virtues of involved grandparenting, issues of cultural transmission and of social inequalities in employment opportunities and in quality day care need to be addressed. Involved grandparenting may not be the first choice of the middle-aged adults or the young-adult parents; it may be the family's only option.

Although all three generations can benefit when grandparents are involved with their grandchildren, benefits should not be assumed. Involved grandparents tend to believe they know best how to raise children, and this may cause conflicts with the young adults.

As immigrant grandchildren grow older within a new country, speaking the language and learning the values, they may no longer respect, obey, or even understand their grandparents (Kolland, 1994). This causes distress on all sides, particularly among grandparents whose hopes for the future are tied to the new generation. As one 60-year-old immigrant from Cambodia explained:

> I'm afraid they might not be what I want them to be because in this country the children are very unpredictable. . . . I don't like to talk too much, because the more you talk the less respect they have toward you.
>
> *[quoted in Detzner, 1996, p. 47]*

Surrogate Parents

surrogate parents Grandparents who take over the raising of their grandchildren as a result of their adult children's extreme social problems.

A range of social problems sometimes catapult grandparents into an extremely involved role. If the parents are poor, young, unemployed, drug- or alcohol-addicted, single, or newly divorced, grandparents may become **surrogate parents.** They take over the work, the cost, and the worry of raising the children.

In 2000, almost 3 percent of all children in the United States were living with their grandparents and without either parent (U.S. Bureau of the Census, 2002). Note that this statistic refers to the children at one point in time. Since most grandparents have several grandchildren, it is estimated that about 20 percent of all grandparents spend some time providing exclusive care of at least one grandchild, sometimes just for a summer vacation but increasingly as full-time surrogate parents.

Children who need extra attention are particularly likely to be sent to Grandma's. Drug-affected infants and rebellious school-age boys, for example, are more likely to live with grandparents than preschool girls are. If the parents are adjudicated as neglectful or abusive, this becomes *kinship care* (see Chapter 8), and the grandparents receive some payment from the state. More often grandparents become surrogate parents out of necessity, with no compensation but increased stress (Bowers & Myers, 1999). Many worry that they are not up to the job, just as many parents do. As one grandmother explains:

> I don't know if God thought I did a poor job and wanted to give me a second chance, or thought I did well enough to be given the task one more time. My daughter tells me she cannot handle the children anymore, but maybe I won't be able to manage them either.
>
> *[quoted in Strom & Strom, 2000, p. 291]*

Middle-aged and older grandparents can provide excellent surrogate care, furnishing the stability, guidance, and patience that distressed parents lack. In fact, children of single parents generally benefit in many ways from living with a

Not Lonely When they were 2, 4, and 6 years old, these boys went to live with their grandparents in Virginia. The family is attending a picnic for grandparents who have become surrogate parents for their grandchildren. Events like this fill a need: Many such grandparents feel isolated from their peers.

? Observational Quiz (see answer, page 562): In two obvious ways, this family is typical of grandparent–grandchild families. Name them.

grandparent, because the grandparent relieves some of the stress and loneliness that single parents feel (Hinton et al., 1995).

Sometimes surrogate parenting impairs the grandparent's own health and well-being, increasing the risk of physical illness, depression, and marital problems (Kelley & Whitley, 2003; Solomon & Marx, 2000). From a developmental perspective, having another child to raise "off-time" is part of the problem. As one surrogate parent says:

> We are participating in a life that in no way resembles that which was anticipated. . . . I grieve for my future, my hopes and aspirations for myself as well as those for my son, my loss of freedom, and my relationship with my husband and daughters. . . . And to make it worse, I cannot give voice to my grief for fear my granddaughter will feel it is her fault.
>
> *[quoted in Baird, 2003, pp. 62, 65]*

After Adult Children Divorce

More than one in three grandparents witness the divorce of an adult child. They typically provide extra help if their newly divorced child receives custody of the grandchildren. They offer emergency housing, extra babysitting, financial support, and sometimes surrogate parenting—all very useful to the child and grandchild, although, as we have just seen, not necessarily to the grandparents. If their child does not have custody, the result may be worse: The parents of the noncustodial ex-spouse are often completely shut out of their grandchildren's lives (Amato, 1999; King, 2003).

If grandparents are shut out, they may sue for visitation rights. Since 1970, every state in the United States has enacted laws that require continuation of a close relationship already formed if a child has lived with the grandparent. Some states go much further, mandating grandparent visitation rights even if no relationship existed, even if the parents were never married, and even if both parents oppose it. In other states, the courts are much more restrictive, ruling that grandparents must prove that the benefit to the child overrides the parents' wishes (Hartfield, 1996).

The problem is that, on the one hand, intergenerational nurturance is an important mainstay for many grandparents and grandchildren, but, on the other

!Answer to Observational Quiz (from page 561): The grandparents are relatively young, and the grandchildren are boys.

sandwich generation A term for the generation of middle-aged people who are supposedly "squeezed" by the needs of the younger and older generations. Some adults do feel pressured by these obligations, but most are not burdened by them, either because they enjoy fulfilling them or because they choose to take on only some of them, or none.

hand, children do not need grandparents in order to develop well. As with some parents, some grandparents are destructive. Usually both parents decide when, how, and even whether children will spend time with their grandparents, cousins, and other relatives. But in the emotional heat of divorce, it is difficult for anyone to know whether a particular association is a blessing or a curse. Legal remedies are available but may not help.

> The law is a very blunt instrument for regulating family relationships and managing family change, and therefore can have unintended as well as intended consequences.
>
> *[Thompson & Wyatt, 1999, p. 214]*

The Myth of the Sandwich Generation

As we have seen, under some circumstances, family relationships can become burdensome and destructive. Because of their position in the generational hierarchy, the middle-aged are expected to help both older and younger generations. That is why they have been called the **sandwich generation**, a term that evokes an image of two slices of bread with a substantial filling—meat, jam, peanut butter—in the middle. The analogy to a sandwich, making it seem as if the middle generation is squeezed by obligations to those younger and older, is vivid—but it is not very accurate.

It is true, as we have seen, that many middle-aged adults provide some support for their children and that one member of the middle generation may become kinkeeper and caregiver to the older generation. Sometimes young-adult children have serious disabilities and remain dependent on their middle-aged parents (Roberto, 1993). This situation has become more common because medical advances have saved the lives of many infants who would have died and adequate, publicly funded homes for disabled adults are scarce.

It is *not* true, however, that all or even most middle-aged adults are burdened by obligations to other generations. To some extent, each member of the middle generation decides whether or not to provide care and to whom.

Most choose *not* to provide financial or caregiving help to any of the older generation. For example, one study of married people aged 51 to 61 with living parents found that less than 20 percent provided help of any kind to any parent. Assistance was more likely to be provided by African-American couples (three times more) and by daughters (Shuey & Hardy, 2003). A detailed breakdown from another study found that in the United States, both husbands and wives tend to tilt toward the wife's parents (Lee et al., 2003) (see Table 22.4). In some other nations, such as China, it is the husband's parents who are more likely to receive support (Lin et al., 2003).

Personality may be as influential as need in determining whether middle-aged adults provide substantial help to either generation. For example, in the

?Observational Quiz (see answer, page 564): Is the typical adult male more attentive to his parents or to his in-laws?

TABLE 22.4 Contacts and Help Provided by Middle-Aged Couples to Parents and In-Laws

	Phone Calls per Month	Visits per Month	Minutes of Help per Week
Wife to own parents	11	6	120
Husband to wife's parents	8	5	70
Total to wife's parents	19	11	190
Husband to own parents	7	4	100
Wife to husband's parents	5	4	58
Total to husband's parents	12	8	158

Source: Lee et al., 2003.

WILL YURMAN / THE IMAGE WORKS

Mother, Father, and Son Outsiders might pity this family because the 40-year-old son has cerebral palsy and is dependent on his parents. However, these three are accustomed to their caregiving interactions, gain comfort from their roles, and are satisfied with their relationship.

study that found only 20 percent of married adults contributing to any of their parents, those 20 percent were also likely to be the ones contributing to their adult children. The researchers suggest that a personality trait (generosity) may be the reason. Culture may be important as well, as is evident from the fact that immigrants and nonwhites provide more intergenerational care than do European-Americans (Shuey & Hardy, 2003).

More important, although any of these family obligations might make middle-aged adults feel squeezed, life satisfaction is likely to increase with caregiving. For example, middle-aged women who are simultaneously employee, wife, mother of a child still at home, and daughter of a parent who needs some assistance tend to be happier with their lives than other women *if* their relationships with the various people are satisfying and no one is too demanding (Barnett & Hyde, 2001; Lawrence et al., 1998). Usually these conditions can be met and the relationship is satisfying, because of the following:

- Although young adult children living at home may not contribute much to the household, their independence reduces their parents' ongoing burden, especially compared to when they were teenagers.
- Disabled adults require less care than when they were children.
- The middle generation may provide some assistance to their parents—but not very much except in unusual circumstances. If major caregiving is required, usually another member of the older generation provides it.

Therefore, middle-aged adults are less "caught in a web of generational obligation" than buoyed by the rewards of each role (Soldo, 1996, p. S272). Most of them are proud of their maturing children, enjoy their grandchildren, take comfort in their relationships with their own parents, and find satisfaction with their family relationships overall. In short, the sandwich generation is not really squeezed by the other generations; this is another myth regarding middle age.

Families are crucial for everyone. Middle-aged adults are often their family's kinkeepers or linchpins, holding the group together. The most important family member for most adults is their intimate partner, typically a spouse, who provides emotional as well as economic support. Usually divorce is disruptive of family ties, and remarriage may also be problematic. Intergenerational

Answer to Observational Quiz (from page 562): His in-laws! Husbands telephoned and visited their parents-in-law more often than they did their own parents. They did help their own parents more—by half an hour per week.

family closeness does not depend on living arrangements. Many adults have households separate from those of the other generations but are nonetheless mutually supportive of aging parents, siblings, and adult children.

Most adults become grandparents during middle age and develop remote, companionate, or involved relationships with their grandchildren, depending on the family's characteristics. The companionate type is the most common. If grandparents become surrogate parents, the grandchildren often benefit but the grandparents may not.

Work in Middle Adulthood

As we saw in Chapter 19, work provides friendship, status, structure, and esteem, as well as a paycheck. In the United States, 90 percent of all middle-aged men and 75 percent of all middle-aged women are employed (U.S. Bureau of the Census, 2002). Percentages are lower in many other nations, though few people are unemployed by choice.

Worldwide, then, for many middle-aged adults, work is a welcome part of life. To a large degree, the rewards and stresses of employment depend more on the demands of the job than on the age, gender, or background of the worker. In general, most jobs provide more joy than stress (Barnett & Brennan, 1997).

Overall Trends

There are some age-related trends in employment. Generally, the "intrinsic rewards of work, satisfaction, relationships with coworkers, and a sense of participation in meaningful work become more important as an individual ages," and extrinsic rewards (salary and benefits) become less crucial (Sterns & Huyck, 2001, p. 452). One reason that wages are less central may be that salary and benefits tend to rise with seniority. Older workers have less reason to worry about income, work hours, and health care.

For whatever reasons, older workers have lower rates of absenteeism, of being fired or quitting, and of seeking another job. Employees over age 35 are half as likely to be actively seeking new jobs as employees under that age (U.S. Bureau of the Census, 2002).

In keeping with these trends, most middle-aged workers have worked for the same employer for more than five years and have settled into work that satisfies them, with routines and coworkers they like. As you saw in Chapter 21, they become experts, doing the job well and able to teach others by example. Many enjoy mentoring younger workers; many advance to a position where they supervise others. Generally, middle-aged workers stay put, with good attendance records, to the satisfaction of their employers.

Many changes in the workplace over the past few decades (reviewed in Chapter 19)—jobs that depend less on physical strength and more on expertise, increased teamwork, greater workplace diversity—are likely to benefit middle-aged workers. Their life experience and maturity generally translate into better human relations skills and less emotional volatility.

One change in the vocational picture may be difficult: unexpected job loss as a result of the restructuring and relocation of major companies. Finding a new job and moving to a new place become more difficult with age. Even those who have a job may be concerned about this possibility.

Uncertainty regarding what present and future employment will offer is true for individuals who presently have job security, stable working conditions, and choice about their retirement. This can change quickly with corporate buyouts, new public policies, and changing attitudes on the part of workers themselves. The possibility of losing one's job, being faced with an early buyout, or uncertainty regarding future prospects are all part of the current scene.

[Sterns & Huyck, 2001, p. 451]

Balancing Work and Family

When young adults enter the job market, they tend to focus on the status, salary, and demands of the job. They are willing to work overtime, to take irregular shifts, or to travel if doing so means promotion or job security. This is less true in middle age, when a major concern is finding a balance among work, family, and self (Werner & Smith, 2001).

Before going further into this topic, we should dispel the myth that men are more concerned with their work than their family life. For both fathers and mothers, the parental role is usually considered more important than the work role (Thoits, 1992). It is still true that, especially when children are young, mothers spend more hours caring for children than fathers do, but that trend is changing as well. Certainly by the time children are school-aged, fathers are very concerned with their well-being and are upset if their hours at work interfere with their ability to be a good father (Milkie & Peltola, 1999). Both sexes report that being a good parent, loving spouse, and loyal friend is more important than being a good worker (Barnett & Hyde, 2001).

Dealing with Job Stress

During early adulthood, a combination of the demands of the workplace and the individual's aspirations for promotion, income, success, and authority can be conducive to "workaholism," an addiction to long hours and challenging work. Indeed, today's workplace, with its high-speed schedules and tight deadlines, expects and rewards such behavior, putting stress on workers (Geurts & Gründemann, 1999). Many corporations want and even require employees to work more than 40 hours a week, including some evenings and weekends (Hochschild, 1997).

As already noted, in general, adults of both sexes are physically and psychologically healthier if they have multiple roles, for example, as workers, spouses, and parents. To deal with job—and home—stresses, it is usually best not to give up any roles but to use the home to buffer the workplace and vice versa (Rogers & May, 2003). A study found that talking to their spouses about work problems and relaxing at home helped employees deal with stressful jobs; more generally, the study found that stress in one area of life can be relieved by the attitudes and companionship of people in some other areas (Grzywacz & Bass, 2003; Rogers & May, 2003).

KATHLEEN MCLAUGHLIN / THE IMAGE WORKS

Stress or Stressor Facing a desk overflowing with income tax forms and checks is stressful, and this woman is new to the job—she began it less than a year ago. Will she quit? Probably not. She is mature enough to establish priorities and to cope with any unreasonable demands from her supervisor.

Scaling Back

Achieving balance involves more than adjusting to work stress; it is also a matter of finding satisfaction in areas of life other than work. According to one study of dual-earner couples, in the "establishment" stage of marriage (aged 35 to 54, with children), both men and women figure out ways to successfully combine work and parenthood (Becker & Moen, 1999).

scaling back A strategy used by middle-aged adults to balance the demands of work and family life. Instead of devoting full time to one or the other, many people reduce their commitment to their work in order to have time for their marriage and children.

A particular strategy that couples use is **scaling back,** deliberately putting less than full effort into their employment (Becker & Moen, 1999). Scaling back is typically a conscious, shared decision to place limits on work hours or responsibilities, which may include refusing jobs that require travel or weekend work. When limits cannot be placed, one spouse may choose to work part time.

In some nations, such as Sweden, where part-timers are well paid and are given responsibility, and where paid maternal and paternal leave are granted with each new birth, scaling back is expected (Drobnic et al., 1999). In the United States, couples come to this solution on their own. They must convince their employers that part-time work is acceptable; they must also budget their own money and time.

In a variation of scaling back, one partner works at a job that pays significant money, while the other has a lower-paying "career" that is personally fulfilling. In families with traditional ideas about gender roles and money, if the man earns less than the woman, this type of scaling back allows her to pay the bills without feeling that she is abandoning her primary role as wife and mother. It also allows him to pursue his vocation or artistic endeavor without feeling inadequate (Milkie & Peltola, 1999). As one married woman said:

> We began to realize . . . that my job was going to be the primary job. He tried to work at other jobs during the year, but he wasn't at all happy. So I told him at that point that he had to try to make a go at a career in coaching. Fortunately, he found a part-time job at a college 40 miles away. He hardly earned anything. It was probably less than our babysitting costs. In the meantime, my job was going very well.

[quoted in Becker & Moen, 1999, p. 1001]

Remember from Chapter 21 that stress can be relieved through cognitive reinterpretation and emotional adjustment; that is what many middle-aged couples do by scaling back in this way.

Especially for Entrepreneurs Suppose you are starting a business. In what ways would middle-aged adults be helpful to you?

In another scaling-back strategy, the partners take turns: One focuses on employment and the other on child care, with the idea of switching at some point. Many parents thus temporarily devote most of their time to family and plan for the time when they will resume their career. Married, middle-aged women are actually more likely to be employed than when they were younger, following this strategy.

All these scaling-back strategies are joint decisions, protecting work and family from unreasonable demands and making sure that the basic tasks get done, both at work and at home. Many middle-aged couples use the same strategy in planning for retirement: It is a joint decision (Kim & Moen, 2001).

Changing Policy

Income and Age

Income is perhaps as much a concern to middle-aged adults as to older and younger ones. This is not because the middle-aged are poor: In fact, average salary and average household income are highest in middle age (see Figure 22.5), and poverty rates are lowest. However, middle-aged adults feel responsible for the rest of their families, as already explained, and also fear that they may be impoverished in old age.

In the United States, the worries of middle-aged adults are fueled not only by publicized statements about Social Security going bankrupt or about pension funds that were promised but not available but also by stories from their parents, who remember the 1960s. Back then, one out of every three elderly residents of the United States was living below the poverty line, and many of the rest were "near poor," living at the edge of poverty. Health care was privately paid, which meant it was beyond the reach of many senior citizens.

Since that time, various economic, demographic, and political changes have raised both the personal income and the living standards of many elderly Americans. Social Security has been extended to more people, and payments begin at the end of middle age when a person retires. A range of medical and social benefits have been established for the aged, reducing the proportion of the elderly below the poverty line to about one in ten (U.S. Bureau of the Census, 2002). Nevertheless, many of the middle-aged remain very concerned about their own elder years. If they become seriously ill or frail, their savings can be depleted quickly.

Ironically, from a developmental perspective, this fear may be misplaced. During the same years that the elderly in the United States were growing richer, children were growing poorer, primarily because young parents had more difficulty finding jobs that paid a living wage. The solution for some couples—for both parents to have jobs—is difficult for families with very young children. In 2000, about one child in six (16 percent) lived below the poverty line (U.S. Bureau of the Census, 2002).

Current fears about the future outlay of Social Security payments to the baby-boom generation (which is now middle-aged and approaching retirement) have reduced the income of young adults, who pay proportionally more Social Security than older workers or than the current elderly ever did. Young adults are also the age group least likely to be covered by health insurance, even though middle-aged people are more worried about their insurance benefits.

A backlash against this economic disparity has led to calls for *generational equity,* defined as equal contributions from, and fair benefits for, each generation. As one researcher, himself approaching late adulthood, explains:

We fear being overthrown by the next generation. . . . We fear not being cared for in our waning years. Greed, too, is involved, not only the financial greed that makes us overstay our years in a high-paying job or resist a reconsideration of government entitlements, but also greed for life, for the extra year or two that extraordinary medicine might bestow. The cost of those extra years may very well compromise medical care for the young.

[Kotre, 1999–2000]

Each nation responds to various generations differently. The U.S. government spends more money on education and hospital care than many other nations. Other developed countries spend more on health care and on housing for the poor. This is not the place to evaluate national priorities, but it explains why many members of the middle generation in the United States, who earn the highest average salaries and who head the wealthiest households, feel obligated to help people of other ages even as they worry about their own old age. They may not be sandwiched personally, but they are concerned about future expenses.

Implicit in a life-span view of human development is the realization that each age and cohort has its own particular and legitimate economic needs that other generations may fail to appreciate. For instance, everyone is affected by the immediate interests of their own age group when they vote about day-care programs, low-interest loans for college, subsidies for farmers or manufacturers, or entitlements for the elderly.

Taking a developmental view, the needs of each generation are balanced with those of the others, with a "sense of mutual responsibility across generations" (Vincent, 2003, p. 108). The interdependence of all generations is a theme the middle generation is in the best position to understand.

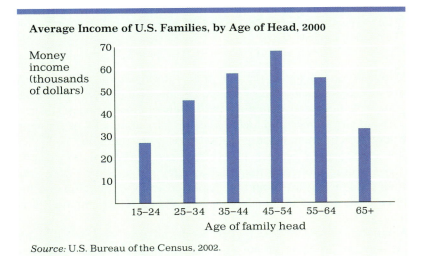

Average Income of U.S. Families, by Age of Head, 2000

Money income (thousands of dollars)

Age of family head

Source: U.S. Bureau of the Census, 2002.

FIGURE 22.5 Middle Age, High Income
According to the U.S. Bureau of the Census, a family consists of at least two related people (e.g., husband and wife, parent and child) living together. In the United States, families that are headed by middle-aged adults have the highest average income.

Response for Entrepreneurs (from page 566):
As employees and as customers. Middle-aged
workers are steady, with few absences and good
"people skills," and they like to work. In addition,
household income is likely to be higher at about age
50 than at any other time, so middle-aged adults
will probably be able to afford your products or
services.

Retirement

Are you surprised to find the topic of retirement from work discussed in the context of middle age? Here we confront other myths. For today's middle-aged adults, retirement planning begins in the 50s, and actual retirement typically starts before age 65, while the person is still middle-aged. Moreover, retirement is anticipated with mixed emotions, but generally more joy than dread (Kim & Moen, 2001).

Many nations are making mandatory retirement illegal and postponing the age at which government pension payments can begin (Bossé, 1998). In theory, these changes encourage people to work past age 65 or 70. Instead, however, adults are retiring at younger and younger ages, some as early as age 55, most before age 65, and almost all by age 70—a change from previous decades (see Figure 22.6). Similar trends are apparent in every developing nation (Ilmarinen, 1995). At the same time, middle age lasts longer today—until age 65 in this text and even longer in some people's view. Thus, retirement is a topic for the middle-aged even more than for the old (Staudinger & Bluck, 2001).

Further, because mandatory retirement is illegal in most jobs and in most nations, the actual age of retirement is more variable. In the United States, about a third of all workers have left the job market completely by age 59, and another third are still working at age 70 (U.S. Bureau of the Census, 2002). Today's workers are no longer pushed out by their employers or by failing health, as was true a few decades ago. Instead, they are pulled out by their own financial assessment and future plans.

Another major change is that, with so many women in the job market, the decision to retire is often made by both husband and wife. Because, on average, wives are several years younger than their husbands, husbands are more likely to retire before wives than vice versa. Many middle-aged women have a retired husband.

Usually the main consideration expressed when couples plan for retirement is financial (Kim & Moen, 2001). Although human relationships are crucial for a happy retirement, people tend to assume that these will be satisfying as long as the money is sufficient. As one man, thinking about his future, said:

> Hopefully then you'll have money and stuff and you can . . . start a new section of your life. . . . You know we've spent eighteen or twenty years raising these girls and we've put all of our time and effort into them and, like I said, we still have a life of our own, and someday once we get our children raised I want to be able to take my wife and have fun.
>
> *[quoted in Townsend, 2002, p. 260]*

Many workers begin to plan for their retirement starting at age 50 and to prepare for it by reducing their work hours, increasing pay to raise a pension, or exploring a change in residence. Further, many of those who are still in the workforce are actually semiretired, perhaps using part-time work or self-employment as a bridge to retirement (Moen, 1998). This is good planning.

Not all is rosy for retirees, especially those who retire before age 60. They tend to be poorer and sicker than their employed age-mates. Many retirees find that their income is lower than they expected and that inflation and health care and other costs are higher than anticipated. That is why planning is crucial (Kim & Moen, 2001).

A particular problem arises when people misread statistics: If people simply look at average life span (about age 76) and ignore the average life span for someone who is already age 65 (age 84), they may seriously underestimate how much money they will need in retirement. If an employer encourages older workers to retire, a generous severance payout can mean pleasure at age 60 but poverty by age 80 (Quadagno & Hardy, 1996).

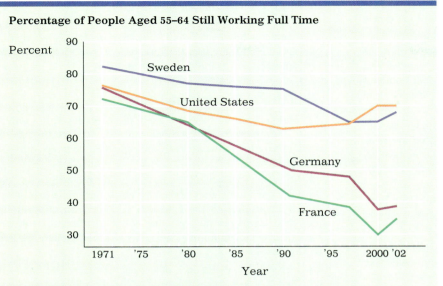

Percentage of People Aged 55–64 Still Working Full Time

Source: Eurostat; Organization for Economic Cooperation and Development, 2003 (http://europa.eu.int/conm/eurostat, accessed 1/27/04). U.S. data from U.S. Census Bureau, *Current Population Survey*, May 20, 2003.

FIGURE 22.6 Opting Out of the Workforce In many developed nations, substantial proportions of the workforce choose to retire or stop working full time before age 65. Such decisions are based on assessments of financial security and on shifts in priorities. Employment opportunity is also a factor, which explains why fewer people retired during the economic boom of 1997–2000.

Groundwork laid in middle adulthood with regard not only to finances but also to health, hobbies, family relationships, and so on can help to make late adulthood busy and happy, as the next chapters will explain.

The joys and stresses of employment continue through most of middle age. There are three aspects that differ. First, the intrinsic rewards of work become more important than the extrinsic ones. Second, employees are more stable and loyal, less likely to change jobs. Third, couples are more likely to seek a balance between home and work life, so men and women take turns, scale back, and adjust schedules to function well as a unit. Financial demands are reduced, but financial planning becomes increasingly important, as retirement begins. Most people actually stop working by age 65, when late adulthood is said to start.

SUMMARY

Personality Throughout Adulthood

1. Several personality traits, referred to as the Big Five, tend to remain quite stable throughout adulthood, because of a combination of genes, culture, and early life experiences. Each adult finds his or her own ecological niche, which supports his or her particular personality configuration.

2. The two sexes may become more alike in personality traits in midlife. Gender convergence may be the result of hormones, context, or cohort—and may not be as apparent now as it was 30 years ago.

3. Although many people reexamine and readjust their lives during middle age, the midlife crisis is more myth than fact.

Family Relationships in Midlife

4. Most middle-aged adults are involved in a satisfying intimate relationship, usually through marriage. Adults whose marriages have survived to middle age generally are happily wed, deriving a strong sense of self-esteem from their marriage. Physical and emotional abuse of a partner is less common in middle age.

5. If a marriage ends in middle age, many family connections are made more complex. Women are less likely than men to find new partners. Remarriage brings new intimacy and new problems.

6. The middle generation often plays a critical role within the family, providing emotional and material support to older and younger family members and serving as the link that connects one relative to another. This is true in all families, particularly in immigrant families with a strong value of familism.

7. Middle-aged adults generally find that their relationships with their own parents and with their young-adult children improve. In recent years in the United States, young adult children have become more likely to live with their parents, while today's elderly parents are more likely to be independent.

8. Siblings often become closer during middle age and later. However, especially if they must provide care for a frail parent, sibling rivalries and resentments may reappear.

9. During middle adulthood, many people become grandparents for the first time. Today grandparents prefer a companionate role over the remote and involved grandparenting roles that were common in the past.

10. A small but increasing number of grandparents act as surrogate parents, raising their grandchildren because the children's parents are unable to. This arrangement often benefits the children but is not necessarily beneficial to the grandparents.

11. Family values sustain and nourish many middle-aged adults, although families are less likely to share a household. Few adults feel squeezed as a "sandwich generation."

Work in Middle Adulthood

12. Middle-aged workers are likely to be employed not only because they need to earn a living but also because they like the work and their coworkers. Consequently, they do not often change jobs.

13. Stress at work is buffered by family life, and vice versa. Many workers learn to balance home and work, becoming less likely to devote themselves to the long hours, promotion opportunities, and time pressures that younger workers tolerate. They scale back their work commitments in order to accommodate the needs of their families.

14. Increasingly, workers in developed nations retire before age 65. Their major worry is financial. Although middle-aged people are usually economically secure, many worry about their future.

KEY TERMS

Big Five (p. 544)
ecological niche (p. 544)
gender convergence (p. 546)
gender crossover (p. 546)
midlife crisis (p. 548)

social convoy (p. 549)
household (p. 553)
kinkeeper (p. 553)
familism (p. 554)

remote grandparents (p. 558)
involved grandparents (p. 558)
companionate grandparents (p. 558)

surrogate parents (p. 560)
sandwich generation (p. 562)
scaling back (p. 566)

APPLICATIONS

1. When do people get "old"? Ask ten people, at least five of them over age 50, when both middle age and late adulthood begin. Social scientists and the public once thought that late adulthood began at about age 55 or 60; many now put it at age 65 or 70. Do your respondents agree?

2. Observe grandparents with grandchildren for at least half an hour. Take detailed notes of what you see and hear. Are the grandparents remote, involved, or companionate? Analyze your observations, comparing the grandparents' behavior with what parents might do.

3. Search the Internet for information about pensions, retirement, and Social Security. How accurately, fairly, and realistically do you think these topics are portrayed? How well informed would you be if the Internet were your only source of information?

4. Find birthday cards intended for middle-aged people. What beliefs and attitudes are reflected?

Part VII   Middle Adulthood

BIOSOCIAL

Normal Changes Changes in the appearance of the skin, hair, and body shape are benign but can be disconcerting. Losses of acuity in hearing and vision are usually gradual, and most individuals learn to compensate quite easily. Overall wellness and secondary aging are influenced by such variables as sex, ethnicity, SES, and long-term health habits. Genetics clearly play a role, but social context and individual choice are more powerful influences on vitality and morbidity than heredity in middle age.

The Sexual-Reproductive System During their late 40s and early 50s, women experience the climacteric, when their body adjusts to changing hormonal levels. Menopause signals the end of a woman's reproductive potential as well as the beginning of reduced natural hormones. Men experience no comparable dramatic decline in hormones or reproductive ability, but the gradual diminution of their sexual responses continues. Both sexes adjust to changes in their sexual interaction.

COGNITIVE

Adult Intelligence Some intellectual abilities improve with age, while others decline. Typically, fluid intelligence decreases and crystallized intelligence increases. Reaction time and speed of thinking slow down; practical intelligence deepens. Overall, cohort differences and individual variations are more important influences on the development of adult intelligence than age alone.

Expertise Adult intelligence tends to flourish in areas of the individual's particular interests, because motivation leads to years of practice and involvement. The result is the development of expertise, characterized by cognitive processes that are intuitive, automatic, and flexible. Each adult becomes an expert at tasks that were once difficult and mysterious, becoming a good cook or a careful driver or an expert surgeon, author, or chess player.

PSYCHOSOCIAL

Changes During Middle Age Middle age is characterized by more stability than change in personality, as the Big Five personality traits combine with each person's ecological niche to engender continuity. Personality changes that do occur, such as a narrowing of the gap between masculine and feminine personality traits, result from historical shifts and personal efforts at self-improvement.

Family Relationships in Midlife Middle-aged adults usually have rewarding relationships with their adult children and grandchildren, without the stress that responsibility for child rearing creates. Marriages tend to become less conflicted. Usually the oldest generation does not require extensive caregiving. However, some middle-aged adults provide caregiving and financial support to both the older and younger generations.

Work in Middle Adulthood Work continues to be an important source of both stress and status in middle age. One of the improvements that occur over the decades of adulthood is that many adults learn how to coordinate the demands of a partner, children, and an employer. A balance of life—which means intense work for some people at some times and early retirement for others—is more likely to be reached in middle age.

Part VIII

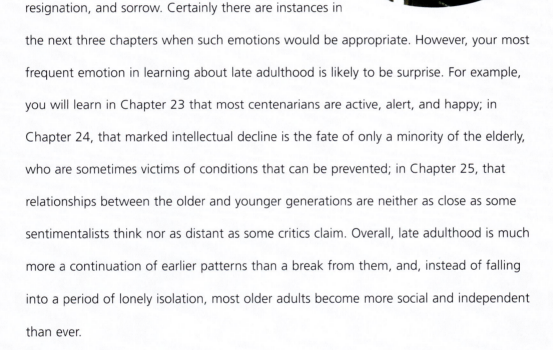

W hat emotions do you anticipate experiencing as you read about development in late adulthood? Given the myths that abound regarding old age, you may well expect to feel discomfort, depression, resignation, and sorrow. Certainly there are instances in the next three chapters when such emotions would be appropriate. However, your most frequent emotion in learning about late adulthood is likely to be surprise. For example, you will learn in Chapter 23 that most centenarians are active, alert, and happy; in Chapter 24, that marked intellectual decline is the fate of only a minority of the elderly, who are sometimes victims of conditions that can be prevented; in Chapter 25, that relationships between the older and younger generations are neither as close as some sentimentalists think nor as distant as some critics claim. Overall, late adulthood is much more a continuation of earlier patterns than a break from them, and, instead of falling into a period of lonely isolation, most older adults become more social and independent than ever.

Nevertheless, this period of life, more than any other, seems to be a magnet for misinformation and prejudice. Why is this so? Think about this question when the facts, theories, and research you read about in the next three chapters turn out to differ from what you expected.

Late Adulthood

Chapter Twenty-Three

Late Adulthood: Biosocial Development

Now we begin our study of the last phase of life, from age 65 or so until death. This chapter describes biosocial changes—in the senses, the vital organs, morbidity, and mortality—and then raises the crucial question: Why does aging occur? The answer might allow everyone to live to age 100 or beyond.

If the thought of living more than a century, or even of reading about this period of the life span, evokes feelings of dread, remember that knowledge usually softens the prejudices (both negative and positive) that many people of all ages have (Palmore, 1998). As one reporter who interviewed dozens of centenarians found, most have "open minds and open hearts. They were curious and generous and fun" (Ellis, 2002, p. 7). Being 100 years old turns out to be less of a problem than getting to that age. This chapter will help you distinguish prejudice from fact. Begin by taking the following quiz.

1. The proportion of the United States population over age 65 is about
   (a) 3 percent.
   (b) 13 percent.
   (c) 25 percent.
   (d) 33 percent.

2. The proportion of the world population over age 65 in the year 2000 was about
   (a) 2 percent.
   (b) 7 percent.
   (c) 12 percent.
   (d) 20 percent.

3. Happiness in older people is
   (a) rare.
   (b) about the same as in younger adults.
   (c) much *less* common than in younger adults.
   (d) much *more* common than in younger adults.

4. The senses that tend to weaken in old age are
   (a) sight and hearing.
   (b) taste and smell.
   (c) varied. Senses improve in some people, decline in others.
   (d) all the senses.

5. The automobile accident rate for licensed drivers over age 65 is
   (a) higher than the rate for those under 65.
   (b) about the same as the rate for those under age 65.
   (c) lower than the rate for those under age 65.
   (d) unknown, because such statistics are not recorded.

6. About what percent of North Americans over age 65 are in nursing homes or hospitals?
   (a) 5 percent
   (b) 10 percent
   (c) 25 percent
   (d) 50 percent

7. Compared with that of younger people, the reaction time of older people is
   (a) slower.
   (b) about the same.
   (c) faster.
   (d) slower for men, faster for women.

8. Lung capacity
   (a) tends to decline with age.
   (b) stays the same among nonsmokers as they age.
   (c) tends to increase among healthy old people.
   (d) is unrelated to age.

9. The most common living arrangement for a person over age 65 in the United States is
   (a) with a husband or wife.
   (b) with a grown child.
   (c) alone.
   (d) with an unrelated elderly person.

10. Compared with people under age 65, an older adult's chance of being a crime victim is
   (a) lower.
   (b) about the same.
   (c) higher.
   (d) lower for men, higher for women.

This quiz is adapted from a much larger one called *Facts on Aging* (Palmore, 1977, 1998).

As you read this chapter, you will find the answers to these questions (1, p. 578; 2, p. 578; 3, p. 601; 4, p. 585; 5, p. 588; 6, p. 580; 7, p. 588; 8, p. 589; 9, p. 580; 10, p. 588). Most college students get more than half these items wrong, sometimes because they simply don't know the correct answer but usually because their prejudices—more often negative than positive—cloud their judgment (Palmore, 1998).

Prejudice and Predictions

Prejudices about late adulthood are held by people of all ages, including children and the very old. As an example of the latter, most people over age 70 think that they themselves are doing quite well compared with other people their age, who have problems far worse than theirs (Cruikshank, 2003). Before discussing some of the specifics of aging and possible ways to extend life, we need to uncover such prejudices, both favorable and unfavorable, and the assumptions that undergird them.

Ageism

Two leading scientists who study old age note that:

> Common beliefs about the aging process result in negative stereotypes—oversimplified and biased views of what old people are like. The "typical" old person is often viewed as uninterested in (and incapable of) sex, on the road to (if not arrived at) senility, conservative and rigid. The stereotype would have us believe that old people are tired and cranky, passive, without energy, weak, and dependent on others.

> *[Schaie & Willis, 1996, p. 17].*

All these stereotypes are false. They arise from a widespread form of prejudice called **ageism,** the tendency to categorize and judge people solely on the basis of their chronological age. "Ageism joins racism and sexism" as terms that refer to unfair stereotyping of human differences (Katz, 2001–2002, p. 27).

You read in Chapter 20 that experts who calculate quality-adjusted life years (QALYs) sometimes devalue a lost year of childhood or of late adulthood but assign a full year's value to a premature death in early adulthood. That approach may be ageist. Some curfew laws require all teenagers, and only teenagers, to be off the streets by 10 P.M. That policy, too, may be ageist. Imagine the outcry if curfew laws applied only to all males (sexist) or all nonwhites (racist), and you can see the similarity to sexism and racism. Ageism is "pigeon-holing people and not allowing them to be individuals with unique ways of living their lives" (Butler et al., 1998, p. 208). It seems obvious that none of us, regardless of our age or our background, should be judged on the basis of some arbitrary characteristic.

Teenagers usually rebel against ageism, and, fortunately, they soon become old enough for it no longer to apply. The elderly are more likely to accept it, and, unfortunately, the older they are, the worse it gets. Restaurant staff patronize them, neighbors do not invite them to parties, employers do not hire them—all merely because they are old. Ageism probably does most damage during late adulthood, because it permits policies and attitudes that reduce pride, activity, health, and social involvement.

Gerontology

Ageism is increasingly being recognized as a prejudice, for two reasons (Huber, 2001–2002; Katz, 2001–2002). One reason is the recent advances made in **gerontology,** the multidisciplinary, scientific study of old age. Gerontology reaches conclusions quite different from **geriatrics,** the traditional medical specialty devoted to aging. Most doctors in geriatrics see patients who are ill and infirm, which leads many geriatricians to consider aging as an illness.

By contrast, most of the participants in gerontology research are healthy and active. As a result, gerontologists, benefiting from the overall life-span perspective, conclude that aging is "socially constructed as a problem" (Cruikshank, 2003, p. 7).

More specialists are needed in both disciplines; the aged are sometimes infirm, but often they are not. Although physicians focus on the "chronic, progressive diseases of 'secondary aging,'" from a "gerontologist's perspective, the twenty-first century will be a time of unprecedented promise and excitement . . . [for] life of great quality, great longevity" (Hazzard, 2001, pp. 452, 455).

Because development is multidirectional, gains as well as losses are evident throughout life. In late adulthood, gains are often masked because aging is perceived only as loss and youth only as gain. Contrary to this cultural belief, many

ageism A term that refers to prejudice against people because of their age. Like racism and sexism, ageism works to prevent elderly people from being as happy and productive as they could be.

gerontology The study of old age. This is one of the fastest-growing special fields in the social sciences.

geriatrics The medical specialty devoted to aging.

now contend that "any gain, at any age, entails a loss, and vice versa" (Staudinger & Lindenberger, 2003, p. 3). Late adulthood is no exception.

Demography

The second reason ageism is decreasing is that there are more aged individuals. When relatively few people survived to late adulthood, demeaning clichés ("second childhood," "dirty old man," "senior moment," "doddering") or patronizing compliments ("spry" and "having all her marbles") were less readily seen as ageist.

In a major demographic shift, a total of 7 percent of the world's population today is over age 65, compared with only 2 percent a century ago (*question 2*). In developed nations, the proportion is larger: 13 percent of the population in Canada, Australia, and the United States (*question 1*); 16 percent in Great Britain; and 18 percent in Italy and Japan. These numbers are rising rapidly; the elderly of the world are projected to make up 9 percent of the population by 2010 (United Nations, 2002). The fastest-growing age group worldwide are those over age 100—still less than 1 percent of the total in any nation, but doubling in the next decade.

Let us look more closely at the relationship between ageism and demography (the study of population numbers). Demographers chart a population in terms of its age groups, which are depicted in a stack with the youngest cohort at the bottom and the oldest one at the top (see Figure 23.1). The resulting picture was usually a *demographic pyramid*. Like a pyramid, the base was widest and each higher level was narrower than the one beneath it, for three reasons. One reason was that many children were born, far more than the "replacement rate" of one per adult. Another was that, before modern sanitation, immunization, and antibiotics, a sizable portion of each cohort died before advancing to the next level. Finally, adult diseases were usually fatal. People did not survive cancer or heart attacks, as many do now. In former decades, after about age 50, each five-year cohort was about 20 percent smaller than the next-younger group (as the pyramid on the left in Figure 23.1 shows).

FIGURE 23.1 The Aging U.S. Population
Unlike earlier times, when each generation was slightly smaller than the one that followed, each cohort today has a unique position that was determined by the reproductive patterns of the preceding generation and by the medical advances that were developed during their own lifetime. As a result of these two factors, the baby boomers, born between 1947 and 1964, represent a huge bulge in the U.S. population. In the next 10 years, the leading edge of the baby-boom generation, largely intact, will begin moving into the upper age group.

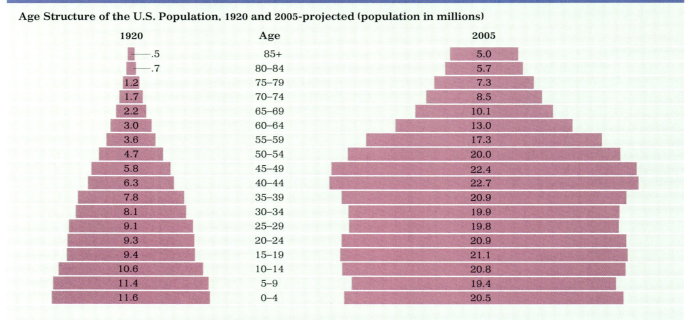

Age Structure of the U.S. Population, 1920 and 2005-projected (population in millions)

1920	Age	2005
.5	85+	5.0
.7	80–84	5.7
1.2	75–79	7.3
1.7	70–74	8.5
2.2	65–69	10.1
3.0	60–64	13.0
3.6	55–59	17.3
4.7	50–54	20.0
5.8	45–49	22.4
6.3	40–44	22.7
7.8	35–39	20.9
8.1	30–34	19.9
9.1	25–29	19.8
9.3	20–24	20.9
9.4	15–19	21.1
10.6	10–14	20.8
11.4	5–9	19.4
11.6	0–4	20.5

Sources: U.S. Bureau of the Census, 1975 (*left*); U.S. Bureau of the Census, International Data Base, 2004 (*right*).

The two age clusters in the diagram that deviate from this pattern are explained by world events: the Great Depression and the end of World War II. Poverty and unemployment during the Depression reduced rates of both marriage and parenthood, so that many fewer babies were born between 1930 and 1941. Postwar prosperity increased rates of marriage, home buying, and births, so that many more babies (the "baby boom") were born between 1947 and 1964.

In recent decades, fewer births and increased survival are changing the shape of the population stack from a pyramid to a square. Unless another unusual event occurs, each cohort will be about the same size as the previous cohort. This is already evident in some nations (the stacks for Germany, Japan, and Spain are already almost square) and will take several generations in others (for example, less than 3 percent of the population is over age 65 in Afghanistan, Angola, Ethiopia, and Syria). In those nations, good medical care is scarce and, although family size has shrunk (from eight to four children, on average), it remains above the replacement level. Malawi has the most children, proportionally. Half its population is younger than 18 (Aldwin & Gilmer, 2003).

By 2030 the proportion of those over 65 is projected to double worldwide, from 7 percent to 15 percent. If current trends continue, the population will eventually be divided into thirds, with only the middle third, aged 30 to 60, active full time in the labor force and thus supporting the older and younger cohorts.

Senior Power These people are waiting in line to cast their ballots in West Palm Beach, Florida. The political power of the elderly is increasing even faster than their numbers, because adults over age 65 are more likely to be politically informed and to vote than are younger adults, especially those aged 18 to 25.

Dependents and Independence

Traditionally, it has been assumed that people participated in the labor force full time from age 15 to 65. Every society has a certain number of self-sufficient, productive adults and a certain number of dependents—that is, people who do not work but instead need care. A **dependency ratio** is calculated by comparing the number of dependents with the number of self-supporting independent people, those who are between ages 15 and 65. The greater the number of dependents compared to workers, the higher the dependency ratio and the greater the burden on the middle generation.

dependency ratio The ratio of self-sufficient, productive adults to dependents—children and the elderly.

In most industrialized countries, the current dependency ratio, about two independent adults for every one dependent person, is lower than it has been for a century, because the birth rate has been declining since 1970 and because those now over age 65 were born during the Depression and make up the smallest cohort of the twentieth century. The poorest developing nations have high birth rates, and the large numbers of children make the current ratio about 1:1.

What will happen as more and more people live past working age? One geriatrician warns:

> America [is] facing financial and sociological destruction, burning in the flash-point of a 76 million megaton age bomb . . . as 76 million aging baby boomers cause an unprecedented crisis in geriatric medicine and in our social and economic support system. . . . The coming juggernaut of the aged and infirm will crush our most beloved and important social support systems—Medicare, Social Security, and quality private health insurance—and, if not deflected, will bankrupt America.

[Klatz, 1997]

RICK SILVA / AP / WIDE WORLD PHOTOS

SONDA DAWES / THE IMAGE WORKS

No Bikinis Body shape and hair color change with age, but these changes in appearance do not mean that active life is over. These women in a water fitness class in Virginia are independent and active, and they plan to stay that way.

young-old Healthy, vigorous, financially secure older adults (generally, those under age 75) who are well integrated into the lives of their families and their communities.

old-old Older adults (generally over age 75) who suffer from physical, mental, or social deficits.

oldest-old Elderly adults (generally, those over age 85) who are dependent on others for almost everything, requiring supportive services such as nursing homes and hospital stays.

Especially as young people worldwide attain more education in high school and college and as old people retire earlier (as discussed in Chapter 22), the entire tax and caregiving burden may fall on the shoulders of a shrinking middle cohort.

Reasons Not to Worry

Fortunately, society is unlikely to be hit by this time bomb, for three reasons. First, technology and science are combining to allow more production with fewer workers. For example, a century ago, 90 percent of the world's workers were farmers, who just barely produced enough food for the population. Now advanced technology makes it possible for a small group of farmers to feed everyone (for example, less than 3 percent of the U.S. labor force work in agriculture). Worldwide, all the basic necessities of life can be produced if less than a third of the population is working.

Second, there is an inverse ratio between birth rates and longevity (Kirkwood, 2003). We have learned from studies of international birth and death rates as well as from animal studies that there are relatively few births per adult in social groups where people live a long time. This means that as more people reach late adulthood, fewer new dependents will be born. Despite the fact that young adults are entering the labor force later and older adults are leaving it earlier, the caregiving requirements may not increase. Adults will not necessarily be burdened by the over-65 generation either, which gets us to the third point.

The assumption that people over age 65 are "dependent" is false. Most members of this age group are independent, providing for their own daily care and expenses and still contributing to society. For example, older adults are more likely than younger people to vote, to obey the law, to participate in community and religious groups, and to donate money and time to help others (Posner, 1995). Most are glad when their adult children no longer need them and are proud that they themselves need no help. One British 86-year-old explains about her children, "They've all got their own little lives, haven't they, when they're married. And that's how we like it" (quoted in Bornat, 2002, p. 126).

Contrary to the idea that most of the elderly are infirm, only 10 percent in developed nations need extensive care, and only half of those (about 5 percent of the total) live in nursing homes or hospitals *(question 6)*. In developed nations, most (about 40 percent) live with a spouse, another third (usually widows) live alone, and about 20 percent live with grown children *(question 9)*.

Generally, elderly married couples take care of each other as they always have and are quite independent of anyone else. Many prefer getting by without governmental programs of assistance that are aimed at the dependent elderly (Bornat, 2002). In poor nations, there are no government programs, and most of the elderly live with their children. They are as likely to contribute to the family as to be cared for by them.

Young, Old, and Oldest

Thus, dependency characterizes only a small group of the aged. Gerontologists distinguish among the **young-old,** the **old-old,** and the **oldest-old,** a distinction based not exclusively on age but also on characteristics related to health and social well-being (Zarit, 1996). The *young-old* make up the largest category of the aging and are healthy, active, financially secure, and independent. The *old-old* suffer from losses in body, mind, or social support, although they still have strengths in some of these areas. The *oldest-old* are dependent on others, at higher risk of every illness and injury (Neugarten & Neugarten, 1986).

Although the oldest-old are only about 10 percent of the elderly population, geriatricians and the general public are more aware of them because they require intense support. In general, the young-old are those under age 75 and the oldest-old are those over age 85. However, age is not an accurate predictor of dependency, so some gerontologists prefer terms that do not refer to chronological age—*optimal aging, usual aging,* and *impaired aging* (Aldwin & Gilmer, 2003; Powell, 1994). The term *successful aging* is also used; it includes optimal aging as well as usual aging (Rowe & Kahn, 1998).

Anti-Aging Measures

Terminology is significant. Once "ageism" was coined, stereotyping by age became more apparent. The "dependency ratio" was a common statistic until the implications of "dependent" were exposed. College students are less likely to stereotype people described as "aged 70–85" than people described as "old" or "elderly," because the latter terms imply impairment (Polizzi & Millikin, 2002). Aging is not supposed to be thought of as bad, yet "anti-aging" advocates are accused of wanting to "die young. As late as possible" (Garreau, 2002, p. 7).

As you will read in detail later in this chapter, aging has many causes—wear and tear, cellular accidents, a declining immune system, or programmed senescence. This suggests that perhaps a gene, a chemical, or another mechanism can be found that alters the aging process and extends the life span. Is this what people want, or is the very idea of anti-aging measures an ageist thought (Holstein, 2001–2002)? Consider this question as you read about the one dramatic success in slowing the aging process.

Calorie Restriction

Mammals can almost double their life span if they eat half as much food throughout adulthood, though not in childhood (Sayer & Cooper, 2000). This has been proven for mice and rats and is probably true for monkeys, chimpanzees, and dogs (Masoro, 2001). Is such a result possible for people? Probably, but it must be carefully done. Obtaining good nutrition becomes more difficult with age, because the need for vitamins and minerals increases at the same time that the body becomes less efficient at digesting food and using its nutrients. Meanwhile, daily caloric requirements decrease by about 100 calories per decade after age 45, so the average 75-year-old should consume at least 10 percent fewer calories (between 2,000 and 2,500 per day) than in middle age in order to maintain weight and energy levels.

Because more nutrients need to be packed into fewer calories, a varied and healthful diet, emphasizing fresh fruits and vegetables, lean meats and fish, and complex carbohydrates (cereals and grains), is even more essential in late adulthood than earlier in life. Indeed, deficits of B vitamins, particularly B_{12} and folic acid, correlate with memory deficiencies (Rosenberg, 2001). Dehydration is also a greater risk in late adulthood because aging cells hold water less efficiently, yet aging digestive systems need more water to function well.

To make it even harder, many older people take drugs that are considered harmless but affect nutritional requirements. Aspirin (taken daily by many who have arthritis or those who are trying to reduce their risk of stroke or heart attack) increases the need for vitamin C; antibiotics reduce the absorption of iron, calcium, and vitamin K; antacids reduce absorption of protein; oil-based laxatives deplete vitamins A and D (Lamy, 1994); caffeine reduces the water in the body. Even multivitamins can do more harm than good—if they include too much iron, for instance. For all these reasons, a good diet is needed to make aging successful, but it is not easy to achieve.

However, mammals with reduced calorie intake are stronger, more vital, and younger in appearance, as long as they consume adequate vitamins and minerals (Clark, 1999). Some people are trying to follow this lead. Nine hundred North Americans belong to the Calorie Restriction Society, whose members eat about 1,000 nutritious calories a day. One is Michael Rae, from Calgary, Canada, who commented to a reporter:

> Aging is a horror and it's got to stop right now. People are popping antioxidants, getting face lifts, and injecting Botox, but none of that is working. At the moment, C.R. [calorie restriction] is the only tool we have to stay younger longer.
>
> *[quoted in Hochman, 2003, p. 5]*

The reporter notes, "Mr. Rae is 6 feet tall, weighs just 115 pounds, and is often very hungry." The article implies that Michael Rae is foolish and that the millions of adults who do not severely restrict their calorie intake are making a wise choice. Most scientists agree.

Prejudice and Delusion

Calorie restriction, like other attempts at slowing the aging process, may arise from prejudice and delusion. One scientist observes:

> An important question to ask about caloric restriction is what impact it may have on the quality of life. This is uniquely a human question, entirely subjective, and not one that can be answered directly from animal studies. Although all of the primates kept on restricted diets so far are certainly healthy, we cannot ask them how they feel about it. Would humans subjected to a calorically restricted diet be constantly hungry, spending all of their free time and energy thinking about food, and how to get it? Would we be constantly agitated and irritable because we're chronically hungry? To achieve an extended life-span, would we have to reduce our total energy expenditure, forgoing many of the energy-expensive activities that enrich our lives?
>
> *[Clark, 1999, p. 144]*

Another says, "The only proven method of life extension for mammals is caloric restriction in infancy, which is impractical for human purposes. Search for a Fountain of Youth has always been a delusion" (Moody, 2001–2002, p. 34).

Maybe the delusion is that comfort and cake today are more important than 20 or more years added to the end of life. That may be ageist thinking—and so may be the opposite view taken by members of the Calorie Restriction Society. In choosing between a happier present and a longer future, does fear of aging affect the choice?

Ageism (in which an entire age group is stereotyped) is commonly applied to older adults; they are all considered confused, infirm, and dependent. However, as more people reach late adulthood (currently 7 percent in the world, 13 percent in North America, 16 percent in most of Europe, and 18 percent in Japan), and as more people are projected to reach age 65 in the future, diversity among the elderly becomes obvious and thus reality undermines prejudice. Despite fears of too many infirm older adults, the reality is that most people over age 65 are quite independent and capable, with only 5 percent (usually the oldest-old) in hospitals or nursing homes at any one time. Terminology is crucial, with the young-old also considered those whose aging is optimal and successful. Many people want a long life, but few want to be "old." This basic contradiction is evident in attempts to slow down aging by severely restricting calorie intake.

Primary Aging in Late Adulthood

To understand the implications of terms that refer to age, remember from Chapter 20 the distinction between **primary aging** (the universal changes that occur with senescence) and **secondary aging** (the consequences of particular diseases). Although secondary aging correlates with age, it is not directly caused by age; secondary aging results in illness, as opposed to usual, optimal, or successful aging. The health habits reviewed in Chapter 20 and the genes inherited at conception are critical factors that make one person enter late adulthood already impaired and another in full physical and cognitive health.

Although secondary aging continues to influence well-being until death, increasingly important throughout the final decades of life is how people cope with primary aging (Vaillant, 2002). If 65-year-olds are in reasonably good health and have long given up cigarette smoking and other destructive habits, their vitality in the remaining decades depends on their attitude and planning.

People vary in *selective optimization with compensation*. They can choose healthy activities and compensate for any primary aging they experience. As in Chapter 17, we continue to describe physiological changes of aging, with particular attention here to compensation—by the individual, his or her friends and family, and the society.

primary aging The universal and irreversible physical changes that occur to living creatures as they grow older.

secondary aging The specific physical illnesses or conditions that are more common in aging but are caused by health habits, genes, and other influences that vary from person to person.

Changes in Appearance

As time passes, primary aging makes everyone look older. In an ageist society, people who look old are treated as old, in a stereotyped way (Butler et al., 1998). Children are quick to see the elderly as old-fashioned; they may ask their own grandparents what life was like before automobiles. When older people notice how they are treated or, for that matter, when they catch an unguarded glimpse in the mirror, they may be surprised by their own internalized ageism, even in late-late adulthood. As one 92-year-old woman related:

> There's this feeling of being out of one's skin. The feeling that you are not in your own body. . . . Whenever I'm walking downtown, and I see my reflection in a store window, I'm shocked at how old it is. I never think of myself that way.
>
> [quoted in Kaufman, 1986, p. 9]

What does the mirror typically show?

The Skin and Hair

The skin often shows the first sign of aging: It becomes drier, thinner, and less elastic; wrinkles, visible blood vessels, and pockets of fat under the skin appear as "irrefutable evidence of the passage of time" (M. Timiras, 2003, p. 397). Dark patches known as "age spots" appear, and the overall reduction of the cells under the skin's surface makes people more vulnerable to cold, heat, and scratches (Whitbourne, 2002).

The hair becomes grayer and, in many people, turns white. Interestingly, loss of hair pigment is the physical change that correlates most closely with chronological age. It is a clearer index to a person's age than skin changes, hearing acuity, blood pressure, heart size, or vital capacity (Balin, 1994), although it does not affect health at all.

For both sexes, hair all over the body becomes thinner with age, and many men experience *male pattern baldness* because of a gene that becomes activated in adulthood. Ironically, although testosterone levels are not related to baldness, many men feel that hair is a signal of virility, just as many older women feel that sexual attractiveness depends on hair color. Accordingly, compensation is frequently sought, and found, for aging hair. Skin is harder to rejuvenate, but

Clean Teeth and More Having cosmetic surgery is "just like going to get your teeth cleaned," according to Sharon Osbourne, manager and wife of Ozzy of MTV and Black Sabbath fame. She has had a face lift, a tummy tuck, liposuction, and breast augmentation. Do you share her matter-of-fact view of elective cosmetic surgery?

DEBBIE VANSTORY-KEYSTONE USA / ZUMA PRESS

GRANTPIX / MONKMEYER

Misleading Appearances This couple may no longer be able to take carefree strolls hand in hand, but that does not mean that romance no longer beats in their hearts. Assumptions based on appearance alone are at the root of ageism, just as they are with racism.

? *Observational Quiz* (see answer, page 587): Who has the more useful walker? Find three reasons for your answer.

billions of dollars are spent annually in the United States on creams, lotions, and minor surgery to make skin more youthful in appearance.

Body Shape and Muscles

Other visible physical changes in late adulthood include changes in the body's shape and muscles (Masoro, 1999). Most older people are shorter than they were in early adulthood, because the vertebrae begin settling closer together in middle age. Body shape is also affected by redistribution of fat, which disappears from the arms, legs, and upper face and collects in the torso (especially the abdomen) and the lower face (especially the jowls and chin).

Older adults often weigh less than they did in middle age, partly because of a reduction in muscle tissue, which is relatively dense and heavy. This difference is notable in men, who have more muscle and less body fat than women. Note that weight reduction during these final years is not necessarily beneficial: In contrast to younger years, when losing weight meant less fat and better health, it now means less muscle, thinner bone, and greater risk (Aldwin & Gilmer, 2003).

Closely related to weight loss is muscle loss, with a reduction in flexibility. Muscles stiffen and atrophy, and as a result there is less range of motion in, for example, kicking from the knee, swinging the arms, and turning the torso (Masoro, 1999). With less flexibility in the muscles holding the vertebrae, a sudden twist might lead to an aching back. For both sexes, reduction in muscle flexibility and strength is especially apparent in the legs, necessitating a slower, stiffer gait and sometimes a cane or walker. Leg muscles, and the heart muscle, are crucial for maintaining independence (Paterson & Stathokostas, 2002).

Self-perception is crucial here. One 92-year-old man who used a cane explained:

> I look like a cripple. I'm not a cripple mentally. I don't feel that way. But I am physically. I hate it. . . . You know, when I hear people, particularly gals and ladies, their heels hitting the pavement . . . I feel so lacking in assurance—why can't I walk that way? . . . I have the same attitude now, toward life and living, as I did 30 years ago. That's why this idea of not being able to walk along with other people—it hurts my ego. Because inside, that's not really me.
>
> *[quoted in Kaufman, 1986, pp. 10–11]*

Self-perception becomes truly debilitating if it leads to a feeling of fragility and a fear of falling, which is "a common and modifiable cause of excess disability" (Lach, 2002–2003, p 37).

Elderly people do sometimes fall and hurt themselves. Bone and muscle loss in and around the vertebrae, which contributes to the fact that some older people stoop instead of standing up straight, is also likely to cause imbalance and therefore falls. A fall can be very serious, partly because bone fragility leads to broken bones. Falls are the leading cause of death from injury after age 60, with mortality rates from falls about one-third higher in men than women and rates 10 times higher at age 90 than at age 70 (Stevens, 2002–2003). However, one longitudinal study of Dutch elderly people who fell found that, although only 6 percent were seriously injured, 35 percent felt less able to get around because of their fall. Functional decline correlated with being female, depressed, and falling at home—not with injury (Stel et al., 2004).

Compensation for a fall may require medical treatment (and surgical hip replacement if need be), but the more effective prevention or treatment involves exercise. Even in the very old, physical activity strengthens the muscles as well as benefiting the cardiovascular, respiratory, digestive, and virtually all other body systems. Compensation must be selective: The pace of exercise must be in keeping with the person's level of heart and lung functioning. For some, this means that jogging replaces running; for others, that brisk walking replaces jogging; for still others, that strolling replaces brisk walking. But for everyone, there is some form of physical activity that is appropriate (Shephard, 2002).

Weight lifting should be part of the exercise routine. Although the elderly lose muscle at an increasingly rapid rate, they can retain or gain muscle if they undertake strength training, including working out with weights and machines that provide resistance, because "strength training has the greatest impact on the most debilitated subjects" (Rice & Cunningham, 2002, p. 138).

How well a person is able to move his or her lower body is one of the best predictors of vitality in old age. Reporting on a 10-week program of muscle training with frail nursing home residents between the ages of 72 and 98, Janet Raloff (1996) notes: "Individuals more than doubled the strength of trained muscles and increased their stair-climbing power by 28 percent when they exercised their legs with resistance training three times a week." Similarly positive results were found in preventing falls via an exercise program for women in their 80s (Campbell et al., 1999).

Dulling of the Senses

For many of the healthy elderly, the most troubling part of aging is isolation from other people. Unless compensation occurs, some distancing is inevitable. Social connection depends partly on the senses, all of which become less sharp with each decade (Meisami et al., 2003) *(question 4)*. This is true for the senses of touch (particularly in the extremities), taste (particularly for sour and bitter), and smell as well as for the more critical senses of sight and hearing.

Up until a century ago, these sensory losses were devastating: Many people who survived to old age were rendered not only lonely but also vulnerable. Today, however, food is processed in such a way that it is less likely to cause food poisoning in someone whose smell and taste have dulled; smoke alarms and carbon monoxide alarms compensate for a diminished ability to smell; and most visual and auditory losses can at least be moderated.

Note that some compensation is always needed. For example, only 50 percent of elderly people pass an odor-discrimination test that 99 percent of 17-year-olds pass (Bornstein & Arterberry, 1999); only 10 percent see well without glasses; and by age 90, the average man is almost deaf, hearing only 20 percent as much as he once did (Aldwin & Gilmer, 2003). But sensory losses need not be debilitating. We now examine specifics for the most vital senses, hearing and seeing.

Vision

Only about 10 percent of the elderly see well, but most visual losses that occur with primary aging are not serious. They can be corrected with glasses, typically both reading and distance glasses or bifocals. About 5 percent of those aged 65 to 80 and about 40 percent of those over age 80 have more serious vision problems, usually cataracts, glaucoma, or senile macular degeneration.

Cataracts involve a thickening of the lens, causing vision to become cloudy, opaque, and distorted. As early as age 50, about 10 percent of adults have such clouding, with 3 percent experiencing a partial loss of vision. By age 70, 30 percent have some visual loss because of cataracts. These losses are initially treatable with eyeglasses and then by outpatient surgery, in which the cloudy lens is removed and replaced with an artificial lens.

Glaucoma is less common, but more devastating if it is not detected. About 1 percent of those in their 70s and 10 percent by age 90 have glaucoma, a buildup of fluid within the eye. This can damage the optic nerve, causing sudden and

SONDA DAWES / THE IMAGE WORKS

Guess Her Age According to the stereotype, muscle-building equipment is for young people, but this 78-year-old grandmother works out at a gym four days a week.

cataracts A common eye disease among the elderly involving a thickening of the lens; it can cause distorted vision if left untreated.

glaucoma A disease of the eye that can destroy vision if left untreated. It involves hardening of the eyeball due to a fluid buildup within the eye.

Current Events If you had to choose between staying informed about current events and being able to see well without glasses, which one would you pick? Most elderly people can no longer choose to see well without glasses, but, like this man reading a newspaper in Cairo, Egypt, older adults tend to be more knowledgeable than people half their age.

senile macular degeneration A disease of the eye involving deterioration of the retina.

Especially for Young Adults Should you always speak louder and slower when talking to a senior citizen?

Wakeup Call This woman is deaf, but her Pomeranian is not. The dog gets her attention, even jumping onto the bed, whenever the alarm clock, telephone, or doorbell rings. Dogs can be trained to compensate for many of the sensory losses experienced by the elderly.

total blindness, but if it is detected early by an eye exam (the person experiences no early symptoms), it can usually be relieved with special eyedrops or, in severe cases, by laser surgery. Glaucoma is partly genetic, and it is more common at earlier ages among African-Americans and people who have diabetes (Whitbourne, 2002).

Senile macular degeneration is deterioration of the retina. It affects one in twenty-five people in the first decade of late adulthood, and one in six over age 80 (Oneill et al., 2001). The primary symptom is partial vision (such as reading with some of the letters missing), and there is no cure. Senile macular degeneration is the leading cause of legal blindness. Fortunately, the remaining vision is usually enough to get by—with bright lights and large print, through auditory and tactile cues, with a computer that scans printed text and "speaks" the words, or with audiotapes of books, magazines, and newspapers.

Hearing

As you remember from Chapter 17, age-related hearing loss, called *presbycusis*, affects every adult to some degree. At first people usually ignore their hearing problems, typically waiting five years or more between the first hint that hearing is fading and a visit to an audiologist. By age 65, 40 percent have difficulty hearing normal conversation. If they wait until hearing loss is major, compensation requires much more adjustment.

Sometimes the audiologist can easily remedy the problem, as by removing impacted earwax. However, most often a hearing aid is recommended, and this is where ageism starts to interfere. Although tiny, digital, personalized aids are now available, many people refuse to use them because they think hearing aids make people look old (Meisami et al., 2003).

Ironically, individuals who frequently mishear and misunderstand conversation may strike others not only as old but also as doddering, and they are excluded from social give-and-take. The hard-of-hearing are likely to withdraw socially and to suspect that inaudible conversations are about them. The net effect is that, compared with the visually impaired, "hard-of-hearing individuals are often mistakenly thought to be retarded or mentally ill . . . [and] are more subject to depression, demoralization, and even at times psychotic symptomology" (Butler et al., 1998, p. 181).

There is one other age-related hearing disorder that, like senile macular degeneration in the eye, has no cure. *Tinnitis* is a buzzing or rhythmic ringing in the ears. It is experienced by 10 percent of the elderly (Coni et al., 1992).

Compensation for Sensory Loss

When people first notice marked sensory loss—when a newspaper is too blurry to read or a dinner conversation is indecipherable—their usual reaction is disbelief, blame, and then depression. Depressed people avoid social situations and resign themselves to their fate, thinking that things will only get worse. With age-related loss of hearing and vision, unless something is done, depression continues—and things actually do get worse.

Compensation, not passive acceptance, is crucial. Those who work with elderly people who have lost vision or hearing are quite optimistic (Horowitz & Stuen, 2003). Many people function well, and happily, for decades with sensory impairments, for three reasons: technology, specialist care, and determination.

First, technology. An array of newly developed devices are available to compensate for sensory losses. These include not only improved hearing aids and lighter glasses but also attachments to televisions, radios, and telephones, headsets for particular occasions, canes that sense when an object is near, infrared lenses that illuminate the darkness, closed-captioned TV programs, and many more.

Second, specialists now connect techniques, technology, and people. Each person's unique sensory needs and personality traits require individualized assistance. People with a new hearing aid, for instance, require several counseling sessions to learn the best settings, positioning, and maintenance procedures. Typically, six sessions and two months enable people to become comfortable with their hearing aids and to develop new patterns of social interaction (Weinstein, 2000).

Specialists also help the visually impaired, because "the technology is not yet so advanced to prescribe itself for the person who needs it, nor does it teach people how to integrate it into their lives" (Goodrich, 2003, p. 69). Simple solutions—making distinctive folds in each denomination of paper money before putting them in a wallet or putting rubber bands on bottles to identify medications—have been developed by thousands of people with low vision but rarely occur to an isolated, depressed person. Both low-tech and high-tech solutions work, but only if people know what they are and how to use them.

The third reason is the key: personal determination. Those who are losing their sight or hearing must heed suggestions and learn new habits. This is hard for anyone—I find myself resistant to mastering a new computer program, or cooking a new vegetable, or even following someone else's suggested route to school. Many older people take particular pride in their independence and have deeply entrenched habits. Yet successful aging depends on a willingness to conquer and compensate for any losses primary aging may bring. A hearing-impaired person needs to make sure the conversation is understood, which may require changing the lighting, reducing background noise, and asking conversation partners to talk more slowly. Similarly, because highways and cars are designed for young adults, an older adult may need to install additional mirrors or a direction locator if, for instance, highway signs cannot be read in time for a safe exit.

As far as driving is concerned, independence and compensation sometimes conflict, and individual action is necessary (McKnight, 2003). Laws in various states sometimes deny license renewal or, more often, grant extensions without retesting driving ability. For this reason, drivers need to monitor their own impairment, compensating and then selecting other means of transportation if need be, long before the law requires them to do so. Determination and compensation are illustrated by a legally blind man, who explains:

> I move about New York as much as ever, but with a healthy caution crossing streets. I slavishly wait for the light to change (I can usually see that) even if there

!*Answer to Observational Quiz* (from page 584): He does. The walkers themselves provide some clues, in that four wheels are more mobile (especially on curbs) than three, and his has a seat for resting while hers merely has a basket. Note that he is leaning into the walker, using it to help him navigate, while she seems to be merely pushing hers along.

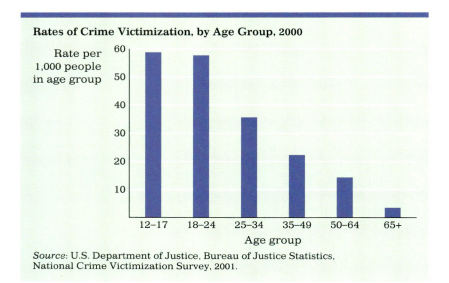

Rates of Crime Victimization, by Age Group, 2000

Rate per 1,000 people in age group

Age group: 12–17, 18–24, 25–34, 35–49, 50–64, 65+

Source: U.S. Department of Justice, Bureau of Justice Statistics, National Crime Victimization Survey, 2001.

FIGURE 23.2 **Victims of Crime** As people grow older, they are less likely to be crime victims. These figures come from personal interviews in which repondents were asked whether they had been the victim of a violent crime—assault, rape, or robbery—in the past several months. This approach yields more accurate results than official crime statistics, because many crimes are never reported to the police.

elderspeak A way of speaking to older adults that resembles baby talk, with simple and short sentences, exaggerated emphasis, a slower rate, higher pitch, and repetition.

is no traffic, and I have taken to crossing alongside other pedestrians—especially women with baby carriages, next to whom I feel safe.

[quoted in Grunwald, 2003, p. 103]

The critical factor is recognition of the problem and willingness to change. Two sets of statistics indicate that many elderly people meet these criteria and are willing to adapt and change their behavior. First, the aged are far less likely to be victims of crime than are younger adults, in part because they become more cautious (see Figure 23.2) *(question 10)*. Second, the elderly are less likely to be the driver in a serious auto accident *(question 5)*: Reaction time is slower *(question 7)*, sign reading is difficult, and night vision is worse, but most older drivers adjust—taking their time, traversing short and familiar routes, getting home before dark (see Figure 23.3). The pedestrian death rate rises in late adulthood, however, because of aspects of the social context—younger drivers, streets without sidewalks or timed traffic lights—that have not made adjustments or been adjusted for aging.

With technology, specialists, and, most important, the attitudes of the elderly themselves making sensory impairments less isolating than they were 30 years ago, the one remaining problem is that younger adults and social practices have not yet caught up. For example, medical insurance (including Medicare) rarely pays for devices or counseling to remedy sensory loss unless that loss occurred suddenly—as the result of an accident, rather than through primary aging (Lidoff, 2003). Even more troubling is the response of passers-by, who may assume that someone with a white cane needs help or that someone who is old needs the patronizingly loud and clear speech called **elderspeak**. Like baby talk, elderspeak uses simple and short sentences, exaggerated emphasis, slower talk, higher pitch, and repetition (See et al., 1999). Some of these features actually reduce comprehension (Kemper & Harden, 1999), including both using higher pitch (lower pitch is more often audible) and stretching out the words (rather than increasing the logical pauses).

FIGURE 23.3 **Get Home Safe** Note that the youngest group of drivers, those aged 15–24, were involved in 25 percent of all fatal motor-vehicle accidents; those aged 65 were involved in only about 10 percent. The main reason for this difference is that older adults tend to be more careful, so they avoid driving when conditions are hazardous.

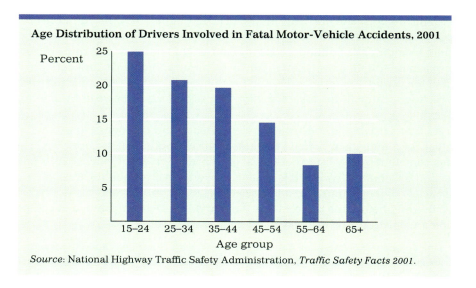

Age Distribution of Drivers Involved in Fatal Motor-Vehicle Accidents, 2001

Percent

Age group: 15–24, 25–34, 35–44, 45–54, 55–64, 65+

Source: National Highway Traffic Safety Administration, *Traffic Safety Facts 2001*.

Elderspeak becomes patronizing when people exaggerate words or call the elderly person "honey" or "dear" or by a nickname instead of a surname ("Johnny" instead of "Mr. White"). The older adult may feel anger or, even worse, self-doubt. In general, unsolicited helpfulness is sometimes appreciated, sometimes not (Smith & Goodnow, 1999), but patronizing communication is ageist, resented, and not effective (See et al., 1999).

Both policies and people need to respond appropriately to the needs of the elderly. For example, public measures (such as longer traffic lights, pedestrian paths, and free blood pressure screening) can be initiated. Family and friends must adjust as well. Adult children can realize that, while a visit from one grandchild may be a joy, a visit from several active youngsters may be exhausting and babysitting for an entire weekend may be overwhelming.

Everyone maintains some strengths with age, and these can be recognized. For example, muscle fibers change, and that "explains why a 10-year-old boy will outrun his 70-year-old grandfather in a 100-meter race, whereas grandpa might still defeat junior in a 10-kilometer march" (Navazio & Timiras, 2003, p. 428). But all too often we cherish speed more than endurance, and put winning the "rat race" over surviving the "march of time."

Response for Young Adults (from page 586): No. Some seniors hear well, and they would resent it.

Major Body Systems

In previous chapters we discussed the vital organs—the cardiovascular, respiratory, digestive, and renal/urinary systems—that sustain life. You are well aware that organ reserve and homeostasis enable each system to function well, even under stress, during most of adulthood, unless some particular chronic problem—such as smoking, obesity, or drug abuse—results in illness. Although cancer, heart disease, and other life-threatening diseases become more common with every decade of life, in most of adulthood primary aging does not directly cause organ failure.

That said, however, we must note that in late adulthood primary and secondary aging combine to make all the major body systems slower and less efficient, eventually causing death. For example, the heart pumps more slowly and the vascular network is less flexible, which raises blood pressure and increases the risk of stroke and heart attacks. The lungs take in and expel less air with each breath (*question 8*), so that the level of oxygen in the blood is reduced. The digestive system slows, becoming less able to absorb nutrients and expel toxins. The kidneys are less efficient at regulating the amount of liquid, potassium, and other substances in the body, making imbalance a greater problem, especially if the older adult drinks less water to ease another problem of the renal/urinary system—incontinence.

It bears repeating that all these developments are affected by past health habits and current exercise. A person who maintains an active life and good health habits ages slowly. Some 70-year-olds have a body like a 40-year-old, as measured by blood pressure or vital capacity. Nonetheless, primary aging slows down everything; no 70-year-old functions as well as a healthy 20-year-old.

As a result of this slowdown and loss of efficiency, serious diseases—coronary heart disease (CHD), strokes, chronic obstructive pulmonary disease (COPD), and most forms of cancer—are much more common in late adulthood. Compared with 25- to 34-year-olds, young-old adults (aged 65–74) in the United States are:

- 200 times more likely to die of COPD
- 200 times more likely to die of cancer

Assessing the Danger The death rate from coronary artery disease is high among adults of all ages, but especially among elderly men. A few decades ago, this Arkansas man with chest pains would probably have had a heart attack and died. Now, thanks to advances in medical treatment, he may live for many years longer.

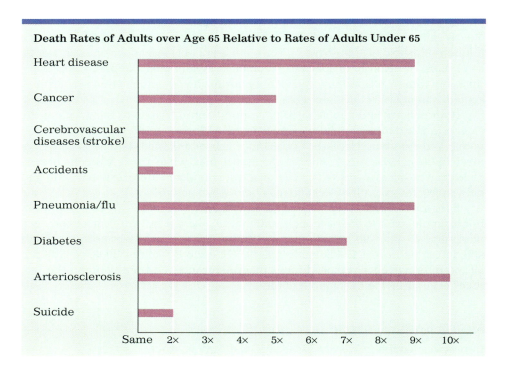

FIGURE 23.4 **Leading Causes of Death Among the Elderly** This chart shows approximate ratios between the death rates for Americans aged 65 and older and those under 65. (The contrast is starker in the text, which compares adults aged 65–74 with those aged 25–34.) The death rate among people over age 65 is higher even for conditions that are not age-related: Older adults do not have more accidents or flu than do younger adults. The main reason is that if an elderly person's organs have lost their reserve capacity, an accident is more likely to cause heat failure, and the flu is more likely to lead to pneumonia.

- 100 times more likely to die of CHD
- 80 times more likely to die of a stroke
- 33 times more likely to die overall

Not only are older persons more susceptible to disease, but they take longer to recover from illness and are more likely to die of any given disease or infection (see Figure 23.4) (Arking, 1998). When young people contract pneumonia, for example, they are almost always fine again in a few weeks; but for people with no organ reserve, pneumonia can cause death. Even the flu can kill, which is why annual flu shots are recommended for everyone over age 65.

Compensation for Aging Organs

As was already explained for sensory loss, compensation entails technology, specialist advice, personal determination, and cultural accommodation. For aging organs, all four of these factors continue to be relevant. Medical technology, including everything from surgery and pacemakers to drugs and home monitors, has tempered the ill effects of every serious condition. Coping with disabilities requires some expert advice and a personal willingness to change. And society can make adjustments that keeps these conditions from being as debilitating as they might be.

Compensation is particularly useful in late adulthood because the overall slowness of the body means that diseases grow more slowly. Many people live for years with diseases that might have killed a younger person. For example, autopsies of the oldest-old usually find cancerous tumors that were never diagnosed and that are not the cause of death (Holliday, 1995). Prostate cancer is evident in virtually every man who dies after age 80, and many older women eventually have slow-growing breast cancer. A diagnosis of almost any form of cancer requires a more aggressive treatment under age 40 than later, if the goal is five-year survival. Of course, old age should not be a reason to stop prevention, detection, and treatment; it is simply one more factor to consider (Kaplan, 2000).

Sleep

The need for adjustment is illustrated by sleep disorders, a common complaint of the elderly. In general, older adults spend more time in bed, take longer to fall asleep, spend less time in deep sleep, wake up more often (about 10 times per night), take more naps, feel drowsy more often in the daytime, and, because of all this, are more distressed by their sleep patterns than younger adults are.

The response of many physicians to insomnia is to prescribe narcotic drugs. This approach may be particularly harmful in late adulthood (Bromley, 1999; Ohayon et al., 1999). The usual narcotic dose is often too much for an older person's metabolism, causing very heavy sleep temporarily and then rebound wakefulness, with confusion, depression, impaired cognition, and even nighttime falls. Another response using technology is surgery to clear air passages. Some elderly insomniacs self-administer alcohol—a solution that creates other problems (Aldwin & Gilmer, 2003).

Actually, the root problem with sleep complaints may be not biological but cognitive—specifically, the mistaken notion that everyone should "sleep like a baby." As Figure 23.5 shows, sleep patterns change with age. Most of the elderly awaken several times a night because of the need to urinate, to move the legs, to adjust the blankets. With advancing years, the brain's electrical activity is reduced, which means less sound sleep, more half-awake time, and shorter dreams (Masoro, 1999). Body rhythms change; older people naturally wake up earlier and are more alert in the morning than at night. Accepting all that as normal may be what is needed. If insomnia is a problem, cognitive therapy is more effective, over time, than drugs (Morin et al., 1999), because specific suggestions can be adapted by the person. Remember, individual determination is key in selective compensation.

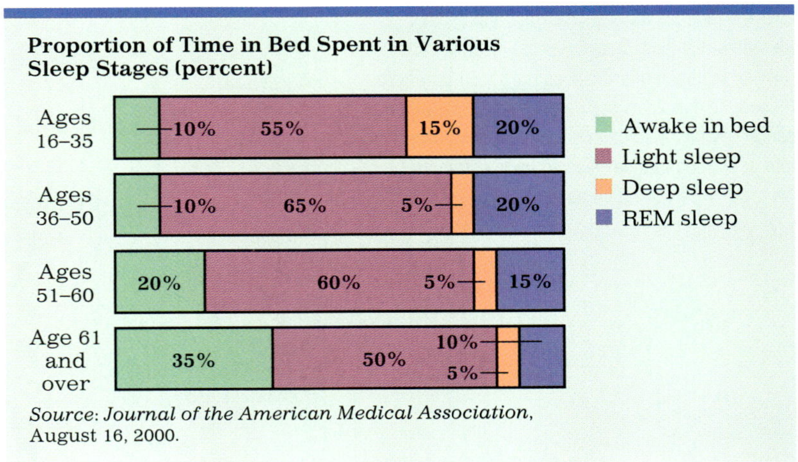

Proportion of Time in Bed Spent in Various Sleep Stages (percent)

Ages 16–35: 10%, 55%, 15%, 20%
Ages 36–50: 10%, 65%, 5%, 20%
Ages 51–60: 20%, 60%, 5%, 15%
Age 61 and over: 35%, 50%, 10%, 5%

■ Awake in bed
■ Light sleep
■ Deep sleep
■ REM sleep

Source: Journal of the American Medical Association, August 16, 2000.

FIGURE 23.5 Don't Just Lie There One of the most common complaints of the elderly is that they spend too much time in bed but not sleeping. The solution is to get up and do something, not wait for sleep to come.

Compression of Morbidity

Although it is impossible to prevent all the diseases that result from primary aging, it is possible to postpone their onset and thus increase the quality of life. The goal is a **compression of morbidity**—that is, reduction of the number of days and months that an aged person is seriously ill, disabled, or in pain.

James Fries (1994) illustrates compression of morbidity with a hypothetical example (see Figure 23.6). A pair of identical twins have the same genetic vulnerabilities to disease and are exposed to the same pathogens, but one "smokes like a chimney, is fat, doesn't exercise, and has a poor diet," while the other has "fairly good health habits" (p. 314). Both get pneumonia at about age 25 (environmental exposure), and both recover quickly, as their organ reserves and immune systems have barely begun to age.

However, both twins are genetically predisposed to the same illnesses—emphysema, heart attack, stroke, and lung cancer. The reckless twin is sick from middle age on, with chronic disease. By his 70s, he has several serious illnesses. Meanwhile, his health-conscious brother has inherited the same conditions, but his lifestyle protects him. Indeed, he dies at about age 80, without his genetic vulnerability to cancer having become apparent. His morbidity is shortened, compressed into a few weeks after a long and healthy life, in contrast to his twin's years of illness, prolonged disability, and reduced quality of life. Their genes are the same, but their QALYs, and the amount of morbidity they experience are

compression of morbidity A limiting of the time a person spends ill or infirm, accomplished by postponing illness and, once morbidity occurs, reducing the amount of time that remains before death occurs.

FIGURE 23.6 Primary and Secondary Aging
The interplay of primary and secondary aging is shown in this diagram of the illness and death of a hypothetical pair of monozygotic twins. Both are equally subject to certain illnesses—so both experience a bout of pneumonia at about age 25. Both also carry the same genetic clock, so they both die at age 80. However, genetic vulnerabilities to circulatory, heart, and lung problems affect each quite differently. The nonexercising smoker *(top)* suffers from an extended period of morbidity, as his various illnesses become manifest when his organ reserve is depleted, beginning at about age 45 and worsening over the next 30 years. By contrast, the healthy lifestyle of his twin *(bottom)* keeps disability and disease at bay until primary aging is well advanced. Indeed, he dies years before the emergence of lung cancer—which had been developing throughout late adulthood but was slowed by the strength of his organ reserve and immune system.

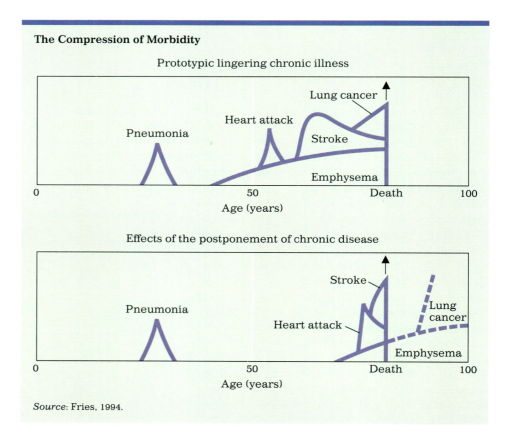

Happy Days Ahead This proud and happy couple in Romania are homeowners and gardeners and are likely to remain quite healthy until a series of illnesses occur in the last year of their lives. This is compression of morbidity at its best.

vastly different, because one suffers from secondary as well as primary aging. In real life, monozygotic twins have dozens of nongenetic differences, and they die five or more years apart (Finch & Kirkwood, 2000).

Compression of morbidity is a psychological as well as a biological blessing. A healthier person is likely to be intellectually alert and socially active—in other words, to experience the optimal aging of the young-old person, not the impaired life of the oldest-old. Medical science has made compression of morbidity possible: Improved prevention, detection, and, most important, treatment allow today's older persons to live with less pain, more mobility, better vision, stronger teeth, sharper hearing, clearer thinking, and enhanced vitality (Bunker et al., 1995). Nonetheless, each individual must do his or her part; a healthier lifestyle in middle age promotes better health in late adulthood and reduces the likelihood of premature death. Continuing our focus on primary aging, we now turn to the questions of what causes aging itself and whether it can be stopped.

Primary aging is inevitable and universal, its effects becoming apparent in many ways as people age. The most obvious signs are superficial—evident in skin, hair, and body shape. Muscles also atrophy, although exercise is an effective way to slow down loss of muscle tissue. Some of the most troubling developments relate to the senses, particularly vision and hearing, because they often result in depression and social isolation. Compensation is available but requires a combination of technology, specialist help, and personal determination. The most ominous consequence of primary aging is that diseases, including fatal ones involving the vital organs, become more likely. The goal is compression of morbidity, so that primary aging does not cause serious disease or severe disability except for a short time, right before death.

Theories of Aging

Can aging and even death itself be postponed, allowing the average person to live 100 healthy years or more instead of 75 or 85? There are many intriguing possibilities but not many definitive answers (Austad, 2001; Clark, 1999; Masoro, 1999). In fact, one expert categorized 300 theories of aging (Medvedev, 1990). Here we describe only two theories (wear and tear and genetic aging) that begin with the entire body, and then several that focus on cells.

Wear and Tear

The oldest, most general theory of aging is the **wear-and-tear** theory (Masoro, 1999). Just as the parts of an automobile begin giving out as the years and mileage add up, so the body wears out part by part after years of exposure to pollution, radiation, toxic foods, drugs, diseases, and other stresses. According to this theory, just by living our lives, we wear out our bodies.

Can this be true? Sometimes. Athletes who put repeated stress on their shoulders or knees have painful joints by middle adulthood; people who regularly work outdoors in strong sunlight damage their skin; industrial workers who inhale asbestos and smoke cigarettes destroy their lungs. By late adulthood, everyone's body shows signs of wear. Scars accumulate, bones reveal past fractures, eyes get cloudy with cataracts, hearing is less sharp, fingernails become ridged, and so on.

Three facts support the wear-and-tear theory. First, women who have never been pregnant tend to live longer than other women, perhaps because they have not worn out their bodies as much as mothers usually do (Finch & Kirkwood, 2000). Second, people who are overweight tend to sicken and die at younger ages, perhaps because they needed to spend more energy maintaining their bodies. Third, one breakthrough of modern medical technology is replacement of worn-out body parts—transplanted organs, artificial knees and hips, implanted dentures.

However, the analogy to a machine's wearing out does not explain all of human aging. A key difference between the human body and a machine is that "unlike inanimate objects, living systems utilize external matter and energy to repair wear and tear" (Masoro, 1999, p. 50). In other words, we eat, we breathe, we move—and we get better! Unlike a machine, the human body benefits from use.

wear-and-tear theory A theory of aging that states that the human body wears out because of the passage of time and exposure to environmental stressors.

LAWRENCE MIGDALE / PHOTO RESEARCHERS

Use It So You Don't Lose It Although wear-and-tear theory might predict otherwise, the single most critical failure of body functions that accelerates aging is loss of mobility. We now know that after a stroke or other mobility-restricting event, the best therapy is to start walking again.

Regular aerobic exercise improves heart and lung functioning; sexual activity stimulates the sexual-reproductive system; digestion is improved by eating raw fruits and vegetables that require vigorous intestinal activity.

The converse is also true: Inactivity breeds illness. People in hospitals get sicker if they do not move. It seems as if people are more likely to "rust out" from disuse or suffer effects of misuse and abuse than to wear out. Thus, although the wear-and-tear theory applies to some aspects of aging, it does not describe primary aging overall (Austad, 2001).

Genetic Aging

Instead of focusing on parts, we need to consider the whole. What could make an entire body age? Some theorists propose that aging is the normal, natural result of the genetic plan for the species.

Life Expectancy

The genetic theory begins with a fact: Every living species seems to have an inherent **maximum life span,** defined as the oldest age to which members of a given species can live. For instance, under ideal circumstances, the maximum that rats live is 4 years; rabbits, 13; tigers, 26; house cats, 30; brown bears, 37; chimpanzees, 55; Indian elephants, 70; finback whales, 80; humans, 122; lake sturgeon, 150; giant tortoises, 180 (Clark, 1999; Finch, 1999).

Maximum life span is quite different from **average life expectancy,** which is the average life span of individuals in a particular group. In humans, average life expectancy varies, depending on historical, cultural, and socioeconomic factors that can cause death in childhood, adolescence, or middle age. In the United States today, average life expectancy at birth is about 74 years for men and 80 years for women (U.S. Bureau of the Census, 2002). Those who are already 65 years old, and thus no longer at risk of an early death, are expected to live to 81 if male and to 84 if female, and those who are already 90 can expect to live another four years. Sometime during very late adulthood the death rate actually stabi-

maximum life span The oldest age to which members of a species can live, under ideal circumstances. For humans, that age is approximately 120 years.

average life expectancy The number of years the average newborn of a particular population group is likely to live. In humans, this age has tended to increase over time, primarily because fewer children die in infancy.

Celebrating a Dozen Decades Only a few people in the world have lived much beyond 100 years. Two of those oldest of the old are shown here: *(left)* Jeanne Calment of France celebrates her 121st birthday, and *(right)* Maria do Carmo Geronimo celebrates her 125th. Geronimo was born in slavery and has no reliable birth records, but several other people are known to have lived to 120. That age seems to be the upper limit for the human species. Even with the best medical care, the majority of people die before age 80.

lizes, so a person who is 105 is no more likely to die within a year than a person who is only 104 (Austad, 2001).

In ancient times, the average life expectancy was about 20 (because so many babies died). In 1900, in developed nations, it was about age 50. The reason for this improvement was the improved odds of survival to age 5 because of new public health measures, including sanitation, immunizations, and the miracle of antibiotics. In recent years, the average life has continued to lengthen because diseases (heart attack, pneumonia, cancer, childbed fever) that once killed many young and middle-aged adults can now be treated, so people who contract them are usually cured, able to live several more years or longer. Secondary aging is also less destructive. Because the average North American now smokes less, exercises more, and takes medication for specific problems that could lead to serious illness (e.g., blood pressure medication that reduces the risk of stroke), he or she lives longer. One estimate projects *average* life expectancy at 100 by 2060 (Oeppen & Vaupel, 2002).

While average life expectancy has increased, the maximum life span has probably remained unchanged: As best we can tell from historical records, the maximum human life span a millennium or two ago was a few years past 100, just as it is today. (The biblical Methuselah's age, 969, was probably measured in "years" that had fewer days.) If so many early Greeks, Egyptians, and Chinese children in the ancient world had not suffered diseases, accidents, infections, warfare, and famine, they would have reached old age, as a lucky few did in those ancient civilizations and as most now do.

At some point, however, for all humans, no matter where or when they live, primary aging takes over. In ancient times those few who survived to late adulthood, by avoiding accidents and illnesses, died of aging-related causes, as people do today. Just as we are genetically programmed to reach sexual maturity during the teen years, we may be genetically programmed to die during late adulthood. Of course, everyone has somewhat different genes. Centenarians are fortunate to inherit genes for a very long life, and they are often healthier than those who are in their 80s (Holden, 2002).

Selective Adaptation

Epigenetic theory (discussed in Chapter 2) provides several genetic explanations for primary aging. One is that since reproduction is essential for the survival of the species, humans had to carry genes that would protect those who might have offspring. Thus, deaths could occur either very early in life (so society didn't expend food and energy raising children who would die before they had children of their own) or after childbearing and child rearing, at age 50 or so—but not from age 15 to 35. Consequently, even today, only nongenetic events (accidents, suicide) are likely to cause death in early adulthood. But at age 50, according to this theory, genes should allow various fatal diseases (Finch & Kirkwood, 2000). Thus, genetic diseases that affected only older people would be passed on from one generation to the next.

Parkinson's disease, Huntington's disease, Alzheimer's disease, type II diabetes, coronary heart disease, and osteoporosis are among the many examples of genetic diseases that evolutionary processes would have no reason to select against (Masoro, 1999). As a result, every person inherits genes that allow survival until middle age and that then cause aging, illness, and death—each in a particular genetic way, but all in one way or another.

Even without genes for various diseases of later life, some genes could cause aging and death in order to "make room" for a new generation. There may be several genes—perhaps 20 or so—that cause aging directly. People would all age sooner or later, because the species required it.

Many scientists are searching for these genes—SIR2, ApoE4, def-2, and several other specific genes or alleles have already been found (Hekimi & Guarente, 2003; Miller, 2001). Success in altering genes in mice and fruit flies has recently bolstered the genetic theory of aging (Miller, 2001; Stearns & Partridge, 2001).

Cellular Aging

Another cluster of theories begin at the cellular level. These theories recognize that humans are not machines destined to wear out but living creatures, made up of millions of aging and regenerating cells. Most cells of the human body reproduce throughout life. An obvious example is the outer cells of the skin, which normally are replaced every few years. When a cut or scrape happens, the process of replacement occurs within a few days. Blood and tissue cells also duplicate rapidly; cells of the ear, eye, and brain, more slowly (if at all). But new cells are being made every minute, each designed to be the exact copy of an old cell.

According to the theories of cellular aging, normal cell duplication eventually allows aging, partly because minor errors accumulate. Mutations occur not only because of toxins and stresses but also in the process of DNA repair. Instructions for creating new cells become imperfect, making new cells that are not quite exact copies of the old or that contain damaged elements that are not easy to repair. Over time, with the rapidly reproducing skin cells, for example, inexact replication results in slower replacement, benign growths, color changes, or skin cancer (P. Timiras, 2003). Similarly, throughout the entire body, cellular imperfections and the declining ability to detect and correct them can result in harmless changes, small reductions in function, or fatal damage.

Too Much Sun The "beauty benefits" of devoted sunbathing are transient; the damage is cumulative. Age spots, wrinkles, and leathery skin texture associated with aging become exaggerated from lengthy exposure to the sun. Worse, tanning and burning greatly increase the risk of skin cancer.

?Observational Quiz (see answer, page 599): Identify several signs visible in this photograph that this woman is high in socioeconomic status.

oxygen free radicals Atoms that, as a result of metabolic processes, have an unpaired electron. They produce errors in cell maintenance and repair that, over time, may cause cancer, diabetes, and arteriosclerosis.

antioxidants Compounds that nullify the effects of oxygen free radicals by forming a bond with their unattached oxygen electron.

Free Radicals

One specific theory that explains how cellular accidents cause aging begins with the fact that electrons of some atoms in our bodies are unattached to their nuclei. The resulting electrons are called *free radicals*. Free radicals are highly unstable, because unpaired electrons can react violently with other molecules, splitting them or tearing them apart.

Damage is especially likely when free radicals of oxygen scramble DNA molecules. These **oxygen free radicals** produce errors in cell maintenance, and repair that, over time, may cause cancer, diabetes, and arteriosclerosis as a result of "oxidative stress," (de Gray, 1999; Grune & Davies, 2001). This process may be slowed down by certain **antioxidants** (substances that bind with the unattached electrons of oxygen radicals, making them no longer freely damaging).

Vitamins A, C, and E and the mineral selenium are all antioxidants, which is one reason a healthy diet slows the rate of various diseases. Ironically, high doses of antioxidants taken in pill form, rather than as food, may actually *increase* oxygen free radicals (Duthie & Bellizzi, 1999), because a certain balance of oxygen and antioxidants is required.

Oxygen free radicals are reproduced in reaction to infections and inflammation of the intestinal tract and as a result of ultraviolet radiation, in addition to being normally produced by the body (Grune & Davies, 2001). It seems, then, that since oxygen free radicals damage cells, affect organs, and accelerate diseases, and since the number of such radicals in the body increases over time and with stress, the gradual accumulation of free-radical damage may cause the aging process.

Errors in Duplication

The idea that cellular aging limits the life span is also supported by laboratory research, particularly the work of Leonard Hayflick (1994; Hayflick & Moorhead, 1961), who believed that cellular aging is a natural process, not the result of damage by oxygen free radicals. Hayflick allowed cells taken from human embryos to age "under glass" by providing them with all the necessary nutrients for cell growth and protecting them from external stress or contamination. In such ideal conditions, it was believed, the cells would double again and again, forever. Instead, cells stopped multiplying after about 50 divisions. Cells from adults divided fewer times than did cells from children, and cells from children doubled fewer times than cells from embryos. The total number of cell divisions roughly correlates with the age of the donor, and it is never infinite.

This research has been repeated by hundreds of scientists, using many techniques and types of cells from people and animals. The result is always that the cells stop replicating at a certain point, referred to as the **Hayflick limit.** Even in ideal laboratory conditions, the replication of cells of living creatures is roughly proportional to the maximum life span of the particular species.

When the Hayflick limit is reached, the aged cells differ from young cells in many ways. One important difference is that the very ends of the cells—called the *telomeres*—are much shorter. In fact, the length of telomeres is thought to index the longevity of a creature, a thought buttressed by the fact that very long-lived creatures, such as lobsters, also have long telomeres (Hayflick, 2001–2002). Because telomeres become shorter every time a cell duplicates, one theory of aging focuses on telomeres, searching for ways to lengthen them (Hornsby, 2001).

Hayflick himself believes that the Hayflick limit, and therefore aging, is caused by the inevitable loss of molecular fidelity—that is, by errors in transcription as each cell reproduces itself (Hayflick, 2001–2002). This raises the possibility that DNA regulates aging, not as a mutation but as a proper function after a certain amount of cell duplication.

Indeed, this version of cellular aging is also a type of genetic theory, focusing on cells rather than on diseases. Humans may have a kind of **genetic clock,** triggering hormonal changes and regulating the cellular reproduction and repair processes. When the genetic clock "switches off" genes that promote growth (at about age 15), it might "switch on" genes that promote aging.

Evidence for genetic regulation of aging comes from diseases that produce premature signs of aging and early death. Down syndrome, or trisomy-21, is the most common: People with this disorder who survive childhood almost always die by middle adulthood, with symptoms of heart disease, cancer, and Alzheimer's disease (Masoro, 1999). Children born with a rare genetic disease called *progeria* have a normal infancy but by age 5 stop growing and begin to look like old people, with wrinkled skin and balding heads. Although their intellects and memories are normal, they develop many signs of premature aging and die by their teens, usually of heart diseases typically found in the elderly (Clark, 1999). All those who have conditions that accelerate aging also have cells that duplicate fewer times than average for that chronological age.

The Immune System

The decline of the immune system is another example of how aging works at the cellular level (Effros, 2001). In a healthy person, the immune system recognizes foreign or abnormal substances in the circulatory system, isolates them, and destroys them. It does this mainly with two types of attack cells. One type of cells, called **B cells** because they are manufactured in the bone marrow, create antibodies to destroy specific invading bacteria and viruses. These antibodies

Hayflick limit The number of times a human cell is capable of dividing into two new cells. The limit for most human cells is approximately 50 divisions, suggesting that the life span is limited by our genetic program.

genetic clock According to one theory of aging, a regulatory mechanism in the DNA of cells regulates the aging process.

B cells Cells manufactured in the bone marrow that create antibodies for isolating and destroying invading bacteria and viruses.

Progeria This 16-year-old South African boy, embraced by his 81-year-old grandmother, has progeria, a genetic disorder that produces accelerated aging, including baldness, wrinkled skin, arthritis, heart and lung difficulties, and early death.

T cells Cells created in the thymus that produce substances that attack infected cells in the body.

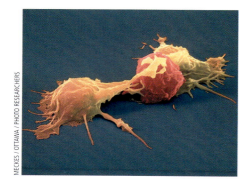

MECKES / OTTAWA / PHOTO RESEARCHERS

Normal Killers The immune system is always at war, attacking invading bacteria, viruses, and other destructive agents. Here two "natural killer" cells are overwhelming a leukemia cell. How healthy we are and how long we live are directly related to the strength and efficiency of our immune system.

Especially for Biologists What are some immediate practical uses for research on the causes of aging?

remain in the system; most people get measles, mumps, or specific strains of influenza only once because a second invasion is immediately thwarted by B cells.

The other type of attack cells, called **T cells** (manufactured by the thymus gland), produce substances to destroy any infected cells. They also help the B cells produce more efficient antibodies and strengthen other aspects of the immune system. B cells and T cells compose only part of the "very complex defense mechanism of the immune response"—a complexity necessitated by the fact that humans are "slow-breeding complex organisms continuously exposed to infection by rapidly growing pathogens or parasites" (Holliday, 1995, p. 31). Among other components of the immune system are NK ("natural killer") cells, K ("killer") cells, and white blood cells.

Many, though not all, aspects of the immune system become less efficient with age (Effros, 2001). Over the years of adulthood, the production and power of T cells and B cells decline, as does the efficiency of the mechanisms that regulate them. These declines are one reason why cancer becomes more common with age and why other infections and illnesses—from a first bout of chickenpox to food poisoning to the latest strain of influenza—are much more serious in an adult than in a child. By late adulthood, the flu can be fatal, because the immune system is too weak to launch an effective, speedy counterattack. Based on such evidence, it has been theorized that the weakened cells of the older immune system permit aging.

Research on Immune Deficiency

Scientific support for this theory comes from research on AIDS, or *acquired immune deficiency syndrome*. HIV (human immunodeficiency virus) can be latent for many years after the person becomes infected with it, but it becomes much more destructive and eventually reaches the point where it is called full-blown AIDS, when the immune system is greatly weakened. Persons of any age whose immune system reaches the point of AIDS are vulnerable to some specific cancers and signs of dementia that rarely occur without AIDS until late adulthood. This suggests a connection between aging and a weakened immune system that has lost the ability to protect and defend, and repair damage.

There is other evidence for this theory. Even if illness does not occur, individuals with weaker immune systems (measured by laboratory analysis of the T and B cells in the blood) do not live as long as those with stronger immune systems. This suggests that decline in immunity is not merely an accompaniment of aging but actually causes aging (Effros, 2001). Evidence also comes from people over age 85, who remain healthy if they have relatively high numbers of natural killer (NK) cells (Mariani et al., 1998). Chronically depressed people tend to have fewer T cells and a higher rate of illness (Gutmann, 1996; Meeks et al., 2000).

Remember that women tend to live longer than men but have more autoimmune diseases. The immune system may explain these sex differences in morbidity and mortality. Throughout life, females tend to have stronger immune systems than males: Their thymus gland is larger, and laboratory tests reveal that their immune responses are more efficient. Consequently, in many families, the father is more likely to be completely incapacitated by flu or a cold than the mother is. This advantage may be a mixed blessing, however, because middle-aged women have higher rates of autoimmune diseases such as rheumatoid arthritis and lupus erythematosus, in which an overactive immune system attacks the person's own body (Carlson et al., 1996). In very late adulthood, when immune-system functioning declines in both men and women, the two sexes have similar vulnerability to almost every disease. Centenarians of both sexes have similarly well-functioning immune systems.

Who Cares About Living Longer?

All these theories of aging, and many others, have shown promise in mice and other species, and they may apply to humans as well. Each theory emphasizes somewhat different causes, but all converge on the idea that something epigenetic—in the genes, cells, and environment—triggers aging and eventually death. For example, the slowdown of the immune system, as just discussed, occurs on the cellular level, but T cells and B cells are obviously under genetic control and respond to the viruses, stresses, and infections that come from the environment.

Thus all theories converge, even though each is different. They share another characteristic, however; Most people are not interested. As with calorie restriction, described earlier, most humans do not want to know why aging occurs and are indifferent about the possibility of extending the average life span much beyond the average (about age 80) or maximum (about age 120). Young adults who are HIV-positive may be willing to take drugs to avoid dying prematurely, but older adults are reluctant to forgo comfort and tradition in order to live longer.

Evidence for this lack of interest is found not only in the daily habits of many adults, who continue overeating and underexercising, but also in the research budgets of many nations and universities. Far more time and money are spent on treating particular diseases than on preventing aging, even though a cure for any lethal disease would add only a few weeks to the average life span (Martin et al., 2003). For example, half the budget of the U.S. National Institute on Aging is spent on Alzheimer's disease, which, if it were eliminated completely, would add only 19 days, but years of quality, to the average life span.

In short, humans seem much more interested in adding to the quality of life than adding to the length of it, in preventing disability instead of preventing mortality, in compensating for losses rather than preventing losses altogether. This may be realistic: Perhaps aging cannot be prevented. It may also be ageism: Perhaps people cannot imagine being old and still enjoying life.

! *Answer to Observational Quiz* (from page 596): She is reading a newspaper, listening to an expensive Walkman, sitting on a hotel beach in Hawaii, and wearing fashionable sunglasses and swimsuit—all of which suggest that she should be too well informed to overexpose her skin to the sun.

> There are hundreds of theories of aging. The wear-and-tear theory proposes that bodies wear out with age. This is apparent in some ways, but the theory does not explain the entire aging process. Genetic theories explain the limits of maximum and average life spans for various species. Survival over the millennia may have required that humans inherit some genes for eventual aging and death. Cellular theories reflect the fact that living organisms are collections of cells, which usually replicate themselves and repair damage—processes that become less effective with age. Some cellular theories focus on damage from oxygen free radicals; others on accumulated errors in cell duplication; others on telomere shortening, when cells no longer reproduce; still others on declines in the immune system

The Centenarians

A centenarian is someone who has lived 100 years or more. Do you hope to become one, as some expect of most babies born today in developed countries (Oeppen & Vaupel, 2002)? What if you were promised that the added years would be active, healthy, and happy instead of a long period of decrepitude, disability, and misery—that compression of morbidity would mean you were infirm only a short while?

(a)

(b)

(c)

(d)

(e)

(f)

Longevity Three remote regions of the world are renowned for the longevity of their people. In Vilcabamba, Ecuador, *(a)* 87-year-old Jose Maria Roa stands on the mud from which he will make adobe for a new house, and *(d)* 102-year-old Micaela Quezada spins wool. In Abkhazia in the Republic of Georgia, companionship is an important part of late life, as shown by *(b)* Selekh Butka, 113, posing with his wife Marusya, 101, and *(c)* Ougula Lodara talking with two "younger" friends. Finally, Shah Bibi *(e)*, at 98, and Galum Mohammad Shad *(f)*, at 100, from the Hunza area of Pakistan, spin wool and build houses. Alexander Leaf, the physician who studied these people, believes that the high social status and continued sense of usefulness of the very old in these cultures may be just as important in their longevity as the diet and exercise imposed by the geographical conditions in each region.

Other Places, Other Stories

Westerners who have traveled to remote regions of the world found three places—one in the Republic of Georgia, one in Pakistan, and one in Peru—that had large numbers of people who enjoyed unusual longevity. In these places, adulthood seemed not only long but also vigorous.

One researcher described the Abkhazia people in Georgia as follows:

> Most of the aged [those about age 90] work regularly. Almost all perform light tasks around the homestead, and quite a few work in the orchards and gardens, and care for domestic animals. Some even continue to chop wood and haul water. Close to 40 percent of the aged men and 30 percent of the aged women report good vision; that is, that they do not need glasses for any sort of work, including reading or threading a needle. Between 40 and 50 percent have reasonably good hearing. Most have their own teeth. Their posture is unusually erect, even into advanced age. Many take walks of more than two miles a day and swim in mountain streams.
>
> *[Benet, 1974]*

Among the people described in this report are a woman said to be over 130 who drank a little vodka before breakfast and smoked a pack of cigarettes a day; a man who sired a child when he was 100; and another man who was a village storyteller with an excellent memory at a reported age of 148.

A more comprehensive study (Pitskhelauri, 1982) found that the lifestyles in the regions famous for long-lived people are similar in four ways:

■ Diet is moderate, consisting mostly of fresh vegetables and herbs, with little consumption of meat and fat. A prevailing belief is that it is better to leave the dining table a little bit hungry than too full.

- Work continues throughout life. In these rural areas, even very elderly adults help with farm work and household tasks, including child care.
- Family and community are important. All the long-lived are well integrated into families of several generations and interact frequently with friends and neighbors.
- Exercise and relaxation are part of the daily routine. Most of the long-lived take a stroll in the morning and another in the evening (often up and down mountains); most take a midday nap and socialize in the evening, telling stories and discussing the day's events.

Furthermore, each of these communities is in a rural, mountainous region, at least 3,000 feet above sea level. This situation minimizes pollution and maximizes lung and heart fitness, because even walking provides aerobic exercise. And, in all three, the aged are respected, and strong traditions ensure that the elderly play an important social role. Perhaps these two factors—exercise and social respect—lengthen life.

The hope that this is true is buttressed by evidence from bumblebees. Genetically, worker bees and queen bees are the same, but worker bees die at about age 3 months and queen bees die at about age 5 years. The reason is that the queen bee is chosen in girlhood and then fed special food and given respect and attention all her life. Only when she dies is another worker bee chosen to become a queen. Could careful diet and social respect extend the human life as well?

Bumblebee research aside, however, there are problems with the reports on remote pockets of human longevity. The regions famous for long-lived humans have no verifiable birth or marriage records from 100 years ago. Beginning at about age 70, many people in these areas systematically exaggerate their age (Thorson, 1995). Persons who claim to be 100 years old may be much younger. In fact, probably every one of those people who claimed to be a centenarian was fibbing. And every researcher who believed them was vulnerable to a kind of ethnocentrism and ageism, the idea that life could be long and wonderful if only the ills of modern civilization could be avoided.

Response for Biologists (from page 598): Although ageism and ambivalence limit the funding of research on the causes of aging, the applications include prevention of AIDS, cancer, senility, and physical damage from pollution—all urgent social priorities.

The Truth About Life After 100

Are you disappointed? Does this mean the testimonies are useless? No. Although the years are exaggerated, it is true that an unusual number of very old people thrive in these isolated areas of the world. While their genetic clocks almost certainly do not allow them to live to age 148, their habits and culture probably allow many to reach 90.

A heartening discovery in recent years has softened the disappointment about the rural centenarians: Active oldest-old people are not that unusual, even in developed nations. Excellent records in many developed countries reveal that an increasing number of people are reaching age 100 or more, with centenarians twice as common as they were 20 years ago and projected to double in number every decade (Oeppen & Vaupel, 2002). Some of them are in very good health.

Moreover, people over age 70—whether they are in excellent health or not—are generally at least as happy and satisfied with their lives as younger adults (Myers, 2000) *(question 3)*, and the oldest of all may be happier than the merely old (Mroczek & Kolarz, 1998). As one woman explained:

> At 100, I have a sense of achievement and a sense of leisure as well. I'm not pushed as much as I was. Old age can be more relaxing and more contemplative. I'm enjoying it more than middle age.
>
> *[quoted in Adler, 1995]*

Mother and Son To celebrate her 100th birthday, Martha Tillotson of Syracuse, New York, dances with her son, Victor, who is an older adult himself. If these two are typical of their age groups, chances are she is just as healthy and even happier than he is.

Researchers in Western Europe, Japan, and North America find similarities between the centenarians in their research and those aged individuals in Peru, Pakistan, and Georgia: moderate diet, hard work, an optimistic attitude, intellectual curiosity, and social involvement. Morbidity, disability, and senility may eventually set in, but many people celebrate a 100th birthday with energy, awareness, and joy (Adler, 1995; Ellis, 2002; Franceschi et al., 1996; Hitt et al., 1999). Centenarians often have strong personalities and deep religious beliefs.

They may even be healthier. Although some data show that the incidence of serious disease (including senility) increases with each decade, people who live past 100 tend to have a shorter period of morbidity before death. This may explain an odd statistic: The U.S. Health Care Financing Administration calculated the average cost of medical care in the last two years of life as $22,600 for people who die at 70 but just $8,300 for people who die after age 100 (cited in Warshofsky, 1999). If this surprises you, you are not alone; many older people themselves would be surprised. Ironically, the older a person is, the less likely he or she is "to imagine large numbers of their peers as favored as they are" (Cruikshank, 2003, p. 11).

Research on centenarians finds no proof that anyone has lived longer than 122 years, but more and more people throughout the world are reaching 100. If people reach late adulthood in good health, their attitudes and activities may be even more important in determining the length and quality of their remaining years than purely physiological factors are. It is ageist to assume that a human will be less happy, less alert, and less interested in life at age 100 than at age 30 or 60. In fact, centenarians may be the happiest and among the healthiest of the old.

SUMMARY

Prejudice and Predictions

1. Contrary to ageist stereotypes, most older adults are happy, quite healthy, and active. Ageism is weakening because gerontologists provide a more optimistic picture of late adulthood than geriatricians do and an increasing percentage of the population is over age 65.

2. The dependency ratio expresses the relationship between the number of self-sufficient, productive adults and the number of children and elderly dependents. Most elderly people are not dependent on the younger generations.

3. Gerontologists sometimes distinguish among the young-old, the old-old, and the oldest-old, according to each age group's relative degree of dependency. Actually, only 10 percent of the elderly are dependent, and only 5 percent are in nursing homes or hospitals.

4. Anti-aging measures may themselves be ageist. One approach to extending life is calorie restriction, an approach successful with many species but rarely attempted by humans.

Primary Aging in Late Adulthood

5. The many apparent changes in skin, hair, and body shape that began earlier in adulthood continue in old age. The senses all become less acute, including vision (90 percent of older people need glasses, and many have cataracts, glaucoma, or senile macular degeneration) and hearing (most older men are significantly hard-of-hearing, as are a smaller number of elderly women).

6. Compensation for sensory losses requires a combination of technology, specialist advice, and personal determination. These three have been underutilized in the past (exemplified by the underuse of hearing aids). The next cohort may compensate more than today's elderly do. The behavior of younger people toward the elderly, such as the use of elderspeak, may impede compensation.

7. Primary aging reduces organ reserve in the major body systems. Although the particulars differ depending on the individual's past health habits and genes, eventually morbidity, disability, and risk of mortality increase. Compensation is possible and

brings many benefits, including compression of morbidity, which means that the person suffers only a short period of infirmity right before death.

Theories of Aging

8. Hundreds of theories address the causes of aging. Wear-and-tear theory suggests that living wears out the body; it applies to some parts of the body, but not to overall aging.

9. Another theory is that genes allow humans to survive through the reproductive years but then to become seriously ill and inevitably die. Each species seems to have a genetic timetable for decline and death, expressed in the length of telomeres. Cell reproduction slows down and eventually stops.

10. Cellular theories of aging include the idea that the processes of DNA duplication and repair are affected by radiation and other factors, causing errors to accumulate as new cells are made.

Oxidative stress, caused by oxygen free radicals, hinders cell maintenance and repair.

11. Age-related decline in the immune system may cause aging, as it contributes to elderly people's increasing vulnerability to disease. Longevity does not seem to be a priority for most people.

The Centenarians

12. It was once believed that many people in certain parts of the world lived long past 100 as a result of moderate diet, high altitude, hard work, and respect for the aged. Such reports turned out to be exaggerated.

13. In developed nations the number of centenarians is doubling every decade. Many of the oldest-old are quite healthy and happy. The personality and attitudes of the very old suggest that long-term survival may be welcomed more than feared.

KEY TERMS

ageism (p. 577)
gerontology (p. 577)
geriatrics (p. 577)
dependency ratio (p. 579)
young-old (p. 580)
old-old (p. 580)
oldest-old (p. 580)

primary aging (p. 583)
secondary aging (p. 583)
cataracts (p. 585)
glaucoma (p. 585)
senile macular degeneration (p. 586)
elderspeak (p. 588)

compression of morbidity (p. 591)
wear-and-tear theory (p. 593)
maximum life span (p. 594)
average life expectancy (p. 594)
oxygen free radicals (p. 596)

antioxidants (p. 596)
Hayflick limit (p. 597)
genetic clock (p. 597)
B cells (p. 597)
T cells (p. 598)

APPLICATIONS

1. Analyze Web sites that have information about aging for evidence of ageism, anti-aging measures, and exaggeration of longevity. To get started, you might look at Hilt & Lipschultz, 2004.

2. Compensating for sensory losses is difficult, because it involves learning new habits. To better understand the experience, reduce your hearing or vision for a day by wearing earplugs or dark glasses that let in only bright lights. (Use caution and common sense: Don't drive a car while wearing earplugs or cross

streets while wearing dark glasses.) Report on your emotions, the responses of others, and your conclusions.

3. Ask five people of various ages if they want to live to age 100, and record their responses. Would they be willing to eat half as much, exercise much more, experience weekly dialysis, or undergo other procedures in order to extend life? Analyze the responses.

Chapter Twenty-Four

Late Adulthood: Cognitive Development

As you saw in the two preceding chapters on adult cognition (18 and 21), during most of adulthood some abilities increase, others wane, and some remain stable. However, decline predominates by the end of adulthood, perhaps at age 65, perhaps not until age 80 or 100. Physical impairment, reduced perception, decreased energy, and slower reactions take an increasing toll on cognitive competence. Yet, even among the oldest-old, decline is not the entire story. The information-processing perspective, a focus of this chapter, makes the complexity and variability of cognition in late adulthood apparent.

When my parents were in their 90s, I visited them often. On learning why I would be away, my friends often asked:

"How are their minds?"

"Good," I would answer.

"Isn't that wonderful?" they sometimes blithely replied.

But it wasn't so simple: I wanted to tell them "no" and lecture about the realities of cognition in late adulthood. My parents' minds were not wonderful—they were sometimes forgetful and repetitive; they could be stuck in the past. But I understood that the implied question was whether or not my parents were senile. Not senile, not wonderful: Late-adulthood cognition is too complex for a brief social exchange or a shorthand summary.

Chapter 23 began to explain this complexity, noting that biosocial development may be optimal, usual, or impaired. This variation is also true for cognition. Severe impairment (dementia) is discussed in this chapter, as is optimal aging (wisdom). Variability is evident: Most old people are neither senile nor wise, but somewhere in between. Before describing the worst and the best, we examine usual aging.

Changes in Information Processing

Most intellectual abilities change little throughout early and middle adulthood (as documented in Chapter 21). At some point, however, everyone experiences some cognitive losses, eventually in every domain. In the Seattle Longitudinal Study, the averages in all five primary mental abilities (verbal meaning, spatial orientation, inductive reasoning, number ability, and word fluency) began to fall at about age 60, a decline particularly notable in the subtests that measured spatial perception and processing speed (Schaie, 1996). Other longitudinal research finds that for some abilities, cognitive decline begins later, perhaps not until age 80 (Singer et al., 2003).

Although researchers differ on specifics of timing or domains of decline, all agree that people do not think as quickly or remember as well at age 80 as they did at age 40. Detailed studies also report significant individual differences: A study of 900 people in their 70s, 80s, and 90s who lived in the community (not in institutions) found great variability, including "both greater-than-expected deterioration as well as less-than-expected deterioration (including improvement)" over a four-year period (Christensen et al., 1999). Another group of researchers explain that "on average, cognition declines in old age. . . . In some people cognition declines precipitously, but in many others cognition declines only slightly or not at all, or improves slightly" (Wilson et al., 2002, p. 179). People over age 80 who tested at a high level in earlier years still surpass their peers and many younger adults. But they do not surpass themselves.

Input: Sensing and Perceiving

The information-processing approach, which was discussed in detail in Chapter 12, starts with input—that is, with sensations, the stimuli taken in by the senses. Remember that the *sensory memory* (or *sensory register*) holds incoming sensory information for a split second after it is received. Small reductions in the sensitivity and power of the sensory register occur naturally with age, making most older people less adept at repeating words they have just heard or retaining the afterimage of a visual display. Compensation for reduction in perceptual ability is not difficult if the person is aware of it: He or she can ask others to speak more slowly or can look longer and more intently at crucial images. Older people readily compensate in such ways.

However, in order for information to reach perception, it must cross the *sensory threshold*; that is, the senses must pick up the relevant sensations. It is here that significant decline in input occurs. Remember that none of the five senses are as sharp at age 65 as at age 16, which means that certain information—such as the details of a road sign 300 feet away or the words of a conversation spoken against a noisy background—never reaches the older person's sensory memory because the senses never detect it. Such deficits, which are progressive, affect some people more severely than others. For those whose vision and hearing are severely affected, even a nearby sign or a loud conversation may be missed.

What Did He Say? No one hears as well as they once did, an especially serious problem for the older members of the audience in this meeting about Medicare. Because we all use our preconceptions to fill in the gaps created by sensory failures, we are likely to appear, and even to be, more stupid than we need to be.

This problem becomes serious because it is insidious. The person is unaware of things not seen or heard (just as you are unaware of a mosquito buzzing before it gets close enough to your ears). To some extent, this is inconsequential. (Who cares about that buzzing mosquito?) But because the deficit occurs before the threshold, after a time the person may miss a substantial amount of information without realizing it. Since cognition depends on perceptions and perceptions depend on sensations, the person might be oblivious to an intellectual handicap.

Research confirms that reduced sensory input (noises, sights, and even smells) impairs cognition (Anstey et al., 2003; Dulay & Murphy, 2002). One study of people of all ages found that 11 percent of the variance in cognitive scores for young adults, and 31 percent of it for older adults, was explained by sensory impairment (Lindenberger & Baltes, 1997). In other words, if one older person scored 100 points higher on a given cognitive test than another, typically about 31 of those points could be attributed to the better sight or hearing of the "smarter" person. The simplest way to predict how much an older person has aged intellectually may be to measure vision, hearing, or smell.

Active Memory

After information reaches the brain, it must be analyzed and placed in the appropriate memory part of the brain. Although many of the elderly ignore sensory deficits because they are unaware of them and discard some input if it comes too fast, the opposite occurs with short- and long-term memory: Fearing memory loss, partly because it is the chief symptom of senility, the elderly tend to overestimate the extent of their memory deficits and to cling to what they do remember. But memory deficits are not as widespread as many think, and people of all ages are poor judges of their own memory (Lane & Zelinski, 2003; Peterson, 2003). More accurate measures come from controlled experiments or standardized tests. We now report some of the conclusions from research comparing a single component of memory in the elderly and in the young.

Working Memory

Of all the aspects of information processing, laboratory research finds that working memory is most likely to decline with age (Briggs et al., 1999; Craik & Salthouse, 2000). Working memory (also called short-term memory) has two functions:

- It temporarily stores information, holding whatever is currently in mind.
- It processes information that is held in mind—reasoning, calculating, inferring, and so on—using other information that is recalled from storage as relevant.

That is, working memory functions as both a repository and a processor. Older individuals have particular difficulty holding several items of new information in working memory while analyzing them in complex ways, especially when distracting material appears. Multitasking is especially difficult for them, because increasing the number of things to be attended to or ignored reduces performance (Anderson, 2001; Kemper et al., 2003; Verhaeghen et al., 2003). This difficulty, as when a person must walk and read or must tap a finger and add, is called the *dual-task deficit.*

In fact, some scholars believe that the inability to screen out distractions and inhibit irrelevant thoughts is the main reason that working memory suffers in late adulthood: The brain cannot handle too much at once (Hasher et al., 2001). Others suggest that a decline in total mental energy—making it too hard to filter and think at the same time—may be at the root of the weakening of working memory (Park & Hedden, 2001). In general, if the person can slow down and focus, performance is as good as in younger years (Verhaeghen et al., 2003).

Learning New Tricks Most older adults readily learn how to use anything that expands their memory capacity, from handwritten to-do lists to computer programs.

Long-Term Memory

Intellectual processing depends not only on input and working memory but also on the knowledge base—that is, the information already stored in long-term memory (do you remember what that was from Chapter 12?). As discussed in Chapter 12, long-term memory is the storehouse of our entire knowledge base. Because attention and working memory are selective, most things are quickly forgotten, never reaching long-term memory. And memories that do reach long-term memory are still subject to alteration. At every age, "it is the rule rather than the exception for people to change, add, and delete things from a remembered event" (Engel, 1999).

An important aspect of the knowledge base is vocabulary. Evidence suggests that long-term memory for words remains unimpaired over the decades. In fact,

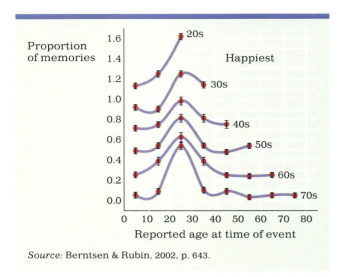

Proportion of memories

Source: Berntsen & Rubin, 2002, p. 643.

FIGURE 24.1 The Memory Bump A sizeable proportion of adults of all ages report having had a "happiness bump" in their mid-20s. Participants in this study ranged in age from their 20s to their 70s, and the curves in this graph are labeled accordingly. To make the graph easier to read, the curve for each age group is offset by 0.2 from the curve for the next-oldest group. As a result, for the group in their 40s, for example, 0.6 is the equivalent of 0. Thus, about 15 percent of participants in their 40s said that they had experienced their happiest memories at age 10 or younger; 15 percent at ages 10–20; 35 percent at ages 20–29; 20 percent at ages 30–39; and about 15 percent at age 40 or older.

Recognition At every age, recognition memory is much better than recall. Chances are that few of my high school classmates could describe how I looked back then, but all of them could point out my picture among the hundreds of photos in our yearbook.

according to two meta-analyses (compilations of the results of many studies), vocabulary increases with age at least until age 80 (Uttl & Van Alstine, 2003; Verhaeghen, 2003).

Also relatively unimpaired are areas of expertise. As you learned in Chapter 21, people become experts in particular areas; their knowledge base holds steady in those areas. Deficits appear in long-term memory, but they are themselves erratic and selective.

Researchers have discovered certain patterns of long-term memory changes over time. Happy events that occurred between ages 10 and 30 are remembered better than events of any kind that happened earlier or later (Berntsen & Rubin, 2002) (see Figure 24.1). Emotions are also remembered better than factual details. For example, people remember how they felt about events ("I was so happy to have had a baby") more than exactly where, how, and when the events occurred. *Source amnesia,* forgetting who or what was the source of a specific fact, idea, or snippet of conversation, is a common problem (Craik & Salthouse, 2000). All these aspects of memory—bias toward happy events in adolescence and young adulthood, emphasis on subjective emotions more than journalistic facts, and source amnesia—are common at every age, but they are increasingly common in late adulthood.

Selective memory can serve the needs of older people. For example, Tina was married 56 years to Tim, who had Parkinson's disease. She says:

> I think of him as a young man. I see him the same. He doesn't look any older to me. . . . I feel sorry that he can't walk. I can't believe it, because he would always be walking ahead of me as if we were from another culture . . . men in front, you know.
>
> [quoted in Koch, 2000, p. 72]

Her children were upset that Tina did not sufficiently protect her own health from the demands of her husband, but she insisted that they did not understand. (And, of course, they didn't; their memories were quite different.)

Does long-term memory stay intact with age? One objective way to study long-term memory might be to ask about public events. This method demonstrates good memory in older adults (Baier & Ackerman, 2001), but it also has inevitable biases. For example, asking for the names of the heads of state at the Yalta conference favors people who were politically aware in 1945; asking for the names of the four Beatles gives an advantage to those who were teenagers in the 1960s; and asking for the names of the stars of the NBA in 2004 gives an edge to those who are relatively young, from the United States, and male. (If you are not in this category, you may not know that NBA stands for National Basketball Association; if you are in this category, you would be amazed that any sentient person would not know.) Further, each of these examples favors people with particular interests—politics, music, and sports, respectively—and each cohort and age tends to have different concerns. Overall, then, no test questions can objectively compare the long-term memory of people who are 15, 45, and 75.

Another approach to assessing long-term memory is to measure knowledge that was learned in high school and used very little in the years since—for example, high school Spanish. One researcher did this and found that young adults who had studied Spanish within the past 3 years remembered it best. Thereafter, forgetting was very gradual: The older persons who had studied Spanish 50 years earlier remembered about 80 percent of what the young adults who had studied 5 years earlier remembered. The most significant variable was not when the language had been studied or how old the person was, but how well the person had learned it in the first place: Those who had earned an A 50 years earlier outscored those who had received a C just 12 months before (Bahrick, 1984). Thus, memories can be stored for decades, and neither age nor the passage of time affects them very much.

Overall, then, several aspects of memory are somewhat weaker in the elderly than in the young, but for some kinds of memory, the elderly can hold their own (Stuss & Binns, 2001). The particulars of the testing process are crucial, as we describe later. Generally, older adults maintain their long-term memory for most things—especially vocabulary, happy experiences, and their area of expertise. Much depends on the specifics. One example is a "lady of 100 years old who could still play (and win) Scrabble in three languages, even though she had marked difficulty remembering what she just had for lunch" (Parkin, 1993). Her Scrabble playing required that she remember not only words in three languages but a vast array of Scrabble skills; she also needed short-term memory to take each turn.

As far as memory in late adulthood is concerned, then, sensory memory is adequate as long as sensory abilities are sharp. Short-term memory may require slower input from one source at a time, and long-term memory is quite good though selective, as it is for all other age groups.

Control Processes

If memory abilities are not generally poor, why is memory loss such a common complaint in old age? One explanation is that the problem is one of control, not memory capacity. When someone says, "I don't remember" or "I never knew that," the root problem may be in the ability to pay attention, to retrieve information when needed, and to organize thoughts. These are **control processes**, part of the executive function of the brain. Control processes include selective attention (as we've discussed in the context of working memory), storage mechanisms, logical analysis, and retrieval strategies.

Older adults "are impaired in controlled cognitive processes" (Jacoby et al., 2001, p. 250). In particular, in their logical analysis and decision making, they seem not to gather and consider all relevant data (Zwahr et al., 1999). They are likely to rely on prior knowledge, general principles, and rules of thumb, applying them even when the specifics require additional information or new approaches. For example, given a diagnosis of cancer, older adults are more likely to arrive at a treatment decision without getting a second opinion or seeking further information on medical options, benefits, and risks (Meyer et al., 1995). This is a "top-down" strategy, using deductive rather than inductive reasoning. In thinking ahead about what should occur next, the older a person is, the greater the chance that intentions will be forgotten before a planned deed is done (West et al., 2003). Everyone walks from one room to another and then wonders what they meant to retrieve, but this happens more often to the old.

Use of retrieval strategies also worsens with age. Trying to recall the name of a childhood acquaintance, for example, a young adult might run through an alphabetical mental checklist or try to associate the person with a specific context—both effective strategies. In contrast, older adults might say, "I forget the name" and then, "It will come to me," or, more ominously, "My memory is failing"—indicating that they are not using effective techniques. Priming, such as giving the first letter of a word, helps, but it does not overcome the age differences (White & Abrams, 2002).

In general, older adults can learn better retrieval strategies, but this does not overcome age-related problems in memory and control. The theory that control processes are the problem more than memory (i.e., that the problem is not the storage capacity of the mind but the ability to recall quickly and correctly) is

Especially for Students If you want to remember something you learn in class for the rest of your life, what should you do?

control processes That part of the information-processing system that regulates the analysis and flow of information. Memory and retrieval strategies, selective attention, and rules or strategies for problem solving are all useful control processes.

Clutter or Control? This man uses notes, photographs, and objects to help him remember not just what he must do but also what he likes to think about. Many older people are attached to specific personal memorabilia—a warning to any younger person who is tempted to organize Grandpa's things.

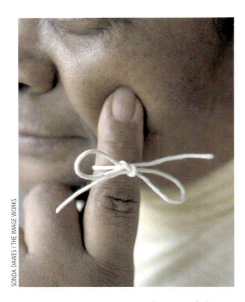

SONDA DAWES / THE IMAGE WORKS

It Really Works! Seeing anything out of place—a shoe by the door, a toothbrush next to the bedside lamp, a string tied around a finger—is enough to remind a person that something needs to be remembered. That thought alone is likely to produce the memory. Apparently, the problem in remembering is not that the memory has disappeared, but that it cannot be recalled at the appropriate time.

explicit memory Memory that is easy to retrieve, usually with words. Most explicit memory involves consciously learned words, data, and concepts.

implicit memory Unconscious or automatic memory that is usually stored via habits, emotional responses, routine procedures, and various sensations.

Response for Students (from page 609): Learn it very well now, and you will probably remember it in 50 years, with a little review.

supported by the fact that older adults' comprehension of vocabulary is far more extensive than that of younger adults. However, they have particular difficulty with tip-of-the-tongue phenomena (they know the word but can't produce it), with names of people (even people they know well), and with spelling (Burke et al., 2000). All these pitfalls suggest that something is amiss with production, not perception—with control, not storage.

Explicit and Implicit Memory

Without adequate control processes, people have particular difficulty recalling information on demand. In other words, **explicit memory** is especially shaky.

Explicit memory involves facts, definitions, data, concepts, and the like. Most of what is in explicit memory was consciously learned, usually through links made with verbal information already in memory and through deliberate repetition and review designed to facilitate later recall. Partly because of this rehearsal, the contents of explicit memory can usually be retrieved in response to questioning. You know your birthdate explicitly.

Implicit memory is less conscious, more automatic. It involves habits, emotional responses, and routine procedures. For the most part, the contents of implicit memory were never deliberately memorized for later recall. Items in implicit memory are, accordingly, difficult to retrieve on demand. However, they are retrievable in other circumstances.

For example, if you were asked to describe the distinctive facial features of your best friend in third grade, you might find the task nearly impossible—but you could immediately recognize that friend in a class photograph. When Jean Piaget asked people how to crawl, most of them gave the wrong verbal directions. (Is it hands and feet, or elbows and knees? Which parts and pairs of the four limbs move together?) However, almost everyone can get down on the floor and correctly demonstrate crawling, because that ability is in implicit, not explicit, memory (Piaget, 1970).

Children, brain-damaged people, and older adults are often much better at implicit memory than explicit memory (Craik & Salthouse, 2000; Schneider & Björklund, 2003). Indeed, on some tests of implicit memory, older adults who are healthy and intellectually sharp overall show no evidence of decline (Cherry & Stadler, 1995; Fastenau et al., 1996). Consider again the test of high school Spanish. Items that require implicit memory—perhaps understanding a Spanish phrase—would be more readily understood than an explicit test—for instance, a list of English words to be translated into Spanish.

Resistance

Some declining control may be the result of refusal to guess, deliberate choice, or resistance to change rather than a direct result of aging. Many older people do not use the memory aids that are available, often resisting others' attempts to teach them those strategies (Cavanaugh, 1999).

In an experiment, adults of various ages were taught a memory technique called the *method of loci,* in which the person creates a mental picture of unusual locations in which the items to be remembered are "placed." Many of the older adults quietly resisted using the new method, even though the experiment required it and, within the narrow confines of the research conditions, the strategy ensured better recall. Instead, the older adults, to the detriment of their memory scores, used their own memory strategies or tried to combine the new strategy with their own. Half the gap between the memory scores of the older participants and the younger ones could be traced directly to this noncompliance rather than to age-related decline (Verhaeghen & Marcoen, 1996).

The same problem may occur in daily life. Many older people of their own accord use strategies such as carrying a grocery list, keeping a calendar, or programming a phone to dial numbers automatically. However, if someone else tells them to do these things, they may refuse, either directly or passively (as by carrying a grocery list but not consulting it).

> Cognitive deficits in late adulthood are neither as extensive nor as devastating as they were once thought to be. There is great variability, not only from one person to another but also from one aspect of information processing to another. Input may be limited if a person has sensory deficits that are not remedied. Once input reaches the brain, memory is usually quite good, although slower processing limits the capacity as well as the speed of working memory. Long-term memory may be very good in the absence of disease, although it is hard to test it accurately. Control processes may be less effective with age, particularly the ability to focus attention and inhibit irrelevant responses.

Does She Need Her Shopping List? A shopping list may help when explicit memory fails. If this shopper wrote a list and then misplaced it, however, she could scan the store shelves and imagine her kitchen cupboards. Implicit memory would probably enable her to choose almost every item she needed.

Reasons for Age-Related Changes

Declines in cognitive functioning may be caused by (1) primary aging, (2) secondary aging, or (3) ageism of two kinds: either reflected in the older person's self-perception or embedded in the way scientists measure cognition. Each of these causes requires a different solution: acceptance, change of health habits, or change of attitudes. Therefore, to find solutions, we need to look at the causes of the declines.

Primary Aging

It was once thought that declines occurred with the gradual destruction of neurons caused by primary aging. However, it now appears unlikely that neural-cell loss is the main factor behind the declines (Stern & Carstensen, 2000). Efforts to connect cognitive deficits with brain atrophy and cell loss have failed. A definitive answer is elusive, partly because over the life span, the brain proves more multifaceted, and thought processes more diversified, than was once imagined. For example, brain scans suggest that many combinations and sequences within the brain can produce the same outcome; when older brains fire differently than younger brains in reaction to a stimulus, that does not mean that the brains are worse—or even that aging has caused the change (Grady, 2001). Primary aging does change brains, just as it changes skin and all the other organs (see Chapter 23). But, as the following explains, the effects are unclear.

Thinking Like a Scientist

Neuroscience and Brain Activity

Research in neuroscience has recently become more exciting, intriguing, and mystifying than ever. It has long been suspected that the brain is the most complex human organ. Half of all human genes are dedicated to brain form and function. Complex interrelationships are evident among neurons, dendrites, axons, and brain areas; the critical distinction between humans and other animals is probably in the brain, not in physical features like thumb grasping or two-legged walking; and split-second coordination of cortex and subcortex, of left and right hemispheres, of frontal/dorsal structures, of various sensory modes, and of emotions and intellect inspire awe as we learn about the brain.

Until recently, most of the brain's complexity over the life span was obscure to scientists. They had only crude measures, such as overall volume (some parts of the brain shrink with age); laboratory analysis at autopsy (which still provides the only definitive proof of Alzheimer's disease), and the effects of massive strokes or surgery (such as severing the corpus callosum to control epilepsy). It was not known whether conclusions from such research applied to healthy people.

Fortunately, in the past few decades, noninvasive neuroimaging in vivo (that is, in living brains) has allowed researchers to see the dynamic workings of the brain. Tantalizing bits of evidence have reaffirmed that the brain is far too complex for simple conclusions. Unfortunately, firm conclusions of any kind are still elusive, partly because data collection is arduous. Both PET and fMRI scans require that research participants lie still, heads surrounded by a large, expensive, sophisticated apparatus, while they respond to various intellectual tasks. Data thus far have been gathered from only hundreds of healthy adults, not from thousands of representative, cross-cultural, diverse individuals.

Although neuroscientists still have much work to do, they have already found that many parts of the brain can be used for almost every task. They no longer believe that the human brain has one or two language areas; dozens of areas might be activated when people listen and talk. Neuroscience has also shown that neurons and dendrites can be formed in adulthood, that intellectual ability does not correlate with brain size, that attention-deficit disorder (ADD) may be caused by an immature prefrontal cortex, and that people use their brains differently as they age.

The new research raises questions that were never asked before. For example, it was assumed that brain activity decreases with age, because older people themselves are less active. This assumption may be false, but not completely. As one expert explains:

When the neuroimaging techniques are applied to . . . young and old adults, there are three possible outcomes in terms of task-related activity in a given brain region: the two groups could have equivalent activity, the young group could have greater activity, or the older group could have greater activity. All three of these outcomes have been found, depending on the task and the particular brain region.

[Grady, 2001, p. 4]

The third outcome, that sometimes older brains show more activity, is unexpected, and researchers are attempting to understand it (Grady, 2001).

One explanation involves compensation: Older adults may naturally compensate for intellectual slowdown by recruiting extra brain areas when they think. This explanation is in accord with the general theory of late adulthood known as selective optimization with compensation. In Chapter 23, you read of many ways older adults keep their senses sharp if unassisted vision and hearing fade, and in Chapter 21 you read that people can become experts when they can choose the tasks they must perform well. Similarly, older brains may naturally select, optimize, and compensate by activating more neurons than they once did for each particular task. For example, in a study that required adults to learn new skills, the brains of older adults were more active at first, when they were learning, but less active once they had mastered the skill (Head et al., 2002).

A second possible explanation for greater brain activity among older adults is that, since control processes become weaker, the brain itself "dedifferentiates"—that is, it no longer uses a different region for each function. Inhibition fails, attention wanders, and thinking becomes more diffuse (Nielson et al., 2002). Like the compensation explanation, the dedifferentiation explanation fits some behavioral data: Older adults do not always stick to one subject when they talk, and they are less able to remember and recount specific details. However, the ability to remember overall themes is unimpaired (Radvansky et al., 2001). When it comes to remembering the particulars, older minds may wander; perhaps their brain activity does, too.

Younger adults usually think within one hemisphere or the other, while older adults use both. This "age-related decrease in lateralization" appears in many cognitive tasks (Cabeza, 2002, p. 97) and may reflect compensation as well as dedifferentiation.

Interpreting any of this evidence is difficult without bringing either benign or hostile ageism into play. Is diffusion of brain function an admirable tendency to combine intellectual and emotional skills, or is it a pathetic loss of focus? Thinking like a scientist means suspending judgment until more data are collected, and avoiding ageist prejudices—favorable as well as unfavorable. Such objectivity is difficult, maybe impossible—except for people whose brains can ignore emotions. (Not my brain. Yours?)

Brain Slowdown

One processing change seems universal and hence is a consequence of primary aging. In every type of laboratory test (pushing a button in response to a light flashing on, and so forth), the elderly react much more slowly than do younger adults. This brain slowdown can be traced partly to reduced production of the neurotransmitters—including dopamine, glutamate, acetylcholine, and sero-tonin—that allow nerve impulses to jump across the synapse from one neuron to another. Other aspects of the brain that decrease with age include the total volume of neural fluid, the speed of the cerebral blood flow, and the pace of activation of various parts of the cortex—all of which affect reaction time (Albert & Moss, 1996; Mattson, 1999).

Speed of thought and reaction is a very powerful factor in many aspects of cognition. If a person cannot process information or ideas quickly, then he or she cannot think about many facts or ideas at once, cannot sequentially analyze information, and cannot fully take in new information, because earlier information is still being processed. When thinking becomes slower, it may also become simpler and shallower because important information gets lost (Salthouse, 1996, 2000).

The significance of speed has been substantiated by various researchers who, in testing adults' ability to learn new materials, allowed adults of all ages additional time to study whatever material was to be learned. Extra time did aid the cognitive performance of older participants—but helped that of younger participants even more (Bryan & Luszcz, 1996). In other words, the aged need more time to reach the level of younger adults, but if the younger adults are required to spend more time, they will further surpass their elders. Not surprisingly, fluid intelligence is particularly affected by the slowdown of processing speed with age (Zimprich & Martin, 2002).

Although slowdown may affect cognition in some ways, especially for learning new material, types of thinking in which speed is not involved are less affected by primary aging. As noted, neuronal loss does not appear to be a significant factor. One reason is that when some brain cells die, others routinely take over their function; also, dendrites continue to grow over time. Such compensation might allow older adults to think as well as they once did.

In short, "aging impairs cognition on some tasks but spares it in others. . . . Individuals adapt, sometimes with great success" (Stern & Carstensen, 2000, p. 3). Thus, in considering primary aging and cognition, we remember the statement earlier in this chapter: Aging does not necessarily impair thinking very much.

This, then, leaves slower processing as the main consequence of primary aging. Slower processing may be chosen by older adults, or it may be inevitable. In any case, speed may be irrelevant in everyday life, especially in familiar situations. The day-to-day decisions that people make are usually complex enough that

> decision time is controlled more by "appropriate programming" that uses our brains efficiently than by raw speed of information processing. . . . In most cases involving everyday activity, the young–old contrast should not be thought of as a contrast between a fast and a slow computer, but as a contrast between a fast computer with a limited library of programs and a slow computer with a large library.
>
> *[Hunt, 1993]*

Compensation

Whenever researchers look for a "common cause" for all the effects of primary aging on cognition, two factors emerge: sensory deficits and slower processing. In Chapter 23, we mentioned the ways adults can compensate for sensory deficits—if they are willing to use them. Here we need to stress compensation for loss of speed.

Using memory tricks and written reminders, allowing additional time to solve problems, repeating instructions that might be confusing, focusing only on meaningful cognitive tasks and ignoring those that are irrelevant—all are methods that older adults use to compensate for slower processing. A meta-analysis of many measures of cognition found that older adults were slower at almost everything but not less accurate (Verhaeghen et al., 2003). Thus, primary aging, including the slowdown discussed here and the reduced seeing and hearing discussed earlier, probably affects cognition, but it does not necessarily do much damage.

Terminal Decline

In some ways, death can be considered an outcome of primary aging, in that each year brings a person closer to death. If death is the result of an overall breakdown in immunity, cell replication, or antioxidant functioning (all of which are discussed in Chapter 23), then primary aging can be said to lead to cognitive decline.

terminal decline An overall slowdown of cognitive abilities in the days or months before death. (Also called *terminal drop*.)

Terminal decline (also called *terminal drop*) is an overall slowdown of cognitive abilities in the days or months before death. Remember from Chapter 23 that a person may experience *compression of morbidity*, with serious problems limited to the last few months before death. Such compression may occur for intellectual factors as well as for physical factors.

Many people demonstrate a marked loss of intellectual power when death is near, even before a physician notices a serious change in blood pressure or blood chemistry, or sees something suspicious on an MRI. Changes in cognition and increased depression often precede rather than follow a visible worsening of health (Rabbitt et al., 2002). Thus, a decline or sudden drop in cognitive ability may be a signal of impending death (Bäckman et al., 2002; Small et al., 2003) and may be a primary consequence of the final aging process. Remember that life expectancy once a person has reached late adulthood is several years, at least. Terminal decline is not the result of being a certain age; it is the result of being close to death (Maier et al., 2003).

Secondary Aging

There is no doubt that secondary aging causes cognitive decline. Several diseases that are common among the elderly impair cognition (Nilsson & Söderlund, 2001). One of them, dementia, will be discussed later, as will other diseases that directly attack the brain. In addition, many systemic conditions affect the brain as well as all the other organs as part of secondary aging. Hypertension, or high blood pressure, during middle age is likely to cause intellectual decline by age 60. Diabetes, arteriosclerosis, and diseases affecting the lungs are similar examples. Poor eating habits, smoking, and lack of exercise can contribute to these diseases, and lack of exercise can itself impair cognition. Feelings of depression and incompetence also slow down cognitive processes—as a cause, not just a result. Thus, good physical and mental health both support cognition in late adulthood (Anstey & Smith, 1999; Caplan & Schooler, 2003):

> Although a slowing of thinking processes seems inevitable with age, it can actually often be halted or even reversed. For example, regular exercise improves blood flow in the brain, aiding cognition in many ways, including faster reaction time and improved memory. Exercise has these effects not only because blood flow is faster at the moment but also because the uptake of neurotransmitters and the branching of dendrites are accelerated.
>
> *[Cotman & Neeper, 1996]*

If people exercise more and improve nutrition to combat diseases such as arteriosclerosis, brain deterioration can be halted. A variety of drugs appear to help, too. For example, long-term use of certain anti-inflammatory steroids, and even aspirin and ibuprofen (often taken daily for arthritis, lung functioning, or heart disease), may have an unexpected side benefit: better and longer-sustained cognitive functioning in old age (Vickers et al., 2000). At least a dozen other drugs may likewise help, although definitive, controlled long-term research has not been completed.

This hopeful note is tempered by data about trends. Fewer and fewer adults in the United States enter late adulthood with none of the diseases or risk factors that lead to secondary aging. Of all 50- to 64-year-olds, 75 percent have at least one risk factor; for half of them, it is hypertension (*MMWR,* January 16, 2004). Thus, if it seems as if most older adults are more cognitively impaired than we have indicated here, secondary aging may be to blame.

Ageism

Finally, let us consider the possibility that cognitive decline is rooted not in the older person's body but in the surrounding social context.

Attitudes of the Elderly

For a person of any age, sex, or ethnicity, stereotypes do most harm when individuals internalize prejudices and react with helplessness, self-doubt, or misplaced anger (as we saw with stereotype threat in Chapter 18). This may happen when the elderly fear losing their intellectual powers (Hess et al., 2003).

Under the influence of expectations, people aged 50 to 70 tend to overestimate the memory skills they had in young adulthood. They selectively forget their earlier forgetfulness! This in itself can create a loss of confidence that impairs memory (as every student who has panicked about an exam can testify). Confidence is further eroded when others interpret an older person's hesitant effort to recall as a sign of impaired memory and react accordingly. If they respond with elderspeak (as explained in Chapter 23), not only does the older person feel less intelligent, but the lack of challenge of the oversimplified context can lead to cognitive slippage (Levy, 2003).

In one experiment, words that expressed either positive or negative ageism were flashed on a screen. The words disappeared so quickly that the participants didn't even know they had seen them. Nonetheless, older adults performed better on cognitive tests after they saw words that reflected positive stereotypes (such as *guidance, wise, alert, sage, accomplished, learned, improving, creative, enlightened, insightful,* and *astute*) than after words that reflected negative stereotypes (*Alzheimer's, decline, dependent, senile, misplaces, dementia, dying, forgets, confused, decrepit, incompetent,* and *diseased*) (Levy, 1996).

When the same experiment was repeated with younger adults, no significant differences in test scores were found. Apparently, negative stereotypes do damage only if a person identifies with them. The researcher concludes:

> Two messages emerge from this research. The pessimistic one is that older individuals' memory capabilities can be damaged by self-stereotypes that are derived from a prevalent and insidious stereotype about aging. Specifically, the stereotype that memory decline is inevitable can become a self-fulfilling prophecy. This research also offers an optimistic message. The findings indicate that memory decline is not inevitable. In fact, the studies show that memory performance can be enhanced in old age.
>
> *[Levy, 1996]*

The influence of stereotyping is also shown by a study that looked at cognitive declines in two groups of people who are somewhat protected from ageist messages: people in mainland China, where the old are traditionally venerated, and deaf people in North America, whose lack of hearing limits their exposure to ageist stereotypes (Levy & Langer, 1994). First, researchers assessed attitudes. Hearing North Americans had the least positive views of aging, Chinese had the most positive, and the deaf were about midway between. Then they compared memory differences between old and young individuals from China, from the deaf community in North America, and from the hearing North American

Especially for Busy People When does "speed reading" make sense?

population. For hearing Americans, the memory gap between old and young was twice as great as that for deaf Americans and five times as great as that for the Chinese.

Other research also makes it apparent that cultural attitudes can lead directly to impaired thinking in the elderly—quite apart from the effects of any neurological deficits caused by primary or secondary aging. This does not mean that *all* cognitive differences between young and old are the result of cultural attitudes. However, attitudes do have some impact, as confirmed by studies of recent and long-ago Chinese immigrants in Canada (Yoon et al., 2001).

Yet another study found no differences between younger and older adults on a test of recognition memory when participants were told it was a test of information, but significant differences when they were told it assessed memory. The latter instruction apparently aroused a stereotype threat, which impaired the older adults' performance (Rahhel et al., 2001).

Ageism in the Context of Laboratory Research

Many of the prejudices people have are indirect and inadvertent. People do not realize that a particular way of doing things may be unfair to a certain group. Such bias is evident when measuring cognition in late adulthood.

The laboratory context of research on aging—usually a university, with experiments often conducted in the afternoon—may favor younger adults (typically students) over older adults, who tend to be at their intellectual best early in the morning, at home.

In the typical laboratory experiment on memory, participants are given meaningless items to memorize (perhaps a string of unrelated numbers or words) within a specific time and then are tested on the accuracy and speed of their retrieval. (Meaningless items are chosen so that items will be culturally neutral.) However, compared to younger adults, older adults are more knowledgeable about, and more dependent on, culturally relevant material (Baltes et al., 1998). In other words, laboratory tests that focus on abstract memory necessarily exclude any benefit that a large knowledge base might provide. Using a familiar setting and memory clues might be considered contaminating or at least confounding from a purely scientific perspective, but doing so might be more realistic and valid (Smith et al., 1996).

Finally, laboratory experiments do not consider each participant's recent practice and his or her attitudes toward exams. Young college students are required to memorize material that is not immediately relevant to their lives, so they have learned how to do so. College students are motivated and practiced at performing under pressure to attain high scores, even when they think they will never need that particular chemistry formula or history date again. Older adults, by contrast, are unpracticed at, and may be suspicious of, exams. If they are conscious of ageist stereotypes, they may decide that the purpose is to prove them stupid. If they expect to fail, they may not try very hard—allowing themselves the face-saving excuse "I didn't really care" or "It didn't really matter."

Beyond Ageism

Even though laboratory results uniformly report some memory loss in late adulthood and even though older adults may become anxious if they think others are judging them, few older adults consider memory problems a significant handicap in their daily lives. They worry about memory lapses

■ At the beginning of late adulthood
■ If they think they are experiencing early symptoms of Alzheimer's disease

Otherwise, they take memory problems in stride. Older people report some explicit-memory problems, such as difficulty remembering names and phone numbers, but they also think that they are better than the young at remembering to pay bills, take medicine on time, and keep appointments. In fact, they may be right (Park & Hedden, 2001; Rendell & Thompson, 1999).

One classic study was designed to mimic the memory demands of daily life (Moscovitch, 1982). Older and younger adults (all living busy lives) were asked to call an answering service every day for two weeks at a specific time they themselves chose. This task was selected partly because remembering appointments is something everyone must do in daily life. Only 20 percent of the younger adults remembered to make every call, but 90 percent of the older adults did.

Why the dramatic difference? Younger adults, it seems, were likely to put excessive trust in their memories ("I have an internal alarm that always goes off at the right time") and therefore were less likely to use memory aids. Older adults, with a heightened awareness of the unreliability of memory, did use reminders, such as a note on the telephone or a shoe near the door.

The experimenters then attempted to increase forgetting. They required only one call per week at a time selected by the researchers; and they made the participants promise not to use any visible reminders. About half of both groups, old and young, failed to call at the appointed time. More old people would probably have forgotten, but some of them bent the rules, using a memory-priming measure (such as carrying the phone number in plain sight in their wallets).

One of the researchers concluded:

> With more effort, we are sure we can bring old people's memory to its knees . . . but that hardly seems to be the point of this research. The main lesson of this venture into the dangerous real world is that old people have learned from experience what we have so consistently shown in the laboratory—that their memory is getting somewhat poorer—and they have structured their environment to compensate.
>
> *[Moscovitch, 1982]*

Many other researchers have assessed memory in older adults, not only in traditional experiments but also in more novel experiments designed to accommodate the special abilities and needs of the elderly. Almost invariably, the more realistic the circumstances, the better an older person remembers. As one series of studies concludes, "Older adults, in their everyday life, are capable of accurate and reliable performance of important tasks" (Rendell & Thompson, 1999).

The structure of the environment is crucial, and most older adults have supportive environments. They use routines, memory strategies, and cues to "help ameliorate, and sometimes eliminate, age-related memory impairment" (Moscovitch et al., 2001). Ordinarily, then, older adults are less likely to forget someone's birthday, forget to take their vitamins, or even forget to brush their teeth than a college student might, because they have developed a context of reminders in their daily lives.

Response for Busy People (from page 615): Faster is not always better, and people who believe a stereotype and develop research to prove it often find what they expect. Therefore, take a skeptical view of any claim that is made about speed reading.

> Cognitive deficits in late adulthood may be caused by primary aging, secondary aging, or ageism. For the most part, primary aging does not limit cognition very much, except in regard to speed of processing and toward the very end of life. Secondary aging does affect cognition in many ways, not only in brain diseases but also in conditions that affect blood circulation or oxygen, such as hypertension, diabetes, and lung diseases. Ageism may make the elderly appear less intelligent if they think it is their memory that is being tested, and laboratory research may inadvertently demonstrate the weaknesses, not the strengths, of cognition in late adulthood.

Dementia

Loss of intellectual ability in elderly people is often referred to as senility. The word *senility* is ageist, however, because *senile,* which means "old," is being used to signify cognitive impairment. The implication is that age itself causes severe intellectual failure. Not so, as you have just read.

A better and more precise term for pathological loss of brain functioning is **dementia**—literally, "out of mind," referring to severely impaired judgment, memory, or problem-solving ability (Edwards, 1993). Traditionally, when dementia occurred before age 60, it was called *presenile dementia,* and when it occurred after age 60, it was called *senile dementia* or *senile psychosis.* However, age 60 is a meaningless marker: A person may have senile dementia at age 40 or age 80. Diagnosis depends on symptoms, not age.

More than 70 diseases and circumstances can cause dementia. The resulting forms of dementia differ in sequence, severity, and particulars, although all are characterized by mental confusion and forgetfulness (Fromholt & Bruhn, 1998). Dementia is chronic, which means it lasts a long time and usually becomes worse as the years go by, unlike *delirium,* the term for acute, severe memory loss and confusion that disappears in hours or days.

Dementia is complex. It is crucial to distinguish dementia from delirium and to avoid the ageist expectation of cognitive confusion in the old but not the young. It is equally crucial to diagnose the particular cause correctly. Yet the precise cause of dementia is difficult to determine, except when the person is dead. Autopsies of brains can reveal plaques and tangles (Alzheimer's disease), selective brain atrophy (strokes), tumors (cancer), Lewy bodies (Parkinson's disease), or other abnormalities.

When adults become confused and memory fails, many assume that Alzheimer's disease is the cause, but autopsies reveal that about 15 percent of the diagnoses were wrong. If someone who is said to have Alzheimer's spontaneously improves, the diagnosis of a progressive brain disease was obviously wrong. Doctors are stuck in a dilemma: The wrong diagnosis may lead to ineffective treatment, but a correct early diagnosis may lead to helpful intervention. More research and better application of research findings are much needed.

dementia Irreversible loss of intellectual functioning caused by organic brain damage or disease. Dementia becomes more common with age, but even in the very old, dementia is abnormal and pathological. Sometimes dementia is misdiagnosed, because reversible conditions such as depression and drug overdose can cause the symptoms of dementia.

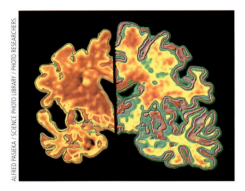

The Alzheimer's Brain This computer graphic shows a vertical slice through a brain ravaged by Alzheimer's disease *(left)* compared with a similar slice of a normal brain *(right)*. The diseased brain is shrunken as the result of the degeneration of neurons. Not viewable in this cross section are tangles of protein filaments within the nerve cells as well as plaques that contain decaying dendrites and axons.

Alzheimer's disease (AD) The most common form of dementia, characterized by gradual deterioration of memory and personality and marked by plaques of B-amyloid protein and tangles in the brain. Alzheimer's disease is not part of the normal aging process.

Alzheimer's Disease

The most common form of dementia (about half of cases worldwide) is **Alzheimer's disease (AD),** a disorder characterized by the proliferation of plaques and tangles, certain abnormalities in the cerebral cortex that destroy brain functioning. Plaques are formed outside the brain cells from a protein called *B-amyloid;* tangles are a twisted mass of protein threads within the cells. In AD, these plaques and tangles usually begin in the hippocampus, the brain region where most memory functions occur.

New techniques for analyzing brain tissue (the only sure way to diagnose AD) show that the amount of plaques and tangles correlates with the degree of intellectual impairment before death but not with the victim's age. Because the analysis of brain tissues can occur only after death, typically a diagnosis is based on reports of symptoms, a medical history, and some cognitive tests. This method is about 85 percent accurate, although autopsies find plaques and tangles in the brains of some very old people who did not have AD symptoms.

Risk Factors for Alzheimer's Disease

Gender, ethnicity, and especially age affect a person's odds of developing Alzheimer's disease. Most studies find that women are at greater risk than men. Alzheimer's is less common in Japan and China than in North America and Europe, and less common among Americans of East Asian descent than among those of European descent (Jellinger, 2002). It may also be less common in Africa, but low life expectancies there mean that relatively few reach late adulthood, so the low rates of AD may be the result of people dying before they develop the disease.

For everyone, everywhere, age is the chief risk factor for AD. According to a compilation of 13 studies from several nations (Ritchie et al., 1992), the incidence rises from about 1 in 100 at age 65 to about 1 in 5 over age 85. Other research finds that the incidence doubles every five years after age 65, with about half of those over age 100 having the disease (Czech et al., 2000; Samuelsson et al., 2001).

As you learned in Chapter 3, Alzheimer's is partly genetic (Selkoe & Podlisny, 2002). When AD appears in middle age, the person has the chromosomal abnormality called trisomy-21 or has inherited at least one of three genes: APP (amyloid precursor protein) gene, presenilin 1, or presenilin 2. In such cases, the disease usually progresses quickly, reaching the last phase within three to five years. This early AD is unusual. Most cases begin in late adulthood and take 10 years or more to progress from first symptoms to final stage (Wilson et al., 2000).

Especially for the elderly, another gene called ALZHS, or a variant of the ApoE gene (allele 4) increases the risk. A person who inherits ApoE4 from one parent, as one-fifth of all people in the United States do, has about a 50/50 chance of developing Alzheimer's by age 80. People who have the gene from both parents usually develop Alzheimer's if they live long enough, although ApoE4 increases the risk of heart disease and stroke, so many such people die before dementia begins. Nevertheless, a few people with the double allele reach age 100 and still do not have Alzheimer's, so ApoE4 is not used diagnostically before symptoms appear.

Genes can also make Alzheimer's disease less likely. Another allele of the same gene, ApoE2, dissipates the amyloid protein that causes plaques. Lifestyle may also decrease the risk, with physical exercise and mental activity said to be protective. There is an allele that protects people from Arctic weather and reduces the risk of Alzheimer's, although it increases the risk of some other diseases (Ruiz-Pesini et al., 2004). People with no known genetic or environmental risk can develop AD, a fact that actually provides hope: "Given that AD is a condition involving multiple genetic, environmental, and pathological factors, there may be many therapeutic strategies that will be useful for delaying or slowing dementia" (Vickers et al., 2000).

> *Especially for Genetic Counselors* Would you perform a test for ApoE4 if someone asked for it?

Stages: From Confusion to Death

Alzheimer's disease usually runs through a progressive course of five identifiable stages, beginning with general forgetfulness and ending in total mindlessness.

Stage One The first stage is characterized by absentmindedness about recent events or newly acquired information, particularly the names of people and places. A person in the first stage of the disease might be unable to remember where he or she just put something or forget people's names after being introduced to them. In this early stage, most people recognize that they have a memory problem and try to cope with it, writing down names, addresses, appointments, shopping lists, and other items much more often than they once did.

This first stage is sometimes confused with normal aging, but recent research finds that it can be distinguished from the normal decline in explicit memory (Peterson, 2003). Failure to remember a common word is a notable sign. One woman described the problem:

> There is embarrassment when I want to say "ocean" and I can't think of the word. It depends on how comfortable I am with the person I'm talking with. Then I can ask, "What's that big water thing?" and they'll guess, "The ocean?" Then I say, "Oh, yeah."
>
> *[Snyder, 1999]*

Response for Genetic Counselors (from page 619): A general guideline for genetic counselors is to provide clients with whatever information they seek; but because of both the uncertainty and the devastation of Alzheimer's disease, the ApoE4 test is not available at present. This may change (as was the case with the test for HIV) if early prevention and treatment become more effective.

Stage Two In the second stage confusion becomes more generalized, with noticeable deficits in concentration and short-term memory. Speech becomes aimless and repetitive, vocabulary is much more limited, and words get mixed up. A person might say *tunnel* when he means *bridge,* for instance. Someone at stage two is likely to read a newspaper article and forget it completely the next moment, or to put down her keys or glasses and within seconds have no idea where they could be. If certain people are suspicious by nature, with Alzheimer's they may accuse others of having stolen what they themselves have mislaid and forgotten. Then, "in the firm conviction of having been robbed, the patient starts hiding everything, but promptly forgets the hiding place. This reinforces the belief that thieves are at work" (Wirth, 1993).

Personality changes are common, as long-standing impulses become more pronounced when rational thought loses control. A person given to tidiness may become compulsively neat; a person with a quick temper may begin to display explosive rages; a person who is asocial may become even more withdrawn.

Memory loss in the second stage is sufficiently severe that people may forget they have a memory problem. Typical is the case of a man who, in stage one, began to run into financial problems because of his fading memory. In stage two, he was forced to turn over all his financial decisions to others, having no responsibility beyond putting his signature on documents. When asked if he was depressed, he replied that he didn't have any reason to be. He knew that he had had problems in the past, but now, he said, "I sign the papers. I'm in charge" (Foley, 1992).

Stage Three In the third stage, memory loss becomes truly dangerous. Individuals can no longer manage their basic daily needs. They may take to eating a single food, such as bread, exclusively, or they may forget to eat entirely. Often they fail to dress properly, or at all, going out barefoot in winter or walking about the neighborhood naked. They are likely to turn away from a lit stove or a hot iron and forget about it, creating a fire hazard. They may go out on some errand and then lose track not only of the errand but also of the way back home. And they cannot ask neighbors for help because they do not recognize them. Getting lost is a serious and valid fear of people in this stage (Sabat, 2001).

For some people with Alzheimer's, visual recognition is a major problem. The particular part of the brain that looks at an object and realizes that it is a *K*, a hat, or a person may become tangled. The person appears more helpless and more incompetent than the overall cognitive losses would indicate.

I Love You, Dad This man, who is in the last stage of Alzheimer's disease, no longer remembers his daughter, but she obviously has fond memories of his fatherly affection.

ALAN ODDIE / PHOTOEDIT, INC.

Stage Four By the fourth stage, people need full-time care. They cannot care for themselves or respond normally to others, sometimes becoming irrationally angry or paranoid. At the end, they can no longer put even a few words together to communicate. They cannot recognize even their closest loved ones. This is not necessarily because they do not remember them at all, but because the part of the brain that recognizes objects and faces has further deteriorated. A man might demand to see his wife but refuse to believe that the person before him is, indeed, his wife.

Stage Five In the fifth stage, people no longer talk, failing to respond with any action or emotion at all. Death usually comes 10 to 15 years after the beginning of stage one (Fromholt & Bruhn, 1998).

Many Strokes

The second most common type of dementia is caused by a stroke or, more often, a series of many strokes, a condition called **vascular dementia (VaD)**, or **multi-infarct dementia (MID)** (Fromholt & Bruhn, 1998). An infarct is a temporary obstruction of the blood vessels that prevents sufficient oxygen from reaching a particular area of the brain. This causes the destruction of brain tissue, which produces immediate symptoms (blurred vision, weak or paralyzed limbs, slurred speech, and mental confusion). In a so-called silent stroke, or ministroke, these manifestations typically disappear in hours or even minutes and may be so slight that no one (including the victim) notices. Nevertheless, brain damage has occurred.

In North America and Europe, VaD causes 10 to 15 percent of all cases of dementia. The incidence is much higher in Japan and China, where VaD is more common than Alzheimer's disease (De la Torre, 2002). Worldwide, both VaD and Alzheimer's disease often occur in a person simultaneously, a combination that accounts for about one-third of all cases of dementia. In fact, some clinicians believe that most older people are affected by both VaD and AD, and that only when it reaches a tipping point is one or the other diagnosed.

The underlying cause of the blood-vessel obstructions that lead to strokes is systemic arteriosclerosis (hardening of the arteries). People who have problems with their circulatory systems, including those with heart disease, hypertension, numbness or tingling in their extremities, and diabetes, are at risk for arteriosclerosis and vascular dementia. Therefore, measures to improve circulation (such as regular exercise) or to control hypertension and diabetes (such as diet and drugs) help to prevent dementia and to slow or halt its progression.

The progression of "pure" VaD is quite different from that of Alzheimer's disease (see Figure 24.2). Typically, the person suddenly loses some intellectual functioning following an infarct. Then, as other neurons take over some of the work of the damaged area, the person becomes better. Therapy to retrain the brain's automatic responses and to repair the damaged links between one neuron and another can sometimes restore the person to intellectual health. Antidepressants can also help if the person feels like giving up and doing nothing, as is often the case (Okamoto et al., 2002).

With successive infarcts, it becomes harder and harder for the remaining parts of the brain to compensate. If heart disease, major stroke, diabetes, or another illness does not kill the VaD victim, and if ministrokes continue to occur, the person's behavior eventually becomes indistinguishable from that of someone suffering from Alzheimer's disease. In pure VaD, autopsy reveals that parts of the brain have been completely destroyed while other parts seem normal; the proliferation of plaques and tangles characteristic of Alzheimer's disease is not apparent.

vascular dementia (VaD)/multi-infarct dementia (MID) The form of dementia characterized by sporadic, and progressive, loss of intellectual functioning. The cause is repeated infarcts, or temporary obstructions of blood vessels, preventing sufficient blood from reaching the brain. Each infarct destroys some brain tissue. The underlying cause is an impaired circulatory system.

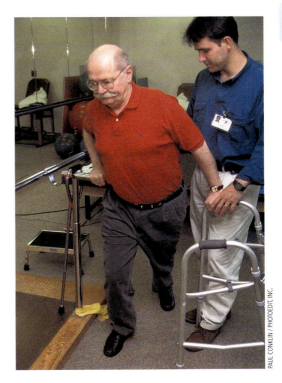

Vascular Dementia Rehabilitation after a stroke is easier for the body than the mind, because progress in physical therapy is more apparent to the patient and the therapist. Mental impairment is also common after a stroke, but the patient's determination to reestablish cognitive connections is less evident.

FIGURE 24.2 The Progression of Vascular Dementia and Alzheimer's Disease Cognitive decline is apparent in both Alzheimer's disease and multi-infarct dementia. However, the pattern of decline for each disease is different. Victims of AD show steady, gradual decline, while those who suffer from VaD get suddenly much worse, improve somewhat, and then experience another serious loss.

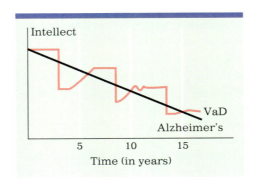

Subcortical Dementias

Many other dementias originate not in the cortex, as with Alzheimer's disease and vascular dementia, but in the subcortex. Because they are below, not inside, the cortex, these conditions do not initially directly involve thinking and memory. At first, **subcortical dementias** cause a progressive loss of motor control.

Subcortical dementias include Parkinson's disease, Huntington's disease, and multiple sclerosis. All begin with a person's realization that a serious, chronic illness has taken hold in the body and that control of the hands, legs, and other body parts is not what it once was. In later stages, when dementia appears, one sign that it is subcortical is that short-term memory and the ability to learn new material are better than long-term memory, exactly the opposite of people with cortical degeneration (Derix, 1994).

The most common subcortical dementia is **Parkinson's disease**, which is initially marked by rigidity or tremor of the muscles. Parkinson's produces degeneration of neurons in a brain region that produces dopamine, a neurotransmitter essential to normal brain functioning. When destruction of neurons and slowed transmission reach a certain threshold, dementia begins, because the brain can no longer compensate for neuron loss. Because cognitive reserve declines with age, older victims of Parkinson's are more likely to become demented than younger ones (Starkstein & Merello, 2002). An estimated 8 percent of newly diagnosed individuals are under age 40, but the majority are over age 60. At any age, dementia is likely to develop in people with Parkinson's, but it is by no means inevitable (Levery & Marder, 2003).

Various infectious agents and toxins can also affect the brain. For instance, almost half of all AIDS patients develop a brain infection that produces dementia, as do many people in the last stages of syphilis. Consumption of beef infected with bovine spongiform encephalitis ("mad cow disease") leads to dementia and death, because of either a slow-acting virus or a prion, a protein particle that acts as a disease agent (Collinge et al., 1996). Any psychoactive drug can produce delirium, and chronic use can lead to dementia. Proof is most evident for the most widely used drug, alcohol. When alcohol abuse is chronic, disruptions in the functioning of the central nervous system impair learning, reasoning, perception, and other mental processes. Over the long term, severe alcohol abuse can lead to *Korsakoff's syndrome,* with loss of short-term memory and increased confusion caused by brain lesions.

Reversible Dementia

The cortical and subcortical dementias already described damage the brain, and brain damage cannot be reversed. However, sometimes a person is assumed to be suffering from such dementias when the symptoms are actually caused by something whose effects can be reversed, such as medication, inadequate nutrition, alcohol abuse (short of Korsakoff's syndrome), or depression or other mental illness. In addition, reversible dementia can be caused by a brain injury, a brain tumor, a stroke, or a head injury. When this occurs, surgery and rehabilitation therapy can often remedy the problem and restore normal cognition.

Overmedication and Undernourishment

Overmedication is the most common cause of reversible dementia. It is particularly likely to occur in a hospital, because many forms of anesthesia can trigger delirium in the aged, and ongoing pain medication can mean ongoing dementia. Further, older adults living at home typically consume five or more different drugs each day, including prescription drugs, over-the-counter drugs, and herbal remedies. Drug interactions can produce symptoms of dementia, from

---

subcortical dementias Dementias, such as Parkinson's disease, Huntington's disease, and multiple sclerosis, that originate in the subcortex. These diseases begin with impairments in motor ability and produce cognitive impairment in later stages.

Parkinson's disease A chronic, progressive disease that is characterized by muscle tremors and rigidity, and sometimes dementia, caused by a reduction of dopamine production in the brain.

confusion to psychotic behavior. An added problem is that the doses may have been determined by tests on younger adults, whose metabolism and digestive system are quite different from those of older adults.

Even without interactions, many drugs commonly taken by the elderly (such as most of those to reduce high blood pressure, to combat Parkinson's disease, or to relieve pain) slow down mental processes (Davies & Thorn, 2002). The solution is simple—moderation or elimination of the problem prescription—but this solution obviously requires that the cause of the dementia first be recognized.

The problem of insufficient nutrition can be closely related to that of too much medication, partly because many medications reduce absorption of vitamins or increase the rate of elimination. Undernutrition can also stem from reduced income, loss of appetite, loneliness, and impaired digestive processes.

Whatever its cause, insufficient nutrition can lead to vitamin deficiencies, which, if extreme, can in turn lead to depression, confusion, and cognitive decline (Rosenberg, 2001). Dehydration can also produce confusion. Simply making sure an older person eats a balanced diet and drinks enough water may be enough to reduce dementia. In any case, balanced nutrition is good for body and mind; yet few residents of nursing homes eat well (Wendland et al., 2003).

Psychological Illness

In general. psychological illnesses are less common in the elderly than in younger adults. Anxiety, antisocial personality disorder, bipolar disorder, schizophrenia, and even depression are less common among the elderly, not only because mortality rates in early and middle adulthood are higher for people with these disorders than for those who are mentally well but also because the illnesses themselves become less severe, for either physiological or psychological reasons.

All the same, whenever a person seems demented, mental illness should always be considered and treated if found. About 10 percent of the elderly who are diagnosed as demented are experiencing psychological, more than physiological, illness.

In some cases, the person is merely unusually anxious (Scogin, 1998). As anyone who has taken a final exam under pressure knows, anxiety can make even a healthy person forget important information. Crippling anxiety is particularly likely when an older person arrives at a hospital or nursing home. The anxiety of such a moment can cause substantial disorientation and loss of memory. If the anxious new patient is tested immediately, a misdiagnosis of organic brain damage is possible. And if psychotropic medicine is prescribed as a result, and perhaps overused, the result can be ongoing, but reversible, dementia. If an older person is depressed, and therefore lonely and inactive, but *not* treated, that can lead to symptoms of dementia as well (Davies & Thorn, 2002).

Although major depression is less common in late adulthood than earlier, many older adults, especially if someone close to them has died, experience symptoms of depression that are sufficiently debilitating to resemble those of dementia (Kasl-Godley et al., 1998). In clinical assessments, even mild depression can diminish overall cognitive performance, although it does not reduce underlying ability. Similarly, one of the main symptoms of schizophrenia is memory loss—another avenue for misdiagnosis of dementia (Vidailhet et al., 2001).

Careful diagnosis can differentiate mental illnesses from dementia. For example, one symptom of depression in late adulthood is exaggerated attention to small memory losses or refusal to answer any questions that measure cognition. Quite the opposite reaction comes from people who truly suffer from dementia, who are often blithely unaware of their serious problems. They try to answer questions and are surprised and embarrassed at their inability to do so (Sabat, 2001). Similarly, people who suffer from schizophrenia are particularly impaired

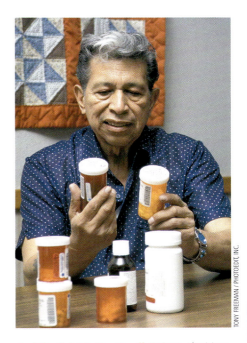

And the Print Is Too Small Patients, physicians, and pharmacists have reason to be confused about the eight or more drugs that the average elderly person takes. Very few patients take their medicines exactly as prescribed. Moreover, in addition to prescription drugs, most elderly people also take over-the-counter medications, vitamins, herbal remedies, and caffeinated or alcoholic drinks. It is no wonder that drug interactions cause drowsiness, unsteadiness, and confusion in about half of all elderly persons.

RICHARD SOBOL / STOCK, BOSTON

Dementia? Mental illness in the elderly often goes unrecognized and untreated because it is mistaken as a natural component of aging or as a sign of dementia.

? *Observational Quiz* (see answer, page 627): Can you see any indications that this woman's problem more likely arises from her concerns and her circumstances than from an inability to think at all?

in episodic memory (memory of what happened) but not in short-term memory, as are people with Alzheimer's disease (Vidailhet et al., 2001). It is quite possible for a person to be both mentally ill and to suffer from dementia, but in this case both conditions need to be treated.

Great strides are being made in the treatment of all sorts of mental illnesses, but not all people who need treatment receive it, especially in late adulthood. Depression, in particular, is one of the most treatable mental illnesses. Psychotherapy and careful use of medication usually bring about noticeable improvement in a few weeks, and the pseudodementia disappears (Davies & Thorn, 2002). However, even more than at younger ages, depressed older people go untreated because no one recognizes their depression as unusual, much less as a curable disease.

Untreated depression can lead to suicide, which occurs more often among those over age 60 than among any other age group. Rates are particularly high for certain subgroups among the elderly—for example, in the United States, males of European background (see Appendix A, p. A-16). The statistics for suicide in themselves suggest that depression can be severe in later life: Phrases such as "I want to die" should be interpreted as signs not of dementia, but of a serious yet treatable problem.

The Current Outlook

A common prediction is that as more people live to a very old age, more will suffer from dementia. Although most making this prediction often fear overcrowded nursing homes or underfunded health insurance, the truth is that usually spouses or adult children care for the victims at home, with little professional help, until the task becomes impossible.

After listing the problems and frustrations of caring for someone who is mentally incapacitated but physically strong, one overview notes: "The effects of these stresses on family caregivers can be catastrophic. Family caregiving has been associated with increased levels of depression and anxiety as well as higher use of psychotropic medicine, poorer self-reported health, compromised immune function, and increased mortality" (Gitlin et al., 2003, p. 362). Reflecting developmentalists' concerns about the health of caregivers, research is moving from describing the many ways such caregivers suffer to identifying more effective interventions than are in common use today (Gitlin et al., 2003).

Scientists are also learning ways to postpone or slow the course of Alzheimer's disease, the most common cause of dementia. If Alzheimer's can be diagnosed earlier, at the stage of mild cognitive impairment, then various drugs might halt or slow the buildup of the plaques and tangles associated with memory loss (Jellinger et al., 2002; Peterson, 2003). Several of these are promising, especially cholinesterase inhibitors. One problem is that some drugs that are sufficiently powerful to affect the brain also have harmful side effects (although treatment may be possible). Moreover, no cure seems forthcoming. Scientists are still far from developing drugs that can stop the disease before the first cognitive deterioration appears (Giacobini, 2002; Peterson, 2003). Stroke prevention is similarly difficult (Okamoto et al., 2002). The early stages of Parkinson's are difficult to diagnose, much less to treat (Starkstein & Merello, 2002).

The quality of life for people with dementia and their families is often grim, but this need not be the case. One person with Alzheimer's said: "I finally said to myself, this is the way it is, deal with it. I still have my creativity. Memory ain't so good, but creativity is there" (quoted in Harris, 2002, p. 165).

> Dementia, characterized by memory loss and mental confusion, is common among the elderly, but is not the usual or necessary result of living a long life. The three main causes of dementia are Alzheimer's disease, multiple strokes resulting in vascular or multi-infarct dementia, and Parkinson's disease. Each condition follows a somewhat different pattern of disablement. There are many other causes of dementias, some of which are reversible if correctly diagnosed. From a developmental perspective, it is crucial that family caregivers, as well as those suffering from dementia, receive adequate help and support.

New Cognitive Development in Later Life

Can older adults develop new interests, new patterns of thought, a deeper wisdom? Many of the major theorists on human development believe that they can.

Erik Erikson finds that people in the older generation are more interested in the arts, in children, and in the whole of human experience. They are "social witnesses" to life, more aware of the interdependence of the generations (Erikson et al., 1986). Abraham Maslow maintains that older adults are much more likely than younger people to reach what he considers the highest stage of development—self-actualization—which includes heightened aesthetic, creative, philosophical, and spiritual understanding (Maslow, 1970).

Both Erikson and Maslow have been criticized for selective perception (they chose whom to interview). But even Paul Baltes, with his data-based study of the elderly in West Berlin, finds that every stage of life has gains as well as losses (Baltes, 2003). What might those gains be?

Aesthetic Sense and Creativity

Many elderly people seem to gain appreciation of nature and aesthetic experiences. As one team of gerontologists explains:

> The elemental things of life—children, friendship, nature, human touching (physical and emotional), color, shape—assume greater significance as people sort out the more important from the less important. Old age can be a time of emotional sensory awareness and enjoyment.
>
> [Butler et al., 1998, p. 65]

For many older people, this heightened appreciation finds active expression. They may begin gardening, bird-watching, pottery, painting, or playing a musical instrument—and not simply because they have nothing better to do. The importance that creativity can have for some in old age is wonderfully expressed by a 79-year-old man, not famous, little educated, yet joyful at his workbench:

> This is the happiest time of my life. . . . I wish there was twenty-four hours in a day. Wuk hours, wake hours. Yew can keep y' sleep; plenty of time for that later on. . . . That's what I want all this here time for now—to make things. I draw and I paint too. . . . I don't copy anything. I make what I remember. I tarn wood. I paint the fields. As I say, I've niver bin so happy in my whole life and I only hope I last out.
>
> [quoted in Blythe, 1979]

For many older people, including this man, the impulse to create did not suddenly arise in late adulthood; it was present, although infrequently expressed, in

It Pleases Me In young adulthood and middle age, many people feel that they must meet social expectations and conform to community values. With a strong hand, a vivid imagination, and bold colors, the elderly are finally free to express themselves as they never did before.

life review The examination of one's own past life that many elderly people engage in. According to Butler, the life review is therapeutic, for it helps the older person to come to grips with aging and death.

earlier years. What does seem to occur in late adulthood is a deepening need to express that impulse, perhaps because, as the years left to live become fewer, people want to defer their dream of creative expression no longer.

One of the most famous examples of late creative development is Anna Moses, who was a farm wife and mother of 10. For most of her life, she expressed her artistic impulses by stitching quilts and doing embroidery during the long winters on the farm. At age 75, arthritis made needlework impossible, so she took to "dabbling in oil" instead. Four years later, three of her oil paintings, displayed in a local drugstore, caught the eye of a New York City art dealer who happened to be passing by. He bought them, drove to Anna Moses's house and bought 15 more, and began to exhibit them. One year later, at age 80, "Grandma Moses" had her first one-woman show in New York, receiving international recognition for her unique "primitive" style. She continued to paint, "incredibly gaining in assurance and artistic discretion," into her 90s (Yglesias, 1980).

For those who have been creative all their lives, old age is often a time of continuing productivity and even of renewed inspiration. There is something called the "old-age style" in the arts, when an established artist changes his or her usual way of creating art, developing a new style that is sometimes more creative then the previous style (Lindauer, 2003). Famous examples abound: Michelangelo painted the amazing frescoes in the Sistine Chapel at age 75; Giuseppe Verdi composed the opera *Falstaff* when he was 80; Frank Lloyd Wright completed the design of the Guggenheim Museum in New York City, an innovative architectural masterpiece, when he was 91.

In a study of extraordinarily creative people, almost none of the subjects felt that their ability, their goals, or the quality of their work was much impaired with age. What had changed was their sense of urgency, which was sharpened by their realization that fewer years lay ahead and that their energy and physical strength were diminishing (Csikszentmihalyi, 1996). As the researcher observed of these individuals, "In their seventies, eighties, and nineties, they may lack the fiery ambition of earlier years, but they are just as focused, efficient, and committed as before . . . perhaps more so" (p. 503).

Another review of artistic expression in late adulthood drew similar conclusions, which the author feels apply to all the aged, artist or not. He writes:

> The study of art in older age increases our awareness of the growth possibilities of aging. . . . A realization that old age can be a time of gains as indicated by the work of aging artists, or a time of cognitive stability, as shown by older non-artists' response to art and arts-related activities, gives a positive perspective on late life potential.
>
> [Lindauer, 1998, p. 248]

The Life Review

In old age, many people become more reflective and philosophical than they once were. Sometimes they think about their own history as they put their lives in perspective, assessing accomplishments and failures (Butler et al., 1998).

One form of this attempt to assess one's own life is called the **life review.** An older person recalls and recounts various aspects of his or her life, remembering the highs and lows and comparing the past with the present. In general, the life-review process helps elders connect their own lives with the future as they tell their stories to younger generations. At the same time, it renews links with past generations as a person remembers what parents, grandparents, and even great-grandparents did and thought. The individual's relationship to humanity, to nature, to the whole of life also becomes a topic of reflection, as various memories are revived, reinterpreted, and finally reintegrated to achieve a better understanding of the entire life course (Kotre, 1995).

One interesting aspect of the life review is that it is more social than solitary. Elderly people want to tell their stories to someone, and they often recount tales that are not solely about them but also about the family, a cohort, a group. Such stories tend to be more interesting when told by elders than by younger adults (Pratt & Robens, 1991). Of course, not everyone, old or young, is a gifted storyteller. The authors of one study explain.

> Most of us can recall older family members or acquaintances from our youth who were legendary (sometimes, perhaps, notorious) as champion storytellers. These individuals shared important cultural and personal knowledge and information on a variety of topics with younger generations through the recounting of their own past experiences. Yet other adults may come to mind who were terrible storytellers. Clearly, adults vary dramatically in their capacities and motivation to engage in such adult storytelling with young persons.
>
> *[Pratt et al., 1999, p. 414]*

! *Answer to Observational Quiz* (from page 624): The visible objects—ashtray, fan, hidden and small photographs, worn sofa cushion, too-large blouse— all suggest that the circumstances of her life are not ideal or even adequate to her needs. More telling are her facial expression, body position, and hands—all of which suggest that she is worried or sad, not mindless. Physical illness may also be a problem here if two symptoms suggested by this photo are actually present: recent weight loss and headache.

Nonetheless, if a listener knows how to hear, the stories are often worth listening to (Kastenbaum, 2003).

Sometimes the life review takes the simple form of nostalgia or reminiscence, which may be quite helpful to the older person, although not always easy for others to listen to. Yet it may be crucial to the person's self-worth that others recognize the significance of these reminiscences. As Robert Butler and his colleagues (1998) explain:

> We have been taught that this nostalgia represents living in the past and a preoccupation with self and that it is generally boring, meaningless, and time-consuming. Yet as a natural healing process it represents one of the underlying human capacities on which all psychotherapy depends. The life review should be recognized as a necessary and healthy process in daily life as well as a useful tool in the mental health care of older people.
>
> *[p. 91]*

In some cases, the reflectiveness of old age may lead to, or intensify, attempts to put broader historical, social, and cultural contexts into perspective (Cohen, 1999). In fact, in a comparison of autobiographical memories provided by young and old adults, the younger people recalled more specific details but the older ones gave more integrative accounts, stressing social roles and broader implications (Levine et al., 2002). In other words, young adults used autobiography to say exactly what occurred, older adults to gain insight and significance to the human experience. No wonder their own life review is meaningful to them.

Wisdom

Wisdom is one of the most positive attributes commonly associated with older people. The idea that wisdom may be common in old age has become a "hoped-for antidote to views that have cast the process of aging in terms of intellectual deficit and regression" (Labouvie-Vief, 1990). Although many people believe that wisdom increases with age, this belief, like the belief that aging inevitably means intellectual decline, may not be generally true.

An interesting dilemma arises among immigrants to the United States from Asia, Southern Europe, and Latin America—all places where respect for the wisdom of the elderly is integral to the culture. When adult children bring their

JAMES SHAFFER / PHOTOEDIT, INC.

So Much to Learn When it comes to computer savvy, these children will probably soon surpass their elderly volunteer teacher. But wisdom includes patience, appreciation of diversity, and willingness to learn, and on these qualities some older adults surpass the typical schoolchild.

wisdom A cognitive perspective characterized by a broad, practical, comprehensive approach to life's problems, reflecting timeless truths rather than immediate expediency; said to be more common in the elderly than in the young.

parents to live with them in the United States, a conflict often arises between the elderly, who feel that their wisdom is devalued, and the younger people, who feel that their parents do not understand the current situation. This is particularly true if the adult child has married someone of another ethnicity. One such spouse complained of his Italian in-laws, "Parents won't let go. They want to bury their child" (quoted in Olson, 2000, p. 201). A Haitian elder said, "The children are not well educated. Yet they make fun of me" (p. 109). Many elders feel that their children and grandchildren are "too American" to respect their elders. In such families, who are the wise ones?

What is wisdom, after all? Wisdom is an elusive concept; any definition is bound to be subjective. Whether any given individual is perceived as wise depends on the immediate social context in which that person's thoughts or actions are being judged (Vaillant, 2002). Given these obstacles to precision, consider one of the more comprehensive, all-purpose definitions of **wisdom,** offered by Paul Baltes: "expertise in the fundamental pragmatics of life, permitting exceptional insight and judgment involving complex and uncertain matters of the human condition" (Baltes et al., 1998, p. 1070).

Wisdom involves elements of both the dialectical thinking that emerges in early adulthood and the expert knowledge that comes with years of personal experience. But is wisdom a typical characteristic of older adults' thinking?

In one study, adults of various ages were asked to assess the lives of four fictitious persons, each of whom faced a difficult decision regarding the future. Here is an example of one story, concerning a dilemma faced by a young adult:

> Elizabeth, 33 years old and a successful professional for 8 years, was recently offered a major promotion. Her new responsibilities would require an increased time commitment. She and her husband would also like to have children before it is too late. Elizabeth is considering the following options: She could plan to accept the promotion, or she could plan to start a family.

The other three stories concerned dilemmas about parental responsibilities at home, accepting early retirement, and intergenerational commitments. After hearing these stories, participants were asked to formulate a course of action for each fictitious person by thinking aloud, indicating when they thought additional information about particular issues was needed. Participants' responses were transcribed and rated by a panel of human service professionals who did not know participants' ages.

Wisdom was in short supply. Of 240 responses, only 5 percent were judged as truly wise. Wise responses came about equally from adults who were young, middle-aged, and old (Smith & Baltes, 1990). More recent research likewise finds wisdom at many ages, although the very wise tend to be in late adulthood. Experience and practice in dealing with the problems of life tend to increase a person's wisdom, but sheer intelligence and chronological age do not (Baltes et al., 1998).

If wisdom includes warm social interactions, humor and perspective, and concern about other people, a study similarly found little correlation between IQ in adolescence and wisdom in middle and late adulthood (Vaillant & Davis, 2000). This study was of men who had low IQ scores (between 60 and 86), some of whom, by late adulthood, were leading wise and good lives. For example, one man, who as a boy had been labeled "slovenly, tardy, and lazy" by his teacher, had become involved with the Salvation Army and eventually became a pastor, first of a small parish, then of progressively larger ones. He loves "helping and teaching" people, and he is excellent at it. Wisely, he appreciates that his wife does the paperwork and math, and he is thrilled that all his children have attended college.

Although not all the men in this study achieved such success, approximately half the low-IQ participants attained levels of joy, connection, devotion, and caring that matched those attained by members of the same cohort who had much higher IQs. Another study found that social interaction is essential to wisdom, that a wise person consults and cooperates with others, as the Salvation Army officer certainly did (Staudinger & Werner, 2003).

What, then, of the relationship between age and wisdom? In a thoughtful longitudinal study of 814 people from adolescence through old age, one of the authors concludes that there is little proof that wisdom is reserved for the old, although some attributes—humor, perspective, altruism—may increase with age. He then writes:

> To be wise about wisdom we need to accept that wisdom does—and wisdom does not—increase with age. Age facilitates a widening social radius and more balanced ways of coping with adversity, but thus far no one can prove that wisdom is great in old age. Perhaps we are wisest when we keep our discussion of wisdom simple and when we confine ourselves to words of one and two syllables. Winston Churchill, that master of wise simplicity and simple wisdom, reminds us, "We are all happier in many ways when we are old than when we are young. The young sow wild oats. The old grow sage."
>
> [Vaillant, 2002, p. 256]

On balance, it seems fair to conclude that the mental processes in late adulthood can be adaptive and creative—not necessarily as efficient as thinking at younger ages, but more appropriate to the final period of life. These qualities are particularly apparent in the work of artists, who seem as creative and passionate about their work in later adulthood as they were earlier. Many others, who are not artistic, also have a strong aesthetic sense and seek to tell their life story to other people. Wisdom is not the sole domain of the old, nor do all older people become wise. Nonetheless, many older people are quite wise, creative, and reflective.

Let us conclude with an exemplary case in point, a poem written by Henry Wadsworth Longfellow at age 80:

> *. . . But why, you ask me, should this tale be told?*
> *Of men grown old, or who are growing old?*
> *Ah, Nothing is too late*
> *Till the tired heart shall cease to palpitate;*
> *Cato learned Greek at eighty; Sophocles*
> *Wrote his grand Oedipus, and Simonides*
> *Bore off the prize of verse from his compeers,*
> *When each had numbered more than four score years,*
> *And Theophrastus, at four score and ten,*
> *Had just begun his Characters of Men.*
> *Chaucer, at Woodstock with the nightingales,*
> *At sixty wrote the Canterbury Tales;*
> *Goethe at Weimar, toiling to the last,*
> *Completed Faust when eighty years were past.*
> *These are indeed exceptions, but they show*
> *How far the gulf-stream of our youth may flow*
> *Into the arctic regions of our lives*
> *When little else than life itself survives. . . .*
> *Shall we then sit us idly down and say*
> *The night hath come; it is no longer day?*
> *The night hath not yet come; we are not quite*
> *Cut off from labor by the failing light;*
> *Some work remains for us to do and dare;*
> *Even the oldest tree some fruit may bear; . . .*
> *And as the evening twilight fades away*
> *The sky is filled with stars, invisible by day.*

SUMMARY

Changes in Information Processing

1. Although thinking processes become slower and less sharp once a person reaches late adulthood, there is much individual variation in this decline, and each particular cognitive ability shows a different rate of age-related decline.

2. The ability to remember stimuli declines relatively little in late adulthood, although, as the senses themselves become dulled, some material never reaches the sensory memory. Working memory shows notable declines, especially when one must simultaneously store and process information in complex ways. Processing takes longer with age.

3. Control processes are less effective with age, as retrieval strategies become less efficient.

4. With increasing age, adults experience greater difficulty accessing information from both short- and long-term memory. Knowledge stored in implicit memory is more easily retrieved than are the facts and concepts stored in explicit memory.

5. Some age-related changes are caused by primary aging, which dulls the senses and slows down every part of the body, including brain reactions. Slower thinking, in some ways, is impaired thinking.

6. Secondary aging also impairs cognition. Hypertension, diabetes, and other chronic conditions eventually take an intellectual toll. Exercise can forestall, or even reverse, some secondary cognitive deficits.

Reasons for Age-Related Changes

7. One reason older adults, on average, do not perform as well as younger adults on tests of cognitive functioning is that more of the older group have negative self-perceptions of their mental skills that undermine their motivation to succeed. Older adults' cognitive performance can be negatively affected by exposure to ageist stereotypes. Some laboratory research creates contexts that impede the efficient use of adult cognition.

8. In daily life, most of the elderly are not seriously handicapped by cognitive difficulties. Usually, once they recognize problems in their memory or other intellectual abilities, they learn to compensate with selective optimization; that is, they learn to build on strengths and shore up weaknesses.

Dementia

9. Dementia, whether it occurs in late adulthood or earlier, is characterized by memory loss—at first minor lapses, then more serious forgetfulness, and finally such extreme losses that recognition of closest family members fades.

10. The most common cause of dementia is Alzheimer's disease, an incurable ailment that becomes more prevalent with age. Genetic factors (especially the ApoE4 gene) play a role in Alzheimer's disease, increasing the amyloid plaques that impair the brain. Drug therapy is beginning to offer some promise for the prevention and treatment of Alzheimer's disease.

11. Vascular dementia (or multi-infarct dementia) is caused by a series of ministrokes that occur when impairment of blood circulation destroys portions of brain tissue. Measures to improve circulation and to control hypertension can prevent or slow the course of this form of dementia.

12. Subcortical abnormalities, such as that leading to Parkinson's disease, are another leading cause of dementia. Other disorders that may lead to dementia are alcoholism and AIDS.

13. Dementia is sometimes mistakenly diagnosed when the individual is actually suffering from a reversible problem. Overuse or misuse of medication, anxiety, depression, and poor nutrition can sometimes cause dementia symptoms.

New Cognitive Development in Later Life

14. Many people become more responsive to nature, more interested in creative endeavors, and more philosophical as they grow older. The life review is a personal reflection that many older people undertake, remembering earlier experiences and putting their entire lives into perspective.

15. Wisdom is commonly thought to increase in life as a result of experience, but this idea has not been confirmed. Apparently, wisdom is not necessarily prevalent at any age. Some of the old are unusually wise or creative.

KEY TERMS

control processes (p. 609)
explicit memory (p. 610)
implicit memory (p. 610)

terminal decline (p. 614)
dementia (p. 618)
Alzheimer's disease (AD)
 (p. 618)

vascular dementia (VaD)/
 multi-infarct dementia (MID)
 (p. 621)
subcortical dementias (p. 622)

Parkinson's disease (p. 622)
life review (p. 626)
wisdom (p. 628)

APPLICATIONS

1. At all ages, memory is selective, and we all forget much more than we remember. Choose someone—a sibling, a past classmate, or a current friend—who went through some public event with you. Sit down together, write separate lists of all the details each of you remembers about the event, and then compare your accounts. What insight does this exercise give you into the kinds of things older adults remember and forget?

2. Many factors affect intellectual sharpness. Think of an occasion when you felt stupid and an occasion when you felt smart. How did the contexts of the two experiences differ? How might those differences affect the performance of elderly and young adults who go to a university laboratory for testing?

3. Visit someone in a hospital. Note all the elements in the environment—such as noise, lights, schedules, and personnel—that might make an elderly patient seem senile.

Chapter Twenty-Five

Late Adulthood: Psychosocial Development

There is a vast array of possibilities and outcomes in development after age 65. As we saw in the previous two chapters, some elderly people run marathons, others hardly move; some write timeless poetry, others cannot speak a sentence. This chapter continues to describe possibilities, particularly how people interact within their social world. It discusses interactions among family members, caregiving for the infirm, and elder abuse. As a preview, consider a couple who have passed their 100th birthdays and have been married 80 years. They live together, without outside help, in their home in Florida, where they retired 40 years ago. Gilbert is proud of his wife, Sadie.

> "She gets out of bed—I timed her this morning, just for fun. I got up first, but while I was in the bathroom, she gets up, she comes out here first and puts the coffee on. Got back and washed up and got dressed and just twelve minutes after she got out bed—*just twelve minutes this morning*—I had her right on the watch."
>
> Sadie chuckles. "I don't have any secrets anymore."
>
> "So then you have breakfast together?" I ask.
>
> "Oh, yes!"
>
> "And then read the paper?"
>
> "After we get the dishes washed, we sit down and read the paper for a couple of hours."
>
> *[Ellis, 2002, pp. 107–108]*

Few centenarians live as Gilbert and Sadie do: Many are widowed, and many are no longer independent. Although Gilbert and Sadie are unusual in some respects, they share with most of the elderly their comfort in their families, their pleasure in their daily routines, and their interest in current events.

In psychosocial development, old age is less likely to level individual differences than to build on them, continuing and extending the diversity of human experience. As we try to comprehend the complexity of development in later life, we begin with theories and then discuss activity levels, social relationships, and frailty.

Theories of Late Adulthood

Dozens of theories focus on psychosocial development in late adulthood. To simplify, we group them in three clusters: self theories, stratification theories, and dynamic theories.

Self Theories

self theories Theories of late adulthood that emphasize the core self, or the search to maintain one's integrity and identity.

Self theories begin with the premise that adults make choices, confront problems, and interpret reality in such a way as to define, become, and express themselves as fully as possible. As Abraham Maslow (1968) described it, people attempt to *self-actualize,* to achieve their full potential. Self theories emphasize "human intentionality and the active part played by the individual in developing selfhood" (Marshall, 1996, p. 9). The idea is that each person ultimately depends on him- or herself, especially as time goes on, so the sense of self becomes even more crucial in late adulthood than earlier. As one person explained:

> I actually think I value my sense of self more importantly than my family or relationships or health or wealth or wisdom. I do see myself as on my own, ultimately. . . . Statistics certainly show that older women are likely to end up being alone, so I really do value my own self when it comes right down to things in the end.
>
> *[quoted in Karger, 2002, pp. 207–208]*

Integrity Versus Despair

integrity versus despair The final stage of Erikson's developmental sequence, in which older adults seek to integrate their unique experiences with their vision of community.

The most comprehensive self theory came from Erik Erikson, who was still writing in his 90s. The eighth and final stage of Erikson's developmental sequence is **integrity versus despair,** when older adults seek to integrate their unique experiences with their vision of community. Many develop pride and contentment with their personal history, as well as a sense of being part of a common community (Erikson et al., 1986). Others experience despair, "feeling that the time is now short, too short for the attempt to start another life and to try out alternate roads to recovery" (Erikson, 1963, p. 269).

As at every stage, tension between the two opposing aspects of the developmental crisis helps move the person toward a fuller understanding. In this eighth stage,

> life brings many, quite realistic reasons for experiencing despair: aspects of the present that cause unremitting pain; aspects of a future that are uncertain and frightening. And, of course, there remains inescapable death, that one aspect of the future which is both wholly certain and wholly unknowable. Thus, some despair must be acknowledged and integrated as a component of old age.
>
> *[Erikson et al., 1986, p. 72]*

On the Same Page This school volunteer, working with "high-risk" children, pays close attention to the picture that has captured the boy's interest. The ability to care for others is one sign of integrity, as older adults realize all the "high risks" they have personally overcome.

Ideally, the reality of death brings a "life-affirming involvement" in the present—for oneself, one's children, one's grandchildren, and all of humanity. As one 82-year-old put it, "Keep busy. Stay in the now. Don't look back. . . . I can make my happiness or break it" (quoted in Melia, 2000, p. 135).

In general, the more positively a person envisions him- or herself, the less depression and despair is felt (Kwan et al., 2003). Thinking positively about oneself becomes increasingly difficult after age 80 or 90: The best way to maintain integrity may be to take pride in being mentally alert, able to care for oneself, or

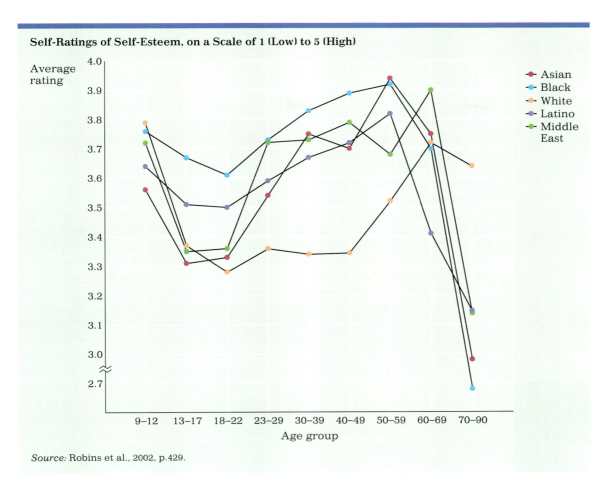

Self-Ratings of Self-Esteem, on a Scale of 1 (Low) to 5 (High)

Source: Robins et al., 2002, p.429.

merely still alive (Erikson et al., 1986; Rothermund & Brandstädter, 2003). Generally, self-esteem is high at the beginning of late adulthood and then drops, especially among nonwhites (see Figure 25.1) (Robins et al., 2002).

Identity Theory

A second self theory originates in Erikson's fifth stage, *identity versus role confusion*. Erikson himself recognized that the search for identity was lifelong, that each new experience, each gain or loss, requires people to reassess and reassert their personal identity. This theme is evident in the work of other developmentalists as well (Cross & Markus, 1991; Kroger, 2000; van der Meulen, 2001; Zucker et al., 2002).

Identity is particularly challenged in late adulthood: The usual pillars of the self-concept begin to crumble, specifically the pillars of appearance, health, and employment (Krauss, 1999; Whitbourne, 1996). As a 70-year-old retired teacher said, "I know who I've been, but who am I now?" (quoted in Kroger, 2000, p. 205).

The basic idea of identity theory is that people of all ages need to know who they are but that personal identity is assaulted by the inevitable experiences of aging. Yet most older people consider their personalities, values, and attitudes quite stable and, except for acknowledging that they may have slowed down a bit, do not feel that much has changed for them (Troll & Skaff, 1997). One researcher described a nursing home resident who,

when asked whether she had changed much over the years, extracted a photo from a stack in her dresser drawer, one taken when she was in her early twenties,

FIGURE 25.1 An Internet Survey on Self-Esteem To the statement "I see myself as someone with high self-esteem," respondents were asked to rate themselves from 1 (disagree strongly) to 5 (agree strongly). Overall, almost 30 percent of the men and 20 percent of the women who responded said that they "agreed strongly." There were clear age-related trends among the 326,641 Internet users who responded. Self-esteem reached a low point at the beginning of adulthood and then rose, only to dip again in later years.

? *Observational Quiz* (see answer, page 636): At what ages and for which ethnic groups is the average self-rating less than 3.0 (the halfway point between "agree strongly" and "disagree strongly")?

and said, "That's me, but I changed a little." She had indeed changed. She was now neither curvaceous nor animated, but was physically distorted from crippling arthritis and sullen from pain. To herself, however, she was still the same person she had always been.

[quoted in Tobin, 1996]

!*Answer to Observational Quiz* (from page 635): Only the 70- to 90-year olds of Asian or African descent. Note that almost all the fluctuations shown on the graph are minimal (between 3 and 4) and that the only group averaging significantly lower than 3.0 was very small, numbering only 13 people of African descent over age 69.

Ideally, the person maintains a firm but flexible identity, finding a balance in the face of the challenges of aging. Some people, however, instead of finding this balance, go to one extreme or the other, either refusing to alter or losing their sense of themselves (Whitbourne, 1996; Whitbourne et al., 2002).

In *identity assimilation,* identity remains what it always was, and new experiences are incorporated, or assimilated, into it. The individual maintains self-esteem by distorting reality and denying that anything significant has changed.

An assimilating older individual might "refuse to acknowledge the weaknesses of the cardiovascular system that may lead to disaster when a highly physically stressful activity is attempted. Or the individual may refuse to buy or use bifocals or hearing aids" (Whitbourne, 1996). This strategy results in rigidity and frequent self-justification, with few self-doubts, although those who use it might readily become angry at any implication that some adjustment is needed.

The opposite strategy is *identity accommodation,* whereby people adapt to new experiences by changing their self-concept, adjusting too much. Accommodating people doubt their values, beliefs, and even themselves, sometimes so intensely that "self-doubting can be an extremely painful process" (Whitbourne, 1996). Aging individuals who use this strategy might decide that all they have ever worked for is lost because, for example, grandchildren no longer go to church, take pride in their ethnic heritage, respect their elders, or—worst of all—listen to their grandparents. Accommodation means giving in to extreme ageist stereotypes. Life is over, integrity is impossible, and all that is left is despair—not only because of impending death but also because of worsening circumstances.

Ideally, a person incorporates long-standing concepts of identity with changing circumstances, so that neither too much assimilation nor too much accommodation occurs. Identity "consists of both more or less enduring, stable beliefs as well as more short-term, variable ones" (van der Meulen, 2001, p. 29). A crucial element of identity theory is that people take action to maintain their identity, that "individuals select pathways, act and appraise the consequences of their actions in terms of their self-identity" (Heinz, 2002, p. 58).

Selective Optimization

As you remember, Paul Baltes emphasizes that people can choose to cope successfully with the undeniable physical and cognitive losses of late adulthood through *selective optimization with compensation,* a concept central to self theories. We saw in previous chapters that the basic idea of this optimization is that individuals set their own goals, assess their own abilities, and then figure out how to accomplish what they want to achieve despite the limitations and declines of later life (Baltes, 2003).

Selective Optimization with Compensation Max Roach has been a leading jazz drummer for over 50 years. His approach to his work at age 73 clearly reflects the idea of selective optimization with compensation: "I joined a health club. . . . I thought I'd tune up, you know, tone up. Playing my instrument is a lot of exercise. All four limbs going. . . . I don't play the way I did back in the 52nd Street days. We were playing long, hard hours in all that smoke. It would kill me now if I played like I did then. Now I play concerts, and the show goes on for just an hour. But I'll tell you something: I'm ready to play until the sticks get too heavy for me to hold up."

As an example of this process, Artur Rubinstein, a world-famous concert pianist who continued to perform in his 80s, explained that he limited his repertoire to pieces he knew he could perform well (selection) and that he practiced before a concert more than he might have when he was younger (optimization). Because he could no longer play fast passages at the same brilliant tempos as before, he deliberately played slow passages more slowly, thereby making his playing of the fast passages seem faster by contrast (compensation) (Schroots, 1996).

More common examples are provided by the many elders who structure their lives so that they can do what they want and do it well. In a study of strategies used by people over age 80, Colleen Johnson and Barbara Barer (1993) tell about a woman who did her food shopping at a distant store because it was near the end of the bus line, so that empty seats were always available for her and her bags of groceries on the return trip. Similarly, two men developed strategies that let them continue to drive: One plans his exact route before setting out in order to avoid getting lost, and the other makes several right turns to avoid having to make a left turn at a dangerous intersection. (Johnson & Barer, 1993).

The readiness to make such selective changes is itself a measure of the strength of the self. People who have a strong sense of self-efficacy (Bandura, 1997) believe that they can master any situation life presents and thus can cope with the various events of aging.

The importance of self-efficacy was confirmed by a study that looked at fear, loneliness, and well-being in 288 people, aged 67 to 87 (Fry, 2003; Fry & Debats, 2002). Surprisingly, there was no correlation between income or even physical health and the psychological health of the participants. However, there was a negative correlation between self-efficacy and fear, loneliness, distress. People who thought they were able to manage their own lives were much less afraid, less lonely, and more satisfied than the others.

In this study, the sexes varied in the choice of self-efficacy domains, though both men and women displayed selective optimization. Women tended to think they were effective at selecting and maintaining friendships and at deepening their spiritual lives; men thought they were effective at managing money and getting things done. In general, as the author of the study explains, "with advancing old age, men and women selectively focus on cultivating areas and domains of positive self-appraisals and competency beliefs . . . in coping with threats, challenges, fears and anxieties of old age" (Fry, 2003, p. 483).

Support from Behavioral Genetics

In recent years, self theories have received substantial confirmation from behavioral genetics. Longitudinal studies of monozygotic and dizygotic twins find that, contrary to the logical idea that genetic influences weaken as life experiences accumulate, some inherited traits seem even more apparent in late adulthood than earlier.

Various life events—from how early a person retires to how often a person marries—seem to be affected at least as much by genetics as by life circumstances (Saudino et al., 1997). This is all the more true in later life. The explanation, developmentalists hypothesize, goes beyond "niche-picking," which was discussed in Chapter 22. When older adults are unharnessed from family and work obligations, their temperament gains free rein and they can become more truly themselves. As one 103-year-old woman observed, "My core has stayed the same. Everything else has changed" (Troll & Skaff, 1997, p. 166).

Obviously, certain stressful events are common in late adulthood (such as the death of a close relative, a serious illness, or a sudden loss of income). But the frequency of such events appears to some extent related to genetic factors, which have been in place since conception (Bergeman, 1997). Certain people seem to have a genetic predisposition to find themselves in difficult circumstances—taking risks, alienating family and friends, and emphasizing fear and anxiety (high in neuroticism and openness, and low in agreeableness, in terms of the Big Five personality traits discussed in Chapter 22).

The power of genetics goes beyond the environments we seek out. Even self-concept, including assessment of abilities, is partly genetic (McCrae et al., 2000). For example, some people are inclined to think well of themselves, their parents, their potential, and so on, while others take the opposite view. The difference arises not primarily because their parents were actually loving or hostile but because each person is always him- or herself, tending to have a particular outlook on childhood (and everything else).

A. RAMEY / PHOTOEDIT, INC.

How They Got That Way Almost 91 years before this photo was taken, a zygote split in half, and these monozygotic twins were the result. Their genetic similarities may be even more apparent now than when they were babies—not only their height and their hair but also less obvious features like the curl of their fingers and the wrinkles on their necks. The fact that they are celebrating their 90th birthday is testimony to shared nature as well as nurture. In their cohort and place of residence (Los Angeles), only one male in 20 reaches age 90.

Remember, however, that behavioral geneticists never claim that any aspect of the self is entirely genetic—the environment always plays a leading role. Although there is much variation, depending on the person and the trait, usually between one-third and one-half of the variation in our personal characteristics (how outgoing, how stressed, or how smart we are) is due to our genetics; the rest is the result of environmental influences (Bergeman, 1997). Proportions change depending on the particular context. For example, variance in children's IQ scores is primarily inherited if the child is from a wealthy family but primarily environmental if the child's family is poor (Turkheimer et al., 2003). In all probability, in the context of old age, genetic variation becomes more expressible, and individuals are quite consistent in genetic personality traits, but they still can and do adjust to changing circumstances (Roberts & Caspi, 2003). Many find that old age gives them the freedom to be more themselves.

Stratification Theories

stratification theories Theories emphasizing that social forces, particularly those related to a person's social stratum or social category, limit individual choices and affect the ability to function. In late adulthood, past stratification continues to limit life in various ways.

A quite different perspective is provided by **stratification theories.** These theories maintain that social forces limit individual choice and direct life at every stage, particularly in late adulthood (Estes, 2001; Hagestad & Dannefer, 2001).

Stratification by Age

One stratification theory focuses on *age stratification*. Industrialized nations tend to segregate their oldest citizens, giving them limited roles and circumscribed opportunities in order to make way for upcoming generations. The elderly are induced or compelled to retire, offered fewer life-saving medical treatments, and encouraged to live in housing restricted to their cohort. Many believe that sociocultural forces thus become even more important, but less supportive, in old age (Smith & Baltes, 1999).

All these policies, when added to ageist assumptions, can have a powerful effect. The effect is felt most deeply by the older people themselves, but "age segregation creates socialization deficits for members of all age groups" (Hagestad & Dannefer, 2001, p. 13).

disengagement theory The view that aging makes a person's social sphere increasingly narrow, resulting in role relinquishment, withdrawal, and passivity.

The most controversial stratification theory is **disengagement theory** (Cummings & Henry, 1961; Johnson & Barer, 1993). This theory holds that a person's social sphere increasingly narrows with age, largely because of the way societies allocate responsibilities and direct social interaction. According to disengagement theory, traditional roles become unavailable or unimportant; the social circle shrinks as friends die or move away; coworkers stop asking for help; children have families of their own. As adults reach their 60s, they anticipate and adjust to this narrowing of the social sphere by disengaging. They give up many of the roles they have played, withdraw from society, and develop a passive style of interaction.

Disengagement theory provoked a storm of protest, particularly from gerontologists who insisted that older people need, want, and find new involvements and new friends to replace the ones they have lost. Some gerontologists developed an opposite theory, called **activity theory,** which holds that the elderly remain active in a variety of social spheres—with relatives, friends, and community groups. If the elderly do disengage and withdraw, activity theorists contend, they do so unwillingly (Rosow, 1985).

activity theory The view that elderly people need to remain active in a variety of social spheres—with relatives, friends, and community groups—and become withdrawn only unwillingly, as a result of ageism.

The dominant view now is that the more active the elderly are and the more roles they play, the greater their life satisfaction and the longer their lives (Rowe & Kahn, 1998). There is extensive evidence supporting this view. For example, a longitudinal study of 77- to 98-year-olds in Sweden found that, over a 10-year period, one-third of those studied actually added activities rather than cutting back,

STEPHANIE MAZE / CORBIS

Silver on Display In the foreground is Layla Eneboldsen, enjoying the company of three other elderly people who live with her. Since more than 90 percent of the elderly in the United States are white (and mostly female), and since the furniture, lights, and artwork date from 60 years ago, this might seem to be a scene from the 1940s in the United States.

? *Observational Quiz* (see answer, page 640): What tells you that this scene is not in the United States and that the photo was not taken long ago?

substituting one activity for another if aging made this necessary. Quality of life was directly related to having many leisure activities (Silverstein & Parker, 2002). According to activity theory, age stratification that leads to disengagement is the result of ageism and should be discredited in the same way, and for the same reasons, that forced segregation by race or sex is discredited.

A more recent view of age stratification suggests that both disengagement theory and activity theory may be too extreme:

> Care providers have reported that their feelings are very mixed when trying to "activate" certain old people. The workers say that while they believe activity is good, they nevertheless have the feeling that they are doing something wrong when they try to drag some older people to various forms of social activity or activity therapy.
>
> *[Tornstam, 1999–2000]*

Rather than either disengaging or needing more activity, most older people become more selective in their social contacts and are happier as a result (Charles & Carstensen, 1999). Age may change how a person thinks and behaves, so that to expect an older person to be as active as ever may mean failing to recognize the distinctive psychosocial position of the oldest generation. In addition, what benefits the young-old may be too much for the oldest-old; age, ability, and personal preference must always be considered (Smith, 2003).

Stratification by Gender and Ethnicity

All stratification theories focus on the ways in which people organize themselves—and are organized by society—according to their particular characteristics and circumstances. Age is a powerful and limiting stratification category, as we have seen, particularly when ageism is its basis. Especially in late adulthood, sex and ethnicity are two other such categories, causing double or even triple "jeopardy" as the problems of stratification by gender and ethnicity compound those of stratification by age (Cruikshank, 2003).

Sexual Discrimination *Feminist theory* draws attention to the gender divisions. From the moment a newborn is given a pink or blue blanket and on through childhood education, adult career choices, family caregiving, and living arrangements

!*Answer to Observational Quiz* (from page 639): Long ago, the elderly lived in multigenerational families. Four older adults would not have shared a residence designed for the elderly, like this one. Much of the old-fashioned furniture was chosen by the people who live in this assisted-living center, subsidized by the government of Denmark. Note the glass and bottle of port, the cigarette, and the candle—all of which would be forbidden in most senior residences in North America.

SONDA DAWES / THE IMAGE WORKS

Dig Deeper A glance at this woman at her outdoor pump might evoke sympathy. Her home's lack of plumbing suggests that she is experiencing late adulthood in poverty, in a rural community that probably offers few social services. Her race and gender put her at additional risk of problems as she ages. However, a deeper understanding might reveal many strengths: religious faith, strong family ties, and gritty survival skills.

in old age, males and females have distinct lives. Feminists are particularly concerned about late adulthood because "the study of aging, by sheer force of demography, is necessarily a woman's issue" (Ray, 1996, p. 674). Currently in the United States, women make up 60 percent of the population over age 65 and 70 percent of the elderly poor (U.S. Bureau of the Census, 2002). Because most men marry women younger than they are and die at a younger age, there are four times as many widows as widowers. Being unmarried doubles an elderly person's risk of living in poverty and ill health (Rank & Hirschl, 1999).

Feminist theorists point out that, because most social structures and economic policies have been established by men, women's perspectives and needs are not always given a high priority, or even recognized. What might women need? Money and independence. Many older women become impoverished because of male-centered economic policies. One example is pension plans that are pegged to a lifetime of continuous employment, which women's focus on caregiving roles makes them less likely to have. Another is medical insurance that pays more for acute illness (more common in men) than for chronic disease (more common in women). A third is the reluctance of adult children to allow an aged widow to live alone, even though men are more vulnerable to violent crime or sudden illness than women (only 1 in 50 victims of violent crime is a woman over age 65; almost half are young men, aged 12 to 19).

Feminist theorists also note that because women are socialized to be nurturant, they are more likely than men to become caregivers for frail relatives (husband, siblings, or handicapped children), even if caregiving strains their own health. Society benefits greatly from this familial caregiving—saving public funds that would otherwise be spent on nursing homes, special services, and home health aides. But caregiving women subsidize this social benefit, sacrificing their own independence and well-being to do so. Indeed, in many ways, social policies and cultural values converge to make later life burdensome for women, and there is "value of considering both gender and age together," because the two interact (Moen, 2001, p. 190).

Ethnic Discrimination Another view of stratification comes from *critical race theory,* which sees ethnicity and race as "social construct[s] whose practical utility is determined by a particular society or social system" (King & Williams, 1995). According to this theory, long-standing ethnic discrimination and racism result in stratification along racial lines. They shape experiences and attitudes not only for minorities but for majorities as well, often without their conscious awareness (Bell, 1992). Remember that today's elderly were raised before 1950, when almost all nonwhite populations were ruled by Europeans and, in the United States, schools, the army, and even hospitals and cemeteries were segregated. In those years, people of color were more likely to be poor, dependent, and less educated.

Decades of ethnic and racial stratification mean that minority elderly, who were excluded from the economic mainstream, are more likely than other elderly people to be poor and frail. In late adulthood, they have less access to senior-citizen centers, clinics, nursing homes, and other social services and amenities; as a result, their health, vitality, and survival are at risk (Williams & Wilson, 2001). This has long been true for nonwhite native-born Americans, and now immigrant elderly experience the same exclusions—partly because of the majority culture and partly because of their own cultural values (Olson, 2000).

Consider the case of an elderly immigrant from Russia, who was placed by his U.S.-born son in a senior-citizen assisted-living center, which he hated and left. He went to live with an 85-year-old Russian widow, to whom he became very attached. But his son moved him out when the landlady became frail; so once again, the elderly man was on his own and unhappy. He says, "Would I like to live with my kids? Of course. But I know that's impossible. They don't want me. . . . It's not that they don't love me. I understand that. In the old days, a hundred years ago, old people stayed at home" (quoted in Koch, 2000, p. 53). As a result of this cultural divide, his life now is described as one of "lonely independence . . . a quintessentially American tragedy" (Koch, 2000, p. 55).

The consequences of past ethnic stratification can be subtle. For example, in North America many elderly benefit from being homeowners: They can continue to live in their home rent free, sell it for profit, or obtain a "reverse mortgage" (receiving a monthly payment in exchange for title to the house when they die). However, decades of housing discrimination mean that fewer elderly African-Americans than European-Americans own their home. Even when they do, the home is usually worth less than the homes of European-Americans of the same income level (Salmon, 1994).

Better Female, Non-European, and Old?

Many contemporary analysts argue that stratification theory yields an unfairly negative picture of women and minority-group members, who often have remarkable strengths in late adulthood. For instance, compared with European-Americans, elderly African- and Hispanic-Americans are often nurtured by multigenerational families and churches. As a result of familism, fewer are in nursing homes, and more feel respected and appreciated by their families than is true for European-Americans.

Similarly, because women tend to be the caregivers and kinkeepers, they are less likely than men to be lonely and depressed. One review finds that because men are socialized to be self-sufficient, they are more vulnerable than women are. As a result, "gender is more problematic for men than women" (Huyck, 1995).

A detailed study of the income of various groups over the life span found that, as expected, minority elders have less income than majority elders in the United States and that poverty impairs their health. But, noting that many minority elders lived in deteriorating places, the study controlled for this neighborhood effect. It then found that the minority elders were actually healthier than majority elders in similar neighborhoods (Robert & Lee, 2002).

Another study compared death rates among Californians over age 65 in various ethnic groups (see Figure 25.2). In all groups, women outlived men, and Latinos, Asian-Americans, and Native Americans outlived non-Hispanic whites—who are financially better off but who have fewer family members to support them (Hayes-Bautista et al., 2002).

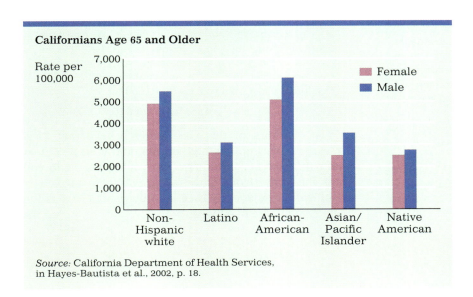

Californians Age 65 and Older

Source: California Department of Health Services, in Hayes-Bautista et al., 2002, p. 18.

FIGURE 25.2 Longevity in California
Greater family support may be one reason that Latino, Asian-American, and Native American Californians over age 65 die at lower rates than do their white peers.

Thus, stratification theories may not be accurate. It seems that the lives of the aged who are also female and of a minority ethnic group can be interpreted in different ways, either as evidence of long-standing problems or as evidence of human resilience. The truth is somewhere in between. The following Case to Study presents Mrs. Edwards as an example.

A Case to Study

Mrs. Edwards, Doing Just Fine

Mrs. Edwards is 76 years old and lives in her small Victorian house in the inner city of San Francisco. Her son Harold and three grandchildren live with her. She has ten children, eight by her first husband and two by her second, as well as several stepchildren and 52 grandchildren, most of whom live nearby. She is a retired practical nurse who has been widowed for "a long time."

When she was 72, Mrs. Edwards developed breast cancer and had surgery. She is now facing a second bout of breast cancer; it is being treated with radiation, and as a result her hair is sparse. Mrs. Edwards has vouchers that enable her to pay only 10 percent when she takes taxis to visit her children and to attend church activities, which are a major factor in her life. She feels busy and blessed, explaining:

> After this interview I will go to my daughter's for dinner. I can get up and go any time I want. I'm not nervous about my health now. I have cancer, so I can't say my health is excellent, but is is not poor. I guess it's fair. I don't worry about it. I'm more concerned about starting my fruitcakes for Thanksgiving dinner than I am about the cancer. The whole family will be here.
>
> I am fortunate that I have enough money. My children help me when I'm sick. I get social security and a pension and my children give me money. The only help I had after surgery was a visiting nurse who stopped by to show my son and daughter-in-law how to change the bandages. The social worker wanted to give me a nurse and someone to clean my house, but why should I pay for that when I have so many children and grandchildren to help me? My daughter gave me four nightshirts. She said she'd kill me if I was sitting in bed in an old sweater. . . .
>
> My eight children by Mr. Houston include my eldest son, who lives in Kentucky. He has a son who is a pediatrician. Next I have a daughter who works for the phone company. My third son has lost two children. A daughter died of crib death and a son died of an automobile accident. My fourth, a son, works for the state. His son got killed. Someone shot him over a drug deal. My fifth is

> Raymond, who has three children. He is a parole officer. His daughter, Angela, is asleep upstairs. Lots of my grandchildren stop by to spend the night. My sixth is David. He has a son who is paraplegic who lives here. His other son is in prison. I don't know when he will get out. My seventh is Kenneth who is also in prison at Vacaville. When I took sick, my doctor wrote a letter requesting he be transferred to a closer prison, but that didn't work out. As it is, I don't get to see him much. He has a wife and two children. My eighth son by Mr. Houston, oh I can't think who it is. Let's see. . . . Oh, it's Richard. Richard came in the other day with a bottle of brandy and passed out on the couch. I took his brandy and hid it. It's what I need for my fruitcake. I talk to his wife every day. My daughter and my son from Mr. Moore are also around here a lot.

[quoted in Johnson & Barer, 2003, pp. 116–117]

On a second visit, the authors of this case study found Mrs. Edwards "much the same. She was still actively involved with her very large family and in the community. Some of her children and grandchildren moved out only to be replaced by other children and grandchildren" (Johnson & Barer, 2003, p. 117). She seemed quite happy, with her church, her family, and her large color television. Her idea of a good day is:

> Nothing hurting and I can lie down and watch TV. I've lost a lot of weight, so I am a little bit depressed. And I am distressed about my son in prison. At least he didn't kill anyone. I read that the punishment is strict for that. But freedom and your health are the best things in life. If your freedom is taken from you, you have nothing.

[quoted in Johnson & Barer, 2003, p. 117]

The authors of this case study believe that Mrs. Edwards is strong, has high spirits, and is in a context that works for her in old age. Do you agree, or do you think she suffers from "triple jeopardy," being harmed by stratification by age, by race, and by gender? Or is the truth somewhere in between?

Cohort shifts will change the meaning of age, gender, and ethnicity for future generations, so current stratification effects may not apply. Today's middle-aged women are employed at almost the same rate as men, so they will have their own retirement income, as Mrs. Edwards does. Being old and female will less often mean being poor (Moen, 2001).

A less beneficial cohort shift is that many younger African-Americans now are less strongly tied to family and church. They usually have only one or two children, unlike Mrs. Edwards and many other women her age. This might mean that their social isolation will increase compared to their elders, who are now over age 65. Another such shift is that elderly Hispanic- and Asian-American immigrants, who are currently well protected by their families, have children and grandchildren who are less devout and less healthy than they are. This, too, may work against these younger generations later on (Williams & Wilson, 2001).

To better understand stratification theory, we need to take a multicultural perspective. In many nations, age stratification is not apparent: The way people are treated depends on factors such as their personality, family connections, and ability to work, not so much on their age (Ahearn, 2001; Makoni & Stroeken, 2002). The general principle of stratification theory is that social institutions and cultural values restrict and guide development, and that those limitations early in life will affect late adulthood. Perhaps gender and ethnicity will not stratify the next generation of the aged, but other characteristics—such as immigration, income, or English fluency—may come to the fore. Social categories and values follow people all their lives, and that is the essence of this theory.

Dynamic Theories

In contrast to self theories and stratification theories, dynamic theories focus on the many variations and changes of late adulthood. **Dynamic theories** view each person's life as an active, ever-changing, largely self-propelled process, occurring within specific social contexts that themselves are constantly changing. In turn, contexts are part of systems, which are ever-changing.

The best-known dynamic theory is called (somewhat ironically) **continuity theory;** it focuses on how selfhood is maintained throughout the social and biological changes the person experiences. Continuity theory "assumes that a primary goal of adult development is adaptive change, not homeostatic equilibrium" (Atchley, 1999). Thus, continuity is possible even as a person changes in response to the outside environment.

One important source of continuity is temperament. Reinforced by the ecological niches that individuals have carved out for themselves, the Big Five personality traits (see Chapter 22) are maintained throughout old age as they were in younger years. Therefore, reactions to any potentially disruptive problem reflect continuity more than change. Attitudes toward everything—drugs, sex, money, neatness, privacy, health, government—similarly reflect lifelong continuity (Binstock & Day, 1996).

In what way is continuity theory dynamic and not merely an extension of behavioral genetics? The explanation lies in the fact that continuity involves people's accommodation to personal circumstances and to changes in their social context.

For example, one woman never had her own career because she put her energy into actively supporting her husband's job. After his retirement, the couple traveled extensively. Such a change may seem like a break from earlier times, but the same core of herself and the same social niche were evident: She was still a companion to her wealthy husband, only now on cruises and visits to exotic places. Then two very disruptive events occurred: Her husband died, and illness made her housebound. Nonetheless, she continued in her social niche, hiring

dynamic theories Theories that emphasize change and readjustment rather than either the ongoing self or the legacy of stratification. Each person's life is seen as an active, ever-changing, largely self-propelled process, occurring within specific social contexts that themselves are constantly changing.

continuity theory The theory that each person experiences the changes of late adulthood and behaves toward others in much the same way as at earlier periods of life.

someone to manage her money, donating to selected charities, and finding satis-faction in supervising her three hired caregivers. These were all dynamic re-sponses to change; continuity required adaptive transformation (Atchley, 1999).

Another example of a person who maintained her core identity even while adjusting to changing circumstances is a retired home economics teacher. She continued helping other people even after leaving the work force—first by doing volunteer work in her community, then, when walking became impossible, by allowing high school seniors to interview her at home. She spent the last days of her life as a much-loved role model in a nursing home (Atchley, 1999).

The dynamic viewpoint stresses that the entire social system works toward individual and community continuity, even as elements of individual lives change. Thus, although the retired teacher's nursing home was located several miles from the town where she had formerly lived, she still had many visitors, and her cheerful determination made her greatly admired by both staff and resi-dents. The specifics of the system are constantly changing as aging affects indi-viduals, but the entire system continues to function to ensure continuity.

As you may have noticed (and remembered from your reading of Chapter 2), self theories echo psychoanalytic theories, especially in the importance they place on childhood self-concept and identity; social stratification theories apply many concepts from sociocultural theory. Dynamic theories, in stressing change, closely relate to epigenetic theory, which attempts to incorporate all the genetic, childhood, and cultural forces into an ever-changing but always productive system. As one researcher wrote, "Human life can be considered as a dynamic system consisting of hierarchically ordered and interacting elements . . . genes, cells, and organs, . . . cognition, motivation, and emotion, . . . social and material contexts" (Staudinger, 1999, p. 363).

> Self theories emphasize that, even in old age, each person defines him- or herself. Erikson's last stage, integrity versus despair, can be seen as a self theory. Stratification theories alert us to the power of social context and in-clude insights from the sociocultural perspective. Disengagement theory and activity theory are opposites, but both focus on age stratification. Adding to both, dynamic theories stress the fluctuations caused by the self, by the con-text, and by personal and historical changes. Continuity theory is one exam-ple. The many changes in psychosocial development in late adulthood are not random; they form patterns, as all three sets of theories describe.

Keeping Active

Disengagement theory observes that older adults reduce their social connec-tions; activity theory insists that social connection is crucial. We are beginning to obtain more extensive data on what actually happens in late adulthood. As dis-cussed earlier, the reality does not correspond exactly with what either theory would predict.

Chosen Activities

Employment has many advantages, as we saw in Chapter 22, but it is not usually something a person has a choice about doing. The freedom to be one's own per-son—to choose one's main activities—is the advantage of retirement. In the pre-vious two chapters we discussed artistic activities and exercise, both of which are done for individual health and pleasure. Here we consider four social activi-ties: education, helping others, religion, and politics.

Continuing Education

For many of the elderly, retirement offers an opportunity to pursue educational interests. Increasingly in the United States, older adults are students. About one out of five adults age 65 and older enrolls in classes of some sort, ranging from courses in the practical arts (carpentry, quilting, and dozens more) to those leading to advanced college degrees (U.S. Bureau of the Census, 2002). Younger adults tend to study to advance their careers, but most elderly students (76 percent) are motivated by a desire for personal or social development, including, for example, the desire to develop hobbies, to manage investment income, or to understand their grandchildren (Jeanneret, 1995).

The eagerness of the elderly to learn is apparent in the rapid growth of **Elderhostel,** a program in which people aged 55 and older live on college campuses and take special classes, usually during college vacation periods. Begun in New England in 1975 with 220 students, Elderhostel now operates more than 1,500 sites throughout the United States and 1,000 sites in 90 other nations. Almost 200,000 students are enrolled each year (Elderhostel, 2003).

Elderhostel A program in which people aged 55 and older live on college campuses and take special classes, usually during college vacation periods.

Thousands of other learning programs throughout the world are filled with retirees. *Universities of the Third Age,* dedicated to older learners, have opened in at least a dozen European nations. A survey in Norway found that 10 percent of those over age 67 had taken a course at one of these institutions in the previous three years (Ingebretsen & Endestad, 1995). The policy of the Chinese government is for all the elderly to study calligraphy and other traditional arts, as well as health practices for themselves and other people, in order to avoid becoming depressed and sickly. Chinese universities have special courses that all the elderly are encouraged to take (Manheimer, 1998).

Many elderly people hesitate to take academic classes populated by mostly younger students. When they do so, however, they usually earn excellent grades because motivation, conscientiousness, and crystallized intelligence compensate for declines in reaction time and fluid intelligence. They also enjoy the experience. One man, who surprised himself by taking drawing, painting, and Spanish classes at a community college, explains:

> When I first retired, I couldn't wait to pack up and go to a warm climate and just goof off. But now, retirement is an enormous challenge. Once you start learning about yourself, you get the feeling that anything is possible.
>
> *[quoted in Goldman, 1991]*

Note, however, that most of the elderly in North America are not in educational programs. Those who become students again generally have already attained some higher education (Pallus, 2002). Many prefer classes that are taught by other elderly people, usually those who have become experts in their field (Manheimer, 1998). Continuity theory is evident in late-life education.

Volunteer Work

Many older adults feel a strong commitment to their community and believe that older people should be of service to others. For example, when a cross section of nearly 3,000 Americans were asked whether older adults have an obligation to help others and serve the community, about twice as many older adults as younger adults strongly agreed. Only 6 percent of those over age 60 strongly disagreed, compared with 12 percent of those under 60 (Herzog & House, 1991).

Older adults are particularly likely to volunteer to assist the young, the very old, or the sick, perhaps because of their perspective on life or because of their patience and experience. Those who are in late middle age or are recently retired (the young-old) are more likely to become involved in volunteer work than are those over age 75 (the old-old) (Caro & Bass, 1997; Guterbock & Fries, 1997).

Especially for Social Workers Your agency needs more personnel but does not have money to hire anyone. Should you go to your local senior-citizen center and recruit volunteers?

SUSAN GREENWOOD / GAMMA LIAISON

Friend-to-Friend Some volunteer programs are trying a new approach known as "timedollars." Volunteer caregivers earn credits for the time they volunteer—visiting, shopping, doing housekeeping, providing transportation, and the like—and are then able to redeem those credits when they themselves are in need of services. Felina Mendoza, shown here visiting a man who is just home from the hospital, is a member of Friend-to-Friend, a timedollar program in Miami, Florida. Its 800 participants earn an average of 8,000 hours of service credits each month.

Response for Social Workers (from page 645): Yes, but be careful. If people want to volunteer and are just waiting for an opportunity, you probably will benefit from their help and they will also benefit. But if you convince reluctant seniors to help you, the experience may benefit no one.

About 40 percent of the elderly in the United States are involved in structured volunteering, often through churches, hospitals, or schools (U.S. Bureau of the Census, 2002).

Many of the other 60 percent volunteer informally. For example, in stable neighborhoods that have a sizable number of elderly, the more capable residents often run errands, fix meals, repair broken appliances, and perform other services that generally make it possible for the disabled elderly to continue to live at home. Such neighborhood help is particularly notable among elderly African-Americans. The elderly also provide a good deal of care for family members. About 30 percent of the elderly provide regular personal care to an elderly relative, and 15 percent provide child care, again usually for relatives (Kincade et al., 1996).

The elderly themselves benefit from volunteering. One large study found that volunteers lived longer than people who did not volunteer (Musick et al., 1999). Those who benefited most volunteered for only one organization. The reason may be that volunteering enables the elderly to gain an important role and to find "new meaning . . . to perform useful services . . . [to] function as mentors, guides, and repositories of experience" (Settersten, 2002, p. 65). This is easier to accomplish if a person commits to just one organization and becomes integral, even essential, to that organization.

Volunteering should not be considered a panacea for the problems of the old. It is true that those who volunteer are happier and healthier than those who do not, but a longitudinal study that included inducing older adults to volunteer more than before and getting nonvolunteers to do some volunteering did *not* find that these efforts increased health and life satisfaction (Pushkar et al., 2002). It seems that the elderly like to be helpful and benefit from volunteering—but not if they are forced to do so.

Religious Involvement

Is it accurate or an ageist stereotype to think, as many young people do, that people become more religious with age? The facts at first seem to the contrary: Older people are less likely to attend weekly religious services. However, church or temple attendance is a poor indicator of spirituality, in part because many religious institutions are inadvertently hostile to the aged—there may be stairs to climb and poor acoustics, and music and prayers may have been updated in ways the elders do not like.

In general, the younger person's hunch is right: Religious faith increases with age, as do prayer and other religious practices (Ingersoll-Dayton et al., 2002). This is fortunate, because religious faith tends to foster health and to counteract fear of death (Chatters, 2000). Because religious activity enhances life for the elderly, it may be worthwhile to physically restructure churches and temples to make religion a more active part of older people's lives. Moreover, as we have seen, the elderly benefit themselves and others through volunteering, and a familiar religious setting is, in theory, ideal for such involvement.

Research on elders from various ethnic groups often reports that religious institutions are particularly important to older Americans who feel alienated from the overall society. For example, one section of Los Angeles, Little Tokyo, has a large population of Japanese elders who stay there because they like being able to walk to churches and Buddhist temples (Shibusawa et al., 2001). African-American elderly find more spiritual and practical activities for them in church than anywhere else (Billingsley, 1999). Many Polish elderly are devout Catholics, sometimes calling Catholicism "the Polish faith" (Berdes & Erdsman, 2001).

Political Activism

By many measures, the elderly are more politically active than any other age group. Compared to younger people, they know more about national and local issues, write more letters to their elected representatives, vote in more elections, feel stronger about party loyalty, and belong to more groups that lobby for their interests (Torres-Gil, 1992). Like Sadie and Gilbert in the ancedote that opens this chapter, many read newspapers as well as watch TV news. The only form of political participation on which they fall short is door-to-door campaigning, although even here many are active pavement pounders.

Political participation translates into considerable power, especially when the elderly organize themselves into political action groups. The major U.S. organization representing the elderly, the AARP (formerly the American Association of Retired Persons), is the largest organized interest group in the United States. In 2003, the AARP had a membership of 35 million (members must be over 50 but need not be retired), employed more than 50 congressional lobbyists, and involved more than 158,000 volunteers in various projects. The political influence of this organization is one reason that Social Security has been called "the third rail" of domestic politics, fatal if touched by any politician who wants to cut benefits.

Among other major senior organizations are the National Committee to Preserve Social Security and Medicare and the National Council for Senior Citizens (5 million members each) as well as the Gray Panthers (400,000 members). Dozens of smaller special-interest groups focus on issues of concern to elders (Binstock & Quadagno, 2001).

All this political activism makes many younger adults suspect that senior citizens wield disproportionate power and use it unfairly to advance their economic interests. This idea is inaccurate. True, elders tend to support financial assistance

DAVID YOUNG-WOLFF / PHOTOEDIT, INC.

Still Politically Active The man with the microphone is Floyd Red Crow Westerman, a Lakota Sioux who is an actor (in *Dances with Wolves*, among many other films) and director. Many members of his cohort fought in Vietnam. Disapproval of the war in Iraq was greater among his generation than among both older and younger cohorts.

AP / WIDE WORLD PHOTOS

Homemade Signs of Protest In the United States, an issue likely to arouse the passion of the elderly is the high cost of prescription medicines. In no other nation does the average elderly person have to spend hundreds of dollars a month on medicine.

for the aged. But, as with people of all ages, most are also interested in wider social concerns—war and peace, the environment, education, and so on—and most are willing to vote against the interests of their age group if a greater good is at stake. When a tax on the Social Security income of wealthier elders was proposed in 1993, for example, the idea received more support from the old than from the young (Kosterlitz, 1993). Questions regarding generational equity—that is, whether each generation contributes and receives its fair share of society's wealth—can be asked about every age group.

Countries outside the United States are also struggling with the notions of generational equity, and the aging are increasingly politically active. In many nations, the increasing numbers of older, retired people, coupled with fears of a declining population of workers to support them, have led to attempts to raise the retirement age. This would save government the costs of health, housing, and income support. In almost every instance, this proposal has led to increased political involvement of the elderly on political issues (Binstock & Quadagno, 2001; Vincent, 2003)

An interesting case study, showing the effectiveness with which older people can mobilize politically, comes from Laguna Woods, California. A state authority was about to build an airport near a senior-citizen community. The residents of this community not only wrote letters and attended rallies but also developed and implemented a successful political strategy. To be specific, they managed to create and incorporate a new town, electing a mayor and city council that opposed the airport (Andel & Liebig, 2002).

Home, Sweet Home

Many elderly people stay busy by maintaining their home and yard. Typically, the amount of housework done by both men and women increases after retirement (Kleiber, 1999; Szinovacz, 2000). Particularly strong is the impulse to do tasks that are *not* necessary household chores: gardening, redecorating, building, and, in some cases, moving. For a minority of the elderly, retirement means a significant move—relocating to a Sunbelt state (in 2000, 18 percent of Florida's population was over age 65) or to a sunny homeland, such as Mexico.

Most elderly people, however, prefer to *age in place,* staying in the same home and adjusting as needed to new health requirements (Nahemow, 2000). This solution is a good one unless the neighborhood has become unsafe (Settersten & Andersson, 2002). If older people do relocate, they usually stay within the same region to remain near their adult children, other family members, or childhood friends (Longino, 2001).

If the children live too far away, however, most elders stay put—which helps to explain why the elderly population in such unlikely places as West Virginia, Maine, and Pennsylvania is above the national average. Rather than moving to a retirement community in the South, they stay in the chilly neighborhoods they moved into 50 years ago with their young children, creating what is known as a *NORC,* or *naturally occurring retirement community.*

The wish to age in place, rather than to find a new home, is evident in U.S. statistics about relocations: Over a recent five-year period, only 1 in 25 persons over age 65 moved, compared to 1 in 3 persons in their 20s (U.S. Bureau of the Census, 2002). It is not simply that the elderly do not like change. In fact, travel is a favorite activity, if they can afford it and if their health allows. They like to get back home, however, because home has become their haven.

Many developers have created alternative living settings with such labels as "shared homes," "congregate living," "granny flats," and "continuous care retirement communities." They have discovered, to their dismay that most of the elderly choose to live in their own homes as long as possible (Folts & Muir, 2002).

One result of aging in place is that many of the elderly live alone. Although, as discussed in Chapter 22, some observers bemoan the demise of the extended family, interviews and studies of the elderly find that most who live alone prefer it that way (Hareven, 2001). They appreciate neighbors, friends, relatives, visiting nurses, and other people who help them maintain their independence. They may allow others to come to stay for a while (as Mrs. Edwards did), but they make it clear that the home is theirs.

> The activities of the retired elderly are many, with four clusters of activities particularly noteworthy. Some of the elderly devote many hours to volunteering, which provides satisfaction and may even protect their health. Some become more religious, reducing fears about death in the process. Some become more politically active. Finally, some spend time fixing up their home, expressing the wish to stay there all their lives. One surprise is that most do not move to retirement communities, preferring instead to age in place, decorating their homes, tending their gardens, and not leaving their old friends in the neighborhood.

The Social Convoy

Remember from Chapter 22 that people travel the life course in the company of others, a reality captured by the phrase **social convoy** (Antonucci et al., 2001). At various points, other people join and leave the convoy. But, just as wagons formed wagon trains to head west and battleships form convoys to cross the high seas, life's journey cannot be completed successfully alone.

social convoy Collectively, the family members, friends, acquaintances, and even strangers who move through life with an individual.

The special bonds formed over a lifetime help in good times and bad. People share triumphs with those who know how important the victory is and rely on familiar confederates when troubles arise. They depend on each other because the relationship is reciprocal. People who were part of a person's past also enable the person to maintain his or her sense of identity. Siblings are particularly useful in this regard, all the more in late adulthood (White, 2001).

Even strangers from the same cohort can participate in the social convoy. Many older adults take comfort in the continued survival of elderly political figures and entertainers. We will begin our examination of the social convoy by looking at the closest relationship of all, the long-term marriage.

Long-Term Marriages

The description of long-term marriages in Chapter 22 also applies to marriages in late adulthood. A spouse is a buffer against many of the potential problems of old age. Married elders tend to be healthier, wealthier, and happier than those who never married or who are divorced or widowed (Myers, 2000). When asked "What is your most important role in life?" almost half of a cross section of older adults said "spouse," compared with about one-fourth who said "parent" and one-eighth who said "grandparent" (Krauss, 1999).

Do marriage relationships change as people grow old? According to longitudinal as well as cross-sectional research, both continuity and discontinuity are apparent (Bradbury et al., 2000). The best predictor of the nature of a marriage in its later stages is its nature early on: While the absolute levels of conflict, sexual activity, and emotional intensity drop over time, couples who start out relatively high or low on any of these dimensions tend to remain so as time goes by.

Generally, marriage changes for the better in late adulthood. One reason is children, who grow from being the prime source of conflict for younger parents

So Happy Together Research suggests that long-term marriages improve with age, and that many long-married older adults are happier with their partners than they were as newlyweds. These blissful couples would no doubt concur.

to being the prime source of pleasure for elderly parents. Another reason is that all the shared contextual factors—living in the same community, raising the same children, and dealing with the same financial and spiritual circumstances—tend to change both partners in similar ways. So, too, does closeness between the partners: "Spouses who have a strong bond with one another may increasingly internalize each other's ideas about appropriate behavior" (Huston, 2000, p. 314).

Although usually the experiences of building a long life together bring a couple closer together, this doesn't mean everything is rosy all the time. Fortunately, even conflicts become less troublesome in later decades. Domestic violence is much more common in young marriages than in old ones. One study that compared both happy and unhappy couples found that when older couples discussed areas of disagreement, they expressed more warmth, humor, and respect than the younger couples did (Carstensen et al., 1995).

Generally, older spouses accept each other's frailties and tend to each other's physical and psychological needs as best they can, usually with feelings of affection rather than of simple obligation. The affection that accompanies caregiving when one spouse is ill was shown in a study which found that wives who cared for their dependent husbands usually felt closer to their spouses and less burdened by the experience in the later stages of caregiving than at the start (Seltzer & Li, 1996). This positive result was a direct consequence of being a spouse rather than of being female or getting used to the role: The study found that, unlike spouses, daughters providing care for aging parents felt more burdened and and more emotionally distance in the later stages of caregiving.

Our focus on mutual caregiving should not distort our understanding of late-life marriages. Intimacy, companionship, and even passionate love are part of the marital relationship for many older couples (Melton et al., 1995). When one happily married elderly couple were asked about their sex life, the husband responded:

> We have sex less frequently now, but it's satisfying to me. Now that we are both home, we could spend all our time in bed. But it's still more amorous when we go away. When we travel, it's like a second honeymoon.

His wife added:

> Sex has been important in our marriage, but not the most important. The most important thing has been our personal relationship, our fondness, respect, and friendship.
>
> *[quoted in Wallerstein & Blakeslee, 1995]*

Sex may or may not be part of a happy long-term marriage. The crucial factor is the relationship between the partners.

Losing a Spouse

Divorce is difficult, emotionally and financially, but rare in late adulthood. By late adulthood, most of those who were divorced in young adulthood have remarried, and they are eventually as healthy and content as those in long-term relationships. Widowhood, however, is common. The death of a spouse eventually occurs for half of all older married people. Adjustment to loss is never easy, but it varies depending on the sex of the surviving spouse.

Widows

There are four times as many widows as widowers, because of choices that were made decades earlier, in young adulthood. Women take better care of their health, so they live longer than men (ranging from an average of 12 years longer in Russia to 2 in Kenya, with the United States about midway at 6 years). Husbands are typically 3 years older than their wives, so wives average 10 or so years of widowhood. As a result, in the United States, of the almost 34 million who were 65 or older in 2000, 8.5 million were widows and only 2 million were widowers (U.S. Bureau of the Census, 2002).

Even though a husband's death is often to some extent expected, it is never easy. The death of a mate usually means not only the loss of a close friend and lover but also lower income, less status, and a broken social circle. In addition, routines such as meal preparation, visiting friends, taking walks, and even going to bed at a regular time typically falter, and the result is substantial physiological stress. Perhaps even more crucial for today's older widows—whose primary roles are likely to have been spouse, caregiver, and homemaker—is the loss of identity (DeGarmo & Kitson, 1996).

Nonetheless, older widows do not usually seek another husband. Many come to enjoy their independence. They are content spending time with other widows and with grandchildren. It could be that "they found it too difficult to anticipate men's new reactions to them as single women. The rules of intergender relations had changed, and the women evidently did not know the new ones" (Van den Hoonaard & Kestin, 2003, p. 193).

Widowers

In general, living without a spouse is somewhat easier for women than for men. Elderly women expect to outlive their husbands and make arrangements for some of the adjustments that widowhood will require. Men, by contrast, often buy insurance to protect their wives rather than thinking about what might happen if their wives die first. In addition, women who are newly widowed usually have friends and neighbors who themselves are widows and who are ready to provide sympathy and support; men who become widowed often lack this social support.

A historical gender difference also makes adjustment more difficult for today's older widowers. Many members of this cohort grew up with restrictive

MARKO HAGERTY / THE IMAGE BANK / GETTY IMAGES

Alone, But Not Lonely Ten million women in the United States are widows. Most, like this woman, are over age 60 and live alone. Many, though not all, are financially secure and well adjusted to their newly independent way of life.

notions of masculine behavior. As a result, men depended on their wives to perform the basic tasks of daily living (such as cooking and cleaning) and to provide emotional support.

Furthermore, over the years of marriage, they tended to be increasingly dependent on their wives for social support of all kinds—from inviting guests to providing confidential advice (Gurung et al., 2003). When their wives die, they often find it hard to reveal their feelings of weakness and sorrow to another person, to ask for help, to care for themselves, or even to ask someone over to chat (Wilson, 1995).

It is not surprising, then, that in the months following the death of their spouse, widowers are more likely to be physically ill than widows or their married contemporaries are. Indeed, they are at a higher risk of death, either by suicide or by natural causes (Hemsrom, 1996; Osgood, 1992). If they overcome their initial depression, many widowers discover that they are sought after by women who would happily fix their meals, clean their houses, and marry them, if possible. Although many widowers, like widows, prefer not to remarry, the sex ratio and their loneliness mean that widowers are far more likely to get married again than widows are.

Differences in Loneliness

As you might expect, there is wide variation in the amount of loneliness suffered in late adulthood. Widows as well as single women or divorced women become less lonely as more and more of their contemporaries become widows. In addition, adult children are more likely to keep in close touch with their mothers than their fathers, bringing grandchildren to visit often. In contrast, men are usually more vulnerable. Many former husbands find themselves isolated from children, grandchildren, and old friends, both because women are typically the kinkeepers and social secretaries of a family and because father–child contact typically dimishes over time, especially in divorce when ex-wives had legal custody (King, 2003).

A study of loneliness in old age (Peters & Liefbroer, 1997) found that generally:

- Men are lonelier than women.
- Adults without partners are lonelier than adults with partners.
- Divorced or widowed adults are lonelier than never-married adults.
- Recent losses are worse than losses experienced 10 or more years ago.
- The more partners a person has lost, the lonelier he or she is.

Thus, the loneliest of all were men who were currently without a partner and who had lost two or more wives through death or divorce within the past few years. The least lonely were wives still in a first marriage. This study also found that the size of the social network was crucial. A major negative effect of recent divorce or widowhood was a smaller network (Peters & Liefbroer, 1997).

Friendship

Of those currently over age 65 in the United States, only 4 percent (1.3 million) have never married, making this the most married cohort in history (U.S. Bureau of the Census, 2002). Most of them also have children and grandchildren. This situation will be quite different in future years, because many more people in subsequent cohorts have never married or had children. Will they be in trouble when they reach the elder years alone?

Probably not. Those of the elder generation who never married are quite content. Since they have spent a lifetime without a spouse, they have usually developed friendships, activities, and connections with other relatives that keep

KEVIN FLEMMING / CORBIS

Good to See You Again Older men, like younger ones, appreciate each other's friendship but seldom get together just to talk. These Delaware farmers met again at a melon auction and took the opportunity to get caught up on their families, their aches and pains, and the price of watermelon.

them busy and happy as long as their health is reasonably good. An unknown portion of the never-married are gays and lesbians, many of whom have long-time companions as well as extensive social networks.

By late adulthood, many members of the social network have been part of a person's convoy for decades. This helps explain a surprising finding: Older people's satisfaction with life bears relatively little relationship to the quantity or quality of their contact with the younger members of their own family but substantial relationship to the quantity and quality of their contact with friends (Lawton et al., 1999; Newsom & Schultz, 1996). Particularly important is the quality of friendship, which generally improves to compensate for losses (Charles & Carstensen, 1999). Having at least one close friend in whom to confide acts as a buffer against the loss of status and roles.

As at younger ages, women seem to do more befriending than men and are more dependent on their friends (Fehr, 1996; Gurung et al., 2003). If an older adult is a married man, typically his closest friends are all relatives. Married women also are usually close to several family members but, in addition, are likely to have a close female friend who is not related. Not surprisingly, unmarried older adults have more close friends who are not relatives than older married adults do. For unmarried men, close friends are equally likely to be male or female; for unmarried women, the closest friend is almost always female (Akiyama et al., 1996).

Even the oldest-old adjust to unwelcome changes in the social convoy, as dynamic theory would predict (Charles & Carstensen, 1999). New intimates are added to the inner circle when death or distance cuts off an old close friend, with the total number of close confidants remaining about the same. After age 85, closest friends are somewhat less likely to be members of the nuclear family and more likely to be nonrelatives or distant younger relatives, in part because at that age many members of the original social convoy have died or become ill.

Overall, all these social-convoy patterns demonstrate selection, compensation, and optimization (Baltes & Carstensen, 2003). Thus, successful aging requires that people keep themselves from becoming socially isolated, a task that most of the elderly manage to accomplish. They have fewer friends and relatives still alive, but they increase their mutual social support (Gurung et al., 2003).

Each person has somewhat different opportunities to reach out, but having a secure social network is a buffer against almost any problem that can arise (Atchley, 1999).

Remember the elderly widower whose son insisted he move out of the home of the Russian widow who had become his friend? The man did not want to leave, but the son "probably couldn't understand because he told me all the time 'She's not your mother. Come on, you're free. You're young enough to live somewhere else.' But I had a very hard time making up my mind what was the right thing to do because my landlady wanted me to stay" (quoted in Koch, 2000, p. 51). At his son's insistence, he moved to Florida and died alone, with one child in Berlin, another in Hong Kong, and the third estranged and angry. He still regretted leaving his landlady friend. This illustrates the well-intentioned bumbling of some younger family members, who do not appreciate the importance of friendship in old age.

Younger Generations

The typical older adult today has many family members, of many ages. Because people are living longer, many families are multigenerational, unlike most families of the past, when the oldest generation usually died before their grandchildren were grown (Uhlenberg, 1996). Some families span five generations, in a pattern called the *beanpole family,* because there are multiple generations but each has only a few members. This may become the pattern of the future, as more families are having only one child. If those children marry and have one child, that child will grow up with no aunts, uncles, cousins, brothers, or sisters— a pattern hard for many of today's elderly to imagine. In such a case, relationships across the generations may become more important (Bengtson, 2001).

Although relationships with younger generations are positive for the most part, they also include tension and conflict, as explained in Chapter 22. Almost all elders who have children and grandchildren devote time and attention to them, sometimes to the frustration of all parties. Few older adults stop parenting simply because their children are fully grown, independent, married, or parents themselves. As one 82-year-old woman succinctly put it: "No matter how old a mother is, she watches her middle-aged children for signs of improvement" (Scott-Maxwell, 1968).

Generally, the mother–daughter relationship, in particular, is simultaneously close and vulnerable. For example, in one study of 48 mother–daughter pairs whose average ages were 76 and 44, respectively, 75 percent of the mothers and almost 60 percent of the daughters listed the other among the three most important persons in their lives. At the same time, 83 percent of the mothers and 100 percent of the daughters readily acknowledged having recently been "irritated, hurt, or annoyed" by the other. The mothers were more likely to blame someone else for the irritation ("Her husband kept on turning up the radio every time I turned it down"); the daughters were more likely to blame their mother and to see the problem as her intrusiveness ("She tells me how to discipline my kids") (Fingerman, 1996).

A family can be very supportive or very independent across the generations, with each pattern welcomed in some families and resented in others (Bengtson, 2001). As a variation, a family can be high in assistance and contact without necessarily being high in warmth and affection. Both satisfaction and resentment depend more on emotional ties than on particulars of communication and help (Hareven, 2001). In general:

- Assistance arises both from need and from the ability to provide it.
- Personal contact depends mostly on geographic proximity.

- Affection is strongly influenced by a family's past history of mutual love and respect.
- Sons feel stronger obligation, while daughters feel stronger affection.
- Cultures and families vary markedly; there is no "right" way for the generations to interact.

Contrary to popular perceptions, since most of the elderly are quite capable of caring for themselves, assistance typically flows from the older generation to their children instead of vice versa. As one expert describes it, the older generation is like a family "National Guard": "Although remaining silent and unobserved for the most part, grandparents (and great-grandparents) muster up and march out when an emergency arises regarding younger generation members' well-being" (Bengtson, 2001, p. 7). In fact, most elders are pleased to be able to buy things for their children and to help out occasionally with the grandchildren, and they do not expect large gifts in return. The older generation enjoys social contact with younger generations, but most prefer that children visit them by invitation and for a relatively short period rather than coming unannounced, staying too long, or expecting the elders to come and pick them up.

Mobility Is Crucial The best help is the kind that permits self-sufficiency. This man's legs can no longer carry him everywhere, but his motorized wheelchair (with room for his furry companion) lets him get around on his own, without having to depend on other people for transportation. Thus, he is not strong, but he is also not frail.

When the older generation needs help and the younger one provides it, ideally the elders accept help gratefully, "minding their own business" about any complaints they have, and their children refrain from any criticisms. The least satisfactory situations are those in which parents want assistance and feel entitled to complain about their children or when children want to provide help and are critical of their parents. The need to balance intergenerational conflict and intergenerational solidarity (both present in every family) means that every family needs to adjust to "changing conditions and circumstances [by] renegotiating relationships" (Connidis, 2002, p. 565).

The price of intergenerational harmony may sometimes be intergenerational distance. This was clearly the case for one couple who felt that they were seen as "outmoded and irrelevant" rather than "wise or expert":

> Our grandson just got married. They both have fancy taste and fancy plans, and they mean to have it all. When we asked about a baby, they said they wouldn't even think about having a child until they could afford a full-time nanny to raise it. Imagine planning to have children so that you won't have time to raise them! Whose children are they, anyway? Why have them? We love him so much, and we don't want to hurt him, so we didn't say anything. As long as we keep rather quiet, he thinks we're sweet and lovable—and rather silly. . . .
>
> [quoted in Erikson et al., 1986, p. 168]

Such distance is impossible to maintain if a family emergency arises, such as an adult child's disruptive divorce, the birth of a handicapped child, or serious illness of an elderly family member. As you will soon see, such circumstances bring out the best and the worst of family ties (Connidis, 2002).

What about those who never had children? Most of the childless elderly have few regrets, whether they were voluntarily or involuntarily childless. For example, when asked to list regrets, older child-free women first mention other areas, such as education, occupation, and artistic expression. Those who deliberately avoided having children put that at the bottom of their list of possible regrets, while those who were involuntarily childless put it halfway down the list. Ironically, children are higher on the list of regrets for those who have children than for those who do not (Jeffries & Konnert, 2002).

In general, having good relationships with one's children enhances well-being, but a poor relationship makes life worse (Koropeckyj-Cox, 2002). Especially if the older generation expected substantial warmth and support from their children but do not get it, they are ashamed as well as sad (Olsen, 2001). Having no children at all does not make life either better or worse. Attitude is crucial; those who have accepted their decision not to have children are quite happy not to have done so; those who wished and expected to have children but did not are likely to be unhappy (Vissing, 2002).

> With age, the social convoy becomes smaller than it once was, but it is no less important for health and happiness: As at younger ages, members of each person's social convoy provide emotional and psychological support as well as practical help. People in long-term marriages typically benefit from their reliance on their spouse. Widows often have close friends to ease the loss; widowers have greater problems initially when their wives die but are also more likely to remarry. Those who never married typically have many friends and activities. Relationships with younger family members, as well as with friends, are generally supportive in late adulthood, although no human relationships are problem-free.

The Frail Elderly

Remember from Chapter 23 that aging can be categorized as optimal, usual, or impaired. So far our discussion has focused on the majority of the elderly: either those who age optimally—fully active, financially secure, well supported by friendship and family ties, and involved in the community—or those who age in the usual way, suffering some losses but maintaining many strengths. These two groups are quite different from the group we focus on now: the **frail elderly,** a group that includes the physically infirm, the very ill, and the cognitively impaired, usually among the oldest-old.

Beyond simple vulnerability and fragility, the crucial sign of frailty is a person's inability to perform, safely and adequately, the various tasks of self-care. Gerontologists often refer to the **activities of daily life,** abbreviated **ADLs,** which consist of eating, bathing, toileting, dressing, and transferring between a bed and a chair. If a person needs assistance with even one of these five tasks, he or she may be considered frail, although for some purposes (such as medical insurance or research on dependency) frailty does not begin until a person is unable to perform three or more of them.

Equally important to independent living, if not more so, are the **instrumental activities of daily life,** or **IADLs,** actions that require some intellectual competence and forethought (Willis, 1996). As one might expect, specific IADLs vary somewhat from culture to culture. For most of the elderly in developed nations, IADLs include shopping for groceries, paying bills, driving a car, taking medications, and keeping appointments (see Table 25.1). In rural areas of other nations, feeding the chickens, cultivating the garden, mending clothes, getting water from the well, and baking bread might be among the IADLs. Everywhere, however, the inability to perform IADLs can make a person frail and dependent on others.

Increasing Prevalence of Frailty

Worldwide, the frail elderly are a minority (Ahearn, 2001). At any given moment, no more than one-fifth of the world's senior citizens overall are frail by any measure, which means that only 2 percent of the total population of the world

frail elderly People over age 65 who are physically infirm, very ill, or cognitively impaired.

activities of daily life (ADLs) Actions that are important to independent living, typically comprising five tasks: eating, bathing, toileting, dressing, and transferring from a bed to a chair. The inability to perform these tasks is a sign of frailty.

instrumental activities of daily life (IADLs) Actions that are important to independent living and that require some intellectual competence and forethought. These are even more critical to self-sufficiency than ADLs.

are frail elders. Most of the elderly can manage their own daily care. However, the number of frail elderly and the degree of their frailty are increasing, for four reasons:

- More people are reaching old age. Those over age 65 are still only 7 percent of the world's population, compared with 30 percent under age 15. Nonetheless, these figures represent a sizable shift: In 1970, only 5 percent of the world's people were over 65, and 40 percent were under 15.
- Medical care now prolongs life. For example, a British study examined the last year of life over an 18-year period. An increasing proportion of those who died were over age 75, were frail, and had been hospitalized several times in their last year of life (Seale & Cartwright, 1994). Older people are far less likely than in the past to die peacefully at home and far more likely to be hospitalized and released several times, before dying in a hospital or nursing home.
- Medical care places a higher priority on prolonging life than on enhancing the quality of life. As a result, morbidity, in the form of chronic problems—ranging from Alzheimer's disease and arthritis to ulcers and varicose veins—is increasing even as mortality rates fall.
- Measures that could prevent or reduce impairment—such as adequate nutrition, safe housing, hearing aids, and hip replacements—are often not available to those with low incomes. Obtaining such benefits requires some mobility, planning, and sometimes co-payment. This combination tends to exclude the poor, the uneducated, and those without family advocates—precisely the people who are most likely to become frail.

The increase in the numbers of frail elderly figures in the argument that we face an "age bomb," which was discussed in connection with ageism in Chapter 23. Gerontologists seek to avoid both ageism and denial, with some arguing that the fact that only 5 percent of the elderly are in nursing homes at any one time is actually a *5 percent fallacy,* because it ignores the facts that one in four of those aged 85 and older are in nursing homes and that this segment of the population is growing the fastest (Folts & Muir, 2002).

TABLE 25.1 **Instrumental Activities of Daily Life**

Domain	Exemplar Task
Managing medications	Determining how many doses of cough medicine can be taken in a 24-hour period Completing a patient medical history form
Shopping for necessities	Ordering merchandise from a catalog Comparison of brands of a product
Managing one's finances	Comparison of Medigap Insurance Plans Completing income tax returns
Using transportation	Computing taxi rates Interpreting driver's right-of-way laws
Using the telephone	Determining amount to pay from phone bill Determining emergency phone information
Maintaining one's household	Following instructions for operating a household appliance Comprehending appliance warranty
Meal preparation and nutrition	Evaluating nutritional information on food label Following recipe directions

Another Test The items in the right-hand column are taken from a questionnaire to assess IADL competence. As you can see, managing daily life is not easy, but most of the elderly do it.

Source: Willis, 1996.

You learned in the discussion of the population pyramid in Chapter 23 (see Figure 23.1) that the proportion of elderly people is small but is increasing just as the proportion of young people is decreasing. These shifting proportions signal that in the future it will no longer be possible for the frail elderly to rely solely on care by younger family members.

Unlike Mrs. Edwards, who has 10 children, many elderly persons will be childless or have only one child. In the "beanpole family" illustrated in Figure 25.3, note that on the mother's side of the family, one adult (the mother) had seven living members of older generations. These are direct ancestors, not counting possible aunts and uncles, great-aunts and -uncles, and so on.

Remember, however, that, like Mrs. Edwards, most of the elderly, most of the time, are quite self-sufficient and proud of it. The long-term solution, described in Chapter 23, is *compression of morbidity*—that is, a reduction in the amount of time during which the elderly require help with ADLs or IADLs. Political and cultural policies may shift to place more emphasis on preventing and reducing impairment. For example, a major effort is required to postpone or prolong the early stages of dementia, when minimal care is needed (Post, 2001). The goal for the elderly, the family, and society is to maintain functioning for decades past age 65.

No culture in the world has solved the problems posed by increasing numbers of the elderly. As we have mentioned, many Asian cultures emphasize family responsibility for the aged and grant great respect and ongoing education to the elderly (Manheimer, 1998). Very few Asians are in nursing homes, either in Asia or in North America. However, gerontologists in almost every Asian country criticize their governments' overreliance on family obligation, noting that many families are unfairly burdened as the sole caregivers (Phillips, 2000).

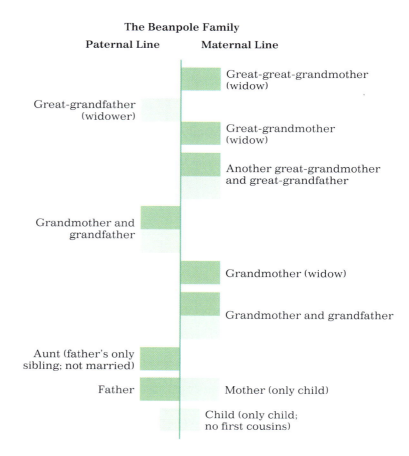

The Beanpole Family

Paternal Line   Maternal Line

Great-great-grandmother (widow)

Great-grandfather (widower)

Great-grandmother (widow)

Another great-grandmother and great-grandfather

Grandmother and grandfather

Grandmother (widow)

Grandmother and grandfather

Aunt (father's only sibling; not married)

Father   Mother (only child)

Child (only child; no first cousins)

FIGURE 25.3 Many Households, Few Members The traditional nuclear family consists of two parents and their children living together. Today, as couples have fewer children, the "beanpole" family is becoming more common. This kind of family has many generations, each typically living in its own household, with only a few members in each generation. (Not shown here are great-aunts and great-uncles.)

BOHEMIAN NOMAD PICTUREMAKERS / CORBIS

Together by Choice Elderly women outnumber elderly men in China by a very wide margin. Chinese cultural traditions include respect for the aged, group spirit, and self-efficacy. These six women in a public park in Guangzhou seek one another out for daily conversation.

Age and Self-Efficacy

Elders of any age differ considerably from one another, as a result of factors including their own characteristics, their background, and the social policies in the place where they live, as well as cultural forces, which are increasingly important with age (Baltes, 2003; Maier & Vaupel, 2003). Thus, for example, there are about 10 times as many homeless elderly in New York City as in London, because of inadequate support for the impoverished aged (Cohen et al., 2001).

Because so many factors are involved, to better understand frailty, we need to look at social forces and their effects, such as the limitations accrued because of ethnicity and gender, and also at each person's choices and interpretations. In other words, we need to draw on insights from both stratification theory and self theory.

An active drive for autonomy and control is one of the best defenses against becoming dependent. Loss of autonomy and control invites further weaknesses in many domains. As one team of researchers notes:

> To a sizable number of chronically ill older persons, their disability is of less salience than might be expected, because they can shift their priorities to other behavioral options. Perceived control and perceived self-efficacy are associated with positive health practices on the one hand, and with the absence of chronic disease . . . on the other.
>
> *[Deeg et al., 1996, p. 143]*

It is for these reasons that, as already mentioned, loss of self-efficacy and control are stronger predictors of future frailty, depression, and dependency than is income or health (Deeg et al., 1996; Fry, 2003; Fry & Debats, 2002). When a disability occurs, a person can, to some extent, choose to overcome it, compensate for it, live with it, or dwell on it. To take a somewhat simplified example, a person who is becoming limited because of weakening leg muscles might start a daily regimen of strength training, might purchase a walker, might adjust by staying on the first floor of the home, or might become a chair-bound invalid, complaining, "I can't do anything anymore because I might fall."

In this example, exercising to remain mobile would be especially appropriate because a fear of falling is one of the best predictors of later functional decline, and lower body strength is one of the best predictors of avoiding dependency (Paterson & Stathokostas, 2002). Equally important is cardiovascular fitness, which itself is related to exercise. Similar choices are involved in virtually every disability, with each choice affecting the degree of frailty that ensues.

Self-efficacy and the choices it leads to are, in short, protective buffers against aging. Background, social policies, and culture can be as well. As dynamic theories remind us, some people enter late adulthood with many buffers in place: family members and friends, past education and continued educational opportunity, employment that gave them a good pension and continued work opportunities, and a lifetime of good health habits within a society that provides crucial help. Others lack these buffers. The following Changing Policy feature shows how this may happen and how policies, too, may affect the outcome.

Changing Policy

Between Fragile and Frail: Protective Buffers

Both advanced years and specific infirmities may make a person more fragile. However, neither of these factors necessarily makes a person frail, because the health and independence of the elderly depend not only on impairment but also on resources, public and private (Hagestad & Dannefer, 2001). Many elderly persons with health problems never become helpless because protective buffers such as attitude, social network, physical setting, and financial resources prevent or postpone the progression from fragility to frailty. To see how this works, consider a hypothetical example of two 80-year-old childless widows, each living on a small pension, who have the same good hearing but failing eyesight and advanced osteoporosis.

One widow lives alone in an old, rundown house in an isolated neighborhood. Among the particulars of her residence and daily life are uneven hardwood floors covered with braided scatter rugs, a flight of steep stairs separating the bedroom and the kitchen, dimly lit rooms and hallways, and rumors of a recent robbery two blocks away. She hears every creak of the old house, listening in terror.

Since falling and fracturing her wrist on the way to the toilet one night, she has been apprehensive about walking without help. She refuses to go downstairs to prepare meals. She never ventures outside and is afraid to answer the door or the phone. Further, she no longer tries to wash or dress herself, or even to eat as much as she should, citing some lingering pain in her fingers and her belief that "no one cares anyway."

Obviously, this widow is very frail, requiring ongoing care. At present, a home attendant comes every morning to bathe her and prepare the day's food, but the attendant is worried about the woman's depression. This is a valid concern, because suicide is particularly common among those over 75 who live alone.

Policies have made her frail. To be specific, home health attendants are among the lowest-paid workers in the United States, so it is unlikely that this aide can do much more than worry. She is neither trained nor expected to act as a social worker or therapist. A professional might set up a program of daily exercise, arrange for transportation to a senior-citizen center, call in a housing consultant who would suggest changes in the home setting, and find a nutritionist who would make sure the woman ate well.

All these services are expensive, and current public policy does not fund them. For the most part, family members are expected to underwrite as well as obtain professional care. Voluntary assistance (e.g., Meals on Wheels) can also be arranged, but this widow is unlikley to do it. She spends almost all her income on the mortgage and heat—even though a reverse mortgage and better insulation would make her financially secure. She is on the waiting list of a nursing home. There she is likely to become even more frail, since nursing homes often discourage independent functioning.

The other widow, by contrast, might have used her financial resources and had the foresight in middle age to purchase, with two old friends, a large co-op apartment near a small shopping center. As all three are aging, they have consulted an expert from the city's Department on Aging who suggested that they reduce their vulnerability by outfitting their home with bright lighting, sturdy furniture strategically placed to aid mobility, secure grab rails in the bathroom to ease bathing and toileting, wall-to-wall carpeting nailed to the floor, a telephone programmed to dial important numbers at the push of one button, a stove that automatically shuts off after a certain time, and a front door that buzzes until it is properly locked with the key. Such accommodations are paid for by public funds in most European nations but not elsewhere. However, in almost every devloped nation, public funds do subsidize housing consultants for people wise enough to call them.

The three housemates compensate for one another's impairments: The one who sees best reads the fine print on all the medicine bottles, legal papers, and cooking directions; the one who is the sturdiest sweeps, mops, and vacuums; and our poorly sighted, osteoporotic widow, who has excellent hearing, listens for the phone, the doorbell, the alarm clock, the oven timer. All three regularly eat, converse, and laugh together—a practice that is good for the digestion as well as the spirit. One feature that makes this arrangement work is that the three friends chose each other; random associations and forced cooperative housing are much less successful (Folts & Muir, 2002).

Unlike the first widow, who will be institutionalized if she does not die soon, the second widow, with the same physical problems, is safe and happy in her apartment, caring for herself, socializing with friends, shopping in the community, and likely to live for 10 years or more. Her buffers will defend her against many factors that could otherwise be disabling. For example, she will be motivated, encouraged, and financially able to obtain good medical care and enabling accessories, such as corrective eyedrops and special glasses, or calcium supplements and a hip replacement, or even, if both major disabilities worsen, home delivery of audiotaped books and the purchase of a motorized wheelchair. Notice that public policy can encourage such buffers by, for example, providing the elderly with specialists who can help them find ways to remain independent. However, current policies assume, wrongly, that the frail elderly are able to navigate a complex public–private set of regulations and subsidies.

The lesson here is that fragility and vulnerability do not necessarily translate into equivalent frailty. Just as a fine crystal goblet—admired, lovingly handled, and carefully stored—is unlikely to break despite its fragility, so an older person, surrounded by crucial buffering, may not become frail.

Caring for the Frail Elderly

Today, as in the past, most of the frail elderly are cared for by relatives, who typically help with both ADLs and IADLs. Indeed, of every ten North American elders who need some assistance, six depend exclusively on family and friends. The other four receive varying combination of family and professional care, half in a nursing home and half in the community. Similar proportions are found in Japan (Saito, 2001) and in Europe (Schroots et al., 1999). In poorer nations there is even more reliance on family and friends.

The current tradition in the United States is that husbands and wives care for each other until it is no longer possible to do so. Many other cultures stress the obligation of children to their parents rather than of the elderly to each other (Weisstub et al., 2001). In Korea, for instance, 80 percent of elderly people with dementia are cared for by daughters-in-law and only 7 percent by a spouse (in contrast 19 and 40 percent, respectively, of Korean-Americans in this situation) (Youn, 1999).

The Demands of Family Care

Although most of the frail elderly benefit from care by loving family members, the demands of caring at home for a frail elderly relative should not be underestimated. The caregiver's physical health suffers and depression increases, especially if the older person suffers from dementia (Pinquart & Sörensen, 2003). In many cases, the caregiver must forgo all other activities, because the physical work and psychological stress are overwhelming. One daughter describes the strain she and her elderly father experienced when her mother developed Alzheimer's disease:

> I worked the entire time through four pregnancies . . . returning to work within six weeks of delivery. It was a piece of cake compared to trying to cope with a combative, frustrated adult who cannot dress, bathe, feed herself; who wanders constantly. A person faced with this situation . . . having to work a full day, raise a family, and take care of an "impaired" relative would be susceptible to suicide, "parent-abuse" . . . possibly murder.

Ageless Love Many women today who reach age 35 hesitate to have a child because they worry they will not be alive when the child grows up. Such concerns are becoming outdated as more and more people live to age 80 and beyond. This Manitoban mother, who is 117, is cared for by her daughter, who was born when the mother was 49.

respite care An arrangement in which a professional caregiver takes over to give the family caregiver of a frail elderly person a break for a few hours each day or for an occasional weekend.

My father tried very hard to take care of her, but a man 84 years old cannot go without sleep, and cannot force her to take care of her personal cleanliness. Up until two years ago, she was taking care of the finances and household. Her signature was beautiful. . . . Now it's just a wavy line. An 84-year-old man does not learn to cook and balance the budget very easily, and he becomes bitter. He did not want to put her in the nursing homes he visited, and so he reluctantly sold his house and moved to a city he didn't like so that his children could help with her care. It has been a nightmare. . . . She obviously belonged in a secondary-care facility because no one can give her 24-hr. care and still maintain their sanity and families.

[quoted in Lund, 1988]

Sometimes caregivers feel fulfilled by their experience because everyone else, from the care receiver and other family members to neighbors and community professionals, appreciates their efforts and helps as much as possible. Even in cases where the care recipient has dementia and a caregiver has provided major care for years, only one-third of caregivers become clinically depressed. All caregivers are at risk for depression, however, more often because they feel trapped and unappreciated than because of the particular behaviors of the older person (Alspaugh et al., 1999). The risk of depression is widely recognized, but there appear to be no easy solutions (Gitlin et al., 2003).

In most cases, caregivers from a younger generation feel that their actions are reciprocation for nurturing that they once received. A notable exception is daughters-in-law, who are likely to give far more care than they received (Ingersol-Dayton & Starrels, 1996). For their part, those receiving care generally try to reciprocate as much as they can, with good humor and a positive attitude, so that they do not feel too burdensome (Gaugler et al., 2002).

Even when caregiving is entered into with a strong sense of reciprocity and the recipient is appreciative, caregivers may still feel resentful, for three reasons:

■ If one relative seems to be doing the job, other family members tend to feel relief or jealousy. They do not do their share, especially in the way the primary caregiver prefers.
■ Care receivers and caregivers often disagree. Does the caregiver have the right to set the daily schedule, regulate menus, arrange doctor's visits, and so forth? Disagreements strain the relationship between the frustrated caregiver and the self-assertive care receiver.
■ Public agencies rarely provide services unless the need is obvious, by which time it may be too late. Especially needed are caregiver support groups and **respite care**, in which a professional caregiver takes over to give the family caregiver a break for a few hours each day or for an occasional weekend. Respite care is more widely available in England than in the United States, where it is particularly difficult to find when an elder is cognitively impaired (Butler et al., 1998; Zarit et al., 1998).

Professionals have recognized the lack of such services, describing "a system that places inappropriate burdens of elder care upon the family" (Seki, 2001, p. 101). Most experts agree that more measures to help family caregivers are needed.

Elder Abuse

When caregiving results in feelings of resentment and in social isolation, usually the caregiver suffers, experiencing stress, depression, and even poor health. These factors alone do not cause elder abuse. However, abuse becomes likely if the caregiver suffers from emotional problems or substance abuse that predates the caregiving (Reis, 2000). Other risk factors include the victim's social isolation and powerlessness, as well as household members' poverty and lack of education (Wolf, 1998). The maltreatment may range from direct physical attack to ongoing emotional neglect. As this description indicates, analysis of elder abuse is complicated because three distinct elements contribute to the problem: the abuser, the victim, and the context of the interaction (Gordon & Brill, 2001).

The frail elderly are particularly vulnerable to abuse. Not only do they depend on others in order to eat, move from place to place, and stay clean, but many of them are confused about many things, from the names of those around them to the state of their finances.

Overall, maltreatment of elders has been shown in "worldwide studies based on community surveys [to be] about a 5% to 6% rate" (Wolf, 1998, p. 161). Because the frail elderly are particularly vulnerable, and because many who are abused or neglected by their family are ashamed to admit it and in some cases admit it but are not believed, it seems certain that the actual rate of maltreatment for the frail elderly is much higher than the overall rate found in studies. Adding to the problem are divergent notions of good care; elders, caregivers, and professionals often disagree.

Although some of the substantiated maltreatment of the elderly is perpetrated by professional caregivers, con artists, and mean-spirited strangers, elder maltreatment is primarily a family affair. For example, a detailed study of every reported case of elder abuse in Illinois found that 87 percent of the perpetrators were family members, most often a middle-aged child (39 percent), sometimes another relative (24 percent), and least often a spouse (14 percent) (Hwalek et al., 1996).

The simplest form of elder abuse is financial, occurring when a relative (or, less often, a stranger) gets an elderly person to sign over his or her savings, or deed to the house, or pension checks, and gives the elder little in return. More often, however, the abuse takes a more complex form, affecting the entire interaction between caregiver and care receiver and increasing over time, all too often ignored by the rest of the family and the public authorities until the problem becomes blatant. As in other forms of domestic abuse, the victim becomes isolated, frightened, and totally dependent on the abuser (Brandl, 2000).

The typical case of elder maltreatment begins benignly, as an outgrowth of a mutual caregiving relationship within the family. For example, an elder may be financially assisting someone of the younger generation, who then gradually takes control of and misuses more and more of the elder's assets; or a younger family member may assume care of an increasingly frail relative, only to become so overwhelmed by the task that gross neglect and abuse occur; or a husband, used to being cared for by his wife, feels both infuriated and at a loss when he has to care for her. This pattern of benign beginnings within a family relationship and gradual development makes elder abuse particularly difficult to recognize and prosecute.

Nursing homes once overmedicated, threatened, or physically restrained patients who were considered difficult; such measures are now illegal in licensed facilities. Families are much less able to cope with difficult patients than trained nurses are, yet family members typically are on duty continuously, with little or no outside help or supervision. It is not surprising that overdrugging, locks, and restraints sometimes seem to families to be their only options. Yet these measures are clearly abuse. Extensive public and personal safety nets for those elderly who are frail or powerless could prevent maltreatment, but few such nets are in place.

Nursing Homes

Many elders and their relatives feel that nursing homes should be avoided at all costs, usually because they believe that all nursing homes are horrible places (Pyke & Bengtsen, 1996). Some nursing homes are indeed horrible. In the United

A Cycle of Abuse This elderly man was found alone, amnesiac and incontinent, tied in his wheelchair at an Idaho dog track. It was later discovered that his own 40-year-old daughter had abandoned him there, hundreds of miles from her home in Oregon, hoping to rid herself of the stress of having to take care of him. The daughter was put on trial on a variety of charges, but her defense describes the kind of tangled family dynamics that often surround elder abuse: The father has late-stage Alzheimer's disease, requiring extensive care and boundless patience, and the daughter says that she was sexually and physically abused by both parents when she was young. Until a year before this incident, she had not seen her father for 20 years. Then one day he arrived at her doorstep, needing help.

Especially for Those Uncertain About Future Careers Would you like to work in a nursing home?

PHOTODISC BLUE / GETTY IMAGES

Strength Provided Here Transferring from a bed to a chair is one of the basic activities of daily life (ADLs). Although nursing homes are often criticized, this room is bright, with a large, insulated window beside the bed, and the aide is cheerfully dressed and skilled (note the positioning of her hands)—all signs of good-quality care. For the frail elderly, such care is preferable to homebound isolation.

Response for Those Uncertain About Future Careers (from page 663): Why not? The demand for good workers will obviously increase as the population ages, and the working conditions will improve. An important problem is that quality varies, so you need to make sure you work in a home whose policies incorporate the view that the elderly can be quite capable, social, and independent.

States, the worst ones tend to be profit-making ventures in which most patients are subsidized entirely by Medicare and Medicaid. Often, the only way for these institutions to make money is to limit expenses; consequently, they tend to be staffed by overworked, poorly trained aides, who all too often provide minimal, even dehumanizing, care. Understandably, family members who see nursing homes as a last resort and, in desperation, admit their frail, aged relative often feel more guilty, depressed, and worried than they did before (Aneshensel et al., 1995).

Overall, however, the abuses that occurred in the United States in the 1950s and 1960s, when the sudden, unregulated expansion of the nursing-home industry triggered widespread shoddy care and maltreatment, have been greatly reduced. Professionals are becoming involved in developing good nursing-home care, with the goal of helping each patient retain as much independence, control, and self-respect as possible (Hill et al., 2002).

Today many nations, such as those in Asia, where culture and policy long dictated that the elderly be cared for at home, are finding that sometimes long-term nursing-home care is needed (Phillips, 2000). This is particularly evident in Japan, where life expectancy is the greatest of any nation and the birth rate is one of the lowest. With more elderly people dependent on fewer children, Japan is seeking to develop a system of long-term-care facilities (Seki, 2001).

In North America and particularly in Western Europe, good nursing-home care is available for those who can afford it and know what to look for. The key elements are independence and privacy for the residents and a sufficient number of well-trained and well-paid staff. The quality and suitability of nursing-home care can make the difference between full, satisfying final years and a dismal end.

A minority of the elderly become frail, unable to perform the activities of daily life (eating, toileting, bathing, dressing, transferring from bed to chair) or the instrumental activities of daily life (such as taking medication, shopping, paying bills). Frailty is not the inevitable result of age or illness, and it can thus be buffered by the attitude of the older person and by social supports from family, friends, and community. If an elderly person needs full-time care, usually the spouse provides it. If he or she is unable to do so, another relative becomes caregiver. Only when illness becomes acute, or when a person has no available relatives, does long-term care in a nursing home begin.

If a family caregiver is psychologically unfit or too stressed to provide care, he or she sometimes becomes abusive. Because abuse generally occurs within a family context and because social safety nets are lacking, maltreatment often goes unnoticed until it becomes severe.

Temperament and financial as well as social supports affect whether or not a person becomes frail, maltreated, or institutionalized as much as or more than does physical health. Public policies are only beginning to improve quality of life for the many people who live to be among the oldest-old.

We close this final chapter about late adulthood with an example of family and nursing-home care at their best. A young adult named Rob related that his 98-year-old great-grandmother "began to fail. We had no idea why and thought, well, maybe she is growing old" (quoted in Adler, 1995, p. 242). The family reluctantly decided it was time to move her from her suburban home, where she had lived for decades, into a nursing home.

MICHAEL WOLF / AURORA PHOTOS

A Nursing Home in Japan Japan has the longest average life span, the highest proportion of elderly people, and the highest proportion of frail elderly who live at home, not in nursing homes. Like those in every other country, the administrators of Japanese nursing homes must weigh the most effective group care against the more labor-intensive individualized care. Note that all the residents shown here appear to be in wheelchairs, are eating the same meal, and are wearing blue plastic sheets that serve as both bib and placemat. On the plus side, many have chopsticks (though large spoons would be more efficient), none appear to be undernourished, and all seem to be wearing their own clothes, not hospital-style gowns and robes.

Fortunately, this nursing home encouraged independence and did not assume that declines in functioning are always signs of "final failing." The doctors there discovered that the woman's pacemaker was not working properly. As Rob explains:

> We were very concerned to have her undergo surgery at her age, but we finally agreed. . . . Soon she was back to being herself, a strong, spirited, energetic, independent woman. It was the pacemaker that was wearing out, not Great-grandmother.
>
> [quoted in Adler, 1995, p. 242]

This story contains a lesson for us all, one that underlies many of the lessons learned throughout this book. Whenever an older person seems to be failing, or a preschooler is unusually aggressive, or a teenager is depressed, or a young adult is torn between work and family, the tendency is to think that such problems "go with the territory" of being at a particular age. There is some truth in that, for each of these possible problems is more common at the stages mentioned. But we can't use people acting their age as an excuse for failing to intervene. The overall theme of the life-span perspective is that, at every age, people can be "strong, spirited, and energetic." We are all able to live life to the fullest, no matter how young or old we are.

SUMMARY

Theories of Late Adulthood

1. Several self theories hold that adults make personal choices in ways that allow them to become fully themselves. Erikson believed that individuals seek integrity that connects them to the human community. Identity theory suggests that people try to maintain a sense of themselves.

2. A dominant interpretation of the goal of later life is that selective optimization with compensation can help in adjusting to physical and cognitive decline. Genetic personality traits may continue to play a major role in the way late adulthood plays itself out.

3. Stratification theories maintain that social forces limit personal choices, especially the disengagement that may come with age. Activity theory predicts the opposite, that older people who are active are also healthier and happier.

4. Lifelong stratification by gender or race may also limit an elder's ability to function well. However, many older members of minority groups function very well, primarily because of strong family and religious connections.

5. Dynamic theories see human development as an ever-changing process, influenced by social contexts, which themselves are constantly changing, as well as by genetic and historical factors that are unique to each person. For instance, continuity theory emphasizes that the changes that occur with age are much less disruptive than they might appear to be.

Keeping Active

6. Many retired people continue their education or perform volunteer work in their communities. Both of these activities enhance the health and well-being of the elderly and benefit the larger society.

7. The elderly are politically active and influential, which is one reason for their success in protecting their economic benefits. For many older people, religious faith increases and thus sustains them.

The Social Convoy

8. A spouse is the most important member of a person's social convoy. Older adults in long-standing marriages tend to be quite satisfied with their relationships and to safeguard each other's health. As a result, married elders tend to live longer, happier, and healthier lives than unmarried elders.

9. The death of a spouse is a serious stressor. Widowers are more likely to experience health problems but are more likely to remarry. Widows are more likely to have financial difficulties but also to find comfort through an expanded network of friends.

10. Friendship continues to be important in late adulthood as a source of happiness and as a buffer against trouble. Particularly among the never-married or the no-longer-married, long-term friendships are particularly valued.

11. Many older people are part of multigenerational families, sometimes with two generations over age 60, each maintaining dependence as well as mutual support. Typically the young-old are more likely to give advice and assistance to younger and older generations than to receive it.

The Frail Elderly

12. Many older people eventually become frail, unable to take care of their daily needs. They need help with the physical or intellectual activities of daily life. As more people reach very late adulthood, the number needing help from family and society will increase.

13. The frail are usually cared for by a close relative—typically their spouse, daughter, or daughter-in-law. Despite the personal sacrifices this care entails, most relatives consider such care an expression of family commitment. For some, caring for an older person may lead to frustration, anger, and maltreatment.

14. For the elderly who enter a nursing home, the quality of their final years of life can vary enormously, depending on the quality of the home. The best homes recognize the individuality of the elderly and encourage their independence.

KEY TERMS

self theories (p. 634)
integrity versus despair (p. 634)
stratification theories (p. 638)
disengagement theory (p. 638)

activity theory (p. 638)
dynamic theories (p. 643)
continuity theory (p. 643)
Elderhostel (p. 645)

social convoy (p. 649)
frail elderly (p. 656)
activities of daily life (ADLs) (p. 656)

instrumental activities of daily life (IADLs) (p. 656)
respite care (p. 662)

APPLICATIONS

1. Attitudes about disabilities are influential. Visit the disability office on your campus, asking both staff and students what they see as effects of attitude on the performance of students. What are your own attitudes? Might they be too rosy or too gloomy for the facts as others see them?

2. People of different ages, cultures, and experiences vary in their values regarding family caregiving. For example, at what point does an elderly person become a burden on his or her children?

When should health concerns (physical or mental) overrule the need for independence and privacy of elders and their offspring? Find four people whose views on this issue will probably differ. Ask their opinions, and analyze the results.

3. Visit a nursing home in your community. Notice details of the physical setting, the social interaction of the residents, and the staff. Would you like to volunteer in this place? Why or why not?

BIOSOCIAL

Ageism Ageism restricts the functioning of the elderly and makes younger people overestimate how many of the aged are impaired. All the same, primary aging is inevitable. Deficits in vision and hearing are widespread, although many elders can prevent or remedy the damage.

Secondary Aging Because of declines in organ reserve, the immune system, and overall muscle strength, older adults are at greater risk of chronic and acute diseases, heart disease, and cancer. However, risk is also related to long-standing health habits and quality of health care.

Postponement of many of the illnesses linked with age is possible, allowing a compression of morbidity. Research on the causes of aging indicates that genes play a prime role. Specific theories of aging related to the immune system, a genetic clock, damage from free radicals, and cellular error are all plausible.

Those who live to age 90 or more are often surprisingly active, happy, and independent.

COGNITIVE

Changes in Information Processing Memory fades in older age, but some aspects are more likely to show deficits. Working (or short-term) memory is the first to slow down; long-term memory is more durable.

Experimental testing of older adults reveals deficits in their ability to receive information, store it in memory, and organize and interpret it. These deficits may result from a decrease of neurotransmitters and blood flow in the brain, a drop in memory self-efficacy, and/or the influence of ageist expectations in the social context. In the tasks of real life, most older adults develop ways to compensate for memory loss and slower thinking.

Dementia Dementia, with its progressive impairment of cognitive functioning, is not inevitable in old age but it does become more common, especially in the very old. Symptoms of dementia may be caused by Alzheimer's disease, problems in the circulatory system, other diseases, depression, or drugs. The underlying causes are primarily genetic or organic. Sometimes a temporary problem or mental illness is misdiagnosed as dementia.

New Cognitive Development Many older individuals develop or intensify their aesthetic and philosophical interests and values in later life. An opportunity to remember and to recount the past, called life review, can be very useful.

PSYCHOSOCIAL

Theories of Late Adulthood The variability of life in late adulthood is even greater than at other periods. Self theories, stratification theories, and dynamic theories all point to sources of variability.

Keeping Active Elders usually remain active whether working or retired. Most find ways to expand their horizons after retirement, with education, volunteering, and political involvement.

The Social Convoy Older adults' satisfaction with life depends in large part on continuing contact with friends and family. Generally, marital satisfaction continues to improve. The greatest source of social support is likely to be other elders, either relatives or friends, particularly those of long-standing importance.

The Frail Elderly As people increasingly live to a very old age, the number needing assistance with the activities of daily life grows. Ideally, this assistance encourages elders to be active and independent. Most caregivers are other elderly people, who sometimes are overwhelmed by their situation. Social support and recognition can reduce caregiver stress. Nursing homes and other modes of care are sometimes very helpful, sometimes not.

Epilogue

Death and Dying

Thinking about death is difficult, because death mirrors and highlights the complexity of all of life (de Vries, 1999). Cultural differences and ethical dilemmas are evident in dying, as well as in all aspects of living. Yet, even though scientific conclusions are uncertain at best, understanding death and dying helps people live their lives to the fullest—one goal of our study of human development. And, as Kit Meshenberg wrote soon after she was diagnosed with terminal cancer, "We *can* learn to talk with each other about these things and support each other and move through this process [of dying], finding joy in every day" (www.lastchapters.org/index.cgi?id-116).

We begin as we did in Chapter 1, with the universals and the variations. Humans worldwide and throughout history have developed practices and rituals related to dying, death, and bereavement. These customs bring *acceptance* of dying, *hope* in death, and then *reaffirmation* of life through bereavement.

As you will see, these practices have taken very different, even seemingly opposite, forms in different cultures: In India, mourners sat on the floor and did not eat or wash until the burning of the funeral pyre; in the southern United States, funerals sometimes seemed like celebrations, with food, music, and dancing; in many Muslim cultures, the dead person was ritually bathed by the next of kin; among the Navajo, no one touched a dead person lest spirits return. But in all cultures death was regarded as a fact of life, a passage to a next phase, and an occasion for family members and neighbors to gather.

Death and bereavement rituals may be changing with globalization, which is causing cultural loss, disruption, and perhaps gains, as "an increasing number of people belong to several cultures" (Braun et al., 2000). Furthermore, medical technology has made death rare among the young and has prolonged dying among the old, allowing hearts to keep beating and lungs to keep taking in oxygen long after the brain is dead. Both cultural fragility and prolonged dying make it even more important to understand the medical options, legal guidelines, and emotional reactions related to death.

Deciding How to Die

One of the first steps in understanding death is to accept it. Over most of human history, acceptance was inevitable because death was relatively common at all ages—unanticipated, unavoidable, and quick: A fever or infection could suddenly progress to a deadly illness; a heart attack was usually fatal; weakness of the lungs or legs or any other body part signaled a downward trajectory; a listless infant or child might soon expire. Every adult had a personal connection with death, as someone had died in almost every home. Dying was accepted as part of life.

In the twentieth century, however, a series of medical miracles rendered death less of an everyday event. Clean drinking water, sterilization, and immunization saved billions of lives, mostly of the young. By the end of the century, surgery, drugs, radiation, and rehabilitation meant that in developed countries, people of all ages got sick, went to the hospital, and did not die, but went home again.

Medical Professionals

As illness came to be perceived as the domain of medicine rather than of religion, people came to believe that physicians could work medical miracles. Doctors and other health care workers came to regard a patient's survival as victory and death as failure. Moreover, the setting for death was increasingly the hospital, so dying itself was hidden. With these changes in attitudes and practices, acceptance of death became elusive.

Largely as a result of the pioneering work of Elisabeth Kübler-Ross, who brought scholarly research and compassionate attention to the psychological needs of dying people (and who will be discussed in more depth later in this chapter), this situation has changed somewhat, but not enough. One researcher reports that in the blood-disorders wing of a large hospital, when patients showed obvious signs of death, "With a few exceptions, health professionals did not indicate that death was imminent. Nor did they provide helpful honest statements that would prepare the patient and the carer" (McGrath, 2002, p. 343). Even in the early years of the twenty-first century, half of all medical textbooks still do not discuss care of the dying (Rabow et al., 2000). Only 20 percent of medical schools in the United States offer a course on the end of life—although that is three times more than the rate in 1975 (Dickinson, 2002).

More generally, physicians in recent years have become more accepting of death—no longer so eager to keep people alive when the quality of life is gone. Medical personnel increasingly realize that part of their job is to prepare the patient and family for the inevitable (Kapp, 2000). But acceptance remains difficult, both for doctors trained to protect life at all costs and for patients and their families in the context of a "technologically-driven health care system that can do much but not everything" (Kapp, 2000, p. 64).

Three innovations of the past half-century seek to counter the problematic consequences of modern medicine and to help the dying achieve a "good death." In the next few pages we will look at hospice care, palliative care, and end-of-life decision making.

Hospice Care

A major disadvantage of traditional hospital care is that once hospital personnel believe that a patient is going to die, they sometimes become less diligent with some aspects of physical and emotional care, such as response to a call button, time spent talking with the patient, and pain medication given. This is especially likely if the person is very old, very young, or culturally different (Hewitt & Simone, 1999; Morgan, 2000). In London during the 1950s, however, a dedicated woman named Cecily Saunders opened the first modern **hospice,** a place in which terminally ill people can spend their last days, receiving a range of care and support. Hospice care provides skilled medical treatment but avoids death-defying intervention in a setting where human dignity is respected (Saunders, 1978).

The dying person and the family are considered "the unit of care" (Lattanzi-Licht & Connor, 1995). In keeping with this view, the dying person's home is sometimes the setting for hospice services. When hospice care is provided in the home, doctors and nurses visit regularly, providing comfort as well as medication and therapy.

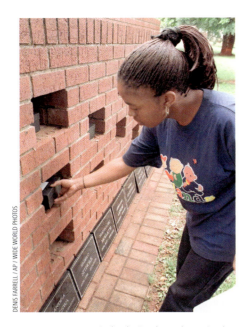

DENIS FARRELL / AP / WIDE WORLD PHOTOS

Not Forgotten Archeologists have determined that remembrance of the dead is one of the oldest rituals of humankind. Each generation and circumstance evoke different rituals. Here, in one of the most recent and tragic circumstances, a worker at the Cotlands Baby Sanctuary of South Africa places the ashes of a young child who died of AIDS into a wall of remembrance in a cemetery. The baby had been found abandoned after both of its parents died of AIDS.

hospice An institution in which terminally ill patients receive palliative care.

Although hospices help many dying patients and their families, they do not reach all who might benefit, for five reasons (Corless & Nicholas, 2003; Wilkinson & Lynn, 2001):

- Hospice patients must be diagnosed as terminally ill, with death anticipated within six months. In the United States, insurance (public and private) does not pay for hospice care unless this diagnosis has been made (Mezey et al., 1999). Such diagnoses can be difficult to make, and doctors often prefer to err on the side of recovery (Wilkinson & Lynn, 2001).
- Patients and caregivers must accept the diagnosis. Understandably, some prefer to maintain hope, no matter how poor the chances of survival. Almost no hospices serve children (Wolfe et al., 2000), because few parents and oncologists (cancer specialists) accept that a child will soon die.
- Hospices were typically designed for adults with terminal cancer, not for older adults with several illnesses, each potentially life-shortening but none necessarily fatal. More and more hospices accept the elderly—and almost half of all hospice patients have a diagnosis other than cancer—but problems arise when patients do not die "on schedule" or within the six-month window allotted by insurance regulations (Lattanzi-Licht & Connor, 1995).
- Hospice care is expensive. Good hospice care requires many skilled workers—doctors, nurses, psychologists, social workers, clergy, and aides—all of whom must be well trained and willing to provide labor-intensive, individualized care around the clock.
- Finally, availability depends primarily on location: Hospice care is more common in England than in the Netherlands (Zylicz, 1999), for example, and more common in the western United States than in the southern states.

Thus, hospices benefit some, but by no means all, dying individuals. In the United States, about one in four deaths occur in the context of hospice care.

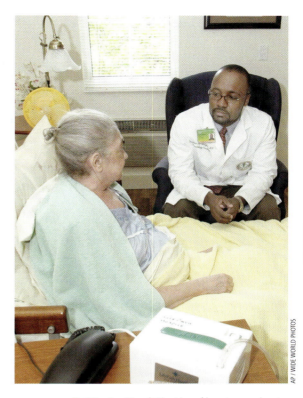

To Meet a Need The idea of hospice care has traveled far from its birthplace in London. Dr. Theodore Turnquest, shown here speaking with a patient in Lifepath Hospice House in Florida, plans to open the first hospice in his native country, the Bahamas.

Palliative Care

The hospice movement has inspired a field of medicine called **palliative care,** which is care designed not to cure but to "relieve physical, emotional, social, and spiritual pain and suffering . . . for patients and their families" (Sherman, 1999). Inadequate palliative care has long been a glaring weakness of modern medicine. As one physician recently complained, "It is criminal the way my colleagues fail to treat pain. . . . Physician-assisted suicide . . . is a problem of physical ignorance and abandonment" (quoted in Curry et al., 2002).

palliative care Care designed not to treat an illness but to relieve the pain and suffering of the patient and his or her family.

The least tolerable physical symptom of fatal illness is pain. Doctors once worried about causing addiction if pain medication were given too freely—but, as palliative care specialists have pointed out, it is absurd to worry about drug dependence in a dying person. Further, research finds that pain destroys health and vitality faster than almost any infection. The resulting science of pain medication has led to gains much appreciated by patients, family members, and medical personnel (Matzo & Sherman, 2001).

Morphine and other opiates, which are usually the preferred analgesics (pain relievers) for dying patients, improve the quality of life but also hasten death by slowing respiration. This phenomenon is called **double effect:** The primary effect is to reduce pain, and the secondary effect is to speed up death. Double effect is now considered acceptable, both in law and in medical and religious codes of ethics.

double effect A situation in which medication has the intended effect of relieving a dying person's pain and the secondary effect of hastening death.

The dying often experience many physical symptoms in addition to those of their primary illness, including nausea, constipation, itchy skin, bedsores, and muscle aches. Palliative care seeks to relieve these relatively minor but bothersome conditions as well (Matzo & Sherman, 2001; Preston et al., 2003).

Much more difficult to treat are the psychological symptoms of patients and their families (Mezey et al., 1999). For example, many patients and family members become depressed or anxious, yet psychotherapy and psychoactive drugs are rarely offered to the dying, perhaps because doctors are unaware that they are needed. Moreover, when psychoactive drugs are prescribed, they may have unpleasant side effects, including confusion and drowsiness (Matzo & Sherman, 2001).

Legal Preparations

Explicit guidelines regarding a person's preferences for end-of-life care are needed, because dying people often become incapable of making and expressing decisions about medical care and "actual death often occurs as a result of a conscious decision" (Mezey et al., 1999). That "conscious decision" should not be made by a stranger. Laws now reflect the awareness that patients may not want to fight death—that they may want to avoid pain and forgo extraordinary measures to prolong life. Part of preparing to die is making decisions about medical care and expressing those desires in writing.

Legally, "all competent individuals have the fundamental right to control decisions related to their own medical care, including the decision to have life-prolonging treatments provided, continued, withheld or withdrawn" (Pietsch & Braun, 2000, p. 38). These decisions can involve accepting or rejecting **passive euthanasia,** in which a seriously ill person is allowed to die naturally, through the cessation of medical interventions (such as a respirator to facilitate breathing, a shock to restart the heart, or a stomach tube to provide nutrition). A *DNR (do not resuscitate) order* on a patient's chart, for example, indicates that if breathing stops, no attempt should be made to restore it.

In contrast to passive euthanasia, **active euthanasia** involves taking action to bring about someone else's death, such as administering a lethal injection or dose of medication, with the intention of ending that person's suffering. As discussed later in this section, active euthanasia is illegal in most places.

Some people, long before death is imminent, sign a **living will,** a document that indicates what medical intervention they want (or don't want) if they become incapable of expressing their preferences. They also designate a **health care proxy,** the person they choose to make decisions for them if need be.

Disagreements About End-of-Life Care

Living wills are only a start. Although hospitals now ask patients on admission about living wills and other advance directives, many people are unfamiliar with such documents and resist signing them. Some low-income, younger, and minority patients, especially, are concerned that they might be deprived of life-support systems and even of routine nursing care (Moulton, 2000).

A more fundamental problem is that end-of-life care involves probabilities, not certainties, until the very last moment. If a particular treatment—itself painful or debilitating—has one chance in five of prolonging life, should it be tried? What about one chance in two, or one in a hundred? Does it matter whether life is prolonged for only a few weeks instead of months or years?

What quality of life is acceptable? Is one doctor, or one clergyperson, or one proxy able to answer for someone else? Even the most detailed living will may not be able to answer all these questions, in part because definitive odds are unknown. Living wills use phrases such as "incurable," "reasonable chance of recovery," and "extraordinary measures," but each of these phrases means quite

passive euthanasia A situation in which a seriously ill person is allowed to die naturally, through the cessation of medical interventions.

active euthanasia A situation in which someone takes action to bring about another person's death, with the intention of ending that person's suffering.

living will A document that indicates what medical intervention an individual wants if he or she becomes incapable of expressing those wishes.

health care proxy A person chosen by another person to make medical decisions if the second person becomes unable to do so.

different procedures to various doctors, lawyers, and family members. In a recent Florida case, the governor overruled the law, which said that a spouse is the one who decides whether a husband or wife is incapable, and allowed the parents to keep their brain-dead daughter on life support against her husband's wishes.

A designated proxy, or key decision maker, is the solution when patients, family members, and doctors disagree. As with living wills, however, three problems are common:

- Many people who are proxies choose measures that they themselves would not want and that the dying person explicitly refused (Kapp, 2000). For example, in some cultures, a wife is expected to keep her husband alive as long as possible, even if she herself would not want life support (Hallenbeck & Goldstein, 1999). She may be torn between her role as proxy and her role as wife.
- Family members may disagree bitterly about how much suffering is acceptable—about whether religion and conscience dictate a natural death through withdrawal of life support or continuing use of medical technology, no matter how small the chance of a miracle. They try to balance the conflicting desires to spare no expense and to provide for the survivors. The proxy may be blamed, no matter what decision is made—and no matter how exact the living will.
- Even when a patient has signed a living will and has provided a health care proxy with explicit advance directives, hospital staff sometimes ignore the patient's preferences. In one such case, a daughter was unable to convince a hospital administrator and attending physician to withdraw life support from her father after brain death until she marshaled various outside professionals and threatened legal measures (Foster, 2003, p. 81).

Euthanasia

Legally, decisions made in living wills and by health care proxies are to be honored, even when there is disagreement about specifics of passive euthanasia. However, active euthanasia is fiercely controversial. Most hospitals, doctors, and laws are opposed to it, and, even if a dying person requests it, active euthanasia is illegal almost everywhere in the world. There are two forms of active euthanasia: **physician-assisted suicide,** in which a doctor enables a patient to end his or her own life (e.g., by prescribing lethal drugs), and **voluntary euthanasia,** in which a patient asks someone else to cause his or her death.

Even when they are illegal, both practices occur almost everywhere. Very few instances are discovered and prosecuted (Prado & Taylor, 1999). Some people fear that allowing active euthanasia or ignoring it when it occurs puts society on a "slippery slope," with extensions and abuses of the practice leading to a landslide of unwarranted deaths (Foley & Hendin, 2002).

Several localities have legalized physician-assisted suicide, voluntary euthanasia, or both, including the Netherlands, Switzerland, Belgium, and the state of Oregon. In these places, legal safeguards attempt to avoid any slippery slope. For example, Oregon's law specifies the following conditions:

- The person must be terminally ill and have less than six months to live.
- The diagnosis of terminal illness must be confirmed by two physicians.
- Both doctors must certify that the person's condition does not impair his or her judgment.
- The person must ask for the prescription for lethal drugs at least twice orally and once in writing.
- Fifteen days must elapse between the first request and the written prescription.

physician-assisted suicide A form of active euthanasia in which a doctor provides the means for someone to end his or her own life.

voluntary euthanasia A form of active euthanasia in which, at a patient's request, someone else ends his or her life.

TABLE Ep.1 Euthanasia in the Netherlands, 2001*

Deaths with no medical decision: 56 percent

Deaths that included withholding intervention: 20 percent

Deaths that resulted from alleviating pain and other symptoms (the double effect): 20 percent

Deaths that involved voluntary euthanasia: 2.6 percent

Deaths that involved physician-assisted suicide (usually taking medication prescribed by the doctor): 0.2 percent

*Percentages do not total 100 because of rounding.
Source: Onwuteaka-Philipsen et al., 2003.

Data from the Netherlands, where voluntary euthanasia and physician-assisted suicide are both permitted, reveal that such deaths are rare (see Table Ep.1). Usually the physician involved is the patient's own family doctor, and physicians perform, on average, less than one euthanasia per year. One Dutch doctor explains:

> The process and procedure take so much emotional energy that physicians hope that nature will take its course before matters reach the point where euthanasia is appropriate. I am grateful when patients die peacefully on their own and do not need euthanasia. Even if the time for euthanasia never comes, just the fact that the physician talks about it with the patient provides an assurance that makes dying a little easier. Patients know they will not be left alone in pain, they will not have to suffer unnecessarily, and they have the comfort of knowing their physician will be there for them no matter what.

> *[quoted in Thomasma et al., 1998]*

Such statements do not sway those who are opposed to euthanasia. Of particular concern is the fact that the Netherlands is small (slightly larger than the state of Maryland) and has universal health care. In other nations, concerns have been raised that euthanasia might be imposed on those who cannot afford medical care—or who are disabled, female, elderly, or members of ethnic minorities (Prado & Taylor, 1999).

Demonstrating Against Euthanasia Ten thousand protesters gathered in April 2001 to urge the Dutch parliament not to legalize euthanasia in the Netherlands. They were partially successful: The law that was passed includes strict guidelines intended to ensure that a patient's decision to die is deliberate, voluntary, and definite.

AP / WIDE WORLD PHOTOS

Other data come from Oregon, which legalized physician-assisted suicide (but not voluntary euthanasia) in 1998 (Wineberg & Werth, 2003). In the following four years, of 28,851 deaths in Oregon, less than 1 percent (91 people, or 0.3 percent) were assisted suicides.

The Oregonians who requested help in dying were somewhat younger and much better educated (43 percent were college graduates) than the average dying Oregon resident. They were more often divorced or had never married (32 percent compared with 18 percent for all Oregon deaths). This may indicate that they were less connected to family or may be a cohort effect, because most of the oldest Oregonians, who died naturally, were married.

Most Oregonians who chose physician-assisted suicide had incurable cancer and were receiving palliative care (Oregon has excellent hospice care). Almost all were European-Americans (97 percent). The rest were Asian-Americans; none were African-Americans, Native Americans, or Latinos. An additional 49 people obtained a lethal prescription but did not use it; of those, 38 died naturally and 11 had not yet made a decision (Wineberg & Werth, 2003).

> As modern medicine has made it more possible to avoid many diseases and has hidden death in hospitals, acceptance of death has become more difficult. In the past few decades, the hospice and palliative care movements have sought to help people achieve a "good death" by relieving pain, discomfort, and deception. In preparing for death, many people sign a living will indicating their preferences regarding medical interventions and designate a health care proxy to make such decisions in the event that they become unable to do so. Although passive euthanasia (allowing a seriously ill person to die) is generally accepted and legal, active euthanasia, whether through physician-assisted suicide or voluntary euthanasia, is illegal in all but a few locales. Despite concerns about a "slippery slope," in the few places where one or both forms of euthanasia are legal, few people choose them and safeguards seem effective in preventing abuse.

Preparing for Death

Although death comes to everyone, responses to death vary greatly. Death has been denied, sought, feared, fought, avoided, and welcomed by families, medical personnel, communities, and the dying themselves. This emotional gamut can occur within a single dying person. Contradictory emotions are to be expected, as was first described in landmark research by Elisabeth Kübler-Ross (1969, 1975).

Avoiding Despair

It is impossible to underestimate the influence that Kübler-Ross has had on our understanding of death. Acceptance of death was so elusive that when Kübler-Ross (1969, 1975) asked the administrator of a large Chicago hospital for permission to speak with dying patients, he informed her that none of the patients were dying! Eventually Kübler-Ross was able to interview a few terminally ill patients, who, to everyone's surprise, were often grateful for the opportunity to talk to her. These and other interviews served as the basis for Kübler-Ross's well-known insight that dying people have many emotions, which typically occur in five stages: denial, anger, bargaining, depression, and acceptance.

Other researchers in **thanatology** (the study of death) have *not* found the same sequence of stages. More typically, denial, anger, and depression appear and reappear; bargaining is a fleeting thought; and acceptance is elusive (Kastenbaum,

thanatology The study of death.

1992). Subsequent attempts to list stages of dying and bereavement deal with generalities. They describe common emotional twists and turns but do not prescribe a course to be followed by everyone (Small, 2001).

Research has elucidated some patterns. Among older people, planning for death is typical (Wilkinson & Lynn, 2001) and may include deciding who will get which heirlooms; reconciling with friends; specifying whether and how burial or cremation should occur; and ending each family visit with loving goodbyes. Such planning, although sometimes unnerving to younger people, is psychologically healthy: Even when merely imagining their death, adults of all ages shift their priorities from pursuing new experiences and excitement to seeking emotional closeness and comfort (Fung et al., 1999). Selective optimization toward the end of life, quite appropriately, makes people draw closer to their family and friends (Baltes & Carstensen, 2003).

The anxiety about death that older adults most commonly express is whether they will have a "good death," one that is swift, painless, and dignified and that occurs at home, surrounded by friends and family (Wilkinson & Lynn, 2001). The likelihood of such a death is, as we have discussed, reduced by modern medicine, which can hold off death with all manner of technological interventions, maintaining organ functioning after brain death has occurred. In developed nations, most people die in hospitals (80 percent in the United States, 70 percent in Great Britain), usually after the person has had days of confused semiconsciousness while attached to an assortment of machines, tubes, and intravenous drips. Preparation becomes impossible in that setting.

Thus far we have discussed preparation for dying primarily from a Western perspective, as something that happens to individuals who have a right to know and determine how their death should occur. When we take a wider view, we find that in many cultures, the family, not the individual, makes decisions. Sometimes death is seen as a welcome relief, a final reward for a life well lived, providing the deceased with a new and exalted role as an ancestor. Focusing only on biological health, or death of an individual, runs counter to some non-Western cultures' appreciation of the soul, the family, and the community (Chatterjee, 2002).

For example, is hope best fostered by not telling individuals that they will soon die? Particularly in some Latin American and Asian cultures, it is feared that telling people that they are dying destroys hope (Talamantes et al., 1999; Yeo & Hikoyeda, 1999). Consider, for example, the experience of Mrs. Y, described in the following Case to Study.

A Case to Study

"Ask My Son and My Husband"

Mrs. Y's case was referred to the ethics committee by a hospital staff person who was concerned about a violation of her autonomy. . . . Mrs. Y was an alert 83-year-old Japanese woman who was admitted to the hospital for shortness of breath. During the evaluation of this symptom, she was found to have an advanced case of lung cancer. Her physician informed her older son and her husband, both of whom told the physician that they did not want Mrs. Y to be informed about the diagnosis. They told the physician that, in Japanese culture, cancer is felt to be a diagnosis that robs the patient of hope. The U.S.-trained hospital staff person, however, felt that by not telling Mrs. Y her diagnosis, she would be robbed of the power to make decisions for herself. A member of the ethics committee recommended that the physician directly ask Mrs. Y whether she would like to be told of her diagnosis when it was discovered and whether she would like to make decisions about her treatment. When asked these questions, Mrs. Y clearly answered, "No, you ask my son and my husband."

[cited in Kogan et al., 2000, p. 320]

This case was brought to the hospital ethics committee because of the common assumption that the dying individual needs to know what is happening and to decide what should be done. Such a supposition, based on the value of individual autonomy, is reflected in the concept of the living will, is inscribed in western law, underlies Elisabeth Kübler-Ross's recommendations, and is implied in the criticism of doctors and hospitals who do not inform, or heed, the patient.

In Mrs. Y's case, this value came into conflict with a Japanese belief related to the value of hope and with a cultural assumption that the family rather than the individual is the appropriate locus for decision making. It may also have conflicted with the greater dependency of females in Japanese culture, which may have made Mrs. Y inclined to defer to her husband and son for a decision.

When should someone be able to impose his or her values on someone else? Are knowledge and self-determination to be valued to such an extent that they override the expressed wish of a patient and a family? Can the emphasis on preserving hope and the reliance on family members as protective decision makers bring peace of mind to individuals? This hospital ethics committee allowed Mrs. Y to die without knowing her diagnosis but with her respect for her husband and son intact. Would you have done the same?

Cultural Variations

Hope often takes the form of the desire that death be held at bay. Surely you have heard stories of people who survived with "incurable" diseases or who survived for years after being told they had only months to live. In actuality, doctors are more likely to overestimate how long a person will live (Wilkinson & Lynn, 2001). Yet hope sustains individuals and their families.

Hope is sometimes expressed as belief in an afterlife or in the significance of a person's life in the context of family and community. Cultures and religions build hope and cohesion for the entire community through beliefs and practices related to death and mourning, but each does it in a distinct way (Lord et al., 2003).

Accordingly, we now present a broad overview. Remember, of course, that no religion or culture is monolithic. Even within one nation and one religion, individuals react very differently. To take one small example, when British doctors, almost all of whom were Christian, were asked about their opinions of the ethics of physician-assisted suicide, their responses differed significantly, depending on their medical specialty but not on any other aspect of their background. The vast majority (80 percent) of the geriatricians thought physician-assisted suicide was never justified, but nearly half (48 percent) of specialists in intensive care could imagine an ethical basis for such a decision (Dickinson, 2002). Thus, the following overview can, at most, attempt to present a very general idea of what people of different faiths and cultures believe.

Death in Religions of Africa and Asia

In many traditional African religions, adults gain new status through death, joining other ancestors who watch over their descendants and their village. Accordingly, the entire village participates in each adult's funeral, preparing the body and providing food and money for the journey to the ancestral realm. Mourning one person's death allows all members of the community to celebrate their connection with one another and with their collective past (Opoku, 1989).

For Muslims, death affirms religious faith. Islam teaches that the achievements, problems, and pleasures of this life are transitory and ephemeral; everyone should be mindful of, and ready for, death at any time. Therefore, caring for the dying is a holy reminder of mortality and of the potential for a happy life in the afterworld. Public and obvious lamenting over death is acceptable in men as well as women (Nobles & Sciarra, 2000), but mourners should not lose sight of

STEVEN M. STONE / PICTURE CUBE

Last Rites This colorful Balinese funeral procession on its way to a Buddhist cremation is a marked contrast to the somber memorial service that is more common in the West. No matter what form it takes, community involvement in death and dying seems to benefit the living.

the fact that the end of mortal life is but the transition to a better world (Hai & Asad, 2000). Specific rituals—including reciting prayers, washing the body, carrying the coffin, and attending the funeral—are performed by devout strangers as well as by relatives and friends.

Among Buddhists, disease and death are among life's inevitable sufferings, which may bring spiritual enlightenment (Nakasone, 2000). The task of the dying individual is to gain insight from the experience, with a clear mind and calm acceptance (Truitner & Truitner, 1993). Thus, in a modern context, family and friends help by ensuring that the person does not receive mind-altering medications or death-defying interventions. Death is not an end to the influence of the person, who remains connected to the family as an ancestor and who will be reborn. Both hope and fear may focus less on the death itself than on rebirth.

Among Hindus, helping the dying to surrender their ties to this world and prepare for the next is a particularly important obligation for the immediate family. A holy death is one that is welcomed by the dying person, who at the last moment should be placed on the ground with water from the sacred Ganges River on the lips and die chanting prayers, surrounded by family members who are reciting sacred texts. Such a holy death is believed to ease entry into the next life. It is difficult to achieve in a modern hospital setting, where, in addition to other problems, the dying person cannot be placed on the floor. Crucial to a Hindu family is knowing when someone is about to die so that preparations can be made and the entire family can be present when the soul leaves (Firth, 2001).

Death in North America

Although the more than 400 tribes of Native Americans (called Aboriginals in Canada and Indians in many places) vary significantly in their customs, all consider death an affirmation of nature and community values. This emphasis is in contrast to the Western emphasis on individualism and science (Brokenleg & Middleton, 1993; Van Winkle, 2000). Unless this contrast is understood by medical personnel, Native Americans may fear and shun hospitals. In one example, the adult sons of a Lakota Sioux man began chanting in his hospital room as soon as he died, a ritual affirmation of their dedication to their father and his legacy:

> A nurse entered the room, heard the chants and called hospital security to remove "those drunken Indians." . . . A doctor arrived to announce that an autopsy should be performed . . . [although the] tribe was firmly opposed to autopsies.
>
> [Brokenleg & Middleton, 1993]

For Jews, who make up about 2 percent of the North American population, the idea that hope for life should be sustained means that death is not emphasized and that the dying person is not left alone. On the day after death, the body is buried, unembalmed and in a plain wooden coffin to symbolize that physical preservation is not possible. The family is expected to mourn at home for a week with the assistance of many visitors, who bring food and comfort, tears and laughter. Then the immediate family recites a prayer (the Kaddish, which does not mention death directly) every day for 11 months and curtails social activities for a year (Katz, 1993).

Many Christians believe that death is not an end but rather the beginning of eternity in heaven or hell; therefore, death may be either welcomed or feared. Particular customs vary from denomination to denomination and from place to place. Thus, funerals may involve bringing relatives and neighbors together to view the body, for visible and vocal expressions of sorrow and for conversation and food; or they may include only those who knew the deceased well, no viewing

ED KASHI / IPN / AURORA PHOTOS

Differences and Similarities An open coffin, pictures of saints, and burning candles are traditional features of a Christian funeral, like this Ukrainian Orthodox ceremony. The look of solemn sorrow on the mourners' faces is a universal element.

of the body, and a restrained and quiet tone. The variability is such that in Mexico, for example, Christianity blends with Aztec customs in the Day of the Dead, the holiday on which people visit the cemetery to bring flowers and food. They tell stories about the dead person, leave sweets on the grave, and eat a festive meal at the graveside, celebrating life and death (Talamates et al., 1999; Younoszai, 1993).

As this brief survey makes clear, religious beliefs and cultural practices related to death offer hope and consolation to the dying and to those who survive them. Contemporary Western practices are no exception. One British commentator writes:

> Since 1960, there has been a fashion in deriding Western mortuary practices as somehow empty or shallow. Locked in cross-cultural envy and nostalgia, we seem to imagine that other people do it better or that we used to be able to throw a good funeral but have somehow lost the knack.
>
> [Bradbury, 2001, p. 224]

This expert cites contemporary Internet postings and other creative memorials as evidence that modern people still find suitable ways to express sorrow and hope.

FIGURE Ep.1 Strong Homeland and Religious Impulses Open-ended interviews with seriously ill Indians who had emigrated to Canada found that the longer they had been away, the more important India and Hinduism became as they thought about their deaths.

Spiritual and Cultural Affirmation

The importance of religion and culture in providing hope is evident in two tendencies among the dying: Religious and spiritual concerns often reemerge at death, and it is common for dying people to return to their roots, through either rituals or an actual journey.

For example, in one study, seriously ill people who had emigrated to Canada from India spoke nostalgically about their origins. As you can see from Figure Ep.1, the longer a person had been away from India, the more strongly he or she wanted to return there and to have a Hindu funeral (Fry, 1999). In the words of one woman who had spent 22 years in Canada:

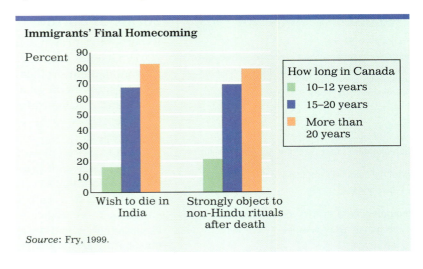

Immigrants' Final Homecoming

Percent

How long in Canada
- 10–12 years
- 15–20 years
- More than 20 years

Wish to die in India

Strongly object to non-Hindu rituals after death

Source: Fry, 1999.

I long to die among my relatives in the old country. . . . I miss the music, the chantings, the smells and sounds and the ringing of the temple bells in my hometown. I worry whether my own Hindu God will take me back or reject me because I am not a pure Hindu any more and have not been in communion with the elders of the Hindu faith for the years and years I have spent in Canada.

[quoted in Fry, 1999]

For many people, spiritual beliefs and a connection to community give hope that is desperately needed at death, a sense "that individual lives cannot be reduced to insignificance, that they can and do make a difference worth making, that the world is better for their existing" (Attig, 2003, pp. 62–63).

> Most Western thanatologists believe that both dying people and their loved ones are less likely to experience despair if they know the truth about the illness and can prepare for death. Although many questions are expressed, there is no prescribed sequence or pattern of emotions that all dying people experience. However, for everyone, pain relief is possible and important. Dying at home, while often longed for, is seldom possible in Western societies. Cultures vary widely in their customs and beliefs regarding death. There is no single, "right" way to die.

TABLE Ep.2 Cremation Rates in Selected Countries, c. 2000*

Country	Percent Being Cremated
Australia	54
Brazil	4
Canada	46
China	47
France	19
Great Britain	71
Italy	7
Japan	99
Netherlands	49
New Zealand	58
Russia	34
Spain	15
Sweden	70
Switzerland	75
United States	27

*These are the latest data. In some cases, the data come from earlier or later than 2000.

Source: Cremation Society of Britain.

bereavement The sense of loss following a death.

grief An individual's emotional response to bereavement.

mourning The ceremonies and behaviors that a religion or culture prescribes for bereaved people.

Coping with Bereavement

Religion and culture result in considerable variations in the practices that follow death—for example, what happens to the body (burial or cremation, and where?) who the mourners are (only immediate family or a wide community?), and how grief should be expressed (quiet tears or loud wailing?). Table Ep.2 shows the variation in the practice of cremation, which is almost universal in Japan but rare in Brazil.

Some universals lie beneath such superficial, albeit dramatic, variations. **Bereavement,** the sense of loss following a death, is a normal and expected response that can lead to a reaffirmation of life. Even when a religion teaches that the dead person is being rewarded in an afterlife, those who loved the person inevitably feel sorrow as well as joy. The reaffirmation that follows death is therefore not automatic but rather is nurtured by culture and custom. To understand this, we need to differentiate between two aspects of bereavement: grief and mourning.

Forms of Sorrow

Experts have drawn a careful distinction between grief and mourning (Small, 2001). **Grief** is a powerful and personal emotion, a sadness that overtakes a person, making ordinary life impossible. Grief includes uncontrollable crying, sleeplessness, irrational and even delusional thoughts. **Mourning** is a more public and ritualistic affair, the ceremonies and behaviors that a religion or culture prescribes for bereaved people; these may include special clothing, food, or prayers.

The two are connected: Mourning is designed by religions and cultures to allow expression of grief and then recovery; grief itself, however personal and private, also follows certain social rules (Anderson, 2001). Ideally, the expression of grief leads to a reaffirmation of life, in which the grieving person may experience a renewed dedication to values held by the deceased, may become involved in personally meaningful activities (gardening, community work, and so on), or may simply arrive at a more general appreciation for family, religion, or nation.

Mourning customs are designed by various cultures to channel grief toward such reaffirmation, which is why, for example, eulogies emphasize the dead person's strengths and successes in life and why many people attend wakes, funerals, or memorial services to help the bereaved, even if they did not know the person who has died. Almost always, mourning customs include an informal timetable as well as an appropriate setting for expression of grief.

Crucial to reaffirmation is people's search for meaning in death, for a reason why the person they grieve for lived and died. In some cases, this search starts with preserving memories: Photographs, personal effects, and anecdotes are central to many memorial services. Sometimes it involves talking with others in a similar situation; people find solace and meaning through organizations for the parents of murdered children, for widows, or for family members of those who died in a particular tragedy. Sometimes "meaning becomes grounded in action" to honor the dead (Armour, 2003, p. 538). For example, one mother carries a bag with personal effects of her murdered son and shows them, item by item, to groups of young gang members.

A. RAMEY / PHOTOEDIT, INC.

The Flowers of Youth In many cultural traditions, mourners bring a token of their presence to funeral rites. Such items as pebbles, stuffed animals, notes, candles, and flowers are left at grave sites throughout the world. These young women are placing flowers on the coffin of a friend who was killed in a drive-by shooting.

> "This is all I had left of my son. A pair of tennis shoes and a pair of underwear that had no blood on them. He loved this little chain he had on. And you see it's broken up, with a shot?" . . . These groups of young kids are sitting there . . . and I tell them exactly about my son. . . . Driving home from that group, I just get warm, like affirmation.
>
> *[quoted in Armour, 2003, p. 532]*

Unexpected and violent deaths are particularly likely to shock and to precipitate a search for meaning. Indeed, there is a very common impulse to believe that unexpected deaths were part of a conspiracy (e.g., Princess Diana), did not really happen (e.g., Elvis Presley), or were meaningful in some way (Browne & Neal, 2001). Following such deaths, the expression of grief can foster understanding, bring communities together, and often, for better or worse, focus blame (against tobacco advertising, or lack of gun regulation, or people of another group or nation). The terrorist attacks of September 11, 2001, triggered donations of far more blood than could possibly be used, widespread displays of the U.S. flag,

AP / WIDE WORLD PHOTOS

Not Alone in Their Grief Family members of people who died in the terrorist attacks of September 11, 2001, gather at the site of the World Trade Center in New York City. Despite their many ethnic and economic differences, the next of kin find comfort in being among other people who have experienced similar losses.

and expressions of grief and consolation almost instantly e-mailed around the world (DeSpelder & Strickland, 2004; Lattanzi-Licht & Doka, 2003).

Contemporary Challenges

In recent times, mourning, especially in North America and Europe, has become more private, less emotional, and less religious. Emblematic of this change are funeral trends in the United States: Whereas older generations prefer burial after a traditional funeral, younger generations are likely to prefer small memorial services after cremation (Hayslip et al., 1999; Tappenden, 1996).

As mourning diminishes, grief becomes "an unwelcome intrusion (or violent intercession) into the normal efficient running of everyday life" (Anderson, 2001, p. 141). This trend concerns many developmentalists who believe that expression of emotion aids growth and that grief is an indispensable part of bereavement.

The most troubling potential result of diminished mourning and grieving is the increased social isolation of those who have lost a loved one—an isolation that is exactly the opposite of what they need. Although physical illness is more common during bereavement (when many people feel sick more often than is usual for them), the bereaved sometimes find themselves seeing a doctor not primarily for medication but for the sympathy and attention—which the shortened mourning period has not provided for them.

Many developmenalists are also concerned about "disenfranchised grief," the practice of excluding certain people from mourning (Doka, 2002). Among those who are often disenfranchised are the unmarried partner (same sex or other sex) of the deceased, the ex-spouse, the young child, or the friend from work. Each of these may have been closer to the person in life than a sibling who had not been in touch for years, but sometimes only adults of the immediate family are "chief mourners," able to make decisions about the funeral, the disposition of the body, and so on.

Any kind of prohibition, restriction, or exclusion can make healing, hope, and affirmation more difficult for the bereaved of all ages (Lamers, 2003). Such interference is all too common, especially with violent deaths. In one case, emergency room staff did not allow the mother of a 17-year-old killed in an auto crash to see her son's body until she answered many questions and promised not to "do anything silly." The mother explains:

> I desperately needed to hold him, to look at him, to find out where he was hurting. These instincts don't die immediately with the child. The instinct to comfort and cuddle, to examine and inspect the wounds, to try to understand, most of all, to hold. But my lovely boy was draped on an altar, covered with a purple robe, and all expressions of love and care were denied to me. And I don't know when that wound will heal.
>
> *[Awoonor-Renner, 1993]*

Murders and suicides, in particular, often trigger police investigations and press reports, which interfere with the grief process. An autopsy complicates grieving for those who believe that the body will ultimately be transported to heaven or that a person's spirit does not leave the body immediately.

Often, if the bereaved were not able to be with the person, they want specific information about the last hours, including any words, gestures, or emotions of

TONY FREEMAN / PHOTOEDIT, INC.

He Died for His Country A family mourns a young Latino serviceman. Hispanic-Americans and African-Americans make up 20 percent of the U.S. population aged 45 and older and 40 percent of those aged 25 and younger. As a result, a disproportionate number of members of the armed services who die are Latino, not so much because of their ethnicity as because of their youth.

the deceased. In some violent deaths, not only is this information unobtainable, but there is no body. Yet placing all, or at least part, of a person's body in a specific location helps the bereaved. This explains why the families of soldiers missing in action seek to have some remains identified and returned, even decades later.

Whatever occasions it, inadequate grief is thought to harm the larger community as well. Rituals after death provide a way to express and share both private sorrow and public loss. As social ceremonies, funerals historically and cross-culturally brought together the community and transmitted culture. The contemporary impulse to omit mourning rituals and to exclude children from grief can curtail expressions of love, concern, and support. It may also prevent children from learning about death and continuity and may hinder all humans in their appreciation and affirmation of life (Lamers, 2003).

Especially for Educators How might a teacher help a young child cope with death?

Responses to Bereavement

What can friends do to help the bereaved person? The first step is simply to be aware that powerful, complicated, and unexpected emotions are likely: A friend should listen and sympathize. Friends and others should not judge a person's sorrow, especially to imply that the person is too grief-stricken or not grief-stricken enough. The bereaved person might or might not want to visit the grave, light a candle, cherish a memento, pray, or sob. In some cases, even so-called absent grief—in which the bereaved refuses to do any of these things (except, perhaps, alone)—might be appropriate. Psychologists now recognize that expecting certain reactions from a bereaved person may be more harmful than helpful (Jordon & Niemeyer, 2003).

As we have seen, culture and cohort play a role in the different responses to death, and this, too, needs to be understood. Those who have been taught to bear grief stoically may be doubly distressed if they are advised to cry and cannot. Those whose cultures expect loud wailing may become confused and resentful if they are told to hush.

Bereavement is an ongoing, often lengthy process; sympathy, honesty, and social support may be needed for months or even years (Mullan et al., 2003). Family sharing of emotions over time, in particular, helps to soothe grief, according to one longitudinal study (Schokatraylor et al., 2003). As time passes, the bereaved usually become involved in other activities, but they do not forget the person they loved, especially on the anniversary of the death. Thus, interspersed with new and productive changes in the bereaved's life, there may be flashbacks, unexpected tears, and other manifestations of sorrow.

The word *recovery,* sometimes used to describe the process, implies that grief over death is an illness to be cured. It is perhaps better to accept such grief and see its potential to lead to a reaffirmation of life. As one counselor explains: "In reality, pain may be tempered by time, but time does not heal. The widowed do not recover . . ." [Silverman, 2003, p. 252]

> Hope and sadness seem to be universal human reactions to the death of a loved one. Every culture and religion has rituals and beliefs regarding death, and all prescribe appropriate mourning, leading to reaffirmation of faith and life. The powerful and long-lasting emotions felt by bereaved people are expressed in various ways. Impulses to grieve, to memorialize, to pray, and to find personal meaning in death are sometimes thwarted by contemporary practices. Yet grief and mourning are basic to the human experience, with the potential to integrate the bereaved into the community and, indeed, to bring communities together.

Conclusion

No matter what method is used to work through emotions of grief, the experience may give the living a deeper appreciation of themselves as well as of the value of human relationships. In fact, a theme frequently sounded by those who work with the bereaved is that people need to learn the lessons that mourners can teach. The most central of these is the value of intimate, caring relationships. As one counselor expresses it:

> I often have heard phrases such as "I wish I had told him I loved him" or "I wish we could have resolved our differences earlier." There may be things we need to say, appreciations that need to be expressed, distances to bridge. . . . Loving and being loved is not just something that happens to us. It is a creative art that must be worked in a variety of ways.
>
> *[Sanders, 1989]*

It is fitting to end this book with just such a reminder of the creative work of loving. As first described in Chapter 1, the study of the process of human development is a science, with topics to be researched, understood, and explained in order to enhance human lives. But the process of actually living one's own life is an art as well as a science, with strands of love and sorrow and resilience woven into each person's unique tapestry. Dying, when accepted, death, when it leads to hope, grief, when allowed expression, and mourning, when it fosters reaffirmation, give added meaning to birth, growth, development, and all human relationships.

Response for Educators (from page Ep-15): Death has varied meanings, so a teacher needs to take care not to contradict the child's cultural background. In general, however, specific expressions of mourning are useful, and acting as if the death did not happen is destructive.

KEY TERMS

hospice (p. Ep-2)
palliative care (p. Ep-3)
double effect (p. Ep-3)
passive euthanasia (p. Ep-4)

active euthanasia (p. Ep-4)
living will (p. Ep-4)
health care proxy (p. Ep-4)

physician-assisted suicide (p. Ep-5)
voluntary euthanasia (p. Ep-5)
thanatology (p. Ep-7)

bereavement (p. Ep-12)
grief (p. Ep-12)
mourning (p. Ep-12)

APPLICATIONS

1. Death is sometimes said to be hidden, even taboo. Survey 10 people, asking them if they have ever been with someone who was dying, in their last days of life. Note not only the proportions but also, for those who say yes, where the deaths occurred. For those who say no, note their reactions to the question.

2. Find statements about death in a book such as *Bartlett's Familiar Quotations*. Do the quotes reflect acceptance, denial, or fear of death? Look for any historical and/or cultural patterns.

3. Every aspect of dying is controversial, with many ethical dilemmas, cultural assumptions, and disputed facts beyond those mentioned in this chapter. Do a search for "hospice" on the Internet, and analyze the conflicting information you find. What is your opinion, and why?

Appendix A
Supplemental Charts, Graphs, and Tables

Often, examining specific data is useful, even fascinating, to developmental researchers. The particular numbers reveal trends and nuances not apparent from a more general view. For instance, many people mistakenly believe that the incidence of Down syndrome babies rises sharply for mothers over 35, or that even the tiniest newborns usually survive. Each chart, graph, or table in this appendix probably contains information not generally known.

Children as a Proportion of a Nation's Population

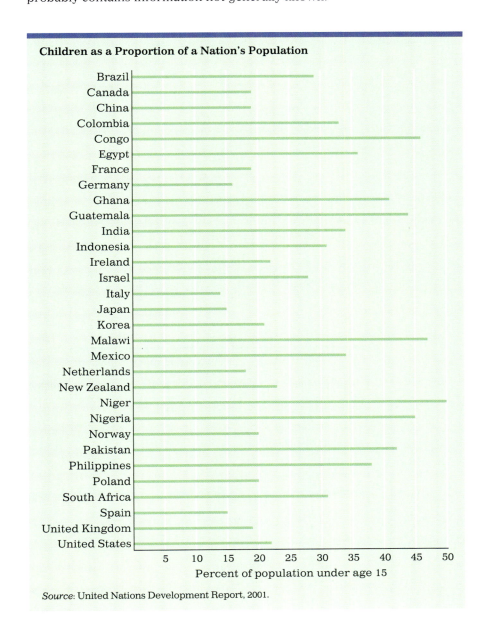

Source: United Nations Development Report, 2001.

More Children, Worse Schools? (Chapter 1)

Nations that have high birth rates also have high death rates, short life spans, and more illiteracy. A systems approach suggests that these variables are connected: For example, the Montessori and Reggio-Emilio early-childhood education programs, said to be the best in the world, originated in Italy, and Italy has the lowest proportion of children under 15 of all the countries in this graph.

Ethnic Composition of the U.S. Population (Chapter 2)

Thinking about the ethnic makeup of the U.S. population can be an interesting exercise in social comparison. If you look only at the table, you will conclude that not much has changed over the past 30 years: Whites are still the majority, Native Americans are still a tiny minority, and African-Americans are still about 11 percent of the population. However, if you look at the chart, you can see why every group feels that much has changed. Because the proportions of Hispanic-Americans and Asian-Americans have increased dramatically, European-Americans see the current nonwhite population at almost one-third of the total, and African-Americans see that Hispanics now outnumber them. There are also interesting regional differences within the United States. For example, Los Angeles County has the largest number of Native Americans (156,000) and the largest number of Asians (1.3 million).

? *Observational Quiz* (see answer, page A-4): Which ethnic group is growing most rapidly?

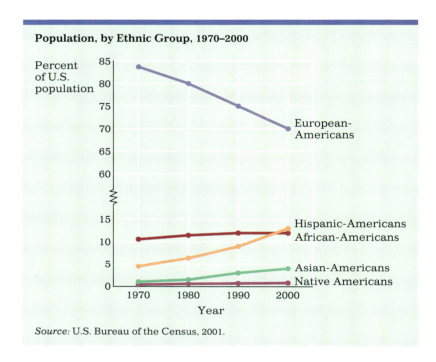

Population, by Ethnic Group, 1970–2000

Source: U.S. Bureau of the Census, 2001.

	Percent of U.S. Population			
Ethnic Origin	**1970**	**1980**	**1990**	**2000**
European (white)	83.7	80	75	70
African (black)	10.6	11.5	12	12
Latino (Hispanic)	4.5	6.4	9	13
Asian	1.0	1.5	3	4
Native American	.4	.6	.7	0.9

The Genetics of Blood Types (Chapter 3)

Blood types A and B are dominant traits, and type O is recessive. The percentages given in the first column of this chart represent the odds that a child born to the parents with the various combinations of genotypes will have the genotype given in the second column.

Genotypes of Parents*	Genotype of Offspring	Phenotype	Can Donate Blood To (Phenotype)	Can Receive Blood From (Phenotype)
AA + AA (100%) AA + AB (50%) AA + AO (50%) AB + AB (25%) AB + AO (25%) AO + AO (25%)	AA (inherits one A from each parent)	A	A or AB	A or O
AA + OO (100%) AB + OO (50%) AO + AO (50%) AO + OO (50%) AB + AO (25%) AB + BO (25%)	AO	A	A or AB	A or O
BB + BB (100%) AB + BB (50%) BB + BO (50%) AB + AB (25%) AB + BO (25%) BO + BO (25%)	BB	B	B or AB	B or O
BB + OO (100%) AB + OO (50%) BO + BO (50%) BO + OO (50%) AB + AO (25%) AB + BO (25%)	BO	B	B or AB	B or O
AA + BB (100%) AA + AB (50%) AA + BO (50%) AB + AB (50%) AB + BB (50%) AB + BO (25%) AO + BO (25%)	AB	AB	AB only	A, B, AB, O ("universal recipient")
OO + OO (100%) AO + OO (50%) BO + OO (50%) AO + AO (25%) AO + BO (25%) BO + BO (25%)	OO	O	A, B, AB, O ("universal donor")	O only

*Blood type is not a sex-linked trait, so any of these pairs can be either mother-plus-father or father-plus-mother.

Source: Adapted from Hartl & Jones, 1999.

Odds of Down Syndrome by Maternal Age and Gestational Age (Chapter 4)

The odds of any given fetus at the end of the first trimester having three chromosomes at the 21st site (trisomy-21) and thus having Down syndrome is shown in the 10-weeks column. Every year of maternal age increases the incidence of trisomy-21. The number of Down syndrome infants born alive is only half the number who survived the first trimester. Although obviously the least risk is at age 20 (younger is even better), there is no year when the odds suddenly increase (age 35 is an arbitrary cut-off). Even at age 44, less than 4 percent of all newborns have Down syndrome. Other chromosomal abnormalities in fetuses also increase with mother's age, but the rate of spontaneous abortion is much higher, so births of babies with chromosomal defects is not the norm, even for women over age 45.

Age (Yrs)	Gestation (Weeks)		Live Births
	10	35	
20	1/804	1/1,464	1/1,527
21	1/793	1/1,445	1/1,507
22	1/780	1/1,421	1/1,482
23	1/762	1/1,389	1/1,448
24	1/740	1/1,348	1/1,406
25	1/712	1/1,297	1/1,352
26	1/677	1/1,233	1/1,286
27	1/635	1/1,157	1/1,206
28	1/586	1/1,068	1/1,113
29	1/531	1/967	1/1,008
30	1/471	1/858	1/895
31	1/409	1/745	1/776
32	1/347	1/632	1/659
33	1/288	1/525	1/547
34	1/235	1/427	1/446
35	1/187	1/342	1/356
36	1/148	1/269	1/280
37	1/115	1/209	1/218
38	1/88	1/160	1/167
39	1/67	1/122	1/128
40	1/51	1/93	1/97
41	1/38	1/70	1/73
42	1/29	1/52	1/55
43	1/21	1/39	1/41
44	1/16	1/29	1/30

Source: Snijders & Nicolaides, 1996.

Saving Young Lives: Childhood Immunizations (Chapter 5)

Recommended Childhood Immunization Schedule, United States, 2004

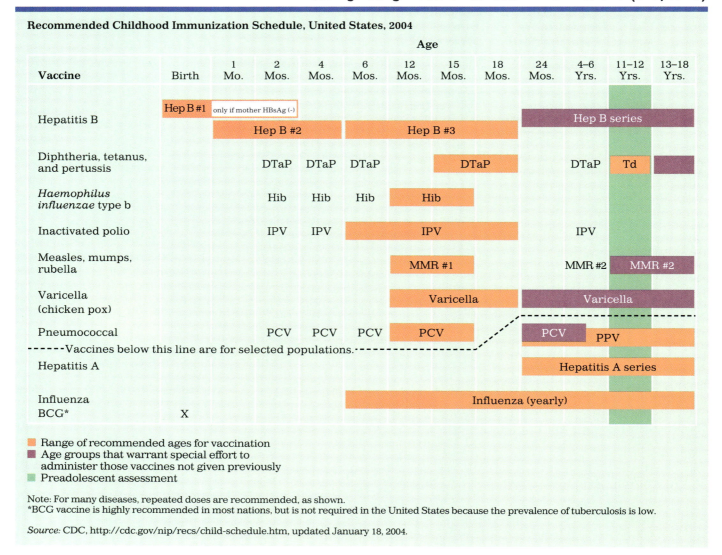

Vaccine	Birth	1 Mo.	2 Mos.	4 Mos.	6 Mos.	12 Mos.	15 Mos.	18 Mos.	24 Mos.	4–6 Yrs.	11–12 Yrs.	13–18 Yrs.
Hepatitis B	Hep B #1 (only if mother HBsAg (-))		Hep B #2			Hep B #3					Hep B series	
Diphtheria, tetanus, and pertussis			DTaP	DTaP	DTaP		DTaP			DTaP	Td	
Haemophilus influenzae type b			Hib	Hib	Hib	Hib						
Inactivated polio			IPV	IPV		IPV				IPV		
Measles, mumps, rubella						MMR #1				MMR #2	MMR #2	
Varicella (chicken pox)						Varicella				Varicella		
Pneumococcal			PCV	PCV	PCV	PCV			PCV	PPV		
Hepatitis A										Hepatitis A series		
Influenza					Influenza (yearly)							
BCG*	X											

- - - - - Vaccines below this line are for selected populations. - - - - - -

- 🟧 Range of recommended ages for vaccination
- 🟪 Age groups that warrant special effort to administer those vaccines not given previously
- 🟩 Preadolescent assessment

Note: For many diseases, repeated doses are recommended, as shown.
*BCG vaccine is highly recommended in most nations, but is not required in the United States because the prevalence of tuberculosis is low.

Source: CDC, http://cdc.gov/nip/recs/child-schedule.htm, updated January 18, 2004.

❗ *Answer to Observational Quiz* (from page A-2): Asian-Americans, whose share of the U.S. population has quadrupled in the past 30 years.

First Sounds and First Words: Similarities Among Many Languages (Chapter 6)

	Baby's Word For:	
Language	Mother	Father
English	mama, mommy	dada, daddy
Spanish	mama	papa
French	maman, mama	papa
Italian	mamma	babbo, papa
Latvian	mama	tēte
Syrian Arabic	mama	baba
Bantu	ba-mama	taata
Swahili	mama	baba
Sanskrit	nana	tata
Hebrew	ema	abba
Korean	oma	apa

Mothering: Knowledge Over Instinct (Chapter 7)

Differentiating excellent from destructive mothering is not easy, once basic needs for food and protection are met. However, as the Toni and Jacob examples in Chapter 7 make clear, psychosocial development depends on responsive parent–infant relationships. Breast-feeding is one sign of intimacy between mother and infant. Regions of the world differ dramatically in rates of breast-feeding, with the highest worldwide in Southeast Asia, where half of all 2-year-olds are still breast-fed.

In the United States, the South is lowest and the West is highest in rate of breast-feeding at one month. The overall rate increased from 39 percent in 1993 to 52 percent in 1999. In the United States, other factors that affect the likelihood of breast-feeding (not shown here) are ethnicity (Latinas are more likely, and African-Americans less likely, to breast-feed than European-Americans); maternal age (a positive correlation between age and breast-feeding); and newborn weight (low-birthweight babies are less likely to be breast-fed). The most marked influence of all is the mother's education.

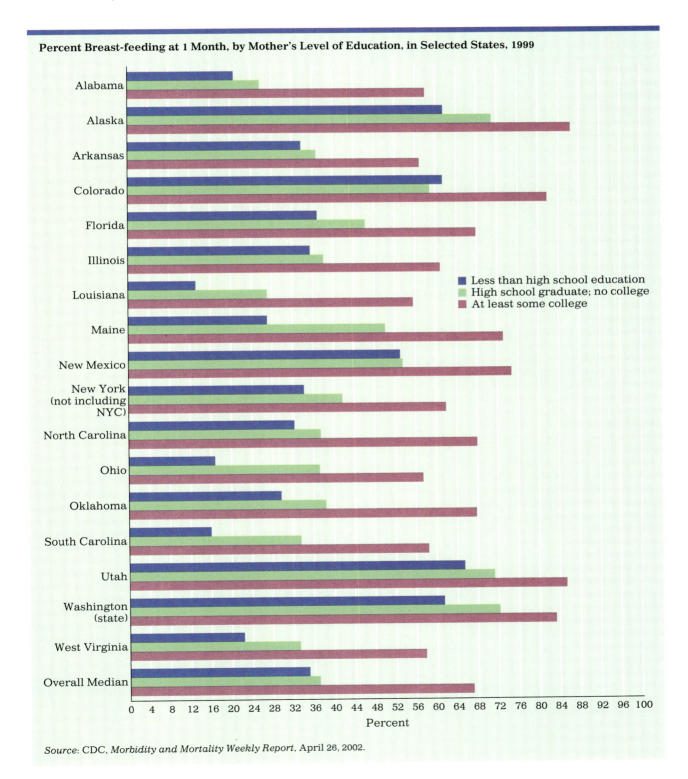

Percent Breast-feeding at 1 Month, by Mother's Level of Education, in Selected States, 1999

Legend:
■ Less than high school education
■ High school graduate; no college
■ At least some college

Source: CDC, *Morbidity and Mortality Weekly Report*, April 26, 2002.

Height Gains from Birth to Age 18 (Chapter 8)

The range of height (on this page) and weight (see page A-7) of children in the United States. The columns labeled "50th" (the fiftieth percentile) show the average; the columns labeled "90th" (the ninetieth percentile) show the size of children taller and heavier than 90 percent of their contemporaries; and the columns labeled "10th" (the tenth percentile) show the size of children who are taller than only 10 percent of their peers. Note that girls are slightly shorter, on average, than boys.

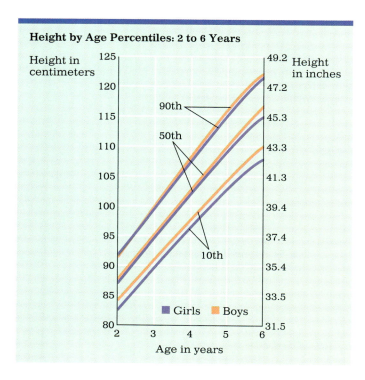

Height by Age Percentiles: 2 to 6 Years

Same Data, Different Form

The columns of numbers in the table at the right provide detailed and precise information about height ranges for every year of childhood. The illustration above shows the same information in graphic form for ages 2–6. The same is done for weight ranges on page A-7. Ages 2–6 are singled out because that is the period during which a child's eating habits are set. Which form of data presentation do you think is easier to understand?

Length in Centimeters (and Inches)

Age	Boys: Percentiles			Girls: Percentiles		
	10th	50th	90th	10th	50th	90th
Birth	47.5 (18¾)	50.5 (20)	53.5 (21)	46.5 (18¼)	49.9 (19¾)	52.0 (20½)
1 month	51.3 (20¼)	54.6 (21½)	57.7 (22¾)	50.2 (19¾)	53.5 (21)	56.1 (22)
3 months	57.7 (22¾)	61.1 (24)	64.5 (25½)	56.2 (22¼)	59.5 (23½)	62.7 (24¾)
6 months	64.4 (25¼)	67.8 (26¾)	71.3 (28)	62.6 (24¾)	65.9 (26)	69.4 (27¼)
9 months	69.1 (27¼)	72.3 (28½)	75.9 (30)	67.0 (26½)	70.4 (27¾)	74.0 (29¼)
12 months	72.8 (28¾)	76.1 (30)	79.8 (31½)	70.8 (27¾)	74.3 (29¼)	78.0 (30¾)
18 months	78.7 (31)	82.4 (32½)	86.6 (34)	77.2 (30½)	80.9 (31¾)	85.0 (33½)
24 months	83.5 (32¾)	87.6 (34½)	92.2 (36¼)	82.5 (32½)	86.5 (34)	90.8 (35¾)
3 years	90.3 (35½)	94.9 (37¼)	100.1 (39½)	89.3 (35¼)	94.1 (37)	99.0 (39)
4 years	97.3 (38¼)	102.9 (40½)	108.2 (42½)	96.4 (38)	101.6 (40)	106.6 (42)
5 years	103.7 (40¾)	109.9 (43¼)	115.4 (45½)	102.7 (40½)	108.4 (42¾)	113.8 (44¾)
6 years	109.6 (43¼)	116.1 (45¾)	121.9 (48)	108.4 (42¾)	114.6 (45)	120.8 (47½)
7 years	115.0 (45¼)	121.7 (48)	127.9 (50¼)	113.6 (44¾)	120.6 (47½)	127.6 (50¼)
8 years	120.2 (47¼)	127.0 (50)	133.6 (52½)	118.7 (46¾)	126.4 (49¾)	134.2 (52¾)
9 years	125.2 (49¼)	132.2 (52)	139.4 (55)	123.9 (48¾)	132.2 (52)	140.7 (55½)
10 years	130.1 (51¼)	137.5 (54¼)	145.5 (57¼)	129.5 (51)	138.3 (54½)	147.2 (58)
11 years	135.1 (53¼)	143.33 (56½)	152.1 (60)	135.6 (53½)	144.8 (57)	153.7 (60½)
12 years	140.3 (55¼)	149.7 (59)	159.4 (62¾)	142.3 (56)	151.5 (59¾)	160.0 (63)
13 years	145.8 (57½)	156.5 (61½)	167.0 (65¾)	148.0 (58¼)	157.1 (61¾)	165.3 (65)
14 years	151.8 (59¾)	63.1 (64¼)	173.8 (68½)	151.5 (59¾)	160.4 (63¼)	168.7 (66½)
15 years	158.2 (62¼)	169.0 (66½)	178.9 (70½)	153.2 (60¼)	161.8 (63¾)	170.5 (67¼)
16 years	163.9 (64½)	173.5 (68¼)	182.4 (71¾)	154.1 (60¾)	162.4 (64)	171.1 (67¼)
17 years	167.7 (66)	176.2 (69¼)	184.4 (72½)	155.1 (61)	163.1 (64¼)	171.2 (67½)
18 years	168.7 (66½)	176.8 (69½)	185.3 (73)	156.0 (61½)	163.7 (64½)	171.0 (67¼)

Source: These data are those of the National Center for Health Statistics (NCHS), Health Resources Administration, DHHS. They were based on studies of The Fels Research Institute, Yellow Springs, Ohio. These data were first made available with the help of William M. Moore, M.D., of Ross Laboratories, who supplied the conversion from metric measurements to approximate inches and pounds. This help is gratefully acknowledged.

Weight Gains from Birth to Age 18 (Chapter 8)

These height and weight charts present rough guidelines; a child might differ from these norms and be quite healthy and normal. However, if a particular child shows a discrepancy between height and weight (for instance, at the 90th percentile in height but only the 20th percentile in weight) or is much larger or smaller than most children the same age, a pediatrician should see if disease, malnutrition, or genetic abnormality is part of the reason.

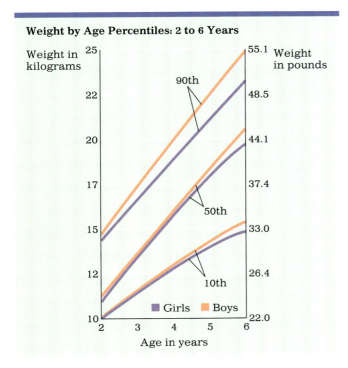

Weight by Age Percentiles: 2 to 6 Years

Comparisons

Notice that the height trajectories in the graph on page A-6 are much closer together than the weight trajectories shown in the graph above. By age 18, the height range amounts to only about 6 inches, but there is a difference of about 65 pounds between the 10th and the 90th percentiles.

? *Critical Thinking Question* (see answer, page A-8): How can this discrepancy between height and weight ranges be explained?

Weight in Kilograms (and Pounds)

Age	Boys: Percentiles			Girls: Percentiles		
	10th	50th	90th	10th	50th	90th
Birth	2.78 (6¼)	3.27 (7¼)	3.82 (8½)	2.58 (5¾)	3.23 (7)	3.64 (8)
1 month	3.43 (7½)	4.29 (9½)	5.14 (11¼)	3.22 (7)	3.98 (8¾)	4.65 (10¼)
3 months	4.78 (10½)	5.98 (13¼)	7.14 (15¾)	4.47 (9¾)	5.40 (12)	6.39 (14)
6 months	6.61 (14½)	7.85 (17¼)	9.10 (20)	6.12 (13½)	7.21 (16)	8.38 (18½)
9 months	7.95 (17½)	9.18 (20¼)	10.49 (23¼)	7.34 (16¼)	8.56 (18¾)	9.83 (21¾)
12 months	8.84 (19½)	10.15 (22½)	11.54 (25½)	8.19 (18)	9.53 (21)	10.87 (24)
18 months	9.92 (21¾)	11.47 (25¼)	13.05 (28¾)	9.30 (20½)	10.82 (23¾)	12.30 (27)
24 months	10.85 (24)	12.59 (27¾)	14.29 (31½)	10.26 (22½)	11.90 (26¼)	13.57 (30)
3 years	12.58 (27¾)	14.62 (32¼)	16.95 (37¼)	12.26 (27)	14.10 (31)	16.54 (36½)
4 years	14.24 (31½)	16.69 (36¾)	19.32 (42½)	13.84 (30½)	15.96 (35¼)	18.93 (41¾)
5 years	15.96 (35¼)	18.67 (41¼)	21.70 (47¾)	15.26 (33¾)	17.66 (39)	21.23 (46¾)
6 years	17.72 (39)	20.69 (45½)	24.31 (53½)	16.72 (36¾)	19.52 (43)	23.89 (52¾)
7 years	19.53 (43)	22.85 (50¼)	27.36 (60¼)	18.39 (40½)	21.84 (48¼)	27.39 (60½)
8 years	21.39 (47¼)	25.30 (55¾)	31.06 (68½)	20.45 (45)	24.84 (54¾)	32.04 (70¾)
9 years	23.33 (51½)	28.13 (62)	35.57 (78½)	22.92 (50½)	28.46 (62¾)	37.60 (83)
10 years	25.52 (56¼)	31.44 (69¼)	40.80 (90)	25.76 (56¾)	32.55 (71¾)	43.70 (96¼)
11 years	28.17 (62)	35.30 (77¾)	46.57 (102¾)	28.97 (63¾)	36.95 (81½)	49.96 (110¼)
12 years	31.46 (69¼)	39.78 (87¾)	52.73 (116¼)	32.53 (71¼)	41.53 (91½)	55.99 (123½)
13 years	35.60 (78½)	44.95 (99)	59.12 (130¼)	36.35 (80¼)	46.10 (101¾)	61.45 (135½)
14 years	40.64 (89½)	50.77 (112)	65.57 (144½)	40.11 (88½)	50.28 (110¾)	66.04 (145½)
15 years	46.06 (101½)	56.71 (125)	71.91 (158½)	43.38 (95¾)	53.68 (118¼)	69.64 (153¼)
16 years	51.16 (112¾)	62.10 (137)	77.97 (172)	45.78 (101)	55.89 (123¼)	71.68 (158)
17 years	55.28 (121¾)	66.31 (146¼)	83.58 (184¼)	47.04 (103¾)	56.69 (125)	72.38 (159½)
18 years	57.89 (127½)	68.88 (151¾)	88.41 (195)	47.47 (104¾)	56.62 (124¾)	72.25 (159¼)

Source: Data are those of the National Center for Health Statistics, Health Resources Administration, DHHS, collected in its Health Examination Surveys.

Day Care and Family Income (Chapter 9)

Note that, in both years, the wealthier families were less likely to have children exclusively in parental care and more likely to have children in center-based care.

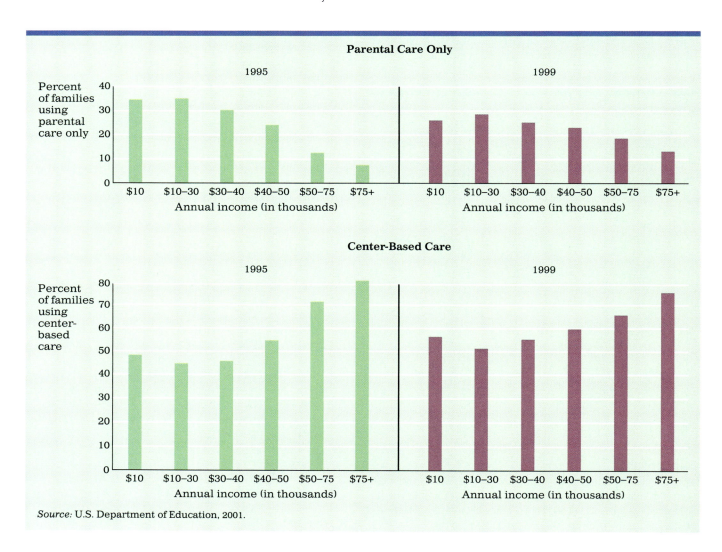

Source: U.S. Department of Education, 2001.

! *Answer to Critical Thinking Question*
(from page A-7): Nutrition is generally adequate in the United States, and that is why height differences are small. But as a result of the strong influence that family and culture have on eating habits, almost half of all North Americans are overweight or obese.

Rates of Poverty, by State and by Age Group

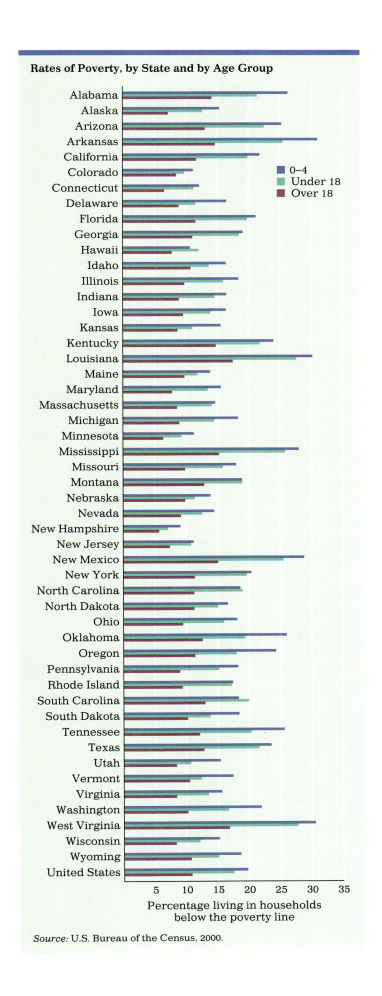

	0–4
	Under 18
	Over 18

Percentage living in households
below the poverty line

Source: U.S. Bureau of the Census, 2000.

Babies Are the Poorest Americans
(Chapter 10)

Is poverty worse for adults than for children? Most developmentalists would say the opposite, and would wonder why every state has more poor children—especially young children—than poor adults.

? *Observational Quiz* (see answer, page A-10): Which state has the highest poverty rate for adults? For children under 18? For children from birth to age 4?

! *Answer to Observational Quiz* (from page A-9): 1. Louisiana, 2. West Virginia, 3. Arkansas. To think about: At which age is poverty the worst and why?

DSM-IV-R Criteria for Attention-Deficit/Hyperactivity Disorder (AD/HD), Conduct Disorder (CD), and Oppositional Defiant Disorder (ODD) (Chapter 11)

The specific symptoms for these various disorders overlap. Many other childhood disorders also have some of the same symptoms. Differentiating one problem from another is the main purpose of DSM-IV-R. That is no easy task, which is one reason the book is now in its fourth major revision and is now 943 pages long. Those pages include not only the type of diagnostic criteria shown here but also discussions of prevalence, age and gender statistics, cultural aspects, and prognosis for about 400 disorders or subtypes, 40 of which appear primarily in childhood. Thus, the diagnostic criteria reprinted here for three disorders represent less than 1 percent of the contents of DSM-IV-R.

Diagnostic Criteria for Attention-Deficit/Hyperactivity Disorder

A. Either (1) or (2):
(1) Six (or more) of the following symptoms of **inattention** have persisted for at least 6 months to a degree that is maladaptive and inconsistent with developmental level:

Inattention

(a) often fails to give close attention to details or makes careless mistakes in schoolwork, work, or other activities
(b) often has difficulty sustaining attention in tasks or play activities
(c) often does not seem to listen when spoken to directly
(d) often does not follow through on instructions and fails to finish schoolwork, chores, or duties in the workplace (not due to oppositional behavior or failure to understand instructions)
(e) often has difficulty organizing tasks and activities
(f) often avoids, dislikes, or is reluctant to engage in tasks that require sustained mental effort (such as schoolwork or homework)
(g) often loses things necessary for tasks or activities (e.g., toys, school assignments, pencils, books, or tools)
(h) is often easily distracted by extraneous stimuli
(i) is often forgetful in daily activities

(2) Six (or more) of the following symptoms of **hyperactivity-impulsivity** have persisted for at least 6 months to a degree that is maladaptive and inconsistent with developmental level:

Hyperactivity

(a) often fidgets with hands or feet or squirms in seat
(b) often leaves seat in classroom or in other situations in which remaining seated is expected
(c) often runs about or climbs excessively in situations in which it is inappropriate (in adolescents or adults, may be limited to subjective feelings of restlessness)
(d) often has difficulty playing or engaging in leisure activities quietly
(e) is often "on the go" or often acts as if "driven by a motor"
(f) often talks excessively

Impulsivity

(g) often blurts out answers before questions have been completed
(h) often has difficulty awaiting turn

(i) often interrupts or intrudes on others (e.g., butts into conversations or games)

B. Some hyperactive-impulsive or inattentive symptoms that caused impairment were present before age 7 years.

C. Some impairment from the symptoms is present in two or more settings (e.g., at school [or work] and at home).

D. There must be clear evidence of clinically significant impairment in social, academic, or occupational functioning.

Diagnostic Criteria for Conduct Disorder

A. A repetitive and persistent pattern of behavior in which the basic rights of others or major age-appropriate societal norms or rules are violated, as manifested by the presence of three (or more) of the following criteria in the past 12 months, with at least one criterion present in the past 6 months:

Aggression to people and animals

(1) often bullies, threatens, or intimidates others
(2) often initiates physical fights
(3) has used a weapon that can cause serious physical harm to others (e.g., a bat, brick, broken bottle, knife, gun)
(4) has been physically cruel to people
(5) has been physically cruel to animals
(6) has stolen while confronting a victim (e.g., mugging, purse snatching, extortion, armed robbery)
(7) has forced someone into sexual activity

Destruction of property

(8) has deliberately engaged in fire setting with the intention of causing serious damage
(9) has deliberately destroyed others' property (other than by fire setting)

Deceitfulness or theft

(10) has broken into someone else's house, building, or car
(11) often lies to obtain goods or favors or to avoid obligations (i.e., "cons" others)
(12) has stolen items of nontrivial value without confronting a victim (e.g., shoplifting, but without breaking and entering; forgery)

Serious violations of rules

(13) often stays out at night despite parental prohibitions, beginning before age 13 years
(14) has run away from home overnight at least twice while living in parental or parental surrogate home (or once without returning for a lengthy period)
(15) is often truant from school, beginning before age 13 years

B. The disturbance in behavior causes clinically significant impairment in social, academic, or occupational functioning.

Diagnostic Criteria for Oppositional Defiant Disorder

A. A pattern of negativistic, hostile, and defiant behavior lasting at least 6 months, during which four (or more) of the following are present:

(1) often loses temper
(2) often argues with adults
(3) often actively defies or refuses to comply with adults' requests or rules
(4) often deliberately annoys people
(5) often blames others for his or her mistakes or misbehavior
(6) is often touchy or easily annoyed by others
(7) is often angry and resentful
(8) is often spiteful or vindictive

Note: Consider a criterion met only if the behavior occurs more frequently than is typically observed in individuals of comparable age and developmental level.

B. The disturbance in behavior causes clinically significant impairment in social, academic, or occupational functioning.

Source: American Psychiatric Association, 2000.

Changes in Ranking of 16 Nations on Science and Math Knowledge Between Fourth and Eighth Grades (Chapter 12)

Only high-scoring nations are included in these rankings. Many other countries, such as Portugal and Iran, rank much lower. Still others, including many nations in Latin America and Africa, do not administer the tests on which these rankings are based. Identical rankings indicate ties between nations on overall scores. International comparisons are always difficult and often unfair, but two general conclusions have been confirmed: Children in East Asian countries tend to be high achievers in math and science, and children in the United States lose ground between the fourth and eighth grades.

Science Knowledge				Math Knowledge			
Nation	Rank in Fourth Grade	Rank in Eighth Grade	Change in Rank	Nation	Rank in Fourth Grade	Rank in Eighth Grade	Change in Rank
Korea	1	2	−1	Korea	1	3	−2
Japan	2	3	−1	Singapore	1	1	0
Netherlands	3	5	−2	Japan	3	2	+1
Australia	5	9	−4	Hong Kong	4	4	0
United States	5	11	−6	Netherlands	5	8	−3
Austria	5	6	−1	Czech Republic	6	5	+1
Czech Republic	7	4	+3	Austria	10	11	+1
Canada	8	10	−2	Hungary	8	6	+2
Singapore	8	1	+7	Australia	7	11	−1
England	10	6	+4	Ireland	10	9	+1
Hong Kong	11	11	0	United States	10	15	−5
Hungary	11	6	+5	Canada	12	9	+3
Ireland	13	11	+2	Israel	13	12	+1
Norway	14	11	+3	England	14	15	−1
New Zealand	14	11	+3	New Zealand	15	13	+2
Israel	16	16	0	Norway	16	13	+3

Source: Third International Mathematics and Science Study (TIMMS), 1998.

Changes in the Average Weekly Amount of Time Spent by 6- to 11-Year-Olds in Various Activities (Chapter 12)

Data can be presented graphically in many ways. The data given here were collected in the same way in 1981 and in 1997, so the changes are real (although the age cutoff in 1997 was 12, not 11). What do you think would be the best way to show this information? What is encouraging and what is problematic in the changes that you see? One possibility is shown below the table: The changes are presented as percentages in a bar graph.

Activity	Average Amount of Time Spent in Activity, per Week		Change in Time Spent
	In 1981	In 1997	
School	25 hrs, 17 min.	33 hrs, 52 min.	+8 hrs, 35 min.
Organized sports	3 hrs, 5 min.	4 hrs, 56 min.	+1 hr, 51 min.
Studying	1 hr, 46 min.	2 hrs, 50 min.	+1 hr, 4 min.
Reading	57 min.	1 hr, 15 min.	+18 min.
Being outdoors	1 hr, 17 min.	39 min.	−38 min.
Playing	12 hrs, 52 min.	10 hrs, 5 min.	−2 hrs, 47 min.
Watching TV	15 hrs, 34 min.	13 hrs, 7 min.	−2 hrs, 27 min.

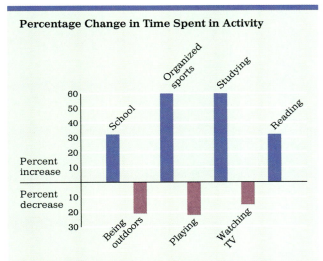

Percentage Change in Time Spent in Activity

Source: University of Michigan Institute for Social Research, Panel Study of Income Dynamics, Child Development Supplement, 1997.

Who Is Raising the Children? (Chapter 13)

Most children still live in households with a male/female couple, who may be the children's married or unmarried biological parents, grandparents, stepparents, foster parents, or adoptive parents. However, the proportion of households headed by single parents has risen—by 500 percent for single fathers and by almost 200 percent for single mothers. (In 2000, 52 percent of U.S. households had *no* children under age 18.)

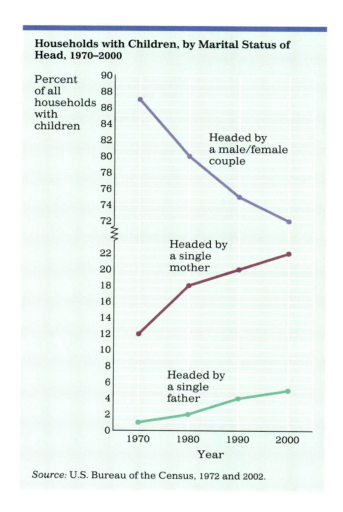

Households with Children, by Marital Status of Head, 1970–2000

Source: U.S. Bureau of the Census, 1972 and 2002.

Smoking Behavior Among U.S. High School Students, 1991–2001 (Chapter 14)

The data in these two tables reveal many trends. For example, do you see that African-American adolescents are much less likely to smoke than Hispanics or European-Americans, but that this racial advantage is decreasing? Do you see that white females smoked more than white males until 2001?

? *Observational Quiz* (see answer, page A-16): If we compare the 2001 data with only the 1991 data, the news about teen smoking is bad: The percentages of current smokers increased overall and for almost every group. However, what evidence is provided by the data that might encourage public-health workers?

Percentage of High School Students Who Reported Smoking Cigarettes

Smoking behavior	1991	1993	1995	1997	1999	2001
Lifetime (ever smoked)	70.1	69.5	71.3	70.2	70.4	63.9
Current (smoked at least once in past 30 days)	27.5	30.5	34.8	36.4	34.8	28.5
Current frequent (smoked 20 or more times in past 30 days)	12.7	13.8	16.1	16.7	16.8	13.8

Percentage of High School Students Who Reported Current Smoking, by Sex, Race/Ethnicity, and Grade

Characteristic	1991	1993	1995	1997	1999	2001
Sex						
Female	27.3	31.2	34.3	34.7	34.9	27.7
Male	27.6	29.8	35.4	37.7	34.7	29.2
Race/ethnicity						
White, non-Hispanic	30.9	33.7	38.3	39.7	38.6	31.9
Female	31.7	35.3	39.8	39.9	39.1	31.2
Male	30.2	32.2	37.0	39.6	38.2	32.7
Black, non-Hispanic	12.6	15.4	19.2	22.7	19.7	14.7
Female	11.3	14.4	12.2	17.4	17.7	14.3
Male	14.1	16.3	27.8	28.2	21.8	15.3
Hispanic	25.3	28.7	34.0	34.0	32.7	26.6
Female	22.9	27.3	32.9	32.3	31.5	26.0
Male	27.9	30.2	34.9	35.5	34.0	27.2
Grade						
9th	23.2	27.8	31.2	33.4	27.6	23.9
10th	25.2	28.0	33.1	35.3	34.7	26.9
11th	31.6	31.1	35.9	26.6	36.0	29.8
12th	30.1	34.5	38.2	39.6	42.8	35.2

Source: CDC, *Morbidity and Mortality Weekly Report,* May 17, 2002, p. 411.

Sexual Behaviors of U.S. High School Students: State-by-State Variations (Chapter 15)

These percentages, as high as they are, are actually lower than they were in the early 1990s. The data in this table reflect responses from students in the 9th to 12th grades. When only high school seniors are surveyed, the percentages are higher. In every state, more than half of all high school seniors have had sexual intercourse, and about 25 percent have had four or more sex partners.

State	Ever had sexual intercourse (%)			First sexual intercourse before age 13 (%)			Four or more sex partners during lifetime (%)			Currently sexually active* (%)			Currently abstinent (%)		
	Female	Male	Total	Female	Male	Total	Female	Male	Total	Female	Male	Total	Female	Male	Total
Arkansas	53.3	57.8	55.5	5.2	14.3	14.3	15.7	25.1	20.5	40.6	39.9	40.2	23.9	30.6	27.4
Colorado	39.9	44.3	42.3	3.9	7.8	6.0	10.0	15.3	12.7	29.9	28.2	29.1	25.0	36.5	31.3
Delaware	49.4	56.1	52.7	4.5	15	9.6	12.8	20.9	16.7	38.4	39.9	39.2	22.2	28.8	25.5
Florida	46.2	53.5	49.9	4.7	13.2	9.1	11.1	21.3	16.3	34.5	38.1	36.4	25.5	28.5	27.0
Hawaii	35.5	30.8	33.6	3.5	6.0	4.8	8.7	7.7	8.4	24.5	21.4	23.2	31.3	30.3	31.0
Maine	48.7	43.6	46.3	3.6	5.0	4.4	10.0	9.8	10.1	38.6	30.5	34.6	20.9	29.3	24.7
Massachusetts	42.3	46.3	44.3	2.5	8.0	5.3	9.4	14.6	12.0	33.1	31.9	32.5	21.9	31.7	26.9
Michigan	42.2	38.0	40.3	3.3	6.3	4.9	9.7	11.1	10.5	33.4	26.0	29.9	20.5	31.3	25.5
Mississippi	58.5	62.9	60.6	6.4	22.1	14.0	17.6	34.2	25.5	44.8	45.0	44.9	23.2	28.2	25.6
Missouri	49.6	52.2	50.9	3.0	10.0	6.5	14.7	19.3	17.0	38.9	38.7	38.8	21.5	25.7	23.7
Montana	43.7	43.9	43.9	3.5	7.0	5.3	13.2	14.4	13.8	32.0	29.3	30.7	27.0	33.1	30.2
Nevada	48.3	50.0	49.1	5.1	11.6	8.3	14.2	18.9	16.6	36.7	32.6	34.6	24.1	34.4	29.3
New Jersey	42.2	52.6	47.4	3.2	12.0	7.6	10.7	23.2	16.8	34.4	37.7	36.1	18.3	28.1	23.6
North Dakota	40.9	43.0	42.0	2.2	6.3	4.4	12.2	11.6	12.1	31.0	30.4	30.8	23.9	29.4	26.7
South Carolina	50.3	60.0	55.0	6.7	20.8	13.6	15.9	27.8	21.7	37.7	41.7	39.7	25.0	29.9	27.6
South Dakota	38.3	41.7	40.0	1.9	5.1	3.5	10.4	12.7	11.5	29.7	28.9	29.4	23.0	30.9	27.0
Tennessee	48.7	53.8	51.3	5.9	12.2	9.0	12.4	20.2	16.3	36.9	35.5	36.2	24.0	33.9	29.3
Texas	47.7	52.9	50.4	4.2	10.7	7.5	12.8	19.8	16.4	36.1	36.1	36.2	24.1	31.4	27.8
Wisconsin	43.9	34.7	39.3	3.0	4.9	4.0	11.5	8.9	10.2	33.5	24.8	29.1	23.9	28.6	25.9
Wyoming	45.9	46.9	46.5	3.6	6.7	5.2	13.4	14.1	13.8	34.0	31.7	32.9	25.8	32.4	29.1

*Active in 3 months prior to survey.
Source: National Center for Chronic Disease Prevention and Health Promotion, Youth Risk Behavior Surveillance System: http://apps.nccd.cdc.gov/YRBSS/ChargeByQuestionV.asp?Cat-4, updated May 29, 2003.

!Answer to Observational Quiz (from page A-15): The main piece of evidence is that the 2001 numbers are much better than those for 1997 and 1999, so the recent trends offer hope. Since cigarette prices skyrocketed and public-service announcements against smoking increased during those years, teenagers may be thinking twice before lighting up. Notice that the percentage of high school students who have never smoked has also increased—another hopeful sign.

United States Homicide Victim and Offender Rates, by Race and Gender, Ages 14–17 (Chapter 16)

Teenage boys are more often violent offenders than victims. The ratio of victimization to offense has varied for teenage girls over the years. The good news is that rates have decreased dramatically over the past ten years for every category of adolescents—male and female, black and white. (Similar declines are apparent for Asian- and Hispanic-Americans.) The bad news is that rates are still higher in the United States than in any other developed nation.

Homicide Victimization Rates per 100,000 Population for 14- to 17-Year-Olds

	Male			Female	
Year	White	Black		White	Black
1976	3.7	24.6		2.2	6.4
1981	4.4	23.6		2.4	6.2
1986	4.2	27.4		2.3	6.6
1991	8.7	73.6		2.6	9.6
1996	8.4	53.3		2.1	8.9
2000	4.1	25.7		1.4	4.5

Source: U.S. Bureau of Justice Statistics, 2004.
Tabulations based on FBI Supplementary Homicide Reports and U.S. Census Bureau, Current Population Reports.

Estimated Homicide Offending Rates per 100,000 Population for 14- to 17-Year-Olds

	Male			Female	
Year	White	Black		White	Black
1976	10.4	72.4		1.3	10.3
1981	10.9	73.1		1.3	8.6
1986	12.3	72.2		1.1	5.6
1991	21.9	199.1		1.3	12.1
1996	17.4	134.8		1.7	7.8
2000	7.9	62.8		1.0	4.9

Source: U.S. Bureau of Justice Statistics, 2004.
Tabulations based on FBI Supplementary Homicide Reports and U.S. Census Bureau, Current Population Reports. Rates include both known perpetrators and estimated share of unidentified perpetrators.

All the charts, graphs, and tables in this Appendix offer readers the opportunity to analyze raw data and draw their own conclusions. The same information may be presented in a variety of ways. On this page, you can create your own bar graph or line graph, depicting some noteworthy aspect of the data presented in the three tables. First, consider all the possibilities the tables offer by answering these six questions:

1. Are white male or female teenagers more likely to be victims of homicide?
2. These are annual rates. How many African-Americans in 1,000 were likely to commit homicide in 2000?
3. Which age group is *most* likely to commit homicide?
4. Which age group is *least* likely to be victims of homicide?
5. Which age group is *almost equally* likely to be either perpetrators or victims of homicide?
6. Of the four groups of adolescents, which has shown the greatest decline in rates of both victimization and perpetration of homicide over the past decade? Which has shown the least decline?

Answers: 1. Boys—at least twice as often. 2. Less than one (actually, only 0.36, if boys and girls are averaged together.) 3. 18–24. 4. 0–13. 5. 25–34. 6. Black males had the greatest decline, and white females had the least (but these two groups have always been highest and lowest, respectively, in every year).
Now—use the grid provided at right to make your own graph.

Overall Rate of Homicide by Age, 1999, United States (Chapter 16)

Late adolescence and early adulthood are the peak times for murders—both as victims and offenders. The question for developmentalists is whether something changes before age 18 to decrease the rates in young adulthood.

Age group	Victims (per 100,000 in age group)	Killers (per 100,000 in age group)
0–13	1.4	0.1
14–17	4.7	9.3
18–24	14.9	27.3
25–34	10.2	11.6
35–49	5.7	4.9
50+	2.5	1.5

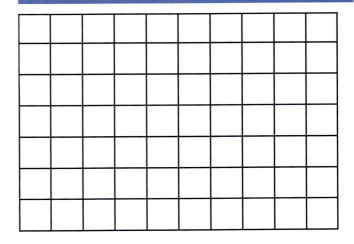

Remaining Childless Longer (Chapter 17)

Women Who Have Not Given Birth, by Age Group and Cohort

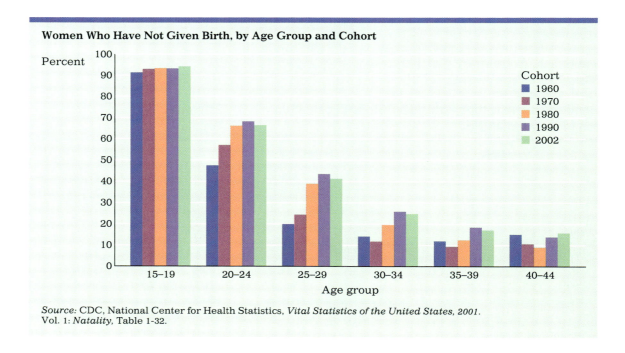

Source: CDC, National Center for Health Statistics, *Vital Statistics of the United States, 2001.*
Vol. 1: *Natality,* Table 1-32.

Education Affects Income (Chapter 18)

Although there is some debate about the cognitive benefits of college education, there is no doubt about the financial benefits. No matter what a person's ethnicity or gender, an associate's degree more than doubles his or her income compared to that of someone who has not completed high school.

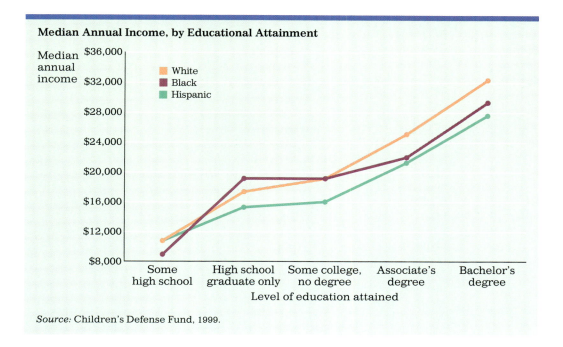

Median Annual Income, by Educational Attainment

Source: Children's Defense Fund, 1999.

Child Support Enforcement, by State, 2002 (Chapter 19)

State	Number of cases	Percent with court order	Percent with collection	Rank
Alabama	259,413	66.2	47.8	42
Alaska	46,385	82.9	53.8	23
Arizona	237,710	66.4	44.5	45
Arkansas	131,109	78.5	50.3	31
California	1,906,364	75.3	42.4	41
Colorado	134,387	83.5	55.0	20
Connecticut	206,731	64.3	55.0	35
Delaware	54,132	70.3	60.7	25
District of Columbia	107,951	29.7	48.0	50
Florida	669,165	65.2	56.4	34
Georgia	476,456	68.2	49.7	38
Hawaii	94,787	59.2	51.1	44
Idaho	79,772	78.6	55.4	24
Illinois	865,936	40.8	39.1	49
Indiana	311,058	70.6	48.5	37
Iowa	170,885	87.8	59.1	9
Kansas	141,158	63.9	55.1	36
Kentucky	312,494	70.0	52.8	33
Louisiana	265,642	67.4	56.4	32
Maine	65,084	87.2	57.8	12
Maryland	309,645	68.6	62.0	26
Massachusetts	245,921	71.2	59.7	27
Michigan	977,654	76.2	59.4	21
Minnesota	240,371	78.0	73.0	6
Mississippi	290,044	49.8	49.5	47
Missouri	390,552	78.9	50.7	30
Montana	40,104	83.1	58.5	15
Nebraska	98,137	76.0	66.5	11
Nevada	94,417	NA	47.0	NA
New Hampshire	37,391	82.0	65.5	8
New Jersey	340,875	78.9	65.0	10
New Mexico	70,294	47.5	46.8	47
New York	899,276	73.1	65.1	17
North Carolina	426,096	73.2	61.3	22
North Dakota	31,113	84.8	71.6	3
Ohio	901,429	71.4	66.8	16
Oklahoma	140,798	69.7	46.5	40
Oregon	246,669	66.9	60.4	29
Pennsylvania	589,847	83.0	74.7	2
Rhode Island	70,085	51.2	61.1	43
South Carolina	224,971	66.7	49.5	39
South Dakota	42,724	92.0	67.7	1
Tennessee	350,470	56.5	50.4	46
Texas	951,631	69.0	59.9	28
Utah	74,795	85.1	58.6	13
Vermont	24,344	85.8	66.3	7
Virginia	361,504	80.2	59.0	18
Washington	302,812	91.0	64.0	4
West Virginia	115,766	74.9	62.1	19
Wisconsin	339,882	79.0	72.7	5
Wyoming	39,299	82.7	60.0	14
United States	**15,805,535**	**70.5**	**57.5**	

Source: Office of Child Support Enforcement, Fiscal Year 2002 Annual Statistical Report, November 2003, Department of Health and Human Services, Administration for Children and Families, Office of Child Support Enforcement, Division of Planning, Research and Evaluation. (http://www.acf.dhhs.gov/programs/cse/pubs/2003/reports/annual_statistical_report, accessed January 30, 2004).

Dying of Lung Cancer: It's Not Just Genes and Gender (Chapter 20)

For lung cancer as well as most other diseases, the male death rate is markedly higher than the female death rate in the United States. Moreover, the death rate for African-Americans is almost twice the average, and for Asian-Americans it is almost half the average. Genes and gender do not explain these discrepancies, however. As you can see, white women are at greater risk than Hispanic or Native American men, and the rate for black men went down as the rate for some other groups rose. (These are "age-adjusted" rates, which means that they reflect the fact that more Asians reach old age and fewer Native Americans do. In other words, the sex and ethnic differences shown here are real—not artifacts of the age distribution.)

Lung Cancer Death Rates, by Ethnicity and Gender

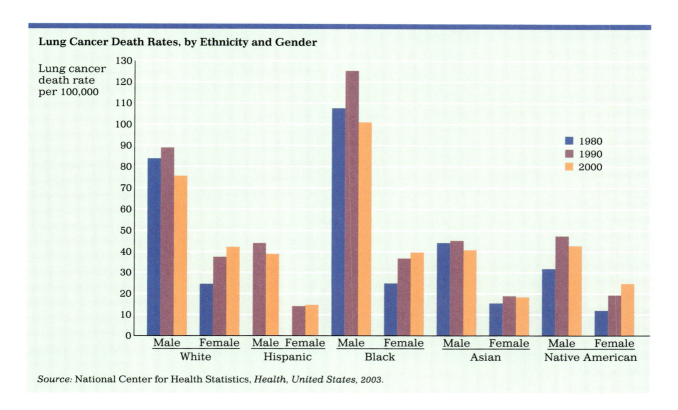

Source: National Center for Health Statistics, *Health, United States, 2003.*

Obesity in the United States, 1976 to 2000 (Chapter 20)

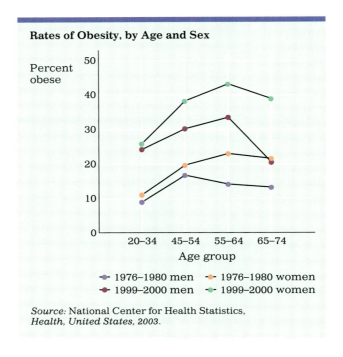

Rates of Obesity, by Age and Sex

Source: National Center for Health Statistics, *Health, United States, 2003.*

Obesity Around the World, 1976 to 2000 (Chapter 20)

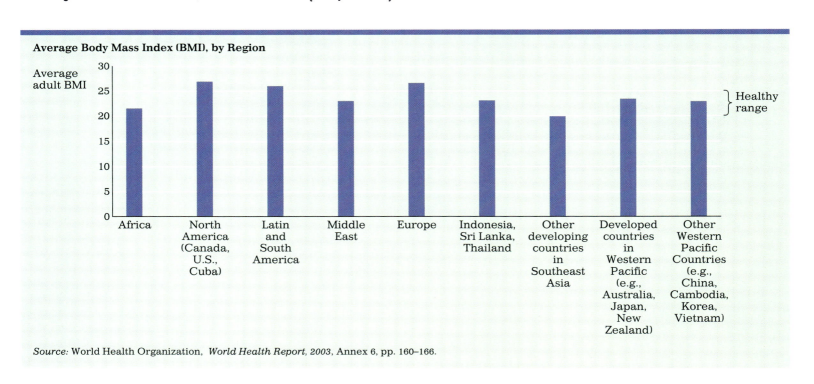

Average Body Mass Index (BMI), by Region

Source: World Health Organization, *World Health Report, 2003*, Annex 6, pp. 160–166.

Continuing Education (Chapter 21)

This chart shows the percentage of adults in certain countries who are enrolled in continuing education related to their work, either through their employment or on their own.

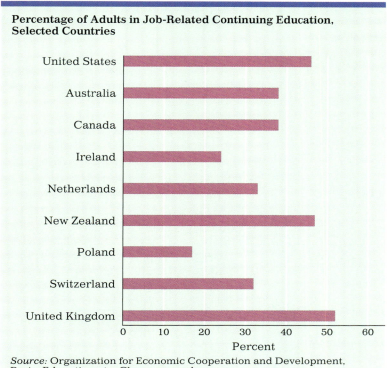

Percentage of Adults in Job-Related Continuing Education, Selected Countries

Source: Organization for Economic Cooperation and Development, Paris, *Education at a Glance*, annual.

Grandparents Parenting Grandchildren (Chapter 22)

In the 2000 census, 3.9 percent of U.S. households included grandparents living with grandchildren. In 40 percent of those households, 2.42 million grandparents were directly responsible for the care of their grandchildren.

Characteristics of U.S. Grandparent–Grandchild Households

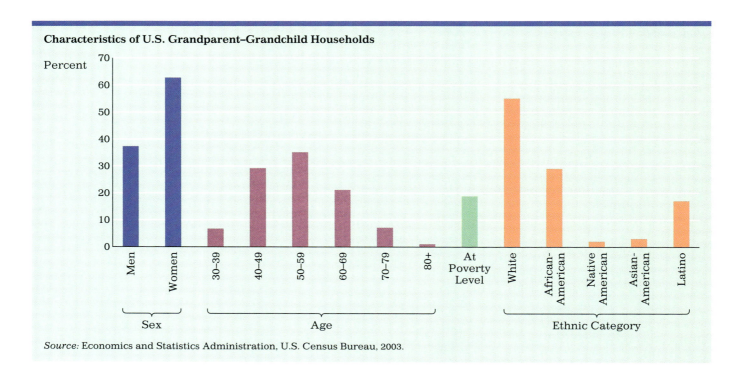

Source: Economics and Statistics Administration, U.S. Census Bureau, 2003.

Disability Rates (Chapter 23)

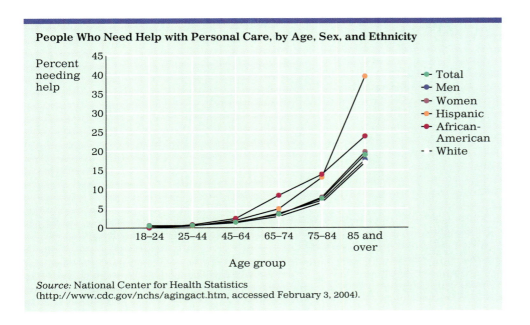

People Who Need Help with Personal Care, by Age, Sex, and Ethnicity

Source: National Center for Health Statistics
(http://www.cdc.gov/nchs/agingact.htm, accessed February 3, 2004).

Alzheimer's Disease Worldwide (Chapter 24)

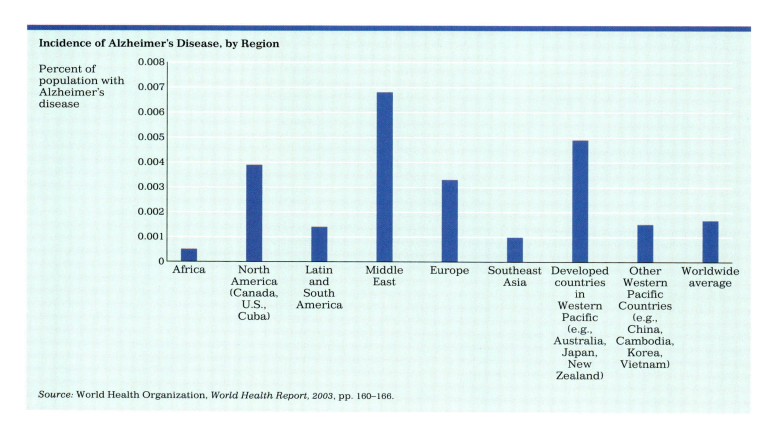

Incidence of Alzheimer's Disease, by Region

Percent of population with Alzheimer's disease

Source: World Health Organization, *World Health Report, 2003*, pp. 160–166.

Suicide Rates in the United States (Chapter 25)

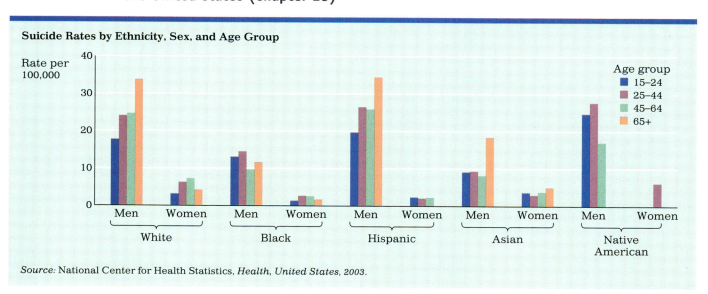

Suicide Rates by Ethnicity, Sex, and Age Group

Rate per 100,000

Age group
- 15–24
- 25–44
- 45–64
- 65+

Source: National Center for Health Statistics, *Health, United States, 2003*.

Suicide Rates Worldwide (Chapter 25)

Suicide Rates for Selected Countries, by Sex

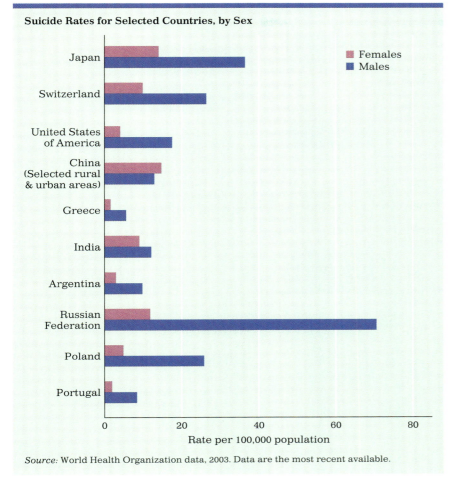

Source: World Health Organization data, 2003. Data are the most recent available.

Aging Around the World (Chapter 25)

Elderly Population in Selected Countries, by Gender

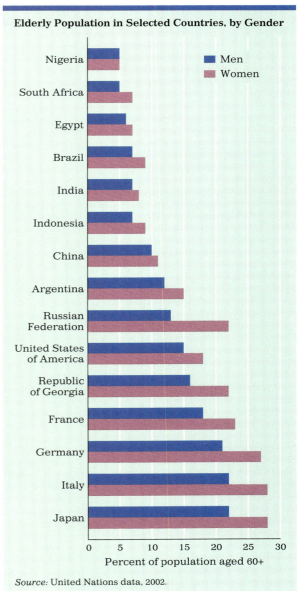

Source: United Nations data, 2002.

People Using Hospice Care, by Age, Sex, and Diagnosis (Epilogue)

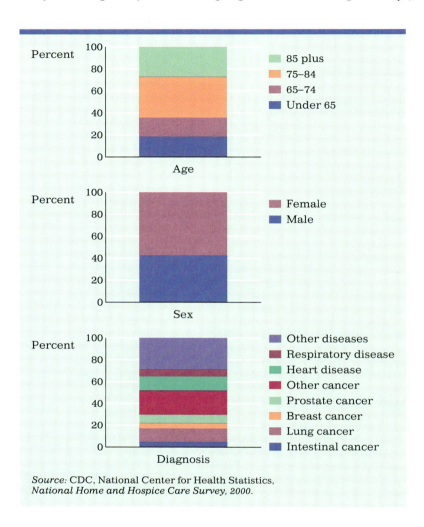

Source: CDC, National Center for Health Statistics, *National Home and Hospice Care Survey, 2000*.

Appendix B
More About Research Methods

The first part of this appendix details some pointers on how to go about gathering more information about human development. The second part expands on Chapter 1's discussion of ways to ensure that research is valid.

Learning More

There are many ways to deepen your understanding of human development, including thinking about your own life and watching the children and adults around you with careful attention to details of expression and behavior. Indeed, such thoughts may become second nature, as you realize how much there is to learn through reflection and observation. But more systematic research, and further book learning, bring insight and understanding that make development even more intriguing.

Library Research

To learn more about a particular topic, focus on readings that are current and scholarly. For instance, if something in a popular magazine or newspaper catches your attention, remember that the writer may have sensationalized, exaggerated, or biased the reporting. You might first check what this textbook says about the topic, and then look at the references cited.

This can begin effective library research. Start with recently published material and then find material from the bibliographies. In addition, there are two collections of abstracts that review current articles from a variety of developmental journals:

- *Psychscan: Developmental Psychology* is published four times a year by the American Psychological Association and includes abstracts of articles from almost 40 scholarly journals, from *Adolescence* to *Psychological Review*. Volume 24 covers the year 2004.
- *Child Development Abstracts and Bibliography* is published three times a year by the Society for Research in Child Development and is organized topically by author. Included are not only journal articles in biology, cognition, education, personality, and theory but also reviews of major books in the field. Volume 78 covers the year 2004. The online address is www.srcd.org.

"Handbooks," which summarize and evaluate research on various topics, are published every ten years or so. The most recent one in child development is in four volumes: *Handbook of Child Psychology* (1998), William Damon (Ed.), New York: Wiley. Relevant handbooks for adulthood and aging include *Handbook of Aging and the Social Sciences* (2001), Robert H. Binstock and Linda K. George (Eds.), San Diego, CA: Academic Press, and *Handbook of Midlife Development* (2001), Margie E. Lachman (Ed.), New York: Wiley.

To find the most current research, even before it appears in these abstracts and handbooks, look at the most recent issues of the many research journals. The three that cover all three domains (biosocial, cognitive, and psychosocial) are *Developmental Psychology*, published by the American Psychological Association (750 First St., NE, Washington, DC 20002); *Child Development*, published by

Blackwell Publishers for the Society for Research in Child Development (Blackwell Publishers: 350 Main St., Malden, MA 02138; Society for Research in Child Development: University of Michigan, 505 East Huron St., Suite 301, Ann Arbor, MI 48104-1522); and *Human Development*, published by Karger (P.O. Box CH-4009, Basel, Switzerland). These three journals differ somewhat in the types of articles and studies they publish; together they provide a good overview of development.

These suggestions are only a start. There are hundreds of other professional journals that focus on one aspect or another of human development; many are devoted to a particular age group or topic or to research from a particular nation. All of us who are professors hope you begin with one topic and soon lose track of time and subject, finding your interest drawn from one journal or book to another.

Using the Internet

The Internet is a boon for every student, from the novice just beginning to learn about a particular issue to the experienced researcher who wants today's data about an arcane topic. However, using the Internet carries certain risks. To maximize the benefits and reduce the costs of your Internet research, keep the following two advantages and two disadvantages in mind.

Advantages

It's All There Virtually everything you might want to know is on the Internet, not only massive government statistics carefully collected and tallied but also very personal accounts of rare maladies. Every journal has a Web site, with tables of contents, usually abstracts of articles, and often full texts. Photos, charts, quizzes, ongoing experiments, newspapers from around the world, videos, and much more are available at the click of a mouse.

Quick and Easy Just by sitting in front of a computer, any time of the day or night, you can research almost any topic. All libraries (especially those in colleges) have computers hooked up to the World Wide Web and librarians who can help you get started. Other students, co-workers, family members, and even strangers are experts in one aspect or another of Internet use, and usually they are flattered to be asked for specific suggestions. On your own, alone with your personal computer, you can access the Web and teach yourself everything you need to know, using on-line tutorials, help buttons, and exploration. This last route takes the most time, but some people learn best by teaching themselves— and do not get discouraged by the inevitable frustration when a particular tactic leads to a dead end.

Disadvantages

There's Too Much You can spend hours sifting through information that turns out to be useless, trash, or tangential. Directories (which list general topics or areas and then move you step by step in the direction you choose) and search engines (which give you all the sites that use a particular word or words) sort information to help you find what you want. Each directory or search engine is different, and each provides somewhat different lists; none provides only the most comprehensive and accurate sites. You can take advantage of several search engines at once by using a metasearch engine (such as www://metacrawler.com or www://dogpile.com), but here, too, the selection process may not yield exactly what you want. With experience and help, you will get better at choosing the best sites for you, but resign yourself to sorting through some junk no matter what you do.

From Quality to Quackery Anybody can put anything on the Web. There is no evaluation of bias, or even of evil; racist hate groups' Web sites and explicit child pornography abound on the Internet. You must evaluate and sift for yourself. Make sure you have several divergent sources for every "fact" you find; consider who put the information on the Internet and for what reason. As the author of a very useful book on psychology on the Web explains: "There is no such thing as a truly free lunch, and there is no such thing as truly neutral information" (Varnhagen, 2002).

Imagine going to your local newsstand and buying a copy of every magazine and newspaper it carries. Then imagine blindly picking one—and reading it uncritically, as if it were the whole truth. You might be lucky and find a publication that is fairly objective, but more often you will find one that was designed for a particular audience that advocates a particular point of view—pro-gun, pro-environment, pro-sex, pro-Catholic, pro-Conservative, and so on. Or you might find one that assumes that sailing or traveling or crossword puzzles or whatever is the most important activity known to humankind. The Internet has the same problem, only much worse. Every controversial issue in development has several sites that advocate radically opposite viewpoints; often they do not even suggest that there might be another side to the issue.

The Bottom Line

What these advantages and disadvantages come down to is that everyone will find the Internet useful for every topic, but anyone can waste time and be led astray. If you use the Web for research, also check print resources and more experienced researchers.

If you write a paper using Internet resources, bear in mind that massive plagiarism and prejudiced perspectives are common problems. Cite every source you use (so your reader can check your references) and evaluate objectivity, validity, and credibility even more carefully than you do for print resources. Expect your readers or your professors to be suspicious of Internet-based papers, and allay their fears by making your sources explicit and using published materials as well as electronic ones.

To help you get started, here are ten Internet addresses. They are all useful, but always remember to read with a critical eye.

- **www.worthpublishers.com/berger**   Includes links to Web sites, quizzes, PowerPoint slides, and activities keyed to every chapter of the textbook.
- **http://www.psych.umn.edu/psylabs/mtfs/**   Describes the findings and ongoing work of the Minnesota Twin Family Study, which seeks to identify the genetic and environmental influences on the development of psychological traits.
- **http://embryo.soad.umich.edu**   The Multidimensional Human Embryo site presents MRI images of a human embryo at various stages of development, accompanied by brief explanations.
- **www.cdipage.com**   A useful site, with links and articles on child development and information on common childhood psychological disorders.
- **http://www.piaget.org/index.html**   The Jean Piaget Society is an international, interdisciplinary organization devoted to "exploring the nature of the developmental construction of human knowledge." Some information about Piaget and his theories is provided, along with references and links to other sites.
- **http://education.indiana.edu/cas/adol/adol.html**   Adolescence Directory Online (ADOL) is an electronic guide to information on adolescent issues. It is a service of the Center for Adolescent Studies at Indiana University.

■ **http://www.nih.gov/nia/**　National Institutes on Aging site includes information on current research on aging.

■ **http://www.alz.org/**　Home page for the Alzheimer's Association contains links to current research, support information, and excellent visual resources on this disease.

■ **http://www.usc.edu/isd/locations/science/gerontology/web_resources.htm**　This directory, sponsored by the University of Southern California, is a clearinghouse for information on aging issues.

■ **http://www.psychREF.com**　Contains an index of references in psychology. Not all of them are relevant to human development, but almost every topic in this text is referenced on this Web site.

Ways to Make Research More Valid

As emphasized throughout this text, the study of development is a science. Social scientists use many methods to make their research more objective and therefore more valid. Several basic techniques are described in Chapter 1, including observation and experiments, correlation and statistical significance, independent and dependent variables, and cross-sectional, longitudinal, and cross-sequential research designs. Six additional terms or techniques pertaining to the validity of research are described here. Understanding them will help you evaluate research read about on the Internet, from library reading, or in textbooks.

Population and Participants

population The entire group of individuals who are of particular concern in a scientific study, such as all the children of the world or all newborns who weigh less than 3 pounds.

participants The people who are studied in a research project.

The entire group of people about whom a scientist wants to learn is called the **population.** Generally, a research population is quite large—not usually the world's entire population of 6 billion, but perhaps all the 4 million babies born in the United States last year, or all the 500,000 Japanese currently over age 65, or even all the 70,000 low-income fifth-graders attending New York City public schools in 2004. The particular individuals who are studied in a specific research project are called the **participants.** Typically, the participants reflect the characteristics of the population. Indeed, every published study reports who the participants were and how they did or did not reflect the population.

Sample Size

sample A group of individuals drawn from a specified population. A sample might be the low-birthweight babies born in four particular hospitals that are representative of all hospitals.

To make statements about people in general, scientists study particular participants chosen from the larger population. Each group of research participants, called a **sample,** must be large enough to ensure that if a few extreme cases happen to be included, they do not distort the statistical picture the sample gives of the population. Suppose, for instance, that researchers want to know the average age at which children begin to walk. Since they cannot include every infant in their study, they choose a sample of infants, determine the age of walking for each subject in the sample, and then calculate the sample average. If the sample is typical, the average walking age will be very close to the average for the entire infant population.

sample size The number of individuals who are being studied in a single sample in a research project.

The importance of an adequate **sample size** can be seen if we assume, for the moment, that one of the infants in the sample had an undetected disability and did not walk until age 24 months. Assume also that all the other infants walked at 12 months, the current norm. If the sample size was smaller than 10 infants, then one late walker would add more than a month to the age at which the "average" child is said to walk; but if the sample contained more than 500 children, the one abnormally late walker would not change the results by one day.

Representative Sample

Data collected from one group of participants may not be valid (that is, applicable and accurate) for other people who are different in some significant way, such as gender or ethnic background. Thus, every sample should be a **representative sample**—that is, should consist of people who are typical of the population the researchers wish to learn about. In a study of the average age of walking, for example, the sample population should reflect—in terms of male/female ratio, socioeconomic and ethnic background, and other characteristics—the entire population of infants. Ideally, other factors might be taken into consideration as well. For instance, if there is some evidence that first-born children walk earlier than later-born children, the sample should also be representative of the population's birth order.

The importance of representative sampling is revealed by its absence in two classic studies of age of walking for infants in the United States (Gesell, 1926; Shirley, 1933). Both studies used a relatively small and unrepresentative sample (all the children were European-American and most were middle-class). Partly because the samples were not representative of the general population of infants, both studies arrived at an average walking age of 15 months. This is 3 months later than the current U.S. norm, which was obtained through research on a much larger, more representative sample that included some low-SES children and some children of African and Latino descent—groups known to have high proportions of early-walking children. Another reason the earlier studies found babies walking 3 months later is that infants 80 years ago received much less physical stimulation, so their motor skill development was slowed down. In other words, infants actually did start to walk somewhat later then, perhaps at 13 months, which the researchers would have found if their sample had been representative.

representative sample A group of research participants who reflect the relevant characteristics of the larger population whose attributes are under study.

"Blind" Experimenters and Subjects

When experimenters have specific expectations about their research findings, those expectations can unintentionally affect the research results. As much as possible, therefore, the people who actually gather the data should be in a state of **"blindness"**—that is, they should be unaware of the purpose of the research.

Suppose we are testing the hypothesis that first-born infants walk sooner than later-borns. Ideally, the examiner who measures the participants' walking ability should not know the hypothesis or the infants' age or birth order. The subjects of the research should also be kept blind to its purpose, especially when the subjects are older children or adults, who might be influenced by their own expectations.

blindness A situation in which data gatherers and their research participants are deliberately kept ignorant of the purpose of the study so that they cannot unintentionally bias the results.

Operational Definitions

When planning a study, researchers establish operational definitions of whatever phenomena they will be examining. That is, they define each variable in terms of specific, observable behavior that can be measured with precision. Even a simple variable, such as whether or not a toddler is walking, requires an operational definition. For example, does "walking" include steps taken while holding onto someone or something, or must the steps be taken without support? Is one unsteady step enough to meet the definition, or must the infant be able to move a certain distance without faltering? For a study on age of first walking to be meaningful, the researchers would need to resolve questions like these through clear and thorough definitions. In fact, the usual operational definition of walking is "takes at least three steps without holding on."

Understandably, operational definitions become much harder to establish when personality or intellectual variables are being studied. It is nonetheless essential that researchers who are investigating, say, "aggression" or "sharing" or "reading" define the trait in terms that are as precise and measurable as possible. Obviously, the more accurately operational definitions describe the variables to be examined, the more objective and valid the results of the study will be.

Experimental and Comparison Groups

To test a hypothesis adequately in an experiment, researchers gather data on two samples that are similar in every important way except one. They compare an **experimental group**, which receives some special experimental treatment, and a **comparison group**, or *control group*, which is matched to the experimental group in every respect but one: It does not receive the experimental treatment.

Suppose a research team hypothesizes that infants who are provided with regular exercise to strengthen their legs begin to walk earlier than babies who do not receive such exercise. In other words, they hypothesize that the independent variable of exercise affects the dependent variable of walking. To find out if this hypothesis is true, the researchers would first select two representative samples of children and examine both groups to make sure they are equivalent in motor skills, such as the ability to roll over and sit up. Then one sample (the experimental group) would receive daily "workouts" devoted to leg-strengthening between, say, their sixth and twelfth months; the other sample (the comparison group) would get no special leg exercise. Results for the two groups would then be compared to test the hypothesis.

To put all this together with the techniques discussed in Chapter 1: A researcher might find 1,000 participants *(sample size)*, randomly chosen from all babies *(population)* born throughout the United States on a particular day *(representative sample)*, and visit them at home once a month from age 8 months to 18 months *(longitudinal research)*, seeing *(naturalistic observation)* which ones take three unaided steps *(operational definition)* at what age. Then, in follow-up research with a similar sample, two groups of participants would be matched on every variable except one: The parents of half the babies *(experimental group)* would be shown how to exercise their infants' legs *(independent variable)* and be encouraged, perhaps even paid, to do this every day. These babies' age of walking *(dependent variable)* could be compared with that of the non-exercised babies *(comparison group)* by a researcher who doesn't know *(blind)* which babies are in which group. If differences between the groups emerge, they could be analyzed to see if they exceed random variability (that is, they could be tested for *statistical significance*).

experimental group Research participants who experience the special condition or treatment that is the crux of the research.

comparison group Research participants who are comparable to those in the experimental group in every relevant dimension except that they do not experience the special condition or treatment that is the key aspect of the experiment. Also called a control group.

Appendix C
Suggestions for Research Assignments

The best way to study human development is to do some investigation yourself, not only by reading the textbook and expressing your ideas in speech and writing but also by undertaking some research of your own. Writing a term paper is the usual mode in most college courses: You and your instructor already know the importance of setting a deadline for each stage (topic selection, outline, first draft, final draft), of asking several readers to evaluate your paper (perhaps including other students or a professor), and of having the final version typed with references correctly cited and listed. Some suggestions for effective use of journals and the Internet are given in Appendix B.

The subject of human development is also ideal for more personal study, so suggestions for conducting observations, case studies, surveys, and experiments are offered here.

Learning Through Observation

Much can be learned by becoming more systematic in your observations of the adults and children around you. One way to begin is to collect observations of ten different children, in differing contexts, during the semester. Each profile should be approximately one page and should cover the following four items:

1. *Describe the physical and social context.* You will want to describe where you are, what day and time it is, and how many people you are observing. The weather and age and gender of those who are being observed might also be relevant. For example:

   Neighborhood playground on (street), at about 4 P.M. on (day, date), 30 children and 10 adults present.
       OR
   Supermarket at (location) on Saturday morning (day, date), about 20 shoppers present.

2. *Describe the specific child who is the focus of your attention.* Estimate age, gender, and so on of the target child and anyone else who interacts with the child. Do not ask the age of the child until after the observation, if at all. Your goal is to conduct a naturalistic observation that is unobtrusive. For example:

   Boy, about 7 years old, playing with four other boys, who seem a year or two older. All are dressed warmly (it is a cold day) in similar clothes.
       OR
   Girl, about 18 months old, in supermarket cart pushed by woman, about 30 years old. The cart is half full of groceries.

3. *Write down everything that the child does or says in three minutes.* (Use a watch with a second hand.) Record gestures, facial expressions, movements, and words. Accurate reporting is the goal, and three minutes becomes a surprisingly long time if you write down everything. For example:

   Child runs away about 20 feet, returns, and says, "Try to catch me." Two boys look at him, but they do not move. Boy frowns. He runs away and comes back in 10 seconds, stands about four feet away from the boys, and says, "Anyone want to play tag?" [And so on.]

OR

Child points to a package of Frosted Flakes cereal and makes a noise. (I could not hear if it was a word.) Mother says nothing and pushes the cart past the cereal. Child makes a whining noise, looks at the cereal, and kicks her left foot. Mother puts pacifier in child's mouth. [And so on.]

4. *Interpret what you just observed.* Is the child's behavior typical of children that age? Is the reaction of others helpful or not helpful? What values are being encouraged, and what skills are being mastered? What could have happened differently? This section is your opinion, but it must be based on the particulars you have just observed and on your knowledge of child development, ideally with specific reference to concepts (e.g., the first may be a rejected child; the second child's language development may not be encouraged).

Structuring a Case Study

A case study is more elaborate and detailed than an observation report. Select one child (ask your instructor if family members can be used), and secure written permission from the caregiver and, if the child is old enough, the child him- or herself. Explain that you are not going to report the name of the child, that the material is for your class, that the child or caregiver can stop the project at any time, and that they would be doing you a big favor in helping you learn about child development. Most people are quite happy to help in your education, if you explain this properly.

Gather Your Data

First, collect the information for your paper by using all the research methods you have learned. These methods include:

1. *Naturalistic Observation.* Ask the caregiver when the child is likely to be awake and active, and observe the child for an hour during this time. Try to be as unobtrusive as possible; you are not there to play with, or care for, the child. If the child wants to play, explain that you must sit and write for now and that you will play later.

    Write down, minute by minute, everything the child does and that others do with the child. Try to be objective, focusing on behavior rather than interpretation. Thus, instead of writing "Jennifer was delighted when her father came home, and he dotes on her," you should write "5:33: Her father opened the door, Jennifer looked up, smiled, said 'dada,' and ran to him. He bent down, stretched out his arms, picked her up, and said, 'How's my little angel?' 5:34: He put her on his shoulders, and she said, 'Giddy up, horsey.'"

    After your observation, summarize the data in two ways: (a) Note the percentage of time spent in various activities. For instance, "Playing alone, 15 percent; playing with brother, 20 percent; crying, 3 percent." (b) Note the frequency of various behaviors: "Asked adult for something five times; adult granted request four times. Aggressive acts (punch, kick, etc.) directed at brother, 2; aggressive acts initiated by brother, 6." Making notations like these will help you evaluate and quantify your observations. Also, note any circumstances that might have made your observation atypical (e.g., "Jenny's mother said she hasn't been herself since she had the flu a week ago," or "Jenny kept trying to take my pen, so it was hard to write").

    Note: Remember that a percentage can be found by dividing the total number of minutes spent on a specific activity by the total number of minutes you spent observing. For example, if, during your 45-minute observation, the child played by herself for periods of 2 minutes, 4 minutes, and 5 minutes, "playing alone" would total 11 minutes. Dividing 11 by 45 yields 0.244; thus the child spent 24 percent of the time playing alone.

2. *Informal interaction.* Interact with the child for at least half an hour. Your goal is to observe the child's personality and abilities in a relaxed setting. The particular activities you engage in will depend on the child's age and temperament. Most children enjoy playing games, reading books, drawing, and talking. Asking a younger child to show you his or her room and favorite toys is a good way to break the ice; asking an older child to show you the neighborhood can provide insights.

3. *Interview adults responsible for the child's care.* Keep these interviews loose and open-ended. Your goals are to learn (a) the child's history, especially any illnesses, stresses, or problems that might affect development; (b) the child's daily routine, including play patterns; (c) current problems that might affect the child; (d) a description of the child's temperament and personality, including special strengths and weaknesses.

    You are just as interested in adult values and attitudes as in the facts; therefore, you might concentrate on conversing during the interview, perhaps writing down a few words. Then write down all you remember as soon as the interview has been completed.

4. *Testing the child.* Assess the child's perceptual, motor, language, and intellectual abilities by using specific test items you have prepared in advance. The actual items you use will depend on the age of the child. For instance, you might test object permanence in a child between 6 and 24 months old; you would test conservation in a child between 3 and 9 years old. Likewise, testing language abilities might involve babbling with an infant, counting words per sentence with a preschooler, and asking a school-age child to make up a story.

Write Up Your Findings

Second, write the report, using the following steps:

1. Begin by reporting relevant background information, including the child's birth date and sex, age and sex of siblings, economic and ethnic background of the family, and the educational and marital status of the parents.

2. Describe the child's biosocial, cognitive, and psychosocial development, citing supporting data from your research to substantiate any conclusions you have reached. Do not simply transcribe your interview, test, or observation data, although you can attach your notes as an appendix, if you wish.

3. Predict the child's development in the next year, the next five years, and the next ten years. List the strengths in the child, the family, and the community that you think will foster optimal development. Also note whatever potential problems you see (either in the child's current behavior or in the family and community support system) that may lead to future difficulties for the child. Include discussion of the reasons, either methodological or theoretical, that your predictions may not be completely accurate.

Finally, show your report to a classmate (your instructor may assign you to a peer mentor) and ask if you have been clear in your description and predictions. Discuss the child with your classmate to see if you should add more details to your report. Your revised case study should be typed and given to your professor, who will evaluate it. If you wish, send me a copy (Professor Kathleen Berger, c/o Worth Publishers, 41 Madison Avenue, New York, NY 10010).

Experiments and Surveys

As you learned in Chapter 1, experiments and surveys are wonderful ways to learn more about development, but each study needs to be very carefully designed and undertaken to avoid bias and to ensure that all the ethical considerations are taken into account. Accordingly, I recommend that an experiment or survey be undertaken by a group of students, not by an individual. Listening carefully to other opinions, using more than one person to collect data, and checking with your professor before beginning the actual study are ways to make sure that your results have some validity.

If you do this, structure your work in such a way that everyone contributes and that contrary opinions are encouraged. (The normal human response is for everyone to agree with everyone else, but, as you learned in Chapter 15, seeking alternate, logical explanations can move an entire group forward to deeper, more analytic thought.) You might designate one person to be the critic, or your group might spend one day designing your study and another day finding problems with the design. (Some problems simply need to be recognized and acknowledged, but some of them can be fixed by changing the design.)

Specific topics for experiments or surveys depend on your group's interests and on your professor's requirements for the course. For ideas, check this book's Subject Index or Study Guide. Since development is multidisciplinary and multicontextual, almost any topic can be related to it. Just remember to consider theory and practice, change and continuity, social interaction and cultural impact . . . and then try to limit your initial experiment or survey to one small part of this fascinating, ever-changing subject!

Glossary

A

23rd pair The chromosome pair that, in humans, determines the zygote's (and hence the person's) sex, among other things.

achievement tests Measures of reading ability, math knowledge, science facts, writing skills, or any other subject matter that has actually been mastered.

activities of daily life (ADLs) Actions that are important to independent living, typically comprising five tasks: eating, bathing, toileting, dressing, and transferring from a bed to a chair. The inability to perform these tasks is a sign of frailty.

activity theory The view that elderly people need to remain active in a variety of social spheres—with relatives, friends, and community groups—and become withdrawn only unwillingly, as a result of ageism.

AD/HD (attention-deficit/hyperactivity disorder) A condition in which a child has great difficulty concentrating for more than a few moments at a time and, as a result, is inattentive, impulsive, and overactive.

adaptation The cognitive processes by which new information is taken in and responded to. Both assimilation and accommodation are kinds of adaptation.

ADD (attention-deficit disorder) A condition in which a child has great difficulty concentrating (but, unlike a hyperactive child, is not impulsive and overactive); the child may be prone to anxiety and depression and may seem lost in thought, spaced out, or distracted.

additive gene A gene that, through interaction with other genes, affects a specific trait (such as skin color or height).

adolescence The period of biological, cognitive, and psychosocial transition from childhood to adulthood, usually lasting a decade or so.

adolescence-limited offender A person whose criminal activity stops by age 21.

adolescent egocentrism A characteristic of adolescent thinking that sometimes leads young people to focus on themselves to the exclusion of others and to believe, for example, that their thoughts, feelings, and experiences are unique.

adoptive family A family that consists of one or more nonbiological children whom an adult individual or couple have voluntarily, legally, and permanently taken to raise as their own.

adrenal glands A pair of glands located above the kidneys that secrete the hormones epinephrine (adrenaline) and norepinephrine (noradrenaline), which help to arouse the body in time of stress.

affordance An opportunity for perception and interaction that is offered by people, places, and objects in the environment.

age of viability The age (about 22 weeks after conception) at which a fetus can survive outside the mother's uterus if specialized medical care is available.

ageism A term that refers to prejudice against the aged. Like racism and sexism, ageism works to prevent elderly people from being as happy and productive as they could be.

aggressive-rejected Referring to children who are actively rejected by their peer group because of their aggressive, confrontational behavior.

allele A slight, normal variation of a particular gene.

Alzheimer's disease (AD) The most common form of dementia, characterized by gradual deterioration of memory and personality and marked by plaques of B-amyloid protein and tangles in the brain. Alzheimer's disease is not part of the normal aging process.

analytic intelligence A form of intelligence that involves such mental processes as abstract planning, strategy selection, focused attention, and information processing, as well as verbal and logical skills.

androgyny A balance, within a person, of traditionally male and female psychological characteristics.

anorexia nervosa A serious eating disorder in which a person restricts eating to the point of emaciation and possible starvation. Most victims are high-achieving females in early puberty or early adulthood.

anoxia A lack of oxygen that, if prolonged, can cause brain damage or death.

antioxidants Compounds that nullify the effects of oxygen free radicals by forming a bond with their unattached oxygen electron.

antipathy A person's feelings of anger, distrust, dislike, or even hatred toward another.

antisocial Behaving in ways that are deliberately hurtful or destructive.

antithesis A proposition or statement of belief that opposes the thesis; the second stage of the process of dialectical thinking.

Apgar scale A means of quickly assessing a newborn's body functioning. The baby's color, heart rate, reflexes, muscle tone, and respiratory effort are scored (from 0 to 2) at one minute and five minutes after birth, and compared with an ideal for healthy babies (a perfect 10).

apprentice in thinking Vygotsky's term for the young child whose intellectual growth is stimulated and directed by older and more skilled members of society.

apprenticeship in thinking In sociocultural theory, the process by which novices develop cognitive competencies through interaction with more skilled members of the society, often parents or teachers, who act as tutors or mentors.

aptitude The potential to learn, or master, a particular skill or body of knowledge.

Asperger syndrome A set of less severe symptoms of autism, in which the individual has fairly normal speech and intelligence but severely impaired social interaction.

assisted reproductive technology (ART) The collective name for the various methods of medical intervention that can help infertile couples have children.

asthma A chronic inflammatory disorder of the airways.

attachment According to Ainsworth (1973), "an affectional tie that one person or animal forms between himself and another specific one—a tie that binds them together in space and endures over time."

authoritarian parenting Baumrind's term for a style of child rearing in which standards for proper behavior are high, misconduct is strictly punished, and parent–child communication is low.

authoritative parenting Baumrind's term for a style of child rearing in which the parents set limits and provide guidance for their child but are willing to listen to the child's ideas and to make compromises.

autism A pervasive developmental disorder marked by an inability to relate to other people in an ordinary way, by extreme self-absorption, and by an inability to learn normal speech.

automatization A process by which thoughts and actions are repeated in sequence so often that they become automatic, or routine, and no longer require much conscious thought.

autonomy versus shame and doubt Erikson's term for the second crisis of psychosocial development, in which toddlers either succeed or fail in gaining a sense of self-rule over their own actions and bodies.

average life expectancy The number of years the average newborn of a particular population group is likely to live. In humans, this age has tended to increase over time, primarily because fewer children die in infancy.

axon A nerve fiber that extends from a neuron and transmits electrical impulses from that neuron to the dendrites of other neurons.

B

B cells Cells manufactured in the bone marrow that create antibodies for isolating and destroying invading bacteria and viruses.

babbling The extended repetition of certain syllables, such as *ba-ba-ba,* that begins at about 6 or 7 months of age.

baby talk The high-pitched, simplified, and repetitive way adults speak to infants; also called *child-directed speech.*

base for exploration The caregiver's role in a relationship of secure attachment, in which the child freely ventures forth and returns.

behavior genetics The study of the genetic origins of psychological characteristics, such as personality patterns, psychological disorders, and intellectual abilities.

behavioral teratogens Teratogens that can harm the prenatal brain, affecting the future child's intellectual and emotional functioning.

behaviorism A grand theory of human development that focuses on the sequences and processes by which behavior is learned. (Also called *learning theory.*)

bickering Petty, peevish arguing, usually repeated and ongoing.

Big Five The five basic clusters of personality traits that remain quite stable throughout adulthood: extroversion, agreeableness, conscientiousness, neuroticism, and openness.

binocular vision The ability to focus the two eyes in a coordinated manner in order to see one image.

blended family A family that consists of two adults, the biological children from a previous union of one or both adults, and any children the adults have together.

body mass index (BMI) The ratio of a person's weight in kilograms divided by his or her height in meters squared.

bulimia nervosa An eating disorder in which the person, usually female, engages repeatedly in episodes of binge eating followed by purging through induced vomiting or use of laxatives.

bully-victim A bully who is or has been a victim of bullying. Also called *provocative victim.*

bullying A child's repeated, systematic efforts to inflict harm on another, particular child through physical, verbal, or social attacks.

bullying aggression Forceful behavior that takes the form of an unprovoked physical or verbal attack on another person, especially one who is unlikely to defend himself or herself.

burden of disease The total reduction in vitality that is caused by disease-induced disability in a given population.

butterfly effect The idea that a small action or event (such as the breeze created by the flap of a butterfly's wings) may set off a series of changes that culminate in a major event (such as a hurricane).

C

carrier A person whose genotype includes a gene that is not expressed in his or her phenotype but can be passed on to his or her children.

case study A research method in which one individual is studied intensively.

cataracts A common eye disease among the elderly involving a thickening of the lens; it can cause distorted vision if left untreated.

centration A characteristic of preoperational thought in which the young child focuses on one aspect of a situation to the exclusion of all others.

cerebral palsy A disorder that results from damage to the brain's motor centers. People with cerebral palsy have difficulty with muscle control, which can affect speech or other body movements.

cesarean section A surgical childbirth, in which incisions through the mother's abdomen and uterus allow the fetus to be removed quickly, instead of being delivered through the vagina.

child abuse Deliberate action that is harmful to a child's physical, emotional, or sexual well-being.

child maltreatment All intentional harm to, or avoidable endangerment of, anyone under 18 years of age.

child neglect Failure to meet a child's basic physical, educational, or emotional needs.

child sexual abuse Any activity in which an adult uses a child for his or her own sexual stimulation or pleasure—even if the use does not involve physical contact. Child pornography, fondling, and lewd comments by strangers are all examples of child sexual abuse.

child with special needs A child who, because of a physical or mental disability, requires extra help in order to learn.

chromosome A carrier of genes; one of the 46 molecules of DNA (in 23 pairs) that each cell of the body contains and that, together, contain all human genes.

classical conditioning The process by which a neutral stimulus becomes associated with a meaningful stimulus, so that the organism responds to the former stimulus as if it were the latter. (Also called *respondent conditioning*.)

classification The logical principle by which things are organized into groups (or categories or classes) according to some property they have in common.

cluster suicides Several suicides committed within the same group in a brief period of time.

code of ethics A set of moral principles that is formally adopted by a group or organization.

cognitive equilibrium In cognitive theory, a state of mental balance in which a person is able to reconcile new experiences with existing understanding.

cognitive theory A grand theory of human development that focuses on the structure and development of thinking, which shapes people's attitudes, beliefs, and behaviors.

cohabitation An arrangement in which a man and a woman live together in a committed sexual relationship but are not formally married.

cohort A group of people whose shared birth year, or decade, means that they travel through life together, experiencing the same major historical changes.

common couple violence A form of abuse in which one or both partners of a couple engage in outbursts of verbal and physical attack.

companionate grandparents Grandparents whose relationships with their children and grandchildren are characterized by independence and friendship, with visits occurring by the grandparents' choice.

comparison group In an experiment, the participants who are not given special treatment but who are similar to the experimental group in other relevant ways. (Also called the *control group*.)

compression of morbidity A limiting of the time a person spends ill or infirm, accomplished by postponing illness or, once morbidity occurs, hastening death.

concrete operational thought Piaget's term for the ability to reason logically about the things and events that one perceives.

conditioning According to behaviorism, any process in which a behavior is learned. See *classical conditioning* and *operant conditioning*.

conservation The principle that the amount of a substance is unaffected by changes in its appearance.

continuity theory The theory that each person experiences the changes of late adulthood and behaves toward others in much the same way as at earlier periods of life.

control processes That part of the information-processing system that regulates the analysis and flow of information. Memory and retrieval strategies, selective attention, metacognition, emotional regulation, and rules or strategies for problem solving are all useful control processes.

conventional moral reasoning Kohlberg's second level of moral reasoning, in which emphasis is placed on social rules.

corpus callosum A long, narrow strip of nerve fibers that connect the left and right hemispheres of the brain.

correlation A number indicating the degree of relationship between two variables, expressed in terms of the likelihood that one variable will (or will not) occur when the other variable does (or does not). A correlation is *not* an indication that one variable *causes* the other.

cortex The outer layer of the brain in humans and other mammals; it is the location of most thinking, feeling, and sensing.

creative intelligence A form of intelligence that involves the capacity to be intellectually flexible and innovative.

critical period In prenatal development, the time when a particular organ or other body part is most susceptible to teratogenic damage.

cross-sectional research A research method in which groups of people who differ in age but share other important characteristics are compared.

cross-sequential research A hybrid research method in which researchers first study several groups of people of different ages (a cross-sectional approach) and then follow those groups over the years (a longitudinal approach). (Also called *cohort-sequential* or *time-sequential research*.)

crystallized intelligence Those types of intellectual ability that reflect accumulated learning. Vocabulary and general information are examples. Some developmental psychologists think crystallized intelligence increases with age, while fluid intelligence declines.

culture The specific manifestations of a social group's design for living, developed over the years to provide a social structure for the group members' life together.

D

deductive reasoning Reasoning from a general statement or principle, through logical steps, to a specific conclusion.

deferred imitation A sequence in which an infant first perceives something that someone else does and then performs the same action a few hours or even days later.

Defining Issues Test (DIT) A series of questions developed by James Rest and designed to assess respondents' level of moral development by having them rank possible solutions to moral dilemmas.

dementia Irreversible loss of intellectual functioning caused by organic brain damage or disease. Dementia becomes more common with age, but even in the very old, dementia is abnormal and pathological. Sometimes dementia is misdiagnosed, since reversible conditions such as depression and drug overdose can cause the symptoms of dementia.

dendrite A nerve fiber that extends from a neuron and receives electrical impulses transmitted from other neurons via their axons.

dependency ratio The ratio of self-sufficient, productive adults to dependents—children and the elderly.

dependent variable In an experiment, the variable that may change as a result of the introduction of or changes made in the independent variable.

developmental psychopathology A field in which knowledge about normal development is applied to the study and treatment of various disorders.

developmental theory A systematic statement of principles and generalizations that provides a coherent framework for studying and explaining development.

***Diagnostic and Statistical Manual of Mental Disorders* (DSM-IV-R)** The American Psychiatric Association's official guide to the diagnosis of mental disorders. The fifth edition will soon be published.

dialectical thought The most advanced cognitive process, characterized by the ability to consider a thesis and its antithesis simultaneously and thus to arrive at a synthesis. Dialectical thought makes possible an ongoing awareness of pros and cons, advantages and disadvantages, possibilities and limitations.

disability Long-term difficulty in performing normal activities of daily life as a result of illness. As a measure of health, disability refers to the portion of the population who cannot perform activities that most others can.

disability-adjusted life years (DALYs) A measure of the impact that disability has on quality of life. DALYs are the reciprocal of quality-adjusted life years: A reduction in QALYs means an increase in DALYs.

diseases of affluence Illnesses, such as lung cancer and breast cancer, that are—or once were—more common in richer people and nations than in poorer ones.

disengagement theory The view that aging makes a person's social sphere increasingly narrow, resulting in role relinquishment, withdrawal, and passivity.

disorganized A category of attachment that is neither secure nor insecure but is marked by the child's and caregiver's inconsistent behavior toward each other.

dizygotic twins Twins who were formed when two separate ova were fertilized by two separate sperm at roughly the same time. Such twins share about half their genes, like any other siblings.

DNA (deozyribonucleic acid) The molecular basis of heredity, constructed of a double helix whose parallel strands consist of both pairs held together by hydrogen bonds.

dominant gene The member of an interacting pair of alleles whose influence is more evident in the phenotype.

dominant–recessive pattern The interaction of a pair of alleles in such a way that the phenotype reveals the influence of one allele (the dominant gene) more than that of the other (the recessive gene).

drug abuse The ingestion of a drug to the extent that it impairs the user's biological or psychological well-being.

drug addiction A condition of drug dependence in which the absence of the given drug in the individual's system produces a drive—physiological, psychological, or both—to ingest more of the drug.

drug use The ingestion of a drug, regardless of the amount or effect.

dynamic perception Perception that is primed to focus on movement and change.

dynamic systems A process of continual change within a person or group, in which each change is connected systematically to every other development in each individual and every society.

dynamic theories Theories that emphasize change and readjustment rather than either the ongoing self or the legacy of stratification. Each person's life is seen as an active, ever-changing, largely self-propelled process, occurring within specific social contexts that themselves are constantly changing.

dyslexia Unusual difficulty with reading.

E

eclectic perspective The approach taken by most developmentalists, in which they apply aspects of each of the various theories of development rather than adhering exclusively to one theory.

ecological niche The particular lifestyle and social context adults settle into that are compatible with their individual personality needs and interests.

ecological-systems approach Research that takes into consideration the relationship between the individual and the environment.

egocentrism Piaget's term for a type of centration in which the young child contemplates the world exclusively from his or her personal perspective.

Elderhostel A program in which people aged 55 and older live on college campuses and take special classes, usually during college vacation periods.

elderspeak A way of speaking to older adults that resembles baby talk, with simple and short sentences, exaggerated emphasis, a slower rate, higher pitch, and repetition.

Electra complex In the phallic stage of psychosexual development, the female version of the Oedipus complex: Girls have sexual feelings for their fathers and accompanying hostility toward their mothers.

embryo The name for the developing organism from about three through eight weeks.

embryonic period Approximately the third through the eighth week after conception, the period during which the basic forms of all body structures develop.

emergent literacy The skills needed to learn to read.

emergent theories Theories that bring together information from many disciplines but that have not yet cohered into theories that are comprehensive and systematic.

emotion-focused coping Dealing with a stressor by changing one's feelings about it. For example, anger can turn into sympathy; frustration can be used to spot a defect in one's own character.

emotional intelligence Goleman's term for the understanding of how to interpret and express emotions.

emotional regulation The ability, beginning in early childhood, to direct or modify one's feelings, particularly feelings of fear, frustration, and anger.

empathy A person's true understanding of the emotions of another, including the ability to figure out what would make that person feel better.

epigenetic theory An emergent theory of development that emphasizes the interaction of genes and the environment—that is, both the genetic origins of behavior (within each person and within each species) and the direct, systematic influence that environmental forces have, over time, on genes.

estrogen A sex hormone, secreted in greater amounts by females than by males.

ethnic group A collection of people who share certain attributes, almost always including ancestral heritage and often including national origin, religion, customs, and language.

ethology The study of patterns of animal behavior, particularly as that behavior relates to evolutionary origins and species survival.

exclusion criteria A person's reasons for omitting certain people from consideration as close friends or partners. Exclusion criteria vary from one individual to another, but they are strong filters.

experience-dependent Refers to brain functions that depend on particular, and variable, experiences and that therefore may or may not develop in a particular infant.

experience-expectant Refers to brain functions that require basic common experiences (which the infant can be expected to have) in order to develop normally.

experiment A research method in which the researcher tries to determine the cause-and-effect relationship between two variables by manipulating one variable (called the *independent variable*) and then observing and recording the resulting changes in the other variable (called the *dependent variable*).

experimental group In an experiment, the participants who are given a particular treatment.

expert Someone who is notably more skilled and knowledgeable about a specific intellectual topic or practical ability than the average person is.

expertise The acquisition of knowledge in a specific area. As individuals grow older, they concentrate their learning in certain areas that are of the most importance to them, becoming experts in these areas while remaining relative novices in others.

explicit memory Memory that is easy to retrieve, usually with words. Most explicit memory involves consciously learned words, data, and concepts.

extended family A family that consists of three or more generations of biologically related individuals.

externalizing problems Emotional difficulties that are manifested outward, when people "act out" by injuring others, destroying property, or defying authority.

F

failure to thrive A situation in which an infant or young child gains little or no weight, despite apparently normal health.

false self A set of behaviors that is adopted by a person to combat rejection, to please others, or to try out as a possible self.

familism The idea that family members should support one another because family unity is more important than individual freedom and success.

family function The ways in which a family works to meet the needs of its members. Children need their families to provide them with food, clothing, and shelter; to encourage them to learn; to develop their self-esteem; to nurture their friendships with peers; and to provide harmony and stability at home.

family structure The legal and genetic relationships among the members of a particular family.

fast mapping The speedy and not very precise process of acquiring vocabulary by mentally "charting" new words into interconnected categories.

fetal alcohol syndrome (FAS) A cluster of birth defects, including abnormal facial characteristics, slow physical growth, and retarded mental development, caused by the mother's drinking alcohol when pregnant.

fetal period The ninth week after conception until birth, the period during which the organs of the developing person grow in size and mature in functioning.

fetus The name for the developing organism from eight weeks after conception until birth. When it is born—even preterm at 22 weeks or post-term at 41 weeks—it is called a baby.

fine motor skills Physical abilities involving small body movements, especially of the hands and fingers, such as drawing or picking up a coin.

fluid intelligence Those types of basic intelligence that make learning of all sorts quick and thorough. Underlying abilities such as short-term memory, abstract thought, and speed of thinking are all usually considered part of fluid intelligence.

Flynn effect A trend toward increasing average IQ, found in all developed nations during the twentieth century.

fMRI Functional magnetic resonance imaging, a measuring technique in which the brain's magnetic properties indicate activation anywhere in the brain; fMRI helps locate neurological responses.

focus on appearance A characteristic of preoperational thought in which the young child ignores all attributes except appearance.

foreclosure Erikson's term for premature identity formation, which occurs when an adolescent adopts parents' or society's roles and values wholesale, without questioning and analysis.

formal operational thought In Piaget's theory, the fourth and final stage of cognitive development; arises from a combination of maturation and experience.

foster care A legally sanctioned, publicly supported plan that transfers care of maltreated children from parents to someone else.

foster family A family in which one or more orphaned, neglected, abused, or delinquent children are temporarily cared for by an adult individual or couple to whom they are not biologically related.

fragile-X syndrome A genetic disorder in which part of the X chromosome is attached to the rest of it by a very thin string of molecules; often produces mental deficiency in males who inherit it.

frail elderly People over age 65 who are physically infirm, very ill, or cognitively impaired.

G

gamete A reproductive cell; that is, a cell that can reproduce a new individual if it combines with a gamete from the other sex.

gateway drugs Drugs—usually tobacco, alcohol, and marijuana—whose use increases the risk that a person will later use harder drugs, such as cocaine and heroin.

gateways to attraction The various qualities, such as appearance and proximity, that are prerequisites for the formation of close friendships and intimate relationships.

gender convergence A tendency for men and women to become more similar as they move through middle age.

gender crossover The idea that each sex takes on the other sex's roles and traits in later life. This idea is disputed, but there is no doubt that maleness and femaleness become less salient in middle age.

gender differences Culturally imposed differences in the roles and behavior of males and females.

gender identity A person's acceptance of the roles and behaviors that society associates with the biological category of male or female.

gene The basic unit for the transmission of heredity instructions.

general intelligence (*g*) The idea that intelligence is one basic trait, underlying all cognitive abilities. According to this concept, people have varying levels of this general ability.

generation gap The distance between generations in values, behaviors, and knowledge, marked by a mutual lack of understanding.

generational stake The need of each generation to view family interactions from its own perspective because each has a different investment in the family scenario.

generativity versus stagnation Erikson's seventh stage of development, in which adults seek to be productive through vocation, avocation, or child rearing. Without such productive work, adults stop developing and growing.

genetic clock According to one theory of aging, a regulatory mechanism in the DNA of cells regulates the aging process.

genetic counseling A process of consultation and testing that enables individuals to learn about their genetic heritage, including conditions that might harm any children they may have.

genome The full set of chromosomes, with all the genes they contain, that make up the genetic material of an organism.

genotype An organism's entire genetic inheritance, or genetic potential.

geriatrics The medical specialty devoted to aging.

germinal period The first two weeks of development after conception; characterized by rapid cell division and the beginning of cell differentiation.

gerontology The study of old age. This is one of the fastest-growing special fields in the social sciences.

glass ceiling An invisible barrier experienced by many women in male-dominated occupations—and by many minority workers in majority-dominated occupations—that halts their advancement and undercuts their power at a level of the organization below that of top management.

glaucoma A disease of the eye that can destroy vision if left untreated. It involves hardening of the eyeball due to a fluid buildup within the eye.

gonads The pair of sex glands in humans. In females, they are called the ovaries; in males, they are called testes or testicles.

goodness of fit A pattern of smooth interaction between the individual and the social milieu, including family, school, and community.

grammar All the methods—word order, verb forms, and so on—that languages use to communicate meaning, apart from the words themselves.

grand theories Comprehensive theories that have traditionally inspired and directed thinking about development. Psychoanalytic theory, behaviorism, and cognitive theory are all grand theories.

grandparent family A family that consists of children living in their grandparents' home, either with their parents (extended family) or without them (grandparents alone).

grandparents alone A family that consists of one or two grandparents and their grandchildren.

gross motor skills Physical abilities involving large body movements, such as walking and jumping.

growth spurt The period of relatively sudden and rapid physical growth of every part of the body that occurs during puberty.

guided participation In sociocultural theory, the process by which a skilled person helps a novice learn by providing not only instruction but also a direct, shared involvement in the learning process.

H

habituation The process of getting used to an object or event through repeated exposure to it.

Hayflick limit The number of times a human cell is capable of dividing into two new cells. The limit for most human cells is approximately 50 divisions, suggesting that the life span is limited by our genetic program.

head-sparing The biological protection of the brain when malnutrition temporarily affects body growth.

heterogamy Defined by developmentalists as marriage between individuals who tend to be dissimilar with respect to such variables as attitudes, interests, goals, socioeconomic status, religion, ethnic background, and local origin.

hidden curriculum The unofficial, unstated, or implicit rules and priorities that

influence the academic curriculum and every other aspect of learning in school.

holophrase A single word that is used to express a complete, meaningful thought.

homeostasis The adjustment of the body's systems to keep physiological functions in a state of equilibrium. As the body ages, it takes longer for these homeostatic adjustments to occur, to that it becomes harder for older bodies to adapt to stresses.

homogamy Defined by developmentalists as marriage between individuals who tend to be similar with respect to such variables as attitudes, interests, goals, socioeconomic status, religion, ethnic background, and local origin.

homosexual family A family that consists of a homosexual couple and the biological or adopted children of one or both partners.

hormone replacement therapy (HRT) Treatment to compensate for hormone reduction at menopause or following surgical removal of the ovaries. Such treatment, which usually involves estrogen and progesterone, minimizes menopausal symptoms and diminishes the risk of osteoporosis in later adulthood.

household A group of people who live together in one dwelling and share its common spaces, such as kitchen and living room.

HPA axis The hypothalamus/pituitary/adrenal axis, a route followed by many kinds of hormones to trigger the changes of puberty and to regulate stress, growth, sleep, appetite, sexual excitement, and various other bodily changes.

Human Genome Project An international effort to map the complete human genetic code.

human immunodeficiency virus (HIV) A virus that gradually overwhelms the body's immune responses, causing AIDS, which makes the individual vulnerable to opportunistic infections.

hypothalamus An area at the base of the brain that, in addition to regulating several maintenance activities (eating, drinking, and body temperature), directs the production of hormones via the pituitary gland.

hypothesis A specific prediction that is stated in such a way that it can be tested and either confirmed or refuted.

hypothetical thought Thought that includes propositions and possibilities that may or may not reflect reality.

I

identification A defense mechanism that lets a person symbolically take on the behaviors and attitudes of someone more powerful than him- or herself.

identity A consistent definition of one's self as a unique individual, in terms of roles, attitudes, beliefs, and aspirations. In logic, the principle that certain characteristics of an object remain the same even if other characteristics change.

identity achievement Erikson's term for the attainment of identity, or the point at which a person understands who he or she is as a unique individual, in accord with past experiences and future plans.

identity diffusion A situation in which an adolescent does not seem to know or care what his or her identity is.

identity moratorium Erikson's term for a pause in identity formation that allows young people to explore alternatives without making final identity choices.

identity versus role confusion Erikson's term for the fifth stage of development, in which the person tries to figure out "Who am I?" but is confused as to which of many possible roles to adopt.

imaginary audience A teenager's false belief, stemming from adolescent egocentrism, that others are intensely interested in his or her appearance and behavior.

immunization A process that stimulates the body's immune system to defend against attack by a particular contagious disease.

implantation Beginning about a week after conception, the burrowing of the organism into the lining of the uterus, where it can be nourished and protected during growth.

implicit memory Unconscious or automatic memory that is usually stored via habits, emotional responses, routine procedures, and various sensations.

in vitro fertilization (IVF) A technique in which ova (egg cells) are surgically removed from a woman and fertilized with sperm in the laboratory. After the original fertilized cells (the zygotes) have divided several times, they are inserted into a woman's uterus.

incidence How often a particular behavior or circumstance occurs.

inclusion A policy under which learning-disabled children are included in the regular class, as in mainstreaming, but are supervised by a specially trained teacher or paraprofessional for all or part of the day.

independent variable In an experiment, the variable that is introduced or changed to see what effect it has on the dependent variable.

individual education plan (IEP) A legally required document specifying a series of educational goals for a child with special needs.

inductive reasoning Reasoning from one or more specific experiences or facts to a general conclusion.

industry versus inferiority The fourth of Erikson's eight crises of psychosexual development, in which school-age children attempt to master many skills and develop a sense of themselves as either industrious and competent or incompetent and inferior.

infant day care Regular care provided for babies by trained and paid nonrelatives.

infertility The lack of a successful pregnancy after one year of regular intercourse without contraception.

information-processing theory A perspective that compares human thinking processes, by analogy, to computer analysis of data, including sensory input, connections, stored memories, and output.

initiative versus guilt The third of Erikson's eight stages of psychosocial development, in which the young child eagerly begins new projects and activities and feels guilt when his or her efforts result in failure or criticism.

injury control/harm reduction The idea that accidents are not random and can be made less harmful with proper control. In practice, this means anticipating, controlling, and preventing dangerous activities.

insecure attachment A relationship that is unstable or unpredictable; in infancy such relationships are characterized by the child's fear, anxiety, anger, clinging, or seeming indifference toward the caregiver.

insecure-avoidant Referring to a pattern of attachment in which one person tries to avoid any connection with another, as an infant who is uninterested in the caregiver's

presence or departure and ignores the caregiver on reunion.

insecure-resistant/ambivalent Referring to a pattern of attachment in which anxiety and uncertainty keep one person clinging to another, as an infant who resists active exploration, is very upset at separation, and both resists and seeks contact on reunion.

instrumental activities of daily life (IADLs) Actions that are important to independent living and that require some intellectual competence and forethought. These are even more critical to self-sufficiency than ADLs.

instrumental aggression Forceful behavior that is aimed at getting or keeping an object or privilege that is also desired by another person.

integrity versus despair The final stage of Erikson's developmental sequence, in which older adults seek to integrate their unique experiences with their vision of community.

interaction effect The condition whereby the risk of a teratogen causing harm increases when it occurs at the same time as another teratogen or risk.

internalizing problems Emotional difficulties that are manifested inward, when troubled individuals inhibit the expression of emotion, become fearful and withdrawn, and inflict harm on themselves.

intimacy versus isolation The sixth of Erikson's eight stages of development. Adults seek someone with whom to share their lives in an enduring and self-sacrificing commitment. Without such commitment, they risk profound aloneness, and isolation.

intimate terrorism Spouse abuse in which the husband uses violent methods of accelerating intensity to isolate, degrade, and punish the wife.

invincibility fable A teenager's false belief, stemming from adolescent egocentrism, that he or she cannot be conquered or even harmed by anything that might vanquish a normal mortal, such as unprotected sex, drug abuse, or high-speed driving.

involved grandparents Grandparents who actively participate in the lives of their grandchildren, seeing them daily.

IQ tests Aptitude tests designed to measure a person's intellectual aptitude, or ability to learn in school. This aptitude was originally defined as mental age divided by chronological age, times 100—hence, intelligence

quotient, or IQ. An example: Actual age of three children: 12, 12, 12 Mental ages of the three: 15, 12, 8 IQ of each of these three:
$15/12 = 1.25 \times 100 = 125$ (superior)
$12/12 = 1 \times 100 = 100$ (average)
$8/12 = 0.75 \times 100 = 75$ (slow learner)

irreversibility A characteristic of preoperational thought in which the young child fails to recognize that reversing a process can sometimes restore whatever existed before the transformation occurred.

K

kangaroo care Care that occurs when the mother of a low-birthweight infant spends at least an hour a day holding the infant between her breasts, like a kangaroo who carries her immature newborn in her pouch. If the infant is capable, he or she can easily breast-feed.

kinkeeper The person who takes primary responsibility for celebrating family achievements, gathering the family together, and keeping in touch with family members who do not live nearby.

kinship care A form of foster care in which a relative of the maltreated child becomes the approved caregiver.

knowledge base A broad body of knowledge in a particular subject area that makes it easier to master new learning in that area.

kwashiorkor A disease of chronic malnutrition during childhood, in which a deficiency of protein causes the child's face, legs, and abdomen to bloat, or swell with water, and makes the child more vulnerable to other diseases, such as measles, diarrhea, and influenza.

L

language acquisition device (LAD) Chomsky's term for a hypothesized brain structure that enables humans to learn language, including the basic aspects of grammar, vocabulary, and intonation.

latency Freud's term for middle childhood, during which children's emotional drives are quieter, their psychosexual needs are repressed, and their unconscious conflicts are submerged.

lateralization Literally, "sidedness," here referring to the differentiation of the two sides of the body so that one side specializes in certain functions. Brain lateralization allows the left side of the brain to control the right side of the body, and vice versa.

learning-disabled Having a marked delay in a particular area of learning that is not associated with any obvious physical handicap, overall mental retardation, or unusually stressful home environment.

least restrictive environment (LRE) A legally required school setting that offers children with special needs as much freedom as possible to benefit from the instruction available to other children; often, in practice, the general classroom.

life review The examination of one's own past life that many elderly people engage in. According to Butler, the life review is therapeutic, for it helps the older person to come to grips with aging and death.

life-course-persistent offender A person whose criminal activity typically begins in early adolescence and continues throughout life; a career criminal.

life-span perspective A view of human development that takes into account all phases of life, not just childhood or adulthood.

little scientist Piaget's term for the stage-five toddler (age 12 to 18 months), who actively experiments without anticipating the results.

long-term memory The component of the information-processing system in which virtually limitless amounts of information can be stored indefinitely.

longitudinal research A research method in which the same individuals are studied over a long period of time.

low birthweight (LBW) A birthweight of less than 5½ pounds (2,500 grams).

M

mainstreaming A policy (mandated by the Education of All Handicapped Children Act in 1975) under which children with special needs must be taught in "the least restrictive environment" available, which usually means that they are taught with other children in the general classroom.

marasmus A disease of severe protein-calorie malnutrition during early infancy, in which growth stops, body tissues waste away, and the infant eventually dies.

maximum life span The oldest age to which members of a species can live, under ideal circumstances. For humans, that age is approximately 120 years.

menarche A female's first menstrual period.

menopause The time in middle age, usually around age 50, when a woman's menstrual periods cease completely and the production of estrogen, progesterone, and testosterone drops considerably. Strictly speaking, menopause is dated one year after a woman's last menstrual period.

metacognition "Thinking about thinking," or the ability to evaluate a cognitive task to determine how best to accomplish it, and then to monitor and adjust one's performance on that task.

middle childhood The period from age 7 to 11.

midlife crisis A period of unusual anxiety, radical reexamination, and sudden transformation that is widely associated with middle age but which actually has more to do with developmental history than with chronological age.

minitheories Theories that focus on some specific area of development and thus are less general and comprehensive than the grand theories.

modeling In social learning theory, the process in which people observe and then copy the behavior of others.

monozygotic twins Twins who have identical genes because they were formed from one zygote that split into two identical organisms very early in development.

morality of care In Gilligan's view, the tendency of females to be reluctant to judge right and wrong in absolute terms because they are socialized to be nurturant, compassionate, and nonjudgmental.

morality of justice In Gilligan's view, the tendency of males to emphasize justice over compassion, judging right and wrong in absolute terms.

morbidity Disease. As a measure of health, morbidity refers to the rate of diseases of all kinds in a given population—physical and emotional, acute (sudden) and chronic (ongoing).

mortality Death. As a measure of health, mortality usually refers to the number of deaths each year per 1,000 members of a given population.

mosaic Referring to a condition in which a person has a mixture of cells, some normal and some with the incorrect number of chromosomes.

multicontextual A characteristic of development, referring to the fact that each human life takes place within a number of contexts—historical, cultural, and socioeconomic.

multicultural A characteristic of development, which takes place within many cultural settings worldwide and thus reflects a multitude of values, traditions, and tools for living.

multidirectional A characteristic of development, referring to its nonlinear progression—gains and losses, compensations and deficits, predictable and unexpected changes.

multidisciplinary A characteristic of development encompassing the idea that dozens of academic disciplines contribute data and insight to the science of development.

multifactorial Referring to inherited traits that are influenced by many factors, including factors in the environment, rather than by genetic influences alone.

myelination The process by which axons and dendrites become insulated with a coating of myelin, a fatty substance that speeds transmission of nerve impulses from neuron to neuron in the brain.

N

naming explosion A sudden increase in an infant's vocabulary, especially in the number of nouns, that begins at about 18 months of age.

nature A general term for the traits, capacities, and limitations that each individual inherits genetically from his or her parents at the moment of conception.

negative identity An identity that is taken on with rebellious defiance, simply because it is the opposite of whatever parents or society expect.

neuron A nerve cell of the central nervous system. Most neurons are in the brain.

norm A standard, or average, measurement, calculated from many individuals within a specific group or population.

nuclear family A family that consists of a father, a mother, and the biological children they have together.

nurture A general term for all the environmental influences that affect development after an individual is conceived.

O

obesity A body weight that is 30 percent or more above the weight that is considered ideal for the person's age and height.

object permanence The realization that objects (including people) still exist even when they cannot be seen, touched, or heard.

objective thought A kind of thinking that follows abstract, impersonal logic.

Oedipus complex In the phallic stage of psychosexual development, the sexual desire that boys have for their mothers and the hostility that they have toward their fathers.

old-old Older adults (generally over age 75) who suffer from physical, mental, or social deficits.

oldest-old Elderly adults (generally, those over age 85) who are dependent on others for almost everything, requiring supportive services such as nursing homes and hospital stays.

one-parent family A family that consists of one parent and his or her biological children.

on–off switching mechanisms Processes in which certain genes code for proteins that switch other genes on and off, making sure that the other genes produce proteins at the appropriate times.

operant conditioning The process by which a response is gradually learned via reinforcement or punishment. (Also called *instrumental conditioning*.)

organ reserve The extra capacity of the heart, lungs, and other organs that makes it possible for the body to withstand moments of intense or prolonged stress. With age, organ reserve is gradually depleted, but the rate of depletion depends on the individual's general state of health.

osteoporosis A loss of calcium that makes bone more porous and brittle. It occurs to some degree in everyone with aging, but serious osteoporosis is more common in elderly women than men. Osteoporosis is the main reason the elderly suffer broken hip bones much more often than do the young.

overregularization The young child's tendency to apply the rules of grammar even when doing so is not necessary or appropriate.

overweight A body weight that is 20–29 percent above the weight that is considered ideal for the person's age and height.

oxygen free radicals Atoms that, as a result of metabolic processes, have an unpaired electron. They produce errors in cell maintenance and repair that, over time, may cause cancer, diabetes, and arteriosclerosis.

P

parasuicide A deliberate act of self-destruction that does not end in death. Parasuicide may be a fleeting gesture, such as a small knife mark on the wrist, or potentially lethal, as when a person swallows an entire bottle of sleeping pills.

parental alliance Cooperation between mother and father because of their mutual commitment to their children. In a parental alliance, both parents agree to support each other in their shared parental roles.

parental monitoring Parents' awareness of what their children are doing, where, and with whom.

parent–infant bond A strong, loving connection that forms as parents hold, examine, and feed their newborn.

Parkinson's disease A chronic, progressive disease that is characterized by muscle tremors and rigidity, and sometimes dementia, caused by a reduction of dopamine production in the brain.

peer group An aggregate of individuals of roughly the same age and social status who play, work, or learn together.

peer pressure Social pressure to conform with one's friends or contemporaries in behavior, dress, and attitude; usually considered a negative force, as when adolescent peers encourage each other to defy adult authority.

peers People who are about the same age and status as oneself.

pelvic inflammatory disease (PID) A common result of recurring pelvic infections in women. Pelvic inflammatory disease often leads to blocked fallopian tubes, which, in turn, can lead to infertility.

percentile Any point on a ranking scale of 1 to 99. For example, the 50th percentile is at the midpoint, with half the subjects ranking higher and half ranking lower.

perception The mental processing of sensory information, when the brain interprets a sensation.

permissive parenting Baumrind's term for a style of child rearing in which the parents seldom punish, guide, or control the child but are nurturant and communicate well with the child.

perseveration The tendency to persevere in, or stick to, one thought or action even when it has become useless or inappropriate.

personal fable A teenager's false belief, stemming from adolescent egocentrism, that he or she is destined to have a unique, heroic, or even legendary life.

pervasive developmental disorders Severe problems, such as autism, that affect many aspects of a young child's psychological growth.

phallic stage Freud's term for the third stage of psychosexual development, which occurs in early childhood and in which the penis becomes the focus of psychological concern as well as physiological pleasure.

phenotype A person's actual appearance and behavior, which are the result of both genetic and environmental influences.

phonics approach The teaching of reading by requiring children to learn the sounds of each letter before they begin to decipher simple words.

pituitary gland A gland that, in response to a biochemical signal from the hypothalamus, produces hormones that regulate growth and control other glands, including the adrenal glands.

plasticity A characteristic of development that indicates that individuals—including their personalities as well as their bodies and minds—change throughout the life span.

polygenic Referring to inherited traits that are influenced by many genes, rather than by a single gene.

possible selves Various ideas of who one might be or might become, each of which is typically acted out and considered as possible identity.

post-traumatic stress disorder (PTSD) A syndrome in which a victim or witness of a trauma or shock has lingering symptoms, which may include hyperactivity and hypervigilance, displaced anger, sleeplessness, sudden terror or anxiety, and confusion between fantasy and reality.

postconventional moral reasoning Kohlberg's third level of moral reasoning, in which emphasis is placed on moral principles.

postformal stage A proposed adult stage of cognitive development, following Piaget's four stages, that is characterized by postformal thought, which is more practical, more flexible, and more dialectical—capable of combining contradictory elements into a comprehensive whole—than is adolescent thinking.

postpartum depression A mother's feelings of sadness, inadequacy, and hopelessness in the days and weeks after giving birth. These feelings are partly physiological (especially hormonal) and partly cultural, particularly if the woman does not receive adequate assistance and encouragement from the baby's father and other helpers.

practical intelligence The intellectual skills used in everyday problem solving.

preconventional moral reasoning Kohlberg's first level of moral reasoning, in which emphasis is placed on getting rewards and avoiding punishments.

preformism The belief that every aspect of development is set in advance by genes and then is gradually manifested in the course of maturation.

prefrontal cortex The area at the front of the cortex of the brain that specializes in the "executive function"—planning, selecting, and coordinating thoughts. (Also called the *frontal lobe* or *frontal cortex*.)

preoperational thought Piaget's term for cognitive development between the ages of about 2 and 6; characterized by centration (including egocentrism), focus on appearance, static reasoning, and irreversibility.

preterm birth Birth that occurs 3 weeks or more before the full term of pregnancy has elapsed—that is, at 35 or fewer weeks after conception.

prevalence How widespread within a population a particular behavior or circumstance is.

primary aging The age-related changes that inevitably take place in a person as time goes by.

primary circular reactions The first of three types of feedback loops, this one involving the infant's own body. The infant senses motion, sucking, noise, and so on, and tries to understand them.

primary prevention Actions that change overall background conditions to prevent some unwanted event or circumstance, such as injury, disease, or abuse.

primary sex characteristics The sex organs—those parts of the body that are directly involved in reproduction, including the vagina, uterus, ovaries, testicles, and penis.

private speech Vygotsky's term for the internal dialogue that occurs when people talk to themselves and through which new ideas are developed and reinforced.

problem-focused coping Dealing with a stressor by solving the problem—e.g., confronting an annoying person, getting the rules changed at work, or changing the habits of a family member.

prosocial Behaving in ways that help other people without obvious benefit to oneself.

protein-calorie malnutrition A condition in which a person does not consume sufficient food of any kind.

psychoanalytic theory A grand theory of human development that holds that irrational, unconscious drives and motives, many of which originate in childhood, underlie human behavior.

puberty A period of rapid growth and sexual change that occurs in early adolescence and produces a person of adult size, shape, and sexual potential.

Q

quality-adjusted life years (QALYs) A way of comparing mere survival without vitality to survival with health. QALYs indicate how many years of full vitality are lost to a particular physical disease or disability. They are expressed in terms of life expectancy as adjusted for quality of life.

R

race A social construction by which biological traits (such as hair or skin color, facial features, and body type) are used to differentiate people whose ancestors came from various regions of the world.

reaction time The length of time it takes a person to respond to a particular stimulus.

reactive aggression Forceful behavior that is an angry retaliation for some intentional or accidental act.

recessive gene The member of an interacting pair of alleles whose influence is less evident in the phenotype.

reciprocity The logical principle that two things may change in opposite ways in order to balance each other out. Also called *inversion.*

reflex A responsive movement that seems automatic, because it almost always occurs in reaction to a particular stimulus.

reinforcement The process in which a behavior is followed by results that make it more likely that the behavior will be repeated. This occurs in operant conditioning.

relational aggression Forceful behavior that takes the form of insults or social rejection, aimed at harming social connections.

REM sleep Rapid eye movement sleep, a stage of sleep characterized by flickering eyes behind closed lids, dreaming, and rapid brain waves.

reminder session A perceptual experience that helps a person recollect an idea or experience, without testing whether the person remembers it at the moment.

remote grandparents Grandparents who are distant but who are honored, respected, and obeyed by the younger generations in their families.

replication The repetition of a scientific study, using the same procedures on another group of participants, to verify or refute the original study's conclusions.

reported maltreatment Maltreatment about which the police, child welfare agency, or other authorities have been officially notified.

resource room A room set aside in some schools for special-needs children to spend part of each day with a teacher who is trained and equipped to work with their disabilities.

respite care An arrangement in which a professional caregiver takes over to give the family caregiver of a frail elderly person a break for a few hours each day or for an occasional weekend.

reversibility The logical principle that sometimes a thing that has been changed can be returned to its original state by reversing the process by which it was changed.

risk analysis The process of weighing the potential outcomes of a particular event, substance, or experience to determine the likelihood of harm. In teratology, risk analysis involves an attempt to evaluate all the factors that increase or decrease the likelihood that a particular teratogen will cause damage.

role buffering A situation in which achievement in one role that an adult plays—spouse, parent, or employee—reduces the impact of disappointments that may occur in other roles.

role overload The stress of multiple obligations that may occur for an adult who is simultaneously a spouse, a parent, and an employee.

rough-and-tumble play Play that mimics aggression through wrestling, chasing, or hitting but that actually occurs in fun, with no intent to harm.

S

sandwich generation A term for the generation of middle-aged people who are supposedly "squeezed" by the needs of the younger and older generations. Some adults do feel pressured by these obligations, but most are not burdened by them, either because they enjoy fulfilling them or because they choose to take on only some of them, or none.

scaffolding A sensitive structuring of the young child's participation in learning encounters.

scaling back A strategy used by middle-aged adults to balance the demands of work and family life. Instead of devoting full time to one or the other, many people reduce their commitment to their work in order to have time for their marriage and children.

scientific method An approach to the systematic pursuit of knowledge that, when applied to the study of development, involves five basic steps: Formulate a research question, develop a hypothesis, test the hypothesis, draw conclusions, and make the findings available.

scientific observation A method of testing hypotheses by unobtrusively watching and recording participants' behavior either in a laboratory or in a natural setting.

scientific study of human development The science that seeks to understand the ways in which people change and remain the same as they grow older.

Seattle Longitudinal Study The first cross-sequential study of adult intelligence. This study began in 1956; the next testing is scheduled for 2005.

secondary aging The specific physical illnesses or conditions that are more common in aging but are caused by health habits, genes, and other influences that vary from person to person.

secondary circular reactions The second of three types of feedback loops, this one involving people and objects. The infant is responsive to other people and to toys and other objects that can be manipulated.

secondary prevention Actions that avert harm in the immediate situation, such as stopping a car before it hits a pedestrian.

secondary sex characteristics Body characteristics that are not directly involved in reproduction but that indicate sexual maturity, such as a man's beard or a woman's breasts.

secure attachment A relationship of trust and confidence; during infancy, a relationship that provides enough comfort and reassurance to enable independent exploration of the environment.

selective adaptation The idea that humans and other animals gradually adjust to their environment; specifically, the process by which the frequency of particular genetic traits in a population increases or decreases over generations, depending on whether the traits contribute to the survival of the species.

selective attention The ability to screen out distractions and to focus on the details that will help in later recall of information.

selective optimization with compensation The theory, developed by Paul and Margaret Baltes, that people try to maintain a balance in their lives by looking for the best way to compensate for physical and cognitive losses and to become more proficient at activities they can do well.

self theories Theories of late adulthood that emphasize the core self, or the search to maintain one's integrity and identity.

self-awareness A person's realization that he or she is a distinct individual whose body, mind, and actions are separate from those of other people.

self-concept People's understanding of who they are. Self-concept usually includes appearance, personality, and abilities.

self-efficacy In social learning theory, the belief that one is effective; self-efficacy motivates people to change themselves and their contexts.

senescence The state of physical decline, in which the body gradually becomes less strong and efficient with age.

senile macular degeneration A disease of the eye involving deterioration of the retina.

sensation The response of a sensory system (eyes, ears, skin, tongue, nose) when it detects a stimulus.

sensorimotor intelligence Piaget's term for the intelligence of infants during the first period of cognitive development, when babies think by using their senses and motor skills.

sensory memory The component of the information-processing system in which incoming stimulus information is stored for a split second to allow it to be processed. Also called the *sensory register*.

separation anxiety Fear of abandonment, exhibited at the departure of a beloved caregiver; usually strongest at 9 to 14 months.

set point A particular body weight that an individual's homeostatic processes strive to maintain.

sex differences Biological differences between males and females.

sexual abuse The use of an unconsenting person for one's own sexual pleasure. Sexual activity is abusive whenever it is not mutual, whenever consent is not freely given, or whenever a person does not understand or feels obligated to agree to a sexual encounter.

sexually active Traditionally, a euphemism for "having had sexual intercourse"; still in use, even though today many adolescents engage in many sexual activities other than intercourse.

sexually transmitted infection (STI) An infection spread by sexual contact, including syphilis, gonorrhea, herpes, chlamydia, and HIV.

shaken baby syndrome A serious condition caused by maltreatment involving shaking a crying infant back and forth, sharply and quickly. Severe brain damage results from internal hemorrhaging and broken neural connections.

small for gestational age (SGA) A birth-weight that is significantly lower than expected, given the time since conception. For example, a 5-pound newborn is SGA if born on time, but not SGA if born two months early. (Also called *small-for-dates*.)

social clock Refers to the idea that the stages of life, and the behaviors "appropriate" to them, are set by social standards rather than by biological maturation. For instance, "middle age" begins when the culture believes it does, rather than at a particular age in all cultures.

social cognitive theory A perspective that highlights how the school-age child advances in learning, cognition, and culture, building on maturation and experience to become more articulate, insightful, and competent.

social comparison The tendency to assess one's abilities, achievements, social status, and other attributes by measuring them against those of other people, especially one's peers.

social construction An idea that is built more on shared perceptions of social order than on objective reality.

social convoy Collectively, the family members, friends, acquaintances, and even strangers who move through life with an individual.

social exchange theory The view that social behavior is a process of exchange aimed at maximizing the benefits one receives and minimizing the costs one pays.

social homogamy The similarity of a couple's leisure interests and role preferences.

social learning theory An application of behaviorism that emphasizes that many human behaviors are learned through observation and imitation of other people.

social mediation A function of speech by which a person's cognitive skills are refined and extended.

social referencing Seeking information about an unfamiliar or ambiguous object or event by observing someone else's expressions and reactions. That other person becomes a reference, consulted when the infant wants to know how to react.

sociocultural theory An emergent theory that holds that human development results from the dynamic interaction between each person and the surrounding social and cultural forces.

sociodramatic play Pretend play in which children act out various roles and themes in stories that they create themselves.

socioeconomic status (SES) An indicator of a person's social and economic standing, measured through a combination of family income, educational level, place of residence, occupation, and other variables.

spermarche A male's first ejaculation of live sperm, whether through masturbation, a wet dream, or sexual contact with another person.

spontaneous abortion The naturally occurring termination of a pregnancy before the fetus is fully developed. (Also called *miscarriage*.)

static reasoning A characteristic of preoperational thought in which the young child assumes that the world is unchanging.

stepparent family A family that consists of a parent, his or her biological children, and his or her spouse, who is not biologically related to the children.

stereotype threat The possibility that one's appearance or behavior will be misused to confirm another person's oversimplified, prejudiced attitude.

Strange Situation A laboratory procedure developed by Mary Ainsworth to measure attachment by evoking an infant's reactions to stress, specifically episodes of a caregiver's or stranger's arrival at and departure from a playroom where the infants can play with many toys.

stranger wariness Fear of unfamiliar people, exhibited fleetingly at 6 months and at full force by 10 to 14 months.

stratification theories Theories emphasizing that social forces, particularly those related to a person's social stratum or social category, limit individual choices and affect the ability to function. In late adulthood, past stratification continues to limit life in various ways.

subcortical dementias Dementias, such as Parkinson's disease, Huntington's disease, and multiple sclerosis, that originate in the subcortex. These diseases begin with impairments in motor ability and produce cognitive impairment in later stages.

subjective thought A kind of thinking that arises from the personal experiences and perceptions of an individual.

substantiated maltreatment Maltreatment that has been reported, investigated, and verified.

sudden infant death syndrome (SIDS) A situation in which a seemingly healthy infant, at least 2 months of age, dies unexpectedly in his or her sleep.

suicidal ideation Thinking about suicide, usually with some serious emotional and intellectual or cognitive overtones.

superego In psychoanalytic theory, the part of the personality that is self-critical and judgmental and that internalizes the moral standards set by parents and society.

surrogate parents Grandparents who take over the raising of their grandchildren as a result of their adult children's extreme social problems.

survey A research method in which information is collected from a large number of people by personal interview, written questionnaire, or some other means.

synapse The intersection between the axon of one neuron and the dendrites of other neurons.

synchrony A coordinated interaction between caregiver and infant, who respond to each other's faces, sounds, and movements very rapidly and smoothly.

synthesis A new idea that integrates the thesis and its antithesis, thus representing a new and more comprehensive level of truth; the third stage of the process of dialectical thinking.

T

T cells Cells created in the thymus that produce substances that attack infected cells in the body.

temperament According to Rothbart and Bates (1998), "constitutionally based individual differences in emotion, motor, and attentional reactivity and self-regulation."

teratogens Agents and conditions, including viruses, drugs, chemicals, stressors, and malnutrition, that can impair prenatal development and lead to birth defects or even death.

terminal decline An overall slowdown of cognitive abilities in the days or months before death. (Also called *terminal drop*.)

tertiary circular reactions The third of three types of feedback loops, this one involving active exploration and experimentation. The infant explores a range of new activities, varying responses as a way of learning about the world.

tertiary prevention Actions that are taken after an adverse event occurs, aimed at reducing the harm or preventing disability. Immediate and effective medical treatment of illness or injury is tertiary prevention.

testosterone A sex hormone, secreted in greater amounts by males than by females.

theory of mind An understanding of human mental processes.

theory-theory Gopnik's term for the idea that children attempt to construct a theory to explain everything they see and hear.

thesis A proposition or statement of belief; the first stage of the process of dialectical thinking.

threshold effect The condition whereby a teratogen is relatively harmless in small doses but becomes harmful once exposure reaches a certain level (the threshold).

time-out A disciplinary technique in which the child is required to stop all activity and sit in a corner or stay indoors for a few minutes.

total immersion An approach to teaching a second language in which instruction occurs entirely in that language and the learner's native language is not used at all.

transient exuberance The great increase in the number of dendrites that occurs in an infant's brain over the first two years of life.

trust versus mistrust Erikson's term for the first crisis of psychosocial development, in which the infant learns whether the world is essentially a secure place where basic needs are always met or an unpredictable arena where needs (for food, comfort, etc.) are sometimes unmet.

V

vascular dementia (VaD)/multi-infarct dementia (MID) The form of dementia characterized by sporadic, and progressive, loss of intellectual functioning. The cause is repeated infarcts, or temporary obstructions of blood vessels, preventing sufficient blood from reaching the brain. Each infarct destroys some brain tissue. The underlying cause is an impaired circulatory system.

visual cliff An experimental apparatus designed to provide the illusion of a sudden dropoff between one horizontal surface and another.

vitality A measure of health that refers to how healthy and energetic—physically, intellectually, and socially—an individual actually feels.

volatile mismatch A lack of fit between a person and his or her environment that causes the person to become angry, hostile, or depressed. Such a situation is said to be typical of teenagers and schools.

W

wear-and-tear theory A theory of aging that states that the human body wears out because of the passage of time and exposure to environmental stressors.

Wechsler Intelligence Scale for Children (WISC) An IQ test designed for school-age children; it is administered by a trained examiner to one child at a time, and the questions are varied to hold the child's interest and to assess many abilities, including vocabulary, general knowledge, memory, and spatial comprehension.

whole-language approach The teaching of reading by encouraging children to develop all their language skills—talking and listening, reading and writing—all with the goal of communication.

wisdom A cognitive perspective characterized by a broad, practical, comprehensive approach to life's problems, reflecting timeless truths rather than immediate expediency; said to be more common in the elderly than in the young.

withdrawn-rejected Referring to children who are actively rejected by their peer group because of their withdrawn, anxious behavior.

working memory The component of the information-processing system in which current conscious mental activity occurs. Also called *short-term memory*.

working model In cognitive theory, a set of assumptions that are used to organize perceptions and experiences.

X

X-linked Referring to a gene that is located on the X chromosome.

XX A 23rd pair that consists of two X-shaped chromosomes, one from the mother and one from the father.

XY A 23rd pair that consists of one X-shaped chromosome from the mother and one Y-shaped chromosome from the father.

Y

young-old Healthy, vigorous, financially secure older adults (generally, those under age 75) who are well integrated into the lives of their families and their communities.

Z

zone of proximal development (ZPD) In sociocultural theory, the range of skills that a learner can exercise and master with assistance but cannot yet perform independently. According to Vygotsky, learning can occur within this zone.

zygote The single cell formed from the fusing of a sperm and an ovum.

Aber, J. Lawrence, Jones, Stephanie M., Brown, Joshua L., Chaudry, Nina, & Samples, Faith. (1998). Resolving conflict creatively: Evaluating the developmental effects of a school-based violence prevention program in neighborhood and classroom context. *Development and Psychopathology, 10,* 187–213.

Aboud, Frances E., & Mendelson, Morton J. (1996). Determinants of friendship selection and quality: Developmental perspectives. In William M. Bukowski, Andrew F. Newcomb, & Willard W. Hartup (Eds.), *The company they keep: Friendship in childhood and adolescence.* Cambridge, England: Cambridge University Press.

Abraido-Lanza, Ana F., Dohrenwend, B. P., Ng-Mak, D. S., & Turner, J. B. (1999). The Latino mortality paradox: A test of the "salmon bias" and healthy migrant hypotheses. *American Journal of Public Health, 89*(10), 1543–1548.

Acton, Kelly J., Burrows, Nilka Rios, Moore, Kelly, Querec, Linda, Geiss, Linda S., & Engelgau, Michael M. (2002). Trends in diabetes prevalence among American Indian and Alaska native children, adolescents, and young adults. *American Journal of Public Health, 92,* 1485–1490.

Adams, Marilyn Jager, & Bruck, Maggie. (1995). Resolving the "great debate." *American Educator, 19,* 7–20.

Adams, Marilyn Jager, Treiman, Rebecca, & Pressley, Michael. (1998). Reading, writing, and literacy. In William Damon (Series Ed.), Irving E. Sigel & K. Ann Renninger (Volume Eds.), *Handbook of child psychology: Vol. 4. Child psychology in practice* (5th ed., pp. 275–357). New York: Wiley.

Adams-Price, Carolyn E. (Ed.) (1998). *Creativity and aging: Theoretical and empirical approaches.* New York: Springer.

Addis, M. E., & Mahalik, J.R. (2003). Men, masculinity, and the contexts of help seeking. *American Psychologist, 58,* 5–14.

Adler, Lynn Peters. (1995). *Centenarians: The bonus years.* Santa Fe, NM: Health Press.

Adler, Nancy E., & Snibbe, Alana Conner. (2003). The role of psychosocial processes in explaining the gradient between socioeconomic status and health. *Current Directions in Psychological Science, 12*(4), 119–123.

Adolph, Karen E., Vereijken, Beatrix, & Denny, Mark A. (1998). Learning to crawl. *Child Development, 69,* 1299–1312.

Agha, Sohail. (2002). A quasi-experimental study to assess the impact of four adolescent sexual health interventions in sub-Saharan Africa. *International Family Planning Perspectives, 28,* 67–70, 113–118.

Aguilar, Benjamin, Sroufe, L. Alan, Egeland, Byron, & Carlson, Elizabeth. (2000). Distinguishing the early-onset/persistent and adolescent-onset antisocial behavior types: From birth to 16 years. *Development and Psychopathology, 12,* 109–132.

Aguirre-Molina, Marilyn, Molina, Carlos W., & Zambrana, Ruth Enid. (Eds.). (2001). *Health issues in the Latino community.* San Francisco: Jossey-Bass.

Ahearn, Frederick L., Jr. (Ed.) 2001. *Issues in global aging.* New York: Haworth.

Ainsworth, Mary D. Salter. (1973). The development of infant–mother attachment. In Bettye M. Caldwell & Henry N. Ricciuti (Eds.), *Review of child development research* (Vol. 3, pp. 1–94). Chicago: University of Chicago Press.

Akhtar, Nameera, Jipson, Jennifer, & Callanan, Maureen A. (2001). Learning words through overhearing. *Child Development, 72,* 416–430.

Akiba, Daisuke, & García Coll, Cynthia T. (2003). Effective interventions with children of color and their families: A contextual developmental approach. In Timothy B. Smith (Ed.). *Practicing multiculturalism: Affirming diversity in theory and practice.* Boston: Allyn & Bacon.

Akiyama, Hiroko, Elliot, Kathryn, & Antonucci, Toni C. (1996). Same-sex and cross-sex relationships. *Journal of Gerontology, 51B,* 374–382.

Albert, Marilyn S., & Moss, Mark B. (1996). Neuropsychology of aging: Findings in humans and monkeys. In Edward L. Schneider & John W. Rowe (Eds.), *Handbook of the biology of aging.* San Diego, CA: Academic Press.

Aldous, Joan, Mulligan, Gail M., & Bjarnason, Thoroddur. (1998). Fathering over time: What makes the difference? *Journal of Marriage and the Family, 60,* 809–820.

Aldwin, Carolyn M. (1994). *Stress, coping, and development.* New York: Guilford Press.

Aldwin, Carolyn M., & Gilmer, Diane F. (2003). *Health, illness, and optimal aging: Biological and psychosocial perspectives.* Thousand Oaks, CA: Sage.

Aldwin, Carolyn M., & Levenson, Michael R. (2001). Stress, coping, and health at midlife: A developmental perspective. In Margie E. Lachman (Ed.), *Handbook of midlife development* (pp. 188–214). New York: Wiley.

Alexander, Robin. (2000). *Culture and pedagogy: International comparisons in primary education.* Malden, MA: Blackwell.

Allen, Mike, & Burrell, Nancy A. (2002). Sexual orientation of the parent: The impact on the child. In Mike Allen, Raymond W. Preiss, Barbara Mae Gayle, & Nancy A. Burrell (Eds.). *Interpersonal communication research: Advances through meta-analysis.* (pp. 125–143). Mahwah, NJ: Erlbaum.

Allwood, Carl Martin, & Selart, Marcus (Eds.). (2001). *Decision making: Social and creative dimensions.* Norwell, MA: Kluwer Academic Publishers.

Alspaugh, M. E. L., Stephens, M. A. P., Towsend, A., & Zarit, S. H. (1999). Objective and subjective primary stress as predictors of longitudinal patterns of risk for depression in dementia caregivers. *Psychology and Aging, 14,* 34–43.

Altbach, Philip (1998). *Comparative higher education: Knowledge, the university, and development.* Greenwich, CT: Ablex.

Alwin, Duane F. (1996). Coresidence beliefs in American society—1973 to 1991. *Journal of Marriage and the Family, 58,* 393–403.

Aman, Christine J., Roberts, Ralph J., & Pennington, Bruce F. (1998). A neuropsychological examination of the underlying deficit in attention deficit hyperactivity disorder: Frontal lobe versus right parietal lobe theories. *Developmental Psychology, 34,* 956–969.

Amato, Paul R. (1999). The postdivorce society: How divorce is shaping the family and other forms of social organization. In Ross A. Thompson & Paul R. Amato (Eds.), *The postdivorce family: Children, parenting, and society* (pp. 161–190). Thousand Oaks, CA: Sage.

Amato, Paul R. (2000). The consequences of divorce for adults and children. *Journal of Marriage and the Family, 62,* 1269–1287.

Amato, Paul R., & Fowler, Frieda. (2002). Parenting practices, child adjustment, and family diversity. *Journal of Marriage and Family, 64,* 703–716.

Amato, Paul R., & Rivera, Fernando. (1999). Paternal involvement and children's behavior problems. *Journal of Marriage and the Family, 60,* 375–384.

Amato, Paul R., Johnson, David R., Booth, Alan, & Rogers, Stacy J. (2003). Continuity and change in marital quality between 1980 and 2000. *Journal of Marriage and Family, 65,* 1–22.

American Psychiatric Association. (2000). *Diagnostic and statistical manual of mental disorders* (4th ed.). Washington, DC: Author.

American Society for Reproductive Medicine. (2002). Assisted reproductive technology in the United States. *Fertility and Sterility, 77,* 18–31.

Ammerman, Robert T., Lynch, Kevin G., Donovan, John E., Martin, Christopher S., & Maisto, Stephen A. (2001). Constructive thinking in adolescents with substance use disorders. *Psychology of Addictive Behaviors, 15,* 89–96.

Ammerman, Robert T., Oh, Peggy J., & Tarter, Ralph G. (Eds.). (1999). Prevention and societal impact of drug and alcohol abuse. Mahwah, NJ: Erlbaum.

Anand, S., & Hanson, K. (1997). Disability-adjusted life years: A critical review. *Journal of Health Economics, 16,* 685–702.

Andel, Ross, & Liebig, Phoebe S. (2002). The city of Laguna Woods: A case of senior power on local politics. *Research on Aging, 24,* 87–105.

Anderman,, Eric M., Griesinger, Tripp, & Westerfield, Gloria. (1998). Motivation and cheating during early adolescence. *Journal of Educational Psychology, 90,* 84–93.

Anderson, Craig A., & Bushman, Brad J. (2002). Human aggression. *Annual Review of Psychology, 53,* 27–51.

Anderson, Daniel R., Huston, Aletha C., Schmitt, Kelly L., Linebarger, Deborah L., & Wright, John C. (2001). Early childhood television viewing and adolescent behavior: The recontact study. *Monographs of the Society for Research in Child Development, 66* (Serial No. 264).

Anderson, Karen. (2002). Perpetrator or victim? Relationships between intimate partner violence and well-being. *Journal of Marriage and Family, 64,* 851—863.

Anderson, Michael. (2001). You have to get inside the person, or making grief private: Image and metaphor in the therapeutic reconstruction of bereavement. In Jenny Hockey, Jeanne Katz, & Neil Small (Eds.), *Grief, mourning, and death ritual* (pp. 135–143). Buckingham, England: Open University Press.

Anderson, Nicole A. (2001). The attentional demands and attentional control of encoding and retrieval. In M. Naveh-Benjamin, M. Moscovitch, & R. L. Roediger III (Eds.), *Perspectives on human memory and cognitive aging: Essays in honour of Fergus Craik* (pp. 208–225). Hove, England: Psychology Press.

Anderson, Robert N. (2001, October 12). Deaths: Leading causes for 1999. *National Vital Statistics Reports, 49*(11).

Andrews, Melinda W., Dowling, W. Jay, Bartlett, James C., & Halpern, Andrea R. (1998). Identification of speeded and slowed familiar melodies by younger, middle-aged, and older musicians and nonmusicians. *Psychology and Aging, 13,* 462–471.

Aneshensel, C.S., Pearlin, L.I., Mullan, J.T., Zarit, S.H., & Whitlatch, C.J. (1995). *Profiles in caregiving: The unexpected career.* San Diego, CA: Academic Press.

Angold, A., & Costello, E. J. (1995). Developmental epidemiology. *Epidemiological Reviews, 17,* 73–82.

Angold, Adrian, Erkanli, Alaattin, Egger, Helen L., & Costello, E. Jane. (2000). Stimulant treatment for children: A community perspective. *Journal of the American Academy of Child and Adolescent Psychiatry, 39,* 975–984.

Anstey, Kaarin J., & Smith, Glen A. (1999). Interrelations among biological markers of aging, health, activity, acculturation, and cognitive performance in late adulthood. *Psychology and Aging, 14,* 605–618.

Anstey, Kaarin J., Hofer, Scott M., & Luszcz, Mary. (2003). A latent curve analysis of late-life sensory and cognitive function over 8 years: Evidence for specific and common factors underlying change. *Psychology and Aging, 18,* 714–726.

Antonucci, Toni C., Akiyama, Hiroko, & Merline, Alicia. *(2001). Dynamics of social relationships in midlife. In Margie E. Lachman (Ed.),* Handbook of midlife development *(pp. 571–598). New York: Wiley.*

Apgar, Virginia. (1953). A proposal for a new method of evaluation in the newborn infant. *Current Research in Anesthesia and Analgesia, 32,* 260.

Aquilino, William S. (1991). Family structure and home-leaving: A further specification of the relationship. *Journal of Marriage and the Family, 53,* 999–1010.

Archer, J. (2000). Sex differences in aggression between heterosexual partners: A meta-analytic review. *Psychological Bulletin, 126*(5), 651–680.

Arfániarromo, Albert. (2001). Toward a psychosocial and sociocultural understanding of achievement motivation among Latino gang members in U.S. schools. *Journal of Instructional Psychology, 28,* 123–136.

Arking, Robert. (1998). *Biology of aging: Observations and principles* (2nd ed.). Sunderland, MA: Sinauer Associates.

Arlin, Patricia K. (1984). Adolescent and adult thought: A structural interpretation. In Michael L. Commons, Francis A.

Richards, & Cheryl Armon (Eds.), *Beyond formal operations: Late adolescent and adult cognitive development.* New York: Praeger.

Arlin, Patricia K. (1989). Problem solving and problem finding in young artists and young scientists. In Michael L. Commons, Jan D. Sinnott, Francis A. Richards, and Cheryl Armon (Eds.), *Adult development: Vol 1. Comparisons and applications of developmental models.* New York: Praeger.

Armour, Marilyn. (2003). Meaning making in the aftermath of homicide. *Death Studies, 27,* 519–540.

Armstrong, Neil, & Welsman, Joanne. (1997). *Young people and physical activity.* Oxford, England: Oxford University Press.

Arnett, Jeffrey J. (1999). Adolescent storm and stress, reconsidered. *American Psychologist, 54,* 317–326.

Arnett, Jeffrey J. (2002). The psychology of globalization. *American Psychologist, 57,* 774–783.

Arnett, Jeffrey J. (2003). Conceptions of the transition to adulthood among emerging adults in American ethnic groups. *New Directions for Child and Adolescent Development* (No. 110), 63–75.

Aron, Arthur, & Westbay, Lori. (1996). Dimensions of the prototype of love. *Journal of Personality and Social Relationships, 70,* 535–551

Aron, David C., Gordon, Howard S., Di Guiseppe, David L., Harper, Dwain L., & Rosenthal, Gary E. (2000). Variations in risk-adjusted Cesarean delivery rates according to race and health insurance. *Medical Care, 38,* 35–44.

Aronson, Joshua, Fried, Carrie B., & Good, Catherine. (2002). Reducing the effects of stereotype threat on African American college students by shaping theories of intelligence. *Journal of Experimental Social Psychology, 38,* 113–125.

Artistico, Danielle, Cervone, Daniel, & Pezzuti, Lina. (2003). Perceived self-efficacy and everyday problem solving among young and older adults. *Psychology and Aging, 18,* 68–79.

Ashman, Sharon B., & Dawson, Geraldine. (2002). Maternal depression, infant psychobiological development, and risk for depression. In Sherryl H. Goodman & Ian H. Gotlib (Eds.), *Children of depressed parents: Mechanisms of risk*

and implications for treatments (pp. 37–58). Washington, DC: American Psychological Association.

Aslin, Richard N., & Hunt, Ruskin H. (2001). Development, plasticity, and learning in the auditory system. In Charles A. Nelson & Monica Luciana (Eds.), *Handbook of developmental cognitive neuroscience* (pp. 149–158). Cambridge, MA: MIT Press.

Aslin, Richard N., Jusczyk, Peter W., & Pisoni, David B. (1998). Speech and auditory processing during infancy: Constraints on and precursors to language. In William Damon, Deanna Kuhn, & Robert S. Siegler (Eds.), *Handbook of child psychology: Cognition, perception, and language* (5th ed., pp. 147–198). New York: Wiley.

Astington, Janet Wilde, & Gopnik, Alison. (1988). Knowing you've changed your mind: Children's understanding of representational change. In Janet W. Astington, Paul L. Harris, & David R. Olson (Eds.), *Developing theories of mind* (pp. 193–206). New York: Cambridge University Press.

Astington, Janet Wilde, & Jenkins, Jennifer M. (1999). A longitudinal study of the relation between language and theory-of-mind development. *Developmental Psychology, 35,* 1311–1320.

Atchley, Robert C. (1999). Continuity and adaptation in aging: Creating positive experiences. Baltimore: John Hopkins University Press.

Attig, Thomas. (2003). Respecting the spiritual beliefs of the dying and the bereaved. In Inge Corless, Barbara B.Germino, & Mary A. Pittman (Eds.). *Dying, death, and bereavement* (pp. 61–75). New York: Springer.

Austad, Steven N. (2001). Concepts and theories of aging. In Edward J. Masuro & Steven N. Austad (Eds.), *Handbook of the biology of aging* (5th ed., pp. 3–22). San Diego, CA: Academic Press.

Aviezer, Ora, van IJzendoorn, Marinus H., Sagi, Abraham, & Schuengel, Carlo. (1994). "Children of the dream" revisited: 70 years of collective early child-care in Israeli kibbutzim. *Psychological Bulletin, 116,* 99–116.

Avis, Nancy. (1999). Women's health at midlife. In Sherry L. Willis & James D. Reid (Eds.), *Life in the middle.* San Diego, CA: Academic Press.

Awooner-Renner, Sheila. (1993). I desperately needed to see my son. In Donna Dickenson & Malcolm Johnson (Eds.), *Dying, death, and bereavement.* London: Sage.

Bachman, Jerald G., & Schulenberg, John. (1993). How part-time work intensity relates to drug use, problem behavior, time use, and satisfaction among high school seniors: Are these consequences or merely correlates? *Developmental Psychology, 29,* 220–235.

Bachman, Jerald G., O'Malley, Patrick M., Schulenberg, John E., Johnston, Lloyd D., Bryant, Alison L., & Merline, Alicia C. (2002). *The decline of substance use in young adulthood: Changes in social activities, roles, and beliefs.* Mahwah, NJ: Erlbaum.

Bachu, A. (1999). Trends in premarital childbearing: 1930 to 1994. *Current Population Reports, 1999,* series P-23, No. 197.

Bäckman, Lars, Laukka, Erika Jonsson, Wahlin, Ake, Small, Brent J., & Fratiglioni, Laura. (2002). Influences of preclinical dementia and impending death on the magnitude of age-related cognitive deficits. *Psychology and Aging, 17,* 435–442.

Badcock, Chrisotpher. (2002). *Evolutionary psychology.* Cambridge, England: Polity.

Bagwell, Catherine L., Schmidt, Michelle E., Newcomb, Andrew, & Bukowski, William M. (2002). Friendship and peer rejection as predictors of adult adjustment. In William Damon (Series Ed.), Douglas W. Nangle & Cynthia A. Erdley (Volume Eds.), *New directions for child and adolescent development: Vol. 91. The role of friendship in psychological adjustment.* (pp. 25–49). San Francisco: Jossey-Bass.

Baier, Margaret E., & Ackerman, Phillip P. (2001). Current-event knowledge in adults: An investigation of age, intelligence, and non-ability determinants. *Psychology and Aging, 14,* 615–628.

Baildam, E. M., Hillier, V. F., Menon, S., Bannister, R. P., Bamford, F. N., Moore, W. M. O., & Ward, B. S. (2000). Attention to infants in the first year. *Child: Care, Health and Development, 26,* 199–216.

Bailey, J. Michael, Kirk, Katherine M., Zhu, Gu, Dunne, Michael P., & Martin, Nicholas G. (2000). Do individual differences in sociosexuality represent genetic or environmentally contingent strategies? Evidence from the Australian twin registry. *Journal of Personality & Social Psychology, 78,* 537–545.

Baillargeon, Renée. (1999). Young infants' expectations about hidden objects: A reply to three challenges. *Developmental Science, 2,* 115–163.

Baird, Annabel H. (2003). Through my eyes: Service needs of grandparents who raise their grandchildren, from the perspective of a custodial grandmother. In Bert Hayslip, Jr., & Julie Hicks Patrick (Eds.), *Working with custodial grandparents* (pp. 59–65). New York: Springer.

Bakan, D. (1966). *The duality of human existence: Isolation and communion in Western man.* Boston: Beacon.

Baker, Jeffrey P. (2000). Immunization and the American way: Childhood vaccines. *American Journal of Public Health, 90,* 199–207.

Baker, Susan P. (2000). Where have we been and where are we going with injury control? In Dinesh Mohan & Geetam Tiwari (Eds.), *Injury prevention and control* (pp. 19–26). London: Taylor & Francis.

Baldwin, Dare A. (1993). Infants' ability to consult the speaker for clues to word referencing. *Journal of Child Language, 20,* 395–418.

Baldwin, Dare A. (2000). Interpersonal understanding fuels knowledge acquisition. *Current Directions in Psychological Science, 9,* 40–45.

Balin, Arthur K. (Ed.). (1994). *Practical handbook of human biologic age determination.* Boca Raton, FL: CRC Press.

Balmford, Andrew, Clegg, Lizzie, Coulson, Tim, & Taylor, Jennie. (2002). Why conservationists should heed Pokémon [Letter to the editor]. *Science, 295,* 2367.

Baltes, Margret, & Carstensen, Laura L. (2003). The process of successful aging: Selection, optimization, and compensation. In Ursula M. Staudinger & Ulman Lindenberger (Eds.), *Understanding human development: Dialogues with lifespan psychology* (pp. 81–104). Dordrecht, Netherlands: Kluwer.

Baltes, Paul B. (2003). On the incomplete architecture of human ontogeny: Selection, optimization, and compensation as foundations of developmental theory. In

Ursula M. Staudinger & Ulman Lindenberger (Eds.), *Understanding human development: Dialogues with lifespan psychology* (pp. 17–43). Dordrecht, Netherlands: Kluwer.

Baltes, Paul B., & Baltes, Margret M. (1990). Psychological perspectives on successful aging: The model of selective optimization with compensation. In Paul B. Baltes & Margret M. Baltes (Eds.), *Successful aging: Perspectives from the behavioral sciences* (pp. 1–34). New York: Cambridge University Press.

Baltes, Paul B., Lindenberger, Ulman, & Staudinger, Ursula M. (1998). Lifespan theory in developmental psychology. In William Damon (Series Ed.) & Richard M. Lerner (Volume Ed.), *Handbook of child psychology: Vol. 1. Theoretical models of human development* (5th ed., pp. 1029–1144). New York: Wiley.

Bamshad, Michael, & Olson, Steve E. (2003). Does race exist? *Scientific American, 289,* 78–85.

Bandura, Albert. (1986). *Social foundations of thought and action: A social cognitive theory.* Englewood Cliffs, NJ: Prentice-Hall.

Bandura, Albert. (1997). The anatomy of stages of change. *American Journal of Health Promotion, 12,* 8–10.

Bandura, Albert. (2001). Social cognitive theory: An agentic perspective. *Annual Review of Psychology, 52,* 1–26.

Bandura, Albert, Barbaranelli, Claudio, Caprara, Gian Vittorio, & Pastorelli, Concetta. (2001). Self-efficacy beliefs as shapers of children's aspirations and career trajectories. *Child Development, 72,* 187–206.

Banerjee, Robin, & Linstern, Vicki. (2000). Boys will be boys: The effect of social evaluation concerns on gender-typing. *Social Development, 9,* 397–408.

Banich, Marie T. (1998). Integration of information between the cerebral hemispheres. *Current Directions in Psychological Science, 7,* 32–37.

Banich, Marie T., & Heller, Wendy. (1998). Evolving perspectives on lateralization of function. *Current Directions in Psychological Science, 7,* 1–2.

Barber, Bonnie L., Jacobson, Kristen C., Miller, Kristelle E., & Petersen, Anne C. (1998). Ups and downs: Daily cycles of adolescent moods. In Ann C.

Crouter & Reed Larson (Eds.), *Temporal rhythms in adolescence: Clocks, calendars, and the coordination of daily life. New directions for child and adolescent development, No. 82* (pp. 23–36). San Francisco: Jossey-Bass.

Barber, Brian K. (Ed). (2002). *Intrusive parenting: How psychological control affects children and adolescents.* Washington, DC: American Psychological Association.]

Barbieri, Robert A. (1999). Infertility. In Samuel S.C. Yen, Robert B. Jaffe, & Robert L. Barbieri (Eds.), *Reproductive endocrinology : Physiology, pathophysiology, and clinical management.* Philadelphia: Saunders.

Barnard, Kathryn E., & Martell, Louise K. (1995). Mothering. In Marc H. Bornstein (Ed.), *Handbook of parenting: Vol. 3. Status and social conditions of parenting* (pp. 3–26). Hillsdale, NJ: Erlbaum.

Barnett, Douglas, & Vondra, Joan I. (1999). I. Atypical patterns of early attachment: Theory, research, and current directions. *Monographs of the Society for Research in Child Development, 64*(3), Serial # 258, 1–24.

Barnett, Rosalind Chait, & Brennan, Robert T. (1997). Change in job conditions, change in psychological distress, and gender: A longitudinal study of dual-earner couples. *Journal of Organizational Behavior, 18,* 253–274.

Barnett, Rosalind Chait, & Hyde, Janet Shibley. (2001). Women, men, work, and family. *American Psychologist, 56,* 781–796.

Barnett, S. Anthony. (1998). *The science of life.* St. Leonards, Australia: Allen & Unwin.

Barnhill, Gena, Hagiwara, Taku, Smith Myles, Brenda, & Simpson, Richard L. (2000). Asperger syndrome: A study of the cognitive profiles of 37 children and adolescents. *Focus on Autism and Other Developmental Disabilities, 15,* 146–153.

Baron-Cohen, Simon. (2000). Is Asperger syndrome/high-functioning autism necessarily a disability? *Development and Psychopathology, 12,* 489–500.

Barrett, Martyn (Ed.). (1999). *The development of language.* Hove, England: Psychology Press.

Basseches, Michael. (1984). *Dialectical thinking and adult development.* Norwood, NJ: Ablex.

Basseches, Michael. (1989). Dialectical thinking as an organized whole: Comments on Irwin and Kramer. In Michael L. Commons, Jan D. Sinnott, Francis A. Richards, & Cheryl Armon (Eds.), *Adult development: Vol. 1. Comparisons and applications of developmental models.* New York: Praeger.

Batalova, Jeanne A., & Cohen, Philip N. (2002.) Premarital cohabitation and housework: Couples in cross-national perspective. *Journal of Marriage and Family, 64,* 743–755.

Bates, Elizabeth, Devescovi, Antonella, & Wulfeck, Beverly. (2001). Psycholinguistics: A cross-language perspective. *Annual Review of Psychology, 52,* 369–396.

Bates, John E., Pettit, Gregory S., Dodge, Kenneth A., & Ridge, Beth. (1998). Interaction of temperamental resistance to control and restrictive parenting in the development of externalizing behavior. *Developmental Psychology, 34,* 982–995.

Bates, John E., Viken, Richard J., Alexander, Douglas B., Beyers, Jennifer, & Stockton, Lesley. (2002). Sleep and adjustment in preschool children: Sleep diary reports by mothers relate to behavior reports by teachers. *Child Development, 73,* 62–74.

Bauer, Patricia J., & Dow, Gina. (1994). Episodic memory in 16- and 20-month-old children: Specifics are generalized but not forgotten. *Developmental Psychology, 30,* 403–417.

Bauer, Patricia J., Liebl, Monica, & Stennes, Leif. (1998). PRETTY is to DRESS as BRAVE is to SUITCOAT: Gender-based property-to-property inferences by 4–10-year-old children. *Merrill-Palmer Quarterly, 44,* 355–377.

Bauer, Ursula E., Johnson, Tammie M., Hopkins, Richard S., & Brooks, Robert G. (2000). Changes in youth cigarette use and intentions following implementation of a tobacco control program. *Journal of the American Medical Association, 284,* 723–728.

Baumeister, Roy F., & Boden, Joseph M. (1998). Aggression and the self: High self-esteem, low self-control, and ego trust. In Russell G. Green & Edward Donnerstein (Eds.), *Human aggression: Theories, research, and implications for social policy.* San Diego, CA: Academic Press.

Baumeister, Roy F., Campbell, Jennifer D., Krueger, Joachim I., & Vohs, Kathleen D. (2003). Does high self-esteem cause better performance, interpersonal success, happiness, or healthier lifestyles? *Psychological Science in the Public Interest, 4,* 1–44.

Baumrind, Diana. (1967). Child-care practices anteceding three patterns of preschool behavior. *Genetic Psychology Monographs, 75,* 43–88.

Baumrind, Diana. (1971). Current patterns of parental authority. *Developmental Psychology, 4* (Monograph 1), 1–103.

Bayley, Nancy. (1966). Learning in adulthood: The role of intelligence. In Herbert J. Klausmeier & Chester W. Harris (Eds.), *Analysis of concept learning.* New York: Academic Press.

Bayley, Nancy, & Oden, Melita. (1955). The maintenance of intellectual ability in gifted adults. *Journal of Gerontology, 10,* Series B(1), 91–107.

Baynes, R. D., & Bothwell, T. H. (1990). Iron deficiency. *Annual Review of Nutrition, 10,* 133–148.

Beach, Lee Roy, Chi, Michelene, Klein, Gary, Smith, Philip, & Vincente, Kim. (1997). Naturalistic decision making and related research lines. In Caroline E. Zsambok & Gary Klein (Eds.), *Expertise: Research and applications: Vol. 2. Naturalistic decision making* (pp. 29–35). Mahwah, NJ: Erlbaum.

Beal, Carole R. (1994). *Boys and girls: The development of gender roles.* New York: McGraw-Hill.

Beal, Susan Mitchell, & Porter, C. (1991). Sudden infant death syndrome related to climate. *Acta Paediatrica Scandinavica, 80,* 278–287.

Bearison, David J., Minian, Nadia, & Granowetter, Linda. (2002). Medical management of asthma and folk medicine in a Hispanic community. *Journal of Pediatric Psychology, 27,* 385–392.

Beauvais, Fred. (2000). Indian adolescence: Opportunity and challenge. In Raymond Montemayor, Gerald R. Adams, & Thomas P. Gullotta (Eds.), *Advances in adolescent development: Vol. 10. Adolescent diversity in ethnic, economic, and cultural contexts* (pp. 110–140). Thousand Oaks, CA: Sage.

Beck, Martha. (1999). *Expecting Adam.* New York: Times Books.

Becker, Gary. (1981). *A treatise on the family.* Cambridge, MA: Harvard University Press.

Becker, Penny Edgell, & Moen, Phyllis. (1999). Scaling back: Dual-earner couples' work–family strategies. *Journal of Marriage and the Family, 61,* 995–1007.

Beckwith, Leila, Cohen, Sarale E., & Hamilton, Claire E. (1999). Maternal sensitivity during infancy and subsequent life events relate to attachment representation at early adulthood. *Developmental Psychology, 35,* 693–700.

Bedford, Victoria Hilkevitch. (1995). Sibling relationships in middle and old age. In Rosemary Blieszner & Victoria Hilkevitch Bedford (Eds.), *Handbook of aging and the family* (pp. 201–222). Westport, CT: Greenwood Press.

Behrend, Douglas A., Scofield, Jason, & Kleinknecht, Erica E. (2001). Beyond fast mapping: Young children's extensions of novel words and novel facts. *Developmental Psychology, 37,* 698–705.

Behrman, Richard E. (Ed.). (1992). *Nelson textbook of pediatrics* (14th ed.). Philadelphia: Saunders.

Belamarich, Peter F., & Ayoob, Keith Thomas. (2001). Keeping teenage vegetarians healthy and in the know. *Contemporary Pediatrics, 18*(10), 89–90, 95–100, 103, 107–108.

Belizan, Jose M., Althabe, Fernando, Barros, Fernando C., Alexander, Sophie. (1999). Rates and implications of caesarean sections in Latin America: Ecological study. *British Medical Journal, 319,* 1397–1400.

Bell, Derrick. (1992). *Faces at the bottom of the well: The permanence of racism.* New York: Basic Books.

Belsky, Jay, Domitrovich, Celene, & Crnic, Keith. (1997). Temperament and parenting antecedents of individual differences in three-year-old boys' pride and shame reactions. *Child Development, 68,* 456–466.

Belsky, Jay, Jaffee, Sara, Hsieh, Kuang-Hua, & Silva, Phil A. (2001). Child-rearing antecedents of intergenerational relations in young adulthood: A prospective study. *Developmental Psychology, 37,* 801–813.

Belsky, Jay, Steinberg, Lawrence, & Draper, Patricia. (1991). Childhood experience, interpersonal development, and reproductive strategy: An evolutionary theory of socialization. *Child Development, 62,* 647–670.

Bem, Sandra. (1993). *The lenses of gender: Transforming the debate on sexual inequality.* New Haven, CT: Yale University Press.

Benes, Francine M. (2001). The development of prefrontal cortex: The maturation of neurotransmitter systems and their interactions. In Charles A. Nelson & Monica Luciana (Eds.), *Handbook of developmental cognitive neuroscience* (pp. 79–92). Cambridge, MA: MIT Press.

Benet, Sula. (1974). *Abkhasians: The long-lived people of the Caucasus.* New York: Holt, Rinehart & Winston.

Bengtson, Vern L. (1975). Generation and family effects in value socialization. *American Sociological Review, 40,* 358–371.

Bengtson, Vern L. (2001). Beyond the nuclear family: The increasing importance of multigenerational relationships in American society. The 1998 Burgess Award Lecture. *Journal of Marriage and Family, 63*(1), 1–16.

Benson, Peter L., Leffert, Nancy, Scales, Peter C., & Blyth, Dale A. (1998). Beyond the "village" rhetoric: Creating healthy communities for children and adolescents. *Applied Developmental Science, 2,* 138–159.

Bentley, Gillian R., & Mascie-Taylor, C. G. Nicholas. (2000). Preface. In Gillian R. Bentley & C. G. Nicholas Mascie-Taylor. (Eds.), *Infertility in the modern world.* Cambridge, England: Cambridge University Press.

Berdes, Celia, & Erdsman, Mary Patrice. (2001). Aging in Polonia: Polish and Polish American elderly. In Laura Katz Olson (Ed.), *Age through ethnic lenses* (pp. 33–44). Lanham, MD: Rowman & Littlefield.

Berg, Cynthia A., & Klaczynski, Paul A. (2002). Contextual variability in the expression and meaning of intelligence. In Robert J. Sternberg & Elena L. Grigorenko (Eds.), *The general factor of intelligence: How general is it?* (pp. 381–412). Mahwah, NJ: Erlbaum.

Berg, Sandra J., & Wynne-Edwards, Katherine E. (2002). Salivary hormone concentrations in mothers and fathers becoming parents are not correlated. *Hormones and Behavior, 42*(4), 424–436.

Bergeman, Cinty S. (1997). *Aging: Genetic and environmental influences.* Thousand Oaks, CA: Sage.

Berger, Klaus, Ajani, Umed A., Kase, Carlos S., Gaziano, J. Michael, Buring, Julie E., Glynn, Robert J., et al. (1999). Light-to-moderate alcohol consumption and the risk of stroke among U.S. male physicians. *New England Journal of Medicine, 341,* 1557–1564.

Berkey, Catherine S., Gardner, Jane D., Frazier, A. Lindsay, & Colditz, Graham A. (2000). Relation of childhood diet and body size to menarche and adolescent growth in girls. *American Journal of Epidemiology, 152,* 446–452.

Berndt, Thomas J. (1999). Friends' influence on children's adjustment to school. In W. A. E. Collins & B. E. Laursen (Eds.), *Relationships as developmental contexts* (pp. 85–107). Mahwah, NJ: Erlbaum.

Berndt, Thomas J., & Murphy, Lonna M. (2002). Influences of friends and friendships: Myths, truths, and research recommendations. In Robert V. Kail (Ed.), *Advances in child development and behavior* (Vol. 30, pp. 275–310). San Diego, CA: Academic Press.

Berntsen, Dorthe, & Rubin, David C. (2002). Emotionally charged autobiographical memories across the life span: The recall of happy, sad, traumatic, and involuntary memories. *Psychology and Aging, 17,* 636–652.

Berrick, Jill Duerr. (1998). When children cannot remain home: Foster family care and kinship care. *The Future of Children: Protecting Children from Abuse and Neglect, 8*(1), 72–87.

Bertenthal, Bennett I., & Clifton, Rachel K. (1998). Perception and action. In William Damon (Series Ed.), Deanna Kuhn, & Robert S. Siegler (Vol. Eds.), *Handbook of child psychology: Vol. 2. Cognition, perception and language* (5th ed., pp. 51–102). New York: Wiley.

Betts, Julian Robert. (1995). Does school quality matter? Evidence from the National Longitudinal Survey of Youth. *Review of Economics and Statistics, 77,* 231–250.

Beunen, Gaston P., Malina, Robert M., Van't Hof, Martin A., Simons, Jan, Ostyn, Michel, Renson, Roland, et al. (1988). *Adolescent growth and motor performance: A longitudinal study of Belgian boys.* Champaign, IL: Human Kinetics Books.

Bialystok, Ellen. (2001). *Bilingualism in development: Language, literacy, and cognition.* Cambridge, England: Cambridge University Press.

Bijou, Sidney W., & Baer, Donald M. (1978). *Behavior analysis of child development.* Englewood Cliffs, NJ: Prentice-Hall.

Billingsley, Andrew. (1999) *Mighty like a river: The black church and social reform.* New York: Oxford University Press.

Binstock, Robert H., & Day, Christine L. (1996). Aging and politics. In Robert H. Binstock & Linda K. George (Eds.), *Handbook of aging and the social sciences* (4th ed.). San Diego, CA: Academic Press.

Binstock, Robert H., & Quadagno, Jill. (2001). Aging and politics. In Robert H. Binstock & Linda K. George, *Handbook of aging and the social science*s (5th ed., pp. 333–351). San Diego, CA: Academic Press.

Birch, Susan A. J., & Bloom, Paul. (2003). Children are cursed: An asymmetric bias in mental-state attribution. *Psychological Science, 14,* 283–286.

Biro, Frank M., McMahon, Robert P., Striegel-Moore, Ruth, Crawford, Patricia B., Obarzanek, Eva, Morrison, John A., et al. (2001). Impact of timing of pubertal maturation on growth in black and white female adolescents: The National Heart, Lung, and Blood Institute Growth and Health Study. *Journal of Pediatrics, 138,* 636–643.

Birren, James E., & Schroots, Johannes J. F. (1996). History, concepts, and theory in the psychology of aging. In James E. Birren, Klaus Warner Schaie, Ronald P. Abeles, Margaret Gatz, & Timothy A. Salthouse (Eds.), *Handbook of the psychology of aging* (pp. 3–23). San Diego, CA: Academic Press.

Bissex, Glenda L. (1980). *GNYS AT WRK: A child learns to write and read.* Cambridge, MA: Harvard University Press.

Bjarnason, Thoroddur, Sigurdardottir, Thordis J., & Thorlindsson, Thorolfur. (1999). Human agency, capable guardians, and structural constraints: A lifestyle approach to the study of violent victimization. *Journal of Youth & Adolescence, 28,* 105–119.

Blanchard-Fields, Fredda. (1986). Reasoning on social dilemmas varying the emotional saliency: An adult developmental perspective. *Psychology and Aging, 1,* 325–333.

Blanchard-Fields, Fredda. (1999). Social schematicity and causal attributions. In Thomas M. Hess & Fredda Blanchard-Fields (Eds.), *Social cognition and aging* (pp. 219–236). San Diego, CA: Academic Press.

Block, Lauren G., Morwitz, Vicki G., Putsis, William P., Jr., & Sen, Subrata K. (2002). Assessing the impact of anti-drug advertising on adolescent drug consumption: Results from a behavioral economic model. *American Journal of Public Health, 92,* 1346–1351.

Bloom, Floyd E., Nelson, Charles A., & Lazerson, Arlyne. (2001). *Brain, mind, and behavior* (3rd ed.). New York: Worth.

Bloom, Lois. (1993). *The transition from infancy to language: Acquiring the power of expression.* New York: Cambridge University Press.

Bloom, Lois. (1998). Language acquisition in its developmental context. In William Damon (Series Ed.), Deanna Kuhn, & Robert S. Siegler (Volume Eds.), *Handbook of child psychology: Cognition, perception, and language* (5th ed.). New York: Wiley.

Bloom, Lois. (2000). Commentary. In George J. Hollich, Kathy Hirsh-Pasek, and Roberta Michnick Golinkoff, *Breaking the language barrier: An emergentist coalition model for the origins of word learning. Monographs of the Society for Research in Child Development, 65*(3, Serial no. 262), 124–135.

Bloom, Lois, & Tinker, Erin. (2001). The intentionality model and language acquisition: Engagement, effort, and the essential tension in development. *Monographs of the Society for Research in Child Development,* Serial No. 267, *66*(4), 1–89.

Bloom, Paul. (2000). *How children learn the meanings of words.* Cambridge, MA: MIT Press.

Blum, Nathan J., Taubman, Bruce, & Nemeth, Nicole. (2003). Relationship between age at initiation of toilet training and duration of training: A prospective study. *Pediatrics, 111,* 810–814.

Blum, Robert W., Beuhring, Trisha, Shew, Marcia L., Bearinger, Linda H., Sieving, Renee E., & Resnick, Michael D. (2000). The effect of race/ethnicity, income, and family structure on adolescent risk behavior. *American Journal of Public Health, 90,* 1879–1884.

Blurton-Jones, Nicholas G. (1976). Rough-and-tumble play among nursery school children. In Jerome S. Bruner, Alison Jolly, & Kathy Sylva (Eds.), *Play: Its role in development and evolution* (pp. 352–363). New York: Basic Books.

Blythe, Ronald. (1979). *The view in winter: Reflections on old age.* New York: Penguin.

Boaler, Jo. (2002). Experiencing school mathematics: Traditional and reform approaches to teaching and their impact on student learning (Rev. ed.). Mahwah, NJ: Erlbaum.

Bock, John, & Johnson, Sara E. (2002). Male migration, remittances, and child outcome among the Okavango Delta peoples of Botswana. In Catherine S. Tamis-LeMonda & Natasha Cabrera (Eds.), *Handbook of father involvement: Multidisciplinary perspectives* (pp. 308–335). Mahwah, NJ: Erlbaum.

Bogin, Barry. (1996). Human growth and development from an evolutionary perspective. In C.J.K. Henry & S.J. Ulijaszek (Eds.), *Long-term consequences of early environment: Growth, development and the lifespan developmental perspective.* Cambridge, England: Cambridge University Press.

Bolger, Kerry E., Patterson, Charlotte J., & Kupersmidt, Janis B. (1998). Peer relationships and self-esteem among children who have been maltreated. *Child Development, 69,* 1171–1197.

Bonner, Barbara L., Crow, Sheila M., & Logue, Mary Beth. (1999). Fatal child neglect. In Howard Dubowitz (Ed.), *Neglected children: Research, practice, and policy* (pp. 156–173). Thousand Oaks, CA: Sage.

Boom, Jan, Brugman, Daniel, & van der Heijden, Peter G. M. (2001). Hierarchical structure of moral stages assessed by a sorting task. *Child Development, 72,* 535–548.

Boonstra, Heather. (2000). Promoting contraceptive use and choice: France's approach to teen pregnancy and abortion. *The Guttmacher Report on Public Policy, 3*(3), 3–4.

Booth, A., & Osgood, D. (1993). The influence of testosterone on deviance in adulthood. *Criminology, 31,* 93–117.

Booth, Alan, & Amato, Paul R. (2001). Parental predivorce relations and offspring postdivorce wellbeing. *Journal of Marriage and Family, 63,* 197–212.

Booth, Tony, & Ainscow, Mel. (1998). *From them to us.* London: Routledge.

Borgaonkar, Digamber S. (1997). *Chromosomal variation in man: A catalog of chromosomal variants and anomalies* (8th ed.). New York: Wiley.

Borkowski, John G., Bisconti, Toni, Willard, Christine C., Keogh, Deborah A., Whitman, Thomas L, & Weed, Keri. (2002). The adolescent as parent: Influences on children's intellectual, academic, and socioemotional development. In John G. Borkowski, Sharon Landesman Ramey, & Marie Bristol-Power (Eds.), *Parenting and the child's world: Influences on academic, intellectual, and social-emotional development* (pp. 161–184). Mahwah, NJ: Erlbaum.

Borland, Moira, Laybourn, Ann, Hill, Malcolm, & Brown, Jane. (1998). *Middle childhood: The perspectives of children and parents.* London: Jessica Kingsley Publishers.

Bornat, Joanna. (2002). Doing life history research. In Anne Jamieson & Christina R. Victor (Eds.), *Researching aging and later life* (pp. 117–134). Buckingham, England: Open University.

Bornstein, Marc H. (2002). Parenting infants. In Bornstein, Marc H. (Ed). *Handbook of parenting: Vol. 1: Children and parenting* (2nd ed., pp. 3–43). Mahwah, NJ: Erlbaum.

Bornstein, Marc H., & Arterberry, M. (1999). Perceptual development. In Marc.H. Bornstein & Michael. E. Lamb (Eds.), *Developmental psychology: An advanced textbook* (4th ed., pp. 231–274). Mahwah, NJ: Erlbaum.

Bossé, Raymond. (1998). Retirement and retirement planning in old age. In Inger Hilde Nordhus, Gary R. VandenBos, Stig Berg, & Pia Fromholt (Eds.), *Clinical geropsychology* (pp. 155–159). Washington, DC: American Psychological Association.

Bosworth, Kris, Espelage, Dorothy L., & Simon, Thomas R. (1999). Factors associated with bullying behavior in middle school students. *Journal of Early Adolescence, 19,* 341–362.

Bouchard, Claude, & Bray, G.A. (Eds.). (1996). *Regulation of body weight: Biological and behavioral mechanisms.* New York: Wiley.

Bouchard, Thomas J. (1994). Genes, environment, and personality. *Science, 264,* 1700–1701.

Bouchard, Thomas J. (1997). Twin studies of behavior: New and old findings. In Alain Schmitt, Klaus Atzwanger, Karl Grammer, & Katrin Schäfer (Eds.), *New aspects of human ethology.* New York: Plenum Press.

Boulton, Michael, & Smith, Peter K. (1989). Issues in the study of children's rough-and-tumble play. In Marianne N. Bloch & Anthony D. Pellegrini (Eds.), *The ecological context of children's play.* Norwood, NJ: Ablex.

Bourgeois, J.-P. (2001). Synaptogenesis in the neocortex of the newborn: The ultimate frontier for individuation? In Charles A. Nelson & Monica Luciana (Eds.), *Handbook of developmental cognitive neuroscience* (pp. 149–158). Cambridge, MA: MIT Press.

Bowerman, Melissa, & Levinson, Stephen C. (2001). Introduction. In Melissa Bowerman & Stephen C. Levinson (Eds.), *Language acquisition and conceptual development* (pp. 1–18). Cambridge, England: Cambridge University Press.

Bowers, Bonita F., & Myers, Barbara J. (1999). Grandmothers providing care for grandchildren: Consequences of various levels of caregiving. *Family Relations, 48,* 303–310.

Bowlby, John. (1969). *Attachment and loss: Vol. 1. Attachment.* New York: Basic Books.

Bowlby, John. (1973). *Attachment and loss: Vol. 2. Separation: Anxiety and anger.* New York: Basic Books.

Bowlby, John. (1988). *A secure base: Clinical applications of attachment theory.* London: Routledge.

Bozik, Mary. (2002). The college student as learner: Insight gained through metaphor analysis. *College Student Journal, 36,* 142–151.

Bradbury, Thomas N., Fincham, Frank D., & Beach, Steven R. H. (2000). Research on the nature and determinants of marital satisfaction: A decade in review. *Journal of Marriage and Family, 63,* 964–980.

Bradbury, Mary. (2001). Forget me not: Memorialization in cemeteries and crematoria. In Jenny Hockey, Jeanne Katz, & Neil Small (Eds.), *Grief, mourning, and death ritual* (pp. 218–225). Buckingham, England: Open University Press.

Bradbury, Thomas N., Fincham, Frank D., & Beach, Steven R. H. (2000). Research on the nature and determinants of marital satisfaction: A decade in review. *Journal of Marriage and Family, 63,* 964–980.

Bradley, Robert H. (1995). Environment and parenting. In Marc H. Bornstein (Ed.), *Handbook of parenting: Vol. 2. Biology and ecology of parenting* (pp. 235–261). Hillsdale, NJ: Erlbaum.

Bradley, Robert H., Corwyn, Robert F., McAdoo, Harriette Pipes, & Garcia-Coll, Cynthia. (2002). The home environments of children in the United States Part I: Variation by age, ethnicity, and poverty status. *Child Development, 73,* 1844–1867.

Brandl, Bonnie. (2000). Power and control: Understanding domestic abuse in later life. *Generations, 24,* 39–45.

Brandtstädter, Jochen. (1998). Action perspectives on human development. In William Damon (Series Ed.), Richard M. Lerner (Volume Ed.), *Handbook of child psychology: Vol. 1. Theoretical models of human development* (5th ed.). New York: Wiley.

Brannen, Julia, Heptinstall, Ellen, & Bhopal, Kalwant. (2000). *Connecting children: Care and family life in later childhood.* New York: Routledge.

Braun, Kathryn L., Pietsch, James H., & Blanchette, Patricia L. (2000). An introduction to culture and its influence on end-of-life decision making. In Kathryn Braun, James H. Pietsch, & Patricia L. Blanchette (Eds.). *Cultural issues in end-of-life decision making* (pp. 1–12). Thousand Oaks, CA: Sage.

Braungart-Rieker, Julia M., Garwood, Molly M., Powers, Bruce P., & Wang, Xiaoyu. (2001). Parental sensitivity, infant affect, and affect regulation: Predictors of later attachment. *Child Development, 72,* 252–270.

Brawley, Otis W. (2001). Prostate cancer screening: A note of caution. In Ian M. Thompson, Martin I. Resnick, & Eric A. Klein (Eds.), *Prostate cancer screening* (pp. 175–185). Totowa, NJ: Humana Press.

Bray, George A. (2003). Low carbohydrate diets and realities of weight loss. *Journal of the American Medical Association, 289,* 1853–1855.

Brazelton, T. Berry, & Cramer, Bertrand G. (1991). *The earliest relationship: Parents, infants, and the drama of early attachment.* Reading, MA: Addison-Wesley.

Breggin, Peter R., & Baughman, Fred A., Jr. (2001, January 26). Questioning the treatment for ADHD [Letter to the editor]. *Science, 291,* 595.

Brendgen, Mara, Vitaro, Frank, Bukowski, William M., Doyle, Anna Beth, & Markiewicz, Dorothy. (2001). Developmental profiles of peer social preference over the course of elementary school: Associations with trajectories of externalizing and internalizing behavior. *Developmental Psychology, 37,* 308–320.

Brennan, P., & Raine, A. (1997). Biosocial bases of antisocial behavior: Psychophysiological, neurological, and cognitive factors. *Clinical Psychology Review, 17,* 589–604.

Bressler, Steven L. (2002). Understanding cognition through large-scale cortical networks. *Current Directions in Psychological Science, 11,* 58–61.

Bretherton, Inge, & Munholland, Kristine A. (1999). Internal working models in attachment relationships: A construct revisited. In Jude Cassidy & Phillip R. Shaver (Eds.), *Handbook of attachment: Theory, research, and clinical applications* (pp. 89–111). New York: Guilford Press.

Briggs, Susan D., Raz, Naftali, & Marks, William. (1999). Age-related deficits in generation and manipulation of mental images: I. The role of sensorimotor speed and working memory. *Psychology and Aging, 14,* 427–435.

Briley, Mike, & Sulser, Fridolin *(Eds.). (2001).* Molecular genetics of mental disorders: The place of molecular genetics in basic mechanisms and clinical applications in mental disorders. *London: Dunitz.*

Brim, Orville Gilbert. (2001). Foreword. In Margie E. Lachman (Ed.), *Handbook of midlife development* (pp. xi–xii). New York: Wiley.

Brody, Leslie R. (1999). *Gender, emotion, and the family.* Cambridge, MA: Harvard University Press.

Brokenleg, Martin, & Middleton, David. (1993). Native Americans: Adapting yet retaining. In Donald P. Irish, Kathleen F. Lundquist, & Vivien Jenkins Nelsen (Eds.), *Ethnic variations in dying, death, and grief : Diversity in universality* (Series in Death Education, Aging, and Health Care) Washington, DC: Taylor & Francis.

Bromley, Rajput V. (1999). Chronic insomnia: A practical review. *American Family Physician, 60,* 1431–1438.

Bronfenbrenner, Urie. (1977). Toward an experimental ecology of human development. *American Psychologist, 32,* 513–531.

Bronfenbrenner, Urie. (1979). *The ecology of human development: Experiments by nature and design.* Cambridge, MA: Harvard University Press.

Bronfenbrenner, Urie, & Morris, Pamela A. (1998). The ecology of developmental processes. In William Damon (Series Ed.) & Richard M. Lerner (Volume Ed.), *Handbook of child psychology: Vol. 1. Theoretical models of human development* (5th ed., pp. 993–1028). New York: Wiley.

Brook, Judith S., Richter, Linda, Whiteman, Martin, & Cohen, Patricia. (1999). Consequences of adolescent marijuana use: Incompatibility with the assumption of adult roles. *Genetic, Social, & General Psychology Monographs, 125,* 193–207.

Brooks-Gunn, Jeanne. (1991). Maturational timing variations in adolescent girls, antecedents of. In Richard M. Lerner, Anne C. Petersen, & Jeanne Brooks-Gunn (Eds.), *Encyclopedia of adolescence* (Vol. 2, pp. 609–618). New York: Garland.

Brown, Bernard. (1999). Optimizing expression of the common human genome for child development. *Current Directions in Psychological Science, 8,* 37–41.

Brown, Larry K., Lourie, Kevin J., & Pao, Maryland. (2000). Children and adolescents living with HIV and AIDS: A review. *Journal of Child Psychology and Psychiatry and Allied Disciplines, 41,* 81–96.

Brown, Nigel A. (1997). Chemical teratogens. In Peter Thorogood (Ed.), *Embryos, genes and birth defects* (pp. 69–88). New York: Wiley.

Browne, Ray B., & Neal, Arthur G. (2001). Introduction. In Ray B. Browne & Arthur G. Neal (Eds.), *Ordinary reactions to extraordinary events* (pp. 1–20). Bowling Green, OH: Bowling Green Press.

Bruner, Jerome. (1996). *The culture of education.* Cambridge, MA: Harvard University Press.

Bryan, Janet, & Luszcz, Mary A. (1996). Speed of information processing as a mediator between age and free-recall performance. *Psychology and Aging, 11,* 3–9.

Buckner, John C., Bassuk, Ellen L., Weinreb, Linda F., & Brooks, Margaret G. (1999). Homelessness and its relation to the mental health and behavior of low-income school-age children. *Developmental Psychology, 35,* 246–257.

Buehler, Cheryl, & Gerard, Jean M. (2002). Marital conflict, ineffective parenting, and children's and adolescents' maladjustment. *Journal of Marriage and Family, 64,* 78–92.

Buekens, Pierre, Curtis, Sian, & Alayon, Silvia. (2003). Demographic and health surveys: Caesarean section rates in sub-Saharan Africa. *British Medical Journal, 326,* 136.

Buhrmester, Duane. (1996). Need fulfillment, interpersonal competence, and the developmental contexts of early adolescent friendship. In William M. Bukowski, Andrew F. Newcomb, & Willard W. Hartup (Eds.), *The company they keep: Friendship in childhood and adolescence.* Cambridge, England: Cambridge University Press.

Bukowski, William M., Newcomb, A.F., & Hartup, W.W. (Eds.). (1996). *The company they keep: Friendship in childhood and adolescence.* New York: Cambridge University Press.

Bukowski, William M., Sippola, Lorrie K., Hoza, B., & Newcomb, Andrew F. (2000). Pages from a sociometric notebook: an analysis of nomination and rating scale measures of acceptance, rejection, and social preference. *New Directions for Child and Adolescent Development, 88,* 11–26.

Bukowski, William M., Sippola, Lorrie K., & Newcomb, Andrew F. (2000). Variations in patterns of attraction to same- and other-sex peers during early adolescence. *Developmental Psychology, 36,* 147–154.

Bulmahn, Eelgard. (1999). Women in science in Germany. *Science, 286,* 2081.

Bumpass, Larry, & Lu, Hsien-Hen. (2000). Trends in cohabitation and implications for children's family contexts in the United States. *Population Studies, 54,* 29–41.

Bunker, John P., Frazer, Howard S., & Mosteller, Frederick. (1995). The role of medical care in determining health: Creating an inventory of benefits. In Benjamin C. Amick, III, Sol Levine, Alvin R. Tarlov, & Diana Chapman Walsh (Eds.), *Society and health.* New York: Oxford University Press.

Burlingham, Dorothy, & Freud, Anna. (1942). *Young children in wartime.* London: Allen & Unwin.

Burr, Jeffrey A., & Mutchler, Jan E. (1999). Race and ethnic variation in norms of filial responsibility among older persons. *Journal of Marriage and the Family, 61,* 674–687.

Buschman, N. A., Foster, G., & Vickers, Pauline. (2001). Adolescent girls and their babies: Achieving optimal birthweight. *Child: Care, Health, and Development, 27,* 163–171.

Bushman, Brad J., & Anderson, Craig A. (2001). Media violence and the American public. *American Psychologist, 56,* 477–489.

Buss, David M., Haselton, Martie G., Shackelford, Todd K., Bleske, April L., & Wakefield, Jerome C. (1998). Adaptations, exaptations, and spandrels. *American Psychologist, 53,* 533–548.

Busse, Ewald W. (1969). Theories of aging. In Ewald W. Busse & Eric Pfeiffer (Eds.), *Behavior and adaptation in late life* (pp. 11–31). Boston: Little Brown.

Butler, Robert N., Lewis, Myrna, & Sunderland, Trey. (1998) *Aging and mental health: Psychosocial and biomedical approaches* (5th ed.). Boston: Allyn & Bacon.

Butler, Samantha C., Berthier, Neil E., & Clifton, Rachel K. (2002). Two-year-olds' search strategies and visual tracking in a hidden displacement task. *Developmental Psychology, 38,* 581–590.

Byrnes, James P. (1998). *The nature and development of decision-making: A self-regulation model.* Mahwah, NJ: Erlbaum.

Cabeza, Roberto. (2002). Hemispheric asymmetry reduction in older adults: The

HAROLD model. *Psychology and Aging, 17,* 85–100.

Cabrera, Natasha J., Tamis-LeMonda, Catherine S., Bradley, Robert H., Hofferth, Sandra, & Lamb, Michael E. (2000). Fatherhood in the twenty-first century. *Child Development, 71,* 127–136.

Cairns, Robert B., & Cairns, Beverley D. (1994). *Lifelines and risks: Pathways of youth in our time.* Cambridge, England: Cambridge University Press.

Cairns, Robert B., & Cairns, Beverley D. (2001). Aggression and attachment: The folly of separatism. In Arthur C. Bohart & Deborah J. Stipek (Eds.), *Constructive and destructive behavior: Implications for family, school, and society* (pp. 21–47). Washington, DC: American Psychological Association.

Calam, Rachel, & Waller, Glenn. (1998). Are eating and psychological characteristics in early teenage years useful predictors of eating characteristics in early adulthood? A 7-year longitudinal study. *International Journal of Eating Disorders, 24,* 351–362.

Caldwell, J. C., & Caldwell, P. (2000). From STD epidemics to AIDS: A socio-demographic and epidemiological perspective on sub-Saharan Africa. In Gillian R. Bentley & C. G. Nicholas Mascie-Taylor (Eds.), *Infertility in the modern world.* Cambridge, England: Cambridge University Press.

Cameron, Judy L. (2001). Effects of sex hormones on brain development. In Charles A. Nelson & Monica Luciana (Eds.), *Handbook of developmental cognitive neuroscience* (pp. 59–78). Cambridge, MA: MIT Press.

Campbell, Darren W., & Eaton, Warren O. (1999). Sex differences in the activity level of infants. *Infant and Child Development, 8,* 1–17.

Campbell, Frances A., Pungello, Elizabeth P., Miller-Johnson, Shari, Burchinal, Margaret, & Ramey, Craig T. (2001). The development of cognitive and academic abilities: Growth curves from an early childhood educational experiment. *Developmental Psychology, 37,* 231–242.

Campos, Joseph J., Hiatt, Susan, Ramsay, Douglas, Henderson, Charlotte, & Svejda, Marilyn. (1978). The emergence of fear on the visual cliff. In Michael Lewis & Leonard A. Rosen-blum (Eds.), *The development of affect.* New York: Plenum.

Cannon, Tyrone D., Huttunen M.O., Lonnqvist J., Tuulio-Henriksson A., Pirkola T., Glahn D., Finkelstein J., et al. (2002). The inheritance of neuropsychological dysfunction in twins discordant for schizophrenia. *American Journal of Human Genetics, 67,* 369–382.

Cannon, Tyrone D., Rosso, Isabelle M., Bearden, Carrie E., Sanchez, Laura E., & Hadley, Trevor. (1999). A prospective cohort study of neurodevelopmental processes in the genesis and epigenesis of schizophrenia. *Development and Psychopathology, 11,* 467–485.

Capaldi, Deborah M., Stoolmiller, Mike, Clark, Sara, & Owen, Lee D. (2002). Heterosexual risk behaviors in at-risk young men from early adolescence to young adulthood: Prevalence, prediction, and association with STD contraction. *Developmental Psychology, 38,* 394–406.

Caplan, Leslie J., & Schooler, Carmi. (2003). The roles of fatalism, self-confidence, and intellectual resources in the disablement process in older adults. *Psychology and Aging, 18,* 551–561.

Caprara, Gian Vittorio, Barbaranelli, Claudio, & Pastorelli, Concetta. (2001). Prosocial behavior and aggression in childhood and pre-adolescence. In Arthur C. Bohart & Deborah J. Stipek (Eds.), *Constructive and destructive behavior: Implications for family, school and society* (pp. 187–204). Washington, DC: American Psychological Association.

Caretta, Carla Mucignat, Caretta, Antonio, & Cavaggioni, Andrea. (1995). Pheromonally accelerated puberty is enhanced by previous experience of the same stimulus. *Physiology and Behavior, 57,* 901–903.

Carlson, Karen J., Eisenstat, Stephanie A., & Ziporyn, Terra. (1996). *The Harvard guide to women's health.* Cambridge, MA: Harvard University Press.

Carlson, Marcia J., & Corcoran, Mary E. (2001). Family structure and children's behavioral and cognitive outcomes. *Journal of Marriage and Family, 63,* 779–792.

Carnegie Council on Adolescent Development. (1989). *Turning points: Preparing American youth for the 21st century.* New York: Carnegie Corporation.

Carnethon, Mercedes R., Gidding, Samuel S., Nehgman, Rodrigo, Sidney, Stephen, Jacobs, David R., & Liu, Kiang. (2003). Cardiorespiratory fitness in young adulthood and the development of cardiovascular disease risk factors. *Journal of the American Medical Association, 290,* 3092–3100.

Caro, F.G., & Bass, S. (1997). Receptivity to volunteering in the immediate postretirement period. *Journal of Applied Gerontology, 16,* 427–431

Carpenter, Siri. (1999, August 14). Modern hygiene's dirty tricks: The clean life may throw off a delicate balance in the immune system. *Science News, 156,* 108–110.

Carr, Janet H. (1995). *Down's syndrome: Children growing up.* New York: Cambridge University Press.

Carstensen, L.L., Gottman, J.M., & Levenson, R.W. (1995). Emotional behavior in long-term marriage. *Psychology and Aging, 10,* 140–149.

Carter, Jimmy. (2001). *An hour before daylight: Memories of a rural boyhood.* New York: Simon & Schuster.

Caruso, David, & Wolfe, Charles J. (2001). Emotional intelligence in the workplace. In Joseph Ciarrochi, Joseph R. Forgas, & John D. Mayer (Eds.), *Emotional intelligence in everyday life: A scientific inquiry.*(pp. 150–159). Philadelphia: Psychology Press.

Cascio, Wayne F. (1995). Whither industrial and organizational psychology in a changing world of work? *American Psychologist, 50,* 928–939.

Case, Robbie. (1998). The development of conceptual structures. In William Damon (Series Ed.), Deanna Kuhn & Robert S. Siegler (Volume Eds.), *Handbook of child psychology: Vol. 2. Cognition, perception, and language* (5th ed., pp. 745–800). New York: Wiley.

Casey, B. J. (2001). Disruption of inhibitory control in developmental disorders: A mechanistic model of implicated frontostriatal circuitry. In James L. McClelland & Robert S. Siegler (Eds.), *Mechanisms of cognitive development: Behavioral and neural perspectives* (pp. 327–352). Mahwah, NJ: Erlbaum.

Caspi, Avshalom, Lynam, Donald, Moffit, Terrie, & Silva, Phil A. (1993). Unraveling girls' delinquency: Biological, dispositional, and contextual contributions to adolescent misbehavior. *Developmental Psychology, 29,* 19–30.

Caspi, Avshalom, McClay, Joseph, Moffitt, Terrie, Mill, Jonathan, Martin, Judy, Craig, Ian W., Taylor, Alan, & Poulton, Richie. (2002). Role of genotype in the cycle of violence in maltreated children. *Science, 297,* 851–854.

Caspi, Avshalom, & Roberts, Brent W. (1999). Personality continuity and change across the life course. In L. A. Pervin & O. P. John (Eds.), *Handbook of personality: Theory and research* (2nd ed., pp. 300–326). New York: Guilford Press.

Caspi, Avshalom, Sugden, Karen, Moffitt, Terrie E., Taylor, Alan, Craig, Ian W., Harrington, HonaLee, et al. (2003). Influence of life stress on depression: Moderation by a polymorphism in the 5-HTT gene. *Science, 301*(5631), 386–389.

Cassidy, Jude, & Shaver, Phillip R. (Eds.). (1999). *Handbook of attachment: Theory, research, and clinical applications.* New York: Guilford Press.

Cassidy, Tony. (1999). *Stress, cognition, and health.* London: Routledge.

Cavanaugh, John C. (1999). Metamemory as social cognition: Challenges for (and from) survey results. In Norbert Schwarz, Denise Park, Barbel Knauper, & Seymour Sudmen (Eds.). *Cognition, aging, and self-reports.* Philadelphia: Psychology Press.

Ceci, Stephen J., & Cornelius, Steven W. (1990). Development of adaptive competence in adulthood: Commentary. *Human Development, 33,* 198–201.

Cepeda, Nicholas J., Kramer, Arthur F., & Gonzalez de Sather, Jessica C. M. (2001). Changes in executive control across the life span: Examination of task-switching performance. *Developmental Psychology, 37,* 715–730.

Chamberlain, Patricia, Fisher, Philip A., & Moore, Kevin. (2002). Multidimensional treatment foster care: Applications of the OSLC intervention model to high-risk youth and their families. In John B. Reid, Gerald R. Patterson, & James J. Snyder (Eds.), *Antisocial behavior in children and adolescents: A developmental analysis and model for intervention* (pp. 203–218). Washington, DC: American Psychological Association.

Champion, Lorna A. (2000). Depression. In Lorna A. Champion & Michael J.

Power (Eds.), *Adult psychological problems* (2nd ed., pp. 29–53). Philadelphia: Psychology Press.

Chan, Evelyn C. W., Vernon, Sally W., O'Donnell, M. S., Ahn, Chul, Greisinger, Anthony, & Aga, Donnie W. (2003). Informed consent for cancer screening with prostate-specific antigen: How well are men getting the message? *American Journal of Public Health, 93,* 779–785.

Chandler, Michael J., Lalonde, Christopher E., Sokol, Bryan W., & Hallett, Darcy. (2003). Personal persistence, identity development, and suicide: A study of native and non-native North American adolescents. *Monographs of the Society for Research in Child Development, 68*(2), vii-130.

Chao, Ruth. (2001). Extending research on the consequences of parenting style for Chinese Americans and European Americans. *Child Development, 72,* 1832–1843.

Charles, Susan Turk, & Carstensen, Laura L. (1999). The role of time in the setting of social goals across the life span. In Thomas M. Hess & Fredda Blanchard-Fields (Eds.), *Social cognition and aging* (pp. 319–342). San Diego, CA: Academic Press.

Charness, Neil, Krampe, Ralf, & Mayr, Ulrich. (1996). The role of practice and coaching in entrepreneurial skill domains: An international comparison of life-span chess skill acquisition. In Karl Anders Ericsson (Ed.), *The road to excellence: The acquisition of expert performance in the arts and sciences, sports and games* (pp. 51–80). Mahwah, NJ: Erlbaum.

Chatterjee, Shuita Chopra. (2002). Death and the discourse of the body. *Omega, 45,* 321–330.

Chatters, Linda M. (2000). Religion and health: Public health research and practice. *Annual Review of Public Health, 21,* 335–367.

Chen, Kevin, & Kandel, Denise. (1995). The natural history of drug use from adolescence to the mid-thirties in a general population sample. *American Journal of Public Health, 85,* 41–47.

Cherlin, Andrew, & Furstenberg, Frank F., Jr. (1986). *The new American grandparent: A place in the family, a life apart.* New York: Basic Books.

Cherry, Katie E., & Stadler, Michael A. (1995). Implicit learning of a nonverbal sequence in younger and older adults. *Psychology and Aging, 10,* P379–394.

Chikkatur, Anita. (1997). A shortcut to independence. In Youth Communications, Andrea Estepa, & Philip Kay (Eds.), *Starting with "I": Personal essays by teenagers* (pp. 12–16). New York: Persea Books.

Children's Defense Fund. (1999). *The state of America's children, yearbook 1999.* Washington, DC: Publications Department.

Chisolm, Kim. (1998). A three-year follow-up of attachment and indiscriminate friendliness in children adopted from Romanian orphanages. *Child Development, 69,* 1092–1106.

Chmiel, Nik. (1998). *Jobs, technology and people.* London: Routledge.

Chobanian, A. V., Bakris, G. L., Black, H. R., Cushman, W. C., Green, L. A., Izzo, J. L., Jr., et al. (2003). The seventh report of the Joint National Committee on prevention, detection, evaluation and treatment of high blood pressure: The JNC 7 report. *Journal of the American Medical Association, 289,* 2560–2572.

Choi, Incheol, Dalal, Reeshad, Kim-Prieto, Chu, & Park, Hyekyung. (2003). Culture and judgment of causal relevance. *Journal of Personality and Social Psychology, 84*(1), 46–59.

Chomsky, Noam. (1968). *Language and mind.* New York: Harcourt, Brace & World.

Chomsky, Noam. (1980). *Rules and representations.* New York: Columbia University Press.

Chow, Gregory E., & Yancey, Michael K. (2001). Labor and delivery: Normal and abnormal. In Frank W. Ling & Patrick Duff (Eds.), *Obstetrics and gynecology: Principles for practice.* New York: McGraw-Hill.

Christensen, H., Mackinnon, A. J., Korten, A. E., Jorm, A. F., Henderson, A. S., Jacomb, P., et al. (1999). An analysis of diversity in the cognitive performance of elderly community dwellers: Individual differences in change scores as a function of age. *Psychology of Aging, 14,* 365–379.

Christoffel, Tom, & Gallagher, Susan Scavo. (1999). *Injury prevention and public health: Practical knowledge, skills, and strategies.* Gaithersburg, MD: Aspen.

Cicchetti, Dante, & Sroufe, L. Alan. (2000). The past as prologue to the future: The times, they've been a-changing. *Development and Psychopathology, 12,* 255–264.

Cicchetti, Dante, & Toth, Sheree L. (1998). Perspectives on research and practice in developmental psychopathology. In William Damon (Series Ed.), Irving E. Sigel, & K. Ann Renninger (Vol. Eds.), *Handbook of child psychology: Vol. 4. Child psychology in practice* (5th ed., pp. 479–483). New York: Wiley.

Cicchetti, Dante, & Walker, Elaine F. (2001). Stress and development: Biological and psychological consequences. *Development and Psychopathology, 13,* 413–418.

Cicirelli, Victor G. (1995). *Sibling relationships across the life span.* New York: Plenum Press.

Clark, Eve Vivienne. (1995). Later lexical development and word formation. In Paul Fletcher, & Brian MacWhinney (Eds.), *The handbook of child language* (pp. 393–412). Cambridge, MA: Blackwell.

Clark, Tim, & Rees, John. (1996). *Practical management of asthma.* London: Martin Dunitz.

Clark, William R. (1999). *A means to an end: The biological basis of aging and death.* New York: Oxford University Press.

Clayton, Richard R., Cattarello, Anna M., & Johnstone, Bryan M. (1996). The effectiveness of Drug Abuse Resistance Education (Project DARE): 5-year follow-up results. *Preventive Medicine, 25,* 307–318.

Clinchy, Blythe McVicker. (1993). Ways of knowing and ways of being: Epistemological and moral development in undergraduate women. In Andrew Garrod (Ed.), *Approaches to moral development: New research and emerging themes.* New York: Teachers College Press.

Cloninger, C. Robert. (2003). Completing the psychobiological architecture of human personality development: Temperament, character, and coherence. In Ursula M. Staudinger, & Ulman Lindenberger (Eds.), *Understanding human development: Dialogues with lifespan psychology* (pp. 159–181). Dordrecht, Netherlands: Kluwer.

Cobb, Paul. (2000). Conducting teaching experiments in collaboration with teach-ers. In Anthony E. Kelly, & Richard A. Lesh (Eds.), *Handbook of research design in mathematics and science education* (pp. 207–334). Mahwah, NJ: Erlbaum.

Cobb, Paul, Wood, Terry, & Yackel, Erna. (1993). Discourse, mathematical thinking, and classroom practice. In Ellice A. Forman, Norris Minick, & C. Addison Stone (Eds.), *Contexts for learning: Sociocultural dynamics in children's development* (pp. 91–119). New York: Oxford University Press.

Cohan, Catherine, & Kleinbaum, Stacey. (2002). Toward a greater understanding of the cohabitation effect: Premarital cohabitation and marital communication. *Journal of Marriage and Family, 64,* 180–192.

Cohen, Carl I., Sokolovsky, Jay, & Crane, Maureen. (2001). Aging, homelessness, and the law. In David N. Weisstub, David C. Thomasma, Serge Gauthier, & George F. Tomossy (Eds.), *Aging: Caring for our elders,* (pp. 219–235). Dordrecht, Netherlands: Kluwer.

Cohen, Deborah, Spear, Suzanne, Scribner, Richard, Kissinger, Patty, Mason, Karen, & Wildgen, John. (2000). "Broken windows" and the risk of gonorrhea. *American Journal of Public Health, 90,* 230–236.

Cohen, G. (1999). Aging and autobiographical memory. In C. P. Thompson, D. J. Herrmann, D. Bruce, J. D. Read, D. G. Payne, & M. P. Toglia (Eds.), *Autobiographical memory: Theoretical and applied perspectives.* Hillsdale, NJ: Erlbaum.

Coie, John D., & Dodge, Kenneth A. (1998). Aggression and antisocial behavior. In William Damon (Series Ed.), & Nancy Eisenberg (Vol. Ed.), *Handbook of child psychology: Vol. 3. Social, emotional, and personality development* (5th ed., pp. 786–788). New York: Wiley.

Cokley, Kevin O. (2003). What do we know about the motivation of African-American students? Challenging the "anti-intellectual" myth. *Harvard Educational Review, 73,* 524–558.

Colder, Craig R., Mott, Joshua A., & Berman, Arielle S. (2002). The interactive effects of infant activity level and fear on growth trajectories of early childhood behavior problems. *Development and Psychopathology, 14,* 1–23.

Cole, David A., Maxwell, Scott E., Martin, Joan M., Peeke, Lachlan G., Seroczynski, Alesha D., Tram, Jane M., et al., (2001). The development of multiple domains of child and adolescent self-concept: A cohort sequential longitudinal design. *Child Development, 72,* 1723–1746.

Cole, Michael. (1996). *Cultural psychology: A once and future discipline.* Cambridge, MA: Belknap Press.

Cole, Pamela M., Zahn-Waxler, Carolyn, Fox, Nathan A., Usher, Barbara A., & Welsh, Jean D. (1996). Individual differences in emotion regulation and behavior problems in preschool children. *Journal of Abnormal Psychology, 105,* 518–529.

Coleman, Marilyn, Ganong, Lawrence, & Fine, Mark. (2000). Reinvestigating remarriage: Another decade of progress. *Journal of Marriage and the Family, 62,* 1288–1307.

Coleman, Peter. (2002). Doing case study research in psychology. In Anne Jamieson & Christine R. Victor (Eds.), *Researching aging and later life* (pp. 135–154). Philadelphia: Taylor & Francis.

Coles, Robert. (1990). *The spiritual life of children.* Boston: Houghton Mifflin.

Coles, Robert. (1997). *How to raise a moral child: The moral intelligence of children.* New York: Random House.

Collaer, Marcia L., & Hines, Melissa. (1995). Human behavioral sex differences: A role for gonadal hormones during early development? *Psychological Bulletin, 118,* 55–107.

Collinge, John, Sidle, Katie C., Meads, Julie, Ironside, James, & Hill, Andrew F. (1996). Molecular analysis of prion strain variation and the aetiology of "new variant" CJD. *Nature* (London), *383,* 685–690.

Collins, W. Andrew. (2003). More than myth: The developmental significance of romantic relationships during adolescence. *Journal of Research on Adolescence, 13,* 1–24.

Collins, W. Andrew, Maccoby, Eleanor E., Steinberg, Laurence, Hetherington, E. Mavis, & Bornstein, Marc H. (2000). Contemporary research on parenting: The case for nature and nurture. *American Psychologist, 55,* 218–232.

Collins, W. Andrew, Madsen, Stephanie D., & Susman-Sullivan, Amy. (2002). Parenting during middle childhood. In Marc H. Bornstein (Ed.), *Hand-*

book of parenting: Vol. 1. Children and parenting (2nd ed., pp. 73–101). Mahwah, NJ: Erlbaum.

Colonia-Willner, Regina. (1998). Practical intelligence at work: Relationship between aging and cognitive efficiency among managers in a bank environment. Psychology and Aging, 13, 45–57.

Comery, Thomas A., Harris, Jennifer B., Willems, Patrick J., Oostra, Ben A., Irwin, Scott A., Weiler, Ivan Jeanne, & Greenough, William T. (1997). Abnormal dendritic spines in fragile-X knockout mice: Maturation and pruning deficits. Proceedings of the National Academy of Sciences, 94, 5401–5404.

Compton, Kristi, Snyder, James, Schrepferman, Lynn, Bank, Lew, & Shortt, Joann Wu. (2003). The contribution of parents and siblings to antisocial and depressive behavior in adolescents: A double jeopardy coercion model. Development and Psychopathology, 15, 163–182.

Comstock, George, & Scharrer, Erica. (1999). Television: What's on, who's watching, and what it means. San Diego, CA: Academic Press.

Conchas, Gilberto Q. (2001). Structuring failure and success: Understanding the variability in Latino school engagement. Harvard Educational Review, 71, 475–504.

Conger, Richard D., Rueter, Martha A., & Elder, Glen H., Jr. (1999). Couple resilience to economic pressure. Journal of Personality and Social Psychology, 76, 54–71.

Coni, Nicholas K., Davison, William, & Webster, Stephen. (1992). Aging: The facts. Oxford, England: Oxford University Press.

Conner, David B., Knight, Danica K., & Cross, David R. (1997). Mothers' and fathers' scaffolding of their 2-year-olds during problem-solving and literacy interactions. British Journal of Developmental Psychology, 15, 323–338.

Connidis, I. A. (2002). Family ties and aging. Thousand Oaks, CA: Sage.

Cook, Thomas D., & Furstenberg, Frank F., Jr. (2002). Explaining aspects of the transition to adulthood in Italy, Sweden, Germany, and the United States: A cross-disciplinary, case synthesis approach. Annals of the American Academy of Political and Social Science, 580, 257–287.

Coontz, Stephanie. (1992). The way we never were: American families and the nostalgia trap. New York: Basic Books.

Coontz, Stephanie (Ed.). (1998). American families: A multicultural reader. New York: Routledge.

Corless, I. B., & Nicholas, P. K. (2003). Hospice and the emergence of palliative care services: A legacy in the making. In I. B. Corless, M. Pittman, & B. Germino (Eds.), Dying, death, and bereavement: A challenge for living (pp. 181–200). New York: Springer.

Cornelius, Llewellyn J., Smith, Pamela L., & Simpson, Gaynell M. (2002). Rural health and women of color: What factors hinder women of color from obtaining preventive health care? American Journal of Public Health, 92(4), 535–539.

Corter, Carl M., & Fleming, Alison S. (1995). Psychobiology of maternal behavior in human beings. In Marc H. Bornstein (Ed.), Handbook of parenting: Biology and ecology of parenting (pp. 141–181). Mahwah, NJ: Erlbaum.

Cosby, Ennis. (1997, January 26). Teaching from the heart. The New York Times, sec. 4, p. 13.

Costello, Anthony, & Manandhar, Dharma. (2000). Improving newborn infant health in developing countries. London: Imperial College Press.

Cotman, Carl W., & Neeper, Shawne. (1996). Activity-dependent plasticity and the aging brain. In Edward L. Schneider, & John W. Rowe (Eds.), Handbook of the biology of aging (4th ed.). San Diego, CA: Academic Press.

Cott, Nancy F. (2000). Public vows: A history of marriage and the nation. Cambridge, MA: Harvard University Press.

Covington, Martin V. (2000). Goal theory, motivation, and school achievement: An integrative review. Annual Review of Psychology, 51, 171–200.

Covington, Martin V., & Dray, Elizabeth. (2002). The developmental course of achievement motivation: A need-based approach. In Allan Wigfield, & Jacquelynne S. Eccles (Eds.), Development of achievement motivation (pp. 33–56). San Diego, CA: Academic Press.

Cowan, Nelson. (Ed.). (1997). The development of memory in childhood. Hove, East Sussex, UK: Psychology Press.

Coward, Raymond T., Horne, Claydell, & Dwyer, Jeffrey W. (1992). Demographic perspectives on gender and family caregiving. In Jeffrey W. Dwyer, & Raymond T. Coward (Eds.), Gender, families and elder care (pp. 18–33). Thousand Oaks, CA: Sage.

Cox, Martha J., & Brooks-Gunn, Jeanne (Eds.). (1999). Conflict and cohesion in families: Causes and consequences. Mahwah, NJ: Erlbaum.

Cox, Maureen V. (1993). Children's drawings of the human figure. Hillsdale, NJ: Erlbaum.

Cox, Maureen V. (1997). Drawings of people by the under-5s. London: Falmer Press.

Craik, Fergus I. M., & Salthouse, Timothy A. (Eds.). (2000). Handbook of aging and cognition (2nd ed.). Mahwah, NJ: Erlbaum.

Cramer, Duncan. (1998). Close relationships: The study of love and friendship. New York: Oxford University Press.

Crane, J., Wickens, K., Beasley, R., & Fitzharris, P. (2002). Asthma and allergy: a worldwide problem of meanings and management? Allergy, 57(8), 663–672.

Crick, Nicki R., Casas, Juan F., & Ku, Hyon-Chin. (1999). Relational and physical forms of peer victimization in preschool. Child Development, 35, 376–385.

Criss, Michael M., Pettit, Gregory S., Bates, John E., Dodge, Kenneth A., & Lapp, Amie L. (2002). Family adversity, positive peer relationships, and children's externalizing behavior: A longitudinal perspective on risk and resilience. Child Development, 73(4), 1220–1237.

Crittenden, Patricia M., Claussen, Angelika H., & Sugarman, David B. (1994). Physical and psychological maltreatment in middle childhood and adolescence. Development and Psychopathology, 6, 145–164.

Cross, S., & Markus, H. (1991). Possible selves across the life span. Human Development, 34, 230–255.

Crouter, Ann C., Bumpus, Matthew F., Maguire, Mary C., & McHale, Susan M. (1999). Linking parents' work pressure and adolescents' well-being: Insights into dynamics in dual-earner families. Developmental Psychology, 35, 1453–1461.

Crow, James F. (2003). There's something curious about paternal-age effects. *Science, 301,* 606–607.

Cruikshank, Margaret. (2003). *Learning to be old: Gender, culture, and aging.* Lanham, MD: Rowman and Littlefield.

Csikszentmihalyi, Mihaly. (1996). *Creativity: Flow and the psychology of discovery and invention.* New York: HarperCollins.

Csikszentmihalyi, Mihaly, & Schneider, Barbara. (2000). *Becoming adult: How teenagers prepare for the world of work.* New York: Basic Books.

Cummings, E. Mark, & Davies, Patrick. (1994). *Children and marital conflict: The impact of family dispute and resolution.* New York: Guilford.

Cummings, E. Mark, Goeke-Morey, Marcie C., & Graham, Marybeth A. (2002). Interparental relations as a dimension of parenting. In John G. Borkowski, Sharon Landesman Ramey, & Marie Bristol-Power (Eds.), *Parenting and the child's world: Influences on academic, intellectual, and social-emotional development.* Mahwah, NJ: Erlbaum.

Cummings, E., & Henry, W. (1961). *Growing old: The process of disengagement.* New York: Basic Books.

Curry, Leslie, Schwartz, Harold, Grumen, Cindy, & Blank, Karen. (2002). Could adequate palliative care obviate assisted suicide? *Death Studies, 26,* 757–774.

Curtis, Patrick A., Dale, Grady, Jr., & Kendall, Joshua C. (Eds.). (1999). *The foster care crisis: Translating research into policy and practice.* Lincoln, NE: University of Nebraska Press.

Czech, Christian, Tremp, Günter, & Pradier, Laurent. (2000). Presenilins and Alzheimer's disease: Biological functions and pathogenic mechanisms. *Progress in Neurobiology, 60,* 363–384.

Dales, Loring, Hammer, Sandra Jo, & Smith, Natalie J. (2001). Time trends in autism and in MMR immunization coverage in California. *Journal of the American Medical Association, 285,* 1183–1185.

Daniluk, Judith C. (1998). *Women's sexuality across the lifespan: Challenging myths, creating meanings.* New York: Guilford Press.

Danis, Agnes, Bernard, Jean-Marc, & Leproux, Christine. (2000). Shared picture-book reading: A sequential analysis of adult-child verbal interactions. *British Journal of Developmental Psychology, 18,* 369–388.

Darling, Nancy E., & Steinberg, Lawrence. (1997). Community influences on adolescent achievement and deviance. In Jeanne Brooks-Gunn, George Duncan, & J. Lawrence Aber (Eds.), *Neighborhood poverty: Vol. 3. Policy implications in studying neighborhoods* (pp. 120–131). New York: Russell Sage.

Darroch, Jacqueline E., Landry, David J., & Susheela, Singh. (2000). Changing emphases in sexuality education in U.S. public secondary schools, 1988–1999. *Family Planning Perspectives, 32,* 204–211, 265.

Dasen, Pierre R., & Mishra, Ramesh C. (2002). Cross-cultural views on human development in the third millennium. In Willard W. Hartup, & Ranier K. Silbereisen (Eds.), *Growing points in developmental science* (pp. 266–286). Hove, East Sussex, England: Psychology Press.

Datan, Nancy. (1986). Oedipal conflict, platonic love: Centrifugal forces in intergenerational relations. In Nancy Datan, Anita L. Greene, & Hayne W. Reese (Eds.), *Life-span developmental psychology: Intergenerational relations* (pp. 29–50). Mahwah, NJ: Erlbaum.

Daulaire, Nils, Leidl, Pat, Mackin, Laurel, Murphy, Colleen, & Stark, Laura. (2002). *Promises to keep: The toll of unintended pregnancy on women's lives in the developing world.* Retrieved September 4, 2003 from http://www.globalhealth.org/news/article/2319.

David, Henry P., & Russo, Nancy Felipe. (2003). Psychology, population, and reproductive behavior. *American Psychologist, 58,* 193–196.

Davies, Chris G., & Thorn, Brian L. (2002). Psychopharmacology with older adults in residential care. In Robert D. Hill, Brian L. Thorn, John Bowling, & Anthony Morrison (Eds.), *Geriatric residential care* (pp. 161–181). Mahwah, NJ: Erlbaum.

Davila, Joanne, & Daley, Shannon E. (2000). Studying interpersonal factors in suicide: Perspectives from depression research. In Thomas E. Joiner, & M. David Rudd (Eds.), *Suicide science: Expanding the boundaries* (pp. 175–200). New York: Kluwer Academic/Plenum Publishers.

Dawson, Geraldine, & Ashman, Sharon B. (2000). On the origins of a vulnerability to depression: The influence of the early social environment on the development of psychobiological systems related to risk for affective disorder. In Charles A. Nelson (Ed.), *The Minnesota symposia on child psychology: Vol. 31. The effects of early adversity on neurobehavioral development* (pp. 245–279). Mahwah, NJ: Erlbaum.

Dawson, Geraldine, Ashman, Sharon B., & Carver, Leslie. (2000). The role of early experience in shaping behavioral and brain development and its implications for social policy. *Development and Psychopathology, 12,* 695–712.

de Beauvoir, Simone. (1964). *Force of circumstances* (Richard Howard, Trans.). New York: Putnam.

De Bellis, Michael D. (2001). Developmental traumatology: The psychobiological development of maltreated children and its implications for research, treatment, and policy. *Development and Psychopathology, 13,* 539–564.

De Bellis, Michael D., Clark, Duncan B., Beers, Sue R., Soloff, Paul H., Boring, Amy M., Hall, Julie, et al. (2000). Hippocampal volume in adolescent-onset alcohol use disorders. *American Journal of Psychiatry, 157,* 737–744.

de Boysson-Bardies, Bénédicte. (1999). *How language comes to children: The first two years.* (Malcolm B. DeBevoise, Trans.). Cambridge, MA: MIT Press.

de Boysson-Bardies, Bénédicte, Halle, Pierre, Sagart, Laurent, & Durand, Catherine (1989). A cross-linguistic investigation of vowel formants in babbling. *Journal of Child Language, 16,* 1–17.

de Gray, Aubrey D. N. J. (1999). *The mitochondrial free radical theory of aging.* Austin, TX: Landes.

De la Torre, Jack C., Kalaria, Raj, Makajima, Kenji, & Nagata, Ken. (Eds.). (2002). Alzheimer's disease: Vascular etiology and pathology. *Annals of the New York Academy of Sciences, 977.*

De Martinis, Massimo, & Timiras, Paola S. (2003). The pulmonary respiration, hemotopoiesis and erythrocytes. In Paola S. Timiras (Ed.), *Physiological basis of aging and geriatrics* (3rd ed., pp. 319–336). Boca Raton, FL: CRC Press.

De Mey, Langha, Baartman, Herman E. M., & Schulze, Hans-J. (1999). Ethnic variation and the development of moral judgment of youth in Dutch society. *Youth and Society, 31,* 54–75.

de Onis, Mercedes, Frongillo, Edward A., & Blössner, Monika. (2000). Is malnutrition declining? An analysis of changes in levels of child malnutrition since 1980. *Bulletin of the World Health Organization, 78,* 1222–1233.

de Róiste, Áine, & Bushnell, Ian W. R. (1996). Tactile stimulation: Short- and long-term benefits for pre-term infants. *British Journal of Developmental Psychology, 14,* 41–53.

de Villiers, Jill G., & de Villiers, Peter A. (2000). Linguistic determinism and the understanding of false beliefs. In Peter Mitchell, & Kevin John Riggs (Eds.), *Children's reasoning and the mind* (pp. 191–228). Hove, England: Psychology Press.

de Vries, Brian (Ed.). (1999). *End of life issues: Interdisciplinary and multidimensional perspectives.* New York: Springer.

Dearing, Eric, McCartney, Kathleen, & Taylor, Beck A. (2001). Change in family income-to-needs matters more for children with less. *Child Development, 72,* 1779–1793.

Deary, Ian J., Leaper, Steven A., Murray, Alison D., Staff, Roger T., & Whalley, Lawrence J. (2003). Cerebral white matter abnormalities and lifetime cognitive change: A 67-year follow-up of the Scottish Mental Survey of 1932. *Psychology and Aging, 18,* 140–148.

Deeg, Dorly J. H., Kardaun, Jan W. P. F., & Fozard, James L. (1996). Health, behavior, and aging. In James E. Birren, & K. Warner Schaie (Eds.), *Handbook of the psychology of aging.* San Diego, CA: Academic Press.

DeGarmo, David S., & Kitson, Gay C. (1996). Identity relevance and disruption as predictors of psychological distress for widowed and divorced women. *Journal of Marriage and the Family, 58,* 983–997.

Degirmencioglu, Serdar M., Urberg, Kathryn A., Tolson, Jerry M., & Rao, Protima. (1998). Adolescent friendship networks: Continuity and change over the school year. *Merrill-Palmer Quarterly, 44,* 313–337.

Deil-Amen, Regina, & Rosenbaum, James E. (2003). The social prerequisites of success: Can college structure reduce the need for social know-how? In

Kathleen M. Shaw, & Jerry A. Jacobs (Eds.). Community college: New environment, new directions. *Annals of the American Academy of Political and Social Science. 586,* 120–143.

DeKeseredy, Walter S., & Schwartz, Martin D. (1998). *Woman abuse on campus: Results from the Canadian National Survey.* Thousand Oaks, CA: Sage.

Delaney, Carol. (2000). Making babies in a Turkish village. In Judy DeLoache, & Alma Gottlieb (Eds.), *A world of babies.* Cambridge, UK: Cambridge University Press.

Demant, Peter. (2003). Cancer susceptibility in the mouse: Genetics, biology, and implications for human cancer. *Nature Reviews Genetics, 4,* 721–734.

DeMaris, Alfred, Benson, Michael L., Fox, Greer L., Hill, Terrence, & Van Wyk, Judy. (2003). Distal and proximal factors in domestic violence: A test of an integrated model. *Journal of Marriage and Family, 65,* 652–667.

Demetriou, Andreas, Christou, Constantinos, Spanoudis, George, & Platsidou, Maria. (2002). The development of mental processing: Efficiency, working memory, and thinking. *Monographs of the Society for Research in Child Development, 67* (1, Serial No. 268).

D'Emilio, Frances. (2002, May 25). Tiny baby spends first day at home. *Associated Press.*

Demo, David H., & Acock, Alan C. (1996). Family structure, family process, and adolescent well-being. *Journal of Research on Adolescence, 6,* 457–488.

Denham, Susanne A. (1998). *Emotional development in young children.* New York: Guilford Publications.

Denham, Susanne A., Blair, Kimberly A., DeMulder, Elizabeth, Levitas, Jennifer, Sawyer, Katherine, Auerbach-Major, Sharon, & Queenan, Patrick. (2003). Preschool emotional competence: Pathway to social competence. *Child Development, 74,* 238–256.

Denney, N. W., & Pearce, K. A. (1989). A developmental study of practical problem solving in adults. *Psychology and Aging, 4,* 438—422.

Dennis, Tracy A., Cole, Pamela M., Zahn-Waxler, Carolyn, & Mizuta, Ichiro. (2002). Self in context: Autonomy and relatedness in Japanese and U.S.

mother-preschooler dyads. *Child Development, 73,* 1803–1817.

Derix, Mayke. (1994). *Neuropsychological differentiation of dementia syndromes.* Berwyn, PA: Lisse.

Dershewitz, Robert A. (2002, December 28). Another good year for immunizations. *Journal Watch.* Retrieved from http://general-medicine.jwatch.org/cgi/content/full/2002/1228/11.

DeSpelder, Lynne Ann, & Strickland, Albert Lee (2004). *The last dance: Encountering death and dying* (7th ed.). New York: McGraw-Hill.

Desruisseaux, Paul (1998, December 4). U.S. trails 22 nations in high-school competition. *Chronicle of Higher Education,* A45.

Detzner, Daniel F. (1996). No place without a home: Southeast Asian grandparents in refugee families. *Generations, 20,* 45–48.

Diamond, Adele. (2000). Close interrelation of motor development and cognitive development and of the cerebellum and prefrontal cortex. *Child Development, 71,* 44–56.

Diamond, Ronny, Kezur, David, Meyers, Mimi, Scharf, Constance N., & Weinshel, Margot. (1999). *Couple therapy for infertility.* New York: Guilford Press.

Dickinson, George E. (2002). A quarter century of end of life issues in United States medical schools. *Death Studies, 26,* 635–646.

Diederich, Paul B. (1973). *Research 1960–1970 on methods and materials in reading.* Princeton, NJ: Educational Testing Service.

Diekstra, Rene F. W. (1995). Depression and suicidal behaviors in adolescence: Sociocultural and time trends. In Michael Rutter (Ed.), *Psychosocial disturbances in young people: Challenges for prevention* (pp. 212–243). New York: Cambridge University Press.

Diekstra, Rene F. W., Kienhorst, C. W. M., & de Wilde, E. J. (1996). Suicide and suicidal behavior among adolescents. In Michael Rutter, & David J. Smith (Eds.), *Psychosocial disorders in young people: Time trends and their causes.* New York: Wiley.

Diener, Marissa. (2000). Gift from the Gods: A Balinese guide to early child rearing. In Judy DeLoache, & Alma Gottlieb (Eds.), *A world of babies* (pp. 91–116). Cambridge, England: Cambridge University Press.

Dietz, Tracy L. (1998). An examination of violence and gender role portrayals in video games: Implications for gender socialization and aggressive behavior. *Sex Roles, 38,* 425–442.

Dietz, William H. (1999). Barriers to the treatment of childhood obesity: A call to action. *Journal of Pediatrics, 134,* 535–536.

Digman, John M. (1990). Personality structure: Emergence of the five-factor model. *Annual Review of Psychology, 41,* 417–440.

DiPietro, Janet A., Hilton, Sterling C., Hawkins, Melissa, Costigan, Kathleen A., Pressman, Eva K. (2002). Maternal stress and affect influence fetal neurobehavioral development. *Developmental Psychology, 38,* 359–668.

DiPietro, Janet A., Hodgson, Denice M., Costigan, Kathleen A., & Hilton, Sterling C. (1996). Fetal neurobehavioral development. *Child Development, 67,* **2553–2567.**

Dishion, Thomas J., & Bullock, Bernadette Marie. (2002). Parenting and adolescent problem behavior: An ecological analysis of the nurturance hypothesis. In John G. Borkowski, Sharon Landesman Ramey, & Marie Bristol-Power (Eds.), *Parenting and the child's world: Influences on academic, intellectual and social-emotional development* (pp. 231–249). Mahwah, NJ: Erlbaum.

Dishion, T. J., Bullock, B. M., & Granic, I. (2002). Pragmatism in modeling peer influence: Dynamics, outcomes and change processes. *Development & Psychopathology, 14,* 969–981.

Dishion, Thomas J., McCord, Joan, & Poulin, Francois. (1999). When interventions harm: Peer groups and problem behavior. *American Psychologist, 54,* 755–764.

Dishion, Thomas J., & Owen, Lee D. (2002). A longitudinal analysis of friendships and substance use: Bidirectional influence from adolescence to adulthood. *Developmental Psychology, 38,* 480–491.

Dishion, Thomas, Poulin, Francois, & Burraston, Bert. (2001). Peer group dynamics associated with iatrogenic effects in group interventions with high-risk young adolescents. In William

Damon (Series Ed.), Douglas W. Nangle, & Cynthia A. Erdley (Vol. Eds.), *New directions for child and adolescent development: Vol. 91. The role of friendship in psychological adjustment* (pp. 79–92). San Francisco: Jossey-Bass.

Dixon, Roger A. (1999). Exploring cognition in interactive situations: The aging of *N* + 1 minds. In Thomas M. Hess & Fredda Blanchard-Fields (Eds.), *Social cognition and aging* (pp. 267–290). San Diego, CA: Academic Press.

Dixon, Roger A., & Lerner, Richard M. (1999). History and systems in developmental psychology. In Marc H. Bornstein, & Michael E. Lamb (Eds.), *Developmental psychology: An advanced textbook* (4th ed., pp. 3–45). Mahwah, NJ: Erlbaum.

Doka, Kenneth J. (Ed.).(2002). *Disenfranchised grief.* Champaign, IL: Research Press.

Douglas, Ann. (2002). *The mother of all pregnancy books.* Indianapolis, IN: Hungry Minds.

Dounchis, Jennifer Zoler, Hayden, Helen A., & Wilfley, Denise E. (2001). Obesity, body image, and eating disorders in ethnically diverse children and adolescents. In J. Kevin Thompson, & Linda Smolak (Eds.), *Body image, eating disorders, and obesity in youth* (pp. 67–98). Washington, DC: American Psychological Association.

Downs, A. Chris. (1990). The social biological constructs of social competency. In Thomas P. Gullotta, Gerald R. Adams, & Raymond R. Montemayor (Eds.), *Advances in adolescent development: Vol. 3. Developing social competency in adolescence* (pp. 43–94). Newbury Park, CA: Sage.

Drobnic, Sonia, Blossfeld, Hans-Peter, & Rohwer, Gotz. (1999). Dynamics of women's employment patterns over the family life course: A comparison of the United States and Germany. *Journal of Marriage and the Family, 61,* 133–146.

Dubowitz, Howard. (1999). Neglect of children's health care. In Howard Dubowitz (Ed.), *Neglected children: Research, practice, and policy* (pp. 109–130). Thousand Oaks, CA: Sage.

Duggar, Celia E. (2001, April 22). Abortion in India is tipping scales sharply against girls. *The New York Times,* pp. A1, A10.

Dulay, Mario F., & Murphy, Claire. (2002). Olfactory acuity and cognitive function converge in older adulthood: Support for the common cause hypothesis. *Psychology and Aging, 17,* 1392–1404.

Duncan, Greg J., & Brooks-Gunn, Jeanne. (2000). Family poverty, welfare reform, and child development. *Child Development, 71,* 188–196.

Duncan, G., & Brooks-Gunn, Jeanne (Eds.). (1997). *Consequences of growing up poor.* New York: Russell Sage Foundation.

Dunifon, Rachel, & Kowaleski-Jones, Lori. (2002). Who's in the house? Race differences in cohabitation, single parenthood, and child development. *Child Development, 73,* 1249–1264.

Dunn, Judy, & Hughes, Claire. (2001). "I got some swords and you're dead": Violent fantasy, antisocial behavior, friendship, and moral sensibility in young children. *Child Development, 72,* 491–505.

Dunphy, Dexter C. (1963). The social structure of urban adolescent peer groups. *Sociometry, 26,* 230–246.

Durbrow, Eric H. (1999). Cultural processes in child competence: How rural Caribbean parents evaluate their children. In Ann S. Masten (Ed.), *The Minnesota Symposia on Child Psychology: Vol. 29. Cultural processes in child development* (pp. 97–121). Mahwah, NJ: Erlbaum.

Durlak, Joseph A. (1998). Common risk and protective factors in successful prevention programs. *American Journal of Orthopsychiatry, 68,* 512–520.

Durrant, Joan E. (1996). Public attitudes toward corporal punishment in Canada. In Detlev Frehsee, Wiebke Horn, & Kai-D. Bussmann (Eds.), *Family violence against children: A challenge for society* (pp. 19–26). Berlin: de Gruyter.

Duster, Troy. (1999). The social consequences of genetic disclosure. In Ronald A. Carson, & Mark A. Rothstein (Eds.), *Behavioral genetics: The clash of culture and biology* (pp. 172–188). Baltimore: Johns Hopkins University Press.

Duthie, G. G., & Bellizzi, M. C. (1999). Effects of antioxidants on vascular health. *British Medical Bulletin, 55*(3), 568–577.

Dutton, Donald G. (1992). Theoretical and empirical perspectives on the etiology and prevention of wife assault. In Ray

D. Peters, Robert J. McMahon, & Vernon L. Quinsey (Eds.), *Aggression and violence throughout the lifespan.* Newbury Park, CA: Sage.

Dutton, Donald G. (2000). Witnessing parental violence as a traumatic experience shaping the abusive personality. In Robert A. Geffner, Peter G. Jaffe, & Marlies Sudermann (Eds.), *Children exposed to domestic violence: Current issues in research, intervention, prevention, and policy development* (pp. 59–67). Binghamton, NY: Haworth Press.

Duval, Thomas Shelley, & Silvia, Paul J. (2002). Self-awareness, probability of improvement, and the self-serving bias. *Journal of Personality and Social Psychology, 82,* 49–61.

Dweck, Carol S. (1999). *Self-theories: Their role in motivation, personality, and development.* Philadelphia: Psychology Press.

Dybdahl, Ragnhild. (2001). Children and mothers in war: An outcome study of a psychosocial intervention program. *Child Development, 72,* 1214–1230.

Dykens, Elisabeth M., Hodapp, Robert M., & Leckman, James F. (1994). *Behavior and development in fragile X syndrome.* Thousand Oaks, CA: Sage.

Eccles, Jacquelynne S., & Barber, Bonnie L. (1999). Student council, volunteering, basketball, or marching band: What kind of extracurricular involvement matters? *Journal of Adolescent Research, 14,* 10–43.

Eccles, Jacquelynne S., Wigfield, Allan, & Schiefele, Ulrich. (1998). Motivation to succeed. In William Damon (Series Ed.) & Nancy Eisenberg (Vol. Ed.), *Handbook of child psychology: Vol. 3. Social, emotional, and personality development* (5th ed., pp. 1017–1095). New York: Wiley.

Edwards, Allen Jack. (1993). *Dementia.* New York: Plenum Press.

Edwards, Carolyn, Gandini, Lella, & Forman, George. (1998). *The hundred languages of children: The Reggio Emilia approach—advanced reflections* (2nd ed.). Greenwich, CT: Ablex.

Edwards, John N. (1969) Familiar behavior as social exchange. *Journal of Marriage and the Family, 31,* 518—526.

Edwards, John R. (1994). *Multilingualism.* London: Routledge.

Effros, Rita B. (2001). Immune system activity. In Edward J. Masoro, & Steven N. Austad (Eds.), *Handbook of the biology of aging* (pp. 324–350). San Diego, CA: Academic Press.

Efron, Robert. (1990). *The decline and fall of hemispheric specialization.* Hillsdale, NJ: Erlbaum.

Egede, Leonard E., & Zheng, Deyl. (2003). Racial/ethnic difference in influenza vaccination coverage in high-risk adults. *American Journal of Public Health, 93,* 2074–2078.

Eggebeen, David J., & Knoester, Chris. (2001). Does fatherhood matter for men? *Journal of Marriage and Family, 63,* 381–393.

Ehrenberg, Ronald G., Brewer, Dominic J., Gamoran, Adam, & Willms, J. Douglas. (2001). Class size and student achievement. *Psychological Science in the Public Interest, 2,* 1–30.

Eid, Michael, & Diener, Ed. (2001). Norms for experiencing emotions in different cultures: Inter- and intranational differences. *Journal of Personality and Social Psychology, 81,* 869–885.

Eisenberg, Nancy. (2000). Emotion, regulation, and moral development. *Annual Review of Psychology, 51,* 665–697.

Eisenberg, Nancy, Cumberland, Amanda, Spinrad, Tracy L., Fabes, Richard A., Shepard, Stephanie A., Reiser, Mark, Murphy, Bridget C., Losoya, Sandra H., & Guthrie, Ivanna K. (2001). The relations of regulation and emotionality to children's externalizing and internalizing problem behavior. *Child Development, 72,* 1112–1134.

Eisenberg, Nancy, Fabes, Richard A., Shepard, Stephanie A., Murphy, Bridget C., Guthrie, Ivanna K., Jones, Sarah, Friedman, Jo, Poulin, Rick, & Maszk, Pat. (1997). Contemporaneous and longitudinal prediction of children's social functioning from regulation and emotionality. *Child Development, 68,* 642–664.

Eisner, Manuel. (2002). Crime, problem drinking, and drug use: Patterns of problem behavior in cross-national perspective. In Frank F. Furstenberg (Ed.), Early adulthood in cross-national perspective. *Annals of the American Academy of Political and Social Science, 580,* 201–225.

Eisner, Mark D., Yelin, Edward H., Trupin, Laura, & Blanc, Paul D. (2002).

The influence of chronic respiratory conditions on health status and work disability. *American Journal of Public Health, 92,* 1506–1513.

Elder, Glen H., Jr. (1998). Life course theory and human development. *Sociological Analysis, 1*(2), 1–12.

Elder, Glen H., Jr., & Conger, Rand D. (2000). *Children of the land: Adversity and success in rural America.* Chicago: University of Chicago Press.

Elkind, David. (1967). Egocentrism in adolescence. *Child Development, 38,* 1025–1034.

Ellis, Bruce J., & Garber, Judy. (2000). Psychosocial antecedents of variation in girls' pubertal timing: Maternal depression, stepfather presence, and marital and family stress. *Child Development, 71,* 485–501.

Ellis, Neenah. (2002). *If I live to be 100.* New York: Crown.

Ellison, Peter T. (2001). *On fertile ground: A natural history of human reproduction.* Cambridge, MA: Harvard University Press.

El-Sheikh, Mona, & Harger, JoAnn. (2001). Appraisals of marital conflict and children's adjustment, health, and physiological reactivity. *Developmental Psychology, 37,* 875–885.

Emery, Robert E., & Forehand, Rex. (1994). Parental divorce and children's well being: A focus on resilience. In Robert J. Haggerty, Lonnie R. Sherrod, Norman Garmezy, & Michael Rutter (Eds.), *Stress, risk, and resilience in children and adolescents: Process, mechanisms, and interventions* (pp. 64–99). New York: Cambridge University Press.

Emler, Nicholas. (1998). Sociomoral understanding. In Anne Campbell, & Steven Muncer (Eds.), *The social child.* Hove, England: Psychology Press.

Engel, Susan. (1999). *Context is everything: The nature of memory.* New York: Freeman.

Engeland, Anders, Bjorge, Tone, Sogaard, Anne Johanne, & Tverdal, Aage. (2003). Body mass index in adolescence in relation to total mortality: 32-year follow-up of 227,000 Norwegian boys and girls. *American Journal of Epidemiology, 157,* 517–523.

Ennett, Susan T., Tobler, Nancy S., Ringwalt, Christopher L., &

Flewelling, Robert L. (1994). How effective is Drug Abuse Resistance Education? A meta-analysis of Project DARE outcome evaluations. *American Journal of Public Health, 84,* 1394–1401.

Epstein, Seymour. (1994). Integration of the cognitive and psychodynamic unconscious. *American Psychologist, 49,* 709–724.

Erdley, Cynthia A., & Asher, Steven R. (1996). Children's social goals and self-efficacy perceptions as influences on their responses to ambiguous provocation. *Child Development, 67,* 1329–1344.

Ericsson, Karl Anders. (1996). The acquisition of expert performance: An introduction to some of the issues. In Karl Anders Ericsson (Ed.), *The road to excellence: The acquisition of expert performance in the arts and sciences, sports and games* (pp. 1–50). Mahwah, NJ: Erlbaum.

Ericsson, K. Anders, & Charness, Neil. (1994). Expert performance: Its structure and acquisition. *American Psychologist, 49,* 725–747.

Erikson, Erik H. (1963). *Childhood and society* (2nd ed.). New York: Norton.

Erikson, Erik H. (1968). *Identity, youth, and crisis.* New York: Norton.

Erikson, Erik H., Erikson, Joan M., & Kivnick, Helen Q. (1986). *Vital involvement in old age.* New York: Norton.

Erwin, Phil. (1998). *Friendship in childhood and adolescence.* London: Routledge.

Eslea, Mike, & Rees, Josette. (2001). At what age are children most likely to be bullied at school? *Aggressive Behavior, 27,* 419–429.

Estes, Carroll L. (2001). *Social policy and aging.* Thousand Oaks, CA: Sage.

Ethics Committee of the American Society for Reproductive Medicine. (2001). Preconception gender selection for nonmedical reasons. *Fertility and Sterility, 75,* 861–864.

Eurostat. (2002). *The life of women and men in Europe: A statistical portrait of women and men in all stages of life.* Luxemburg: Statistical office of the European communities.

Eurostat, Statistical Office of the European Communities. (2002). *Total employment rate of older workers.* Retrieved February 19, 2004, from http://europa.eu.int/comm/eurostat/

Evans, Jonathan, Heron, Jon, Francomb, Helen, Oke, Sarah, & Golding, Jean. (2001). Cohort study of depressed mood during pregnancy and after childbirth. *British Medical Journal, 323,* 257–260.

Eveleth, Phyllis B., & Tanner, James M. (1990). *Worldwide variation in human growth* (2nd ed.). Cambridge, England: Cambridge University Press.

Everaerd, Walter, Laan, Ellen T. M., Both, Stephanie, & van deer Velde, Janneke. (2000). Female sexuality. In Lenore T. Szuchman, & Frank Muscarella (Eds.), *Psychological perspectives on human sexuality.* New York: Wiley.

Eyer, D. (1992). *Maternal-infant bondings: A scientific fiction.* New Haven, CT: Yale University Press.

Fackelmann, Kathy A. (1994, November 5). Beyond the genome: The ethics of DNA testing. *Science News, 146*(19), 298–299.

Fagot, Beverly I. (1995). Parenting boys and girls. In Marc H. Bornstein (Ed.), *Handbook of parenting: Vol. 1. Children and parenting* (pp. 163–183). Mahwah, NJ: Erlbaum.

Fairburn, Christopher G., & Wilson, G. Terence. (Eds.). (1993). *Binge eating: Nature, assessment and treatment.* New York: Guilford Press.

Falcón, Angelo, Aguirre-Molina, Marilyn, & Molina, Carlos W. (2001). Latino health policy: Beyond demographic determinism. In Marilyn Aguirre-Molina, Carlos W. Molina, & Ruth Enid Zambrana (Eds.), *Health issues in the Latino community* (pp. 3–22). San Francisco: Jossey-Bass.

Falk, Ruma, & Wilkening, Friedrich. (1998). Children's construction of fair chances: Adjusting probabilities. *Developmental Psychology, 34,* 1340–1357.

Farkas, Janice I., & Hogan, Dennis P. (1995). The demography of changing intergenerational relationships. In Vern L. Bengtson, Klaus Warner Schaie, & Linda M. Burton (Eds.), *Adult intergenerational relations: Effects of societal change* (pp. 1–29). New York: Springer.

Farrington, David P. (1994). Interactions between individual and contextual factors in the development of offending. In Rainer K. Silbereisen, & Eberhard Todt (Eds.), *Adolescence in context: The interplay of family, school, peers, and work in adjustment* (pp. 366–389). New York: Springer-Verlag.

Fastenau, Philip S., Denburg, Natalie L., & Abeles, Norman. (1996). Age differences in retrieval: Further support for the resource-reduction hypothesis. *Psychology and Aging, 11,* 140–146.

Fehr, Beverley. (1996). *Friendship processes.* Thousand Oaks, CA: Sage.

Feldman, Ruth, Weller, Aron, Sirota, Lea, & Eidelman, Arthur I. (2002). Skin-to-skin contact (kangaroo care) promotes self-regulation in premature infants: Sleep-wake cyclicity, arousal modulation, and sustained exploration. *Developmental Psychology, 38*(2), 194–207.

Felson, Richard B., Ackerman, Jeff, & Yeon, Seong-Jin. (2003). The infrequency of family violence. *Journal of Marriage and Family, 65,* 622–634.

Fenson, Larry, Dale, Philip S., Resnick, J. Steven, Bates, Elizabeth, Thal, Donna J., & Petchick, Stephen J. (1994). Variability in early communicative development. *Monographs of the Society for Research in Child Development, 59* (5, Serial No. 242).

Ferguson, Mark W. J., & Joanen, Ted. (1982). Temperature of egg incubation determines sex in *Alligator mississippiensis. Nature, 296,* 850–853.

Fergusson, David M., & Horwood, L. John. (2002). Male and female offending trajectories. *Development and Psychopathology, 14,* 159–178.

Fergusson, David M., & Woodward, Lianne J. (1999). Maternal age and educational psychosocial outcomes in early adulthood. *Journal of Child Psychology and Psychiatry and Allied Disciplines, 40,* 479–489.

Ferrari, Michel, & Sternberg, Robert J. (1998). The development of mental abilities and styles. In William Damon (Series Ed.), Deanna Kuhn, & Robert S. Siegler (Vol. Eds.), *Handbook of child psychology: Vol. 2. Cognition, perception, and language* (5th ed., pp. 899–946). New York: Wiley.

Field, Tiffany. (2001). Massage therapy facilitates weight gain in preterm infants. *Current Directions in Psychological Science, 10*(2), 51–54.

Finch, Caleb E. (1999). Longevity without aging. In Jean-Marie Robin, Bernard

Forett, Claudio Franceschi, & Michel Allard (Eds.). *The paradoxes of longevity.* New York: Springer.

Finch, Caleb E., & Kirkwood, Thomas B. I. (2000). *Chance, development, and aging.* Oxford, England: Oxford University Press.

Fingerman, Karen L. (1996). Sources of tension in the aging mother and adult daughter relationship. *Psychology and Aging, 11,* 591–606.

Finkel, Deborah, Pedersen, Nancy L., Plomin, Robert, & McClearn, Gerald E. (1998). Longitudinal and cross-sectional twin data on cognitive abilities in adulthood: The Swedish Adoption/Twin Study of Aging. *Developmental Psychology, 34,* 1400–1413.

Finkelhor, David. (1994). Current information on the scope and nature of child sexual abuse. *The Future of Children, 4,* 31–53.

Finn, Jeremy D., Gerber, Susan B., Achilles, Charles M., & Boyd-Zaharias, Jayne. (2001). The enduring effects of small classes. *Teachers College Record, 103,* 145–183.

Firth, Shirley. (2001). Hindu death and mourning rituals: The impact of geographic mobility. In Jenny Hockey, Jeanne Katz, & Neil Small (Eds.), *Grief, mourning, and death ritual* (pp. 237–246). Buckingham, England: Open University Press.

Fiscella, Kevin, Kitzman, Harriet J., Cole, Robert E., Sidora, Kimberly, & Olds, David. (1998). Delayed first pregnancy among African-American adolescent smokers. *Journal of Adolescent Health, 23,* 232–237.

Fischer, Kurt W., & Bidell, Thomas R. (1998). Dynamic development of psychological structures in action and thought. In William Damon (Series Ed.) & Richard M. Lerner (Vol. Ed.), *Handbook of child psychology: Vol. 1. Theoretical models of human development* (5th ed., pp. 467–561). New York: Wiley.

Fischer, Kurt, Yan, Zheng, & Stewart, Jeffrey. (2003). Adult cognitive development: Dynamics in the developmental web. In Jaan Valsiner, & Kevin J. Connolly (Eds.), *Handbook of developmental psychology* (pp. 491–516). Thousand Oaks, CA: Sage.

Fishbein, Martin, Hall-Jamieson, Kathleen, Zimmer, Eric, von Haeften,

Ina, & Nabi, Robin. (2002). Avoiding the boomerang: Testing the relative effectiveness of antidrug public service announcements before a national campaign. *American Journal of Public Health, 92,* 238–245.

Fisher, Barbara C. (1998). *Attention deficit disorder misdiagnosis: Approaching ADD from a brain-behavior/neuropsychological perspective for assessment and treatment.* Boca Raton, FL: CRC Press.

Fisher, Jennifer O., & Birch, Leann L. (2001). Early experience with food and eating: Implications for the development of eating disorders. In J. Kevin Thompson, & Linda Smolak (Eds.), *Body image, eating disorders, and obesity in youth* (pp. 261–292). Washington, DC: American Psychological Association.

Fitness, Julie. (2001). Intimate relationships. In Joseph Ciarrochi, Joseph R. Forgas, & John D. Mayer (Eds.), *Emotional intelligence in everyday life: A scientific inquiry* (pp. 98–112). Philadelphia: Psychology Press.

Flannery, Daniel J., Vazsonyi, Alexander T., Liau, Albert K., Guo, Shenyang, Powell, Kenneth E., Atha, Henry, et al. (2003). Initial behavior outcomes for the PeaceBuilders universal school-based violence prevention program. *Developmental Psychology, 39,* 292–308.

Flavell, John H., Miller, Patricia H., & Miller, Scott A. (2001). *Cognitive development* (4th ed.). Upper Saddle River, NJ: Prentice-Hall.

Flegal, Katherine M., Carroll, Margaret D., Ogden, Cynthia L., & Johnson, Clifford L. (2002). Prevalence and trends in obesity among U.S. adults, 1999–2000. *Journal of the American Medical Association, 288,* 1723–1727.

Fleming, Alison S., Ruble, Diane, Krieger, Howard, Wong, P. Y. (1997). Hormonal and experiential correlates of maternal responsiveness during pregnancy and the puerperium in human mothers. *Hormones and Behavior, 31 (2),* 145–158.

Fletcher, Anne C., Darling, Nancy, & Steinberg, Laurence. (1995). Parental monitoring and peer influences on adolescent substance use. In Joan McCord (Ed.), *Coercion and punishment in long-term perspectives* (pp. 259–271). New York: Cambridge University Press.

Flores, Glenn, & Zambrana, Ruth Enid. (2001). The early years: The health of children and youth. In Marilyn Aguirre-Molina, Carlos W. Molina, & Ruth Enid Zambrana (Eds.), *Health issues in the Latino community.* San Francisco: Jossey-Bass.

Flynn, James R. (1984). The mean IQ of Americans: Massive gains 1932 to 1978. *Psychological Bulletin, 95,* 29–51.

Flynn, James R. (1987). Massive IQ gains in 14 nations: What IQ tests really measure. *Psychological Bulletin, 101,* 171–191.

Foley, Joseph M. (1992). The experience of being demented. In Robert H. Binstock, Stephen G. Post, & Peter J. Whitehouse (Eds.), *Dementia and aging: Ethics, values, and policy choices.* Baltimore: Johns Hopkins University Press.

Foley, Kathleen, & Hendin, Herbert (Eds). (2002). The case against assisted suicide: For the right to end of life care. Baltimore, MD: Johns Hopkins.

Folts, W. E., & Muir, K. B. (2002). Housing for older adults: New lessons from the past. *Research on Aging, 24* (1), 10–28.

Fonzi, Ada, Genta, Maria Luisa, Menesini, Ersilia, Bacchini, Dario, Bonino, Silvia, & Costabile, Angela. (1999). Italy. In Peter K. Smith, Yohji Morita, Josine Junger-Tas, Dan Olweus, Richard F. Catalano, & Phillip T. Slee (Eds.), *The nature of school bullying: A cross-national perspective.* London: Routledge.

Fordham, Signithia, & Ogbu, John U. (1986). Black students' school success: Coping with the burden of "acting White." *Urban Review, 18,* 176–206.

Foster, Zelda. (2003). The struggle to end my father's life. In Inge Corless, Barbara B. Germino, & Mary A. Pittman (Eds.), *Dying, death, and bereavement* (pp. 79–85). New York: Springer.

Fowler, James W. (1981). *Stages of faith: The psychology of human development and the quest for meaning.* New York: Harper & Row.

Fowler, James W. (1986). Faith and the structuring of meaning. In Craig Dykstra, & Sharon Parks (Eds.), *Faith development and Fowler.* Birmingham, AL: Religious Education Press.

Fowles, Don C., & Kochanska, Grazyna. (2000). Temperament as a moderator of pathways to conscience in children: The contribution of electrodermal activity. *Psychophysiology, 37,* 788–795.

Fox, Nathan A., Henderson, Heather A., Rubin, Kenneth H., Calkins, Susan D., & Schmidt, Louis A. (2001). Continuity and discontinuity of behavioral inhibition and exuberance: Psychophysiological and behavioral influences across the first four years of life. *Child Development, 72,* 1–21.

Franceschi, Claudio, Monti, Daniela, Barbieri, Daniela, et al. (1996). Immunosenescence: Paradoxes and new perspectives emerging from the study of healthy centenarians. In Suresh I. S. Rattan, & Olivier Toussaint (Eds.), *Molecular gerontology: Research status and strategies.* New York & London: Plenum Press.

Frankenburg, William K., Fandel, A., Sciarillo, W., & Burgess, D. (1981). The newly abbreviated and revised Denver Developmental Screening Test. *Journal of Pediatrics, 99,* 995–999.

Freda, B. (1997). *Personal communication.*

Fredricks, Jennifer A., & Eccles, Jacquelynne S. (2002). Children's competence and value beliefs from childhood through adolescence: Growth trajectories in two male-sex-typed domains. *Developmental Psychology, 38,* 519–533.

Freedman, Vicki A., & Martin, Linda G. (1998). Understanding trends in functional limitations among older Americans. *American Journal of Public Health, 88,* 1457–1462.

Frensch, Peter A., & Buchner, Axel. (1999). Domain-generality versus domain-specificity in cognition. In Robert J. Sternberg (Ed.), *The nature of cognition* (pp. 137–172). Cambridge, MA: MIT Press.

Freud, Anna. (1958/2000). Adolescence. In *The psychoanalytic study of the child: Vol. 13* (pp. 255–278). New York: International Universities Press.

Freud, Sigmund. (1933/1965). *New introductory lectures on psychoanalysis* (James Strachey, Ed. & Trans.). New York: Norton.

Freud, Sigmund. (1935). *A general introduction to psychoanalysis* (Joan Riviere, Trans.). New York: Liveright.

Freud, Sigmund. (1938). *The basic writings of Sigmund Freud* (A. A. Brill, Ed. & Trans.). New York: Modern Library.

Freud, Sigmund. (1964). An outline of psychoanalysis. In James Strachey (Ed. & Trans.), *The standard edition of the complete psychological works of Sigmund Freud* (Vol. 23). London: Hogarth Press. (Original work published 1940.)

Friedman, Michael K., Powell, Kenneth E., Hutwagner, Lori, Graham, LeRoy M., & Teague, Gerald. (2001). Impact of changes in transportation and commuting behaviors during the 1996 Summer Olympic Games in Atlanta on air quality and childhood asthma. *Journal of the American Medical Association, 285,* 897–905.

Friedrich, William N. (1998). Behavioral manifestations of child sexual abuse. *Child Abuse and Neglect, 22,* 523–531.

Fries, James F. (1994). *Living well: Taking care of your health in the middle and later years.* Reading, MA: Addison-Wesley.

Fries, James F., & Crapo, Lawrence M. (1981). *Vitality and aging.* San Francisco: Freeman.

Fromholt, Pia, & Bruhn, Peter. (1998). Cognitive dysfunction and dementia. In Inger Hilde Nordhus, Gary R. VandenBos, Stig Berg, & Pia Fromhold (Eds.), *Clinical geropsychology.* Washington, DC: American Psychological Association.

Frone, M. R. *(2003). Work–family balance. In J. C. Quick, & L. E. Tetrick (Eds.),* Handbook of occupational health psychology *(pp. 143–162). Washington, DC: American Psychological Association.*

Fry, Christine L. (1995). Kinship and individuation: Cross-cultural perspectives on intergenerational relations. In Vern L. Bengtson, Klaus Warner Schaie, & Linda M. Burton (Eds.), *Adult intergenerational relations: Effects of societal change* (pp. 126–173). New York: Springer.

Fry, Prem S. (1999). The sociocultural meaning of dyng with dignity: An exploratory study of the perceptions of a group of Asian Indian elderly persons. In Brian de Vries (Ed.), *End of life issues: Interdisciplinary and multidimensional perspectives.* New York: Springer.

Fry, Prem S. (2003). Perceived self-efficacy domains as predictors of fear of the unknown and fear of dying among older adults. *Psychology and Aging, 18,* 474–486.

Fry, Prem S., & Debats, Dominique, L. (2002). Self-efficacy beliefs as predictors

of loneliness and psychological distress in older adults. *International Journal of Aging and Human Development, 55,* 233–269.

Fuhrer, R., Shipley, M. J., Chastang, J. F., Schmaus, A., Niedhammer, I., Stansfeld, S. A., et al. (2002) Socioeconomic position, health, and possible explanations: A tale of two cohorts. *American Journal of Public Health, 92,* 1290–1294.

Fuligni, Andrew J. (1997). The academic achievement of adolescents from immigrant families: The roles of family background, attitudes, and behavior. *Child Development, 68,* 351–363.

Fuligni, Andrew J. (1998). Authority, autonomy, and parent–adolescent conflict and cohesion: A study of adolescents from Mexican, Chinese, Filipino and European backgrounds. *Developmental Psychology, 34,* 782–792.

Fuligni, Andrew J. (2001). A comparative longitudinal approach to acculturation among children from immigrant families. *Harvard Educational Review, 71,* 566–578.

Fung, Helene H., Carstensen, Laura L., & Lutz, Amy M. (1999). Influence of time on social preferences: Implications for life-span development. *Psychology and Aging, 14,* 595–604.

Furstenberg, Frank F., Cook, Thomas D., Sampson, Robert, & Slap, Gail. (2002). Preface. In Frank F. Furstenberg (Ed.), Early adulthood in cross-national perspective. *Annals of the American Academy of Political and Social Science, 580,* 6–15.

Gabrieli, John D. E. (1998). Cognitive neuroscience of human memory. *Annual Review of Psychology, 49,* 87–115.

Galambos, Nancy L., Barker, Erin T., & Almeida, David M. (2003). Parents do matter: Trajectories of change in externalizing and internalizing problems in early adolescence. *Child Development, 74,* 578–594.

Galambos, Nancy L., & Leadbeater, Bonnie J. (2000). Trends in adolescent research for the new millennium. *International Journal of Behavioral Development, 24,* 289–294.

Gall, Stanley A. (1996). *Multiple pregnancy and delivery.* St. Louis, MO: Mosby.

Gallo, Robert C., & Montagnier, Luc. (2002). Historical Essay: Enhanced prospects for the future. *Science, 298,* 1730–1731.

Gallup, George, Jr. (1996). *The Gallup Poll public opinion 1995.* Wilmington, DE: Scholarly Resources. Copyright © 1996 by the Gallup Organization.

Ganong, Lawrence H., & Coleman, Marilyn. (1994). *Remarried family relationships.* Thousand Oaks, CA: Sage.

Ganong, Lawrence H., & Coleman, Marilyn. (1999). *Changing families, changing responsibilities: Family obligations following divorce and remarriage.* Mahwah, NJ: Erlbaum.

Gantley, M., Davies, D. P., & Murcett, A. (1993). Sudden infant death syndrome: Links with infant care practices. *British Medical Journal, 306,* 16–20.

Garbarino, James, & Collins, Cyleste C. (1999). Child neglect: The family with a hole in the middle. In Howard Dubowitz (Ed.), *Neglected children: Research, practice and policy* (pp. 1–23). Thousand Oaks, CA: Sage.

García Coll, Cynthia T. (2001). Cultural influences on children and families' well-being. In Arland Thornton (Ed.), *The well-being of children and families: Research and data needs.* Ann Arbor, MI: University of Michigan Press.

Gardner, Howard. (1983). *Frames of mind: The theory of multiple intelligences.* New York: Basic Books.

Gardner, Howard. (1993). *Multiple intelligences: The theory in practice.* New York: Basic Books.

Gardner, Howard. (1998). Are there additional intelligences? The case for naturalist, spiritual, and existentialist intelligences. In Jeffrey Kane (Ed.), *Education, information, and transformation: Essays on learning and thinking.* Englewood Cliffs, NJ: Prentice-Hall.

Garner, Pamela W., & Spears, Floyd M. (2000). Emotion regulation in low-income preschoolers. *Social Development, 9,* 246–264.

Garofalo, Robert, Wolf, R. Cameron, Wissow, Lawrence S., Woods, Elizabeth R., & Goodman, Elizabeth. (1999). Sexual orientation and risk of suicide attempts among a representative sample of youth. *Archives of Pediatrics and Adolescent Medicine, 153,* 487–493.

Garreau, Joel. (2002, October 13). Forever young: Suppose you soon can live to well over 100, as vibrant and energetic as you are now: What will you do with your life? *Washington Post,* p. 7.

Gathercole, Susan E. (1998). The development of memory. *Journal of Child Psychology and Psychiatry and Allied Disciplines, 39,* 3–27.

Gaugler, Joseph E., Kane, Robert, & Kane, Rosalie. (2002). Family care for older adults with disabilities: Toward more targeted and interpretable research. *International Journal of Aging and Human Development, 54,* 205–231.

Gauvain, Mary. (1998). Cognitive development in social and cultural context. *Current Directions in Psychological Science, 7,* 188–192.

Gdalevich, Michael, Mimouni, Daniel, & Mimouni, Marc. (2001). Breastfeeding and the risk of bronchial asthma in childhood: A systematic review with meta-analysis of prospective studies. *Journal of Pediatrics, 139,* 261–266.

Ge, Xiaojia, Conger, Rand D., & Elder, Glen H., Jr. (2001). Pubertal transition, stressful life events, and the emergence of gender differences in adolescent depressive symptoms. *Developmental Psychology, 37,* 404–417.

Ge, Xiaojia, Kim, Irene J., Brody, Gene H., Conger, Rand D., Simons, Ronald L., Gibbons, Frederick X., et al. (2003). It's about timing and change: Pubertal transition effects on symptoms of major depression among African American youth. *Developmental Psychology, 39,* 430–439.

Geiger, Brenda. (1996). *Fathers as primary caregivers.* Westport, CT: Greenwood Press.

Gelles, Richard J. (1999). Policy issues in child neglect. In Howard Dubowitz (Ed.), *Neglected children: Research, practice, and policy* (pp. 278–298). Thousand Oaks, CA: Sage.

Gelman, Rochel, & Williams, Earl M. (1998). Enabling constraints for cognitive development and learning: Domain specificity and epigenesis. In William Damon (Series Ed.), Deanna Kuhn, & Robert S. Siegler (Vol. Eds.), *Handbook of child psychology: Vol. 2. Cognition, perception, and language* (5th ed., pp. 575–630). New York: Wiley.

Gelman, Susan A. (2003). *The essential child: Origins of essentialism in everyday thought.* New York: Oxford University Press.

Genesee, Fred. (1998). A case study of multilingual education in Canada. In Jason Cenoz, & Fred Genesee (Eds.), *Beyond bilingualism: Multilingualism and multilingual education.* Clevedon, England: Multilingual Matters.

Gennetian, Lisa A., & Miller, Cynthia. (2002). Children and welfare reform: A view from an experimental welfare reform program in Minnesota. *Child Development, 73,* 601–620.

Gentner, Dedre, & Boroditsky, Lera. (2001). Individuation, relativity, and early word learning. In Melissa Bowerman, & Stephen C. Levinson (Eds.), *Language acquisition and conceptual development* (pp. 215–256).

Georgieff, Michael K., & Rao, Raghavendra. (2001). The role of nutrition in cognitive development. In Charles A. Nelson, & Monica Luciana (Eds.), *Handbook of developmental cognitive neuroscience* (pp. 149–158). Cambridge, MA: MIT Press.

Gergely, Gyoergy, & Watson, John S. (1999). Early socio-emotional development: Contingency perception and the social-biofeedback model. In Philippe Rochat (Ed.), *Early social cognition: Understanding others in the first months of life* (pp. 101–136). Mahwah, NJ: Erlbaum.

Gershoff, Elizabeth Thompson. (2002). Corporal punishment by parents and associated child behavior and experiences: A meta-analytic and theoretical review. *Psychological Bulletin, 128,* 539–579.

Gerstel, Naomi. (2002). Review of *Talk of Love. Marriage and the Family, 64,* 554–556.

Geurts, Sabine A. E., & Gründemann, Robert G. W. (1999). Workplace stress and stress prevention in Europe. In Michiel Kompier, & Cary Cooper (Eds.), *Preventing stress, improving productivity: European case studies in the workplace* (pp. 9–32). London: Routledge.

Giacobini, Ezio. (2002). Long-term stabilizing effect of cholinesterase inhibitors in the therapy of Alzheimer's disease. *Journal of Neural Transmission Supplement, 62,* 181–187.

Gibson, Eleanor. (1969). *Principles of perceptual learning and development.* New York: Appleton-Century-Crofts.

Gibson, Eleanor Jack. (1988). Levels of description and constraints on perceptual development. In Albert Yonas (Ed.), *Perceptual development in infancy.* Hillsdale, NJ: Erlbaum.

Gibson, Eleanor Jack. (1997). An ecological psychologist's prolegomena for perceptual development: A functional approach. In Cathy Dent-Read, & Patricia Zukow-Goldring (Eds.), *Evolving explanations of development: Ecological approaches to organism-environment systems* (pp. 23–54). Washington, DC: American Psychological Association.

Gibson, Eleanor Jack, & Walk, Richard D. (1960). The visual cliff. *Scientific American, 202,* 64–72.

Gibson, James Jerome. (1958). The registering of objective facts: An interpretation of Woodworth's theory of perceiving. In G. H. Seward, & J. P. Seward (Eds), *Current psychological issues: Essays in honor of Robert S. Woodworth* (pp. 39–52). Oxford, England: Henry Holt.

Gibson, James Jerome. (1979). *The ecological approach to visual perception.* Boston: Houghton Mifflin.

Gibson-Cline, Janice (Ed.). (2000). *Youth and coping in twelve nations.* London: Routledge.

Giele, Janet. (2000). Careers and the theory of action. In Richard A. Settersten, Jr., & Timothy J. Owens (Eds.), *New frontiers in socialization* (pp. 65–88). Amsterdam: JAI.

Gilhooly, Mary. (2002). Ethical issues in research on later life. In Anne Jamieson, & Christine R. Victor (Eds.), *Researching aging and later life* (pp. 211–225). Philadelphia: Taylor & Francis.

Gilligan, Carol. (1981). Moral development. In Arthur W. Chickering (Ed.), *The modern American college: Responding to the new realities of diverse students and a changing society.* San Francisco: Jossey-Bass.

Gilligan, Carol. (1982). *In a different voice: Psychological theory and women's development.* Cambridge, MA: Harvard University Press.

Gilligan, Carol, Murphy, John M., & Tappan, Mark B. (1990). Moral development beyond adolescence. In Charles N. Alexander, & Ellen J. Langer (Eds.), *Higher stages of human development: Perspectives on adult growth* (pp. 208–225). New York: Oxford University Press.

Gilliom, Miles, Shaw, Daniel S., Beck, Joy E., Schonberg, Michael A., & Lukom, JoElla L. (2002). Anger regulation in disadvantaged preschool boys: Strategies, antecedents, and the development of self-control. *Developmental Psychology, 38,* 222–235.

Ginn, Jay, & Arber, Sara. (1994). Midlife women's employment and pension entitlement in relation to co-resident adult children in Great Britain. *Journal of Marriage and the Family, 56,* 813–819.

Ginsburg, Herbert P., Klein, Alice, & Starkey, Prentice. (1998). The development of children's mathematical thinking: Connecting research with practice. In William Damon (Series Ed.), Irving E. Sigel & K. Ann Renninger (Vol. Eds.), *Handbook of child psychology: Vol. 4. Child psychology in practice* (5th ed., pp. 401–476). New York: Wiley.

Girouard, Pascale C., Baillargeon, Raymond H., Tremblay, Richard E., Glorieux, Jacqueline, Lefebvre, Francine, & Robaey, Philippe. (1998). Developmental pathways lending to externalizing behaviors in 5-year-olds born before 29 weeks of gestation. *Journal of Developmental and Behavioral Pediatrics, 19*(4), 244–253.

Gitlin, Laura N., Belle, Steven H., Burgio, Louis D., Czaja, Sara J., Mahoney, Diane, Gallagher-Thompson, Dolores, et al. (2003). Effect of multicomponent interventions on caregiver burden and depression: The REACH multisite initiative at 6-month follow-up. *Psychology and Aging, 18,* 361–374.

Glass, Jennifer. (1998). Gender liberation, economic squeeze, or fear of strangers: Why fathers provide infant care in dual-earner families. *Journal of Marriage and the Family, 60,* 821–834.

Glauber, James H., Farber, Harold J., & Homer, Charles S. (2001). Asthma clinical pathways: Toward what end? *Pediatrics, 107,* 590–592.

Glazer, Deborah F., & Drescher, Jack (Eds.). (2001). *Gay and lesbian parenting.* New York: Hawthorne.

Glazier, Anne M., Nadeau, Joseph H., & Aitman, Timothy J. (2002). Finding genes that underlie complex traits. *Science, 298,* 2345–2349.

Glenn, Norval D. (1991). The recent trend in marital success in the United States. *Journal of Marriage and the Family, 53,* 261–270.

Glick, Jennifer E., Bean, Frank D., & Van Hook, Jennifer V. W. (1997). Immigration and changing patterns of extended family household structure in the United States. *Journal of Marriage and the Family, 59,* 177–191.

Goetzel, Laura, & D'Alton, Mary. (2001). Prenatal diagnosis. In Frank W. Ling, & Patrick Duff (Eds.), *Obstetrics and gynecology: Principles for practice* (pp. 69–80). New York: McGraw-Hill.

Gogate, Lakshmi J., Bahrick, Lorraine E., & Watson, Jilayne D. (2000). A study of multimodal motherese: The role of temporal synchrony between verbal labels and gestures. *Child Development, 71,* 878–894.

Gold, Deborah T. (1996). Continuities and discontinuities in sibling relationships across the life span. In Vern L. Bengtson (Ed.), *Adulthood and aging: Research on continuities and discontinuities* (pp. 228–243). New York: Springer.

Gold, Rachel Benson, & Nash, Elizabeth. (2001). State-level policies on sexuality, STD education. *The Guttmacher Report on Public Policy, 4*(4), 4–7.

Goldberg, Susan, Muir, Roy, & Kerr, John (Eds.). (1995). *Attachment theory: Social, developmental, and clinical perspectives.* Hillsdale, NJ: Analytic Press.

Goldman, Connie. (1991). Late bloomers: Growing older or still growing? *Generations,* 15, 41–44.

Goldman, Herbert I. (2001). Parental reports of "MAMA" sounds in infants: An exploratory study. *Journal of Child Language, 28*(2), 497–506.

Goldscheider, Frances K., & Goldscheider, Calvin. (1998). The effects of childhood family structure on leaving and returning home. *Journal of Marriage and the Family, 60,* 745–756.

Goleman, Daniel. (1998, August). *Building emotional intelligence.* Keynote address presented at the 106th Annual Convention of the American Psychological Association, San Francisco, CA.

Golub, Sharon. (1992). *Periods: From menarche to menopause.* Newbury Park, CA: Sage.

Gomes, Uilhi A., Silva, Antonio A., Bettiol, Heloisa, Barbieri, Marco A. (1999). Risk factors for the increasing caesarean section rate in Southeast Brazil: A comparison of two birth cohorts, 1978–1979 and 1994. *International Journal of Epidemiology, 28*(4), 687–694.

Goodman, Sherryl H., & Gotlib, Ian H. (1999). Risk for psychopathology in the children of depressed mothers: A developmental model for understanding mechanisms of transmission. *Psychological Review, 106,* 458–490.

Goodman, Sherryl H., & Gotlib, Ian H. (2002). Transmission of risk to children of depressed parent: Integration and conclusions. In Sherryl H. Goodman & Ian H. Gotlib (Eds.), *Children of depressed parents: Mechanisms of risk and implications for treatments* (pp. 307–326). Washington, DC: American Psychological Association.

Goodrich, Gregory L. (2003). Available and emerging technologies for people with visual impairment. *Generations, 27*(1), 64–70.

Gopnik, Alison. (2001). Theories, language, and culture: Whorf without wincing. In Melissa Bowerman & Stephen C. Levinson (Eds.), *Language acquisition and conceptual development* (pp. 45–69). Cambridge, UK: Cambridge University Press.

Gordon, Debra Ellen. (1990). Formal operational thinking: The role of cognitive-developmental processes in adolescent decision-making about pregnancy and contraception. *American Journal of Orthopsychiatry, 60,* 346–356.

Gordon, Richard A. (2000). *Eating disorders: Anatomy of a social epidemic* (2nd ed.). Oxford, England: Blackwell.

Gordon, Robert M., & Brill, Deborah. (2001). The abuse and neglect of the elderly. In David N. Weisstub, David C. Thomasma, Serge, Gauthier, & George F. Tomossy (Eds.), *Aging: Caring for our elders,* (pp. 203–218). Dordrecht, Netherlands: Kluwer.

Gorenstein, Ethan E., & Comer, Ronald J. (2002). *Case studies in abnormal psychology.* New York: Worth.

Gorman, Elizabeth H. (1999). Bringing home the bacon: Marital allocation of income-earning responsible job shifts, and men's wages. *Journal of Marriage and the Family, 61,* 110–122.

Gorski, Peter A. (2002). Racing Cain. *Journal of Developmental and Behavioral Pediatrics, 23,* 95–101.

Gottlieb, Alma. (2000). Luring your child into this life: A Beng path for infant care. In Judy DeLoache & Alma Gottlieb (Eds.). *A world of babies.* Cambridge, England: Cambridge University Press.

Gottlieb, Gilbert. (1992). *Individual development and evolution.* New York: Oxford University Press.

Gottlieb, Gilbert. (2002). *Individual development and evolution: The genesis of novel behavior.* Mahwah, NJ: Erlbaum.

Gottlieb, Gilbert. (2003). Probabilistic epigenesis of development. In Jaan Valsiner & Kevin J. Connolly (Eds.), *Handbook of developmental psychology* (pp. 3–17). Thousand Oaks, CA: Sage.

Gottlieb, Gilbert, & Halpern, Carolyn Tucker. (2002). A relational view of causality in normal and abnormal development. *Developmental Psychopathology, 14,* 421–436.

Gould, Duncan C., Petty, Richard, & Jacobs, Howard S. (2000). The male menopause—does it exist? *British Medical Journal, 320,* 858–861.

Graber, Julia A., Brooks-Gunn, Jeanne, Paikoff, Roberta L., & Warren, Michelle P. (1994). Prediction of eating problems: An 8-year study of adolescent girls. *Developmental Psychology, 30,* 823–834.

Gradin, Maria, Eriksson, Mats, Holmqvist, Gunilla, Holstein, Asa, & Schollin, Jens. (2002). Pain reduction at venipuncture in newborns: Oral glucose compared with local anesthetic cream. *Pediatrics, 110,* 1053–1057.

Grady, Cheryl L. (2001). Age related changes in the functional neuroanatomy of memory. In M. Naveh-Benjamin, M. Moscovitch, & R. L. Roediger III (Eds.), *Perspectives on human memory and cognitive aging: Essays in honour of Fergus Craik* (pp. 325–333). East Sussex, UK: Psychology Press.

Graham, John W., & Beller, Andrea H. (2002). Nonresident fathers and their children: Child support and visitation from an economic perspective. In Catherine S. Tamis-LeMonda & Natasha Cabrera (Eds.), *Handbook of father involvement: Multidisciplinary perspectives* (pp. 431–453). Mahwah, NJ: Erlbaum.

Grantham-McGregor, Sally M. & Ani, C. C. (2001). Undernutrition and mental development. In John D. Fernstrom, Ricardo Uauy, & Pedro Arroyo (Eds.), *Nutrition and brain* (pp. 1–18). Basel, Switzerland: Karger.

Gratton, Brian, & Haber, Carole. (1996). Three phases in the history of American grandparents: Authority, burden, companion. *Generations, 20,* 7–12.

Green, Jonathan, Gilchrist, Anne, Burton, Di, & Cox, Anthony. (2000). Social and psychiatric functioning in adolescents with Asperger syndrome compared with conduct disorders. *Journal of Autism and Developmental Disorders, 30,* 279–293.

Green, Michael F. (2001). Teratology. In Frank W. Ling & Patrick Duff (Eds.), *Obstetrics and gynecology: Principles for practice.* New York: McGraw Hill.

Greenberger, Ellen, & Chen, Chuansheng. (1996). Perceived family relationships and depressed mood in early and late adolescence: A comparison of European and Asian Americans. *Developmental Psychology, 32,* 707–716.

Greenough, William T. (1993). Brain adaptation to experience: An update. In Mark H. Johnson (Ed.), *Brain development and cognition* (pp. 319–322). Oxford, ENGLAND: Blackwell.

Greenough, William T., & Volkmar, Fred R. (1973). Pattern of dendritic branching in occipital cortex of rats reared in complex environments. *Experimental Neurology, 40,* 491–504.

Greenough, William T., Black, James E., & Wallace, Christopher S. (1987). Experience and brain development. *Child Development, 58,* 539–559.

Greydanus, Donald Everett. (1997). Disorders of the skin. In Adele Dellenbaugh Hofmann & Donald Everett Greydanus (Eds.), *Adolescent medicine* (3rd ed.). Stamford, CT: Appleton and Lange.

Greydanus, Donald Everett. (1997). Neurological disorders. In Adele Dellenbaugh Hofmann & Donald Everett Greydanus (Eds.), *Adolescent medicine* (3rd ed.). Stamford, CT: Appleton and Lange.

Griffin, Kenneth E., Scheier, Lawrence M., Botvin, Gilbert J., & Diaz, Tracy. (2001). Protective role of personal competence skill in adolescent substance use: Psychological well-being. *Psychology of Addictive Behaviors, 15,* 194–203.

Grilo, Carlos M., & Pogue-Geile, Michael F. (1991). The nature of environmental influences on weight and obesity: A behavior genetic analysis. *Psychological Bulletin, 110,* 520–537.

Grolnick, Wendy S., Deci, Edward L., & Ryan, Richard M. (1997). Internalization within the family: The self-determination theory perspective. In Joan E. Grusec & Leon Kuczynski (Eds.), *Parenting and children's internalization of values: A handbook of contemporary theory* (pp. 135–161). New York: Wiley.

Grossmann, Klaus E., & Grossmann, Karin. (1990). The wider concept of attachment in cross-cultural research. *Human Development, 33,* 31–47.

Grotevant, Harold D. (1998). Adolescent development in family contexts. In William Damon (Series Ed.) & Nancy Eisenberg (Volume Ed.), *Handbook of child psychology: Vol. 3. Social, emotional, and personality development* (5th ed., pp. 1097–1149). New York: Wiley.

Gruber, Jonathan. (2001). Introduction. In Jonathan Gruber (Ed.), *Risky behavior among youth: An economic analysis* (pp. 1–28). Chicago: University of Chicago Press.

Grune, Tilman, & Davies, Kelvin J. A. (2001). Oxidative process in aging. In Edward J. Masoro & Steven N. Austad (Eds.), *Handbook of the biology of aging* (pp. 25–58). San Diego, CA: Academic Press.

Grunwald, Henry. (2003). Twilight: Losing sight, gaining insight. *Generations, 27*(1), 102–104.

Guberman, Steven R. (1996). The development of everyday mathematics in Brazilian children with limited formal education. *Child Development, 67,* 1609–1623.

Gullone, Eleonora, Moore, Susan, Moss, Simon, & Boyd, Candace. (2000). The Adolescent Risk-Taking Questionnaire: Development and psychometric evaluation. *Journal of Adolescent Research, 15,* 231–250.

Gunnar, Megan R. (2000). Early adversity and the development of stress reactivity and regulation. In Charles A. Nelson (Ed.), *The Minnesota symposia on child psychology: Vol. 31. The effects of early adversity on neurobehavioral development* (pp. 163–200). Mahwah, NJ: Erlbaum.

Gunnar, Megan R., & Vasquez, Delia M. (2001). Low cortisol and a flattening of expected daytime rhythm: Potential indices of risk in human development. *Development and Psychopatholoy, 13,* 515–538.

Gurung, Regan A. R., Taylor, Shelley E., & Seeman, Teresa. (2003). Accounting for changes in social support among married older adults: Insight from the MacArthur studies of successful aging. *Psychology and Aging, 18,* 487–496.

Guterbock, T.M., & Fries, J.C. (1997). *Maintaining America's social fabric: The AARP survey of civic involvement.* Washington, DC: American Association of Retired Persons.

Gutmann, David. (1994). *Reclaimed powers: Men and women in later life* (2nd ed.). Evanston, IL: Northwestern University Press.

Gutmann, David. (1996). Psychological immunity and late onset disorders. In Vern L. Bengston, (Ed.), *Adulthood and aging: Research on continuity and discontinuity.* New York: Springer.

Grzywacz, Joseph G., & Bass, Brenda L. (2003). Work, family and mental health: Testing different models of work—family fit. *Journal of Marriage and Family, 65,* 248–262.

Hack, Maureen, Flannery, Daniel, J., Schluchter ,Mark, Cartar, Lydia, Borawski, Elaine, & Klein Nancy. (2002). Outcomes in young adulthood for very-low-birth-weight infants. *New England Journal of Medicine, 346*(3), 149–157.

Hack, Maureen, Klein, Nancy, & Taylor, H. Gerry. (1995). Long-term developmental outcomes of low-birth-weight infants. *The Future of Children: Low Birth Weight, 5,* 176–196.

Hacker, Karen A., Amare, Yared, Strunk, Nancy, & Horst, Leslie. (2000). Listening to youth: Teen perspectives on pregnancy prevention. *Journal of Adolescent Health, 26,* 279–288.

Haden, Catherine A., Ornstein, Peter A., Eckerman, Carol O., & Didow, Sharon M. (2001). Mother–child conversational interactions as events unfold: Linkages to subsequent remembering. *Child Development, 72,* 1016–1031.

Hagerman, Randi J. (1996). Biomedical advances in developmental psychology: The case of fragile X syndrome. *Developmental Psychology, 32,* 416–424.

Hagestad, Gunhild O., & Dannefer, Dale. (2001). Concepts and theories of aging: Beyond microfication in social science approaches. In Robert H. Binstock & Linda K. George (Eds.), *Handbook of aging and the social sciences* (5th ed., pp. 3–21). San Diego, CA: Academic Press.

Hai, Hamid Abdul, & Asad, Husain. (2000). Muslim perspectives regarding death, dying, and end-of-life decision making. In Kathryn Braun, James H. Pietsch, & Patricia L. Blanchette (Eds.), *Cultural issues in end-of-life decision making* (pp. 199–212). Thousand Oaks, CA: Sage.

Haier, Richard J. (2001). PET studies of learning and individual differences. In James L. McClelland & Robert S. Siegler (Eds.), *Mechanisms of cognitive development: Behavioral and neural perspectives* (pp. 123–145). Mahwah, NJ: Erlbaum.

Hala, Suzanne, & Chandler, Michael. (1996). The role of strategic planning in accessing false-belief understanding. *Child Development, 67,* 2948–2966.

Hallenbeck, James, & Goldstein, Mary K. (1999). Decisions at the end of life: Cultural considerations beyond medical ethics. *Generations, 23,* 24–29.

Halterman, Jill S., Aligne, C. Andrew, Auinger, Peggy, McBride, John T., & Szilagyi, Peter G. (2000). Inadequate therapy for asthma among children in the United States. *Pediatrics, 105,* 272–276.

Hamer, Dean. (2002). Rethinking behavior genetics. *Science, 298,* 71–72.

Hamil, P. (1991). Triage: An essay. *The Georgia Review, 45,* 463–469.

Hamilton, Stephen A., & Lempert, Wolfgang. (1996). The impact of apprenticeship on youth: A prospective analysis. *Journal of Research on Adolescence, 6,* 427–455.

Hamm, Jill V. (2000). Do birds of a feather flock together? The variable bases for African American, Asian American, and European American adolescents' selection of similar friends. *Developmental Psychology, 36,* 209–219.

Hanish, Laura D., & Guerra, Nancy G. (2002). A longitudinal analysis of patterns of adjustment following peer victimization. *Development & Psychopathology, 14*(1), 69–89.

Hankin, Benjamin L., & Abramson, Lyn Y. (2001). Development of gender differences in depression: An elaborated cognitive vulnerability—transactional stress theory. *Psychological Bulletin, 127,* 773–796.

Hansen, David M., Larson, Reed W., & Dworkin, Jodi B. (2003). What adolescents learn in organized youth activities: A survey of self-reported developmental experiences. *Journal of Research on Adolescence, 13,* 25–55.

Hanushek, Eric A. (1999). The evidence on class size. In Susan E. Mayer & Paul Peterson (Eds.), *Earning and learning: How schools matter* (pp. 131–168). Washington, DC: Brookings.

Hardy, John, Singleton, Andrew, & Gwinn-Hardy, Katrina. (2003). Ethnic differences and disease phenotypes. *Science, 300,* 737.

Hareven, Tamara K. (2001). Historical perspectives on aging and family relations. In Robert H. Binstock & Linda K. George (Eds) *Handbook of aging and the social sciences* (5th ed., pp. 141–159). San Diego, CA: Academic Press.

Harlow, Clara Mears (Ed.). (1986). *From learning to love: The selected papers of H. F. Harlow.* New York: Praeger.

Harlow, Harry F. (1958). The nature of love. *American Psychologist, 13,* 673–685.

Harnack, Lisa, Stang, Jamie, & Story, Mary. (1999). Soft drink consumption among U.S. children and adolescents: Nutritional consequences. *Journal of the American Dietetic Association, 99,* 436–441.

Harris, Judith Rich. (1998). *The nurture assumption: Why children turn out the way they do.* New York: Free Press.

Harris, Judith Rich. (2002). Beyond the nurture assumption: Testing hypotheses about the child's environment. In John G. Borkowski, Sharon Landesman Ramey, & Marie Bristol-Power (Eds.), *Parenting and the child's world: Influences on academic, intellectual, and social-emotional development* (pp. 3–20). Mahwah, NJ: Erlbaum.

Harris, Russell, & Kinsinger, Linda S. (2002). Routinely teaching breast self-examination is dead: What does this mean? *Journal of the National Cancer Institute, 94,* 1420–1421.

Hart, Betty, & Risley, Todd R. (1995). *Meaningful differences in the everyday experience of young American children.* Baltimore: Brookes.

Hart, Sybil, Field, Tiffany, & Nearing, Graciela. (1999). Depressed mothers' neonates improve following the MABI and a Brazelton demonstration. *Journal of Pediatric Psychology, 23,* 351–356.

Harter, Susan. (1998). The development of self-representations. In W. Damon (Series Ed.), Nancy Eisenberg (Volume Ed.), *Handbook of child psychology: Vol. 3. Social, emotional and personality development* (5th ed., pp. 553–618). New York: Wiley.

Harter, Susan. (1999). *The construction of the self: A developmental perspective.* New York: Guilford Press.

Harter, Susan, Marold, Donna B., Whitesell, Nancy R., & Cobbs, Gabrielle. (1996). A model of the effects of perceived parent and peer support on adolescent false-self behavior. *Child Development, 67,* 360–374.

Harter, Susan, Waters, Patricia L., & Whitesell, Nancy R. (1997). Lack of voice as a manifestation of false-self behavior: The school setting as a stage upon which the drama of authenticity is enacted. *Educational Psychologist, 32,* 153–173.

Hartfield, Bernadette W. (1996). Legal recognition of the value of intergenerational nurturance: Grandparent visitation statutes in the nineties. *Generations, 20,* 53–56.

Hartl, Daniel L. & Jones, Elizabeth W. (1999). *Essential genetics,* 2nd Edition. Sudbury, MA: Jones & Bartlett.

Hartman, Donald P., & George, Thomas P. (1999). Design, measurement, and analysis in developmental research. In Mark H. Bornstein & Michael E. Lamb (Eds.), *Developmental psychology: An advanced textbook* (4th ed., pp. 125–195). Mahwah, NJ: Erlbaum.

Hartup, Willard W. (1996). The company they keep: Friendships and their developmental significance. *Child Development, 67,* 1–13.

Hartup, Willard W. (2002). Growing points in developmental science: A summing up. In Willard W. Hartup & Ranier K. Silbereisen (Eds.)., *Growing points in developmental science* (pp. 329–344). Hove, East Sussex, England: Psychology Press.

Hartup, Willard W., & Stevens, Nan. (1999). Friendship and adaptation across the life span. *Current Directions in Psychological Science, 8,* 76–79.

Haselager, Gerbert J. T., Cillessen, Antonius H. N., Van Lieshout, Cornelius F. M., Riksen-Walraven, J. Marianne A., & Hartup, Willard W. (2002). Heterogeneity among peer-rejected boys across middle childhood: Developmental pathways of social behavior. *Developmental Psychology, 38,* 446–456.

Hasher, Lynn, Tonev, S. T., Lustig, C., & Zacks, Rose T. (2001). Inhibitory control, environmental support, and self-initiated processing in aging. In M. Naveh-Benjamin, M. Moscovitch, & R. L. Roediger III (Eds.), *Perspectives on human memory and cognitive aging: Essays in honour of Fergus Craik* (pp. 286–297). East Sussex, UK: Psychology Press.

Hashima, Patricia Y., & Finkelhor, David. *(1999). Violent victimization of youth versus adults in the National Crime Victimization Survey.* Journal of Interpersonal Violence, 14*(8), 799–820.*

Hassan, M. A., & Killick, S. R. (2003). Effect of male age on fertility: Evidence for the decline of male fertility with increasing age. *Fertility and Sterility, 79,* Suppl.3.

Hassold, Terry J., & Patterson, David (Eds.). (1999). *Down syndrome: A promising future, together.* New York: Wiley.

Hattery, Angela. (2001). *Women, work, and family: Balancing and weaving.* Thousand Oaks, CA: Sage.

Haugaard, Jeffrey J. (2000). The challenge of defining child sexual abuse. *American Psychologist, 55,* 1036–1039.

Haugaard, Jeffrey J., & Hazan, Cindy. (2002). Foster parenting. In Marc H. Bornstein (Ed.), *Handbook of parenting: Vol. 1. Children and parenting* (2nd ed., pp. 313–329). Mahwah, NJ: Erlbaum.

Hawley, Patricia H. (1999). The ontogenesis of social dominance: A strategy-based evolutionary perspective. *Developmental Review, 19,* 97–132.

Hay, Dale F., Pawlby, Susan, Sharp, Deborah, Asten, Paul, Mills, Alice, & Kumar, R. (2001). Intellectual problems shown by 11-year-old children whose mothers had postnatal depression. *Journal of Child Psychology and Psychiatry and Related Disciplines, 42,* 871–889.

Hayes-Bautista, David E., Hsu, Paul, Perez, Aide, & Gamboa, Cristina. (2002). The "browning" of the graying of America: Diversity in the elderly population and policy implications. *Generations, 26*(3), 15–24.

Hayflick, Leonard (1994). *How and why we age.* New York: Ballantine Books.

Hayflick, Leonard. (2001–2002). Anti-aging medicine: Hype, hope, and reality. *Generations, 15,* 20–26.

Hayflick, Leonard, & Moorhead, Paul S. (1961). The serial cultivation of human diploid cell strains. *Experimental Cell Research, 25,* 585.

Hayslip, Bert, Jr., & Patrick, Julie Hicks. (2003). Custodial grandparenting viewed from a life span perspective. In Bert Hayslip Jr. & Julie Hicks Patrick (Eds.), *Working with custodial grandparents* (pp. 3–11). New York: Springer.

Hayslip, Bert, Servaty, Heather L., & Guarnaccia. (1999). Age cohort differences in perceptions of funerals. In Brian de Vries (Ed.), *Kinship bereavement in later life: A special issue of Omega-Journal of Death and Dying.* Amityville, NY: Baywood.

Hazzard, William R. (2001). Aging, health, longevity, and the promise of bio-medical research: the perspective of a gerontologist and geriatrician. In Edward J. Masoro & Steven N. Austad (Eds.), *Handbook of the biology of aging* (pp. 445–456). San Diego, CA: Academic Press.

Head, Denise, Raz, Jaftali, Cunning-Dixon, Faith, Williamson, Adrienne, & Asker, James D. (2002). Age-related differences in the course of cognitive skill acquisition: the role of regional cortical shrinkage and cognitive resources. *Psychology and Aging, 17,* 72–84.

Heath, Andrew C., Bucholz, Kathleen K., Madden, Pamela A. F., Dinwiddie, Stephen H., Slutske, Wendy S., Bierut, Laura J., et al. (1997). Genetic and environmental contributions to alcohol dependence risk in a national twin sample: Consistency of findings in women and men. *Psychological Medicine, 27,* 1381–1396.

Heckhausen, Jutta. (2001). Adaptation and resilience in midlife. In Margie E. Lachman (Ed.), *Handbook of midlife development* (pp. 345–394). New York: Wiley.

Heimann, Mikael, & Meltzoff, Andrew N. (1996). Deferred imitation in 9- and 14-month-old infants: A longitudinal study of a Swedish sample. *British Journal of Developmental Psychology, 14,* 55–64.

Heiner, Maier, & Vaupel, James W. (2003). Age differences in cultural efficiency: Secular trends in longevity. . In Ursula M. Staudinger & Ulman Lindenberger (Eds.), *Understanding human development: Dialogues with lifespan psychology* (pp. 59–78). Dordrecht, Netherlands: Kluwer.

Heinz, Walter R. (2002). Self-socialization and post-traditional society. In Richard A. Settersten, Jr., & Timothy J. Owens (Eds.), *New frontiers in socialization* (pp. 41–64). Amsterdam: JAI.

Hekimi, Siegfried, & Guarente, Leonard. (2003). Elderly Americans and the Internet: E-mail, TV news, information, and entertainment websites. *Educational Gerontology, 30,* 1351–1354.

Held, Richard. (1995). Binocular vision. In P. D. Gluckman and M. A. Heymann (Eds.), *Developmental physiology: A pediatric perspective* (2nd ed.). London: Edward Arnold Publishers.

Helmuth, Laura. (2001). Where the brain tells a face from a place. *Science, 292,* 196–198.

Helson, Ravenna, Stewart, Abigail J., & Ostrove, Joan. (1995). Identity in three cohorts of midlife women. *Journal of Personality and Social Psychology, 69,* 554–557.

Helwig, Charles C. (1995). Adolescents' and young adults' conceptions of civil liberties: Freedom of speech and religion. *Child Development, 66,* 152–166.

Helwig, Charles C., & Jasiobedzka, Urszula. (2001). The relation between law and morality: Children's reasoning about socially beneficial and unjust laws. *Child Development, 72,* 1382–1393.

Hemsrom, Orjan. (1996). Is marriage dissolution linked to differences in mortality risks for men and women? *Journal of Marriage and the Family, 58,* 366–378.

Herman-Giddens, Marcia E., Wang, Lily, & Koch, Gary. (2001). Secondary sexual characteristics in boys: Estimates from the national health and nutrition examination survey III, 1988–1994. *Archives of Pediatrics and Adolescent Medicine, 155,* 1022–1028.

Hernandez, Jeanne. (1995). The concurrence of eating disorders with histories of child abuse among adolescents. *Journal of Child Sexual Abuse, 4,* 73–85.

Hertz, Rosanna, & Marshal, Nancy L. (Eds.) (2001). *Working families: The transformation of the American home.* Berkeley, CA: University of California Press.

Herzog, Regula A., & House, James S. (1991). Productive activities and aging well. *Generations, 15*(1), 49–54.

Hess, Thomas M., Auman, Corinne, Colcombe, Stanley J., & Rahhal, Tamara A. (2003). The impact of stereotype threat on age difference in memory performance. *The Journals of Gerontology, 58B,* 3–11.

Hetherington, E. Mavis, & Kelly, John. (2002). *For better or for worse: Divorce reconsidered.* New York: Norton.

Hetherington, E. Mavis, Bridges, Margaret, & Insabella, Glendessa M. (1998). What matters? What does not? Five perspectives on the associations between marital transitions and children's adjustment. *American Psychologist, 53,* 167–184.

Heuveline, Patrick. (2002). An international comparison of adolescent and young adult mortality. *Annals of the American Academy of Political and Social Science, 580,* 172–200.

Hewitt, M., & Simone, J.V., (Eds.). (1999). *Ensuring quality cancer care.* Washington, DC, National Academy Press.

Heyman, Bob, & Henriksen, Mette. (2001). *Risk, age, and pregnancy: A case study of prenatal genetic screening and testing.* New York: Palgrave.

Heyman, Gail D., & Gelman, Susan A. (2000). Beliefs about the origins of human psychological traits. *Developmental Psychology, 36,* 663–678.

Heyman, R.E., & Slep, A.M.S. (2002). Do child abuse and interparental violence lead to adulthood family violence? *Journal of Marriage and Family, 64,* 864–870.

Hill, Nancy E., Bush, Kevin R., & Roosa, Mark W. (2003). Parenting and socialization strategies and children's mental health: Low-income Mexican-American and Euro-American mothers and children. *Child Development, 74,* 189–204.

Hill, Robert D., Thorn, Brian L., Bowling, John, & Morrison, Anthony (Eds.). (2002.) *Geriatric residential care.* Mahwah, NJ: Erlbaum.

Hinde, Robert A. (Ed.). (1983). *Primate social relationships: An integrated approach.* Oxford, England: Blackwell.

Hinton, Ivora D., Wilson, Melvin N., Solomon, Hope, Smith, Ursula, Phillip, Di-Ann, & Boyer, Jennifer. (1995). Effect of familial composition on parent–child interactions in African American families. In Melvin N. Wilson (Ed.), *African American family life: Its structural and ecological aspects* (pp. 73–84). San Francisco: Jossey-Bass.

Hobbs, Frank, & Stoops, Nicole. (2002). *U.S. Census Bureau, Census 2000 Special Reports, Series CENSR-4: Demographic trends in the 20th century.* Washington, DC: U.S. Government Printing Office.

Hodges, Ernest V. E., Boivin, Michel, Vitaro, Frank, & Bukowski, William M. (1999). The power of friendship: Protection against an escalating cycle of peer victimization. *Developmental Psychology, 35,* 94–101.

Hofer, Myron A. (2002). The riddle of development. In David J. Lewkowicz & Robert Lickliter (Eds.), *Conceptions of development* (pp. 5–29). Philadelphia: Psychology Press.

Hoff, Erika, & Naigles, Letitia. (2002). How children use input to acquire a lexicon. *Child Development, 73,* 418–433.

Hofferth, Sandra L., & Anderson, Kermyt G. (2003). Are all dads equal? Biology versus marriage as a basis for paternal investment. *Journal of Marriage and Family, 65,* 213–232.

Hofmann, Adele Dellenbaugh. (1997). Adolescent growth and development. In Adele Dellenbaugh Hofmann & Donald Everett Greydanus (Eds.), *Adolescent medicine* (3rd ed.). Stamford, CT: Appleton & Lange.

Hogan, Dennis P., Sun, Rongjun, & Cornwell, Gretchen T. (2000). Sexual and fertility behaviors of American females aged 15–19 years: 1985, 1990, and 1995. *American Journal of Public Health, 90,* 1421–1425.

Hoh, Josephine, & Ott, Jurg. (2003). Mathematical multi-locus approaches to localizing complex human trait genes. *Nature Reviews Genetics, 4,* 701–709.

Hokado, R., Saito, T. R., Wakafuji, Y., Takahashi, K.W., & Imanichi, T. (1993). The change with age of the copulatory behavior of male rats age 67 and 104 weeks. *Experimental Animal, 42,* 75.

Holden, Constance. (2000, July 28). The violence of the lambs. *Science, 289,* 580–581.

Holden, Constance. (2002). The quest to reverse time's toll. *Science, 295,* 1032–1033.

Hollich, George J., Hirsh-Pasek, Kathy, Golinkoff, Roberta Michnick, Brand, Rebecca J., Brown, Ellie, Chung, He Len, Hennon, Elizabeth, Rocroi, Camille. (2000). Breaking the language barrier: An emergentist coalition model for the origins of word learning. *Monographs of the Society for Research in Child Development, 65*(3, Serial 262), v–123.

Holliday, Robin. (1995). *Understanding aging.* Cambridge, England: Cambridge University Press.

Holme, Jennifer Jellison. (2001). Buying homes, buying schools: School choice and the social construction of school quality. *Harvard Educational Review, 72,* 177–205.

Holstein, M. B. (2001–2002). A feminist perspective on anti-aging medicine. *Generations, 25*(4), 38.

Holtzman, Neil A. (2003). Expanding newborn screening: How good is the evidence? *Journal of the American Medical Association, 290,* 2606–2608.

Horan, Michael A., Barton, Roger N., & Lithgow, Gordon J. (2000). Aging and stress, biology of. In George Fink (Ed.), *Encyclopedia of stress* (pp. 111–117). San Diego, CA: Academic Press.

Horan, Patricia F., Phillips, Jennifer, & Hagan, Nancy E. (1998). The meaning of abstinence for college students. *Journal of HIV/AIDS Prevention and Education for Adolescents and Children, 2,* 51–66.

Horn, John L., & Cattell, Raymond B. (1967). Age differences in fluid and crystallized intelligence. *Acta Psychologica, 26,* 107–129.

Horn, John L., & Hofer, Scott M. (1992). Major abilities and development in the adult period. In Robert J. Sternberg & Cynthia A. Berg (Eds.), *Intellectual development* (pp. 44–99). New York: Cambridge University Press.

Horn, John L., & Masunaga, Hiromi. (2000). New directions for research into aging and intelligence: The development of expertise. In Timothy J. Perfect & Elizabeth A. Maylor (Eds.), *Models of*

cognitive aging (pp. 125–159). New York: Oxford University Press.

Hornsby, Peter J. (2001). Cell proliferation in mammalian aging. In Edward J. Masoro & Steven N. Austad (Eds.), *Handbook of the biology of aging* (pp. 207–245). San Diego, CA: Academic Press.

Horowitz, Amy, & Stuen, Cynthia. (2003). Introduction: Aging and the senses. *Generations, 27*(1), 6–7.

Horwitz, Allan V., & White, Helene Raskin. (1998). The relationship of cohabitation and mental health: A study of a young adult cohort. *Journal of Marriage and the Family, 60,* 505–514.

Houts, Renate M., Robins, Elliot, & Huston, Ted L. (1996). Compatibility and the development of premarital relationships. *Journal of Marriage and the Family, 58,* 7–20.

Howe, Christine J. (1998). *Conceptual structure in childhood and adolescence.* London: Routledge.

Howson, Geoffrey. (2002). Some questions on probability. *Teaching Statistics, 24,* 17–21.

Hsu, Hui-Chin, Fogel, Alan, & Cooper, Rebecca B. (2000). Infant vocal development during the first 6 months: Speech quality and melodic complexity. *Infant and Child Development, 9,* 1–16.

Hu, Frank, Li, T.Y., Colditz, G.A., Willett W.C., & Manson J.E. (2003). Television watching and other sedentary behaviors in relation to risk of obesity and Type 2 diabetes mellitus in women. *Journal of the American Medical Association, 289,* 1785–1791.

Hubbs-Tait, Laura, Culp, Anne McDonald, Culp, Rex E., & Miller, Carrie E. (2002). Relation of maternal cognitive stimulation, emotional support, and intrusive behavior during Head Start to children's kindergarten cognitive abilities. *Child Development, 73,* 110–131.

Huber, Carole. (2001–2002). Anti-aging: Why now? A historical framework for understanding the contemporary enthusiasm. *Generations, 8,* 9–14.

Huesmann, L. Rowell, Moise-Titus, Jessica, Podolski, Cheryl-Lynn, & Eron, Leonard D. (2003). Longitudinal relations between children's exposure to TV violence and their aggressive and violent behavior in young adulthood:

1977–1992. *Developmental Psychology, 39,* 201–221.

Hughes, Edward G., & Giacomi, Mita. (2001). Funding in vitro fertilization treatment for persistent subfertility: The pain and the politics. *Fertility and Sterility, 76,* 431–442.

Hulanicka, Barbara. (1999). Acceleration of menarcheal age of girls from dysfunctional families. *Journal of Reproductive and Infant Psychology, 17,* 119–132.

Hulbert, Ann. (2003). *Raising America: Experts, parents, and a century of advice about children.* New York: Knopf.

Hunt, Earl. (1993). What do we need to know about aging? In John Cerella, John Rybash, William Hoyer, & Michael L. Commons (Eds.), *Adult information processing: Limits on loss.* San Diego, CA: Academic Press.

Hurst, Laurence D. (1997). Evolutionary theories of genomic imprinting. In Wolf Reik & Azim Surani (Eds.), *Genomic imprinting* (pp. 211–237). Oxford, England: IRL Press.

Huston, Ted L. (2000). The social ecology of marriage and other intimate unions. *Journal of Marriage and the Family, 62,* 298–320.

Huttenlocher, Janellen, Levine, Susan, & Vevea, Jack. (1998). Environmental input and cognitive growth: A study using time-period comparisons. *Child Development, 69,* 1012–1029.

Huyck, Margaret Hellie. (1995). Marriage and close relationships of the marital kind. In Rosemary Blieszner & Victoria Hilkevitch Bedford (Eds.), *Handbook of aging and the family.* Westport, CT: Greenwood Press.

Huyck, Margaret Hellie. (1999). Gender roles and gender identity in midlife. In Sherry L. Willis & James D. Reid (Eds.), *Life in the middle: Psychosocial and social development in middle age* (pp. 209–232). San Diego, CA: Academic Press.

Hwalek, Melanie A., Neale, Anne Victoria, Goodrich, Carolyn Stahl, & Quinn, Kathleen. (1996). The association of elder abuse and substance abuse in the Illinois elder abuse system. *Gerontologist, 36,* 694–700.

Hyde, Kenneth E. (1990). *Religion in childhood and adolescence: A comprehensive review of the research.* Birmingham, AL: Religious Education Press.

Iacovou, Maria. (2002). Regional differences in the transition to adulthood. *Annals of the American Academy of Political and Social Science, 580,* 40–69.

Ibrahim, Said A., Whittle, Jeff, Bean-Mayberry, Bevanne, Kelley, Mary E., Good, Chester, & Conigliaro, Joseph. (2003). Racial/ethnic variations in physician recommendation for cardiac revascularization. *American Journal of Public Health, 93,* 1689–1693.

IFFS Surveillance . (2001). A survey of 39 nations. *Fertility and Sterility, 76,* Supplement 2, No. 5.

Ilmarinen, Juhani. (1995). A new concept for productive aging at work. In Eino Heikkinen, Jorma Kuusinen, & Isto Ruoppila (Eds.), *Preparation for aging.* New York: Plenum Press.

Ingebretsen, Reidun, & Endestad, Tor. (1995). Lifelong learning experiences from Norway. In Eino Heikkinen, Jorma Kuusinen, & Isto Ruoppila (Eds.), *Preparation for aging.* New York, Plenum Press.

Ingersoll-Dayton, Berit, Krause, Neal, & Morgan, David. (2002). Religious trajectories and transition over the life course. *International Journal of Aging and Human Development, 55,* 51–70.

Ingersoll-Dayton, Berit, Neal, Margaret B., Ha, Jung-Hwa, & Hammer, Leslie B. (2003). Redressing inequity in parent care among siblings. *Journal of Marriage and Family, 65,* 201–212.

Ingersoll-Dayton, Berit, Starrels, Marjorie E., & Dowler, David. (1996). Caregiving for parents and parents-in-law: Is gender important? *The Gerontologist, 36,* 483–491.

Inhelder, Bärbel, & Piaget, Jean. (1958). *The growth of logical thinking from childhood to adolescence.* New York: Basic Books.

Institute of Medicine. (2003). *Testosterone and aging: Clinical research directions.* Washington, DC: Institute of Medicine of the National Academies.

Irwin, Julia R., Carter, Alice S., & Briggs-Gowan, Margaret. (2002). The social-emotional development of "late-talking" toddlers. *Journal of the American Academy of Child and Adolescent Psychiatry, 41*(11), 1324–1332.

Isolauri, Erika, Sutas, Yelda, Salo, Matti K., Isosonppi, Riitta, & Kaila, Minna. (1998). Elimination diet in cow's milk allergy: Risk for impaired growth in young children. *Journal of Pediatrics, 132,* 1004–1009.

Jaccard, James, & Dittus, Patricia J. (2000). Adolescent perceptions of maternal approval of birth control and sexual risk behavior. *American Journal of Public Health, 90,* 1426–1430.

Jackson, Yo, & Warren, Jared S. (2000). Appraisal, social support, and life events: Predicting outcome behavior in school-age children. *Child Development, 71,* 1441–1457.

Jacob's father. (1997). Jacob's story: A miracle of the heart. *Zero to Three, 17,* 59–64.

Jacobs, Janis E., Lanza, Stephanie, Osgood, D. Wayne, Eccles, Jacquelynne S., & Wigfield, Allan. (2002). Changes in children's self-competence and values: Gender and domain differences across grades one through twelve. *Child Development, 73,* 509–527.

Jacobson, Joseph L. & Jacobson, Sandra W. (1996). Methodological considerations in behavioral toxicology in infants and children. *Developmental Psychology, 32,* 390–403.

Jacoby, Larry L., Marsh, Elizabeth J., & Dolan, Patrick O. (2001). Forms of bias: Age-related changes in memory and cognition. In Moshe Naveh-Benjamin, Morris Moscovitch, & Henry L. Roedinger III (Eds.), *Perspectives on human memory and cognitive aging: Essays in honour of Fergus Craik* (pp. 240–252). East Sussex, UK: Psychology Press.

Jaffee, Sara, Caspi, Avshalom, Moffitt, Terrie E., Belsky, Jay, & Silva, Phil. (2001). Why are children born to teen mothers at risk for adverse outcomes in young adulthood? Results from a 20-year longitudinal study. *Development and Psychopathology, 13,* 377–397.

Jahns, Lisa, Siega-Riz, Anna Maria, & Popkin, Barry M. (2001). The increasing prevalence of snacking among US children from 1977 to 1996. *Journal of Pediatrics, 138,* 493–498.

Janson, Christer, Chinn, S., Jarvis, D., Zock, J. P., Toren, K., Burney, P., & European Community Respiratory Health Survey. (2001). Effect of passive smoking on respiratory symptoms, bronchial responsiveness, lung function, and total serum IgE in the European Community Respiratory Health Survey: A cross-sectional study. *The Lancet, 358,* 2103–2109.

Jayakody, Rukmalie, & Kalil, Ariel. (2002). Social fathering in low-income, African American families with preschool children. *Journal of Marriage and Family, 64,* 504–516.

Jeanneret, René. (1995). The role of preparation for retirement in the improvement of the quality of life for elderly people. In Eino Heikkinen, Jorma Kuusinen, & Isto Ruoppila (Eds.), *Preparation for aging.* New York: Plenum Press.

Jeffries, Sherryl, & Konnert, Candace. (2002). Regret and psychological well-being among voluntarily and involuntarily childless women and mothers. *International Journal of Aging and Human Development, 54,* 89–106.

Jellinger, Kurt A., Schmidt, Reinhold, & Windisch, Manfred. (Eds.) (2002). *Ageing and dementia: Current and future concepts.* Vienna: Springer Verlag.

Jenkins, Jennifer M., & Astington, Janet Wilde. (1996). Cognitive factors and family structure associated with theory of mind development in young children. *Developmental Psychology, 32,* 70–78.

Jensen, Arthur R. (1998). *The g factor: The science of mental ability.* Westport, CT: Praeger.

Jensen, Peter S., & Hoagwood, Kimberly. (1997). The book of names: DSM-IV in context. *Development and Psychopathology, 9,* 231–249.

Johanneson, Magnus, & Johansson, Per-Olov. (1997). Is the valuation of QALYs gained independent of age? Some empirical evidence. *Journal of Health, 16,* 589–599.

Johnson, Byron R., Jang, Sung Joon, Li, Spencer De, & Larson, David. (2000). The 'invisible institution' and black youth crime: The church as an agency of local social control. *Journal of Youth and Adolescence, 29,* 479–498.

Johnson, Colleen L. (1995). Cultural diversity in the late-life family. In Rosemary Blieszner & Victoria Hilkevitch Bedford (Eds.), *Handbook of aging and the family* (pp. 307–331). Westport, CT: Greenwood Press.

Johnson, Colleen L., & Barer, Barbara M. (1993). Coping and a sense of control among the oldest old. *Journal of Aging Studies, 7,* 67–80.

Johnson, Colleen L., & Barer, Barbara M. (2003). Family lives of aging black Americans. In Jaber F. Gubrium & James A. Holstein (Eds.), *Ways of aging* (pp. 111–131). Malden, MA: Blackwell.

Johnson, Dana E. (2000). Medical and developmental sequelae of early childhood institutionalization in Eastern European adoptees. In Charles A. Nelson (Ed.), *The Minnesota symposia on child psychology: Vol. 31. The effects of early adversity on neurobehavioral development.* Mahwah, NJ: Erlbaum.

Johnson, Jeffrey G., Cohen, Patricia, Smailes, Elizabeth M., Kasen, Stephanie, & Brook, Judith S. (2002). Television viewing and aggressive behavior during adolescence and adulthood. *Science, 295,* 2468–2471.

Johnson, Mark H. (1997). *Developmental cognitive neuroscience: An introduction.* Cambridge, MA: Blackwell.

Johnson, Mark H. (1998). The neural basis of cognitive development. In William Damon (Series Ed.), Deanna Kuhn & Robert S. Siegler (Volume Eds.), *Handbook of child psychology: Vol. 2. Cognition, perception, and language* (pp. 1–49). New York: Wiley.

Johnson, Mark H. (1999). Developmental neuroscience. In Marc H. Bornstein & Michael E. Lamb (Eds.), *Developmental psychology: An advanced textbook* (4th ed.). Mahwah, NJ: Erlbaum.

Johnson, Michael P., & Ferraro, Kathleen J. (2000). Research on domestic violence in the 90s: Making distinctions. *Journal of Marriage and Family, 63,* 948–963.

Johnson, Norine G. (2003). Psychology and health. *American Psychologist, 58,* 670–677.

Johnson-Powell, Gloria, Yamamoto, Joe, Wyatt, Gail E., & Arroyo, William (Eds.). (1997). *Transcultural child development: Psychological assessment and treatment.* New York: Wiley & Sons.

John-Steiner, Vera. (1986). *Notebooks of the mind: Explorations of thinking.* Albuquerque, NM: University of New Mexico Press.

Johnston, Lloyd D., O'Malley, Patrick M., & Bachman, Jerald G. (2001). *Monitoring the future: National survey results on drug use, 1975–2000: Vol. 1. Secondary school students* (NIH Publication No. 01-4924). Bethesda, MD: National Institute on Drug Abuse.

Johnston, Lloyd D., O'Malley, Patrick M., & Bachman, Jerald G. (2002). *Monitoring the future: National survey results on drug us, 1975-2001.* Bethesda, MD: National Institute of Drug Abuse.

Johnston, Timothy D., & Edwards, Laura. (2002). Genes, interactions, and the development of behavior. *Psychological Review, 109,* 26–34.

Joiner, Thomas E., Jr. (1999). The clustering and contagion of suicide. *Current Directions in Psychological Science, 8,* 89–92.

Jones, Constance J., & Meredith, William. (1996). Patterns of personality change across the life span. *Psychology and Aging, 11,* 57–65.

Jones, Harold E., & Conrad, Herbert S. (1933). The growth and decline of intelligence: A study of a homogeneous group between the ages of ten and sixty. *Genetic Psychology Monographs, 13,* 223–298.

Jones, Robin, Schlank, Anita, & Le Guin, Louis. (1999). Assessment of adolescent sex offenders. In Jon A. Shaw (Ed.), *Sexual aggression.* Washington, DC: American Psychiatric Press.

Jongbloed, Ben, Maassen, Peter, A. M., & G. Neave, Guy (Eds.). (1999). *From the eye of the storm: Higher education's changing institution.* Hingham, MA: Kluwer.

Jordon, John R., & Neimeyer, Robert A. (2003). Does grief counseling work? *Death Studies, 27,* 765–786.

Joseph, Rhawn. (2000). Fetal brain behavior and cognitive development. *Developmental Review, 20,* 81–98.

Jung, Carl Gustav. (1933/1961). *Memories, dreams, reflections.* New York: Vintage.

Jusczyk, Peter W. (1997). *The discovery of spoken language.* Cambridge, Mass.: MIT Press.

Kachur, S. Patrick, Potter, Lloyd B., James, Stephen P., & Powell, Kenneth E. (1995). *Suicide in the United States: 1980–1992* (Violence Surveillance

Summary Series No. 1). Atlanta: Centers for Disease Control and Prevention, National Center for Injury Prevention and Control.

Kahana-Kalman, Ronit, & Walker-Andrews, Arlene S. (2001). The role of person familiarity in young infants' perception of emotional expressions. *Child Development, 72,* 352–369.

Kahn, Jeffrey P., Mastroianni, Anna C., & Sugarman, Jeremy (Eds.). (1998). *Beyond consent: Seeking justice in research.* New York: Oxford University Press.

Kail, Robert. (2000). Speed of information processing: Developmental change and links to intelligence. *Journal of School Psychology, 38,* 51–61.

Kaiser, Jocelyn. (2003). How much are human lives and health worth? *Science, 299,* 1836–1837.

Kalmuss, Debra, Davidson, Andrew, Cohall, Alwyn, Laraque, Danielle, & Cassell, Carol. (2003). Preventing sexual risk behaviors and pregnancy among teenagers: Linking research and programs. *Perspectives on Sexual and Reproductive Health, 35,* 87–93.

Kamp Dush, **Claire M., Cohan, Catherine L., & Amato, Paul R.** (2003). The relationship between cohabitation and marital quality and stability: Changes across cohorts? *Journal of Marriage and Family, 65,* 539–549.

Kanaya, Tomoe, Scullin, Matthew H., & Ceci, Stephen J. (2003). The Flynn effect and U.S. policies: The impact of rising IQ scores on American society via mental retardation diagnoses. *American Psychologist, 58,* 778–790.

Kandel, Denise B., & Davies, Mark. (1996). High school students who use crack and other drugs. *Archives of General Psychiatry, 53,* 71–80.

Kanner, Leo. (1943). Autistic disturbances of affective contact. *Nervous Child, 2,* 217–250.

Kaplan, Bonnie J., Crawford, Susan G., Dewey, Deborah M., & Fisher, Geoff C. (2000). The IQs of children with ADHD are normally distributed. *Journal of Learning Disabilities, 33,* 425–432.

Kaplan, Robert M. (2000). Two pathways to prevention. *American Psychologist, 55,* 382–396.

Kapp, Marshall B. (2000). Ethical considerations and court involvement in end-of-life decision making. In Kathryn Braun, James H. Pietsch, & Patricia L. Blanchette (Eds.)., *Cultural issues in end-of-life decision making,* (pp. 55–68). Thousand Oaks, CA: Sage.

Karoly, Lynn A., Greenwood, Peter W., Everingham, Susan S., Houbé, Jill, Kilburn, M. Rebecca, Rydell, C. Peter, Sanders, Matthew, & Chiesa, James. (1998). *Investing in our children: What we know and don't know about the costs and benefits of early childhood interventions.* Santa Monica, CA: RAND.

Karpov, Yuriy, & Haywood, H. Carl. (1998). Two ways to elaborate Vygotsky's concept of mediation: Implications for instruction. *American Psychologist, 53,* 27–36.

Kasl-Godley, Julia E., Gatz, Margaret, & Fiske, A. (1998). Depression and depressive symptoms in old age. In I.H. Nordhus, G.R. VandenBos, S. Berg, & P. Fromholt (Eds.), *Clinical geropsychology* (pp. 211–217). Washington, DC: American Psychological Association.

Kastenbaum, Robert J. (1992). *The psychology of death.* New York: Springer-Verlag.

Kastenbaum, Robert J. (2003). Where is the self in elder self-narratives? *Generations, 27*(3), 10–15.

Katz, Jeanne Samson. (1993). Jewish perspectives on death, dying and bereavement. In Donna Dickenson & Malcolm Johnson (Eds.), *Death, dying & bereavement.* London: Sage.

Katz, Stephen. (2001–2002). Growing older without aging? Positive aging, anti-ageism, and anti-aging. *Generations, 15, 27–32.*

Kaufman, Alan S., & Lichtenberger, Elizabeth O. (2000). *Essentials of WISC-III and WPPSI-R assessment.* New York: Wiley.

Kaufman, Joan, & Charney, Dennis. (2001). Effects of early stress on brain structure and function: Implications for understanding the relationship between child maltreatment and depression. *Development and Psychopathology, 13,* 451–471.

Kaufman, Sharon R. (1986). *The ageless self.* Madison: University of Wisconsin Press.

Keating, Daniel P., & Hertzman, Clyde (Eds.). (1999). *Developmental health and the wealth of nations: Social, biological, and educational dynamics.* New York: Guilford.

Keil, Frank C., & Lockhart, Kristi L. (1999). Explanatory understanding in conceptual development. In Ellin Kofsky Scholnick, Katherine Nelson, Susan A. Gelman, & Patricia H. Miller (Eds.), *Conceptual development: Piaget's legacy* (pp. 103–130). Mahwah, NJ: Erlbaum.

Keiley, Margaret K., Howe, Tasha R., Dodge, Kenneth A., Bates, John E., & Pettit, Gregory S. (2001). The timing of child physical maltreatment: A cross-domain growth analysis of impact on adolescent externalizing and internalizing problems. *Development and Psychopathology, 13,* 891–912.

Keith, Jennie. (1990). Age in social and cultural context: Anthropological perspectives. In Robert H. Binstock & Linda K. George (Eds.), *Handbook of aging and the social sciences* (3rd ed.). San Diego, CA: Academic Press

Keller, Sally, & Stricker, George. (2003). Links between custodial grandparents and the psychological adaptation of grandchildren. In Bert Hayslip Jr. & Julie Hicks Patrick (Eds.), *Working with custodial grandparents* (pp. 27–43). New York: Springer.

Kelley, Sue A., Brownell, Celia A., & Campbell, Susan B. (2000). Mastery motivation and self-evaluative affect in toddlers: Longitudinal relations with maternal behavior. *Child Development, 71,* 1061–1071.

Kelley, Susan J., & Whitley, Deborah M. (2003). Psychological distress and physical health problems in grandparents raising grandchildren: Development of an empirically based intervention model. In Bert Hayslip Jr. & Julie Hicks Patrick (Eds.), *Working with custodial grandparents* (pp. 127–144). New York: Springer.

Kellman, Philip J., & Banks, Martin S. (1998). Infant visual perception. In William Damon (Series Ed.), Deanna Kuhn, & Robert S. Siegler (Volume Eds.), *Handbook of child psychology: Cognition, perception, and language* (5th ed.). New York: Wiley.

Kelly, Karen. (1998). Working teenagers: Do after-school jobs hurt? *The Harvard Education Letter, 14,* 1–3.

Kemper, Susan, & Harden, Tamara. (1999). Experimentally disentangling what's beneficial about elderspeak from what's not. *Psychology and Aging, 14,* 656–670.

Kemper, Susan, Herman, Ruth E., & Lin, Cindy H. T. (2003). The costs of doing two things at once for young and older adults: Talking while walking, finger tapping, and ignoring speech or noise. *Psychology and Aging, 18,* 181–192.

Kendler, Howard H. (2002). Unified knowledge: Fantasy or reality? *Contemporary Psychology, 47,* 501–503.

Kerig, Patricia K., Fedorowicz, Anne E., Brown, Corina A., & Warren, Michelle. (2000). Assessment and intervention for PTSD in children exposed to violence. In Robert A. Geffner, Peter G. Jaffe, & Marlies Sudermann (Eds.), *Children exposed to domestic violence: Current issues in research, intervention, prevention, and policy development* (pp. 161–184). Binghamton, NY: Haworth Press.

Keshet, Jamie. (1988). The remarried couple: Stresses and successes. In William R. Beer (Ed.), *Relative strangers.* Totowa, NJ: Rowman & Littlefield.

Kessler, Seymour. (2000). *Psyche and helix: Psychological aspects of genetic counseling.* New York: Wiley.

Keyes, Corey Lee M., & Ryff, Carol D. (1999). Psychological well-being in midlife. In Sherry L. Willis & James D. Reid (Eds.), *Life in the middle* (pp. 161–180). San Diego, CA: Academic Press.

Khaleque, Abdul, & Rohner, Ronald P. (2002). Perceived parental acceptance-rejection and psychological adjustment: A meta-analysis of cross-cultural and intracultural studies. *Journal of Marriage and Family, 64,* 54–64.

Kim, Jungmeen E., & Moen, Phyllis. (2001). Moving into retirement: Preparation and transitions in late midlife. In Margie E. Lachman (Ed.), *Handbook of midlife development* (pp. 487–527). New York: Wiley.

Kim, Kenneth, & Smith, Peter K. (1998). Retrospective survey of parental marital relations and child reproductive development. *International Journal of Behavioral Development, 22,* 729–751.

Kincade, Jean E., Rabiner, Donna J., Bernard, Shulamit L., Woomert, Alison, Konrad, Thomas R., DeFriese,

Gordon H., et al. (1996). Older adults as a community resource: Results from the national survey of self-care and aging. *Gerontologist, 36,* 474–482.

King, Gary, & Williams, David R. (1995). Race and health: A multi-dimensional approach to African-American health. In Benjamin C. Amick III, Sol Levine, Alvin R. Tarlov, & Diana Chapman Walsh (Eds.), *Society and health.* New York: Oxford University Press.

King, P.M., & Kitchener, K.S. (1994). *Developing reflective judgment: Understanding and promoting intellectual growth and critical thinking in adolescents and adults.* San Francisco: Jossey-Bass.

King, Valerie. (2003). The legacy of a grandparent's divorce: Consequences for ties between grandparents and grandchildren. *Journal of Marriage and Family, 65,* 170–183.

Kirkwood, Thomas B. (2003). Age differences in evolutionary benefits. In Ursula M. Staudinger & Ulman Lindenberger (Eds.), *Understanding human development: Dialogues with lifespan psychology* (pp. 45–57). Dordrecht, Netherlands: Kluwer.

Kitzinger, Sheila. (2001). *Rediscovering birth.* New York: Simon & Schuster.

Klaczynski, Paul A. (2000). Motivated scientific reasoning biases, epistemological beliefs, and theory polarization: A two-process approach to adolescent cognition. *Child Development, 71,* 1347–1366.

Klaczynski, Paul A. (2001). Analytic and heuristic influences on adolescent reasoning and decision-making. *Child Development, 72,* 844–861.

Klatz, Ronald M. (1997). Introduction. In Ronald M. Klatz and R. Goldman, *Anti-aging medical therapeutics.* Marina Del Rey, CA: Healthquest.

Klaus, Marshall H., & Kennell, John H. (1976). *Maternal-infant bonding: The impact of early separation or loss on family development.* St. Louis: Mosby

Kleiber, Douglas A. (1999). *Leisure experience and human development: A dialectical interpretation.* New York: Basic Books.

Klepinger, Daniel H., Lundberg, Shelly, & Plotnick, Robert D. (1995). Adolescent fertility and the educational attainment of young women. *Family Planning Perspectives, 27,* 23–28.

Klug, William S., & Cummings, Michael R. (2000). *Genetics* (6th ed.). Upper Saddle River, NJ: Prentice-Hall.

Kluwer, Esther S., Heesink, Jose A. M., & van de Vliert, Evert. (2002). The division of labor across the transition to parenthood: A justice perspective. *Journal of Marriage and Family, 64,* 930—943.

Koch, Tom. (2000). *Age speaks for itself.* Westport, CT: Praeger.

Kochanska, Grazyna, Coy, Katherine C., & Murray, Kathleen T. (2001). The development of self-regulation in the first four years of life. *Child Development, 72,* 1091–1111.

Kochanska, Grazyna, Murray, Kathleen, & Coy, Katherine C. (1997). Inhibitory control as a contributor to conscience in childhood: From toddler to early school age. *Child Development, 68,* 263–277.

Kochenderfer-Ladd, Becky, & Wardrop, James L. (2001). Chronicity and instability of children's peer victimization experiences as predictors of loneliness and social satisfaction trajectories. *Child Development, 72,* 134–151.

Kogan, Shari L., Blanchette, Patricia L., & Masaki, Kamal. (2000). Talking to patients about death and dying: improving communication across cultures. In Kathryn Braun, James H. Pietsch, & Patricia L. Blanchette (Eds.). *Cultural issues in end-of-life decision making* (pp. 305–325). Thousand Oaks, CA: Sage.

Kohlberg, Lawrence. (1963). The development of children's orientations toward a moral order: I. Sequence in the development of moral thought. *Vita Humana, 6,* 11–36.

Kohlberg, Lawrence. (1973). Continuities in childhood and adult moral development revisited. In Paul B. Baltes & K. Warner Schaie (Eds.), *Life-span developmental psychology: Personality and socialization.* New York: Academic Press.

Kohler, Julie K., Grotevant, Harold D., & McRoy, Ruth G. (2002). Adopted adolescents' preoccupation with adoption: The impact on adoptive family relationships. *Journal of Marriage and Family, 64,* 93-104.

Kojima, Hideto, Fujimiya, Mineko, Matsumura, Kazuhiro, Younan, Patrick, Imaeda, Hirotsugu, Maeda, Makiko, et al. (2003). NeuroD-betacellulin gene therapy induces islet neogenesis in the liver and reverses diabetes in mice. *Nature Medicine, 9,* 596–603.

Kolland, Franz. (1994). Contrasting cultural profiles between generations: Interests and common activities in three intrafamilial generations. *Aging and Society, 14,* 319–340.

Kompier, Michiel, & Cooper, Cary (Eds.) (1999). *Preventing stress, improving productivity: European case studies in the workplace.* London: Routledge.

Koropeckyj-Cox, Tanya. (2002). Beyond parental status: Psychological well-being in middle and old age. *Journal of Marriage and Family, 64,* 957–971.

Kosslyn, Stephen M., Cacioppo, J.T., Davidson, R.J., Hugdahl, K., Lovallo, W.R., Spiegel, D. & Rose, R. (2002). Bridging psychology and biology. *American Psychologist, 57,* 341—351.

Kosterlitz, J. (1993). Golden silence? *National Journal,* pp. 800–804.

Kotre, John. (1995). *White gloves: How we create ourselves through memory.* New York: Free Press.

Kotre, John. (1999–2000). Generativity and the gift of meaning. Reasons to grow old: Meaning in later life. *Generations, 23,* 65–71.

Kovacs, Donna M., Parker, Jeffrey G., & Hoffman, Lois W. (1996). Behavioral, affective, and social correlates of involvement in cross-sex friendship in elementary school. *Child Development, 67,* 2269–2286.

Kozol, Jonathan. (1991). *Savage inequalities.* New York: Crown.

Kraft, Joan Creech & Willhite, Calvin C. (1997). Retinoids in abnormal and normal embryonic development. In Sam Kacew & George H. Lambert (Eds.), *Environmental toxicology and human development.* Washington DC: Taylor & Francis.

Krauss, J.B. (1999). Educational innovation and responsibility. *Archives of Psychiatric Nursing, 13,* 225–226.

Krieger, Nancy. (2002). Breast cancer: A disease of affluence, poverty, or both? The case of African American women. *American Journal of Public Health, 92,* 611–613.

Kroger, Jane. (1989). *Identity in adolescence: The balance between self and other.* London: Routledge.

Kromelow, Susan, Harding, Carol, & Touris, Margot. (1990). The role of the father in the development of stranger sociability during the second year. *American Journal of Orthopsychiatry, 60,* 521–530.

Kübler-Ross, Elisabeth. (1969). On death and dying. New York: Macmillan.

Kübler-Ross, Elisabeth. (1975). Death: The final stage of growth. Englewood Cliffs, NJ: Prentice-Hall.

Kuh, D., & Ben-Shlomo Y. (1997). *A life course approach to chronic disease epidemiology.* New York: Oxford University Press.

Kuller, Jeffrey A., Strauss, Robert A., & Cefalo, Robert C. (2001). Preconceptual and prenatal care. In Frank W. Ling & Patrick Duff (Eds.), *Obstetrics and gynecology: Principles for practice.* New York: McGraw Hill.

Kurdek, Lawrence A. (1992). Relationship status and relationship satisfaction in cohabiting gay and lesbian couples. *Journal of Social and Personal Relationships, 9,* 125–142.

Kurdek, Lawrence. (1998). Relationship outcomes and their predictors: Longitudinal evidence from heterosexual married, gay cohabiting, and lesbian cohabiting couples. *Journal of Marriage and the Family, 60,* 553–568. .

Kwan, Christine Man Lai, Love, Gayle Dienberg, Ryff, Carol D., Essex, Marilyn J. (2003). The role of self-enhancing evaluations in a successful life transition. *Psychology and Aging, 18,* 3–12.

La Leche League International. (1997). *The womanly art of breastfeeding.* New York: Plume.

Labouvie-Vief, Gisela. (1990). Wisdom as integrated thought: Historical and developmental perspectives. In Robert J. Sternberg (Ed.), *Wisdom: Its nature, origins, and development.* Cambridge, England: Cambridge University Press.

Labouvie-Vief, Gisela. (1992). A neo-Piagetian perspective on adult cognitive development. In Robert J. Sternberg & Cynthia A. Berg (Eds.), *Intellectual development.* New York: Cambridge University Press.

Lach, Helen W. (2002–2003). Fear of falling: An emerging public health problem. *Generations, 26*(4): 33–37.

Lachman, Margie E. (2001). Preface. In Margie E. Lachman (Ed.), *Handbook of midlife development* (pp. xvii–xxvi). New York: Wiley.

Lachman, Margie E., & Bertrand, Rosanna M. (2001). Personality and the self in midlife. In Margie E. Lachman (Ed.), *Handbook of midlife development* (pp. 279–309). New York: Wiley.

Lacourse, Eric, Nagin, Daniel, Tremblay, Richard E., Vitaro, Frank, & Claes, Michel. (2003). Developmental trajectories of boys' delinquent group membership and facilitation of violent behaviors during adolescence. *Development and Psychopathology, 15,* 183–197.

Ladd, Gary W. (1999). Peer relationships and social competence during early and middle childhood. *Annual Review of Psychology, 50,* 333–359.

Ladd, Gary W., & Pettit, Gregory S. (2002). Parenting and the development of children's peer relationships. In Marc H. Bornstein (Ed.), *Handbook of parenting: Vol. 5. Practical issues in parenting* (2nd ed., pp. 269–309). Mahwah, NJ: Erlbaum.

Lagattuta, Kristin Hansen, & Wellman, Henry M. (2002). Differences in early parent-child conversations about negative versus positive emotions: Implications for the development of psychological understanding. *Developmental Psychology, 38,* 564–580.

Lamb, Michael E. (1982). Maternal employment and child development: A review. In Michael E. Lamb (Ed.), *Nontraditional families: Parenting and child development.* Hillsdale, NJ: Erlbaum.

Lamb, Michael E. (1997). The development of father-infant relationships. In Michael E. Lamb (Ed.), *The role of the father in child development* (3rd ed., pp. 104–120). New York: Wiley.

Lamb, Michael E. (1998). Nonparental child care: Context, quality, correlates, and consequences. In William Damon (Series Ed.), Irving E. Sigel, & K. Ann Renninger (Volume Eds.), *Handbook of child psychology: Vol. 4. Child psychology in practice* (5th ed., pp. 73–133). New York: Wiley.

Lamb, Michael E. (1999). Noncustodial fathers and their impact on the children of divorce. In Ross A. Thompson & Paul R. Amato (Eds.), *The postdivorce family: Children, parenting, and society* (pp. 105–125). Thousand Oaks, CA: Sage.

Lamb, Michael E. (2000). The history of research on father involvement: An overview. In H. Elizabeth Peters, Gary W. Peterson, Suzanne K. Steinmetz, & Randal D. Day (Eds.), *Fatherhood: Research, interventions, and policies* (pp. 23–42). New York: Haworth.

Lambert, Wallace E., Genesee, Fred, Holobow, Naomi, & Chartrand, Louise. (1993). Bilingual education for majority English-speaking children. *European Journal of Psychology of Education, 8,* 3–22.

Lamers, Elizabeth P. (2003). Helping children during bereavement. In Inge Corless, Barbara B. Germino, & Mary A. Pittman (Eds.), *Dying, death, & bereavement* (pp. 267–286). New York: Springer.

Lamy, Peter P. (1994). Drug–nutrient interactions in the aged. In Ronald R. Watson (Ed.), *Handbook of nutrition in the aged.* Boca Raton, FL: CRC Press.

Lan, Pei-Chia. (2002). Subcontracting filial piety: Elder care in ethnic Chinese immigrant families in California. *Journal of Family Issues, 23,* 812–835.

Landau, Simha F., Björkqvist, Kaj, Lagerspetz, Kirsti M. J., Österman, Karin, & Gideon, Lior. (2002). The effect of religiosity and ethnic origin on direct and indirect aggression among males and females: Some Israeli findings. *Aggressive Behavior, 28,* 281–298.

Landry, David J., Singh, Susheela, & Darroch, Jacqueline E. (2000). Sexuality education in fifth and sixth grades in U.S. public schools, 1999. *Family Planning Perspectives, 32,* 212–219.

Lane, Christianne J., & Zelinski, Elizabeth M. (2003) Hierarchical linear models of the memory functioning questionnaire. *Psychology and Aging, 18*(1), 38–53.

Langer, Jonas M. (2001). The mosaic evolution of cognitive and linguistic ontogeny. In Melissa Bowerman & Stephen C. Levinson (Eds.), *Language acquisition and conceptual development* (pp. 19–44). Cambridge, UK: Cambridge University Press.

Lansford, Jennifer E., Cebello, Rosario, Abbey, Antonia, & Stewart, Abigail J. (2001). Does family structure matter? A comparison of adoptive, two-parent biological, single-mother, stepfather, and stepmother households. *Journal of Marriage and Family, 63,* 840–851.

Lapsley, Daniel K. (1993). Toward an integrated theory of adolescent ego development: The "new look" at adolescent egocentrism. *American Journal of Orthopsychiatry, 63,* 562–571.

Largie, Shay, Field, Tiffany, Hernandez-Reif, Maria, Sanders, Christopher E., & Diego, Miguel. (2001). Employment during adolescence is associated with depression, inferior relationships, lower grades, and smoking. *Adolescence, 36,* 395–401.

Larivee, Serge, Normandeau, Sylvie, & Parent, Sophie. (2000). The French connection: Some contributions of French-language research in the post-Piagetian era. *Child Development, 71,* 823–839.

Larner, Mary B., Stevenson, Carol S., & Behrman, Richard E. (1998). Protecting children from abuse and neglect: Analysis and recommendations. *The Future of Children: Protecting Children from Abuse and Neglect, 8*(1), 4–22.

Larsen, William J. (1998). *Essentials of human embryology.* New York: Churchill Livingstone.

Larson, David E. (Ed.). (1990). *Mayo Clinic family health book.* New York: Morrow.

Larson, Reed W. (2001). Commentary. In Daniel R. Anderson, Aletha C. Huston, Kelly L. Schmitt, Deborah L. Linebarger, & John C. Wright (Eds.). Early childhood television viewing and adolescent behavior. *Monographs of the Society for Research in Child Development, 66* (Serial No. 264), 148–154.

Larson, Reed W., & Almeida, David M. (1999). Emotional transmission in the daily lives of families: A new paradigm for studying family processes. *Journal of Marriage and the Family, 61,* 5–20.

Larson, Reed W., & Gillman, Sally. (1999). Transmission of emotions in the daily interactions of single-mother families. *Journal of Marriage and the Family, 61,* 21–37.

Larson, Reed W., & Richards, Maryse Heather. (1994). *Divergent realities: The emotional lives of mothers, fathers, and adolescents.* New York: Basic Books.

Lattanzi-Licht, Marcia, & Connor, Stephen. (1995). Care of the dying: The hospice approach. In Hannelore Wass & Robert A. Neimeyer (Eds.), *Dying: Facing the facts.* Washington, DC: Taylor & Francis.

Lattanzi-Licht, Marcia, & Doka, Kenneth J. (Eds.) (2003). *Living with grief: Coping with public tragedy.* New York: Brunner-Routledge.

Laumann, Edward O., Gagnon, John H., Michael, Robert T., & Michaels, Stuart. (1994). *The social organization of sexuality: Sexual practices in the United States.* Chicago: University of Chicago Press.

Lavender, Tony. (2000). Schizophrenia. In Lorna A. Champion & Michael J. Power (Eds.), *Adult psychological problems* (2nd ed., pp 201—230). Philadelphia: Psychology Press.

Law, James. (2000). Factors affecting language development in West African children: A pilot study using a qualitative methodology. *Child: Care, Health, and Development, 26,* 289–308.

Lawrence, Renée H., Tennstedt, Sharon L., & Assmann, Susan F. (1998). Quality of the caregiver–care recipient relationship: Does it offset negative consequences of caregiving for family caregivers? *Psychology and Aging, 13,* 150–158.

Lawton, M. P., Winter, L, Kleban, M. H., & Ruckdeschel, K. (1999). Affect and quality of life: Objective and subjective. *Journal of Aging and Health, 11,* 169–198.

Leach, Penelope. (1997). *Your baby and child: From birth to age five* (3rd ed.). New York: Knopf.

Leaper, Campbell. (2002) Parenting girls and boys. In Marc H. Bornstein (Ed.), *Handbook of parenting: Vol. 1. Children and parenting* (2nd ed., pp. 189–220). Mahwah, NJ: Erlbaum.

Leaper, Campbell, & Anderson, Kristin J. (1997). Gender development and heterosexual romantic relationships during adolescence. In Shmuel Shulman & William A. Collins (Eds.), *Romantic relationships during adolescence: Developmental perspectives. New directions for child development,* No. 78 (pp. 85–103). San Francisco: Jossey-Bass.

Leaper, Campbell, Anderson, Kristin J., & Sanders, Paul. (1998). Moderators of gender effects on parents' talk to their children: A meta-analysis. *Developmental Psychology, 34,* 3–27.

Lear, Dana. (1997). *Sex and sexuality: Risk and relationships in the age of AIDS.* Thousand Oaks, CA: Sage.

Lee, Eunju, Spitze, Glenna, & Logan, John R. (2003). Social support to parents-in-law: The interplay of gender and kin hierarchies. *Journal of Marriage and Family, 65,* 396–403.

Lee, K. (2000). Crying patterns of Korean infants in institutions. *Child: Care, Health and Development, 26,* 217–228.

Lemaitre, Rosenn N., Siscovick, David S., Raghunathan, Trimellore E., Weinmann, Sheila, Arbogast, Patrick, & Lin, Dan-Yu. (1999). Leisure-time physical activity and the risk of primary cardiac arrest. *Archives of Internal Medicine, 159,* 686–690.

Lenneberg, Eric H. (1967). *Biological foundations of language.* New York: Wiley.

Leone, Tiziana, Matthews, Zoë, & Dalla Zuanna, Gianpiero. (2003). Impact and determinants of sex preference in Nepal. *International Family Planning Perspectives, 29,* 69–75.

Lerner, Janet. (2000). *Learning disabilities: Theories, diagnosis, and teaching strategies* (8th ed.). Boston: Houghton Mifflin.

Lerner, Richard M. (1998). Theories of human development: Contemporary perspectives. In William Damon (Series Ed.) & Richard M. Lerner (Volume Ed.), *Handbook of child psychology: Vol. 1. Theoretical models of human development* (5th ed., pp. 1–24). New York: Wiley.

Leroy ,Valériane, Karon, John M., Alioum, Ahmadou, Ekpini, Ehounou R., Meda, Nicolas, Greenberg, Alan E., et al., & The West Africa PMTCT Study Group. (2002). Twenty-four month efficacy of a maternal short-course zidovudine regimen to prevent mother-to-child transmission of HIV-1 in West Africa. *AIDS, 16,* 631–641.

Levery, Gilberto, & Marder, Katen. (2003). Prevalence, incidence, and risk factors for dementia in Parkinson's disease. In Marc-Andre Bedard (Ed.), *Mental and behavioral dysfunction in movement disorders* (pp. 259–270). Totowa, NJ: Humana Press.

Levine, B., Svoboda E.M., Hay, J.F., Winocur, G., & Moscovitch, M. (2002). Aging and autobiographical memory: Dissociating episodic and semantic retrieval. *Psychology & Aging, 17,* 677–689.

Levinson, Daniel J., Darrow, Charlotte N., Klein, Edward B., Levinson, Maria H., & McKee, Braxton. (1978). *The seasons of a man's life.* New York: Knopf.

Levinson, David. (1989). Physical punishment of children and wife beating in cross-cultural perspective. *Child Abuse and Neglect, 5,* 193–195.

Levy, Becca. (1996). Improving memory in old age through implicit self-stereotyping. *Journal of Personality and Social Psychology, 71,* 1092–1106.

Levy, Becca, & Langer, E. (1994). Aging free from negative stereotypes: Successful memory in China and among the American deaf. *Journal of Personality and Social Psychology, 66,* 989–997.

Lewis, Hunter. (2000). *A question of values* (Rev.). New York: Axios Press.

Lewis, Lawrence B., Antone, Carol, & Johnson, Jacqueline S. (1999). Effects of prosodic stress and serial position on syllable omission in first words. *Developmental Psychology, 35,* 45–59.

Lewis, Michael. (1997). *Altering fate: Why the past does not predict the future.* New York: Guilford Press.

Lewis, Michael, & Brooks-Gunn, Jeanne. (1978). Self-knowledge and emotional development. In Michael Lewis & L. A. Rosenblum (Eds.), *The development of affect: Vol. 1. Genesis of behavior.* New York: Plenum Press.

Lewit, Eugene M., & Kerrebrock, Nancy. (1998). Child indicators: Dental health. *The Future of Children: Protecting Children from Abuse and Neglect, 8*(1), 133–142.

Lidoff, Lorraine. (2003). Public policy and age-related sensory loss. *Generations, 27*(1), 78–82.

Liebkind, Karmela, & Jasinskaja-Lahti, Inga. (2000). Acculturation and psychological well-being among immigrant adolescents in Finland: A comparative study of adolescents from different cultural backgrounds. *Journal of Adolescent Research, 15,* 446–469.

Lieu, Tracy A., Ray, G. Thomas, Black, Steven B., Butler, Jay C., Klein, Jerome O., Breiman, Robert F., Miller, Mark A., & Shinefield, Henry R. (2000). Projected cost-effectiveness of pneumococcal conjugate vaccination of healthy infants and young children. *Journal of the American Medical Association, 283,* 1460–1468.

Lightfoot, Cynthia. (1997). *The culture of adolescent risk-taking.* New York: Guilford Press.

Lillard, Angeline. (1998). Ethnopsychologies: Cultural variations in theories of mind. *Psychological Bulletin, 123,* 3–32.

Lin, I-Fen, Goldman, Noreen, Weinstein, Maxine, Lin, Yu-Hsuan, Gorrindo, Tristan, & Seeman, Teresa. (2003). Gender differences in adult children's support of their parents in Taiwan. *Journal of Marriage and Family, 65,* 184–200.

Lindauer, Martin S. (1998). Artists, art, and arts activities: What do they tell us about aging? In Carolyn E. Adams-Price (Ed.), *Creativity and successful aging.* New York: Springer.

Lindauer, Martin S. (2003). *Aging, creativity and art: A positive perspective on late-life development.* New York: Plenum.

Lindenberger, Ulman. (2001). Lifespan theories of cognitive development. In N. J. Smelser & Paul B. Baltes (Eds.), *International encyclopedia of the social and behavioral sciences* (pp. 8848–8854). Oxford, England: Elsevier.

Lindenberger, Ulman, & Baltes, Paul (1997). Intellectual functioning in old and very old age: Cross-sectional results from the Berlin Aging Study. *Psychology and Aging, 12,* 410–432.

Linver, Miriam R., Brooks-Gunn, Jeanne, & Kohen, Dafna E. (2002). Family processes as pathways from income to young children's development. *Developmental Psychology, 38,* 719–734.

Lisak, David. (1997). Male gender socialization and the perpetuation of sexual abuse. In Ronald F. Levant & Gary R. Brooks (Eds.), *Men and sex: New psychological perspectives.* New York: Wiley.

Little, Peter (Ed.). (2002). *Genetic destinies.* Oxford, England: Oxford University Press.

Liu, Li, Parekh-Olmedo, Hetal, & Kmiec, Eric B. (2003). The development and regulation of gene repair. *Nature Reviews Genetics, 4,* 679–689.

Lockhart, Kristi L., Chang, Bernard, & Story, Tyler. (2002). Young children's beliefs about the stability of traits: Protective optimism. *Child Development, 73,* 1408–1430.

Loeber, Rolf, & Farrington, David P. (2000). Young children who commit crimes: Epidemiology, developmental origins, risk factors, early interventions, and policy implications. *Development and Psychopathology, 12,* 737–762.

Loeber, Rolf, Drinkwater, Matthew, Yin, Yanming, Anderson, Stewart J., Schmidt, Laura C., & Crawford, Anne. (2000). Stability of family interaction from ages 6 to 18. *Journal of Abnormal Child Psychology, 28,* 353–369.

Longino, Charles F., Jr. (2001). Geographical distribution and migration. In Robert H. Binstock & Linda K. George (Eds.), *Handbook of aging and the social sciences* (5th ed., pp. 103–124). San Diego, CA: Academic Press.

Lord, Janice Harris, Hook, Melissa, & English, Sharon. (2003). Different faiths, different perceptions of public tragedy. In Marcia Lattanzi-Licht & Kenneth J. Doka (Eds.) (2003). *Living with grief: Coping with public tragedy* (pp. 91–107). New York: Brunner-Routledge.

Lorenz, John M., Wooliever, Diane E., Jetton, James R., & Paneth, Nigel. (1998). A quantitative review of mortality and developmental disability in extremely premature newborns. *Archives of Pediatric & Adolescent Medicine, 152,* 425–435.

Lund, Dale. (1988). *Longitudinal study on caregivers.* Salt Lake City: University of Utah, Gerontology Center.

Luthar, Suniya S., Cicchetti, Dante, & Becker, Bronwyn. (2000). The construct of resilience: A critical evaluation and guidelines for future work. *Child Development, 71,* 543–562.

Lutz, Donna J., & Sternberg, Robert J. (1999). Cognitive development. In Marc H. Bornstein & Michael E. Lamb (Eds.), *Developmental psychology: An advanced textbook* (4th ed., pp. 275–311). Mahwah, NJ: Erlbaum.

Lye, Stephen J., & Challis, John R. G. (2001). Parturition. In Richard Harding & Alan D. Bocking (Eds.), *Fetal growth and development.* New York: Cambridge University Press.

Lynam, Donald R., Milich, Richard, Zimmerman, Rick, Novak, Scott P., Logan, Tamra Kinkner, Martin, Catherine, et al. (1999). Project DARE: No effects at 10-year follow-up. *Journal of Consulting and Clinical Psychology, 67,* 590–593.

Lyons, Peter & Rittner, Barbara. (1998). The construction of the crack babies phenomenon as a social problem. *American Journal of Orthopsychiatry, 68,* 313–320.

Lyons-Ruth, Karlen, Bronfman, Elisa, & Parsons, Elizabeth. (1999). Chapter IV. Maternal frightened, frightening, or atypical behavior and disorganized infant attachment patterns. *Monographs of the Society for Research in Child Development, 64*(3), 67–96.

Maccoby, Eleanor E. (1998). *The two sexes: Growing up apart, coming together.* Cambridge, MA: Belknap Press of Harvard University Press.

Maccoby, Eleanor E. (2000). Parenting and its effects on children: On reading and misreading behavior genetics. *Annual Review of Psychology, 51,* 1–27.

Maccoby, Eleanor E. (2002). Parenting effects: Issues and controversies. In John G. Borkowski, Sharon Landesman Ramey, & Marie Bristol-Power (Eds.), *Parenting and the child's world: Influences on academic, intellectual, and social-emotional development* (pp. 35–46). Mahwah, NJ: Erlbaum.

Macfie, Jenny, Cicchetti, Dante, & Toth, Sheree L. (2001). The development of dissociation in maltreated preschool-aged children. *Development and Psychopathology, 13,* 233–254.

MacIntyre, U. E., de Villiers, F. P., & Owange-Iraka, J. W. (2001). Increase in childhood asthma admissions in an urbanising population. *South African Medical Journal, 91*(8), 667–672.

MacMillan, Ross & Gartner, Rosemary. (1999). When she brings home the bacon: Labor-force participation and the risk of spousal violence against women. *Journal of Marriage and the Family, 61,* 947–958.

Macpherson, Alison, Roberts, Ian, & Pless, I. Barry. (1998). Children's exposure to traffic and pedestrian injuries. *American Journal of Public Health, 88,* 1840–1843.

Macrae, C. Neil, & Bodenhausen, Galen V. (2000). Social cognition: Thinking categorically about others. *Annual Review of Psychology, 51,* 93–120.

MacWhinney, Brian, & Bornstein, Marc H. (2003). Language and literacy. In Marc H. Bornstein, Lucy Davidson, Corey L. M. Keyes, & Kristin A. Moore (Eds.), *Well-being: Positive development across the life course* (pp. 331–339). Mahwah, NJ: Erlbaum.

Madden-Derdich, Debra A. & Arditti, Joyce A. (1999). The ties that bind: Attachment between former spouses. *Family Relations, 48,* 243–249.

Madsen, Kreesten Meldgaard, Hviid, Anders, Vestergaard, Mogens, Schendel, Diana, Wohlfahrt, Jan, Thorson, Poul, Olsen, Jorn, & Melbye, Mads. (2002). A population-based study of measles, mumps, and rubella vaccination and autism. *New England Journal of Medicine, 347,* 1477–1482.

Maguen, Shira, Floyd, Frank J., Bakeman, Roger, & Armistead, Lisa. (2002). Developmental milestones and disclosure of sexual orientation among gay, lesbian, and bisexual youths. *Applied Developmental Psychology, 23,* 219–233.

Maguire, Kathleen, & Pastore, Ann L. (Eds.). (1998). *Sourcebook of criminal justice statistics, 1997.* Washington, DC: U.S. Government Printing Office.

Mahler, Margaret S., Pine, Fred, & Bergman, Anni. (1975). *The psychological birth of the human infant: Symbiosis and individuation.* New York: Basic Books.

Mahoney, Joseph L., Stattin, Hakan, & Magnusson, David. (2001). Youth recreation centre participation and criminal offending: A 20-year longitudinal study of Swedish boys. *International Journal of Behavioral Development, 25,* 509–520.

Mahowald, Mary B., Verp, Marion S., & Anderson, R. R. (1998). Genetic counseling: Clinical and ethical challenges. *Annual Review of Genetics, 32,* 547–559.

Maier, H., McGue, Matthew, Vaupel, James W., Cristensen. K. (2003). Cognitive impairment and survival at older age. In Caleb Finch, Jean-Marie Robine, & Yves Christen (Eds.), *Brain and longevity.* (pp. 131–144). Berlin: Springer-Verlag.

Maier, Susan E., Chen, Wei-Jung A., & West, James R. (1996). The effects of timing and duration of alcohol exposure on development of the fetal brain. In Ernest L. Abel (Ed.), *Fetal alcohol syndrome: From mechanism to prevention.* Boca Raton: CRC Press.

Makoni, Sinfree, & Stroeken, Koen. (2002). *Ageing in Africa: Sociolinguistic and anthropological approaches.* Burlington, VT: Ashgate.

Males, Mike A. (1999). *Framing youth: Ten myths about the next generation.* Monroe, ME: Common Courage Press.

Malina, Robert M. (1990). Physical growth and performance during the transitional years (9–16). In Raymond Montemayor, Gerald R. Adams, & Thomas P. Gullotta (Eds.), *Advances in adolescent development: An annual book series: Vol. 2. From childhood to adolescence: A transitional period?* (pp. 41–62). Newbury Park, CA: Sage.

Malina, Robert M., & Bouchard, Claude. (1991). *Growth, maturation, and physical activity.* Champaign, IL: Human Kinetics Books.

Mange, Elaine J., & Mange, Arthur P. (1999). *Basic human genetics.* Sunderland, MA: Sinauer Associates.

Manheimer, Ronald J. (1998). The promise and politics of older adult education. *Research on Aging, 20,* 391–414.

Manly, Jody Todd, Kim, Jungmeen E., Rogosch, Fred A., & Cicchetti, Dante. (2001). Dimensions of child maltreatment and children's adjustment: Contributions of developmental timing and subtype. *Development and Psychopathology, 13,* 759–782.

Mansfield, Christopher J., Wilson, James L., Kobrinski, Edward, & Mitchell, Jim. (1999). Premature mortality in the United States: The roles of geographic area, socioeconomic status, household type, and availability of medical care. *American Journal of Public Health, 89,* 893–898.

Manson, J.E., Hu, F. B., Rich-Edwards, J. W., Colditz, G. A., Stampfer, M. J., Willett, W. C., et al. (1999). A prospective study of walking as compared with vigorous exercise in the prevention of coronary heart disease in women. *New England Journal of Medicine, 341,* 650–658.

Marcia, James E. (1966). Development and validation of ego identity status. *Journal of Personality and Social Psychology, 3,* 551–558.

Marcia, James E. (2002). Identity and psychosocial development in adulthood. *Identity: An International Journal of Theory and Research, 2,* 7–28.

Marcia, James E., Waterman, Alan S., Matteson, David R., Archer, Sally L., & Orlofsky, Jacob L. (Eds.). (1993). *Ego identity: A handbook for psychosocial research.* New York: Springer-Verlag.

Marcus, Gary F. (2000). *Pabiku* and *Ga Ti Ga:* Two mechanisms infants use to learn about the world. *Current Directions in Psychological Science, 9,* 145–147.

Margolis, Mitchell M., Christie, Jason D., Silvestri, Gerald A., Kaiser, Larry, Santiago, Silverio, & Hanson-Flaschen, John. (2003). Racial differences pertaining to a belief about lung cancer surgery: Results of a multi-center survey. *Annals of Internal Medicine, 139,* 558–563.

Mariani, Erminia, et al. (1998). Natural immunity and bone and muscle remodeling hormones in the elderly. *Mechanisms of Aging and Development, 102,* 270–302.

Markus, Hazel R., Cross, Susan, & Wurf, Elissa. (1990). The role of the self-system in competence. In Robert J. Sternberg & John Kolligian, Jr. (Eds.), *Competence considered* (pp. 205–225). New Haven, CT: Yale University Press.

Markus, Hazel R., & Nurius, Paula. (1986). Possible selves. *American Psychologist, 41,* 954–969.

Marsh, Herbert E., Hau, Kit-Tai, & Kong, Chit-Kwong. (2000). Late immersion and language of instruction in Hong Kong high schools: Achievement growth in language and nonlanguage subjects. *Harvard Educational Review, 70,* 302–346.

Marsh, Herbert W. (1989). Age and sex effects in multiple dimensions of self-concept: Preadolescence to early adulthood. *Journal of Educational Psychology, 81,* 417–430.

Marsiglio, William, Amato, Paul, Day, Randal D., & Lamb, Michael E. (2000). Scholarship on fatherhood in the 1990s and beyond. *Journal of Marriage and the Family, 62,* 1173–1191.

Marsiske, Michael, & Willis, Sherry L. (1995). Dimensions of everyday problem-solving in older adults. *Psychology and Aging, 10,* 269–283

Marsiske, Michael, & Willis, Sherry L. (1998). Practical creativity in older adults' everyday problem solving: Lifespan perspectives. In Carolyn E. Adams-Price (Ed.), *Creativity and aging: Theoretical and empirical approaches* (pp. 73–113). New York: Springer.

Martin, Carol Lynn. (2000). Cognitive theories of gender development. In Thomas Eckes & Hanns M. Trautner (Eds.), *The developmental social psychology of gender* (pp. 91–121). Mahwah, NJ: Erlbaum.

Martin, Carol Lynn, Eisenbud, Lisa, & Rose, Hilary. (1995). Children's gender-based reasoning about toys. *Child Development, 66,* 1453–1471.

Martin, Carol Lynn, & Fabes, Richard. (2001). The stability and consequences of young children's same-sex peer interactions. *Developmental Psychology, 37,* 431–446.

Martin, George M., LaMarco, Kelly, Strauss, Evelyn, & Kelner, Katrina L. (2003). Research on aging: The end of the beginning. *Science, 299,* 1339–1341.

Martin, Joyce A., Hamilton, Brady E., Ventura, Stephanie J., Menacker, Fay, & Park, Melissa M. (2002). Births: Final data for 2000. *National Vital Statistics Report, 50*(5), 1–104.

Martin, Joyce A., Hamilton, Brady E., Ventura, Stephanie J., Menacker, Fay, Park, Melissa M., & Sutton Paul D. (2002). Births: Final data for 2001. *National Vital Statistics Reports, 51*(2).

Martin, Todd F., White, James M., & Perlman, Daniel. (2003). Religious socialization: A test of the channeling hypothesis of parental influence on adolescent faith maturity. *Journal of Adolescent Research, 18,* 169–187.

Marvin, Robert S. (1997). Ethological and general systems perspectives on child–parent attachment during the toddler and preschool years. In Nancy L. Segal, Glenn E. Weisfeld, & Carol C. Weisfeld (Eds.), *Uniting psychology and biology: Integrative perspectives on human development* (pp. 189–216). Washington, DC: American Psychological Association.

Masaro, Edward J. (1999). *Challenges of biological aging.* New York: Springer.

Masataka, Nobuo. (1992). Early ontogeny of vocal behavior of Japanese infants in response to maternal speech. *Child Development, 63,* 1177–1185.

Mascie-Taylor, C. Nicholas, G. & Karim, Enamul. (2003). The burden of chronic disease. *Science, 302,* 1921–1922.

Maslow, Abraham H. (1968). *Toward a psychology of being* (2nd ed.). Princeton, NJ: Van Nostrand

Maslow, Abraham H. (1970). *Motivation and personality* (2nd ed.). New York: Harper & Row.

Masoro, Edward J. (1999). *Challenges of biological aging.* New York: Springer.

Masoro, Edward J. (2001). Dietary restriction: An experimental approach to the study of the biology of aging. In Edward J. Masoro & Steven N. Austad (Eds.), *Handbook of the biology of aging* (pp. 396–420). San Diego, CA: Academic Press.

Masten, Ann S. (2001). Ordinary magic: Resilience processes in development. *American Psychologist, 56,* 227–238.

Masten, Ann S., & Coatsworth, J. Douglas. (1998). The development of competence in favorable and unfavorable environments: Lessons from research on successful children. *American Psychologist, 53,* 205–220.

Masterpasqua, Frank, & Perna, Phyllis A. (1997). *The psychological meaning of chaos: Translating theory into practice.* Washington, DC: American Psychological Association.

Masters, William H., & Johnson, Virginia E. (1966). *Human sexual response.* Baltimore: Lippincott Williams & Wilkins.

Masters, William H., Johnson, Virginia E., & Kolodny, Robert C. (1994). *Heterosexuality.* New York: HarperCollins.

Masunaga, Hiromi, & Horn, John. (2001). Expertise and age-related changes in components of intelligence. *Psychology and Aging, 16,* 293–311.

Masuro, Edward J. (1999). *Challenges of biological aging.* New York: Springer.

Matsuda, Fumiko. (2001). Development of concepts of interrelationships among duration, distance, and speed. *International Journal of Behavioral Development, 25,* 466–480.

Mattson, M. P. (1999). Cellular and neurochemical aspects of the aging brain. In William R. Hazzard (Ed.), *Principles of geriatric medicine and gerontology* (4th ed., pp. 1193–1217). New York: McGraw-H:11.

Matzo, Marianne & Sherman, Deborah W. (2001). *Palliative care nursing: Quality care toward the end of life.* New York: Springer.

Maughan, Angeline, & Cicchetti, Dante. (2002). Impact of child maltreatment and interadult violence on children's emotion regulation abilities and socioemotional adjustment. *Child Development, 73,* 1525–1542.

Maxwell, Jan Carlisle. (2000). Changes in drug use in Australia and the United

States: Results from the 1995 and 1998 national household surveys. *Drug and Alcohol Review, 20,* 37–48.

Mayberry, Rachel I., & Nicoladis, Elena. (2000). Gesture reflects language development: Evidence from bilingual children. *Current Directions in Psychological Science, 9,* 192–196.

Maydol, Lynn, Moffitt, Terrie E., Caspi, Avshalom, & Silva, Phil A. (1998). Hitting without a license: Testing explanations for differences in partner abuse between young adult daters and cohabitors. *Journal of Marriage and the Family, 60,* 4–55.

Mayer, Karl Ulrich. (2003). The sociology of the life course and lifespan psychology: Diverging or converging pathways? In Ursula M. Staudinger & Ulman Lindenberger (Eds.), *Understanding human development: Dialogues with lifespan psychology* (pp. 463–481). Dordrecht, Netherlands: Kluwer.

Maynard, Ashley E. (2002). Cultural teaching: The development of teaching skills in Maya sibling interactions. *Child Development, 73,* 969–982.

McAdams, Dan P. (2001). Generativity in midlife. In Margie E. Lachman (Ed.), *Handbook of midlife development* (pp. 395–443). New York: Wiley.

McAdams, Dan P., & de St. Aubin, Ed. (1998). *Generativity and adult development: How and why we care for the next generation.* Washington, DC: American Psychological Association.

McAdams, Dan P., Hart, Holly M., & Maruna, Shadd. (1998). The anatomy of generativity. In Dan P. McAdams & Ed de St. Aubin (Eds.), *Generativity and adult development: How and why we care for the next generation.* Washington, DC: American Psychological Association.

McBride-Chang, Catherine, & Treiman, Rebecca. (2003). Hong Kong Chinese kindergarteners learn to read English analytically. *Psychological Science, 14,* 138–143.

McCabe, D. L., & Trevino, L. K. (1996) What we know about cheating in college. *Change, 28,* 28—33.

McCabe, Kristen M., Hough, Richard, Wood, Patricia A., & Yeh, Mary. (2001). Childhood and adolescent onset conduct disorder: A test of the developmental taxonomy. *Journal of Abnormal Child Psychology, 29,* 305–316.

McCarthy, William J., Caskey, Nicholas H., Jarvik, Murray E., Gross, Todd M., Rosenblatt, Martin R., & Carpenter, Catherine. (1995). Menthol vs. nonmenthol cigarettes: Effects on smoking behavior. *American Journal of Public Health, 85,* 67–72.

McCarty, Michael E., & Ashmead, Daniel H. (1999). Visual control of reaching and grasping in infants. *Developmental Psychology, 35,* 620–631.

McCloskey, Laura Ann, & Stuewig, Jeffrey. (2001). The quality of peer relationships among children exposed to family violence. *Development and Psychopathology, 13,* 83–96.

McCrae, Robert R., & Allik, Juri (Eds.). (2002). *The five-factor model of personality across cultures.* New York: Kluwer.

McCrae, Robert R., & Costa, Paul T., Jr. (1994). The stability of personality: Observations and evaluations. *Current Directions in Psychological Science, 3,* 173–175.

McCrae, Robert R., & Costa, Paul T., Jr. (2003). *Personality in adulthood: A five-factor theory perspective* (2nd ed.). New York: Guilford Press.

McCrae, Robert R., Costa, Paul T., Jr., de Lima, Margarida Pedroso, Simões, António, Ostendorf, Fritz, Angleitner, Alois, et al. (1999). Age differences in personality across the adult life span: Parallels in five cultures. *Developmental Psychology, 35,* 466–477.

McCrae, Robert R., Costa, Paul T. Jr., Ostendorf, F., Angleitner, A., Hrebrikova, M., Avia M. D., et al. (2000). Nature over nurture: Temperament, personality, and life span development. *Journal of Personality and Social Psychology, 78,* 173–186.

McDevitt, Thomas M. (1998). *World population profiles: 1998.* Washington, DC: U. S. Commerce Department.

McEwen, Bruce S. (2000). Effects of adverse experiences for brain structure and function. *Biological Psychiatry, 48,* 721–731.

McGinnis, Sandra L. (2003). Cohabiting, dating, and perceived costs of marriage: A model of marriage entry. *Journal of Marriage and Family, 65,* 105—116.

McGrath, Pam. (2002). Are we making progress? Not in haematology! *Omega, 45,* 331–348.

McGue, Matthew. (1995). Mediators and moderators of alcoholism inheritance. In J. Rick Turner, Lon R. Cardon, & John K. Hewitt (Eds.), *Perspectives on individual differences: Behavior genetic approaches in behavioral medicine* (pp. 17–44). New York: Plenum Press.

McGuffin, Peter, Riley, Brien, & Plomin, Robert. (2001). Toward behavioral genomics. *Science, 291,* 1232–1249.

McKelvie, Pippa, & Low, Jason. (2002). Listening to Mozart does not improve children's spatial ability: Final curtains for the Mozart effect. *British Journal of Developmental Psychology, 20,* 241–258.

McKusick, Victor A. (1994). *Mendelian inheritance in humans* (10th ed.). Baltimore: Johns Hopkins University Press.

McLanahan, Sara S., & Sandefur, Gary. (1994). *Growing up with a single parent: What hurts, what helps.* Cambridge, MA: Harvard University Press.

McLoyd, Vonnie C. (1998). Socioeconomic disadvantage and child development. *American Psychologist, 53,* 185–204.

McLoyd, Vonnie C., & Smith, Julia. (2002). Physical discipline and behavior problems in African American, European American, and Hispanic children: Emotional support as a moderator. *Journal of Marriage and Family, 64,* 40–53.

McMichael, A. J., Butler, C. D., & Folke, Carl. (2003). New visions for addressing sustainability. *Science, 302,* 1919–1920.

McNally, Richard J., Bryant, Richard A., & Ehlers, Anke. (2003). Does early psychological intervention promote recovery from posttraumatic stress? *Psychological Science in the Public Interest, 4*(2), 45–79.

McNight, A. James. (2003). The freedom of the open road: Driving and older adults. *Generations, 27*(2), 25–31.

Medved, Michael. (1995, October). Hollywood's 3 big lies. *Reader's Digest, 147,* 155–158.

Medvedev, Z. A. (1990). An attempt at a rational classification of theories of aging. *Biological Reviews, 60,* 375–398.

Meeks, Suzanne, Murrell, Stanley A., Mehl, Rochelle C. (2000). Longitudinal relationships between depressive symptoms and health in normal older and middle-aged adults. *Psychology and Aging, 15,* 100–109.

Meisami, Esmail. (1994). Aging of the sensory systems. In Paola S. Timiras (Ed.), *Psysiological basis of aging and geriatrics* (2nd ed.). Boca Raton, FL: CRC Press.

Meisami, Esmail, Brown, Chester M., & Emerle, Henry F. (2003). Sensory systems: Normal aging, disorders, and treatment of vision and hearing in humans. In Paola S. Timiras (Ed.), *Physiological basis of aging and geriatrics* (3rd ed., pp. 141–165). Boca Raton, FL: CRC Press.

Melia, Susan Perschbacher. (2000). Generativity in the lives of elder Catholic women religious. In Timothy J. Owens (Ed.), *Self and identity through the life course in cross-cultural perspective.* Stamford, CT: Jai Press.

Menon, Usha. (2001). Middle adulthood in cultural perspectives: The imagined and the experienced in three cultures. In Margie E. Lachman (Ed.), *Handbook of midlife development* (pp. 40–74). New York: Wiley.

Mercy, James A., Sleet, David A., & Doll, L. (2003). Applying a developmental approach to injury prevention. *American Journal of Health Education, 34*(5), 87–88.

Merrell, Kenneth W., & Gimpel, Gretchen A. (1998). *Social skills of children and adolescents: Conceptualization, assessment, treatment.* Mahwah, NJ: Erlbaum.

Merrill, Susan S., & Verbrugge, Lois M. (1999). Health and disease in midlife. In Sherry L. Willis & James D. Reid (Eds.), *Life in the middle.* San Diego, CA: Academic Press.

Merriman, William E. (1998). Competition, attention, and young children's lexical processing. In Brian MacWhinney (Ed.), *The emergence of language* (pp. 331–358). Mahwah, NJ: Erlbaum.

Merzenich, Michael M. (2001). Cortical plasticity contributing to child development. In James L. McClelland & Robert S. Siegler (Eds.), *Mechanisms of cognitive development: Behavioral and neural perspectives* (pp. 67–95). Mahwah, NJ: Erlbaum.

Meyer, Bonnie J. F., Russo, Connie, & Talbot, Andrew. (1995). Discourse comprehension and problem solving: Decisions about the treatment of breast cancer by women across the life span. *Psychology and Aging, 10,* 84–103.

Meyer, Daniel R. (1999). Compliance with child support orders in paternity and divorce cases. In Ross A. Thompson & Paul R. Amato (Eds.), *The postdivorce family: Children, parenting, and society* (pp. 127–157). Thousand Oaks, CA: Sage.

Mezey, Mathy, Miller, Lois L., & Linton-Nelson, Lori. (1999). Caring for caregivers of frail elders at the end of life. *Generations, 23,* 44–51.

Michaud, Catherine M., Murray, Christopher, J. L., & Bloom, Barry R. (2001). Burden of disease—implications for future research. *Journal of the American Medical Association, 285,* 535–539.

Michaud, Catherine. (1999). The global burden of disease and injuries in 1990. *International Social Science Journal, 161,* 287–296.

Midobuche, Eva. (2001). More than empty footprints in the sand: Educating immigrant children. *Harvard Educational Review, 71,* 529–535.

Milkie, Melissa A., & Peltola, Pia. (1999). Playing all the roles: Gender and the work—family balancing act. *Journal of Marriage and the Family, 61,* 476—490.

Miller, Brent C., Fan, Xitao, Christensen, Mathew, Grotevant, Harold D., & van Dulmen, Manfred. (2000). Comparisons of adopted and non-adopted adolescents in a large, nationally representative sample. *Child Development, 71,* 1458–1473.

Miller, M., Bowen, J. R., Gibson, F. L., Hand, P. J., & Ungerer, Judy A. (2001). Behaviour problems in extremely low birthweight children at 5 and 8 years of age. *Child: Care, Health, and Development, 27,* 569–581.

Miller, Orlando J., & Therman, Eeva. (2001). *Human chromosomes* (4th ed.). New York: Springer.

Miller, Patricia H. (2001). *Theories of developmental psychology* (4th ed.). New York: Worth.

Miller, Patricia Y., & Simon, William. (1980). The development of sexuality in adolescence. In J. Adelson (Ed.), *Handbook of adolescent psychology* (pp. 383–407). New York: Wiley.

Miller, Richard A. (2001). Genetics of increased longevity and retarded aging in mice. In Edward J. Masoro & Steven N. Austad (Eds.), *Handbook of the biology of aging* (pp. 369–395). San Diego, CA: Academic Press.

Mills, James L., McPartlin, Joseph M., Kirke, Peadar N., & Lee, Young J. (1995). Homocysteine metabolism in pregnancies complicated by neural-tube defects. *Lancet, 345,* 149–151.

Min, Pyong Gap. (2000). Korean Americans' language use. In Sandra Lee McKay & Sau-ling Cynthia Wong (Eds.), *New immigrants in the United States* (pp. 306–332). Cambridge, England: Cambridge University Press.

Mindel, Charles H., Habenstein, Robert W., & Wright, Roosevelt, Jr. (Eds.). (1998). *Ethnic families in America: Patterns and variations* (4th ed.). Upper Saddle River, NJ: Prentice-Hall.

Mintz, Laurie B., & Kashubeck, Susan. (1999). Body image and disordered eating among Asian American and Caucasian college students. *Psychology of Women Quarterly, 23,* 781–796.

Mitchell, Jean & McCarthy, Helen. (2000). Eating disorders. In Lorna Champion & Mick Power (Eds.), *Adult psychological problems* (2 nd ed., pp. 103–130). Philadelphia: Psychology Press.

Mitchell, Katherine. (2001). Education for democratic citizenship: Transnationalism, multiculturalism, and the limits of liberalism. *Harvard Educational Review, 71,* 51–78.

Mitchell, Peter, & Kikuno, Haruo. (2000). Belief as construction: Inference and processing bias. In Peter Mitchell & Kevin John Riggs (Eds.), *Children's reasoning and the mind* (pp. 281–299). Hove, England: Psychology Press.

Mitka, Mike. (2003). Surgery for obesity: Demand soars amid scientific and ethical questions. *Journal of the American Medical Association, 289,* 1761–1762.

Mix, Kelly S., Huttenlocher, Janellen, & Levine, Susan Cohen. (2002). *Quantitative development in infancy and early childhood.* New York: Oxford University Press.

MMWR. (1995, March 24). Youth risk behavior surveillance—United States, 1993. *Morbidity and Mortality Weekly Report, 44*(No. SS–1), 1–56.

MMWR. (1996, September 27). Youth risk behavior surveillance—United States, 1995. *Morbidity and Mortality Weekly Report, 45,* 20.

MMWR. (1998, August 14). Youth risk behavior surveillance—United States, 1997. *Morbidity and Mortality Weekly Report, 47.*

MMWR. (2000, June 9). Youth risk behavior surveillance—United States 1999. *Morbidity and Mortality Weekly Report, 49,* 1–96.

MMWR. (2000, August 18). Surveillance for characteristics of health education among secondary schools—School health education profiles, 1998. *Morbidity and Mortality Weekly Report, 49,* 1–41.

MMWR. (2002, February 8). Progress toward elimination of perinatal HIV infection—Michigan, 1993–2000. *Morbidity and Mortality Weekly Report, 51,* 93–97.

MMWR. (2002, April 26). Prevalence of selected maternal behavior and experiences, Pregnancy risk assessment monitoring system (PRAMS), 1999. *Morbidity and Mortality Weekly Report, 51,* SS-2, 1–27.

MMWR. (2002, May 17) Trends in cigarette smoking among high school students—United States, 1991–2001. *Morbidity and Mortality Weekly Report, 51*(19), 409–412.

MMWR. (2002, June 28). Youth risk behavior, surveillance—United States, 2001. *Morbidity and Mortality Weekly Report, 51*(No. SS-4).

MMWR. (2002, July 12) Hysterectomy Surveillance—United States, 1994–1999, *Mortality and Mortality Weekly Report, 51,* No. 55-5.

MMWR. (2002, August 16).. Prevention of perinatal group B streptococcal disease. *Morbidity and Mortality Weekly Report, 51,* No. RR-11, 1–18.

MMWR. (2002, September 13). Folic acid and prevention of spina bifida and anencephaly. *Morbidity and Mortality Weekly Report, 51,* No. RR-13.

MMWR. (2002, October 25). Nonfatal choking-related episodes among children—United States, 2001. *Morbidity and Mortality Weekly Report, 51,* 945–948.

MMWR. (2002, December 6). State specific trends in U. S. live births to women born outside the 50 states and the District of Columbia—United States, 1990 and 2000. *Morbidity and Mortality Weekly Report, 51* (48), 1091–1095.

MMWR. (2003, March 21). Public health dispatch: Absence of transmission of the d9 measles virus—Region of the Americas, November 2002–March 2003. *Mortality and Morbidity Weekly Report, 52*(11), 228–229.

MMWR. (2003, August 22). State-specific prevalence of selected chronic disease-related characteristics—Behavioral risk factor surveillance system, 2001, *52,* No. SS-8.

MMWR. (2003, October 10). Cigarette smoking among adults—United States, 2001, *52.*

MMWR. (2003, November 21). Health-related quality of life among low-income persons aged 45–64 years—United States, 1995–2001. *Morbidity and Mortality Weekly Report, 52.* 1120–1124.

MMWR. (2004, January 16). Declining prevalence of no known major risk factors for heart disease and stroke among adults—United States 1991–2001. *Morbidity and Mortality Weekly Report, 53,* 4–7.

Moats, Louisa C. (2001). Overcoming the language gap: Invest generously in teacher professional development. *American Educator, 25*(2), 4–9.

Moen, Phyllis. (1996). Gender, age, and the life course. In Robert H. Binstock, Linda K. George, Victor W. Marshall, George C. Myers, & James H. Schulz (Eds.), *Handbook of aging and the social sciences* (4th ed., pp. 171–187). San Diego, CA: Academic Press.

Moen, Phyllis. (1998). Reconstructing retirement: Careers, couples, and social capital. *Contemporary Gerontology, 4,* 123–125.

Moen, Phyllis. (2001). The gendered life course. In Robert H. Binstock & Linda K. George (Eds.), *Handbook of aging and the social sciences* (5th ed., pp. 179–196). San Diego, CA: Academic Press.

Moen, Phyllis, & Yu, Y. (1999). Having it all: Overall work/life success in two-earner families. In T. Parcel (Ed.), *Research in the sociology of work, Volume 7.* Greenwich, CT: JAI Press.

Moffitt, Terrie E. (1997). Adolescence-limited and life-course-persistent offending: A complementary pair of developmental theories. In Terence P. Thornberry (Ed.), *Developmental theories of crime and delinquency* (pp. 11–54). New Brunswick, NJ: Transaction.

Moffitt, Terrie E., Caspi, Avshalom, Belsky, Jay, & Silva, Paul A. (1992). Childhood experience and the onset of menarche. *Child Development, 63,* 47–58.

Moffitt, Terrie E., Caspi, Avsholem, Rutter, Michael, & Silva, Phil. (2001). *Sex differences in antisocial behavior: Conduct disorder, delinquency, and violence in the Dunedin longitudinal study.* New York: Cambridge University Press.

Mohan, Dinesh. (2000). Injury control and safety promotion: Ethics, science, and practice. In Dinesh Mohan & Geetam Tiwari (Eds.), *Injury prevention and control* (pp. 1–12). London: Taylor & Francis.

Molina, Brooke S. G., & Chassin, Laurie. (1996). The parent-adolescent relationship at puberty: Hispanic ethnicity and parent alcoholism as moderators. *Developmental Psychology, 32,* 675–686.

Moody, H. R. (2001–2002). Who's afraid of life extension? *Generations, 15,* 33–37.

Moon-Howard, Joyce. (2003). African American women and smoking: Starting later. *American Journal of Public Health, 93,* 418—420.

Moore, Celia L. (2002). On differences and development. In David J. Lewkowicz & Robert Lickliter (Eds.), *Conceptions of development: Lessons from the laboratory* (pp. 57–76). New York: Psychology Press.

Moore, Keith L., & Persaud, T. V. N. (1998). *The developing human: Clinically oriented embryology.* Philadelphia: W. B. Saunders.

Morgan, Elaine R. (2000). Care of children who are dying of cancer. *New England Journal of Medicine, 342,* 347–348.

Morgenstern, Hal, Bingham, Trista, & Reza, Avid. (2000). Effects of pool-fencing ordinances and other factors on childhood drowning in Los Angeles County, 1990–1995. *American Journal of Public Health, 90,* 595–601.

Morin, Charles M., Colecchi, Cheryl, Stone, Jackie, Sood, Rakesh, & Brink Douglas. (1999). Behavior and pharmacological therapies for late-life insomnia. *Journal of the American Medical Association, 281,* 991–999.

Morita, Yohji, Soeda, Haruo, Soeda, Kumiko, & Taki, Mitsuru. (1999). Japan. In Peter K. Smith, Yohji Morita, Josine Junger-Tas, Dan Olweus, Richard F. Catalano, & Phillip T. Slee (Eds.), *The*

nature of school bullying: A cross-national perspective (pp. 309–323). London: Routledge.

Morrison, Donna Ruane, & Coiro, Mary Jo. (1999). Parental conflict and marital disruption: Do children benefit when high-conflict marriages are dissolved? *Journal of Marriage and the Family, 61,* 626–637

Morrison, Frederick J., Griffith, Elizabeth M., & Alberts, Denise M. (1997). Nature–nurture in the classroom: Entrance age, school readiness, and learning in children. *Developmental Psychology, 33,* 254–262.

Morrongiello, Barbara A., Fenwick, Kimberley D., & Chance, Graham. (1998). Crossmodal learning in newborn infants: Inferences about properties of auditory-visual events. *Infant Behavior & Development, 21,* 543–553.

Morrow, Daniel G., Ridolfo, Heather E., Menard, William E., Sanborn, Adam, Stine-Morrow, Elizabeth A. L., Magnor, Cliff, et al. (2003). Environmental support promotes expertise-based mitigation of age differences on pilot communication tasks. *Psychology and Aging, 18,* 268–284.

Mortensen, Preben Bo, Pedersen, Carsten Bocker, Westergaard, Tine, Wohlfahrt, Jan, Ewald, Henrik, Mors, Ole, et al. (1999). Effects of family history and place and season of birth on the risk of schizophrenia. *New England Journal of Medicine, 340,* 603–608.

Mortimer, Jeylan T., Finch, Michael D., Ryu, Seongryeol, Shanahan, Michael J., & Call, Kathleen T. (1996). The effects of work intensity on adolescent mental health, achievement, and behavioral adjustment: New evidence from a prospective study. *Child Development, 67,* 1243–1261.

Morton, J. Bruce, & Trehub, Sandra E. (2001). Children's understanding of emotion in speech. *Child Development, 72,* 834–843.

Moscovitch, Morris. (1982). Neuro-psychology of perception and memory in the elderly. In Fergus I.M. Craik & Sandra Trehub (Eds.), *Aging and cognitive processes.* New York: Plenum Press.

Moshman, David. (1999). *Adolescent psychological development: Rationality, morality, and identity.* Mahwah, NJ: Erlbaum.

Moshman, David. (2000). Diversity in reasoning and rationality: Metacognitive and developmental considerations. *Brain and Behavioral Science, 23,* 689–690.

Moshman, David, & Geil, Molly. (1998). Collaborative reasoning: Evidence for collective rationality. *Thinking and Reasoning, 4,* 231–248.

Moster, Dag, Lie, Rolv T., Irgens, Lorentz M., Bjerkedal, Tor, & Markestad, Trond. (2001). The association of Apgar score with subsequent death and cerebral palsy: A population-based study in term infants. *Journal of Pediatrics, 138,* 798–803.

Moulton, Charles P. (2000). Cultural and religious issues for African Americans. In Kathryn Braun, James H. Pietsch, & Patricia L. Blanchette (Eds.), *Cultural issues in end-of-life decision making* (pp. 71–82). Thousand Oaks, CA: Sage.

Mpofu, Elias, & van de Vijver, Fons J. R. (2000). Taxonomic structure in early to middle childhood: A longitudinal study with Zimbabwean schoolchildren. *International Journal of Behavioral Development, 24,* 204–212.

Mroczek, D. K. & Kolarz, C. M. (1998). The effect of age on positive and negative affect: A developmental perspective on happiness. *Journal of Personality and Social Psychology, 75,* 1333–1349.

Mrug, Sylvie, Hoza, Betsy, & Gerdes, Alyson C. (2001). Children with attention deficit/hyperactivity disorder: Peer relationships and peer-oriented interventions. In William Damon (Series Ed.) & Douglas W. Nangle & Cynthia A. Erdley (Volume Eds.), *New directions for child and adolescent development: Vol. 91. The role of friendship in psychological adjustment* (pp. 51–77). San Francisco: Jossey-Bass.

Msall, Michael E., Avery, Roger C., Tremont, Michelle R., Lima, Julie C., Rogers, Michelle L., & Hogan, Dennis P. (2003). Functional disability and school activity limitations in 41,300 school-age children: Relationship to medical impairments. *Pediatrics, 111,* 548–553.

Mueller, Margaret M., & Elder, Glen H., Jr. (2003). Family contingencies across the generations: Grandparent–grandchild relationships in holistic perspective. *Journal of Marriage and Family, 65,* 404–417.

Mullan, Joseph T., Skaff, Marilyn M., & Pearlin, Leonard I. (2003). The bereavement process: Loss, grief, and resolution. In Inge Corless, Barbara B. Germino, & Mary A. Pittman (Eds.) *Dying death and bereavement* (pp. 247–265). New York: Springer.

Mumme, Donna L., & Fernald, Anne. (2003). The infant as onlooker: Learning from emotional reactions observed in a television scenario. *Child Development, 74,* 221–237.

Murphy, J. Michael, Wehler, Cheryl A., Pagona, Maria E., Little, Michelle, Kleinman, Ronald E., & Jellinek, Michael S. (2001). Relation between hunger and psychosocial functioning. In Margaret E. Hertzig & Ellen A. Farber (Eds.), *Annual progress in child psychiatry and child development, 1999* (pp. 215–228). New York: Brunner/Routledge.

Murphy, Shane. (1999). *The cheers and the tears: A healthy alternative to the dark side of youth sports today.* San Francisco: Jossey-Bass.

Musick, Kelly. (2002). Planned and unplanned childbearing among unmarried women. *Journal of Marriage and Family, 64,* 915–929.

Musick, Marc A., Herzog, Regula, & House, James C. (1999) Volunteering and mortality among older adults: Finding from a national sample. *Journal of Gerontology, 54B,* S173–S180.

Mustillo, Sarah, Worthman, Carol, Erkanli, Alaattin, Keeler, Gordon, Angold, Adrian, & Costello, E. Jane. (2003). Obesity and psychiatric disorder: Developmental trajectories. *Pediatrics, 111*(4), 851–859.

Muuss, Rolf E. (1996). *Theories of adolescence* (6th ed.). New York: McGraw-Hill.

Myers, David G. (1993). *The pursuit of happiness.* New York: Avon Books.

Myers, David G. (2000). The funds, friends, and faith of happy people. *American Psychologist, 55,* 56–67.

Myers, David G. (2002). *Intuition: Its powers and perils.* New Haven, CT: Yale University Press.

Nahemow, Lucille. (2000). The ecological theory of aging: Powell Lawton's legacy. In Robert L. Rubinstein, Miriam Moss, & Morton H. Kleban (Eds.), *The many dimensions of aging,* pp. 22–40. New York: Springer.

Naito, Mika, & Miura, Hisayoshi. (2001). Japanese children's numerical competencies: Age- and school-related influences on the development of number concepts and addition skills. *Developmental Psychology, 37,* 217–230.

Nakamura, Suad, Wind, Marilyn, & Danello, Mary Ann. (1999). Review of hazards associated with children placed in adult beds. *Archives of Pediatrics and Adolescent Medicine, 153,* 1019–1023.

Nakasone, Ronald Y. (2000). Buddhist issues in end-of-life decision making. In Kathryn Braun, James H. Pietsch, & Patricia L. Blanchette (Eds.), *Cultural issues in end-of-life decision making* (pp. 213–228). Thousand Oaks, CA: Sage.

Nantais, Kristin, & Schellenberg, E. Glenn. (1999). The Mozart effect: An artifact of preference. *Psychological Science, 10,* 370–373.

Nasser, Mervat. (1997). *Culture and weight consciousness.* London and New York: Routledge.

Nation, Kate, & Snowling, Margaret J. (1998). Individual differences in contextual facilitation: Evidence from dyslexia and poor reading comprehension. *Child Development, 69,* 996–1011.

National Academy of Sciences. (Eds: Andrews, Lori B., Fullarton, Jane E., Holtzman, Neil A., & Motulsky, Arno G.) (1994). *Assessing genetic risks: Implications for health and social policy.* Washington, DC: National Academy Press.

National Center for Education Statistics, U.S. Department of Education. (2001). *Digest of education statistics: 2000.* Washington, DC: U.S. Department of Education.

National Center for Education Statistics, U.S. Department of Education, (2002). *Digest of education statistics, 2001* (NCES 2002–130). Washington, DC: U.S. Government Printing Office.

National Center for Education Statistics, U.S. Department of Education. (2003). *Digest of education statistics, 2002* (NCES 2003–060). Washington, DC: U.S. Government Printing Office.

National Center for Health Statistics. (1995). *Health, United States, 1994.* Hyattsville, MD: Public Health Service.

National Center for Health Statistics. (2000). *Health, United States, 2000.*

Hyattsville, MD: Centers for Disease Control and Prevention.

National Center for Health Statistics (2001). Births to teenagers in the United States, 1940–2000. *National Vital Statistics Reports, 49*(10), entire issue.

National Center for Health Statistics. (2002). Deaths: Leading causes for 2000. *National Vital Statistics Reports, 50*(16), (PHS) 2002–1120.

National Center for Health Statistics. (2002). *Vital statistics of the United States, 2002.* Washington DC: U.S. Government Printing Office.

National Center for Health Statistics. (2003). Births, marriages, divorces, and deaths: Provisional data for Oct.—Dec. 2002. *National Vital Statistics Reports, 51*(10), June 17

National Heart, Lung, and Blood Institute. *Clinical guidelines on the identification, evaluation, and treatment of overweight and obesity in adults: The evidence report.* National Institutes of Health: www.nhlbi.nih.gov.

National Highway Traffic Safety Administration. (2001). *Traffic safety facts 2001.*

National Research Council and Institute of Medicine. (Eds.: Jack P. Shonkoff, & Deborah A. Phillips) (2000). *From neurons to neighborhoods: The science of early childhood development.* Washington, DC: National Academy Press.

National Task Force on Fetal Alcohol Syndrome and Fetal Alcohol Effect. (2002). Defining the national agenda for fetal alcohol syndrome and other prenatal alcohol-related effects. *Morbidity and Mortality Weekly Report, 51,* RR-14, 9–12.

Navazio, Frank, & Timiras, Paola. (2003). Healthful aging: Nutrition and exercise and experimental strategies in dietary restriction. In Paola S. Timiras (Ed.) *Physiological basis of aging and geriatrics* (3rd ed., pp. 415–442). Boca Raton, FL: CRC Press.

Nazareth, Irwin, Boynton, Petra, & King, Michael. (2003). Problems with sexual function in people attending London general practitioners: A cross-sectional study. *British Medical Journal, 327,* 423–420.

Neisser, Ulric (Ed.). (1998). *The rising curve: Long-term gains in IQ and related* *measures*. Washington, DC: American Psychological Association.

Nelson, Adie. (2000). The pink dragon is female: Halloween costumes and gender markers. *Psychology of Women Quarterly, 24,* 137–144.

Nelson, Katherine. (1996). *Language in cognitive development: The emergence of the mediated mind.* New York: Cambridge University Press.

Nemy, Enid, with Alexander, Ron. (1998, November 2). Metropolitan diary. *New York Times,* p. B2.

Neugarten, Bernice L., & Neugarten, Dail A. (1986). Changing meanings of age in the aging society. In Alan Pifer & Lynda Bronte (Eds.), *Our aging society: Paradox and promise.* New York: Norton.

Newsom, Jason T., & Schultz, Richard. (1996). Social support as a mediator in the relation between functional status and quality of life in older adults. *Psychology and Aging, 11,* 34–44.

NICHD Early Child Care Research Network. (1996). Characteristics of infant child care: Factors contributing to positive caregiving. *Early Childhood Research Quarterly, 11,* 269–306.

NICHD Early Child Care Research Network. (1998). Early child care and self-control, compliance, and problem behavior at twenty-four and thirty-six months. *Child Development, 69,* 1145–1170.

NICHD Early Child Care Research Network. (1999). Child care and mother-child interaction in the first 3 years of life. *Developmental Psychology, 35,* 1399–1413.

NICHD Early Child Care Research Network. (2000). The relation of child care to cognitive and language development. *Child Development, 71,* 960–980.

NICHD Early Child Care Research Network. (2001). Child care and children's peer interaction at 24 and 36 months: The NICHD study of early child care. *Child Development, 72,* 1478–1500.

NICHD Early Child Care Research Network. (2002). Parenting and family influences when children are in child care: Results from the NICHD study of early child care. In John G. Borkowski, Sharon Landesman Ramey, & Marie Bristol-Power (Eds.), *Parenting and the child's world: Influences on academic,*

intellectual, and social-emotional development (pp. 99–123). Mahwah, NJ: Erlbaum.

Nichol, Kristin L. (2001). Cost-benefit analysis of a strategy to vaccinate healthy working adults against influenza. *Archives of Internal Medicine, 61,* 749–759.

Nicotera, Anne Maydan. (1997). *The mate relationship: Cross-cultural applications of a rules theory.* Albany, NY: SUNY Press.

Nielson, Kristy A., Langenecker, Scott A., & Garavan, Hugh. (2002). Differences in functional neuoranatomy of inhibitory control across the adult life span. *Psychology and Aging, 17,* 56–71.

Nieto, Sonia. (2000). *Affirming diversity: The sociopolitical context of multicultural education* (3rd ed.). New York: Addison Wesley Longman.

Nilsson, Karina, & Strandh, Mattias. (1999). Nest leaving in Sweden: The importance of early educational and labor market careers. *Journal of Marriage and the Family, 61,* 1068–1079.

Nilsson, Lars-Göran, & Söderlund, Hedvig. (2001). Aging, cognition, and health. In Moshe Naveh-Benjamin, Morris Moscovitch, & Henry L. Roedinger III (Eds.), *Perspectives on human memory and cognitive aging* (pp. 253–264). East Sussex, UK: Psychology Press.

Nisbett, Richard E., Peng, Kaiping, Choi, Incheol, & Norenzaan, Ara. (2001). Culture and systems of thought: Holistic versus analytic cognition. *Psychological Review, 108,* 291–310.

Nixon, James. (2000). Injury prevention and children's rights. In Dinesh Mohan & Geetam Tiwari (Eds.), *Injury prevention and control* (pp. 167–180). London: Taylor & Francis.

Nobles, A., & Sciarra, D. T. (2000). Cultural determinants in the treatment of Arab Americans: A primer for mainstream therapists. *American Journal of Orthospsychiatry, 70*(2), 182–191.

Nunan, David, & Lam, Agnes. (1998). Teacher education for multilingual contexts: Models and issues. In Jasone Cenoz & Fred Genesee (Eds.), *Beyond bilingualism: Multilingualism and multilingual education.* Clevedon, England: Multilingual Matters.

O'Connor, Thomas G., Rutter, Michael, Beckett, Celia, Keaveney, Lisa, Kreppner, Jana M., & English and Romanian Adoptees Study Team. (2000). The effects of global severe privation on cognitive competence: Extension and longitudinal follow-up. *Child Development, 71,* 376–390.

O'Donoghue, Ted, & Rabin, Matthew. (2001). Risky behavior among youths: Some issues from behavioral economics. In Jonathan Gruber (Ed.), *Risky behavior among youth: An economic analysis* (pp. 29–67). Chicago: The University of Chicago Press.

O'Hara, Michael W. (1997). The nature of postpartum depressive disorders. In Lynne Murray & Peter J. Cooper (Eds.), *Postpartum depression and child development.* New York: Guilford.

O'Neill, C., Jamison, J., McCulloch, D., & Smith, D. (2001). Age-related macular degeneration: Cost of illness issues. *Drugs and Aging, 18,* 233–241.

O'Rahilly, Rona & Muller, Fabiola. (2000) *Human embryology and teratology* (3rd ed.). New York: Wiley.

Oeppen, Jim, & Vaupel, James W. (2002). Broken limits to life expectancy. *Science, 296,* 1029–1031.

Ogbu, John U. (1993). Differences in cultural frames of reference. *International Journal of Behavioral Development, 16,* 483–506.

Ohayon, M. M., Caulet, M., Arbus, L., Bilard, M., Coquerel, A., Guieu, J. D., et. al. (1999). Are prescribed medications effective in the treatment of insomnia complaints? *Journal of Psychosomatic Research, 47,* 359–368.

Ohring, Richard, Graber, Julia A., & Brooks-Gunn, Jeanne. (2002). Girls' recurrent and concurrent body dissatisfaction: Correlates and consequences over 8 years. *International Journal of Eating Disorders, 31,* 404–415.

Okamoto, Koichi, Tanaka, Makoto, & Kondo, Susumu. (2002). Treatment of vascular dementia. In Sergio Starkstein & Marcelo Merello (Eds.), *Psychiatric and cognitive disorders in Parkinson's disease.* Cambridge, England: Cambridge University Press.

Olausson, Petra Otterblad, Haglund, Bengt, Weitoft, Gunilla Ringbäck, & Cnattingius, Sven. (2001). Teenage childbearing and long-term socioeconomic consequences: A case study in Sweden. *Family Planning Perspectives, 33,* 70–74.

Olson, Laura Katz (Ed.). (2000). *Age through ethnic lenses: Caring for the elderly in a multicultural society.* Lanham, MD: Rowman & Littlefield.

Olson, Sheryl L., Kashiwagi, Keiko, & Crystal, David. (2001). Concepts of adaptive and maladaptive child behavior: A comparison of U.S. and Japanese mothers of preschool-age children. *Journal of Cross-Cultural Psychology, 32,* 43–57.

Olweus, Dan. (1992). Bullying among schoolchildren: Intervention and prevention. In Ray DeV. Peters, Robert Joseph McMahon, & Vernon L. Quinsey (Eds.), *Aggression and violence throughout the life span* (pp. 100–125). Newbury Park, CA: Sage.

Olweus, Dan. (1993). Victimization by peers: Antecedents and long-term outcomes. In Kenneth H. Rubin & Jens B. Asendorpf (Eds.), *Social withdrawal, inhibition, and shyness in childhood* (pp. 315–341). Mahwah, NJ: Erlbaum.

Olweus, Dan. (1999). Norway. In Peter K. Smith, Yohji Morita, Josine Junger-Tas, Dan Olweus, Richard F. Catalano, & Phillip T. Slee (Eds.), *The nature of school bullying: A cross-national perspective* (pp. 28–48). London: Routledge.

Ono, Hiromi. (2003). Women's economic standing, marriage timing, and cross-national contexts of gender. *Journal of Marriage and Family, 65,* 275–286.

Onwuteaka-Philipsen, Bregje D., van der Heide, Agnes, Koper, Dirk, Keij-Deerenberg, Ingeborg, Rietjens, Judith A. C., Rurup, Mette L., et al. (2003). Euthanasia and other end-of-life decisions in the Netherlands in 1990, 1995, and 2001. *Lancet,* (Published online June 17, 2003. Retrieved from http://image.thelancet.com/extras/03art3297web.pdf.

Oosterlaan, Jaap, Logan, Gordon D., & Sergeant, Joseph A. (1998). Response inhibition in AD/HD, CD, comorbid AD/HD + CD, anxious, and control children: A meta-analysis of studies with the stop task. *Journal of Child Psychology and Psychiatry and Allied Disciplines, 39,* 411–425.

Opoku, Kofi Asare. (1989). African perspectives on death and dying. In Arthur Berger, Paul Badham, Austin H. Kutsch-er, Joyce Berger, Ven. Michael Petty, & John Beloff (Eds.), *Perspectives on death and dying: Cross-cultural and multidisciplinary views.* Philadelphia: Charles Press.

Oppenheim, David. (1998). Perspectives on infant mental health from Israel: The case of changes in collective sleeping on the kibbutz. *Infant Mental Health Journal, 19,* 76–86.

Orford, Jim. (2001). *Excessive appetites* (2nd ed.). New York: Wiley.

Osgood, Nancy J. (1992). *Suicide in later life.* Lexington, MA: Lexington Books.

Osterling, Julie A., Dawson, Geraldine, & Munson, Jeffrey A. (2002). Early recognition of 1-year-old infants with autism spectrum disorder versus mental retardation. *Development and Psychopathology, 14,* 239–251.

Ostrom, Elinor, Dietz, Thomas, Dolsak, Nives, Stern, Paul C., Weber, Elke U., & Stonich, Susan (Eds.). (2002). *The drama of the commons.* Washington, DC: National Research Council, National Academy Press.

Pahl, Ray, & Spencer, Liz. (1997). The politics of friendship. *Renewal, 5,* 100–107.

Pallus, Aaron M. (2002) Educational participation across the life course: Do the rich get richer? In Richard A. Settersten, Jr., & Timothy J. Owens (Eds.), *New frontiers in socialization* (pp. 327–354). Amsterdam: JAI.

Palmore, Erdman, B. (1977). *The facts on aging quiz.* New York: Springer.

Palmore, Erdman, B. (1998). *The facts on aging quiz.* New York: Springer.

Panchaud, Christine, Singh, Susheela, Feivelson, Dina, & Darroch, Jacqueline E. (2000). Sexually transmitted diseases among adolescents in developed countries. *Family Planning Perspectives, 32,* 24–32, 45.

Pang, Jenny W. Y., Heffelfinger, James D., Huang, Greg J., Benedetti, Thomas J., Weiss, Noel S. (2002). Outcomes of planned home birth in Washington State. *Obstetrics & Gynecology, 99* (4), S70-S71.

Panksepp, Jaak. (1998). Attention deficit hyperactivity disorders, psychostimulants, and intolerance of childhood playfulness: A tragedy in the making? *Current Directions in Psychological Science, 7,* 91–98.

Papernow, Patricia L. (1993). Becoming a stepfamily: Patterns of development in remarried families. San Francisco: Jossey-Bass.

Park, Denise C., & Hedden, Trey. (2001). Working memory and aging. In M. Naveh-Benjamin, M. Moscovitch, & R. L. Roediger III (Eds.), *Perspectives on human memory and cognitive aging: Essays in honour of Fergus Craik* (pp. 148–160). East Sussex, UK: Psychology Press.

Parke, Ross D. (1995). Fathers and families. In Marc H. Bornstein (Ed.), *Handbook of parenting: Vol. 3. Status and social conditions of parenting* (pp. 27–63). Hillsdale, NJ: Erlbaum.

Parke, Ross D. (1996). *Fatherhood.* Cambridge, MA: Harvard University Press.

Parke, Ross D., Ornstein, Peter A., Rieser, John J., & Zahn-Waxler, Carolyn. (1994). The past as prologue: An overview of a century of developmental psychology. In Ross D. Parke, Peter A. Ornstein, John J. Rieser, & Carolyn Zahn-Waxler (Eds.), *A century of developmental psychology.* Washington, DC: American Psychological Association.

Parker, Richard. (2002). The global HIV/AIDS pandemic, structural inequalities, and the politics of international health. *American Journal of Public Health, 92,* 347–351.

Parkin, Alan J. (1993). *Memory: Phenomena, experiment and theory.* Oxford, England: Blackwell.

Pascarella, Ernest T., & Terenzini, Patrick T. (1991) *How college affects students: Findings and insights from twenty years of research.* San Francisco: Jossey-Bass.

Pasupathi, Monisha, Staudinger, Ursula M., & Baltes, Paul B. (2001). Seeds of wisdom: Adolescents' knowledge and judgment about difficult life problems. *Developmental Psychology, 37,* 351–361.

Patel, Dilip R., & Luckstead, Eugene F. (2000). Sport participation, risk-taking and health risk behaviors. *Adolescent Medicine: State of the Art Reviews, 11,* 141–155.

Patel, Vimla L., Arocha, Jose F., & Kaufman, David R. (1999). Expertise and tacit knowledge in medicine. In Robert J. Sternberg & Joseph A. Horvath (Eds.), *Tacit knowledge in professional practice:*

Researcher and practitioner perspectives (pp. 75–99). Mahwah, NJ: Erlbaum.

Paterson, Donald H., & Stathokostas, Liza. (2002). Physical activity, fitness, and gender in relation to morbidity, survival, quality of life and independence in old age. In Roy J. Shephard (Ed.), *Gender, physical activity, and aging* (pp. 99–120). Boca Raton, FL: CRC Press.

Patterson, Charlotte J. (2002). Lesbian and gay parenthood. In Marc H. Bornstein (Ed.), *Handbook of parenting: Vol. 3. Being and becoming a parent* (2nd ed., pp. 317–338). Mahwah, NJ: Erlbaum.

Patterson, Gerald R. (1998). Continuities—a search for causal mechanisms: Comment on the special section. *Developmental Psychology, 34,* 1263–1268.

Paulesu, E., Demonet, J. F., Fazio, F., McCrory, E., Chanoine, V., Brunswick, N., Cappa, S. F., Cossu, G., Habib, M., Frith, C. D., & Frith, U. (2001). Dyslexia: Cultural diversity and biological unity. *Science, 291*(551), 2165–2167.

Pearson, J. D., Morell, C. H., Gordon-Salant, S., Brant, L. J., Metter, E. J., Klein, L., et al. (1995). Gender differences in a longitudinal study of age-associated hearing loss. *Journal of the Acoustical Society of America, 97,* 1196–1205.

Pechmann, Cornelia, Dixon, Philip, & Layne, Neville. (1998). An assessment of U.S. and Canadian smoking reduction objectives for the year 2000. *American Journal of Public Health, 88,* 1362–1367.

Pedersen, William C., Miller, Lynn Carol, Putcha-Bhagavatula, Anila D., & Yang, Yijing. (2002). Evolved sex differences in the number of partners desired? The long and the short of it. *Psychological Science, 13,* 157–161.

Peeters, Anna, Barendregt, Jan J., Willekens, Frans, Mackenbach, Johan P., Al Mamun, Abdullah, & Bonneux, Luc. (2003). Obesity in adulthood and its consequences for life expectancy: A life table analysis. *Annals of Internal Medicine, 138,* 24–32.

Pellegrini, A. D., & Long, Jeffrey D. (2002). A longitudinal study of bullying, dominance, and victimization during the transition from primary school through secondary school. *British Journal of Developmental Psychology, 20,* 259–280.

Pellegrini, Anthony D., & Smith, Peter K. (1998). Physical activity play: The nature and function of a neglected aspect of play. *Child Development, 69,* 577–598.

Pellegrini, Anthony D., & Smith, Peter K. (2001). Physical activity play: The nature and function of a neglect aspect of play. In Margaret E. Hertzig & Ellen A. Farber (Eds.), *Annual progress in child psychiatry and child development, 1999* (pp. 1–36). New York: Brunner Routledge.

Peltonen, Leena, & McKusick, Victor A. (2001). Genomics and medicine: Dissecting human disease in the postgenomic era. *Science, 291,* 1224–1229.

Peng, Kaiping, & Nisbett, Richard E. (1999). Culture, dialectics, and reasoning about contradiction. *American Psychologist, 54,* 741–754.

Pennington, Bruce F. (2001). Genetic methods. In Charles A. Nelson & Monica Luciana (Eds.), *Handbook of developmental neuroscience* (pp. 149–158). Cambridge, MA: MIT Press.

Penninx, Brenda W. J. H., & Deeg, Dorly J. H. (2000). Aging and psychological stress. In George Fink (Ed.), *Encyclopedia of stress* (pp. 104–110). San Diego, CA: Academic Press.

Pennisi, Elizabeth, & Roush, Wade. (1997). Developing a new view of evolution. *Science, 277,* 34–37.

Pepler, Debra, Craig, Wendy M., & O'Connell, Paul. (1999). Understanding bullying from a dynamic systems perspective. In Alan Slater & Darwin Muir (Eds.), *The Blackwell reader in developmental psychology* (pp. 440–451). Malden, MA: Blackwell.

Perfect, Timothy J., & Maylor, Elizabeth A. (Eds.). (2000). *Models of cognitive aging.* New York: Oxford University Press.

Perkins, H. Wesley (Ed.) (2003). *The social norms approach to preventing school and college age substance abuse.* San Francisco: Jossey-Bass.

Perlmutter, Marion, Kaplan, Michael, & Nyquist, Linda. (1990). Development of adaptive competence in adulthood. *Human Development, 33,* 185–197.

Perner, Josef, Lang, Birgit, & Kloo, Daniela. (2002). Theory of mind and self-control: More than a common problem of inhibition. *Child Development, 73,* 752–767.

Perriello, Vita. (2001). Aiming for healthy weight in wrestlers and other athletes. *Contemporary Pediatrics, 18*(9), 55–74.

Perry, William G., Jr. (1981). Cognitive and ethical growth: The making of meaning. In Arthur W. Chickering (Ed.*), The modern American college: Responding to the new realities of diverse students and a changing society.* San Francisco: Jossey-Bass.

Persaud, T. A., Chudley, S. R., & Skalko, R. G. (1985). Basic concepts in teratology. New York: Liss.

Peters, Arnold, & Liefbroer, Aart C. (1997). Beyond marital status: Partner history and well-being in old age. *Journal of Marriage and the Family, 59,* 687–699.

Petersen, Anne C., Compas, Bruce E., Brooks-Gunn, Jeanne, Stemmler, Mark, Ey, Sydney, & Grant, Kathryn E. (1993). Depression in adolescence. *American Psychologist, 48,* 155–168.

Peterson, James C. (2001). *Genetic turning points: The ethics of human genetic intervention.* Grand Rapids, MI: Eerdmans.

Peterson, Ronald C. (Ed.). (2003). *Mild cognitive impairment.* Oxford, England: Oxford University Press.

Petitto, Laura A., & Marentette, Paula F. (1991). Babbling in the manual mode: Evidence for the ontogeny of language. *Science, 251,* 1493–1496.

Petrou, Stavros, Sach, Tracey, Davidson, L. (2001). The long-term costs of preterm birth and low birth weight: Results of a systematic review. *Child: Care, Health and Development, 27*(2), 97–115.

Pettit, Gregory S., Laird, Robert D., Dodge, Kenneth A., Bates, John E., & Criss, Michael M. (2001). Antecedents and behavior-problem outcomes of parental monitoring and psychological control in early adolescence. *Child Development, 72,* 583–598.

Pew Environmental Health Commission. (2000). Attack asthma: Why America needs a public health defense system to battle environmental threats. Baltimore, MD: Johns Hopkins School of Public Health.

Pfeifer, Marcie, Goldsmith, H. Hill, Davidson, Richard J., & Rickman, Maureen. (2002). Continuity and change in inhibited and uninhibited children. *Child Development, 73,* 1474–1485.

Phillips, David R. (Ed.). (2000). *Ageing in the Asia-Pacific region.* London: Routledge.

Phipps, Maureen G., & Sowers, MaryFran. (2002). Defining early adolescent childbearing. *American Journal of Public Health, 92,* 125–128.

Piaget, Jean. (1952). *The child's conception of number* (C. Gattegno & F. M. Hodgson, Trans.). London: Routledge & Kegan Paul.

Piaget, Jean. (1962). *Play, dreams, and imitation in childhood.* New York: Norton.

Piaget, Jean. (1970). The child's conception of movement and speed (G.E.T. Holloway & M.J. Mackenzie, Trans.). New York: Basic Books.

Piaget, Jean. (1970). *The child's conception of movement and speed.* (G. E. T. Holloway & M. J. Mackenzie, Trans.). New York: Basic Books.

Piaget, Jean. (1970). *The child's conception of time.* (A. J. Pomerans, Trans.). New York: Basic Books.

Piaget, Jean, & Moreau, Albert. (2001). The inversion of arithmetic operations. In Robert L. Campbell (Ed. and Trans.), *Studies in reflecting abstraction* (pp. 69–85). Hove, England: Psychology Press.

Piaget, Jean, Voelin-Liambey, Daphne, & Berthoud-Papandropoulou, Ioanna. (2001). Problems of class inclusion and logical implication. In Robert L. Campbell (Ed. and Trans.), *Studies in reflecting abstraction* (pp. 105–137). Hove, England: Psychology Press.

Pietch, James H., & Braun, Kathryn. (2000). Autonomy, advance directives, and the Patient Self-Determination Act. In Kathryn Braun, James H. Pietsch, & Patricia L. Blanchette (Eds.), *Cultural issues in end-of-life decision making* (pp. 35–46). Thousand Oaks, CA: Sage.

Pinker, Steven. (1994). *The language instinct.* New York: Morrow.

Pinquart, Martin, & Sörensen, Silvia. (2003) Associations of stressors and uplifts of caregiving with caregiver burden and depressive mood: A meta-analysis. *The Journals of Gerontology Series B: Psychological Sciences and Social Sciences, 58,* P112–P128.

Pirozzo, Sandi, Papinczak, Tracey, & Glaszion, Paul. (2003). Whispered voice test for screening for hearing impairment in adults and children: Systematic review. *British Medical Journal, 327,* 967–970.

Pitskhelauri, G.Z. (1982). *The long-living of Soviet Georgia* (Gari Lesnoff—Caravaglia, Trans.). New York: Human Sciences Press.

Plank, Stephen B., & MacIver, Douglas J. (2003). Educational achievement. In Marc H. Bornstein, Lucy Davidson, Corey L. M. Keyes, & Kristin A. Moore (Eds.), *Well-being: Positive development across the life course. Crosscurrents in contemporary psychology* (pp. 341–354). Mahwah, NJ: Erlbaum.

Plomin, Robert. (2002). Behavioural genetics in the 21st century. In W. W. Hartup & R. K. Silbereisen (Eds.), *Growing points in developmental science: An introduction* (pp. 47–63). Philadelphia: Psychology Press.

Plomin, Robert, DeFreis, John C., McClearn, Gerald E., & McGuffin, Peter. (2001). *Behavioral genetics* (4th ed.). New York: Worth.

Pogrebin, Letty. (1996). *Getting over getting older: An intimate memoir.* Boston: Little Brown.

Polivy, Janet, & Herman, C. Peter (2002). If at first you don't succeed: False hopes of self-change. *American Psychologist, 57,* 677–689.

Polizzi, Kenneth B., & Millikin, Richard J. (2002). Attitudes toward the elderly: Identifying problematic use of ageist and overextended terminology in research instructions. *Educational Gerontology, 28,* 367–377.

Pollack, Harold A., & Frohna, John G. (2001). A competing risk model of sudden infant death syndrome in two U.S. birth cohorts. *Journal of Pediatrics, 138,* 661–667.

Pollak, Seth D., Cicchetti, Dante, Hornung, Katherine, & Reed, Alex. (2000). Recognizing emotion in faces: Developmental effects of child abuse and neglect. *Developmental Psychology, 36,* 679–688.

Pong, Suet-Ling, Dronkers, Japp, & Hampden-Thompson, Gillian. (2003). Family policies and children's school achievement in single- versus two-parent families. *Journal of Marriage and Family, 65,* 681–699.

Ponsoby, Anne-Louise, Dwyer, Terence, Gibbins, Laura E., Cochrane, Jennifer A., & Wang, Yon-Gan. (1993). Factors potentiating the risk of sudden infant death syndrome associated with the prone position. *New England Journal of Medicine, 329,* 377–382.

Posner, Michael I., & Rothbart, Mary K. (2000). Developing mechanisms of self-regulation. *Development and Psychopathology, 12,* 427–441.

Posner, Richard A. (1995). *Aging and old age.* Chicago: University of Chicago Press.

Post, Stephen G. (2001). Dementia care ethics. In David N. Weisstub, David C. Thomasma, Serge Gauthier, & George F. Tomossy (Eds.), *Aging: Caring for our elders,* (pp. 177–190). Hingham, MA: Kluwer Academic Publishers.

Powell, Douglas H. (1994). *Profiles in cognitive aging.* Cambridge, MA: Harvard University Press.

Prado, C.G., & Taylor, S.J. (1999). *Assisted suicide: Theory and practice in elective death.* Amherst, NY: Humanity Books.

Pratt, Michael W., Arnold, Mary Louise, Norris, Joan E., & Filyer, Rebecca. (1999). Generativity and moral development as predictors of value-socialization. Narratives for young persons across the adult life span: From lessons learned to stories shared. *Psychology and Aging, 14,* 414–426.

Pratt, Michael W., & Norris, Joan E. *(1999). Moral development in maturity: Life-span perspectives on the processes of successful aging. In Thomas M. Hess & Fredda Blanchard-Fields (Eds.),* Social cognition and aging. *San Diego, CA: Academic Press.*

Pratt, Michael W., & Robins, S. (1991). That's the way it was: Age differences in the structure and quality of adults' personal narratives. *Discourse Processes, 14,* 73–85.

Presser, Harriet B. (2000). Nonstandard work schedules and marital instability. *Journal of Marriage and the Family, 62,* 93–110.

Preston, Fredrica, Tang, Stephanie, & McCorkle, Ruth. (2003). Symptom management for the terminally ill. In Inge Corless, Barbara B. Germino, & Mary A. Pittman (Eds.), *Dying, death, and bereavement* (2nd ed., pp. 145–180) New York: Springer.

Previti, Denise, & Amato, Paul R. (2003). Why stay married: Rewards, barriers, and marital stability. *Journal of Marriage and Family, 65,* 561–573.

Pridemore, William Alex. (2002). Vodka and violence: Alcohol consumption and homicide rates in Russia. *American Journal of Public Health, 92,* 1921–1930.

Proos, L. A., Hofvander, Y., & Tuvemo, T. (1991). Menarcheal age and growth pattern of Indian girls adopted in Sweden. I. Menarcheal age. *Acta Paediatrica Scandinavica, 80,* 852–858.

Putnam, Samuel P., Sanson, Ann V., & Rothbart, Mary K. (2002). Child temperament and parenting. In Marc H. Bornstein (Ed.), *Handbook of parenting: Vol. 1. Children and parenting* (2nd ed., pp. 255–278). Mahwah, NJ: Erlbaum.

Pyke, Karen. (1999). The micropolitics of care in relationships between aging parents and adult children: Individualism, collectivism, and power. *Journal of Marriage and the Family, 61,* 661–672.

Pyke, Karen D., & Bengtson, Vern L. (1996). Caring more or less: Individualistic and collectivist systems of family eldercare. *Journal of Marriage and the Family, 58,* 379–392.

Quadagno, Jill, & Hardy, Melissa. (1996). Work and retirement. In Robert H. Binstock, Linda K. George, Victor W. Marshall, George C. Myers, & James H. Schulz (Eds.), *Handbook of aging and the social sciences* (4th ed., pp. 325–345). San Diego, CA: Academic Press.

Rabin, Bruce S. (2003). Healthy aging begins with the fetus. *American Journal of Public Health, 93,* 1202.

Rabow, Michael W., Hardie, Grace E., Fair, Joan M., & McPhee, Stephen J. (2000). End-of-life care content in 50 textbooks from multiple specialties. *Journal of the American Medical Association, 283,* 771–778.

Radvansky, Gabriel, Zwaan, Rolf A., Curiel, Jacqueline M., & Copeland, David E. (2001). Situation models and aging. *Psychology and Aging, 16,* 145–160.

Rahe, Richard H. (2000). Coping, stress and. In George Fink (Ed.), *Encyclopedia of stress* (pp. 541–546). San Diego, CA: Academic Press.

Rahhal, Tamara A., Hacher, Lynn, & Colcombe, Stanley J. (2001). Instructional manipulations and age differences in memory: Now you see them, now you don't. *Psychology and Aging, 16,* 697–706.

Raloff, Janet. (1996). Vanishing flesh: Muscle loss in the elderly finally gets some respect. *Science News, 150,* 90–91.

Ramey, Craig T., Ramey, Sharon Landesman, Lanzi, Robin Gaines, & Cotton, Janice N. (2002). Early educational interventions for high-risk children: How center-based treatment can augment and improve parenting effectiveness. In John G. Borkowski, Sharon Landesman Ramey, & Marie Bristol-Power (Eds.), *Parenting and the child's world: Influences on academic, intellectual, and social-emotional development.* (pp. 125–140). Mahwah, NJ: Erlbaum.

Ramey, Sharon Landesman. (2002). The science and art of parenting. In John G. Borkowski, Sharon Landesman Ramey, & Marie Bristol-Power (Eds.), *Parenting and the child's world: Influences on academic, intellectual, and social-emotional development* (pp. 47–71). Mahwah, NJ: Erlbaum.

Rank, Mark R., & Hirschl, Thomas A. (1999). Estimating the proportion of Americans ever experiencing poverty during their elderly years. *Journal of Gerontology, 54B,* 5184–5193.

Ranyard, Rob, Crozier, W. Ray, & Svenson, Ola (Eds.). (1997). *Decision making: Cognitive models and explanations.* New York: Routledge.

Rao, Raghavendra, & Georgieff, Michael K. (2000). Early nutrition and brain development. In Charles A. Nelson (Ed.), *The Minnesota Symposia on Child Psychology: Vol. 31. The effects of early adversity on neurobehavioral development.* Mahwah, NJ: Erlbaum.

Raskin-White, Helene, Loeber, Rolf, Stouthamer-Loeber, Magda, & Farrington, David P. (1999). Developmental associations between substance use and violence. *Development and Psychopathology, 11,* 785–803.

Rauscher, Frances H., & Shaw, Gordon L. (1998). Key components of the Mozart effect. *Perceptual and Motor Skills, 86,* 835–841.

Rauscher, Frances H., Shaw, Gordon L., & Ky, Katherine N. (1993). Music and spatial task performance. *Nature, 365,* 611.

Rawlins, William K. (1992). *Friendship matters.* Hawthorne, NY : Aldine de Gruyter.

Ray, Ruth E. (1996). A postmodern perspective on feminist gerontology. *The Gerontologist, 36,*(5), 674–680.

Raymo, James M. (2003). Premarital living arrangements and the transition to first marriage in Japan. *Journal of Marriage and Family, 65,* 302–315.

Rayner, Keith, Foorman, Barbara R., Perfetti, Charles A., Pesetsky, David, & Seidenberg, Mark S. (2001). How psychological science informs the teaching of reading. *Psychological Science in the Public Interest, 2,* 31–74.

Reid, John B., Patterson, Gerald R., & Snyder, James J. (2002). *Antisocial behavior in children and adolescents: A developmental analysis and model for intervention.* Washington, DC: American Psychological Association.

Reis, Myrna. (2000).The IOA screen: An abuse-alert measure that dispels myths. *Generations, 24,*13–16.

Reiss, David. (2000). *The relationship code: Deciphering genetic and social influences on adolescent development.* Cambridge, MA: Harvard University Press.

Reiss, David, & Neiderhiser, Jenae M. (2000). The interplay of genetic influences and social processes in developmental theory: Specific mechanisms are coming into view. *Development and Psychopathology, 12,* 357–374.

Reiter, Edward O., & Lee, Peter A. (2001). Have the onset and tempo of puberty changed? *Archives of Pediatrics and Adolescent Medicine, 155,* 988–989.

Remez, Lisa. (2000). Oral sex among adolescents: Is it sex or is it abstinence? *Family Planning Perspectives, 32,* 298–303.

Rendell, Peter G., & Thompson, Donald M. (1999). Aging and prospective memory: Differences between naturalistic and laboratory tasks. *Journal of Gerontology: Psychological Sciences, 54B,* 256–269.

Renninger, K. Ann, & Amsel, Eric. (1997). Change and development: An introduction. In Eric Amsel & K. Ann Renninger (Eds.), *Jean Piaget symposium series: Vol. 25. Change and development: Issues of theory, method, & application.* Mahwah, NJ: Erlbaum.

Renshaw, Domeena C. (1998). Women's sexual function and dysfunction. In Regina A. Casper (Ed.), *Women's health, hormones, emotions, and behavior* (pp. 36–52). Cambridge, England: Cambridge University Press.

Research Advisory Committee of the National Council of Teachers of Mathematics. (1989). The mathematics education of underserved and underrepresented groups: A continuing challenge. *Journal for Research in Mathematics Education, 20,* 371–375.

Rest, James R. (1993). Research on moral judgment in college students. In Andrew Garrod (Ed.), *Approaches to moral development: New research and emerging themes.* New York: Teachers College Press.

Rest, James R., Narvaez, Darcia, Bebeau, Murel J., & Thoma, Stephen J. (1999b). *Postconventional moral thinking: A neo-Kohlbergian approach.* Mahwah, NJ: Erlbaum.

Reynolds, Arthur J. (2000). *Success in early intervention: The Chicago child–parent centers.* Lincoln, NE: University of Nebraska Press.

Rhodes, Frank H. T. (2001). *The creation of the future: The role of the American university.* Ithaca, NY: Cornell University Press.

Rice, Amy L., Sacco, Lisa, Hyder, Adnan, & Black, Robert E. (2000). Malnutrition as an underlying cause of childhood deaths associated with infectious diseases in developing countries. *Bulletin of the World Health Organization, 78,* 1207–1221.

Rice, Charles L., & Cunningham, David A. (2002). Aging of the neuromuscular system: Influences of gender and physical activity. In Roy J. Shephard (Ed.), *Gender, physical activity, and aging,* (pp.121–150). Boca Raton, FL: CRC Press.

Rich, Lauren M., & Kim, Sun-Bin. (2002). Employment and the sexual and reproductive behavior of female adolescents. *Perspectives on Sexual and Reproductive Health, 34,* 127–134.

Richards, Marcus, Jarvis, Martin, Thompson, Neil, & Wadswroth, Michael E. J. (2003). Cigarette smoking and cognitive decline in midlife: Evidence from a prospective birth cohort study. *American Journal of Public Health, 93,* 994–998.

Richards, Maryse H., Crowe, Paul A., Larson, Reed, & Swarr, Amy. (1998). Developmental patterns and gender differences in the experience of peer companionship during adolescence. *Child Development, 69,* 154–163.

Ridley, Matt. (1999). *Genome.* London: Fourth Estate Limited.

Riegel, Klaus F. (1975). Toward a dialectical theory of development. *Human Development, 18,* 50–64.

Rigby, Ken, & Slee, Phillip T. (1999). Australia. In Peter K. Smith, Yohji Morita, Josine Junger-Tas, Dan Olweus, Richard F. Catalano, & Phillip T. Slee (Eds.), *The nature of school bullying: A cross-national perspective.* London: Routledge.

Rind, Bruce, Tromovitch, Philip, & Bauserman, Robert. (1998). A meta-analytical examination of assumed properties of child sexual abuse using college students. *Psychological Bulletin, 124,* 22–53.

Ro, Marguerite. (2002). Moving forward: Addressing the health of Asian American and Pacific Islander women. *American Journal of Public Health, 92,* 516–519.

Robert, Stephanie A., & Lee, Kum Yi. (2002). Explaining race differences in health among older adults. *Research on Aging, 24.* 654–683.

Roberto, Karen A. (1993). Family caregivers of aging adults with disabilities: A review of the caregiving literature. In Karen A. Roberto (Ed.), *The elderly caregiver: Caring for adults with developmental disabilities* (pp. 3–18). Thousand Oaks, CA: Sage.

Roberts, Brent W., & Caspi, Avshalom. (2003). The cumulative continuity model of personality development: Striking a balance between continuity and change in personality traits across the life course. In Ursula M. Staudinger & Ulman Lindenberger (Eds.), *Understanding human development: Dialogues with life-span psychology* (pp. 183–214). Dordrecht, Netherlands: Kluwer.

Robin, Daniel J., Berthier, Neil E., & Clifton, Rachel K. (1996). Infants' predictive reaching for moving objects in the dark. *Developmental Psychology, 32,* 824–835.

Robins, Lee N. (1995). Editorial: The natural history of substance abuse as a guide to setting drug policy. *American Journal of Public Health, 85,* 12–13.

Robins, Richard W., Trzesniewski, Kali H., Gosling, Samuel D., Tracy, Jessica L.,& Potter, Jeff (2002). Global self-esteem across the life span. *Psychology and Aging, 17,* 423–434.

Robinson, Thomas N., & Killen, Joel D. (2001). Obesity prevention for children and adolescents. In J. Kevin Thompson & Linda Smolak (Eds.), *Body image, eating disorders, and obesity in youth* (pp. 261–292). Washington, DC: American Psychological Association.

Robitaille, David F., & Beaton, Albert E. (Eds.). (2002). *Secondary analysis of the TIMSS data.* Boston: Kluwer Academic Publishers.

Rochat, Philippe. (2001). *The infant's world.* Cambridge, MA: Harvard University Press.

Rodier, Patricia H. (2000, February). The early origins of autism. *Scientific American, 282,* 56–63.

Rogers, Kathleen Boyce. (1999). Parenting processes related to sexual risk-taking behaviors of adolescent males and females. *Journal of Marriage and the Family, 61,* 99–109.

Rogers, Stacy J., & May, Dee C. (2003). Spillover between marital quality and job satisfaction: Long-term patterns and gender differences. *Journal of Marriage and Family, 65,* 482–495.

Rogoff, Barbara. (1990). *Apprenticeship in thinking: Cognitive development in social context.* New York: Oxford University Press.

Rogoff, Barbara. (1998). Cognition as a collaborative process. In William Damon (Series Ed.), Deanna Kuhn & Robert S. Siegler (Volume Eds.), *Handbook of child psychology: Vol. 2. Cognition, perception, and language* (5th ed., pp. 679–744). New York: Wiley.

Rolls, Edmund T. (2000). Memory systems in the brain. *Annual Review of Psychology, 51,* 599–630.

Romaine, Suzanne. (1999). Bilingual language development. In Martyn Barrett (Ed.), *The development of language* (pp. 251–275). Hove, England: Psychology Press.

Roosa, Mark W., Reinholtz, Cindy, & Angelini, Patti Jo. (1999). The relation of child sexual abuse and depression in young women: Comparisons across four ethnic groups. *Journal of Abnormal Child Psychology, 27,* 65–76.

Roschelle, Anne R. (1997). *No more kin: Exploring race, class, and gender in family networks.* Thousand Oaks, CA: Sage.

Rose, Amanda J., & Asher, Steven R. (1999). Children's goals and strategies in response to conflicts within a friendship. *Developmental Psychology, 35,* 69–79.

Rosegrant, Mark W., & Cline, Sarah A. (2003). Global food security: Challenges and policies. *Science, 302,* 1917–1919.

Rose-Jacobs, Ruth, Cabral, Howard, Posner, Michael A., Epstein, Jennifer, Frank, Deborah A. (2002). Do "we just know?" Masked assessors' ability to accurately identify children with prenatal cocaine exposure. *Journal of Developmental and Behavioral Pediatrics, 23*(5), 340–346.

Rosenberg, Elinor B. (1992). The adoption life cycle. Lexington, MA: Lexington Books.

Rosenberg, James H. (2001). Aging, B vitamins, and cognitive decline. In J.D. Fernsterom, R. Vavy& P. Arroyo (Eds.) *Nutrition and the brain* (pp. 201–217). Basel, Switzerland: Karger.

Rosow, Irving. (1985). Status and role change through the life cycle. In Robert H. Binstock & Ethel Shanas (Eds.), *Handbook of aging and the social sciences* (2nd ed.). New York: Van Nostrand.

Rosser, Pearl L., & Randolph, Suzanne M. (1989). Black American infants: The Howard University normative study. In J. Kevin Nugent, Barry M. Lester, & T. Berry Brazelton (Eds.), *The cultural context of infancy: Vol I. Biology, culture, and infant development* (pp. 133–165). Norwood, NJ: Ablex.

Rossi, Alice S. (1994). *Eros and caritas: A biopsychosocial approach to human sexuality and reproduction.* Chicago: University of Chicago Press.

Rossi, Alice S. (Ed.). (1994). *Sexuality across the life course.* Chicago: University of Chicago Press.

Rossi, Alice S. (Ed.). (2001). *Caring and doing for others: Social responsibility in the domains of family, work, and community.* Chicago: University of Chicago Press.

Rothbart, Mary K., & Bates, John E. (1998). Temperament. In W. Damon (Series Ed.), N. Eisenberg (Volume Ed.), *Handbook of child psychology: Vol. 3. Social, emotional, and personality development* (5th ed., pp. 105–176). New York: Wiley.

Rothbaum, Fred, Pott, Martha, Azuma, Hiroshi, Miyake, Kazuo, & Weisz, John. (2000). The development of close relationships in Japan and the United States: Paths of symbolic harmony and generative tension. *Child Development, 71,* 1121–1142.

Rothermund, Klaus, & Brandtstädter, Jochen. (2003). Coping with deficits and losses in later life: From compensatory action to accomodation. *Pyschology and Aging, 18,* 896–905.

Rovee-Collier, Carolyn K. (1987). Learning and memory in infancy. In Joy Doniger Osofsky (Ed.), *Handbook of infant development* (2nd ed., pp. 98–148). New York: Wiley.

Rovee-Collier, Carolyn K. (1990). The "memory system" of prelinguistic infants. In A. Diamond (Ed.), *The development and neural bases of higher cognitive functions.* Annals of the New York Academy of Sciences, Vol. 608. (pp. 517–542). New York: New York Academy of Sciences.

Rovee-Collier, Carolyn K. (2001). Information pick-up by infants: What is it, and how can we tell? *Journal of Experimental Child Psychology, 78,* 35–49.

Rovee-Collier, Carolyn K., & Gerhardstein, Peter. (1997). The development of infant memory. In Nelson Cowan & Charles Hulme (Eds.), *The development of memory in childhood: Studies in developmental psychology* (pp. 5–39). Hove, UK: Psychology Press.

Rovee-Collier, Carolyn K., & Hayne, Harlene. (1987). Reactivation of infant memory: Implications for cognitive development. In H. W. Reese (Ed.), *Advances in child development and behavior* (Vol. 20, pp. 185–238). New York: Academic Press.

Rowe, John Wallis, & Kahn, Robert L. (1998). *Successful aging.* New York: Pantheon.

Royal College of Obstetricians and Gynecologists. (2001). *The national sentinal caesarean section audit report.* London: ROCG Press.

Rozin, Paul, Kabnick, Kimberly, Pete, Erin, Fischler, Claude, & Shields, Christy. (2003). The ecology of eating: Smaller portion size in France than in the United States help explain the French paradox. *Psychological Science, 14,* 450–454.

Rubin, Kenneth H., Bukowski, William, & Parker, Jeffrey G. (1998). Peer interac-

tions, relationships, and groups. In William Damon (Series Ed.) & Nancy Eisenberg (Volume Ed.), *Handbook of child psychology: Vol. 3. Social, emotional, and personality development* (5th ed., pp. 619–700). New York: Wiley.

Rubin, Kenneth H., Burgess, Kim B., & Hastings, Paul D. (2002). Stability and social-behavioral consequences of toddlers' inhibited temperament and parenting behaviors. *Child Development, 73,* 483–495.

Ruble, Diane N., & Martin, Carol Lynn. (1998). Gender development. In William Damon (Series Ed.) & Nancy Eisenberg (Volume Ed.), *Handbook of child psychology: Vol. 3. Social, emotional and personality development* (5th ed., pp. 933–1016). New York: Wiley.

Ruffman, Ted, Slade, Lance, & Crowe, Elena. (2002). The relation between children's and mothers' mental state language and theory-of-mind understanding. *Child Development, 73,* 734–751.

Ruiz-Pesini, Eduardo, Mishmar, Dan, Brandon, Martin, Procaccio, Vincent, & Wallace, Douglas C. (2004). Effects of purifying and adaptive selection on regional variation in human mtDNA. *Science, 303,* 223–226.

Rumbaut, Rúben G., & Portes, Alejandro. (2001). *Ethnicities: Children of immigrants in America.* Berkeley, CA, and New York: University of California Press and the Russell Sage Foundation.

Russell, Mark. (2002). Institute helps spread use of vaccines in Asia. *Science, 295,* 611–612.

Rust, John, Golombok, Susan, Hines, Melissa, Johnson, Katie, Golding, Jean, & ALSPAC Study Team. (2000). The role of brothers and sisters in the gender development of preschool children. *Journal of Experimental Child Psychology, 77,* 292–303.

Rutstein, Shea O. (2000). Factors associated with trends in infant and child morality in developing countries during the 1990s. *Bulletin of the World Health Organization, 78,* 1256–1270.

Rutter, Michael. (1998). Some research considerations on intergenerational continuities and discontinuities: Comment on the special section. *Developmental Psychology, 34,* 1269–1273.

Rutter, Michael. (2002). Nature, nurture, and development: From evangelism through science toward policy and practice. *Child Development, 73,* 1–21.

Rutter, Michael, Giller, Henri, & Hagell, Ann. (1998). *Antisocial behavior by young people.* New York: Cambridge University Press.

Rutter, Michael, & Rutter, Marjorie. (1993). *Developing minds: Challenge and continuity across the life span.* New York: Basic Books.

Rutter, Michael, & Sroufe, L. Alan. (2000). Developmental psychopathology: Concepts and challenges. *Development and Psychopathology, 12,* 265–296.

Rutter, Michael, Thorpe, Karen, Greenwood, Rosemary, Northstone, Kate, & Golding, Jean. (2003). Twins as a natural experiment to study the causes of mild language delay: I: Design; twin-singleton differences in language, and obstetric risks. *Journal of Child Psychology and Psychiatry and Allied Disciplines, 44,* 326–341.

Ryalls, Brigette Oliver. (2000). Dimensional adjectives: Factors affecting children's ability to compare objects using novel words. *Journal of Experimental Child Psychology, 76,* 26–49.

Ryalls, Brigette Oliver, Gul, Robina, & Ryalls, Kenneth R. (2000). Infant imitation of adult and peer models: Evidence for a peer model advantage. *Merrill-Palmer Quarterly, 46,* 188–202.

Ryan, Sarah. (1998). Management by stress: The reorganization of work hits home in the 1990s. In Stephanie Coontz (Ed.), *American families: A multicultural reader.* New York: Routledge.

Rybash, John M., Hoyer, William J., & Roodin, Paul A. (1986). *Adult cognition and aging: Developmental changes in processing, knowing, and thinking.* New York: Pergamon Press.

Ryff, Carol D., Singer, Burton, Love, Gayle Dienberg, & Essex, Marilyn J. (1998). Resilience in adulthood and later life: Defining features and dynamic processes. In Jacob Lomranz (Ed.), *Handbook of aging and mental health: An integrative approach* (pp. 69–96). New York: Plenum Press.

Sabat, Steven R. (2001). *The experience of Alzheimer's disease: Life through a tangled veil.* Oxford, England: Blackwell.

Sackett, Paul R., Hardison, Chaitra M., and Cullen, Michael J. (2004). On interpreting steroetype threat as accounting for African American–white differences on cognitive tests. *American Psychologist, 59,* 7–13.

Sadeh, Avi, Raviv, Amiram, & Gruber, Reut. (2000). Sleep patterns and sleep disruptions in school-age children. *Developmental Psychology, 36,* 291–301.

Sagi, Abraham, Koren-Karie, Nina, Gini, Motti, Ziv, Yair, & Joels, Tirtsa. (2002). Shedding further light on the effects of various types and quality of early child care on infant-mother attachment relationship: The Haifa study of early child care. *Child Development, 73,* 1166–1186.

Saito, Masahiko. (2001). Decision-making in social and medical services for patients with dementia in Japan. In David N. Weisstub, David C. Thomasma, Serge, Gauthier, & George F. Tomossy (Eds.), *Aging: Caring for our elders* (pp. 191–202). Dordrecht, Netherlands: Kluwer.

Salazar, Lilia P., Schludermann, Shirin M., Schludermann, Eduard H., & Huynh, Cam-Loi. (2001). Filipino adolescents' parents' socialization for academic achievement in the United States. *Journal of Adolescent Research, 15,* 564–586.

Salmon, Mary Anne P. (1994). *Double jeopardy: Resources and minority elders.* New York: Garland.

Salthouse, Timothy A. (1984). Effects of age and skill in typing. *Journal of Experimental Psychology: General,* 113, 345–371.

Salthouse, Timothy A. (1996). General and specific speed mediation of adult age differences in memory. *Journals of Gerontology, 51B,* 30–42.

Salthouse, Timothy A. (2000). Steps toward the explanation of adult age differences in cognition. In Timothy J. Perfect & Elizabeth Maylor (Eds.), *Theoretical debate in cognitive aging.* London: Oxford University Press.

Salzarulo, Piero, & Fagioli, Igino. (1999). Changes of sleep states and physiological activities across the first year of life. In A. F. Kalverboer, Maria Luisa Genta, & J. B. Hopkins (Eds.), *Current issues in developmental psychology* (pp. 53–73). Dordrecht, Netherlands: Kluwer.

Sampaio, Ricardo C., & Truwit, Charles L. (2001). Myelination in the developing human brain. In Charles A. Nelson & Monica Luciana (Eds.), *Handbook of developmental cognitive neuroscience* (pp. 35–44). Cambridge, MA: MIT Press.

Sampson, Paul D., Streissguth, Ann P., Bookstein, Fred L., Little, Ruth E., Clarren, Sterling K., Dehaene, Philippe, et al., (1997). Incidence of fetal alcohol syndrome and prevalence of alcohol-related neurodevelopmental disorder. *Teratology, 56,* 317–326.

Sampson, Robert J., & Laub, John. (1993). *Crime in the making: Pathways and turning points through life.* Cambridge, MA: Harvard University Press.

Sampson, Robert J., Raudenbush, Stephen W., & Earls, Felton. (1997). Neighborhoods and violent crime: A multilevel study of collective efficacy. *Science, 277,* 918–924.

Samuelsson, G., Dehlin, O., Hagberg, B., & Sundstrom, G. (2001). Incidence of dementia in relation to medical, psychological and social risk factors: A longitudinal cohort study during a 25-year period. In Caleb Finch, Jean-Marie Robine, & Yves Christen (Eds.), *Brain and longevity* (pp. 131–144). Berlin: Springer Verlag.

Sanchez, Laura. (1994). Gender, labor allocations, and the psychology of entitlement within the home. *Social Forces, 73*(2), 533–553.

Sanchez, Maria del Mar, Ladd, Charlotte O., & Plotsky, Paul M. (2001). Early adverse experience as a developmental risk factor for later psychopathology: Evidence from rodent and primate models. *Development and Psychopathology, 13,* 419–450.

Sanders, Catherine M. (1989). *Grief: The mourning after.* New York: Wiley.

Sanders, Stephanie A., & Reinisch, Jane Machover. (1999). Would you say you "had sex" if . . . ? *Journal of the American Medical Association, 281,* 275–277.

Santelli, John S., Lindberg, Laura Duberstein, Abma, Joyce, McNeely, Clea Sucoff, & Resnick, Michael. (2000). Adolescent sexual behavior: Estimates and trends from four nationally representative surveys. *Family Planning Perspectives, 32,* 156–165, 194.

Sapp, Felicity, Lee, Kang, & Muir, Darwin. (2000). Three-year-olds' difficulty with the appearance-reality distinction: Is it real or is it apparent? *Developmental Psychology, 36,* 547–560.

Sarroub, Loukia A. (2001). The sojourner experience of Yemeni American high school students: An ethnographic portrait. *Harvard Educational Review, 71,* 390–415.

Satcher, David. (2001). *The Surgeon General's call to action to promote sexual health and responsible sexual behavior.* Washington, DC: U.S. Government Printing Office.

Satcher, David. (2001). *Women and smoking: A report of the surgeon general.* Rockville, MD: U. S. Department of Health and Human Services.

Saudino, Kimberly J., McClearn, G.E., Pedersen, Nancy L., Lichtenstein, Paul, & Plomin, Robert. (1997). Can personality explain genetic influences on life events? *Journal of Personality and Social Psychology, 72,* 196–206.

Saunders, C.M. (1978). *The management of terminal disease.* London: Edward Arnold.

Savage, Felicity, & Lhotska, Lida (2000). Recommendations on feeding infants of HIV-positive mothers. WHO, UNICEF, UNAIDS guideline. In Nathan Back, Irun R. Cohen, David Kritchevsky, Abel Lajtha, & Rodolfo Paoletti (Series Eds.), & Berthold Koletzko, Kim Fleischer Michaelsen, & Olle Hernell (Vol Eds.), *Advances in experimental medical biology, Vol. 478: Short and long-term effects of breast feeding on child health* (pp. 225–230). Dordrecht, The Netherlands: Kluwer Academic/Plenum.

Savin-Williams, Ritch C., & Diamond, Lisa M. (1997). Sexual orientation as a developmental context for lesbians, gays, and bisexuals: Biological perspectives. In Nancy L. Segal, Glenn E. Weisfeld, & Carol C. Weisfeld (Eds.), *Uniting psychology and biology: Integrative perspectives on human development* (pp. 217–238). Washington, DC: American Psychological Association.

Saxe, Geoffrey B. (1991). *Culture and cognitive development: Studies in mathematical understanding.* Hillsdale, NJ: Erlbaum.

Saxe, Geoffrey B. (1999). Sources of concepts: A cultural-developmental perspective. In Ellin Kofsky Scholnick, Katherine Nelson, Susan A. Gelman, & Patricia H. Miller (Eds.), *Conceptual development: Piaget's legacy* (pp. 253–268). Mahwah, NJ: Erlbaum.

Sayer, Avan Aihie, & Cooper, Cyrus. (2000). Early undernutrition: Good or bad for longevity? In Ronald R. Watson (Ed.), *Handbook of nutrition on the aged* (3rd ed., pp. 97–106). Boca Raton, FL: CRC Press.

Schacter, Daniel L., & Badgaiyan, Rajendra D. (2001). Neuroimaging of priming: New perspectives on implicit and explicit memory. *Current Directions in Psychological Science, 10,* 1–4.

Schaffer, H. Rudolph. (2000). The early experience assumption: Past, present, and future. *International Journal of Behavioral Development, 24,* 5–14.

Schaie, K. Warner. (1989). Perceptual speed in adulthood: Cross-sectional and longitudinal studies. *Psychology and Aging, 4,* 443–453.

Schaie, K. Warner. (1996). *Intellectual development in adulthood: The Seattle Longitudinal Study.* New York: Cambridge University Press.

Schaie, K. Warner. (2002). The impact of longitudinal studies on understanding development from young adulthood to old age. In Willard W. Hartup & Rainer K. Silbereisen (Eds.), *Growing points in developmental science: An introduction* (pp. 307–328). Philadelphia: Psychology Press.

Schaie, K. Warner, & Willis, Sherry L. (1996). *Adult development and aging.* New York: HarperCollins.

Schaie, K. Warner, & Willis, Sherry L. (2000). A stage theory model of adult cognitive development revisited. In Robert L. Rubinstein, Miriam Moss, & Morton H. Kleban (Eds.), *The many dimensions of aging* (pp. 175–193). New York: Springer.

Schardein, James L. (1976). *Drugs as teratogens.* Cleveland: CRC Press.

Scharf, Miri. (2001). A "natural experiment" in childrearing ecologies and adolescents' attachment and separation representation. *Child Development, 72,* 236–251.

Scheuffgen, Kristina, Happe, Francesca, Anderson, Mike, & Firth, Uta. (2000). High "intelligence," low "IQ"? Speed of processing and measured IQ in children with autism. *Development and Psychopathology, 12,* 83–90.

Schiller, R. (1998). The relationship of developmental tasks to life satisfaction, moral reasoning, and occupational attainment at age 28. *Adult Development, 5,* 239–254.

Schmader, Toni. (2002). Gender identification moderates the effects of stereotype threat on women's math performance. *Journal of Experimental Social Psychology, 38,* 194–201.

Schmidtke A., Weinacker B., Apter A., Batt A., Berman A., Bille-Brahe U., et al. (1999). Suicide rates in the world: Update. *Archives of Suicide Research, 5,* 81–89.

Schneider, Edward L., & Davidson, Lucy. (2003). Physical health and adult well-being. In Marc H. Bornstein, Lucy Davidson, & Corey L. M. Keyes (Eds.), *Well-being: Positive development across the life course* (pp. 407–423). Mahwah, NJ: Erlbaum.

Schneider, Wolfgang. (1998). The development of procedural metamemory in childhood and adolescence. In Guiliana Mazzoni & Thomas O. Nelson (Eds.), *Monitoring and control processes in metacognition and cognitive neuropsychology* (pp. 1–21). Mahwah, NJ: Erlbaum.

Schneider, Wolfgang, & Björklund, David. (2003). Memory and knowledge development. In Jaan Valsiner & Kevin J. Connolly (Eds.), *Handbook of developmental psychology* (pp. 370–403). London: Sage.

Schneider, Wolfgang, & Pressley, Michael. (1997). *Memory development between two and twenty* (2nd ed.). Mahwah, NJ: Erlbaum.

Schokatraylor, Elaine, Hayslip, Bert, Kaminski, Patricia, & York, Christina. (2003). Relationships between grief and family system characteristics: A cross lagged longitudinal analysis. *Death Studies, 27,* 575–601.

Schooler, Carmi, Mulatu, Mesfin Samuel, & Oates, Gary. (1999). The continuing effects of substantively complex work on the intellectual functioning of older workers. *Psychology and Aging, 14,* 483–506.

Schrag, Stephanie J., Zywicki, Sara, Farley, Monica M., Reingold, Arthur L., Harrison, Lee H., Lefkowitz, Lewis B., Hadler, James L., Danila, Richard, Cieslak, Paul R., & Schuchat, Anne. (2000). Group B streptococcal disease in the era of intrapartum antibiotic prophylaxis. *New England Journal of Medicine, 342,* 15–20.

Schreibman, Laura. (2000). Intensive behavioral/psychoeducational treatment for autism: Research needs and future directions. *Journal of Autism and Developmental Disorders, 30,* 373–378.

Schroots, Johannes J.F. (1996). Theoretical developments in the psychology of aging. *Gerontologist, 36,* 741–748.

Schroots, Johannes J. F., Fernandez-Ballesteros, Rocio, & Rudiner, Georg. (1999) *Aging in Europe.* Amsterdam: IOS Press.

Schulman, Kevin A., Berlin, Jesse, William Harless, Kerner, Jon F., Sistrunk, Shyril, Gersh, Bernard J., et al. (1999). The effect of race and sex on physician's recommendations for cardiac catherization. *New England Journal of Medicine, 340,* 618–625.

Schulz, Richard, Musa, Donald, Staszewski, James, & Siegler, Robert S. (1994). The relationship between age and major league baseball performance: Implications for development. *Psychology and Aging, 9,* 274–286.

Schwab, Jacqueline, Kulin, Howard E., Susman, Elizabeth J., Finkelstein, Jordan W., Chinchilli, Vernon M., Kunselman, Susan J., et al. (2001). The role of sex hormone replacement therapy on self-perceived competence in adolescents with delayed puberty. *Child Development, 72,* 1439–1450.

Schwartz, David, Proctor, Laura J., & Chien, Deborah H. (2001). The aggressive victim of bullying: Emotional and behavioral dysregulation as a pathway to victimization by peers. In J. E. Juvonen & S. E. Graham (Eds.), *Peer harassment in school: The plight of the vulnerable and victimized* (pp. 147–174). New York: Guilford Press.

Schweder, Richard A., Goodnow, Jacqueline, Hatano, Giyoo, LeVine, Robert A., Markus, Hazel, & Miller, Peggy. (1998). The cultural psychology of development: One mind, many mentalities. In William Damon (Series Ed.) & Richard M. Lerner (Volume Ed.), *Handbook of child psychology: Vol. 1. Theoretical models of human development* (5th ed., pp. 865–937). New York: Wiley.

Schweinhart, Lawrence J., & Weikart, David P. (1997). *Lasting differences: The High/Scope preschool curriculum comparison study through age 23.* Ypsilanti, MI: High/Scope Educational Research Foundation.

Scott, Stephen, Spender, Quentin, Doolan, Moira, Jacobs, Brian, & Aspland, Helen. (2001). Multicentre controlled trial of parenting groups for childhood antisocial behavior in clinical practice. *British Medical Journal, 323,* 194–198.

Scott-Maxwell, Florida. (1968). *The measure of my days.* New York: Knopf.

Scovel, Thomas. (1988). *A time to speak: A psycholinguistic inquiry into the critical period for human speech.* New York: Newbury House.

Scribner, R. (1996). Paradox as paradigm: The health outcomes of Mexican Americans. *American Journal of Public Health, 86,* 303–305.

Seale, Clive, & Cartwright, Ann. (1994). *The year before death.* Aldershot, England: Avebury.

See, Sheree, Kwong, T., & Ryan, Ellen Bouchard. (1999). Intergenerational communication: The survey interview as a social exchange. In Norbert Schwarz, Denise C. Park, Barbel Knauper, & Seymour Sudman (Eds.), *Cognition, aging, and self reports.* Philadelphia: Psychology Press.

Segalowitz, Sidney J., & Schmidt, Louis A. (2003). Developmental psychology and the neurosciences. In Jaan Valsiner & Kevin J. Connolly (Eds.), *Handbook of developmental psychology* (pp. 48–71). London: Sage.

Seibel, Machelle M. (1993). Medical evaluation and treatment of the infertile couple. In Machelle M. Seibel, Ann A. Kiessling, Judith Bernstein, & Susan R. Levin (Eds.), *Technology and infertility: Clinical, psychosocial, legal and ethical aspects.* New York: Springer-Verlag.

Seki, Fusako. (2001). The role of government and the family in taking care of the frail elderly. In David N. Weisstub, David C. Thomasma, Serge Gauthier, & George F. Tomossy (Eds.), *Aging: Caring for our elders,* (pp. 83–105). Dordrecht, Netherlands: Kluwer.

Selkoe, Dennis J., & Podlisny, Marcia B. (2002). Deciphering the genetic basis of Alzheimer's disease. *Annual Review of Genomics and Human Genetics, 3,* 67–99.

Seltzer, Judith A. (2000). Families formed outside of marriage. *Journal of Marriage and the Family, 62,* 1247–1268.

Seltzer, Marsha M., & Li, Lydia Wailing. (1996). The transitions of caregiving: Subjective and objective definitions. *The Gerontologist, 36.*

Sena, Rhonda, & Smith, Linda B. (1990). New evidence on the development of the word *big. Child Development, 61,* 1034–1052.

Senechal, Monique, & LeFevre, Jo-Anne. (2002). Parental involvement in the development of children's reading skill: A five-year longitudinal study. *Child Development, 73,* 445–460.

Senior, B. (1997). Team roles and team performance: Is there really a link? *Journal of Occupational and Organisational Psychology, 70,* 241–258.

Settersten, Richard A., Jr., & Andersson, Tanetta. E. (2002) Moving and still: Neighborhoods, human development, and the life course. In Richard A. Settersten, Jr., & Timothy J. Owens (Eds.) *New frontiers in socialization,* (pp. 197–227). Amsterdam: JAI.

Settersten, Richard A. Jr., & Hagestad, Gunhild. (1996). What's the latest? Cultural deadlines for educational and work transitions. *Gerontologist, 36,* 602–613.

Shahin, Hashem, Walsh, Tom, Sobe, Tama, Lynch, Eric, King, Mary-Claire, Avraham, Karen B., et al. (2002). Genetics of congenital deafness in the Palestinian population: Multiple connexin 26 alleles with shared origins in the Middle East. *Human Genetics, 110,* 284–289.

Shanley, Mary Lyndon. (2001). *Making babies, making families: What matters most in an age of reproductive technologies, surrogacy, adoption, and same-sex and unwed parents.* Boston: Beacon Press.

Shapiro, Jeremy P., Burgoon, Jeolla D., Welker, Carolyn J., & Clough, Joseph B. (2002). Evaluation of the Peacemakers Program: School-based violence prevention for students in grades four through eight. *Psychology in the Schools, 39,* 87–100.

Shatz, Marilyn. (1994). *A toddler's life: Becoming a person.* New York: Oxford University Press.

Shaw, Daniel S., Vondra, Joan I., Hommerding, Katherine Dowdell, Keenan, Kate, & Dunn, Marija G. (1994). Chronic family adversity and early child behavior problems. A longitudinal study of low income families. *Journal of Child Psychology and Psychiatry and Allied Disciplines, 35,* 1109–1122.

Shea, John B., & Powell, Geoffrey. (1996). Capturing expertise in sports. In K. Anders Ericsson (Ed.), *The road to excellence: The acquisition of expert performance in the arts and sciences, sports and games.* Mahwah, NJ: Erlbaum.

Sheehy, Gail. (1976). *Passages: Predictable crises of adult life* (1st ed). New York: Dutton.

Sheinberg, Marcia, & Fraenkel, Peter. (2001). *The relational trauma of incest.* New York: Guilford Press.

Shephard, Roy J. (2002). Constitution or environment: The basis of regional and ethnic difference in the interactions among gender, age, and functional capacity. In Roy J. Shephard (Ed.), *Gender, physical activity, and aging* (pp. 41–77). Boca Raton, FL: CRC Press.

Sherman, D.W. (1999). End-of-life care: Challenges and opportunities for health care professionals. *Hospital Journal, 14,* 109–121.

Shibusawa, Tazuko, Lubben, James, & Kitano, Harry H. L. (2001). Japanese American elderly. InLaura Katz Olson (Ed.) *Age through ethnic lenses* (pp 33–44). Lanham, MD: Rowman & Littlefield.

Shuey, Kim, & Hardy, Melissa A. (2003). Assistance to aging parents and parents-in-law: Does lineage affect family allocation decisions? *Journal of Marriage and Family, 65,* 418–431.

Shute, Nancy, Locy, Toni, & Pasternak, Douglas. (2000, March 6). The perils of pills. *U.S. News and World Report,* pp. 45–49.

Sicker, Martin. (2002). *The political economy of work in the 21st century.* Westport, CT: Quorum Books.

Sickmund, Melissa, Snyder, Howard N., & Poe-Yamagata, Eileen. (1997). *Juvenile offenders and victims: 1997 update on violence.* Washington, DC: Office of Juvenile Justice and Delinquency Prevention.

Siegel, Judith M., Yancey, Antronette K., Aneshensel, Carol S., & Schuler, Roberleigh. (1999). Body image, perceived pubertal timing, and adolescent mental health. *Journal of Adolescent Health, 25,* 155–165.

Siegler, Ilene C., Kaplan, Berton H., Von Dras, Dean D., & Mark, Daniel B. (1999). Cardiovascular health: A challenge for midlife. In Sherry L. Willis & James D. Reid (Eds.), *Life in the middle.* San Diego, CA: Academic Press.

Siegler, Robert S., & Jenkins, Eric A. (1989). *How children discover new strategies.* Hillsdale, NJ: Erlbaum.

Silk, Jennifer S., Nath, Sanjay R., Siegel, Lori R., & Kendall, Philip C. (2000). Conceptualizing mental disorders in children: Where have we been and where are we going? *Development and Psychopathology, 12,* 713–735.

Silverman, Phyllis R. (2003). Social support and mutual help for the bereaved. In Inge Corless, Barbara B.Germino, & Mary A. Pittman (Eds.). *Dying, death, and bereavement* (pp. 247–265). New York: Springer.

Silverstein, Merril, & Chen, Xuan. (1999). The impact of acculturation in Mexican American families on the quality of adult grandchild–grandparent relationships. *Journal of Marriage and the Family, 61,* 188–198.

Silverstein, Merril, & Parker, Marti G. (2002). Leisure activities and quality of life among the oldest-old in Sweden. *Research on Aging, 24,* 528–547.

Simon, Herbert A. (2001). Learning to research about learning. In Sharon M. Carver & David Klahr (Eds.), *Cognition and instruction* (pp. 205–226). Mahwah, NJ: Erlbaum.

Simonton, Dean K. (1998). Career paths and creative lives: A theoretical perspective on late-life potential. In Carolyn E. Adams-Price (Ed.), *Creativity and successful aging: Theoretical and empirical approaches* (pp. 3–18). New York: Springer.

Singer, Lynn T. (1999). Advances and redirections in understanding effects of fetal drug exposure. *Journal of Drug Issues, 29*(2), 253–262.

Singer, Lynn T., Arendt, Robert, Minnes, Sonia, Farkas, Kathleen, Salvator, Ann, Kirchner, H. Lester, Kliegman, Robert. (2002). Cognitive and motor outcomes of cocaine-exposed infants. *Journal of the American Medical Association, 287*(15), 1952–1960.

Singer, Mark I., Slovak, Karen, Frierson, Tracey, & York, Peter. (1999). Viewing preferences, symptoms of psychological trauma, and violent behaviors among children who watch television. *Journal of the American Academy of Child and Adolescent Psychiatry, 37,* 1041–1048.

Singer, Wolf. (2003). The nature–nurture problem revisited. In Ursula M. Staudinger & Ulman E. R. Lindenberger (Eds.), *Understanding human development: Dialogues with lifespan psychology* (pp. 437–447). Dordrecht, Netherlands: Kluwer.

Singh, Gopal K. (2003). Area deprivation and widening inequalities in US Mortality, 1969–1998. *American Journal of Public Health, 93,* 1137–1143.

Singh, Gopal K., & Yu, Stella M. (1996). Adverse pregnancy outcomes differences between U.S.- and foreign-born women in major U.S. racial and ethnic groups. *American Journal of Public Health, 86,* 837–843.

Singh, Susheela, Wulf, Deirdre, Samara, Renee, & Cuca, Yvette P. (2000). Gender differences in the timing of first intercourse: Data from 14 countries. *International Family Planning Perspectives, 26,* 21–28, 43.

Sinnot, Jan D. (1998) *The development of logic in adulthood: Postformal thought and its applications.* New York: Plenum Press.

Siperstein, Gary N., Leffert, James S., & Wenz-Gross, Melodie. (1997). The quality of friendships between children with and without learning problems. *American Journal on Mental Retardation, 102,* 111–125.

Siqueira, Lorena, Rolnitzky, Linda M., & Rickart, Vaughn I. (2001). Smoking cessation in adolescents: the role of nicotine dependence, stress, and coping methods. *Archives of Pediatrics and Adolescent Medicine, 155,* 489–495.

Skinner, Burrhus Frederic. (1953). *Science and human behavior.* New York: Macmillan.

Skinner, Burrhus Frederic. (1957). *Verbal behavior.* New York: Appleton-Century-Crofts.

Sliwinski, Martin J., Hofer, Scott M., Hall, Charles, Buschke, Herman, & Lipton, Richard B. (2003). Modeling memory decline in older adults: The importance of preclinical dementia, attrition, and chronological age. *Psychology and Aging, 18,* 658–671.

Slobin, Dan I. (2001). Form-function relations: How do children find out what they are? In Melissa Bowerman & Stephen C. Levinson (Eds.), *Language acquisition and conceptual development* (pp. 406–449). Cambridge, UK: Cambridge University Press.

Small, Brent J., Fratiglioni, Laura, von Strauss, Eva, & Bäckman, Lars. (2003). Terminal decline and cognitive performance in very old age: Does cause of death matter? *Psychology and Aging, 18,* 193–202.

Small, Neil. (2001). Theories of grief: A critical review. In Jenny Hockey, Jeanne Katz, & Neil Small (Eds.), *Grief, mourning, and death ritual* (pp. 19–48). Buckingham, England: Open University Press.

Smeeding, Timothy M., & Phillips, Katherin Ross. (2002). Cross-national differences in employment and economic sufficiency. In Frank F. Furstenberg (Ed.), *Early adulthood in cross-national perspective. Annals of the and American academy of Political and Social Sciences, 580,* 103–133.

Smetana, Judith G., & Asquith, Pamela. (1994). Adolescents' and parents' conceptions of parental authority and adolescent autonomy. *Child Development, 65,* 1147–1162.

Smil, Vaclav. (2003). *Energy at the crossroads.* Cambridge, MA: MIT Press.

Smith, Glenn E., Petersen, Ronald C., Ivnik, Robert J., Malec, James F., & Tangalos, Eric G. (1996). Subjective memory complaints, psychological distress, and longitudinal change in objective memory performance. *Psychology and Aging, 11,* 272–279.

Smith, Gregory C. (2003). How caregiving grandparents view support groups: An exploratory study. In Bert Hayslip, Jr., & Julie Hicks Patrick (Eds.), *Working with custodial grandparents* (pp. 69–91). New York: Springer.

Smith, Jacqui, & Baltes, Paul B. (1990). Wisdom-related knowledge: Age/cohort differences in response to life-planning problems. *Developmental Psychology, 26,* 494–505.

Smith, Jacqui, & Baltes, Paul B. (1999). Trends and profiles of psychological functioning in very old age. In P. B. Baltes & K. U. Mayer (Eds.), *The Berlin aging study: Aging from 70 to 100.* New York: Cambridge University Press.

Smith, Jacqui, & Goodnow, Jacqueline J. (1999). Unasked-for support and unsolicited advice: Age and the quality of social experience. *Psychology and Aging, 14,* 108–121.

Smith, Leslie. (2002). *Reasoning by mathematical induction in children's arithmetic.* Amsterdam, Netherlands: Pergamon/Elsevier Science.

Smith, Linda B. (1995). Self-organizing processes in learning to learn words: Development is not induction. In Charles Alexander Nelson (Ed.), *Basic and applied perspectives on learning, cognition, and development.* The Minnesota Symposium on Child Psychology, Vol. 28. (pp. 1–32). Mahwah, NJ: Erlbaum.

Smith, Peter K., Morita, Yohji, Junger-Tas, Josine, Olweus, Dan, Catalano, Richard F., & Slee, Phillip T. (1999). *The nature of school bullying: A cross-national perspective.* London: Routledge.

Smock, P. J. (2000). Cohabitation in the United States: An appraisal of research themes, findings, and implications. *American Review of Sociology, 26,* 1–20.

Snarey, John R. (1993). *How fathers care for the next generation: A four-decade study.* Cambridge, MA: Harvard University Press.

Sniezek, Janet A. (1999). Issues in self-control theory and research: Confidence, doubt, expectancy bias, and opposing forces. In Robert S. Wyer (Ed.), *Advances in social cognition: Vol. 12. Perspectives on behavioral self-regulation* (pp. 217–228). Mahwah, NJ: Erlbaum.

Snijders, R. J. M., & Nicolaides, K. H. (1996). *Ultrasound markers for fetal chromosomal defects.* New York: Parthenon.

Snow, Catherine E. (1984). Parent-child interaction and the development of communicative ability. In Richard L. Schiefelbusch & Joanne Pickar (Eds.), *The acquisition of communicative competence* (pp. 69–107). Baltimore: University Park Press.

Snowden, David. (2001). *Aging with grace.* New York: Bantam.

Snyder, Howard N. (1997). *Serious, violent, and chronic juvenile offenders: An assessment of the extent of and trends in officially recognized serious criminal behavior in a delinquent population.* Pittsburgh: National Center for Juvenile Justice.

Snyder, Lisa. (1999). *Speaking our minds.* New York: Freeman.

Society for Research in Child Development (SRCD). (1996). Ethical standards for research with children. *SRCD Directory of Members,* 337–339.

Sofie, Cecilia A., & Riccio, Cynthia A. (2002). A comparison of multiple methods for the identification of children with reading disabilities. *Journal of Learning Disabilities, 35,* 234–244.

Soldo, Beth J. (1996). Cross pressures on middle-aged adults: A broader view. *Journals of Gerontology: Series B: Psychological Sciences & Social Sciences, 51B,* S271–S273.

Solomon, Jennifer Crew, & Marx, Jonathan. (2000). The physical, mental, and social health of custodial grandparents. In Bert Hayslip Jr. & Robin Goldberg-Glen (Eds.), *Grandparents raising grandchildren: Theoretical, empirical, and clinical perspectives* (pp. 183–205). New York: Springer.

Sourcebook of Criminal Justice Statistics Online. (Kathleen Maguire & Ann L. Pastore, Eds.). (2003). *Sourcebook of Criminal Justice Statistics, 2002* [Electronic version]. Retrieved February 3, 2004, from http://www.albany.edu/sourcebook/

Spearman, Charles. (1927). *The abilities of man.* New York: Macmillan.

Spelke, Elizabeth S. (1993). Physical knowledge in infancy: reflections on Piaget's theory. In Susan Carey & Rochel Gelman (Eds.), *The epigenesis of mind: Essay on biology and cognition.* Hillsdale, NJ: Erlbaum.

Spock, Benjamin. (1976). *Baby and child care.* New York: Pocket Books.

Springer, Sally P., & Deutsch, Georg. (1998). *Left brain, right brain: Perspectives from cognitive neuroscience* (5th ed.). New York: Freeman.

Sputa, Cheryl L., & Paulson, Sharon E. (1995). Birth order and family size: Influences on adolescents' achievement and related parenting behaviors. *Psychological Reports, 76,* 43–51.

Sroufe, L. Alan. (1996). *Emotional development: The organization of emotional life in the early years.* Cambridge: Cambridge University Press.

Stack, Charles D., & Burton, Linda M. (1993). Kinscripts. *Journal of Comparative Family Studies, 24,* 157–170.

Stack, Steven, & Eshleman, J. Ross. (1998). Marital status and happiness: A 17-nation study. *Journal of Marriage and the Family, 60,* 527–537.

Stanovich, Keith E. (1999). *Who is rational? Studies of individual differences in reasoning.* Mahwah, NJ: Erlbaum.

Stanovich, Keith E. (2000). *Progress in understanding reading: Scientific foundations and new frontiers.* New York: Guilford.

Starkes, Janet L., Deakin, Janice M., Allard, Fran, Hodges, Nicola J., & Hayes, April. (1996). Deliberate practice in sports: What is it, anyway? In Karl Anders Ericsson (Ed.), *The road to excellence: The acquisition of expert performance in the arts and sciences, sports and games* (pp. 81–106). Mahwah, NJ: Erlbaum.

Starkstein, Sergio E., & Merello, Marcelo. (2002). *Psychiatric and cognitive disorders in Parkinson's disease.* Cambridge, England: Cambridge University Press

Stattin, Hakan, & Kerr, Margaret. (2000). Parental monitoring: A reinterpretation. *Child Development, 71,* 1072–1085.

Stattin, Hakan, & Trost, Kari. (2000). When do preschool conduct problems link to future social adjustment problems and when do they not? In Lars R. Bergman, Robert B. Cairns, Lars-Goran Nilsson, & Lars Nystedt (Eds.), *Developmental science and the holistic approach* (pp. 349–375). Mahwah, NJ: Erlbaum.

Staudinger, Ursula M. (1999). Social cognition and a psychological approach to an art of life. In Thomas M. Hess & Fredda Blanchard-Fields (Eds.), *Social cognition and aging.* San Diego, CA: Academic Press.

Staudinger, Ursula M., & Bluck, Susan. (2001). A view on midlife development from a life-span theory. In Lachman, Margie E. (Ed.) *Handbook of midlife development.* New York: Wiley.

Staudinger, Ursula M. & Lindenberger, Ulman. (2003). Why read another book on human development? Understanding human development takes a metatheory and multiple disciplines. In Ursula M. Staudinger & Ulman Lindenberger (Eds.), *Understanding human development: Dialogues with life-span psychology.* (pp 1–13). Dordrecht, Netherlands: Kluwer.

Staudinger, Ursula M., & Werner, Ines. (2003). Wisdom: Its social nature and lifespan development. In Jaan Valsinger & Kevin J. Connolly (Eds.), *Handbook of developmental psychology* (pp. 584–600). London: Sage.

Stearns, Stephen C., & Partridge, Linda. (2001). The genetics of aging in *Drosophila.* In Edward J. Masoro & Steven N. Austad (Eds.), *Handbook of the biology of aging* (pp. 353–368). San Diego, CA: Academic Press.

Stecher, Brian M., & Bohrnstedt, George W. (2000). *Class size reduction in California: The 1998–99 evaluation findings.* Sacramento, CA: California Department of Education.

Steele, Claude M. (1997). A threat in the air: How stereotypes shape the intellectual identities and performance of women and African-Americans. *American Psychologist, 52,* 613—629.

Steele, Kenneth M., Bass, Karen E., & Crook, Melissa D. (1999). The mystery of the Mozart effect: Failure to replicate. *Psychological Science, 10,* 366–369.

Steinberg, Adria. (1993). *Adolescents and schools: Improving the fit.* Cambridge, MA: Harvard Education Letter.

Steinberg, Laurence, & Morris, Amanda Sheffield. (2001). Adolescent development. *Annual Review of Psychology, 52,* 83–110.

Steinberg, Lawrence, & Dornbusch, Sanford M. (1991). Negative correlates of part-time employment during adolescence: Replication and elaboration. *Developmental Psychology, 27,* 304–313.

Stel, Vianda S., Smit, Johannes H., Pluijm, Saskia M. F., & Lips, Paul. (2004). Consequences of falling in older men and women and risk factors for health service use and functional decline. *Age and Ageing, 33,* 58–65.

Stern, Daniel N. (1985). *The interpersonal world of the infant: A view from psychoanalysis and developmental psychology.* New York: Basic Books.

Stern, Paul C., & Carstensen, Laura L. (Eds.). (2000). *The aging mind: Opportunities in cognitive research.* Washington, DC: National Academies Press.

Sternberg, Robert J. (1988). Intellectual development: Psychometric and information-processing approaches. In M.H. Bornstein & M.E. Lamb (Eds.), *Developmental psychology: An advanced textbook* (2nd ed.). Hillsdale, NJ: Erlbaum.

Sternberg, Robert J. (1988). *The triarchic mind: A new theory of human intelligence.* New York: Viking Press.

Sternberg, Robert J. (1996). *Successful intelligence.* New York: Simon & Schuster.

Sternberg, Robert J. (2002). Everything you need to know to understand the current controversies you learned from psychological research: A comment on the Rind and Lilienfeld controversies. *American Psychologist, 57,* 193–197.

Sternberg, Robert J. (2003). *Wisdom, intelligence, and creativity synthesized.* New York: Cambridge University Press.

Sternberg, Robert J., Forsythe, George B., Hedlund, Jennifer, Horvath, Joseph A., Wagner, Richard K., Williams, Wendy M., et al. (2000). *Practical intelligence in everyday life.* New York: Cambridge University Press.

Sternberg, Robert J., & Grigorenko, Elena L. (Eds.). (2002). *The general factor of intelligence: How general is it?* Mahwah, NJ: Erlbaum.

Sternberg, Robert J., Grigorenko, Elena Y., & Bundy, Donald A. (2001). The predictive value of IQ. *Merrill-Palmer Quarterly, 47,* 1–41.

Sternberg, Robert J., Grigorenko, Elena L., & Singer, Jerome L. (Eds.). (2004). *Creativity: From potential to realization.* Washington, DC: American Psychological Association.

Sternberg, Robert J., & Horvath, Joseph A. (Eds.). (1999). *Tacit knowledge in professional practice: Researcher and practitioner perspectives.* Mahwah, NJ: Erlbaum.

Sterns, Harvey L., & Huyck, Margaret Hellie. (2001). The role of work in midlife. In Margie E. Lachman (Ed.), *Handbook of midlife development* (pp. 447–486). New York: Wiley.

Stevens, Judy A. (2002–2003). Falls among older adults: Public health impact and prevention strategies. *Generations, 26*(4): 7–14.

Stevenson, Harold W., Hofer, Barbara K., & Randel, Bruce. (2000). Mathematics achievement and attitudes about mathematics in China and the West. *Journal of Psychology in Chinese Societies, 1*(1), 1–16.

Stevenson, Jim. (1999). The treatment of the long-term sequelae of child abuse. *Journal of Child Psychology and Psychiatry and Allied Disciplines, 40,* 89–111.

Stewart, A. W., Mitchell, E. A., Pearce, N., Strachan, D. P., & Weiland, S. K. (2001). The relationship of per capita gross national product to the prevalence of symptoms of asthma and other atopic diseases in children (ISAAC). *International Journal of Epidemiology, 30*(1), 173–179.

Stewart, Abigail J., & Ostrove, Joan M. (1998). Women's personality in middle age: Gender, history, and midcourse corrections. *American Psychologist, 53,* 1185–1194.

Stewart, Anita L., & King, Abby C. (1994). Conceptualizing and measuring quality of life in older populations. In Ronald P. Abeles, Helen C. Gift, & Marcia C. Ory (Eds.),. *Aging and quality of life.* New York: Springer.

Stewart, Deborah A. (1997). Adolescent sexual abuse, sexual assault, and rape. In Adele Dellenbaugh Hofmann & Donald Everett Greydanus (Eds.), *Adolescent medicine* (3rd ed.). Stamford, CT: Appleton & Lange.

Stewart, Sunita Mahtani, & Bond, Michael Harris. (2002). A critical look at parenting research from the mainstream: Problems uncovered while adapting Western research to non-Western cultures. *British Journal of Developmental Psychology, 20*(3), 379–392.

Stewart, Susan D., Manning, Wendy D., & Smock, Pamela J. (2003). Union formation among men in the U. S.: Does having children matter? *Journal of Marriage and Family, 65,* 90–104.

Stigler, James W., & Hiebert, James. (1999). *The teaching gap: Best ideas from the world's teachers for improving education in the classroom.* New York: Free Press.

Stiles, Joan. (1998). The effects of early focal brain injury on lateralization of cognitive function. *Current Directions in Psychological Science, 7,* 21–26.

Stipek, Deborah J., Feiler, Rachell, Daniels, Denise, & Milburn, Sharon. (1995). Effects of different instructional approaches on young children's achievement and motivation. *Child Development, 66,* 209–223.

Stones, Michael J., &Kozma, Albert. (1996). Activity, exercise and behavior. In James E. Birren and K. Warner Schaie (Eds.), *Handbook of the psychology of aging.* San Diego, CA: Academic Press.

Storch, Eric A., & Storch, Jason B. (2002). Fraternities, sororities, and academic dishonesty. *College Student Journal, 36.*

Strachan, D. P. (1999). The epidemiology of childhood asthma. *Allergy, 54,* 7–11.

Straus, Murray A., & Donnelly, Denise A. (1994). *Beating the devil out of them: Corporal punishment in American families.* New York: Lexington Books.

Straus, Murray. A., & Gelles, Richard. J. (Eds.). (1995). *Physical violence in American families: Risk factors and adaptations to violence in 8,415 families.* New Brunswick, NJ: Transaction.

Strauss, David, & Eyman, Richard K. (1996). Mortality of people with mental retardation in California with and without Down syndrome, 1986–1991. *American Journal on Mental Retardation, 100,* 643–653.

Strawbridge, William J., Wallhagen, Margaret I., & Shema, Sarah J. (2000). New NHLBI clinical guidelines for obesity and overweight: Will they promote health? *American Journal of Public Health, 90,* 340–343.

Streissguth, Ann P., & Connor, Paul D. (2001). Fetal alcohol effects and other effects of prenatal alcohol: Developmental cognitive neuroscience implications. In Charles A. Nelson & Monica Luciana (Eds.), *Handbook of developmental cognitive neuroscience.* Cambridge, MA: MIT Press.

Strom, Robert D., & Strom, Shirley K. (2000). Goals for grandparents and support groups. In Bert Hayslip Jr. & Robin Goldberg-Glen (Eds.), *Grandparents raising grandchildren: Theoretical, empirical, and clinical perspectives* (pp. 289–303). New York: Springer.

Stuss, Donald T., & Binns, Malcolm A. (2001). Aging: Not an escarpment, but multiple slopes. In M. Naveh-Benjamin, M. Moscovitch, & H.L. Roediger III (Eds.), *Perspectives on human memory and cognitive aging: Essays in honour of Fergus Craik* (pp. 334–347). East Sussex, UK: Psychology Press.

Suarez-Orozco, Carola, & Suarez-Orozco, Marcelo M. (2001). *Children of immigration.* Cambridge, MA: Harvard University Press.

Suarez-Orozco, Marcello M. (2001). Globalization, immigration and education: The research agenda. *Harvard Educational Review, 71,* 345–365.

Sullivan, Sheila. (1999). *Falling in love.* London: Macmillan.

Sulloway, Frank J. (1997). *Born to rebel: Birth order, family dynamics, and creative lives.* New York: Vintage Books.

Suls, Jerry, Lemos, Katherine, & Stewart, H. Lockett. (2002). Self-esteem, construal, and comparison with the self, friends, and peers. *Journal of Personality and Social Psychology, 82,* 252–261.

Suomi, Stephen. (2002). Parents, peers, and the process of socialization in primates. In John G. Borkowski, Sharon Landesman Ramey, & Marie Bristol-Power (Eds.), *Parenting and the child's world: Influences on academic, intellectual, and social-emotional development* (pp. 265–279). Mahwah, NJ: Erlbaum.

Susman, Elizabeth J. (1997). Modeling developmental complexity in adolescence: Hormones and behavior in context. *Journal of Research on Adolescence, 7,* 283–306.

Sutherland, Lisa. (2003). Report presented at Conference on Experimental Biology, San Diego, CA.

Sutton-Smith, Brian. (1997). *The ambiguity of play.* Cambridge, MA: Harvard University Press.

Swain, Merrill, & Johnson, Robert K. (1997). Introduction. In Robert K. Johnson & Merrill Swain (Eds.), *Immersion education: International perspectives.* Cambridge, England: Cambridge University Press.

Swain, S. O. (1992). Men's friendships with women: Intimacy, sexual boundaries, and the informant role. In P.M. Nardi (Ed.), *Gender in intimate relationships.* Belmont, CA: Wadsworth.

Swanson, H. Lee. (1999). *Interventions for students with learning disabilities: A meta-analysis of treatment outcomes.* New York: Guilford.

Swenson, Nora C. (2000). Comparing traditional and collaborative settings for language intervention. *Communication Disorders Quarterly, 22,* 12–18.

Szatmari, Peter. (2001, Spring). Thinking about autism, Asperger disorder, and PDD-NOS. *Newsletter of the Centre for Studies of Children at Risk, 34,* 24–34.

Szinovacz, Maximiliane E. (2000). Changes in housework after retirement: A panel analysis. *Journal of Marriage and the Family, 62,* 78–92.

Szkrybalo, Joel, & Ruble, Diane N. (1999). "God made me a girl": Sex-category constancy judgments and explanations revisited. *Developmental Psychology, 35,* 392–402.

Takahashi, T., Nowakowski, Richard S., & Caviness, Verne S., Jr. (2001). Neocortical neurogenesis: Regulation, control points, and a strategy of structural variation. In Charles A. Nelson & Monica Luciana (Eds.), *Handbook of developmental cognitive neuroscience.* Cambridge, MA: MIT Press.

Talamantes, Melissa A., Gomez, Celine, & Braun, Kathryn L. (2000). Advance directives and end-of-life care: The Hispanic perspective. In Kathryn Braun, James H. Pietsch, & Patricia L. Blanchette (Eds.), *Cultural issues in end-of-life decision making* (pp. 1–12). Thousand Oaks, CA: Sage.

Talukder, M. Q.-K. (2000). The importance of breastfeeding and strategies to sustain high breastfeeding rates. In Anthony Costello & Dharma Manandhar (Eds.), *Improving newborn infant health in developing countries.* London: Imperial College Press.

Tamis-LeMonda, Catherine S., Bornstein, Marc H., & Baumwell, Lisa. (2001). Maternal responsiveness and children's achievement of language milestones. *Child Development, 72,* 748–767.

Tanaka, Takeo. (2001). The identity formation of the victim of "shunning." *School Psychology International, 22,* 463–476.

Tangney, June Price. (2001). Constructive and destructive aspects of shame and guilt. In Arthur C. Bohart & Deborah J. Stipek (Eds.), *Constructive and destructive behavior: Implications for family, school and society* (pp. 127–145). Washington, DC: American Psychological Association.

Tannen, Deborah. (1990). *You just don't understand.* New York: Morrow.

Tanner, James M. (1978). *Fetus into man: Physical growth from conception to maturity.* Cambridge, MA: Harvard University Press.

Tappenden, Eric C. (1996). Ethical questions in changing funeral and burial practices. In John D. Morgan (Ed.), *Ethical issues in the care of the dying and bereaved aged.* Amityville, NY: Baywood.

Tarter, Ralph E., Vanyukov, Michael, Giancola, Peter, Dawes, Michael, Blackson, Timothy, Mezzich, Ada, et al. (1999). Etiology of early age onset substance use disorder: A maturational perspective. *Development and Psychopathology, 11,* 657–683.

Tatar, Moshe. (1998). Teachers as significant others: Gender differences to secondary school pupils' perceptions. *British Journal of Educational Psychology, 68,* 217–227.

Tatz, Colin. (2001). *Aboriginal suicide is different: A portrait of life and self destruction.* Canberra: Aboriginal Studies Press.

Taylor, Donald H., Hasselblad, Vic, Henley, Jane, Thun, Michael, & Sloan, Frank A. (2002). Benefits of smoking cessation for longevity. *American Journal of Public Health, 92,* 990–996.

Taylor, H. Gerry, Klein, Nancy, & Hack, Maureen. (2000). School-age consequences of birth weight less than 750 grams: A review and an update. *Developmental Neuropsychology, 17,* 289–321.

Tebbutt, Tom. (2003, December 24). Injury, Henin-Hardenne clip Serena's wings. *The Globe & Mail* (Toronto), p. S4.

Teicher, Martin H. (2002). Scars that won't heal: The neurobiology of child abuse. *Scientific American, 286*(3), 68–75.

Teitelbaum, Philip, Teitelbaum, Osnat, Nye, Jennifer, Fryman, Joshua, & Maurer, Ralph G. (1998). Movement analysis in infancy may be useful for early diagnosis of autism. *Proceedings of the National Academy of Sciences, 23,* 13982–13987.

Teitler, Julian. (2002). Trends in youth sexual initiation and fertility in developed countries: 1960–1995. *The Annals of the American Academy of Political and Social Science, 580,* 134–152.

Tenenbaum, Harriet R., & Leaper, Campbell. (2002). Are parents' gender schemas related to their children's gender-related cognition? A meta-analysis. *Developmental Psychology, 38,* 615–630.

Thelen, Esther, Corbetta, D., Kamm, K., Spencer, J.P., Schneider, K., & Zernicke, R.F. (1993). The transition to reaching: Mapping intention and intrinsic dynamics. *Child Development, 64,* 1058–1098.

Thoits, Peggy A. (1992). Identity structures and psychological well-being. Gender and marital status comparisons. *Social Psychology Quarterly, 55,* 236–256.

Thomas, Alexander, & Chess, Stella. (1977). *Temperament and development.* New York: Brunner/Mazel.

Thomas, Alexander, Chess, Stella, Birch, Herbert G., Hertzig, Margaret E., & Korn, Sam. (1963). *Behavioral individuality in early childhood.* New York: New York University Press.

Thomasma, David C., Kimbrough-Kushner, Thomasine, Kimsma, Gerrit K., & Ciesielski-Carlucci, Chris (Eds.). (1998). *Asking to die: Inside the Dutch debate about euthanasia.* Dordrecht, Netherlands: Kluwer Academic Publishers.

Thompson, Richard F. (2000). *The Brain* (3rd ed.). New York: Worth.

Thompson, Ron A., & Sherman, Roberta. (1993). *Helping athletes with eating disorders.* Bloomington, IN: Human Kinetics Books.

Thompson, Ross A. (1992). Developmental changes in research risk and benefit: A changing calculus of concerns. In Barbara Stanley & Joan E. Sieber (Eds.), *Social research on children and adolescents: Ethical issues* (pp. 31–64). Newbury Park, CA: Sage.

Thompson, Ross A. (1998). Early sociopersonality development. In William Damon (Series Ed.), Nancy Eisenberg (Volume Ed.), *Handbook of child psychology: Vol. 3. Social, emotional, and personality development* (5th ed., pp. 24–104). New York: Wiley.

Thompson, Ross A., & Nelson, Charles A. (2001). Developmental science and the media: Early brain development. *American Psychologist, 56,* 5–15.

Thompson, Ross A., & Wyatt, Jennifer M. (1999). Values, policy and research on divorce: Seeking fairness for children. In

Ross A. Thompson & Paul R. Amato (Eds.), *The postdivorce family: Children, parenting, and society.* Thousand Oaks, CA: Sage.

Thorson, J.A. (1995). *Aging in a changing society.* Belmont, CA: Wadsworth.

Timiras, Mary Letitia. (2003). The skin. In Paola S. Timiras (Ed.), *Physiological basis of aging and geriatrics* (3rd ed., pp. 397–404). Boca Raton, FL: CRC Press.

Timiras, Paola S. (2003). The adrenals and pituitary. In Paola S. Timiras (Ed.), *Physiological basis of aging and geriatrics* (3rd ed., pp. 167–188). Boca Raton, FL: CRC Press.

Timiras, Paola. (2003). Cardiovascular alterations with aging: Atherosclerosis and coronary heart disease. In Paola S. Timiras (Ed.), *Physiological basis of aging and geriatrics* (3rd ed., pp. 375–395). Boca Raton, FL: CRC Press.

Timiras, Paola S. (2003). The skeleton, joints, and skeletal and cardiac muscles. In Paola S. Timiras (Ed.) *Physiological basis of aging and geriatrics* (3rd ed., pp. 375–395). Boca Raton, FL: CRC Press

Tobin, Sheldon S. (1996). Cherished possessions: The meaning of things. *Generations, 20,* 46–48.

Toledo, J. Rafael, Hayslip, Bert, Jr., Emick, Michelle A., Toledo, Cecilia, & Henderson, Craig E. (2000). Cross-cultural differences in custodial grandparenting. In Bert Hayslip Jr. & Robin Goldberg-Glen (Eds.), *Grandparents raising grandchildren: Theoretical, empirical, and clinical perspectives* (pp. 107–123). New York: Springer.

Tomasello, Michael. (2001). Perceiving intentions and learning words in the second year of life. In Melissa Bowerman & Stephen C. Levinson (Eds.), *Language acquisition and conceptual development* (pp. 132–158). Cambridge, UK: Cambridge University Press.

Torff, Bruce, & Gardner, Howard. (1999). The vertical mind—The case for multiple intelligences. In M. Anderson (Ed.), *The development of intelligence* (pp. 139–159). Hove, England: Psychology Press.

Torff, Bruce, & Sternberg, Robert J. (Eds.). (2001). *Understanding and teaching the intuitive mind: Student and teacher learning.* Mahwah, NJ: Erlbaum.

Torney-Purta, Judith, Lehmann, Rainer, Oswald, Hans, & Schulz, Wolfram. (2001). *Citizenship and education in twenty-eight countries: Civic knowledge and engagement at age fourteen.* Amsterdam: IEA (International Association for the Evaluation of Educational Achievement).

Tornstam, Lars. (1999–2000). Transcendence in later life. *Generations, 23*(4), 10–14.

Torres-Gil, Fernanda M. (1992). The new aging. New York: Auburn House.

Townsend, John Marshall. (1998). *What women want–What men want: Why the sexes still see love and commitment so differently.* New York: Oxford.

Townsend, John W. (2003). Reproductive behavior in the context of global population. *American Psychologist, 58,* 197–204.

Townsend, Nicholas. (2002). Cultural contexts of father involvement. In Catherine S. Tamis-Lemonda & Natasha Cabrera (Eds.), *Handbook of father involvement: Multidisciplinary perspectives* (pp. 249–277). Mahwah, NJ: Erlbaum.

Toyama, Miki. (2001). Developmental changes in social comparison in preschool and elementary school children: Perceptions, feelings, and behavior. *Japanese Journal of Educational Psychology, 49,* 500–507.

Tremblay, Richard E. (2000). Quoted in Constance Holden. The violence of the lambs. *Science, 298,* 580–581.

Troll, Lillian E. (1996). Modified-extended families over time: Discontinuity in parts; continuity in wholes. In Vern L. Bengston (Ed.), *Adulthood and aging: Research on continuities and discontinuities* (pp. 246–268). New York: Springer.

Troll, Lillian E., & Skaff, Marilyn McKean. (1997). Perceived continuity of self in very old age. *Psychology and Aging, 12,* 162–169.

True, Mary McMahan, Pisani, Lelia, & Oumar, Fadimata. (2001). Infant-mother attachment among the Dogon of Mali. *Child Development, 72,* 1451–1466.

Truitner, Ken, & Truitner, Nga. (1993). Death and dying in Buddhism. In Donald P. Irish, Kathleen F. Lundquist, & Vivian Jenkins Nelsen (Eds.), *Ethnic variations in dying, death, and grief.* Washington, DC: Taylor & Francis.

Tucker, G. Richard. (1998). A global perspective on multilingualism and multilingual education. In Jasone Cenoz & Fred Genesee (Eds.), *Beyond bilingualism: Multilingualism and multilingual education.* Clevedon, England: Multilingual Matters.

Tuomilehto, J., Lindstorm J., Eriksson J.G., Valle T.T., Hamalainein H., Ilanne-Parikka P., et al, for the Finnish Diabetes Prevention Study Group. (2001). Prevention of Type 2 diabetes mellitus by changes in lifestyle among subjects with impaired glucose tolerance. *New England Journal of Medicine, 344,* 1343–1350.

Turkheimer, Eric, Haley, Andreana, Waldron, Mary, D'Onofrio, Brian, & Gottesman, Irving I. (2003). Socioeconomic status modifies heritabilty of IQ in young children. *Psychological Science, 14,* 623–628.

Turkheimer, Eric, & Waldron, Mary. (2000). Nonshared environment: A theoretical, methodological, and quantitative review. *Psychological Bulletin, 126,* 78–108.

Turley, Ruth N. Lopez. (2003). Are children of young mothers disadvantaged because of their mother's age or family background? *Child Development, 74,* 465–474.

Twenge, Jean M., Campbell, W. Keith, & Foster, Craig A. (2003). Parenthood and marital satisfaction: A meta-analytic review. *Journal of Marriage and Family, 65,* 574–583.

Uhlenberg, Peter. (1996). The burden of aging: A theoretical framework for understanding the shifting balance of caregiving and care receiving as cohorts age. *Gerontologist, 36,* 761–767.

Umberson, Debra. (1992). Relationship between adult children and their parents: Psychological consequences for both generations. *Journal of Marriage and the Family, 54,* 664–674.

Ungar, Michael T. (2000). The myth of peer pressure. *Adolescence, 35,* 167–180.

United Nations. (1991). *Human development report, 1991.* New York: Oxford University Press.

United Nations. (2002). *Statistical Yearbook.* Paris: UNESCO.

United Nations Development Program. (2001). *Human Development Report.* New York: Oxford University Press.

U.S. Department of Health and Human Services. (2002, February 14). Annual update of HHS poverty guidelines. *Federal Register, 67,* 6931–6933.

U.S. Bureau of the Census. (1972). *Statistical abstract of the United States, 1972* (92nd ed.). Washington, DC: U.S. Department of Commerce.

U.S. Bureau of the Census. (1975). *Statistical abstract of the United States, 1975* (95th ed.). Washington, DC: U.S. Government Printing Office

U.S. Bureau of the Census. (1999). *Statistical abstract of the United States, 1999* (119th ed.). Washington, DC: U.S. Government Printing Office.

U.S. Bureau of the Census. (2000). *Statistical abstract of the United States, 2000* (120th ed.). Washington, DC: U.S. Department of Commerce.

U.S. Bureau of the Census. (2001). *Statistical abstract of the United States, 2001* (121st ed.). Washington, DC: U.S. Department of Commerce.

U.S. Bureau of the Census. (2002) *National Vital Statistics Reports, 50*(5).

U.S. Bureau of the Census. (2002). *Statistical abstract of the United States, 2002* (122nd ed.). Washington, DC: U.S. Government Printing Office.

U.S. Bureau of the Census. (2003, May 20). *Current Population Survey.*

U.S. Bureau of the Census. (2004). International Data Base

U.S. Bureau of Labor Statistics. (2001, November). *Monthly Labor Review.*

U.S. Bureau of Labor Statistics. (2002). *Comparative civilian labor force statistics, ten countries, 1959–2001.*

U.S. Centers for Disease Control and Prevention (2001, August). Vaccines: An issue of trust. *Consumer Reports,* p. 19.

U.S. Department of Education. National Center for Education Statistics. (2000.) *Digest of education statistics, 1999* (NCES 2000-031). Washington, DC: U.S. Government Printing Office.

U.S. Department of Education. National Center for Education Statistics. (Eds.: Thomas D. Snyder, & Charlene M. Hoffman) (2001). *Digest of Education Statistics, 2000* (NCES 2001-034). Washington, DC: U.S. Government Printing Office.

U.S. Department of Health and Human Services. (2000). *Trends in the well-being of America's children and youth* (No. 017-022-01484-0). Washington, DC: U.S. Government Printing Office.

U.S. Department of Health and Human Services. (2002, February 14). Annual update of HHS poverty guidelines. *Federal Register, 67,* 6931–6933.

U.S. Department of Health and Human Services, Administration on Children, Youth and Families. (2001). *Child maltreatment 1999: Reports from the states to the national child abuse and neglect data system.* Washington, DC: U.S. Government Printing Office.

U.S. Department of Health and Human Services. Administration on Children, Youth and Families. (2003). *Child Maltreatment [1990-]2001.* Washington, DC: U.S. Government Printing Office.

U.S. Department of Justice (2001). Bureau of Justice Statistics, National Crime Victimization Survey, 2001.

U.S. Department of Justice. (2001). *Justice sourcebook, 2001.* Washington, DC: Bureau of Justice Statistics.

U.S. Department of Justice (2004). *Source book of Criminal Justice Statistics.* Washington DC.

United States Preventive Task Force. (2002). Postmenopausal hormone replacement therapy for primary prevention of chronic conditions: Recommendations and rationale. *Annals of Internal Medicine, 137,* 834–839.

Uttl, B., & Van Alstine, C.L. (2003). Rising verbal intelligence Scores: implications for research and clinical practice. *Psychology and Aging. 18,* 616–621.

Uttal, William R. (2000). *The war between mentalism and behaviorism: On the accessibility of mental processes.* Mahwah, NJ: Erlbaum.

Vaillant, George E. (2002). *Aging well.* Boston: Little Brown.

Vaillant, George E., & Davis, J. Timothy. (2000). Social/emotional intelligence and midlife resilience in schoolboys with low tested intelligence. *American Journal of Orthopsychiatry, 70,* 215–222.

Vandell, Deborah Lowe, Hyde, Janet S., Plant, E. Ashby, & Essex, Marilyn J. (1997). Fathers and "others" as infant-care providers: Predictors of parents' emotional well-being and marital satisfaction. *Merrill-Palmer Quarterly, 43,* 361–385.

Vandell, Deborah Lowe, McCartney, Kathleen, Owen, Margaret Tresch, Booth, Cathryn, & Clarke-Stewart, Alison. (2003). Variations in child care by grandparents during the first three years. *Journal of Marriage and Family, 65,* 375–381.

Van den Hoonaard, & Deborah Kestin. (2003). Expectations and experiences of widowhood.. In Jaber F. Gubrium & James A. Holstein (Eds.), *Ways of aging* (pp. 182–199). Malden, MA: Blackwell.

Van der Meulen, Matty. (2001). Development in self-concept theory and research: Affect, context, and variability. In Harke Bosma, E. Saskia Kunne, Keith Oatley, & Antony Manstead (Eds.), *Identity and emotion: Development through self-organization* (pp. 10–32). Cambridge, England: Cambridge University Press.

Van Geert, Paul. (2003). Dynamic systems approaches and modeling of developmental processes. In Jaan Valsinger & Kevin J. Connolly (Eds.), *Handbook of developmental psychology* (pp. 640–672). London: Sage.

Van Winkle, Nancy Westlake. (2000). End-of-life decision making in American Indian and Alaska native cultures. In Kathryn Braun, James H. Pietsch, & Patricia L. Blanchette (Eds.), *Cultural issues in end-of-life decision making* (pp. 127–144). Thousand Oaks, CA: Sage.

Vartanian, Lesa Rae. (2001). Adolescent reactions to hypothetical peer group conversations: Evidence for an imaginary audience? *Adolescence, 36,* 347–393.

Veldhuis, Johannes D., Johnson, Michael L., Keenan, Daniel, & Iranmanesh, Ali (2003). The ensemble male hypothalamo-pituitary-gonadal axis. In Paola S. Timiras (Ed.) *Physiological basis of aging and geriatrics* (3rd ed., pp. 213–231). Boca Raton, FL: CRC Press.

Veldhuis, Johannes D., Yoshida, Kohji, & Iranmanesh, Ali. (1997). The effects of mental and metabolic stress on the female reproductive system and female reproductive hormones. In John R. Hubbard & Edward A. Workman (Eds.), *Handbook of stress medicine: An organ system approach.* Boca Raton, FL: CRC Press.

Verhaeghen, Paul, & Marcoen, Alfons. (1996). On the mechanisms of plasticity in young and older adults after instruction in the methods of loci: Evidence for an amplification model. *Psychology and Aging, 11,* 164–178.

Verhaeghen, Paul, Marcoen, Alfons, & Goossens, Luc. (1992). Improving memory performance in the aged through mnemonic training: A meta-analytic study. *Psychology and Aging, 7,* 242–251.

Verhaeghen, Paul, Steitz, D.W., Sliwinski, M.J., & Cerella J. (2003). Aging and dual-task performance: A meta-analysis. *Psychology and Aging, 18*(3), 443–460.

Vickers, James C., Dickson, Tracey C., Adlard, Paul A., Saunders, Helen L., King, Carolyn E., & McCormack, Graeme. (2000). The causes of neural degeneration in Alzheimer's disease. *Neurobiology, 60,* 139–165.

Victora, Cesar, Bryce, Jennifer, Fontaine, Liver, & Monasch, Roeland. (2000). Reducing deaths from diarrhea through oral rehydration therapy. *Bulletin of the World Health Organization, 78,* 1246–1255.

Vidailhet, P., Christensen, B.K., Danion, J.M., & Kapur, S. (2001). Episodic memory impairment in schizophrenia: A view from cognitive psychopathology. In M. Naveh-Benjamin, M. Moscovitch, & R. L. Roediger III (Eds.), *Perspectives on human memory and cognitive aging: Essays in honour of Fergus Craik.* East Sussex, UK: Psychology Press.

Vincent, John A. (2003). *Old age.* New York: Routledge.

Vinden, Penelope G. (1996). Junin Quechua children's understanding of mind. *Child Development, 67,* 1707–1716.

Vissing, Yvonne. (2002). *Women without children.* New Brunswick, NJ: Rutgers University Press.

Vizmanos, B., & Marti-Henneberg, C. (2000). Puberty begins with a characteristic subcutaneous body fat mass in each sex. *European Journal of Clinical Nutrition, 54,* 203–206.

Volling, Brenda. (2003). Sibling relationships. In Marc H. Bornstein, Lucy Davidson, Corey L. M. Keyes, & Kristin A. Moore (Eds.). *Well-being: Positive development across the life course* (pp. 205–220). Mahwah, NJ: Erlbaum.

Vygotsky, Lev S. (1934/1994). The development of academic concepts in school-aged children. In René van der Veer & Jaan Valsiner (Eds.), *The Vygotsky Reader.* Malden, MA: Blackwell.

Vygotsky, Lev S. (1978). *Mind in society: The development of higher psychological processes* (Michael Cole, Vera John-Steiner, Sylvia Scribner, & Ellen Souberman, Eds.). Cambridge, MA: Harvard University Press.

Vygotsky, Lev S. (1987). *Thinking and speech* (N. Minick, Trans.). New York: Plenum Press.

Vygotsky, Lev S. (1994). Principles of social education for deaf and dumb children in Russia. In René van der Veer & Jaan Valsiner (Eds.) & Theresa Prout (Trans.), *The Vygotsky Reader* (pp. 19–26). Cambridge, MA: Blackwell. (Original work published 1925)

Wachs, Theodore D. (1999). Celebrating complexity: Conceptualization and assessment of the environment. In Sarah L. Friedman & Theodore D. Wachs (Eds.), *Measuring environment across the lifespan: Emerging methods and concepts.* Washington, DC: American Psychological Association.

Wachs, Theodore D. (2000). *Necessary but not sufficient: The respective roles of single and multiple influences on individual development.* Washington, DC: American Psychological Association.

Wachs, Theodore D. (2000). Nutritional deficits and behavioral development. *International Journal of Behavioral Development, 24,* 435–441.

Wadden, Thomas A., & Stunkard, Albert J. (Eds.). (2002). *Handbook of obesity treatment.* New York: Guilford.

Wadsworth, Michael. (2002). Doing longitudinal research. In Anne Jamieson & Christina R. Victor (Eds.), *Researching aging and later life* (pp. 94–116). Philadelphia: Taylor & Francis.

Wahlstein, Douglas. (2003). Genetics and the development of brain and behavior. In Jaan Valsiner & Kevin J. Connolly (Eds.), *Handbook of developmental psychology* (pp. 18–47). Thousand Oaks, CA: Sage.

Wainryb, Cecilia, & Turiel, Elliot. (1995). Diversity in social development: Between or within cultures? In Melanie Killen & Daniel Hart (Eds.), *Morality in everyday life: Developmental perspectives.* Cambridge, England: Cambridge University Press.

Walberg, Peder, McKee, Martin, Shkolnikov, Vladimir, Chenet, Laurent, & David, A Leon. (1998). Economic change, crime, and mortality crisis in Russia: Regional analysis. *British Medical Journal, 317,* 312–318.

Walcott, Delores D., Preatt, Helen P., & Patel, Philip R. (2003). Adolescents and eating disorders: Gender, racial, ethnic, sociocultural, and socioeconomic issues. *Journal of Adolescent Research, 18,* 223–243.

Waldron, Nancy L., & McLeskey, James. (1998). The effects of an inclusive school program on students with mild and severe learning disabilities. *Exceptional Children, 64,* 395–405.

Walker, Lawrence J. (1988). The development of moral reasoning. *Annals of Child Development, 55,* 677–691.

Walker, Lawrence J., Gustafson, Paul, & Hennig, Karl H. (2001). The consolidation/transition model in moral reasoning development. *Developmental Psychology, 37,* 187–197.

Walker-Barnes, Chanequa J., & Mason, Craig A. (2001). Ethnic differences in the effect of parenting on gang involvement and gang delinquency: A longitudinal, hierarchical linear modeling perspective. *Child Development, 72,* 1814–1831.

Wallerstein, Judith S., & Blakeslee, Sandra. (1995). *The good marriage.* Boston: Houghton Mifflin.

Walsh, Froma. (2002). A family resilience framework: Innovative practice applications. *Family Relations, 51,* 130–137.

Wannametheen, S. Goya, & Shaper, A. Gerald. (1999). Type of alcoholic drink and risk of major coronary heart disease events and all-cause mortality. *American Journal of Public Health, 89,* 685–690.

Ward, Russell A., & Spitze, Glenna. (1996). Gender differences in parent–child coresidence experiences. *Journal of Marriage and the Family, 58,* 718–725.

Wardley, Bridget L., Puntis, John W. L., & Taitz, Leonard S. (1997). *Handbook of child nutrition* (2nd ed.). New York: Oxford University Press.

Warshofsky, Fred. (1999). *Stealing time: The new science of aging.* New York: TV Books.

Wartella, Ellen A., & Jennings, Nancy. (2000). Children and computers: New technology—old concerns. *The Future of Children, 10*(2), 31–43.

Watson, John B. (1998/1924). *Behaviorism.* New Brunswick, NJ: Transaction. (Original work published 1924)

Watson, John B. (1928). *Psychological care of infant and child.* New York: Norton.

Weinstein, B. (2000). *Geriatric audiology.* New York: Theime Medical Publishers.

Weisfeld, Glenn. (1999). *Evolutionary principles of human adolescence.* New York: Basic Books.

Weissbluth, Marc. (1999). *Healthy sleep habits, happy child* (Rev. ed.). New York: Fawcett.

Weisstub, David N., Thomasma, David C., Gauthier, Serge, & Tomossy, George F. (Eds.). (2001). *Aging: Caring for our elders.* Dordrecht, Netherlands: Kluwer.

Weizman, Zehave Oz, & Snow, Catherine E. (2001). Lexical input as related to children's vocabulary acquisition: Effects of sophisticated exposure and support for meaning. *Developmental Psychology, 37,* 265–279.

Wellman, Henry M. (2003). Enablement and constraint. In Ursula M. Staudinger & Ulman Lindenberger (Eds.), *Understanding human development: Dialogues with lifespan psychology* (pp. 245–263). Dordrecht, Netherlands: Kluwer.

Wellman, Henry M., Cross, David, & Watson, Julanne. (2001). Meta-analysis of theory-of-mind development: The truth about false belief. *Child Development, 72,* 655–684.

Wendland, Barbara, Greenwood, Carol E., Weinberg, Iris, & Young, Karen W. H. (2003). Malnutrition in institutionalized seniors: The iatrogenic component. *Journal of the Geriatrics Society, 51,* 85–90.

Wendland-Carro, Jaqueline, Piccinini, Cesar A., & Millar, W. Stuart. (1999). The role of an early intervention on enhancing the quality of mother-infant interaction. *Child Development, 70,* 713–721.

Wentzel, Kathryn R. (2002). Are effective teachers like good parents? Teaching styles and student adjustment in early adolescence. *Child Development, 73,* 287–301.

Werner, Emmy E., & Smith, Ruth S. (1982). *Vulnerable but invincible: A study of resilient children.* New York: McGraw-Hill.

Werner, Emmy E., & Smith, Ruth S. (1992). *Overcoming the odds: High risk children from birth to adulthood.* Ithaca, NY: Cornell University Press.

Werner, Emily E., & Smith, Ruth S. (2001). *Journeys from childhood to midlife: Risk, resilience, and recovery.* Ithaca, NY: Cornell University Press.

Wertsch, James V. (1985). *Vygotsky and the social formation of mind.* Cambridge, MA: Harvard University Press.

Wertsch, James V., & Tulviste, Peeter. (1992). L. S. Vygotsky and contemporary developmental psychology. *Developmental Psychology, 28,* 548–557.

West, Robin L., Thron, Roxanne M., & Bagwell, Dana K. (2003). Memory performance and beliefs as a function of goal setting and aging. *Psychology and Aging, 18,* 111–125.

Wethington, Elaine. (2002). The relationship of turning points at work to perceptions of psychological growth and change. In Richard A. Settersten Jr. & Timothy J. Owens (Eds.), *New frontiers in socialization* (pp. 93–110). Amsterdam: JAI.

Whitaker, Daniel J., Miller, Kim S., & Clark, Leslie F. (2000). Reconceptualizing adolescent sexual behavior: Beyond did they or didn't they? *Family Planning Perspectives, 32,* 111–117.

Whitbourne, Susan Krauss. (1996). *The aging individual: Physical and psychological perspectives.* New York: Springer.

Whitbourne, Susan Kraus. (2001). The physical aging process in midlife: Interactions with psychological and sociocultural factors. In Margie E. Lachman (Ed.), *Handbook of midlife development* (pp. 109–155). New York: Wiley.

Whitbourne, Susan Krauss. (2002). *The aging individual* (2nd ed.). New York: Springer.

Whitbourne, Susan Krauss, Sneed, Joel R., & Skultety, Karyn M. (2002). Identity processes in adulthood: Theoretical and methodological challenges. *Identity, 2,* 29–46.

White, Aaron M., Ghia, Amol J., Levin, Edward D., & Swartzwelder, H. Scott. (2000). Binge pattern ethanol exposure in adolescent and adult rats: Differential impact on subsequent responsiveness to ethanol. *Alcoholism: Clinical & Experimental Research, 24*(8), 1251–1256.

White, Katherine K., & Abrams, Lee. (2002) Does priming specific syllables during tip-of-the-tongue states facilitate word retrieval in older adults? *Psychology and Aging, 17,* 226–235.

White, Lynn. (2001). Sibling relationships over the life course: A panel analysis. *Journal of Marriage and Family, 63,* 555–568.

White, Lynn K., & Rogers, Stacy J. (1997). Strong support but uneasy relationships: Coresidence and adult children's relationships with their parents. *Journal of Marriage and the Family, 59,* 62–76.

Whiteman, Shawn D., McHale, Susan M., & Crouter, Ann C. (2003). What parents learn from experience: The first child as a first draft. *Journal of Marriage and Family, 65,* 608–621.

Whitley, Bernard E., & Keith-Spiegel, Patricia. (2002). *Academic dishonesty.* Mahwah, NJ: Erlbaum.

Whittington, L. A., & Peters, H. E. (1996). Economic incentives for financial and residential independence. *Demography, 33*(1), 82–97.

Wicker, Allan W., & August, Rachel A. (1995). How far should we generalize? The case of a workload model. *Psychological Science, 6,* 39–44.

Wiener, Judith, & Schneider, Barry H. (2002). A multisource exploration of the friendship patterns of children with and without learning disabilities. *Journal of Abnormal Child Psychology, 30,* 127–141.

Wierson, Michelle, Long, Patricia J., & Forehand, Rex L. (1993). Toward a new understanding of early menarche: The role of environmental stress in pubertal timing. *Adolescence, 28,* 913–924.

Wigfield, Allan, & Eccles, Jacquelynne S. (2002). The development of competence beliefs, expectancies for success, and achievement values from childhood through adolescence. In Allan Wigfield & Jacquelynne S. Eccles (Eds.), *Development of achievement motivation* (pp. 91–120). San Diego, CA: Academic Press.

Wigfield, Allan, Eccles, Jacquelynne S., Yoon, Kwang Suk, Harold, Rena D., Arbreton, Amy J. A., Freedman-Doan, Carol, et al. (1997). Change in children's competence beliefs and subjective task values across the elementary school years: A 3-year study. *Journal of Educational Psychology, 89,* 451–469.

Wilkie, Janme R., Ferree, Mayra M., & Ratcliff, Kathryn S. (1998). Gender and fairness: Marital satisfaction in two-earner couples. *Journal of Marriage and the Family, 60,* 577–594.

Wilkinson, Anne M. & Lynn, Joanne. (2001). The end of life. In Robert H. Binstock & Linda K. George, (Eds.), *Handbook of aging and the social sciences* (5th ed., pp. 444–461). San Diego, CA: Academic Press.

Willatts, Peter. (1999). Development of means-end behavior in young infants: Pulling a support to retrieve a distant object. *Developmental Psychology, 35,* 651–667.

Willett, W.C., & Trichopoulos, D. (1996). Nutrition and cancer: A summary of the evidence. *Cancer Causes Control, 7,* 178–180.

Williams, Benjamin R., Ponesse, Jonathan S., Schachar, Russell J., Logan, Gordon D., & Tannock, Rosemary. (1999). Development of inhibitory control across the life span. *Developmental Psychology, 35,* 205–213.

Williams, David R. (2002). Racial/ethnic variation in women's health: the social embeddedness of health. *American Journal of Public Health, 92,* 588–597.

Williams, David R. (2003). The health of men: Structured inequalities and opportunities. *American Journal of Public Health, 93,* 724–731.

Williams, David R., & Wilson, Colwick M. (2001). Race, ethnicity, and aging. In Robert H. Binstock & Linda K. George, *Handbook of aging and the social sciences* (5th ed., pp. 160–178). San Diego, CA: Academic Press.

Willis, Sherry L. (1996). Everyday cognitive competence in elderly persons: Conceptual issues and empirical findings. *Gerontologist, 36,* 595–601

Wills, Thomas Ashby, Dandy, James M., & Yaeger, Alison. (2001). Time perspective and early-onset substance use: A model based on stress-coping theory. *Psychology of Addictive Behaviors, 15,* 118–125.

Wilson, Gail. (1995). "I'm the eyes and she's the arms": Changes in gender roles in advanced old age. In Sara Arber & Jay Ginn (Eds.), *Connecting gender and aging.* Buckingham, England: Open University Press.

Wilson, Melvin N., Lewis, Joyce B., Hinton, Ivora D., Kohn, Laura P., Underwood, Alex, Phuong Hogue, Lan

Kho, et al. (1995). Promotion of African American family life: Families, poverty, and social programs. In Melvin N. Wilson (Ed.), *African American family life: Its structural and ecological aspects* (pp. 85–99). San Francisco: Jossey-Bass.

Wilson, Robert S., Beckett, Laurel A., Barnes, Lisa L., Schneider, Julie A., Bach, Julie, Evans, Denis A., et al. (2002). Individual differences in rate of change in cognitive abilities of older persons. *Psychology and Aging, 17,* 179–193.

Wilson, Robert S., Gilley, David W., Bennett, David A., Beckett, Laurel A., & Evans, Denis A. (2000). Person-specific paths of cognitive decline in Alzheimer's disease and their relation to age. *Psychology and Aging, 15,* 18–28.

Wineberg, H., & Werth, J. L., Jr. (2003). Physician-assisted suicide in Oregon: What are the key factors? *Death Studies, 27,* 501–518.

Winsler, Adam, Carlton, Martha P., & Barry, Maryann J. (2000). Age-related changes in preschool children's systematic use of private speech in a natural setting. *Journal of Child Language, 27,* 665–687.

Winsler, Adam, Díaz, Rafael M., Espinosa, Linda, & Rodríguez, James L. (1999). When learning a second language does not mean losing the first: Bilingual language development in low-income, Spanish-speaking children attending bilingual preschool. *Child Development, 70,* 349–362.

Wirth, H.P. (1993). Caring for a chronically demented patient within the family. In W. Meier-Ruge (Ed.), *Dementing brain disease in geriatric medicine.* Switzerland: Karger.

Wise, Phyllis M. (2003).The female reproductive system. In Paola S. Timiras (Ed.) *Physiological basis of aging and geriatrics* (3rd ed., pp. 189–212). Boca Raton, FL: CRC Press.

Wishart, Jennifer G. (1999). Learning and development in children with Down's syndrome. In Alan Slater and Darwin Muir (Eds.), *The Blackwell reader in developmental psychology* (pp. 493–508). Malden, MA: Blackwell.

Wolf, Rosalie S. (1998). Domestic elder abuse and neglect. In Inger Hilde Nordhus, Gary R. VandenBos, Stig Berg, & Diane Fromhold (Eds.), *Clinical feropsychology.* Washington, DC: American Psychological Association.

Wolfe, David A., Wekerle, Christine, Reitzel-Jaffe, Deborah, & Lefebvre, Lorrie. (1998). Factors associated with abusive relationships among maltreated and nonmaltreated youth. *Development and Psychopathology, 10,* 61–85.

Wolfe, Joanne, Grier, Holcombe, E., Klar, Neil, Levin, Sarah B., Ellenbogen, et al.(2000). Symptoms and suffering at the end of life in children with cancer. *New England Journal of Medicine, 342,* 326–333.

Wolfson, Amy R., & Carskadon, Mary A. (1998). Sleep schedules and daytime functioning in adolescents. *Child Development, 69,* 875–887.

Wollons, Roberta (Ed.). (2000). *Kindergartens and cultures: The global diffusion of an idea.* New Haven, CT: Yale University Press.

Wolraich, Mark L., Hannah, Jane N., Baumgaertel, Anna, & Feurer, Irene D. (1998). Examination of DSM-IV criteria for attention deficit hyperactivity disorder in a county-side sample. *Journal of Developmental and Behavioral Pediatrics, 19,* 162–168.

Wong, Sau-ling Cynthia, & Lopez, Miguel G. (2000). English language learners of Chinese background: A portrait of diversity. In Sandra Lee McKay & Sau-ling Cynthia Wong (Eds.), *New immigrants in the United States* (pp. 263–305). Cambridge, England: Cambridge University Press.

Wong, Shelia, Chan, Kingsley, Wong, Virginia, & Wong, Wilfred. (2002). Use of chopsticks in Chinese children. *Child: Care, Health and Development, 28,* 157–161.

Wong, Siu Kwong. (1999). Acculturation, peer relations, and delinquent behavior of Chinese-Canadian youth. *Adolescence, 34,* 108–119.

Woods, Stephen C., Schwartz, Michael W., Baskin, Denis G., & Seely, Randy, J. (2000). Food intake and the regulation of body weight. *Annual Review of Psychology, 51,* 255—277.

Woodward, Amanda L., & Markman, Ellen M. (1998). Early word learning. In William Damon (Series Ed.), Deanna Kuhn, & Robert S. Siegler (Volume Eds.), *Handbook of child psychology: Vol. 2. Cognition, perception and language* (5th ed., pp. 371–420). New York: Wiley.

Woolley, Jacqueline D., & Berger, Elizabeth A. (2002). Development of beliefs about the origins and controllability of dreams. *Developmental Psychology, 38,* 24–41.

World Health Organization. (2000). *The world health report: 2000: Health systems: Improving performance.* Geneva, Switzerland: World Health Organization, United Nations.

World Health Organization. (2001). *The world health report, 2001.* Geneva, Switzerland: World Health Organization.

Wright, William. (1998). *Born that way: Genes, behavior, personality.* New York: Knopf.

Wyman, Peter A., Cowen, Emory L., Work, William C., Hoyt-Meyers, Lynne, Magnus, Keith B., & Fagen, Douglas B. (1999). Caregiving and developmental factors differentiating young at-risk urban children showing resilient versus stress-affected outcome: A replication and extension. *Child Development, 70,* 645–659.

Wysong, Earl, Aniskiewicz, Richard, & Wright, David. (1994). Truth and DARE: Tracking drug education to graduation and as symbolic politics. *Social Problems, 41,* 448–472.

Xu, Fujie, Schillinger, Julia A., Markowitz, Lauri E., Sternberg, Maya R., Aubin, Mark R., & St. Louis, Michael E. (2000). Repeat *chlamydia trachomatis* infection in women: Analysis through a surveillance case registry in Washington State, 1993–1998. *American Journal of Epidemiology, 152,* 1164–1170.

Yeh, Christine, & Inose, Mayuko. (2002). Difficulties and coping strategies of Chinese, Japanese and Korean immigrant students. *Adolescence, 37*(145), 69–82.

Yeo, Gwen & Hikoyeda, Nancy. (2000). Cultural issues in end-of-life decision making among Asians and Pacific Islanders in the United States. In Kathryn Braun, James H. Pietsch & Patricia L. Blanchette (Eds.), *Cultural issues in end-of-life decision making* (pp. 101–125). Thousand Oaks, CA: Sage.

Yerkes, Robert M. (1923). Testing and the human mind. *Atlantic Monthly, 131,* 358–370.

Yeung, W. Jean, Linver, Miriam R. & Brooks-Gunn, Jeanne. (2002). How money matters for young children's development: Parental investment and family processes. *Child Development, 73,* 1861–1879.

Yglesias, Helen. (1980). Moses, Anna Mary Robertson (Grandma). In Barbara Sicherman & Carol Hurd Green (Eds.). *Notable American women: The modern period.* Cambridge, MA: Belknap Press.

Yoder, Kevin A., Hoyt, Dan R., & Whitbeck, Les B. (1998). Suicidal behavior among homeless and runaway adolescents. *Journal of Youth & Adolescence, 27,* 753–771.

Yoon, Carolyn, Hasher, Lynn, Feinberg, Fred, & Rahhal, Tamara A. (2001). Cross-cultural differences in memory: The role of culture-based stereotypes about aging. *Psychology and Aging, 15,* 694–704.

Yoos, H. Lorrie, Kitzman, Harriet, & Cole, Robert. (1999). Family routines and the feeding process. In Daniel B. Kessler & Peter Dawson (Eds.), *Failure to thrive and pediatric undernutrition* (pp. 375–384). Baltimore: Brooks.

Yoshikawa, Hirokazu. (1994). Prevention as cumulative protection: Effects of early family support and education on chronic delinquency and its risks. *Psychological Bulletin, 115,* 28–54

Yoshikawa, Hirokazu, & Hsueh, JoAnn. (2001). Child development and public policy: Toward a dynamic systems perspective. *Child Development, 72,* 1887–1903.

You, Roger X., Thrift, Amanda G., McNeil, John J., Davis, Stephen M., & Donnan, Geoffrey A. (1999). Ischemic stroke risk and passive exposure to spouses' cigarette smoking. *American Journal of Public Health, 89,* 572–575.

Youn, Gahyun. (1999). Differences in familism values and caregiving outcomes among Korean, Korean American, and White American dementia caregivers. *Psychology and Aging, 14,* 355–364.

Younoszai, Barbara. (1993). Mexican American perspectives related to death. In Donald P. Irish, Kathleen F. Lundquist, & Vivian Jenkins Nelsen (Ed), *Ethnic variations in dying, death, and grief: Diversity in universality* (Series in Death Education, Aging, and Health Care). Washington, DC: Taylor & Francis.

Zahn-Waxler, Carolyn, Friedman, Ruth J., Cole, Pamela M., Mizuta, Ichiro, & Hiruma, Noriko. (1996). Japanese and United States preschool children's responses to conflict and distress. *Child Development, 67,* 2462–2477.

Zahn-Waxler, Carolyn, Schmitz, Stephanie, Fulker, David, Robinson, Joann, & Emde, Robert. (1996). Behavior problems in 5-year-old monozygotic and dyzygotic twins: Genetic and environmental influences, patterns of regulation, and internalization of control. *Development and Psychopathology, 8,* 103–122.

Zarit, Steven H. (1996). Continuities and discontinuities in very late life. In Vern L. Bengston (Ed.), *Adulthood and aging: Research on continuities and discontinuities.* New York: Springer.

Zarit, Steven H., Dolan, Melissa M., & Leitsch, Sara A. (1998). Interventions in nursing homes and other alternative living settings. In Inger Hilde Nordhus, Gary R. VandenBos, Stig Berg, & Pia Fromholt (Eds.), *Clinical geropsychology.* Washington, DC: American Psychological Association.

Zavodny, Madeline. (1999). Do men's characteristics affect whether a nonmarital pregnancy results in marriage? *Journal of Marriage and the Family, 61,* 764–773.

Zeifman, Debra, Delaney, Sarah, & Blass, Elliott. (1996). Sweet taste, looking, and calm in two- and four-week-old infants: The eyes have it. *Developmental Psychology, 32,* 1090–1099.

Zigler, Edward F. (Ed.). (1996). *Children, families, and government: Preparing for the twenty-first century.* New York: Cambridge University Press.

Zigler, Edward, & Styfco, Sally J. (2001). Can early childhood intervention prevent delinquency? A real possibility. In Arthur C. Bohart & Deborah J. Stipek (Eds.), *Constructive and destructive behavior: Implications for family, school, and society* (pp. 231–248). Washington, DC: American Psychological Association.

Zimprich, D., & Martin, M. (2002). Can longitudinal changes in processing speed explain longitudinal changes in fluid intelligence? *Psychology and Aging, 17,* 690–695.

Zucker, Alyssa H., Ostrove, Joan M., & Stewart, Abigail J. (2002) College-educated women's personality development in adulthood: Perception and age differences. *Psychology and Aging, 17,* 236–244.

Zwahr, Melissa D., Park, Denise C., & Shifren, Kim. (1999). Judgments about estrogen replacement therapy: The role of age, cognitive abilities, and beliefs. *Psychology and Aging, 14,* 179–191.

Zylicz, Zbigniew. (1999). Innovations in end-of-life care. An international journal and on-line forum of leaders in end-of-life care. Retrieved from http://www.edc.org/lastacts/

Subject Index